SEXUALITY AND HOMOSEXUALITY

A New View

SEXUALITY AND HOMOSEXUALITY

A New View

ARNO KARLEN

W · W · NORTON & COMPANY · INC ·

NEW YORK

SBN 393 01087 2
Library of Congress Catalog Card No. 70-116103
ALL RIGHTS RESERVED
Published simultaneously in Canada
by George J. McLeod Limited
PRINTED IN THE UNITED STATES OF AMERICA

Contents

v

Preface

This book is an act of presumption. I can only plead that at first it was the presumption of ignorance.

In 1965 an editor and my literary agent suggested that I consider writing a very different book. The mass media insisted that we were increasingly surrounded by microboppers who took the Pill at puberty, suburban swappers, rodentlike college students, homosexuals and kinky undergrounds. The sexual revolution had allegedly reached a new peak, and with it the more baroque forms of sexuality. The press claimed that a homosexual Mafia was taking over the American culture establishment and breaking down whatever sex distinctions remained in our society. I declined to write a book rounding up the evidence for all these arguments, because I had doubts that they were true. In fact, my scientific reading suggested the contrary.

The more I read and talked to serious students of the subject, the more convinced I became that what passes for an informed, enlightened view of sex among educated laymen is twenty to fifty years out of date. The sexological truisms of intellectual cocktail parties are just a few cuts above phlogiston theory in accuracy and relevance. I proposed writing a very different sort of book, and thus began a five-year venture that changed many of my own ideas and feelings. It took me from primate-behavior laboratories to luncheons with transvestites, from interviewing heterosexual college students to sifting through the intellectual backbiting of opposed schools of scientists. I rapidly learned that the important revolution of our time is not in sexual behavior but in the scientific study of sex. The widely publicized work of Kinsey and Masters and Johnson is only a fraction of it. Most lies buried in fragments in specialized journals. If one begins to assemble the contributions of psychiatry, anthropology, animal behavior, genetics and a half dozen other fields, there are dramatic congruences and contradictions among them. Some new answers emerge, and many of the old questions we asked seem so naïvely conceived that they must be scrapped. I looked for books summarizing and relating this research and found none. Only a handful of scientists are trying to join the pieces in a coherent whole, in guarded essays in specialized texts. Most lay writers report on sexology and sex in society without even knowing such developments exist. As a result, a revolutionary interdisciplinary view of human sexuality remains unknown even to the majority of researchers, physicians, teachers and writers.

This begs explanation, for talk of interdisciplinary study is fashionable in most fields today. After I had interviewed many people involved in sex research, I saw why the book I was seeking didn't exist. Many very different specialties are involved, and each is full of polemics and intellectual partisan politics. In a time of extreme specialization, when so much scientific literature consists of minute mutual criticism, the words "general" and "eclectic" have a bad odor in the academies. Scientists who venture outside their fields are likely to be attacked by their colleagues as presumptuous, uncritical and unprofessional (which is eventually costly in terms of grants and promotions). And the few scientists who write about their fields for laymen tend to receive scorn from their peers as mere showmen and financial opportunists. Most professional writers simply cannot afford to spend enough time studying to do an adequate job with such material, even if they have the desire and ability to do so. Probably only a layman would write the book I had sought, knowing that on each page he dealt with questions to which a scholar could devote his life. It was a presumptuous, perhaps an impossible task, but by now I was too fascinated and committed to back off from the project. Certainly the book was badly needed, for as I had learned, even most of the best existing ones were in some way outmoded, inaccurate or limited in scope. One had only to see the summaries of anthropological knowledge in psychiatrists' books, perpetuating ideas dead for a half century among anthropologists; or assumptions about the biology of sex in anthropologists' books, which no biologist would touch with a stick today.

Somehow a narrowed focus had to be found. One can no more write a book about sex than about life, not without oversimplifying to the point of obscuring the subject. The idea originally suggested to me—increased homosexuality and sex-role confusion as a symptom of sexual revolution—was ideal. It demanded confronting all the fundamental questions about human sexuality, since the normal and abnormal mutually define each other. What is biologically programed into us at birth as male and female? As heterosexual or homosexual? What is culturally determined, and how? How do family structure and child-rearing relate to sexual behavior and attitudes? Do changes in attitudes really alter what happens in the bedroom? Or to put it in formal terms, what is the relationship between overt mores, covert mores and behavior?

So I decided that I would take three statements widely held as common knowledge today: (1) there is a sexual revolution in progress or nearly complete; (2) there is more homosexuality and/or more open homosexuality; (3) these first two developments are related. I would subject these statements to the most advanced perspectives of medical and social science, in as broad a context as possible, as a case study in human sexuality. I would use the results of this as a framework for social reportage. When I began, I could not predict the results, for no one had taken on such a foolhardy task. I was still naïvely underestimating the job.

I worked for five years, usually with one or more research assistants. Even so, I had to draw arbitrary limits to my studies in some fields because of their inexhaustible complexity. On the other hand, I discovered startling gaps in our sexual knowledge, many of them due to emotional fears of studying sex, let alone deviant sex. For instance, when I began to seek sources for what I expected to be a forty-page chapter on sexual deviance in the Western past, I found that not one half-reliable book existed. The half-truths and clichés that pass for sexual history of the West are not only accepted by laymen but influence the theories of specialized researchers in sexology. I ended up writing what amounts to a book in itself—the first section of this volume—to rediscover our sexual legacy and examine our myths about it.

I could not responsibly write this book without constantly checking my own accuracy against the knowledge of specialists, and checking their knowledge against what turned up in observation and reporting. At first my interviews were not meant to be part of the book, but as I proceeded, they demanded a place in it. I spoke to psychiatrists, ethologists, homosexuals, heterosexuals, students, teachers, people sitting next to me on trains and planes. I heard experts try to demolish each others' work and personalities; homosexuals telling secrets long kept from their families and friends; sometimes heterosexuals literally weeping with relief at finally talking to someone about the uncertainty and suffering in their sex lives. Then I had to assess what I had heard and resolve the intellectual and moral problems that fell on me.

The easiest problem to solve was protecting deviant informants. I have altered their names, residences, professions, looks and other identifying details if they wished (use of only a first name in an interview shows that the subject's identity has been disguised, and use of a surname as well indicates that such details are unchanged). More difficult was the problem of the knowledge I gained of many public and academic experts on sex. Some are secret homosexuals, their "research" disguised apologetics. Other researchers and clinicians reveal, in private, a vengeful hatred toward sexual deviants that they would never display in print or in public, and which makes their "research" equally suspect. Such people speak as authorities to troubled laymen and influence our laws and social policies. Like anthropologists who write about race and poverty, they bear a special ethical responsibility; I bear an equal responsibility not to leave them unchallenged. If I have erred in this book, it is toward protectiveness in naming names. Fortunately most biased writings can be adequately criticized on an impersonal level.

Another problem, a quite serious one, was my presuming to judge so much specialized knowledge, if only indirectly by my selection of material. Initially my qualifications to write this book were three. I had written in a variety of forms and fields, from fiction and poetry to journalism on many subjects. I had been interested enough in biology, medicine and social science to have considered them as careers, and possessed at least more than the usual lay background in these fields. And for several years I had been thinking and writing about sex behavior and sex role. It was for these reasons that I had been asked to write a book in the first place.

Painfully aware of my vast task and my inadequacies, I approached scientists as a suppliant at founts of arcane knowledge. It became dramatically clear to me, as never before, that research is as unbiased, intelligent and reliable as those who perform it. Some scientists were marvelously scrupulous, cogent and imaginative. Others turned out to be zealots trying to explain all human activity with one theory of genetics or learning or psychodynamics. If I used my perceptions and general rules of logic and evidence, more than half the "scientific" material I had to consider dropped out of view, and my choices narrowed. Now I had to try to show what was fact and what was theory, and what my own evaluations were. I am fairly confident that my conclusions, if not above argument, are at least not arbitrary or born of utter ignorance. Throughout the entire writing of the book, I have kept checking it against a wide variety of expert opinions, yet tried to avoid the intellectual cowardice of dodging basic issues.

Finally, the most difficult problem was not scientists' occasional weakness for fad, bias or special pleading, but my own intellectual and emotional limits—to which I am surely as blind as anyone is about his own. I felt it was my responsibility to explore, with the help of an analytically oriented psychiatrist, any prejudices, fears, hostilities or other irrational feelings I might harbor about the subject, and I did so in detail.

When I began this book, many people I knew predicted that I would have a difficult time getting people to talk freely about their personal lives or give me their valuable professional time. I wanted the help of closet queens, overworked researchers and strangers, many with a well-earned disrespect for anything like a journalist. I spoke to hundreds of people and received perhaps a dozen refusals. Only a small handful had second thoughts, scientists terrified in retrospect of having spoken *ex cathedra*. Many people with a lot to lose extended their trust to me; many scientists provided examples of dedication, intellectual rigor and human compassion. Meeting many of these people has been the book's gift to me, and I hope it is worthy of the help they generously gave. I have included some of the interviews in the book, though there are a dozen or so for each one printed here. I have put them at the ends of certain chapters. In some cases, they amplify or illustrate the text. Interviews with homosexuals and other laymen sometimes dramatically illuminated what may otherwise seem like fanciful theories or speculations. Interviews with scientists gave them a chance to talk informally, as they rarely do in print, and to reveal their personal experiences and convictions, describe their ongoing projects, and talk of future work. Sometimes a few interviews are used to approximate the informal discussion that follows the reading of a paper at a scientific meeting. And last but not least important, I have hoped by the direct juxtaposition of past and present, theory and reportage, data and commentary, to take the reader along with me on my search for a wide-ranging synthesis.

Naturally I cannot thank most of my informants by name, nor is there space to list all the scientists and friends who gave me help, encouragement and criticism. Among those not named in the text are Howard Becker, Dr. Irving Bieber, Jeff and Madeline David, Philip Fried, Dr. Evelyn Hooker, Christine Howard, Dr. A. D. Jonas, Dr. Abram Kardiner, Bennet Kremen, Dr. Howard Kremen, Birgitta Linner, James MacGibbon, Dr. Judd Marmor, Lynn Nesbit, Mrs. Michael Rau, Prof. Henry Sams, Eric Swenson, Dr. Konrad Van Emde Boas, Nahum Waxman, Stephan Wilkinson and, in their special ways, my parents, my wife and my children.

Within the limits of the possible, I have tried to write a book I'd hoped someone had written for my information five years ago. I hope it is a book for others as well.

Introduction

It has become a journalistic commonplace that the 1960s were a decade of sexual revolution. Even the reporting and discussion of homosexuality became frequent and open. In 1960 the subheading *Homosexuality*, under *Sex*, in the *New York Times Subject Index* covered only three entries, all cross-references. Just five years later that would seem scandalously scant attention to an American minority of ten to twenty-five million people, about as large as blacks and twice as large as Jews.

The category *Sex* first appeared in the *Index* in the 1920s, during America's first great stride toward emancipation from traditional mores. Only token freedom followed; in 1936 the word still stood over a mere seven entries and a list of *Sex Crimes*, and for many years the *Index*'s heading read *SEX, See also Glands*. The word homosexual appeared in a headline once in 1937, but not again until 1950. Over those years, homosexuality was sometimes involved in criminal cases, but such phrases as "indecent behavior" and "immoral practices," along with a generally official, fastidious tone, often left readers wondering what gender had done what to whom. Occasionally psychiatrists spoke out for treatment rather than life sentences or sterilization for sex offenders, but more often doctors, clergymen and legislators talked with horror and outrage about stamping out "degenerates" and "unnatural acts." The press presented a picture of a stable society sporadically threatened by disgusting, rare mutants who were beyond understanding, help, toleration or even pity.

KINGS COUNTY SHERIFF RECOMMENDS SHOOTING CHILD ATTACKERS ON SPOT
August 24, 1936

MEDICAL AND CHURCH LEADERS PROTEST OHIO STATE PENITENTIARY ACTION ON REPORT THAT 6 SEX CRIMINALS HAVE BEEN EMASCULATED IN ORDER TO GET PAROLES
September 5, 1941

DR. L. S. LIPSCHUTZ SEES BRAIN SURGERY [PREFRONTAL LOBOTOMY] ON MORAL DEGENERATES AS POSSIBLE PREVENTIVE
May 17, 1946

A change began slowly in the late forties and early fifties. The appearance of the Kinsey reports in 1948 and 1953 caused the *Sex* category of the *Index* to expand immensely. Many of the items were explanations, praise or criticism of the Kinsey studies, but even after the *Sexual Behavior* volumes ceased to be news, the number of articles on sex still grew larger each year. Through the early fifties, there was a *Homosexuality* heading under *Sex*, but this rose from allegations of homosexual security risks by Senator McCarthy and others. In 1953 the word homosexual appeared for the first time in the list of *Sex Crimes* articles. (The case had occurred in England, but the existence of homosexual offenses—somewhere else—was finally being admitted.) And now it became more common to see such headlines as:

Dr. D. Abrahamson says term "sexual psychopath" should be dropped; holds offenders are not oversexed but emotionally underdeveloped; calls for special research and treatment

In the mid-fifties the heading *Homosexuality* almost disappeared from the *New York Times Subject Index* again. In 1960 it stood over just three cross-references to other subjects. But in 1964 the *Homosexuality* entries filled a column of fine print. The words transvestite and lesbian appeared in headlines. By 1966 it was reported that homosexuals were insisting on their right to serve in the armed forces; staging "sip-in" demonstrations at bars that had refused their patronage; talking about organizing as a voting bloc in California. The new police chief of New York City swore not to harass or entrap them. Their frank novels and autobiographies were more widely read and admired than ever; their plays, films and clothing styles were prominent, sometimes dominant, in their fields. They were financing an Off-Broadway play on lesbianism in the interest of public enlightenment. They were the subject of network television programs (in 1967, two in one month). Now, it was being said, the "love that dared not speak its name" would not shut up.

The tone of articles describing these events was usually neutral. Sometimes it was sympathetic. At worst it showed judicious concern, mild irritation or gentle, tongue-in-cheek amusement. Where a few years earlier one would have found in the *New York Times* a filler item on crop rotation in East Pakistan, this item appeared:

EXECUTION OF A HOMOSEXUAL
VIEWED BY 6,000 IN YEMEN

SANA, Yemen, Aug. 1 (AP) A condemned homosexual was executed before 6,000 people in the main square of Sana today. A religious court sentenced the accused man, Ahmed a-Osmany, a 60-year-old municipal employee.

An Islamic law requires that a man convicted of homosexuality be thrown from the highest point in the city, but the court said the condemned man could be beheaded instead.

When the hour of execution arrived, the official executioner did not show up. After waiting 20 minutes, a religious judge asked the condemned man if he would consent to being shot. He nodded and a police officer executed him.

"They thought of throwing him from a plane, but that's expensive," said the Minister of Education, Mohammed el Khalidy. It was the first time a homosexual had been executed in Yemen, he said.

In this report, homosexuality is anecdotal material in a story without broad medical or legal significance. Most readers were probably amazed by the harsh sentence, amused by the exoticism and backwardness of the whole business, and shocked by the macabre mixture of ineptitude and etiquette. A decade earlier they would have been shocked mostly by the mention of homosexuality.

In 1968 reporting was even wider. Homosexual organizations were larger, more vocal and more noticed. Columbia University awarded a charter to a campus group seeking equal rights for homosexuals. An exposé of Philadelphia prisons as "sodomy factories" engaged national attention and brought a cry for reform—not by stamping out perversion, but by instituting conjugal visits. Two New Yorkers were suing the city for having denied them jobs as social caseworkers on grounds of homosexuality; the American Civil Liberties Union was backing them.

More than a dozen major films appeared dealing with homosexuality, including *The Fox, Therese and Isabelle, The Killing of Sister George* and *The Queen*, the last a documentary on female impersonators in a transvestite Miss All-America contest. *The Killing of Sister George* and *Staircase* were successful on Broadway, and *Fortune and Men's Eyes* and *The Boys in the Band* Off-Broadway; all subsequently became popular films. (An Off-Off Broadway play was most succinctly titled *The Faggot*.) On television, Johnny Carson was making frequent, thinly veiled allusions to homosexuality, transvestism, sado-masochism and fetishism. There was a new network show, *The Ugliest Girl in Town*, whose central character was a male dressed as a girl; *Newsweek* said that the lead resembled Mickey Rooney in drag. And "art theaters" in major cities were starting to show homosexual as well as heterosexual nudie movies—one place in San Francisco exhibited one of each simultaneously.

There was hardly a magazine that didn't discuss homosexuality and casually mention it often—*Time, Newsweek, Life, Look, Esquire*. It was weekly fare in the *Village Voice* and the underground press. Women's magazines talked about it constantly as a grave problem their readers must face; they gave advice on how to know and avoid homosexuals (allegedly ubiquitous, especially in New York) when seeking a boyfriend or mate, how to use them as "safe" escorts or to make boyfriends jealous. People wrote letters signed "Gay" to *Dear Abby* in major newspapers, and psychologists writing columns and answering readers' letters told parents how to prevent homosexuality and effeminacy in their sons. In 1967 a regularly recurring advertisement in the *Village Voice* for a computerized introduction service had begun, "WE'D LIKE TO SAY A FEW WORDS ABOUT HETEROSEXUALITY. It's coming back." A year later underground newspapers were offering computerized dating services to homosexuals.

It has been generally assumed that homosexuality is more common. Still, the attitude of most articles and references is benign, protective or like that taken toward alcoholism—considering it an emotional disturbance to be treated, not punished. There was significant contrast between the McCarthy-era headlines on homosexual security risks and the press's attitude toward the 1965 case of presidential assistant Walter Jenkins. After Jenkins was arrested in the course of a homosexual incident in a YMCA lavatory in Washington, D.C., the press treated him with more sympathy than indignation. It was assumed to be common knowledge that some married men with children have homosexual episodes in their lives. Jenkins' chronic fatigue from overwork was mentioned repeatedly as an extenuation, and his family was pitied along with him because of the damage to their lives. A few attempts to make political use of Jenkins' trouble met with such moral contempt that they were quickly dropped. The press and much of the public had apparently taken the attitude that a man's sexual life, even his homosexual acts under some circumstances, were his own business, and not a toxin threatening to poison society.

Many Americans have long equated homosexuality with artists, intellectuals, liberals of all kinds, and a general decline into permissiveness. The educated liberal, on the other hand, has prided himself on not taking a persecutory view of deviance. He has viewed homosexuality more in sorrow than anger or has even defended it as a separate but equal way of life. Though the old, conservative view is still predominant—especially in some small-town, inland-America areas, in some ethnic groups and in lower social-economic levels—it is losing ground. At least lip-service is increasingly paid to the liberal position.

Some educated liberals, especially those younger than thirty, see increased homosexual behavior and the breakdown of old sex-role distinctions as healthy. They presume that men are naturally bisexual, and that old sex-role requirements have been a tyranny. "Man Talk" in *Mademoiselle*, "The Step After Muscle" in *Cosmopolitan*, the book *The Masculine Mystique*, by Myron Brenton, are examples of some of the popular writing that says traditional ideas of masculinity only breed unhappiness —that we are headed, luckily, toward an end of the war between the sexes, which will no longer be polarized in emotional style and role. The idea is especially popular among people in their teens and early twenties. Just as rebellious youths of the past wanted freedom for heterosexual adventure, today's dissident youth culture wants freedom from traditional sex-role demands.

Others, however, are upset at what seems a rising tide of deviance in the arts, professions, fashion, entertainment and public life. They have felt that their attempts to understand psychological and social forces, to avoid inherited prejudice, oblige them to stand for freedom for sexual as well as racial and political minorities. But they now find themselves protecting sexual deviance with the same doubts they feel when protecting the freedom of the radical right or the goals of the new radical feminism.

Though they believe that openness about sex is healthy, they dislike and worry about what is happening to traditional standards of masculinity and femininity. They see homosexuals and unisex enthusiasts becoming tastemakers, from national magazines to cultural foundations, and giving society new paradigms in dress, behavior, mores and art. They say that the staffs of many leading art museums and galleries have become predominantly homosexual, and art politics has to a large extent become homosexual politics. In recent years actors have complained that many more theatrical agents are homosexual, bringing the homosexual casting couch to still another part of their profession. The change in style of male film heroes has been written about constantly, from the Bogarts and Coopers of the past to petulantly boyish or androgynous stars of the fifties and sixties. At the same time, frankly homosexual cliques have dominated large areas of the theater and film industry.

Who's Afraid of Virginia Woolf? and other plays have been damned by reviewers as homosexual allegory. The underground film is in large part a compendium of homosexual and sado-masochistic fantasies, from Kenneth Anger's *Scorpio Rising* and Jack Smith's *Flaming Creatures* to many of the productions of Andy Warhol. Further, novels by or about homosexuals have increased in number and popularity. The works of Jean Genet, James Baldwin, John Rechy and Charles Wright are only a few of the better-known. Reading them, seeing such films as Shirley Clarke's *Portrait of Jason*, it sometimes seems that the homosexual Negro junkie has become a culture hero. The Reverend Alvin Carmines of Judson Memorial Church in Greenwich Village, where many avant-garde productions are staged, was quoted in the *New York Times*: "There's something else about Off-Off-Broadway. A certain amount of homosexual influence is good, I think, particularly when it's practiced by nonhomos."

Homosexuality is often powerful even when not explicit. "Camp" was once homosexual argot for anything overtly homosexual in manner, from gait to artistic taste. First came apologists and theoreticians of camp, then popularizers and promoters. In a diluted form it became widespread, respectable and profitable in the mid-sixties. Soon came "kink"—such rarer deviance as sado-masochism and shoe and leather fetishism. Kink, like camp, became transformed into a fashionable, salable item. Early in 1965 an editor of *Esquire* sought a writer to do an article on its new prominence, from the Profumo affair to the raid of a brothel in northern New Jersey that specialized in whipping and other kinky services, and the sudden appearance of kink in fashion. The spring 1965 *New York Times Fashion Supplement*, some issues of *Harper's Bazaar* and many subsequent fashion displays and ads showed an unmistakable resemblance to kinky pornography in poses, facial expressions, situations, clothing design and general emotional tone. In the past, homosexual couturiers, photographers, fashion writers and advertisers had done their work for the heterosexual public and kept their tastes more or less to themselves. Now they were dressing much of the nation in their fantasy clothes, with the help of the media—especially the women's magazines, many of whose editors and contributors show, at least in their product, an inversion of traditional sex-role values. The great rush of kinky fashions subsided to a steady influence. Then in 1968 *Queen* magazine in England showed female impersonator Danny la Rue in five fashion photos of women's clothes, and Hess's Department Store, in Allentown, Pennsylvania, advertised formal, floor-length evening skirts for men as part of their line of "Clothing for the Emancipated Male." Purses are becoming a common men's accessory in the Village.

So today the heterosexual with traditional sex-role values is increasingly torn between those values and his liberalism. One of the most important personal and intellectual issues in his life is the widespread sexual malaise and crisis in sex role that has existed since the twenties. He is disturbed not only by the new public influence of homosexuality, but by the way homosexual values and tastes are less and less distinguishable from those of society at large.

Some of his confusion arises from the fact that the sexual revolution is spoken of as a settled fact, which is far from true. The sexual revolution is, in fact, the great aborted revolution of the West. From teenagers to middle-aged divorcees to retired widows and widowers, sexual behavior and role behavior remain troubling and subject to conflicting standards. We still ask uneasily, "What should I be like in order to be a normal, happy man or woman?" Whether or not homosexuality is really more common, it seems likely that for each such major sexual casualty, there are many more marginal ones who suffer less obvious or acute disturbances in sex behavior and sex roles—unassertive men, unresponsive and sexually competitive women, people unable to free sensuality and affection at the same time in order to create a rewarding love life. The sexual revolution is hardly even half won when our books, magazines, newspapers and personal lives are full of discussions of the same behavior and role problems as forty years ago. It makes homosexuality seem only the most dramatic symptom of a mounting state of sexual confusion, in which principles and expectations of freedom have far exceeded most people's ability to live freely.

All this shows in the continuing debate over female orgasm; over passive men and controlling women; the continuing conflict of women trying to be wives, mothers, lovers and workers at once; a persistently high rate of divorce; increased problems of psychosexual identity in the dissident youth culture; shifting yet still uncertain views on virginity, affection, and promiscuity; radical attacks on old feminine patterns; popular models of masculinity that fail old tests, such as the "frankly beautiful young man" of women's magazines and the nonaggressive, long-haired males of the young cultural left. And, most clearly, the fact that after a half century of psychiatry, mass education and apparently shriveling inhibitions, the amount of secret sexual doubt and suffering seems hardly less today than a half century ago, as any psychotherapist or marriage counselor knows.

Some people try to deny this with fake sophistication; they insist the revolution is all over. As in another emotion-laden revolution, the black man's fight for equality, the smug cant of progress lets people evade deep, difficult change. *Redbook* had Max Lerner analyze college girls' views on premarital sex, and *Newsweek* ran interview features on the subject—both asking the same questions and getting much the same answers as four decades ago. The brag of a new freedom covers an old bewilderment and fear.

One reason for the widespread and premature optimism about sexual revolution is that much youthful rhetoric is taken at face value. A mere fifteen years ago, the people then still called Bohemians felt that free premarital and perhaps extramarital sex were the goals of a battle for a sane, rewarding sex life. Their hip counterparts today consider the issue passé. They speak with lofty pity of their elders' inhibitions and naïveté. They say they fear neither heterosexual nor homosexual experience; and associated with long hair for boys, baggy clothes for girls, a search for heightened experience through hallucinogens, is a call for the breakdown of old sex roles. But in fact there is often a heartbreaking gap between what they preach and what they do. A psychiatrist who treats hippies and flower children on New York's Lower East Side says, "Lots are shacked up, but in sibling relationships. They want love, and downgrade sex. They tend to be passive and dependent. Sex without love is a problem, but love without sex is no improvement." A Philadelphia clinical psychologist says, "They come in my office wearing beads, old dresses and soldier coats, with beautiful façades of love and freedom. They verbalize well, but they don't know how to live or love. Even the girls with lots of experience usually have no capacity for pleasure."

The over-all picture is one of a society more aware than ever of its dissatisfactions, but unable to find new satisfying patterns. On our bookshelves stand Mead, Kinsey, Masters and Johnson, de Beauvoir, Freud, Brown—and for each of these there are ten superficial popularizers, such as Helen Gurley Brown, Betty Friedan, Myron Brenton and Jess Stearn. A new book appears, and people rush to read, compare their lives to the books and rate themselves. For it is to sex that we turn for salvation today. It is our religion, our Golden Land—for many, a purgatory where one waits for failure or bliss, hoping that the time to love has not been, will not be, spent loving badly, the ultimate waste of life.

Sex is the touchstone by which we define and judge ourselves. In the Middle Ages a man was seen as first of all a religious being. To sum up a person's character, one might say, "He's a good Christian" or "He just confesses to be free to sin again." In the nineteenth century man was defined economically; the phrases "typical bourgeois" and "real proletarian" were supposed to express a person's basic characteristics. Today it is sex that defines, gives the essence of a personality. When we say, "She's a castrating woman" or "He's a Don Juan trying to prove his masculinity," we feel we have exposed the mainspring of a person's life.

Therefore we believe that if we straighten out our sex lives—sex acts, sex role, love relationships—the good life will follow as a matter of course. Conversely, we feel that failure in these things means a failed life. Even those who decry the "cult of sex" often analyze character and relationships in terms of sex and sex role, and see one's love life as the test of one's virtue and wisdom. To them, too, health and happiness mean freedom and serenity in one's manhood and womanhood.

While individuals in private, and journalists in print, thrash in a vast welter of conflicting information, events and values, men in many scientific fields have been producing new information on human sexuality, in fact a new perspective on it. Even most people who consider themselves knowl-edgeable and open about such things are quite ignorant of it. Some of the most important work has been in research on homosexuality, for this sub-ject touches the basic issues about sex: definitions of abnormal masculinity, femininity and sex-love relationships all implicitly bear definitions of the normal. Homosexuality is not only important as a phenomenon in itself, but raises pressing questions about the nature of man, from sex, love, marriage and child-rearing to mores, laws and civil restraint. The purpose of this book is to bring together the two sexual revolutions, social and scientific, by focusing on homosexuality as a case in point.

PART ONE

1

The Myth of the Patriarchs

The keystone of the homosexual's defense of homosexuality is historical.
To himself, to the straight world, to the psychiatrist, he argues: "Freud had
to teach the West what it had once known but then forgot—that man is
naturally bisexual. Homosexuality was practiced by the ancient Babylonians and Egyptians, the first civilized men. Among the Greeks it was not
only accepted as a natural expression of the sexual instinct but praised as
being even more genuine and tender than heterosexual love. The Romans
practiced it widely and openly. Among the famous homosexuals and bisexuals of the ancient world were Socrates, Plato, Sappho, Pindar, Alexander
the Great, Virgil, Catullus, Julius Caesar . . . the list is pages long. Homosexuality has existed in all places and times, and the periods of greatest
artistic and cultural vitality have been those when men could exercise their
natural bisexuality freely. No puritanical society, vengeful toward homosexuality, could have produced the great men of the Italian Renaissance and
Elizabethan England—the great princes and generals and popes, Da Vinci
and Michelangelo, Marlowe and Shakespeare. Since then, Frederick the
Great, Goethe, Beethoven, Tchaikovsky, Verlaine, Wilde, Gide, Whitman,
Hart Crane, Maugham. . . ."

The case can be condensed or expanded like an accordion, from a paragraph to a long volume. At its most artful and reasoned, it is Gide's *Corydon*; at its most silly and crude, such books as Plummer's *Queer People*.
The liberal heterosexual may agree with several of the points but want to
reject or qualify the conclusion. He has probably read Freud second-hand
and believes man is naturally bisexual; he probably agrees that artistic,
intellectual and social vitality are greatest at times of unfettered self-
expression, in sex as in ideas, art and politics. Furthermore, one of his most
deeply held values is sexual freedom; he wants legal and social liberty to
sleep with whom he chooses, without shame, secrecy or penalties, to have
the right to practice birth control and divorce; he believes in sexual equality and perhaps in the arbitrariness of monogamy and marital fidelity. It
seems likely that such freedoms will come only with general sexual permissiveness, so he must stand for freedom for homosexuals and other deviants
if he is to have it himself. Still, beneath all these intellectual opinions he

3

may have a basic belief that homosexuality is in some way pathological; given a choice, he would much prefer to be heterosexual, and not just for the sake of convenience.

If he is ferociously consistent, he ends up in a wonderland of sexual values that makes his own seem inverted. If our strictures against homosexuality are just the prejudice of a restrictive society, then homosexuality isn't properly an offense, a neurosis or even a nuisance; it is a natural impulse every man should express. It means, in fact, that the homosexual is right in saying that the exclusive heterosexual unhealthily denies his nature; that just as whites, not Negroes, make of color a "race problem," so it is only the defensive fear of militant heterosexuals that creates a "homosexual problem." It means that heterosexuality is a damaging, repressive myth.

Even if the homosexual's view of history did not have to be dealt with, one would still have to look to the past for information on the nature of heterosexuality and homosexuality. Social and biological sciences agree that human sexual behavior is very plastic and follows the path of a sex role learned from society, largely through the agency of the family. The so-called "third sex" has a role, just as the others do, and it has changed with them through history in some ways, and remained significantly constant in others. And if it is true that homosexuality is, contrary to homosexual apologetics, a reaction against heterosexual roles, it can only be understood in juxtaposition with them.

Take, for instance, the homosexual style—walk, mannerisms, tastes, banter—we call effeminate. It is sometimes said that "effeminacy" is an imitation or parody of femininity, but most homosexuals identify strongly as males—as homosexual men, but still as men, not as women. No woman walks with limp wrists, mincing, gliding, wagging her bottom, drawling and squealing. If imitation were intended, it could be done more accurately; if parody, more pointedly. An actor imitating or parodying a woman would do so very differently. If we can understand this homosexual style and its relation to heterosexual style, we will know a great deal about both. How alike in dress, walk, emotional character are the homosexuals of New York today, Victorian London, Renaissance Florence, medieval Provence, Nero's Rome and an ancient Canaanite settlement? Did the poet Agathon, whom Aristophanes loved to mock, walk and talk and make love like a Negro queen in New Orleans today? This has the same importance as would knowing, in the study of female sexuality, whether women of those times and places were more or less assertive than today, did or didn't expect and experience orgasm, felt emotionally deprived or content.

It is generally agreed now that sex role and sex behavior are formed by the joint influences of biology, family and society; to grasp any one period we must know not only its sexual behavior but its family structure, mores, child-rearing methods—a whole constellation of social, moral, religious and scientific attitudes. Otherwise we are collecting anecdotes, not evidence. Unfortunately, such a history must begin with reservations and proceed with carping. Despite all the entertaining books that pretend otherwise, man's sexual history is known only in tantalizing scraps and tatters. Few documents survive, and only despite every attempt of zealots to destroy them through burning, censorship and falsification. Sex and its regulation are so basic to man and his society that deviation has often been equated with heresy and treason, from the ancient Hebrews to Senator McCarthy. Deviants—from whatever norm—have often been persecuted and murdered, their literature and defense brief destroyed with them. The testimony of the accusers can rarely be trusted.

In milder times, internal self-censorship has usually been enough to divert study from sex; one simply didn't give one's time, reputation and career to such things. This is still largely true. Our knowledge would be immensely greater if fifty years ago and even now scholars felt there was as much to learn from the forms of man's sexuality as from the forms of his economy; or if they would give to sex the time and energy devoted to such topics as the fluctuation of cotton prices during the War of 1812. Those with the scholarly ability to study sexual history effectively have usually shunned it, leaving it to the irresponsible, inept or partisan.

Besides, our questions and standards of evidence are now very different than in the past. Sex is too secret, emotion-laden an issue for us to accept any but hard, dispassionate evidence. If we apply the same rigorous historical tests to documents on the history of sex as we do in other areas of history, our body of knowledge is much smaller than most people think. The Kinsey reports proved that one man's guess about sexual behavior is as good as another's until broad, objective studies are made. Every scientist, journalist and common citizen knew all about American sex behavior— until the Kinsey reports left no one unsurprised in some way. If we know so little about our own society, we know a thousand times less about the past. We can only make cautious inferences from snatches of literature and chronicle, as one would from the scattered patches of an almost obliterated fresco. While doing so, it is good to bear in mind the picture of our society that would emerge if posterity dug up from the ruins of a bombed city only *The Scarlet Letter* and *Sanctuary* or the poems of Emily Dickinson and Genet's *The Balcony*.

Most writers have guessed, filled in, clung to any theory that will liven and fatten a book. To their advantage, the facts are so scanty that with careful selection and handling they can be made to prove almost anything. More scholarly hobby horses than deserve to be named have been driven over these fields. Some are still racing on, remounted again and again by writers on sex, love and the family. The liveliest is still the theory of the Great Mother (or White Goddess, to Robert Graves), a collective name for the fertility goddesses of the ancient Mediterranean and Near East.

The eastern end of the Mediterranean in the millennium before the great period of Greco-Roman civilization is the earliest time and place about which we have any sexual information. The reliable facts on the original, preclassical cults are very thin. Most of our information comes from accounts written third-hand, by hostile or foreign observers, or many centuries later, after the cults may have undergone changes. With confidence we can say this: for centuries or even millennia before the Greeks, many peoples from the eastern Mediterranean to Sumeria worshiped a goddess whose rites included both heterosexual and homosexual intercourse. The goddess was known as Artemis in Ephesus, Aphrodite in Corinth, Astarte in Phoenicia, Ishtar in Babylon, Isis in Egypt, Atargatis in Canaan, Anaitis in Persia, Rhea in Crete, Cybele in Phrygia, Bendis in Thrace, and in Cappadocia, in what is now Turkey, just plain Mā. Beyond this, few single details are certain, but the mass of stories have enough similarities to enable us to add some more strokes to the picture.

Herodotus, writing of the temple of Mylitta, said, "The Babylonians have one most shameful custom. Every woman born in the country must once in her life go and sit down in the precinct of Venus, and there consort with a stranger." Herodotus is a typical source on the Great Mother— credulous, uncritical, a magpie of gossip and sensational anecdote, and then, suddenly, quite reliable. But similar stories are told by Strabo, Athenaeus, Lucian and Church fathers about their own and earlier times. They variously said that in some places women sacrificed their virginity to the goddess in the temple, to a priest or any stranger. That the money people paid for the service was dedicated to the deity. That in ancient Armenia, Cyprus and Lydia the money went to the girl, and she might spend a long period as a prostitute in the temple accumulating her dowry. That such practices were known in the worship of Isis in Egypt. That such practices were *not* known in Egypt. That in some places there were both priests and priestesses. That the priests might be eunuchs, transvestites or both. That priests or hieroduli (literally, servants of the goddess)—"male temple prostitutes"—existed among the devotees of Ishtar and Astarte in Syria, the Albanians and Babylonians, the Canaanite neighbors of the ancient Hebrews, and in Cos, Crete and Ephesus in the Greek world. That such men performed sexual acts with other men, and perhaps also with women, as the female temple prostitutes did.

There are a lot of or's and perhaps's. We can never put ourselves in the minds of the ancient Babylonians, but if we accept parallels from non-Western cultures—and many have ritual intercourse and eunuch or transvestite priests—it is likely that although the religion provided an outlet for homosexuality, the temple practices were at least as much holy as hedonistic. Christianity, Judaism and Islam, the religions close to our understanding, separate the body and worship, physical and spiritual love; but sex as worship is not rare in the world. Just as the Catholic, when he takes the Host, is united with God through the medium of the priest, the worshiper of the Great Mother may have united himself with the deity by joining his body to that of the priest, the goddess' vessel. The act may have been seen as a magical invocation of her fecundity or as a re-enactment of her impregnation, to insure the fertility of the individual, tribe, crops and flocks. Gordon Rattray Taylor writes in *Sex in History*: "When men visited the temple to perform ritual intercourse with the deity, if the hierodule was biologically male, the intercourse was technically homosexual. Some historians have described this practice as homosexual prostitution—a doubly misleading description, as the attitudes involved were appropriate neither to homosexuality nor to prostitution."

However, it is equally true that sodomy could hardly exist as a religious rite if most people found it as repugnant as most of the West does today. The eminent scholar Raphael Patai deduces that there was actually little distinction between profane and sacred prostitution. There are many important facts we do not know. How often did worshipers go to the temple for intercourse? Was there a choice between priest and priestess? Did all or only a few have homosexual relations there? Was ritual sodomy mutual, or did only one partner take the role of penetrator? What emotions were experienced during the act by both parties? Were any distinctions made between homosexual and heterosexual intercourse in the temple? Outside the temple? About these things, and about day-to-day sex life and attitudes, we know nothing.

Of all the fragmentary chapters of our sexual history, this earliest one is among the most fascinating and frustrating. It is also one of the most important, for one can already see in it much that still remains in Western sexuality. The Great Mother cults will disillusion those who think of mother-worship and paganism as carefree celebrations of the flesh. The myths of the Great Mother say that she gave grain, love and fruitfulness, but also that she seduced or held in thrall a male who was variously her husband, son or lover, whom she castrated and killed (in some versions he was nailed to a tree), and who was then reborn. The tales reflect a phobic attitude toward the female, terror of her power to sexually pollute man, to maim and destroy him. This feeling was so strong among the mother-worshiping peoples that the extreme solution of self-castration existed, and may not even have been rare. Celibacy, which can be seen as functional castration, was associated with some of the Great Mother cults in Roman times and may have been practiced earlier. Homosexuality and transvestism, which are other answers to the threat of the sexual female, were also widespread among these cultists. When Latin poets retold the myths of the Great Mother, they made it clear that she saw desexing oneself as a step toward grace. The idea that sex sullies the soul, making it unfit for religious perfection, went from these cults into Christianity, along with castration and celibacy, horror of woman as a destroying temptress, and worship of a holy mother and her asexual son who died nailed to a cross and was reborn.

The Great Mother has become a historical specialty in herself. One can spend years wandering through the historical, archeological and linguistic tangles of her province, where fanatical pedants have planted as many exot-

ica as Sartre did in the land of Saint Genet. The study of the Great Mother
led to a theory of patriarchal and matriarchal societies that is still held by
some psychiatrists, journalists and historians. It began a century ago with a
Swiss scholar named Bachofen, who on the basis of sketchy anthropological and historical evidence decided that all societies pass through a series of
stages according to an evolutionary formula. Man's earliest state, he said,
was one of sexual promiscuity and common ownership of property; since
man's role in reproduction was not understood, woman was regarded as the
great life-giver, splendidly wrapped in veneration; then society was
matriarchal, and the great supernatural power was seen as a female. Eventually, though, man realized his paternal importance, his power of continuing himself through his descendants. He usurped woman's glory and
power. Woman was downgraded, and private property developed along
with the customs of descent and inheritance through the male. The female
became merely a vessel, a chattel, an instrument of the male in a man's
world. The Great Mother gave way to a Great Father.

The idea of a matriarchal utopia of the past appealed to many people,
especially feminists and socialists seeking the source of women's and workers' sorrows. Engels called the arrival of the patriarchal stage of civilization
"the great historical defeat of the feminine sex." Writers tried to explain
sex, economics, religion and most of the rest of human history through the
ascendancy at various periods of matriarchal or patriarchal characteristics.
Patriarchal cultures worshiped a male god and were authoritarian, puritanical, compulsive-obsessive, believing in reason over sensuality and instinct.
Matriarchal, mother-worshiping cultures were permissive, expressive, close
to nature and the irrational. To some, such as Robert Graves, the ancient
matriarchy was the time of noble savagery; the decline of the West into an
age of mass production, antibiotics and indoor plumbing began with the
ascendancy of the father. Simone de Beauvoir, in *The Second Sex*, rejects
some of the theory, keeps some, and adds similar pseudo-anthropology of
her own. Gordon Rattray Taylor, one of the more imaginative historians of
sex, has created a "matrist-patrist" theory of Western history, a psychological elaboration of the "matriarchal-patriarchal" tradition of interpretation.

Robert Briffault was the last social thinker to take Bachofen's theory
seriously, with his book *The Mothers* in 1927. Scientific anthropology and
critical history reduced every aspect of it to rubble by the mid-thirties. It is
a metaphysical system built about a period of which we know so little that
it can never be proved right or wrong. However, one of the best pieces of
evidence against it is the fact that no matriarchal society has ever been discovered anywhere in the world. Still, the idea appeals to the feminist, to the
backward-looking utopian, to the mystical historian, to people looking for
neat dualistic schemes of history. Many self-styled archeologists, historians
and experts on sex still try to force new evidence into its creaking framework, and rummagers in history from other fields—for instance, psychia-

trists writing on homosexuality and attempting to sketch its history—
sometimes borrow the theory entire.

The turning point of Western history, according to the theory's advocates, was the dominance of the patriarchal ancient Hebrews over the earlier mother-worshipers of the Near East. Actually, references to homosexuality in the Old Testament range from scanty to ambiguous. One of the earliest gives us the word sodomy:

> But before they lay down, the men of the city, the men of Sodom, both
> young and old, all the people . . . surrounded the house; and they called to
> Lot, "Where are the men who came to you tonight? Bring them out to us,
> that we may know them."
>
> Genesis 19

The name of the city survives in the word sodomy, as synonymous with
anal intercourse and, loosely, with homosexuality. But where the King
James version of the Bible says, "Sodomite," the original Hebrew says
kedeshim, which the New Revised version translates more accurately as
"male cultic prostitute"—one of the eunuch, transvestite or homosexual
servants of the Great Mother. The word "harlot" in the King James version
is sometimes a rendering of the feminine form of the same word, and
should more properly be translated as "priestess of the Great Mother" or
"temple prostitute." The Revised version renders Deuteronomy this way:

> A woman shall not wear anything that pertains to a man, nor shall a man
> put on a woman's garment; for whoever does these things is an abomination
> to the Lord your God. . . . There shall be no cult prostitute of the daughters
> of Israel, neither shall there be a cult prostitute of the sons of Israel. You
> shall not bring the hire of a harlot or the wages of a dog into the house of the
> Lord your God in payment of any vow.
>
> Deuteronomy 22, 23

It has been guessed that "dog" in this context is a term of contempt for
male cult prostitutes. The passage certainly seems a prohibition of sexual
worship of the kind practiced by followers of the Great Mother. The chronicles of the Kings of Israel say:

> . . . they also built for themselves high places and pillars, and Asherim
> [phallic poles used to honor the goddess of fertility] on every high hill and
> under every green tree; and there were also male cult prostitutes in the land.
>
> I Kings 14

> And Asa did what was right in the eyes of the Lord, as David his father had
> done. He put away the male cult prostitutes out of the land. . . .
>
> I Kings 15

> Now the rest of the acts of Johosaphat . . . the remnant of the male cult
> prostitutes who remained in the days of his father Asa, he exterminated from
> the land.
>
> I Kings 22

Josiah, King of Judah, "broke down the houses of the male cult prostitutes which were in the house of the Lord" (2 Kings 23). The prophet Hoseah complained that "the men themselves go aside with harlots and sacrifice with cult prostitutes" (Hoseah 4).

But back in Leviticus, in what may be the most ancient shalt-nots of the Hebrews, although homosexuality is among the crimes punishable by death, there is no reference to cult prostitutes, only a vague one to the crimes of peoples less favored by God—which to the Hebrews meant everyone.

> If a man lies with a man as with a woman, both of them have committed an abomination; they shall be put to death, their blood is upon them.
> Leviticus 20

> You shall not lie with a male as with a woman; it is an abomination. . . . Do not defile yourselves by any of these things, for by all these the nations I am casting out before you defiled themselves. . . .
> Leviticus 18

The sure facts are that the Jews had a long-standing and strict prohibition against both male and female homosexuality, which they associated at later dates, but not necessarily at first, with worshipers of the Great Mother. Nevertheless, there was enough cultic and perhaps plain secular homosexuality among them to make necessary periodic cleansings of temple and town. Homosexuality came to be equated with ungodliness, heresy and moral subversion by neighboring enemies—shades of the homosexual security risk who would betray us to godless Communism! The partisans of the matriarchal-patriarchal theory say that the early Hebrews were sexually permissive mother-worshipers and that their indignant attitude toward homosexuality dates from their change to worshiping the authoritarian, male Jahweh. Others say that when the Jews became monotheistic, they turned against homosexuality precisely because it was associated with matriarchal polytheism.

It is difficult to believe that a value as deep as the approval or disapproval of homosexuality could change on political grounds. It could, however, be put to political use if it already existed. Did the Old Testament bans represent nationalistic propaganda of priests, scribes and chiefs, aimed at mother-worshiping political enemies, or did it just reflect popular sentiment? Did the Jews themselves once worship a Great Mother, then change, and in changing reverse their attitude toward homosexuality? For that matter, not all mother-worshipers practiced cultic or noncultic homosexuality. The cult of the male Baal, at least in Roman times, had homosexual and eunuch priests and worshiped before *asherim*. It could even be that the Jews were originally mother-worshipers, yet never condoned homosexuality. Were those biblical homosexuals—mysteriously tolerated and persecuted in turn, so that they had to be driven out again and again—Jews who worshiped non-Jewish gods or were they enclaves of non-Jews in Jewish settlements?

The relationship between law and daily life is always a touchy historical problem. If archeologists of a distant time ever dig up the laws of the United States, they may assume that the people of many states made love only in "missionary position" (or prone-supine, as textbooks call it), since any other technique could send even a married couple to jail for years. England allows a sentence of life imprisonment for sodomy with a youth; if future times assume this prevented it from happening, or that most offenders were caught, innumerable British buggerers know better today. What the ancient Hebrews proscribed and what they practiced may have been very different.

With the Hebrews, as with the ancient mother-worshipers, we end on questions, not answers—unless one accepts the matriarchal-patriarchal theory, which still gives handy theoretical reassurance to many. In 1966 Dr. Robert Ollendorff, a psychiatrist, began his book *The Juvenile Homosexual Experience* with: "That the earliest recording of history coincides with that of homosexuality is no mere coincidence. Both are the products of a patriarchal society." Rattray Taylor says categorically, "In societies that conceive of their deities as mother-figures, incest is regarded as the overwhelming danger and is hedged with taboos, whereas homosexuality has little importance. Conversely, in societies that conceive of their deities as father-figures, homosexuality is regarded as the overwhelming danger and is surrounded with taboos and condemnation." If this matriarchal-patriarchal theory distorts the historical picture of sexual behavior, it utterly garbles the contemporary scene. But it continues to have appeal because of its dramatic and orderly dualism. Fortunately, life is more confusing, disorderly and exciting than such intellectual double-column book-keeping. Human behavior follows laws to a large extent, but it is also creative, always a little new and different, its solutions to life as many as men.

2

The Greek Revision

When an age writes history, it paints its self-portrait. By selecting and interpreting evidence it reveals its own obsessions and creates a mythology that justifies them. The Middle Ages, for instance, have been made a paragon of every sort to succeeding times. The Augustans considered them a black pit of barbarism; nineteenth-century earth-and-folk utopians portrayed them a serene arts-and-crafts colony; Romantic Decadents made them thrillingly brutal and erotically perverse, admirably preserving paganism in the form of witchcraft.

Ancient Greece, though, has remained unchanged in the West's imagination for centuries. Since the early Renaissance, it has stood for spiritual daring, intellectual excellence, esthetic and erotic genius, for discipline and abandon mixed with strict sensual perfection. Since it was the world's most gifted civilization, what it did must be right: one had only to explain why. Fortunately, recent historians have portrayed Greece as more than a gaggle of bearded sages in white drapes wandering among white columns and talking wisdom—when they were not making rapturous love to women and boys alike. The reason for Europe's veneration, perhaps, was that Greece seemed to combine all the desirable opposites between which Christianity forced choices—virility and sensitivity, action and contemplation, spiritual refinement and sexual impulsiveness, moral discernment and unashamed love of the body. Many who find homosexuality disgusting forgive it in the Great Pagans. Many who call it a sickness feel that in Greece it managed to be a sign of joyful sexual exuberance. It is the strongest item in homosexual apologetics, and one to which many heterosexuals accede, theoretically admitting that we would be better off today if we were like that. Kinsey accepted the traditional view of Greek sexuality, in his chapter on homosexuality in *Sexual Behavior in the Human Male*, and many otherwise knowledgeable sexologists continue to do so today.

But one can no more talk inclusively about the Greeks than about the Christians. They were of many traditions and cultures, and underwent frequent, dramatic changes through their long history. We first know the Greeks as the Mycenaeans of about 1200 B.C., whom Homer described several centuries afterward—a very different people from the Peripatetics of homosexual apology. Technologically the Mycenaeans were on a level with the Incas and Aztecs the Conquistadors encountered—if anything, perhaps a bit lower. After a few minutes in their midst, any of us would categorize them as savages. They had not performed the psychological leap that would make them closer to us than to the non-Western primitives of today. The Homeric Greek projected his feelings outside himself. He saw not only danger and good luck as the work of gods, but also his own anger, sexuality and creativity. It was not he who was irrational, but the gods he had formed in the image of his own fears and impulses. Ethics in the modern sense did not exist for him. He was ruled not by conscience, or internalized guilt, but by shame, the praise and scorn of his tribe. What was good was what won wealth, success, victory and praise in his neighbors' eyes; the best man was the most powerful and honored. A schemer and betrayer like Odysseus was a good man, for his schemes and betrayals worked. In the same ruthlessly pragmatic view, what was bad was what failed.

The *Iliad* and *Odyssey,* like the Bible, are not sociological documents. The author was retelling in legendary form the events of a long-past war, not describing the contemporary life of ordinary people in ordinary circumstances. Guessing at Mycenaean life and attitudes from Homer is like trying to reconstruct an eleventh-century Tuscan town from *The Divine Comedy.* But Homer did tell what people of his time thought their great forebears were, ideally, likely to feel and do.

Homer's women were underprivileged by our standards, but perhaps not much better or worse off than those of an Italian village today. They lived separate lives from men, under strong male authority, and men, at least powerful ones, might openly keep concubines. But women were often respected, and in practice somewhat independent; they had some freedom of movement and perhaps strong domestic and personal influence. Fidelity was expected but could not be counted on; wifely adultery was a subject of frequent comment.

When Agamemnon said he preferred his mistress to his wife for her understanding and skill as well as her beauty, he was hardly talking about mere chattel; he was describing a human being whose virtues he had come to prize in intimacy. There was often devotion, tenderness and perhaps even companionship between spouses or lovers. Hector and Andromache were justifiably used as an example of a deeply loving and mutually respectful couple. When Hector is preparing to leave for battle, Andromache makes a speech that with change of idiom could go into a contemporary film, spoken by a wife to a husband going off to the front. "When I lose you I might as well be dead. There will be no comfort left, when you have met your doom—nothing but grief. . . . You, Hector, are father and brother and mother to me, as well as my beloved husband." Between her and Hector there was not merely the obligation of a social contract or the force of erotic passion, but also devoted friendship. Marriage was a reward as much as a duty. Ulysses, wishing Nausicaa a happy marriage, told her: "There is nothing better or more precious than the perfect sympathy between husband and wife at the domestic hearth. In it the jealous are confounded, the friends of the family delighted and the couple themselves at the pinnacle of happiness." When the beautiful goddess Calypso tempted Ulysses to stay with her on her island, he answered, "Revered goddess, hear me and pardon. I know well that prudent as Penelope may be, compared with you she is neither great nor fair. She is but mortal, and you will never age nor die. . . . And yet the only desire I have each day is to come again into my own, to see the hour, in my own house, of my return."

Homer makes clear that friendship was as much or more to be expected between comrades in arms, such as Achilles and Patroclus, than between men and women. But he did not discount women as loving companions. And nowhere in his work is there a mention of homosexuality. If there was any among the Mycenaeans, he ignored it. Alleged "homosexual sentiment" and "latent homosexuality" are like witches and subversives; one who believes in them makes them appear through his self-fulfilling prophecy. We will examine the concept of latency later; for the moment, let us note that everyone has homicidal impulses, but the person who acts out such impulses is importantly different from those who do not. Or, as psychiatrist Stanley Willis wrote in his book on homosexuality, "To categorize behavior as homosexual unless that behavior is specifically directed toward achieving orgasm is to obscure an ultimate understanding of the problem. Many homoerotic activities, in the sense of love and affection toward the same sex, are not directed toward orgasm, and many homophilic activities, in the sense of attraction by members of the same sex, have neither homoerotic nor homosexual components." None of the Homeric heroes went to bed together or seemed to want to. That was only suggested centuries after Homer, when Classical Greece rewrote its past.

The Mycenaeans had entered Greece around 2000 B.C. They were at the height of their power, prosperity and refinement when the siege of Troy took place. Their little empire soon tottered, and Dorian invaders came, conquering and displacing them. The Dorians may have had the use of iron for their weapons, against the Mycenaeans' bronze, but generally their culture was probably lower. Their supremacy began what is called ancient Greece's dark age. One should be careful about dark ages; they often reflect the ignorance not of the times but of later historians. Almost no records exist of Greek life between the twelfth and seventh centuries B.C. It is assumed from later records of Sparta and other cities apparently of Dorian stock that the Dorians were culturally limited but rigidly disciplined, their society structured to produce a tough military elite that institutionalized homosexuality for the first time in Greece.

The record resumes in bits and pieces around the end of the eighth century B.C. Homer, who expressed the devotion of Hector and Andromache, Ulysses and Penelope, was now followed by such misogynist poets as

Hesiod. His *Works and Days* show women as vain, extravagant and burdensome. Another of his poems told the story of Pandora, whose amorality and foolishness were designed by the gods to let loose everlasting pain in a once happy world:

> As the price of fire I will give men an
>   evil, and all men shall fondle
> this, their evil, close to their hearts. . . .
> Aphrodite was to mist her head
>   in golden endearment
> and the cruelty of desire and longings
>   that wear out the body,
> but to Hermes, the slayer of Argos,
>   he gave instructions
> to put in her the mind of a hussy,
>   and a treacherous nature . . .
> lies, and wheedling words,
>   of falsehood . . . and gave her
>   the name of woman,
> Pandora, because all the gods
>   who have their homes on Olympus
> had given her each a gift, to be a sorrow
>   to men who eat bread. . . .

Between Homer's day and Hesiod's, the Greeks' almost religious regard for the bond of comradeship had grown stronger, but now woman was thought an inferior being, incapable of such fine feelings. She had become a slave—mistrusted, feared and despised like all slaves. In Sparta and some other Dorian settlements, women had some freedom of movement; however, the upper-class woman of Athens lived confined to the women's quarters of her home, enjoined to be silent, industrious, asexual and stupid. Pericles said, "The woman who goes out of her home ought to be in that time of life when men ask not, Whose wife is she? but, Whose mother is she?"

At seven an Athenian boy started to go to school, later to the gymnasium. At seventeen or eighteen he became an *ephebus*, a young citizen, and spent even more time away from home than before—in conversation, physical training, business, public affairs and amusement. When he married, it was an arranged match with a young girl who passed from the women's quarters of her father's house to those of her husband. She always remained under the authority of her father, never becoming part of her husband's family in our sense. Sequestered from ideas and men, prepared to accede to demands, not express her own, she had learned only to run a household, perhaps also to write a little. Her currents of will, intellect and sexuality had been subverted from birth. Her husband, back from a day of male gossip, amateur philosophizing, political debate, could hardly have found her sparkling in conversation or in bed, or even thought of discussing with her his interests and activities. A wife was a necessary social evil, demanded by society and the state for producing heirs and citizens. (So distasteful was marriage to some men that in the sixth century B.C. the legislator Solon suggested, and may have had passed, a law making it compulsory.) The poet Palladas wrote:

> Marriage brings a man only two happy days:
> The day he takes his bride to bed, and the day he lays
>   her in her grave.

Euripides was only one of many Greek poets who bristled with misogyny. The tragic poet Carcinus said, "Oh Zeus, what need is there to abuse women? It would be enough if you only said the word 'woman.'"

Like most people in the Mediterranean world today, the ancient Greeks saw woman much as the southern white has traditionally viewed the Negro—inferior in intelligence and spirit. Bitter, contemptuous and phobic misogyny runs through every aspect of Greek culture; the lack of information on households, marriage and women's lives shows how little they were valued. Men married as late as they could and found their pleasures elsewhere. A wife could be the object of approval, but only that. For infatuation one turned to whores or boys, and for friendship to men. Demosthenes said: "Mistresses we keep for pleasure, concubines for daily attendance upon our persons, and wives to bear us legitimate children and be our housekeepers." He omitted boys, but many Greek men of his class did not.

Anyone who has been in modern Greece and glimpsed beneath the thin façade of twentieth-century Europeanization has seen a sexual life possibly not very different from that of Demosthenes' Athens. Throughout childhood, Greek boys are pampered, girls taught to obey, serve and suffer in silence. The father spends his spare time with other men in cafes; society is a male club, and there all true companionship lies. Women live separate, sequestered lives. Girls' virginity is carefully protected, and the majority of homicides are committed over the "honor" of daughters and sisters. In some Greek villages a woman does not leave her home unaccompanied by a relative between puberty and old age. Women walk the street, even in Athens, with their eyes down; a woman who looks up when a man speaks to her is, quite simply, a whore. The young male goes to prostitutes and may carry on homosexual connections; it is not unusual for him to marry at thirty having had no sexual experience save with prostitutes and male friends.* When he does marry, it is in an arranged match, with a dowry. During his engagement, the upper- and middle-class Greek complains bitterly about Greek women. "They're cows. They're mercenary. You can't talk to them about anything, all they do is gabble and gossip and try to make profitable

---

*One enlightened urban family I knew in Greece was delighted that their son had found a pretty and charming young woman to live with him and relieve his loneliness while he was in the army. They treated the girl with kindly hospitality. When the two young people decided to marry, the parents were furious and scandalized, for the bride-to-be was not a virgin.

matches." Yet if the girl is in any way assertive, he is resentful, shocked and disapproving. He says only foreign women are worthwhile, for they can talk interestingly and make love with pleasure instead of shame. But he still truly thinks that any woman who would do so is a whore, so in the end he marries the virtuous, boring Greek girl he despises. Even after marriage, he will think of her as a whore if she is sexually responsive, and any sign of personal independence will be seen as insubordination. He will continue to chase foreign women, go to prostitutes, keep a mistress of a lower social class, perhaps have sporadic affairs with younger males. No woman can win all his approval, for her functions have been split; sex and affection are irrevocably separated for him.

His wife, of course, has grown up in the same culture, and her attitudes are a mirror image of his. She has been badly prepared to win his intellectual and erotic interest. Despairing of a full relationship with a man, she simply tries to make the most comfortable and successful arrangement she can. Her only weapons against her authoritarian husband are nagging, acquisitiveness, hypochondria, hysteria and religion, to which she turns for comfort. Her only emotional outlet is her children, especially her sons, whom she pampers and "protects" from the father. All this makes her even less attractive to the man, so the separation of the sexes is constantly reinforced on both sides.

The male, then, suffers, the classic "mama's boy" syndrome of the Latin Lover, a conflicting desire for maternal pampering, feminine submission, chastity and libidinousness. A psychologist might explain it as arising from his dependent, incestuously flavored relationship with his mother, and the distance and authoritarianism of his father. He denies his dependency needs with a jock-strapping, *macho* attitude that downgrades women, so that sex and deep feeling can never unite in a re-enactment of his hidden fantasy life. He never finds himself in the arms of the whore-mother of his dreams. Every woman is dangerous who may arouse in him tenderness and sexuality at once.

Some writers—for instance, Robert Flacelière in *Love in Ancient Greece* and Morton Hunt in *The Natural History of Love*—make a direct, causal relationship between the downgrading of women from Mycenaean to Classical times and the simultaneous appearance of homosexuality. To make the theory hold, one would have to show that in other times and other cultures anti-feminine feeling, as reflected in subjugation and contempt for women, is in direct proportion to homosexuality. It cannot be done. In fact, homosexuality flourished more in the ancient world as woman's position improved and her freedom increased.

Like most writers on sex, Flacelière and Hunt tend to look for a single cause of homosexuality, a decisive condition or event. They say it was the low status of women; others say it was the arrival of Dorians or Near Eastern influence; still others blame the development of a monetary, commercial and slave society. Any or all of these may have been involved, but until we can examine in depth the biological, psychological and cultural bases of homosexuality, it is best to assume that it is not a single, simple entity but a group of complex variations on a theme, with different characteristics in different times and places. It is more accurate to say that in the West, and especially around the Mediterranean, mistrust and hostility between the sexes, with the downgrading of women, has been part of the *background* of homosexuality. It has meant segregated women deprived of men's warmth; men clubbing together away from women they desired, despised and feared; an unfilled need that encouraged erotically tinged companionships within each sex; a belief in the opposite sex as a destroyer, denier and exploiter who subverts the good life the other could have had.

The first recorded homosexual voice to come from this society, and the first in the Western world, was that of Sappho of Lesbos. It was also the first recorded voice of a woman, and the first cry of romantic love. But her name and birthplace quickly became generic words for female homosexuality, not woman or love. Sappho was born around 612 B.C. in the town of Mytilene, on the island of Lesbos, off the coast of Asia Minor. The island's inhabitants were Aeolians, a people whose life had probably changed less since Mycenaean times than had that of Athenians and most other mainland Greeks. Sappho's very literacy and physical freedom of movement suggest the less repressive attitude toward women that faded with the Mycenaean era. Sappho had a circle of women about her who may have been friends, a lesbian coterie, a circle of poetic disciples—or, one nineteenth-century theory said, students at a sort of finishing school she ran for upper-class girls.

No picture of Sappho has survived that was made before her death. Some ancient writers called her "beautiful Sappho," and others said she was short, swarthy and ugly. She was possibly married, for she was the mother of a girl whom she named Kleis after her own mother. But she fell passionately in love with one woman after another. Her poems to and about them are direct and self-revealing like nothing before them in Greek literature. She was lyric, lustful, bitter, ecstatic and sulky by turns. It was she who first gave shape to the Western concept of romantic love. Hector's love for Andromache was tender and sometimes passionate, but it was not the gnawing, frenzied, self-destructive yearning of Sappho's *Seizure*:

> . . . as I look at you my voice fails,
> my tongue is broken and thin fire
> runs like a thief through my body.
> My eyes are dead to light, my ears
> pound, and sweat pours down over me.
> I shudder, I am paler than grass
> and am intimate with dying—but
> I must suffer everything, being poor.

Catullus, and later innumerable others, would imitate her frustrated, engulfing need, the demand that can be satisfied in verse as never in life.

She was jealous, tender, nostalgic, wheedling, furious, as she lay awake all night, lamenting that her body aged while her passions burned as strongly as ever. The emotional ambiance is familiar to anyone who has felt romantic love, and especially to anyone who has spent time with lesbians of a certain temperament—mercurial, tense, going from one idealized love to another with mixed sublimity, bitterness and hysterical desperation.

Sappho wrote more than five hundred poems totaling twelve thousand lines. Today we have only seven hundred lines, many isolated or forming short, barely intelligible fragments. The majority describe her love for girls, though some express love for men, celebrate marriage and address lovers whose gender is unclear. There is not one direct mention of homosexual love-making. One often-quoted poem goes:

> Then I said to the elegant ladies:
> "How you will remember when you are old
> the glorious things we did in our youth!
>
> We did many pure and beautiful things.
> Now that you are leaving the city,
> love's sharp pain encircles my heart."

This poem about "pure and beautiful things" and the lack of explicit sex made many writers claim that Sappho of Lesbos was not, except in the most "Platonic" way, a Sapphist, or lesbian. At the end of the second century B.C. Maximus of Tyre wrote: "If it is right to argue from one age to another, the Lesbian's love was nothing else but that which Socrates practiced. Both seem to me to have engaged in the same kind of friendships, she of women, he of men, and both said they could fall in love many times and all beautiful people attracted them."

The most important question is, as Maximus said, whether it is right to argue from one age to another. Sappho's life and character were hazy with legend by a short time after her death, and the only surviving sources of her work and life were written much later, when ideas about sex were different. One authority said she was "slanderously accused of being attached in a shameful love," but Horace called her "the manly Sappho," and Ovid asked, "What did Sappho teach other than how to love girls?" They may have had works of hers we don't possess, but they may also have been arguing on the basis of widespread homosexuality in their own times. A legend arose that there had actually been two Sapphos, one a poet and one a prostitute; another said that she had fallen in love with a ferryman named Phaon and hurled herself from a cliff after he spurned her.

One possibility is that Christian zealots destroyed all the poems that were directly erotic. Around A.D. 380 Saint Gregory of Nazianzus, Bishop of Constantinople, ordered her books burned wherever they were found, calling her *gynaeon pornikon erotomanes*—roughly, "lewd nymphomaniac," but without specifying whether heterosexual or homosexual. Pope Gregory VII had many of her surviving works burned in 1072. By the Renaissance about all that remained were fragmentary quotations in the essays of scholiasts. Then in the nineteenth century some of her poems were found written on papyri at Fayum and Oxyrinchus in Egypt—they had been torn into strips and used as mummy wrappings. Sentences, lines, words, broke off in the middle, and the pieces did not form a complete manuscript. Sappho's surviving work was now about 5 per cent of the original, a small but readable body of writing—and still no concrete evidence of physical homosexuality.

Writers today assume Sappho was an active homosexual just as confidently as nineteenth-century writers made her a teacher or priestess innocent of "impure" love. Both parties prove that every age finds what it wants in its past. Certainly Sappho had intense love and erotic feelings for women, and probably heterosexual inclinations and activity as well. That she was a practicing homosexual is quite likely, but not certain.

A Sappho could not have existed in much of Greece in her time, nor for centuries after; generally women had no such freedom or education. Lesbianism did exist though, and Plato explained in the speech he put in Aristophanes' mouth in the *Symposium* that lesbians appeared for the same natural reason as male homosexuals—a fact of bisexual creation. Plutarch wrote in his life of Lycurgus, "At Sparta love was held in such honor that even the most respectable women became infatuated with girls."

Opportunities for adultery must have been hard to come by for the strictly isolated Greek women. Since their husbands neglected them for whores and boys, some consoled themselves and even each other. Some used an artificial phallus, called an *olisbos*. *Olisboi* are shown in vase paintings and discussed enthusiastically in a work by Herondas in the third century B.C. In Aristophanes' *Lysistrata,* women mourn not having any more of the leather *olisboi* which the women of Miletus specialized in making and using. In the *Amores* attributed to Lucian, tribadism is discussed— female homosexuality practiced in imitation of heterosexual intercourse, one woman atop the other, with an artificial phallus or with the enlarged clitoris the lesbian was believed to possess. A homosexual and a heterosexual argue for their preferences, and the heterosexual says:

> If you concede homosexual love to men, you must in justice grant the same to women; you will have to sanction carnal intercourse between them; monstrous instruments of lust will have to be permitted, in order that their sexual congress may be carried out; that obscene term, tribade, which so rarely offends our ears—I blush to speak it—will become rampant, and Philaenis [a lesbian erotic writer whose works have been lost] will spread androgynous orgies throughout our women's quarters.

Lucian of Samosata is one of our best sources on the ancient world's sexual life. He lived in the second century A.D., when many Greeks had become urbane agnostics, citizens of the multinational Roman Empire, who could view their own and other societies from a distance. He has been compared to Swift and Voltaire, but his attitude toward every excess, from the metaphysical to the sexual, was one of amusement, not horror. If he resembles anyone else, historian Crane Brinton rightly suggests, it is Diderot. Without restraint, moral outrage, false piety or reverence for conventions, his *Dialogues of the Gods* and *Dialogues of the Courtesans* take his society over the coals. In the fifth of the *Dialogues of Courtesans,* Leaena and Clonarium discuss a woman named Megilla from Lesbos—the island's name had already become generic for female inversion. Clonarium begins, "We've been hearing strange things about you, Leaena. They say that Megilla, the rich Lesbian woman, is in love with you just like a man, that you live with each other, and do goodness knows what together. What! Blushing? Tell me if it's true." Leaena answers, "Quite true, Clonarium. But I'm ashamed, for it's unnatural." Clonarium presses for details, and Leaena can't keep the story to herself. Megilla and another rich woman, Demonassa, from Corinth,* hired Leaena to provide music at their dinner party—a common service for her class of prostitute. At the end of the party, Megilla and Demonassa were drunk, and Megilla invited Leaena to sleep between them. Leaena recounts:

> At first they kissed me like men, not simply bringing their lips to mine, but opening their mouths a little, embracing me, and squeezing my breasts. Demonassa even bit me as she kissed, and I didn't know what to make of it. Eventually Megilla, being now rather heated, pulled off her wig, which was very realistic and fitted very closely, and revealed the skin of her head, which was shaved close, just as on the most energetic of athletes. This sight gave me a shock, but she said, "Leaena, have you ever seen such a good-looking young fellow?" "I don't see one here, Megilla," said I. "Don't make a woman out of me," said she. "My name is Megillus, and I've been married to Demonassa here for ever so long; she's my wife." I laughed at that, Clonarium, and said, "Then . . . you have everything that a man has, and can play the part of a man to Demonassa?" "I haven't got what you mean," said she, "I don't need it at all. You'll find I've a much pleasanter method of my own." "You're surely not a hermaphrodite," said I, "equipped both as a man and a woman, as many people are said to be?" For I still didn't know, Clonarium, what it was all about. But she said, " . . . I was born a woman like the rest of you, but I have the mind and the desires and everything else of a man . . . just give me a chance . . . I have a substitute of my own. Only give me a chance, and you'll see."

Clonarium begs, "What did she do? How?" Leaena replies, "Don't inquire too closely into the details; they're not very nice, so, by Aphrodite in heaven, I won't tell you." There the dialogue ends, to the distress of Clo-

---

*Demonassa's birthplace is as significant as Megilla's. Corinth was famous for temple prostitution under the protection of Aphrodite. This may once have been like temple prostitution in the Great Mother cults, but in historical times it was merely that the numerous prostitutes of the city worshiped the goddess, and the cultic significance that may once have existed had given way to the commercial. But there are a few hints in Greek literature that then, as in later times, prostitution and lesbianism were associated, and Lucian may have had this in mind.

narium and history. But it sounds as though the two lesbians had an *olisbos.*

We can't know whether this story of Lucian's was largely imagination or dirty joke, or whether it came from real familiarity with lesbians. It is one of the very few mentions of lesbianism in surviving Greek literature. One or two lost works are referred to in extant works. Greek vase paintings and decorative carvings show heterosexual intercourse—genital, oral and anal, in all possible numbers and positions. They show bearded men giving presents to youths, kissing and caressing them, and having sex with them. But to my knowledge there are no surviving depictions of two women making love. (Some experts say there are, and others say no; I have come across none.) When a vase shows two complementary love scenes, one shows the loves of gods, the other the loves of men. Or one shows men making love to women, the other men making love to boys. Male and female homosexuality did not appear as counterparts. Greek art was by, for and about men. Greek men didn't bother much about the lives of the menials of their households or of their whores. Only men were worth an expense of interest, feeling, intelligence and effort.

But the record of male homosexuality is vast. The historian Pausanius said that Anacreon of Teos, who lived from 560–475 B.C., "was the first poet after Sappho of Lesbos to make love the main subject of his poetry." So the first male poet of love also celebrated homosexuality. Sappho and Anacreon became for later Greeks and Romans what Dylan Thomas and e. e. cummings are today for romantic undergraduates. Five hundred years after Anacreon, Plutarch wrote, "We were the first to be displeased with and condemn the new custom, which was imported into Rome, of reading from Plato as an after-dinner entertainment and listening to his dialogues over the dessert, perfume and wine, so that now when they recite Sappho or Anacreon I think I should put down my cup out of shame."

Although Anacreon wrote some love poems about women, it was *ephebi* who truly won his ardor. Tradition says that he lived in the court of Polycrates, ruler of the island of Samos, who surrounded himself with pretty youths. Anacreon wrote songs praising many of them, but he was especially infatuated with a Thracian boy named Smerdis. "Oh boy with a maiden's look, I seek thee, but thou dost not hear, not knowing that thou ridest thy chariot over my heart." Polycrates became jealous of Smerdis' flattered response to Anacreon's verse, and in a rage cut off the hair that the poet doted on in the boy. Anacreon cannily pretended the haircut had been the boy's own idea and chided, "he cut off the irreproachable bloom of his soft hair, whereas before he was wont to throw it back so saucily." Hans Licht, the pseudonymous German author of an exhaustive and apologetic account of Greek homosexuality, commented with owlish accuracy, "Of the boyish ideal of Anacreon we can even today form a living idea."

After Anacreon came a flood of homosexual writings, from philosophy to lyric poetry. Classical Greece set about rewriting Mycenaean myth to fit its very different sensibility. The new cosmology showed not Homer's sweep and forthrightness but elegiac charm and lyric delicacy. In Homer, Ganymede was the son of King Tros, who gave Troy its name; Zeus abducted Ganymede to make him cup-bearer for the Olympian gods because he was the most beautiful youth on earth. Homer never even hinted that the reason was homosexual infatuation; it was, rather, the primitive Greek awe of physical beauty. But in Classical Greece, Ganymede's abduction was recast: now it was said that Zeus, in love with the boy, disguised himself as an eagle, swooped down and carried him to heaven to be his lover. Plato and many others used Zeus and Ganymede as an example of the force, charm and divine precedent for male homosexuality. (Later, when he decided that homosexuality was a bad thing, Plato called this version of Zeus-Ganymede "a wicked Cretan invention.") Ganymede's name passed into Latin as Catamitus, giving English the word catamite for the receiver in sodomy. In the Greco-Roman world, the job of cupbearer was symbolically given to a household homosexual minion.

Lucian, who on the balance showed homosexuality more contempt than liking, devoted one of his sly, deliciously irreverent *Dialogues of the Gods* to the couple, whose affair was now as predictable a reference in Greek love literature as Tristan and Iseult would be in the Middle Ages. Lucian made Zeus a lecherous old man and Ganymede an obstinately heterosexual little hayseed. Zeus keeps inveigling the boy, who doesn't know what the god wants and keeps asking to go home. Zeus wheedles that on Olympus he will have fun, games, and even a playmate, little Eros.

GANYMEDE: Where shall I sleep tonight. With Eros, my playmate?
ZEUS: No, that's why I carried you off up here; I want us to sleep together.
GANYMEDE: Can't you sleep alone? Will you prefer sleeping with me?
ZEUS: Yes, when it's with a beautiful boy like you.
GANYMEDE: But how will you sleep better because of my beauty?
ZEUS: It's sweet and soothing, and brings softer sleep.
GANYMEDE: But daddy would get annoyed with me when I slept with him, and kept telling us first thing in the morning how he couldn't sleep for me tossing and turning, kicking out and talking in my sleep; so he usually sent me to sleep with mummy . . . the sooner you put me back down on earth again, the better, or you'll have a terrible time with sleepless nights. For I'll be an awful nuisance to you, tossing and turning all night long.
ZEUS: That's just what I like best—staying awake with you, kissing and hugging you again and again.
GANYMEDE: You can find out by yourself. *I'll* go to sleep and leave the kissing to *you*.

Lucian's zestful cynicism was exceptional, even for someone with predominantly heterosexual tastes. Homosexuality had become a conventional, romantic revision of Greek myth. Poseidon, it was now said, had loved Pelops. Apollo had loved Hypnos, Hyacinthus, Endymion and some twenty more. Zeus had loved Ganymede, Chrysippus and innumerable others. Hercules became a bisexual swiver of heroic proportions. In other representations he was a transvestite or effeminate. Legend said he had once had to serve Queen Omphale dressed in a gown and do women's work; he was depicted as a transvestite spinning wool at her feet.

Two-sexed gods exist in many societies. In Greece some of them were associated with the Great Mother and were probably Near Eastern borrowings: the Phrygian Agdistis, whose followers castrated themselves and dressed as women, was known on Lesbos and perhaps Greek Asia Minor—a bisexual being that castrated itself to become female. The oldest native Greek theogonies also show twofold deities that procreated without a partner. The Cypriots worshiped a bearded Aphrodite called Aphroditos, with a woman's body and clothes, a beard and male genitals. When they sacrificed to Aphroditos, they cross-dressed, men as women and women as men. Archaic Greek vases show a bearded Dionysos wearing a women's veils, and a virile Priapus with breasts. Hermaphrodite, offspring of Hermes and Aphrodite, was then a quite masculine figure with breasts or a grandly maternal woman with large male genitals. We are no longer sure what these gods meant to those who worshiped them, but the very representations show that there was no question of an intersexual being. The Crypian Aphroditus was a very feminine being other than the genitals; the Dionysus with breasts was not effeminate. These were twofold gods, doubly powerful, capable of infinite generation and immortality. They may have been fertility figures, and almost surely protected sex and marriage. In Plutarch's time, bridegrooms at Cos still wore women's robes at their weddings, and at Argos brides wore false beards on their wedding nights; the exact reasons for these practices were no longer clear even then, for the old worship and traditions had changed.

The image of a double being, symbol of total abundance and eternal life, was subject to revision like the rest of Greek religion, myth and legend. By the fourth century B.C., the representations of these gods had changed. Hermaphroditus was now a gently lovely figure neither clearly male nor clearly female in any way, but a creature between the sexes, and more an object of erotic esthetics than of serious worship. Dionysos, in Hellenistic art, was not a man-and-woman but an effeminate—Ovid and Seneca called him "girl-faced." The once-bearded Priapus was beautified into a sensual, effeminate adolescent, eventually equated with Hermaphroditus.

When Ovid told the story of Hermaphroditus in his *Metamorphoses,* he revealed how his era explained itself in explaining its past. It was a lyric tale of reluctant male sexuality. The beautiful offspring of Hermes and Aphrodite was a youth of dazzling beauty, and he was craved by a water nymph to whom he was indifferent. The nymph wanted to be one with him, and against his will he was united with her by the gods. As he entered the water where she dwelled, he became half woman, and he prayed to his father and mother to make every man who bathed in it *semivir,* a half-man, like himself. (The *semivir* is similar in conception to the virago, a woman with a man's soul.) Hermaphrodite was shown in graphic art as an effeminately pretty, pensive youth. His bisexuality was not double fertility but diminished maleness. From this time on the esthetic ideal of Greek art was the rounded youth and the small-breasted, waistless goddess. Modern restorers have sometimes mistakenly restored *ephebi* as girls and given beards to vase paintings of women.

Throughout Greek and Roman history, physical hermaphrodites were held in horror, disgust or amusement. For many centuries, children whose sex was doubtful at birth or whose sex seemed to change at puberty were destroyed by exposure, drowning or burning. As late as the first century B.C. Pliny was able to say, "Hermaphrodites were considered as terrifying apparitions, but today only as objects of jest." The twofold god was a symbol, and the change in the symbol reflected a profound change in belief and in sensibility. Marie Delcourt, a French scholar who has studied the hermaphroditic god in detail, says that starting in the fourth century in Greece, it was as if "an androgynous figure had haunted their imagination . . . a homosexual dream expresses itself . . . in these ambiguous forms." In a relatively agnostic age of widespread homosexual and bisexual behavior in the upper classes, the twofold deities became trifles of sentimental and comic literature. Now Hercules, probably once a seriously worshiped god who undergoes a cross-dressed penitence, as appears in many cultures, was shown in comedy as a ridiculous effeminate or a henpecked husband. Writers made him the tender lover of Iolas, Admetus and some ten other boys, including "sweet Hylas of the curling locks." Hylas' death at the hands of sexually voracious nymphs,* and Hercules' grief at losing him, became a stock reference in Classical literature. The poet Diotimus, in the third century B.C., retold the story of Hercules, showing all his labors as performed out of love for the youth Eurystheus.

The word pederasty means, literally, love of boys, and mostly Greek homosexuality was between men and adolescents, not adult males. To the Greeks, a boy was someone between puberty and close to twenty. A common and fond phrase was *ta paedika*—boyish things—referring to looks and behavior characteristic of adolescence. The coarse, muscular (we would say butch) type was rarely admired. Rather it was the hermaphroditic youth. Great poetic debate was held on whether a youth was most beautiful before he had any beard, when the first down appeared on his face, or a bit later. The half-manly state of the early teens was most favored. The appearance of hair on legs and body was called "horrid" and "ugly"; it usually signaled the end of the affair. Boys in the Greek world did not

---

*The rape or destruction of a sexually cool youth, such as Hermaphroditus or Hylas, was frequent in Greek tales of the period. Just as popular were the themes of self-adoring Narcissus, cold and priggish Hippolytus, lascivious old hags who lusted for young men. All reflected the same phobic reaction to female sexuality that was now so deeply engrained in upper-class Greek culture.

remove their pubic hair, as women did, but those with homosexual inclinations carefully depilated their legs. Typical praise was of "a beardless, tender and beautiful youth" with "sweet and lustrous" thighs, "flashing eyes and blushing cheeks," and long hair. The hair on the head was sometimes left very long; this, along with depilation of the body, must have produced an appearance somewhere between the sexes. Most of the comparisons and metaphors used by homosexual lovers evoke a picture either of a slender sapling or a boy-girl creature, coquettish yet naïve, or a fuzzy little blooming peach.

The love of beautiful youths was responsible for the rewriting of history as well as myth, and the change over the centuries of Homer's story of Achilles and Patroclus is a thumbnail history of Greek homosexuality. To Homer they were devoted brothers-in-arms, but not homosexual lovers. Aeschylus, who was said to be an avid boy-lover, wrote about them in his *Myrmidons* as though they were bed partners: Achilles reproaches dead Patroclus for leaving him alone, "Despite our kisses, cruel one, to save those lustrous thighs thou didst not think, alas!" When Plato produced his philosophic justification of pederasty, he took issue with Aeschylus: Achilles, he said, had not been the lover of Patroclus, for Patroclus had been handsomer and younger—it was the other way around, Patroclus had been the lover of Achilles! After him, Lucian, Plutarch, Xenophon and Martial, all of whom denigrated pederasty to some degree, assumed from the practices of their own times that two men so close must have been lovers.

The chief justification of pederasty was Cretan and Dorian homosexuality. Among those peoples the relationship between man and boy was supposed to be pedagogic and to produce brave men and good citizens. The older lover was called "the inspirer," the boy beloved "the listener." Virtue was supposed to be reinforced by the lover's need to impress the boy, the boy's need to prove himself worthy of the man. In Crete a man would "kidnap" the boy he wanted, just as in Sparta and many places in the non-Western world men ritually abducted their brides. The man declared his intentions to the boy's family, and with their consent went through the motions of abduction; he then brought the boy to his house, gave him a present, and took him away to the countryside for a two-month honeymoon. After they had returned to the city, the man presented to him a drinking cup, a bull for sacrifice and a military outfit.

Now, if the relationship continued, it was the man's job to mold the boy into a good citizen and brave warrior. Here, as in Sparta, says Plutarch, it was considered shameful for a wellborn boy of twelve or thirteen not to have a lover. The phrase "wellborn," like the assumption of having city and country homes and time for a long honeymoon, indicates an upper-class phenomenon. In fact, it sounds as though these military cultures split boys from their families when young and encouraged only enough contact with women to allow for the production of new citizens. They grew up in a barracks culture that would produce a tight-knit warrior elite with tremendous cohesion and morale. Sexual relations between man and wife were carried on with haste and shame among the Spartans, in the dark, during brief visits home. Women had more freedom of movement than in Athens, but it was chiefly to allow them to be physically fit so that they could bear healthy young warriors.

Similar pairing of men, without abduction, took place not only in Sparta but in Boeotia and other Dorian areas. Everything in Dorian society seems to have been aimed at idealizing the military homosexual relationship. Plutarch said, "Once Eros has entered into the souls of a pair of lovers, no enemy ever succeeds in separating them. They display their ardor for danger and risk their lives even when there is no need for it. The Thessalian Theon, for instance, once laid his hand against a wall, drew his sword and cut off his thumb, challenging his rival in love to do the same. Another such lover, having fallen face downward in battle, begged his enemy to wait a moment before stabbing him, lest the youth whom he loved should see him wounded in the back." Plutarch told similar stories about the warlike Chalcidians and Lacedaemonians. The famous "sacred band of Thebes" was a force of elite shock troops composed of pairs of lovers. They were defeated by Philip of Macedon, himself perhaps a lover of boys as much as women. When Philip inspected the bodies and found them all wounded in front, not the back, he is said to have wept, saying, "Cursed be those who imagine that heroes could ever do or suffer a deed of shame!" His words have been seen as praise of pederasty, though they could just as well mean the opposite.

Ancient writers claimed that in some of these military societies a boy who had no lover was punished, and fined if he chose a rich lover over a poor one. If he showed cowardice in the gymnasium or on the battle field, his older mentor was allegedly punished. Before troops went into battle, they sacrificed to Eros, the god of physical love. It is certainly possible that among the Cretans and Dorians bravery, civic virtue and *esprit de corps* existed and were furthered by homosexual bonds in what amounted to a select warrior fraternity. The question is whether homosexuality was the cause of courage and virtue or just a coexisting phenomenon that needed public justification and therefore received it. How automatic and conventional this rationalization for homosexuality became shows in a silly poem by Seleucus, written in the beginning of the second century B.C. "I also love boys; this is more beautiful than languishing in the yoke of marriage; for in murderous battle your friend still stays as a protector at your side."

Solon, who created the democratically reformed constitution of Athens in 594 B.C., and who wrote poems of homosexual love ("Boys in the flower of their youth are loved; the smoothness of their thighs and soft lips is adored"), made it illegal for a slave to have homosexual relations with a freeborn boy. Homosexual writers said that Solon had thus meant to encourage homosexuality among the upper classes and discourage it among the low, as a support of virtue and democracy (which were the preserve of the privileged). This became a standard theme in homosexual apologetics. Homosexual love was called an instrument of freedom from despots. Poets, painters and sculptors wore thin the tale of Harmodius and Aristogiton, who in 514 B.C. killed the tyrant Hipparchus as the result of a jealous three-way homosexual intrigue.

Like negrophiles speaking of negritude, Arab nationalists of Moorish influence on Europe—and like many homosexuals today—Athenian peder-asts attributed everything virtuous and desirable to homosexuality. Love, liberty, courage and sincerity were all eminently homosexual traits. For proofs and examples they used the newly homosexual gods and heroes, the homosexuality of the Dorian military caste, pederastic pedagogy, the polit-ical assassinations performed by homosexuals. It remained for Plato, in the *Symposium*, to put them all together in a grand, long paean to homosexual love.

The argument could exist only on a dual base of misogyny and the Greek cult of beauty. Grecophiles throughout Western history have admired Greece for its awe of physical beauty. Schiller said, "At that time nothing was sacred but the Beautiful." He was half right; the cult of beauty did exist, but it reflected Greek primitivism, not Greek civilization. Guided by shame rather than guilt, the Greeks saw in beauty a powerful gift of the supernatural powers that bestow luck and bad fortune. They saw in ugli-ness, as in weakness and bad luck, an object of contempt before the Might that makes right.

Their horror at physical unattractiveness was such that invalids and the dying covered their faces to hide the distortions of suffering. The oboe was played only by slaves, because it made the cheeks puff out unattractively. The word *kalos* meant both beautiful and noble; *aeschros* meant both ugly and shameful. In the fourth century B.C. the Athenian orator Isocrates said (I condense): "Helen shared the privileges of beauty, the most revered, precious and divine of boons. Everything which lacks beauty is devoid of charm. Virtue itself is only appreciated because it is the fairest habit of the mind. The moment we perceive beautiful persons we feel well disposed to them. They and the gods are the sole beings whom we never cease to serve." When the famous courtesan Phryne was brought to trial in Athens for debauchery in holy places, a crime punishable by death, her lawyer tore away her robe, revealing her breasts, and the judges acquitted her. They felt that such beauty must be a gift of Aphrodite, a sign of divine grace. The incident may charm the Schillers who see in Greece an esthetic utopia, but they probably wouldn't really enjoy living with it. No matter how they may deplore certain Anglo-Saxon scruples about eroticism, they also take for granted the impersonal Anglo-Saxon ideal of due process for all, and would hate a court that made its decisions as the Athenian one did— especially if they themselves were being sued or accused by a Phryne.

Socrates, Plato and their followers incorporated the equation of beauty and good into their philosophic systems. Plato's basic argument is this: The beautiful is good; love is love of the good-and-beautiful; men are better and more beautiful than women; hence one should love men. To some Greeks, with their ambivalent feelings toward women, it might seem reasonable or even natural. Even in his *Republic*, when Plato spoke more against than for homosexuality, and became liberal (for a Greek) toward women, he said: "The gifts of nature are alike diffused in both men and women; all the pursuits of men are the pursuits of women also, but in all of them a woman is inferior to a man."

This was hardly the creature in whom to seek the ideal, beautiful and true—when a barely developed boy looked similar enough and had no threatening *vagina dentata*. What distinguishes Socrates (or Plato) is that misogyny and the primitive cult of beauty are slightly transcended. But this may have to some extent reflected a concession to convention, too. It was common for Greek poets to say that at forty the fires of love started to burn low, and gray hairs made the love-chase unseemly. Now one should philosophize, free at last of love, "a mad and furious master." Socrates' and Plato's many past male lovers suggest that only with age did they find sexual worship of beautiful male flesh a bit shallow.

Plato's *Symposium* was held in honor of the poet Agathon, who had won a prize for tragedy. Agathon has been the lover of Euripides and of Plato: a poem attributed to Plato in the *Greek Anthology* says, "My soul, when I kissed Agathon, crept up to my lips as though it wished (poor thing!) to cross over to him." Also present are Phaedrus, who was a favorite of Plato at one time; Pausanius, another lover of the ubiquitous Agathon; Alcibiades, a notorious bisexual rake and political adventurer; the dramatist Aristophanes, and a few others. They decide to pass the time discussing love. Phaedrus begins with the Dorian pedagogic argument, saying that love—homosexual love, of course—is a spur to virtue. "A lover who is detected in doing any dishonorable act, or submitting through cowardice when any dishonor is done to him by another, will be more pained at being detected by his beloved than at being seen by his father. . . . The beloved too, when he is found in any disgraceful situation, has the same feeling about his lover. And if there were only some way of contriving that a state or any army should be made up of lovers and their loves, they would be the very best governors of their own city."

Next Pausanius says that there are two kinds of love, common and heavenly. The common

> has no discrimination, being such as the meaner sort of men feel, and is apt to be of women as well as of youths. . . . But the offspring of the heavenly Aphrodite is derived from a mother in whose birth the female has no part— she is from the male only; this is that love which is of youths. . . . Those who are inspired by this love turn to the male, and delight in him who is the more valiant and intelligent nature; anyone may recognize the pure enthusiasts in the very character of their attachments. For they love not boys, but intelligent beings whose reason is beginning to be developed, much

> about the time at which their beards begin to grow. . . . The good are a law
> to themselves, and the coarser sort of lovers ought to be restrained. . . .
> These are the persons who bring a reproach on love; and some have been
> led to deny the lawfulness of such attachments because they see the im-
> propriety and evil of them.

After this admission that homosexuality is condemned by many, he argues
that male love is inimical to tyranny and promotes purity of spirit.

Next comes Eryximachus, who gives a medical lecture on love. He is followed by Aristophanes, who tells about the origin of the sexes in the fission
of the original bisexual being. As a result, each man and woman comes
from a male or female mold and tries to unite with its other half.

> Men who are a section of the double nature which was once called androg-
> ynous are lovers of women; adulterers are generally of this breed, and also
> adulterous women who lust after men: the women who are a section of the
> woman do not care for men, but have female attachments; the female com-
> panions are of this sort. But they who are a section of the male follow the
> male, and while they are young, being slices of the original man, they hang
> about men and embrace them, and they are themselves the best of boys
> and youths, because they have the most manly nature. Some indeed assert
> that they are shameless, but this is not true; for they do not act thus from
> any want of shame, but because they are valiant and manly, and have a manly
> countenance, and they embrace that which is like them. And these when they
> grow up become our statesmen, and these only, which is a great proof of
> the truth of what I am saying. When they reach manhood they are lovers
> of youth, and are not naturally inclined to marry or beget children—if at all,
> they do so only in obedience to the law.

He goes on to talk about the "amazement of love and friendship and intimacy" of such men when they find each other and live together.

Agathon delivers a flowery panegyric on beauty and love, and then at
last it is Socrates' turn. He argues that man loves beauty, beauty is the
good, man is better than woman, etc.—but adds two provisos. First, he
praises parenthood by saying that men love their offspring, in whom the
beautiful is generated and immortality glimpsed. Second, he makes the
point that real beauty, he now realizes in his philosophic old age, is moral
and not fleshly. Alcibiades comes in at this point; there is a lot of homoerotic banter, and Alcibiades says that despite all his attempts to become
Socrates' lover, all he has got from him is philosophic lectures. The others
joke on, accusing each other of really liking nothing but pretty faces, and
soon the party ends.

Much of the *Symposium* is devoted to answering those who criticize
homosexuality and repeating conventional defenses of it. The Aristophanes
who is made to defend homosexuality was, in truth, a harsh mocker of it.
The entire production has the unmistakable air of a minority polemic. Only
Socrates' position distinguishes it much from the writings of the early
Stoics, whose homosexual philosophizing was shamelessly simplistic. The

Stoics of the Porch, as they were called, followed Zeno in practicing and recommending homosexuality with this argument: "The wise should love the young. For the latter's beauty proves that they are well equipped for virtue." Ariston of Chios wrote, "A virtuous and noble mind may be discerned in the bloom and grace of a body, just as a well-made shoe reveals the beauty of a foot." At least Plato had said that outer and inner beauty were not necessarily synonymous. Among the Stoics, a boy with moral beauty and acne apparently had to shift for himself.

The pederastic vein grew richer and richer. Theognis, in the sixth century B.C., wrote poems to a favorite named Cyrnus, complaining of unreturned love, threatening suicide and offering to teach him to have a virtuous character. Sophocles was a notorious flirter with boys and probably wrote at least one play (now lost) with a homosexual theme. Aeschylus was known as a confirmed pederast. Euripides was claimed by both heterosexual and homosexual writers. The Boeotian Pindar wrote, "I pine when I look upon the blooming youth of lads." Theocritus, in the third century B.C., wrote a series of sentimental *Idylls,* many devoted to tender and imploring homosexual love. A whole flock of imitators of Anacreon created a body of delicately erotic homosexual love poems called *Anacreontea.* The entire twelfth book of the *Greek Anthology* is devoted to the love of boys and their superiority over girls.

The debate between proponents of heterosexual and homosexual love became a literary set piece. Even such writers as Plutarch and Lucian, who had little use for boy-love, sometimes felt obliged to recite the formula of homosexuality's virtues before expressing what seem to be their more heartfelt views. Some Greeks ascribed the earliest homosexuality to the Cretans, others to the Dorians. Aristotle suggested that the Cretans used it as a form of population control. Then, as in our times, some said homosexuality was an Eastern importation, perhaps associated with the Great Mother cults, with their traditions of castration, transvestism and cultic homosexual intercourse. Others reversed the argument. Herodotus and Xenophon said the Persians had borrowed homosexuality from the Greeks and effeminacy from the Medes. Xenophon added that the Medes were soft and sybaritic, and kept fancily made-up favorites. Clearchus claimed that they castrated boys for sexual purposes.* Plutarch, on the other hand, said that the Persians had had eunuchs before encountering the Greeks.

One thing is certain: homosexuality was associated in the Greek mind

*Castration provided safe domestic servants for wealthy men's wives and concubines, and also sexual objects for homosexual men. Sometimes little harems of castrated minions were maintained in the ancient world, and a poem in the *Greek Anthology* attributes one such collection to a wealthy eunuch. Castration usually meant removing the testicles. If done after puberty it destroyed fertility but not sexual desire or competence; actually, a eunuch of this kind made an eminently safe lover for a married woman. If the operation was performed before puberty, it prevented sexual maturation and resulted in an utterly safe (from the husband's viewpoint) servant for women or a soft, hairless catamitic favorite.

with the separation of the sexes, the military ethos, male nudity, physical culture and gymnasia. The education of boys consisted of physical training as much as scholarship and the arts, and it took place in the gymnasia. The word comes from *gymnos*, which means naked. Boys spent a great part of the day racing and wrestling there, naked or lightly clad. No gymnasium was without statues of Hermes, who represented youthful masculine beauty, of Hercules, Apollo and Eros—a powerful gathering of bisexual erotic deities. In Athens no woman could set foot in the gymnasium. As boys and youths worked out there, males of all ages gathered in its colonnades to idle, gossip and conduct business. The gymnasium was also a place for forming homosexual liaisons, often of a kind Plato would have frowned on.

Some proponents of homosexuality realized that despite their revision of myth and history, male nudity and pederasty were relatively new to Greece. Plato said in the *Republic*: "Not long ago, the Hellenes were of the opinion, which is still generally received among the barbarians, that the sight of a naked man was ridiculous and improper; and when first the Cretans and the Lacedaemonians introduced the custom, the wits of that day might equally have ridiculed the innovation." Herodotus agreed with him, and Thucydides pointed out that in 720 B.C. the runner at the Olympian games wore an apron around his hips rather than going naked.

Plutarch puts the case more strongly.

> Homosexuality resembles a son born late, of parents past their maturity, or a bastard child of darkness seeking to supplant his elder brother, legitimate love. For it was only yesterday or at best the day before yesterday that the pederast came slinking into our gymnasia, to view the games in which youths then first began to strip for exercising. Quite quietly at first he started touching and embracing the boys. But gradually, in these arenas, he grew wings [a reference to the statues of Eros in the gymnasia] and then there was no holding him. Nowadays he regularly insults conjugal love and drags it through the mud.

He mentions a man named Pisias who was in love with a youth called Bacchon; Pisias tried to stop Bacchon from marrying a rich widow and "imitated ill-conditioned lovers of the ordinary sort in trying to prevent his friend from marrying. The man's only object was to prolong the pleasure he took in watching the boy strip in the arena."

Plutarch's and other writers' frequent allusions to lovers' wealth and high birth are significant. A nontechnological society such as Athens cannot afford idle hands, and only a wealthy few could have spent their days in the gymnasium. Attica, of which Athens was the center, had 25,000 citizens, 10,000 free noncitizens, and 150,000 to 300,000 slaves. Even most citizens and freemen must have lacked time to split hairs of love's dogma with Plato or hurl the discus in the cool of each morning. Did any but the well-born in Sparta and Crete have homosexual mentors? Greece's literature, like that of most of the West till a century ago, was by and about a tiny upper crust of society. About the only evidence of nonaristocratic homosexuals in ancient Greece is mention of freeborn male prostitutes, whom some Athenian men hired to live with them like kept mistresses. Boys with long hair, depilated bodies, coquettish manners and make-up congregated at the shops of barbers, surgeons, perfumers and flower sellers, plied the dark hills outside Athens, roamed its streets, worked in bordellos and even made house calls. Like female prostitutes, they were probably freeborn foreigners and lower-class citizens. Robert Flacelière, probably the most painstaking and unbiased scholar of Greek sexual life, says that "inversion was never very prevalent except in one class of society and over a quite limited period. . . . And finally there is no evidence that homosexuality met with any general social approval. . . . The Greeks never 'canonized' the physical act of sodomy. They always kept up the fiction of 'educational' pederasty."

Flacelière's view is supported by a close look at the place of homosexuality in upper-class life and the response it provoked. As we have seen, upper-class marriages were social arrangements which failed to fulfill a new ideal of romantic fulfillment that was coming into existence in life and in literature, as exemplified by the poetry of Sappho and Anacreon. Poems to courtesans and boys contain all the sentiments we would associate today with heterosexual romance. Many Greek men shuttled between whores and boys, often without satisfaction in either camp—Meleager wrote verse renouncing the love of women and lads by turn. The pattern was to fall in love with a *hetaira*, discover she wasn't faithful, and flee in disappointment and disgust to boys, only to discover they could be just as fickle, silly, coy, unstable and mercenary as any female whore. The literature revealing this cycle was full of infatuations, high expectations and a great deal of self-conscious literary gesturing. Many poems of heartsick homosexual love seem more conventional than felt. Doubtless some lovers did what they recorded in their poems—getting drunk, moping in loneliness outside a boy's home at night, carving his name on trees, stammering, blushing and mooning. But many of the poems remind one of formalized eighteenth-century poetry, full of Eros' little stinging arrows, bittersweet conceits and clever puns. Although some of the homosexual relationships were doubtless benevolent, protective or deeply loving, one gets an over-all impression of shallow adolescent romanticism in grown men, and often of mercenary affairs and callous bed-hopping by a psychosexually disturbed leisure class.

Such switching back and forth between boys and women would create a crisis of masculine identity and potency problems in the majority of men today. The upper-class Greeks at least claimed that it did not for them. In fact, some poets were so casual about the gender of their beloved that they failed to make it clear in their verse. They achieved this ambidextrous ease by lumping women and young boys together as soft, passive, not-male. In sex with either, a man was not cohabiting with his own kind. When a Greek boy grew a beard, he was supposed to become *muy macho*, give up the passive homosexual role and look in his turn for courtesans and boys.

The Greek interest in buttocks and sodomy is significant, for the act has symbolic overtones of dominance and submission, which are equated with masculinity and femininity. Sodomy was popular with the Greeks, practiced on both women and boys, as was intercourse *a tergo,* from behind. Sodomy and coitus *a tergo* were frequently written about and depicted on vases. In *Plutus,* Aristophanes writes, "And they say of the *hetairae* of Corinth that if a poor man longs for their love, they pay no attention to him, but that if he is rich they at once turn their buttocks to him." Athenaeus records Machon's anecdote about Demophon, a minion of Sophocles who was in turn keeping a female mistress. "Now the woman in question is said to have had a very beautiful bottom, which Demophon once desired to possess. And she said with a laugh, 'Very good; take it from me and pass it on to Sophocles.' "

To the bisexual Greek, women and boys were both "the ones who are fucked," submissive nonmales. Many non-Western societies have similar attitudes and behavior patterns, and one finds this in slightly diluted form in much of the Mediterranean world today. A man can have boys as well as women without his masculinity being questioned by himself or others, as long as he takes a clearly dominant role and "womanizes" partners of both genders. Relations with another adult male would be a different matter, as would taking a passive sexual role. Such a sexual-dominance pattern tends to contain a strong element of psychic sadism, and can hardly be called a sign of untrammeled naturalness or psychosexual health.

In ancient Greece as in modern Greece, the exclusive homosexual was considered laughable and despicable. The French scholar H. I. Marrou, in his exhaustive history of education in antiquity, says:

> We can imagine the difficulty which sociologists of the future will have when they try to decide just what place adultery had in the lives of twentieth-century Frenchmen. Just as for us, there is contradictory evidence from ancient times . . . but the very vocabulary of the Greek language and the laws of most city-states show that homosexuality was always regarded as something "abnormal." . . . It is described in terms that mean "to dishonor," "to outrage," "a shameful act," "infamous conduct," "impurity," "despicable habits." The contempt is more explicitly directed against the passive partner. . . . It does not seem to have been legal except in Elis.

Solon set a death sentence on men who sneaked into gymnasia and boys' schools in Athens. In Sparta, Lycurgus made sexual relations with a youth punishable by exile or death. In Ionia, says Plato, pederasty was thought a disgrace. Elis, where homosexual acts may not have been illegal, was condemned for sexual indulgence by Plato and Maximus of Tyre. Homosexuality was not only illegal but, to many people, immoral and ridiculous. The word effeminate was loosely used to mean debauched and lazy. The distance between literary idealizations and everyday life was nowhere more striking than in the pederastic pursuit of boys by both bisexuals and homosexuals.

Pederastic lovers were called not only "inspirer" and "hearer" but "wolf" and "lamb." For every alleged Socratic mentor there was an amatory cynic sweet-talking eleven-year-olds at the gymnasium. Poems tell of their seduction with gifts, flattery and fees. The poet Addaeus frankly warned, "If you see a beauty, strike while the iron is hot . . . if you say, 'I reverence you and will be like a brother,' shame will close your road to accomplishment." Xenophon was thoroughly skeptical about Spartan pedagogic rationalizations: "Homosexuals who claim that sensuality plays no part in their affairs do so because they are ashamed of themselves and fear punishment. They have to have some excuse for approaching good-looking boys, so they make a show of friendship and virtue." The corruption of boys by homosexual tutors was a common theme. Plutarch said that no wise father would allow one of the great ancient philosophers near his sons. Hard-headed Lucian assumed that both Socrates and Plato were ordinary hypocritical buggerers, and that Socrates' corruption of Athenian youth was anal, not philosophical. In one of his dialogues, the courtesan Drosis complains of an excellent young customer whose tutor, Aristaenetus, "is the sort who's fond of boys and, by pretending to teach them, keeps company with the handsomest youths. . . . Besides that, he's reading with them amorous discourses addressed by the old philosophers to their pupils. . . . If only you can help me fight that old imposter Aristaenetus!"

Plutarch commented on how many boys were deserted by their lovers as soon as their beards sprouted, and said this showed the selfish inconstancy of homosexual love. Maturity was in fact a common reproach of homosexual poets. So was the spoiled arrogance and petulance of boys. Diocles wrote: "And so Damon, who excels in beauty, does not even say good-day now! A time will come that will take vengeance for this. Then, grown all rough and hairy, you will give good-day first to those who do not give it back to you." There seemed to be little illusion about the mercenary ways of the adolescent boys who took men as lovers. A good-looking boy of twelve might be surrounded by men competing for his company in bed, and he quickly graduated from demanding flattering poems and sweet cakes to cash gifts. Some were little male Lolitas. Strato wrote, "My neighbor's quite tender young boy provokes me not a little, and laughs in no novice manner to show me that he is willing. But he is not more than twelve years old."

Once one looks beyond the literary apologists for homosexuality in ancient Greece, one finds a widespread attitude of mockery and disgust. Homosexual behavior was probably often practiced with shame, false bravado or secrecy. As today, many a homosexual married to put up a heterosexual front and escape scorn. Lucilius wrote of one such man: "To avoid suspicion, Apollophanes married and walked as a bridegroom through the middle of the market, saying, 'Tomorrow at once I will have a child.' Then when tomorrow came, he appeared carrying the suspicion instead of a child." Plato himself, in his later years, condemned homosexual relations as unnatural and degrading. The poet Agathius also called them contrary to nature, and swore, "Let Aphrodite herself, let all the company of Love curse me, shrivel my sick heart with their hate, if ever I turn to the love of boys."

Probably the best source of ancient Greek attitudes toward homosexuality is Aristophanes. His plays were popular comedies aimed at the mass theater-going population, not at a small coterie of philosophers. His withering satire of pederasts, effeminates and secret homosexuals probably represents common Greek opinion far more than Plato's *Symposium* does. His *Lysistrata* hardly suggests that homosexuality or even bisexuality was universal in Athens. In his first play, *The Guests*, he contrasts an exemplary young man with an invert and treats the latter with harsh sarcasm. In *The Birds*, he ironically puts this speech in the mouth of a man dreaming of the ideal city:

> I should like to live in a town where the father of some pretty boy might come up to me and say angrily: "Well, this is a nice state of affairs, you damned swaggerer! You meet my son just as he comes out of the gymnasium, all fresh from his bath and you don't kiss him, you don't say a word to him, you don't hug him and you don't feel his testicles! And yet you're supposed to be a friend of ours!"

Aristophanes says that no homosexual poet has the spunk to write great poetry; he can only make prettily affected phrases. In *The Clouds* he shows Socrates and his disciples as pasty-faced, unmanly jugglers of words, pours scorn on their pedagogy, and says it is used only to confound common sense and seduce the morals of young men. Poets, orators, philosophers—these, to Aristophanes, are the sorriest of men. Here, to my knowledge, is the first statement of the West's equation of homosexuality with sedentary, verbal and artistic professions. In *The Knights*, Aristophanes has Cleon say, "Is it not I who curbed the pederasts by erasing Gryttus' name from the lists of citizens?" He is answered, "Ah! noble Inspector of Asses, let me congratulate you. Moreover, if you set yourself against this form of lewdness, this pederasty, it was for sheer jealousy, knowing it to be the school for orators."

His most protracted and virulent attack, worthy of an antihomosexual routine in a modern burlesque house, is in the *Thesmophoriazusae*. Euripides is being discussed by a crowd of furious Athenian women because of his misogynous plays. Afraid, he goes with Mnesilochus to visit the poet Agathon—the same Agathon who delivered the panegyric on male love in the *Symposium*, lover of Plato and apparently just about everybody. He gets Agathon to disguise himself as a woman, join the crowd and speak in Euripides' favor. First Agathon's servant appears, proclaiming his master's arrival. Mnesilochus delivers sarcastic comments in counterpoint.

SERVANT: . . . Agathon, our master, the sweet-voiced poet, is going . . .
MNESILOCHUS: . . . to be made love to?

SERVANT: . . . is going to construct the framework of a drama . . .

MNESILOCHUS: . . . and sway his buttocks amorously.

Then Agathon appears, lying on a bed and wearing a saffron tunic, with feminine toilet articles spread about him. Mnesilochus says:

Whence comes this androgyne? What is his country? his dress? What contradictions his life shows! A lyre and a hairnet! A wrestling school oil flask and a girdle! . . . What relation has a mirror to a sword? And you yourself, what are you? Do you pretend to be a man? Where is your tool, pray? Where is the cloak, the footgear that belong to that sex? Are you a woman? Then where are your breasts? Answer me. But you keep silent. Oh! just as you choose; your songs display your character quite sufficiently.

Agathon explains: "My dress is in harmony with my thoughts. A poet must adopt the nature of his characters. Thus if he is placing women on the stage, he must contract all their habits in his own person. If the heroes are men, everything in him will be manly. What we don't possess by nature, we must acquire by imitation." Mnesilochus answers, "When you are staging Satyrs, call me; I will do my best to help you from behind."

Euripides begs Agathon to speak for him in disguise; he would go himself, he says, but he has white hair and a long beard, and Agathon is fair, delicate and has a woman's voice. Agathon replies that one must meet adversity by submitting to fate, and Mnesilochus breaks out: "You fairy! That's why your ass is so accessible to lovers," Agathon finally accedes, and Euripides starts to disguise him. He insists that Agathon supply women's clothes, saying, "You cannot say you haven't got them." Agathon hands over a robe, and Mnesilochus parodies him: "By Aphrodite! what a sweet odor! how it smells of young male tools! Hand it to me quickly."

This could hardly win a prize in a society that approved of homosexuality. Often in Greek literature, if a man was being criticized, and he was homosexual or bisexual, his penchant for males was used against him as a sign of his poor character. When Lucian lampooned a teacher of public speaking, he insultingly equated the man's flowery speech and effeminate appearance:

. . . a wholly clever and handsome gentleman with a mincing gait, a thin neck, a languishing eye, and a honeyed voice, who distills perfume, scratches his head with the tip of his finger and carefully dresses his hair, which is scanty now, but curly and raven-black—an utterly delicate Sardanapalus, a Cinyras, a very Agathon (that charming writer of tragedies, don't you know?) . . . tossing back what hair is still left him, faintly smiling in that sweet and tender way which is his wont, and rivaling Thais herself of comic fame, or Malthace, or Glycera, in the seductiveness of his tone, since masculinity is boorish . . . . To become a public speaker you should have a shameless singing delivery, and a gait like mine . . . let your clothing be gaily colored . . . so that your body will show through; and wear high Attic sandals of the kind that women wear . . . do not be ashamed to have the name of being an effeminate . . . use depilatories, preferably all over . . . let your mouth be open for everything indifferently; let your tongue serve you not only in your speeches, but in any other way it can . . . it can perform other services, even at night . . . soon you will turn out an excellent speaker, just like myself.

Greek literature is full of such mockery and denunciation of homosexuality. Aeschines, himself a sometime lover of boys, attacked Timarchus for having "debauched his body by womanly acts of lust . . . who against the law of nature has given himself to lewdness." If early Stoics praised homosexuality, later ones condemned it strongly as unnatural. The Cynics generally saw it unfavorably. Epictetus assumed that some of his readers were bisexual in behavior, and he mourned their womanly ways. He said that Plato had not meant "Dress your locks, and pluck the hairs out of your legs," but rather, "Make beautiful your moral purpose." He ranted against depilation, saying that women are delicate and are exhibited as prodigies of nature if they are hairy; men are naturally hairy, and one who dipilates himself is as dreadful a spectacle as a hirsute woman. "What reason have you to complain against your nature? Because it brought you into the world as a man?"

Epicurus did not encourage homosexuality, and his disciple Philodemus condemned it. Aristotle felt that "Love and friendship are found most and in their best form between men," but he considered homosexual acts a morbid depravity, and more prevalent among foreigners than among Greeks. Lucian made a female character say, "I do not care for a man who himself wants one." Some writers of Alexandrian prose romances were neutral about homosexuality, some did not mention it, and many were disgusted by it. Plutarch was the first ancient writer to say that the highest love is conjugal affection. If he had thought a step farther, he would have put the question we would naturally ask today: why is it necessarily another man, and one with whom there is a sexual relationship, who becomes one's moral juror? The whole pedagogic defense of homosexuality stands on the base of Greek disgust at women, wives, family and home. A man like Menander—who wrote, "No one is so wretched as a father, except another father who has more children than he"—would not look to a female lover or a wife as the witness of his virtue. But that is no sign of exuberant psychosexual health.

The point of all this is not to prove that homosexuality is vicious or pernicious, but that in ancient Greece homosexuality was considered a deviation; it was given positive value only by a minority of homosexuals, bisexuals and apologists. Neither did its presence in Greece have any relationship to social, artistic or political health. The fact that homosexuality was a factor in the lives of many great men only speaks for its prevalence among the leisured, literate elite from which artists and statesmen came. A permissive or positive view of homosexuality must find other grounds than the myth that made everything Greek praiseworthy. Even today it is difficult for people to think of Plato's and Agathon's buggery as the same act that is performed by two 42nd Street "queers." If the social and historical facts of ancient Greece had the label of any other time and place, we would respond differently—perhaps with the clinical condescension we usually give to societies that solve their problems no better than we.

In the Hellenic and subsequent periods, the position of women improved, and they appeared more in literature, painting and sculpture. The heterosexual romance gained popularity, and marriage and family life entered literature. Homosexual and bisexual behavior were still common, but the context had changed. From the third century B.C. on, Greece ceased to be a loose constellation of small states living out of local cultural traditions and entered the various, cosmopolitan world of the Roman Empire.

INTERVIEWS

Jack and Larry insistently proclaim that they have a relationship like that of homosexual lovers in ancient Greece, as portrayed by novelist Mary Renault and others. It is quite probable that they do. I meet them by accident in the course of another interview. I am in a large apartment in a grand, high-ceilinged house in Chicago's fashionable Near North. Jack and another homosexual live here; their lovers and a large crowd of friends frequently visit, party and sleep over. The dozen who wander in and out this evening vary from long-haired hippie types in jeans and polo shirts to very effeminate little guys and a couple of stolid-looking males one wouldn't take to be homosexual. A sign on the bathroom door changes as you walk by it, from MEN *to* WOMEN *or vice versa, depending on the angle from which you see it.*

Jack is a husky, slightly paunchy man of thirty, very successful in the entertainment industry. We pass when I enter, but don't stop to talk; I've come to talk to his roommate's lover, Fred. Fred and I talk for a half hour. Then we hear yelling through the closed doors that separate us from the big living room. Fred excuses himself twice to speak to someone in the other room. He comes back more agitated each time. Then he leaves again, in the middle of a sentence. This time he doesn't quite close the door to the living room, and I hear a deep, angry voice shouting, "How would you like it if I walked in to your boss and told him you're a faggot? I'll protect you as long as you protect me! Wait till you make my kind of money, and then you can blow it!"

I walk into the living room. Fred—slim, delicate, nineteen—is sitting tensely in a big armchair. Jack—big, masculine and aggressive-looking—turns to me and says angrily:

Look, I didn't know you were coming here. I thought Fred was going to your place to talk to you. If I'd known you were coming, I wouldn't have been here. It's too late now. You may as well hear this. I want you both to get this straight. [*He continues his angry, admonitory lecture to Fred, who at moments seems about to cry.*]

You still have to learn this. Being homosexual is like being black or a Jew. In the concentration camps the Nazis had yellow stars for Jews and pink stars for homosexuals—except for all the homosexuals who were in the SA. Look, X [*a famous playwright*] can be an open faggot all over New York and get away with it. He can afford it. Until you're where he is, you play it cool.

[*Fred nods, swallows to keep back tears. Jack is talking to Fred still, but I feel this is meant for me as much as for Fred.*] You just have to learn this. Look, I don't have any big bond with homosexuals just because they're homosexuals, but you have to learn to protect the people around you. When you make a hundred G's a year like I do, you see whether you can afford to have it blown to somebody who walks in here. [*He leans back in the chair, a little more benign. I am now wondering how long he will go on if no one stops him. He is past the first spurt of rage; the talk is now more instructional.*]

When I was twenty-one, I used to go to gay bars and give a fake name, because I was so paranoid I was afraid my father could be blackmailed. Now sometimes I walk into a bar and see one of those people I met there years ago, and he calls me by the fake name I used to use. So the only answer for me now is, I don't go to bars! [*He lectures Fred for ten minutes more. Finally he turns to me and says almost genially,*] Well, I guess it's all right. I had to make this point to him. The biggest hang-up dealing with gay people is that they're all children.

[*Fred soon excuses himself, and almost sails out of the room. Jack haggles with me about the waiver form I use as a legal guarantee of anonymity. It is all an immense production. Meanwhile, his boyfriend, Larry, has arrived. Larry is nineteen, tall, with shoulder-length pageboy hair and a perfect, slightly androgynous beauty, with finely molded features that could have come off an Italian Renaissance cameo. He wears jeans and a striped sweater. His manner is archhip—very slow, passive and detached. He slouches in an easy chair, a leg thrown over one side, smoking hashish, strumming his guitar and sometimes stopping to stroke or brush his hair with unabashed sensual interest.*

Through most of the conversation, Jack leads, lectures, dominates. Larry chimes in, echoing him, repeating his arguments, sometimes making token gestures of independence in his views, but leaving no doubt who's the leader.]

Why do you think there are so many homosexuals in the entertainment business?

JACK: The homosexual is like the Jew in feudal Europe. He's prohibited from so many fields, he gravitates to those where people are empathic enough not to limit him as a human being because he's homosexual. Then people go screaming that homosexuals dominate this or that.

But when homosexuals work in the same field or the same company, like you and Fred, do they tend to support each other?

JACK: At work, when I have to choose between another Jew and a Gentile, I choose a Jew, because I know how he thinks. But if I have to choose between a homosexual and a heterosexual, I choose the heterosexual. Who needs trouble?

But there is a homosexual ideology, a group ideology.

JACK: I used to be turned off by the whole homosexual argument. Now I see more in it. You must read Mary Renault's *Last of the Wine*. It shows the real, legitimate homosexual relationship. I think some homosexuals are that way from the day they're born; they'll be homosexual aside from any influences.

Some are homosexual because of psychoneurotic problems—it's their choice. Those are probably the majority. To exist, to avoid death of the ego, it must be chosen; it's the alternative to the Oedipal mother. Larry is a good case of that. His mother complains and dominates, just turns him into jelly. But the more I read, the more I believe in genetic studies. Almost every homosexual I know, including myself, has a gay sibling, or maybe a gay cousin.

LARRY: Yes, my mother was my buddy when I lost my father. She was my friend for years, till she remarried. God, is she a nag!

JACK: Homosexuality is normal because it occurs in nature. My dog will do it. I think it's probably a naturally occurring kind of attraction, which in fact may have helped at various times in history to produce a better society. If it weren't for society, most homosexuals would be heterosexual, and would have occasional homosexual experiences.

Why don't homosexuals usually have lasting relationships?

JACK: There's no pressure, no requirements to bind them. If those pressures and requirements didn't exist, no more heterosexuals would stay together than homosexuals. Now, Larry and I can be heterosexual sometimes, as long as it doesn't interfere with our relationship. We both have sexual freedom, but we rarely use it. Sometimes we slip. We both intend to get married if the right chick comes along. I've had three long, satisfying relationships with women, and Larry has had good heterosexual relationships. We may go out together with a couple of chicks and end up in the rack with them. [*Larry nods.*] But the girl can't interfere with our relationship. We even took the same girl to bed together once.

I mean, in this society we have to get back to the Greek pattern. Women for home and children, but not for friendship. For that you need a man. He thinks and feels the way you do. It's American and Western sexual relationships that are twisted. The problem is that the American girl wants liberation, but she wants the old privileges.

LARRY: Right. I'm perverse in the eyes of society. Then fuck society! After all, there's nothing unhealthy about homosexuality, medically. And I've had a good heterosexual life. But the more I think about it, the more I see I was homosexually inclined from the beginning. Every man has this if he'll admit it. I didn't start with girls till I was fifteen, didn't get laid till I was sixteen, which was late for a guy in my prep school. I didn't really feel much for girls, but I'd go home after school with a copy of *Playboy* and jack off. But once I'd had girls, I went like a house on fire. I'm truly bisexual. This went on till I was sixteen or seventeen, just screwing. Then I wanted a relationship. I mean, I can swing both ways. I've been homosexual for about a year; the last heterosexual sex I had was . . . [*he stops to calculate in his head*] . . . about seven months ago.

You don't really prefer men or women?

LARRY: The most satisfying thing about homosexuality is the emotional side. It's easiest to be a friend with someone of the same sex. Women have a whole different psychology.

[*When Larry speaks of women, sex with women, his mother, his tone is one of disdain and disgust. Jack's voice, manner and choice of words always show bottled-up rage about to break loose, but it is especially strong when he is speaking of women.*]

JACK: The problem he's talking about is American momism at its worst. Homosexuality became a way to fight it. I mean, Philip Wylie described it so well. Larry, have you read Philip Wylie? He's really one of the greatest writers of our time. [*Larry shakes his head.*] I wonder whether the incipient homosexual doesn't pick out girls who are easy to screw. He doesn't get involved, and he proves his social point.

LARRY: That's a lot of where I'm at. I like to direct things in a heterosexual relationship, but I like to be directed in homosexual ones. I like to get advice, have a father confessor. I *like* to get laid. I mean, wow, it's really great. But the important thing is friendship. The average homosexual relationship is a burning love affair, not a friendship. Being in love is wanting to spend most of your time with one person. My homosexual love knows my innermost thoughts. A woman never could, she has a whole other psychology.

JACK: That's the way I feel. If I ever have a son, it should be like Larry. Or if I could pick a father. If I could be born again, I'd like to be like Larry.

LARRY: That's just the way I feel about Jack.

JACK: We aren't like most homosexuals. The magic in-love stuff they write about is bullshit.

LARRY: That's right. It all started with some feudal guy writing poems to a woman because she didn't want to be seduced until she had this cat in the palm of her hand!

Jack, when were you aware of being homosexual?

JACK: It began when I was sixteen, lying in bed masturbating, and I realized what I was fantasying. I thought, "Son of a bitch, Jack, you're queer!" In just those words. My problem later became, "How do I deal with those idiots who don't want to let me live?" I went into therapy because in my sophomore year at college I started going to gay bars. I was upset, was sleeping instead of going to classes. I went to a rabbi, who got me to a psychiatrist, and I went for a while, and let me tell you that it takes a lot of guts to make the homosexual decision and step outside the pale. I got into the same avoiding-class trouble in graduate school and went for therapy again. Together, I had three years of intensive therapy, and got an MS in clinical psychology. My analyst taught me the attitude that homosexuality is a positive alternative to ego death.

I said it before—I still don't feel any bond with a homosexual because he's homosexual. There's a kind of Jew I call a kike, and there's a kind of homosexual I call a faggot, and neither reflects well on me. Actually, I'm a chicken hawk, I just like young bodies. If I ever get sent to jail, it'll be for screwing a teeny-bopper. It hangs me up, because I like an older head. My outlet has varied over the years, totally heterosexual sometimes, and totally homosexual sometimes. When I was with a woman, it was 99 per cent heterosexual. Now it's 99 per cent homosexual because of Larry.

Larry, what about you?

LARRY: I met Jack four years ago, when I was fifteen. I've known him since then, and I traveled back and forth between here and home to visit him, and, then between here and college. This past year, we're really making it together, as friends and in the rack. The problem is, when you say you're homosexual, you find yourself in a gay bar and ask, "What do I have to do with this bunch of faggots?" I was in therapy, too, for a few months.

JACK: I sent him, because he was young, and I was introducing him to homosexuality, and I was responsible. And because of the army. He's passive, and he went CO. As for cure, I object to the term. Homosexuality is a symptom.

LARRY: [*Angrily.*] It's not a disease!

Do you come across fag hags, the girls who hang around with men who are homosexual? [They both nod.] What are they like? Why do they do it?

JACK: They aren't openly homosexual, but the homosexual men are safe for them. If they engage in sex, it's oral.

LARRY: It's a boost to their egos to see men bow to the almighty cunt.

JACK: A faggot treats the girl like his mother, and she gets an ego boost.

What patterns do you see in homosexuals in terms of background?

JACK: Most homosexuals are middle class. They may not make much money, but they're of middle-class origin. Working-class homosexuals are prostitutes or have polymorphous behavior and don't consider themselves homosexuals. A lot of southern boys are like that, and lots of them are available; you find that out when you drive around down there, and friends of mine have said the same thing.

LARRY: The hippies are either or both, but they just aren't up tight.

[*We talk on for a while, and finally the conversation trickles out. I feel that Jack threw his initial rage in order to steal the spotlight and get me to listen to him, not because of anger at the threat of exposure. I come back later to talk more to Fred and his lover, and several more times over the next month to talk to people in their group. I will find that the opinion of several people is that Larry is really just a kept boy, with girlfriends on the side, who will skip out on Jack if ever the big allowance and supply of hashish give out. And that despite Jack's insistence to the contrary, almost everyone he works with knows he is homosexual.*]

3

Homosexual and Pansexual

We learn our official cultural heritage from books; as a result, our idea of our vital past tends to narrow to the small part that survives on paper. But our deepest heritage, lived each moment of our lives, is the total emotional style of our society, and often that is reflected only obliquely in recorded culture. We start to learn it the day we are born. We begin with nursing, weaning, toilet training and discipline. We continue to learn from children's games, gestures without words, smiles, frowns, an averted eye or an unthinking nod. The total complex of feelings and values, of each civilization at each time in history, is distinctive; therefore the pattern of sexual expression is probably in some ways unique in each.

Our total inheritance is as much Celtic, Teutonic, Iberian and Slavic as it is Hebrew, Roman or Greek. The loves of ancient Celtic heroes may explain as much about us as do those of Homeric chiefs, but just how much, and in what way, we cannot tell: only the Hebrew, Greek and Roman traditions were extensively committed to paper. Greek colonizers, for instance, carried their sexual style with them to Italy, France, Spain. There they met people who may have had similar or very different sexual patterns and attitudes. The kind and degree of mutual influence is a piquant unknown. Massilia, the ancient Marseilles, was notorious in classical literature for homosexuality. Whether that homosexuality was a Greek transplant, a native practice or a combination of the two will probably always remain a gap in our knowledge.

Classical literature sometimes describes the sex lives of non-Greek and non-Roman peoples, but between ignorance and malice, it has little credibility. Aristotle, Strabo and Diodorus Siculus all claimed that the ancient Celts practiced homosexuality; Diodorus credited them with playing a homosexual version of "Lucky Pierre"—a sexual sandwich of two catamites for each man. Unfortunately, many ancient writers understood their neighbors about as well as medieval Christians did the Jews in their midst. Stories of Celts bedding down in homosexual trios may be true or they may mean as little as medieval tales of Jews breakfasting on Christian babies.

This same uncertainty clouds ancient writings on the sexual life of the Etruscans, who strongly influenced the technology, the art and possibly the mores of the Romans. Roman sexual life was very different from that of the Greeks, and it might be clearer to us if we knew more about their Etruscan relatives. A little before the time of Homer, the Etruscans, Latins and other tribes that spoke Indo-European languages entered Italy from the east and displaced the neolithic peoples there. In the sixth century B.C. the warlike and mercantile Etruscans had absorbed influences from all over the Mediterranean and developed a refined and artistic culture; they dominated the Italian peninsula and ruled the Latins and many other of their neighbors. But before long the Etruscan empire mysteriously declined; the Latins escaped their rule, defeated them, and finally exterminated them. The Etruscan language is still largely undecoded, and it is to Etruscan art and non-Etruscan writers that we must look for information. Plato, Herodotus, Aristotle, Timaeus, Theopompus and many others wrote that the Etruscans were wild hedonists, distinguished for their open drunkenness, debauchery, effeminacy and homosexuality. In fact, these writers draw a picture that somewhat resembles Rome in the days of the Empire. Scholars today question or discount ancient stories of Etruscan homosexuality; they do not correspond with the evidence of Etruscan art, with its deep obeisance to heterosexual pleasures and marital devotion. Equally uncertain is D. H. Lawrence's version of them as joyous sensualists. The ancient Greek views of the Etruscans may be due to the fact that Etruscan women seem to have had relative freedom and esteem. A parallel can be seen in Mediterranean countries today, where men tend to assume that female tourists are all promiscuous, because only a promiscuous woman of their own society would travel alone or speak to strangers. In the same way, the legend of Etruscan bisexual libidinousness may have been created by Greeks who thought that a society where women were not locked away must be orgiastic.

The origins of the Romans and Etruscans may have been similar, and the Etruscan influence on Rome was powerful, yet there is a dramatic difference between the ancient accounts of Etruscan and early Roman mores. The later Romans talked constantly about the simplicity, self-discipline and strict morality of their forebears, and compared them to the so-called degeneracy of their own times. In 300 B.C. the Latins had still been unimportant to the rest of the world; a century and a half later they were the West's greatest power, soon to control the entire European and African Mediterranean, the Near East, and parts of northern Europe. Now they looked back to their past with nostalgia, blaming every ill, from the economic to the sexual, on the loss of their rigid rural virtue. Seneca, Cato, Tacitus and others complained that civic corruption, religious mania, adultery and effeminacy were results of the loss of the original Latin spirit as wealth, empire and foreign influence arrived. They especially deplored the influence of the Greeks, whom they viewed with envy and suspicion and thought of as Americans and Englishmen have traditionally stereotyped Parisians—cunning, effeminate and degenerate.

This view has been perpetuated by scholars ever since—that the fall of Rome was implicit in its rise, and that growth, prosperity, cosmopolitanism and sexual freedom are all signs of decadence. It is sometimes called, especially in regard to the United States, Rome's lesson for the twentieth century. Whether in fact these things make people less moral or fit to survive is an important question, but not one solved by Senecan clichés. Explaining today's difficulties by the loss of yesterday's virtue is a sport as old as the second generation of man. According to patriotic myth, the Romans were once hard-working, dutiful, straightforward and chaste. We have only myth to assure us that they were truly hardier than homosexual Dorian warriors, more dutiful or hard-working or chaste than peasant societies anywhere.

It is true that they apparently began as a dour, no-nonsense people who praised *gravitas, pietas, simplicitas* and *virtus*—dignity, respectfulness, simplicity and manliness. However, as much as they praised straightforwardness, their history usually shows its use only as a last resort, and disingenuousness is not a gift of advanced civilization. Like any undeveloped, rural people, the early Romans probably led rather predictable lives much of the time, but that does not mean they were simple or good. They always seemed less complex in character than, say, the Greeks, but the myth of simple people, as individuals or as a society, always disappears with close knowledge. The Roman myth of early virtue sounds like that of conservative Americans today, who point yearningly to pre-urban, pre-industrial America as a sadly lost world of virtue and contentment; one wishes they could spend just a week in the real, not the mythical, small-town America of the nineteenth century, with its lawlessness, bigotry, cultural barrenness—and doubtless human relationships as complex as those of any other place or time. An American especially should suspect the Greek view of the Romans, for it resembles contemporary European clichés about the United States—"simpler and less mature." The Romans, like us, were restless, aggressive, eclectic; shocking one moment in their lack of finesse, clever and complicated the next; constantly experiencing terrific change and strain as their society underwent cataclysmic alteration; and reduced, in the eyes of their jealous neighbors, to a race of silly, rich children.

The farmers and herdsmen of early Rome may or may not have practiced homosexuality; discounting the retrospective piety of later writers, we know terribly little about them. Women were legally more enslaved even than in Greece, but in practice they were probably less despised and restricted. They were accepted and even admired as human beings because of their work as mothers, helpmates and sometimes as active members of their society. The family and its close relationships were highly valued. The power of the husband-father was very great in theory, but no one can say just how harshly it was usually exercised. Certainly as time went on, women won equality in law and in daily life as they never did in Greece.

The increasing freedom of women was only part of a complex, massive social change that took place as the empire grew, and a closed village society became an open urban one. In the first century A.D. Rome had more than a million inhabitants. Peasants flocked into the cities, and the old culture crumbled; there were social upheaval and deep personal bewilderment. The mores of the city children were not those of their country-bred parents. Citizens went to foreign countries to fight, rule or trade and came back with new tastes, views, religious beliefs. The legions borrowed the Mithraic cult from the Near East; Greco-Roman art was carried to the edge of the far Orient. Rome was mobbed with the uprooted not only of Italy but of the whole empire—Syria, Egypt, Germany, France, Spain, the Balkans. The old patrician families were pushed aside by *nouveaux riches*—a new middle class of freeborn speculators, of drifters and adventurers, of newly freed foreign slaves who became millionaires and powerful politicians.

Traditional ideas of class, morality and manners changed, and so did those of family and sex. In the first century the emancipation of the Roman woman was complete. Her free consent was necessary for marriage; she received an education; she had liberty of movement and full economic rights. The *hetaira* was unnecessary, for a wife, lover or single woman of one's own class might have all the freedom, charm and sexual expressiveness that Greeks allowed only to "bad" girls. Adultery became common; so did contraception and abortion, and the birth rate dropped in the middle and upper classes. Men and women might marry several times for financial, political or emotional reasons.

Like their modern American counterparts, Roman women suffered because they had cast off old standards of femininity, but had nothing to take their place. They had not been raised to participate seriously in professions, art, politics and public life; unable to use their freedom to purpose, they often retreated to a frantic search for fulfillment in their sex lives. A woman was not merely a mother, nor merely a wife, nor merely a lover—but neither was she a man, dedicated to a vocation and proud of fulfilling traditional male obligations. Neither men nor women were very sure any more what was or was not womanly; therefore neither could they be sure what was masculine. The idea of a satisfying life centered not on family and vocational involvement, but on pleasure and passion—whose satisfaction does not seem enough to anchor most people's sense of identity in the long run.

Family and parental roles probably lost importance and clarity in the lower as well as upper social classes, but Roman writings tell us mostly about the well-to-do, so we have a fairly detailed picture of their problems. Upper-class children were raised by slaves and by the Greek chambermaids it was fashionable to own or hire, while the parents pursued evanescent sexual satisfactions and labored at social climbing. Judging by what psychiatrists see today in family patterns, one would expect certain characteristics to appear fairly frequently as a result. The lack of dependable, warm, nurturing parents may produce children with frozen emotions and poorly developed superegos—that is, people who are cold and conscienceless. Parents whose sexual identity is shaky may produce children with poorly defined sexual identities and, sometimes, vague discrimination among sexual objects. Roman life was, in fact, marked by bisexuality, homosexuality, brutality and emotional caprice.

An excellent example is the poet Catullus. Literary history usually emphasizes his importance in developing the idea of romantic love; his verses are the high point in lyrical love poetry between Sappho and medieval courtly literature. He came to Rome from Verona as a young man around 61 B.C. and fell in with a fashionable set of young intellectuals, politicians, society people and poets. He met a woman named Clodia, wife of the governor of Cisalpine Gaul, and wrote love poems to her in which she was disguised by the name Lesbia—which may suggest either the poetic influence of Sappho or bisexuality. Catullus' rage of love is exceptional in classical literature; it was he who invented the phrase "*odi et amo*"—"I hate and I love." When Clodia's husband died, Catullus hoped to have her wholly, but she began a career of random promiscuity. The more she deceived and humiliated him, the more he needed her. It was as though his love were a madness that could feed only on frustration and fury.

But there was another, and equally important, side to Catullus. Without Clodia around, he wrote love poems to boys, as tender and contradictory as those to her—demanding and pleading, craving and disgusted. Although he indulged in homosexuality, he mocked it in others. Sometimes he withdrew emotionally from both women and boys into caprice, flippancy, a cold-blooded search for impersonal physical satisfaction that brings to mind the tortured, driven rakes of Restoration England.

> O Cato listen, here's something so fantastic
> it deserves your laughter,
> laugh then as heartily as you love your Catullus.
>
> I saw a boy and girl (the boy on top) so I fell,
> chiefly to please Dione,
> upon the boy and pierced him,
> held him to his duty with my rigid spearhead.

Like Tibullus, Propertius and many other Roman poets, he could love only with alternating rapture and revulsion, driven by a rage that made the object seem almost irrelevant. Sex was an act of vengeance as much as love, and the threat he makes to two homosexuals is, "I'll blow you and bugger you, pathic Aurelius and fairy Furios." As in Greece, men suffered such uneasiness in their love relationships that they withdrew to whores and to superficial dalliances with boys, carrying on with both a brutal game of dominance and submission. It was not healthy pansexuality, any more than in Greece, that made them bisexual or homosexual, but fearful avoidance. Tibullus fell in love with sluttish Delia and mercenary Nemesis, then with a young man named Marathon, who deceived him for a wealthier man and then for a girl. The poet showed all three as greedy and full of cruel whims. Propertius, during his violent and unhappy affair with his Cynthia, wrote, "A woman's love? My enemies may have it. I wish my friends the love of some young boy. For him no griefs; an easy tranquil journey on little waves that bring no pain but joy. Him can you soften with a single word; die, and you have her cold heart still unstirred."

The cool-headed Epicurean poet Lucretius gave typical Roman advice on love. He said that though sex is a hygienic necessity, love is a disgusting disease that makes men plead, moan, grovel and stupidly rub their bodies against women's in fits of weakening emotion. Whenever a man finds himself caught in this madness, he should think of everything ugly and disgusting about the girl—bowel, smells, stupidity, avarice—and be cured, like Swift's lover fleeing in obsessive horror:

> Thus finishing his grand Survey,
> Disgusted Strephon stole away
> Repeating in his amorous Fits,
> Oh! Celia, Celia, Celia shits!

Horace, who wrote love poems to both boys and girls, scoffed at all emotional involvement. Adultery and whores, he said, are just trouble, so "When your passions urge, and a young slave girl or boy for whom you long is at hand, would you rather be consumed with desire than possess it? Not I." His poems, full of tender but quite literary love, tell less of Roman life than does this offhand practical advice; they are verbal wreaths to pieces of attractive and frustrating flesh from which he wanted submission and compliance, but not complexities or intimacy.

A psychiatrist today might say of lovers of Horace's and Catullus' type that in childhood they had failed to develop affectional bonds or a firm idea of their sexual identity; that the results were cold, mechanical, angry indulgence of the senses, pansexuality, hidden or open sadism, and other psychosexual disorders. Sadism, in fact, apparently became almost universal. Flogging with birch switches and leather whips was a common punishment in schools and homes; frustrations could be vented by cruelty to slaves. Rome's most popular diversion was the arena, where men were burned alive, dismembered, flogged with chains, disemboweled, decapitated, torn apart by beasts. People whose emotions are frozen need extreme stimulation; Ovid—detached, charming, graceful—recommended the arena as a fine place for flirtations and the beginning of a love affair. One thinks again of the London gentlemen of the seventeenth and eighteenth centuries who assaulted and mutilated people in the streets and sought sexual release with every sort of sexual object in cold frenzy.

Suetonius' biographies of the twelve Caesars from Julius Caesar through Domitian is a catalog of astounding psychosexual disease, from incest to transvestism. Julius Caesar slept his way to early success in the bed of King Nicomedes of Bithynia; he depilated his body and was dandyish to the point of effeminacy; he was variously called "the Queen of Bithynia" and "every woman's man and every man's woman." Tiberius retired to a pleasure palace on Capri where he kept *spintriae*—effeminate homosexuals—who performed in groups; he trained little boys, whom he called his "minnows," to lick and nibble between his legs while he swam; he had unweaned babies suck at his penis. A list of Tiberius' tortures and atrocities would nauseate anyone but a psychopath.* Mad, epileptic boy-emperor Caligula was equally sadistic, committed incest with his three sisters, indulged in both heterosexual and homosexual acts, and often appeared in public dressed as a woman. Claudius kept favorite freedmen and eunuchs; Nero was introduced to homosexuality by Seneca, his tutor. He slept with his mother and then had her assassinated. Suetonius says:

> Not satisfied with seducing freeborn boys and married women, Nero raped the Vestal Virgin Rubria. . . . Having tried to turn the boy Sporus into a girl by castration, he went through a wedding ceremony with him—dowry, bridal veil and all. . . . He was released from a den dressed in the skins of wild animals, and attacked the private parts of men and women who stood bound to stakes. After working up sufficient excitement by this means he was despatched—shall we say?—by his freedman Doryphorus. Doryphorus now married him—just as he himself had married Sporus—and on the wedding night he imitated the screams and moans of a girl being deflowered.

Vitellius came next; he advanced toward the throne by being a *spintria* for Tiberius at Capri in his boyhood; he was notorious for his murders and tortures, and depended for political advice on his catamite Asiaticus. Titus kept a troop of inverts and eunuchs. Domitian at first forbade castration, enforced laws against adultery and child prostitution, and had many men convicted under the old Scantinian Law that forbade homosexual relations with freeborn boys, but soon sadism and indiscriminate bisexuality dominated him too.

Not one of these emperors was exclusively homosexual; their homosexual behavior was only one expression of their psychopathic characters. Homosexual behavior in Rome went the full range from occasional and casual indulgence through transvestism. Among the moneyed, it was often carried on in fashionable imitation of the Greeks, with pretty long-haired boys serving wine as Sappho and Anacreon were read aloud. There was, however, none of the Greek pedagogic rationalization. Roman sexuality was more frank and aggressive, even when it protested its love.

Female homosexuality existed, but apparently far less than among males. The *olisbos* was frequently mentioned in Latin literature, usually as used

---

*It must be made clear that never in the ancient world, to our knowledge, was violence consciously practiced to bring orgasm. There was no sexual sadism, in the strict sense, until the Renaissance. The Roman brutality, though, was part of the character disorder that manifested itself in other sexual deviations.

by women for masturbation, but sometimes allegedly for tribadic inter-course. Seneca, Juvenal and Lucian mentioned lesbianism, but the only physical details from the Greco-Roman world are in the epigrams of Martial. He believed that the tribade was created with an abnormally large cli-toris with which she penetrated other women—a myth that did not die till the twentieth century. Two of his epigrams say:

> As no one, Bassa, ever saw you go with men; as rumor never assigned you a lover, as every office about you was fulfilled by a troop of women, no man ever coming nigh you, you seemed to us, I admit, a very Lucretia. But, oh! shame on you, Bassa, you were a fornicator all the time! You dare to con-join the private parts of two women together, and your monstrous organ of love feigns the absent male. You have contrived a miracle to match the The-ban riddle: that where no man is, there adultery should be!

> Philaenis the tribade pedicates boys, and stiffer than a man, in one day works eleven girls. . . . After all that, when she is in good feather, she does not suck, that is too feminine; she devours right out girls' middle parts. May all the gods confound you, Philaenis, who think it manly work to lick cunt.

We can say little about the backgrounds of male and female homosex-uals or of their origins by class and by ethnic, urban or rural background. However, the poets Juvenal and Martial give a vivid picture of homosexual behavior in their society, more detailed and specific than is available for any other period in our distant past.

At the end of the first and beginning of the second centuries A.D., Juv-enal wrote sixteen verse satires on the vices of his times. There is a story that he had been banished from Rome for many years by Domitian for obliquely slighting in a poem one of the homosexual actors among Domi-tian's favorites. Prostitution and homosexuality were common among the actors and mimes of Rome—the first record of the long Western associa-tion between the theater and homosexuality.

After Juvenal returned from exile, he lived in poverty and bitterness, writing attacks on the decay of the Roman people, especially the ruling class. It is easy to believe the story of his banishment, for the dominant theme of his satires is that the perverted—in sex, moral principle and life style—were taking over Rome and destroying it. In the first satire he painted the streets of the capital thronging with crude *nouveaux riches,* criminals, transvestites, gigolos, and eunuchs who got rich by cunning and took wives for appearance's sake. Many Romans responded to the con-fused society they lived in with cynicism, stoicism or hedonism; the moral-istic Juvenal was implacably furious.

Juvenal's second satire is devoted entirely to male homosexuality. Like Horace and Catullus, he was not against homosexual acts *per se,* but he found exclusive homosexuality absurd and effeminacy disgusting. Most important, he feared that the high echelons of government, business and social life were riddled with irresponsible, greedy deviants who contributed to the ills of society instead of curing them. He begins the second satire by saying that some men are born homosexual and should be pitied, but goes on to attack homosexuals with disgust and indignation. He says that some men who seem rough, taciturn Stoics are, in fact, homosexuals:

> What street is not filled, overflowing
> With these glum-looking queers? You rail at foul practices, do you,
> When you're the ditch where they dig, the Socratic buggering perverts?
> Hairy parts, to be sure, and arms all covered with bristles
> Promise a rough tough guy, but the pile doctor smiles; he knows better
> Seeing that smooth behind, prepared for the operation. . . .

One of these fake Stoics gives a lecture against the immorality of modern Roman women; a woman answers, saying that the very men who make such speeches are often homosexuals, more immoral than any female, and the law that should be invoked is not the Julian, forbidding adultery, but the Scantinian, forbidding homosexuality.

> Some of us do eat raw meat, and a few might be lady-wrestlers,
> But look at you, spinning the wool, and mincing along with full baskets.
> Don't think I don't know why Hister bequeathed to his freedman
> All he owned; why, in life, he rewarded his consort so richly.
> She who sleeps third in a big wide bed is certain to prosper.
> Marry, and shut your mouth; the wages of silence are jewels!

But worse than these hyprocrites, says Juvenal, are the homosexuals who meet secretly, dress as women and hold services for the Great Mother (whose worship was now common in Rome) that turn into homosexual orgies.

> Here's a lad making his eyebrows long, with damp soot on a needle,
> Here's one taking a swig from a goblet shaped like a phallus,
> Another one fixing his eyes, with a golden net on his long hair.
> Here's one in sky-blue checks, another in pale-green satin
> With a male maid who swears, as does the master, "By Juno!"

Something still worse can be found—a Gracchus, member of a noble old Roman family, who married another man in a secret wedding ceremony, as Nero married his favorites. Juvenal ends by saying that Rome's corruption will corrupt all its subject people.

> So, we have come to this. Our arms have invaded the Orkneys,
> Ireland, the northern lands where the light dwells long in the summer,
> But the acts that are done in this proud city of victors
> Never were done by the men we have beaten down. Wait! They tell us
> Here's an Armenian prince, softer than all of our fairies,
> Said to have given himself to some tribune's passionate ardor.
> An innocent hostage he came here, but Rome is where we make men.

In the third satire he speaks of widespread homosexuality among actors and of the alleged Greek homosexual influence on Rome. In the sixth he gives the classic argument of Rome's moral degeneration. In the old days women were chaste and frugal, stayed at home, and had babies whom they raised to be responsible citizens of a healthy state. Now patrician women keep sterile but sexually competent eunuchs on their household staffs, sleep with actors and gladiators and even lie in brothels. They are driven into furies of lust at the cult celebrations of the Bona Dea, and when they cannot satisfy each other sexually any more, they send for slaves, water carriers off the streets, even a burro. Yet like Horace and Lucretius, he advises:

> Surely you used to be sane. Postumus, are you taking a wife?
> Tell me what Fury, what snakes, have driven you on to this madness?
> Can you be under her thumb, while ropes are so cheap and so many,
> When there are windows wide open and high enough to jump down from,
> While the Aemilian bridge is practically in your back yard?
> Or if no such way out appeals to you, isn't it better
> To get some young boy in your bed to sleep with you in the night-time
> Without threatening suits or insisting on costlier presents,
> Uncomplaining if you refuse to breathe hard at his bidding?

In the ninth satire Juvenal meets Naevolus, a pathetic little homosexual prostitute. Juvenal asks why Naevolus, once busy and prosperous, now looks so unkempt. It turns out that he has been the paid lover of a wealthy catamite named Virro. Naevolus took care to send gifts—a parasol, amber balls—on the day for sending presents to sweethearts, but Virro has been stingy with him.

> Does he think this job is so easy,
> Shoving it in to the point where it meets with yesterday's dinner?
> Ploughing the master's field pays more than ploughing his person. . . .

He even fathered a son and daughter on Virro's wife so that Virro could keep up public appearances. But now he knows too much, and Virro fears scandal or blackmail, and it isn't beyond him to have his former whore assassinated.

The tenth satire contains a passage that has been copied and expanded many times by subsequent poets; it is the source of Samuel Johnson's *The Vanity of Human Wishes*. This satire warns mothers to lock up their sons because perversion is so common that a boy is bound to end up degraded or in trouble—a gigolo, an adulterer, a rich man's eunuch. Juvenal's own tastes are given in the eleventh satire, in which he tells of inviting a friend to dine at his simple country home, where Latin is spoken, not affected Greek, and the serving boys are real boys.

> Any service you want you'll have to ask for in Latin.
> All my boys dress alike; their hair is straight and close-cropped. . . .
> One is a sheepherder's son. . . .
> He has an honest look, natural, simple, and modest,
> Such as those should have with the crimson stripe on their togas.
> He doesn't go to the baths with an oil flask over his members,
> Showing his armpits all shaved, an exhibitionistic loudmouth.

Juvenal paints a world in which men have become emasculated and corrupt, the women tough and domineering bawds, both so busy serving their various greeds and perversions that society is an unpiloted ship drifting toward calamity. He often seems too angry to be trusted as a reliable historical source, but Martial and other cool-headed writers confirm much of what he says, from the general state of society to the details of a drag queen's cosmetics.

Martial and Juvenal were friends; much that we know of the latter's life comes from poems written to him by Martial. They shared little, though, except a poet's hard life and the satiric genre. Roman writers had incomes and worked for their own pleasure or were dependent on patrons. In the booming Rome of the first and second centuries, the majority of patrons were no longer men of old noble families, but the vastly wealthier *nouveaux riches*—often crude collectors of parasites and motivated by social ambition rather than love of art. In return for flattering verses they gave money, clothes and meals; the relationship became so mechanical that sometimes the poet, instead of dining with his patron, was handed the price of dinner by a servant and sent off. He had to be servile and persistent—tramping from mansion to mansion, shuffling in waiting rooms crowded with other parasites of the rich—just to get mere food, clothes and lodging. He observed the crudity and vice of the new society with the anger of the outraged poor. He usually became either a bitter moralist, like Juvenal, or a thorough cynic, like Martial.

Spanish-born Martial was a professional survivor, willing to write verse of slobbering flattery to anyone, from the bloody Domitian on down. He had fewer hopes or just less severe expectations than Juvenal. His shrewd, polished epigrams poke fun with cold malice, not reformist rage. Still, his satire always contains at least implied moral standards, or it would have no bite.

Martial assumed that any good-looking young household slave was a homosexual favorite. As in Greece, boy lovers, whether slave or freeborn, could become trying and expensive—Cato was indignant that a pretty youth could cost as much as a farm. Their whims and greed were frequent poetic themes. Many extracted cash and gifts as shrewdly as any grown female prostitute, and Martial describes men ruined by their mercenary wiles. He himself had often been their mark:

> For the purpose of asking and exacting presents, Clytus, your birthday falls eight times in one year. . . . Though your face is smoother than the polished stones of the dry shore; though your hair is blacker than the mulberry ready to fall; though the soft delicacy of your flesh surpasses the feathers of the dove, or a mass of milk just curdled; and though your breast is as full as that which a virgin reserves for her husband . . . let there be some limit to your rapacity; for if you still carry on your joke, and it is not enough for you to be born once a year, I shall not, Clytus, consider you born at all.

Boys normally let their hair grow long until adolescence, when they cut off their locks and began to wear the toga. Long hair after puberty was a mark of the confirmed minion in the slave, of foppishness or homosexuality in the free. After cutting his locks, the former boy minion became a regular adult slave; as in Greece, the freeborn boy who had taken a passive homosexual role was supposed to start pursuing women and perhaps young boys who would be passive to him. Some boys remained homosexual, and a number became prostitutes; there were many in Rome, and some, like Juvenal's Naevolus, were capable of serving men or women as the occasion demanded.

Homosexuals gathered at the baths, along with prostitutes of both sexes, for flirting and pickups. Some men maintained the more traditional Roman style of dress, now associated with Stoicism, but fashions under the first emperors became more exhibitionistic. As today, men's and women's clothing styles drew close, and homosexual style went one step further toward feminine modes than did advanced heterosexual fashions. Silk and shorter clothes became the rage; homosexuals and minions wore revealing or even semitransparent clothes, as did female prostitutes. Frequently they dressed in yellow, *galbus* in Latin; *galbinus*, the diminutive form of the word, became synonymous with homosexuality. Dandies began using perfume and wearing white lead on their faces. Long hair on the head, and depilation of the body except for the pubes and buttocks, became common; but removing the pubic hairs, as many female prostitutes did, and depilating the buttocks were considered marks of homosexuality.

Martial, like many of his contemporaries, considered the new dandyism effeminate, halfway to faggotry, as is evident in the following epigram, in which he makes fun of someone for secret homosexuality—one of his favorite gibes: "Pluck out the hair from breast and legs and arms; keep your member cropped and ringed with short hair; all this, we know, you do for your mistress' sake, Labienus. But for whom do you depilate your buttocks?"

To Martial, as to our society, any marked display of passivity, vanity or narcissism meant masculine inadequacy. In two of his epigrams he compares his own Spanish-provincial virility to the effeminacy of Roman dandies. One says:

Cotilus, you are a pretty fellow. . . . But tell me, what is a pretty fellow? A pretty fellow is one who arranges neatly his curled locks; who continually smells of balsam, continually of cinnamon; who hums catches from the Nile and Gades; who waves his depilated arms in time to varied measures; who all the day lolls amid the women's chairs, and is ever whispering in some ear; who reads billets sent from one quarter to another, and writes them; who shrinks from contact with the cloak or his neighbor's elbow; who knows who is the lover of whom; who hurries from one party to another. . . .

The other asks:

> ... why, for heaven's sake, call me Brother—
> Me, born in Celteberia's land,
> A citizen from Tagus' strand?
> Say, is't that everybody traces
> A wondrous likeness in our faces?
> You walk with sleek and flowing hair,
> While my rough Spanish crop I wear;
> Your polished skin of pumice speaks
> While I have hairy limbs and cheeks;
> You lisp—your tongue's so plaguey weak,
> My infant child could louder speak:
> Are doves like eagles, prithee tell,
> Or like strong lion lithe gazelle?
> From saying Brother then desist, or,
>   Charmenion, I may call you Sister.

Martial mocked sodomy, but when his wife caught him buggering a boy and said she had a posterior too, he answered that women and boys are separate pleasures. He seems too sexually sophisticated to have scorned oral sex, but of the homosexual Zoilus he wrote, "Zoilus, why spoil the bath by bathing your bottom in it? If you would make it still dirtier, plunge your head in." He also gibed at cunnilingus—implying, like Norman Mailer today, that it is done only by eunuchs who are capable of no more. In equally contradictory fashion he composed flattering poems to boys yet wrote scathingly of other men who enjoyed them, and he praised marriage but then called it a worse fate than being a drag queen.

Martial and his Roman audience, like the Greeks, equated masculinity with aggressiveness and dominance; one could use a younger male as a passive sexual object without loss of maleness. Oral sex and sodomy have always, in the West, suggested submission to another's will and pleasure, implying femininity and inferiority. The historian and sociologist Fernando Henriques has suggested that oral sex has been looked down on in the West because of its association with homosexuality; he may have had the equation backward. Martial's ambivalence about oral sex is no different from ours. Our society officially condemns it, and its existence is usually publicly ignored, but many people practice it. Still, even to many who enjoy it, it carries guilty undertones of dominance and submission. Like schoolboys full of desire and shame, we express our ambivalence about oral sex in negative humor. We consider anal sex more deviant than oral sex, homosexual behavior more deviant still. To Martial and his society, oral and anal sex were apparently about as deviant as with us, but casual sex with younger boys less so.

Only a living norm can be violated and create ambivalence. There must have been many people, perhaps a majority, who believed in the traditional values of the society and utterly disapproved of such things. And many

more who, like Martial, alternated between shame and zest. It is easy to
forget that the empire was not a continual three-ring circus of sex, sadism
and psychopathy. Most people must have continued to feel, to at least some
small degree, as Seneca did:

> Virtue you will find in the temple, in the forum, in the senate-house . . .
> pleasure you will more often find lurking out of sight, and in search of
> darkness, around the public baths and sweating-rooms and the places that
> fear the police—soft, enervated, reeking with wine and perfume, and
> pallid, or else painted and made up with cosmetics like a corpse. . . . Scipio
> would disport his triumph and soldierly person to the sound of music,
> moving not with the voluptuous contortions that are now the fashion, when
> men even in walking squirm, with more than a woman's voluptuousness,
> but in the manly style in which men in the days of old were wont to dance.

When we read Suetonius, Juvenal, Martial and others of the period, it
seems that the empire was about to crumble out of sheer mismanagement,
but it went on for centuries more. There were the five "good emperors"
topped by Marcus Aurelius. There were poets, statesmen, bureaucrats, military officers and private citizens who continued to live and work with
bourgeois propriety and devotion to duty; they may have been very like the
Victorian gentlemen who held together and sometimes almost justified the
British Empire, despite its core of greed, brutality and social injustice.
These men of conscience, restraint or mere dullness did not make the pages
of historical scandalmongers and satirists; some lived out the Stoic ideal at
its best. Even Martial believed it, or wanted to, and he put it perfectly in a
lovely epigram:

> . . . the things for to attain
> The happy life be these, I find:
> The riches left, not got with pain;
> The fruitful ground; the quiet mind;
> The equal friend; no grudge, nor strife;
> No charge of rule nor governance;
> Without disease, the healthful life;
> The household of continuance;
> The mean diet, no delicate fare;
> Wisdom joined with simplicity;
> The night discharged of all care,
> Where wine may bear no sovereignty;
> The chaste wife, wise, without debate;
> Such sleeps as may beguile the night;
> Contented with thine own estate,
> Neither wish death, nor fear his might.

There were also great numbers of more or less stable people among the
more or less poor and undistinguished, who had no time, inclination or
opportunities for more than family and work. There must have been countless villages and small towns in the provinces, from Spain and England to

the Middle East, where life went on in a fairly familiar groove for most people. Their presence makes one think, at times, that the entire version of Rome's fall because of license and luxury is a moralistic or propagandistic invention of Christianity. In part it probably is, and we still tend to think that if people are having as much sex as they want and living without hardship, they are in a moral trough and headed for an apocalyptic end.

Still, there must have been some real destructive process at work for so many people to feel that the death of society and the state was imminent. The institution of slavery, with all its demoralizing effects, including unfeeling sexual exploitation of human chattel, went on without opposition. There were sudden wrenchings of life style at all levels of society. There were great masses of poor, uprooted people crowded in all the empire's major cities, living on state dole; perhaps as many more lived in perpetual migration, often unemployed, *luftmenschen* subsisting by cleverness or crime. These bewildered and disgruntled hordes sought inner and outer stability or despaired of finding it. In this atmosphere of upheaval, the institution of the family shattered; men and women were confused about their roles, and children poorly raised.

One of the most convincing proofs of profound and widespread psychosexual malaise is the spread of Great Mother cults all over the empire. The old Latin religion had ceased to engage the minds of the educated by the end of the republic, and it had little power or relevance to the growing urban masses. The Persian cult of Mithraism was adopted by the legions in the Near East and carried all over the empire: the remains of a Mithraic temple have been found even in London, at the site of a Roman settlement. The traditional Roman religion had been hazy about the afterlife; Mithraism, with its dramatic bath in the blood of a bull and its promise of a glorious rebirth, became widespread even though it was never officially adopted into the state religion, as many Greek gods and cults were.

The Bacchanalia arrived in Rome from Greece via southern Italy. Its ceremonies were highly secret, and it was stamped out by the state in 186 B.C. after a scandal that was recorded in detail by Livy. It is possible that the actual issue was more political conspiracy than sexual misconduct—or, more accurately, the misconduct was exploited for political reasons. Livy says, "The men were guilty of more immoral acts among themselves than the women." Similar vague accusations of orgiastic rites involving homosexuality were made against adherents of the Bona Dea, or Good Goddess. She may have originally been a Phrygian version of the Great Mother, and she was worshiped only by women. Plutarch described her rites as being a dignified affair of matrons, rising to its quite moderate heights when "interspersed with gaiety and music." However, Juvenal describes the worshipers as a bunch of sexually crazed women coupling with each other, men and beasts.

Isis, the Egyptian goddess of the moon and of fertility, was also imported to Rome. In 58 B.C. altars dedicated to her were destroyed, and later Tiberius had her image cast into the Tiber because a noblewoman had been sexually "defiled" in her rites. Her cult was finally officially recognized by Caligula, and she had many devotees. Scholars still disagree about whether it was an ascetic cult or promoted sexual license. Apuleius' *Metamorphoses*—or *The Golden Ass*, as it is also known—is, among other things, propaganda for the cult of Isis, and it contains a magnificent description of a procession in her honor—garlanded women in white garments, the music of pipes, the sprinkling of flowers and balsam, priests with shaven heads and white linen robes bearing holy objects and tinkling sistrums. This cult, like Mithraism, promised an afterlife and included baptism—in water, not blood. It particularly attracted women, and it is still open to argument whether temple prostitution had a place in its rites. Juvenal called its priestesses "bawds." Ovid said, "Do not ask what could happen in the temple of linen-clad Isis . . . she makes many women become what she became for Jupiter." A period of chastity was demanded of women before ritual occasions, and Ovid said that this could provide them with a good excuse for putting off lovers. "Often deny your favors. Now pretend a headache, and let Isis be your excuse." The annoyance some men must have felt toward such displays of piety may account in part for the hostility the cult generated.

The most shocking and significant cultic newcomer to Rome was the Great Mother in her castrating forms—Cybele, Atargatis, Astarte. These were versions of the same goddess the Hebrews deplored and whose eunuch or homosexual priests served in temples over much of the Near East. She arrived in Rome in 204 B.C., and at first her adherents were few. The Galli, her priests, were all immigrants from Asia Minor, for Roman men were not allowed to emasculate themselves in emulation of Attis to serve her. In the middle of the first century A.D., the emperor Claudius incorporated the worship of Cybele into the state religion. (When the basilica of St. Peter's on Vatican Hill was enlarged around 1607, inscriptions were found showing that a sanctuary of Cybele had once stood there.) Before long the goddess had a huge following in Rome, and her shrines stood not only in Italy but in Africa, Spain, Portugal, France, Germany and Bulgaria. In the third century baptism in the blood of a bull or ram was added to her ritual of initiation, and Roman citizens were permitted to become neophytes. In the fourth century St. Augustine said that the idol of the goddess was bathed in the Tiber and carried along in a boat that aristocratic matrons pulled by ropes from the shore, while Galli danced alongside in a frenzy, shaking their tambourines.

Ovid and Catullus both wrote poems explaining why the servants of Cybele castrated themselves. According to Ovid, the Phrygian youth Attis pledged himself to the goddess' chaste service, but was overwhelmed by passion for the tree-nymph Sagaritis. The goddess destroyed the tree, and thus the nymph; then she drove Attis into a madness in which he slashed his body with a sharp stone, dragged his long hair through the dust and finally castrated himself, crying:

> "Confounded be those parts that did transgress!
> Confounded be they!" And so off he reft
> His shame; no symptoms of his sex were left.
> This is their pattern; her gelt priests from hence
> Pluck off their locks and cut their pudiments.

Catullus told the ending differently:

> Attis . . . his blood gone mad, seized a sharp stone, divorced his
>   vital members from his body,
> then rising (the ground wet with blood) he was transformed, a
>   woman with her delicate white hands
> sounding the tympanum, the tympanum singing praise through sacred
>   trumpets raised to goddess Cybele,
> mysterious mother of a sexless race.
> Then in his sweet falsetto Attis sang: Now follow me, O priests of
>   Cybele, come follow, we are creatures
> of this goddess, wind, dance, unwind the dance again, O exiles
>   from a far land, come with me
> across the rapid salt sea wave. Your bodies shall be clean; no
>   more shall Venus
> stain you with foul disease and move your limbs with power of love. . . .
> Attis, leaving sweet Pasithea wife of sleep, awoke,
> looked back and saw what he had done, how his mad brain deceived
>   him, saw how he lost
> his manhood—all this in passionless clarity seized his mind, and
>   with his eyes turned homeward
> across the sea, she wept, poor creature, neither man nor woman. . . .
> Great goddess, spare me, never haunt my home—take others for your
>   slaves, those creatures
> that you have driven mad and those who in their madness wake again your
>   passionate cruelty.

By the end of the Republic, the Galli were a common sight in Rome, dressed in Oriental costumes, religious images on their breasts, chanting hymns to the music of cymbals, tambourines, flutes and horns, bearing the idol of Cybele, sometimes begging for alms. Drawing on many classical sources, Frazer, in *The Golden Bough*, says that on March 24 "the Archigallus or high priest drew blood from his arms and presented it as an offering . . . the inferior clergy whirled about in the dance with waggling heads and streaming hair, until, rapt into a frenzy of excitement and insensible to pain, they gashed their bodies with potsherds or slashed them with knives . . . the novices sacrificed their virility. Wrought up to the highest pitch of religious excitement they dashed the severed portions of themselves against the image of the cruel goddess. . . . Goddesses thus ministered to by eunuch priests were the great Artemis of Ephesus and the great Syrian

Astarte of Hierapolis." Frazer gives Lucian's famous description of the rites at Hierapolis, in which the novices slashed and castrated themselves, ran through the city with the bloody organs, and finally cast them into houses. The inhabitants would give the novices women's clothes, which they wore from that time on.

Many of those who had not been won over by the hysteria and pageantry of the Great Mother cults despised everything connected with them— ecstasy, self-mutilation, penance, castration, astrology, fortune telling, mendicancy, the hordes of women who became devout and often gullible followers. All this represented the baleful East. When the Greeks had looked East, they'd done so with suspicion and contempt. The Romans in turn saw Greece and the lands beyond with increasing degrees of distaste. Both Greek and Roman writers used the name of the Persian Sardanapalus as a synonym for refinement, degeneracy, homosexuality and luxury. This idea about the Near East, Middle East and Orient has had a long life. When a British gentleman decades ago said "Levantine," he probably meant pretty much what a Roman meant by "Greek," and what both Greek and Roman meant by "Phrygian."

Homosexuality was constantly imputed to the Galli. It must be remembered that men who lose their testicles after sexual maturity tend to lose their fertility, but nothing else—at least not for a good many years afterward. Apuleius, in his *Metamorphoses*, describes the attempted rape of a youth by a gang of mendicant priests of Cybele, who are portrayed as lubricious old frauds using their cult as an excuse for their laziness, greed and homosexual lust. Martial tells a similar story of a troop of eunuch priests trying to emasculate a handsome young soldier.

The equation of eunuchism, homosexuality and Eastern religious cults is also suggested in Petronius' *Satyricon*. It is believed that Petronius Arbiter, after some years as a government administrator, became a sort of professional sensualist at Nero's court, organizing the emperor's entertainments. Denounced in a court intrigue, he committed suicide, but before dying he made a list of Nero's debaucheries, including the names of the emperor's male and female sexual partners, and sent it to Nero himself. The *Satyricon* must have been tremendous, for the part that survives comprises only the fifteenth and sixteenth sections of the original. It is a pastiche of forms and styles, a parody of epic and rhetorical romance; the heroes are homosexuals stumbling through a series of comic misfortunes in the service of minor lubricious deities. William Arrowsmith points out, in his preface to his brilliant translation of the book, that the *Satyricon* definitely is not an ebullient celebration of homosexuality suited for "adepts in search of classical precedents." It is a work of unremitting irony, satire and parody in which homosexuality provides one more opportunity for comic inversion. It gives minute details of homosexual life—the career of a boy hustler, scenes at the baths, portraits of the entourages of wealthy perverts, homosexual love scenes and quarrels. The hysteria and sentimentality of the affairs is instantly familiar to anyone today who has spent time in homosexual milieux.

Many other writers mocked the cults' eunuchs, and not just for homosexuality. In the fourth century Saint Jerome told how women ordered grown, handsome slaves castrated for their pleasure. A eunuch, said Martial, could be useful even if his penis had been removed with the testicles. "What have you Baeticus, a priest of Cybele, to do with the female pit? That tongue of yours by right should lick men's middles. For what was your member amputated with a Samian potsherd, if the woman's parts had so much charm for you? You must have your head castrated."

It was in association with such cults that emperors' deviance became most flagrant. Commodus, who took the throne in 180, appeared in public dressed as a woman and was strangled by a catamitic favorite; Hadrian deified his homosexual lover Antinous. But neither matched Elegabalus, who began his rule at the age of fourteen in 218, after having been raised in Syria as a priest of Baal. He entered Rome amid Syrian priests and eunuchs, dressed in silks, his cheeks painted scarlet and his eyes made up. Various Roman historians say that he assembled the homosexuals of Rome and addressed them garbed as a boy prostitute; put on a wig and solicited at the door of a brothel; tried to get doctors to turn him into a woman; offered himself for buggery while playing the role of Venus in a court mime; kissed his male favorites' genitals in public and, like Nero, formally married one of them. The phallic sun cult of Baal, like the Great Mother cults, demanded the service of effeminates who joined themselves, as in marriage, to the deity. Elegabalus erected in Rome the great phallic *asherim* which the Hebrew kings had kept trying to purge from their land.

Elegabalus was completely mad. Herodian says the army was appalled by his effeminacy. Finally he was assassinated in a latrine. But during his four years' reign, he made Rome more accustomed than ever to the religious-sexual exports of the East. Until his madness became insupportable to enough people, he was very popular among the masses, and the pageantry of the cult of Baal was welcomed by large crowds.

INTERVIEWS

Clichés and established reputations govern many of our assumptions about life style in various times and places, from ancient Rome to modern-day Dayton. I chose to look into the homosexual subculture of Dayton, Ohio, precisely because it is one of those cities whose name represents the sticks to dwellers in capital cities. If one mentioned the gay world of Dayton to New Yorkers or San Franciscans, they would grin at the very idea. When I arrived there, the first thing I noticed was in character with its reputation; the city had won a national

*award for civic cleanliness, and all over town were posters announcing that this
was* THE CLEANEST CITY IN AMERICA.

*Dayton has about three hundred thousand people; the three major popula-
tion groups are descendants of old North European settlers, white crackers up
from the rural South, and blacks. Local gossip attributed widespread homosexuality to all three, depending on whom one spoke to. Within a five-minute walk
of my downtown hotel were several conspicuous gay bars. Every evening men
cruised the streets nearby in noticeable numbers. Not long ago the city had been
stirred up by the arrest of twenty-six men who had been photographed in the
lavatory of the county courthouse in nearby Xenia, among them a lawyer and a
minister from Dayton. Fifteen of them were originally charged with indecent
exposure and eleven with "sodomy," which could bring a maximum prison sentence of twenty years. Some of the men were later allowed to plead guilty to
lesser charges, and most received only fines and suspended sentences. Their
names had appeared in local newspapers several times during the hearings and
trials, but the* Dayton Daily News, *which had covered the scandal in detail, edi-
torialized: "What innocent person has been harmed? Whom is the law protecting? Does not the law aggravate the problem by pushing it to clandestine
extremes and opening it to blackmail? England recently has joined some European countries in repealing laws against sexual contacts between consenting
adults in private. It seems a sensible course."*

A HIGH SCHOOL TEACHER: I know of four gay bars; one sometimes has female
impersonators. One pick-up area is at 5th and Main and for several blocks
around, near the bars and hotels and the burlesque house. Another is in the
black ghetto on the West Side. The prostitution pattern here for both sexes is
black prostitutes and white customers. The whites cruise in cars on the West
Side—roughly in an area near Roosevelt High, at 3rd and Broadway. The black
women are hustling the white men, and the black men are hustling the white
fags. By the way, fags seem to be almost acceptable on the West Side, but
bulldykes are rare there, and they're treated with a lot of hostility.

I hear that recently the police broke up a group of kids who were hustling;
they made their contacts through ham radio operations. A white Appalachian
boy was a ham, and men contacted him on his set and arranged to pick him up.
He was absent from school so much that he was followed and questioned.
Finally he named men, who were arrested and named more boys, and so on.
About fifteen or sixteen boys were involved. Personally I know that the star athletes in one high school got spending money by hustling fags. They weren't gay,
and they weren't really a gang, just some guys who ran around together. They
were sixteen and seventeen, I'd say. It broke up when some of them started
squealing on each other to the coach.

I've seen gay boys in school, though never an obviously dykey girl. The
schools' attitude is just like that of the general public. There's no active punishment if nothing happens in the open, but there's no counseling, no referral for
help. Administrators and teachers mostly don't even try to teach gay kids. They
just make them pariahs. And that's something, because I personally know of one
man who's highly placed in the school system who's homosexual—it's common
knowledge, a sort of public secret. And another man, a teacher, is a pretty
obvious case. Years back he got married, but he went around everywhere with

his wife and boyfriend. And the system tolerated it. I don't know, you figure it out.

A POLICEMAN: There are at least four fag bars. I think the number could go up to ten if we didn't keep it down. We use harassment to prevent the spread. Usually if people do what they do in private, and there's no violence, they're left alone. But you know, the fags get the young, and we have to stop that. And since there's a lack of laws to prosecute, we have to catch them right in the act. We get some hustlers who work bars on the West Side and around 3rd and Ludlow, but usually people get off with suspended fines and sentences. There just aren't facilities to imprison them all. So there's a high prosecution rate but light punishment. I hear lots of stories about incest among the crackers, and for months I've heard rumors about a so-called erotic club in town, but I don't know anything about it for sure.

A REPORTER: People get arrested at the Y, and there's entrapment at the Mayfair Burlesque—the police use peepholes. Don't bother talking to — [*a police-official*]. He knows a lot and says damn little. Anyway, these things are often pretty complicated. For instance, there's a big hood in town who makes a living just on the blackmail of two prominent homosexuals. He tagged these two guys, got photos and so on. The hood, the two men, the police—everyone knows the story, but there are photos involved, and if the guys prosecute, they'll be ruined. Actually, I don't think there are too many fags here. It's a tough town for homosexuals, they can get in real trouble. You know, last year there was that big bust over at the county courthouse in Xenia, when they got all these guys sword-fighting in the men's room. It's pretty bad when you can't even take a leak unmolested in the county courthouse.

ANOTHER REPORTER: Sure, boys hustle at the bus station and at rough joints on Salem Avenue, and there are couple of classy gay bars downtown. One cop has caught fifteen men in the last few months in the men's room of a department store. He says fifteen guys reached underneath the partitions dividing the stalls and fondled his privates. Now how in hell did he get fifteen guys to do that? Is there really so much homosexuality or do they use entrapment? Anyway, we don't report things like that. They're so common.

LETTER TO "THE PLAYBOY FORUM" IN PLAYBOY MAGAZINE, FEBRUARY, 1967: The vice squad of Dayton, Ohio, has been doing a marvelous job of ridding our town of scandalous activities—that is, rounding up homosexuals. Meanwhile, the Dayton newspapers have been covering their pages with the names, addresses and occupations of those caught in the raids, thereby wrecking the victims' homes, families and careers. . . .

DOUGLAS FAVRE, MANAGING EDITOR OF THE DAYTON DAILY NEWS: Frankly, we were ambivalent about the bust at the county courthouse. As you saw, our editorial said at the time that we are against the present laws, and that our beliefs stand with English law: what consenting adults do in private should be their own business. However, we also happen to be a newspaper, and our job is to keep the public record. The law is as it is, arrests were made and names released, and we printed them. Interestingly, the results were as ambivalent as our position. The mail we received was overwhelmingly against our having printed the names and addresses; but there was also a hostile reaction by many people to our liberal editorial stand. Unfortunately, homosexuality isn't a matter of much public discussion around here. Tomorrow we will print a full-page piece on prison homosexuality in Ohio, to open things up. At the moment many of the cases of the Xenia bust are still pending. One man who was arrested was a prominent lawyer. Another man has already moved away from town. The Mattachine Society picketed us, and they went on TV in Cincinnati to say our printing names was a violation of homosexuals' civil rights.

A LAWYER: Dayton and Cincinnati are the two big towns for homosexuality in this area. You know about the bars, the private club with dancing, the hustling. There are also one or two places where lesbians hang out on East 8th Street. I have a private theory that one of the reasons homosexuality is so big in Dayton is its history during World War II. You know, there are Wright-Patterson Air Force Base and several big plants here, some of which turn out defense products. Women worked in the plants during the war. I think that between the military and the plants, this became a stopping-off and employment point for homosexuals. My personal knowledge tells me that there are few straight women on the night shift at one major factory here that has women on the assembly line.

Actually, when you compare the number of homosexuals and homosexual hustlers with the number of arrests, you have to conclude that this city is pretty easy on homosexuals. There are apartment houses that specialize in renting to male and female homosexuals. Recently there have been big crackdowns on prostitution, but aside from the bust in Xenia, the pressure on homosexuals isn't terrific. Really, I think the only reason for that bust was that so many people come from all over the county and state to the courthouse, and there were so many people being solicited all damn day in there, that the complaints finally forced a police action. By the time it had all gotten under way, and some of the names were out, lots of people wished it had never started.

A TEACHER OF ONE OF THE ARTS FROM THE CINCINNATI AREA: Last year I got an invitation from one of my students to go to a gay St. Valentine's Day party in Dayton. I didn't know any of the people, just this kid, who was a friend of the person giving the party. I was on sabbatical that semester, and I wanted to visit some friends in Dayton anyway, so I drove there and dropped in at the party. Well, here I am, a man in my early fifties, and I walk in on this party of local eighteen-year-old pansies. It was like any silly, innocuous teenage party, with hats and favors and cut-out hearts at each place at the table. It was all pretty funny and sweet to an old queer like me.

4

The Christian Bedrock

Our culture's restraints on sex are usually referred to as Judeo-Christian, as opposed to the alleged free sensuality of "pagans." But Christianity was a syncretic religion, and most of its major elements, from philosophy through ritual to sexual taboos, had long been familiar to the ancient world—baptism, blood communion with the deity, a dualistic view that separated the universe into pure, good spirit and evil, impure matter. Flesh lay on the side of evil, asceticism and impulse-control on the side of virtue. Though Christian polemics made paganism synonymous with untrammeled sex, materialism and worldliness, this very linking of pleasure, luxury, evil and sex had existed all over the ancient West and Near East.

Flight from sex, aggression and worldliness were eminent in many Great Mother cults, which had masses of converts all over the Greco-Roman world. Zoroastrianism and its offspring sects were baldly dualistic and antisexual. The complex religious philosophies of the time made sex an unfortunate backsliding into the animal realm. Stoicism and Epicureanism both preached *ataraxia*—detachment, freedom from passion, control of impulse, withdrawal from the world and from ambition. Epicurus wrote, "Nobody was ever better for the carnal act." Epictetus said, "Suffer and renounce." Apollonius of Tyana looked down on even conjugal love. Neo-Platonism and Gnosticism, which influenced many of the Church Fathers, sided with eternal spirit over transient matter. The Pythagoreans' motto was *soma sema*—the body is a tomb. All these philosophies, which took the place of cults for educated agnostics, promised to save man by denaturing him, curing him of sexual desire and other passions.

The important exception was the Hebrews' naturistic view. They believed that when God looked on the world He had created, He said it was good, and that man should embrace it with praise and thanks. Much of the Old Testament's greatest poetry is celebration of the material world, of love and the flesh, rather than a prayer for the soul's escape from an ignominious shell of matter. It condemns adultery, homosexuality and bestiality, but it contains no paeans to celibacy, no exhortations to preserve virginity. The sin of Adam and Eve was not sex but rebellion against God.

When Protestant fundamentalism arose, Calvin was puzzled by the absence of "Thou shalt not fornicate" from the Hebrew scriptures.

The Babylonian captivity in the sixth century B.C. and the disasters that followed made Jews think of themselves as punished by God for insufficient piety. Their thoughts turned more to sin, repentance and a better world after this one; the mild strain of dualism in Judaic culture grew deeper. The Jewish sectarians called Essenes, whose influence on Jesus was powerful, retired to a simple communal life that was probably a model for Christian monasticism. This new asceticism increased as Jews turned from the chaotic, cosmopolitan Roman world that had shattered their nation. On the other hand, many Jews joined that cosmopolitan society and absorbed the dualistic ideas of Greco-Roman culture.

Christianity rather than Judaism or the Great Mother cults finally won out and became the major religion of the West. We do not know why; history is not a predictive science, and we cannot reconstruct the past, experimentally add or remove elements, and see the results. We can only note the special refraction that Christianity gave to the ancient world's ubiquitous dualism and disdain for the flesh, lay it like a transparency over the picture of the empire's dissolution, and see the congruences.

In 180 A.D., when Marcus Aurelius died, Rome was at its greatest power and apparent stability. But it was already seething with disorder and off keel from abrupt social change. Between 235 and 250 there was almost constant civil war, and a dozen emperors flitted across the throne. In 248, when Rome celebrated what by legend was her thousandth year, the presiding emperor was Philip, son of a Bedouin chief who had married a Christian. The armies he commanded were predominantly German. The capital's population was predominantly Near Eastern and Greek-speaking. The streets thronged with Syrians, Berbers, Iberians, Gauls, Dacians, Scythians, Teutons and Greeks; white-robed, tonsured priests of Isis; Jews, Christians and the eunuch priests of Cybele; the uprooted of three continents.

By the fourth century, only six million of the empire's seventy million inhabitants were Romans. As moralists of the Republic and satirists of the early Empire had feared, the Roman family had shattered, the birth rate declined, and sexual deviance seemed commoner. The upper classes were increasingly devoted to power struggles, hedonism and religious hysteria rather than responsible rule. Assassinations were frequent, and rulers might last as little as a month. One mad, brutal or incompetent despot followed another; the occasional wise emperor could not reverse the empire's course. Civil service, tax collecting, policing, courts and road repair broke down. Warlordism replaced politics; mercenary armies were often busy supporting their generals for the throne instead of guarding a ten-thousand-mile frontier that stretched from Persia to Scotland. Bandits plagued the countryside, and pirates swarmed the Mediterranean. Old provincial patriotisms and hostilities asserted themselves, and one area after another revolted; every time troops were shifted to a trouble spot, the border they had just left unguarded was trampled. In short, the forms of government, social institutions and family life were disintegrating, and people's personal lives had less and less social rootedness. They experienced uncertainty, apathy, frenzy or indifference—something that we today, with our own unrest, spiritual hungers and social atomization, can understand.

A bellicose migration fever had spread over Europe and Asia. People everywhere were on the move—fighting, pillaging, resettling. Goths from southern Sweden fought to the heart of eastern Europe; Persia revived under the Sassanid rulers and overran Syria; Saharan tribes sacked the Roman cities of North Africa; Vandals swept through France, occupied Spain and took Carthage. Angles, Saxons, Jutes, Franks, Thuringians, Burgundians, Suevi, Lombards, Numidians, Libyans and Alemanni all killed, burned and plundered in the Balkans and the Rhine Valley, in the Near East, North Africa and the British Isles. By the fifth century, Europe was a maelstrom of warring hordes. There were probably few people who got through a long life without some shattering experience like that known by the DPs of the Second World War.

Rome was sacked by Goths in 410 and by Vandals in 455. In a century its population had dropped from one and a half million to three hundred thousand. After another century it would be more like fifty thousand, and peasants would be carrying off the charred fragments of great buildings to fortify their crude villages nearby. The empire was dead, and every old tribal, political and linguistic border of Europe had shattered. The bloodletting and reruralization of Europe went on. By 600 centuries of urban culture had been lost, tribes had parceled up the West, and literacy was almost the sole possession of the elite of the Christian clergy. The Dark Ages had arrived. The Eastern Empire, with its capital at Constantinople, went on as a Christian power till the fifteenth century, but its life was more relevant to the Near East than to Europe.

Christianity arose during this confusion, upheaval and slaughter, absorbed the values of a dozen different tribal cultures, and won out over many similar competing faiths. The reason for its triumph may lie in the social disorganization and brutal misfortunes of the late Roman world. Like the Jews in Babylon, many people wondered what they had done to bring on such disaster; they felt guilt and wanted relief from it. Social flux had created a mood of emotional deprivation. Petronius portrayed great masses who lived not only with practical insecurity but also with alienation, frustration, a lack of belief or purpose in their lives; many must have been grateful for a faith demanding deep commitment. The people like Catullus and Clodia who had been raised without developing a capacity for lasting affectional ties or a secure sexual identity must finally have needed relief from the emptiness and anger at the center of their lives.

Christianity said, "Surrender anger, abandon the sterile struggle, receive forgiveness and purpose." Other religions offered this, but few with such fervent radicalism. The Church first attracted many fanatics, and their example must have impressed the undecided who sought the security of true belief. In one gesture, converts felt they had become as children are sometimes imagined to be—free of fear, pain, anger and lust.

The great personalities that shaped Christianity would fare badly in the hands of psychiatric analysis; it takes great understanding not to see this as a bad reflection on either camp. Later we will examine how the emotional dynamics of conversion resemble those of the "coming out" into a homosexual identity. For the moment, we can see that Christianity rose in a world full of violence, guilt, anxiety and internal anger and lust that had no reassuring limits on them. The two chief controls of impulse that Christianity offered in a world made miserable by unchecked impulse were phobia and reaction formation.

Phobia is irrational fear; it keeps people away from situations that arouse their conflicts and anxieties. A person full of buried fantasies of rape and mayhem may become afraid of means of transportation, of even walking out on the street; thus he is neatly protected from encountering people and situations that will rouse his anger and lust. Reaction formation is a defense that sometimes becomes a personality trait; the conscious mind stands firmly and diametrically opposed to feared unconscious urges. A person seething with angry feelings but afraid of their destructive force or of retribution may become oversolicitous; someone full of sexual urges that fill him with guilt and self-contempt may become a protector of public morals. Phobia controls troubling impulses by avoiding situations where they will be activated; reaction formation denies their existence.

The writings of the Church Fathers sometimes seem one mass of phobia and reaction formation against sexual and aggressive impulses. One should be a gentle lamb, turn the other cheek, avoid worldly competition and power; sex is hurtful to both parties, soiling, dangerous. In fact, self-assertion, aggression and sexuality, as we shall see, are inseparable; one cannot be controlled without controlling the other. In many homosexuals, the avoidance of both is conspicuous, and homosexuality is sometimes successfully treated by regarding it as a phobia—fear of female genitals as a way of avoiding heterosexual assertion. Those who accept the concept of latent homosexuality will find it plentifully in the lives and writings of the Church Fathers. One classical psychoanalyst has described Paul's conversion as a "homosexual solution" to his emotional problems. Rather let us say that a person painfully haunted by hostile and sexual feelings he cannot accept may find many solutions, a variety of attitudes and life styles that bring reassurance. Homosexuality is one; conversion to an antisexual and nonviolent life is another. Many similar feelings and emotional dynamics may be involved.

At first Christianity comprised many splinter groups with very different styles of sexual control. All sought justification in the words of Christ, the apostles and the earliest Church Fathers. They made cases for clerical marriage, for castration, for marriage by mutual consent, for chastity. Actually, Jesus' remarks on sex were brief and sketchy. [Like other Jews before and during his time, he took marriage for granted and did not condemn sex or praise chastity.] But he did condemn divorce except on grounds of adultery, and he forbade remarriage. The Pharisees objected that this made marriage a dismal prospect. Jesus answered, in contradiction to his previous words, that "all men cannot receive this saying, save they to whom it is given. For there are some eunuchs, which were so born from their mother's womb; and there are some eunuchs, which were made eunuchs of men; and there be eunuchs, which have made themselves eunuchs for the kingdom of heaven's sake. He that is able to receive it, let him receive it." Some scholars guess that this contradictory passage was inserted later into the Gospel by another hand, and it seems likely.

Jesus made one other important statement on sex, that "whosoever looketh on a woman to lust after her hath committed adultery with her already in his heart." Here is the crucial difference between Christianity and other sects of the time. Christianity would not accept mere outer conformity to rules of moral behavior. It said that one's actions, one's outer life, can only be pure if they reflect one's intentions and inner life. [Christianity marked the West's full transformation from a shame culture to a guilt culture, in which prohibitions are fully internalized and man is ruled by conscience rather than by others' disapproval.]

There was hardly enough in the Gospels to build a full code of sexual behavior on, but the Church Fathers used what there was to support their hysteria, guilt, prurience and masochism. It is all as morbidly fascinating as anything Suetonius chronicled in the lives of the emperors. Some took literally the mysterious business about "eunuchs for the kingdom of heaven's sake" and castrated themselves. An early Christian sect variously called Valesians and Valerians were said to castrate not only themselves but anyone on whom they could enforce their spiritual surgery. Origen, the great Church Father from Alexandria, and Leontius, Bishop of Antioch. also voted with the knife. Pope Sextus II advocated castration, and St. Justin Martyr approved it, but finally the Church forbade sexual mutilation. One consideration may have been that it made Christianity seem just another Eastern cult, like that of Cybele. But the idea kept reappearing from time to time—in Russia, for instance, in the eleventh century, the two famous Greek-born metropolitans of Kiev, John and Ephriam, castrated themselves, and in the eighteenth century men and women of the Skoptzi sect mutilated their genitals.

Even though castration had been officially condemned, Christianity expressed obsessively and frantically the idea that woman and sex are pollutions, barriers to religious grace. The predominant emotional mood of Christian antisexuality took shape in the Church Fathers' diatribes against loss of inner control. If one gave in to the slightest pleasure, they said, the floodgates of impulse would fly open to loose an unstoppable tide of sin.

There is a sensual beast within man, and if you give him an inch, he will lope on forever in furious, destructive rut. Cassian said that the sinfulness of Sodom arose from the fact that "through fullness of bread they were inflamed with uncontrollable lust of the flesh." Some fled to the desert to starve, whip and mutilate themselves; they lived on crusts, in rags, sometimes ulcerated and literally crawling with maggots. Sin was pleasure, pleasure sin. The words fornication, lust and whoredom were used indiscriminately for all physical enjoyments. By their own implication, sex was the greatest pleasure of all, so the one most feared. Ideas of savagery were often coupled with it, and the violence that was not acted out on religious principle was shifted to the war against sin.

The ancient world's negative attitude toward women sharpened. St. John Chrysostom held that "among all savage beasts none is found so harmful as woman." His fear and hatred were thinly masked as disgust, and he spoke of women's bodies in much the same tone as homosexuals do among themselves. "The groundwork of this corporeal beauty is nothing else but phlegm and blood and humor and bile . . . when you see a rag with any of these things on it, such as phlegm or spittle, you cannot endure looking at it; are you then in a flutter of excitement about the storehouses and repositories of these things?" The millennium of progressive emancipation of women in the Greco-Roman world was lost; they were held in more contempt than ever. As late as 858 it was seriously debated whether women had souls.

Paul was a vengeful man, devoted to persecuting Christians until he experienced a hallucination and three days of hysterical blindness and emerged a fanatical convert to the faith he had hated. On Jesus' sketchy sexual code he built a system of misogyny and antisexuality that in turned provided a base for wilder extremes. "In my flesh dwelleth nothing good. . . . I see another law in my members, warring against the law of my mind, and bringing me into captivity to the law of sin which is in my members. . . . It is good for a man not to touch a woman. Nevertheless . . . it is better to marry than to burn." But Paul's rejection of heterosexuality does not imply homosexuality as the alternative. He had scorn for effeminate manner or dress and spoke of those who indulged "vile affections; for even their women did change the natural use into that which is against nature: And likewise also the men, leaving the natural use of the woman, burned in their lust one toward another; men with men working that which is unseemly . . . filled with all unrighteousness, fornication, wickedness, covetousness, maliciousness; full of envy, murder, debate, conceit, malignity." Though Jesus had not suggested celibacy, and Paul grudgingly decided it was preferable but not obligatory, celibacy remained a major Church issue.

The Church could not resolve the question; it looked down on sex but allowed it, praised chastity yet approved marriage. In 362 the provincial council of Gengra declared heretical the view that sex and marriage are sinful; but the theoretical lash kept falling on woman, sex and marriage, and pressure for at least clerical celibacy remained strong. Agapetism, or continent marriage, was attempted from Egypt to Ireland, but the effort often failed. Some people apparently followed the letter but not the spirit of the agapetist contract. Cyprian, Bishop of Carthage, wrote in 249 that many a virgin companion of the clergy "may have sinned in some other part of her body which may be corrupted and yet cannot be examined." Agaptism, like castration, was declared a heresy, but agapetist experiments in "spiritual marriage" continued into the late Middle Ages, and as late as the tenth century an Anglo-Saxon queen was canonized for refusing to consummate her marriage.

St. Jerome, who had spent years in the Ethiopian desert dressed in sackcloth and fasting for a week at a time to banish visions of bevies of dancing girls, declared, "He who too ardently loves his own wife is an adulterer." His position became Church doctrine; laymen must settle for the lesser state of marriage, but with an appropriate sense of incomplete virtue. Pope Siricius decreed in 385 that priests might not marry, and after a decade or so the rule was fairly well observed. The rule never took hold in the Eastern church, but at the turn of the seventh century Pope Gregory the Great finally decided that clerical celibacy must be thoroughly enforced. But only in the eleventh century were the lower orders of the clergy enjoined to celibacy, and clerical celibacy was not a totally dead issue till a few centuries after that.

So it was decided: marriage had been made a sacrament, and one could reach heaven *despite* it. Surely to die a virgin was superior—some people being more morally equal than others. But in case any doubt remained, in 1563 the Council of Trent condemned to anathema anyone who said marriage was as virtuous as celibacy. As Bertrand Russell has put it, sex for believers must have been rather like drinking during prohibition. After all, the great Tertullian had pointed out in a letter to his wife that since sex was for procreation, not pleasure, a widow's remarriage would be piggishly licentious. In the better world to follow ours, "There will be . . . no resumption of voluptuous disgrace between us."

After Jesus and Paul, the crucial figure in the development of Christian sexual attitudes was St. Augustine. His *Confessions* is the first intimate autobiography in Western literature. It is also the *locus classicus* of Christian sexual morality, for which it provided a lasting vocabulary and rationale. And it presents many of the basic sexual conflicts that still trouble Western man. Augustine was born in 354 in Tagaste, a little south of the Algerian coastal city of Bône. North Africa then contained a mixture of Romans, Phoenicians, Numidians, Berbers and others; they were devotees of the cult of Cybele, Christianity, Manicheanism and probably various indigenous cults. Augustine's father was a worldly, hot-tempered pagan—according to Augustine, untroubled by guilt over his many extramarital affairs. His mother, later canonized as St. Monica, was a devout

Christian pacifist and, on the domestic scene, a conspicuous martyr to her husband's temper and infidelities. The parents competed for the boy's allegiance, and during his youth he was constantly torn between being a righteous mama's boy and a comrade-in-misbehavior of his assertive father. When he was seventeen, he went to Carthage to pursue his studies; his mother's parting advice to him was to avoid fornication. He describes himself then:

> Love and lust seethed together within me . . . swept me away over the precipice of my body's appetites and plunged me into the whirlpool of sin . . . floundering in the broiling sea of my fornication . . . a frenzy gripped me and I surrendered myself entirely to lust. . . . One day at the public baths [my father] saw the signs of active virility coming to life in me and this was enough to make him relish the thought of having grandchildren. He was happy to tell my mother about it, for his happiness was due to the intoxication which causes the world to forget you, its Creator. . . . But in my mother's heart you had already begun to build your temple. . . . So, in her piety, she became alarmed and apprehensive.

Throughout the *Confessions*, Augustine keeps bewailing the sinfulness of his youth, but this seems the product of bad conscience and overready scruples, not sensual abandonment. One of the terrible crimes to which he devotes detailed analysis and morbid contrition is having stolen some pears with his playmates. His description of himself suggests that actually he was bookish and priggish, desperately wanting to prove to his father and male peers that he was virile and bad, but held back by guilt toward his mother. Sometimes he trod in his father's footsteps, feeling hopeless about filling them poorly; his mother followed, plucking at his sleeve and filling his ear with tears, prayers and pious nagging. He managed to take a concubine when fairly young; he was faithful to her for fifteen years, raised a child with her, and then cravenly allowed his mother to throw her out and move in with him. His conflict was one that is often involved in a choice between homosexuality and heterosexuality: each parent said, in effect, "to have my love, you must reject the other parent." He must renounce his mother's approval and identify solely with his father, or renounce his father's esteem and win his mother's love. Either choice can mean homosexuality, with different emotional underpinnings. But such a conflict can have other resolutions than homosexuality. Augustine symbolically posed the conflict in terms of his parents' religious conflict—worldly, assertive, pleasure-loving paganism against ascetic, nonaggressive Christianity.

Augustine spent many years traveling, studying and trying on religions, like an ideological bed-hopper of 1930s leftism. His irrepressible sexual impulses kept him from feeling he had attained spirituality each time. First he joined Manicheanism, a relatively new religion founded by Mani, who had been crucified in Persia in 277. It borrowed from Zoroastrianism, resembled Christianity in some ways, but denied that God would manifest Himself in anything so tainted as human flesh. It forbade marriage and procreation as aiding the powers of evil by trapping still another soul in matter. To become pure, one must practice vegetarianism and celibacy. Those like Augustine, who could not attain such control, remained mere "aspirants" to the faith.

Augustine remained a Manichee for nine years in Carthage. Finally he decided to go to Rome. He was restless, disillusioned, hoped a better life lay abroad. His wailing mother tried to go with him, but he gave her the slip and left her standing at the empty pier from which his ship had sailed. He spent some time in Rome, and in 383, at the age of twenty-nine, left for Milan. There he associated briefly with the Skeptics, who at their most extreme felt that since nothing in this world was certain, one should withdraw to the desert as a hermit and avoid action entirely. But Augustine was too much in need of certainty and self-justification to settle for that. He became a student of Plotinus' Neo-Platonism, which took an important place in his thinking and, through his later writings, in Christian theology.

All these years Augustine had been a teacher of public speaking, ambitious to achieve and distinguish himself, as are many people whose mothers accepted them only on special terms. He always had one or several close male friends, usually men more assertive than he, as though he were still seeking a model for masculinity to take the place of the father he never dared accept. But all this time his mother was dogging his steps; she followed him to Italy, ousted his concubine and moved in with him. She never stopped showing her grief that he was not a chaste, baptized Christian. Augustine tells God (as though He needed reminding) that she "wept to you for me, shedding more tears for my spiritual death than other mothers shed for the bodily death of a son."

Augustine began to study the writings of St. Paul, attend Christian services and listen to the preaching of Bishop Ambrose of Milan. A "voice of Truth" was suggesting to him the path of those who made themselves eunuchs for the sake of the kingdom of heaven. Still, he could not give up sex, and he felt that until he could do that, he could not accept baptism. Finally, in 386, he experienced a crisis that resolved his conflicts about sex and religion in one swift stroke.

One day Augustine was at home with a boyhood friend from Carthage named Alypius, who was also flirting with Christianity. Alypius had tried sex, found it wanting, and become celibate; he could not understand why Augustine did not do the same. They were visited by a Christian named Ponticianus, who spoke to them at length about St. Anthony and the Desert Fathers, their torments of asceticism and sexual self-denial. Augustine thought how he had always prayed, "Give me chastity and continence, but not yet." He became deeply ashamed and angry at himself. He flushed, the pitch of his voice changed, he broke off in the middle of some words to Alypius and went out to the garden. He felt he was mad, dying, "overcome by violent anger with myself . . . tore my hair and hammered my forehead with my fists; I locked my fingers and hugged my knees . . . lashed with the twin scourge of fear and shame." He felt the tug of his old desires, suggesting "things so sordid and shameful that I beg you in your mercy to keep the soul of your servant free from them!"

Then he experienced a vision: "While I stood trembling at the barrier, on the other side I could see the chaste beauty of Continence in all her serene, unsullied joy, as she modestly beckoned me to cross over and to hesitate no more. She stretched out loving hands ... Continence herself, not barren but a fruitful mother of children." He broke into a fit of weeping and flung himself down beneath a tree. Suddenly he heard a child's voice repeating to him, "Take it and read. Take it and read." He took the writings of Paul and opened by chance to the words, "Not in reveling and drunkenness, not in lust and wantonness, not in quarrels and rivalries. Rather, arm yourself with the Lord Jesus Christ; spend no more thought on nature and nature's appetites." Immediately he became calm. His decision was made. He told Alypius what he had been feeling, and his experience moved Alypius to the same conclusion. "Then," says Augustine, "we went in and told my mother, who was overjoyed. And when we went on to describe how it had all happened, she was jubilant with triumph ... you had granted her far more than she used to ask in her tearful prayers and plaintive lamentations. You converted me to yourself, so that I no longer desired a wife or placed any hope in this world. And you turned her sadness into rejoicing, into joy far fuller than her dearest wish."

As the autobiographical part of the *Confessions* nears its end, a serene Augustine stands awaiting baptism on Easter Sunday, 387, before Ambrose. With him are his mother, his friend Alypius, and his bastard son Adeodatus. It must have been the ideal family Augustine had craved in childhood fantasies—a mother who finally loved him without reservation, a male companion who did not challenge him to disobey her, and Augustine, all three at peace instead of in competition and conflict. Augustine lived with his mother like a chaste lover until her death not long after, and then returned to Africa to live another thirty-four years in celibate obscurity.

Augustine's writings show acute fear of losing conscious controls. To him, the serene exercise of reason and will was the way to God; the mindless tempest of orgasm, the most uncontrolled of states, was farthest from God. And since every loss of control threatened general loss of control, blanket restriction must become a way of life. Augustine theorized that before the Fall, Adam and Eve would have begotten children through a special paradisical intercourse in which there was no passion or pleasure—an act of cool, rational choice rather than sensuality. They fell by giving in to concupiscence, or willfulness, which is strongest in sexual desire, for in it the mind follows the body instead of the body following the mind.

All men, Augustine concluded, are born as the result of concupiscence; that is, they are conceived in sin. They also live their early years in sin, because children are not reasonable beings. Christ, being the product of virgin birth, bore no stain of original sin; ordinary mortals stand in constant danger that concupiscence will set their genitals in rebellion against God-given reason. The task of each man is to make up for his original sin by giving his will control over his impulses. In Augustine's thought we can see the equation of logic, sanity, asexuality and virtue on one hand, and on the other impulse, unreason, sex and sin. This makes sexual restraint a cornerstone, even a synonym, for moral behavior.

The Church adopted the ideas of concupiscence and original sin, and most of Augustine's other thoughts on sex and marriage as well. He called celibacy the most blessed state; but physical celibacy is meaningless when the mind is full of desire, so constant self-policing is needed. Marriage is a rung on the ladder to salvation, but a lower one than chastity. It would be best if man and wife lived without sex, but if they cannot, they should couple for procreation, not pleasure. Therefore oral sex, masturbation, sodomy—which cannot lead to conception—are forbidden; they could only be practiced for the sake of pleasure alone. The same is true of sex during menstruation, lactation and after menopause. And, of course, homosexuality.

Augustine's argument became the West's official sexual code. Birth control is still used today as a pretext for sex control—birth control means practicing sex for pleasure. Augustine said that when motherhood is not the aim of sex, the wife becomes a mistress. When it was objected that the attainment of true virtue by mankind would thus be the end of mankind, Augustine replied that the preservation of the race could be left to pagans, and if they should fail, the Kingdom of Heaven would be reached all the sooner.

In the thirteenth century, Thomas Aquinas systematized and expanded Augustine's thinking, and the result became doctrine by papal decree. Aquinas agreed with Augustine that reason is the distinctive human characteristic, its exercise the state of virtue. He categorized strayings from the unpassionate life with exquisite finesse. For instance, if a woman has been raped but did not enjoy it, or felt "involuntary pleasure in her body alone," she is still a virgin before God. Pleasure experienced in a dream is no sin, for in sleep one's reason is suspended; but pleasure due to failure of reason and will calls for penance. Thomas defined as unnatural those sex acts that do not lead to conception. In order of increasing unnaturalness, and thus sinfulness, they are masturbation, oral and anal heterosexual acts, homosexual sodomy and bestiality. Masturbation omits the partner; oral and anal heterosexuality join the right species and the right sex, but by the wrong apertures; homosexuality joins the right species but the wrong sex; bestiality joins the wrong species. Thomas added a particularly repellent fillip to Christian sexual law by what he probably intended as a stroke of generosity. He said that if a man or woman is so beset by lust that adultery is imminent, the other spouse should "render the marriage debt" (without pleasure, of course) to protect the tempted one from the greater sin of adultery. To demand the debt is a venial sin, but to pay it anesthetically a moral obligation.

The Church gave final definition and authority to these doctrines at the Council of Trent in 1563, in response to the challenges of the Reformation. Questions on which there had been room for some conflict of opinion crystallized into dogma, so Augustine and Aquinas became unshakable law for the faithful: sex, even in marriage, shows a degree of moral abasement; the ideal state is freedom from impulse; the deepest and most dangerous impulse is sex.

This sort of basic attitude was not, as we have seen earlier, anything new in the West; the Christian, as compared to pre-Christian, view of sex was a variation on an old theme. The traditional Western hostility to homosexuality went on with little change in rationalization. Christianity simply showed somewhat greater vengefulness and punitive fervor, as it did generally in moral controls. The emperor Constantine converted to Christianity in 323, and it was on the way to becoming the state religion. Early Christians, like Greeks and Romans, thought of effeminacy, homosexuality, luxury and general lack of hardiness as unmasculine and "unnatural." Augustine had grown up seeing painted eunuchs of Cybele in the streets, and despite his agonies over sex, he had a quite traditional view of deviations from the masculine norm. "Sins against nature, like the sin of Sodom, are abominable and deserve punishment wherever and whenever they are committed. . . . In fact, the relationship which we ought to have with God is itself violated when our nature, of which he is the Author, is desecrated by perverted lust." Tertullian said succinctly, "So far as sex is concerned, the Christian is content with the woman." The Council of Elvira, in 305, had already denied communion to homosexuals and prostitutes, even *in extremis*.

In 342, the sons of the emperor Constantine, named Constans and Constantius, decreed in their respective Eastern and Western empires: "When a young man 'marries' in the manner of a woman, a 'woman' about to renounce men, what does he wish, when sex has lost its significance; when the crime is one which it is not profitable to know; when Venus is changed into another form; when love is sought and not found? We order the statutes to arise, the laws to be aimed with an avenging sword, that these infamous persons who are now, or who hereafter may be, guilty may be subjected to exquisite punishment." The actual sentence was to be death, and the emperor Valentinian, in 390, specified that the mode of execution should be burning at the stake. In 438 the Eastern emperor Theodosius II had all the laws of the empire since the accession of Constantine codified, and this Theodosian code, including the edicts on homosexuality of Constans, Constantius and Valentinian, was accepted in both East and West.

The great Byzantine emperor Justinian decided in 538 that the great jumble of accumulated Roman law was again due to be winnowed down—this time to a logical code in accord with Christian doctrine. The result was a vengefully orthodox system that remained the law of the Byzantine empire until its fall almost a millennium later. It was cast aside in the West by the Lombards when they conquered Italy in 568, but its influence remained strong in Europe through various survivals and revivals over many centuries.

Novella 77 of the Code warned that famine, earthquake, plague and even total destruction awaited cities harboring homosexuals—as demonstrated by the fate of Sodom. Therefore homosexuals were to be tortured, mutilated, paraded in public and executed. We have some information on the enforcement of this law from Procopius, a historian employed by the emperor.

Procopius hated Justinian and his empress, and he composed a *Secret History,* or *Anecdota,* hidden till after his death, full of tales of such imperial brutality and dissoluteness that its honesty is sometimes, rightly or not, held in doubt. The prosecution of homosexuals, says Procopius, "was carried out in reckless fashion, since the penalty was exacted even without an accuser, for the word of a single man or boy, and even, if it so happened, of a slave compelled against his will to give evidence against his owner, was considered definite proof. Those who were thus convicted had their privates removed and were paraded through the streets." Significantly, Procopius adds, "Not in all cases, however, was this punishment inflicted in the beginning, but only upon those reputed to be greens [a political faction] or to be possessed of great wealth or those who in some way chanced to have offended the rulers." As Gibbon put it more than a thousand years later, "Pederasty became the crime of those to whom no crime could be imputed."

The laws and attitudes toward sex that developed in Europe reflected the slow coalescence of various tribal traditions with Christian doctrine. During the Dark Ages, between 600 and 1000, "barbarians" adopted Christianity one by one—some moved by missionaries, some forced by military conquest, others obeying chiefs who had converted for personal or political reasons. Historical cliché says that these people, like the Greco-Roman non-Christians, were sexually unrestrained and gradually fell under the yoke of Christian repression. Another cliché says that they were examples of abstemious rigor. The two contradictory clichés have lived on together.

For instance, in the fifth century, the Christian writer Salvian praised the Vandals for their restraint, morality and noble savagery when they conquered Carthage. That city, he said, wallowed in luxury and crawled with effeminates, to the point where "nothing seemed worse to certain men than having something masculine about them." They traipsed the streets in women's veils, practiced incest and homosexuality, and had boy campfollowers attending their armies. When the Vandals came upon this city, they might have jumped in with both feet, "yet in so great abundance and luxury, none of them became effeminate. . . . They entered the richest towns where all these vices were rampant . . . avoiding the filth and the bad. . . . They have abominated the impurities of men."

These military Boy Scouts are the very people whose sexual freedom is said to have been smothered by the pall of Christian guilt. Salvian himself was born in pagan Gaul, where Celts had allegedly indulged in homosexual threesomes for amusement. In fact, the various peoples of Europe, like "foreigners" of all sorts at all times, were made into whatever polemics required. We know very little about the sex lives of the barbarians, and most of that only from laws and by inference. Though they varied greatly, they seemed to share with the Christianized Mediterranean world certain sexual strictures, among them a scornful and punitive attitude toward homosexuals.

Records of the Anglo-Saxons and Vikings suggest a life, even at court, that would shock anyone but Hell's Angels. *Beowulf* presents the heroic ideals of a people who drank and brawled a lot, lived by a rigid, primitive code of honor and combat, but were masters and admirers of fine trickery. Men and dogs gnawed their bones together; plumbing, courtesy and subtlety were as rare as lice were common. It must also be remembered that these nontechnological, violent people also had complex social, legal and artistic traditions. In fact, with them we are back in the same sort of world as that of Homer's Mycenaeans.

In some tribes women were apparently assertive, fairly free and sometimes sexually aggressive. In others, they lacked all legal or economic rights; but even in some of these, shrewish domestic tyrants and influential ladies of rank existed. There were also variations in sexual permissiveness, but there was general agreement with Latin and Christian codes that homosexuals, adulterous women and some other sexual offenders deserved harsh punishment. Among the Visigoths, the *Breviarium* enacted by Alaric II in 506 remained in effect until the revival of Latin law in the late Middle Ages. It condemned sodomites to burn at the stake. In the seventh century, King Chindasvinds relented and changed the punishment to castration. Among some Scandinavian peoples, law provided that either spouse could obtain divorce if the other dressed in clothes of the opposite sex. Laws do not necessarily reflect behavior, but the free love, or free lust, of barbarian tribes seems more disproved than proved by the total evidence. Christianity and non-Christian custom and law all over the West agreed on what we today still know as the basic sexual offenses.

Church and civil powers divided between them jurisdiction over investigating and punishing various offenses. Many sexual crimes came under ecclesiastic rather than civil courts; but since the Church could only assign penance and not itself spill blood, it "relaxed" the convicted offender to civil authorities for punishment under civil law. In effect, barbarian rulers, once Christianized, made an easy accommodation to Christian law and undertook to carry out sanctions. Of course many of the Christian leaders themselves came from tribal backgrounds. There are few records of strong civil and ecclesiastic conflict in the matter of homosexuality.

The Church said that homosexuality, along with murder and adultery, was one of the *clamantia peccata,* "sins that cry to heaven." Its seriousness as compared to other crimes is revealed by penitential handbooks, the lists of penances for various sins that were drawn up by Church theorists for use by parish priests. Some were inconsistent, offering several different penances for the same sin, apparently leaving the choice to each priest.

The canonical letters of St. Basil of Caesaria, written around 375, said that "They who have committed sodomy with men or brutes, murderers, wizards, adulterers, and idolators, have been thought worthy of the same punishment . . . thirty years [penance] for the uncleanness which they committed through ignorance." In another place he equated the adulterer and homosexual, assigning to each fifteen years' penance, as was ordered for bestiality.

The Penitential of Theodore called in one place for one year's penance for fornication with a virgin, four for fornication with a married woman, ten or fifteen for bestiality and sodomy; in another place it decreed seven years alike for sodomites, effeminates and adultresses. In another place it prescribed three years for both lesbianism and female masturbation; it then made an exception of fellatio, "the worst of evils," and charitably called for merely seven years, noting that others had demanded twelve years or even a lifetime of penance.

The Penitential of Columban, written about 600, prescribed for monks ten years' penance for homicide and sodomy, three for fornication. *The Penitential of Cummean,* a half century later, demanded one hundred days for masturbation the first time, a year for repetitions; a year for bestiality; three years for incest with one's mother; four for oral sex ("those who befoul their lips") the first time, seven for repeaters; seven for sodomy. *The Penitential of St. Bede,* early in the eighth century, listed effeminacy and sodomy as capital offenses.

A detailed section on lesbianism appeared in the canonical writings of Bishop Burchard of Worms in the early eleventh century. He advised that women should be questioned closely in confession to make sure they hadn't used "a certain engine or mechanical device in the form of the male sexual organ, the dimensions being calculated to give you pleasure, and binding it to your own or another woman's pudenda, and have you thus committed fornication with other evilly disposed women or they, using the same or some other apparatus, with yourself." If the answer was yes, the prescribed penance was five years' fasting during all Church festivals. If the woman had been "sitting upon the aforesaid instrument or some other device of similar construction, and thus committing fornication upon yourself in solitude," the penance was only a year. (Burchard promptly contradicted himself by assigning three years for both offenses.) A nun who engaged in tribadism was to suffer seven years' penance.

In various other penitential handbooks, a man was sentenced to seven years' penance for intercourse with his wife "like a dog," and excommunication and lifelong fasting for sodomy with his wife. Penalties were also assigned to men who saw their wives naked; had sex on Sunday; had nocturnal emissions; thought about fornication; sang lascivious songs; loitered around church after midnight; had intercourse during the forty days preceding Easter and Christmas; to a woman who attended religious ceremonies while menstruating, and to men who had intercourse with her. According to some, even marriage and childbirth called for penance and abstinence from Mass.

The terms in the handbooks did not always have the same meaning as today. Intercourse with a non-Christian might be called bestiality, and intercourse with an in-law incest. Sleeping with a nun might be adultery (because she is a bride of Christ) or incest (because she is a sister of mankind). We don't know whether these varying penances come from precedents reflecting real attitudes or from theological nicety. Nor whether the plethora of prohibitions reflected real attempts to control people's lives or just obsessive concern by some churchmen. Had Bishop Burchard seen tribades and *olisboi* or had he been reading classical erotica? Did his restrictions reflect abstract system-making, an attempt to enforce Christian ideals on tribal peoples, or the absorption of tribal traditions by the Church? We can only be fairly sure that certain attitudes were jointly held by the Church and the peoples of Europe, had been about for thousands of years, and are alive today. Premarital sex, adultery, homosexuality, and oral and anal intercourse may have been practiced, but they were frowned upon, and perhaps severely punished. The Church and the barbarians probably inherited these values from common cultural ancestors, and have passed them on to us.

INTERVIEWS

The Reverend Edward Lee is a tall man in his middle thirties. He wears horn-rimmed glasses, clerical black shirt and white collar, and a white-and-black cord summer suit. He is one of the three full-time Protestant clergymen available to students of Temple University in Philadelphia: his official title is Episcopal Adviser of the University Christian Movement. And he is one of a small but growing number of clerics who are trying to modify traditional religious strictures on sexuality. He says:

When a student comes in for counseling, he may say, "I'm homosexual" or "I think I'm homosexual." I always ask him, "How do you know?" He's almost always shocked by the question. He asks what I mean. I say, "How do you know? Is it something you're afraid of, is it fantasies you have, or is it something you've done?" I had one case of a kid who said he was homosexual, he just knew it. I kept asking, "What evidence do you have?" He finally admitted that he masturbated twice a day, so he knew he must be homosexual. I asked what his masturbation fantasies were about. He burst out, "Why, they're girls!" I told him I didn't think the masturbation frequency was *per se* abnormal. The question was, what anxiety made him need such frequent release. I told him, "We just ought to find out what purpose the masturbation is serving."

I spent five years at Holy Trinity Church, on Rittenhouse Square. Of course I already knew about homosexuality—everyone who has been to a seminary does. When clergymen are out of town at a conference and they go out for an evening, they're constantly propositioned. Then in my parish I had to try to help men who were struggling with homosexual problems. I really got involved in 1963, when I helped a homosexual group hold a conference on the church and homosexuality. The hotel where they had booked space backed out the day before. I was asked by a mutual connection to intercede, and I think my association with a fashionable church did it. I went to the meeting, expecting to see people who were like alcoholics at an AA meeting, trying to kick the habit. And I saw I was wrong. I had to face the problem of the church's position on sex and homosexuality squarely.

You see, a guy can stand up in church and say he's an alcoholic and be supported; he gets sympathy and help. But if he says, "I'm homosexual," he'll be ostracized. The church has had a long-standing hypocrisy about these things, and a patronizing attitude. You know, laymen and the average clergyman feel safer dealing with heterosexual deviance than with homosexual deviance. When we say, "He's an adulterer," we mean, "He's wrong, but at least he's normal." When we say, "He's homosexual," we make a statement about the state of his soul. I'm one of a few here who are willing to talk about deviance; I want to move back to the central question of the nature of human sexuality and its place in human life.

Now we have a small informal group of clergymen and psychiatrists who work together. Fortunately, a new generation of clergymen is coming up who get clinical training in psychology. More seminarians are getting psychotherapy. Episcopals, some Lutherans and others are becoming more comfortable with problem areas. They counsel more and moralize less.

My personal interest comes from my own feelings. These things always do. I grew up in an Anglo-Saxon Protestant culture that is very up-tight about male affection. It is also up-tight about sex—the church's position on sexuality itself needs rethinking. In 1961 the National Council of Churches had a big conference on family life and sexuality. Dr. Evelyn Hooker was the resource person on homosexuality, and she spoke of the alliances homosexuals make with parents that rob them of the ability to feel male enough. The lack of identity with male groups is critical in a person's development. A guy thinks, "I play football, I read *Playboy*, but I don't feel male enough, I don't feel at home with men." Our idea of masculinity puts strict limits on male feelings toward other males; even fathers won't show emotion to their sons. Women can touch and embrace, but our culture frowns on this for men. From the father-son relationship through adult life, male relatedness is stunted.

If we're to repair this, we must do it without creating homosexuality; but I might even be willing to say that limited homosexual experience isn't the worst thing in the context of expanding relationships with men. The trouble is that we equate homosexual acts and homosexual identity. We say that if a kid wins the ejaculation contest at Boy Scout camp when he's thirteen, he's homosexual. Certainly that's the impression Kinsey helped create with his figures.

We have the ideas of crime, sin and sickness attached to many sex acts. Well, I don't think homosexuality should be a crime. An illness? Is the orientation itself pathological? I think not. The problem is sin. I come from a tradition that says it is a sin, and I've been indoctrinated enough to still be ambivalent about that.

If you want to see what sort of thing the church can do if it takes a more liberal stance, you should see Ted McIlvenna at the Council on Religion and the Homosexual in San Francisco. They're really the national model for all of us who are thinking in new directions.

Father Ted McIlvenna is a Methodist minister in his late thirties. In his work at the Glide Urban Center, a private Methodist foundation in San Francisco's Tenderloin, he became involved in work with homosexuals, homosexual prostitutes and drug users, all of which abound in the neighborhood. In 1964 he helped various Protestant groups and homophile associations to form the Council on Religion and the Homosexual. In 1968 he and a physician, Dr. Joel Fort, founded the National Sex and Drug Forum. Father McIlvenna is active in all three organizations as an organizer, counselor, and liaison man between scientists, clergymen, and those needing their help. A large part of this work at the Glide Foundation is making the counselors realistically aware of the lives and problems of homosexuals and drug users. He systematically keeps in touch with leading sex researchers around the country.

My interest hasn't been serving the homosexual. In San Francisco homosexuality was there. Like most people who are rather compulsive, I wanted to find out about what I didn't know, and understand homosexuals. I met them. I went to the so-called experts and read about "how they got that way"—which is not something we ask about heterosexuals. I feel that people with different sexual identifications aren't that different otherwise. Sexual identification just isn't the most important thing about a person, and his value shouldn't be based on it any more than on his economic or political identification.

I think we need research on how people make their sexual identification, and many tend to start from the viewpoint of pathology. Homosexuality is usually spoken of in the language of sickness, which has largely replaced the language of sin. People live in fear of sexual things that they've surrounded with mythology. It's our job in the church to set people free. I shudder when I think of people going to most clergymen and psychiatrists with problems such as homosexuality. They're branded, because homosexuality is a scapegoat for society's sex problems. When we see someone doing something more, sexually, than what we're doing, we scapegoat him—the fairies on Market Street, the bulldykes, they carry society's guilt. A lot of people remain very hung up about this. They ask themselves, "Is what I just did normal? Is masturbation a sin against God?" I'd like to demythologize and radically humanize sexuality; there are just so many openings in the body, just so many socio-sexual relationships. I think the only abnormal act is the one you can't perform. I only object to hurting people. But as for branding them, putting them in a ring with the whole crowd booing—how would you react?

It's interesting, in a training session here I used a film showing two very attractive boys kissing and making love. A couple of psychiatrists who were watching were really bugged. They nearly climbed the walls. Until then, they'd imagined homosexuality as something that involved just encounters in a public toilet.

You see, we work on an action-research concept. We experiment in producing confrontations between professionals and nonprofessionals and see what happens. Those who come and work with us usually have great expectations about what they'll learn; then they see that we know little. What we do is provide exposure to what people say and feel. We use a multimedia concept. We sit them in a room on cushions on the floor, and they listen to Indian music and see a six-way projection around the walls of the varieties of sexual experience. Then we show them to a select library—the Institute for Sex Research helped us with it—showing more about various physical acts. The people who come are mostly professional people—doctors, clergymen, social workers, educators, some interested citizens. It's amazing what demythologizing about sex most of them still have to do.

Of course counseling people with problems is part of our work. It's 11 A.M. now, right? I've already had two calls. We get couples with marital problems. Maybe he wants to screw around, and she doesn't, or vice versa; but they don't want to break up the marriage. Maybe they come for specific information, because they've looked elsewhere and gotten no help. A homosexual comes here after a bad lovers' quarrel. A mother brings a daughter who's been screwing all over town, and she wants to know what to do. Someone comes because he wants to be bisexual and is looking for a bisexual group. When we get people with deep emotional problems, we refer them to psychiatrists.

But probably the most important task we have in our various groups is getting people to confront other people—professionals and nonprofessionals, homosexuals and heterosexuals, the people and the experts—so that they experience each other as human beings.

5

The Capital Sin

No sooner had feudalism become a firm code, giving order and security to the settling barbarians, when urbanization, the Crusades and other social cataclysms subverted it. The isolated, self-sufficient manor broke down as trade, travel and a money economy reappeared. Escaped and freed serfs, beneficiaries of the manpower shortage caused by wars and plagues, became merchants and artisans in the swelling towns. The Crusades sent nobles, merchants, chroniclers and camp-followers traveling about Europe and the Near East. Their absence disrupted the life of their homelands; their return brought contact with Byzantine and Arab civilizations. Literacy increased, the status of women improved, society became more varied and polished. Much of life was still crude and brutal, but changes were under way that would lead to a complex urban society, capitalism, the modern state and the Renaissance.

Historians usually portray the Middle Ages, between about 1000 and 1450, as torn between radical Christianity and easy peasant bawdiness. There is support for this in martyrologies, chronicles, farces and graphic art. Life often seemed intensely ascetic and roughly unbridled by turns. But as the cities grew, a new sort of life began there, and with it came an apparent increase in homosexuality and prostitution. Commentators then and now have usually preferred the infection theory to explain it.

Streetwalkers crowded European cities; by the fifteenth century civic morality (and the civic treasury) had to be protected by herding them into state and municipal whorehouses. Public baths, or bagnios, or stews, arose for the first time since the Roman Empire, and many were open brothels. Late in the twelfth century, the Norman poetess Marie de France said that any man who ignored a woman's advances risked being suspected of homosexuality. In 1230 the prelate Jacques de Vitry described the students of Paris as being "more dissolute than the people. They counted fornication no sin. Prostitutes dragged passing clerics to brothels almost [*sic*] by force, and openly through the streets; if the clerics refused to enter, the whores called them sodomites. . . . That abominable vice sodomy so filled the city that it was held a sign of honor if a man kept one or more concubines." In 1292 there was a homosexual scandal at the University of Paris that led to the banishment of many theologians and scholars. Complaints of homosexuality occurred in Spain and Switzerland. There were mentions of homosexual prostitution, lesbianism and transvestism in Rome and Venice. Fairly reliable charges of homosexuality were made against many distinguished nobles, kings and clerics all over Europe.

One common explanation then had been used a thousand years before, and is still used by writers today: the East was the source of Western sexual deviance. The Greeks and Romans blamed Asia for dumping homosexuality on their land. In the Middle Ages and today it is has been widely said that the Crusades, by renewing contact and trade with the Near East, infected the Spaniards, Italians, Normans and others who did business with the Muslims instead of pursuing the Holy War. One thinks of the English calling syphilis the French disease, the French calling it the Italian disease, the Russians calling it the Polish disease. But homosexuality is not an infectious disease, and people who do not practice it are not likely to borrow it from military invaders, like children presented an irresistible sweet.

We are asked to believe by medieval chroniclers and many modern historians that Norman homosexuality spread in England as syrup is stirred into water. There is little reference to homosexuality among the Anglo-Saxons, but after the Norman Conquest of 1066, homosexuality seems to have become more common, more open, or both, especially among the Normans but progressively among the other English as well. In 1102 a church council in England declared that priests should be degraded for committing sodomy and anathematized for "obstinate sodomy." That year St. Anselm wrote to an archdeacon not to be too hard on all sodomites, since "this sin has been so public that hardly anyone has blushed for it, and many, therefore, have plunged into it without realizing its gravity." Ordericus Vitalis, a Norman-English chronicler, wrote in 1141 that the Normans had become very effeminate, and that after William the Conqueror's death sodomy became common in both Normandy and England. The homosexuality of William's son and successor, William Rufus, is almost certain; it may have been the reason he was not buried in consecrated ground. During his reign, men wore their hair long, and male fashions became extravagant. Edward II was almost surely homosexual—perhaps the reason his murderers, in 1327, used as their weapon a hot poker "putte thro the secret place posteriale." Havelock Ellis said, "Among the Normans, everywhere, homosexuality was markedly prevalent; the spread of sodomy in France about the eleventh century is attributed to the Normans, and their coming to England seems to have rendered it at times almost fashionable, at all events at court."

One of the much-quoted documents to this effect is the *Policraticus* of the ecclesiastic and scholar John of Salisbury, written in 1159. He spoke of parents who pander for their wives and daughters and even make an offering of their sons to Venus . . . effeminate as the result of vice and corruption of morals. . . . When the rich lascivious wanton is preparing to satisfy his passion he has his hair elaborately frizzled and curled; he puts to shame a courtesan's make-up, an actor's costume. . . . Thus arrayed he takes the feet of the figure reclining by him in his hands, and in plain view of others caresses them and, not to be too explicit, the legs as well. The hand that had been encased in a glove to protect it from the sun and keep it soft for the voluptuary's purpose extends its exploration. Growing bolder, he allows his hand to pass over the entire body with lecherous caress, incites the lascivious thrill that he has aroused, and fans the flame of languishing desire. Such abomination should be spat upon rather than held up to view. . . . The many laws directed against this evil are held in no respect nor are they feared, although the Emperor had decreed that it be severely punished.

At first this seems an explicit enough document. It happens to be a pastiche of quotations and paraphrases from Juvenal, St. Jerome and other ancient writers—even to such details as the curled and frizzled hair. The emperor is Justinian, dead six centuries before. We will never know how much John was using classical sources to describe his own times or indulging the medieval delight in synopsis of ancient literature. [In any case, the accusations of clerical moralists aren't the best historical documents.]

It is difficult to say just how much homosexual fire produced all this smoke. Were Norman homosexuals a conspicuous minority at courts? Were they 2 or 10 or 20 per cent of the population? How did they so easily infect an allegedly staunchly heterosexual Anglo-Saxon nation? And one wonders just how the Normans became so effeminate. They were descendants of Vikings who had not long before settled in France. The Gallic culture to which they adapted was an amalgam of Celtic and Germanic elements. The Celts, Germans and Vikings were hardly notorious for effeminacy or homosexuality.

A much better explanation of the apparent increase in homosexuality exists than mysterious contagion. Rural, Anglo-Saxon England may have had much or little homosexuality, but little has been recorded, and there's no reason to suspect it was very widespread among them. The Norman conquerors, despite similar roots in a North European warrior culture, had recently become far more urban, refined and prosperous. The Anglo-Saxons saw their conquerors as sophisticated and hedonistic. In Rome two thousand years ago, in Chicago today, one still hears that foppish but supersexed urban Fancy Dans have corrupted pure, straight small-town folk. It was doubtless believed by the Anglo-Saxons and Normans. All over Europe at that time, rapid urbanization was under way, and rural and tribal traditions were suffering economic and social shocks. Life was changing for both the invaded and the conquerors of England, but the Normans were concentrated in courts and cities, where prostitution and homosexuality were perhaps a bit more widespread and conspicuous.

We don't know surely whether cities create much more sexual activity and deviance than the country and small towns. Anyone who has lived in small towns knows that they may harbor much promiscuity and deviance as open secrets—accommodated by the community and even protected from prosecution by outsiders. Kinsey's studies did show that in the United States a slightly larger number of people are involved in all kinds of sex activities in urban areas, and they perform these acts a little more often than rural people. The difference is distinct but not staggering, generally within a range of 5 to 10 per cent. These findings may or may not apply to other societies and eras, but they are the only factual guideline we have. In addition, though, we have seen in our century that urbanization creates new patterns of family life, sex role, courting and sex behavior—and probably the people caught in conflict between old and new patterns tend to be more sexually active. Cities not only provide a wider choice of sexual partners but have enough deviants for subcultures to arise, which increase deviants' visibility and provide examples for the sexually developing person.

We should probably take the writings about Norman effeminacy and homosexuality not as literal truth but as reflections of a slow and complex social development. Literature also gives the impression of increased homosexuality in other parts of Europe throughout the Middle Ages, probably for the same reasons as in England—not cultural contact of Christian with Muslim, Anglo-Saxon with Norman, but continuing urbanization, with its mild increase in deviance and marked increase in deviant visibility.

The fact that homosexuality and prostitution were more open does not mean that they were tolerated. Against the Middle Ages' frank bawdiness and growing urban sophistication, there ran a strong countercurrent of antisexuality and orthodox persecution. Families walked naked through towns to the bagnios, and high nobles and clerics owned brothels; nevertheless, people were flogged through the streets for fornication, and prostitutes were ducked, pilloried, whipped, their noses slit and their pubic hair burned off with torches in public. Men were burned alive for bestiality; there are records in England of people dying at the stake with such paramours as dogs, goats, cows, pigs and geese.

Adultery and bestiality were the business of civil courts; homosexuality was investigated by ecclesiastical courts. (The *Compendium of Canon Law* declared *sodomia imperfecta*—defined as unnatural coitus between a couple either male or female—to be a matter for the Church; acts that fell under the unexplained and intriguing rubric *sodomia perfecta* went to civil courts.) The Lateran Council of 1179 prescribed that clerical sodomites would suffer degradation and partial confinement in a monastery, which may have been carrying coals to Newcastle. Secular law called for burning in France and Germany. By the time of Richard I in England—the later twelfth century—homosexuality had been designated "the nameless crime not fit to be named by Christians," to be punished by burning, drowning, hanging or being buried alive. Laws enacted by Alphonso X of Spain in the thirteenth century spared boys of fourteen or younger the full penalty—to be castrated and then stoned to death. Under Ferdinand and Isabella, at the end of the fifteenth century, the punishment was changed to burning. There are records of executions at the stake for homosexuality in Bourges in 1445 and in Zurich in 1482. Actual cases show that in fifteenth-century Venice the punishment for sodomy with a woman, even one's own wife, varied from a week in jail to four years in jail followed by banishment. Sodomy with a man could result in lifelong banishment or decapitation and burning.

Startling extremes of sexuality and antisexuality also existed among the clergy. Many were devout and ascetic; others were totally unhindered by sexual scruples. Homosexuality seems to have occurred most at the highest and lowest levels of the hierarchy, among popes, cardinals and bishops at the top, and monks and nuns at the bottom. The papacy was a scandal between the tenth and sixteenth centuries. Many popes and high-ranking clerics won their posts through nepotism, bribery, power politics and assassination. They lived as powerful nobles did, engaging in every worldly activity from hawking to warfare. The Vatican frequently entertained concubines, courtesans and prostitutes. Popes Paul II and Sixtus IV were almost surely homosexual, and the imputation has been made of other popes as well. There is a story that a cardinal, with a fine blend of presumption and whimsy, successfully petitioned Pope Sixtus for an indulgence to commit sodomy during the warm months of the year. Two successive archbishops of Tours were homosexuals, the second the lover of the first; the second in turn rewarded his young lover by obtaining the See of Orléans for him.

The priests, at the middle of the hierarchy, were notorious chiefly for their heterosexual randyness and their bastards by concubines and parishioners. Clerical marriage had been stamped out in the greater part of Europe, so many priests took to concubinage—man and woman living together outside marriage, a state recognized by law in much of Europe till the end of the Middle Ages. Though it was officially forbidden to priests, parishioners in parts of Spain and Switzerland demanded their priest take a concubine to safeguard their wives, and in Germany *Pfaffenkind,* "parson's child," was a synonym for bastard. The cliché of the time, whether justly or not, was that the offending parish priest was goatish but not homosexual.

From the middle of the Dark Ages on, charges of sexual misconduct in monasteries and nunneries increased. At first they were of heterosexual sin. In 756 St. Boniface wrote that many English nobles, including King Ethelbald, lived in adultery with nuns, and for another thousand years nunneries would be described figuratively and literally as brothels. People of our time find it difficult to imagine such communities of one sex existing without homosexual activity, but the accusation was relatively rare until about A.D.

1000. Monasticism had reached its peak around the tenth century. Then the number of monasteries decreased, but their size and wealth grew. They were often major landholders, centers of literacy and artisanship, famous for good food, good wine and comfortable living in an uncomfortable age. Now charges of luxury, greed and homosexuality increased. The timing is roughly parallel with the increased accounts of homosexuality in cities and courts.

For instance, around the end of the Middle Ages, a noble of Parma named Salimbene di Adamo wrote that homosexuality was common in his day, "especially among scholars and clerks"; he suggested it was practiced by nuns as well. The Italian cardinal St. Peter Damiani presented to Pope Leo IX a volume he had written on the vices of the clergy, *Liber Gomor-rhianus,* or *The Book of Gomorrah,* with a full chapter titled "On the Diversity of Sins Against Nature." In response to such criticisms, waves of monastic and clerical reform began in the eleventh century—Clunaic, Cistercian, Carthusian, Franciscan. Nevertheless, mendicants of these new orders wandering about Europe brought more such accusations on the lower levels of the Church in turn. We will never know how many of those charges were accurate and how many reflect anticlerical sentiment over the growing riches and power of monastic elites; it is probably wisest to divide the responsibility.

A new and significant twist to accusations of homosexuality appears in the case of a man named Segarello; according to di Adamo, he founded a sect of roving evangelists who were accompanied in their travels by whores and boy catamites. Segarello was burned alive for heresy, but the charge of sodomy was an important factor in the case. Soon vast numbers of people would be tortured and burned on the joint accusation of sexual and religious deviance. In fact, the two sins were used interchangeably; sodomites were heretics, heretics were sodomites, and one charge was sometimes a way of getting at a person suspected of the other. Because of the strange psychosexual upheavals of the late Middle Ages, this could be done with a mixture of expedience and sincere religious zeal.

Large numbers of people at this time suffered psychosexual disorders that found convenient expression in religious terms. Children were raised on martyrologies full of stories like that of St. Perpetua, who while being torn apart by a wild bull managed to arrange her clothes so as to die modestly. Christians were reminded each day that they had been conceived in sin between bladder and bowel, and that even sex with one's spouse meant less than grace. Hysterical seizures like those described by Freud became epidemic in some places. People obsessed by sexual guilt concluded, with paranoid logic, that the devil and his minions were attacking them sexually. Christine Ebner, on the other hand, thought she had been impregnated by Jesus, and Mechthild of Magdeburg felt God's hands fondling her breasts. Self-punishment went to fantastic extremes, sometimes with sexual content and sometimes without. Christine of St. Trong lay in a hot oven, had herself racked, hanged on a gallows with a corpse and partly buried in a grave. The Blessed Angela de Fulgina had to be stopped by her confessor from laying hot coals in her crotch to burn out concupiscence.

Some clerics and laymen looked on such behavior with disgust, indignation or mere curiosity. Others found that it struck a sympathetic chord in them, and bestowed admiration, awe and sometimes canonization. But when such masochism reached cultic proportions, became widespread and threatened established institutions, the Church declared it heretical and stamped it out, when necessary, with fire and sword.

In the eleventh and twelfth centuries, for instance, flagellation was introduced as a form of penance. In the wake of plagues and earthquakes in the thirteenth and fourteenth centuries, great processions of flagellants calling themselves the Disciplinata di Gesu Cristo whipped themselves through the streets of Italy, Germany and Bohemia, weeping and praying for mercy. In 1348 bubonic plague—the Black Death—swept over Europe, wiping out whole cities and almost rending the social fabric of the continent. In an age abounding with acute guilt, masochism and hysteria, this set off astonishing mass phenomena. Choromania, or hysterical dancing, seized people and made them rip off their clothes, leap, dance, cry out they were dying, beg others to stop them. Pope Clement VI ordered a penitential procession at Avignon, where the papal court now resided. Priests and laymen, barefoot and naked to the waist, paced through the streets, ashes on their heads, crying *"Mea culpa! Mea maxima culpa!"* and whipping themselves. It didn't prevent some of them from collapsing on the way, in the last throes of the plague. During the next two years bands of flagellants wandered in Austria, Switzerland, Germany, Bohemia, the Netherlands, Italy and England, imitating the sufferings of Christ and driving out the devil of concupiscence by whipping themselves with scourges of knotted leather fitted with nails. They were now officially organized as the Brotherhood of the Cross.

There was nothing heretical in any of this at first, and Pope Clement encouraged the Brethren. But soon it became apparent that the nudity and near nudity of the Brethren, their hysteria and their bloodshed, excited even greater hysteria and disruption wherever they went. And worse, they were claiming that self-punishment could free men of sin, without confession and penance; they were on the way to becoming a self-sufficient sect outside the structure of the Church. A violent campaign by Church and civil authorities broke up the Brethren; they reappeared a few years later, and were finally destroyed by the sword. Flagellation, like castration, had been damned for being "more royalist than the king." Whether from the left flank or the right, attacks on the dominant mores and institutions of society would be smashed as heresy, treason, the work of evil Others.

The charge of homosexuality was linked with most major "heresies" other than the flagellants'. The most important was the Albigensian heresy, which in fact gave English the word "bugger" for anal intercourse—a curious development, since the Albigensian heresy was closely linked to the rise of women's status and the spread of the concept of romantic love.

Since the fall of the Roman Empire, the Church's misogyny had continued full force. Man had been made in the image of God; ideally, he was reasonable, controlled and pure. In an extraordinary act of projection, the whole burden of sexual concupiscence was thus thrown upon woman. She was called a stinking rose, a deadly fascination, the devil's mirror; she was a vampire of depthless guile and malice.

Nevertheless, during the late Middle Ages many women were living far better than their forebears had. Around the tenth century, ladies at court, castle and town started joining their husbands at the table instead of just serving them. By the fourteenth and fifteenth centuries, letters between husbands and wives showed mutual affection and respect. Literature and chronicles portrayed women who openly ruled their husbands, and noble ladies distinguished themselves in government and the arts more than any Roman matron. And if women could be figures of evil, responsible for sin and misfortune, now they could also become magically beneficent, wielders of white rather than black power. This happened with the development of courtly love.

There had been precedents for courtly love, in Sappho and Catullus, the erotic mystical traditions of Platonism, Christian agapetism and Muslim Sufism. *L'amour courtois* was all these and more. In the eleventh century, troubadours appeared in Provence who proclaimed they had entered ladies' service as one gave fealty to a feudal overlord, swearing loyalty and indebtedness. This *amor purus* was spiritual and didactic, like Platonic love, but it was heterosexual. Though agapetist, it was clearly erotic; the beloved might not be one's wife, for marriage was a social obligation, and the service of love was a voluntary exercise of renunciation and sacrifice. It was not possession that ennobled a lover but yearning and trials of worthiness, bravery, kindness and virtue.

The idea spread to Germany, throughout the Mediterranean, to England, and eventually throughout the entire European upper class. Men swore oaths, sang their humble love, endured pilgrimages, crusades and self-abnegation—all to rise from aspirant to suppliant to suitor to lover, and receive at last one kiss. With supreme luck they might lie naked with their ladies and caress them.

Modern historians have variously called courtly love a literary convention, a cultural revolution, an aristocratic diversion, a masochistic derangement, and a cover for Ovidian adulteries. It was probably all these things to various people, and yet more. The ruling class of Europe had been illiterate louts given to brawling, rape and piggish squalor. Their wives gave them heirs, their concubines gave them pleasure, and for amusement they hawked, fought and guzzled. Now they learned to sit and talk to women as equals or even superiors. They tried to exercise grace and wit, to sing and rhyme. Even to ape mercy and gentleness in a brutal, competitive warrior society was a great change. Courtly love introduced introspection, moral self-consciousness and awareness of others' feelings as the Church never had. A courtly lover might rape a peasant girl after serenading his lady, but at least he now knew two ways of loving rather than one.

Even though *l'amour courtois* usually equated chastity and love, it angered many clerics. It made love a law unto itself, the purpose and guide of life; it put a positive moral value on erotic attachment; it praised adulterous bonds. Worst of all, it was associated with Mariolatry and the Albigensian heresy. Many troubadours called their ladies Madonna and wrote poems to the Virgin as though she were a lover. Denis de Rougemont's great scholarly work *Love in the Western World* argues that courtly love, Mariolatry and Albigensianism were three facets of the same heretical cult—in fact, that courtly love was a disguise for Albigensianism. Whether or not this is true, all three rose from the same ground—rising respect for woman and the love bond, the birth of a new style of love, and elevation of a benign virgin as compared to the destructive Liliths and witches of the medieval imagination. The Albigensian heresy contained many things that disturbed the Church, and soon it was linked with sodomy, the sexual act the West has most feared and despised. Extreme religious deviation was paired with extreme sexual deviation.

The Crusades and trade with the East had brought Christians in touch with related dualistic religions; also, Christianity was still only superficial in parts of Europe, a thin veneer over hardy pagan survivals. By conversion, survival or both, new cults rose up. In Bulgaria and Bosnia there appeared the Bogomiles, or Friends of God, whose dualism resembled Manicheanism and perhaps was actually descended from or influenced by it. A similar cult arose in southern France, perhaps imported from Bogomile areas through Mediterranean trade. Those of the Provençal sect were called Cathari (pure ones) and Albigensians (for Albi, where they were numerous). Many troubadours were Cathari, and the Virgin was prominent in Cathar belief, as in courtly love. The Cathari preached chastity, nonviolence, vegetarianism and the end of private property. They saw all matter, flesh and sexual activity as sinful, and believed that even the married should remain chaste, loving in agapetist fashion.

Angry Inquisitors claimed that the Albigensians rejected the sacraments, Mass, Trinity and Virgin Birth, and that to retain technical chastity they sodomized their wives. In this they were said to be like the Bogomiles in Bulgaria. The French word *bougre* came into use, a corruption of the Latin Bulgarus, or Bulgar; it meant, quite simply, sodomite. From French it passed into English as "bugger." Today the most common English word for anal intercourse, interchangeable with "homosexual," is an old word for heretic.

Many nobles and clerics of Provence professed or protected Catharism, but Pope Innocent II launched a crusade of a half million men against it—led by barons of northern France and Germany who were eager to loot and to have easy access to the Mediterranean. For almost thirty years they burned, slaughtered and tortured in Provence. People's eyes were gouged out, their noses cut off; they were burned, hanged and stoned. When the Crusaders took Béziers, their leaders asked their spiritual guide, the Abbot of Citeaux, how to tell the orthodox Catholics from the Cathari and were told, "Kill them all. God knows his own."

The radical side of the Mariolatry-agapetism complex was stamped out. But in its mild aspect, as courtly love, it quietly conquered all Europe, rousing only mild, temporary disapproval. Some clerics called courtly love an instrument of heresy, and Dante, who did nothing without reflection, put troubadours in the same circle of hell with sodomites. But Danta himself wrote one of the great works influenced by *l'amour courtois*. European ideas of love and the sexes would never go back to old ways.

Other forms of heresy arose, and often sexual issues were interjected by the Church whether or not they were genuinely involved—usually a charge of homosexuality, buggery, incest or bestiality. A sect called Adamites had tried in the second century to recreate the sinless, paradisical love of Adam and Eve by celebrating Mass naked and practicing *coitus reservatus*, intercourse without orgasm. They reappeared among the Hussites of Bohemia in the late Middle Ages as the Taborite sect. The Brethren of the Free Spirit, in fifteenth century Germany, said that no one who could be excited or ashamed of the body was pure; they practiced nudity and agapetism. The Taborites and the Brethren of the Free Spirit were massacred and burned at papal command—accused of sexual misbehavior, among other things. Similar practices existed among the Josephists, Apostolici, Beghards and Beguines; they too were accused of sexual deviations. The Waldensians were prosecuted for sexual promiscuity. The Stedingers, in a case more political than religious, were accused of communion with devils and "indiscriminate debauchery." All the horrors of the penitential handbooks—sodomy, incest, bestiality—were coupled regularly with charges of blasphemy and heresy. The extent to which this was cynically done for political and economic motives is clearest in the case of the destruction of the Templars.

The Order of the Knights Templars had been founded after the First Crusade and become Christianity's elite troops in the Near East. Their rigid military organization was pledged not only to poverty and warfare against heathens but to chastity. They were not permitted even to kiss their own mothers and sisters. For two centuries the Templars grew in numbers and wealth, and built headquarters all over Europe. They became successful bankers and money lenders, perhaps the biggest single source of credit and loans in the West.

In 1307 Philip IV of France, desperate for funds, pressured Pope Clement V into bringing charges of heresy against the Templars, much of whose wealth lay in France. Philip was able to do so because he had helped dispose of Clement's predecessor, Boniface VIII, and his influence in selecting a successor made Clement, in effect, Philip's puppet. Philip immediately seized the Templars and their treasure; he kept the treasure and turned over the Knights to the Inquisitors. Their confessions under torture were remarkably alike, probably because they had all been asked the same list of questions. They admitted that in their initiation rites new members must spit, urinate or trample on the cross, kiss the officiating Templar on the mouth, navel (or penis) and back (or anus), and agree to sodomy with any Templar who should demand it. They further admitted that they worshiped a cat and an idol named Baphomet; that they profaned the cross, even on Good Fridays; that they had been corrupted into such sacrileges by making a pact with Muslims (again the Evil East). Many Templars protested their innocence after signing confessions but were burned at the stake. The Pope dissolved the order, and King Philip kept its wealth. Not long after, when King Philip got Pope Clement, for political reasons, to conduct a post-mortem trial of his predecessor, Pope Boniface VIII, the charges that were invented were exactly those used against the Templars—that he was an infidel, sorcerer, idolater, adulterer and sodomite. This had become a well-worn accusatory formula.

George Legman has written an ingenious but unconvincing book called *The Guilt of the Templars*, alleging that the order really was guilty of many of the charges against it, including homosexuality—though the Templars were destroyed, he agrees, only to get their wealth.* After listing the identical, almost ritual string of accusations made against the Templars and Boniface, he comments: "These accusations have not been detailed here for purposes of comedy, but to show what was the temper of the times in the way of accusations intended to discredit an enemy, living or dead. Different centuries, different accusations. In our own century not one of the accusations brought against the Templars . . . would be employed, with the significant exception of homosexuality. . . . All else would be changed today to match the centuries' changing shibboleths: from religious blasphemy to economic, from heresy to Communism." He demonstrates the nature of such charges by quoting a masterpiece of the genre, a Chinese attack on Jesuit missionaries and white Christians in general,

*This book, like Gordon Rattray Taylor's widely read *Sex in History*, twists evidence and makes devious interpretations in order to prove rather crankish theories, but both contain many fascinating facts and astute observations.

written after the massacres of Chinese during the Opium War in the 1840s. A British gentleman copied it around 1870, with many stars signifying expurgations.

> Every seventh day they [Christians] perform worship which they call the Mass. . . . When the ceremony is over all give themselves up to indiscriminate sexual intercourse. This is the height of their enjoyment. They call it the "Great Communion," or the "Love-gathering."
>
> The bride is required to spend the first night with her religious teacher. This is called "holy introduction to the net of pleasure." . . . When a father dies his son may marry his mother. . . . They also suck in with their mouths the seminal fluid from youths who have arrived at puberty; and in the same manner obtain the corresponding principle from virgins. . . . It is impossible to enumerate all their practices. If we seek for the general motive which leads to them, it is a fixed determination utterly to befool our people, and under the false pretence of religion to exterminate them.

Of course these are just the sort of charges the Roman Catholic hierarchy brought against the Cathari, Waldensians and Templars. Most historians have exonerated the Templars; it is worth noting that less than twenty years before their destruction, the Templars were also charged with supporting fourteen thousand female prostitutes. Legman may be adding a needed grain of realism in his argument; in an elite organization of soldiers sworn to avoid heterosexual commitments, there may well have been some cultism and homosexuality. But the extent and type were almost surely not of the kind "confessed" by them.

As the Middle Ages progressed, Europe seemed to be swept by more and more manifestations of sexual neurosis, and of neurosis with sexual content—often paranoid nightmares about destructive sexuality urged by the Devil and acted out by women. That is, witchcraft. The ancients and many barbarians had believed in witches; both Roman and Teutonic law listed punishments for witchcraft. Yet in 758 the Synod of Paderborn called belief in witches a delusion caused by the Devil, and ordained death for anyone who should cause a person to be burned as a witch. Despite the Church's fight against superstition in this matter, many people continued to believe in witches, and Aquinas and many men of the Renaissance took their existence for granted.

Trials and lynchings for witchcraft and heresy occurred sporadically during the eleventh and twelfth centuries. In the thirteenth century, organized persecutions began. Roman law had meanwhile been revived in Europe; it called for an *inquisitio*, or inquiry, into suspect persons and incidents, and it provided the death penalty for heresy, blasphemy and treason. In 1298 the Church—citing the Old Testament injunction "Thou shalt not suffer a witch to live"—set out in earnest to discover witchcraft and hand the guilty to the "secular arm" for burning under Roman-style civil law.

In the course of a witchcraft trial in Toulouse in 1335, there occurred the first known report of a Witches' Sabbath, and over the next few centuries it became a common feature of witch hunts. This night-gathering of witches was said to give their leader, the Devil, the "obscene kiss" on the buttocks or anus (in some cases he had a second face there, whose lips they kissed). Then anti-Christian rites were performed, usually Mass in reverse, with a nude woman's buttocks for an altar. The Sabbath ended with an orgy among the witches or between them and the Devil. One sixteen-year-old girl, by her own confession, had been deflowered by the Devil and witnessed incest and the violation of every natural law. A nun who said she had regularly attended Sabbaths reported: "On Sundays they polluted themselves with their abominable intercourse with devils. On Thursdays they fouled themselves with sodomy. On Saturdays they prostituted themselves with abominable bestialities. On other days they used the customary method." However, another account claimed that Sundays were devoted to elaborate perversions, Mondays and Tuesdays to simple fornication, Wednesdays and Fridays to blasphemies, and Thursdays and Saturdays to bestiality and sodomy.

Two German Dominicans named Sprenger and Kramer conducted merciless witch hunts and raised so much popular opposition that they could not continue without papal support. In 1484 they got Pope Innocent VIII to issue a bull, *Summa desiderantes*, which said, "It has indeed lately come to Our ears . . . that in some parts of northern Germany . . . many persons of both sexes . . . have abandoned themselves to devils, incubi and succubi, and by their incantations, spells and conjurations . . . have slain infants yet in their mother's womb, as also the offspring of cattle, have blasted the produce of the earth, the grapes of the vine, the fruit of the trees . . . they hinder men from performing the sexual act and women from conceiving, whence husbands cannot know their wives, nor wives receive their husbands." Soon it was asserted that to deny the existence of witchcraft was heresy. That witches fly at night became dogma. In much of Europe intercourse with the Devil became a civil crime punishable by death.

Shortly after *Summa desiderantes* was issued, Sprenger and Kramer wrote a handbook for discovering witches, *Malleus Malleficarum—The Witch's Hammer*. It went through twenty-eight editions over the next two centuries and was the source of a whole literature on the nature of witchcraft. Six of the seven chapters dealt with sex, and they are a paradigm of the witch-hunt mentality, with its vengeful sexual paranoia. "All witchcraft comes from carnal lust, which in women is insatiable. . . . But if it be asked why the devil is allowed to cast spells upon the venereal act . . . the power of the devil lies in the privy parts of men." It explained that impotence, satyriasis and nymphomania could be explained as the work of witches. On the basis of even trivial anonymous complaints hundreds and then thousands of people, mostly women, were tortured until they admitted having become witches by performing coitus and sodomy with the Devil. Many were persuaded to agree with their questioners that the Devil had a forked penis so that he could commit fornication and sodomy simultaneously; that his phallus was two feet long and covered with scales; that his sperm was ice cold; that he commanded witches to commit blasphemy, sodomy, bestiality and incest. In Spain, Torquemada sent more than ten thousand people to the stake and almost ten times that number to the galleys. One bishop of Geneva had five hundred people burned in three months. In 1518 inquisitors had seventy witches burned near Brescia and held thousands of suspects in prison. For two centuries more, trials and burning for witchcraft occurred all over Europe, from Italy to Sweden, and in the American colonies. This was not during the Dark Ages, but at the height of the Renaissance.

The similarity of witchcraft confessions has led a few historians to claim that a medieval cult existed based on pagan survivals and anti-Christian rebellion. It is true that some people believed in and practiced magic, and that there were sects incorporating pre-Christian material. But it is also true that witches' confessions were exacted under torture, and from the same prepared sets of questions. Furthermore, the results make a curiously consistent picture not of paganism but of Christianity in reverse. Tales of witches shrieking blasphemies, beshitting the cross, and programmatically violating every basic rule of sexual behavior sound like infantile fantasies of acting out the forbidden. From superstition and projections there probably grew up in the Middle Ages a stock picture of a radical antisocial conspiracy, like that invented by anti-Semitism. [Witches and their sabbaths were largely inventions of a disordered time, a classic example of paranoia, in which people ascribe to others the feelings and urges they loathe in themselves.] This picture of radical deviance drew together all the most feared and despised ideas of the medieval mind.

The preoccupation with sodomy is consistent with the rest of the syndrome. The anus is the most despised part of the body, surrounded with taboos through toilet training even before genital prohibitions are imposed. Its enjoyment is rank sexual heresy, as great a threat to sexual normality and morality as witchcraft is to religious orthodoxy. The witch became the minion of evil by being buggered by the Devil, and was ordered by him to perform sodomy with other humans. The witch showed loyalty to the devil with the age-old symbol of submission and degradation—kissing his ass. When Salimbene di Adamo wanted to tell the most shocking possible tale of blasphemy, he described a priest who, having lost his hawk while hunting, dropped his breeches, turned his backside to the heavens of the ungenerous Lord, and galloped home to shit upon the altar of his private chapel.

Facile anti-Christianity, by writers as different as Nietzsche and Mencken, has seen Christian ideals and ideology as a tyranny from above, with a few twisted fanatics destroying society's freedom and health. Debased Freudianism has been used to support the idea, with the sexually tinged religious fanaticisms of the Middle Ages pointed out as proofs that when the sex drive is blocked, it finds twisted substitute expressions. Both ideas are simplistic distortions. Hysterical and masochistic behavior tend to have powerful sexual conponents, but they are not just disguises of sex; a disturbed personality is usually disturbed in ways other than merely the sexual. Furthermore, sexual regulation is not an arbitrary decree by one element in society. Sexual regulation is basic to human society; different societies have different ideas of normality and deviance, to a degree, but all have norms, and these are expressed in all of society's institutions— religion, civil law, ethical values, customs, humor, folkways, art. All express the same complex of values and feelings, the same psychosexual climate. If formal religion no longer speaks authoritatively to many people today about sexual conduct, it is because some of the power to do so has passed to customs, science and laic institutions. In the Middle Ages, though, the Church was in harmony with the dominant mores and most other institutions.

The ancient Hebrews made cultic prostitution and homosexuality synonymous with heresy and tribal disloyalty. The Romans spoke of homosexuality, treason and sacrilege in the same breath. It is no surprise that the medieval Church, and much of medieval society, equated religious and sexual nonconformity. The deviant—sexual, religious or political— is always seen as stabbing at his community's vitals by disregarding its self-defining principles. Those who hold the dominant views tend to see him as part of a conspiracy or hostile clique out to destroy the most cherished values, and to control society as society wants to control him. The deviant may be called a homosexual security risk, a sodomitic diabolist, or any other combination of fundamentally antisocial names. He may be laughed at and treated as a harmless crank, but if he strikes a point of emotional or political sensitivity during unstable times, if he seems to have social advantages or power, if he starts a principled opposition and claims a right to his behavior—he becomes a menace to the majority. Witch hunts, anathemas and persecutions follow.

INTERVIEWS

Homosexual-hunting has occurred sporadically in the United States over recent decades. Often it has had thinly veiled political motivation or has resulted from a breach of public decorum or a case involving a youngster. Immigration officials are notoriously severe with homosexuals or people with any history of homosexual acts. But generally, considering the number of such people and acts, there are few prosecutions. To get an idea of how the armed services routinely deal with the matter, I speak to three men who served in the navy at the same time, during the mid-sixties, one as a psychiatrist, another as an intelligence officer, the third as a legal officer.

Ted is a psychoanalyist in his thirties, a few years past his hitch in the navy. He says:

I saw many guys who tried to put on a homosexual act to get discharges from the navy. I don't think one faker ever got by me. It was because they were obviously ambivalent about posing. They hedged the act, as though to tip off that although they wanted to get out of the navy, they weren't really fags. Probably guys who were less ambivalent about putting on a homosexual act did it at the recruiting station instead of waiting till they were in the service. When I dealt with someone who really was homosexual, I always tried to give him a medical discharge, "for emotional reasons," which didn't label him as negatively.

The attitude toward homosexuality among the navy officers wasn't so much punitive as evasive. They just didn't want to have to deal with it. I had one case of a sailor, a lower-middle-class white boy from the South, who turned out to be an acting homosexual without any heterosexual experience. He'd gotten into the navy and done okay for a while. Until he was put on submarine duty and spent a couple of months down under on a nuclear sub near a Russian port. Undergoing confinement and psychological pressure, he got into emotional trouble. When his ship returned he talked to a senior officer, who referred him to me. The officer said, "He's been a good sailor, and his father is a navy man. He's a good kid, really." He wanted the boy off his ship, because he had vague visions of demoralization, and he was uncomfortable. I think his was the commonest sort of attitude. I got the kid a medical discharge.

Stuart is a consultant, an intelligent and urbane man in his thirties. In a restaurant near his office in midtown Manhattan, he describes his years in the Office of Naval Intelligence.

I was an administrative officer in an ONI unit containing five investigative squads of seven to ten men each. Our job was security investigations for clearances, and one squad worked almost exclusively at checking on suspected deviants.

What sort of deviants?

Almost all were homosexuals and transvestites. Information or a tip would come from witnesses or barracks-mates, and an effort would be made to see whether the accusation was legitimate. Remember, these were administrative investigations, not judicial ones, to preserve security. The investigators weren't servicemen; they were civilian employees of the navy, drawn from the civil service.

What were they like?

Most from middle- and lower-middle-class backgrounds, generally a bit crude, and tending to be politically reactionary. But in my experience, this just made them like most investigators. Their pay scale was relatively low, so no man with really high intellectual qualifications would be attracted to it. To say nothing of the atmosphere and the criteria that were used.

Had they volunteered for the work?

Most had, though there wasn't a set policy that one must be a volunteer to do it.

Did anyone ever suspect them of being homosexual themselves?

No one but me. I thought one was a latent homosexual who fulfilled himself through the investigations. Actually, their attitudes covered a big range. Some were very hostile to homosexuals. They were all trained investigators, and entrapment is an illegal means of getting evidence, even in administrative proceedings. But they used what I'd call psychological entrapment, which isn't illegal, but it's pretty awful. They'd talk to a man, draw him out, and get him to give himself away. This squad took a certain glee in uncovering a homosexual. I remember an officer who was caught by the local police wearing women's clothes. The chief of the squad made him march through the office in front of all the clerical workers, and made a big display of handing over the clothes item by item—one bra, one woman's panties, etc.

Did the men on the squad ever discuss homosexuality?

Not only didn't they discuss homosexuality, they wouldn't countenance it from outsiders. If it ever came up, they'd say emotionlessly, "That's none of our business. We have a job to do." You'd hear fear in that deadness in their voices, I think.

What did they consider evidence of homosexuality?

A homosexual act was proof. But they'd note it if a guy seemed effeminate to them, if he had no beard and didn't shave, if he minced or in any other way seemed not masculine to them. I can't tell you what they thought, really, because I considered the whole damn thing so absurd. They just didn't know what it's about. The one good thing was that there was an officialese informally required in reports, a way of putting things that left very little room for opinions and elaborations. The reports were largely he-said, I-said, and so on.

Do you feel from your experience there that a homosexual is a security risk?

Well, in many of the most famous and some not so well-known spy cases of recent years, homosexuality was involved. In one case, a man who had access to our secret codes defected; the Russians knew he was homosexual and the ONI didn't. Whether homosexuality was a crucial factor in the case, I don't know. Ideological sympathies or greed may have been more important. I think that finally there's no sure knowledge about whether homosexuality itself constitutes a risk. The information just isn't adequate. Therefore I think it's reasonable of the military to consider it a risk in matters of importance. That's what risk means—we aren't sure.

What I do object to is the lack of perception of those who investigate—their attitudes, their narrow approach. Like metropolitan police, they deal with complex problems for which they have no background. Their focus on homosexuality is a pair of blinders. There were people right in that investigative office who were risks. One man was having an affair with a married woman who had two children; he could have been threatened with blackmail. There was a girl with an unconsummated marriage, building up tension, ripe for an irrational act of some kind. There were all the things that go on in any office, that make people potentially as much security risks as many homosexuals.

Did they miss some homosexuals and brand others wrongly?

I'm sure they missed a lot of people, but I don't know of a case in which a man was labeled unjustifiably. I suppose there must be a few, but they're rare. There are probably also some guys who didn't defend themselves too well so that they could get out of the service, but I suspect that that's very rare too. The real hotbed for homosexuality was the WAVEs. I'd guess that on a *per capita* basis there were many more lesbians in the WAVEs than male homosexuals in the navy.

What happened to the record of a man who was investigated and found not to be homosexual?

It didn't go into his service record, but a file was kept in the ONI. If the officer of a unit called to check on a man in his command, he'd be informed of the investigation. Or if a man wanted a new job, and a background check was done for security clearance, they'd see that he had been investigated. As in political investigations, this alone could be seen by some as making him suspect. It tends to create doubts about reliability.

Alan spent his four years in the navy as a legal officer, at the same time as Ted and Stuart. He is now a corporate lawyer in New York City.

I don't know of anyone who was given a long sentence for a homosexual offense in the navy. The officers didn't want to send men to jail, they just wanted them out of the navy. They couldn't verbalize why very easily; it was just assumed that the homosexual has no place in the service. Few thought homosexuality loathsome. The usual reaction was, "Gee, it's a tragedy"—a recognition by them that although a homosexual act is a criminal act, it isn't one that harms another person except in cases of a nonconsenting partner. I saw one man who had been caught by two New York City policemen performing a homosexual act in a subway station. At a civilian court in Brooklyn a charge of sodomy was dismissed, and he pleaded guilty to disorderly conduct. The navy merely processed him for administrative discharge.

It used to be that a homosexual act performed before entering the service was grounds for discharge. That changed while I was in the navy, around 1964. Now there must be a homosexual act while in the service. I've seen men freely admit to homosexual acts to get out of the service. If a homosexual act was proven, the result was usually an administrative discharge, not a court-martial proceeding. There are three types of administrative discharge—undesirable, administrative and dishonorable. Administrative includes anything that doesn't result from a court martial or expired time; it covers everything from a medical discharge for wounds received in combat to criminal acts. Homosexuality is specified in the records, but not on the face of the discharge certificate. But the certificate does mention the section of the manual involved, and that indicates homosexual acts to someone who knows the manual.

If a man is faced with administrative discharge for homosexuality and wants to prove his innocence, he can insist on a court martial. Twice I defended men at court martials who almost surely would have been processed out by an administrative tribunal. Both were found innocent and stayed in the service. After four years in the navy, I'm convinced that military justice is a more enlightened criminal procedure than one finds in civilian courts. The officers at a court martial are a sophisticated jury.

For instance, I had one case involving three men. A and B swore that C had approached them with the thought of performing a homosexual act. All three were given lie-detector tests, and A and B said their accusations had been false. A soon went AWOL, and I had the job of prosecuting B for false statements.

When he got on the stand, he said his original accusation had been true. I put C on the stand, and he turned out to be very effeminate. The minute he opened his mouth, the case was lost; my man, B, was acquitted. One officer wanted to prosecute C for homosexuality. But finally there was agreement that there was doubt about who might be telling the truth, so they were bound not to convict, and the whole matter was dropped. I'm still not sure to this day what the truth was.

6

The Bisexual Glory

The Renaissance is spoken of as a sunbeam dispelling dank, gloomy primitivism; a time of rebellious, exuberant gusto in art, philosophy and public life; of picaresque heroes, brilliant rogues and adventurer-scholars. And, many people add, a time of "healthy, guiltless bisexuality, as in ancient Greece." The homosexuality or bisexuality of the great creative figures of the Renaissance has become a commonplace, and so meticulously exact a work as the special 1966 *UCLA Law Review* study of homosexuality and the law says flatly that "homosexual behavior was prevalent among the intellectuals of the Renaissance."

It is true that the Renaissance was a time of change, and often of confident joy at the expansion of knowledge and the known world. However, the Renaissance was also characterized by anxiety, confusion and contradiction. It was less a revolution than an unstable point in a long continuum of change between the Dark Ages and the later eighteenth century, full of hesitations, backslidings, and anticipations of the future. Pico della Mirandola believed in succubi, and the exasperatingly rational Sir Thomas More assumed the existence of witches. Witch hunting began in the late Middle Ages but reached its height during the Renaissance and continued into the first half of the eighteenth century. Coarseness and refinement existed side by side in society and within individual men. Religious war, civil unrest, famine and plague were normal events—for many, life was adventurous of necessity, not by choice. Voltaire justly compared the sixteenth century, with its tumult, violence, crudity, elegance and high culture, to a silken robe smeared with blood.

We tend to think of the Renaissance as involving a socially important change in sexual values and behavior. But much of the frank sexuality of the time merely continued the forthrightness the Middle Ages had shown in fabliaux, public nudity and open prostitution. The medieval association of sex, flesh and pleasure with the Devil also survived, more than most modern glorifiers of the period care to note. We know that the cities' populations grew, but not their walls; the streets were more crowded, dirty and dangerous than ever. The new urban milieu may have created continuing, slow change in life style, family structure, sex role and possibly sex behavior. We know very little about the beliefs and lives of the rural and the poor; if there was great change in their mores and behavior, it went unrecorded. The middle and upper class—as tiny a fraction of the population as in ancient Athens—recorded a little about their values and their lives. It is to the fragmentary record of this handful of nobles, clerics, merchants and artisans that we must turn for signs of change and of continuity during the Renaissance.

There was no more a typical Renaissance man than there is a typical Catholic or typical American, but to the extent that a type can be constructed, he was an aristocrat or a bourgeois aping aristocrats who wanted to create an elite of learning, manners and statecraft based on a Christian reinterpretation of classical culture. The masses of Europe were touched little or not at all by this. A host of social, economic, political and psychological forces caused Renaissance man to rediscover himself, as in a distorting mirror, in Greek and Latin writings, but he no more wanted to reform society or alter the power structure than had medieval ascetics. Neither did he desire to revive pagan sexuality: there were a few freethinkers and erotic revolutionaries ahead of their time, but most Renaissance men, like their medieval forebears, were good Christians in theory if not in practice. Attitudes about sex, women and marriage began to find authority in sources other than the Church, but that does not mean that they basically changed.

The Renaissance man saw that the ancients had praised combined excellence of mind, body and manners; he rather self-consciously tried to emulate them—to practice art, philosophy and the always messy business of politics with leisured dilettantism. The whole business was more often literary than lived. Even among the Greeks there had been some break between cerebral and active life—an assumption that intellectual, artistic and sedentary pursuits are less masculine than aggressively physical ones. ⌈The nineteenth and twentieth centuries have wanted to see in the Renaissance what the Renaissance wanted to see in Greece and Rome.⌋ In both cases there was just enough justification to allow the distortion to pass. A few men, such as Cellini, Raleigh and Montaigne, actually lived much of the neoclassical ideal. More were mildly cultured brawlers or reclusive scholars forced by violent times to violent lives.

Now that feudal chiefs were being replaced by educated, leisured courtiers and burghers, courtly love underwent a transformation. It made an alliance with Neo-Platonism. A new literature of "Platonic love" sprang up, descended from that of the troubadours; it spread as quickly and met with as much enthusiasm as had its predecessor. It traveled from Italy to France around 1540, and during the next century its influence grew steadily in England. The Court of Love was replaced by meetings at villas and chateaus where gentlemen and ladies discussed attaining the Divine through chaste contemplation of the Beautiful and Good as manifest in one's beloved. This was more cerebral and denatured in theory than courtly love, but the lady was not the impassive *dame* of the Middle Ages. She had to meet her lover soul to soul, mind to mind. The noblewoman, the wealthy bourgeois wife, the expensive courtesan, was often intelligent and witty, a musician and poetess. Men might court with intellectual wit, graceful banter, songs and verse. This was the gallantry not of knights on horseback but of charm and cleverness.

Plato had said that this love of soul for soul could only exist between men, and the old Western mistrust of women was far from dead. Although many of the Neo-Platonic love poems were from men to women, many were from men to men, following courtly tradition by mixing the vocabularies of religion, philosophy and eroticism. Some were direct imitations of classical poems of male comradeship or male love; Zeus and Ganymede became common props in the works of many heterosexual artists. Sometimes it is impossible to tell whether the motive for a given poem is literary imitation of ancient writers, male friendship or homosexuality.

Neo-Platonic gallantry eventually became as much a veneer for cynical sexuality as Plato's theories had for ordinary buggery. In practice, Platonic love ranged from intellectual sibling attachments to ordinary seduction. Donne sometimes took it seriously; the Cavalier poets made it a light erotic game. One person might be capable of both. The love life of many a Renaissance man was full of contradictions anyway. He may have been raised more by servants than parents, his marriage arranged when he was three or seven. The marriage was a duty to produce money, alliances and heirs; pleasure would be sought elsewhere. Wives had few legal rights, and were told to be dependent and submissive; there were still many Griseldas around. And men still tended to divide women into wives and whores, witches and saints. From Italy to England, for every Renaissance song to woman's beauty and goodness, there was a verse or tract on her silliness, cupidity, malice and lust. Just as the medieval lover might recite verses of chaste yearning to his lady's barred door and then rape a peasant, the Platonic lover might go from the salon to a brothel. Continuing social change created a chaotic atmosphere, and family life ceased to be important to many people. The same sort of delinquent became common that had arisen in the Roman Empire—angry, pansexual, almost without a superego. Many biographies of the time abound with casual, callous incidents of random violence and murder, obsessive sex, rape, incest and homosexuality. Catullus and Martial might have been at home among the Medici and Borgias. We can afford to see the *condottiere* and Elizabethan "rogue" as fascinating rascals. Their contemporaries, their victims, could not.

Gallantry, open bawdiness and obsessive sex helped produce a new pornographic literature. *Novelle* became popular, short prose tales about seduction, adultery, perversion, lecherous monks and insatiable ladies. Boccaccio's *Decameron* is today the most-read work of the genre, if far from the most pornographic. The *novelle* traveled from Italy to France,

England and the rest of Europe along with respectable Renaissance culture. The complexity of the time is revealed by the fact that one great collection of bawdy tales, the *Heptameron*, was written by Marguerite of Navarre, a leading theoretician of Platonic love.

Imitations of Juvenal and classical erotic poets became very popular. Valla and Beccatelli in Italy, Choirier in France and a host of lesser writers turned out compendia of sexual adventure and experiment to which very little could be added today; they included oral and anal sex, heterosexual and homosexual, orgies and flagellation and bestiality. In the late fifteenth century, Pico della Mirandola described a man who could enjoy sex only if beaten bloody with a whip dipped in vinegar. This was the first mention of sexual sado-masochism as a distinct entity in Western history; it soon had a regular place in pornography and in life.* In the early 1650s there appeared the first Western novel of homosexuality since the *Satyricon*, a book called *L'Alcibiade Fanciullo a Scuola* (*The Boy Alcibiades at School*), variously attributed to one Antonio Rocco or to Ferrante Pallavicino. *Alcibiade* was a literary blend of Platonic philosophy and homosexual erotica, the revival of a classical literary genre.

Just as the abominations and rantings of many clerics can't be accepted as historical documents, neither can pornography. Ariosto said all humanists were homosexuals, and at roughly the same time San Bernardino claimed that Naples deserved the fate of Sodom. Both may have been right, but neither can be trusted for accuracy. The pornographic spirit sees life through sex-colored glasses, just as the prurient, inquisitorial spirit does; the difference is that one savors what it imagines, and the other loathes it. In *The Waning of the Middle Ages*, Johann Huizinga points out that pornography is as much utopian fantasy as the poetry of Platonism and courtly love:

> Erotic thought never acquires literary value save by some process of transfiguration of complex and painful reality into illusionary forms. The whole genre of *Les Cent Nouvelles Nouvelles* and the loose song, with its wilful neglect of all the natural and social complications of love, with its indulgence toward the lies and egotism of the sexual life, and its vision of never-ending lust, implies, no less than the screwed-up system of courtly love, an attempt to substitute for reality the dream of a happier life.

The idea that the artists and scholars of the Renaissance were "bisexual" is largely the invention of homosexual apologists of the late nineteenth and early twentieth centuries. At that time writers gathered from memoirs and pornography as many homosexual incidents as they could and classified the people in them or the authors as homosexual and bisexual, and the judgment has been commonly accepted. If one combs through the source material without a desire to find homosexual precedents, however, the picture changes radically.

*It is less unrealistic than one might first think to say that sado-masochism, like romantic love, hardly existed until it had a name and a history.

For instance, Pietro Aretino, who lived in the first half of the fifteenth century, is often spoken of as an uninhibited Renaissance bisexual. He left his home in Arezzo when he was about thirteen to work at various trades; bookbinding and painting were among them, and his detractors added pimping and a stint in the galleys. He became a prolific writer of verse, especially satire, and for years wandered about in search of patronage from princes and churchmen. Fame first came to him when he was in his early thirties; he caused a scandal with a set of obscene sonnets to accompany engravings that showed various positions of sexual intercourse.

A decade later his satire was so famous and so feared that he could blackmail men or win their support by threatening to write against them or by becoming their publicist. He was wily at flattery and intrigue, a good storyteller and drinking companion, and he obtained the patronage of popes, monarchs and powerful princes. He was as well known for his whoring, numerous mistresses and unabating lust as for his verse.

Aretino's work includes plays, dialogues and satires; it was best when he was poking fun, like Martial, at the libertine world he enjoyed. His *Ragionamenti*, dialogues in imitation of Lucian, described with mixed relish and contempt the infidelity of wives, lubricity of nuns, ways of prostitutes, flagellation, bestiality; they include a description of an orgy of seven (six participants and a masturbating observer), with various sorts of sex *à trois* and the use of *olisboi*. His scathing comedy *Il Marescalco* (*The Master of the Horse*) satirized the sex lives of cardinals and their mistresses, whores, cuckolds and transvestites. The central figure was allegedly modeled after a homosexual at the court of Aretino's patron, the Marquess (later Duke) of Mantua; in the play he suffered horrified anticipation of marriage till he joyfully discovered his spouse was really to be a boy.

It is commonly said that Aretino was bisexual. He was once accused of blasphemy and sodomy—by the husband of a lady he had allegedly seduced. Aretino praised buggery in his pornography, but so did most pornographers of the time, with humor and bravado. There were few neutral witnesses to Aretino's life; he was a charming, ruthless man who is said to have died of apoplexy while laughing at a dirty joke. It is easy to imagine him, like Catullus, indulging in a push with a boy now and then, and the one sure homosexual incident we know of in his life sounds like that sort of thing. He wrote to the Marquess of Mantua, asking help in obtaining the favors of a pretty youth at the court, for Aretino had propositioned him unsuccessfully. The Marquess refused, and Aretino was apparently too shrewd to pursue the matter. Though Aretino's heterosexual preference is unquestioned, he did pursue boys on occasion. This sort of aggressive, pansexual personality was probably not rare in his time and level of society, but it is misleading to suggest that "bisexuality" was common.

Cellini is often given as another example of the Renaissance bisexual.

He says in his autobiography that twice detractors unjustly accused him of homosexuality. What we know of his personality suggests a temperament somewhat like Aretino's; but there is no evidence of even one casual homosexual act in his life. Michelangelo is also usually named. During his later years, he wrote Platonic love poems to young men; no lover, female or male, was ever known to exist in his life. Similar is the case of Leonardo da Vinci's alleged homosexuality. Freud's book on Leonardo, claiming to show latent homosexuality sublimated in his art, is in wide disrepute among all but the most devoutly Freudian psychiatrists for its methods and conclusions. The evidence suggests that both Leonardo and Michelangelo, unless they had secret, unrecorded homosexual lives, were mostly sexually inactive. They may or may not have identified as homosexuals. To describe either as homosexual with confidence reflects a desire to believe them homosexual. In fact, there is only one Italian painter of the Renaissance who was surely homosexual—Giovanni Bazzi, popularly know as Sodoma. Vasari contemptuously described Sodoma's effeminacy in his *Lives of the Artists*; since he did not mind doing so, one can assume he probably would have mentioned other artists' homosexuality had he known of it.

Among the humanist scholars of the time, Strozzi and Politian were generally suspected of homosexuality; Dante claimed a large number would end up with his former teacher in the Inferno. Some such remarks of that period, such as Ariosto's statement that all humanists were homosexual, were obviously satire (like Niccola Franco's claim that "the Pope buggers, and so do all his cardinals, and so do all the other clerics"). They reflect the old Western contempt for "unmasculine" artists and scholars, frequently expressed by artists and scholars themselves—about their colleagues. But the assumption was so widespread at the time that homosexuality was very common among scholars (not artists) that it may have had a basis in fact.

The final tally. Sodoma and an unspecified number of churchmen and scholars—homosexual. Strozzi and Politian—almost surely homosexual. Aretino—some homosexual episodes. Da Vinci, Michelangelo—mysterious, possibly homosexual and possibly not. It is not a long or impressive list. If one makes a list of all the painters, sculptors, writers, scholars and philosophers of the time, starting with the lower rank of Politian, Strozzi and Sodoma, and works up to the summit, it would surely fill a page. The proportion of homosexuals and even of heterosexuals with bisexual behavior is tiny. If one doubles the number of homosexuals on principle, to allow for secret and unrecorded homosexuality, it is still strikingly small.

In fact, when one reads descriptions of Italian cities at the time, one gets the impression that homosexuality was quite visible, perhaps relatively common. There seem to have been fewer homosexuals among the creative men of the Italian Renaissance than among the urban population at large. The usual attitude toward homosexuality—outside pornography and satire—was apparently that of Castiglione, who said that the perfect courtier was not soft and feminine, like some men one saw, with fancy hair-dos and made-up eyebrows, behaving like "the most lascivious and dishonorable prostitutes. . . . These, since Nature did not make them women, as they make clear they desire, should be driven away like courtesans, not only from the courts of great nobles but from the company of all gentlemen."

The number of known homosexuals among creative men in Renaissance France is even smaller. The most famous homosexual of the time was Henri III, who was born in 1551, took the throne in 1574, and from then until his death in 1589 built one of the least appetizing reputations in French history. Until his early twenties he was known as a profligate woman-chaser; then his desires turned to men. He had a series of *mignons*, or homosexual favorites, whose names and descriptions have survived in journals and lampoons of the time. Henri's court gives us the first reliable accounts, outside Italy, of homosexual transvestism and sadomasochism in Christian Europe. Henri wore women's clothes and make-up much of the time, collected miniature dogs and ran shrieking at the sound of thunder. He and his *mignons* were publicly very devout and took part in penitential processions; satires spoke with salacious knowingness of his pleasure in whipping his lovers under cover of piety. The diarist Pierre de l'Estoile wrote in 1576:

> At this time the word *mignons* began to be heard in the mouths of the people, to whom they were quite odious, as much for their ways, which were waggish and haughty, as for their effeminate and indecent paint and apparel, but especially for the king's boundless gifts and generosity to them, which the people thought were the cause of their ruin, even though the truth was that such gifts could not stay in their savings for one moment, and were immediately transmitted to the people as is water in a pipe.
>
> These pretty *mignons* wore their hair pomaded, artificially curled and recurled, flowing back over their little velvet bonnets, like those of whores in a bordello, and the ruffs of their starched linen shirts were a half foot long, so that seeing their heads above their ruffs was like seeing Saint John's head upon a platter. The rest of their clothes were made the same way. Their exercises were playing, blaspheming, jumping, dancing, fencing, fighting and whoring and following the king everywhere.

While civil war and foreign invasion threatened, Henri appeared at parties, masquerades and tourneys dressed as an Amazon or wearing a ball gown, make-up, earrings and extravagant jewelry, attended by homosexual parasites whose behavior outraged an already contemptuous public. Mocking songs, jokes and poems were passed by word of mouth, printed and handed about, scrawled on the walls of churches and public buildings. They had such titles as "The Isle of Hermaphrodites" and "Penitent's Sonnet." They spoke of Henri's special liking for blond Gascon boys; the fact that when a *mignon* married one couldn't tell bride from groom; that the *bougres* were taking over; that bleeding France was being destroyed by an Elegabalus, and by his courtesan warriors who blonded and curled their hair; that Ganymedes who made love from behind were draining the treasury with their extravagance; that the king would lose his crown for masquerading as a woman when he should be pursuing the holy war against the Huguenots. In short, there was the outcry about unnaturalness, decay and perdition that is still heard when homosexuality steps into public view.

Protestants and other enemies of the Valois court made hay of the king's behavior. The most skillful was the Huguenot poet Agrippa d'Aubigné. In his *Princes*, he accused the royal family of being false to nature, false to their country, false to Christianity—a masterpiece of character assassination, linking, in traditional fashion, sexual deviance with political and religious deviance. By the time d'Aubigné was done, Henri's homosexuality seemed malicious defiance of everything his society believed. The poet said that Henri's mother, Catherine de Medici, was one of the many Italian Catholics who were politically and sexually corrupting France. In order to rule through her three sons, she had made them all weak monsters. To François II she assigned a tutor, the maréchal de Retz, who was an "atheistic sodomite, a pimp, a traitor"; as a result, François was an utter good-for-nothing. She created in Charles IX an unnatural taste for blood, so he became a slaughterer (he gave the order for the St. Bartholomew's Day massacre of Protestants). Her favorite son, Henri III, ended up homosexual. With all three so depraved and feminized, their mother was free to rule France as though she were a man. D'Aubigné threw in for good measure that the brothers had committed incest with their sister Marguerite.

If Henri's homosexuality hadn't existed, d'Aubigné might have invented it. He carefully wove together charges of perversion, foreignness, treason and Catholicism. Italy was known for Machiavellian politics and for super-elegance; the latter has always suggested diminished masculinity in the West. Soon sodomy would be referred to in France as *le vice Italien*. D'Aubigné, like a Roman noting an effeminate's use of Greek words and Eastern fashions, pointed out that Henri wore an Italian cap and clothes of Spanish cut, and that many of his advisers were both foreign-born and homosexual. This bias, and the presence of literary echoes of Juvenal and Suetonius, create doubts about much in the *Princes*, but many details of effeminacy and homosexuality at court are corroborated by other sources.

Suspicion of homosexuality fell on Louis XIII, who took the throne in 1610. Though some called him "Louis the Chaste," others said homosexuality was the reason his wife had produced his heir only after twenty years of marriage. That Louis was homosexual is still uncertain, but there is no doubt that much sexual experiment and deviance existed in his court. A revealing light on the times is the list of the volumes in the library of the Duchesse de Montpensier in 1587; her collection included books on incest, on "the sin against nature," and a *Lexicon de Fouteries* (*Lexicon of Fucking*) written by the Duchesse d'Uzès.

Only three prominent artists and scholars of the French Renaissance were charged with homosexuality. The one sure case was that of the Flemish sculptor Jerome Duquesnoy, whose brother François made the *Mannekin Pis* of Brussels. He was burned in 1654 for seducing into sodomy two acolytes who had modeled for him at a church where he was executing a commission. The other two cases show how accusations of homosexuality continued to be weapons in religious and personal vendettas.

Theodore de Bèze was born in 1519. In 1548 he experienced a serious illness that shook him deeply. In its aftermath he married his mistress, underwent a profound religious experience, and turned from Catholicism to Calvinism. He became a leader of the Reformation in France and a friend and collaborator of Calvin; after Calvin's death is 1564 he became the ruler of Geneva and lived on for forty years more as a respected religionist and scholar.

In the year of his conversion, de Bèze had published a book of poems entitled *Juvenilia*, and among them was one called *His Affection for Candide and Audebert*. It described his conflict between following "love" and going to see friend Audebert in Paris, and following "pleasure" by seeking out the woman Candide in Orleans. He called both of them his *mignons* and said he burned for each, but if he had to choose, he would give a heartfelt kiss to Candide and go to Audebert. It sounds like a conventional Neo-Platonic verse praising deep soul-companionship between men, as compared to mere carnal infatuation with women. It is straining things to call it a poem of homosexual versus heterosexual love, since it followed a then-popular literary convention and remains the only evidence of homoeroticism in de Bèze's life. In fact, it probably reflected homosexuality as much as poems about milkmaids and shepherds showed a real liking for farm life. But Catholic polemicists, who saw this promising theologian become an effective apologist for Calvinism, preferred the sexual interpretation. One said, "He was tortured by a burning lust for this young Audebert, a remarkably handsome boy, with whom he was united in a sodomitic love." Another lectured: "Instead of your Audebert, now you have embraced Calvin, and so have substituted a spiritual male whore for a carnal one; thus being still what you were—a sodomite." Books by and for homosexuals regularly list de Bèze as one of the great homosexuals of the Renaissance.

Marc Antoine Muret was a contemporary of de Bèze, the most respected humanist scholar of his day in France. In 1553 he was arrested

and imprisoned at Chatelet on a charge of sodomy. He was soon released, thanks to some friends' intervention. He went to Toulouse to live,
but was there again accused of sodomy. This time the charge of being a
Huguenot was added. He fled, was tried *in absentia*, found guilty and
burned in effigy. In 1558, this time in Padua, he was again charged with
sodomy. Friends helped him escape to Venice, but soon he faced the
same accusations there. Shortly afterward, his luck changed. He won the
protection of the powerful Cardinal d'Este, prominent in the Catholic
hierarchy in Rome and France. He finally returned to France and spent
the rest of his life in high repute there as a churchman, writer and
Latinist. It is doubtful that he was ever a Huguenot. Although his letters
reveal deep emotional friendships with men, they contain harsh disapproval of homosexuality. There is no evidence of homosexuality in his
life, and in his youth he wrote erotic poems to women. Perhaps vengeful
clerics made charges follow him through Europe's network of ecclesiastic
courts. It is possible, of course, that both de Bèze and Muret managed
respectively to rule Calvinist Geneva and hold high rank and respect in
the Church for decades and yet be secret homosexuals. It is much more
likely that both were, for political-religious reasons, stamped with the
most damaging accusation their age could imagine, the dual sins of religious and sexual heresy.

The Renaissance in England, as in Italy and France, was characterized by a classical revival, social and political upheavals, exhibitionistic
fashions, and the existence side by side of sexual forthrightness and powerful sexual guilt. Those who disliked the changes in society often blamed
Italy for them. Travel was now common among the wealthy and well-to-
do; Englishmen had brought back from Italy such customs as elaborate
gallantry and eating with a fork instead of fingers. It was now that northern
and southern Europe started becoming self-consciously different, embark-
ing on a complex love-hate relationship full of envy, contempt and indignation. The erotic *novelle* were widely translated and imitated, and Roger
Ascham, Queen Elizabeth's tutor, complained that "they introduce such
refinements of vice as the simple head of an Englishman is not able to
invent." He was indulging what would become an English mental habit—
pious underestimation of British erotic and political ingenuity. Such
skills were allegedly the monopoly of darker southern peoples. To a degree, all northern Europe came to feel this way, but England seems to
have mothered and perfected the idea.

Despite such complaints, everything Italian became fashionable. When
reading Thomas Nash, one could be listening to the prurient plaint of
Romans about Greeks, Peorians about Parisians. "When Englishmen
come back from Italy they are full of smiles; they have a ready wit and
delight in vain talk. They give up all idea of getting married, love and no
marriage is their only wish; they arrange assignations; they behave quite

improperly. They be the greatest makers of love, the daylie dalliers, with much pleasant words, with such smiling and secret countenances. . . ." The Italianate dandy, the court fop, was an object of contempt. However, to use the modern idioms, he was a show-off and a sissy, but not a fairy. In the eighteenth century, Englishmen would sometimes, like the French, call homosexuality the Italian vice. But during the sixteenth and seventeenth centuries, the Italian villain of English literature, though guilty of popery, political treachery, adultery, even incest, was not shown as homosexual. And the notorious cases of homosexuality in the artistic and noble worlds of England at the time were impeccably native figures.

The known homosexuals of the English Renaissance were few, but as in France the most famous was a king. When James VI of Scotland succeeded Elizabeth to become James I of England, he was already known for love affairs with men. People passed about the Latin joke, *"Rex Elizabeth fuit, nunc Jacobus regina est"*—Elizabeth was king, now James is queen. James was a bearlike, bandy-legged man with a pedantic but hysterical personality. Though he married and had several children, his true love was a page named Robert Carr. Carr later become the lover of Lady Essex and drew away from James; justly or not, he was implicated in the still mysterious Overbury poisoning case, with its tangle of intrigues and revenges, and he spent the rest of James's reign in the Tower. His place in James's life was taken by George Villiers, who in 1614 became, in Greek tradition, cupbearer to the king. By 1623 he had been made Duke of Buckingham and become immensely rich and the greatest power behind the throne. James called him Steenie because he resembled a then famous painting of St. Stephen. James carried his lover's portrait next to his heart. His love for all his favorites was doting, dependent, demanding and mercurial.

James was a fairly good scholar and writer. He wrote poetry, composed tracts on witchcraft, tobacco and divorce, and was responsible for the version of the Bible that bears his name (probably the only masterpiece ever to issue from a committee). His court, though, was full of crudeness, heavy drinking, and open sexuality of several varieties. After his son Charles took the throne in 1625, a lady of the court wrote that now it was "temperate, chaste and serious so that the fools and bawds, mimics and catamites of the former court, who did not quite abandon their debaucheries, yet so reverenced the king as to retire into corners to practice them."

Charles' love for his wife, Henrietta Maria of France, was like that of his father for Buckingham—tender and uxorious. When he was about to be beheaded, it was found that he wore a medallion bearing her portrait, as James had carried Buckingham's. But when the Cromwellians tried to justify having beheaded the king, John Milton, Secretary for Foreign Tongues, announced to England that Charles had been "a monster who had also been nasty with his father's own catamite, the Duke of Buckingham, the very instrument by which he had poisoned his own father." It is a touch of historic justice that H. R. Hays, a contemporary writer, has paid Milton back in his own coin by calling him a passive homosexual who sublimated his perversion in the Platonic idealism of his poetry.

Only two English artists of the period were surely homosexual, Nicholas Udall and Francis Bacon. Udall, author of the earliest extant English comedy, *Ralph Roister Doister,* was headmaster of Eton from 1534 till 1541, where he gained a reputation for enjoying the infliction of corporal punishment. In 1541 he was accused of "unnatural crime" with a boy, confessed to the Privy Chamber, and wrote to them a letter full of repentence and promised to reform. He lost his post at Eton and was committed for a while to Marshalsea Prison. However, he kept his sinecure as Vicar of Braintree, received Queen Mary's patronage for his playwriting, and in 1554 was made headmaster of another school, Westminster. The homosexual scandal seems to have permanently ruined neither his professional nor literary fortunes. It seems that then, as today, good connections could sometimes win immunity for deviants, and a properly put admission of guilt soothe social indignation.

Such protection certainly helped Francis Bacon. He married at forty-six and had a dry, childless union. John Aubrey stated flatly in his *Brief Lives* that Bacon was a pederast, and the diary of antiquarian Sir Simonds d'Ewes mentioned Bacon's affairs with his male servants, especially one "very effeminate-faced youth . . . his catamite and bedfellow." In the 1870s a letter written to Bacon by his mother came to light, in which she reproved him for the young Welshmen he kept as servants and lovers. Aubrey says that there was once a possibility of Bacon being publicly accused and tried for sodomy. It is possible that when Bacon entered high-level politics, his enemies threatened to make public what was fairly common knowledge about him in tolerant court circles. Eventually a bribe-taking charge forced Bacon to step back from the center of political infighting and content himself with safer literary, scientific and public-service occupations. His public life was always circumspect, and there is no hint of his homosexuality in his writings. In fact, in his *New Atlantis* he followed utopian tradition by making his ideal community as asexual as possible. "It is the virgin of the world . . . marriage is ordained a remedy for unlawful concupiscence . . . unlawful lust being like a furnace, that if you stop the flames altogether it will quench, but if you give it any vent it will rage; as for masculine love, they have no touch of it."

Homosexuality has been imputed to Richard Barnfield, a poet good enough for some of his sonnets to have been confused with Shakespeare's. In 1594, when he was twenty, Barnfield wrote a poem called *The Affectionate Shepherd*, about the love of Daphnis for Ganymede—probably,

despite his denial of it, an imitation of Virgil's homosexual Second Eclogue.
His poem contained the lines:

> If it be sin to love a lovely lad,
> Oh, then sin I.

In some of his later poems there are less direct expressions of love for
men. There is no record of Barnfield's personal life except that he married in 1599 and, when he died twenty years later, left behind a son.
Some have argued that he was homosexual, especially as part of an attempt
to prove that Shakespeare was homosexual. Others say that the poems in
question were just neoclassical literary exercises. The likelihood of such
a charge will be clearer when examining the evidence about Shakespeare.

The theater was the only circle of English society besides the court
that was associated with homosexuality. Women were not allowed on
stage, and female roles were played by boys. This was one reason for the
Puritan rage against theaters as a moral slum. Philip Stubbes wrote in 1583
that "players and play-haunters in their secret conclaves play the Sodomites," and went on to name men who had fallen in love with boy
actors.

The two greatest dramatists of the time, Marlowe and Shakespeare,
have been called homosexual or bisexual. Marlowe comes closer than any
other Englishman to our romanticized picture of the Renaissance man
—a spy and an artist, a brawler and a philosopher, a passionate, rebellious
and impulsive man, yet author of some of the most tender love poetry in
our language. In short, he combined the aggressive, intellectual and lyrical
qualities that have always conflicted in the Western image of masculinity. Actually, almost nothing is known of his life except that he was a
poet, probably a paid political agent, and was knifed to death in a tavern.

The idea of Marlowe's homosexuality derives from testimony at the inquest after his death. Richard Baines, or Bames, was a government informer who had been following Marlowe; probably he was one of several men involved in murdering him for political reasons now unknown,
under cover of a put-up tavern brawl. Baines's note, submitted at the inquest, accused Marlowe chiefly of atheism and blasphemy, with running
hints of treason. It listed "the opinion of one Christopher Marly Concerning his Damnable Judgment of Religion, and scorn of gods word." Among
Marlowe's views, claimed Baines, were:

> He affirmeth that Moyses was but a Juglar, & that one Heriots being Sir
> W Raleighs man can do more than he.
>   That the first beginning of Religioun was only to keep men in awe.
>   That Christ was a bastard and his mother dishonest.
>   That if there be any god or any good Religion, then it is in the papistes
> because the service of god is performed with more Cerimonies, as Elevation

of the mass, organs, singing men, Shaven Crownes & cta. that all protestants are Hyprocriticall asses.

. . . That all the new testament is filthily written.

That St. John the Evangelist was bedfellow to Christ and leaned always in his bosome, that he used him as the sinners of *Sodoma*.

That all they that love not *Tobacco* & Boies were fooles.

. . . he perswades men to *Atheism* willing them not to be afeared of bug-beares and hobgoblins. . . .

To be called soft on atheism or Catholicism when England teetered on the edge of religious civil war, and witches and heretics were still commonly burned, was a serious matter; a schoolfellow of Marlowe's was burned as a heretic. The Baines statement, now generally referred to by historians as "the Baines libel," tried to link Marlowe with everything disreputable from religion through politics to sex. He was accused of both Catholic and atheist leanings! Tobacco was mentioned twice, probably to reinforce the recurring implication of a link with Raleigh; smoking was a new and still rare practice, introduced in England by Raleigh only seven years earlier, and its mention probably made people think at once of that poet and adventurer whose politics and skeptical views were in bad odor at court. The statement that Marlowe claimed only fools didn't like tobacco and boys seems a throwaway, an extra stone cast in case the assassinated character should twitch. It is the only thing that has ever linked Marlowe and homosexuality.

John Bakeless, author of the authoritative biography of Marlowe, says that the Baines libel reads like "the jottings of a horrified and rather literal-minded listener to the rather wild conversation of a radical young man who took an intense pleasure in making his listeners' flesh creep." He fails to note that the charges against Marlowe were the old Roman-law and Christian trinity of heresy, treason and sexual deviance. The basis for the charges can be estimated by the fact that although writer Sir Thomas Kyd was tortured into giving what evidence could be wrung from him to defame Marlowe, the Baines libel was still thought necessary by the prosecution.

During the decades following Marlowe's death, Puritan rhetoric used him as a moral example. Here was a sign of the times—an atheist, wencher, sodomite and murderer who was himself killed in a tavern brawl! Marlowe's perversity became common knowledge. Later, homosexual apologists, followed by Freudian critics, sought homosexuality in Marlowe's writings. Whether they would have found it without prior conviction that Marlowe was homosexual or bisexual is doubtful. Homosexual attraction occurs in *Dido* and *Hero and Leander,* but it occurs in much literature of the time, in the same context of classical allusion. The play *Edward II* is about homosexual infatuation; it is also a historical work, recounting the pathetic downfall of Edward through his love of Gaveston.

It can more easily be read as a condemnation of homosexuality than as a defense of it.

The theory that Shakespeare was homosexual was first stated in 1889 by Oscar Wilde. Samuel Butler, Frank Harris and a few other writers agreed (Butler also decided on the basis of internal, stylistic evidence that Homer was really a woman). Within a few decades many people proclaimed Shakespeare's homosexuality, bisexuality or "homosexual temperament." Like Marlowe, he was now one of the healthy, ambidextrous Elizabethans. Malcolm Muggeridge suggests that the instant popularity of the idea was due to the fact that "homosexuals were heartened to feel that there was no *prima facie* reason why they should not have written *Hamlet.*" Some of the proofs of Shakespeare's homosexuality are as ingenious as those that Shakespeare was really German—which has been proved many times by German scholars.

The greatest evidence for this theory is the sonnets written to a man whose initials were W. H. In Shakespeare's time, as we have seen, such poems were common all over Europe. Ben Jonson—who has never been called homosexual—signed a letter to a male friend "your true lover" and dedicated his eulogy to Shakespeare "To the memory of my Beloved." Shakespeare himself describes his dead friends as "my lovers gone." Shakespeare and W. H. were no more likely to have been homosexual lovers than de Bèze and Audebert. Those out to make a case for Shakespeare's homosexuality have grouped together the facts that Barnfield's and Shakespeare's sonnets were confused with each other, both wrote poems of Platonic love to men, and Barnfield did an imitation of Virgil's *Second Eclogue.* We know nothing of Barnfield except that he was married and, when young, wrote fashionable Platonic verses. Hesketh Pearson says:

> Most of the Sonnets may be read as literary exercises . . . there was a craze for that sort of thing. . . . They were not meant to be taken *too* seriously; the love-making in them was literary love-making; and the flattery of some young nobleman was part of the game; as in Richard Barnfield's *Certaine Sonnets,* where a youth of "worship," who arouses the correct amount of jealousy in the poet, is addressed as "my love," "Nature's fairest work," "sweet boy."

But by 1640 Platonic male love and its expression in sonnet form were dead literary traditions. That year Benson edited the sonnets and changed some of the pronouns, apparently trying to protect the author or readers. A few others read the sonnets over succeeding centuries without allowing for changes in the conventions of amatory poetry; in 1780 George Steevens said that Sonnet 20 could not be read without "an equal admixture of disgust and indignation." The great Shakespeare scholar Edmond Malone explained to readers a decade later that the use of loving terms among men had been a mere literary habit in Shakespeare's time, but the suspicions of the Bensons and Steevenses have continued. For instance, a doubting Leslie Fiedler says, "The poet admits to, even boasts of, sleeping with women and considering it filthy, while chastely (but passionately) embracing an idealized male beloved." Fiedler also considers the relationship between Huck Finn and Nigger Jim to be homosexual.

The arguments against Shakespeare being homosexual are numerous. First, there is no record of homosexuality in his life; all the so-called proofs are from internal literary evidence. Second, the sonnets to W. H. are like those written all over Europe by heterosexual poets. Third, all his other works show heterosexual preoccupation, and every direct reference to homosexuality in his plays shows pitying scorn (for the complete list see Eric Partridge's *Shakespeare's Bawdy*.) Fourth, it is far from certain that any of the sonnets are directly autobiographical; the one in which he called himself an old leafless tree was written when he was thirty. And most important, deducing the life or even the personality of a writer from his work—*pace,* Freud—is sometimes difficult, sometimes doubtful, and sometimes impossible.

When St. Augustine spreads out his life and feelings in his *Confessions* or Catullus brags in first person of a homosexual fling, some direct and indirect conclusions are justified. It's another matter to claim to know someone's secret life or alleged latent, repressed or otherwise hidden feelings from his fiction or verse. On the same grounds that lead one to believe from the sonnets that Shakespeare was homosexual or bisexual, one is obliged to declare Kafka a paranoid schizophrenic—and in fact one critic has stated that this was so. We know, in fact, that Kafka was not blatantly paranoid. For that matter, Sir Thomas Browne, father of ten, wrote, "I could be content that we might procreate like trees, without . . . this trivial and vulgar way of union." There is doubtless some orthodox Freudian or homosexual apologist to argue that Browne was a latent homosexual.

It is possible that Shakespeare had a roaring homosexual secret life; after all, Bacon was homosexual, but one would never know it from his writings. The sonnets to W. H. may, indeed, reflect a homosexual episode in Shakespeare's life. But as Edward Hubler says, "The charge of homosexuality can neither be proved nor disproved on the available evidence, but the balance of probabilities discredits it."

I have discussed this matter with several Shakespeare scholars and found that it made some of them uneasy and argumentative. I personally feel that they want to preserve the possibility of Shakespeare's bisexuality for several reasons. First, they believe theoretically that a healthy, uninhibited life would probably be bisexual, and they think Shakespeare, being great, must have been so. Second, they share the brittle false sophistication that seizes on the least durable aspects of Freudianism to prove the nasty "real story"—the same cynicism that claims all troubadours must have been sleeping with their *dames.* Third, they share the current commonplace that a great artist must have "feminine" sensitivity: as the Shakespeare scholar G. Wilson Knight writes, the female element is an integral part of the male, especially the creative male, and "our greatest writers all have this share of supersexual understanding." Whether sensitivity and creativity are feminine, let alone homosexual, is an idea that, like latency, should be carefully studied before it is indiscriminately applied to biography.

The "homosexuality," "homosexual temperament," "latent homosexuality" or "bisexuality" of Erasmus, Montaigne and others has been alleged on grounds more slender than Shakespeare's sonnets. Using such techniques, almost anyone living or dead can be turned into a case of secret or latent homosexuality. Some years ago, the *New Statesman* ran a competition, asking people to submit poems that might have been written back to Shakespeare by W. H. The winning poem is probably closer to historical truth than the speculative ingenuities of Knight and Fiedler.

> Whenas—methinks that is a pretty way
>   To start—my father spoke to you anent
> The precious note I got the other day,
>   The perfum'd posy and the poet of scent,
> My drowned eyes are constantly bedewed,
>   The cruel rod of wrath I have not 'scaped;
> My mother has been cool, my brother rude,
>   Honest, you'd think I was already raped.
> —You really think I'm like a summer's day?
>   Really and truly? Thank you ever so—
> Behind the Globe, if I can get away,
>   I'll show my weals and tell thee all my woe.
> In your next po'm, an thou wouldst give me joy,
>   Will you make it clear I'm not that sort of boy?

The idea of the bisexual creative man of the Renaissance collapses even more foolishly than that of the happily homoerotic philosopher of ancient Greece. In France and England, as in Italy, the number of homosexuals among artists and intellectuals was, if anything, smaller than one would expect at that level of society; the inclusion of borderline or doubtful cases hardly changes the picture. Though we have no idea of the exact number or percentage of deviants, homosexuality was not an extreme rarity, and permissiveness, experimentation and possibly sexual kinks were increasingly common among the noble and wealthy, in cities and courts, from the later Middle Ages through the Renaissance. What needs understanding is not homosexuality among creative men of the time, but its relative absence, and the insistence during the past century on reversing the balance of historical evidence.

To the law, the church and society at large, homosexuality remained a ghastly breach of the social order—as did heterosexual sodomy. Both continued to be punished by death in most of Europe, from Italy to Sweden to England. There are records of burnings in England and Scot-

land for the "wyld, filthie, execrabill, detestabill and unnaturall crime" of
sodomy. A former provost of the University of Paris, Jean Badon, was
burned in 1586 for injuring a boy in the act of anal rape. In Venice, in
1492, a nobleman and a priest were publicly beheaded and burned for
committing homosexual acts.

These records are not indices of the prevalence of deviance. Homosexuality was doubtless kept even more secret than today because of
the severity of the penalties. On the other hand, rank and wealth often
protected deviants, and prosecution apparently depended in many cases
on whether there was a desire to use homosexuality against a person hated
for other reasons, or who was politically annoying, or whose involvement
in public scandal made action unavoidable.

With the Reformation, power to investigate and prosecute passed steadily from ecclesiastic to civil courts; civil law usually just perpetuated old
legal sanctions and Church attitudes. When Henry VIII seized authority
from the Church in 1533, he made sodomy a civil felony punishable by
death (adding that "there is not yet sufficient and condign punishment"
for this "detestable and abominable vice"). In countries that remained
Catholic, the transition was slower and sometimes involved a bitter power
struggle. The state often insisted on dealing with such matters as adultery
and rape, which involved property and personal rights; the Church argued
strongly that homosexuality and suicide, which were sins against God
rather than property or citizens, were its concern.

In Spain, for instance, the controversy dragged on for two centuries; it
was settled differently in various parts of the country. Sometimes a compromise was reached, and the Church carried out the trial, but under
the rules of local civil law. In any case, the punishment was death,
always executed by the civil authorities. In 1506 twelve men were burned
in Seville as the result of a special ecclesiastical inquest; three years later
the Suprema firmly told the Inquisition there to limit itself to matters of
faith, and to try only cases in which heresy was involved. But as the argument went on all over Spain, accused homosexuals fell to the tortures of
the Inquisition. If those found guilty were older than twenty-five, they
were burned; if younger, they were whipped and sent to the galleys. Between 1598 and 1602 twenty-seven men were convicted of sodomy in
Valencia—the city where, in 1519, a priest had preached that the plague
there was God's wrath for the prevalence of sodomy, and five men were
burned by mobs.

There is no way to know whether the large number of trials and burnings indicates much homosexuality or the eagerness and efficiency of the
Inquisition. Nor can we know, on the other hand, how many clergymen
and powerful laymen were protected from exposure. To guess at the
prevalence of homosexuality one must make an impressionistic mosaic of
legislation, trial records, sermons, diaries, travel books, letters and so on.
Homosexual prostitution is a good indication that deviance exists to a sig-

nificant degree. It was not recorded in Renaissance England; there the theater and court alone had reputations for homosexuality. But it was open in Paris at least as early as the thirteenth century. Bussy-Rabutin, who wrote a famous *Amorous History of the Gallic People* in 1665, said that in Henri II's time the "Camp Flory" was a rendezvous for prostitutes of both sexes; in the following century, Mirabeau wrote that Henri's contemporaries had made homosexual pickups around the Louvre.

Italy seems to have deserved its reputation for sexual deviance; England and France didn't catch up, at least in public activity, for a century or two. In 1455 the Venetian Council of Ten pronounced that "the abominable vice of sodomy multiplies in this city" and appointed two men in each quarter of the city to stamp it out, and thus "avert the wrath of God." In 1480 a law was passed there forbidding female prostitutes to dress as boys; one interpretation is that they were soliciting sodomy. In 1492 the Council said that some men in the city wore women's clothes, and some women dressed as men, which was "a species of sodomy." English and French visitors were shocked at the prevalence and openness of homosexuality. William Lithgow, an English traveler, wrote in the early seventeenth century that the Romans practiced "unnatural vices" and that "beastly sodomy [is] rife [in Padua] as in Rome, Naples, Florence, Bullogna, Venice, Ferrara, Genoa, Parma, not being exempted, nor yet the smallest village of Italy; a monstrous filthinesse, and yet to them a peasant pastime, making songs and singing sonets of the beauty and pleasure of their Bardassi, or embuggered boyes."

A French visitor said in 1694:

> ... however easy may be the commerce with women and however beautiful they may be, would you believe it but the Venetians mistrust them, and attach themselves rather to a boy, even if he as ugly as a monkey, rather than to the most pleasant girl. It is the dominant vice of the nation, to which they are so attached it is quite horrible, and they do not breathe day or night but for that, and squandering time and money to satisfy their horrible passions. There are even those who go to the infamous excess of paying porters and gondoliers to bestialise themselves. All their activities are directed toward this end, and where in France conversation between young men may revolve round the love of women, here it revolves round that between men. The Turks are also active in this direction but I do not think more so than the Italians. The Monks also have a terrible reputation as regards this, as well as regards women.

Many such accusations can be chalked up to clerical hysteria, the hostility or incomprehension of foreigners, and exaggeration. But in sum they are convincing. It remains impossible to say whether homosexual acts were performed by one or twenty out of a hundred men, with what variations by class, origin and personality, with what frequency or what feelings. But homosexuality was clearly commonplace in urban Italy, present in France, and less public, probably less common, in England. In all these places it remained a capital crime and, to many or most people, an object of contempt.

Accounts of lesbianism began to appear for the first time since the ancient world. The Renaissance brought tentative female emancipation, and in the upper and middle classes there were women who dressed and lived in what were considered rather masculine ways. However, the number of verified cases of lesbianism is tiny. It first appeared not in life but in literature. In the medieval romance *Huon of Bordeaux,* a girl disguised as a man was forced to marry another woman; after her discovery, the king said she should be burned, "for he sayd he wold not suffre suche boggery to be used." Similar situations, with clear implications of familiarity with lesbianism, occur in Ariosto's *Orlando Furioso*; in a sixteenth-century French version of Eastern tales called *La Fleur Lascive Orientale*; in Sir Philip Sidney's *Arcadia* ("an uncouth love, which nature hateth most"); and in d'Urfé's *Astrée*. Cross-dressing became very popular in Renaissance drama; Shakespeare used it in *Twelfth Night* and *As You Like It*, but as in most plays of the period, it carried no suggestion of lesbianism. Usually it seemed meant to provoke that peculiar titillation and uneasy eroticism which sexual disguise provokes in our society.

Two English plays of the period were based on the lives of real female transvestites. Middleton and Dekker's *Roaring Girl* was a romanticized version of the life of Mary Frith. In reality she was a robber, forger and fence known by the alias Moll Cutpurse; she had no known attachment to anything living save her pet mastiff. In the play she became a sort of daring tomboy feminist. In Spain a disciple of Lope de Vega, Juan Pérez de Montalban, produced a play in 1616 called *La Monja Alférez*; its subject was a Basque woman much like Moll Cutpurse, and she was similarly gilded by the playwright.

Lesbianism existed, in fact was common, in Renaissance erotic writings, but how widely it was practiced is a mystery. Montaigne's *Journal of a Voyage in Italy*, written in 1581, told about seven or eight women weavers who dressed as men to seek work. One passed as a man so well that she married another woman. She was exposed by someone from her native village and condemned to be hanged. "She said she would even prefer this to living again as a girl, and was hanged for using illicit inventions to supply the defects of the sex."

The story smells of exaggeration. So-called real cases often turn out to be literary inventions or just dirty jokes with real names and places attached. A French poem of 1581 called *La Frigarelle* told about the lovemaking of a great French lady and a girl. At first glance it seems the tale of a current scandal; it is actually a close imitation of Lucian's dialogue between the prostitutes Leaena and Clonarium. We will never know whether the *olisboi* in Aretino's literary orgy were objects the author had seen or had merely read about in Lucian.

7

Marrieds and Libertines

The Reformation, and especially Puritanism, helped create the morality by which we live today; it did so chiefly by changing the family, which is the seedbed of mores. The new urban middle class did not go off on crusades or live in leisure and legal immunity. Many worked at home, with their wives and children; they expected more from their families than had medieval men or their upper-class contemporaries. In the past, lonely exceptions had written of woman as man's friend, partner and full equal, but not until the sixteenth century did many books appear which, instead of damning woman as the soulless snare of the Devil, gave two-sided debate on her nature. Volumes on love, marriage and women became a thriving industry, and some seriously discussed marrying for love. Men were beginning to imbue family ties with the idealization that courtly and Platonic love had reserved for mistresses. This revolution, making love, sex and marriage compatible, was more profound than any we are witnessing today. It found its voice with the Reformation.

Martin Luther had been raised by harshly moralistic parents who beat him for the smallest transgression. All his life he harbored two opposing selves—an angry parent who raged against impulsiveness, and a rebel who defended spontaneity and the flesh. As a monk, he scourged and starved himself to maintain his chastity; he also suffered anxiety, rages and hallucinations, in which he was sometimes tempted by Satan himself—whom he characteristically drove away by farting at him or by shouting "Lick my ass!"

When this pious, angry young Augustinian from provincial Germany visited Rome, he was horrified. The old complaints of Pico della Mirandola and Boccaccio were still true—fornication and prostitution flourished in nunneries, and sins "natural and sodomitical" were widespread among clerics. Celibacy was enforced only among the lower clergy, and then often weakly. Why, Luther wondered, had he prayed, fasted and whipped himself, when the very leaders of the Church didn't even try to contain themselves?

When Luther later broke with Rome and somewhat inadvertently found himself in the center of a vast religious and political upheaval, sex and marriage became crucial issues. Like Augustine and most subsequent Christians, Luther viewed sex as a base, raging bestiality; he differed in his idea of how to manage it. He agreed that the desire for sexual pleasure was awful to God, and that to marry for passion was sin: had Adam and Eve not stained themselves with concupiscence, they would never have had to suffer "epileptic and apoplectic lust." But the power of lust was so great, its taint so deep, that no human could resist. Attempting celibacy was an invention of the Devil to create sin on earth—as the behavior of the Roman clergy made clear. God, in His wisdom, had provided marriage as a necessary remedy; even heathens knew this, for they all had the institution. The alternatives to marriage—fornication and celibacy—were respectively sinful and futile. Even marital sex was unclean, but, said Luther, "God winks at it." In fact, even polygamy was better than fornication and adultery; in one case, Luther recommended it. Anyone married to a frigid woman or impotent man was not truly married; to insist on their union was provoking adultery. If necessary, a discreet *à trois* arrangement could be made by common consent. "If the wife refuse, let the maid come "

In all, Luther's view of sex and marriage was pretty much what one would expect from a pious but lusty German provincial. He insisted on family solidarity, wifely submission, the sinfulness and necessity of sex— and the shamefulness of deviance. In his commentary on the story of Lot, he wrote:

> I for my part do not enjoy dealing with this passage, because so far the ears of Germans are innocent of and uncontaminated by this monstrous depravity; for even though this disgrace, like other sins, has crept in through an unholy soldier and a lewd merchant, still the rest of the people are unaware of what is being done in secret. The Carthusian monks deserve to be hated because they were the first to bring this terrible pollution into Germany from the monasteries of Italy. Of course, they were trained and educated in such a praiseworthy manner at Rome. . . .
>
> In Rome I myself saw some cardinals who were esteemed highly as saints because they were content to associate with women. . . . Whence comes this perversity? Undoubtedly from Satan, who, after people have once turned away from the fear of God, so powerfully suppresses nature that he blots out the natural desire and stirs up a desire that is contrary to nature.

Calvin's theology was not much different from Luther's, but his personality was—ascetic, legalistic and rigid. At twenty-six he wrote his *Institutes*, a blueprint for a community based on primitive Christianity; a few years later he began to turn Geneva into the theocracy of his dreams. Luther's authoritarian streak was balanced by an earthy sense of the physical and impulsive life—and the democratic humility it implies. Calvin's was not, and his cold word became law. In the course of two years, 414 people were prosecuted for singing, swearing and extravagant dress. Fornication became punishable by exile, adultery by drowning or beheading; some offenders got off with fines or imprisonment, but many paid the full penalty. Torture and execution for sexual offenses and heresy were common in this city ruled by the *Institutes'* ban on "the licentiousness of the flesh, which unless it be rigidly restrained, transgresses every bound." Calvin noted the passage in Deuteronomy that says a woman's hand should be cut off if she accidentally touches the genitals of a man against whom she helps her husband fight; he admitted it was a bit harsh, but thought it showed how pleasing is modesty to God.

Luther was a virgin when he married at forty-two, but he then enjoyed his wife and family as though made for them. Calvin married at thirty; nine years later his wife died, and he remained a widower. All records describe him as icily controlled. He had an obsessive concern about the sin of adultery, but an even greater loathing for sodomy, since, he said, even beasts do not commit such violations of nature. Yet with all this thinly concealed horror of sex, of spontaneity of any kind, he went even farther than Luther in idealizing marriage. Like Luther, he said that few men are capable of celibacy; he was probably thinking of homosexuality when he said that men should not take vows they cannot live up to, for God would then send them "secret flames of lust" and "horrible acts of Filthiness." Echoing Luther's "God winks," he called marital intercourse "pure, honorable and holy . . . a veil by which the fault of lust is covered over, so that it no longer appears in the sight of God." But where Luther saw in woman a redeeming receptacle of man's lust, Calvin saw a companion, a friend, a partner. He liked to dwell on the words in Genesis, "It is not good that man should be alone." God, he said, had created woman so that "there should be human beings on the earth who might cultivate mutual society between themselves." He propounded the idea that sexual reformers three centuries later called companionate marriage.

Calvin had imitators and supporters in many places. John Knox remade Scotland on the Genevan model by the 1560s. During the reign of Queen Elizabeth, the Puritans in England raged against drinking, dancing, the theater and ornate dress. The conflict between their middle-class, family-oriented morality and upper-class permissiveness grew so sharp that James I tried to solve it by shipping Puritans off to New England. The split kept widening; the Puritans were mocked as killjoys and hypocrites, and they in turn found unrestrained Anglicans as frivolous and pernicious as Italian Papists. Such clash of life style always finds political expression. There was a civil war, and in 1649 King Charles I was beheaded and a Puritan regime installed. Theaters were closed, church attendance made compulsory. Nude statues were plastered into decency, and "idle sitting at doors and walking in churchyards" banned. Adultery became a capital crime.

The laws of Puritan New England were as harsh as those of the Puritan mother country. The Massachusetts and Plymouth colonies demanded death for murder, witchcraft, sodomy, rape and bestiality. As in England, offenders over fourteen were to be hanged for buggery, those under fourteen "severely punished." Puritanism, with its scarlet letters and paternal dictatorship in family and government, seemed to have found in America a perfect soil, unrestrained by opposition.

In fact, Puritan controls were more praised than practiced. Geneva was full of forced marriages and bastards, and Calvin's own daughter and sister-in-law were caught in adultery. The elaborate and severe sexual regulations were so repellent to many people in England that there were few prosecutions and fewer convictions. Rape, incest, fornication and homosexuality went on unabated. In the American colonies, there were illegitimacy, premarital and extramarital sex, bestiality and homosexuality. Attempts to enforce the death penalty for adultery failed after a few decades, and it was removed from the books. The American Puritans tried to blame the sexual lapses in their utopia on newer arrivals: their realm was now a dumping ground not only for Old World utopians and zealots but for criminals and undesirables of all kinds. In 1642 Governor William Bradford of Plymouth complained that although sins were nowhere more severely punished than in his colony, "all of this could not suppress the breaking out of sundrie notorious sins . . . especially drunkenness and unclainnes; not only incontinencie between persons unmarried . . . but that which is even worse, even sodomie and bugerie (things fearfull to name,) have brook forth in this land, oftener than once." Cotton Mather reassures us of the Colonial sexual imagination by telling of a man considered saintly by his community until his son caught him "hideously conversing with a sow."

There exist court records from the colonies of executions for sodomy, and other cases may be disguised by official charges of "uncleanness" or "defiling." A curious problem of jurisdiction arose when "5 beastly Sodomiticall boyes" were discovered on the ship Talbot en route to Massachusetts from England in 1629. No one knew what to do with them on the high seas. One Reverend Francis Higgeson recorded, "The fact was so fowle wee reserved them to bee punished by the governor when he came to new England, who afterward sent them backe to the company to bee punished in ould England, as the crime deserved."

The usual view today is that Puritanism was the triumph of an anti-life force, a tyranny enforced with such tools of public humiliation as the ducking stool, pillory and badge of guilt. In fact, in its extreme form, it was so excessive a piece of repressiveness that it soon lost power everywhere—it lasted only a century even in Geneva. The Puritans are supposed to have been hypocrites, witch hunters, latent homosexuals, haters of women and sex, and full of what classical psychoanalysis calls anal characteristics—acquisitive, obsessive-compulsive, paranoid, full of righteousness that was really a reaction formation. If Puritanism and all such attempts to contain sexuality are hopeless, how did the Puritan legacy dominate the West for centuries after its last political strongholds crumbled? On the other hand, if its grip has been so great, how did it suddenly vanish in the course of a decade, as we are constantly assured happened between 1960 and 1970? Such questions cannot be sensibly answered because the premise behind them is barely a half-truth. The Puritans were not uniformly as they have been portrayed; they have been made a whipping boy in the rhetoric of sexual liberation since the beginning of the anti-Victorian reaction.

There were Puritan dandies who insisted on ruffles, laces, courtliness and fine manners. Aside from stronger sanctions on adultery, the Puritan penalties for sexual offenses were the same ones that had been in effect all over Europe for centuries. Pillories, ducking stools and branding had been common for sexual offenses through the Catholic Middle Ages. People were burned for witchcraft, sodomy and adultery in non-Puritan countries and colonies as in the Puritan ones. We don't know that the father's power was in practice greater than in early Rome, twelfth-century Germany or most Catholic countries of the same period. Nor do we know how much neurosis, psychosis and sexual disorder resulted from Puritan efforts at control—it could hardly have been much more than existed during the late Middle Ages. Nor is there evidence that Salem held more guilt-ridden hysterics and paranoids than a town of ancient Great Mother worshipers or Levittown. No evidence suggests striking changes in sexual behavior or basic shifts in attitudes toward sex during the Puritan age.

As for homosexuality in particular, court records, memoirs and other sources only hint at its degree among the Puritans. The records of Plymouth colony show that between a fourth and a fifth of all prosecutions for sexual offenses were for homosexual acts, but this unusually high figure may be due to special local enforcement or chains of accusations. There were also many cases of homosexuality in non-Puritan colonies; New York had a number of them, complete with burnings at the stake. (Lord Cornbury, Governor of New York during the reign of Queen Anne, was a demented transvestite, and a portrait of himself in drag that he commissioned is still in existence.) We know only that Puritan homosexuals existed. Theories about latent homosexuality in father-dominated Puritan families are like Great Mother theories: they are convenient and pat, and if we ever have a hundred times the evidence we now possess, we can guess whether they are accurate. We can safely make few generalizations of that kind even about our own society.

Radical Puritanism did leave us an important legacy, but it is not the scarlet letter, which both preceded and survived Calvin and Knox. Its really revolutionary aspect was its insistence that love and marriage should be inseparable, and could free sex of much of its taint. In a sense, Puritanism was the last great medieval movement, sacrificing pleasure and utility to create heaven on earth, in heaven's terms. Perhaps that is why the Puritan makes us so uncomfortable; we have no such other-worldly commitment. He embarrasses us, as all moral radicals do. At his worst, he became smug, repellent and boorish in his piety, like all moral radicals, scorning all who failed to police themselves as harshly as he did himself. In his failures to live his principles, he might become guiltily devious or melodramatically repentant, and thus laughable. In either case, he was easy prey for satirists. But the Puritan was often courageous, and dignified by his belief; perhaps this firm dignity and moral commitment, which most people would call manly, are the reason it is so difficult to imagine Puritan effeminates, though they certainly existed.

Among the Puritans there were, of course, stern paternal hypocrites with thunderous no's tumbling from their lips, but the Puritans had no monopoly on them; they existed among Hebrews, Romans, Catholics and among other Protestant sectarians, some of whom were more puritanical than the Puritans. In many ways the usual Puritan—not the ruling zealot but the *homme moyen antisensuel*—resembled the firmer Roman Stoics. He was repelled by the worldly self-indulgence of his times, and he sought to create within his own life a zone of discipline, morality, responsibility and committed personal attachments. He believed in the great power of sex, feared it as all believing Christians did, and tried to control and even enjoy it by limiting it to marriage . . . this last belief was truly revolutionary, and the Catholic hierarchy murdered vast numbers of people for this heresy. He demanded power over his wife and children; like most Westerners, he believed women were mentally and spiritually children, and that it was his responsibility to protect them even if they were so silly as not to wish it. But he made his family the center of his life. That is our true Puritan inheritance: the belief that one's greatest fulfillment can come from the love expressed in one's marriage and family.

In Puritan New England, a woman could win a divorce if her husband beat her. The congregation of the First Church of Boston expelled a member as unnatural and un-Christian for denying his wife sex for two years on grounds of punishing himself for his sins. The Puritan Daniel Rogers wrote, "Husbands and wives should be as two sweet friends," their love a "sweet compound" of the spiritual and physical. In an age of egocentric sensuality in the upper classes, when the Don Juan legend had become a common reality among society's leaders, the Puritans transformed the tradition of romantic love by moving it from the adulterous to the conjugal bed. The Puritan who sternly refused to use diminutive endearments to his fiancée or wife was proving that he truly loved her, not merely bent on indulging frivolous sensuality. His love letters were often more touching, and rang more true, than those of the courtier.

John Milton was the movement's greatest spokesman. He urged Parliament—in vain—to allow divorce on grounds of "contrariety of mind." He called celibacy the work of Antichrist, and said the goal of man and wife was "a human society; where that cannot be had there is no true marriage . . . not in a forced cohabitation, and counterfeit performance of duties, but in unfeigned love and peace."

No homosexual of the fifteenth century would have defended his deviance by saying that homosexual love was just as sincere, profound and worthy as that of man and wife. Marriage was a necessity, a way to produce profit and heirs, not an act of love; the failure of marriage was not viewed as a failing of character. Today we feel that anyone who cannot find satisfaction in marriage and family is emotionally (or morally) deficient. The heterosexual has a grand idealization to try to live up to; the homosexual feels barred from ever approaching it. No matter how he argues to others and himself that it isn't vitally important, he is not convincing. The belief that married love is the happiest human fate has become too deep and pervasive in our society. That is true Puritanism. As for sex behavior and basic taboos, all the fighting with words and weapons clears away like smoke to reveal that the drama of Western sexuality is probably more one of continuity than of change.

While these new values grew slowly in the middle class and began to percolate through other social levels and religious groups, another development was taking place—first in the upper classes and eventually elsewhere. The Puritans were forced from power in 1660, and Cromwell's body was dug up and exposed to the hatred of people sick of civil war and so many attempts at social control. Charles II returned from exile in France, and he and his court brought with them the elegant manners and flippant sexuality of Versailles. The theaters reopened—with actresses in female roles—and the boards were full of Sir Fopling Flutter's siblings. The dandy and the rake arrived on the scene.

The Cavalier gentleman of earlier decades had seen women largely as instruments of his capricious indulgence. John Suckling spoke for him:

> Out upon it, I have lov'd
>   Three whole days together;
> And am like to love thee more,
>   If it prove fair weather. . . .
>
> Had it any been but she,
>   And that very Face,
> There had been at least ere this
>   A dozen dozen in her place.

There was scapegrace charm is this, capable of zest and superficial good nature. But the dalliance was hardening beneath the surface. By 1748, Lord Chesterfield would advise his son, "Women, then, are only children of large growth. . . . A man of sense only trifles with them, plays with them, humors and flatters them . . . they have in truth but two passions, vanity and love." Intellectually, the educated were turning to a "rationalism" that said only ignorance, pride or fear could prevent a reasonable human animal from appeasing its letch: this was the message behind many graceful poems inviting Phyllis to be kind and join in pleasure. It was probably a realistic code for a man dealing with courtesans, actresses and the ladies of Charles' court. Behind the philosophy and poetry lie the misogyny and mistrust of the icy Don Juan: since women are exploiters, they should be exploited first.

Today there is a tendency to make of Don Juan, as of da Vinci, a latent homosexual. It is one of our more burdensome debts to early psychoanalysis. Pioneer analyst Otto Fenichel wrote that "after [Don Juan] knows he is able to excite a specific woman, his doubts also arise concerning other women . . . an unconsciously homosexual man, for example, may be aroused by sexual contact with women but not satisfied; he then vainly seeks satisfaction in more and more sexual activity." This is a primitive, two-spigot sexual theory: if a man doesn't truly love women, he must love men.

There is no need for recourse to Fenichel's sort of preoccupation with alleged latent emotions. It reflects his age more than the Restoration. From examining the Roman Empire and the Renaissance, we are familiar with a type of pansexual, angry, coldly pleasure-seeking man in the upper classes—mistrustful of women and indulging occasionally in deviant acts. The extreme of the type was Mervin Lord Audley, who in 1631 was the center of a scandalous trial for having set up in his home at Castlehaven a bisexual circus of his servants, wife and twelve-year-old daughter. He was found guilty and executed for "abetting a Rape upon his Countess, Committing Sodomy with his servants, and Commanding and Countenancing the Debauching of his Daughter." This is a preview of the Restoration rakehell at his worst.

The Restoration's furious life of the nerve endings had its most brilliant representative in John Wilmot, Earl of Rochester—a great poet, whoremaster, vicious prankster and, according to his own braggadoccio, bisexual. He was one of the most disreputable men even at Charles' court. (When the king was addressed as "the father of his people," Rochester added, "Of a good many of them.") Anthony Hamilton said of Rochester in the *Memoirs of the Count de Grammont* that "his delight was to haunt the stews, debauch women, to write filthy songs and lewd pamphlets. . . . For five years together he was said to be drunk. . . . Once with the Duke of Buckingham he rented an inn on the Newmarket Road, and turned innkeeper, supplying the husbands with drink and defiling their wives."

Some such tales probably weren't true, but for each one recorded, there were surely genuine ones never put to paper. In a viciously sensual age, Rochester matched most of his peers in cruelty and promiscuity. As a result, his name became a magnet for every floating story of Restoration debauchery, cynicism and violence for decades after his death; and thus he became a pretext for moralistic preachings and inflated accusations, as had Marlowe before him.

The brittle bravado of Rochester's poems bring to mind Catullus at his most hurt and angry. He bragged in a pathetic rage that he would do anything with anybody. In *The Debauchee,* he wrote:

> I rise at Eleven, I dine about two,
> I get drunk before Sev'en, and the next Thing I do
> I send for my Whore, when, for fear of a Clap
> I fuck in her Hand, and I spew in her Lap;
> Then we quarrel and scold, till I fall asleep,
> When the Bitch growing bold, to my Pocket does creep;
> Then slily she leaves me and to revenge the Affront,
> At once she bereaves me of Money and Cunt.
> If by Chance then I wake, hot-headed and drunk,
> What a Coil do I make for the Loss of my Punk?
> I storm and I roar, and I fall in a Rage,
> And missing my Whore, I bugger my Page.
> Then Crop-sick all Morning, I rail at my Men,
> And lie in Bed yawning till Eleven again.

He claimed that untrustworthy women had made him turn—in scorn, he said—to wine, friendship and boys:

> Farewell Woman, I entend,
> Henceforth ev'ry Night to sit
> With my lewd well natur'd Friend,
> Drinking, to engender Wit.
> Then give me Health, Wealth, Mirth, and Wine;
> And if busy Love, intrenches,
> There's a sweet soft Page, of mine,
> Does the trick worth Forty Wenches.

How much of Rochester's talk of buggery was bragging and how much reality is a guess. There is no verified homosexual incident in Rochester's life, though books by and for homosexuals regularly list him among the great deviants. Some have attributed to him a play called *Sodom, or The Quintessence of Debauchery.* It is about a king who decreed sexual freedom for all and himself turned to homosexuality, so that the queen and her ladies had to make do with *godmichés* (*olisboi*) and each other. It is unlikely that Rochester wrote *Sodom,* but it resembles his poetry in being relentlessly, angrily pornographic. Like many writings by Martial and Aretino, it is not so much homosexual as unboundedly sexual. One can imagine the audience who enjoyed it—rakes and dandies who followed foppish fashions, drank and gambled and pranked and whored, and some of whom perhaps buggered a page now and then—but ready to crucify with their malice anyone effeminate or predominantly homosexual.

As usual, we have only impressions of the upper classes, and almost no information at all about the lower classes who made up the vast majority of the population. Nor do we know much about the probable majority who simply never made it into the chronicles of scandal. But it seems that

Rochester and his circle give a preview of psychosexual disturbance that by the eighteenth century became widespread among the wealthy and other classes as well. As the seventeenth century neared its end, exhibitionism, sado-masochism, fetishism, transvestism and homosexuality were mentioned more and more in literature, memoirs and public documents. Until then, all these deviations except homosexuality were rare or unnamed, perhaps barely known. When Samuel Pepys said in his diary that homosexuality was common at court, this was hardly news in the Western world. But it was news when an impotent old masochist and perhaps shoe fetishist appeared in Otway's play *Venice Preserved*. In Shadwell's comedy *The Virtuoso*, old Snarl, a fossil from the Puritan period who damned the day's degenerate morals, turned out to be a masochist—and to have acquired the passion while a student at Westminster, where Nicholas Udall had once been headmaster. He and his old friend Mrs. Figgup are commiserating on the degenerate times they live in:

SNARL: In sadness, it's a very wicked age. . . . In the last age we were modest and virtuous. . . . By the mass, my heart bleeds to see so great a decay of conjugal affection in the nation.

MRS. FIGGUP: Out upon 'em, filthy wenches. I wonder they dare show their hardened faces. They are so bold 'tis a burning shame they should be suffer'd, I vow.

SNARL: Nay, the young coxcombs are worse: nothing but swearing, drinking, whoring, tearing, ranting, and roaring. In sadness, I should be weary of the world for the vices of it but that thou comfortest me sometimes, buddy.

MRS. FIGGUP: Prithee dear numps, talk no more of 'em. I spit at 'em, but I love m 'own buddy man. Perdie, kiss me. . . . I love thee; thou art a civil, discreet, sober person of the last age.

SNARL: Ah poor little rogue. In sadness, I'll bite thee by the lip, i'faith I will. Thou has incens't me strangely; thou hast fir'd my blood; I can bear it no longer, i'faith I cannot. Where are the instruments of our pleasure? Nay, prithee, do not frown; by the mass, thou shalt do't now. . . . But dost hear, thou art too gentle. Do not spare thy pains. I love castigation mightily. So here's good provision.

[*Pulls the carpet; three or four great rods fall down.*]

One can imagine the delight of a Restoration audience at seeing the crusty old Cromwellian moralist revealed as a secret pervert. It was taken for granted for the first time in English literature that sado-masochism was something most playgoers had heard of. There is a hint in the play that brothels already existed specializing in flagellation.

Lesbianism was also mentioned with increasing frequency. Anthony Hamilton told of Lord Rochester's rivalry with a Miss Hobart, maid of honor to the Duchess of York, for the love of a young court beauty named Anne Temple. Miss Hobart reached the goal first, but lost the game; she tried to embrace Miss Temple, the girl screamed, other ladies-in-waiting came running, and "this was sufficient to disgrace Miss Hobart at court and totally ruin her reputation in London."

The libertine atmosphere had developed farther and earlier among the French upper class and court circle. Women at the top of society lived even more independent lives than those in England; many were distinguished by wit, literary ability and great political influence. Louix XIV was a true *galant* of the time—correct, graceful, flattering, domineering and cold. His court resembled him in cynicism, intrigue and indiscriminate sex. But despite his own sexual adventurousness, Louis intensely despised homosexuals, and at one time planned to scour them from the realm. He reneged, because the first to go would have been his own brother, the Duc d'Orléans.

The duke, popularly known simply as Monsieur, consciously emulated the homosexual Henri III. Monsieur was a good and brave soldier, but he rode into battle wearing paint, powder, eye make-up, ribbons and jewelry, but no hat, for fear of flattening his wig. He married to produce heirs, but his first wife, Henriette of England, could never rival the Chevalier de Lorraine and the Marquis d'Effiat in his heart. It was rumored, probably without truth, that Monsieur and his closest homosexual companions directly or indirectly caused her death by poison. Monsieur's second wife, Princess Elizabeth-Charlotte of the Palatinate, stayed with him till his death, though they slept apart after producing a few heirs. She was known simply as Madame. She was a huge, blonde, active woman, and she dwarfed her swarthy little husband. After riding and hunting, her favorite occupation was letter writing, and her correspondence is one of the chief records of court life in her day. Of the homosexuals there she wrote:

> Those who give themselves up to this vice, which believing in Holy Scripture, imagine that it was only a sin when there were few people in the world, and that now the earth is populated it may be regarded as a divertissement. Among the common people, indeed, accusations of this kind are, so far as possible, avoided; but among persons of quality, it is publicly spoken of; it is considered a fine saying that since Sodom and Gomorrah, the Lord has punished no one for such offenses. . . . [Monsieur] has the manners of a woman rather than those of a man. He likes to play, chat, eat well, dance and perform his toilet—in short, everything that women love. . . . He loves finery and he takes care of his complexion. He dances well, but he dances like a woman. Except in time of war, he could never be prevailed upon to mount a horse. The soldiers said of him that he was more afraid of the heat of the sun, or the black smoke of gunpowder, than he was of musket bullets.

Other witnesses said he liked to appear in public dressed in full drag, wearing bracelets, rings, perfume, rouge and very high heels. He enjoyed attiring women and dressing their hair. According to the Abbé de Choisy, himself a transvestite, this may have been because of a court conspiracy to deliberately feminize him by dressing him as a girl and doing his hair like a girl's when he was a child. On the other hand, Madame de Sévigné said that Monsieur's homosexuality was due to early seduction by the Duc de Nevers, who practiced "the Italian vice."

Whatever the reason for Monsieur's homosexuality, he never did cause the king or anyone else serious trouble. He was just an embarrassment to the throne and a nuisance to his burly wife. He surrounded himself with homosexuals, and Madame catalogued them in her letters—Prince Eugene of Savoy, the general Duc Claude de Villars, the Grand Condé. Homosexual visitors from abroad sometimes joined the group. After the English ambassador, William Bentinck, Earl of Portland, arrived with a group of attendants, one of them told Madame that Portland had been lover to William III, now king of England. Portland had been shipped away because his place had been taken by a former page, Arnould van Keppel, who for his special skill as royal kept boy had been made Earl of Albemarle. Madame wrote that King William "is said to have been with Albemarle as with a woman, and they say he used to kiss his hands before all the Court."

Homosexuality was odious to Louis XIV, and it haunted him. First there was his brother. Then there was his son by his mistress Louise de La Vallière; he was involved in a homosexual scandal when still quite a young boy, and the king ignored his existence from then until his death at the age of sixteen. The two Princes de Conti, nephews of the Grand Condé, were homosexual; they and Eugene of Savoy were among a group of courtiers who fell into strong disfavor when Louis discovered their love letters. And then, if the story is to be believed, there came the worst scandal of all. Louis found that some of the nation's highest nobility had formed a secret society sworn to avoid women except to produce one heir. This so-called Order of Sodomites had meetings and perhaps homosexual orgies at a rural estate, and they all wore beneath their coats a cross that bore a picture of a man trampling on a woman. The group included the elder Prince de Conti, the Duc de Grammont, and the great court composer from Italy, Raimond Lully. The ugly scandal was recorded in detail by Bussy-Rabutin in his erotic history, in a chapter headed "France Turned Italian." The story is almost too wild and dramatic to be true, but it may be—or at least in part. Strangely, Louis favored through all these events the Duc de Vendome, a good general but a fat, dirty old man, his nose eaten away by syphilis, and a flagrant homosexual.

In this society the transvestite Abbé de Choisy caused little shock. His mother had wanted a daughter; she dressed him in girl's clothes, had his ears pierced, and adorned his face with beauty spots (he continued to wear them all his life). Most of his life, like many transvestites, he did not conceive of himself as homosexual. He generally avoided oral and anal sex with other men, or so his memoirs say. He entered the Church and therefore was always in skirts, either feminine or ecclesiastic. He once ran off to Bordeaux for five months, where he passed as a woman and worked as an actress. In the fragments of his memoirs that have survived, he said that "everybody was taken in. I even had lovers to whom I granted small favors, while remaining extremely reserved on the subject of more important ones. I was praised for my virtues!" Another time he lived in Paris as "Mademoiselle de Sancy," and at Bourges as the "Comtesse de Barres," and was proposed to by a *chevalier*. Once he impregnated an actress and adopted and supported the child, but to the end of his life, in 1724, when he was eighty, he delighted in wearing the dresses and jewelry his mother had left to him. De Choisy was a distinguished scholar and became a member of the French Academy, which then lacked the scruples that more recently made it bar André Gide because of his homosexuality.

One of the most exhaustive, or at least most lengthy, sources on the sexual life of the time is Pierre de Brantôme's *Lives of Gallant Ladies,* written in 1665. Brantôme was a rambling, witty collector of scandal and gossip; he claimed that all his stories were true, but many of the incidents about a "person of quality whom I know" seem rehashings of *novelle,* vehicles for pornographic invention or just dirty jokes. It is impossible to know when to believe him. Though apparently nothing shocked him, his own morals, at least in print, were often quite conventional. He was disgusted by homosexuals and by sodomy, either homosexual or heterosexual.

He said that the first time he was in Italy he heard a tale in Ferrara about a man who fell in love with a handsome youth. He persuaded his own wife to go to bed with the youth, pretended to capture them in the act, put a dagger to the boy's throat, and got him to save his life by acceding to his desires. Further, he had heard of a married lady who comforted her worried lover by saying that if the husband made trouble she would accuse him of sodomy, which carried the death penalty. He added, "How many women there be in the world, which if they were examined by midwives and doctors and expert surgeons, would be found no more virgin one way than another, and which could at any moment bring action against their husbands."

He also said that lesbianism was common in France, and that the "love which is called *donna con donna"* had arrived there from Italy with "a person of noble rank" (perhaps he meant Catherine de Medici). It was especially widespread in the courts of Naples and Sicily, and existed in Spain, Turkey, Greece and wherever women were secluded. He then got down to cases—some of which have a ring of authenticity.

> I have heard of an honorable gentleman who, desiring one day at Court to seek in marriage a certain very honorable damsel, did consult one of her kinswomen thereon. She told him frankly he would be wasting his time; for as she did herself tell me, such and such a lady, naming her ('twas one I had already heard talk of), will never suffer her to marry. Instantly

I did recognize the hang of it, for I was well aware how she did keep this damsel at bed and board, and did guard her carefully. . . .

'Tis said how that weasels are touched with this sort of love, and delight female with female to unite and dwell together. And so in hieroglyphic signs, women loving one another with this kind of affection were represented of yore by weasels. I have heard tell of a lady which was used always to keep some of these animals for that she did take pleasure in watching her little pets together.

He told stories about women using *godmichés* and being injured by them, and speculated on whether the allegedly lesbian Marguerite of Austria really had affairs with other women. In all, he was amusedly tolerant of lesbianism. Lesbianism wasn't bad for widows and unmarried girls, he thought; at least it was less a sin than fornication. "Moreover they deem they do not so much offend God, and are not such great harlots, as if they had to do with men, maintaining there is a great difference between throwing water in a vessel and merely watering about it and round the rim." Lesbians weren't as odious as male homosexuals, for it was much better "for a woman to be masculine and a very Amazon and lewd after this fashion, than for a man to be feminine, like Sardanapalus or Heliogabalus, and many another their fellows in sin. For the more manlike she is, the braver she is."

Brantôme is usually spoken of as a libertine writer. Whatever he expected from courtesans, he felt wives should be kept ignorant of the refined pleasures of sex; sexual pleasure and freedom could only lead to a search for more of the same, and thus to adultery and the breakdown of social and moral restraints. Some men, he said, urged their wives to have lesbian affairs to insure that they wouldn't commit adultery; but they were wrong, for no woman could really satisfy another woman, just inflame her to go on to more fulfilling pleasures. Brantôme's picture of lesbianism, like that of most writers until relatively recently, was a projection of male heterosexuality. He could not imagine that some women actually fell in love with other women, formed deep emotional attachments with them and found real sexual fulfillment with them.

He also mentioned a few cases of sexual sadism—the first, to my knowledge, to do so after Pico della Mirandola and the observers of Henri III's circle. He described one "world-renowned lady, very great indeed," who had her ladies and maids undress to slap and switch their buttocks, "and then her fascination was to see them move and make contortions of their bodies and buttocks, which, in accord, with the blows they received, were quite strange and pleasing. . . . And with these sights and contemplations her appetites were so sharpened that she satisfied them with some gallant and robust young man." He also had heard a story he considered even worse—a great lord who could not have sex with his wife without being whipped. Brantôme said, "I would greatly like some competent physician to tell me the reason for this."

Many of Brantôme's anecdotes sound like pornography, and some are probably quite genuine; many, though doubtless considered genuine, were third- and fourth-hand reports. Truth, half-truth, gossip and invention all seem mixed in his work. As for how common male homosexuality, sodomy, lesbianism and sado-masochism were in his time, one is at a loss. But many of the sexual kinks he considered strange and rare would be documented widely only a century after his death, in the eighteenth century.

8

Mollies and Roarers

The eighteenth century is called the century of libertinage. The rake and *galant* became common, the record of sexual deviation more copious, detailed and extravagant. In the upper classes, many people married for wealth and position, then continued their old round of flirtation, seduction and whoring. Children were raised by servants, instructed by tutors, shipped off to boarding schools and convents; they knew their caretakers better than their parents. They learned to trust no one's love, and so never to be disappointed. Like all emotionally parched people, they would be compelled to re-enact all their lives their early drama of deprivation, anger and compensation. As Morton Hunt put it in *The Natural History of Love*:

> If the parent-child relationship is cold, barren and distant, the child will remain psychologically a self-centered, angry infant, his concept of love being that of a struggle to grasp, seize and hurt the unloving beloved . . . love can mean at best a sensual delight with a modicum of friendliness; at worst, the sodomy, tortures and obscene self-gratifications of the Marquis de Sade; and between these extremes, the half-genial, half-hostile lecheries of the actual Don Juans.

The pornography of the time was full of force and trickery, of virgin and unresponsive women made to suffer, submit and finally be reduced to begging for pleasure—an angry little boy's fantasy of conquering an indifferent mother. Women were widely viewed as cunning, grasping bawds—as Swift put it, "a species hardly a degree above a monkey." In the nineteenth century, the French essayist Taine would say of the English Don Juan: "Unyielding pride, the desire to subjugate others, the provocative love of battle, the need for ascendancy, these are his predominant features. Sensuality is but of secondary importance compared with these."

An intricate code of manners masked all emotion—charming and elegant and frigid. Lord Chesterfield advised his son to smile, but never to laugh out loud. To show love was bourgeois, vulgar, gauche. Monsieur d'Épinay told his clinging, adoring young wife, "Amuse yourself. Go out into society—to the theater. Have liaisons, live like all the other women of your age." Intellectuals used the new science to rationalize their untrusting view of humanity. Vulgarized utilitarianism explained love quite simply: it was, said Chamfort, "the contact of two epidermises." Buffon, the greatest naturalist of the century, said, "There is nothing good in love but the physical part."

Beneath the libertine's manner of graceful dalliance and zestful lechery there lay a wrecker's malice. When the façade broke down, what appeared could charm no one. Adult, upper-class delinquents made assault, rape, drunkenness and whoring a way of life. In 1709 Ned Ward, in *The Secret History of Clubs,* described the Ballers, the Dancing Club, the Beau's Club and other groups of leisured young men who met to drink, whore and play sadistic pranks. The Mohocks were out nightly in 1712 to flatten or slit people's noses, gouge out their eyes, stand women and girls on their heads and roll them down hills inside casks. The Bold Bucks specialized in rape, the Sweaters in slashing people with swords. There was a furious desire to outrage every moral convention. Private clubs arose devoted to sexual indulgence, blasphemy and satanic ritual. In our century many have written with fascination about the Hellfire Club and its like, with their black masses and orgies. Actually, their parties and childish rites sound rather like today's ugliest expense-account parties of executives and call girls, with tasteless costumed games added.

One of the clubs Ward described was the Mollies, who met in women's clothes to drink and party. The word "mollies" was used generally for homosexuals, and there were "molly houses" that catered to them and provided quarters for homosexual prostitution. One of the most famous was that of Margaret Clap—or Mother Clap, as she was known—in Holborn, a resort popular with homosexuals. She had thirty to forty clients on weekday nights and as many as fifty on weekends. One account makes it sound like an unrestrained homosexual bar today:

> . . . men would sit in one another's laps, kissing in a lewd manner and using their hands indecently. Then they would get up, dance and make curtsies, and mimic the voices of women, "Oh, fie, sir"—"Pray, sir"—"Dear sir"— "Lord, how can you serve me so?"—"I swear I'll cry out"—"You're a wicked devil"—"And you're a bold face"—"Eh, ye dear little toad"—"Come, bus." They'd hug and play and toy and go out by couples into another room, on the same floor, to be "married," as they called it.

Was homosexuality more common or just less restrained? A diarist at the turn of the century claimed it was dangerous "to send a young man who is beautiful to Oxford . . . among the chief men in some of the colleges sodomy is very usual." In 1729 the anonymous *Hell upon Earth: or the Town in an Uproar* said:

> They also have their Walks and Appointments, to meet and pick up one another, and their particular Houses of Resort to go to, because they dare not trust themselves in an open Tavern. . . . It would be a pretty scene to behold them in their clubs and cabals, how they assume the Air and affect the name of Madam or Miss, Betty or Molly, with a chuck under

the chin, and "Oh, you bold pullet, I'll break your eggs," and then frisk and walk away.

Surely these were not aristocrats, or not the majority of them. With the growth of industrialization, cities were growing faster than ever, and there was more mention of middle- and lower-class homosexuals in them. In 1749 there appeared a book called *Satan's Harvest Home: or the Present State of Whorecraft, Adultery, Fornication, Pimping, Sodomy, etc.* The section headed "Reasons for the Growth of Sodomy" spoke of the "Game of Flats," or lesbianism; the author claimed it had originated in Turkey but was now just as common in Twickenham, and was gaining ground among prostitutes and gentlewomen alike. There were many police drives against homosexuals in the 1780s, with the discovery of homosexual rings in London and Exeter. Smollett's Roderick Random, new to London, was almost taken in by a homosexual who was after both his body and his money. Earl Strutwell's speech to Roderick is a perfect parody of clichéd homosexual apologetics and seduction pieces, including a statement that although homosexuality "is generally decried, and indeed condemned by our laws . . . it prevails not only over all the East, but in most parts of Europe; in our own country it gains ground apace, and in all probability will become in short time a more fashionable vice than simple fornication."

The apparent increase in homosexuality was only part of a general efflorescence of psychosexual deviation. Transvestism was recorded extensively for the first time since Roman days. The *Annual Register* shows fifteen cases of women dressing as men between 1761 and 1815, surely a tiny fraction of the number of existing transvestites, since generally only a small proportion of people are prosecuted for sexual offenses, and the vast majority of transvestites are males. The most famous case of the century was that of the Chevalier d'Eon, a Burgundian noble. He was a small, slight, delicate child, and his parents dressed him as a girl. He grew up to be a great swordsman, a good musician and scholar, a distinguished diplomat and a successful secret agent. In his work as a spy, he often disguised himself as a girl. Eventually he left government service and spent all his time in women's clothes. Toward the end of his life he lived entirely as a woman. When he died in 1810, some people thought he'd been a woman who sometimes dressed as a man. An autopsy was done to prove that he had been a physically normal male. There is no record of his ever having had sex with either a woman or a man. When Havelock Ellis wrote his pioneer studies of sexual deviance at the end of the nineteenth century, he called transvestism Eonism, after Europe's most famous transvestite.

Sex became furious trophy hunting for many people, and there now appeared a widespread interest in defloration and sado-masochism. A book published in 1760 said that a virgin cost fifty pounds, but the demand for virgins soon became so great that procuring them turned into a widely organized activity, and the price fell to a tenth of that. Brothels full of ten- and eleven-year-old girls were numerous until 1869, when Parliament outlawed prostitution for females under thirteen. Flagellation became known as "the English vice," and the birch rod as England's national emblem. Pornographic works on flagellation had first appeared during the Restoration; now they became widespread—for instance, *The Exciting and Voluptuous Pleasures to be Derived from Crushing and Humiliating the Spirit of a Beautiful and Modest Young Lady*. Special brothels were set up to cater to sado-masochists. Mrs. Collet's establishment was so famous that George VI visited it. Mrs. Theresa Berkeley had a house where people could be whipped, beaten, stuck with pins, strangled, scrubbed with nettles, and mounted on the "Berkeley horse"—a special rack for whipping. Mrs. Berkeley became wealthy enough to retire after eight years.

Charlotte Hayes catered to men with every specialized taste or in need of unusual stimulation. One of her handbills showed through code words and pseudonymns which of her girls specialized in masturbating their clients, whipping them, allowing intermammary intercourse and selling their oft-repaired virginity. (Because of the passion for young girls and defloration, a craft developed of "restoring" lost hymens through suturing.) The code is not much different in erotic ads in the underground press today.

> A girl of 19 years, not older, for Baron Harry Flagellum. Nell Hardy from Bow Street, Bat Flourish from Berners Street or Miss Birch from Chapel Street   10 guineas

> For Colonel Tearall, a gentle woman. Mrs. Mitchell's servant, who has just come from the country and has not yet been out in the world 10 guineas

> For Dr. Frettext, after consultation hours, a young agreeable person, sociable, with a white skin and a soft hand. Polly Nimblewrist from Oxford, or Jenny Speedyhand from Mayfair   2 guineas

> For Lord Pyebald, to play a game of piquet, for *littillatione mammarum* and so on, with no other object. Mrs. Tredrille from Chelsea   5 guineas

Clandestine magazines appeared that gave erotic gossip and the names, anatomical specifications and prices of female flagellants who could be hired; they had such names as *The Bon Ton Magazine, Englishwoman's Domestic Magazine* and *The Annals of Gallantry, Glee and Pleasure*. Unfortunately, it is impossible now to know which stories in them were factual and which pornographic invention—for instance, an item in *The Bon Ton Magazine* of December, 1792, describes a female flagellation club. "These female members are mainly married women. . . . [The club] never has fewer than twelve members. At each meeting six are chastised by the other six . . . the whipping starts on the calves and goes up to the posterior."

Outlets existed for every special sexual interest and commodity. There was a heavy trade in dildoes and aphrodisiacs. Increased literacy allowed pornography to become a big industry, especially toward the end of the century. Many books were alleged lives of whores and courtesans, whose careers provided opportunities for erotic scenes of every sort— heterosexual, homosexual, sado-masochistic, fetishistic, voyeuristic. *Fanny Hill*, one of the better-written of these, included flogging, hair fetishism, homosexuality, transvestism and voyeurism.

However, even in this "age of libertinism" in the upper class and its bourgeois imitators, deviation was still viewed with amusement or disgust by most of society. The penalty for homosexual relations remained death, and it was sometimes carried out. In 1726 Mother Clap was charged with keeping a "sodomitical house" and sentenced to a fine, the pillory and two years' imprisonment. Even attempted homosexual acts were similarly punished, and often severe injury or death resulted from missiles hurled by angry mobs. The records of the Old Bailey show a range of judicial attitudes running from casual to very severe. Sometimes if a man could bring witnesses to testify to his general good character, he got off. In 1721 a young married man, said to be very religious, was convicted of attempting sodomy and placed in the pillory and imprisoned for two months. In 1730 another man was sentenced to death for sodomy inflicted on his young apprentice, with some physical damage.

During the 1720s the police were at work entrapping homosexuals. A detective reported at the Old Bailey that he had snared a suspect while walking in Upper Moorfields, a homosexual pick-up area.

> I takes a turn that way and leans over the wall. In a little time the prisoner passes by, and looks hard at me, and at a small distance from me stands up against the wall as if he was going to make water. Then by degrees he sidles nearer and nearer to where I stood, till at last he was close to me. "This is a very fine night," says he. "Aye," says I, "and so it is." Then he takes me by the hand, and after squeezing and playing with it a little, he conveys it to his breeches,

The detective promptly seized the man by his genitals and held him there till a constable arrived.

Those who got off lightly in court might still be disgraced or ruined. From the 1760s on, the *Annual Register* showed not only many cases of sodomy but also of homosexuals being blackmailed. A deviant could be made a laughing stock in the same way, and over the same things, as in Martial's and Juvenal's Rome. The poet Samuel Foote was ruined by pamphlets accusing him of homosexuality, though the case has all the marks of calculated character assassination. Poet Thady ("Fribble") Fitzpatrick, a friend of the great actor Garrick, became a victim of his society's contempt for effeminacy. Garrick quarreled with friend Fribble and in 1761 wrote a defamatory poem called "The Fribbleriad."

> A *Man* it seems—'tis hard to say—
> A *Woman* then?—a moment pray—
> Unknown as yet by sex or feature,
> Suppose we try to guess the creature;
> Whether a *wit*, or a *pretender*?

Of *masculine* or *feminine* gender? . . .
Nor male? nor female? then on oath
We safely may pronounce it *Both*.

At which, *ONE* larger than the rest
With visage sleek, and swelling chest,
With stretch'd out fingers, and a thumb
Stuck to his hips, and jutting bum,
Rose up!—All knew his smirking air—
They clap'd, and cry'd—the *chair*, the *chair*!
He smil'd—and to the honour'd seat,
Padle'd away on mincing feet.

The unfortunate poet's nickname became so popular that Dr. Johnson included the verb "to fribble" in his *Dictionary,* quoting from the *Spectator* the explanation that "a *fribbler* is one who professes rapture for a woman, and dreads her consent." In 1763 Charles Churchill, a much better poet than Garrick, wrote a poetic satire called "The Rosciad" in which he expanded Garrick's attack on Fribble. Like Westerners of all times, he held the man in contempt for qualities that belong to the stereotype of female seductiveness—fleshiness, softness, narcissism, coyness. He also used the old charge that such men produce art as spunkless, mannered and gabbling as themselves. In another poem, "The Times," he imitated Juvenal to decry the debauchery and perversion of London. He started, of course, by blaming Italy, and went on to complain that sodomites were taking the bread from honest whores. If anyone bore a son, he should go into mourning, weep and drape his house in black. He must lock his son up and send rumors about town that the boy is ugly, pocked and maimed, "An Antidote to Lust!"

Let Him not have one Servant that is male;
Where Lords are baffled, Servants oft prevail. . . .
Give him no Tutor—throw him to a punk,
Rather than trust his morals to a Monk. . . .
. . . Ourselves have liv'd to see
More than one Parson in the Pillory.
Should he have Brothers, (Image to thy view
A scene, which, tho' not public made, is true)
Let not one Brother be to t'other, known,
Nor let his Father be with him alone.
Be all his Servants, Female, Young, and Fair. . . .
. . . 'mongst such a race,
To have a bastard is a sign of grace. . . .

Writings in France also gave a picture of more common and more open deviance in all classes. Erotic literature had a long, refined tradition there, and the eighteenth century produced it in torrents, giving more emphasis than ever to homosexuality and various kinks. Mirabeau, Mairobert, Rétif de la Bretonne and many lesser writers made erotica their profession or avocation. Such works are usually treated as historical documents, though it is clear, for instance, that Churchill's poem is a case of a clever man enjoying the momentum of his satire. The important fact about all this deviant erotica is not its details but its quantity, ubiquity and popularity.

Lesbianism was more widely documented than ever, but the quasi-pornographic sources of much of the information leave us doubtful about details. Casanova said that the women of Provence were especially inclined to it, and that it was so common among nuns that some confessors didn't even impose penance for it. Its existence in convents was frequently mentioned in fiction and plays; Diderot's novel *La Réligieuse* dealt with lesbianism and sexual sadism in a nunnery. The Comte de Tilly mentioned a lady who was "suspected of having habits once much in vogue in Lesbos and which to the shame of our time have made alarming progress even in the provinces." Mairobert's *Apologie de la Secte Anandryne* alleged the existence of a lesbian organization, something like the old Order of Sodomites, with branches all over France and members largely from the upper class. Actresses and courtesans were commonly suspected of lesbianism.

What is all this worth? Mairobert's secret society may be fact, gossip or pornography. Diderot's novel, though allegedly based on a real case, was as much anticlerical as reportorial. And, of course, if homosexuality really multiplied in every generation, as most generations have claimed, Western man would have been extinct long ago. Again, we must admit the presence of a forest without being able to distinguish the trees. The eighteenth century's pornography, memoirs and historical writings do show that lesbianism was a familiar fact of life in the upper classes. For every wild generalization and piece of hearsay evidence, there is a reliable case—say, Countess Sarolta Vay of Hungary, who dressed as a man and married another woman, and Catharina Margaretha Lincken, who was executed in 1721 for "sodomy," or homosexual intercourse with the use of an artificial phallus.

Writings about homosexuality among the clergy show the same mixture of spurious and reliable accounts. Proponents of enlightenment and revolution felt that Christian morality had destroyed the possibility of sexual happiness in Europe. They and even many believers attacked religious institutions not only for their reactionary political-economic role, but with accusations of sexual perversion. Their writings bring to mind religious conformists' charges of heresy and sodomy in the late Middle Ages; sexual defamation is not the exclusive tool of either the left or the right wing.

The Jesuits received particular attention; enemies had accused them of homosexuality since 1600, but now the attacks multiplied. The Lisbon earthquake of 1755 was believed by many devout people to be a punishment from God. The Chevalier de Oliveyra, a Portuguese gentleman who had moved to England and converted to Protestantism, argued the contrary. God, he said, had sent the earthquake to destroy the Inquisition in his native country. He addressed the Holy Office, "Ye have taken great pains to use indulgence, and spare openly, all those who are capable of that abominable crime [sodomy]. . . . Whence is this partiality but that you are yourselves guilty of that crime which modesty forbids me to name? I could furnish you with many incontestable truths."

Revolutionary propaganda in France was full of obscene satires of clerics and aristocrats as buggerers. Organized religion became the scapegoat of reformers—as did, in later times, "Victorians" and the "double standard" and "bourgeois morality" and "squares." It is always easiest to blame one class or institution for attitudes deeply embedded in the social fabric.

Rousseau's *Confessions* give an interesting view of homosexuality among clerics. When he was considering conversion to Catholicism in his youth, someone at the hospice where he was receiving instruction tried violently to seduce him. He spoke about the incident, and the next day "one of the principals came very early and read me a sharp lecture, accusing me of impugning the honor of a sacred establishment and making a lot of fuss about nothing." The man explained homosexuality to Rousseau, though he didn't really believe the boy had been as ignorant as he claimed, just that he'd been unwilling.

> He told me gravely that it was a forbidden and immoral act like fornication, but that the desire for it was not an affront to the person who was its object. There was nothing to get so annoyed about in having been found attractive. He told me quite openly that in his youth he had been similarly honored and, having been surprised in a situation where he could put up no resistance, he had found nothing so brutal about it all. He carried his effrontery so far as to employ frank terminology and, imagining that the reason for my refusal had been fear of pain. assured me that my apprehensions were groundless.

Actually, Rousseau may not have been as ingenuous as he claimed; it stretches the imagination to believe some of his claims of sexual ignorance in the incident. It may merely be that by the time he recorded the incident, he had done some mental editing. But it's hardly surprising that the cleric's complaisance made him suspicious about both priests and homosexuals.

Other writings of the period also suggest that there must have been considerable homosexuality among churchmen as well as general familiarity with homosexuality at many levels of society. Homosexual prostitution remained widespread in Paris, and in 1702 an organized system was discovered there, catering to a clientele that included priests and marquises. In the 1770s Mirabeau said that the Paris police allowed certain public places for such activity, and

> young people who consign themselves to the profession are carefully classified—so far do the regulatory systems extend. They are inspected. Those who can act as active and passive, who are handsome, ruddy, well built, filled out, are reserved for the great lords or get very good fees from bishops and financiers. Those who are deprived of their testicles—or in the terms of the profession (for our language is more chaste than our morals),

who do not possess their "weaver's weights"—but who give and receive, form the second class. They too are expensive, for women use them as well as men. Those who are so worn out that they are no longer capable of erection, though they have all the necessary organs of pleasure, set themselves down as pure passives and compose the third class; but the person who presides over their pleasures verifies their impotence. To this end they are placed entirely naked on a mattress with their lower half exposed; two girls caress them the best they can, while a third gently strikes with budding nettles the seat of venereal desires. After a quarter hour of this attempt, a long red pepper is introduced into their anus, which causes considerable irritation. On the blisters caused by the nettles is placed fine Caudebec mustard, and the glans is annointed with camphor. Those who can stand these ordeals and give no sign of erection serve as passives at a mere third of fee.

This sounds like the usual blend of fact and fiction. State supervision of prostitutes existed through much of Western history, and it quite likely occurred in Mirabeau's Paris, but one wonders whether the police went to the trouble and expense of such refined tests.

In England and France, upper-class delinquency and public deviance neither caused nor resulted from a change in basic sexual values. Burnings for homosexuality were rare, but they occurred in France until a few years before the Revolution. Some of the prominent men arrested in the Paris homosexual-prostitution scandal of 1702 had been burned, and others cut their own throats to avoid punishment or disgrace. Gustavus III of Sweden was homosexual, but the Swedish penal code of 1734 prescribed as punishment for sodomy decapitation followed by exposure or burning of the body—worse than the sentences for murder, sorcery and treason. In Haarlem, in Holland, the names of convicted homosexuals were published, and their wives became free to remarry or resume their maiden names. For every homosexual or alleged homosexual in the upper class—Catharine II of Russia, the German archeologist Winckelmann—there existed many who felt anger, contempt, fear or amusement toward homosexuality.

Even that brilliant and freaky pornographer Rêtif de la Bretonne, himself something of a foot-and-shoe fetishist, scorned

those who sodomize with males. The reason for the preference for this over women is that *You don't serve leg of lamb without the bone.* In this class must be included schoolboys who do it for mischief, soldiers for lack of money, and monks of necessity. As for *mignons,* it is certain that they do so only from avarice, for they derive no pleasure from it whatever, and they expose themselves to much more contempt and sarcasm than do buggerers. Xolange is known to have said to an Italian with whom he had a fight: "Mademoiselle, if I did not respect our sex, I would strike you with my cane."

Voltaire probably represented liberal opinion on the subject. When he was at the court of Frederick the Great, he and an English gentleman decided to go to bed together as a scientific experiment in what he called the *pêche philosophique*. Voltaire found it unsatisfactory, but a few days later the Englishman returned to say that he had repeated the experiment. Voltaire declared, "Once a philosopher, twice, a sodomite!"

Frederick the Great himself may have experimented with homosexual relations, but he rated them low. Rather, like Louis XIV, he had to accept as a family embarrassment the homosexuality of his younger brother. Prince Henry of Prussia was a notorious homosexual, and Mirabeau, who was a special envoy at the Prussian court, wrote in his *Secret History of the Court of Berlin,* "An old servant of Prince Henry, apt in serving his master's passion for pederasty, became his favorite at first and was then made canon of Magdeburg where the prince was bishop. . . . The aristocracy of the army knows that with Prince Henry the Ganymedes have always made and shall always make the decisions." When Americans were considering the importation of a noble to head their new nation as a constitutional monarch, Prince Henry was put forward as a candidate by a group of European aristocrats. The idea of a constitutional monarchy was dropped, and the United States lost their chance to have a Prussian homosexual as the father of their country.

The growth of science in the eighteenth century did not clarify sexual problems. Without being aware of the contradiction, people tended to think of homosexuality as being simultaneously a disease, a matter of national custom, and a sin. No distinction had been made yet between physical feminization, effeminate behavior, and homosexual object choice—that is, between physical and psychological aspects of sexuality. This is clearest in the writings on castrati.

Castration was still a common operation. It had been known for millennia that if it was performed before puberty, physical masculine development was prevented. Many castrati, for obvious psychological reasons, were notorious homosexuals (castration in itself does not affect sexual object choice). The castrati of whom we know most today were those of classical opera. Until the eighteenth century women were not permitted on the stage in most of Europe, and female opera parts were taken by male sopranos, men who had been castrated just before their voices were about to break. The result was a pure boy-tenor quality supported by adult chest and diaphragm; it was quite different in quality and range from any female voice, and very beautiful. Händel and many other great composers wrote parts for castrati throughout the eighteenth century. Castrati remained on the stage into the nineteenth century, and some were among the great musical stars of their time. Little is known today of their sex lives, but they were spoken of as feminine, vain, hysterical and homosexual.

In one part of his great *Spirit of the Law*, Montesquieu spoke of homosexuality variously as the result of national custom; as willful immorality; as a physical condition identical with emasculation. His exact words are worth examining for their particular illogic, which is typical of the times.

In Rome women do not appear on the stage; castrati dressed as women are used instead. This has a very bad effect on morality; because there is nothing that I know of which does more to inspire Socratic love among the people of Rome. . . . During my time at Rome there were, at the Capranica theater, two little castrati, Mariotti and Chiostra, dressed as women, who were the most beautiful creatures I have ever seen in my life, and who would have inspired the tastes of Gomorrah in people least prone to this form of depravity.

A young Englishman, believing that one of them was a woman, fell madly in love with him and for more than a month remained the victim of this passion. Formerly in Florence the Grand Duke Cosimo III, out of infatuation, drew a similar inference. Imagine the effect this must have produced in Florence, which was in this respect the new Athens!

An anonymous pamphlet on the subject published in London in 1787 added the familiar themes of foreign vice and insipid art by ball-less artists. "By supporting these emasculated foreign singers, we are promoting general moral degeneration and effeminacy, which is contagious like the pestilence." Both Montesquieu and the English writer made the usual set of contradictory assumptions. Castration makes men homosexual. Nevertheless, it is contagious and can easily be caught by the uncastrated. Its influence is almost irresistible, and those who give in are guilty of a ghastly moral lapse. Yet those to whom this happens are pitiable.

What we call emotional disorder was still more within the philosopher's and theologian's province than the doctor's. Christian theology had always said that reason, will, virtue and chastity were one. Sin, sex, anger, unreason and impulse made up the other side of the coin. Reason shows what is moral, and will enables one to act on it, which is virtue. Loss of reason leads to loss of control over impulses, and the result is sin, sex, rage. Insanity, by traditional definition, is "loss of reason." We show this sort of thinking when we tell an emotionally disturbed person to "pull himself together," as though he need only think logically and try hard, and his anxiety will vanish. He isn't really ill, he is unreasonable and undisciplined. Significantly, English and French use the same word for insanity as for anger—mad, *fou*. The word madness tends to evoke pictures of a beast foaming at the mouth and wreaking destruction.

Sin, insanity, rage, unreason and lust all tend to be equated with almost any sort of undesired or antisocial behavior. Between about 1600 and 1800, the Bicêtre in France housed not only the psychotic but homosexuals, victims of venereal disease, political undesirables, "incorrigible girls, debauchers, imbeciles and ungrateful sons." It also eventually held beggars, the aged, any who offended the mores or taxed the resources of society. The Bastille was also used as a lockup for the delinquent and abnormal of all kinds, and in the eighteenth century overt homosexuals were detained there. It was only in the late eighteenth century that there were more than a few institutions solely for the mentally disturbed, for the concept of mental illness as we know it hardly existed. Even to most of the better minds of the eighteenth century, the trinity of madness, vice and unreason defined extreme deviance just as witchcraft, blasphemy and sodomy had in the Middle Ages.

Many people still believed mental disorders were the work of devils. Others followed Greco-Roman medical traditions that had been revived during the Renaissance; refinements of ancient humoral theory and similar concepts of "animal spirits" were used to explain everything from digestion to personality. Occasionally a prophetic note would be struck, as when Johann Weyer, a sixteenth-century pioneer of psychology, noted that homosexuality sometimes accompanies delusionary feelings of persecution. ("I know another sodomite who complained that he always heard passers-by come to cause noise in his ears; even his parents, he said, were doing it; he wrote to me on his own behalf, quite secretly, asking me whether I could not give him some advice since some people had told him that his trouble was in his organ of hearing.") But even at the end of the eighteenth century no fruitful attempt had been made to observe mental illness and emotional disturbances. Instead, intricate systems of classifications were devised on various theoretical grounds, and soon abandoned for others. The nosologists, or classifiers, built their procession of castles. In 1763 Boissier de Sauvages listed *Vices* among mental illnesses; one of the other categories, *Bizarreries*, included "depraved appetite," excessive thirst, satyriasis and panic. An English physician studied the inmates of Bedlam and gave as the causes of their madness hereditary disposition, drunkenness, excessive study, fever, venereal disease, love, jealousy and excessive devotion to the Methodist religion. In 1804 Giraudy said that of the 476 inmates of Charenton, where de Sade was incarcerated, fifty-two were mad because of hereditary disposition, twenty-eight because of masturbation, and twelve because of "abuse of the pleasures of Venus."

The scientific study of sex would not begin till the latter half of the nineteenth century. However, the general development of science was in various important ways preparing groundwork for twentieth-century views of sex. Utilitarianism, with its universe of impersonal cause and effect, its rules of pleasure and avoidance, became popular in an age marked by cool, angry, self-seeking personalities: fashions in science have sources as irrational as all other fashions. Now it was said that God, if He existed, had created a clockwork world and retired, leaving man to figure out the ticking. Divine will and miraculous intervention were no longer good enough explanations of material and human behavior. In fact, the practical successes of science made it seem that man might soon be able to control his environment, and cure individual suffering and social ills by rational intervention. Locke and his heirs convinced many that human life must be explained in terms of gratification, not morality; man, like all animals, seeks pleasure and avoids pain. The physiology of the senses became a subject of wide interest, from which experimental psychology eventually grew.

Some went so far as to say that the soul was merely a function of the central nervous system, love the vapor of an overheated brain.

Conservatives and the devout feared that without belief in superhuman moral sanctions, mankind would revert to hedonism or savagery. They needn't have worried so. People do not throw off a lifetime of acculturation on logical grounds. As conservatives hoped, and a few radical speculators feared, the customs and morals learned in childhood couldn't just be scrapped and replaced by others. What happened, predictably, was that traditional mores and experimental science made a mutual accommodation, each filling in where the other left gaps.

Simple utilitarianism left many questions unanswered. If people did only what gave them pleasure, why had they ever developed morals and social restraints at all? Why weren't they still living in savage, egocentric anarchy? An ingenious answer was devised that was not far out of line with either convention or science. Savage man, it was said, had realized that he was happiest in the long run if he cooperated with others. Social organization and restraints had arisen, with division of labor, pooling of skills and resources, limits on power, property and sexual behavior, the protection of law and order, etc. As Bentham put it, social restraint (and the morality it creates) gave the greatest happiness to the greatest number. Thus was invented what Voltaire—half mocking but also half believing—called the best of all possible worlds.

But there was also a powerful wind of antisocial anger sweeping through European intellectual life. The English cult of sensibility, German *Sturm und Drang,* French pre-Romanticism, all showed the the irrational side of man calling for gratification in the first age of scientism. Eighteenth-century fiction increasingly depicted men who found happiness among primitive people or on desert islands; it told of Hurons, Persians and Tahitians whose naïve purity showed up the corruption of European society. Kant declared that primitive man was "subject to very little insanity or stupidity" because he was "free in his movements." He was kinder and happier than European man, free of the tortures of possessiveness and perversions. Swift wrote of the Houyhnhmns, "I expected every moment that my master would accuse the Yahoos of these unnatural appetites in both sexes, so common among us. But nature it seems has not been so expert a school mistress; and these politer pleasures are entirely the productions of art and reason, on our side of the globe." Let science and reason say what they wished, an inner restlessness was calling for a Return to Nature.

And for a return as well to feeling. Some people had had enough of the rake and of the naturalist's *l'homme machine.* Sensibility, or sensitivity, was increasingly fashionable all over Europe. There appeared *romans larmoyants,* weepy tales of sweet suffering love, that became as much a problem of hygiene as of literature. Fashionable people wept, had vapors, were bled in order to look wan, fainted promiscuously. Mackenzie's novel *The*

Man of Feeling did for the period what beat-hip chronicles did for our fifties and sixties. People gathered in salons to read it aloud and weep together. They were no more or less silly than those who today meet to smoke marijuana and feel euphoric, oceanic love. Both are experiments in feeling, proof that affectation is the very stuff of civilization.

People can entertain very contradictory ideas, yet feel that their beliefs are of a piece. Generations brought up on scientific utilitarianism now had to reconcile their logic with the search for feeling; believers in progress had to make it compatible with love of the primitive. The reconciliation was usually something like this. Nature is orderly. When we are reasonable, we are in accord with nature. That brings about pleasure, goodness, and attainment of every moral and practical goal. It is natural to seek pleasure, and Nature is so arranged that if we do so, we will find individual happiness and in fact contribute to the well-being of others. Illogical strayings from Nature produce perversions, poverty and every other major ill. Unfortunately, such institutions as church, law and sexual mores have become so perverted in Europe, have so twisted people, that men no longer recognize their best interests. They seek despotic rule, wealth, ascetic ideals. They have forgotten that these cannot truly bring happiness. If the search for gratification is resumed, and a reasonable selfishness sends men once again in pursuit of love and sensual fulfillment, health and happiness will return to both individuals and society.

There are too many questionable axioms in this for us to analyze it—in these pages I am hopping from stone to stone over a deep stream. Suffice to say that from aspects of this whole complex of ideas and feelings would soon develop the rationales for feminism, democracy, social engineering and many other facts of our life, and to it can be traced descendants as different as Skinner's behaviorism and the love cults of New York's Lower East Side. Today's "sexual revolution" is implicit in this complex, anticipated in almost every way by Diderot, Rousseau and de Sade, with their insistence on reason and their dark revolutionary fervor. We are today acting out the ideas of the eighteenth century as the eighteenth century could never have imagined.

During his life and long after, Denis Diderot was known as one of the great voices of Rationalism, and his name was most of all linked to the *Encyclopedia*, his century's great testament to reason and the perfectibility of mankind. Nevertheless, his fiction was full of ribaldry, passion, irony, defiance and wild imaginativeness.* Today he is considered one of the

*The story of Diderot's literary work would make a fascinating book of cultural history. Much of his fiction was published only after his death, and it was dismissed as tasteless by most French nineteenth-century critics. Goethe read the daring and funny *Jacques le fataliste* early in the nineteenth century and translated it into German in a fit of enthusiasm; it was ignored as pointedly in Germany as in France. During the last few decades Diderot has been re-evaluated along with the other pre-Romantics. In the 1970s, he often sounds more contemporary than most writers of the 1930s.

great Pre-Romantics, with all the Romantic desire for the exotic, the anti-social, the sensual and the extreme. Both sides of him showed in the sexual utopia he created.

Now, someone looking for proof of man's tragic nature need only read the paradises he has imagined. The most famous—Plato's *Republic,* More's *Utopia,* Bacon's *New Atlantis*—are tedious and grim. The very countryside where they stand lacks character ("The city lay upon a broad plain. . . ."). The buildings, customs and inhabitants are fiercely drab and uniform. There are no factions or dissent, no weeping or laughter, no spontaneity or sensuality. Browbeating and brainwashing guarantee that men shall be as angels. This turnkey's view of humanity exalts control over expressiveness, reason over feeling—assuming, of course, that man's unrestrained feelings are destructive. An elite of the controlled and reasonable are in com-mand—a committee of intellectual tyrants. The good life is based on the careful restriction and allotment of those things which make men behave unreasonably—subsistence, property, power and sexual gratification.

In the eighteenth century, erotic utopias began to appear, saying that the key to attaining the good life was not control but expressiveness; that man, given free rein, was good and loving, not destructive; that the vital drive in man was not for property or power, but sexual happiness. Diderot and some others of his century, long before Freud, said that man is above all a sexual being, and the repression of his sexuality is the key to his personal unhappiness and his social dilemmas.

Diderot was by nature spendthrift. He wrote about science, politics, esthetics, religion, everything, and he never stopped to audit what he pro-duced, he just spent on. (His work contains such throwaways as, "If your little savage were left to himself and to his native blindness, he would in time join the infant's reasoning to the grown man's passion—he would strangle his father and sleep with his mother.") He believed, with Rous-seau and others of his age, that salvation would come from freeing impulse, not from throttling it; that is what makes him our contemporary. In 1781, three years before Diderot's death, Bougainville published an account of his voyage around the world. His description of Tahiti became for Diderot the basis of an erotic utopia that might upset Albert Ellis. It is what the West still likes to imagine the non-Western world to be. Diderot's *Supplement to Bougainville's Voyage* asks:

> Is there anything so senseless as a precept that forbids us to heed the changing impulses that are inherent in our being? . . . May a father sleep with his daughter, a mother with her son, a brother with his sister, a hus-band with someone else's wife? Why not? . . . Jealousy is practically un-known here in Tahiti. Tenderness between husband and wife, and maternal love? We have put in their place another impulse, which is more universal, powerful and lasting—self-interest. . . . When we are born we bring noth-ing into the world with us except a constitution similar to that of other human beings—the same needs, an impulsion toward the same pleasures,

a common dislike for the same pains: that is what makes man what he is, and the code of morality appropriate to men should rest on no other foundation . . . the sweetest, most important and most universal of enjoyments. . . . Marital fidelity is a will-of-the-wisp . . . modesty, demureness and propriety are part of the whole retinue of imaginary devices . . . the gap which divides a man from a woman would be crossed first by the more amorously inclined of the two. . . . Religious institutions have attached the labels "vice" and "virtue" to actions that are completely independent of morality. . . . But the untamed heart will not cease to cry out against its oppressors. . . . Once upon a time there was a natural man; then an artificial man was built up inside him. Since then a civil war has been raging continuously within his breast. . . . But whichever gains the upper hand, the poor freak is racked and torn, tortured, stretched on the wheel, continually suffering, continually wretched. . . . If you want to become a tyrant, civilize him; poison him as best you can with a system of morality that is contrary to nature. Devise all sorts of hobbles for him, contrive a thousand obstacles for him to trip over, saddle him with phantoms and terrify him, stir up an eternal conflict inside him, and arrange things so that the natural man will always have the moral man's foot upon his neck.

Rousseau also called for renovation of sexual relationships. He said that love was a natural bond, the only reason for people to live together; society's preoccupation with property had corrupted love. In *La Nouvelle Héloïse* he showed how a girl, married off for economic reasons against her will, suffered because of her love for another man. In *Émile* he called for great reforms in education—like others who combined Enlightenment ideas with what would later be called Romanticism, he wanted impulse and emotion to create a new life in sex, education and politics. Like Diderot, he believed that "every age has its dominant idea; that of our age seems to be Liberty."

Diderot, Rousseau and the like-minded overestimated the power of instinct and the contractual basis of society, which they considered the warring extremes in man's struggle for liberty. They underestimated the degree to which people internalize society's values at an early age, and feel them as truly their own. They themselves were victims of this. Finally, though Rousseau's sex life was masochistic and infantile, his ideals of sex role and sex behavior were quite conventional. He wanted women to be submissive and forbearing. He never called for divorce or the abolition of private property. His unhappily married heroine was providentially saved from the sins of deserting or cuckolding her husband by a noble death. Monogamy, said Rousseau, is more pleasurable in the long run than promiscuity and polygamy: despite its minor frustrations, it saves one from domestic discord and venereal disease. Rousseau's natural man turned out to be a good bourgeois husband, father and Christian after all. Diderot was more daring, but only in fits. He alternated between advocating utterly free love and writing plays about happy bourgeois families that Marie Antoinette called "insipid as milk soup." Like most sexual revolutionaries they ultimately showed how little sudden liberty people can bear in such matters, and how much more continuity there is than change.

The greatest of the revolutionary paper tigers was the Marquis de Sade. He was the angry pansexual in extreme form, obsessive and psychopathic, a Rochester without any trace of humor, flexibility or emotional variety. He was born in 1740 of a noble and distinguished family. His father was considered a very cold and stern man; when the boy was five he was sent off to board with an uncle, at ten to a Jesuit school in Paris. His childhood was utterly lacking in tenderness and lasting ties. By the time he was in his early thirties he had been in and out of many scrapes, and kept heading into more. Though married and the father of three children, he was imprisoned and fined several times for sexual offenses. Once he severely flogged a girl he had picked up in the street. Another time he gave poisonously powerful cantharides—"Spanish fly"—to five prostitutes. He was accused of sodomy with his valet, fled the country, was tried *in absentia*, found guilty and burned in effigy. He went on an escapade with his sister-in-law and was involved in a scandal with several of his servants, female and male. It is impossible to know now which of the alleged crimes he actually committed, and to what extent, as a brutal young rake, he made himself vulnerable to false accusations with potential for cash settlement.

De Sade's life was not rare in his class and time, just a little more cruel and extreme than most—several Restoration rakes and eighteenth-century roarers left records like his. But he had become a nuisance and disgrace, and his uncle demanded he be locked up for life as a madman. He was incarcerated in one prison after another, often in solitary confinement, without exercise, visitors, books or writing materials. His appeals were ignored, and he spent more than a decade in prison, writing when he was able. After the Revolution he was released along with many others who had been arbitrarily detained. He was now fat, middle-aged and half blind. His wife left him, and he settled into a calm, close affair with a woman that lasted until his death. He enjoyed a mildly distinguished career as a playwright and government official, and saw the anonymous publication of some of his erotica. However, he had bad luck in the political turbulence of the 1790s, and in 1801 he was arrested and charged with authorship of obscene and politically offensive works. He was committed to Bicêtre and then the Charenton asylum. He remained there, sometimes writing and directing plays for inmates, until his death in 1814.

During his young manhood de Sade had been a cruel and unstable libertine, during his later freedom a capable official and dramatist. However, he spent twenty-seven years in prisons and asylums, battling solitude, despair and physical disintegration. He poured out on paper a glacial world of compulsive anger, sex and argument. In *Justine* and *Juliette* he told about two orphaned sisters, one of whom became rich through vice, the other who aimed at virtue but was sexually and sadistically abused by man after man. The moral was that vice always triumphed, and should. In all de Sade's books, sexual scenes alternate with philosophical lectures that attempt to justify them. In the orgies, characters mechanically, monotonously, perform intercourse, fellatio, cunnilingus, sodomy, flogging, strangling, dismemberment, burning, incest, castration, cannibalism, necrophilia, coprophilia, zoophilia, sex with dwarfs and hermaphrodites, in every combination, position and manner. They are truly pornographic, devoid of content or significance aside from the sexual acts. The divorce of sex from all emotions but anger gives them the rigid and private quality of ritualized masturbation fantasies. Literarily, the distance between content and diction creates unintentional comedy ("In this posture, Madame, my prick is well within your reach. Condescend to frig it, I beg you, while I suck this heavenly ass.") The philosophical arguments are based on the axioms that gratification is the aim of life; that man's deepest pleasures are, in descending order, sodomy, sacrilege and cruelty; that love, virtue and morality are the invention of the timid; that if perversion exists, it is a fact of nature, and nature must have her due. He uses the same sort of arguments to prove the essential evil and cruelty of life as Diderot used to prove its essential sweet goodness: scientific materialism, the degradation of Western social institutions, accounts of primitive peoples. Diderot said nature's command was to love; de Sade said it was to bugger, beat, mutilate and murder.

The line between the author and his characters is never very strong. The arguments of de Sade's mouthpieces are as hollow and obsessive as the sexual scenes—like all obsessive harangues, not so much stating anything as allaying the speaker's anxiety. They dwell on the same themes like a mad bird circling over the same dark spot again and again. Most of all they show how men cannot live without somehow justifying themselves to themselves.

A literary cult developed around de Sade's books in the early nineteenth century and has grown steadily. Yet most of his work is poor literature, and as philosophy it brings to mind Hobbes's dictum that an evil man is only a child grown strong. However, it is interesting as a concentrated document of the psychological nature of certain kinds of deviance. Dolmance, the protagonist and philosopher of *Philosophy in the Bedroom*, hates women; he loathes their vaginas especially. He will not have intercourse with a woman; he aristocratically looks down on it, as on anything suggesting impregnation or children. As diversion, he will use and even enjoy any part of a woman's body, but his real preference is for men. He loves, for instance, to be whipped by a man, buggered by another, and, at the moment of orgasm, having a third shit in his mouth. His true pleasure with women comes when, worked up to the height of excitement, he subjects them—cowering, shrieking, pleading—to agonizing and bloody tortures that culminate in murder. It is best if they are virginal *ingenues*. He lives in a world of buttocks, excrement, blood, shrieks and death. He is Catullus or Rochester gone mad.

De Sade was of course far more perverse and sadistic on paper than in life—as most men are, even sexual radicals. So are most of the men who have written of him with fascination and respect. The realization of de Sade's fantasies and philosophy does exist in this world. It was carefully documented at Treblinka, Maidanek, Buchenwald and Auschwitz. I suspect that even the paper tigers of the cult of The Divine Marquis would not really enjoy that spectacle.

INTERVIEWS

Accounts of places and groups where kinky behavior are common tend to have an air of melodrama and the bizarre; they evoke pictures of some sort of vile social bilge—or sometimes of glamorous hedonism. In actuality, many people who have kinky patterns are quite modest, inconspicuous or even dull, and their behavior exciting, in reality, to no one but themselves. For instance, I do not learn that Harvey is a leather freak until well into my second visit to his apartment. He and Fred are roommates, and they seem like a quiet, conventional couple except when they are having their larger homosexual parties. Their big, pleasant apartment has a domestic and cozy air, and they keep a cute little dog there, which they have named Camp. Their social crowd—mostly Fred's friends —are delicate, fey and apparently rather quiet fellows of eighteen and twenty.

Harvey is still at work; while Fred and I wait for him, Fred tells me about his past. He is about twenty, short, slim, wears tight slacks, a close-fitting jersey and love beads. He has a faunlike face that reacts like a delicate barometer to his own and others' emotions, turning in an instant from boyish glee to boyish malice. I ask him what he thinks causes homosexuality.

I don't accept all the psychiatric views. Homosexuality could happen to anyone, and the influences that cause it aren't necessarily parental. In my case, at first I felt hero worship for men. Then I began to run with a crowd that was gay, though I didn't know it at first. They were all stagestruck. They worshiped Barbra Streisand and used to wait in a crowd outside the theater for her after shows. I hung out with them. I'd been very lonely, and to stay in the group I went along with homosexuality.

Did you ever see a psychiatrist?

Yes, a couple of them, over a period of about four years.

Why?

Because I was suicidal. I had no rapport with the first one, when I was seventeen, and I didn't tell him anything. The second one was earthy and used four-letter words. I could discuss anything with him. He didn't want to change me. He wanted me to be happy as I was.

What sort of people are you attracted to?

I can be attracted to people who are fifteen to fifty. But after a year as a homosexual I started avoiding the very attractive ones. They tend to love themselves more than they love other people. I also avoid the very tough. I've read about sado-masochists, and I'm not a masochist . . . [*he smiles*] . . . at least not a physical one. I hate the leather crowd. I didn't like drag queens at first, but that doesn't bother me any more.

Do you think homosexuals are different, as a group, in things besides sex?
Such as what?

Anything. From personalities to the way they vote.

Well, I think homosexuals are more liberal-minded, but I'd bet they vote less than average; they move around so much. Few are prejudiced about having a Negro in their school or neighborhood, but few of the young really cross the race line. It's the older ones who do that, the ones who have to take anything they can get.

Are there other differences?

There are more unhappy homosexuals, because they're a small group. And they're narcissistic and hypersexual. They'll do anything to get the guy they want, and you don't see many couples stick together for very long. You feel that in the atmosphere in most of the gay bars. I've learned to really despise those places, where people hang around and appraise each other like pieces of meat. I used to go to them a lot. There was one lesbian bar on University Place, the One-Two-Three, where I used to go. [*He laughs.*] I've never felt so safe in my life!

Do your parents know that you're homosexual?

They know everything. In fact, my mother almost encouraged one affair.

How did they find out?

When I first saw a doctor, a psychiatrist. My father and I haven't spoken since the doctor told him. The doctor said to him that he was partly responsible, because he didn't play with me when I was a boy, and he was absent from home. Now we can't bear to be in the same room with each other. I live at home, but I'm rarely there. When my father and I have to be together, we patronize each other.

[*Harvey comes in, tired from a day's work. He is in his late twenties, medium height, narrow-shouldered and unmuscular, already a little round in the belly. His features are small, his face soft. Straight black hair falls over his forehead and the top of his dark-rimmed glasses. His manner is sober, quietspoken; he gives the impression of an earnest, hard-working young man, a little prematurely middle-aged in style. That is, in fact, just what he's like, and it has made him quite successful in the technical field in which he works. Despite this, there remains an obvious boyish streak in his face and manner. Both he and Fred tend to avert their eyes and overcontrol their speech; and both give the impression that they contain huge reserves of stubborn anger, like unforgiving children.*]

HARVEY: I grew up in a very small town in Indiana. My father owned a business in town, but where we lived it was so rural that it was like growing up alone. When I did have playmates, they happened to be girls. I didn't have friends in high school either; I did almost no dating. I was always very interested in my profession, and I was very precocious in that. But I was ignorant in other ways. I had no sex education of any kind, and even through college I hardly dated. In my home town the leading social lady was a lesbian, and there were a few homosexual high school teachers, male and female. And everyone knew. But I didn't even know I was homosexual when I got out of college four years ago. I came to New York to work, and I still had no sexual experience.

I made friends at work, and I used to go driving around with one guy in particular. We'd drive around at night and just talk. One night we stopped the car and sat listening to the radio. I remember that I thought, "I wonder if he's homosexual and whether he'll try anything." Well, soon we decided to take an apartment, and before we signed the lease, we went driving one night, and he told me about himself. He explained that he was gay and told me about his life—he wanted me to know before signing the lease. When I heard his account, I knew that this was me. A little after that I met another guy and ended up in the back seat of the car with him. Our legs touched, and he winked. That was the beginning. We kissed. Then we drove back to the city and went to bed together. God, it was the most nervous night of my life. That was four years ago, and I was twenty-four. I was about eight years late starting my sex life. But I had no information about it at home; the word sex was just never used there.

Do you and your friends talk much about homosexuality, as we're doing now?

HARVEY: No, it's not discussed, as a topic. It's very rare that I hear such conversations. But I don't meet many people at all, anyway. I'm meeting Fred's friends now, and I'm very grateful for it. They're a nice bunch of guys, and it's hard for me to meet people. I don't like effeminate things, whether in girls or in guys. I've never had any relationship with a girl. I don't seek them out, so it doesn't happen.

If you had a choice of being homosexual or heterosexual, would you choose either?

FRED: Most homosexuals could be heterosexual if they really wanted the responsibility of living in the heterosexual world. They don't want it or they don't have the time to try.

HARVEY: I don't agree. I'm very happy being homosexual. I don't think I have any major problems, and I don't think I need psychotherapy.

FRED: But what about things like family responsibility? Homosexuals don't have that.

HARVEY: But look at our life together. God knows what sort of lives people think homosexuals live. We live a pretty quiet life, and we spend a lot of time working things out in the relationship; and a lot of it is domestic, things like who takes out the garbage and who washes the dishes, and so on. Like any couple who love each other and live together.

FRED: I don't think it's true, Harvey. But I do think that except for being gay I live a normal life. And I'd never fornicate with a person if it was his first homosexual experience. I wouldn't precipitate trouble for him. It's true that homosexual couples don't stay together for long, and there are unhappy older homosexuals. But look at the heterosexual of forty-five or fifty-five who's single or has a bad marriage. And heteros are just as preoccupied with sex. Just listen to men as they talk about women. And homosexuals are cleaner. They have to be, they're always on the make. They'd never go three days without a shower.

Have you ever belonged to any homosexual organizations?

FRED: I went up to the Mattachine Society here in New York once. I thought I'd do volunteer work. I found out that they aren't seriously fighting, it's really social. The library had bad sex paperbacks. It's a front for flaming fags who want to meet each other.

Fred, you have some lesbian friends, don't you?

FRED: Yes. Despite the myth, most homosexuals and lesbians get along. They don't need each other sexually. I used to go to a lesbian bar and hang out with the crowd there. I felt safe. But any man can seem like a competitor to some of them. Once a dyke suspected her femme had made a pass at me, and it got ugly.

Is there anything I haven't asked about that you think I should mention?

HARVEY: Before, you said that you want to meet all sorts of people—fruit flies, drag queens, closet queens, leather freaks. Well . . . [*he pauses, ducks his head a little, raises his eyes with a shy little smile*] . . . I'm a leather freak.

How convenient of you. Tell me more.

HARVEY: Oh, nothing bizarre. I've never ever engaged in any of the s-m things, just being dressed in it. It's something that has increased in the last year and a half.

Exactly how would you describe the pleasure in it?

HARVEY: The feel is a great part of it to me. Someone I used to know used an oiled rubber sheet. The idea appeals to me. I used to have a rubber suit, the kind they advertise for water skiing. It was very tight. Wearing it was one of my first sexual thrills, in the first year of college. The leather has a feel and touch and smell that are wonderful. Leather gives me a very masculine feeling, especially leather pants. Actually, it's only the last year and a half that I go out in the street in leather. I used to drive to the leather bars down on Christopher Street—like Danny's, that's *the* leather bar. Then my car was stolen, so I started walking there. I did that some in Europe, wearing leather in the street, and the reaction was more liberal. The motorcycle types are thrilling to me. I'd like to learn to ride one. Simply seeing someone in a leather jacket gets me thinking about the leather thing; just going to a bar in leather and seeing others in leather is as exciting as sex itself. I've had a lot of leather suits made. But you know, there's no one type; the leather types are very different. I've only had sex with a few because there wasn't always that much attraction; I'm very particular about who I go to bed with. And the last three months, since I've met Fred, I really don't go out. Our relationship is the sort of thing I've always dreamed of.

But just what is the pleasure of dressing in leather?

HARVEY: I had it in mind for years before I did it, and I was sensitive and ashamed about it. But it's preference, not really a fetishism. The heterosexual leather thing is sado-masochistic. But the homosexual leather thing isn't, necessarily. It isn't for me. It's a need for masculinity. When I put on leather, I just feel so . . . so . . . so *masculine*!

9

The Victorians

The French revolutionaries associated libertinage and deviance with the aristocracy. They detested both the class and its behavior. Madame de Pompadour's grave was opened, and her remains scattered in the streets. Crowds execrated the severed head of Madame de Lamballe, who was said to have been a lesbian. To protect marriage and promote virtue, they tried to stop prostitution.

On the other hand, they harbored a romantic, anarchic impulse. Love must be protected as well as the family, individual rights as well as the rights of society. They secularized marriage, legalized divorce and eased old laws restricting sexual behavior. The Civil Code enacted by Napoleon made homosexual acts illegal only if they involved force or public display. Conservatives predicted orgies in the streets and dissolution of families.

They were disappointed, of course. Laws do not transform mores; they reflect and reinforce them. Mores survive and are enforced only if they have been emotionally internalized at a young age by the members of a society. So there were divorces, but not a vast number. There is no record of homosexuality being more open; despite the Code, police continued to harass homosexuals, and homosexuals to hide their deviance. Sexual behavior had come under secular control, and the penalties for sexual offenses made lighter. Homosexuality was no longer a sin, nor even a crime, but it was still antisocial and subject to informal sanctions. Napoleon himself showed this ambivalence. He defended the family and bourgeois morals (at least for others). He accepted the open homosexuality of his assistant Cambracères, but sometimes mocked him. Once Cambracères came late to a meeting and explained the delay had been caused by a lovely visitor. The Emperor said, "Next time, my friend, be so good as to tell this lady, 'Take your hat and stick and shove off!' "

Before long, a political and social counterrevolution began. Until the middle of the nineteenth century, reaction had center stage, and liberalism fretted in the wings. Many of the revolutionaries' liberal laws were repealed. During the Restoration and Empire, police were actively enforcing traditional controls. In 1826 the Paris police closed down a homosexual club that had two doors, one leading to a men's section, the other to women's. In 1845 some fifty homosexuals were arrested in the "Rue Basse des Ramparts scandal." As usual, people complained that homosexuality was increasing. And, as usual, they found outsiders to blame it on—this time the Arabs. France had seized an empire in Africa, and for a century afterward French writers would claim that the occupation of Algiers had infected French troops with Arab homosexuality.

In England, in 1811, the anonymous work *The Prevalence of Vice* complained of growth in the "shocking depravity of men's *unnatural passions, sodomitical.*" This may have been prompted by a scandal that had begun with the arrest of a Mr. Cook, keeper of the White Swan Inn on Vere Street. He was charged with letting his place be used for immoral purposes. Hoping to get off lightly, Cook offered to tell the court the names of the famous and wealthy homosexuals who frequented his place. The Home Secretary intervened, trying to hush up the case. Cook was hustled off to the pillory, and when he returned was told by a turnkey, "It was not intended that you should have come back alive."

A lawyer named Holloway was angry at the whitewash and made a personal investigation. In 1813 he produced a book called *The Phoenix of Sodom, being an Exhibition of the Gambols Practiced by the Ancient Lechers of Sodom and Gomorrah, embellished and improved with the Modern Refinements in Sodomitical Practices by the members of the Vere Street Coterie of detestable memory.* He was amazed to discover that homosexual prostitutes were often not effeminate men "but butchers, blacksmiths, coal-merchants, police runners, who do it and have favourite women. . . . These odious practices are not confined to one, two or three houses, either public or private; for there are many about town; [including one] kept by a fellow known by the title of the Countess of Camomile."

Holloway called for a way of "restraining this vice, either by castration or some other cogent preventative, without waiting for completion of the offense." He was not heeded, nor were others who suggested castration or infibulation* for sexual offenders during the eighteenth and nineteenth centuries. But the legal penalties remained severe enough. Though capital punishment was abolished in England for many crimes in 1837, it was retained for murder, rape, intercourse with girls younger than ten, and sodomy. Punishment, of course, did not prevent the crime. In the 1840s London had brothels that supplied young boys as well as young girls for ten pounds. *The Yokel's Preceptor,* a guide to the city published in 1850, warned of "the increase of these monsters in the shape of men, commonly designated as Margeries, Pooffs, &c, of late years in the great metropolis." The author said that homosexuality was widespread in the theatrical

*Fastening of the pierced foreskin, prepuce or labia with a wire or ring to prevent sexual activity. It is referred to by many Roman writers and reported among some non-Western peoples. The Romans did it to keep slaves chaste, and in vain to create male sopranos (perhaps believing that sexual activity hastens sexual maturity). The English navigator Thomas Cavendish said in the sixteenth century that some natives he saw on his travels used this "nail of Sodom" to keep men from homosexual acts.

profession, and he described the signs by which homosexuals revealed themselves to each other—the same ones listed by another English writer seventy-five years earlier.

During this period, many English ship captains let prostitutes on board when in port; they defended the practice to the outraged by saying it prevented homosexuality. In 1821 an irate group volunteered to the Lords Commissioners of the Admiralty a *Statement of Certain Immoral Practices Prevailing in His Majesty's Navy.* Their argument was: "What can be more *unnatural* . . . than the open, undisguised, unblushing, promiscuous concubinage, which now takes place? . . . It is either when the appetite is palled or sated with enjoyment, or when a familiarity with gross pollution has prepared the mind for further grossnesses, that such enormities [homosexuality] are to be apprehended. Indeed, all crimes are progressive."

If one crack appears in the floodgates, tides of lust will bear men away, making them monsters. Each pleasure leads to another more outrageous, until one is a mad and half-spent beast forever in rut, shambling to the farthest reaches of sexual imaginings. This is the voice of Victorianism, which by 1821 was at its height. It said little new. It was one more variation on the ideas of the ancient world, of St. Augustine, the Puritans and Rousseau (who said that the contortions of the face in sexual excitement resemble those of anger, and must make men disgusting to women). It expressed fear of sex, anger and all impulse. It tried to dam up sexual activity within monogamous marriage; everything from childhood masturbation to adultery must be prevented, and one slip could be enough. This attitude is as old as the recorded West; since we are living in reaction against its last severe public campaign, associated with Queen Victoria, we call it Victorian—a simplistic distortion as much as calling it Puritan or Judeo-Christian.

Victorianism was in full force well before Queen Victoria took the throne in 1837, and it was on its way out in the upper classes decades before she died in 1901. The silly part of it we know—a pious and smug denial of sex. It arose in a wave of prudery, guilt and religious reformism in the second half of the eighteenth century. At that time the Protestant domestication of romantic love was becoming entrenched. There was revulsion at the arid *galant* and cruel libertine, the world of Casanova and Laclos. Diaries of the time are full of religious and moral hesitations about sex. Early in the eighteenth century, Italians had felt at home in London, and French writers spoke of the natural frankness of English women. In 1790, a German traveling there, apparently in middle-class circles, commented on the reserve among gentlemen and especially among ladies, and on how many churchgoers and reform movements there were. He said that "unnatural pleasures are held in great abhorrence with the men. In no country are such infamous pleasures spoken of with greater detestation. The custom of embracing each other, so common among the men in other

European countries, is for this reason displeasing to the English. A foreigner who did so would be in risk of insult from the populace." Rigid fear of all sensual and impulsive expression was becoming a national characteristic.

The middle class had been strongly touched by Methodism. John Wesley started putting the fear of hell in merchants, shopkeepers and clerks in 1738, damning such moral horrors as drinking tea and lying abed in the morning. The middle and lower middle classes, unable to put moral pressure on libertine aristocrats, turned on the new masses of urban workers, trying in their genuine but misguided way to save them. In 1692 the Society for the Reformation of Manners had been founded; in 1725, when young titled rakes were terrorizing the streets, the Society was responsible for almost a hundred thousand arrests—mostly of the poor. By the end of the eighteenth century, this somewhat diluted Calvinism took root among the poor (as it did soon after in rural America) through evangelical movements. By the early nineteenth century, the morals of Wesley, tent-revival preachers, the rigid romance of monogamy and good appearances, had won much of England and the United States.

This new campaign for restraint differed from Puritanism in its emphasis on social rather than spiritual sanctions—the eye of the neighbor mattered as much as the eye of God. Class distinctions partly replaced theological ones; in the 1790s satirists were already pointing out that though the poor sweated, the refined perspired. Until this time much of even the urban West had accepted nudity and excretion casually; now a veil was drawn over the body, the bathroom door locked. In 1818 Thomas Bowdler presented to England *The Family Shakespeare*, all sexual references removed, and gave his name to verbal prudery. When Tennyson published *The Wreck of the Hesperus*, he had to change "bull" to "gentleman cow."

Many Victorians, like early Christians and Puritans, quaked in fear of all strong feelings; they condemned great laughter and great grief as well as sex. They moralized each act, each moment, waking and even sleeping. Some doctors said that wet dreams showed lack of purity and will, which even Aquinas had hesitated to affirm. There had also been a shift in handling sexual impulse and sexual control. In the Middle Ages, Europe had projected the burden of sexual impulse onto woman—the witch, the stinking rose, the vessel of the Devil who lured men to sin. The nineteenth century allayed its sexual anxiety by putting the burden on man. Woman was desexualized, domesticated. She became a friend, a sister, a mother, a homemaker, an overgrown prepubertal girl. She was supposed to be shy, delicate, easily disconcerted, the potential victim of males, who now had a monopoly on sex and sin.

This clinging vine who flourished in domestic air was glorified by Coventry Patmore as *The Angel in the House*. She was to lean on man, adore him, serve him and shame him. Since his brutality and lust could smash this frail thing or drag her through the slime of sex, he must protect her by controlling himself. She was his moral arbiter, manipulating and controlling him through guilt. Outside, in business or in the colonies, man might be crude, combative and lustful; at home his coarse nature would be softened by browsing in the tender foliage of feminine society. Women, of course, must control and desexualize themselves: everything that hinted of flesh and animality was unfeminine.

Delicacy and refinement were virtues by 1790, a tyranny by 1820. A century earlier, women could visit taverns and lead active lives. Now they were supposed to be utterly incorporeal; they were advised that "the luxury of eating is beyond expression indelicate and disgusting." Dr. Gregory, a famous writer on domestic manners, said, "If you love your husband, do not ever say so." A writer in *The Westminster Review* said that women's sexual urges were dormant or nonexistent. "Nature has laid so many burdens on the delicate shoulders of the weaker sex: let us rejoice that this, at least, is spared them." If they realized how great their sexual potential was, "sexual irregularities would reach a height of which, at present, we have happily no conception." This was unlikely as long as a frail, unsensual constitution invalided them out of the beastly sexual fray. The distinguished writer on sex, Dr. William Acton, said that to claim women were capable of sexual impulses was a "vile aspersion." William Hammond, U.S. Surgeon-General, said that nine-tenths of the time decent women had no pleasure from intercourse, and the famous Swiss gynecologist, Dr. Fehling, called sexual desire in young women pathological.

The left wing of Victorianism was Romanticism. The Pre-Romantics of the later eighteenth century had stocked literature—and to a degree life—with cynical libertines who finally converted to weepy sensibility. Romanticism further desexualized love, and as sex waned, emotion soared. Love became a mad trembling of spirit, fantasy, ethics, of scruples so strong that only frantic passion swept one beyond them. Keats, who probably died a virgin, looked on wan Victorian woman and said fervently:

> God, she is like a milk-white lamb that bleats
> For man's protection.

Man, said Tennyson, should feel "a maiden passion for a maid." Otherwise one became a Byron or Heathcliffe, a dark sinister destroyer who ruined women like a brute shredding blossoms with his terrible paws. If right-wing Victorianism was a wall of guilt and restraint, Romantic love was a thing of tears, impossibility and woe.

In the works of many Romantic writers—and in the lives of many as well —sexual identity became shaky. The eighteenth century's attempt to balance the rational, pragmatic life with passionate primitivism was carried further; emotion spun off into high-pitched fantasy where sex distinctions broke down. Men and women loved like brothers and sisters, parents and children, souls without bodies. Men cultivated their "feminine" sensitivity, renounced aggressiveness, became as yearningly impotent as Cathar poets.

Women wore trousers, smoked cigars and developed their "individuality" —George Sand and George Eliot, writing under male pseudonyms, were notorious cases. German Romanticism was full of the idea of exchanged sex roles. Schleiermacher spoke of becoming a woman, and his wife replied, "You are not a man to me, but a sweet pure virgin." Despite her trousers, cigars and male pen name, George Sand was not a lesbian, but she suffered from a confused sexual identity and resulting problems in sex role and sexual behavior. Some of the earlier Romantics were homosexual—William Beckford, Matthew Lewis, August von Platen—but for a long roster of deviant artists one must look to the second half of the century. Allegations have occasionally been made that Byron, Tennyson, Beethoven, Goethe, Hölderlin and Kleist were homosexual or bisexual, but they are highly speculative.

Psychologists, historians and popular writers have analyzed Victorians and their behavior with varying degrees of crudity and ingenuity. They usually find in right-wing Victorianism a pattern much like that ascribed to the Puritans—"anal," guilty, acquisitive, obsessive, rigid, authoritarian, afraid of sex, homosexuality and all spontaneity. They often find in left-wing Victorianism an "oral," passive and permissive character. It is true, to a degree, that both types evoke inhibited children who overidentified, respectively, with their fathers and their mothers. But the psychological and social forces involved are too complex to make such concepts more than rough metaphors, and total reliance on them oversimplifies issues we would benefit from understanding in deeper detail.

For instance, one must clarify the Victorians' hypocrisy and concern for appearances—which is what later generations have most held against them. This hypocrisy has overshadowed the positive aspects of Victorianism: the social idealism that went with the sexual idealism; the spirit of reform, democracy and humanitarianism; the attempt to counteract a competitive, mercantile culture with feeling and morality; the stress on devotion and regard for others.

Often the preoccupation with appearances was really quite frank. *The Lady's Magazine* said in 1818, "A woman without delicacy is a beast; a woman without the *appearance* of delicacy is a monster." To understand this, one must consider the class structure and urban life of the period. People were flooding into urban slums and mining and mill towns, and multiplying there. They were impoverished, overworked, desperate, many living continually in semistarvation or starvation. Prayer, gin, violence and sex were the only outlets and comforts available. Families broke up in large numbers. The squalor and brutality were greater than that in any ghetto in England or the United States today. In order to survive, mill girls prostituted themselves, and unemployed men stole to put bread in their families' mouths. Many workers lived like serfs; in 1828 a French visitor to a Lancashire mill was casually told to take his pick of the women working there.

The middle and upper classes lived far above the workers, in a stratosphere of privilege and choice.

The only way out of this jungle was to conform to nonslum standards and creep into the lower middle class. One must learn to control impulses—to discuss rather than fistfight, not get drunk, avoid pregnancy, not be shocking or drop "aitches." Then one could move from mine or mill to shop counter or office, from streetcorner to servants' quarters. One thus became more than a short-lived piece of meat. In the stinkholes of London's slums, a man could buy a hungry fourteen-year-old girl for the price of a meat tart. In *The Other Victorians*, Steven Marcus points out that "in the degree to which that young girl succeeded in denying her sexuality . . . in the degree to which she even made her own sexuality inaccessible to herself, in that degree might she have the chance of extending her humanity in other directions."

So Victorian morals separated the slum dwellers from the respectable middle and lower middle classes. Methodism and other reform and religious movements helped "respectable" values to percolate downward. And as the middle class came to dominate society economically, its values spread upward as well. Aristocrats and factory hands were both adjusting to a bourgeois society. By 1850 Victorianism had invaded the aristocracy, the countryside and the fringes of the slums; a countermovement was already stirring in parts of the upper and upper middle classes.

Victorianism flourished all over the West. The French bourgeoisie was just as Victorian as the British. The author of *Madame Bovary* was prosecuted for indecency. Middle-class French, German, Swedish and Italian girls were raised and married off as ignorant as possible of sex. In the United States, despite less rigid class lines and the greater social freedom of women, there was almost as much lashing-the-waves to drive away sex as in England and on the Continent. Frances E. Willard wrote, "When I was first a boarding school pupil in Evanston, in 1858, a young woman who was not chaste came to the college there through some misrepresentations, but was speedily dismissed; not knowing her degraded status I was speaking to her when a school-mate whispered a few words of explanation that crimsoned my face suddenly: and grasping my dress lest its hem should touch the garments of one so morally polluted, I fled the room." Frederick Marryat, at about the same time, gave his oft-quoted (and perhaps tongue-in-cheek) description of finding the "limbs" of a piano clad in a proper American family living room.

We blame and mock the nineteenth century middle class for blighting sex. If the clichés are true, there must have been little of it—and what there was, tense and hurried, shaming to the man and endured by the woman. (We are still speaking, of course, of the minority of affluent city dwellers and their imitators.) The fact remains that for every case of Victorian frigidity or inhibition one can point to a scandal, a whore, a homosexual, a love affair, a defiance of convention. Even in our own day, it is extremely difficult to generalize about a society's sexual practices; accurate studies always contain surprises such as Kinsey's. But two interesting guesses have been widely made about Victorian sexuality, and they tell a great deal about our thinking, if not about the Victorians.

Some people argue that sexual practices never really vary much. For instance, the distinguished historian Crane Brinton wrote, "I think it extremely likely that on the whole there was, in the nineteenth century West at least . . . the usual difference in sexual behavior of a few percent-age points." Dr. Richard Lewinsohn, author of the popular *A History of Sexual Customs,* writes, "No one knows how many sexual anomalies there are, but it is improbable that the number varies greatly from one generation to another." If Brinton and Lewinsohn are right, we should draw three conclusions. First, Victorianism was merely a set of social conventions without much real effect on sexual behavior. Second, it therefore cannot have left behind a significant sexual burden. Third, verbal freedom and changing sexual etiquette has probably changed behavior no more today than it did a century ago. Neither Brinton nor Lewisohn explains why these things are likely, and neither produces evidence to back up his opinion.

On the other hand, the hydraulic theory of sex says that blocking usual outlets will cause sex to manifest itself in deformed, substitutive ways. It is a view so simplistic that it obscures rather than clarifies important questions about social forces and behavior. It is cherished by many people who seek a cynical and leveling rationale to fit their emotional view. They need to feel that appearances, especially of altruism and self denial, are hoaxes. They live in a land of fantasy and folklore where all monks are lechers; nuns are sluts; censors are secret deviants; prostitutes have better hearts than any housewife; genteel Victorians all had minds like de Sade novels and chased sex in back alleys like crazed goats. This is the realm of para-noia, not fact.

At first it seems easy to make a case for superabundant secret deviance among the Victorians, nature's revenge on repressive conventions. A cen-tury ago London, Paris and Berlin were full of deviants, scandal and pros-titution. Pornography of all kinds became a progressively bigger business; and now it was full of secretive, obsessive sniggering and highly deviant fantasties as never before—an erotic periodical of 1822 listed twenty-five deviations with distinct cant names, about twenty of them specifically known to modern psychiatry. During the first half of the nineteenth cen-tury, fetishism became a generally recognized deviation rather than a spo-radically noted peculiarity. Flagellation as a sexual specialty especially increased, and England was generally acknowledged to be its capital. Flagel-lation brothels were flourishing in London at the end of the eighteenth century. The Goncourts recorded in their journal in 1862 that they had met a calm, mad young English gentleman who explained to them his passion for witnessing executions and displayed his treasured copy of the earliest classic of sado-masochistic pornography, Meibomius' seventeenth-century *Utility of Flagellation in the Pleasures of Love and Marriage.*

Swinburne was a famous case of flagellomania—a small, odd-looking man who went to brothels to be whipped and allegedly had little sexual desire otherwise. Among his clandestine writings were *The Flogging Block* and *The Whippingham Papers.* In the latter he said, "One of the great charms of birching lies in the sentiment that the floggee is the powerless victim of the furious rage of a beautiful woman." He blamed his masochistic penchant on the whippings he had received at Eton. It was now a ritual part of sado-masochistic pornography that the author, often signed "Etonensis," had become deviant because of whippings at "Birchminster" or some other school

The association of England with whipping was probably as real and unreal as previous linkings of homosexuality with Italy—that is, a grain of truth was probably blown up into a grotesque exaggeration. And the cliché of a high-born Eton boy being whipped by servants and schoolteachers is probably a symbolic rather than literal explanation of apparently increasing sexual masochism. In the early eighteenth century, Ned Ward had complained that the young of the upper classes tended to grow up like weeds, running wild, indulged, without strong affectional ties; the most visible type of sexual neurotic in their class was the angry pansexual. Predictably, sexual sadism became a fixture of pornographic writing at this time, in fact a pornographic specialty in itself—indicating an audience for it. In the nineeenth century, child-rearing methods became more restrictive, with a new emphasis on obedience and control, but in many homes without any greater tenderness and warmth to the child. The effects of boarding-school life must have been very different on these children than on their ancestors.

It is likely that a person becomes sexually deviant because of basic emotional and developmental deficits; his choice of a specific deviant style is probably determined by details of family background, social milieu and chance. To a child prepared for a deviant adaptation to life, school whippings must have become a symbol, almost a scapegoat, for all that predisposed him (deviants tend to name specific traumatic events or situations as the reason for their deviance, without explaining why such things should have affected them so). The uncontrolled, angry children of one century may have turned to a sadistic psychosexual orientation when subjected to corporal discipline; the overcontrolled children of another time may have reacted by becoming masochistic. Such patterns conform with what is seen today in psychiatric practice. Certainly the school-whipping situation conforms to the basic emotional experience of masochism—helplessness, humiliation, punishment. Sado-masochistic pornography usually sets up a difference in class, age or status between punisher and punished; they are woman and boy, teacher and student, master and slave. The Etonensis of

Birchminster in pornographic ritual was probably a symbolic expression of the guilt- and power-laden aspects of masochism, not a direct reflection of hordes of boys turned into masochists by Eton.

This explanation of why masochism apparently replaced sadism as the most visible deviation during the nineteenth century is speculation, of course, but I think it is likely in terms of modern clinical experience—more so, at least, than just calling it another leak sprung in sexual conduits blocked by Victorianism. And if certain sexual kinks did become commoner in the upper classes, as it seems they did, the answer may lie more in new patterns of child rearing produced by complex social change than by purely sexual factors. Demoralizing urbanization may have also created much more sexual disturbance in the lower classes. But finally, in an over-all view, we don't know that sex during the Victorian period was less frequent or more deviant than during the fourteenth century, the eighteenth century or the middle of the twentieth century. It is easy and convenient to blame certain kinds of sexual problems, which were much written about, on "Victorianism," but one could just as well lay widespread sexual disturbance in the Middle Ages to "Christianity"—and be no wiser in either case.

A broad psychosocial perspective makes it seem that Victorianism—like Romanticism, feminism, increased sado-masochism and fetishism—was not the cause of sexual malaise but one of many factors involved in it, perhaps more a symptom than a cause. Even in the last twenty years, since the Kinsey studies and much other research, we are just making crude beginnings at sorting out the factors that determine sexual behavior and attitudes, and how attitudes affect behavior. We are not ready to make many definitive statements about ourselves, let alone past centuries. We just don't know what happened in most Victorian bedrooms: that is, we do not yet fully understand the relationship between overt mores, covert mores, and behavior.

People with double lives did exist then, as today. We possess the diary of one who tells us much about sex and homosexuality in his time. The tone of *My Secret Life* is so frank and convincing that after Greek apologists, Church fathers, Brantôme, Casanova and Frank Harris, it is like a sudden breeze cutting through stale halls of bragging and myth. Here, finally, is a detailed sexual autobiography that is fairly trustworthy and allows for modern interpretation. It shows in detail much one has to guess at or infer when dealing with earlier periods.

The author—let us call him X—was born into an upper-middle-class family in the early 1820s. Like many of the affluent young of his time, he was introduced to sex by servants. When, as an adolescent, X tried to go to bed with a housemaid, she strung him along and always stopped just short of intercourse, mocking the size of his penis. All his life fear of such ridicule haunted him. Finally he got to bed with a servant nearer himself in age and inexperience. From then on his life was a frantic, consuming search for sex. He recorded forty years of this in a diary, which he finally transformed into the privately printed confession *My Secret Life*. The book was not pornography, but an earnest attempt to record, explain and justify his life. It was his life that was pornographic—a mechanical, obsessive enactment of sexual fantasies.

Like many people of his social level, he equated class, money, domination and sex. Most of his women were domestic servants, whores and poor girls. In his world, the affluent and poor were as different in each other's eyes as are blacks and whites to a racist. In fact, the upper class saw the lower much as the bigoted white sees someone dark—not quite human in the same way as himself, not feeling the same emotions, needs and outrages he would feel in their place. X believed, "as to servants and women of the humbler class . . . they all took cock on the quiet and were proud of having a gentleman to cover them." After raping a farm worker, he tried to shut off her misery by paying her. When that failed, he threatened her with the loss of her job. She was not a suffering human, just an inconvenience pretending to be one. X even thought his whores took pleasure in selling themselves to him. Since he saw sex as a struggle for domination—with status and money the artillery backing up his penis—he could not afford to humanize his partners. That would make the game break down into a human encounter.

Until he was about thirty, X's sex life was active but uncomplicated. As he got older, he developed more and more kinks, including homosexual and transvestite acts. Many of them are explainable by the barely contained rage that lay behind his sexual fever, the rage of a child whose parents are distant shadows, who learned from mocking or merely acquiescent servants what it was to be held by a woman. Rage and sexual activity tend to exclude each other. Two situations caused X occasional impotence throughout his life. One was the intrusion of affection or pity into a sexual situation; then it would almost dawn on him that what he needed most was not sex but love. The other was the threat of his hostility breaking out into the open; that happened when he tried to deflower little girls and to commit buggery. He also had a mania for inspecting women's genitals. X thought of his penis as a weapon of assault and subjugation; it was his gun, his spear. A person as angry as he is likely to assume that others are like himself, and he expects retaliation. The female counterpart of the penile weapon is the *vagina dentata* which children create in fantasy, a toothed vagina that destroys the invading penis. X's need to inspect women's cunts can be interpreted as a need to reassure himself that he was not facing castration inside his female counterpart.

In *The Other Victorians*, Steven Marcus has analyzed X, X's book and their social context with subtle intelligence and broad imagination. However, he uses traditional and sometimes almost mechanical Freudian formulas to explain some of X's kinks, especially his homosexual ones, when the concept of identity confusion explains them better. Identity panic is what someone would feel if awakened in the night with a deluge of ice water, to find himself in a strange bed, a strange room, a strange world. For a moment he would wonder not just where he was, but whether this was real or a dream, whether he was sane or mad, whether at this moment he himself was a creature being dreamed by someone else. Many terror films dealing with shifting identities play on this sense of a crumbling or nonexistent self. Many so-called homosexual panics are identity panics. A staunch, hyperaggressive heterosexual who considers homosexuals to be contemptible faggots may feel a homosexual impulse or have a flash homosexual fantasy. With panic, he demands to know, "Am I homosexual?" A homosexual may feel the same panic when, in psychotherapy, he is faced with the possibility of a heterosexual life. Identity panic may occur whenever one's accustomed, conscious self is threatened by unacceptable impulses or fantasies.

X needed not only to inspect women but to exhibit his penis to them; Marcus explains this in the usual terms of exhibitionism as aggression. But significantly, this usually happened when X was involved in a violent seduction, with all his buried rage coming close to enactment. In fact, a whole complex of infantile feelings and fantasies then threatened to get out of control and engulf him—murderous rage at an ungiving woman, fear of retribution by castration, a sense of inner desolation. He may have suddenly pulled out his penis for himself to see, not for the woman, to remind himself that he was an adequate, whole man, not a raging monster or a rejected and castrated offender. Eventually X found his greatest pleasure in intercourse with a woman immediately after another man had had her, while her vagina was still wet with the other man's sperm. He had brothels arrange for him to watch other customers through peepholes and then used the whores immediately after. He wanted the other men to be young and virile-looking, with large sex organs. Steven Marcus calls this a distorted Oedipal re-enactment; it can also be explained as X's attempt to affirm his male identity by sharing another man's—as primitive people magically share an animal's qualities by incorporating or identifying with it.

Sex as a power struggle; fear of retributive rage; identity confusion, with uncertainty of maleness; incorporating other men's maleness; identifying with them—all these things will come up again in present-day psychiatric study of homosexuality. X did work himself up to dabbling in homosexual relations, but it took years, for he had many fears and doubts about it, as about the rest of his sex life. He suffered frequent depression, impotence, fear of inadequacy. In any age he would have been troubled; in the studied silence of middle- and upper-class Victorian England, he was tortured. With frankness and sometimes desperation he kept asking: Do other men act as I do in bed? What do they think and feel? What do women think, feel, desire? Most people ask themselves these questions fleetingly or infrequently. X's sexual obsessiveness made them his central concern. But none of the psychological concepts we take for granted were available to him, and he lacked even a useful vocabulary for posing the questions fruitfully. To maintain any shred of self-love, X had to brazen out for himself a self-justifying science and morality of sex. It was very like that of educated liberals today. He decided that only social custom made any sex act improper. "Why, for instance . . . may a man, and a woman handle each other's privates, and yet it be wrong for a man to feel another's prick, or a woman to feel another's cunt?"

X had one of his whores set him up with a male prostitute. He found, when the time came, that the man repelled him. X trembled with nervousness, but "pride, bravado, and the curiosity of handling another man's prick, of seeing his emotions in spending kept me going." The male prostitute asked, "Are you fond of a bit of brown? . . . We always say a bit of brown among ourselves, and a cunt's a bit of red." X felt nauseated and wanted to masturbate the man instead. But the man wanted to be buggered. X was impotent.

> "Shall I suck it?"—"You?"—"Yes."—"Do you do so?"—"Lord yes, I have had it so thick in my mouth, that I've had to pick it out of my teeth with a toothpick."—I turned sick, but after a time I turned his arse towards me, and got my prick stiff by hard frigging, determined to try what buggery was like. But the moment I put it against his arsehole down it drooped. . . . Again I frigged him, curious to see his emotions, and watched his face when with difficulty he spent lightly.—But my cock would not stand.— So I went into the room to Betsy . . . I mounted her, and fucked, feeling his prick whilst I did so—that either suggested itself to me, or he suggested it—and it seemed to increase my pleasure.

X had the woman while holding the other man's penis like a talisman. For a while now he tried other sexual fantasies and inventions, including staging lesbian scenes with prostitutes. His activities continued to be frequent, frenzied and impersonal; unable to release his feelings, he sought sexual excitement as a substitute for them, to avoid total depersonalization. Marcus calls it "an endless search for what cannot be found, for a gratification that does not exist . . . the grounds of any compulsive repetitive activity are unconscious . . . so long as these grounds remain undisturbed so long will the monotonous search for the same variety persist."

X finally worked up courage for homosexual experiment again. Now he was a more experienced and, in some ways, a more assured man. He also had more entrenched rationalizations. But the prospect again filled him with anxiety. One of his whores procured a man for him—this time an apprentice carpenter who had been near starvation for weeks and would do anything for money. Like X, he lacked homosexual experience and felt ashamed and scared. X masturbated the apprentice, played with him and the whore as though they were toys, and finally used the whore while holding the apprentice's penis. Then he let the apprentice have her, and followed him immediately, mixing his semen with the apprentice's—bathing in another man's manhood.

Later X felt guilty, but soon he was ready again to seek his own maleness through another man. His chief interest was not another male's body or affection, but his virility and his ability to reassure X that he existed by being a mirror for him. X wanted "once more to make him spend, and to watch his prick from its stiffening to its shrinking. To watch his face and see how pleasure affected it." He got the man and woman together many times again, staging various erotic scenes and finally practicing mutual fellatio with the apprentice.

The usual intellectual reflex today is to call X a latent homosexual who played the compulsive seducer with women but sporadically slipped into his "real" homosexuality. Actually, men did not interest him in a directly erotic way much or often. His homosexual experiments were a small part of his sexual career. Rather, he experimented with other men in search of a double whose maleness would fortify his own, through magical, childlike incorporation and identification. This makes less mysterious the psychiatric truism that often a homosexual act is a man's desperate attempt to establish his own masculinity. Many of the psychological factors that operated in X's homosexual ventures lie behind those of the exclusive homosexual— just as paranoid thinking sometimes occurs in people who are not paranoiacs. But basically X was a troubled heterosexual whose inner rage, pansexual impulses and lack of a firm male identity occasionally led him to homosexual acts.

Over the years, X's sexual life became more sadistic, impersonal and controlling. The later stages of his play with the apprentice and the whore showed this blatantly. "I frigged him four times, and had no end of amusement with him—I had a taste that night for rolling over him as if he were a woman." He dressed the apprentice in women's silk clothes, delighting in the feeling of power at manipulating and exciting him, yet identifying with him. He gave the apprentice an erection and "looked at his naked rigidity—feeling it, kissing it, glorying in my power—with my own prick upright." Then he decided again that he wanted to try the ultimate act of sexual domination—buggery. He did so, and immediately felt disgust and loathing for the apprentice.

Over the following years he occasionally experimented with men, sometimes practicing mutual fellatio and masturbation, but usually taking turns with them inside women. Once he used a whore as bait to get an adolescent boy to perform with them. While the three of them were in bed, he decided at last to consent to being buggered, and "at one thrust he went half way up. A revulsion came instantly, 'Pull it out,' I cried,—Out it came, she laughed and there it ended.—I did not feel pleased with myself at all.— What is the good of my philosophy?"

INTERVIEWS

Howard is a writer in his fifties, a small, slight man from a "good family" and the right schools. He is charming and exquisitely articulate, with a fastidious manner that usually stays just this side of overfine. He sometimes seems to have stepped out of the nineteenth-century upper middle class, with its equation of sex, race, class and dominance. He lives in a pretty little apartment in London with a guardsman. When I arrive, he is alone. His guardsman friend, Will, is on duty, at a parade. I want to ask Howard and his friend about the traditional homosexual prostitution in the mounted guards—it came to public notice in 1960, when writer Simon Raven's article "Boys Will Be Boys" appeared in Encounter. *While we wait for Will, Howard talks about himself and his travels.*

I knew I was homosexual when I was five, and I was never a bit ashamed. Some years ago I saw a famous psychoanalyst because of very troubling dreams. I told him, "I have a problem, and I want you to help me with it, but don't touch my structure, I want to remain homosexual." It helped me greatly, and my homosexuality wasn't touched; and if there was any shame in me, it was gone after that.

I'm sure homosexuality is genetic, or in some way biological. My analyst was wrong on some counts. For instance, when I was five I started falling in love with bus conductors. I used to lie awake nights, thinking of "my young men," as I called them. I imagined five of them, naked, handing me around from one to another. The doctor said this was just an idea I'd had. Well, it soon turned out that he was quite wrong. There was a scandal about the bus conductors, and it turned out that many of them were former guardsmen!

Yes, I'm more and more convinced that it's biological. My brother is homosexual. But he's different from me. He has no emotional life. He just pays a fiver to a guardsman, and that's that. On the other hand, I need someone like Will. It's peaceful having a strong person around, having a man in the house. It's like the Russian novelists marrying peasant women. Homosexuality is based on the attraction of opposites, just as with men and women—white and black, upper class and guardsman, and so on.

I've been in love with girls, but I've never been able to penetrate anyone, male or female. Why that is, I can't tell you. I don't think it's fear of having it snapped off, and all that nonsense. I think it's that I'm not a very positive person, except in my work. And that's why I like having a strong man in the house. Actually, Will and I have very little sex. My only regret in all this is not being able to have a son.

Did you go to a public school?

Oh yes. Here boys are all shut up in them from nine to seventeen without seeing girls. It's a very strong element in English life, and it's perpetuated in men's clubs. It's also a class thing, of course. I think comprehensive schools are better. They don't create those terrible boyhood crushes. I used to take one of my public-school master's cufflinks, carry them around in my pocket and kiss them.

Has the change of law here made much difference in many people's lives, do you think?

Oh, it hasn't changed much. The illegality was very important and exciting, but if a homosexual who works in an insurance office becomes known, he'll be dismissed despite the law. Here it's the suburban middle class that really looks down on one. The lower class and the aristocrats are never surprised—certainly not the aristocrat. If anything is changing, it's because of the young generation. I've had some of these lovely young chaps, fifteen and sixteen, and they say to me, "I'm not homosexual or heterosexual, I'm just sexual."

How does all this compare with what you've seen when traveling?

Oh, it's very different from place to place. In America I think there's more prejudice than here. Last year I had American soldiers and marines who were on R and R in Hong Kong. They'd pretend not to be there when they woke up in my bed the next morning. They deny it to themselves, try to believe it didn't happen. You've got to let them off. With the Chinese, I found just what Maugham told me to expect when we discussed it eight years ago. The Chinese adore older people, just adore them. I had a young Chinese boy, and on the third night he said he was glad I was older. I said I was forty-three, and he said, "I was afraid you were thirty. Papa-san much wiser than boy." He wanted me to have a big belly, be a sort of Buddha figure. I had boys in Borneo and Japan, Malaya, the Arab world. In Nigeria and Ghana the boys in hotels are surprised if you don't want to go to bed with them. It's the same in the West Indies; it's left over from colonialism. To them, your being white is like being a woman—having you is a conquest.

[Will arrives—a big, strapping man in his early or middle twenties. He has a way of sitting on the sofa next to Howard that makes him seem to still be mounted on a horse, on parade. He has a provincial accent; he comes from an industrial city in the North. He generally speaks only when spoken to, and for a long time gives an impression of patiently bearing the entire proceedings.]

HOWARD: We were talking about the things that go on in various parts of the world, Will. I was going to mention those supermasculine fellows in New York and San Francisco, the ones with the leather and chains and sombreros. They all just want to be fucked, don't let them fool you. They are really feminine. The sadists wore their key chains hanging out of their back pockets; that's how one recognized them. I was wearing this ring in San Francisco, which has a buckle on it—you see? It turns out that this is a sign there; I was taken for an advertising masochist. I think all this business is American. You don't find all these signs and signals here. Do you, Will?

WILL: Wearing a pinkie ring on the left hand is a signal.

HOWARD: Oh, is it? I didn't know that.

It has been for a long time in New York.

HOWARD: It is here, too?

WILL: Yes, it is.

HOWARD: I suppose you want to know about the guardsman scene.

Yes. All I know is what I read in Simon Raven's article.

HOWARD: That was the first time it was written about, but there's a lot he didn't know. You see, there are the Household Cavalry; then there are the Blues, the Horse Guards, who were set up by Cromwell, a very violent and nasty gang; and there are the Life Guards, set up by Charles I. They all have an old tradition, perhaps going back to their beginnings, of selling themselves. It may also go on in the Mechanized Household Cavalry, though some deny it. Years ago, when the horse guards came off duty at Whitehall, ladies and men both used to come and drop their telephone numbers into the tops of those great high boots they wear. Once someone suggested the guards make signs, one for each boot, MALE and FEMALE.

You see, the guards are taught to look marvelous. They become like actors, learn to admire themselves. They do it for a fiver and say they don't enjoy it. Actually, many of them marry young because they've got a girl pregnant, and come down to London and join the service. Then the guard mixes with the upper classes, sees a different life, and he and his wife grow apart, so a lot of the marriages blow up.

Will, is that what happened to you?

WILL: Sort of, yes. I'm from up north. I never heard about these things up there. I got married and she had a child, and we moved down here. Up home, 99 per cent of the writing in pub lavatories was about women. Here it was about men. I got so that if a man asked me for a light on the street, I'd wonder, "What's the bloke up to?" Well, I joined the guards, and for two years I didn't do anything with men. I fought the idea. I felt very square, you know, all these blokes going out for dinner with sirs and barons and such, and sometimes they got as much as eight pounds. It was a big temptation.

Was Howard the first man you went out with?

WILL: I tried once before. Finally, after about two years, I did it out of curiosity. I went to the meat-market pub they all go to, to find out—then it was Tattersall's, now it's the Pig and Whistle. But I just couldn't go through with it. I punched the guy. Then later I met Howard and came here, and he talked and put me completely at ease about it. My wife and I are getting divorced, and now I have a girl. Sometimes I bring her here to Howard's, she doesn't care.

How many of the guards do go out with men?

WILL: I'd say about half. But not more than 5 per cent of them who do it are that way themselves. They just do it for money. About 15 per cent of them who do it loathe it, and they loathe the men they do it with. Our blokes just hate the guys like Howard's brother, who pay out a fiver and that's that.

Are any of the guardsmen effeminate?

WILL: All of them that does it, oh, 99 per cent, they're very masculine. They only let the gentleman go down on them. The female-type guardsman is very unpopular, and he's made fun of. We have one big strapping one who likes to take the woman's role, though.

[*The atmosphere is a little more relaxed than before. Will still habitually sits as though on horseback, but he offers more comments and opinions. Howard becomes campy and flirtatious at moments. A subtle interplay goes on as we continue to talk. As Howard becomes slightly more playful, more seductive, often touching Will and me on the arm or shoulder, Will occasionally shoots glances at me as though to signal that he is not really part of such business. Once or twice he even shakes his head a little while Howard is talking.*]

Will, now that you know more about what goes on than you used to, are you aware of more homosexuality aside from the guards?

WILL: Oh, now I hear stories about Manchester, for instance, of bars with female impersonators. And stories about Sheffield and Leeds. That they're centers.

HOWARD: A little while ago I got a boy up here, a fantastic little boy of fifteen in black leather with dyed hair, and he said he'd been used by forty men by the time he was fourteen. And he told me that Leeds was a very important center for homosexuality on a money basis. And Glasgow is said to be another center.

WILL: I'll tell you something else. The WRACs are just about all lesbians. I was going with a girl a couple of years ago, a big ugly thing, but very funny and a great sport. We had sex a few times, and she asked me once should she join the army. I said that after six months she'd turn lesbian if she did. And that's exactly what happened. Just like with policewomen. In fact, I almost got bashed by one of those WRACs once. We had summer camp in the country, and we went to a town nearby to drink. We saw a bunch of WRACs in the pub there, so I asked a girl for a date. Another one stood up with a pint pot in her fist and says, "You talk to her and I'll smash your teeth in. She's mine!"

HOWARD: Montgomery's Desert Rats wouldn't be disbanded because they were all in love with each other. You know, of course, about the Greek military ethos, and how homosexual love holds a military group together and raises their morale.

[*Will is shooting me looks again. It is getting late. Will and Howard are getting involved in an argument about whether Will's son should go to a comprehensive school or be sent by Howard through a public school. Howard is arguing for giving the boy the best start in the world, and Will is saying, almost in so many words, that he will not have his son turned into one of those high-class effeminate twots. Both are trying to get me to voice an opinion. I think it is time to leave. Howard smiles and presses a hand on my shoulder.*]

HOWARD: Well, Arno, I must say, you're a very attractive man. I just know that before you finish this book you're going to be gay yourself.

Thanks, Howard, I have about six months to go, and I'll let you know if anything changes.

PART TWO

10

The Scientific Overture

The scientific study of sex began just after the middle of the nineteenth century, as an anti-Victorian movement began in the European upper classes. Since science is no more disinterested than those who practice it, it showed a fumbling revolt against established sexual values and hidden special pleading to that end. Educated Victorian man, even more than his Enlightenment grandfather, was turning to the underbelly of psychic and social life. The development of psychiatry, anthropology, artistic Naturalism and Decadence all reflected the feeling that one must probe beneath the surface of a highly organized, repressive society to find the impulsive, primitive bedrock of life. Sex became a "problem," like poverty, and could no longer be taken for granted; it was time for investigation, reform and a new idealism.

Eighteenth-century studies of sex had been few, and mostly based on theories of physical constitution. The ideas of instinct, reflex, adaptation and association were unknown or just coming into use among philosophers and scientists. No one applied them yet to sexual life. De Sade reflected advanced thinking in his time, matching up physical traits and sexual behavior. For instance, he mentioned a pansexual woman who was hirsute, with a long clitoris and "virile anus." He assumed that sexual assertiveness was a masculine trait and must result from physical mannishness. De Sade predicted that when anatomy became a perfect science, the connection between constitution and sexual life would be clear. A pervert, he said, was " a sick person, like an hysterical woman." This sounds like a modern psychological view till one recalls that hysteria was then thought to be caused by displacement of the womb.

In the late eighteenth and early nineteenth centuries, there were occasional books and essays on sex, sexual offenses, nymphomania, satyriasis, hermaphroditism and homosexuality, mostly based as much on classical literature as on observation. In 1824 the German classicist Forberg collected erotic writings from antiquity and the Renaissance in his *Manual of Classical Erotology.* He said that the passive partner in sodomy must feel the same pleasure in his rectum that the active one felt in his penis. The best explanation he could find was that of Renaissance physician Coelius Rho-

181

diginus: "With people whose seminal ducts are not in a normal condition, be it that those leading to the mentula are paralyzed, as in the case with eunuchs and the like, or for any other reason, the seminal fluid flows back to its source. If this fluid is very abundant with them, it accumulates in great quantities, and then the part where the secretion is accumulated longs for friction."

The few scattered essays on deviance were less important sources of later scientific thinking about homosexuality than was the voluminous literature on masturbation. Men everywhere have explained in various ways that after orgasm they experience not only tension release but sometimes a slump of passivity and tiredness. If they feel guilt and anxiety about sex, they may experience this as depression, fatigue or disgust. Therefore men have often thought of sex as an experience of loss, debility or pollution—from the warnings of Hippocrates about depletion from loss of sperm, to the officer in *Doctor Strangelove* who feared the leaking away of his "precious bodily fluids." But masturbation was the subject of little medical or other attention until about 1717, when the *Urtext* of masturbation scare literature appeared anonymously in London—*Onania, or the Heinous Sin of Self-Pollution.*

The author was probably a cleric turned quack doctor. Onan's sinful act had really been coitus interruptus, not masturbation, but that was the least of the book's errors. It said that sex, but especially masturbation, sullied body, mind and soul. "Onanism" produced several diseases, vapors, epilepsy, madness, "lying, forswearing, perhaps murder." A half century later the book was in its eightieth edition, and the word onanism had become general for masturbation. At first, few medical men accepted the book unreservedly, but one who did was the famous Swiss physician Samuel Tissot. In 1758 there appeared his *Onania, or a Treatise upon the Disorders Produced by Masturbation.* Tissot said sexual excess, and especially the "flagrant crime of masturbation," caused dangerous loss of semen and thus opened the door to consumption, eye trouble and impotence. Since sexual activity sent blood rushing to the brain, too much of it produced melancholy, catalepsy, imbecility, numbness and nervous weakness.

This medical rationalization of masturbation guilt struck a sympathetic chord in the European psyche in the days leading up to Victorianism. Scientists and laymen alike made bogeys of masturbation and "sexual excess," as the Middle Ages had of witchcraft-*cum*-sodomy. When Benjamin Rush wrote the first American text on mental disorders in 1812, he said that masturbation had fearsome effects from consumption to "fatuity and death." Doctors thought there was a special type, "The Masturbator"—a male with downcast eyes, pallid skin and brooding, vacant air—whom they could spot on sight. The French psychologist Lallemand wrote in 1842, "He has no other interests; he loves no one; he is attached to no one; he shows no emotion before the grandeur of nature or the beauties of art . . . dead to the call of his family, his country or humanity." In 1863 the Scots physician David Skae defined a specific form of madness caused by masturbation.

By the middle of the nineteenth century it had become almost universal medical doctrine that sexual "excess" of any kind, but masturbation in particular, led to impotence, "masturbatory insanity" or perversion. Even liberal sex reformers argued that masturbation caused homosexuality. Lord Acton said that the "ordinary practice of sleeping with the hands bound behind one's back should not be ignored even by grown men." Others suggested infibulation. Doctors recommended cages, bandages, mittens and straitjackets to restrain the weak-willed. Though the tide of fright began to ebb at the turn of this century, such liberal sexologists as Havelock Ellis and Albert Moll suggested chastity devices for boys as late as the early 1920s.

Equally important to early scientific thinking about homosexuality was the work of Darwin. He began his notebooks on the transmutation of the species in 1836, at the age of twenty-seven, as a result of his observations as a naturalist aboard the H.M.S. *Beagle*. The next year he discovered the work of Malthus, and there he found a concept that helped him interpret his findings. Malthus, a prim English clergyman, had argued in his *Essay on Population* that a species' birth rate exceeds its food supply, so the weak perish in the competition for survival. The human birth rate, he argued, was now outstripping the world's food supply; as defense against this creeping peril, Malthus prescribed abstention and late marriage. He set an example by marrying at forty, still a virgin himself. He had already fathered, if nothing else, a movement. After the Malthusians came the Neo-Malthusians, who agreed on the need for population control but denied that sex was meant only for reproduction. From Neo-Malthusianism grew the modern birth-control movement.

But not until the 1880s did birth control become a widespread campaign and part of a general call for sexual emancipation. Darwin, in 1837, was concerned only with the idea that nature solved overpopulation by what he called "natural selection." Creatures whose deviations from the normal gave them a competitive advantage would perpetuate themselves and eventually create a better-adapted species. Those whose deviations put them at a disadvantage would die out.

Darwin found support in the geology of Lyell, who had shown the evolution of the planet through natural processes. Comparative anatomy and embryology would also bear him out. There were structural relationships between species, and each human embryo, as it develops, repeats the evolution of the whole animal kingdom. In 1859, after years of scrupulous documentation, Darwin published *On the Origin of the Species by Means of Natural Selection, or the Preservation of Favored Races in the Struggle for Life.*

"Social Darwinism," the interpretation of society in the light of Darwin's theory, was in tune with the era's outlook. Those poorly adapted to their environment would fail in life. To be colonizer or colonized, rich or poor, was itself a judgment of Nature. The terms fit and unfit, higher and lower, became moral values, invaded politics, literature and social science. Darwin himself tried to avoid glib analogies between biological and social life, but he did believe mankind had evolved from savagery to civilization. He presented the idea in 1871 in *The Descent of Man*, with a typically Victorian bias toward monogamy, sexual control and conformity. He argued that just as the amoeboid blobs of the primordial sea had developed into Lyells and Darwins, mankind had risen from an amoral, primitive horde right up the ladder of perfection to the Victorian middle class. Savages, said Darwin, demonstrate "intemperance, licentiousness and unnatural crimes." As among all creatures, the males compete for the females, and those with most power and attractiveness win out. Thus "sexual selection" sorts out the fit and unfit. The male is by nature competitive, selfish, ambitious, aggressive and lustful; the female, made for maternity, is more passive, tender and altruistic. (Apparently the sexes had always been Victorian.) Savages remained mired in this sort of life because their selfishness prevented cooperation. But mankind, in certain places and times, had learned that conscience and cooperation were to their practical advantage. Selfishness led to marriage, which created jealousy, which gave birth to a "moral sense," which created in turn monogamy, chastity and temperance.

So from Darwin's work the conclusion was drawn that Victorian sexual and social morality represented Nature's best judgment. The poor man, the criminal, the deviant, the prostitute, were hereditary, adaptive failures sliding backward to destruction amid the ranks of a progressing species. The idea that such "failures" owed their problem to degeneration of their genes gave rise to the term "degenerate." It soon had the same overtones as "sodomite." Science had replaced religion as a justification of traditional mores.

Meanwhile, the science of psychiatry was developing. The term had first been used in 1808. At the turn of the nineteenth century, Pinel in France and Tuke in England had unfettered the insane and tried to treat them. Only now did the idea lose ground that mental disorders were caused by witchcraft or humors. The new view was that insanity rose from injury or disease of the central nervous system. There were few effective treatments. Science kept largely to theorizing and classifying. The borderline between sanity and insanity seemed sharp; few people thought that those on both sides of it might share the same mental processes. After Darwin's work appeared, it was generally believed that the insane were biological failures, cursed through hereditary weakness with "neuropathy"—weakness of the nervous system—which made them hopeless drop-outs from the normal world of middle-class evolutionary success.

However, it remained difficult to explain that some people seemed normal except for one compulsion; though their reason was intact, they had irresistible impulses to murder, rape, arson or homosexual acts. In

1835 the English psychologist Pritchard introduced the concept of "moral insanity"—a "morbid perversion" of the feelings and impulses without delusion or loss of intellect. For almost a century scientists would classify homosexuality as a form of moral insanity.

Psychiatry gained ground quickly toward the end of the century. Such syndromes as manic-depression and catatonia were defined. The "masturbatory insanity" of Skae was redefined by Hecker in 1871 as hebephrenic schizophrenia, a psychosis that usually occurs at puberty, with rapid mental deterioration. Many hebephrenics masturbate constantly; Skae, in an age of acute masturbation-guilt, had confused cause and symptom. Despite such developments, old views on psychosexual life took a long time to break down. Until Freud's work became widely known, very few people sought the causes of sexual problems in the emotional and social environments. The concept of personality, as we use it, did not exist yet. Freud's professor of neurology at the Medical School in Vienna still objected to the very term psychiatry; he created a theory of mental disorders based on circulatory changes in the brain.

The one area of research that held some promise for treating sexual disorders was the one embracing hypnosis, hysteria and epilepsy. In the eighteenth century Anton Mesmer had "magnetized" into health people suffering from hysterical blindness. The phenomenon he discovered had been discredited and largely ignored until the middle of the nineteenth century, when it was revived and named hypnosis. The French physician Jean Charcot, director of the Saltpetrière asylum, tried to use it in treating hysteria. But he and his co-worker, Magnan, lumped epilepsy and hysteria together, confused by the common symptom of convulsions. They thought "hystero-epilepsy" was caused not by a displaced womb alone, as tradition said, but displaced ovaries as well, and so they treated it with hypnosis and an "ovarian compressor." Other doctors, also assuming (like the ancient Egyptians, Greeks and Romans) that convulsive disorders were connected with sex, treated them by castration in men and cauterization of the clitoris and ovariectomy in women. It was in this scientific atmosphere that Charcot and Magnan, as we shall see, eventually tried to cure fetishists and homosexuals with hypnosis.

Considering the general state of knowledge, it is often amusing but not surprising to read what passed for advanced scientific views of homosexuality. The two most quoted writers on the subject just after mid-century were the leading medico-legal experts of Germany and France, the doctors Casper and Tardieu. Both were chiefly concerned with whether the disgusting breed of pederasts could be physically identified for courts and whether they should be held legally responsible for their acts.

In 1852 and 1863 Casper put forth a distinction between "innate" and "acquired" homsexuality, an idea that would have long popularity. The majority of homosexuals, he said, were congenital; there was no "depraved fancy" at work in their case. But in others "the taste for this vice has been acquired in life, and is the result of oversatiety with natural pleasures. People of this stamp sometimes indulge their gross appetites alternately with either sex." The born pederast could be distinguished only where there had been long-term prostitution, for frequent sodomy brought certain changes in the appearance of the rectum.

This was an ancient observation. In Latin satires there were many jokes about it. Martial made puns about the *ficus*, which means both fig and hemorrhoid, to imply someone practiced sodomy. Juvenal similarly referred to "knobs"—papillary growths of the anus. Paulus Zacchius, in a medico-legal treatise of 1726, referred to obliteration of the radial folds around the anus as a sign of sodomy. In the nineteenth century, Casper, Tardieu and many others devoted essays to whether lack of radial folds, a "funnel-shaped" rectum and syphilitic chancres of the anus invariably resulted from sodomy and could be taken as legal proof of it.

In some ways, though, Casper took an innovative view of homosexuality. He was one of the first scientists to stress that some homosexuals felt true love for each other—even, he said, "a warmth of passion more fervent than is common in the relations of the opposed sexes." He also broke tradition by pointing out that homosexuality and sodomy are not synonymous, for many homosexuals never in their lives experience anal intercourse.

The other great expert, Tardieu, in his text on forensic medicine of 1857, was far more typical of his times; he portrayed homosexuals as degraded monsters, not only morally but physically different from other men. The active pederast, he said, has a slender, underdeveloped penis with a small glans, tapering from root to tip like a dog's. (He also believed that sensual women were hirsute.) He maintained that even before sodomy ever took place, the homosexual's rectum was smooth and lacked radial folds.

The first* serious major work exclusively about homosexuality was written by a homosexual, and it had a long influence on scientific thought. The author was Karl Heinrich Ulrichs, a lawyer and writer born in Hanover in 1825. Between 1862 and his death more than three decades later, he turned out numerous books and pamphlets explaining and defending homosexuality—first under the pseudonym Numa Numantius, and then under his own name.

The homosexual, said Ulrichs, is neither criminal nor insane. He is the product of abnormal embryonic development. Ulrichs pointed out that at an early stage of development the genital tissue of the human embryo is undifferentiated; only after a few months does it develop as male or as female. In the male homosexual, he said, the genitals became male, but the same differentiation failed to take place in the part of the brain that determines sex drive. The result is an *animal muliebris virile corpore inclusa*—a female soul in a male body. This is inborn and unchangeable, but not any more pathological than color blindness. Freud, a half century later, would

---

*Heinrich Hössli, a homosexual Swiss milliner, wrote a two-volume work on homosexuality in the 1830s, but it was largely an apologia based on classical literature.

look to the sexually undifferentiated embryo to show why, as he thought, everyone contains at least latent homosexual drive. Ulrichs gave case histories in which homosexuals said they had been so as far back as they could remember—proof, said Ulrichs, that they'd been born that way. This argument would be accepted for a long time—as would his assertion, based on his own observations, that most homosexuals whistle poorly or not at all.

The word homosexual hadn't been coined yet, and Ulrichs would not accept sodomite or pederast. He turned to Plato's *Symposium,* where it was said that "those dedicated to the goddess Urania feel themselves drawn exclusively to males." He Germanized the word Uranian into *urning,* and it was widely used for fifty years, along with his intricate classification of homosexuals into active or passive and then by preference in sexual partner—for instance, a *mannling* is an active urning attracted to effeminate men, and a *zwischen-urning* one who prefers adolescents.

Ulrichs concluded that since homosexuals were different but not inferior or sick, persecuting them was a brutal injustice, like punishing the left-handed. Since homosexuality was inborn, the fear of homosexuals seducing heterosexuals was absurd—after all, he said, congenitally heterosexual boys healthily throw off boarding-school homosexuality. Anyway, the ancient Greeks were standing proof that homosexuality was not destructive to society. Homosexual love was as pure, elevated and elevating as heterosexual love. The reason for antihomosexual prejudice, said Ulrichs, was that all sex was in some way repugnant. With that quaint argument, he embarked on pamphleteering for full legal rights for homosexuals, including their right to legally marry one another.

In 1869, when Ulrichs was defending Uranian love as separate but equal, a Hungarian doctor named Benkert was writing another pamphlet on the subject, under the pseudonym Kertbeny. He coined the word homosexual from the Greek *homos,* meaning same. The pamphlet and the word went largely unnoticed at the time, but that same year, in Berlin, there appeared in the journal *Archiv für Psychiatrie* a study of transvestites more systematic and objective than anything yet written on sexual deviance. The author was the journal's editor, Dr. Karl Westphal, a distinguished professor of psychiatry and one of the first men to describe obsessional states and agoraphobia.

Westphal's paper on what he dubbed "contrary sexual feeling" said that it was a kind of moral insanity due to "congenital reversal of sexual feeling." The paper drew tremendous attention. Doctors began to send papers on perversions to the journal, and the phrase "contrary sexual feeling" remained in use in Germany and other countries for decades. Westphal himself went on to study more than two hundred cases of homosexuality. During the next two decades the trickle of writings on sexual behavior, and especially on deviant sexuality, would become a flood.

The next crucial paper was "Inversion of the Genital Sense," by Charcot and Magnan, in 1882. These French doctors, already famous for their work with hysteria and hypnosis, claimed to have had some therapeutic success with sexual deviants. They got into a theoretical mess trying to explain why hypnosis should help a congenital condition, but they had that problem dealing with hysteria, too, and they found ways around it. Like most doctors of the time, they said the cause of psychosexual problems was constitutional nervous weakness due to hereditary degeneration. Magnan, echoing Ulrichs, said the male homosexual had a woman's brain in a man's body; he never showed how male and female brains differ. Still, Charcot's and Magnan's work provoked a flood of studies, and others adopted their terms "invert," "inversion" and "stigmata of degeneration."

The great psychiatrist Janet and other luminaries of the day joined the hunt for proofs of hereditary inferiority in deviants. The eminent Dr. Moreau wrote that homosexuals form "an intermediate class . . . a real link between reason and madness . . . explained by one word: Heredity." Like most forward-looking doctors, he wanted to save sexual offenders from prison and put them under medical care—in asylums. The distinguished Swiss scientist August Forel agreed that homosexuals were not vice-ridden and depraved, but victims of degenerated genes; they should not be punished, even though "nearly all inverts are in a more or less marked degree psychopaths or neurotics. . . . The excesses of female inverts exceed those of the male. One orgasm succeeds another, night and day, almost without interruption."

Where did this damage to the genes come from? Certainly from nervous disorders, perhaps alcoholism, too. One authoritative explanation came from Russia, where many works on deviance were written between the mid-nineteenth century and the First World War. The most famous Russian sexologist was Benjamin Tarnowski, a St. Petersburg doctor and expert in forensic medicine. He was the trusted physician of many homosexuals, and his practice gave him a glimpse of homosexual life in urban Russia. He decided that in some cases homosexuality was acquired—these people read dirty books, kept bad company, lived luxuriously, and were so jaded by sexual excess that they took up homosexuality and other bizarre practices for kicks. It was only such "real vice, acquired sex perversion in a healthy man . . . that deserves fitting punishment." Born homosexuals couldn't help themselves. Their condition came from damage to their parents' genes resulting from hysteria, epilepsy, alcoholism, anemia, typhus, debauchery, soil, climate and altitude.

Many theoreticians concentrated on the "bisexuality" of the human embryo. Some lower animals have both male and female sex organs; higher animals have evolved into two monosexes, male and female. Human beings repeat in embryo the development from undifferentiated (or "bisexual") to either male or female. Two Chicago psychiatrists, Kiernan and Lydston, in papers between 1884 and 1892, made a detailed classification of types of homosexuals and claimed that they had not moved fully from the lower, hermaphroditic stage of evolution to the higher monosexual stage. Gley and

Chevalier in France built similar theories of bisexuality and a resulting "psychic hermaphroditism." Scientists everywhere agreed, attributing homosexuality to a failure to pass beyond a primitive, ancestral condition of bisexuality.

This idea was taken to its logical extreme by the Italian psychiatrist and criminologist Cesare Lombroso. His theory was that acts called criminal in civilized society are natural among animals and common among primitive men. With the growth of civilization, humans outgrow robbery, murder, promiscuity and perversion. Each child is a savage at birth; he must repeat society's evolution and become civilized. If he fails to do so, he becomes a criminal, a deviant, a prostitute, a mental defective. He is an atavism—in the civilized world, a case of moral insanity.

To prove his point and establish a science of "criminal anthropology," Lombroso measured the skulls, bodies and features of criminals, prostitutes, idiots, arsonists, the poor, and homosexuals. In *Criminal Man*, in 1876, he revealed that he had found in them such primitive characteristics as jutting jaws, malformed craniums and close-set eyes. Once discovered, he said, these people should be separated from the rest of humanity and kept from reproducing. In *The Female Offender,* in 1893, he said that prostitutes and female criminals are mannish, implying that criminality, prostitution, lesbianism and physical masculinization are identical.

Lombroso's work stimulated tremendous enthusiasm and research. All over Europe, and especially in Italy and Germany, scientists studied prostitutes and lesbians. Some found that the facts didn't bear out Lombroso, but others did.* One researcher discovered that the fingerprints of prostitutes were "inferior" to those of "normal women." Since women were by nature sexually unaggressive, the sensual woman and prostitute must be mannish. Studies revealed masturbation and lesbianism among prostitutes, and that was evidence of their masculinity. Someone suggested that prostitutes were a subgroup of congenital homosexuals.

Lombroso and most scientists of his time, having been raised in the Victorian middle class, were shocked by working-class life, with its lack of impulse control. Poverty, crime, perversion and mental disorders tended to coalesce in their thinking. Lombroso eloquently said that the "born prostitute" and the criminal, identical and morally insane, had "the same lack of. moral sense, the same hardness of heart, the same precocious taste for evil . . . for facile pleasures, for the orgy and for alcohol." Inspired by such thinking, a London magistrate wrote in the *Ethnological Journal* of the "same deteriorated physique and decadent moral fibre" of male tramps, petty thieves, beggars and prostitutes. Even animals did not escape such

*There is a story that Lombroso took the anthropologist Westermarck on a tour of an Italian prison, explaining as they walked that the criminal type always has a projecting big toe. Lombroso removed the shoes of two prisoners, but neither had the predicted equipment. Westermarck tactfully decided not to exhibit his own projecting big toes and thus proffer a third exception to the rule.

study. In 1896 a French scientist named Cornevin published in the *Archives d'anthropologie criminelle* a monograph called "Contribution to the study of criminality in animals; perversion of the genital sense in a stallion."

Even many of Lombroso's critics shared his basic approach. Scientists who did not stress atavism and degeneracy went on seeking a constitutional basis for sexual deviance. They studied the skulls, blood chemistry and sex organs of homosexuals. Ulrichs had said that many homosexuals could not whistle; case histories taken all over Europe dutifully noted whether the subject could whistle. Lesbians' ability to whistle was considered a sign of mannishness—as were their smoking, drinking and masturbating. Many scientists looked for lack of differentiation or reversal of sexual characteristics—narrow hips and big hands in lesbians, the opposite in male homosexuals—and found what they had expected. Hirschfeld and Fliess in Germany studied left-handedness in homosexuals; they thought it an important sign of "inverted secondary sexual characteristics." Studies were made of homosexuals' facial and body hair. (This was being done with all mental problems: two French scientists in 1901 studied a thousand sane and a thousand insane women and found abundant facial hair in 23 per cent of the sane, 50 per cent of the insane.) When one Dr. Bernhardi of Berlin found an absence of spermatozoa in five effeminate homosexuals, he felt he had discovered the solution to an "enigma of many thousand years." The passive pederast was a "monster of the feminine sex, having nothing else in common with the male than the male genitals, which in some cases are only imperfectly developed."

Meanwhile, truly important contributions were made to the study of sex. During the last decades of the nineteenth century, research increased in Germany, France, Italy and Russia. Papers began to appear in Spain and the United States. In France, Lasegue defined exhibitionism as a distinct perversion, and Binet wrote the first study of fetishism. The German Näcke and the English Havelock Ellis developed the concept of narcissism. Although Näcke looked for a "homosexual center" in the brain at one time, he also wrote about homosexual dreams in heterosexuals well before Freud. Unfortunately, most of this work remained unread by the general public. Instead they were likely to read the books of someone like Paola Mantegazza.

Mantegazza was an Italian doctor and anthropologist who wrote several books calling for scientific sexology, public frankness, sex education and equality of the sexes. His *Sexual Relations of Mankind* and other books—farragoes of medicine, psychology and anecdotal anthropology—hedged every liberal call with reservations and cries of disgust. Even so, they created such scandal in the 1870s and 1880s that he almost lost his professorship and his seat in the Italian senate.

Mantegazza began his section on homosexuality in *Sexual Relations of Mankind* by calling it "one of the most terrifying facts to be met in human psychology." It had three possible causes. In some cases, the genital nerves were distributed around the rectum. In others, homosexuality was not a vice but a passion of psychic origin, "specific to intelligent men, cultivated and frequently neurotic." And last, there was a group whose homosexuality was caused by the *larghezza desolante,* or desolating largeness, of the human vagina, which made some men turn to the cozy tightness of the male rectum!

The pinnacle of the period's sexology was Richard von Krafft-Ebing's *Psychopathia Sexualis—A Medico-Forensic Study.* This ponderous, pedantic volume on sexual perversions became the West's most widely read and influential scientific treatise on sex, the Old Testament of its field. Krafft-Ebing was born in Mannheim, Germany, in 1840. He became a specialist in nervous diseases, director of a mental institution, and an expert in medico-legal problems. In 1887 his great book appeared, and three years later he moved to Vienna as a professor of psychiatry and neurology. When he died in 1902, *Psychopathia Sexualis* was in its twelfth edition, revised and expanded—in fact, it contained cases of deviants who had visited Krafft-Ebing for help after reading earlier editions of the book.

Krafft-Ebing began with a review of current knowledge of sex. As the subtitle shows, he was concerned with whether deviants were willful lawbreakers or victims of innate drives. He tried to be objective, but he spoke of "unnatural practices," because he believed that sex was meant for reproduction and that "man puts himself on a level with the beasts if he seeks to gratify lust." With Darwin, he believed that only tempering lust with altruism and restraint made civilization possible, and that "in the sunny balm of Christian doctrine," monogamy and woman's "divine virtue" would finally flourish. Like most Victorians, he believed that sexual "excess" weakened the body, especially masturbation. He defined the process in detail, making a coherent theory of various ideas then current about excess, heredity and perversion.

Krafft-Ebing held that climate and social circumstances influence sexuality—witness the "greater sensuality of southern races." However, since sex drive rises from the brain and the sex glands, sexual disorders must have their origins in either or both those parts of the body. Hormones had not yet been discovered, and no sexual center had been found in the brain; so Krafft-Ebing had to spend many pages on learned-sounding fumbling about the precise nature of normal and abnormal sexual physiology. But at least the genetic and evolutionary theories worked out in recent years provided a basic groundwork for explanations of the perversions.

The bulk of *Psychopathia Sexualis* consists of hundreds of cases of "paresthesia," or "perversion of the sexual instinct," with descriptions of sexual acts in Latin to protect the imperfectly educated. Each case begins with an evaluation of the subject's heredity, noting the presence of insanity, epilepsy, hysteria, convulsions, alcoholism and severe physical disorders in his family. Some of these people, because of genetic flaws, had failed to differentiate properly at the time of fetal bisexuality. The result was physical and mental feminization in men and masculinization in women.

The congenital urning had no heterosexual feelings, was physically feminized and showed an interest in cooking, sewing, *belles-lettres* and other feminine occupations, "even to the extent of giving himself entirely to the cultivation of the beautiful." The female congenital invert was physically mannish and showed an interest in "manly sports." The majority of innate male homosexuals showed no physical resemblance to the opposite sex; it was only their brains that had been feminized. There were also people who practiced both homosexuality and heterosexuality—"psychic hermaphrodites" who had differentiated normally in their bodies but remained bisexual in their nervous systems. Unfortunately, Krafft-Ebing never did locate the genes that determine interest in soccer and embroidery.

Throughout the book, Krafft-Ebing distinguished such innate paresthesia from acquired perversion, for medical and legal reasons. However, he argued that even acquired homosexuality could exist only if there was some hereditary weakness of the nervous system, for it was "questionable whether an untainted individual is capable of homosexual feelings at all." Some people, because of genetic flaws, had weakened and super-irritable nervous systems. These neuropaths were highly excitable sexually; their precocious and excessive sex activity did further damage to their fragile nerves; then they needed stronger stimulation to satisfy their failing nervous systems, and so on in a vicious cycle that took them from masturbation to homosexuality to impotence. This was more likely to occur in man, because woman, "if physically and mentally normal, and properly educated, has but little sexual desire. . . . She remains passive. Her sexual organization demands it, and the dictates of good breeding come to her aid."

There was nothing revolutionary in most of this, but the book did contain many new ideas, including some shrewd if undeveloped psychological insights. For instance, Krafft-Ebing grasped well the psychological aura of fetishism and compulsive masturbation, the withdrawal from human contact into fantasy, isolation and obsession. Sadism was a long-accepted term; Krafft-Ebing named and defined its counterpart as masochism, after the contemporary German writer Leopold van Sacher Masoch, who was then turning out stories about men whose sexual pleasure came from tortures and humiliations inflicted on them by booted and furred female sadists. Krafft-Ebing explained sadism and masochism as distortions of natural male aggressiveness and female passivity—again, innate or acquired, but always with a hereditary, neuropathic basis. If masochism was just an exaggeration of female submissiveness, he theorized, it must represent "partial effemination" in a man. "Observation shows that masochists really possess feminine traits of character. This renders it intelligible that the masochistic element is so frequently found in homosexual men." He further saw that shoe-and-foot fetishism was often combined with masochism; he called it a form of "latent masochism."

It had been noticed before that several perversions can coexist in one person; Magnan and the famous German doctor Albert Moll had recorded cases of homosexuals who were also sado-masochists or fetishists. But in this, as in everything else, Krafft-Ebing presented a more complete and systematic explanation than anyone before him. The book's great strength was its exhaustiveness and authoritative voice. The scattered fragments of sexual study had finally been fitted together into a patchy but nevertheless broad system. Of course it is easy now to find fault with the book. It contained all the cultural prejudices of its day. It is laced with ominous warnings against masturbation and cries of disgust at any but the most limited sex life. The statements of patients were taken at face value. Some of the diagnoses are curious by our standards. But the book had a great impact on both the public and scientists.

Laymen saw for the first time a world some had hardly dreamed existed. This fat volume in German and Latin, impeccably medical, contained cases of lust-murder, sexual cannibalism and necrophilia; of a man who visited a Paris brothel to have prostitutes laid out in white shrouds; of coprophiliacs and fetishists; of a man whose great sexual delight was gathering pubic hair from brothel beds with his teeth. One typical case history begins:

> Workman, aged twenty-seven, [genes] heavily tainted, tic in the face, troubled with phobia (especially agoraphobia) and alcoholism. He experiences the greatest pleasure if the prostitutes defecate and urinate into his mouth. He pours wine over the bodies of whores and catches it in his mouth, which he applies to the prostitute's genitals. His delight is intense if he can suck the menstrual blood as it flows out of the vagina. He is a fetishist of ladies' gloves and slippers; he kisses his sister's shoes when her feet perspire. His desire achieves the greatest satisfaction only when prostitutes tread on him: more so, if he is flagellated to the effusion of blood. When flagellated, on his bent knees, he asks the prostitute's pardon and mercy; then he begins to masturbate.

Many such people were gentlemen and ladies with respectable family and public lives. Behind their social façade lay a cesspool of secret perversion and madness. A bizarre new sexual reality was being displayed, and it was difficult even for Dr. Krafft-Ebing to say whether it was more revolting or more pitiful. Deviation was no longer a subject for gossip and anecdote, as in Brantôme. It was a ghastly, haunting deformity for science to study. Many of Krafft-Ebing's patients had visited him because they were on the verge of suicide over their sexual problems. *Psychopathia Sexualis* contained a letter from a homosexual to the author that has often been quoted. It was a new sort of document to many doctors and laymen. The author could not be seen merely as a joke or a social or moral outrage; he was a suffering human being. It said (I condense):

You have no idea what a constant struggle we all must endure, and how we suffer under the prevailing false ideas about us and our so-called "immorality." The youthful urning, when he feels the first sexual promptings and naïvely expresses them to his comrades, soon finds that he is not understood; he shrinks into himself. If he tells his parents or teacher what moves him, he is told it must be fought and overcome at any price. Then an inner conflict begins. Some continue the conflict for a longer or shorter time, and thus injure themselves; others at last cease to try to do the impossible—the repression of instinct. Then, however, begin constant suffering and excitement. He sees men that attract him, but he dares not say—nay, not even betray by a look—what his feelings are. He thinks that he alone of all the world has such abnormal feelings. Onanism is practiced inordinately, and followed by all the evil results of that vice. Or let us suppose the urning has had the rare fortune to soon find a person like himself. But he cannot be approached openly, as a lover approaches the girl he loves. In constant fear, both must conceal their relations. Even in this relation is forged a chain of anxiety and fear that the secret will be betrayed or discovered, which leaves them no joy in the indulgence. Another less fortunate man falls into the hands of a blackmailer, and the more he gives, the more voracious the vampire becomes. The nerves give way, insanity comes on. I do not think I err when I declare that at least half of the suicides of young men are due to such conditions. By far the great number of cases of mental disturbance in urnings are caused by the existing notions concerning urnings, and the resulting laws, and dominant public sentiment. Anyone with an adequate idea of the mental and moral suffering, of the anxiety and care that the urning must endure; of the constant hypocrisy and secrecy he must practice; of the difficulties that meet him in satisfying his natural desire—can only be surprised that more insanity and nervous disturbance does not occur.

At the end of the book, Krafft-Ebing called for tolerance and legal reform. He asked for the repeal of the harsh antihomosexual Article 175 of the German criminal code. One should not punish a sickness, he said, especially one for which there was little hope of cure. Krafft-Ebing did hope to at least encourage the heterosexual side of the bisexual. Perhaps hypnosis could help homosexuals and fetishists. He put one patient in a deep hypnotic trance and told him repeatedly to give up masturbation, abhor homosexuality, stop finding men handsome, and fall in love with a virtuous woman. He had some limited, short-range success with hypnosis, but no definite permanent cures. The important action one could take, he concluded, was to protect young homosexually predisposed people from blossoming into perverts. Masturbation must be prevented, and boys should not be allowed to sleep or swim together unsupervised.

Krafft-Ebing had to stop several times in his book to argue with another school of scientific thought. The French psychologist Binet, who had made the pioneer study of fetishism, put great stress on the mental process of association; for instance, a boy might have an erection while watching a woman who held a handkerchief scented with lilac perfume, the two cognitions (sexual arousal and a lilac-scented hanky) became linked in his mind, and he developed into a fetishist who felt pleasure only in the presence of lilac-scented hankies. Krafft-Ebing, Moll and most of the scientific world seized on the idea. For instance, Krafft-Ebing gave this case history in his section on "Acquired Masochism." "At the age of seven he was taught to masturbate by a servant girl. X first experienced pleasure in these manipulations when the girl happened to touch his member with her shoe-clad foot. Thus, in the predisposed boy, an association was established."

The key word is "predisposed." Why did accidents become associated with sex in one person but not in another? Did constitution or environment matter more? Binet stressed environment. A few famous psychiatrists supported him—the eminent Germans Näcke, Bloch and Schrenk-Notzing. They said general nervous weakness was predisposition enough; "acquired homosexuality" was essentially a matter of association. Here Krafft-Ebing drew the line. It was logical, he said, to explain fetishism or masochism by an environmental accident, but when it came to homosexuality, "Psychological forces are insufficient to explain manifestations of so thoroughly degenerated a character."

A controversy raged in books and journals for a couple of decades, and opinion fell progressively behind Krafft-Ebing rather than Binet. The idea of environment rather than constitution could not yet marshal much evidence. The famous and prolific French psychiatrist Charles Féré said that the very idea of acquired homosexuality was a delusion; there had to be an inborn leaning. The equally famous Moll agreed. In 1898 the Frenchman Thoinot settled the question to many people's satisfaction by presenting the idea of "retarded inversion"; actually, what people called acquired homosexuality was really congenital inversion that did not show itself until late in life. Näcke and Bloch finally abandoned Binet's view. The environmental school had lost the day.

The other great controversy through these decades was whether homosexuality was a kind of biological failure or just a nonpathological oddity like left-handedness or color-blindness. A great victory came for the oddity argument when the master, Krafft-Ebing, wavered. In 1901, a year before he died, he wrote a paper in which he conceded that his lifelong stress on "degeneracy" had been wrong. Although many deviants showed mental disorders and neuropathy, homosexuality was not itself a disease; it was a congenital anomaly compatible with psychic health. Iwan Bloch, first a serious psychiatrist and later a sloppy, silly popularizer, agreed with this. Havelock Ellis, Magnus Hirschfeld and other prominent men of the generation after Krafft-Ebing reached a wide public with their argument for anomaly rather than pathology.

By the turn of this century, a majority scientific view had emerged and began to filter down to laymen. Homosexuality was congenital, caused by hereditary damage that appeared as neuropathy, and was exacerbated by masturbation. Probably the embryonic bisexual stage had never been surmounted. (It was becoming common for books on reproduction and sex to contain such statements as "all individuals are potentially bisexual.") There was a good chance that homosexuality, though, was not pathological; in any case, it should not be punished. Since it was congenital, it was incurable. The early hope for hypnosis, held by Krafft-Ebing and a few others, disappeared. In fact, said Féré, trying to "cure" a homosexual of his innate drive was an attempt to pervert his true instincts. Besides, it was dangerous, for if he married, he would pass on his hereditary taint. The homosexual, said Féré, should make chastity his ideal.

INTERVIEWS

Dr. Gerald Feigen is a proctologist, a specialist in disorders of the rectum and colon. In Krafft-Ebing's day, his field was considered first in knowledge of homosexuality. And it is true that he has acquired a great deal of special knowledge about homosexuals, though not what Krafft-Ebing would have expected. Dr. Feigen has also worked with emotionally disturbed children, been a writer, consultant and sort of guru to the staff of Ramparts. *He is a slender man of medium height with a bushy black mustache and deep-set, dark eyes. We sit at a table at Enrico's, a cafe that has long been a meeting place for artists and intellectuals in San Francisco. I bring up the question of the old forensic studies of homosexuality, which talked about changes in the rectum due to sodomy—obliteration of the folds around the anus, the "funnel-shaped" rectum, piles and so on. He says:*

The only change in the ano-rectal region due to sodomy is that the rectal canal will dilate if the anus is touched. The external sphincter has enough muscle tone to close, but if you touch it, the whole lower canal opens up immediately. And people who practice sodomy often show the common ano-rectal disorders two decades earlier than usual—at twenty or thirty instead of forty or fifty. They get hemorrhoids, fissures, fistulas. You also see condylomas, what are sometimes called venereal warts. Often these are associated with gonorrhea, but sometimes they occur without it. Actually, they're caused by a virus, to which some people have immunity, while others don't. I've seen venereal warts cause real sexual paranoia among homosexuals. A man gets warts or rectal gonorrhea, and his partner yells, "You've been shacking up with somebody behind my back!" And then there's a big fight.

One thing about homosexual sodomy. Alfred Kinsey and I once discussed the reaction of the passive partner. Kinsey believed that the passive one only gets his prostate tickled, without experiencing orgasm. I've often asked male patients who perform passive sodomy, "Do you enjoy it, and do you have an orgasm? Or are you just servicing your partner so that you'll get serviced in return?" About 50 per cent enjoyed sodomy and actually had an orgasm from it. The rest didn't like sodomy but allowed it as a favor to the active partner. They didn't experience orgasm. Of course, some homosexuals practice sodomy exclusively, some occasionally, some rarely.

I learned a great deal during my years as a consultant to the state prisons. The rectum is the biggest salable item in jail. I once saw a kid whose ribs had been cracked from being grabbed and raped from behind. Some of the men in prison gussy up their anal areas to make themselves look female—parting the hair and so on.

Back in the fifties all prisoners who confessed to homosexuality, whether it was true or not, were put in a common compound. Some straights said they were queer so that they could steal commissary checks from the queers. They were called "commissary punks." Other straights said they were queer so that they'd be put among queers and get some kind of sex; they felt it was better than none.

A great deal that the proctologist learns about homosexuals comes from the fact he is the one to treat them for rectal damage and rectal VD—especially rectal gonorrhea and syphilis. The rise in veneral disease in recent years is largely due to two groups, teeny-boppers and homosexuals. There are public-health campaigns to teach the symptoms of rectal VD, but they're sometimes easy even for a doctor to miss. Especially in the case of syphilis. A homosexual guy may get involved without any preliminaries and have contact with ten or twelve different men in a week. Because of soreness from sodomy, he may not realize that he has a syphilitic chancre in his rectum. And unless his doctor does a very careful examination, including the dark-field test, he may miss it, too.

Many homosexuals go to homosexual doctors, who know about rectal VD and send the patient to a proctologist for diagnosis and treatment. But some doctors, especially in small communities, aren't familiar with the problem and may overlook rectal VD. Worse, even in a large city, a straight doctor may get anxious dealing with homosexuals and lecture more than he examines. The patient may be antagonized and not finish the examination or come back for treatment. So the primary syphilitic lesion is missed, and it disappears. The secondary lesion is at least as easily missed, and it disappears in turn. Then over the next ten years you see tertiary syphilis and locomotor ataxia—paralysis.

Is there anything special you've noticed in recent years besides the rise in VD?

Generally, patients are more frank today about admitting to homosexuality. They used to cop out more about how they got infected. There has also been a slight shift in occupations, I think. Most of my homosexual cases have always been white-collar workers. A decade ago they were mostly hairdressers, florists, decorators and so on. Lately there have been more who hold clerical jobs, personnel jobs, work in cybernetics. I think their bosses are mostly unaware, because the man doesn't act campy on the job. Of course I do get others, at both ends of the scale—a small number of rich men who keep male mistresses, and a few indigents who are male prostitutes.

I should say, too, that I've treated quite a few male homosexuals who are married to women. I'm amazed that so few of the wives knew their husbands were practicing homosexuals, although I did have a woman patient recently who complained frantically because some man was flirting with both her and her husband.

I've come to the conclusion that most homosexuals are latent heterosexuals. I made a careful survey of several hundred, and I found that the main common denominator was a weak or absent father and a shrewish mother. The notion of "male" and "female" partners is inaccurate. A small percentage always take the female role; another small percentage are muscle men, homosexual pin-ups, who always take the active role. But for the most part, they often switch roles.

What bothers me is that if you've written papers on this subject, you're called on by an assortment of homosexual societies to give talks. I don't mind giving talks before groups of doctors, students or members of the American Social Health Society, but talking to homosexual groups is out with me. They really want to talk about how more folks than meet the eye are homosexual, and that there should be a revision of the law.

I agree about the law. At present it's absurd, and allows for blackmail and harassment. Homosexuality should be taken out of the police and prison system and moved over to public health and psychiatry. But I don't think homosexual clubs should have a booth at the state fair to distribute literature, as they've requested. I think unhappiness is the key word in the homosexual life. Homosexuality has to be accepted, but not approved of. Society doesn't improve with an increase in homosexuality. And we have to be wary of psychologists who claim that homosexuals are no different from anyone else. I believe that as society and psychiatric technique advance, the number of homosexuals will dwindle to the irreducible minimum of emotional derelicts.

11

The Witch Reborn

A nightmare vision of sex appeared more and more frequently in Western literature through the nineteenth century, darker and more frightful even as the anti-Victorian reaction gained momentum. It showed spectacularly in the late Romantics and Decadents. Mario Praz, in *The Romantic Agony*, describes the rise of the cult of Medusean beauty, a cult of "hospitals, brothels, purgatory, hell, anguish without end." Literature was full of grotesques, hags, prostitutes, impotent diabolists, vampires, graveyards, dungeons, agony, perversity, bats, lizards and rot. More and more, sex appeared as open or suggested homosexuality, sado-masochism, incest and necrophilia.

The new character on the literary forestage was a female destroyer who consumed delicate and chaste young men, a charnel house to which they stumbled in fatal fascination. She had her beginnings in Keats's *Belle Dame Sans Merci*, in Mérimée's *Carmen* and *Venus d'Ille*, a woman of stone who crushed young bridegrooms to death in her arms. This literary attack on woman as a sexual ghoul had no parallel since the witch hunts. Schopenhauer sourly declared, "It is only the man whose intellect is clouded by his sexual impulses that could give the name of *the fair sex* to that undersized, narrow-shouldered, broad-hipped and short-legged race." Poe, Baudelaire, Novalis, Pater, Swinburne, Wilde, D'Annunzio, Huysmann, Mendès and Schwob turned woman into a harpy, a succubus. She was the Salomé of Beardsley,* the rotting animal with sprawled legs that reminded Baudelaire of a woman in rut, the lady of the House of Usher in her world of madness, ruin, death and necrophilia. At this time a violent wrenching of traditional sex roles was occurring, and the increasingly frequent depiction of woman as destroyer and as lesbian seems to have been related to it.

During the first three quarters of the century, lesbianism occurred most commonly in French art and literature. In paintings, lesbians were usually seen as written pornography had always tended to show them—sensual and uninhibited, like the unfettered pagans of libidinous imagination, who would indulge any and all desires. They were female Casanovas and roués

---

*Beardsley was long suspected of having been homosexual, but his most recent and thorough biographer, Stanley Weintraub, concludes that he was impotent or, in effect, asexual, rather than homosexual.

who went from pleasure to pleasure, excess to excess. This type appeared in literature as well—for instance, as Daudet's Sappho. But there was also the tradition that lesbians were hermaphrodites or mannish, and Gautier observed this in *Mademoiselle de Maupin*. Like Dekker's *Roaring Girl*, it was loosely based on the life of an actual transvestite. Though not explicitly homosexual. Mlle. de Maupin was the first of a lesbian type that would soon be common in literature—tall, wide-shouldered and narrow-hipped, skilled in riding and fencing, aggressive, domineering, the mannish counterpart of the effeminate male. She described herself as "of a third sex, one that has as yet no name above or below," and she went out into the world dressed as a man to live a man's life.

Another touch of more realistic psychological portraiture came from Baudelaire. His publisher announced the coming appearance of a book of poems called *Les Lesbiennes*, but it seems that threat of censorship stopped the project. Later, the original edition of the *Fleurs de mal* was to have contained three poems dealing with lesbians (probably those announced in the earlier, abortive volume), but the longest was removed, along with five other poems. They were not publicly printed until 1911. Baudelaire romanticized lesbianism as a defiant state of damnation, but he had some psychological understanding of it. One of his poems is a shrewd emotional portrait of a clever, aggressive lesbian seducing a passive and unhappy girl as the latter dreams of being loved by a man.

Paul Verlaine led a life of alternating heterosexuality and homosexuality. His famous affair with Arthur Rimbaud was recently the subject of Christopher Hampton's play *Total Eclipse*. In 1867 Verlaine had printed in Brussels a book of six poems entitled *Les Amies, Scènes d'Amour Sapphique*. They were more explicit than Baudelaire's poems, and they showed lesbianism as a lonely and futile way of life. Lesbianism was also mentioned more or less openly by Coleridge, Christina Rossetti and a few other writers, but the first attempt in Western literature to treat lesbianism seriously as a subject in itself was a second-rate novel by a hack quasi-pornographer, *Mlle Giraud, Ma Femme*, by Adolph Belot.

Belot was a prolific writer of titillating novels, including one about a male homosexual organization in Germany that achieved great notoriety. Perhaps capitalizing on the fact that Westphal's pioneer studies of homosexuality around 1870 had made a stir that went beyond scientific circles, he wrote a novel about a lesbian. *Le Figaro* started to print it in serial form, but soon stopped "in the interest of morality." Nevertheless, *Mlle Giraud* came out as a book and was reprinted several times within a decade.

Mlle. Giraud was a young lady who refused sexual consummation to her husband. He found out why when he discovered her lesbian love nest, an apartment significantly containing such books as *La Réligieuse*, *Mlle Maupin* and Balzac's *The Girl with the Golden Eyes*, all of which deal with lesbianism. Mlle. Giraud's lover was also a married woman, and M.

Giraud sought out her husband. The two men tried to separate their wives, but without success. Mlle. Giraud explained that lesbianism was caused by the segregation of girls in boarding schools, where loneliness drove them together. Her husband saw she was not merely "depraved" but "morally ill"—for the times, a radically kind concession. Despite discussions, intrigues and consultations with doctors, the affair between the women couldn't be stopped. Finally Mlle. Giraud died of meningitis caused by sexual excess (a medical truism of the 1880s). M. Giraud later heard that his wife's old lover was seducing another girl. He drowned her in a rigged accident and reported to her widower that he had done the world a service by ridding it of "this reptile."

Today the novel seems a mixture of folklore, moralizing and melodrama. Nevertheless, it was the first book to deal with lesbianism as a distinct phenomenon, as a social and medical problem, and as a love relationship rather than an erotic caprice shaped by male sexual imaginings. Other books and stories followed quickly, some Naturalistic, some Decadent, some satiric, some pornographic.

The Naturalists claimed they were cameras out to record life, biologists of social man. Instead of writing grandly of heroes, they wrote of the poor, the antisocial and the insignificant in the language of the slums, streets and farms. Behind their claim to describe things as they really were—each literary generation claims that—lay a pessimistic bias. They felt that the real truth of life was pain, poverty, crime, perversion and ruin. Like their contemporaries the Decadents, with whom they seemed to share so little, they tended to see sex as a dark flood waiting to drown mankind, and woman as a destroyer of men.

Maupassant's story *Paul's Mistress* tells about a shy boy named Paul who takes a girl called Madeleine to an amusement park. There they see four lesbians, two wearing men's clothing. The crowd shouts at them, "Lesbos! Lesbos!"—an interesting indication of the familiarity of the sight. Paul is disgusted by them, but even more shocked to see that his disgust infuriates Madeleine. He realizes that she too is a lesbian. She disappears from his side, and he hunts feverishly for her. He finds her in a thicket, making love with one of the mannish lesbians; he throws himself into the river and drowns. Madeleine weeps over his body, but she goes home with her head on the other lesbian's shoulder. The implication is that a fine and delicate youth has been crushed by an evil woman.

Zola, the greatest of the Naturalists, described in novel after novel people ground to nothingness by brutality, bad heredity, money, sex, their own character. In 1880 his *Nana* appeared, the story of a courtesan, a blonde Venus who destroyed men with her greed and cruelty. Her progress to total depravity included growing amounts of lesbianism, usually with other prostitutes. Zola was the first person to portray prostitutes' lesbianism in detail, showing it not as mere pansexuality but as the touch of warmth and trust that could not exist in their exploitative relationships with men.

Nana despised and manipulated men, used and ruined them with cold glee. Her only true friend was a poor streetwalker named Satin, who introduced her to lesbianism. Satin revealed that one of her customers was a lesbian named Madame Robert, whom she met at Laure's, a restaurant where lesbians and lesbian prostitutes gathered. Zola's description of a lesbian hangout is the first in literature.

> The majority were nearing the age of forty: their flesh was puffy, and so bloated by vice as almost to hide the outlines of their flaccid mouths. But amid all these gross bosoms and figures, some slim, pretty girls were observable. These still wore a modest expression, despite their impudent gestures, for they were only beginners in their art, who had started life in the ballrooms of the slums, and had been brought to Laure's by some customer or other. Here the tribe of bloated women, excited by the sweet scent of their youth, jostled one another, and, whilst treating them to dainties, formed a perfect court around them, much as old amorous bachelors might have done . . . . [Nana] was momentarily interested, however, at the sight of a young man, with short curly hair and insolent face, who kept a whole tableful of vastly fat women breathlessly attentive to his slightest caprice. But when the young man began to laugh, his bosom swelled.
>   "Good God, it's a woman!"

Zola's disapproval came through clearly, but the description of the room full of heavy-set, older lesbians and pretty, slim femmes could fit many lesbian bars today. Nana had one relationship with a man—the brutal pimp she served. One night, after being badly mistreated by him, she took refuge with Satin and found solace in going to bed with her. Satin cleverly offered sexualized mothering while she played on Nana's resentment toward men. "Oh, the pigs, the pigs! Look here, we'll have nothing more to do with them . . . Let's go to bed as fast as we can, pet. We shall be better off there! Oh, how silly you are to get this way about things! I tell you they're dirty brutes. Don't think any more about them. I—I love you very much. Don't cry, and oblige your own little darling girl."

All along Zola had showed Nana as an irresistible, poisoned confection. Her sexuality was the revenge of the poor, oppressed and outcast on "good" society—the middle class seems to have always projected its fantasies of sex and violence onto the poor. Zola, like the Decadents, thought of uncontrolled sex as a fatal malignancy; his intellectual view was that sexual deviation was due to a degenerative hereditary taint. When Nana died of the plague, she was one big pustulant wound, an emblem of infection and death, a witch finally shed of her princess disguise. "Scientific" Naturalism was not far behind the Desert Fathers in its negative view of sex.

Pierre Louys's *The Songs of Bilitis* was a book of prose poems about a courtesan of ancient Greece, a driven, romantic bisexual like Sappho as she appears in certain versions of her life. Barbey d'Aurevilly, in *Les Diaboliques*, showed lesbians as masculine and aggressive, like Mlle. de Maupin;

he and some other Decadents made sexual deviance a symbol of tragically fated defiance of bourgeois convention. But generally lesbianism was shown as a kind of female monstrousness. The German playwright Wedekind created Lulu—like Nana, a symbol of unbounded and malignant female sexuality, a prostitute and lesbian, a beautiful, beastly destroyer. Catulle Mendès' *Mephistophelia* was a long and detailed novel about a lesbian, Sophie, who is shown at the beginning as a pathetic drug addict. As a girl, Sophie had loved another girl so passionately that she fled from marriage. But it had been a secret love. She was later initiated into lesbian lovemaking and the lesbian world by a showgirl, and started a long series of affairs and encounters with other women. Finally she went back to see her girlhood love, and found her the mother of four children. She was disgusted and then scornful when, spying through a window, she saw the breast she'd dreamed of kissing given to nursing a baby. "Now Emmaline was no longer worthy of her passion. Was her own life wrong? Must one be like such clods to be happy? . . . No! She repudiated such spineless notions. She was what she was. She thrust from her her old dreams of Emmaline's breast, she jeered at Emmaline's bovine happiness." Mendès hated lesbians because they rejected the feminine role. He made clear that he thought failure to accept maternity was central to Sophie's lesbianism and consequent self-destruction.

To some writers of that day, the worst villain in the drama of normality and deviance was the feminist movement, which revealed the same sex-role confusion so common in literature. The founding father of feminism was Mary Wollstonecraft. She grew up in England at the end of the eighteenth century, with a violent, alcoholic father, a favored older brother and a martyr of a mother who defended her brutal husband to the children. Mary saw the world as composed of cruel, exploiting men and spineless, oppressed women. She had contempt for her mother; no woman, she felt, should be the willing victim of these golden boys who callously had their way with the world.

The world about her mirrored her inner conflict. Women's relative freedom had been progressively curtailed as the Victorian pattern became firmer. Women were supposed to be helpless, obedient and dependent. They were legal nonpersons, unable to make wills and contracts, own property or vote. They had no right to employment, education or self-determination in sex or marriage. They couldn't even keep custody of their children if that were contested by the husband. In France, when Revolutionary reforms were reversed, a husband would be able to get a divorce for adultery; he could even murder his wife with impunity if he caught her in the act. A woman had no legal redress against adultery unless her husband actually brought another woman to live under the same roof.

In 1792 Mary Wollstonecraft wrote her *Vindication of the Rights of Women*, the bible of feminism from which spring the books of Simone de

Beauvoir and much of what one reads currently in American women's magazines. It is also the source, as much as any other single work, of the rationale for this century's sexual revolution. It said that women were in every way equal to men, with a right to the same freedom, choices and prerogatives. They should not be property or house serfs, controlled through a double standard foisted on them by greedy, fearful men.

Many of the just parts of her argument have slowly been heeded and put into practice, and the process is continuing. But rational, democratic principles are not the only matters involved; Mary Wollstonecraft's ideology was as much an expression of her emotional bias as St. Augustine's was of his. The phrase "penis envy," despite the oversimplifications it has suffered, inevitably comes to mind. According to Mary Wollstonecraft, man, "the lustful prowler," had guaranteed his selfish desires for sexual and domestic slaves by tricking, shackling, and brainwashing women throughout history. Under his tutelage they had been demeaned, trivialized, weakened, kept ignorant and silly. All female failing and all female depravity, she said, "branch out of one grand cause—want of chastity in men." For woman, sexual acquiescence had been synonymous with humiliation and slavery.

Beneath her apparent scorn of men and ennobling of women lay a contrary feeling. She admired and envied men, as slaves mentally magnify their conquerors. To Mary Wollstonecraft, men were possessors of magical power. She said bitterly that women were burdened by their smaller size, weaker muscles, menstruation, pregnancy and childbirth. To her, liberty meant freedom from these biological facts, from nagging little dependents, freedom to compete with men on their own grounds. We are so accustomed today to this emotional viewpoint and its intellectual defense that we usually fail to see it in logical perspective. It is no different from a man saying that he wishes to be free of his muscles, his penis and his aggressiveness, free of responsibility to be self-reliant and protective. One would take such a man for a passive mama's boy, afraid of his maleness, overidentifying with his mother. Mary Wollstonecraft hated her femininity and all that went with it, and was an angry and envious believer in male superiority.

Lundberg and Farnham, in *Modern Woman, The Lost Sex*, give a biased and sometimes glibly inaccurate rebuttal to the extreme feminist position. But they do analyze its emotional coloring well—hostile to heterosexual love, hostile to sex, hostile to motherhood and most of all hostile to women. They say, "What the feminists were actually aiming for was definitely not justice. It was, as Mary Wollstonecraft flatly said . . . *masculinity*. And a female who attempts to achieve masculinity is psychically ill in the same way as a male who attempts to achieve femininity."

A few radical intellectual circles agreed that women should be considered people, not merely mistresses, homemakers and mothers. As descendants of the Puritans and Rousseau, they agreed that a match should not be a property merger but a sharing based on mutual love and respect.

Many Romantics, with their idealization of women, democratic views and empathy with the underdog, became allies of the feminists.

During the first decades of the nineteenth century, feminism was chiefly represented by a small number of flamboyant female artists and adventurers. The most notorious was George Sand, who dressed like a man, smoked cigars, believed in free love, wrote under a male pseudonym and said, "I doubt not that marriage will be abolished if the human race makes any progress toward justice and reason." Like many feminists, she wanted children cared for by specialists and nurseries, to end "binding in eternal fetters the freedom of the parents." The rights of women took precedence over a child's right to a mother, a father and a home.

George Sand exercised her sexual freedom, but it did not make her happy—nor did it gladden Mérimée, Musset, Chopin and the rest of her lovers. *Gamiani*, a famous erotic novel with a destructive lesbian for a protagonist, is said by some to be have written about her by Musset in revenge. After a disastrous amatory encounter with Mérimée—a champion seducer of Paris high society—Sand publicly denigrated his masculinity, but privately she wrote, "If he had loved me, he would have subjected me; and had I been able to subject myself to a man, I had been saved, for my freedom gnaws at me and slays me."

George Sand had an English counterpart in Marian Evans, who published her novel *Adam Bede* under the pseudonym George Eliot. She once involved herself in a free-love experiment based on the ideas of Godwin, Shelley and Fourier—the first was Mary Wollstonecraft's husband and champion, the second a believer in her ideas, the third a utopian of great originality. But her talk of freedom, like that of many feminists, was largely just talk. Mary Wollstonecraft herself had shown she wasn't immune to the values she fought; she tried to commit suicide after bearing an illegitimate child, then married when she learned she was pregnant a second time.

In its early days, feminism was often inseparable from other radical and utopian movements; they had mutual influence in the matters of sex, marriage and sex role. The first half of the last century was as rich in cults as Southern California is today. There were communities of socialists, anarchists, Mormons, free-lovers, nudists, vegetarians, freed slaves; there were tribes of adherents to new fads from phrenology to hydrotherapy. Many utopian experiments that called for communal living also demanded the same social reforms as the feminists—contraception, divorce, a free and single sexual standard. Lovers, children, property should all be shared. Fourier, for instance, stressed individuality and self-fulfillment, and believed frustration of desire was the source of all evil. He wanted division of labor based on preference, and choice of work partners based on love. In his communities women would be free agents, and sexual counselors would advise, console and "pleasure" the erotically disappointed. To Fourier, bourgeois marriage was a frost on the blossom of humanity. "Let us

liberate all our passions," he said. "Then we shall know what true joy in
life is." In 1825 Robert Owen started the colony of New Harmony, Indiana, a short-lived experiment in communism, free thought and equal marriage. He defined chastity as "sexual intercourse with affection." Soon there
were nine more Owenite communities. Brook Farm, Hopedale and some
thirty other Fourierist communities arose and died in America in the next
few decades. The most interesting and long-lived was John Noyes's Perfec-
tionist settlement at Oneida, New York, which successfully did away with
exclusiveness in sex as in property and performed some extraordinary pioneer experiments in eugenics.

So even while Victorianism and political reaction were reaching their
height, Romanticism, feminism, socialism, free love, anarchy and birth control were all bubbling together in a world of underground protest and
experiment. Each sect had at least a few things in common with the others;
socialism, feminism and Romanticism especially drew strength from each
other. Convinced feminists—almost all middle class—made a spiritual alliance with oppressed workers. Besides, women were now working in factories in great numbers, earning only a quarter to half as much as men. Marx
spoke in one breath of the liberation of workers and of women. Engels
became a spokesman for feminism; he said the lot of woman was tied to
the history of property, and borrowed Bachoven's proto-anthropology
about matriarchies to prove it.

In the 1840s there was still almost universal mockery of feminism. It was
one more tassel on the lunatic fringe. But changes were gaining momentum,
and by mid-century women started to go around unchaperoned again, as
they had a century before; they began to wear low-cut evening dresses, to
ride bicycles and play lawn tennis. Amelia Bloomer provoked a howl of
outrage by showing her reformed costume for women—long baggy trousers
covered by a short skirt, to allow women to be physically active. In the
1860s women were no longer isolated freaks if they entered universities.
They involved themselves in social reform and even entered professions.
The angel in the house was replaced by an ideal of red-cheeked, unaffected
vigor. Dorothea Dix, Florence Nightingale and many other active women,
though not themselves feminists, set new models for feminine behavior.
Ladies went to work in slums and prisons, helping the young, the
orphaned, the mentally ill, the alcoholic, the sick and destitute. American
reformers who had devoted themselves to abolition turned to the "female
problem" after the end of the Civil War; as a result, feminism gained in
strength and militance. Victorianism was waning among the educated, and
an increasing number of social and political liberals began to support
feminism.

Equal rights for women and sexual permissiveness had been inseparable
from the start of the movement. As feminism grew, there was disagreement
about whether political and legal aims (legal autonomy, the vote, custody

of children, divorce) should be endangered by the even more explosive issues of free love and contraception. In 1871 Victoria Claflin Woodhull, the beautiful sideshow star of the American feminist movement, shouted to a frenzied, booing audience in New York's Steinway Hall, "Yes, I am a free lover! I have an inalienable, constitutional and natural right to love whom I may, to love as long or as short a period as I can, to change that love every day if I please!" That was no way to sway state legislatures; the movement split. The political rather than the sexual-freedom faction controlled the movement in most places. Gradually, from this time on, women gained the right to legal independence, property, the vote, education, public office, child custody and divorce.

Between 1870 and 1900 female employment rose rapidly. Single girls could support themselves away from home, and many mobile, urban young people lived on their own. As self-support became easier, divorce began to rise. Upper-class women began to smoke, to enter professions, to adopt such tailored, mannish items of clothing as the shirtwaist, and to cultivate boyish hair styles. These fashions soon became standard in the middle class. By the 1920s women had won their chief legal goals in much of the West, and the remaining distinctions are now being whittled away. In Catholic and Mediterranean countries the changes are slower, but even there the idea is taking hold that man and woman are equal before the law, and, to a lesser degree, before society. After the 1920s, when the greatest legal hurdles blocking women were on their way down, the battle for sexual autonomy once again came to the fore.

Feminism always retained Mary Wollstonecraft's ambivalence toward traditional—even biological—differences between the sexes. Leaders of the movement said: "The lowest prostitute is yet better than the best of men. . . . Idiots are more numerous among males than among females. . . . Hairiness denotes a low stage of development. . . . All the generations of women who knelt down in the straw and let the neighbour woman hold them there, while they shrieked and watched their bodies in the shambles of child-birth, know what it was to go through with something as inescapable as death."

In France, Victor Hugo had publicly supported the League of Women's Rights. In England, John Stuart Mill wrote *The Subjection of Women* and gave the movement more respectability there. He said, "Women have proved themselves capable of everything, perhaps without a single exception, which is done by men, and of doing it successfully and creditably." Lundberg and Farnham commented: "Such as impregnate another woman? Founding an empire? Creating a religion? Elaborating a major— or minor—philosophical system?" Their first point, at least, is unarguable.

There was public fury at Lucy-Stoners, who, like their namesake, kept their maiden names after marriage; at women who wore bloomers; at the first women in pants; at liberal and radical circles of "brawling women and Aunt Nancy men." Some men were hostile because they failed to see the elementary social justice of many feminist demands. Others were hostile because the feminists were hostile. And some were either sensibly or lazily habit-bound, as one wishes to see it.

Several scientists and reformers admitted that there were a large number of masculine women and even lesbians in the movement. Edward Carpenter, one of the earlier writers on homosexuality in England, who knew many sex-reform and feminist leaders, said in the early years of this century: "The women of the new movement are naturally drawn from those in whom the maternal instinct is not especially strong; also from those in whom the sexual instinct is not preponderant. . . . Some are rather mannish in temperament . . . to many, children are more or less a bore; to others, man's sex-passion is a mere impertinence, which they do not understand, and whose place they frequently misjudge."

There was one temperate and extremely shrewd analysis of feminism in its more ferocious and crippling aspect. It was somewhat passed over when it appeared in 1885; today it is undiminished in relevance, for the feminist spirit is a major factor in Western sex-role problems today. Henry James's *The Bostonians* cannot be reduced to a précis without brutalizing it, for it is long, complex and subtle. Essentially, it tells of the rivalry between Olive Chancellor, a spinster feminist, and her cousin Basil Ransom for a passive and overpliant girl named Verena Tarrant.

Ransom represents everything James admires as "the masculine attitude"—forthright, steadfast, courageous. Olive has a tense, cramped, angry personality; she is obsessed by the wrongs women have suffered and treats men as an enemy she must fight or isolate herself from. She binds the passive, talented Verena to her and uses her as a showpiece in the feminist movement. Basil Ransom tells Verena that the age needs less feminization, not more, and that she needs a man more than a cause. Philip Rahv calls the book a fine analysis of "the emotional economy of the Lesbian woman." There is no explicit sexual relationship between Olive and Verena,* but it is constantly implied that the bond between them is, at best, a failure for them and for society's best interests. Ransom steals Verena away from Olive at the end, but James hints that her passive, narcissistic, little-girl quality will mean more unhappiness for them both in the future. Olive is too rigid to be womanly, Verena too formless and in need of a mother. James was too sensitive and intelligent to take some of the acrimonious polemics over feminism at face value. He knew that the bitterest fights were not over the real issues but the emotional forces they represented.

Romanticism, Victorianism, socialism, feminism, urbanization, utopian-

---

*James was explicit about lesbianism in *The Turn of the Screw*, and he might have been in *The Bostonians* had he wished. But generally, out of personal taste or fear of censorship, he usually avoided mention of sexual activity in a direct way. He was far from naïve, though, and when sexual implications seem strong in his description of a relationship, it is no accident.

ism, rapid economic and family-structure changes—all make a confused picture of forces affecting sexual behavior in the nineteenth century. There is no convenient unifying principle, but they all converged, like tremors from many directions, on the West's old sex-role and behavior patterns. Science began to study sex, and the first courageous efforts were often firmly based on folklore and fear. The first literary and scientific efforts to bring sex from the realms of theology and pornography to public places and the laboratory show how far we have come, and how far we still have to go.

INTERVIEWS

The women I speak to about their homosexual experience range from committed, mannish lesbians to heterosexuals who have dabbled with the gay of both sexes. In all of them, elements of "masculine protest," competitiveness, antimaternal feelings and feminine inadequacy are variously represented.

Maureen Duffy is the author of the novels The Microcosm *and* That's How It Was; *the former describes the Gateways Club, the only major lesbian gathering place in London, where part of* The Killing of Sister George *was filmed. She meets me for lunch at a Soho restaurant; she is a handsome woman in a white pants-suit and dark glasses, with short-cropped hair. From a distance I am not sure whether she is a mannishly dressed woman or a man with striking and slightly sinister good looks. Speaking of the gay life in London, she says:*

The Gateways hasn't changed since my book came out. Other clubs come and go, but the Gateways remains. A lot of people who've read my work write to me and ask what to do for a social group, and I put them in touch by taking them there. There's also the MRG, the Minorities Research Group; they put out the magazine *Arena 3*, which is more or less like *The Ladder** in America. There are some other small lesbian organizations, but here the homosexual groups tend to be aggressively middle class, dominated by teachers and professionals, the old-fashioned tweeds-and-brogues set.

Lesbians have a terrible problem about places to meet. The office is the heterosexually oriented marriage bureau of society, so you have to keep up a front there. But some people do meet other lesbians at work. Some women head for certain professions. Teaching gives equal pay with men, and status and social prospects. Many lesbians go into nursing. There aren't that many lesbian policewomen, to my knowledge, but I've known four or five who were in the armed forces. Some working-class women take jobs on buses and in garages, where they can wear pants without being too obvious.

It's still rough for a woman to be a homosexual. Sometimes butches are beaten up by young roughs, spat at in the street, fired from their jobs. Publishing is usually a pretty liberal profession, but I know a girl who lost her job at a publishing house because she was seen with me in a pub at lunchtime.

*The publication of the Daughters of Bilitis, the major lesbian organization in the United States.

The cause of homosexuality? I'm Freudian. If people think it's innate, they can say, "I'm not guilty, not responsible." It's a way out.

A LOS ANGELES PSYCHIATRIST: I have two lesbian patients right now, both in their twenties. One sleeps with a lot of men to prove she can have an orgasm, but they don't really interest her. She has an overprotective mother and several brothers. She envied her brothers for being free of the mother's oppressive over-protection. She talks tough, acts tough and wants male freedom and privilege. The other girl was AC-DC for a while; then she copped out and became lesbian. She has a very feminine sister, and she says, "I could never be frilly like that." Her feeling of feminine inadequacy is really powerful.

Edna and Carol are in their late twenties and live together in London. Both are easy-mannered, friendly, slatlike girls with short hair. Both are freelance professionals in the arts.

CAROL: I almost got married once. It took me a long time to admit that I could never have a good relationship with a man. I'd had my lesbian crushes, and I realized that if I gave in to social pressures, I should never be happy. There had been boys I'd felt involved with, but if they'd said they were passionately fond of me, I'd have run a mile.

EDNA: It was very different for me; I couldn't have been fixed as a homosexual from a younger age. I was always with boys and never liked girls at all till I grew up. I was a sort of tomboy bluestocking as an adolescent. I thought girls were a pain in the neck. I reckon I had a hereditary disposition that was strongly reinforced by my upbringing. But I suppose that for most people it's environmental. I did have an older brother who died soon after birth, and I was raised somewhat as a boy. I had a very mothering mother; from the age of two or three I wanted to be all dirty, and she tried to get me into dresses, so I guess she must have had the right instincts.

CAROL: There's no single cause, I think, but I believe I'm homosexual because of my mother. She's a repressed homosexual herself. Her attitude toward sex and men shows it. If one doesn't have a mother who can accept her femininity enough to be a mother, one lacks the mothering influence. But in Edna's case, it seems to be genetic. You can understand a pairing like her and me. My type is due to bad mothering and isn't masculine, and we're usually attracted to women who take a masculine role early in life for genetic reasons.

EDNA: I usually find that the femmes of butch-femme pairs are bisexual. Some couples consist of two butches. In any case, the butch-femme distinction doesn't mean much in bed, and once one is homosexual such distinctions may be beside the point. I think it must be dreadful to have such a fragmented, sorry self-image that you want to be cured. The idea of behavior therapy gives me a feeling of abhorrence, but I'm in favor of psychoanalysis—it has benefited many of my friends.

CAROL: Aversion is a failure if you don't live up to their presuppositions. Psychoanalysis is open-ended, you find out where you are going as it proceeds. They don't sit you down and say, "All right, my dear, we're going to make you a nice little heterosexual mother."

At a large outdoor cafe in Amsterdam all the men keep staring at a sullen beauty who sits alone in a back corner. She is about twenty-five, tall, with long blonde hair, high cheekbones and an eerie resemblance to the young Ingrid Bergman. But her vernal freshness is contradicted by an air of defensive ferocity. Sitting in rigid discomfort, face taut, lips locked tight, she intently avoids each look as though it were an assault; after a while she puts on dark glasses, which make her seem even icier. Obviously she is awaiting someone, and his arrival is becoming a matter of public drama.

Finally she is joined by a big square woman in her mid-forties with close-cropped hair and a tailored suit; her cheeks and jowls are full, her features coarse, her hands like a wrestler's. Both women wear identical gold wedding bands. The blonde removes her dark glasses and leans across the table attentively, listening and nodding. Now her face is transformed, eyes wide and soft, lips slightly parted. Everything about her is open, gentle, flowerlike. A silent, wondering sigh passes through the cafe. She is the most beautiful and poignant of sights—a lovely woman in love.

Jennifer is a professional woman of thirty, very successful in her highly competitive field. She is the youngest child in a family that includes an aggressive father and several older brothers. She is quite attractive, but one can imagine that she was a flat-bodied, gangling adolescent. She has had no homosexual experience but spent several years associating only with homosexual men, followed by a period of unhappy promiscuity. She has developed strong feminist sympathies. Now, about to be married, she recalls:

I went with gay boys because I wasn't attractive. I was gawky and very competitive, so most guys in high school never bothered with me. In college I learned to dress and use make-up. I met lots of homosexuals in the college theater group, and they just doted on me. I began to dress for them—very chic, with shift dresses and big hats, the campier and more outrageous the better. They gave me the queen-bee role, and I lived up to it. People started telling me that Larry, my boyfriend, was homosexual, and I didn't believe it. He was absolutely beautiful. I was a virgin and we just necked. I finally found out he was gay at the first gay party I went to. Larry begged me not to go, but I insisted, because I was curious. There was a room full of people from college whom I hadn't known were homosexual. One girl from my history class was there in full drag. I tried to be inconspicuous, but this butch type came over and asked me to dance. I said no, and she said, "You think I'm gonna rape you?" The girl from my history class came up to me after the butch left and said, "You're not supposed to say no, even if you're straight. It's a terrible slap in the face." Then she asked me to dance, even though she had a girlfriend with her. It was excruciating for both of us, it was so embarrassing. Anyway, later on she told me, "Your boyfriend is in the next room kissing another boy."

I just said, "Oh." She said, "Do you want to see?" I said, "No," and started for the door. Larry showed up then, very drunk, and said, "Don't think ill of us because of this." I just stood there and wept. Finally I left. And can you believe it, I was saying to myself, "Well, he doesn't have to be homosexual just because of that. We can work things out."

A week later Larry and I talked, and he said we couldn't go together any more. But I knew I could do something to bring him back, and it worked. I dyed my hair pink. Larry heard and came to my class to see, and he flipped over me. We went out again for a while, and then it petered out. But I'd done this wild, campy thing, and everyone talked about it for a while, and I was at the center of the gay group again.

Later I had a long relationship with Andy. He was gay and wasn't interested in me sexually, though he did have another girlfriend whom he slept with some-times, a big-breasted motherly girl. He and I became friends after I accepted no sexual relationship was possible. When he was miserable or in a panic, he'd come to my apartment and we'd sleep together. He just wanted the warmth of being held, and really so did I. When he was twenty-two, he committed suicide. At his funeral, the priest started, "This man . . ." His mother started screaming hysterically, "Not a man! A boy! A boy! My little boy!" By the way, Larry, my first gay boyfriend, also committed suicide later on.

To me those relationships were idyllic. Sexual demands and real men terrified me, so I pretended to myself that these relationships were normal. Also, as I see now, not being sexually threatened gave me more control in the relationships. One of the things that finally led me to a psychiatrist was why I surrounded myself with homosexuals. When I finally lost my virginity, I stopped hanging around with gay boys. For a number of years I went to the other extreme and was very promiscuous. With gay boys I got sexual rejection and fed on it, because I was even more afraid of *not* being rejected. Then I slept with guys I cared nothing about, nor they for me. It's only recently that I can look back on some of this and think it's pretty funny.

12

The Apologists

At the turn of the twentieth century a Berlin doctor was becoming the world's leading scientific expert on homosexuality. Dr. Magnus Hirschfeld's first publication was the pamphlet "Sappho and Socrates," presented under a pseudonym in 1896. His writings and activities were prodigious over the next few decades. His first major project was to devise a questionnaire on sexual behavior, including homosexuality, and get ten thousand people to fill it out. This was the first large statistical study of sex behavior. The results were used in his book *The Uranian* in 1903 and in his two-volume study the following year, *Berlin's Third Sex*. His phrase "the third sex" became popular, but the book brought the author a fine from Berlin authorities. Hirschfeld went on with research, writing and reform. He insisted to scientists, courts and the public that homosexuality was congenital and nonpathological, probably due to the interplay of hormones and the nervous system. He fought for the legal and social rights of deviants, and to get the antihomosexual Section 175 of the penal code repealed.

Hirschfeld founded a periodical that became a major locus for studies of deviance. In 1910 he coined the term transvestism in his book *Transvestites: An Investigation into the Erotic Impulse of Disguise*. Shortly after, he published his masterwork, *Homosexuality in Men and Women*. In 1918 he founded the Institute for Sex Research in Berlin, the first organization of its kind. With Forel and Ellis, he set up the world's first international congress for sex reform in 1921. Meanwhile, his institute developed a library and a marriage-counseling service, worked for legal reforms, and gave advice on birth control and sex problems.

Today Hirschfeld's theories and data are mostly discredited, his works as much relics as *Psychopathia Sexualis*. His importance was as a pioneer in research methods and reform. He fought hard, and to much effect, for the idea that homosexuality (innate, incurable and nonpathological) should be tolerated. In fact, he said, homosexuals have special virtues: their world has less regard for caste and status than the heterosexual, so they are more democratic. But this and other of Hirschfeld's theories are discounted because he was himself a homosexual and occasional transvestite, known affectionately in Berlin's gay world as "Auntie Magnesia."

Hirschfeld was not alone in having a special stake in a sexual revolution. Many apparently sober scientific works and liberal sermonizings came from such secret deviants, and special pleading lay behind a number of landmark works in sexology. England produced a particularly large number of covert apologies disguised as scholarship and science. Many were by men of intelligence and talent. One of the earliest was Sir Richard Burton. He was not homosexual, just exceedingly sexual. His life and work are in many ways typical of those men who used science as a polemic tool for breaking the Victorian silence on sex and creating a more permissive atmosphere.

Burton was born in 1821, one of three children of a retired officer whose wanderlust made him hustle his family about the world. Richard grew up a cultured delinquent without permanent home or school, always adventuring and learning new languages. All his life he was rebellious and unconventional, but capable of immense labor at what interested him— travel, writing, languages, sex. In 1842 he became an officer of the East India Company and went to Bombay. There he took a native mistress, studied Hindustani twelve hours a day, disguised himself as an Indian, opened a shop and used it to learn local lore. Either he was ordered or he took it upon himself (it still is not clear) to investigate and write an official report on male bordellos in Karachi, where boys and eunuchs served men. In 1851 he published a book on the Sind region, a ragbag of geography, customs and travelogue. Here he set forth a theory that women in warm countries are more passionate than the men, but that in cold countries the opposite holds true. It was a quasi-scholarly variation on the myth of the hot-blooded south, and he would use it again when he got to writing on homosexuality.*

Burton spent decades traveling and writing; he was a mixture of scholar, prankster, adventurer and artist. Knowing native languages and customs, he was able to enter in disguise the forbidden cities of Medina and Mecca; he was the first European to see the slave-trade city of Harar in Ethiopia. At close to forty he married a devout Catholic Englishwoman. Then he was off again, to discover Lake Tanganyika and travel in South America, the Near East and the western United States. His books about these voyages made him the most famous travel writer of all time. But all this while, wherever he went, he was privately busy taking notes on local peoples' sex lives—on sexual positions, castration, female circumcision, polygamy, aphrodisiacs, homosexuality, prostitution, bestiality. Some of his knowledge went into papers for anthropological societies, safe snippets into his travel works. Most had to be saved for use in the last decades of his life, when he turned his attention almost fully to erotica.

Behind Burton's life and work lay griping discontent with Western

---

*He had many antecedents. Voltaire, writing on "Socratic Love," said: "It is well known that this mistake of nature is much more common in mild climates than among the snows of the North, for the blood runs hotter there and the occasion arises more frequently."

sexual life. He was a terror to Victorian drawing rooms, where he made no secret of his belief that English women were sexual cripples, deformed by their education, and their men amatory oafs. Like X of *My Secret Life*, he was a hypersexual man in an antisexual society. He preached for frankness and sex education, and championed polygamy as the natural state of man. Society did not understand him, and in his frustration he used everything from anthropology to Greek classics to try to convince it that it must.

Burton spent his later years translating Arabic and Indian books on sex. His greatest labor was his translation—in ten volumes, with a six-volume supplement—of the *Book of the Thousand and One Nights*. Its appearance in 1886 sent indignation and disgust through English society. Many of the stories mentioned intercourse, homosexuality, bestiality and female orgasm. Most offensive of all were the painstaking notes and the long "Terminal Essay," into which Burton poured a lifetime of information on sex gleaned from study and travel. One part of the "Terminal Essay" was a long section on homosexuality, mostly from a historical and anthropological point of view. Like all his work, it was a jumble of scholarship, observation, gossip and wild hypothesis. It contained classical and Oriental lore; scandal about homosexual life in London, Dublin and Berlin; ancient Greek slang for homosexual practices; things he had seen and heard about in the Near East.

Burton concluded that homosexuality was "geographic and climatic, not racial." It existed primarily in an area he called the Sotadic Zone, after a homosexual poet of ancient Greece named Sotades. This zone was bounded roughly by the northern and southern shores of the Mediterranean and went around the world, including southern France, Spain, Italy, Greece, North Africa, Turkey, Afghanistan, the Punjab, Kashmir, Turkestan, China, Japan, South Sea Islands, and parts of the New World.

> Within the Sotadic Zone, the vice is popular and endemic, held at the worst to be a mere peccadillo, whilst the races to the north and south of the limits here defined practise it only sporadically amid the opprobrium of their fellows who, as a rule, are physically incapable of performing the operation and look upon it with the liveliest disgust.

Sporadically or Sotadically, even Burton knew that geography was not really explanation enough; in support, he quoted Paola Mantegazza on physiological anal-eroticism, and claimed that in the Sotadic regions the genital nerves probably deviated toward the rectum. Burton said that "this perversion of the erotic sense, one of the marvelous list of amorous vagaries, deserves not prosecution but the pitiful care of the physician and the study of the psychologist." He was apparently unaware of the newer theories that had become current in recent years, such as the degenerative, but his ideas were not much more inaccurate than many then in scientific fashion. His work was read by many, and it succeeded in rubbing "shocking" reality into Victorian faces. Like a lush in a Mormon meeting defending his passion for the bottle, he argued the naturalness of sex, its power and variety in human life. His crude proto-anthropology, with its examples of exotic eroticism, was aimed at making a case for the sexual freedom his temperament demanded.

When Burton was almost seventy years old, he was living in Trieste translating Latin erotic poetry and annotating his translation of the Arab love book *The Perfumed Garden.* He finished the last page of the *Garden* and died the next day. His pious wife had him baptised while he was delirious, persuaded a priest to give the corpse extreme unction, and spent sixteen days burning everything she didn't want him remembered by, including his translation of the Garden and decades of an intimate diary. Then she gave him the monument she thought he deserved—a great marble tent in a Catholic cemetery in England.

A similar posthumous cleansing was made of the life and work of John Addington Symonds, one of the better poets, essayists and translators of his generation in England. He had been aware of homosexual desires at an early age, but he married, fathered four daughters and kept his homosexuality to romantic feelings and restrained caresses. As he traveled about Europe in his thirties, he became more frankly sexual with men, began to move in homosexual circles, and met and talked with the homosexual Karl Ulrichs. In 1883 Symonds had privately and anonymously printed a long essay called "A Problem in Greek Ethics, Being an Inquiry into the Phenomenon of Sexual Inversion." This was the first serious attempt in England to write about homosexuality—and, incidentally, the first English use of the word inversion. Symonds argued that homosexuality was an Asiatic luxury which the Greek genius turned into a "chivalrous enthusiasm" like courtly love—ennobling, didactic and preferably chaste. Symonds dismissed the vulgar act of sodomy and idealized Greek homosexuality. "I need scarce add that none but a race of artists could be lovers of this sort. . . . The Greeks admitted, as true artists are obliged to do, that the male body displays harmonies of proportion and melodies of outline more comprehensive . . . than that of women." Symonds expressed sorrow and indignation that science had neglected so widespread a condition. Despite his homosexual bias, much of the essay is both learned and shrewd.

Symonds and his wife eventually agreed to live separate lives so that he could follow his homosexual desires. Though his love life was probably kept secret from the general public and at least some of his children, it was common knowledge in literary circles. While he romanticized the spiritual nobility of homosexual comradeship, his life went a different route. His sexual preference was for choirboys and handsome lower-class men; during his last ten years he kept an Italian peasant, who traveled everywhere with him. Swinburne called him "Soddington." He exchanged homosexual pornography with other homosexuals in the literary world—for instance the famous critic Edmund Gosse, who, according to one of Symonds' biographers, was "driven to steal glances at a photograph Symonds had sent him, all through Robert Browning's funeral services at Westminster Abbey."

Symonds also read widely on the scientific study of homosexuality—Casper, Tardieu, Burton, Ulrichs, Moll, Krafft-Ebing, Lombroso. In 1891 he had printed—again privately and anonymously—a companion essay to his work on the Greeks, "A Problem in Modern Ethics." With all its bias, the essay is still readable, interesting and often acute. Symonds saw through the fashionable scientific clichés of his time, and picked out the basic flaws in the theories of Krafft-Ebing, Lombroso and other famous scientific experts. It was absurd to say masturbation caused homosexuality; what about those who masturbate but don't become homosexual, and those who never masturbate but do become homosexual? If homosexuality was the result of hereditary neuropathy, why did even scientists call it a mere "custom" in ancient Greece? And if it was hereditary, why hadn't the children of homosexuals who married so tainted the world's genetic pool that everyone was homosexual? Were schoolboys and prisoners who indulged in homosexual acts tainted? Were homosexual geniuses tainted? Symonds concluded that "theories of disease are incompetent to explain the phenomenon in modern Europe." Considering the theories of mental disease in his time, he was more right than wrong.

Unfortunately, Symonds had little to offer in the place of what he debunked. Like Hirschfeld and many other homosexuals, he wanted to believe that the condition was in all cases innate, nonpathological, not involving hereditary taint or any disorder at all. Homosexuality, he said, is a "recurring impulse of humanity . . . in the majority of cases compatible with an otherwise normal and healthy temperament." It was monstrous to punish inverts; the only results could be secrecy, blackmail and suffering, because then their love must be acted out "furtively, spasmodically, hysterically." Symonds said that sexual deprivation of young heterosexuals was also damaging, and he made a call for general sexual freedom. He got in touch with Havelock Ellis, whom he knew was writing a vast, encyclopedic work on sex, and suggested that they collaborate on a volume on homosexuality. Symonds would supply the historical and literary material, Ellis the scientific. They did collaborate, but in 1893 Symonds died, and the volume did not appear until 1897—printed in Germany to avoid English censorship. Symonds and Ellis were named as coauthors. Symonds' family bought up most of the edition and destroyed it. They insisted his name be removed from forthcoming editions, and Ellis agreed. Symonds' ideas, shorn of his name, would remain embedded in the most influential book on sex in the English language, Havelock Ellis' *Studies in the Psychology of Sex.*

Ellis, whom one of his biographers dubbed the Sage of Sex, was born in 1859, and for fifty of his eighty years wrote learned, humane and essentially propagandist texts on sex. His father was a sea captain, rarely at home; he grew up with a shy, nervous, devout mother and four sisters. The atmosphere of the house was loftily religious and emotionally reserved. However, when Havelock was twelve, his mother urinated in his presence with what seemed unconscious but deliberate coquetry, and Ellis always blamed this event for what he called "a germ of perversion" in his make-up. All his life he had a touch of what he called urolagnia—sexual fascination with the act of urination. This was the least of his sexual problems.

During his youth, his sex life consisted only of occasional nocturnal emissions unaccompanied by dreams. He was timid, introverted, unathletic and intellectually precocious. He withdrew into books and became very devout. Havelock's father, afraid the boy was being feminized in a household of women, twice took him on sea voyages. The second time, when Havelock was nineteen, he stayed in Australia to work as a school teacher. Isolated and lonely, he found consolation in religion for his passivity, his shyness, his living as an observer rather than a participant. His great virtue, he told himself, was his ability to suffer in silence. Still, he dreamed of giving his journal, full of his yearnings for mutual love and devotion, to some girl who would understand it and love him. During this period he had his first waking sexual sensations—a spontaneous orgasm while reading Brantôme.

Not long after, he had a religious experience that gave his life its direction. It occurred while he was reading a book by James Hinton, a doctor who had turned to religion, philosophy and sexual utopianism and become the center of a small intellectual-religious cult. As Ellis was reading Hinton's attempt to reconcile Christianity and science, he was suddenly overcome by euphoria and a sense of harmony with the world. After this ecstatic experience, he knew what to do with his life. He would accept his own inadequacies and cease to seek happiness. He was destined for something higher: to give happiness to others. He would become a doctor, like Hinton, and use his knowledge to advise, comfort, heal. His study would center on sexual behavior.

Burton had fought for sexual enlightenment because he was hypersexual. Ellis decided to do so because he was sexually inadequate. It is possible to offer many interpretations of what happened emotionally to Ellis at this time. One thinks of Augustine's crisis of sex, morality and conversion. In lonely despair, with his sexual urges becoming conscious for the first time, Ellis seems to have decided on unraveling his own inner conflicts by objectifying them, studying them scientifically in other people. He remained a shy, bookish man all his life, theoretically plunging into the tangle of sexual deviance but never using emotional probes on himself, as did his near-contemporary Freud. Ellis saw others as he saw himself—a man with a buried mystery. Later in life, in his autobiography, he wrote:

Of Nature I have never been afraid. But the world has always seemed to me to be full of strange human beings, so unknown, mysterious and awe-inspiring, so apt to give joy or pain, so apt also to receive either. I have always felt a mixed reverence and fear of human creatures so that I have sometimes even been afraid to look into the eyes of strangers; they seemed to me gates into chambers where intimate and terrible secrets lie bare.

Ellis returned to England—a handsome young man with a short beard and a grand brow, but awkward and shy, with a high, thin voice. He joined the Hinton group and began to associate with other circles of utopians. During the next decade, from his twentieth to his thirtieth year, he became involved in myriad activities. He became a doctor; corresponded with progressive and utopian thinkers; edited a series of scientific books and the famous Mermaid Series of Elizabethan plays; wrote scientific and literary works. Gradually he gained a reputation as an intellectual rebel. He insisted on leaving the Elizabethan plays he edited uncensored, and in preparing his volume on Marlowe discovered the Baines Libel. His science series included such influential new works as those of Lombroso. His literary essays praised Diderot, Whitman and other still unfashionable artistic mavericks. Ellis was the perfect idealistic progressive, calling for more imaginative, informed and humane ideas in art, science and sex. He was supported and influenced by a large circle of friends who were socialists, feminists, homosexuals and devout anti-Victorians, such as Swinburne, Symonds, Margaret Sanger and Olive Schreiner.

Among these friends was the young novelist Edith Lees, a lesbian. When Ellis grew close to her, he had a firmly set view of himself—physically unlike most men, lamed by urolagnia and impotence. He hoped only for the love of kindred spirits, affairs of souls. Though he idealized women and love in Victorian fashion, he believed that Victorian ideas of "normality" and "purity" were foolish. Normality was a social convention; God created anomalies such as himself, Edith, Swinburne, Symonds and the masochistic Olive Schreiner out of his grand wisdom. They, like everything that lived, had their own particular value in creation. They were not just freaks, but fascinating varieties of humanity, like four-leaf clovers in a field of three-leaf clovers.

When Edith revealed her lesbian tendencies to Ellis he was not shocked or condemning. He said that obviously neither of them was capable of a normal sex life. Both had very "advanced" ideas about marriage—an equal partnership of two independent beings, without economic or sexual possessiveness. Edith had been told by doctors not to have children; Havelock wanted to devote himself to his work, not a family. Despite their advanced views on the degradation of traditional marriage, they did not enter a "free union." They were legally wed in 1891, at Edith's insistence.

Edith was a talented writer, but emotionally and sexually troubled. She suffered progressively acute manic-depressive swings throughout her life. Like all the women to whom Ellis was attracted, she was mercurial, vital, but in need of an adviser and protector. The excessively reasonable, moderate Havelock calmed her. In turn, she stimulated and buoyed him. He told her she was not inferior because of her lesbianism, merely a hereditary sport. She had a lesbian affair, and Ellis gave it his Olympian blessing. If she accepted it, as he accepted his urolagnia and impotence, they could both be happy. Edith sometimes complained that he was pushing her into homosexuality, to which she was not utterly committed; she wanted him to save her. He declined to do so, more upset than he admitted at such a call to masculine assertiveness. They lived progressively separate lives, she with other women, he with other female soul-companions. She finally became deeply depressed, paranoid and suicidal.

Ellis' high-minded tolerance of all deviant sexuality, his justification of it as equal to heterosexual normality, was the covert message of his great work, *Studies in the Psychology of Sex*, which appeared in seven volumes between 1897 and 1928, during his marriage to Edith. His bias was bolstered by several friends, especially Symonds and Edward Carpenter. When Arthur Symonds entered collaboration on the first volume, on homosexuality, his material and many of his own apologetic arguments joined Ellis' in the text. Edward Carpenter was a poet, socialist and reformer who in 1896 had privately printed a book called *Love's Coming of Age*, championing women's rights and sex education. It contained a chapter entitled "The Intermediate Sex," which called for a new, important role in society for homosexuals as well as for women. He said homosexuals can best rise above mere sex to spiritual comradeship, and are therefore especially fitted for leadership in a progressive, democratic society. Later Carpenter combed history, literature and anthropology for evidence to prove the special spirituality of the urning temperament, and presented it in 1914 in *Intermediate Types among Primitive Folk*. Carpenter argued that many great religious leaders of humanity had "feminine traits" and were "somewhat bisexual in temperament." After all, he said, homosexual men are not warlike, and lesbians are not domestic; both seek other channels of expression and become innovators. Their bisexual mixture of traits gives them intuition and complexity far beyond heterosexuals. In 1916 Carpenter disingenuously "confessed" that he "had once been" homosexual.

In 1897 the first volume of *The Psychology of Sex* had appeared—*Sexual Inversion*. Like all Ellis' writings, it was graceful, convincing and encyclopedically complete, and the over-all tone attractively balanced and compassionate. Ellis' method was to review all known information and theories and then give his own tempered judgments and views. He seems a learned, reasonable man inviting the reader to join his circle of the curious and unprejudiced, to examine all the evidence with him, and draw a likely conclusion. Was homosexuality inborn or acquired? Physical or psychic? Was it, as Carpenter and Hirschfeld said, an intermediate sex? Was it pathological? Ellis characteristically said there was perhaps a bit of truth in each view. But finally he believed it most likely that homosexuality was an inborn constitutional abnormality—quite nonpathological even though

there were a fair number of neurotics among deviants. The hereditary element was strong, but perhaps some day the study of internal secretions
(hormones, they were later called) would reveal more about the constitutional aspects of deviance.

Often Ellis' balanced presentation makes all the views and evidence seem
to cancel each other out, and it is difficult to know just what Ellis believed.
Yet the reader comes away with a very definite point of view. In fact, *The
Psychology of Sex* is a covert polemic. Ellis viewed all deviance as he did
his own—harmless, unblameworthy, perhaps even specially valuable. When
he discussed the idea that it was like color-blindness, as Symonds had
claimed, he said with apparent scientific objectivity that perhaps it was
more like synesthesia, such as "color-hearing," which makes some people
equate visual and aural impression and say that a sound is "red." He then
ended by saying that "the subjects of such sensations sometimes, though by
no means invariably, show minor neurotic characters or a neurotic heredity, while at the same time it is possible to argue (as some of the subjects
of such sensations do argue) that color-hearing indicates a further step of
human development." Then, going on to whether "abnormality" meant
pathology, he pointed out that although congenital abnormality was due to
a "peculiarity" of genes or development, "the same may doubtless be said
of the normal dissimilarities between brothers and sisters." The reader
comes away from a complex welter of arguments and evidence with a
strong subliminal impression that heterosexuals and homosexuals differ no
more than red and yellow roses.

As one of Ellis' biographers points out, "The unwholesomeness one feels
... arises from the uneasy sense that the author's real meaning is different
from his apparent meaning, like a woman talking about the need to satisfy
one's biological urges when she really means she wants you to take her to
bed." The real message of the book is that all sexual acts, particularly the
more unusual, and, to many people, unattractive ones, are alike before God
and should be alike before man. His reasonable way of saying so was more
effective than a dozen fervent crusades against "hypocrisy" and "persecution." It convinced. One can read all seven volumes and hardly stop to
think that there is almost no mention of the commonest marital problems,
but a whole volume on homosexuality. In 1958 the English sex researcher
J. A. Hadfield wrote: "Havelock Ellis maintained that homosexuality was
of a constitutional type, but he admitted to me in person that he made this
statement only because he wanted to emphasize that the individual could
not help being what he was."

Ellis said, quite accurately, that the majority of sexual case histories in
previous studies had been garnered from prisons and asylums, and that if
heterosexuality were represented from such sources, it would seem just as
bizarre. But his case histories came from his friends and their acquaintances, also a very loaded sample. They were highly educated, self-aware,
articulate and deviant—writers, doctors and social reformers who elo-

quently described their suffering and often displayed admirable qualities. By using such subjects and quoting liberally from Symonds, Carpenter and other apologists, Ellis buttressed the idea of the homosexual's artistic and moral superiority. The sections on history and on the occupations of homosexuals give a strong impression that any touch of homosexual inclination or "temperament" makes one capable of greater spiritual and artistic heights. Exactly what Ellis meant by homosexuality is not clear; he claimed, in effect, that any man who felt affection for another man was showing repressed homosexuality. Where there was no evidence of homosexual behavior, he spoke of a "bisexual temperament." He further said that "distinguished women in all ages and in all fields . . . have frequently displayed some masculine traits," though he never said which ones.

Using such arguments, Ellis concluded that Shakespeare "narrowly escapes inclusion in the list of distinguished inverts." (This is like a judge reminding the jury thrice to disregard something, thus reinforcing their memory of it.) Though he himself had discovered the Baines Libel, he concluded on internal literary evidence that Marlowe had a "bisexual temperament." He gave a list of homosexual kings and said that "kings, indeed, seem peculiarly inclined to homosexuality." He stated it was even possible that musical or dramatic talent sprang from the same abnormal streak in the constitution as did homosexuality.

When *Sexual Inversion* appeared, an attempt to suppress it made it famous. As further volumes appeared, Ellis superseded Krafft-Ebing as the great public authority on sex—especially for the great majority who then rejected the budding field of psychodynamic theory. Deviants wrote to Ellis from all over the world—lonely and desperate, unable to talk to family, doctor or priest. Ellis counseled them. This was his mission in life, to bring peace and a feeling of worth to the "anomalies" of the world. He criticized Freud for charging his patients money. His work put him in contact with other reformers. Margaret Sanger, the Irish-American leader of the birth-control movement, sought him out and became a good friend. Ellis advised and defended Radclyff Hall when she wrote and published *The Well of Loneliness,* the first widely read work on lesbianism in English.

After his wife Edith's death, when Ellis was in his sixties, he won the love of a younger woman. He wrote to her, "I am not a bit like the virile, robust men of the people in your dreams! I have several dear loving women friends . . . we can be perfectly free and natural and like children together. But there is not one to whom I am a real lover. I don't ever want to be." Nevertheless, an affair began, and Ellis found himself for the first time in his life a perfectly normal, potent man. When they were separated, and she had an affair with another man, he found he could not keep to the "advanced" views he had held through his sterile marriage; he was deeply hurt and jealous. But the rift was mended, and they lived happily together for almost twenty years. If this had happened to Ellis in 1880 instead of 1920, *Studies in the Psychology of Sex* might have been just as finely written, just as scholarly and just as beautifully compassionate, but it might also have been less deviously deviant.

INTERVIEWS

Dr. Albert Ellis is a clinical psychologist, psychotherapist and Director of the Institute for Rational Living, which has headquarters in New York and branches in several cities. Though he vigorously defends the right to be deviant, he writes energetically against homosexual apologetics. He has devised a technique he calls "rational-emotive therapy," which treats people with emotional disturbances by uncovering the "irrational" beliefs and values that underlie and maintain the disturbances. It emphasizes examining self-defeating attitudes and working actively at solving life problems. Dr. Ellis has written many books and articles for laymen and many scientific papers—including an excellent critical essay on various theories about the alleged biological basis of homosexuality. Through his writings for laymen, he has become widely known as a vigorous radical spokesman for a free, guiltless sex life.

I gather that you don't believe in the idea of a well-adjusted homosexual.
No, I'm afraid I don't. Much of that sort of thinking is sparked by the new hippie point of view, and by the well-meaning but not very scientific views of Thomas Szasz and Ronald D. Laing. They say there's no such thing as an emotionally ill person, that people whom psychologists and psychiatrists call sick are just idiosyncratic and creative, and it's our own hang-ups that make us call them sick. Maybe so—but maybe the shoe is really on the other foot, with certain hung-up professionals myopically afraid to see that there are people with severe disturbances.

Of course, there are homosexuals who are better adjusted than others; usually they're less guilty about their deviation and don't condemn themselves for it. But every gay person I've seen is still pretty nutty. I used to think that most homosexuals were neurotic. Now I think that maybe 50 per cent of them are borderline psychotics. When I get one who isn't—a classic neurotic—I find that he tends to move quickly in therapy, to give up fixed homosexuality and enjoy heterosexual relations within a few weeks or months. But most homosexuals I see are like my exceptionally shy, self-hating heterosexuals—seriously disturbed. And since they wrongly prefer to believe they were born as they are, they often refuse to work very hard at tackling their basic problems.

The usual fixed homosexual is a severe phobic. He may contend that he's homosexual by choice or preference, but he has little or no heterosexual experience. Where's the choice if he hasn't tried both? Not that he should be persecuted for anxieties; we don't persecute people with nonsexual phobias. It's foolish and inhuman to make homosexuality a legal offense. But that hardly means it's wrong to acknowledge that it's a pronounced psychological disorder.

What about nonpatient homosexuals? And nonpatients in general? Do therapists only learn about "the sick ones"?
A good point. But remember that some of the sickest people in the world are

so defensive that they never admit they're disturbed, so they never go for treatment. Actually, the homosexuals we see in therapy are often less disturbed than those who refuse to come for help. Besides, I know scores of homosexuals personally who've never had any type of treatment and are just as disturbed as those I regularly see for psychotherapy. There are several recent studies that purport to show that homosexuals are no more disturbed than heterosexuals. But these studies have been uniformly done in a naïve, biased, careless way. Dr. Evelyn Hooker's famous study unjustifiably compared a few highly selected, better-adjusted, bright, working, unguilty homosexuals to an unselected group of heterosexuals. For testing, it mainly used the Rorschach test, which has no proven validity. Does this kind of study truly show that homosexuals aren't disturbed?

Dr. Harry Benjamin and some others claim they've dealt with people who are relatively normal aside from being transvestites and transsexuals.

First of all, I've never seen a transvestite who wasn't a serious neurotic. And, again, I've known a good many socially who weren't any therapist's patients. As for transsexuals, who want their penises and testicles amputated to make them "true" women, can anyone doubt whether practically all of them are out of their minds? I've interviewed a dozen, all of whom tried to get me to help them be castrated. They were all paranoid schizophrenics. Dr. Benjamin is an old friend of mine, and he's indubitably heterosexual. But I'm sorry to say that many of the other authorities who claim homosexuality is innate, that homosexuals can't change and should be adjusted to their handicap, are homosexual themselves. They're more than slightly biased. In an essay I wrote for one of the homosexual society's journals, I only named dead writers of this kind, such as Magnus Hirschfeld, who wouldn't admit that homosexuals are disturbed because of their own deviance. But I know of a good many who are around today—and from your interviews you probably know a few yourself. It's sad to say that I've had patients who picked up homosexual psychiatrists and psychologists in public parks and baths. Many homosexuals feel safe with these professionals, who only want to adjust them. Then these same professionals authoritatively write that fixed homosexuals can't be cured!

Do you get the impression that lesbians, as a group, are either more or less disturbed than male homosexuals?

Yes, in some respects. Frequently they not only love other women but hate males; you don't necessarily find that much hostility to women among male homosexuals. Maybe some very hostile women find in butch-type lesbianism an outlet for their anger. Women can be heterosexual despite frigidity, since they don't have to achieve and maintain erection. And if they want to have heterosexual relations, they can get laid more easily. A male trying to cure himself of homosexuality may not be able to get a girl so easily. Or he has to risk displaying his initial impotence with her. So women who cop out on the female role and become lesbians are giving up on a relatively easy role to assume; and they're often exceptionally disturbed.

You hear a lot of nonsense about "all women are lesbians" because they embrace and kiss each other and so on. But it's a lot different being a confirmed lesbian, compulsively driven to other women. The confirmed lesbian tends to come to psychotherapy mainly at a time of crisis—"I lost my girlfriend and I hurt terribly" or "I can't win any girl I love, and I want to commit suicide." She is so disturbed, and goes with other girls who are so self-hating and angry, that her life is often melodramatic. When she dares leave a lesbian lover, she's often threatened with harassment, the lover's suicide, or even threats of murder. But when a lesbian gets over her current emotional crisis, she tends to discontinue psychotherapy.

Many males are driven by itching penises to engage in easily available homosexual relations, as compared to the difficulties of making it with women in our society. Males may be very sexy, but because they're afraid of failure with women they tend to drift into the gay life instead of withdrawing from sex altogether. Women are less imperiously driven into sex, more prone to emphasize the social and familial assets of a stable married life. So when they avoid heterosexual relations entirely and become ccnfirmed lesbians, they're often as disturbed as they can be.

How do you treat homosexuals?

I've explained it in detail in my book, *Homosexuality: Its Causes and Cure.* Briefly, we see fixed homosexuals for individual therapy sessions and also often put them into therapy groups—one or two, usually, in a group that's otherwise heterosexual. If too many homosexuals are in the same group, they may be upset at seeing a member change and try to drag him back to homosexuality.

We give all clients lessons in straight thinking, and also specific homework assignments. Classical analysis provides a cop-out; a person can just talk for several years, so that he can avoid working to get better. We try to give the individual three kinds of insight. First, we show him that his present symptoms have antecedents—specifically, that to *feel* anxious, guilty, depressed or angry he must be telling or signalling to himself some irrational ideas, some perfectionistic demands on himself or others. Second, we show him that no matter where his rigid, self-defeating thinking originated, it only exists today because *he* is actively, if perhaps unconsciously, carrying it on. Third, we convince him that there's no way but hard work and practice to give up this nonsense. He must keep challenging his own irrational thinking and force himself to do some risk-taking in his activity. So in group therapy we show the homosexual that he is right now, in the present, convincing himself that he can't make it with girls, that it would be terrible if he failed, and he must be supermasculine by supposedly winning other males' approval. We do more, too. We give him graduated homework assignments. Try to make a date with several girls. Actually go out on some dates. Make overtures of affection and sex to at least one girl. Masturbate with the image of females in mind. Try to have intercourse with a girl. The group and I check up on the assignments to see whether they were done, and why not if they were avoided, and so on.

Almost all homosexuals can function with females if they persist at trying, but often they don't try. My associates and I actively get them to. For example, I saw a man who'd been married ten years but had mainly avoided intercourse with his wife while steadily having it with many men. I persuaded him to think of the real disadvantages of going to bed with men, picture the pleasures of going to bed with women, and have intercourse with his wife almost every night, whether he wanted to or not at first, for thirty days. After a month he was really lusting after his wife—and other girls too! His homosexual desire had dropped enormously, and all his compulsive cruising for men stopped.

We use some behavior methods along with others. Wolpe says if you're afraid of a snake, think of one twenty miles away, then ten miles, and so on, till the fear disappears. Skinner, with his operant conditioning idea, is closest to what we do. We insist, if you're afraid of snakes, go to the zoo, see one, touch it. Take some risks and challenge irrational ideas. We also teach clients to be long-range instead of short-range hedonists. Fixed homosexuals, quite typically, have low frustration tolerance. They believe it's too hard or impossible to do something—such as succeed with women—rather than the truth, which is that it's often damned hard, but it can be done. We teach them to forgo pleasures of today, and give up their childish, goofing philosophies of life, to behave with more self-discipline and enjoy tomorrow and the day after.

How successful do you think the treatment of homosexuals is?

As you know, psychotherapists rarely follow up their cases, partly because it's very expensive. In my own unofficial follow-ups, I find that some fall back to their old patterns, most continue their new and improved patterns, and some go on to really cure themselves, working at making themselves less and less disturbed over the years. Most of my improved homosexual clients continue to enjoy heterosexual relations after therapy has ended. A minority find it "too hard" to get female partners in our prudish society, find it easier to get male companionship, and largely slip back into homosexual pathways.

I think we must face the fact that people are both born and raised to be seriously disturbed, and they have great difficulty getting and remaining better. There are probably twenty vectors, genetic and other, that make a person susceptible to neurosis and a deviant pattern of some kind. Some of the most seriously disordered improve greatly, though they're never completely cured. I probably have more ex-schizophrenic individuals walking the streets of New York today than any other psychotherapist. Once emotionally crippled, now they work, are reasonably happily mated, live pretty good lives. I think few, if any, are completely cured. They still tend toward cognitive slippage, crooked thinking, but they're doing immensely better than when I first saw them. Now homosexuals, like other seriously disturbed people, have tremendous resistance to working to overcome their inborn and acquired tendencies to be neurotic, borderline psychotic or psychotic. Although they weren't born homosexual, they generally have innate tendencies toward severe general disturbance. Even when they give up fixed homosexuality and enjoy heterosexual relations immensely, they still have slippery thinking in other respects. They aren't totally cured, but they are improved. This isn't to say it's impossible for easily upsettable people to stay rational and un-self-destructive. But it's certainly hard.

Do you think deviations other than homosexuality are very common?

Not in the usual sense of the term. Compulsive sadists, masochists, peepers, exhibitionists—there are probably more fixed homosexuals than all of them combined. But the number of people who engage in unconventional forms of sex behavior but aren't truly deviant seems to be increasing. Take people who participate in wife-swapping or orgies; as long as they aren't compulsive, phobic, fixated on one form of sex, they aren't actually deviant. They're hardly in the millions, but more and more people are experimenting, and as long as they're able to enjoy regular sexual intercourse and one-to-one love relationships with the other sex, this is in some ways a healthy addition to the oldtime forms of sex, love and marriage.

I get the impression that many of the so-called sexual revolutionaries on the campuses are actually practicing a sort of gentle, lyrical, barely sexual sex.

Yes, just because they have free-love unions doesn't mean that they're truly sexually liberated. Many follow a neopuritan line that says sex isn't really good in itself, but has to be deodorized by love. They ignore or deny the fact that hordes of people can have a great time in bed whether or not they're amatively attached to their partner. Some of them take Martin Buber's I-Thou philosophy to obnoxious extremes and say that it alone makes sex legitimate—which isn't what Buber said. Going by this unrealistic standard, they keep asking themselves whether they *really* love their sex partners, whether they aren't vilely exploiting them when wanting an orgasm for themselves. They make themselves continually anxious and guilty. If sex partners keep demanding, "Do I really love her enough? Am I doing the right thing? Am I exploiting?" they become incapable of enjoying themselves. These college kids often have too little healthy self-interest. Without enlightened self-interest, what's sex really worth—or almost anything else, for that matter?

13

Beyond the West

Most of the early writers on homosexuality sought evidence on sex norms and deviations in non-Western societies. Since the great age of voyage and discovery in the sixteenth century, explorers had brought back to Europe erotic accounts that disgusted and delighted their listeners. They reported nudity, polygamy, wife lending, bestiality, homosexuality and transvestism. Some so-called savages were more rigorously controlled about sex than Christians, but most were portrayed as naked hordes abandoned to promiscuity and perversion. Depending on whether one was conventionally devout or a sexual utopian, these stories were a smirch on mankind or a hint of paradise.

Some of these crude accounts are still all the information we have about the sexuality of certain peoples. Of homosexuality in much of Asia, Africa and the Arab world, we know little or no more than such anecdotalists as Burton and Mantegazza did. This has done little to stop the use of China, Japan, India, North Africa, black Africa and the Near East as support for various theories of sexuality and homosexuality. Scientific anthropology has done surprisingly little to clarify and add to this slim knowledge.

Most of the early accounts of non-Western homosexuality were sweeping but brief. Samuel Purchas, the Elizabethan compiler of travel writings, said that the Tartars were "addicted to Sodomie or Buggerie." In the late 1580s, Thomas Cavendish, the third man to circumnavigate the world, reported that he had discovered homosexuality in the islands north of Japan. Many of the Conquistadors found it in various parts of Central and South America. Leo Africanus, an Arab-born voyager and geographer of the first half of the sixteenth century, said there was organized lesbian prostitution at Fez, in Morocco, and that male witches there had "a damnable custome to commit unlawful Venerie among themselves." William Lithgow, a Scot who roamed thirty-six thousand miles back and forth across Europe and the Middle East between 1609 and 1622, recorded in his *Rare adventures and painefull peregrinations* that the Turks were "generally addicted, besides all their sensuall and incestuous lusts, unto Sodomy, which they account as a daynty to digest all their other libidinous pleasures."

Many explorers, traders, missionaries and colonists misinterpreted what they saw, believed hearsay, took folklore literally and generalized from splinters of knowledge. What in their writings can one believe? Imagine trying to determine the facts about homosexuality in Burundi from three letters by a Chicago-bred nun working in a clinic there; two anecdotes passed second-hand from a Southport-*cum*-Smith deb who stopped over for two days during a plane trip; the recollections, years after, by the wife of a Marine security man at the U.S. embassy; the diary of a visiting Milanese importer; three paragraphs in a book on tribal politics by a sociologist from the University of Grenoble. The Marine's wife might be the most perceptive observer, the sociologist most blinded by ideology or inhibition—but one would have no way of knowing that.

Some reports of sexual life in China, for instance, describe modest restraint, and others tell of uninhibited and exquisite sexual refinement. The *Historie of China* written in 1585 by the Augustinian father Juan Gonzales de Mendoza called the Chinese decorous, closely bound to their families, and quite virtuous in European terms. But if one reads Sir John Barrow, the picture is very different. Barrow was secretary to the English ambassador to China in the late eighteenth century, a writer, geographer and, later, founder of the Royal Geographical Society. In his *Travels in China,* in 1806, he said that the Chinese were a moderate people and generally observed premarital and extramarital chastity, but since women were kept in total submission, and marriage was a social rather than a passionate bond, the poor Chinese man went to prostitutes for excitement, and the wealthy kept a seraglio of up to ten concubines. Furthermore, this temperate heterosexual climate seemed to promote

> that sort of connection . . . that sinks the man many degrees below the brute. The commission of this detestable and unnatural act is attended with so little shame, or feelings of delicacy, that many of the first officers of state seemed to make no hesitation in publicly avowing it. Each of these officers is constantly attended by his pipe-bearer, who is generally a handsome boy from fourteen to eighteen years of age, and is always well dressed. In pointing out to our notice, the boys of each other, they made use of signs and motions, the meaning of which was too obvious to be misinterpreted.

Actually, homosexuality had been noticed by foreigners in China long before Barrow's day. Two Arab travelers trekked through India and China in the ninth century, and in their chronicle said the Chinese were addicted to sodomy and even performed it in their shrines. Like Barrow, they noticed many eunuchs, and linked them with homosexual practices. There is evidence from other sources that a century or so later there was a class of male prostitutes in China who were made subject to legal penalties but then formed a guild and walked the streets dressed like women. In later centuries, the boys and men who played women's parts in the all-male Chinese theater were notorious for homosexuality and homosexual prostitution.

A still less inhibited picture appeared in a book written late in the nineteenth century by a French physician named Matignon. According to him, Chinese women were such docile, homebound dullards that the men, like those of ancient Greece, sought courtesans and boys. Most people were casual about homosexual acts, and the law made little distinction between homosexual and heterosexual offenses—it was age and consent that mattered most. Some of the wealthy even considered homosexuality a rather chic distraction, said Matignon, and used the emperor's proclivities as a precedent.

Some travelers said sodomy was most common in northern China, where there were brothels stocked with poor boys from Peking. The Chinese poor sometimes sold their children into prostitution, and Matignon claimed that male bordellos acquired boys as young as four to train them for the profession. The boys received depilation, dilation of the anus, massages to develop the buttocks and training in singing, drawing and poetry. They were effeminate and luxuriously dressed. Waiters at restaurants would direct clients to them or to less refined homosexual prostitutes. Simone de Beauvoir, describing Peking in 1955, said that in the ring between the Forbidden City and the Chinese City "one used to find the localities dedicated to amusements and debauchery: theaters, public baths, renowned restaurants which still exist, and opium dens and brothels which exist no more. Hereabout, until 1911, there were even houses of male prostitution legally tolerated and frequented by the Manchu nobility."

There were also male bordellos in Canton, in the south, into the nineteenth and early twentieth centuries, and in other parts of Asia. Homosexual prostitutes among the Sarts of Turkestan were called by the Chinese name *batsha*. In what was then French Indo-China, Annamite boys prostituted themselves to Europeans living in Saigon. Male homosexuality was described by travelers among the Malaysians and the Bataks of Sumatra, and lesbianism in Bali.

When Burton spoke of China in his "Terminal Essay," he far outdid even Matignon, citing a number of Western writers who had reported male prostitution, tribadism, aphrodisiacs, "French ticklers," devices for female masturbation, and erotic literature and art. He called the Chinese "the chosen people of debauchery, and their systematic bestiality with ducks, goats and other animals is equalled only by their pederasty."

Finally, a Western reader couldn't be sure whether most Chinese preferred the shrine and family fireside or the brothel, barnyard and opium den. Were they homebound, industrious, judicious and rather prim? Or sensual, amoral and addicted to ingenious lubricity? It depended on which writer one read, or even which pages of a single writer. Undoubtedly homosexuality and homosexual prostitution existed, but how much, and what place they had in Chinese society, are uncertain. The extreme descriptions either way sound like parodies of a Chinese family laundry and repetitions of the old European belief that the East is the world's fount of "luxury and vice."

A similar but not quite as severe contradiction appeared in writings about Japan. There, too, women were subservient, sexual attitudes permissive, and homosexuality described as a pleasure of the rich and of priests. When Hagenaar and Frans Caron went to Japan for the Dutch East India Company in the 1630s, they observed that "all the priests and some of the nobility are strongly attached to unnatural lusts; they do not make any sin of this propensity, and neither feel shame or remorse on account of it." They described pleasure parties at Shinto shrines, to which laymen brought courtesans; the priests, "being forbidden the use of women, have recourse to unnatural practices."*

In the closing years of that century, Englebert Kaempfer, physician to the Dutch embassy in Japan, wrote that there was no homosexual soliciting in the streets, but one had only to enter an inn, tea booth or cookshop, even in a village, to find a homosexual partner, often a prostitute. The priests might be luxurious and slothful, said Kaempfer, but they weren't especially given to homosexuality—on this the Carons had erred.

From other writers the West heard that three groups were traditionally linked with homosexuality in Japan—monks, actors and samurai. Buddhist monasticism spread there in the ninth and tenth centuries, and homosexuality allegedly developed as a result, especially between religious masters and their disciples. Shinto priests also received their share of accusations. Japanese actresses became known as prostitutes, and in 1629 they were banned from the stage. As a result, men and boys took female roles; soon they were put under the regulations applying to prostitutes. And in medieval Japan, the samurai, or warrior class, were said to have institutionalized homosexuality along ancient Greek lines. They considered the love of women contemptible and took young men as pages and lovers. Despite attempts to limit this by the Tokugawa shogunate from the early seventeenth century on, it remained a familiar part of samurai tradition until the revolution of 1868, when Japan banned homosexual acts along with many other things that embarrassed her before Western eyes.

We lack reliable evidence about the incidence of homosexuality in even the West's theaters, monasteries and military elites; how precisely talk of homosexual monks, actors and samurai reflected reality is anyone's guess. But it does seem—from Japanese fiction of the seventeenth and eighteenth centuries and from other sources—that in the cities there was a fairly tolerant attitude toward homosexual behavior—at least in certain contexts, such as the samurai affair and the bisexual pleasure-seeking of well-to-do young men on the town.

In India there was a great difference in attitude and behavior between the Hindus and the Muslims. Hinduism puts a very heavy emphasis on

*If reports of homosexuality among priests and monks in Japan are correct, they may, like the Arab chronicle of China, point to temple prostitution like that of the ancient Near East. If not true, they may merely be the product of the usual tendency to link foreignness, nonbelief and sexual deviance.

abstinence and self-control, and the Laws of Manu protect the family zealously. They prescribe that if a married woman seduces an unmarried girl, her head should be shaved, two of her fingers lopped off, and that she be ridden through town on a donkey. The *Kama Sutra* mentions dildoes in harems, but whether these refer to a common practice we cannot tell. When hundreds of English colonials wrote about India in the eighteenth and nineteenth centuries, there was almost unanimous agreement that the Hindus abhorred homosexuality just as much as they did, and that if many practiced it, they did so in secrecy and shame. There was a class of boys called *hinjras* who were said to prepare for their trade as homosexual prostitutes by stretching the anus with a conical piece of wood or metal; they were held in deep contempt by other Hindus.

The Indian Muslims, on the other hand, were constantly accused by English and French writers of homosexuality, both male and female. An English traveler, Peter Mundy, said back in the second quarter of the seventeenth century that Muslim aristocrats kept handsome pages for their pleasure, and that Sufi mystics, whose idea of spiritual love was perhaps a parent of the *amor purus* of the Albigensians, really carried on secret homosexual affairs. In 1845 Burton discovered three brothels of boys and eunuchs in the small town of Karachi alone. In his "Terminal Essay" he said he had found

> the Sikhs and Moslems of the Panjáb much addicted to *le vice*, although the Himalayan tribes to the north and those lying south, the Rájputs and Marathás, ignore it. The same may be said of the Kashmirians. . . . M. Louis Daville describes the infamies of Lahore and Lakhnau where he found men dressed as women, with flowing locks under crowns of flowers, imitating the feminine walk and gestures, voice and fashion of speech, and ogling their admirers with all the coquetry of bayadères. Victor Jacquemont's *Journal de Voyage* describes the pederasty of Ranjít Singh, the "Lion of the Panjáb," and his pathic Guláb Singh whom the English inflicted upon the Cashmir as ruler by way of paying for his treason. Yet the Hindus, I repeat, hold pederasty in abhorrence and are as much scandalized by being called Gándmárá (anus-beater) or Gándú (anuser) as Englishmen would be.

However, there were also accounts of scorn and avoidance of homosexuality in Muslim India. Mundy himself had reported that when a Muslim boy killed an officer under whom he served for inflicting a homosexual act on him, the boy spent only six months in prison, because "the Governor did not dare to condemn him, as he feared the people, who maintained that the young man had acted rightly." The Muslims, like Christians, officially condemned homosexuality but enforced the ban inconsistently—sometimes harshly and sometimes hardly at all. Yet as long as Europe has been in contact with Islam, it has accused it of carefree sodomy, with attitudes varying from horror to amused contempt. Furthermore, it has confused the concepts of Islam and Arab, attributing "*le vice*" to both and thinking of them interchangeably.

After its beginning in the sixth century, Islam, or the Muslim faith, spread west from Arabia to the Near East and North Africa. It went eastward though India to southeast Asia, and for a while embraced part of southern Europe. (For several centuries Hindu and Muslim kingdoms stood side by side in India, but Muslim control grew steadily and was almost complete from about 1300 till the middle of the eighteenth century, when the British took over. Muslim and Hindu retained their separate ways of life, and the latter remained concentrated in greater numbers in the north.) By conversion and conquest, Islam took in many peoples with very different cultural, linguistic and physical characteristics. "Arabs" are only a part of Islam. The term Arab is variously used for people of the Muslim faith, those who speak the Arabic languages, and loosely for cultural and physical traits common in North Africa and the Near East. None of these categories quite overlap; the word is an unfortunate artifact for which no substitute exists. Even within the narrowest definition, the term Arab includes great differences in culture and sexual mores and practices. The only thing common to it and societies often associated with it is the official code of Islam.

Islam set up many of the same sexual restrictions as Judaism and Christianity; it differed chiefly in allowing a man up to four legal wives, and concubines besides. Like Judaism, and unlike Christianity, it put no premium on celibacy for its own sake. All forbidden sexual acts fall into the category called *Zîna*; among them are sodomy, tribadism, bestiality and prostitution. The punishment for *Zîna*, as for murder, theft and usury, is death, usually by stoning; but an airtight case is required, and the sentence has rarely been carried out.

"Arab homosexuality" is often said to be largely the result of the separation of the sexes called for by the Koran. As a system it is called *purdah*, and in practice it requires a harem—literally, a forbidden place—a part of each house where the women live, protected from contact with all males but certain close relatives. *Purdah* has usually gone along with low status for women, even contempt for them. No one is sure where *purdah* originated; some say Persia, others India. It was well established in much of the Muslim world by the turn of the ninth century, and it continued widely into the twentieth. People have assumed that this seclusion of women created lesbianism in their quarters and made frustrated males turn to each other for sexual satisfaction. Europeans visiting Egypt, Turkey and Muslim India have claimed in recent centuries that lesbianism abounded in harems and women's baths there, even that every woman who lived in a harem had a "friend."

But since harems were kept isolated and secret, most information on them is unreliable gossip. There are also many references to prohibitions against homosexuality and the punishments it might bring. It is said that when the early caliph al-Hadi found two female attendants in his palace making love, he beheaded them on the spot. The great harem built by

Muhammed II in Constantinople in the fifteenth century contained many European women captured in war, and they were supervised by other women and by eunuchs. Lesbianism was said to exist there, and in the seventeenth century male homosexuality was said to be rife in the sultan's palace also. However, homosexuality was far from approved. According to Sir Paul Rycaut, in 1687, the homosexual pages there had a sign language among themselves because "in the event of discovery they were nearly beaten to death and expelled from the Seraglio."

Accounts of male homosexuality and male homosexual prostitution showed contrasts of official disapproval and informal indulgence all over North Africa and the Near and Middle East. In the Middle East in the early eighth century there was a class of homosexual prostitutes called Mukhannath who dressed and acted like women, plaited their hair and hennaed their nails. Those in Mecca were castrated on the order of Caliph Suleiman.

Various parts of the Arab and Muslim world were named as paradigms of homosexual riot. Europeans told of homosexual prostitution in the nineteenth century in Mecca and Zanzibar, transvestite dervishes in Jerusalem, sodomy in Syria and Iraq. Burton said that the Afghans took "traveling wives," as they called them, on their caravans with them—boys with kohl about their eyes, henna on their fingers and toes, and rouged cheeks. He also indicted the Kurds and Georgians, and claimed that though Armenians preferred women, they would prostitute themselves to men. Persia acquired a special reputation. One traveler reported the presence of male brothels and the absence of female brothels. Boys were said to be used by men, then to grow up, marry to produce heirs, and go to boys for pleasure in their turn.* Here Burton found a practice noted for some time in parts of the Arab world—mass sodomitic rape as a punishment and humiliation. This was almost surely done to Lawrence of Arabia by his Turkish captors, and during the Napoleonic conquest, the Orientalist Jaubert had said that "The Arabs and Mamlukes did to our prisoners what Socrates is said to have done to Alcibiades. They had to go along with it or die." Burton said a

---

*Although Persia was often called the nucleus of homosexuality within the Arab world, many Persians are not Muslims but Zoroastrians. According to the Zoroastrian *Vendidâd*, "There is no worse sin than this in the good religion, and it is proper to call those who commit it worthy of death in reality. If anyone comes forth to them, and shall see them in the act, and is working with an axe, it is requisite for him to cut off the heads or to rip up the bellies of both, and it is no sin for him. But it is not proper to kill any person without the authority of high-priests and kings, except on account of committing or permitting unnatural intercourse." Capital punishment in this world would be followed by torments in the next. The Zoroastrians held sodomy a sin created by wicked demons, and its commission put one utterly outside the faith. If an infidel committed it in ignorance, he might submit to Zoroastrianism, swear never to repeat it and be absolved. But for a Zoroastrian there was no atonement. Like the Jews and Christians, the Zoroastrians saw sodomy as an act of unbelief, heresy, outsideness.

favorite Persian punishment for strangers caught in the harem was to strip them and throw them to male slaves for anal rape:

> I once asked a Shirazi how penetration was possible if the patient resisted with all the force of the sphincter muscle: he smiled and said, "Ah, we Persians know a trick to get over that; we apply a sharpened tent-peg to the crupper-bone (os coccygis) and knock till he opens." A well-known missionary to the East during the last generation was subjected to this gross insult by one of the Persian Prince-governors, whom he had infuriated by his conversion-mania: in his memoirs he alludes to it by mentioning his "dishonoured person"; but English readers cannot comprehend the full significance of the confession.

Turkey and North Africa ran a close second to Persia in European reports. In Turkey, nineteenth-century visitors said, men commonly had homosexual relations with boys of twelve to eighteen, and prostitution was prevalent. Attendants of all-night baths in Constantinople would masturbate their clients. Homosexuality was said to be common not only in such big cities as Cairo, Algiers, Tunis and Tripoli, where there were male bordellos and effeminates who haunted the baths, but also among Egyptian peasants, Tunisian villagers and the Arab-speaking mountaineers of northern Morocco. Westermarck said that a Moroccan boy learning the Koran was thought to do so properly only if he had relations with the scribe who taught him, and the same applied to apprentices learning trades from masters.

A special form of transvestism and male prostitution was described in Cairo in the 1830s by an Englishman named E. W. Lane. He told of a group, who sound rather like a special caste, perhaps Gypsies, who worked as entertainers and prostitutes. A woman of this group was called a Ghawazee, a man a Ghazee. In 1834 public female dancing and prostitution were both prohibited by law, so the Ghawazee were put out of work. Their place was taken by Khawals and Ginks. The Khawals were males who dressed as women, grew their hair long, plucked their beards, wore kohl and henna, and often went veiled in the streets. They did the Ghawazee dances at marriages, circumcisions and other celebrations, and doubled as male prostitutes. The Ginks were also female impersonators and male prostitutes. Both types must have been masters of transvestism; when Gérard de Nerval visited Egypt and saw Khawals dance, it was not till after their performance that he realized they were men.

There is no doubt that eunuchs, boy prostitutes and homosexuals of both sexes existed through much of the Arab world and Muslim Asia, probably more than in much of Europe. Descriptions varied from a lurid stew of gleeful perversion to a pattern that existed in ancient Greece and much of Mediterranean Europe for thousands of years into our own times—a minority of exclusive homosexuals, and scorn for the grown male who took a passive role or had frequent relations with other men instead of with woman and boys. Scandalized Europeans reported the extreme aspects of homosexual behavior, too rarely distinguishing whether homosexuality was an open minority activity or a majority practice—and, if common, whether exclusive or secondary.

In fact, when assessing these reports it helps to stop and think of someone from another planet visiting London in 1750, Berlin in the early thirties or New York in 1971. He would see areas of the city where transvestites and young male prostitutes parade the street in great numbers; learn of influential politicians, artists and businessmen with homosexual or bisexual behavior patterns; perhaps find more or less what Kinsey did, that a significant percentage of males have at least one or a few homosexual experiences; see homosexual bars for both sexes; learn of sado-masochism, of festishism, of brothels and prostitutes that specialize in deviant pleasures. The report the visitor from space sent home might be as full of "shameless" deviance as are European accounts of some other cultures. To understand a people's life, one needs not just simple observations and a jumble of gossip, but an understanding of how many people do what to whom, when, in what circumstances, and how they and others feel about it. We still lack such careful study of most of the Arab world.

The same confusing ancedote gathering occurred when Europeans discovered Africa, the Pacific and the Americas. The laws of the Aztecs of Central Mexico and the Mayas of Yucatan and Central America both condemned homosexuals to death by stoning. Nevertheless, Bernal Diaz, chronicling Cortez's conquest of Mexico, described homosexuality and male brothels. Other Spaniards found the same in Nicaragua and Panama. Among the Aztecs, the younger sons of prominent men were sometimes castrated and sent to temples to serve as *bijanas,* "dedicated to the gods." This sounds somewhat like the male prostitution that accompanied the worship of Ishtar and Artemis.

The Spaniards did not distinguish ritual from secular prostitution, if such a distinction actually existed, and they had no more use for male brothels in Mexico than they did in their homeland. Those whom the Mexican natives had stoned, the Spaniards roasted. The high-handed ruler of Mexico Nuño de Guzman wrote in 1530, "The last which was taken, and which fought most couragiously, was a man in the habite of a woman, which confessed that from a childe he had gotten his living by the filthinesse, for which I caused him to be burned." Two centuries later men were still being reported in the Mexican provinces who dressed as women and married other men. Several writers confirmed the presence of male homosexuality, lesbianism, transvestism and temple homosexuality in the Peruvian Inca kingdom, which had its capital at Cuzco. The Spanish soldier and chronicler Cieza de Leon said that "the Devill so farre prevayled in their beastly Devotions that there were Boyes consecrated to serve in the Temple; and at the times of their Sacrifices and Solemne Feasts, the Lords and principall men abused them to that detestable filthinesse." It was said that in the hill country every temple had priests who had been dressed and raised as females since childhood.

Nevertheless, according to Garcilaso de la Vega, sodomy was an abomination to the Incas, and they had strong legal sanctions against it. Garcilaso was a mestizo, the son of an Inca princess and a Spaniard, born about eight years after the conquest of Peru. He wrote the *Royal Commentaries of Peru,* based on the history and legends of his mother's people. He said that when an Inca commander conquered a valley village, he looked into the local customs and found that homosexuality was practiced in secret there and in other valley communities. He reported to the Inca ruler, who told him to burn the homosexuals alive, and their trees and houses with them, and to visit this fate upon any village in its entirety if homosexuality were discovered in it. In Cuzco, said Garcilaso, if one as much as said the word sodomite to another man, one was considered to have fouled one's mouth.

Later colonial writers mentioned male and female homosexuality in this area. Even in the nineteenth and twentieth centuries, male concubinage and transvestism were found among tribes descended from the Incas, Aztecs and Mayas—for instance, among the Aymara of Bolivia, who are direct descendants of the Incas. Homosexuals of both sexes were reported in other parts of Latin America as well; among the Gandavo of Brazil, for instance, there were said to be lesbians who refused to be touched by men, wore their hair in male fashion, fought with bow and arrow, and married other women.

While all this information and misinformation accumulated, scientific anthropology was germinating. Since Hobbes in the seventeenth century, men had occasionally spoken of creating a "social physics" that would apply the precise techniques of physical science to the study of society. And like Hobbes, many people assumed that man is by nature selfish and aggressive, and that civilization progressively curtails brute, amoral urges. Therefore anthropology developed largely around the question of sexual controls and family structure. Hume's belief, which became quite popular, was that sex brought human beings together; this created families, which led to mutual protection, sympathy and aid; this in turn gave rise to fixed social customs. So sex led to love, love to marriage, marriage to civilization. With grand arrogance and grander naïveté, Westerners assumed that preliterate peoples were simple folk dragging anchor at an early stage of social development equivalent to Europe's distant past. The problem, as they saw it, was to figure out how Europe had risen above such savage disorder, sin and silliness.

So as biblical accounts of creation faded, "natural philosophers" (as many scientists still called themselves) theorized at length on the evolutionary stages of human progress. Turgot, in France, said that men go from hunting to pastoral to agricultural societies. Condorcet, Hume and others had their own versions of the ladder to civilization; eventually Darwin,

Marx and others would produce other such theories in turn. All these evolutionary theories make two assumptions. One is that aggregates of men obey rules of nature just as asteroids and migrating swallows do. The other is that mankind has risen from savagery, selfishness and unreason to logic, altruism and restraint. Implicit in the second assumption is the West's old nightmare vision of man as a feral, slavering creature of unbridled sex and aggression.

The systematic study of folklore became popular in the second half of the eighteenth century. Gradually it moved from collecting curiosa and bizarre anecdotes to the systematic comparison of mores, sex behavior, the family, law, languages, religion and political institutions. In the 1840s anthropological societies appeared in Europe. During the decades that followed, the first masterpieces of modern anthropology appeared. Henry Maine published the first great study of comparative law, and William Lecky his vast *History of European Morals.* In 1853 John Jacob Bachofen's *Das Mutterrecht (Matriarchal Law)* helped determine the course of cultural anthropology by setting up a controversy with Maine.

Two years earlier Maine had claimed in his great work that the original social unit of mankind was the patriarchal family. From such families grew clans, and from clans grew tribes. Bachofen said that, to the contrary, there had first been a promiscuous, anarchic Primitive Horde. Women had controlled the family, culture and government. This epoch, said Bachofen, "is the poetry of history because of the sublime character, the heroic majesty and beauty, it lends to women." Then, he said, came the catastrophe of the patriarchal coup, when men realized their role in procreation. Private property replaced common property, gods replaced goddesses, men instead of women ran society, and modesty developed as a male instrument of protecting his female chattel. Bachofen, like Maine, drew on ethnology, myth and Western history to support his theory.

The Bachofen idea of matriarchies and patriarchies has had extraordinary durability. One of Bachofen's advocates, the Scot John MacLennan, produced another theory with a gift for survival. On the basis of folk customs, history and ethnology he decided that all societies go through a period of marriage by capture, the male overcoming and abducting his intended. This is the source of those comic-book jokes about men in fur suits clubbing ladies and dragging them off by the hair. MacLennan did make a great contribution to anthropology, though. He drew attention to totemism, totemic social organizations and exogamy, the practice of marrying outside one's social group. The controversies that followed focused anthropology closely on the question of kinship. Who is a relative, what constitutes a family, and therefore what constitutes incest? From all this there emerged one of the few statements that can be made about human social behavior in all cultures. Wherever there are people, there are families, and where there are families, there is a rule against incest. Families may be defined somewhat differently from society to society, and therefore the definition of incest varies, but the basic incest-tabooed unit always includes at least the nuclear family of parents, children and siblings.

Most writers on the subject of sex, family, kinship and exogamy at that time were intent on proving or disproving certain Victorian assumptions about morality. One of the great pioneer anthropologists, Henry Lewis Morgan, sometimes tended to make Presbyterian monogamy seem a law of nature. But he also did some of the great early studies of kinship, and went to great pains to show that the European bourgeois family was not the only possible one, and that progress and monogamy were not exactly synonymous. He developed many ideas now considered self-evident: that technical and economic factors influence cultural developments; that all people have rules about sex and marriage; and that even among people with rudimentary material culture these rules may be fantastically complex.

In 1871 Edward Tylor's *Primitive Culture* appeared, and this is usually considered the starting point of modern scientific anthropology. Tylor underscored the cultural relativity of values, and he raised the crucial question of whether similarities between societies are due to contact and transmission or to a "psychic unity of mankind" that makes the same ideas and institutions arise independently. (In other words, to what extent is there a basic human nature? It is still an important question.) Tylor also refined the methods of comparative ethnology. He used statistical techniques on his information more extensively than any anthropologist before him, and thus made theories more susceptible to proofs.

It was at this point that an anthropologist wrote the first serious study of homosexuality. Edward Westermarck was born in Finland and lived his adult life in England. By the time he was in his early thirties he was a world-famous scholar. Until that time most sexual anthropology had been in the Mantegazza-Burton style—grab-bags of anecdote, folklore and rumor. Westermarck, after the fashion of Tylor, tried to be careful and systematic with his evidence before generalizing. His *History of Human Marriage*, which appeared in 1891, was a mountainously documented attack on the primitive-promiscuity theory. He showed that there is no evidence that a society has ever existed, present or past, that didn't have a system of marriage and family. Early evolutionists had said marriage was a way of legally restricting the previously untrammeled sex instinct. Westermarck said that the basis of marriage and the family was not the desire for exclusive sexual property, but the fact that the human infant, with its long period of helpless dependency, needs a stable and nurturing adult group in which to grow up. This is the position of most scientists today. Within a few years after Westermarck's book appeared, Bachofen's *Mutterrecht* theory began to fall from regard. In 1927, when feminist and communist Robert Briffault wrote *The Mothers* as a last-ditch defense of Bachofen, he had to concentrate on trying to discredit Westermarck.

Westermarck's *The Origin and Development of Moral Ideas* appeared between 1906 and 1908. It contained a section on "Homosexual Love" and was the most complete, thoughtful cross-cultural study ever made of the subject. It was also markedly uncondemnatory. When Lecky had written his early comparative study of European morals, he had called homosexuality "the lowest abyss of unnatural love." In a quietly stubborn way, Westermarck broke with most authorities of his day by taking a truly neutral tone.

This is not to say that his attitude was like liberal and psychiatrically oriented ones of today. He was a contemporary of Freud, but his thinking about homosexuality was closer to that of Havelock Ellis, whom he quoted freely. Before he got into cross-cultural comparisons, he stopped to separate the congenital sheep from the acquired lambs. It was true, he said (inaccurately), that homosexuality occurred among animals, and that it probably appeared at least sporadically "among every race of mankind." The great Krafft-Ebing, Moll and Ellis had all said so. Why was it common in some places and rare in others? Scientists had invoked everything from the genes to climate. But the cultural variety of incidence, said Westermarck, suggested the reason was custom (culture, we would say) rather than heredity or physical environment.

Although Westermarck slithered around the nature-nurture question, he kept emphasizing cultural influence. He bowed to Ellis by saying that homosexuality was sometimes a matter of instinctive preference, sometimes due to circumstances inhibiting normal intercourse. He quoted Ellis' opinion that social influences "required a favorable organic predisposition to act on." But then he said that perhaps William James had been right, in his *Principles of Psychology,* in calling homosexuality a germinal possibility in all men, the predisposition to it part of man's ordinary constitution. In fact, Westermarck added, "our chief authorities on homosexuality have underestimated the modifying influence which habit may exercise on sexual instinct." Granted that homosexuality occurred from Arab-influenced Africa to Tahiti, where the *mahus* dressed like women and did women's work. But widespread homosexuality in both sexes, he stressed, went hand in hand with isolation of women and a premium on chastity. He suggested that freer relations between men and women would reduce its frequency.

Westermarck had lived in Morocco, and he pointed out that there homosexuality was most common among scribes, who from childhood lived closely with their fellow students. Among the Arabs of the plains, who gave unmarried girls considerable freedom, there was little boy-love. But among the mountain people of the north, who segregated females and had a high regard for chastity, homosexuality was extensive. He added, "It should be noticed that the most common form of inversion, at least in Mohammedan countries, is love of boys and youths not yet in the age of puberty, that is, of male individuals who are physically very like girls."

Among the natives of the Kimberley District of western Australia, he said, where older men had a monopoly on marriageable girls, many young

men used boys as wives. Separation of the sexes among such warrior societies as the Sikhs, Afghans, Dorians, Japanese samurai and some North
American Indians accounted for their high rates of homosexuality.
Westermarck dismissed the idea, which has come up sporadically since
Aristotle, that homosexuality was practiced as a form of birth control;
abortion, infanticide, celibacy and contraception achieve the same goal
without radical sexual reorientation. He felt that the real reason for the
hostility toward homosexuality in the West was its traditional connection
with heresy and unbelief.

Havelock Ellis, in his volume on homosexuality, had quoted Westermarck's work almost as much as Westermarck had quoted him. Ellis had
begun the anthropological discussion of homosexuality in his book:
"Traces of homosexual practices, sometimes on a large scale, have been
found among all the great divisions of the human race . . . we seem bound
to recognize that there is a widespread natural instinct impelling men
toward homosexual relationships." At first Ellis and Westermarck seem to
be saying pretty much the same thing. But one leaves Ellis with the feeling
that homosexuality just can't be kept down; one leaves Westermarck with
the impression that homosexuality would be rare if people would stop
trying to fetter heterosexuality.

Today Westermarck's work is merely a historical document to working
anthropologists. He, Ellis and most of their contemporaries were soon left
behind, and the two men who particularly made their approach obsolete
were Emile Durkheim and Franz Boas. Durkheim is considered the
founder of modern sociology. He insisted that studies of social institutions
should have the rigorous exactitude of biological observation. He wanted to
avoid the sweeping metaphysical schemes of evolution and the grand armchair comparative surveys that were so popular then. He preferred to concentrate on more immediate and limited social problems such as suicide,
alcoholism, education, politics and educational reform. He also introduced,
to some degree, the modern functional approach. He said that society is a
complex yet coherent organism, its members the cells that comprise it, and
that one must empirically study and treat its malfunctions. Though he carried the biological metaphor too far, made some ambitious generalizations
of his own, and overestimated man's ability to rationally put his knowledge
to good use, he was successful in calling for an end to the pursuit of philosophic whys and got people to begin asking simply how things work. He
sought statistical correlations between various conditions in society. This
hard-headed, problem-oriented approach in sociology found very receptive
ground in the United States. Unfortunately, it was rarely applied to the
problem of sexual deviance until many decades later.

Anthropology did study sex, though, and it too was transformed into an
empirical social science. The most important person in its coming-of-age
was the German-American Franz Boas. He pressed even farther than
Durkheim in insisting on limited, careful, precise studies of societies. He

and his students drove the armchair evolutionists and theory makers out of business. For instance, one of Boas' projects demolished the use of skull shape as a criterion of race. Boas studied the skulls of American immigrants and their American-born children and found differences that according to old standards should have meant a difference in race. Climate, nutrition and perhaps other factors had Americanized the immigrants' children's skulls. For several decades American anthropology, under Boas' leadership, did social science the service of becoming a persistent nay-sayer. Boas-trained researchers insisted on proofs, not just emotionally attractive theories. Worshipers of goddesses? It was shown that within historical times god-worshiping peoples became goddess worshipers, reversing Bachofen's evolutionary schedule. Furthermore, no matriarchal society had ever been discovered. True, some societies are matrilocal (a married couple live with the wife's people), and some are matrilineal (name and some goods pass through the maternal line). But in no known society, past or present, have women had chief control over goods, decision-making, politics and personal relationships. And since no matriarchies have existed, all theories based on the idea of their existence must be dropped. Nor is there any relationship between matrilocal or matrilineal patterns and homosexuality. Nor is there a consistent relationship between women's status and male homosexuality—*pace* Westermarck. Nor is there a consistent pattern relating private property with hunting or agricultural systems, nor any of these with sexual patterns. Uncontrolled sexual communism has never been discovered, nor is there evidence it has ever existed. About the only big generalizations one can make is that all societies have rules of sexual behavior, have families consisting of some variation of the biological nuclear family, practice exogamy on the family and, usually, a larger social level, and proscribe exclusive homosexuality.

The show-me attitude of the Boas tradition has sometimes been carried to hard-nosed extremes. But on the whole its influence has been good. It has made it impossible for people to pass off their emotional biases about sex, morals and the family as science, and thus give them social and even legal authority. Unfortunately, many of the theoretical cloud cathedrals of nineteenth-century anthropology are still commonly accepted by educated laymen and even scientists outside anthropology. Westermarck, to many people, still represents a modern anthropological view of homosexuality. Many psychiatrists who write on the subject are no better informed. This is a curious failure to know their own professional traditions, for anthropology finally told a great deal about homosexuality when it absorbed psychodynamic concepts and used them on a broad social scale. Some of the earliest and best studies of this kind were done with the shamans of the North American Indians, who were variously homosexual, transvestites, epileptics, schizophrenics, prophets and priests. That could not happen until ego psychology developed and anthropology became much more sophisticated than Westermarck could have conceived. Meanwhile, at least, the idea had been established that the sexual way of the West was not the only way.

INTERVIEWS

Many homosexuals in Europe and the United States have discovered Amsterdam, and it has become the favorite homosexual resort of the Western world. Homosexuals of both sexes and many nationalities arrive there in chartered plane-loads. Homosexual acts among consenting adults are legal in Holland (an inheritance of the Napoleonic Code). In 1967 a candidate appeared on national television representing the Bachelors Party; he complained about the high income tax paid by unmarried men and about unfair treatment of homosexuals. That year newspapers and magazines all over the world reported a wedding mass for two male homosexuals, performed by a Roman Catholic priest. Some of the clergy in Rotterdam have begun pastoral work with homosexuals.

The homosexual city-within-the-city in Amsterdam is about what one finds in other easy-going cities of approximately a million people—some thirty bars for male homosexuals, a few for lesbians. They have drinking, some have dancing, and some a show; one club has female impersonators. The tone varies from chic and restrained to very campy. Homosexuals, male and female, go around central Amsterdam arm in arm without receiving a great deal of attention. They abound in the Rembrandtplein and around the smaller Leidseplein, where the C.O.C.—the largest homosexual organization in Holland—and many homosexual bars are located. If you sit at 11 P.M. at Reynders or Hoopman, two famous old Leidesplein cafes, you see the C.O.C. crowd pass by—homosexuals of both sexes, all races and nationalities, in business suits, in cerise bell-bottomed trousers, in shades, with spitcurls, and many with no distinguishing marks whatever. There are also two areas, in other parts of the city center, for homosexual prostitution. At one, along a canal, there may be a dozen to fifteen teenage boys standing on a single block.

If, as some claim, the problems and neuroses of many homosexuals are due to social pressure, this let-live atmosphere should produce a carefree, healthy homosexual population. I speak to a number of psychiatrists and homosexuals, and a wide range of ordinary citizens. I find that Holland's let-live atmosphere and "healthy" homosexual life are as much mythical oversimplifications as Swedish Sin. Though homosexual acts are not illegal, the social consequences of being a known homosexual are like those in other Western countries. Homosexual prostitutes are known to rob customers under threat of exposure. On a recent television panel discussion of homosexuality by homosexuals, the only person willing to sit facing the camera was the president of the C.O.C. Homosexuals are sometimes beaten up in the streets by adolescent gangs. Police are suspected by some of keeping unofficial records of deviants. I ask people, "How likely is it for a known homosexual to be hired as a middle-level executive, or if discovered, to keep his job and be promoted?" Almost without exception, they say the chances are minuscule. And they distinctly dislike their reputation as a deviant Mecca.

Homosexuals can be as open in Amsterdam as in New York or London, per-
haps a bit more. Foreign visitors anywhere, of course, feel less fear and pressure
than those who must live and work in the place. The Dutch do not accept homo-
sexuality, but to a degree they tolerate it—a very important distinction.

The Dutch national myth is tolerance. Americans consider themselves inde-
pendent, egalitarian and inventive; the French consider themselves rational; the
Dutch see themselves as tolerant. Asked about Amsterdam's red-light district,
the last in the metropolitan West, and her slight edge over other countries in
freedom and openness for homosexuals, the Dutch say, "We fought the Span-
iards for eighty years for our freedom. We took in the Spanish Jews, the French
Huguenots, the Pilgrim dissenters, all those who also had to fight to be free. We
make a place for everyone. We don't persecute homosexuals, we accept them."
Like other such national self-images, it is quite true in some ways and utterly
untrue in others.

Holland is half Roman Catholic and half Dutch Reform (one of the harshest
hellfire Protestant denominations). Dutch sexual values are not different from
those in the rest of northern Europe and North America. It is a country with
many splinter faiths, splinter political parties and strong regional differences.
The national ethic is, "I don't have to like you, but I'll treat you decently and
not tread in your garden if you'll do the same with me." One thinks of territo-
rial animals respecting each others' turfs. The Dutch regard homosexuals as
they do the religious and political groups they have no use for: they are as toler-
ant as they can manage to be. Homosexuals are far from accepted, and have
much more toleration to win in the future. In the homosexual world, I see only
a little that is different from the same world in metropolitan America. Among
scientists I find lack of information, inertia and hopelessness about treatment of
deviants.

In London, before I had gone to Amsterdam to investigate the scene for
myself, Phillip had given me his impression of the city:

Amsterdam is the one place where queers can live openly, with self-respect.
Let me tell you my first experience there. I went to the big homosexual organization, the C.O.C. It has dancing, a bar and so on—it's a club, but anyone who
pays the admission fee can join up at the door. The first time I went there I was
terribly embarrassed. I don't go to queer pubs in London because it's so terrible
to stand around like an old auntie and be turned down by all the kids. I decided
I'd go in for just ten minutes.

I stood at the sidelines of the dance floor like a wallflower for a while. Then
this fat little German man came up, about sixty and shaped just like a barrel.
He clicked his heels, bowed, and said like a Prussian drillmaster at a cotillion,
"May I haff diss tance?" I thought, God, this is awful, but I just can't say no, it
would be too cruel, it's happened to me so many times. So I bowed back and
said yes.

Well! that fat little man just took me in his arms and whisked me away on the
maddest waltz of my life! Fantastic! At the end, he whirled me back to the sidelines as though I were a feather. Then he bowed, clicked his heels, said *"Danke*
schön" and started to walk away. I stopped him and asked where he'd learned
to dance like that. It turned out he had been the male lead of the X ballet troup
during its greatest years, in the thirties. We talked for an hour. There was no

tension, no games, no flirting and jockeying, as in the queer pubs and clubs in every other country. I found out how *normal* homosexual life can be. Just talking, drinking and dancing with people like myself. Just being *people*.

The C.O.C. has a bar and dance hall, and carries on social, educational and legal programs. When I visited, president Benno Premsela was on vacation; the presiding officer was reluctant and uncooperative at first, though I produced references from my English and American publishers and a major homophile group. He finally agreed to call the trustees and ask whether I should be granted some time. I returned the next day and was grudgingly told I could speak to the C.O.C. secretary, an amiable man in his middle or late twenties. We sat and talked in an office full of scrolls and pennants bearing the yang-yin symbol. I tell him:

I'm surprised at the reluctance to speak to me when I came here. Since you're here to help and educate people, mightn't you discourage some of them that way?
You must understand that many people come here claiming they are journalists because they are homosexual and are afraid to ask outright for information. We are always cautious. [*Considering the circumstances, this is very implausible, but I feel little will be gained by belaboring the point.*]
Why do you think Amsterdam has become known as a sort of Mecca for homosexuals?
We don't like that Mecca phrase. I'd like to see someone prove that there are more homosexuals here than in Hamburg or San Francisco! We don't want to be a Mecca. We want other countries to be like us. What we have here is two big homosexual clubs—the C.O.C. and the D.O.K.—twenty-five or thirty bars, and the beginning of a breakdown of the ghetto walls for homosexuals. The press is very middle class here, and they're the ones who say this is a Mecca. They say that what's happening in Amsterdam is a warning of what will happen to Holland.
How is the ghetto wall breaking down?
Look at the C.O.C. itself. We began in 1946 in an undergound atmosphere, even though homosexual acts weren't illegal. People used fake names or first names only. Now it has fifty-five hundred members and it's much more open. There are C.O.C. clubs in eight major sections of the country.
Are the members all male homosexuals?
About 20 per cent are female. We have big branches in Utrecht and Rotterdam. The Hague has no clubs or society, just some homosexual bars. But within the last few months three homosexual bars opened in Arnhem, with licenses that allow dancing.
These are all homosexual institutions, and yet you say that you want to do away with the homosexual ghetto.
Yes. We want to integrate and get rid of hush-hush attitudes. But that takes time. Now fewer people join under fake names or refuse to get our publications at their homes, though not enough of them read our periodical or share the official goal of integration and emancipation. As I said, that will take time.
Aside from the bar and dancing, what do you do?
We have readings, a drama club, a record club and a bridge club. We allow

people to get in contact in a more normal way than the erotic one of bars, where contact means a proposition.

It still creates a separate homosexual community.

Yes, it would be better if our member was in a heterosexual bridge club or a heterosexual choir. But he can't reveal himself. You see, a heterosexual can say, "Isn't that soprano beautiful?" But a homosexual can't say, "Isn't that tenor wonderful?" And you don't know except in a homosexual group who else is homosexual, so there's no public touching or speaking out.

Do you offer any sort of counseling or referral to counselors?

We're starting to work on that. We've begun discussion groups for members, with help from the Dialoog Foundation. This is an organization set up and subsidized by the C.O.C. The C.O.C. also chooses Dialoog's board of directors—about a third of them are heterosexual.

And the C.O.C. board?

Nine men and one woman, all homosexual.

What does Dialoog do?

It gathers information and puts out a publication to inform heterosexuals. But mostly homosexuals read it. Dialoog acts as our specialist, and can give advice about where to go if you want information or counseling. But C.O.C. isn't for therapy, it's for the secure. These groups we're forming are to let people talk about their problems—maybe later that can be done on an individual basis. We assume that the new member is a normal homosexual, not a psychopathic personality, but that he does need to talk to people.

You try to get them to accept their homosexuality.

Yes. A study showed that people who have a negative attitude and don't accept their homosexuality usually don't live normal, happy lives. This psychiatrist says one should get homosexuality out in the open and into action. It's better than trying to convert the patient.

What do you assume to be the cause of homosexuality?

We don't take on that question. We just say, there are so many homosexuals, how can they live well? There have always been homosexuals, in all times, places and classes. We're pragmatic. We say we must do something for them.

Can it be that you help solidify a homosexual way of life for someone standing on the borderline?

At sixteen a person has to have a chance to experiment, to experience life, find out what a homosexual life means. Dialoog also says it isn't right to push a person in either a heterosexual or homosexual direction. If a boy can love a girl or another boy, he'll take his choice. For instance, when I was twelve, I saw boys in locker rooms and found them exciting. Then when I was sixteen and seventeen I kissed girls.

Did you ever do more with a girl than kiss?

No. But then at nineteen I kissed a boy, had an erection and found out I was homosexual. I experimented and found out.

Are many of the C.O.C. members quite young?

Twenty-one is the age of legal consent. Until you're that age, you can't go anywhere publicly or join the C.O.C. There's no problem with the law if two sex partners are under twenty-one, but if one is well under that age and the other well past it, there can be real trouble. There's a new homosexual group starting now for people between sixteen and twenty-three, the Z.O.S.S. I think it has a hundred members now, maybe more.

I am taken to meet Mr. van Bekkum, a young man who is Dialoog's only full-time salaried worker—he says it has about fifty volunteers. We go half a dozen blocks from the C.O.C. to the Dialoog office, to sit and talk amid books, clippings and film cans.

We gather press clippings, scientific papers and books on homosexuality. We try to reach priests, doctors and police and educate them on the subject. We also lobby for teaching police and servicemen about homosexuality. For instance, the army speaks little of sex and says nothing at all about homosexuality. There's no regulation against it, but it can be made very uncomfortable for you if you're discovered, and you may end up discharged for psychological reasons.

Do homosexuals tend to work in certain professions in Holland?

No.

Hairdressing, decorating, the arts—none have associations with homosexuality?

The C.O.C. did a study and found the usual range of occupations.

How open can you be about yourself at work in Holland if you're homosexual?

It depends on your boss, but it's rarely public knowledge. If you're homosexual, you prefer a job where you can be as you are.

Such as?

Oh, the usual ones.

Is it possible to live without secrecy in a small town in Holland?

I lived in Arnhem. You can be yourself there without too much bad reaction. I was able to get written permission from the officials to go to the annual town festival with my partner. People don't like you if you're shy and secretive. Then they don't know what you're doing, and they worry about the children.

Do you think it's better here than in other countries?

Yes, not quite as bad as elsewhere. The church is changing, and the public has more information. The gay life isn't quite as separate and secret as before. People are more informed, and you run into less trouble. It's the frightened people who have the most trouble. We try to inform the community and convince the homosexuals not to be ashamed.

What are they afraid of?

Losing their jobs. When it's a matter of hiring a Jew or a homosexual, they're just like everyone else.

There was quite a stir a year or so ago when a Roman Catholic priest here married two homosexuals.

Yes, and it turned out to have been a publicity stunt they'd put over on him. I think they weren't even Dutch, but German. I know couples who get sympathetic Protestant priests to do simple ceremonies to bless their unions. I don't believe in it. It's a way of trying to imitate heterosexuals and be like them.

14

The Life

Between the end of the nineteenth century and the start of the First
World War, scientific studies, confessions, apologetics, novels and plays
dealing with homosexuality came out in the thousands. Still, there was no
systematic study of homosexuality. Only by going through a broad range of
these writings and piecing together bits of information from them can one
begin to make a picture of the homosexual world. One element of it to be
described at this time was male prostitution, which had not been portrayed
since Juvenal's *Ninth Satire.* Female prostitution had become a subject of
medico-social study and reform in the middle of the nineteenth century,
and sidelights about male prostitution appeared as a result. Forensic studies
mentioned it, and works in the new field of scientific criminology touched
on it. F. Carlier, chief of the Department for Morals of the Paris police
between 1860 and 1870, revealed in a book called *The Two Prostitutions*
that the Paris police had a list of 6,432 prostitutes. There were doubtless
others who escaped police notice or weren't steady professionals. Carlier
said that pimps trained and kept boys of twelve and fourteen to work as
streetwalkers. Soldiers, he claimed, were much sought after by homosexuals, and in French garrison towns there were male bordellos where soldiers picked up extra money in their off-duty time. Female brothels would
obtain male prostitutes for clients who wanted them.

Havelock Ellis confirmed that similar types of male prostitutes were
common in England; soldiers solicited in Hyde Park and Albert Gate,
competing with full-time professionals to earn pocket money to spend on
themselves and their girls. In Germany there were homosexual *kniepen,* or
small bars, that were fronts for male brothels. The staff were working-class
men and boys out of work and money. These establishments were considered safe by the customers, because the owners allowed no robbery or
extortion and prevented raids by paying off the police. The *pupenjunge,* or
young male prostitutes, who frequented other cafes were often experts at
rolling and blackmail. Hirschfeld said that three thousand of ten thousand
homosexuals he studied had been blackmailed. In the major cities of

France and Russia, steam baths were centers for homosexual prostitution, with all the attendant dangers.

Informed guesses could now be made about the frequency of homosexuality. Tarnowski said the Russian poor called it "gentlemen's games," but it was apparently far from rare among the English poor and the peasants of Switzerland. It was said to be most common in Germany; the French called it *le vice allemand*. Moll said he had seen six to seven hundred homosexuals in Berlin and heard of a few hundred more. When Abraham Flexner made his famous study of prostitution in Europe just before the First World War, he said Berlin had between one and two thousand male prostitutes, about forty homosexual hang-outs, and some thirty thousand homosexuals. But Magnus Hirschfeld, with his personal contacts in the homosexual world, claimed that he himself had known more than ten thousand homosexuals in Germany. He guessed that the percentage of homosexuals varied by region and occupation from 1 per cent to 10 per cent, with an over-all average above 2 per cent in a large population. Ellis guessed at 5 per cent male and 10 per cent female homosexuals in the English middle class, with the ratio diminishing as one went down the social scale. Like Hirschfeld, he put the over-all average somewhere above 2 per cent. After reading the Kinsey reports and similar studies, we might guess that these estimates were low, but at that time such a figure seemed shockingly high. Even at 2 per cent, homosexuals were not a handful of depraved freaks whom one saw in certain neighborhoods or beheld revealed in occasional scandals; they numbered one, two or three million in each major country in Europe.

More and more details of homosexual life and society were recorded. It had always been known that homosexuality existed in boarding schools, and now a larger number of people than ever sent their children away to be educated. Accounts appeared of widespread homosexual behavior in schools, sometimes highly organized in dormitories in England, France and Germany. In Russia, Tarnowski was called in by a boys' school because of an outbreak of syphilis there, spread by homosexual relations.

Burton named specific pick-up places for homosexuals in Paris, and he gave the dates and addresses of drag balls, where homosexuals partied in female dress. Ellis said Paris, Nice, Florence, Naples and Cairo were the favored resorts of English homosexuals. Every major city in Europe, it turned out, had cafes, restaurants and hotels where homosexuals gathered; often the employees at these places were all homosexual. Certain professions had an extra share of homosexuals—hairdressing, the performing arts, perhaps writing. Homosexuals had codes and signals that varied from place to place and time to time. In France, said one writer, the homosexual emblem was the handkerchief; worn in the front pocket it indicated an active homosexual, in the back pocket a passive one. Chevalier mentioned a homosexual group in Paris who wore green cravats; English observers told of men wearing green carnations who congregated at London's Holborn Casino, Argyll Rooms and Empire Theatre.* In Frankfurt there was a homosexual society called The Black Cravats, which became the basis of a novel by Belot. After the turn of this century, red also was mentioned as an identifying color.

Information accumulated about other sexual abnormalities. Bizarre deviations were more common than most people had believed. Readers learned that most experienced prostitutes kept whips as a matter of course. Books mentioned parks favored by exhibitionists. Newspapers carried ads in code for deviant contacts. In 1895 Hanover newspapers commonly ran ads from masochistic men seeking partners. Hirschfeld told of a governess in Moscow who innocently put an ad in the papers there offering English lessons and received frantic missives from masochists craving flagellation.

The most surprising revelation was what doctors and homosexuals told about deviants' sexual behavior. Since Casper and Ulrichs, sexologists had constantly repeated that homosexuality was not synonymous with sodomy: homosexuality was a choice of sexual object, with as much variation in sex practices as among heterosexuals. Now statistical confirmation was offered. Hirschfeld, who knew the homosexual world better than anyone else, said that only 8 per cent of the homosexuals in Germany practiced sodomy. Ellis, working with a far smaller sample in England, claimed 25 per cent there. Then what did homosexuals do? Hirschfeld said mutual masturbation was the exclusive activity of 40 per cent of all homosexuals, male and female. Among the males, oral sex, one-way or mutual, accounted for another 40 per cent. Another 12 per cent preferred interfemoral intercourse. Furthermore, there were many homosexuals who didn't do much of anything except perhaps kiss and caress each other.

Hirschfeld's and Ellis' writings on transvestites were just as startling. The most important thing for cross-dressers, they revealed, was change of clothing; it did not necessarily include homosexual object choice. One third of all transvestites, said Hirschfeld, were heterosexual; another third were homosexual; and the remaining third variously bisexuals, autosexuals who only masturbated, and a few asexuals. Some transvestites, said Hirschfeld, think of themselves as women and are dominated by fantasies of pregnancy and childbirth; the fantasies are often very specific, such as wanting to be a servant girl or a courtesan or an aristocratic *grande dame*. Frequently they change their names, from Emil to Emilia, George to Georgette. These are the transvestites people usually see, but many others are heterosexual and married, and practice their dressing-up only at home, in secrecy away from home, or by wearing female underclothes beneath their masculine street clothes.

---

*In ancient Rome, homosexuals were called *galbanati* because green and yellow were their favored colors. Was the nineteenth-century practice a revival based on classical educations or even a survival? Jokes about wearing green on Thursday still exist among homosexuals in the United States.

Lesbianism had always been less studied and less understood than male homosexuality. In 1901 Krafft-Ebing said that less than fifty case histories were on record. Therefore every scrap of information was significant. Although there was little to go on, guesses were made at the frequency of lesbianism. Krafft-Ebing, Ellis and many others said it was just as common as male homosexuality, but this was a logical deduction rather than an empirical fact. If homosexuality was a hereditary or developmental fluke, it should occur equally in both sexes. The relative invisibility of lesbianism was explained by the idea that although the tendency was equally common in men and women, the latter, being less sensual and assertive, less often became acting-out deviants. Kissing, affection and devotion took the place of sex between many lesbians, as it would by preference with many women in their relationships with men.

Still, there was more active lesbianism about than had usually been thought. It was reputedly common among actresses, and even more so among dancers. Lombroso and many others pointed out that there was much lesbianism among prostitutes; Moll said that about a quarter of them had lesbian tendencies, and another Germany study declared forty-one of sixty-six prostitutes studied were homosexual. Hirschfeld said lesbians were apt to turn to prostitution; others claimed that the degradation of hetero-sexual relations made prostitutes turn to their own sex for love.

Moll had included a chapter on lesbianism in his *Contrary Sexual Feelings*, as had Krafft-Ebing in his great book. Ellis devoted a section to it in *Sexual Inversion*. Hirschfeld, in his major book on homosexuality, was the first to treat male and female homosexuality as complementary phenomena and with equal emphasis. He claimed that among English and German feminists, the percentage of lesbians was high—somewhere under 10 per cent. He also wrote about female cross-dressing, citing some of the famous cases of the nineteenth century—for instance, that of "James Barry," a woman who got through medical school and into the English army disguised as a man, and died in 1865 after forty-six years in a high position in the army medical service.

There was a lesbian subsociety, smaller than the male homosexual world, but discernible in big cities. Berlin and Paris had many lesbian hangouts—the Rat Mort, in the Place Pigalle, attracted artists and poets during the day, lesbians at night. In 1887 the Municipal Council of Paris received a report on lesbian prostitution, which Zola would soon describe in *Nana*. In Germany, Näcke collected ads placed by lesbians in Munich newspapers, just like those placed by male homosexuals: "Actress with modern ideas desires to know rich lady with similar views for the sake of friendly relations." "Young lady of 19, a pretty blonde, seeks another like herself for walks, theater, etc."

Studies were made of lesbian attachments in schools, factories and prisons. Belot, the lesbian Pauline Tarn (under the pseudonym René Vivien) and Zola wrote on the subject; Colette, in the Claudine series of novels, described lesbian love in detail. Tradition had it that lesbians rubbed their genitals together, or that one used her large clitoris or an artificial phallus to penetrate the other. The Mantegazza-Burton school of thought was that the homosexual had genital nerves around the rectum, and assumed sodomy was the logical flagrant delight of lesbians as well as of male homosexuals. But Ellis said that most lesbians found their greatest pleasure in kissing, embracing, sleeping together and "lying spoons"—lying on their sides, one embracing the other from behind, bodies curled together with knees bent, so that the *mons veneris* of one rubbed against the other's buttocks. Cunnilingus was less common, and "not usually mutual, but practiced by the more active and masculine partner." Rarest of all was tribadism, or mutual contact of the genitals.

Of course the enlarged clitoris of lesbians was a folklore tradition, probably based on a few rare cases of physical abnormality. If penetration was desired, an artificial penis would have to be used. Hirschfeld supported Ellis in saying this was the least frequent of all lesbian acts. When it was practiced, he said, the way (at least in Germany) was to wrap a stick in cotton wool, bind it with linen and fix it to a sanitary belt.

Early in this century, lesbianism was said to be increasing not only in France, Germany and England, but in the United States as well, where information on deviance was accumulating for the first time. In the eighteenth century and the first half of the nineteenth, there had been almost no mention of it. If homosexuality was part of the male society of the frontier and mining and logging camps, it was not recorded. The early mentions of deviance that exist are questionable or vague. In the 1790s Moreau de Saint Méry, a French politician and lawyer who lived in Philadelphia, wrote about that city's domestic and sexual life. He spoke of the chastity and respectability of the upper and middle classes, the promiscuity of the poor and rural. He also damned what he considered the cold, passionless character of American women and added, "I am going to say something that is almost unbelievable. These women give themselves up at an early age to the enjoyment of themselves; and they are not at all strangers to being willing to seek unnatural pleasures with persons of their own sex." But in context it isn't clear which social class the author was talking about, and his statement is as problematic as assertions in France at the same time that lesbianism was "making progress even in the provinces."

Estimating American morals and behavior has always been especially difficult, for our society is uniquely mobile, changing and pluralistic. When speaking of Americans does one mean frontier men and women or the settled East Coast middle class? Negroes, Orientals, Indians or Latin Americans? Mormons, Catholics, city Protestants, rural evangelistic Protestants or southern Jews? Swedes, Slavs or Greeks? Such differences are still greater today than many people realize, and were probably stronger then, when more people were strongly rooted in a variety of ethnic traditions.

Much of America did go through a "Victorian" phase that equaled England's, if without quite the same emphasis on class differences. There was the same spate of books denying female sexuality and warning against masturbation. (Catherine Beecher and Harriet Beecher Stowe wrote in 1869, in their *The American Woman's Home*, that masturbation leads to "disease, delirium and death.") There was also the same social toleration of "back door" sexuality; prostitution was widespread, not only on the frontier but in every large city. Until early in this century New York, Boston, Philadelphia, Chicago, New Orleans and many other large cities had big red-light districts and hordes of streetwalkers, female and male.

There remains extremely little hard knowledge about sex behavior before the Civil War, and almost none permitting generalizations. We know that deviations existed then only by pornography and occasional brief references. Mentions of it became common only in the late decades of the century. One intriguing specimen of late-nineteenth-century American pornography was entitled *Raped on the Elevated Railway: A true story of a lady who was first ravished, then flagellated on the Uptown Express, illustrating the perils of travel in the New Machine Age.* Around this time, accounts of deviants appeared in American medical journals. Drs. Kiernan, Lydston and a few others were publishing case histories and theoretical studies; between 1880 and the outbreak of the First World War, there were reports of cases of homosexuality, lesbianism, sadism and transvestism. They occurred in Chicago, Memphis, Philadelphia and small midwestern towns, in the working class and in eastern high society. A number, though, were recorded only because they involved murder, suicide or scandal and had no particular scientific interest.

Magnus Hirschfeld said that when he visited America, he saw hardly any open homosexuality in Philadelphia and Boston. It's hard to imagine that he didn't know where to look, but people there assured him that its extent was colossal, and someone sent Havelock Ellis a description for his big sex opus. In this anonymous dispatch, it was said that most men in American cities knew what homosexuals were and had been approached by them on the street or even had inverts among their friends. "The public attitude toward them is generally a negative one—indifference, amusement, contempt." Their world, he said, was organized, with its own words, customs and traditions, its churches, meeting places, cafes and streets where at night "every fifth man is an invert." They had their own so-called clubs— actually dance halls attached to saloons, presided over by the saloon's proprietor, who was invariably homosexual and hired homosexual waiters and musicians. The customers were homosexuals of about seventeen to thirty, feminine in manner but, probably because of police pressure, never in female clothes. Nevertheless, "it is not unusual for the inquiring stranger to be directed there by a policeman."

Another American told Ellis that red—especially a red tie—had been adopted as the homosexual badge. It was worn by many "fairies," as they were now called, in New York. "A friend told me once that when a group of street-boys caught sight of the red necktie he was wearing, they sucked their fingers in imitation of fellatio. Male prostitutes who walk the streets of Philadelphia and New York almost invariably wear red neckties."

A Baltimore doctor named William L. Howard published a paper in 1904 called *Sexual Perversion in America*. Many of his views were standard for the medical profession then: oral and anal sex are perversions whether practiced homosexually or heterosexually; homosexuality is associated with artistic ability; perversions may be congenital or acquired. (Unlike most doctors of the time, he felt that most deviants had some element of normal sexuality and could be cured if detected early enough.) Dr. Howard said that the number of deviants in America was astonishing to any but the knowing. They stood in the pulpit and before the bar, sat at the editorial desk and by the sickbed. They were both male and female, had clubs and societies, and "are well read in literature appertaining to their condition; they search for everything written relating to sexual perversion; and many of them have devoted a life of silent study and struggle to overcome their terrible affliction. They have but little faith in the general practitioner; in fact, in our profession; and their past treatment justifies their lack of confidence." Howard told of a fairly well-off man in New York, a former candidate for the ministry, who went about at night searching for hoodlums of the Gas House and Hell's Kitchen gangs to sodomize him; they often beat him up, but he once lived with a gang leader as his "loved one."

It was just such anecdotal cases that made people in the United States and all over the West more realistically aware of homosexuality. Most of the scientific literature was read only by scientists, most of the apologetics by homosexuals. Krafft-Ebing, Ellis, Mantegazza and a few others reached a growing upper- and upper-middle-class public, and newspapers related scandals that had a great impact at lower social levels. There were scandals enough—in St. Petersburg, Paris, London, Philadelphia—often involving the upper ranks of society, the clergy, the military and government. The airing of these cases made some people realize that homosexuals were not, as even many of the so-called experts had believed, an odd species apart, like a rare and grotesque breed of monkeys. None of these scandals matched the Oscar Wilde case, which remains a paradigm of the vindictiveness, hysteria and official dishonesty that so often motivates such convulsions of public morality.

In 1895 Oscar Wilde was forty years old, married and the father of two sons; his novel *Dorian Gray* had been acclaimed; two of his plays were running successfully in London. He was a well-known public figure, notorious for his wit, dandyism and radical opinions about art, esthetics and politics. For some years he had secretly indulged in homosexual liaisons, including an affair with young Lord Alfred Douglas, his beloved "Bosie." A few days after *The Importance of Being Earnest* had opened triumphantly, Wilde received at his club an insulting card from Bosie's father,

Lord Queensberry, a cruel and loutish man whose name survives for his boxing code. The card accused Wilde of sodomy. Bosie, obsessed by hatred for his father and the desire to destroy him, encouraged Wilde to make the quarrel public by suing Queensberry for criminal libel. Wilde did so, and the action attracted wide attention. Wilde lost, Queensberry was acquitted, and the audience in the court broke into cheers. Wilde was immediately put under arrest and imprisoned without bail.*

Wilde's books immediately disappeared from print; his plays, after running briefly with no author's name on the programs, were closed down. He was bankrupted, his home sacked. His two sons had to be removed from their school. The press almost unanimously acted as though the entire nation had been raped, calling Wilde a villain and monster. Frank Harris justly said that "his arrest was the signal for an orgy of Philistine rancor such as even London had never known before. The Puritan middle class, which had always regarded Wilde with dislike as an artist and an intellectual scoffer . . . now gave free scope to their disgust and contempt."

At his trial Wilde gave a definition of "the love that dare not speak its name," citing Plato and other writers on ennobling, chaste affection between men; he was so eloquent that he won spontaneous applause. The jury, perhaps influenced by this, could not come to a decision. Wilde had already been ruined, but the case was not dropped; he was held for a second trial. A kind-hearted parson named Stewart Headlam stood bail for Wilde on principle and was almost stoned by a mob outside his home. The press kept up a daily barrage of vilification. Wilde was deserted by most of his friends; many fled the country for fear of sharing his fate in court and in the press, whether guilty or innocent. People who had corresponded with him burned his letters. Any man in the street who dressed or spoke elegantly risked jeering yells of "Oscar!"

The second trial was a kangaroo court. The witnesses against Wilde, who swore they'd been to bed with him, all testified under threat of prosecution, and one of them was a professional blackmailer. Wilde was found guilty and given the maximum sentence, two years at hard labor. George Bernard Shaw tried to start a petition calling for Wilde's freedom, but only Headlam, who had stood bail for Wilde, was willing to sign it. Three years after his release from prison, Wilde died, impoverished, in a hotel room in Paris. Not long before his death he said, "I never came across anyone in whom the moral sense was dominant who was not heartless, cruel, vindictive, log-stupid and entirely lacking in the smallest sense of humanity. Moral people, as they are termed, are simple beasts. I would sooner have fifty unnatural vices than one unnatural virtue."

*Wilde was accused not of sodomy but of "gross indecency," a charge that had become law only a decade earlier. In 1885, when a law to prevent white-slaving was in committee, an M.P. tacked on an irrelevant amendment to punish "outrages on decency" between males, whether occurring in public or private. It was automatically passed with the rest of the bill.

England had stained itself with a cruel injustice in a class with France's Dreyfus affair and America's McCarthy purge. There was only one social benefit in the whole catastrophe. Until now homosexuality, when spoken of at all, was "the unspeakable vice," a bizarre and mysterious bogey. Now it was daily fare in newspapers; the unmentionable was in everyone's conversation, and some people began to realize that, as editor W. T. Stead wrote, "If all persons guilty of Oscar Wilde's offences were to be clapped into gaol, there would be a very surprising exodus from Eton and Harrow, Rugby and Winchester, to Pentonville and Halloway."

Similar scandals brought Germany to public discussion of homosexuality—the Krupp and Eulenberg-Moltke affairs. The German police had a secret file about highly placed homosexuals who might be liable to scandal and blackmail. It included dossiers on the armaments king Friedrich Krupp, one of the Kaiser's brothers, the Kaiser's aide Prince Eulenberg, the Kaiserin's private secretary, Count Kuno von Moltke and others. In 1902 the Krupp scandal brought some of the file's secrets into the open.

The Krupp armaments company was so vast and so vital to Germany's economy and military strength that it was in effect a junior partner in the government. When Friedrich Krupp was thirty-three, his father died, and he took over the great business. He was married, but he and his wife lived separately so that he could lavishly indulge his homosexual desires. At his Grotto of Fra Felice, a cave above the sea on Capri, he created a private pleasure palace where he brought the young fishermen, muleteers, barbers and beggers he wanted. Eventually local clerics complained, the issue took on political overtones, and details of Krupp's life on Capri leaked to the Italian press. There were photographs showing that Krupp had violated the law—not by homosexual acts, which were not an offense in Italy, but by seducing minors. Krupp had to leave Italy, *persona non grata*. Soon a German paper picked up the story, and Krupp's homosexual ventures hit Germany as the Wilde trial had struck England. The government tried to cover up for Krupp, but newspapers—especially opposition papers—obtained and printed more evidence. When Krupp's wife asked the Kaiser for help in handling the scandal, the Kaiser and her husband had her locked away in an asylum to silence her.

Krupp brought a suit against the German newspaper that had first printed the Capri story, but soon afterward he was found dead, almost surely by suicide. The Kaiser tried to quell the public uproar and defend the house of Krupp (and his association with it) by following Krupp's coffin in a state funeral. But the case became a political football for pro- and antigovernment factions. Its reverberations went on long after Krupp's death.

Four years later, other names that had been in the secret police files appeared in the press. Maximilian Harden, publisher of the periodical *Die Zukunft*, had been told by Bismarck about the "perversions" of the Kaiser's personal aide, Prince Eulenberg. It is still uncertain whether Eulenberg was homosexual, though there was probably some abnormality in his sex life; but Eulenberg was marked for destruction for political reasons, as was his friend Count Kuno von Moltke, Adjutant to the Kaiser and Governor of Berlin. Harden ran an editorial saying that the imperial court was controlled by a clique of "catamites," a shadow government who had the king's ear more than his own ministers did. Homosexuals, said Harden, formed an international conspiracy, "a comradeship which is stronger than that of the monastic orders and of free-masonry, which holds closer and throws a bond across all the walls of creed, State and class, which unites the most remote, the most foreign, in a fraternal league of offense and defense. . . . All rally together against the common enemy. Many of them look down on normal men as beings of another kind, insufficiently 'differentiated.' "

Liberals in Germany were against dismissing men from government jobs for their sexual tastes; besides, the political motives behind Harden's crusade were obvious. There was a terrific controversy, a flurry of charges and countercharges. Millions read the details as the trials of Eulenberg and Moltke dragged on for years. Magnus Hirschfeld was called in by the court as an expert in 1909, and he declared Moltke a homosexual. Homosexuality and homosexual-hunting became common facts of life. The Munich humorous journal *Simplizissimus* ran a cartoon of the Weimar Poets' Monument, in which Goethe and Schiller stand hand in hand: Goethe was withdrawing his hand from Schiller's and saying, "Fritz, let go! Here comes Magnus Hirschfeld!"

Similar cases arose in other countries. The alleged homosexuality of Walt Whitman was debated in print in America, England and Germany. (It is still without positive solution.) The Danish writer Herman Bang produced many prohomosexual writings, arguing among other things that "homosexuality is notably and unexplainably related to artistic inclination." Johannes Jensen, a Danish poet and novelist who later won a Nobel Prize for literature, attacked Bang furiously in the press, suggesting that homosexuals be locked up and taught needlework. The dispute about Bang and homosexuality went on in Denmark for years. All over Europe, sex research, reform movements, a new apologetic literature and public scandal were preparing a revolution in sexual attitudes. A new sexual ideology in which to frame it was being shaped by Sigmund Freud.

15

The Age of Irony

In school we learn of such great moments as Archimedes leaping from his bath, Watts observing a steaming tea kettle, and Newton being struck by an apple. We are considered too young for the equally great moment when the young Viennese neurologist Sigmund Freud first witnessed "Fraulein Anna O." at what she called chimney-sweeping—talking out memories under hypnosis to alleviate her hysteria. Until then, Freud's work had been conventional and moderately distinguished. He had been born into a middle-class Jewish family in Freiberg in 1856; they moved to Vienna, and he became a doctor there. In the early 1880s, when he was in his middle and late twenties, he was already earning a name as a talented diagnostician, researcher in neuro-anatomy, and lecturer on nervous diseases.

Among Freud's acquaintances was a respected internist named Josef Breuer. Between 1880 and 1882 Breuer treated "Fraulein Anna O." (as she was called in print), whose case is now probably the best-known in medical history. She suffered from phobias and such hysterical conversion symptoms as paralysis, anesthesia, neuralgia, tremors and disorders of vision, speech and hearing. Breuer told Freud that he was curing her of symptom after symptom by what she called "chimney-sweeping" or "the talking cure." Freud joined Breuer on the case and saw that under hypnosis she could remember the first occurrence of a hysterical symptom and the feelings associated with it; when she awoke, bringing the memory into waking life, the syptom was gone. Breuer called this release of a symptom's roots in hidden memories and feelings catharsis.

Freud began to experiment with hypnosis and catharsis, and in 1885 he went to Paris to see the famous Dr. Charcot's demonstrations with hypnosis. Charcot showed in his own, slightly different way that hysterical symptoms re-enacted or symbolically expressed forgotten mental shocks, or traumas. Freud was deeply impressed, and he carried away Charcot's passing remark, "In such cases it's always the sexual thing—always, always, always!" As he continued to treat hysterics, the memories they revealed made him suspect that Charcot had been more right than he'd known: early sexual trauma was common in hysterics, perhaps almost universal. Now Freud began to lean toward the ancient idea that hysteria results from unspent sexual drive. Thomas Sydenham, S. Weir Mitchell and a few other great physicians of the past had guessed the psychological rather than physical nature of hysteria, but in this they remained outside the main-stream of medical thought. Freud joined them and embarked on a course that nearly destroyed his career.

In 1895 Freud and Breuer published their book, *Studies in Hysteria*, stating that hysterical symptoms could be cured by the recall and catharsis of repressed traumas. But soon the two men ended their collaboration. Apparently Breuer was put off by Freud's insistence that the decisive trauma of hysterics not only was sexual but predated puberty. It was then almost universally accepted that sex life began at puberty. To say that small children had sexual feelings was considered a nauseating sacrilege. Also, Breuer had been disturbed by Anna O.'s attraction to him as treat-ment proceeded. After Breuer turned away from the case, Freud went on investigating. He theorized that this attachment was an inevitable transfer-ence of repressed childhood erotic feeling to the doctor; he decided that he had become a "father figure." He began to believe that there existed in everyone a vast area of such hidden mental activity, much of it sexual and normally hidden by repression, that affects day-to-day emotional life.

Now, independent of Breuer, Freud dropped hypnosis as his chief tool of analyzing patients' feelings, for in using it he always eventually met resis-tance to uncovering more repressed material. Though hypnosis first dis-solved resistance, it often failed before later, more powerful blocks. Also, by dissolving resistance, hypnosis concealed it and thus lessened the doc-tor's insight into the patient's habitual mental processes. Freud gradually came to feel that it was in fact necessary for the patient to do the work of breaking down his own resistances and unearthing his buried feelings; having them handed to him by the doctor might give intellectual insight, but it brought little change in symptoms. Now Freud had his patients lie down, relax and say whatever entered their minds. This "free association" allowed many clues to repressed material to filter through the barrier of repression. Patients volunteered accounts of dreams, and these too turned out to be packed with oblique evidence of unconscious thoughts: another analytic tool had fallen into Freud's hands. In sleep, Freud decided, uncon-scious material appeared in symbolic disguise, only half hidden by the groggy force of repression. In 1900 Freud published *The Interpretation of Dreams*, based on analysis of his own and patients' dreams. Four years later he produced *The Psychopathology of Everyday Life*, in which he showed that slips of the tongue and pen, like dreams, were lapses of repression that allowed a glimpse of unconscious feelings.

By 1905, when his *Three Essays on the Theory of Sexuality* appeared, Freud had already produced enough new ideas to change Western thought as dramatically as had Darwin and Marx. All human behavior, he said, has a cause, and usually an unconscious one. The unconscious is vast, complex, mysterious. It guides us secretly, and just when we think we are most rational. It is primitive, wily, amoral, protean, roiling with lust, greed and violence. The lid that holds it down is repression, the inner censorship one forms during early childhood. Without repression and other such mechanisms for handling impulses, man would be a mere beast. On the other hand, overdeveloped controls make one emotionally sick. Therefore every man walks a delicate line between primitivism and neurosis. The same sort of unconscious, said Freud, and the same mechanisms for controlling it, exist in us all. There is no neat line between normal and abnormal humans, no comforting distance between normal and abnormal psychology. The neurotic, the pervert, the psychotic are not another breed. They express in exaggerated form what every child feels, and what continues to exist in the child buried within each man.

It was natural that the man who tried to map what lay behind the surface of rationality and inherited attitudes was a Jew. For centuries Jews had stood outside the mainstream of society, watching its contradictions and hypocrisies. Men preached love, piety and virtue—then turned to the ghetto to burn, plunder, rape and murder. Irony became a habit of mind to Western Jewry. Typically, the Yiddish joke is a wrecker of appearances; Freud used it as a chief means of understanding the unconscious roots of all humor. In Freud's day, the urban, educated, nonreligious Gentile was becoming more and more like the Jew in his intellectual perspective—standing outside society's old institutions and traditional pieties, deciding that the true nature of man and culture were not to be found in appearances and inherited ideas. Franz Kafka had in mind the outsider's doubt, irony and search for hidden motives when he told a group of non-Jewish intellectuals in Prague, "Ladies and gentlemen, you are all more Jewish than you think."

Freud looked at everything, from morality to puns to dreams to slips of tongue and pen, and said that really they all meant something more than the obvious—in fact, they usually meant the opposite of what they seemed to say. To a society ready to applaud when traditional appearances were stood on their heads, Freud gave a viewpoint and a vocabulary. Among those who have hated the Freudian perspective most have been defenders of tradition, those comfortably in the traditional mainstream. They have not been of a temperament to believe that within man is a child, or that behind solicitude may lurk hostility, or that a laugh can express hate. They believe that they say what they mean, and do as they say. Few Jews—and few intellectuals of the last hundred years—have been so trusting of appearances, so lacking in a sense of ambiguity and irony.

One of the early findings that most disturbed Freud, as he tried to see beyond the "obvious," was that the most crucial traumatic event in so many patients' lives was a complex of incestuous conflicts. Freud had heard from one patient after another tales of childhood seduction, usually by an older relative of the opposite sex. He began to think that this was the key to hysteria and many other abnormal states. Then he realized with despair that the stories were mere fabrications. He had earned contempt and isolation in his profession for espousing the idea of childhood sexuality, only to learn that the mentally ill had duped him into believing their delusions and lies. For a while he was deeply shaken. Then he made a decisive reinterpretation. The stories of family seduction were neither memories nor lies, but wishful fantasies. Neuroses result from the patient's defense against his own forbidden, shameful incestuous imaginings. Like Oedipus, every child wants to possess its parent of the opposite sex and destroy the rival parent of the same sex. Freud eventually concluded that this complex of Oedipal feelings exists not just in neurotics but in all people. The neurotic simply has not made peace with the conflict and remains pained and preoccupied by it.

Freud was a tough-minded experimentalist. He felt that if certain feelings exist in all people, crucial not only to neurosis but to the course of everyone's development, they must have a biological cause and follow some blueprint within the organism. He felt that the next job of psychiatry would be to chart that course of development and see how disturbances to the process cause emotional illness. Instinct theory then dominated medical and biological research, and the new science of genetics provided an explanation for the transmission of instincts. It was natural for Freud to seek explanations through these ideas. The sequence of psychosexual development, Freud thought, must be set hereditarily, and the individual driven to follow it by instinct. The libido, or sexual instinct, said Freud in the *Three Essays,* is second only to the instinct of self-preservation. Its aim is not merely genital but the attainment of pleasure and a sense of well-being, as opposed to pain, frustration and discomfort. Like many of his contemporaries, Freud thought of this instinct as resembling electricity or hydraulic power, a force that the body must keep in equilibrium.

As electricity can flow to any spot and charge it, libido can flow to any part of the body and sexualize it, making it an "erogenous zone." The skin and body orifices, with their heavy concentration of nerve endings, are libido's main targets, and the preordained path of libido leads from mouth to anus to genitals. Certain life experiences and feelings coincide with each period of libidinal focus and are fused with it, determining much in adult sexuality and personality. If libido follows its course properly, one attains healthy adulthood—the urge to heterosexual intercourse, which perpetuates the species. If for some reason libido is fixated at a pregenital stage, or if under stress a person regresses to an early libidinal stage, the result is neurosis or perversion. Freud decided that hysteria and anxiety are, respectively, converted and outpouring libido, homosexuality the result of its early fixation.

During the first year of infancy, libido is not felt as sexual urge in the adult sense, nor its discharge as adult sexual pleasure. It flows to the mouth and eroticizes sucking and feeding; the contentment that follows nursing is the model for later feelings of sexual satiation. The child as yet has no sense of his separate existence; pleasure to him is a passive, self-centered experience. Freud's disciple Karl Abraham later defined a late substage of the oral phase, which he called cannibalistic. As the child gets his first teeth, he begins to realize that the breast is separate from him, beyond his will; if he bites, it is taken away. He experiences frustration and a separate sense of self for the first time. Since his life is lived chiefly through his mouth, he expresses his anger by biting. The prohibition against biting further frustrates him, and creates in turn more fantasies of oral aggression.

Between the ages of one and three, the child abandons sucking and biting as his chief sensual experiences. Some libido remains invested in his mouth, and all his life he will take pleasure in feeding, kissing, sucking and biting. But most of his libido now switches to his anus. Withholding feces and releasing them has the pleasurable sexual pattern of tension and relief. Still "uncivilized," he likes the warmth and smell of his own wastes, and treasures them as part of himself. As he is toilet-trained, he learns that he can defy his parent by withholding his stools or by refusing to control his sphincter. He can also win their approval by complying with what they want. Finally his defiance and narcissistic body-love must be repressed; passive compliance gets the upper hand. The child creates his first big reaction formation—denying to himself that he likes his body products by learning to be "disgusted" by them.

When the child is about three, his libido moves on to another zone; it now eroticizes the genitals. At first he experiences a short "phallic" phase. Pleasure now centers in the penis for boys, the clitoris for girls. But this pleasure is still narcissistic, self-centered. Between the ages of about four to seven, the child for the first time feels his libido reaching for a goal outside his own body. He wants as his sexual object his parent of the opposite sex—and also, perhaps, an older sibling of the opposite sex. He expects to be punished for this forbidden desire, especially by the parent (and siblings) of the same sex. He especially fears castration. Masturbation, because it is loaded with fantasies of incest, jealousy and revenge, also creates guilt and fear of castration. Finally, at about seven, the child represses the entire struggle and enters a "latency period," during which his libido is sublimated—turned into such nonsexual channels as learning and play. The conflict and guilt of the Oedipal phase are so massive that when latency begins, most or all sexual experience until this time is repressed. That is why most people recall such things only with the help of hypnosis or psychoanalysis.

At puberty, between twelve or fourteen, the body ripens, genital libido presses for expression, and the buried Oedipal conflict briefly revives. Now interest shifts from the parents and sibling of the opposite sex to someone outside the family. The girl's interest shifts from her clitoris to her vagina. Adult heterosexuality begins.

Actually, Freud constructed this theory not only from the often bizarre symptoms of perversion but from the fantasies—homosexual, sado-masochistic, narcissistic, fetishistic—that eventually came from everyone he psychoanalyzed. Like tales of childhood seduction, they reflected childish thinking. ⌈Children—and the child inside every adult—think magically, without adult ideas of cause and effect, and from partial knowledge.⌉ Freud, as no one before him, reconstructed the magical and primitive mind of inner man. A boy who sees menstrual blood thinks the vagina is a bleeding wound; unable to understand differences in people, he thinks there was once a penis there, which has been cut off. He suspects that the rectum and vagina, like the mouth, conceal teeth. He sees his mother swelling where he thinks there is only the stomach, and is told that a baby will soon emerge from lower in the mother's body; by analogy, he assumes babies are conceived through the mouth and dropped from the rectum like turds. He is angry at a parent, wishes to hurt him, and then one day sees that parent injured or unhappy; not understanding that wishes don't always come true, he believes he is responsible. He fears that an angry thought is equal to assault, even murder. This primitive, infantile mode of thought remains the mode of much of the unconscious all one's life, and childhood ideas formed in this way remain functioning underground in the adult.

If libido becomes fixated at, say, the anal stage, the ideas and feelings of the anal stage will dominate the personality. The person may be openly anal-erotic or his defenses against his "shameful" anality may be foremost. In the latter case, he is rigid, neat, controlled, stingy and stubborn, controlling and denying the child within who wants to release his feces and play in them. Since the inner duel of compliance and defiance is fought by the child during the anal stage, sado-masochism will be part of the anal personality. There are also oral and phallic personalities, created by too heavy investment of libido at those stages of development. Many character traits and perversions, said Freud, can be explained by the concepts of oral, anal and phallic personality.

Perversion, then, is really infantile, "pregenital" sexuality. This is just the definition put forth for neurosis. In fact, said Freud, with a healthy sex life there is no neurosis; a neurosis is the negative image of a perversion. A pervert, deprived of his perversion, will be a neurotic. Similarly, a neurotic is fleeing a repressed perversion. Even in one person, perversion and neurosis may take turns: Freud quoted the old proverb *Junge Hure, alte Betschweste*r—a young whore makes an old nun.

So the pervert is not insane or degenerate. Every person is originally "polymorphous perverse," capable of enjoying all sexual acts. "There is something innate lying behind the perversions," he said, "but it is something innate in *everyone*." In the normal adult, infantile pregenital pleasures remain as foreplay and sexual *divertissements*—oral and anal sensuality. The pervert has made one of these preliminaries to adult sexuality his chief goal. We all bear the seed of every perversion. Freud said that childhood seduction does not produce a pervert, but rather it tends to make a person pansexual and hypersexual—focused too much and too early on indiscriminate sexual release. Much more damage, he said, can come from a fantasy—a repressed pregenital urge that has never or rarely been expressed, over which there is great guilt.

A few of these ideas were not in *Three Essays* but in subsequent papers; I have telescoped material for the sake of economy. Even so, *Three Essays* plus these other works do not comprise a complete, systematic theory of sex, and they are heavier on guesses than on evidence. Freud was pioneering, and he knew that the best he could do was put forth hypotheses, test them against cases, and revise. He did this all his life, so his works are full of changes, contradictions and gaps. In various essays between 1905 and the early 1920s he wrote about homosexuality in both sexes, fetishism, sado-masochism and narcissism (in which one "treats his own body in the same way as otherwise the body of a sexual object is treated"). He set forth many important ideas. Masochism, he said, is not different from sadism; it is sadism turned upon oneself, like the other side of a reversible jacket. The environmental event Binet had believed to be the cause of fetishism was often a "screen memory," a way of avoiding acute Oedipal conflict with a symbolic substitution of an inanimate object for the Oedipal goal. The same might be said of homosexuality: it represented an avoidance form of sex. The mind of the child said, "Anything—feet, shoes, people of the same sex—anything rather than incest."

It is impossible to give more than a brief and oversimplified account of Freudian theory about homosexuality. Like Marxist theory, it is a fantastically baroque, even rococo, edifice of inference and speculation. Freud's writings do not present a full, final theory of homosexuality, but they do sketch out a new picture of its origin and nature quite different from anything before it. As in all things, Freud tried to find ultimate reasons in biology, especially instinct theory. He felt he must assume as a scientist that there was a physical cause for mental events, if only one still to be discovered in the future. Meanwhile, he must look for specific conditions and events in a person's life that account for his state. It was a necessary paradox, he said, to assume the presence of constitutional factors in theory, and to look for unique and environmental ones in each case. One could not in reality separate constitutional and environmental causes. Perhaps in the future, chemical processes would better explain sexual and emotional life—when research on hormones began, Freud thought they might be the key. Meanwhile, he had to see what tortuous path libido had taken in each patient, and where it was fixated, assuming that probably heredity or constitution favored one erogenous zone.

Therefore, he said, the question of innate and acquired homosexuality, which had dominated thought on the subject for decades, was a waste of time. Theories about psychic hermaphroditism remained oversimplified guesses, unsupported by medical evidence. Homosexuality was probably produced by environment working on some unknown degree of constitutional propensity. Analysis showed homosexual thoughts or images in all neurotics, without exception, no matter what their salient problems. Freud always found, if only in dreams or bits of fantasy, what he interpreted as homosexual content: like Ellis, he attached the label homosexual to all attachments to a person of the same sex, for he believed that all attachments are to a degree sexual. He said that just as the libido can charge any organ, it can choose any object: everyone is potentially pansexual. But just as people grow beyond their intense orality and their Oedipal conflicts, they repress and sublimate their infantile homosexuality to make way for adult heterosexuality. So, said Freud, there are three forms of homosexuality—latent (constitutional, existing in everyone), repressed (unconscious, perhaps involving emotional problems) and overt. Homosexuality is often an exaggerated factor in the mental life of the emotionally disturbed, but even in a normal person's adult life, libido oscillates between male and female objects.

Freud believed that two childhood events can increase one's capacity for adult homosexuality, the "inverted" Oedipal complex and narcissism. A small boy identifies with both parents, sees them both as nurturing him. When his relationship with his mother grows more intense and sexual, his father is seen more as a rival. There is love-lust for the mother, fear and hatred of the father. But a contrary set of feelings is at work. The boy resents his mother for preferring the father, and rejects her for that. And because of his bisexual nature, he has feminine urges for his father and is jealous of the mother for winning him. A boy's first homosexual love is his father, as a countercurrent to his Oedipal desire for his mother. If a boy is constitutionally more feminine and passive than is normal, said Freud, and the Oedipal conflict is intense, he will retain this inverted Oedipal crush and become a homosexual.

Narcissism, according to Freud, plays a crucial role in homosexual development, especially if a boy is overattached to his mother, and the father is absent. The boy performs an act of narcissistic projection—seeks in other boys an idealized image of himself, to love as he wants his mother or father to love him. In homosexual attraction and love-making, the narcissistic male projects himself into another male and gives to him the mother-love he wants for himself. This sort of love may show first in hero worship or in crushes on other boys.

Later Freud said that paranoid projection also plays a big role in homosexuality: in fact, he eventually decided that homosexuality is a defense against paranoia. He described the case of a female patient who claimed that the man with whom she was becoming sexually involved plotted against her. Analysis revealed that she was deeply attached to her mother and secretly longed for women like her. As a man led her toward heterosexuality, she did an intricate piece of emotional juggling to avoid it, with paranoid delusion as the result. In analyzing other cases, Freud took the idea further. In extreme delusional jealousy, he said, a man's unconscious train of thought is, "I do not love other men, she does." In classic paranoid fashion, he projects onto someone else an urge he cannot tolerate in himself. The patient whose analysis gave Freud this idea showed powerful repressed homosexuality and had many emotional qualities frequently seen in homosexuals. He had been overattached to his mother. His narcissism made him overvalue the male sex organ and downgrade people who lacked it—the basis of an aversion for women. He was afraid of his father, and any attempt at heterosexual assertion made him feel threatened by castration. He had had rivalries with his older brothers that duplicated the one with his father; this reinforced his fear of competition with males and the resulting fear of castration. Freud summed up: "Attachment to the mother, narcissism, fear of castration—these are the factors that we have hitherto found in the psychic etiology of homosexuality, and on them is superimposed the effect of any seduction bringing about a premature fixation of the libido, as well as the influence of the organic factor favoring the passive role in love."

In 1920 Freud published a fascinating, detailed case of lesbianism—a beautiful girl of eighteen from a proper middle-class family. The parents asked the girl to see Freud. She complied, but told him she felt no need to give up homosexuality. Still, she said, she would try to be helped for her parents' sake. Freud was doubtful she could be cured. Psychoanalysis had had little clear success with confirmed homosexuality. Freud said that with the more hopeful cases one could make the way open to the opposite sex and to bisexuality, and then "it lay with themselves to choose . . . to undertake to convert a fully developed homosexual into a heterosexual is not much more promising than to do the reverse." Usually, he felt, the homosexual goes to a psychiatrist because of external pressure. Secretly he hopes to fail; then he can claim to himself and to others that he has done everything possible and "resign himself with an easy conscience."

This patient, like so many homosexuals, showed no physical traits of the opposite sex. As she spoke about her past, Freud found that early in her life, during the Oedipal period, she had felt deeply betrayed by her father because he preferred the mother to her. Hurt, she held back the flowering of her femininity. At puberty she felt a revival of this conflict; at that time her mother became pregnant and gave birth to the girl's third brother. The betrayal had been repeated. She utterly renounced her femininity, which she felt had brought her only bitter rejection and disappointment. This girl, like most neurotics, found many "advantages through illness"—or "secondary gains," as they are now called. By becoming a lesbian she enraged her stern father, left him hurt and helplessly angry; thus she had her revenge on him. The mother was still young, pretty and sexually very competitive with her daughter (though indulgent with her sons). So the patient retired from sexual competition and left the field to her mother—and, by extension, to all women. It was just like the male homosexual retreating from competition with his father and older brothers. Freud pointed out that the patient's latest female lover reminded her of her older brother, so in this affair she satisfied both her homosexual and her heterosexual impulses.

Freud felt that he understood her history but would have little success treating her. Behind her apparent considerateness toward her parents lay defiance and vengefulness—especially toward her father. She seriously considered all explanations offered her, said Freud, "as though she were a *grande dame* being taken over a museum and glancing through her lorgnon at objects to which she was completely indifferent." Before, she had made sure her father learned of her lesbianism to enrage him, and secondarily to assure her competitive mother that she was out of the fray. Now, with the same quiet, stubborn anger, she dug in against Freud and against cure. Freud said, "Bitterness against men is as a rule easy to gratify upon the analyst; it need not evoke any violent emotional manifestations, it simply expresses itself in rendering futile all his endeavors and in clinging to the neurosis." Freud advised that if she continued treatment, it should be with a female analyst.

All along, Freud had been speaking of her lesbianism as a meander in her psychic development, caused by the unfolding of family relationships. But, true to instinct theory, he added, "we suspect some special factor which has definitely favored one side or the other, and which perhaps only waited for the appropriate moment in order to turn the choice of object finally in its direction." That was the constitutional factor. Freud concluded that this case, like most or all cases of homosexuality, was one of "inborn homosexuality which, as usual, becomes fixed and unmistakably manifest only in the period following puberty."

Last, Freud added some important final observations. Not enough writers on homosexuality, he pointed out, distinguished sufficiently between a person's sexual identity and his choice of sexual object. Many a homosexual thinks of himself as a man and is masculine in his life; it is only his choice of sexual object that is not normally masculine. There are also men with very feminine characters whose sexual choice is heterosexual. The same variety and distinctions exist among women. "The mystery of homosexuality is therefore by no means so simple as it is commonly depicted in popular expositions, e.g., a feminine personality, which therefore has to love a man, is unhappily attached to a male body; or a masculine personality, irresistibly attracted by women, is unfortunately cemented to a female body." There are three separate factors—physical gender, mental sexual identity and choice of sexual object—which occur in various combinations and balances. Since all people show "a very considerable measure of latent or unconscious homosexuality . . . the supposition that nature in a freakish mood created a 'third sex' falls to the ground."

In all, it is a confusing picture. At the end of the essay on the lesbian, Freud said that at that time one could only trace the ways people acquired their sexual identities and made their object choices, and hope that biology would some day clarify things further. The new research in hormones and gland-transplant gave promise, he thought. For that matter, he admitted, the vague and complex ideas of masculinity as active and femininity as passive were conventions that needed critical study.

While Freud developed these theories between 1905 and the early 1920s, most people considered him worse than de Sade. As they saw it, he had said all children are perverts, craving incest and parenticide; all adults have a swampland for a soul. At the Hamburg Psychiatric Congress of 1910 someone wanted to discuss Freud's theories, and the chairman said, "That is no fit subject for a scientific congress. It is a matter for the police."

Scientists were scandalized and laymen horrified; apologists for deviance felt attacked by the assertion that homosexuality was at least partly developmental—after Ellis and Krafft-Ebing had begun convincing the world it was innate. Freud said they were not a highly evolved third sex sprouting Platos and Tchaikovskys. His contention that everyone bears some kind or degree of homosexuality hardly mollified them, but it antagonized many heterosexuals.

Hirschfeld borrowed a few snippets from Freud, but said that if his theory had any truth, it applied to only a handful of homosexuals. In 1912, when the great Dr. Moll wrote a book called *The Sexual Life of the Child*, he began it by saying, "To speak of 'the sexual life of the child' seems at first sight to involve a contradiction in terms." He admitted childhood sexuality existed, but basically rejected what Freud had to say about it. Ellis said Freud was reviving the "antiquated conception of homosexuality as an acquired phenomenon." He admitted that Freud had made a few good points, but said he was basically paddling upstream. As for erotic attachments to one's mother, that happened not because of sexual feeling, but because a boy's "feminine disposition" made the society of males unpleasant to him (and, in fact, that explained Ellis to Ellis). Freud was referred to variously as a madman, a sex fiend and a "Viennese libertine."

A small group of people read Freud's work, followed his leads and corresponded with him. Bleuler, Fliess, Sadger, Jung, Adler, Abraham, Ferenczi, Stekel and Rank all entered psychoanalytic research and began to publish. In the second decade of this century, journals and societies appeared dedicated to the new science. The flowering of psychoanalysis in the study of sex was still to come.

16

New Expectations

Much of the twenties' "revolt of modern youth" was self-conscious and deliberate. Except for the past decade, there is probably no period in history when so many young people congratulated themselves so much on their public image and worked so hard to live up to it. And like youth in the sixties, they did not really so much live a revolution as dramatize and publicize one that had been brewing for decades. Early in the century, Freud, Einstein, Heisenberg and others destroyed traditional scientific perspectives. Religious belief began to wane. People had moved in great numbers from Europe to America and from small towns to big cities; their children knew a generation gap greater than any spoken of a half century later.

During the decade following the First World War, new living conditions, mores and intellectual concepts swept through Europe and the United States. What had once been radical, minority causes reached the educated middle class and began to filter down through the new mass media. If one watched newspapers, magazines and films, the dominant new social and moral ideals seemed to be rational hedonism and studied iconoclasm. This was the time of H. L. Mencken and Dorothy Parker, the Scopes trial, the rapid spread of labor and socialist organizations. It was the age of flappers and career women, emancipated youth, hip flasks, dating and petting, films and radio, a rising divorce rate, the first popularization of psychology. At one social level, young Americans careened around in their automotive "brothels on wheels," spooning at shockingly young ages and drinking bootleg whisky. Their counterparts in another milieu discussed Freud, Picasso, Gertrude Stein, sexual equality and free love. When the "Flaming Youth" reached their thirties, they would be renamed the Lost Generation; they wore that sobriquet as well with bravado and affected weariness. They had demanded the right to sin, and now alternately claimed to enjoy and be bored by it.

The same wave of modernism and emancipation was taking place all over the West. The English "Bright Young Things" of whom Waugh and Huxley wrote were smoking, drinking, discussing "advanced ideas," bubbling cynical chatter, experimenting in the forbidden. In France drugs, cocktails and programmatic revolt in art, politics and sex became fashionable. In Russia the Communist regime wiped away traditional sexual controls; young revolutionaries praised the new age of science, reason and change.

Feminism was transformed from a radical to a liberal-in-power. By the early twenties women could vote in England, the United States and several other Western countries. During the next twenty-five years they would gradually come close to being man's equal before the law. They were more mobile, unrestrained and financially independent than ever. The career woman and the independent young miss became common types; the feminine ideal was more energetic, less passive. With the new social image came a new physical one: women were supposed to be flat-chested, stick-legged, short-haired, pouty, blasé—as curveless and pertly petulant as spoiled little boys.

With the vote won, feminism turned to the fight for birth control and a single sexual standard. At first Margaret Sanger in the United States, Marie Stopes in England, Elise Ottesen-Jensen in Sweden and their counterparts in other countries had a tough time promoting contraception. But by the mid-twenties it was common in the upper and middle classes and making headway among the rural and poor. Pressure for sex education became stronger. Diatribes against "puritanism" were common. Those who wanted to free sex attitudes and behavior used biology and Freud for support. Sex was just a biological urge, like hunger and sleepiness; to thwart it was unhygienic. Hadn't Freud said that blocked libido was the cause of neurosis? And that man is instinctually bisexual?

It was a logical extension of such thinking to dissociate sex from such "outmoded" values and institutions as the double standard, the limitation of sex to marriage, marriage itself. Isadora Duncan was one of many feminists who defended free sexual choice and the right to bear children out of wedlock. She was also one of a smaller number who lived their principles. D. H. Lawrence, H. G. Wells, Bertrand Russell and "moderns" everywhere called for a new sexual code. Wells said that if a man and woman shared "friendship, clear understanding, absolute confidence," they could indulge anything—love, sex, perhaps even marriage. Writers called for trial marriage and polygamy. Judge Ben Lindsay, author of *The Revolt of Modern Youth*, asked in *Companionate Marriage* for a union that included birth control, the end of "the law of sexual property," and the right to dissolve childless marriages at will. Havelock Ellis, now a world-famous authority on sex, claimed that love would absorb adultery. Fannie Hurst expressed this idea more brightly by proposing "visiting marriages," with separate households and meetings by appointment. In France Léon Blum's book *Free Love*, which had been greeted with shrieks of execration in 1903, enjoyed a big revival. Crusaders in the French press and parliament advocated free love as a cure for jealousy, crime and mental illness.

In Russia, where socialist-feminist ideology had become law, contraception and abortion were easily available, marriage and divorce matters of mutual consent. Writer Boris Pilnyak portrayed an emancipated young Soviet lady saying of her pregnancy:

> "In the center of attention was neither love nor my partner, but I myself and my emotions. I chose men, different men, in order to learn everything. I did not want to become pregnant; sex is joy; I did not think of the child. But I will manage it, and the State will help me. As to morals, I don't know what it means, I have been taught to forget it. Or perhaps I have my own morals. I am responsible only for myself."

Here was the core of the sexual revolution: maternity and wifehood were no longer the unquestioned goals of life, and women had a right, in fact a duty, to enjoy sex. It could no longer be a burden borne for the sake of men. It must become a joy and a gesture of independence. With contraception and economic freedom available, women *would* have fun in bed—or judge themselves failures. In 1918 Marie Stopes said in her influential book *Married Love* that a wife should always receive full sexual gratification. In 1926 the Dutch physician Theodoor H. van de Velde published *Ideal Marriage*, a typical text of the period that is still widely read. Van de Velde was a Kahlil Gibran of sex, his work a *This Is My Beloved* of female orgasm. He presented coitus as a lyric flight, orgasm a hygienic necessity and a Wagnerian implosion. "Every considerable erotic stimulation of their wives that does not terminate in orgasm, on the woman's part, represents an injury . . . to both body and soul." Van de Velde, Stopes and many others described female orgasm with metaphors of breaking waves, dancing lights, waves of electricity and various celestial events. Gilbert V. Hamilton, an eminent American psychiatrist and author of a pioneer study of sexual behavior, said that absence of female orgasm was a cause of illness, infidelity and divorce. Writers echoed Havelock Ellis on the trauma of the wedding night and the Western male's crude incompetence in bed. Now husbands were exhorted to awaken their brides by being Paganinis of sex. They were advised to engage in acts of foreplay that only a generation ago doctors had described as perversions.

The call for general sexual expressiveness rose louder. Once "sexual excess" had been thought a cause of madness; now Dr. Binet Sanglé in France claimed that two thirds of the inmates of the Salpêtrière asylum were celibates. In 1926 the German psychiatrist Wilhelm Reich produced *Function of the Orgasm*, the first major step in his campaign for sex as the universal cure; he later went so far as to claim that masturbation, by releasing sexual energy, would cure cancer. This was the age, said Viennese satirist Karl Kraus, in which if a man walked the boulevard with a woman he was considered her lover; if with a man, a homosexual; if alone, a masturbator.

It had once been an act of courage to speak at all of sexual deviance, let

alone practice it. Now it was chic to take it for granted or even claim to
have dabbled in it. In New York, deviance became associated with Greenwich Village. Since the turn of the century artists and intellectuals had been
moving there because it was a pleasant, tolerant and inexpensive neighborhood, once an Irish ghetto and now a Little Italy. After the war, the colony
there swelled with pseudo-bohemians and social drop-outs of all kinds.
Cabarets, clubs and tea houses sprang up, some of which became pickup
joints and homosexual hangouts. Newspapers were full of titillating stories
about the "flaming youth" and deviants there, and busloads of tourists went
to gawk at them. In her account of Greenwich Village in the twenties,
Caroline Ware described a little nightclub in the basement of a tenement
building:

> By 1930, promiscuity was tame and homosexuality had become the ex-
> pected thing. One girl who came nightly was the joke of the place because
> she was trying so hard to be a Lesbian, but when she got drunk she forgot
> and let the men dance with her. A favorite entertainer was a "pansy" whose
> best stunt was a take-off on being a "pansy." To lend a touch of intellectual-
> ity and to give people a sense of activity, the proprietor set aside two nights
> each week for discussion or performance by regular patrons. These evenings,
> however, did not interrupt the group's major preoccupation, for the subjects
> chosen for discussion were such things as "the social position of a gigolo"
> and "what is sex appeal?" On the latter subject, the views of the Lesbians
> present were especially called for.

Similar neighborhoods existed in major cities all over Europe, and in
them homosexuals moved freely and openly. Homosexuality was also being
written about more, and censorship barriers started to fall. In England and
America novels, plays and stories dealt with or mentioned deviance. In
1915 D. H. Lawrence's *The Rainbow* presented lesbianism as a force
against love and life; a British court ordered it withdrawn from circulation.
In 1917 Clemence Dane's *The Regiment of Women* described a sadistic
lesbian schoolmistress; a popular film on the same theme appeared in Germany, *Mädchen in Uniform*. Male and female homosexuality appeared in
the works of Ronald Firbank, Sherwood Anderson, James Gibbon
Hunecker and Wyndham Lewis—Lewis' *Apes of God* contained an acidly
satiric chapter called "The Lesbian Ape." In 1924 *Harper's* magazine seri-
alized a novel, a sort of dramatized psychiatric case history, that included
lesbian fantasies. The play *The Drag* opened in Boston in 1927, with Mae
West, created a furor, and promptly closed down.

Finally two works made homosexuality an acceptable subject for the
general public in England and America. One was Bourdet's play *The Captive*, which appeared in Paris in 1925. Within eight months it was also
playing in Berlin, Vienna, Budapest and New York. It was a conventional
domestic-triangle melodrama, but the rival was a lesbian. It lacked artistic
or documentary value, but it appeared when the public was ready to accept
an author thus capitalizing on the new freedom for sexual frankness. The

New York showing resulted in the enactment of a law making the dramatic presentation of homosexuality an offense, but to no lasting effect.

In 1928 *The Well of Loneliness* appeared in England; it is best described as the *Uncle Tom's Cabin* of lesbianism—earnest, improbable, drably written and polemical. Havelock Ellis had encouraged the author, Radclyffe Hall, through her work on the book, and contributed a preface. Today it seems tame, and Rose Macaulay described it as "a most gentlemanly book," but it was viciously attacked in the press and by the Home Secretary, Sir William Joynson-Hicks, who tried to protect England from it. Literary and scientific leaders fought the ban and won. The book had an effect almost like that of the Kinsey reports two decades later. Those who believed in sexual emancipation rejoiced that puritanism was dead, the New Morality ascendant.

Publications also brought homosexuality increasingly into public view in Germany, Denmark, Sweden and France. One of the most popular books in France during the twenties was *La Garçonne*, the story of a girl who lived "the new freedom" and had both heterosexual and homosexual affairs. In Germany there were many magazines dedicated solely to homosexuality—*Friendship and Freedom, Eros, Transvestite*—some with circulations of many thousands. One such publicaion in France, *Marges*, sent a questionnaire to leading writers asking what they considered the cause and significance of so much literature about homosexuality since the war. Thirty replies came back, naming as causes the war, Freud and general social decadence. They variously recommended whipping, imprisonment and confinement to asylums for homosexual writers. The editor went into a snit over this display of illiberalism and suggested that some other magazine conduct a similar study of heterosexuality and ways to combat it.

So far we have been seeing the twenties as the period saw itself, and therefore as later decades have. People believed that science, iconoclasm and hedonism had destroyed traditional taboos. When Kinsey and his associates produced their landmark studies of sexual behavior in 1948 and 1953, they gave proof that the sexual revolution of the twenties was not as great as most people had then thought.

In his study of males, Kinsey compared people born in each decade between the 1890s and the 1940s. He found only moderate change, and most of that in the twenties. Those who believed during the thirties and forties that the sexual revolution was continuing could find no support in these statistics. In the twenties, men began to go to prostitutes less frequently and had more sexual contact with girls of their own social background. Necking and petting had become common practices among the college-educated population, but coital patterns were not greatly changed.

The real sexual revolution of the twenties had occurred among females. Kinsey concluded that a person's life pattern of sex behavior is largely determined by economic and social class, religion, peers and, of course, the family. Signs of one's pattern are already becoming apparent at three or four; it is set by the middle teens, and there is very little chance that it will change after that despite individual development and environmental shifts. So if a revolution did occur during the late teens and twenties, its origin must lie in the formative years of those people who grew to maturity and became the statistics of revolution at that time. In other words, it occurred in the growing-up years of children between 1900 and 1910. Indeed, the profile of the twenties' sexual revolution appeared in comparative figures of the two generations of women born before 1900 and between 1900 and 1910. Women of the latter generation engaged in more sexual activities and began them sooner. The dramatic changes were:

	Pre–1900	1900–1910
Masturbated at some time during their lives	40%	50%
Practiced deep kissing	44	74
Petted to orgasm	26	44
Ever reached orgasm	72	80
Unmarried females, manipulated male genitals	12	31
Unmarried females, premarital coitus before 25	14	36
Married females, coitus with woman above	33	50
Married females, practiced fellatio	29	46
Married females, allowed cunnilingus	42	53

Of ten single girls in the older generation, only one would have petted to orgasm by the age of twenty; three out of ten would have done so in the later generation. If still unmarried at twenty-five, one or two of the older generation would be nonvirgins, but three or four of the younger. Once married, women contributed more to coital foreplay; they expanded their sexual repertoires. Fewer women abstained from sex entirely before marriage, and there were fewer spinsters.

But the change in most practices beyond petting was not great—ten or fifteen percentage points for a given act at a given age. Taboos on oral sex, from deep-kissing to oral-genital acts, became markedly weaker, and an emphasis on female orgasm began to appear strongly among the better educated. Still, the majority of girls who had premarital coitus did so entirely or mostly with the men they were engaged to marry. Though incidences changed (the number of people who have performed an act), frequencies for most acts did not increase. Girls of the younger generation were more likely to pet to orgasm for the first time at sixteen, as compared to eighteen for the older; but once they began, they did not do so any more often, perhaps once a month or less. A slightly larger number of women had extramarital sex, but those who did so revealed the same frequency—rarely. The proportion of women engaged in premarital coitus who reached orgasm did not change. In fact, the frequency of marital coitus decreased from a statistical average of 3.2 times per week to 2.6 times per week, probably because of greater regard for wives' sexual desires.

The antisexual tradition had been significantly eroded, but there was no vast revolution in behavior. The greatest changes, in fact, were not in coitus but in petting, a tentative step by females toward sex before marriage. Considering how stable sexual mores have been in the West, how deeply rooted they are, how early in life and how firmly they are learned, a crash reversal is very unlikely. The greatest revolution in the twenties was in attitudes, expectations and values. In 1910 most college girls would say premarital sex was a sin. In 1925 they would say it was all right if one loved a man, and everyone was doing it; most would then add, "I just haven't met the right boy yet myself." Gut reactions still hadn't caught up with ideology. It took a great deal of talk for people to work themselves up to a relatively small change in behavior. People believed a great revolution had taken place because petting had become conspicuous and talk boastful.

So as women were more likely to allow limited sex with men they loved, the men went to prostitutes less frequently; sex took on a more positive value, especially for women. There was a moderately large but sharp upswing on graphs of sexual behavior. By 1930 the graphs almost leveled off, and a slight, almost imperceptible rise continued for another few decades. Yet during the thirties and forties so-called experts insisted that a revolution was continuing. The mass media had as much to do with ideas of change as what people did in private.

One tends to forget that most people could not afford automobiles, and that those who owned them didn't all use them for orgy and riot. Many people never saw a flapper or hip flask. Most people still spent their time working, keeping homes and raising children; few have ever spent most of their time at drinking, partying and sex. Some people lived unconventionally; some always had. It was fashionable to talk about change, especially at higher social and educational levels. But as Kinsey said later,

> Upper level individuals like to think that they have become more liberal, sexually emancipated, free of their former inhibitions, rational instead of traditional in their behavior, ready to experiment with anything. It is notable, though, that such emancipated persons rarely engage in any amount of actual behavior which is foreign to the pattern laid down in their youth . . . the change in the form of a generation's rationalizations has not affected its overt behavior one whit.

The divorce rate did rise steadily from the late nineteenth century through the first half of the twentieth, but that does not mean ideas of love and marriage had died. When the Lynds, in the mid-twenties, published their famous sociological study of Muncie, Indiana, disguised as *Middletown*, they found a 600 per cent increase in divorce since 1890. But they pointed out that the old pattern of unbroken marriage had been replaced by one of divorce and remarriage. Marriage was more than ever considered an act of love, not a social contract; if a first marriage failed to be rich in love, a second attempt should be made. The old axiom that sex, love and marriage should go together was, if anything, stronger than ever.

This was the reason for the increase in petting and premarital coitus that formed the mini-revolution of sex in the twenties. The twenties were actually a time of heightened individualistic romanticism. Around the turn of the century vast numbers of people arrived in the United States from Europe, and people migrated in hordes from small towns to big cities. The childen born to these people were conscious of being very different from their parents; these Anglicized, city-bred young knew a "generation gap" much greater than that of the sixties. For the first time, a distinct, self-conscious youth culture arose, with expectations of arranging one's own marriage through adolescent experimentation at love. The dating-petting syndrome came into existence. The idea that sex is validated by marriage was extended by some people to the love that leads to marriage, and by very few more to affection without expectation of marriage. In a social milieu that offered few supports as the extended family began to disappear, people felt a stronger need than ever for close love bonds, the intimate companionate marriage the Puritans and Ben Lindsay had extolled. The age of boasting about free love was also the age of the birth of the soap opera.

Many of the very authorities to whom the "rebels" pointed for support had not stood for unrestrained sex. Freud was a controlled and monogamous man in his life and values; he felt that repression and sublimation were the necessary basis of civilized life. D. H. Lawrence deplored people who were now, out of bravado and defiance of their parents, "*doing it on purpose*—as unpleasant and hurtful a repression [of feelings], just as much a sign of secret fear." Ben Lindsay wanted companionate marriage to end in blissful monogamy; for even such mild revisionism in sex and marriage he was dismissed from his position as magistrate of a juvenile court in Denver. Probably the great majority of society remained unchanged at heart about basic values on the conduct of love and sex.

Conventional writers, and there were many, went on stressing the evil effects of "sexual excess" and premarital intercourse. By the thirties a counterrevolution had begun among people who felt that the twenties emancipation movement had brought not only freedom for few but grief and complications for many. In many "emancipated" couples only one of the partners really wanted emancipation, and the other reluctantly acquiesced, often with an aftermath of frustration or bitterness.

In Russia a great majority of people never took part in the new freedom made available by middle-class revolutionaries. Certainly much of the devout peasantry had no use for it, and sometimes it failed to satisfy even those who had originally wanted it. The great satirist Mikhail Zoshchenko portrayed a modern bridegroom who couldn't find his bride at the wedding—after all, he'd only seen her once, on a streetcar. He had fun at the party and got divorced the following morning, without ever having spotted his "wife." In the thirties divorce and abortion once again became almost impossible to obtain, homosexuality again became a crime, and Russians settled back to their traditional morality. There, as in other countries where a sexual "revolution" had taken place, the masses no more really engaged in free love than queens had swished in hordes along the boulevards when the Napoleonic Code made homosexuality legal. The heroine of *La Garçonne*, that novel of emancipated bisexual love, no more represented the average French girl of the twenties than the heroine of *Bonjour Tristesse* personified the French girl of the fifties.

Typical of the partial, or arrested, revolution of the twenties were Marcel Proust and André Gide. Proust had been a sickly boy, deeply attached to his mother. He became a frail, brilliant young society wit. He pretended to be, or tried to be, attracted to women, but he became exclusively homosexual and in his twenties had a number of casual and somewhat squalid homosexual encounters. As the years went on, he secluded himself to write his vast seven-volume novel *Remembrance of Things Past*. He kept a series of young men, who were virtually imprisoned in his household while in his service. Among them was an Albert, his lover and procurer, whom Proust eventually rewarded by setting him up in business as proprietor of a Turkish bath that fronted for a homosexual brothel.

In conversations with friends and in his private notebooks, Proust said that he did not dare be frank in his great work about his homosexuality. The aim of the books was ambitious psychological and social portraiture of a quite new kind. The public, he said, would be so prejudiced, so mentally fixated on the homosexuality involved, that the real point would be missed. Proust switched his homosexual experiences and emotions, especially the more tender ones, into the female mode, attributing them to a lesbian named Albertine. The character Baron de Charlus was a homosexual dirty-old-man; Albert, with his bath-house-brothel, appeared as Jupien.

Proust relegated to his notebooks, which appeared in fragments long after his death, some brilliant comments on homosexuality. He described the loneliness, the feeling of differentness and threat that so often go with homosexuality. Some few homosexuals, Proust thought, were not congenitally so and could be cured. The others, innately inverted, had to live their agony, as he had. In the notebooks he characteristically described homosexuality with beautiful, subjective precision. When one is young, he said, one is no more aware that one is homosexual than that one is a snob. "The snob is not a man who loves snobs, but merely a man who cannot set eyes on a duchess without finding her charming. A homosexual is not a man who loves homosexuals, but a man who, seeing a soldier, immediately wants to have him for a friend."

At first, said Proust, the homosexual thinks it is the object of his desire that has special qualities. Finally he sees himself from the outside, realizes it is a quality within himself that creates the attractiveness. It is then that he finally says to himself, "I am a homosexual." After that, he may decide that traffic with women has dulled the minds of most men. He interprets literature and history in the light of his obsessions, and, if he finds a phrase in Montaigne or Stendhal that seems to show a particularly ardent friendship, he will "feel convinced that what [he finds] to love in these authors is a shared taste, though the authors themselves had probably not been conscious of it, and had needed someone like their latest reader to open their eyes to the truth." Such a person, said Proust, becomes a zealot trying to convert the young to his obsession.

But another man, he said, after finding a homosexual identity, may be overwhelmed by terror and guilt. Instead of proselytizing, he retires into isolation, reaching out only tentatively from his secret gloom. Still another may go to the extreme of homosexuality, a world of mixed furtiveness and melodrama. People who do this, said Proust, "haunt the waiting rooms of stations, delicate creatures with sickly faces and strange flamboyant clothes, scanning the crowd for the return of an assumed look of lazy disdain." The search for a partner by such "addicts" is so dangerous that they feel their sort of love can't be like that of heterosexuals, born of the moment. It must be

> far more deeply rooted in the life of him who thus responds, in his temperament, maybe in his heredity, that the answer to their call has come from somewhere far beyond the passing minute, that the "beloved" thus miraculously given has been his affianced love from days before his birth, has found his way to this moment of meeting from the depths of limbo, from those stars where all our souls inhabit before they are incarnate. Such love, they will be more than tempted to believe, is the only true love. For among the special, pre-established harmonies that it implies there can be no room for mere caprice, but only for the working of destiny.

Proust understood the subtle complexities of feeling in a particular sort of homosexual life. His oblique presentation of his experience and knowledge in his novel had a wide public effect, and in some circles "Proustian" became a polite circumlocution for "homosexual."

Gide, though he lacked Proust's probing subtlety, became the first self-professed homosexual of great literary standing in our time to address the public about deviance. Like Proust, he was one of the great innovative geniuses of modern literature; unlike Proust, he was a morally obsessed Calvinist. During a trip to North Africa in his twenties he had a joyless introduction to heterosexuality, and several homosexual encounters that filled him with lust and lyrical abandon for the first time in his life. He tried to ignore the homosexual interlude and returned to France to marry a cousin whom he loved deeply. In 1902 he wrote *The Immoralist*, a book about the marriage of a homosexual. It was not an exact portrait of his own marriage, but it dealt with his type of situation and included incidents from his North African experiences. When it was dramatized on Broadway in the fifties, its subject and attitude could still cause an uproar.

Gide could not live without his wife, nor could he do without beautiful adolescent boys. He stayed with his wife in abiding companionship; he also traveled alone a great deal, and on these occasions led a very different life. By the mid-twenties he had become one of the great men of French literature, and now he dared publish two books written years before and kept from public circulation, which revealed his own homosexuality. He had hesitated for fear of the public embarrassment to his wife, and because the times had not yet been ripe. Now, with his usual rebellious rectitude, he claimed that he cared not at all about losing honors, acclaim, public esteem.

The first edition of *Corydon* had numbered twelve copies; they were privately printed in 1911 without the author's name, and promptly locked away in Gide's desk. In 1924, against his friends' advice, Gide let the works appear in the influential *Nouvelle Revue Française* under his name, and then as a book. It consisted of dialogues between a narrator and his friend Corydon, a homosexual physician. The narrator takes traditional antihomosexual positions, and Corydon corrects and instructs him with evidence from biology, sociology and history. The book's theory of homosexuality is an ingenious piece of literary theory building based on fragments of research that fit the author's purpose. It explains male homosexuality badly, lesbianism not at all. It includes several good and well-taken points, but also such chestnuts of homosexual apology as the statement that homosexuality always accompanies periods of high culture. The entire work reflects Gide's puritanical temperament, his belief in ethical feeling and control: "Whether lust is homo- or hetero-sexual, virtue consists in dominating it."

Later that year Gide published his autobiographical work *If It Die*. It described in detail his first homosexual experiences and his decision to marry. Like *Corydon,* it had previously been printed in a small edition. The book explains little about homosexuality, but it is a well-written and moving personal account. It was the first voluntary, detailed, public avowal of homosexuality by a prominent man since Greco-Roman times. Gide's friends warned him not to publish either *Corydon* or *If It Die*. The novelist Roger Martin du Gard argued with Gide, and recorded in his diary that he had told him:

> . . . the fact that certain moral principles are less vigorously defended does not mean that they are weaker at the roots. We may seem less strict, in such matters, in France; there may be greater freedom of expression in print; the police may be less rigorous; conventional people may be less prudish. But essentially nothing—nothing at all—has changed, neither in the repressions of the law nor in the attitude of the great majority of our contemporaries.

Gide did not listen. The books brought both scandal and praise. He died in 1951, world-famous and admired, his homosexuality public and taken for granted. Many accepted him in spite of it. He received the Nobel Prize for literature, but he never became a member of the French Academy—a decade later Jean Cocteau would break that barrier.

It is difficult to say whether Gide or Martin du Gard was more right. Gide was not pilloried, as Wilde had been, but the circumstances of their revelations were different. The public climate had certainly changed some-what, and a superficial new liberalism allowed Gide's books to be published; but most homosexuals were not as privileged as Gide, and they still lived in fear of loneliness, disgrace, mockery and blackmail. Like the rest of the twenties revolution, the change regarding homosexuality was great in talk and apparent public tolerance, but slight at gut level. Accord-ing to Kinsey, there was no difference between the pre-1900 and 1900–1910 generations in the amount of male or female homosexuality. One wonders whether any of the "emancipated" dabbled in anything they wouldn't have dabbled in anyway, with different rationales. When it came to extreme deviance, the revolution had made only the tiniest dent.

INTERVIEWS

Probably no one knows more about measuring a society's sex behavior than the staff of the Institute for Sex Research at Indiana University, in Bloomington, founded by Alfred Kinsey. The present director is Dr. Paul Gebhard, professor of anthropology at the university and a member of the Institute since Kinsey's days. Gebhard is a man in his fifties, with light eyes behind dark-rimmed glasses, a small mustache, and a strong current of nervous energy beneath a genial surface.

Dr. Gebhard, I've found that it makes people uncomfortable when I say that we still need data about sex behavior in our own society. They usually say we all know what's going on, we don't need any more nose-counting, or whatever. Why is there still this anxious refusal to admit that we don't know what goes on around us, let alone in other places or the past?

⌈Well, data curbs speculation, so there's terrific resistance to it. You just can't have fun guessing when you know the facts.⌋

Or justify your own life and emotions with those guesses.

Right. There's a conflict between evidence and emotion. When there's emo-tional content, people resist counting, and the reaction seems to be proportional. No one objected to the Institute's figures on wet dreams or onset of menstrua-tion. But when it came to premarital sex and homosexuality, they picked at the figures and then said they didn't mean much anyway.

I know you've been asked this many times, but how sure can you be of accu-rate answers in your studies? Not because people lie, but because they have inhi-bitions and selective memories.

No, people don't lie much; after all, they'll never see us again, and what they say won't affect their lives. It is true that we're vulnerable to people's inner inconsistencies. But our questionnaires and interviews have lots of internal checks for inconsistencies, and when we spot one, we peck away at it. For instance, in the questionnaire we may see that a woman practiced masturbation pretty frequently in her early teens. At another point she says her masturbation was down to once a week at nineteen, but that there was no premarital intercourse or homosexual activity. We point out the inconsistency—that pattern is an unlikely one. We have her rethink the thing; usually, she'll start remembering things and correct herself.

Or say we ask a former GI about his sex activity when he was in the service. We may get something like:

How often did you have intercourse while you were stationed overseas?

Oh, every night.

All the time you were in Europe?

Well, I mean, when I was in Naples.

Were you in active combat during that period?

Yes.

Then you weren't in Naples every night.

No, about half the time.

Did you have sex every night you weren't in combat?

Well, not every night. . . .

A skilled interviewer who knows his techniques can produce pretty reliable information.

What do studies here and elsewhere show in terms of the sexual revolution talked about in the media?

William Simon and John Gagnon did a study here before they left the Institute, and the results coincide in general direction with most of the smaller ones in recent years. They show that the same trend lines of slow change in sex behavior that existed decades ago are continuing pretty much unchanged. I'm sure they're right. I'd be amazed to see trends change as drastically as current talk suggests, at least in so short a time.

There has been a lot of talk about large numbers of homosexuals, sado-masochistic networks, swapping clubs, undergrounds, communes, group marriages, and so on. Do these really involve significant numbers of people?

It's hard to tell, of course, because such people don't seek to be known. Except some homosexuals—they're a mixed group. There's danger for some of them in being honest, but also many are desperately interested in educating non-homosexuals. Half want to hide, and half are anxious to be open. As for the other deviants, they're very small groups, though they don't like to think so. There may be psychological sado-masochism operating in a lot of people, but practicing s-m's and so on may number only in the thousands. When you find an s-m who's knowledgeable, you discover that he knows many of the others you've talked to. It's a small fraternity. One indication of the smallness of the group is how hard it is to get partners. There are lots of masochists—at least among men—but not many sadists. When masochistic men hear about a female sadist whose services are available, they come flocking from hundreds of miles around.

Who joins swinging groups? A sexually uninhibited person has a whole city in which to find partners. Why a group?

This is just an impression, but I find that the majority of females in swinging groups aren't terribly attractive. That may be a motive for joining. I agree that a sexually well-adjusted guy probably isn't making noise or joining groups; he's just living his life—successfully. The groups may serve special functions for people with special problems. One of the basic hang-ups in deviant behavior is that it can become the pivotal point of one's life, making everything else peripheral.

I'd like to ask you about the famous 37 per cent in Sexual Behavior in the Human Male. *That figure, the number of men who've had "homosexual contact to orgasm" at some time in their lives, is used to show the prevalence and alleged normality of homosexuality. But isn't it misleading? Does an act of mutual masturbation at thirteen or one homosexual experience at eighteen have anything to do with what we usually mean when we talk about homosexuality?*

God, sometimes I wish we'd never published that statistic! Of course there are a lot of homosexual acts that occur outside the hard-core homosexual population. Many people have one or two homosexual experiences, and there are those whose homosexual activity varies throughout their lives. When people are young, they can have fairly extended homosexual episodes and then maintain a heterosexual pattern for the rest of their lives; as you get older, into your thirties, you don't go in and out of homosexuality with such freedom. In the two behavior volumes, homosexuality was put on a scale from 1 to 6, based on both behavior and psychological factors. Earlier in life there may be some sliding up and down, as I said; sometimes it may be due to, say, a prison situation—someone is a Kinsey 1 outside prison but a Kinsey 5 inside prison. I think we should divide these ratings into two factors, psychological and behavioral. We could fractionate them—for instance, a $1/3$ would be a psychological 1 and an overt 3. Most people would have the same numbers, $1/1$, $2/2$, etc. My guess would be that when you get a spread of two or more points between the two factors, such as $1/4$ or $2/0$, you'd find you're dealing with someone under stress—such as a prison situation.

The word bisexual is often used. My feeling is that I've met many homosexuals who have heterosexual experience, and vice versa, but few or no people without a basic leaning one way or the other.

Yes, it's rare to be fifty-fifty. My own impression is that there are two kinds of people who don't care so much about the sex of their partners. One is cosmopolitan and sophisticated, and cares a great deal about love and affection. The other is lower class, and willing to just stick it into anything.

Isn't homosexuality—I mean exclusive adult homosexuality—considered deviant in every society?

Yes. Homosexuals are always apart, in a special niche, even when they're said to have special talents and powers. There are societies that consider being exclusively heterosexual or exclusively homosexual abnormal, but I don't know of a culture where homosexual orientation is a majority thing.

Have you done studies of homosexual populations in this country?

We've finished the field work on one, and are pulling the data together. And now we will do the biggest study of homosexuality ever tried. It will be our major job here for the next few years.

The first study was meant to give information about homosexuals' general life adjustment. How do they get along in a heterosexual society that's by and large unsympathetic?

Who were the subjects?

Nearly five hundred male homosexuals, mostly in Chicago. I suspect a town has to get up to about fifty thousand to support a gay bar; small-town patterns may be quite different from what we found. Our sample was pretty much limited to young, white, urban, fairly well-educated males who were relatively open and belonged to the homosexual community. We missed the closet queen, the older conservative businessman, the lower-middle-class boy, and many who live outside the homosexual community. We missed those who can't afford to be seen in homosexual gathering places or who have stable relationships. I think that having a circle of homosexual friends and entertaining at home is probably the most common social pattern.

We started by looking at institutions that shape the subculture and give support to individuals—bars, stores and so on. We wanted to see how many signs of stress showed in the subjects' lives, such as suicide attempts and psychosomatic ailments. We wanted to know how many friends people had. Whether their parents knew, and how they related to them. How they got on with brothers and sisters. How they made peace with religion. How many heterosexual friends they had, and whether these friends knew about the subjects' homosexuality.

The data aren't fully analyzed yet, but generally I'd say we found a large number of the homosexuals coping, though paying a price in terms of employment, depression and other problems. Our second study will replicate the first study and expand to the San Francisco Bay area and other locales. This time we'll have a broader approach—including blacks, lesbians and family background. We'll test out Bieber's hypothesis that the absent or hostile father is a common crucial factor.

17

Instincts and Analysts

After the First World War, Freud's ideas were popularized and became fashionable among the educated and liberal. As today, more read about Freud than actually read his works. Probably the majority of laymen went on reading Krafft-Ebing, Havelock Ellis and others who were intellectually pre-Freudian, such as Moll and Forel. Meanwhile, psychoanalysis was moving in new directions, and for the first time it began minutely plotting the development and emotional dynamics of homosexuality.

In 1902, when Freud was still relatively obscure and derided, he sent postcards to Alfred Adler, Wilhelm Stekel and two other doctors interested in his new perspective on neurosis, inviting them to his home to discuss it. This was the nucleus of the Vienna Psychoanalytic Society. It soon drew the attention of Jung, Bleuler, Sadger, Ferenczi, Abraham, Brill and others who would eventually carry Freudianism to their own cities and countries and lead analytic movements there.

Freud was flexible in changing his own ideas, but often rigidly opposed to innovations by his adherents. Many of the brilliant men he attracted weren't meant to be anyone's disciple. Rivalries and quarrels broke out, with the development of cultic splinter groups and mutual excommunications. Freud once said to Stekel, "When I look at my pupils, I get the impression that psychoanalysis liberates the worst instincts in human beings." This was shortly before the first disciple began to go his own way. In 1911 Alfred Adler found himself so intellectually at odds with Freud that he became the first major apostate of the psychoanalytic movement.

Adler had come to reject the idea that libido or any other "instinct" is the force behind neurosis. He developed instead an outlook that offered brilliant insights into the emotions in general and homosexuality in particular; they anticipated the best modern interpretations of deviance. He gave the central place in human development to the need for mastering one's environment and personal fate. Everyone is born helpless and has a long period of dependence; therefore his first experience of life is being small, weak and helpless. This is both unpleasant and threatening. From the start, the ways in which he is fed, handled and spoken to make him feel secure or insecure, timid or defiant. With such characteristics forming, he must progressively deal with not only parents but siblings, peers and the world outside his home.

He learns that society equates masculinity with courage, freedom, the right and ability to assert will and aggression. It equates femininity with obedience, dependence and inhibition. These stereotypes influence him as he develops a set of life goals and a life style for reaching them. If he falls short in his struggle for superiority, dominance and power, he has a sharp sense of dis-ease. His feeling of inferiority predisposes him to neurosis. He must protect his masculinity (superiority); to do so he denies his weakness (femininity) and overcompensates for it. "The Jerusalem of every neurosis," said Adler, is "I want to be a real man."

Adler's approach was significantly different from Freud's not only in theory but in therapeutic practice. He proposed that one's destiny is shaped more by social than by biological forces; the source of personality and behavior lies not in a closed system of instincts but in family and social interaction. In fact, instincts become subsidiary to life style, which is fashioned as a means of coping with the environment. Adler stressed "social embeddedness," by which he meant involvement with social values, friends, vocation, status. He believed that if the Oedipus complex is powerful, pernicious and lasting, it is because the person was a pampered child who couldn't give up his mother and face reality without her protection. He sees the world as a threat to the vulnerable fiction of his strength and superiority. When his power to cope breaks down, he shows neurotic symptoms. Treatment, then, should not be a tortuous excavation of traumas, but a re-education in dealing with the world—relatively short, with the doctor taking an active teacher's role. A patients' distortion in life goals and life style should be pointed out, his feelings of inferiority and his compensations made clear.

Adler viewed homosexuality as one of many types of failure to cope with life, with a heterosexual world. As a life style, he said, it reflected low self-esteem. As for the belief in homosexuality being innate and unchangeable, this was "scientific superstition." Freud had said that where a perversion is acted out, there is no neurosis to treat, because of the instinctual mechanics involved. Adler said, "There can be no sexual perversion without training. Only those who have noted this training will understand that sexual perversion is an artificial product."

Physical constitution, he claimed, is involved in the "training" only in that a child who is physically inadequate feels inferior. If a boy is weak, awkward or overdelicate, he may feel girlish; he then may feel that he isn't man enough to stand up to his environment, and become shy, clinging, submissive. A girl who feels gawky, ugly, and undelicate doubts that she can master the world about her as a female, with the female means of charm, seductiveness and compliance. Her goals and life style become deformed. Soon such children may renounce their masculinity and femininity because they feel utterly hopeless about winning in life as men and women. As this goes on, the mind influences the body, and posture, facial expression, voice quality, and muscle tone reflect a personality that is basically fearful.

A girl who thinks she cannot succeed as a girl—perhaps feeling defeated by her mother, sisters, father or brothers—substitutes the "fictional triumphs" of neurosis. She may accept that maleness is better, like a Negro accepting the myth of white superiority. She feels, "I am *only* a girl." Then she tries to equal or outdo men on their own terms—power, dominance, aggression. This "masculine protest," as Adler called it, may produce an angry, mannish feminist with menstrual troubles and relative frigidity. Or it may produce a lesbian or prostitute—both, said Adler, are women who felt from early childhood that they could never win any man's real love and interest.

Similarly, a boy who feels insufficiently masculine may become homosexual. In many such people one finds in the background a family in which females were preponderant; early discomfort over the difference between male and female genitals; unsurenss of sex role; and the thwarted "ambition that seeks its triumphs in a roundabout way." The boy retreats from women and from society's demand that he perform as a heterosexual. At the same time, like all neurotics, he does a salvage job on his self-esteem through fictional triumphs. One of Adler's homosexual patients grew up dominated by sisters who played sexual games with him. As an adult homosexual, his greatest pleasure was his power to excite other men and thus control them. (One thinks of X in *My Secret Life*, with his pleasure in reducing others to a state of helpless, lustful need.) Such a person, said Adler, shows "the training of a discouraged individual from childhood to avoid a normal solution to the sexual problem by eliminating the possibility of defeat."

Adler became as rigid about his theory as Freud was about his own. Freud and his followers derided Adler for decades, and in the thirties Freud said scathingly and with some justice: "Whether a person is homosexual, or a necrophilist, or an anxiety-ridden hysteric, or a shut-in obsessional, or a raving madman—in every case [the Adlerian] will assign as the motive of his condition the fact that he wants to assert himself, to overcompensate for his inferiority, to be on top, to move over from the feminine to the masculine role."

But Adler's obsession was as fruitful as Freud's, and some of his ideas have become just as much a part of our intellectual stock—inferiority and superiority complexes, life style, life goals, masculine protest and overcompensation. Many of his pioneering concepts were prophetic of psychiatry today. He removed the emphasis from instinct and moved it to social adaptation. He got others to follow him in trying more active, short-term therapy, which today has generally taken the place of classical psychoanalysis. He stressed aggression, competition and personal interaction, which are major concerns of psychiatry now. And long before anyone else, he said what most knowledgeable specialists say today—that homosexuality is not the expression of a constitutional error or an instinctual jumble, but of a person's total emotional development in relation to his family and society.

In 1912 Carl Jung broke with Freud. Like Adler, he felt that Freud overstressed instinct, especially sexual instinct. In some ways, he was running parallel to Adler. He wanted to focus less on causes, more on present behavior and life aims. He said that if a person retains his Oedipus complex, it must be to serve a present need. Therapy must not only remove infantile patterns but help create new ones in their place.

Jung never wrote much or systematically about homosexuality, but he made some brilliant passing comments. He claimed that much we tend to call feminine in a man—his "soft" emotional life—is no more homosexual than is a woman's firm inner strength. But there is, he said, an unconscious feminine self in each man, and a masculine self in each woman. (He eventually spoke of these as inherited archetypes, but more psychiatrists would speak of them as simply arising from a child identifying in turn with both his parents.) Jung wisely said that modern Western man is afraid of his "feminine weakness" and his "female shadow," but that the more he tries to keep them unconscious for his own comfort, the greater a toll the avoidance exacts.

Jung also anticipated the idea that many mothers consciously or unconsciously connive in creating their children's deviance. The "mother complex," said Jung, can produce Don Juanism, impotence or homosexuality. "The homosexual's masculinity is tied to his mother; Don Juan seeks his mother in every woman he meets." But this is not just due to the child. A mother, he said, can teach a son devotion, loyalty and fidelity to her in order to protect him from life. If he learns the lesson too well, he will always be true to her. "This naturally causes her the deepest anxiety (when, to her great glory, he turns out to be a homosexual, for example) and at the same time affords her an unconscious satisfaction that is positively mythological."

Wilhelm Stekel also went his own way in psychoanalysis before the First World War. He was a gifted writer, an energetic reformer, and a widely read author for both specialists and laymen. His genius was less in theory than in therapeutic insight, description and practice. His ability to feel a neurosis as the patient did, to find useful interpretations of dreams and recollections, was full of intuitive brilliance; he was shrewd and compassionate, and eloquent in describing what he saw. Many of his books, though theoretically outmoded, are more readable today than most of the baroque, overintellectualized theory of early psychoanalysis.

Stekel's ten volumes on *Disorders of the Instincts and Emotions* dealt in large part with sexual problems. Their therapeutic optimism was unfashionable in analytic circles then. According to Freud, deviations were rarely if ever curable, because libido is expressed rather than blocked, as in hysteria or phobia. And as the analyst Fenichel put it, the symptoms are pleasant. But Stekel claimed all neuroses and sexual disorders rise from mental conflict, not blocked instinct, and are therefore potentially curable. Although he accepted the idea of instinctive bisexuality, his approach was different from Freud's. One sometimes sees a homosexual who seems free of conflict—in fact, generally normal apart from his homosexuality. Stekel believed that such a man has completely sublimated his heterosexuality, and analysis will reveal neurosis. The clue to this, he said, is that almost all homosexuals show disgust at women, and disgust is a reaction formation against lust.

In many ways, Stekel's picture of the deviant resembles Adler's. He has isolated himself and chosen a tortuous path through life to avoid challenges he can't handle. Adler caught the magical quality of this in his metaphor of the "witch's circle," a line of defenses the neurotic draws about himself to avoid spontaneous interchange with people. Stekel vividly showed in case histories how sexual deviance can act as such a magical barrier against life's challenges and threats.

One of his patients was a female transvestite of thirty-four. When she first saw Stekel, she did not want to change, only to get his help in obtaining a police permit for wearing men's clothes in public. She told Stekel she wore men's clothes because dressing as a woman made her feel "like a dressed-up monkey." She said that though she'd never felt like a female, her lesbianism and cross-dressing hadn't crystallized till she had entered her twenties. Her love affairs were nonphysical, and her real pleasure came from cross-dressing.

As session followed session, the picture changed through the airing of memories, dreams and associations. Like most people, she found with a little probing that her sexual feelings and experiences went back farther than she had first remembered. Now it seemed that she had reached orgasm through completing the act of cross-dressing in her early teens. Then she recalled that her rejection of her gender and her terror of contact with men went back to her earliest childhood.

Her father had died when she was two; her mother remarried and bore two sons by a second husband. The girl's stepfather often told her how unattractive she was; she generally felt that he rejected her. She also believed her mother rejected her in favor of her stepfather and stepbrothers. Her dreams and associations showed a vast, thwarted craving for affection, especially from her mother.

With a child's reasoning, she believed that if she were a boy, her mother and stepfather would love her. She resented maleness as the thing that had deprived her of love, yet she envied and desired it as the way to a better life. When she was nine, she saw her stepbrother's penis and wanted to cut it off in fury. At about that time she began to believe that as she grew up her clitoris would develop into a penis. When her stepfather tried to get her to do housework and play with girls' toys, she refused. She was secretly waiting for the magic cure of growing up to be a man and thus being thought lovable. When she began to menstruate, the dream crashed. She would never be male, she would never be beautiful, her mother would never love her. And as her stepfather kept telling her, she had no hope of winning love as a woman.

Now she found another magical solution. One day she dressed in the clothes of a stepbrother toward whom she had strong erotic feelings. She had an orgasm. Once she had seen the penis as the important difference between the sexes; now that she had no hope of getting a penis, she clung to the new fantasy that the difference between the sexes was clothes. She gave up entirely on femininity. Having lost in the competition with males to win love, she worked according to the principle, "If you can't beat them, join them."

At thirty-four she still felt femininity meant ugliness and rejection. Her avoidance of men was based on fear that her old fantasies of castrating them in fury would come to the surface and get out of control (she fantasied fellatio followed by biting). In her homosexual affairs she sought madonna types, at whose breasts she wanted to suck. This girl, said Stekel, had only wanted what any woman wants: to be pretty and loved. She had seen a harsh and confusing environment as blocking the path to such fulfillment in heterosexuality; it put anxiety and disgust in her way. So, said Stekel, with the wondrous resilience of the human mind, "her injured narcissism found a way to pleasure and beauty"—transvestism.

Like Adler, Stekel said that the deviant feels unable to win in love and life through the usual route, so he wins by renouncing or changing. But Stekel remained closer than Adler to certain analytic ideas. Like most analysts, he stressed the important role of narcissistic projection in homosexuality—how deviants, as Stekel put it, "staging their eternal scene, always switch both their own and their partners' roles." As a blatant example he told of one of his patients who had been seduced by his stepmother at thirteen and had had intercourse with her for a period of a year. He was obsessed by the memory of her and avoided all other women. In his fantasies, he identified with her while in bed with other men. Soon he was in bed with other men in reality, fantasying that the other was himself, he the stepmother.

In all his writings, Stekel showed extraordinary, unsentimental empathy for people with sexual problems. In his volume on fetishism, he wrote a classic description of what fetishism feels like to the fetishist, what it means to him. He showed how the fetish stands symbolically for an Oedipal partner, and therefore the search for pleasure is never quite satisfied, the real goal never reached. The fetish is like a screen memory, symbolic of a whole trend in emotional development but not really a cause. The fetishist withdraws progressively from real sexual contact, and the fetish becomes a god, so loaded with feelings and symbolic meanings that the fetishist himself no longer really understands it. It has become the deity of an "erotic monotheism" that carries the believer farther and farther from reality, like any consuming faith. Not until Vladimir Nabokov wrote *Lolita* did anyone show so well how compulsive dramas of sexual substitution fill a person's life, crowding out all else, until he divides all the world into two categories, his sexual deity and useless furniture.

One other man, Sandor Ferenczi, made important contributions to the understanding of homosexuality in the early days of analysis. He never broke with Freud, but he came very close to it several times, chiefly because he swung away from an impersonal, authoritarian attitude toward patients to the view that a doctor should be the permissive "good parent" most patients had lacked. Sometimes when patients were in the throes of reliving childhood conflicts, he took them in his arms or on his lap. He insisted that analysts should admit mistakes and shortcomings to analysands, and did much to humanize the doctor-patient relationship. He was also sometimes an acute theoretician, and shortly before the First World War he wrote a paper that permanently marked analytic thinking about homosexuality.

In "The Nosology of Male Homosexuality" Ferenczi called useless the traditional division of homosexuals as sexually active and passive. Instead he made the distinction between inverted gender identity and inverted choice of sexual object; he used the categories subject and object homosexuals. The subject homosexual identifies as a woman. From early childhood he was emotionally passive and tended toward inverted gender identity. He loved his father; he wanted the mother's beauty, her clothes, the tenderness she won from her husband. Such a homosexual, said Ferenczi, is comfortable with women and drawn to mature, powerful men. He makes relative peace with his homosexuality and rarely wants treatment or change. He probably owes his state to an anomaly of development that has a constitutional basis, and he cannot be cured. At best, analysis can relieve his anxieties and other problems.

The object homosexual identifies as a man. In many cases he was a spoiled, narcissistic only child or his father's favorite. He was probably sexually and intellectually precocious. He was also obsessive, and in childhood may have worked out private sexual theories to account for his own behavior, and these theories are the subject of his adult obsessions. Basically, he is a frustrated, frightened heterosexual. His heterosexual urges were punished or impeded—especially at puberty, by his mother. For him, homosexuality is a way of living up to his parents' sexual interdictions by the letter of the law (no sex with women, but no one mentioned men), and of removing the Oedipal rivalry between himself and his father. He releases much of his angry feeling in the act of sodomy; analysis may reveal that unconsciously he magically equates buttocks with breasts. One of Ferenczi's patients acted out this drama in perfect accord with the theoretical paradigm. Whenever he felt insulted by another man, especially a superior, he sought a male prostitute to sodomize. Some of the details of Ferenczi's theories have not stood up, but he made clear the difference between inverted identity and inverted object choice, removed the old active-passive cliché, and won support for the idea that there is not a single entity, homosexuality, but that there are many homosexualities.

Around 1920 psychoanalysis had worked itself into a dead end. It still cured only a fairly small percentage of neurotics, and the sexual perversions and psychoses were usually considered beyond its reach, as, in terms of instinct theory, they were. But now Freud revised many of his ideas and branched out into new areas. All his life he was able, with one imaginative stroke, to provide science with new ideas that could be fruitfully explored for decades. He did so now with a new description of the mind as consisting of id, ego and superego, and a new perspective on the problem of anxiety. From this work sprang ego psychology and a new era in the study and treatment of psychosexual problems.

The id, said Freud, is composed of basic drives and instincts, such as hunger, lust and aggression. An infant is almost pure id. Then the environment starts saying *no* to him when he acts out his impulses. When he bites his mother's nipple, she takes it away; when he ignores his father's command, he is spanked or temporarily rejected. As he realizes that he has a separate identity, and that the world does not exist only for his gratification, his ego develops through the construction of defenses—denial, repression, projection, reaction formation. He finds new, safer channels for his impulses. Id and ego are like horse and rider, the brute power of the one reined and guided by the other. In all this, of course, a child's magical perceptions and fantasies are at work. The sense of time isn't developed, and a brief withdrawal of love may be forever, the beginning of eternal isolation. Or punishment may be imagined as a murderously destructive swipe of the parent's huge hand, an attack by the huge adult genital. The ego mediates between the id and these real and imagined threats of abandonment, loss, rape, castration and death.

When the child is five or six, his superego forms. Until now he has reined his impulses because he learned to fear the consequences of releasing them. But now he introjects his parents' voices, makes them part of his own being. The superego is roughly equivalent to "conscience." From now on many of the worst threats he feels will come from within himself. He has become so frightened by the Oedipal conflict and its imagined consequences that he renounces his primitive urges, adopts the moral code of his parents (and thus of society). To defy the introjected parental voices brings shame, self-contempt, feelings of ugliness and unlovability. Actually, the superego is more unconscious than conscious. Its nay-saying is so familiar, so automatic and taken for granted, that it isn't recognized much of the time. And it is often irrational, for it is based partly on a child's perceptions and fears.

With this new topography of the mind, Freud revised his thinking about anxiety. Before, he had thought of it as repressed libido pushing for release. Freud now said, "It is not repression that creates anxiety, but anxiety that creates repression." That is, anxiety is the warning signal of an ego afraid of being overwhelmed by id impulses that it and the superego fear. The symptoms of the neurotic are ways of avoiding anxiety. For instance, a situation threatens to provoke a reaction of strong lust or anger. There is a lifelong habit of expecting that the release of these feelings will result in rejection or retaliation. Anxiety is felt, like a warning buzzer: "Get rid of the offending impulse, hold the fort." Various neurotic processes and symptoms can do the job. Projection can be the way: "I'm not angry, it's other people who want to attack me." Or phobia: "I'm not dangerous, but closed spaces are."

With neurotic symptoms seen as ways of allaying anxiety, and anxiety in turn as a warning against unacceptable impulses breaking forth, castration-fear takes on a wide, metaphoric meaning. It means not only fear of actual physical damage but fear of general disaster, of punishment, of ostracism—mental or physical injury in general. In this sense, it also has a place in women's emotional lives—as Ernest Jones called it, aphanasis, a generalized dread of destruction and death.

This opened up what became known as ego psychology. Until this time, analysis centered on explaining symptoms by tracing the increase, discharge, fixation and equilibrium of biological energy. It had demanded the invention of such contradictory ideas as "desexualized libido" to explain friendship and art. Soon the major psychiatric question would be not how libido is fixated or discharged, but how the ego develops—how weak, vague or brittle it is, and how psychotherapy might affect it. Emphasis would soon shift away from traumas and the earliest years to how the adult ego copes with present threats to emotional and social security. One of the key transitional figures was Wilhelm Reich. When he broke with Freud in 1932 he had already pioneered a shift in psychiatric thought with his work on what he called character neurosis.

Character neurosis is a disorder consisting of ego defenses so stable that they seem a fixed part of the personality. Usually it is seen by the person who suffers from it as a set of traits, not a disorder. If blocked rage is expressed by phobia, the result is a sense of discomfort and illness. But if an oversolicitous manner has long been the way the ego deals with inner rage, the result is seen as "just the way I am." In fact, it can be rationalized as normal or even a virtue—as can other such neurotic traits as perfectionism, obstinacy, obedience, belligerence and shyness.

Much of a patient's resistance to analysis, said Reich, is his "character armor." A person brings to the doctor the same character he brings to the rest of the world; if his armor can be broken through in therapy, this will lead to change in the rest of his life. At first, attempts to pierce his defensive armor will be fought, ignored or taken in stride. Reich became very interested in the now fashionable field of nonverbal communication. He was the first to be deeply aware of how posture, facial expression and other physical reactions reveal character. Reich said that what the patient says often matters less than how he says it—whining, evasive, denying, defiant, overpolite. The therapist therefore never lacks material. Even silence is material: hysterical patients are anxiously silent, but compulsives are spitefully silent.

Reich held on to a good bit of Freudian instinct theory, but soon a number of other psychiatrists did not. They became more involved in mapping the growth of the ego and its defenses. Reich's "character neurosis" was, after all, the total arsenal of a threatened ego. Study should now aim at seeing how defensive habits arise and become fixed life patterns. Treatment should aim at making more strong and flexible an ego that is stunted, brittle or burdened with uneconomical defenses. There was new attention to the effects of weaning, toilet training and general permissiveness. It seemed that a very permissive upbringing didn't force a child to develop his ego enough to deal well with his feelings and the rest of the world. Yet a very controlling and frustrating atmosphere created a very rigid and therefore vulnerable ego.

Theories about phases and mechanisms of ego growth multiplied. Some have remained, and some have not. One series of important revisions and new contributions came from the presence of a number of female psychiatrists, such as Anna Freud, Melanie Klein, Helene Deutsch and Clara Thompson. Freud's idea of femininity had been largely negative. He believed that little girls envy boys their penises and think their vulvas are wounds resulting from castration. By their nature, he said, little girls have inadequate superegos and arrive at heterosexuality through a devious path, often incompletely. This happens because they feel their mothers deprived them of boys' wondrous equipment, so they bitterly turn to their fathers, and fall in love with them. There were elements of truth in specific aspects of this, but female analysts pointed out that many of Freud's ideas made human universals out of his own rather Victorian, patronizing attitude toward women. Penis envy, they said, is in some cases as much male grandiosity as female reality. Girls' superegos aren't lesser, just different.

Analytic writings between the First World War and the middle thirties contained some of the first long scientific studies of lesbianism. Many psychiatrists said homosexuality was as common in women as in men, perhaps more common. But they often found it difficult to draw the line between friendship and homosexual love—the basic problem created by the theories of instinctual bisexuality and latency. The number of cases of overt female homosexuality that were described was still relatively small. However, some trends and common interpretations did emerge.

There was wide agreement that the key to much lesbianism was obsession or fixation on the mother, due to inadequate warmth and attention from her. Some lesbians play the passive, submissive little girl and get into mother-daughter relations with other women. Their sexual life may involve a lot of "mothering"—kissing, caressing, comforting and fondling—and much mouth-breast and mouth-genital activity, as though making up some early deprivation in infantile gratification. Some lesbians deny this need by taking the opposite pose—they become aggressive and dominating, and play the psychologically enslaving mother instead of the dependent, enslaved little girl. Beneath the tough façade is a little girl fighting the urge to cry for mothering. Since the early decades of psychiatry this pattern of dependence and the denial of dependence, with a background of deficient mothering, has been confirmed over and over in a large percentage of lesbians. Helene Deutsch, in writing about this, quoted Colette: "two women embracing are a melancholy and touching picture of two weaknesses; perhaps they are taking refuge in each other's arms in order to sleep there, weep, flee from a man who is often wicked, and to taste what is more desired than any pleasure, the bitter happiness of feeling similar, insignificant, forgotten."

Problems from later childhood and the relationship with the father may also be crucial to lesbian development. Obviously, there is Oedipal feeling, which brings a girl into conflict with her mother and siblings. If the father is seductive, this becomes acute. As Freud first pointed out, a girl may avoid her rivals' retaliation by saying to herself as well as to them, "I don't hate and envy my mother and sister, I wouldn't dream of competing with them." At this point she may regress back to being a compliant mama's girl, and later re-enact this mother-daughter relationship homosexually.

In some cases a girl feels threatened by her father before or around puberty. At a young age she may fantasy being skewered by her father's huge penis in vaginal or anal rape (the distinction may not be very clear to her). Instead of fleeing back to mother, she may "identify with the aggressor" and model herself on her father. She tries to be as strong and masculine as he. She may try to win his love by being tomboyish. Later she may enter a sadistic relationship with another woman, who lets her act out the threats and aggression she feared from her father. Or after menstruation has put an end to fantasies of maleness, she may love another woman as a son loves a father—as Helene Deutsch put it, with "all the gallantry of a boy in love with a mature woman." Or she may seek out younger girls—projected images of herself as a young girl—whom she loves as she wishes her father had loved her.

Many other variations were described. The question still remains of how many describe particular cases, how many represent a common element in sexual deviation, and whether the things described were really causative or just part of a larger picture. But it was significant that the analysis of lesbians commonly showed the things frequently noted in analyses of male homosexuals—incest avoidance, narcissistic projection and role exchange, indirect struggles for power and dependency. Many lesbians, like many male homosexuals, came from homes where sexuality was strongly disapproved of, limited or punished.

Psychiatrists seemed more sure about male homosexuality. Until the early thirties, most psychoanalytic writings elaborated what had already been sketched out by Freud and the early pioneers. In some cases, a boy identified with his mother and wanted to be possessed by men as she was by the father—the typical "subject" homosexual of Ferenczi's theory. Some analysts claimed that boys confronting severe Oedipal conflict regressed back to this "pre-Oedipal" mama's-boy stage. Some analysts, however, began to see that hostility and competition often lay beneath the "subject" homosexual's effeminate manner and female identification. The boy had fantasied decoying father away from mother, and thus also putting him sexually out of commission. Now, as an adult, he felt that playing the female role was really a way of mastering other males. One psychiatrist described a patient with a strong incestuous tie to his sister; whenever her boyfriend came to visit, the brother seduced the boyfriend to make him impotent with the sister. Other "subject" homosexuals reported efforts to seduce men who had girlfriends, to take the girls' place. Adler probably would have said that being unable to compete directly with their fathers and other men, they retrieved their sense of mastery through "fictional triumphs." It was also noticed that such homosexuality sometimes involved "identifying with the aggressor"—a boy adopting the role of a cold mother and getting the love of boys who represent himself.

In other cases, incest avoidance seemed powerfully clear. During the period of Ocdipal competition, the boy imagined the father's revenge and tried to appease him—"I love you, so why would I want your woman?" He fended off attack by camouflaging himself—"Don't worry about me, I'm not even male." Even Moll, who generally resisted psychoanalytic interpretations, agreed that if one questions a homosexual who says he has always been thus, he eventually recalls heterosexual desires in childhood. Just as the girl in Oedipal conflict must choose between her father and her femininity, the boy must choose between his mother and his masculinity. The homosexual male is often a latent heterosexual hounded by literal and figurative fears of castration.

Male homosexuality could also be a symbolic way of saying, "Father, love me as you love mother" or "Mother, love me as you love sister" or many other things. If homosexuality was not established very early and deeply, a man may choose girlish boys or even boyish girls, and marry one of the latter. The girlish boy is like (but "not really") a girl; the boyish girl is a "girl made safe." Similar substitutions, reversals and disguises began to appear in analysis of all the perversions. The sadist was often doing what he feared might be done to him. The masochist, with fantasies of punishment for an unspecified disobedience, was using the screen of a "lesser evil" for incestuous desires and the terror of annihilating punishment.

Still, most of the psychiatrists sketching out these patterns in their patients were trying to fit them into the old instinct-theory framework and the already huge verbal edifice of analytic speculation. The very attempts to carry their work further sometimes tangled them up worse than ever. Psychiatrists were finding similarities between many neurotics and homosexuals. It was said that many alcoholics had overprotective mothers who indulged in unconscious coquetry with them; they tended to marry maternal women to whom they clung emotionally, having been put out of commission sexually by alcohol. Homosexual undercurrents, according to some theorists, played a role in acute depression. Freud's idea that paranoia is a defense against homosexuality was still canon law. Sometimes it seemed that "latent homosexuality" accounted for alcoholism, Don Juanism, war, peace and psychoanalysis itself.

In the early thirties it was still heretical to most analysts to deny innate bisexuality, to really talk to a patient, to treat homosexuals with therapeutic optimism. In 1935 an American woman wrote to Freud asking whether he could treat her homosexual son. In the often-reprinted reply, Freud said, "In a certain number of cases we succeed in developing the blighted germs of heterosexual tendencies which are present in every homosexual, in the majority of cases it is no more possible."

But at that very time a new movement was giving psychiatry broader vision and opening the way to treating the perversions and psychoses. Significantly, this happened in the United States. Until now, most leading analysts had come from German-speaking and Middle European countries. However, psychodynamic thinking had made its strongest mark in English-speaking countries, especially the United States. The unstable social amalgam of American society, its cultural hyphenation (Irish-American, Afro-American, Jewish-American, German-American) made people especially aware of the bonds and conflicts between an individual and his social environment. The "interpersonal" and "dynamic-cultural" schools of psychiatry grew up here.

Freudians had looked to the "vicissitudes of the libido" and its fixations at various points to explain character development. Society was a by-product of the need to control the inchoate lust and aggression of the id. With Erich Fromm, Karen Horney, Clara Thompson and Harry Stack Sullivan the emphasis began to shift from constitution, childhood and trauma to environment, family interaction and social influences.

Fromm and Horney were both trained as analysts before emigrating to the United States. Fromm was especially struck by the recent findings of anthropologists showing how different societies produce different patterns of childhood development and adult personality. He said that "man's nature, his passions, and anxieties are a cultural product; as a matter of fact, man himself is the most important creation and achievement of the continuous human effort." He and others began to talk less of instinct, more of the need for security and mastering one's environment, of family life as an interplay of relationships. Ego psychology, with its concentration on the development of defenses and character, provided the language for examining the ways a culture's values are internalized through interaction with parents and peers.

Karen Horney was one of the major heretics of this movement, and the doctrinaire Freudians therefore labeled her "superficial." She said a child's first need is not instinctual release or equilibrium but security in relation to his parents. Furthermore, his early experiences are not definitive; they are modified as he grows. If he was submissive with his parents, he will be submissive with his peers and invite their domination. Thus he reinforces what began with his parents. His experiences with father figures throughout life go on changing or reinforcing the pattern he developed with his own father. Finally, when he comes for psychiatric treatment as an adult, he is not just compulsively repeating his early past, and his current life situation requires attention. He has a gap between his idealized self-image and his actual self; he may have several neurotic goals that conflict with each other, such as exaggerated needs to conquer yet to be loved; his vicious circles of conflict and defense produce secondary defenses, which produce further problems in turn.

Horney treated patients whose behavior was bisexual and concluded that they were driven not by bisexual instincts but by emotional needs so bitterly imperative that sex distinctions became secondary. In some, the need to subdue men and women, sexually and otherwise, was predominant. Others, "prone to yield to sexual advances from either sex, are driven by an unending need for affection, especially by a fear of losing another person through refusing a sexual request"—or any request, for that matter, whether just or unjust. She found that during treatment "the seemingly homosexual trends disappear as soon as a sound self-assertion has taken the place of anxiety." And she added that although homosexuality was a varying, complex condition, she had "not yet seen a homosexual person in whom the factors mentioned in the 'bisexual' group were not also present."

More and more people, in Adler's footsteps, were turning to the patient's "social embeddedness" as vital to his development and treatment. Treatment became more brief and directive, and there were some successes with those patients Freudians had claimed were untreatable—the very narcissistic, the schizophrenic, the sexually deviant. One of the great clinicians and thinkers of this period was Harry Stack Sullivan, who developed an "interpersonal" theory of development based on the conviction that man is a product more of his relationships with people than of his drives.

Sullivan, like Horney, put a strong emphasis on the need for security. He also stressed self-esteem as one sees it measured in other people's reactions. He was aware of the importance of very early experiences, the ways mothers convey their warmth or tensions to an infant, their "emotional contagion and communion" with the child. He also spoke of the imaginary people to whom one relates—the "dream girl" and "the man who will take me away from all this," even personifications of society and government. But he also stressed the corrective nature of relationships with peers during preadolescence. In fact, his picture of "preadolescent chumship" is one of the most important and still underresearched areas in psychosexual development.

Sullivan said that just as the age of puberty varies, so does the preadolescent period, but usually it is roughly the years between eight and a half and twelve. This is when one leaves the nuclear family to form important relationships and becomes fully socialized. A boy finds a chum whose welfare and happiness are as important to him as his own, with whom he shares intimacies as well as thoughts and activities. Freudians would have spoken of latent homosexuality. Sullivan spoke of this as one's first love and added, "I still find that some people imagine that intimacy is only a matter of approximating genitals one to another. And so I trust that you will finally and forever grasp that interpersonal intimacy can really consist of a great many things ... that intimacy in this sense means, just as it has always meant, closeness."

Sullivan never wrote systematically about homosexuality, but he made several significant observations about it, and its relationship to preadolescent and adolescent chumship. In clinical practice he had many male patients who were tense and vigilant in all relationships and dealings with other men. "I have found without exception that each one has lacked anything like good opportunities for preadolescent socialization. Some are heterosexual, others homosexual: in either case, they aren't at ease with strange men."

Such men had not had chums and been part of a preadolescent "gang." The loner who couldn't find a chum his own age sometimes made a relationship with an adolescent instead. In many cases, Sullivan thought, this had a considerable role in creating a homosexual or bisexual behavior pattern later in life. Of course the varying ages of reaching puberty put various members of the preadolescent group out of step with each other, but they usually arrived there close enough together to make heterosexuality their last "preadolescent collaboration—the topic of who's who and what's what in the so-called heterosexual world." Gang sexual activity might be part of this.

Sullivan said that our society puts a severe handicap on the person trying to deal with the lust that comes with puberty. It must be satisfied without a loss of security and self-worth. If a boy is lonely to begin with and can't keep up with his peers, he can't reach out toward the other sex. One of the most damaging things that can happen now is ridicule and denigration by his elders. Many parents do this without conscious malice because they are uncomfortable about the child's budding sexuality. They jokingly minimize it or even set rules that stand in the way of the switch from same-sex to other-sex intimacy. The double standard, said Sullivan, makes lust and the rest of personality development stand totally at odds. Bad girls are unworthy, and good girls will reject the lust. As the boy splits girls into sexy and nice, he is split within himself. Masturbation is the commonest release, but sometimes this collision of lust and self-esteem leads to "homosexual" play (the quotation marks are Sullivan's). He didn't seem to consider such adolescent behavior homosexual in terms of life pattern or identity. In any case, Sullivan didn't consider homosexuality a problem in itself, but a way of adjusting to anxiety.

Sullivan had a homosexual patient who recounted his life at a boys' boarding school. He said that many boys, the "regular" guys who lived in the chumship gang, had experimented with homosexual acts. He, a loner, an outsider, had never done so. None of the guys in the gang had, to his knowledge, grown up to be homosexual. There was another boy who, like himself, had been a loner and not participated in the homosexual play. Much later Sullivan had a chance to check up on the other boy. He, like the patient, was homosexual.

INTERVIEWS

In the United States, orthodox Freudianism—with its instinct theory and, usually, therapeutic pessimism about homosexuality—is becoming unpopular and relatively rare. An eclectic psychodynamic approach has taken its place, centering on problems of ego development and general adaptation to life. In England the balance is more like that found in the United States a few decades ago. And in England a larger number of psychiatrists treat emotional disturbances medically—with drugs, electric shock and other drug and physical therapies.

I am introduced to two distinguished English analysts. One, a man, is a leading member of the famous Tavistock Clinic; the other, a woman, is a Kleinian analyst. He says:

About 8 per cent of the psychiatrists in England are analysts. They really have quite limited acceptance. The rest of the psychiatrists are medically oriented.

What sort of advice does a homosexual usually get, then, when he picks a psychiatrist at random?

Generally, I should think he'd be told to learn to live with his condition. [*Turning to the other analyst.*] Wouldn't you say so?

SHE: Yes. Analysis isn't meant to be a tool for conformity.

A number of studies, such as Irving Bieber's,* say cure is possible in many cases. Can't the idea that homosexuality is unchangeable be a self-fulfilling prophecy for a therapist?

HE: I wouldn't call a so-called cured patient homosexual.

You mean, if he was cured, he wasn't really homosexual?

HE: Yes. And I think you'll find a consensus among my colleagues that homosexuality is incurable.

* An important recent American study depicting a common family background for male homosexuals of a "close-binding-intimate" mother and absent or withdrawn father, and claiming about 25 per cent cure and 50 per cent improvement in the subjects treated. It involves major revision of old Freudian concepts. See Chapter 30.

SHE: I'm willing to bet that if one of those so-called cured homosexuals showed up on my couch, he would produce associations and dreams with at least latent or symbolic homosexual content.

Suppose a man has heterosexual identity, fantasies and behavior? You wouldn't call it cure? [He shakes his head in the negative.]

SHE: A man may go to bed with women, but that doesn't mean he relates well to them. Behavior is no measure of cure.

When a homosexual appears in your office for help, what is your immediate reaction?

HE: What I'd really like to tell him is, "Come on, don't waste my time!"

Dr. Ismond Rosen has treated sexual deviants individually and in groups, and edited one of the best scientific volumes on deviation published in England in recent years. I tell him:

Talking to people in London, I get the impression that a homosexual seeking treatment is likely to get drugs, conditioning treatment or classical analysis. The odds seem to be against the eclectic but analytically oriented approach more common in America.

That's probably true whatever a person's emotional problems. Lots of psychiatrists are medically oriented, kept busy as custodians of institutions, or haven't had analysis themselves. There are about two hundred analysts in England, mostly in London. Actually, the chance of getting any sort of treatment is small. There's only one clinic for deviants—the Portman Clinic, where I've worked—and that also deals with delinquents.

I'm an analyst, as you know. I think that if you're brought up with a father and mother, you have—you need to have—libidinal relationships with both, and that's the place to look in dealing with homosexuality, not to the genes or medical therapy. But I also think that experience after childhood is very important in determining the tone and style of a person's sex life. What patterns develop? Does a homosexual seek someone who resembles himself or someone who has the masculine qualities he desires? Does he have love affairs or is he a very disturbed, deeply narcissistic person who forms no attachments and gets no real pleasure from all his experiences? Or is he one of those people who avoids the gay scene, goes to baths for mutual masturbation and watching, and never makes a homosexual relationship of any kind?

Do you feel there has been an increase in homosexuality?

We have no reliable figures, but I think there's an increase generally in deeply disturbed people. We have so improved infant care that many survive who wouldn't have in the past—infants that won't grow in a healthful home or who start life with a weakness or defect, predisposed to have problems. Besides, there is a clear-cut relationship between cultural change and the sorts of emotional defense systems you find in people, and this needs more study.

How does your experience here compare to the findings of Bieber and his collaborators?

Similar. Of course there are many complex patterns of homosexuality, but there is a classic picture, and Bieber shows it very well. The relationship with the father is crucial. The mother has conspired in the problem by pushing father and son apart.

There are similarities in the backgrounds of many homosexuals and schizo-phrenics, aren't there?

Yes, in that both may have suffered acute early deprivation in maternal care. They end up with strong oral fixation, and a magical symbolic confusion of penis and breast. The conditions are complex and varied, and may overlap. I think the idea we must examine in depth is self-esteem and ego strength—crucial to both conditions. In fact, I think self-esteem may be the central issue in all the perversions. It certainly seems so in the course of successful treatment. As therapy progresses, heterosexual interest appears alongside homosexual inter-est. The balance changes bit by bit, till there is heterosexual intercourse—often with homosexual acts continuing. But slowly the patient's general confidence and assertiveness grow with his confidence in his maleness. He works through his relationships with his mother, father, sister, brother. As a matter of fact, I've seen a number of cases where the patient confronted the father, a man-to-man relationship formed for the first time, and the father's assertiveness improved! The whole constellation of family dynamics shifts. Until now, the patient has idealized male fellowship, making up for the father-son relationship the mother helped undermine. Now he can drop that idealization, stand up for himself, and not be appeasing with other men. Finally he can go into a room with a girl, and when a good-looking chap comes along, he isn't terrified the other fellow will take her away.

What is the biggest factor in cure?

Motivation. And the biggest threat to an established homosexual is identity change. The homosexual is often a person who suffered intense inner desolation, and uncertainty about his identity. Homosexuality gave him an identity, a way of life, a way out of the desolation. Treatment is a threat to all this, it seems to him a request to give up everything for an uncertainty. The only alternatives he has known are homosexuality and the desolation from which it was an escape, and change seems a threat of loss of identity, of barrenness and pain. He must be so motivated that he is willing to take that risk, and discover that these are not really the only alternatives.

One thing I've noticed and would like to be able to verify is that homosex-uals, exhibitionists, voyeurs, all seem to have very strong reactions to object loss—the death of a relative or loss of a lover. I suspect that many who are picked up by the police are suffering from severe depression following object loss. They wander around in need of excitement, however painful, to relieve their depression, doing things that fairly ask for any sort of action or attention to take them out of themselves.

If the situation in England resembles that in the United States two or three decades ago, much of the Continent is a decade or so behind England. I speak to a young Dutch psychiatrist who has worked in the United States and returned to his own country. At his home in Amsterdam, he says:

All over the Continent neurology and psychiatry have remained much more linked than in your country. Our professional society here is the Dutch Society for Psychology and Neurology—you see the point. When someone here becomes disturbed, people ask, "Is it nerves or is it emotions?" They mostly still prefer to say it's nerves. I would never put the title "Psychiatrist" on my door. I put "Neurologist." Here one doesn't admit to seeing a psychiatrist, as one does in America. Except for the educated, emancipated upper middle class, people don't accept psychodynamic thinking. Till recently pre-Freudian nosologists had a hold on our university departments; now Freudians have a lock on the academies. At the other end of the scale, behaviorists work in the state hospitals. Eclectics are still attacked. Finally, about a decade ago, sex entered the nerve-doctor's province. Sex education in Holland is at the discretion of each community; it varies, and some give none at all. People say, "Oh, sex is just the same old problem it always was."

Only a tiny number here are progressive enough to shift from the old medical model of "mental illness" and "mental health" to an adaptational view of degrees of coping. Talk about maladjustment and psychosis is labeling, stigmatizing. When psychiatry began, it was a good, liberating idea to tell the public that disturbed people are sick, not criminals or inferior creatures. Now that we've switched our frame of reference from the prison to the hospital, we have to switch it again, and stop using diagnostic concepts to stand for a whole person, We don't call a lady with appendicitis an appendicitic, but we call someone with a neurosis a neurotic, and someone who performs homosexual acts a homosexual. Our job is to see the whole person and his total style of adaptation to the world around him.

Jan Foudrayne is a psychoanalyst who spent a number of years in the United States, working at Chestnut Lodge, an institution famous for its innovative work in the psychotherapy of schizophrenia. He hasn't been back in Holland long, but he is unhappy, almost despairing, about the practice of psychiatry there and is considering returning to the United States to work.

In Holland a homosexual can't find a competent psychotherapist—nor can the person who's been labeled delinquent, schizophrenic or just neurotic. There is classical psychoanalysis, and then the great lot of psychiatrists who run hospitals, in charge of ninety or a hundred people each, so that they can barely give medical supervision. I think full analysis is necessary for a therapist, but not for many patients. So the analytic approach is inappropriate in many cases. As for the strictly medical—I have a homosexual and schizophrenic patient who's had eight or nine years of despair going in and out of hospitals receiving electro-shock and no other treatment at all!

We have to release psychoanalysis from its tie to the medical idea of disease. Back in the thirties, Freud himself said in *Lay Analysis* that psychiatry is really tied to social science. When that happened, even doctors in America said Freud had got too old to know what he was saying! They decided psychiatry must remain a medical specialty. I think that some day neuropsychiatrists will separate somewhat from those who treat the dynamics of families, groups. As we develop the art of analysis maybe we'll get rid of asylums and create schools for life. Maybe we'll take the burden of the word "patient" from people who already have difficulty living.

In this country no sociologist has ever got the right to enter an asylum. Old Kraepelinian nosologists and classical Freudians are still around, the latter just replacing the former as the academic power group. We're a full thirty years behind. It's true in our work with schizophrenia, homosexuality, all sorts of problems. The big problem in schizophrenia is an overwhelming sense of ego weakness. Ego strength is really a mysterious concept, a feeling of competence and self-esteem. The schizophrenic needs it, needs an exhilarating sense of self, of success and confidence. Each little task well done helps him, and each failure threatens to send him down the slide. Insight isn't enough—that's where classical analysis fails. Analysis has to be joined to support outside the treatment sessions. And we need faster methods that can reach more people. Maybe the answer is therapeutic communities, the schools for living I was talking about. I think that in many ways, in the sexual sphere especially, the homosexual needs what the schizophrenic needs—success. Not just in sex acts, either, but in all expressions of manliness, assertion, taking a stand. We don't know how many men have been saved from homosexuality by a successful experience—a woman who made him feel effective, that he fulfilled and satisfied her, that his penis is big enough. Maybe when a male homosexual can stand up to his male analyst and give him hell, and he sees that he isn't killed as a result, he can go out and perform with a woman. Success. People need human success.

18

The Life Till the Fifties

According to popular opinion, the revolution of the twenties continued through the next two decades. Psychiatric terms and formulas became journalistic cant. Contraception, marriage counseling and sex education had entered American life, approved and practiced even by many churches. Female emancipation went on; the girl away from home, the lady bachelor, the career woman, were now cultural fixtures. The headings *Homosexuality* and *Sex Perversions* appeared sporadically in the *Guide to Periodical Literature*; the twenties' air of sophistication, scientific enlightenment and self-congratulation had become entrenched.

In serious literature Djuna Barnes, Henry Miller, Thomas Wolfe, Mary Renault and many others dealt with homosexuality. The homosexuality of such artists as Gide, Proust, Gertrude Stein and Hart Crane was widely assumed and accepted in intellectual circles. The 1932 court decision to allow James Joyce's *Ulysses* to appear in America marked the slow, steady erosion of old rules of public morality. Then in 1934 Lillian Hellman's *The Children's Hour* became a great success on Broadway—a play about two girls'-school teachers unjustly charged with lesbianism, and how one committed suicide because the scandal made her realize that she was in fact lesbian in feeling. Drama critic George Jean Nathan caricatured contemporary British drama, probably with special reference to Noel Coward's work, by proposing a play whose cast included "Lord Derek, a hermaphrodite; his father, an onanist; his mother, a lesbian; his sister, a flagellant; Lady Vi Twining, his sister's friend and auto-eroticist with tribade tendencies; his servant, a homosexual and transvestite."

As during the twenties, much of the change was more hope and verbal bravado than fact. Later statistical studies showed little loosening of sexual behavior; great masses of people lived relatively tradition-bound lives. Each artist who dealt frankly with sex had to fight censorship that remained general and stifling. Though homosexuals were mentioned in novels and articles, it was always at some risk. When *Esquire* used the words backside, behind and bawdy-house in 1944, there was a spate of protests. After a wealthy lady in New York cafe society was murdered by her husband, newspapers avoided saying that the defendant had proclaimed himself homosexual and had made that vital to his defense. *PM*, the great experiment in liberal mass journalism, finally mentioned "indications of an abnormal psychological nature"; a few days later the other papers finally, by common consent, broke down and said "homosexual." Most significant of all, novels and plays that presented homosexuals usually showed the males as lank and limp, lesbians as shrill and hipless; like *The Children's Hour*, such works progressed from lofty tolerance to suicide, dementia and other bad endings.

Two forces worked against a study of the homosexual world being made in the thirties and forties. One was the moderate increase in permissive attitudes and the new knowing manner; flip knowledgeability always makes research seem unnecessary. Second, traditional attitudes still underlay this seeming liberation, distorting most writings on deviance. A good example is a book published in 1937 called *Mentality and Homosexuality*, by a Dr. Samuel Kahn, psychiatrist for the New York City Department of Correction. In the thirties, everyone arrested in New York City who was even suspected of being homosexual landed at the Women's Workhouse or at the County Penitentiary for men on Blackwell's Island. At the Women's Workhouse lesbians were not set apart—as usual in the West, they weren't considered so awful a contaminant to society as male deviants. But at the penitentiary, male homosexuals lived in a section called the South Prison, along with psychotics, mental defectives and syphilitics. Even there they were scrupulously segregated. They worked separately, lived separately, ate separately, even saw movies separately.

Kahn's book gave the results of his study of these homosexuals. They varied from native New Yorkers to Italian immigrants to southern Negroes. Many came from broken families, had never finished grammar school and revealed histories of general psychosocial instability. Many were alcoholics and drug addicts; a large proportion had been arrested on narcotics charges, and many others for prostitution, shoplifting and other minor offenses. From this information Kahn drew many conclusions, but without pointing out that imprisoned homosexuals—the majority arrested for nonsexual offenses—were by definition an atypical group. He never thought to ask whether they had more in common with other homosexuals or with other prisoners. Throughout, he paid lip service to psychiatric theory and the tolerance that sometimes grew from it; but his attitude was contemptuous and authoritarian, and his methods make most of his data doubtful. The prisoners knew he could recommend their indefinite detention in state mental institutions, and he capitalized on this by using obvious manipulation, browbeating and even open threats. He established initial rapport by asking, "Of course, you are a homosexual or degenerate?" The doctor sadly reported that although many male homosexuals were "suggestible" and pliant, the more intelligent and strong-willed ones remained uncooperative; most of the lesbians were just as hostile as the men. In order to extract case histories, Kahn had to threaten extended prison terms, asylums, and forced physical examinations, presumably for signs of sodomy.

Apart from the author's accidental self-disclosures, the most interesting part of the book was the prisoners' love letters—half-literate, sentimental missives to men named Diana, Dolly, Jennie, Queen Mary, Cinderella and Princess Wee Wee. They promised Honey and Sweetheart to be father, mother, lover, brother and sister, separately or at once. A male inmate who had been released wrote back to his lover in jail, "You are a real wife and I think I am showing you I am a real daddy ... sticking to you as good as any daddy you had, am I, so sweetheart don't worry about when you come out if you knew what is waiting for little wife when she comes."

The value today of most thirties and forties books on homosexuality is the clues they give about the otherwise unrecorded homosexual subculture of the time. Hundreds and then thousands of detailed case histories piled up in books and in journals. One doctor's cases were largely queens jailed on narcotics charges, another's upper-middle-class professional people; one history revealed bits of homosexual argot, another the fact that a city had organized homosexual prostitution. If one combs enough cases for these scattered fragments, a rough sketch of the homosexual world emerges—a little clearer and more detailed than that of any period before.

Homosexual slang, for instance, had been used in pornography for homosexuals, but now it appeared in psychiatric case histories. Some from the thirties has died out, but the majority of it is still used today.* Some of the words—*queer, queen, fairy, fag, homo, les, dyke*—have long been the common property of homosexuals and heterosexuals, and it is no longer clear which group used them first. *Homo, les* and *lesbo* were widely used in the thirties and after. *Quean* meant whore in sixteenth-century England. Just when its spelling and meaning shifted is uncertain; but by 1880 it meant effeminate homosexual in Australia, and according to one theory it passed from there to the United States by 1905 and to England by 1915. It occurred commonly in print in all these places by the thirties. *Queer*, on the other hand, may have originally been American hobo slang that spread into general use. By the twenties it was seen in books about tramps, prisons and homosexuals, and it became common in England.

Fag and *faggot* have raised several etymological arguments, for it isn't clear whether the long or short form was the original, let alone whether it arose as a derogatory term by heterosexuals or spread to general use from homosexual slang. Over the last century and a half it has variously meant in England a pickpocket, a cigarette, and a young public-school boy who serves and runs errands for older boys. One guess is that it came from the use of younger students not only as lackeys but as sexual partners. Another

*Dictionaries of slang disagree on the origin and earliest use of many of these words. Usually they take as date of first use the earliest appearance in print; but slang may be spoken for a short or a very long time before its written debut, so these estimates are always debatable.

is that it came from the fact that when cigarettes became popular around the First World War, they were considered less manly than pipes and cigars. Fag and faggot meant male homosexual to many people by the early twenties, especially in the United States, where one term for a homosexual brothel or gathering place was a "fag factory."

Similarly, some of the most common words for female homosexuals have been current among homosexuals and heterosexuals for decades. *Dyke* (or *dike*) was in use by the twenties to indicate any lesbian; *bulldyke* (and *bulldyker, bulldagger* and other variations) particularly meant an aggressive lesbian with mannish appearance. Its origin is unsure; some guess it came from a garbling of the word hermaphrodite and originated on America's West Coast.

Names have also been homo- and heterosexual slang. *Nancy* meant buttocks in nineteenth-century English slang, but by the First World War it meant a sissy, effeminate or homosexual in both England and America. *Mary* has also been in use for a long time in the United States with the same meaning; perhaps this is just because the name is so common, and for that reasons many homosexuals address each other as Mary.

A few words for homosexuals are used almost entirely by heterosexuals—for instance *pansy* and *fruit. Pansy* was probably used in the United States at least as early as the thirties, and is now somewhat dated. *Fruit* was teenage and student slang by 1910 and quite common by 1930. A few other terms probably passed from the heterosexual to the homosexual world. *John* has long been used by the underworld and among prostitutes for a prostitute's client; among homosexuals it may also mean an elderly, well-to-do man who supports a young homosexual. *Angel*, long used in the theater for a private financial backer, became underworld slang by 1935 for a male homosexual, usually butch, who buys gifts for or keeps a more effeminate partner.

There is another language, essentially homosexual, though some knowledgeable heterosexuals are acquainted with it and have made bits of it general property. This argot has great social and psychological significance, but for the moment its existence and established use in the twenties and thirties is the most important point, for this shows a strong continuity that can come only from an established subculture.

The homosexual word for anything homosexual is *gay*; a queen and a lesbian are both gay, a homosexual bar is a gay bar, the homosexual world the gay world. Something or someone heterosexual is *straight*, and an obviously heterosexual man is *butch*. The effeminate male homosexual is a *queen*, a very extreme one a *flaming* or *screaming queen*, use of female clothes or accessories being *in drag*. A fussy, middle-aged homosexual is an *aunt* or *auntie. Trade* (*rent* in England) is a person who will "be done" but will not "do" someone else—allows fellation but won't perform it, commits sodomy but won't allow it on himself. Sometimes he is openly homosexual, sometimes a bisexual or a virile-seeming male prostitute, sometimes heterosexual. *Rough trade* is a strapping, muscular, aggressive man, sometimes tattooed and hairy-chested and sadistic, who will only be trade. It is traditional that real trade is not a homosexual, only a "real man" indulging (though it is also traditional that "today's trade is tomorrow's queen"). A mannish lesbian (like an apparently virile male homosexual) was called a *butch* by the early forties, and her more feminine-seeming partner a *femme*. The pair might also be called *lady lover* and *bitch*.

Some such gay words have become known and used by a limited number of heterosexuals. One is *daisy chain*, the term for mass sex: the original image is of three or more men in a circle, linked in buggery. Actually, a real daisy chain might involve masturbation and fellation instead of or along with sodomy, and therefore has occasionally been reported in groups of lesbians. A daisy chain of men and women can be made, but the first appearance of the word in print was in a homosexual context.

Probably the homosexual word most recently and widely used by heterosexuals is *camp*. Originally it meant effeminate behavior, and in the twenties it was common in the theater, especially vaudeville and burlesque, where comic travesties of homosexuals were described by the word. *Variety* in the twenties and thirties contained ads by comedians who specialized in high camp or low camp; the former was imitation or parody of extreme effeminacy, the latter a subtler, refined, mincing manner—its greatest masters were Jack Benny and Edward Everett Horton.

There was a special slang about homosexuality in prisons, which came to light in case histories and books on prisons. In men's prisons, the aggressive, dominant male was a *jocker*—a word that as far back as 1890 meant a homosexual hobo who lived off the begging of a boy companion. His younger passive partner was a *punk*. In women's prisons during the thirties the bulldyke might also be called a *mantee, jockey* or *top sergeant*. Dykes and femmes, it was then said, were also called *mamas* and *papas*—a half-truth clarified by sociological researchers only in recent years.

Some slang reported in the thirties died or changed meaning. *Nola* meant a homosexual; a *brilliant* or *jam fag* was a vain and effeminate male homosexual; a *chocolate lover* preferred Negro partners, the homosexual equivalent of today's heterosexual *spade-baller*; *fairy lady* meant the femme of a lesbian couple; *boy* and *peg boy* indicated an effeminate male, *peg house* a male brothel; a *fish* was a male homosexual who performed cunnilingus on lesbians, *fishing* a general term for oral sex. These have all dropped from use, except for *fish*, which has been adopted by lesbians as a term for bisexual femmes. Other words shifted meaning. *Bird* originally meant female prostitute in England, but by 1920 it meant a male homosexual or any bizarre person; now, like *chick* in the United States, it refers to any girl or young woman. Another changeling word was *gunsel*. Since 1915 tramps and prisoners had used the German and Yiddish word *gänsel*, or gosling, corrupted to gunsel, for a passive sodomite, especially a young, inexperienced boy companion. From the mid-twenties on it gradually came to mean a sneaky or disreputable person of any kind. By the mid-thirties it meant a petty gangster or hoodlum. One wonders whether Humphrey Bogart knew what he was really calling Elisha Cook, Jr., in *The Maltese Falcon* when he dubbed him a gunsel.

Standard dictionaries never mentioned such things; they even omitted such ancient, established Anglo-Saxon words as fuck, cunt and prick. The 1933 *Oxford English Dictionary* gave no homosexual meanings for the words queer, queen, fairy, invert or lesbian. Homosexuality was not entered. Fortunately, dictionaries of slang existed not only in English but in other languages. A French dictionary of argot published in the 1870s gives many of the words still used in France for homosexuals; some duplicate or parallel English slang. The most common words then and today are *tapette* and *pédé* (or *pédéro*, from *pédéraste*). *Tante* (aunt) was and is used as in English. The dictionary also listed *il en est*—exactly like the English "he's one," the source of countless jokes (men sounding off in the army—"One!" "Are you one?" "Yes, are you one, too?"). Also given was *gosselin*, or gosling, like *gänsel-gunsel*.

In many of the books and papers of the thirties that revealed the gay argot, it became clear how homosexuals conducted their lives, and where their subculture lay within a city. The homosexuals who were professionally successful and usually passed for straight tended to avoid obvious homosexual hangouts. Some had heterosexual marriages as covers. Some had other "bachelors" as roommates and in effect settled into gay "marriages." However, despite the risks of exposure, entrapment and blackmail, some did go outside private homosexual cliques. The search for partners, when not conducted through friends and parties, was done by *cruising*—walking the streets and using lavatories and bars for pickups.

Every city had its known cruising areas. In a small town, it was almost always the main street. In Boston, the Common and Fenway Park were notorious cruising grounds. In New York the same ones were used that are still popular today—Riverside Drive, Central Park, Bryant Park, the midtown section of Fifth Avenue. Other contact points were public lavatories, train stations, subway washrooms, YMCAs, Turkish baths and certain bars and restaurants. The public lavatories often had extensive homosexual data and phone numbers written on the walls. In the gay world they were called "tea rooms," and one at 47th Street and Broadway in Manhattan was dubbed the "Sunken Gardens." In Turkish baths, the masseurs, seeing that a patron had an erection, would masturbate him to orgasm. In some establishments, steam rooms and cubicles were sites for random encounters of every sort from masturbation and rimming (oral-anal sex) to daisy chains of three, four or more.

Bars had gradations by economic class and degree of effeminacy. The two factors tended to be in accord, for "flaming fags" and "screaming bitches" tended to be progressively unstable, marginal and exhibitionistic, thus making regular jobs and normal social contacts out of the question.

Discreet, middle-class homosexuals who were professionally successful tended to use straight bars—without most heterosexual customers being aware that the place was a respectable pick-up spot for the gay as well as the straight. In some openly homosexual bars there might be much shrieking, petting, "groping," dancing and open propositioning, yet little or no transvestism. Some bars and clubs allowed customers to enter in drag; many of these might be male prostitutes (as are some "customers" in most types of homosexual bars). Some bars that let men come in drag, wearing stuffed brassieres, switches, painted nails and perfumes, were functioning male brothels. One in Brooklyn was full of painted boys, and sailors went there to find partners to sodomize. In New York, homosexual bars of many kinds were numerous between 43rd and 49th streets, both east and west. In Harlem and the Little Italy in Greenwich Village there were homosexual "clubs"; one need only be obviously homosexual to join on the spot for a small fee. Clubs of the same sort exist in the Village today.

The clubs in Harlem were frequented by white homosexuals with a penchant for black partners, either amateur or professional. Like many large cities, New York had its big drag balls; one such event in the thirties was held in a rented hall near Columbus Circle, but a large number took place in Harlem. Some of these balls were attended by hundreds or even thousands of people. An account of one says that it was three quarters black and one quarter white, with some lesbians in the audience but only men (in drag) on the dance floor, and policemen on hand in great numbers to oversee the event and prevent goings-on in the lavatories. Many drag balls had beauty contests, with prizes for the winners.

Cruising streets, lavatories and bars was full of risks—raids and entrampment by police, beating and robbery and blackmail by prostitutes, venereal disease, assaultive heterosexuals. That did not prevent cruising from being extensive. And wherever the gay cruised, there would be professional hustlers. Some were effeminate, and mixed with female prostitutes and bums on the Bowery near Chinatown. They lived in flophouses and gathered at the Bowery bars and food counters. This was the training ground from which they hoped to graduate to Times Square and 42nd Street, which thronged with effeminate hustlers.

The majority of hustlers ranged from their middle teens to middle or late twenties. Youthful good looks were at a premium, and the boys would say, "As soon as a gray hair shows, I'm through." During the thirties they worked the streets, bars and brothels for fees ranging between two and ten dollars—occasionally twenty or more. Some hustlers of a better class took from a customer's apartment not only a ten- or twenty-dollar bill but clothes and other gifts. Apparently the commonest wish of customers was for "trade," though sometimes the opposite was wanted. Occasionally a man just wanted to caress and hold another man's body. Or to be beaten. The butch type of hustlers, the rough-trade hoods who claimed to be heterosexual and to hate queers, were often sought out by such masochists. The customers knew they ran the risk of being beaten, abused and robbed—which was just what they wanted. Sometimes they fell into the hands of sailors, some really hustling and some not, who walked Riverside Drive to get cash either by being trade or by beating and rolling homosexuals.

Many of the hustlers were delinquents, petty hoods or tough lower-class boys; they were, or claimed to be, bisexual or heterosexual, and consented only to be trade. They denied pleasure in the act and had girlfriends or wives. Some worked for a few months or a few years and quit—to live heterosexually afterward, it was said. But some continued to be bisexual in behavior, and others, finding the money good and having little energy left over for women, became habituated to homosexuality. (It is difficult to believe that some became involved in hustling without some degree of conscious or unconscious interest to begin with.) But such hustlers objected violently if anyone called them homosexual, and they occasionally beat, robbed and blackmailed customers, whom they considered contemptible faggots.

Usually male prostitution was not highly organized, nor was there the servitude to pimps that female hustlers endured. But there were "call houses" where a customer could pick a prostitute or meet one he had ordered in advance. There were male brothels on Third Avenue in Manhattan where high school boys worked, allegedly to make money to spend on girls or to buy baseball uniforms. A procurer might have four, eight or even a dozen boys and young men for customers to choose from, and he might even send the boys out cruising. Often these hustlers were about twenty, strongly built butch types with girlfriends or wives, who were trade only, charged two to five or ten dollars, and gave half to the procurer. But most male brothels, or peg houses, were just set-ups where a queen used personal contacts to put customers in touch with prostitutes and, for a split of the fee, provided the use of an apartment. Such peg houses existed in Chicago, the Deep South and possibly many other parts of the country.

There was far less description of the lesbian world, for the simple reason that it was far less organized and extensive. As with male homosexuals, case histories and reportage showed that every sort of background was represented in the lesbian world—Harlem lower class, poor small-town Down Easters, wealthy southern girls, artists, singers and executives, middle-class Italian-Americans and midwesterners. Only New York had a highly developed subculture, but it functioned mostly in private places, for lesbians hardly ever cruise as male homosexuals do. But wandering groups of lesbians were not a rare sight in the Village in the thirties, and some lesbian bars existed downtown and midtown. The midtown lesbian bars were sometimes attended by heterosexual men fascinated by lesbians. A few rare references exist to lesbian prostitution and to bisexual or lesbian women being kept by other women. Blackmail of lesbians was hardly mentioned. Some lesbians were married to heterosexual men and had children or kept up marriages of convenience with bisexual or homosexual men.

Single lesbians might seek partners at lesbian bars, but more often it was through friends, work or other normal social connections. The one-night stand was apparently rarer than among male homosexuals. Sometimes two women settled in a long-term domestic relationship, even wearing wedding rings, the femme signing her name with Mrs. before it. Some such couples adopted children to raise. Many lesbians, married and unmarried, worked as nurses, teachers, businesswomen and performing artists. The extreme butches, though, who formed the hard core of the lesbian subculture, were notorious for jealous brawls, complete with slugging, hair-pulling and the breaking of furniture. They would wear T-shirts, socks, a flattening or binding bra to hide their breasts, pants slung low on their hips. Many had heavy, muscular bodies and wore their hair short, combed back like a man's, with the neckline shaved. Their only jewelry would be wedding rings given them by their "bitches." In the gay bars, butches would hover jealously over their bitches—frilly, feminine-looking women wearing jewelry and playing the flirtatious little girl. In the privacy of their bedroom the two might progress from kissing and breast-fondling to grinding (rubbing vulvas together in simulation of intercourse), masturbation, cunnilingus. Some tough bulldykes were known to be sadistic; they beat up their partners or tied them to beds and whipped them. As with male homosexuals, though probably more rarely, there were people with particular quirks, such as urinating on their partners or having others urinate in their mouths.

The fact that such things were being described did not mean that real sexual libertarianism made life much easier for homosexuals during the thirties and forties. If anything, public toleration of deviant behavior had diminished in some ways. By the twenties, red-light districts had been destroyed in most American cities. There was no longer a *zona*, an area cordoned off especially for officially illicit sexual activities. This made cruising and gathering in public places more difficult and risky for homosexuals. Periodic "cleanups" kept parks and certain neighborhoods from replacing the red-light districts. Every so often a van was backed up, for instance, to Bryant Park in New York, and the homosexuals and exhibitionists there loaded in and packed off to jail. A week later the park would be teeming with deviants again, and such mass arrests sometimes bagged an affluent, influential person, to everyone's embarrassment, and the whole business then had to be covered up.

During the thirties police in many cities took payoffs from owners of homosexual hangouts, but raided them sporadically so that the establishment had to keep changing name and location. They entrapped men in lavatories, movie houses and public cruising areas. Sometimes they shook down and went on blackmailing men they had entrapped. There were organized extortion rings, some of which had liaison with police vice squads and had their help in blackmailing the wealthy and prominent. When such a ring was cracked in New York in the late thirties, one lawyer made a plea for clemency for his convicted client on grounds that the extortionist had done a public service by revealing to the world a pervert who had debauched American youth.

Smaller cities sometimes went on rampages of sexual virtue. Typical of such convulsions of purity was one in the late thirties: the city is not named, but the account comes from a reliable source. An eminent citizen was questioned by the police; he had been married and a family man for many years, but occasionally, in his wife's absence from town, compulsively went in search of a homosexual partner. The police called him in, assured him they only wanted information to help in an investigation, got him to make a detailed statement and, as soon as it was signed, jailed him. Soon thirty men had been arrested, many of them quite prominent townsmen. When the original victim's lawyer tried to introduce psychiatric evidence at the trial, the judge interrupted: "It isn't going to do these fellows any good to listen to that rubbish." The judge handed out six-month sentences on the road gangs, but graciously offered surgical emasculation as an alternative. He said that in the previous five years many men had chosen the operations, and the results had been "100 per cent perfect"; they had lost "the unnatural tendencies that were causing them to commit wretched crimes." The offer was accepted by no one. Finally a leading local physician was arrested; he pleaded not guilty, went home and committed suicide, leaving a widow and three children. The crusade ended.

In the late thirties some judges began to recommend psychiatric treatment for sex offenders, but in many cases this just meant detention in overcrowded, understaffed state institutions—after which a man was released with his name tarnished for life, facing the same social threats as before. "Sophistication" and "enlightenment" meant little when society and the law got into action against them. The somewhat larger number of psychiatrists, lawyers and other educated people who began calling for tolerance and treatment only made a small dent in traditional mores. It took the political nightmare of Nazi Germany to show just how deep a hatred of deviants lay within society waiting to be mobilized.

Germany had seemed even more permissive about open homosexuality than most other Western countries during the twenties. It has often been said that the Nazi Party was a haven for sexual deviants; there is no doubt that a number of homosexuals helped Hitler in his rise to power. Göring liked to attend parties in drag, and Walter Funk was both an alcoholic and a homosexual. Many tales about homosexuals in the SA, SS and concentration-camp system have gained currency (a recent account of Treblinka says that the assistant commandant there was a sadistic homosexual who kept a harem of boy prisoners mincing about the place in drag). Actually, one cannot be sure that the Nazi Party had more homosexuals than other political parties in Germany or elsewhere. But there is no question that they were allowed to indulge their interests as long as they served Hitler, and then were publicly immolated on charges of perversion when Hitler no longer needed them.

Ernst Röhm joined the German Workers' Party before Hitler. He was a short, stocky bullnecked professional soldier, part of whose face had been shot away during the First World War. As Hitler built up the Nazi Party, Röhm was at his side organizing unemployed veterans and young toughs into the brown-shirted *Sturm Abteilung* (Storm Troopers), or SA. Röhm was widely known in Nazi circles to be homosexual, and he gave many leading posts in his organization to homosexuals. Among these was Lieutenant Edmund Heines, head of the Munich SA, who had Storm Troopers scouring Germany in search of male lovers for Röhm.

In William L. Shirer's description of Röhm and the SA, it is difficult to separate hatred for Nazis and contempt for homosexuals. In his *Rise and Fall of the Third Reich* he calls Röhm "a tough, ruthless, driving man— albeit, like so many of the early Nazis, a homosexual." He claims that Röhm, Heines and dozens of others in the SA, "quarreled and feuded as only men of unnatural sexual inclination, with their peculiar jealousies, can." But the downfall of the SA was not caused by any such bickering. By 1933 the SA numbered eight hundred thousand and held great power. Meanwhile, Himmler's black-shirted SS had been created, and a struggle between the two organizations began. Complicated political maneuvering among these and other military and political groups forced Hitler to make choices among them. In June 1934 he decided to destroy the SA. The charge he used surprised the public, but it should not surprise historians—treason and homosexuality.

On June 30, Röhm, Heines and other SA chiefs were to meet with Hitler at a Bavarian resort. The night before, the SA chief had a party. Hitler rushed there just before dawn, hours ahead of schedule, and with him came an SS contingent. As he must have known in advance, the scene he found was of empty bottles, unwashed dishes, Röhm in bed with his chauffeur, and Heines and others asleep in various men's arms—some of them male prostitutes brought down from Berlin. Heines and his lover of the night were hauled outside and shot. The rest were arrested as traitors. Röhm was shipped to Stadelheim Prison in Munich, given a gun and told to shoot himself. Ten minutes later the guards returned and found him still alive. He said to them, "Let Adolf do his own dirty work," and he was shot down on the spot. Meanwhile about 150 SA leaders had been rounded up and shot in Berlin.

That same day party headquarters in Munich had released a statement announcing that Germany was being cleansed of men who were both traitors and perverts. These storm troopers had been conspiring against the government; furthermore, they were guilty of "such immorality that any trace of pity was impossible. . . . Der Führer gave orders for this plague to be done away with ruthlessly. In the future he will not permit millions of decent people to be compromised by a few sick men." It did not mention that Hitler had known of these men's homosexuality for fifteen years.

There were several fantastic footnotes to this purge of real and alleged homosexuals. Hitler issued a pamphlet against homosexuals—in which he quoted the work of Wilhelm Stekel, the pacifist Jewish psychiatrist whom he had forced to flee the country. Then Himmler, Göring and others used a frame-up of homosexuality charges to destroy Werner von Fritsch, commander in chief of the army and a leader of the old conservative military faction that had remained hostile to Hitler. The Fritsch case was almost surely total fabrication. It served to prevent an anticipated "revolt of the generals" against Hitler; the Führer finally had the armed forces safely in his pocket, making his control of Germany complete. At about that time Hitler also used charges of "sexual immorality" to destroy Catholic opposition to his regime. The years 1937 and 1938 saw a series of campaigns by the government that resulted in the trials and convictions of priests, monks and lay brothers all over the country for homosexual offenses.

Meanwhile, in the United States, the Second World War did not seem to bring immediate changes in mores and behavior. Many men were refused places in the armed forces on grounds of homosexuality; many other homosexuals entered the service, controlled or discreetly satisfied their homosexual desires, and completed their stints. I have several times heard stories from veterans of World War II of mess companies and other units that somewhat openly consisted mostly or entirely of homosexuals; they claim to have been direct witnesses.

Psychiatrist George Henry, an eminent expert on homosexuality during the thirties and forties, examined some two thousand men excluded or discharged from the service because of homosexuality. He concluded that "more homosexuals served with the armed forces than were eliminated before or after induction. Many men had their first overt homosexual experience while in the armed forces." One of Henry's subjects listed twenty-five homosexual partners when he'd been in the army.

Some homosexuals, though, found themselves in psychological or practical difficulties, confessed to chaplains or psychiatrists in hope of help—and were reported. If an officer, a homosexual was usually allowed to resign "under conditions other than honorable for the good of the service," though court martial was a possibility. Enlisted men were given army "blue" or navy "green" discharges—dishonorable, depriving them of the right to vote, barring them from all GI benefits, and marking them for life.

INTERVIEWS

Phillip is amused when he meets me at my hotel near South Kensington tube station. I'd neither heard nor noticed that the station, its lavatory and the surrounding area are among the better-known cruising spots in London.

Phillip is a long, lean, relaxed and casually elegant man in his fifties, an accomplished composer, charming, articulate and an obsessive talker. He has known the gay scene in London for decades. He has agreed to take me on a tour tonight. But first we will get acquainted over dinner. He takes me a few blocks away to a fine, cozy little Italian restaurant where the owner and waiters greet him like old friends. They are all unobtrusively but unmistakably homosexual. The clientele is mixed. Phillip tells me about his personal background, his travels, his experiences in other countries.

I've lived with one man for thirty years now. He and I are open with each other about infidelities, which we allow each other, but I'm afraid it's mostly on my part. Homosexuals are really more promiscuous, I think, but they usually deny it if you say so. They say, "Oh, look what heterosexuals do." As for why I'm homosexual, I simply couldn't say. When I was a kid, I went for women's breasts. Then I changed to men's bottoms. I had great religious guilt about masturbation; I still don't like it. I didn't do it at all till I was seventeen. My father? He died when I was fourteen. I was one of twins, and my brother died as a small child. Sometimes I wonder whether I'm looking for my lost brother, my other half. I went for counseling once because my relationship with my lover has always been very stormy, but I have no desire to explain my nature, as they say.

My lover and I live in a little village of a few thousand, and we never have any trouble there. What we are is clear to everyone, and they couldn't care a damn. In fact, we're very popular. Of course, I come to London a good bit for my work, and my partner is very jealous, but he has adjusted to my promiscuity as long as he doesn't have to hear much about it. It's a very difficult relationship. No, I wouldn't suggest talking to him or many of our friends. Most couples would take it amiss if you suggested they meet an American writer and talk about it. They'd say, "Really, it isn't on to go talking about homosexuality."

It's different with some of the working-class people. Many of the young men today say their birds are too complicated, and take each other on instead. Recently I was in a lorry bar in the country, unshaven and wearing old clothes, and a man came in and started talking in such a way that he established indirectly but quite clearly that he was interested in men. I bought him tea, we talked a few minutes, and he said, "Cor, I'm cold tonight." I said, "You'll need someone to sleep with." And he asked right out, "How about you?" We went outside, found a private place, he leaped on me and went down on me. He didn't have an orgasm. That was all he wanted. I asked him why, and he said, "Me and my mates, we've fallen out with our birds and have a go with each other." I asked him where he and his friends gathered, and he named a pub. I went there later, and it turned out to be an ordinary working-class pub full of guys with their girls. I tried to catch one man's eye, then another's, and another's. I drew a total blank. I'll never know whether the fellow's story was a fraud or not.

I travel a good bit, and I've met all sorts. You just go to the middle of any town you're in, and if you're homosexual, you have a built-in Geiger counter. You find out where things are. But I always call friends first and find out. Now, in Paris it's Saint Germain. It's just crawling with whores, around the Deux Magots and the Flore. Most of the *pissoirs* have been removed now, but the two that remain near those cafes are the hub of activity on the boulevard. The big indoor place is the Drugstore—I hear that the other Drugstore, on the Champs-Elysées, is for female whores. Anyway, the queer hustlers go inside and perambulate the horseshoe, with no pretense of doing anything else.

It's always a problem knowing the professionals from the amateurs. You can only tell by the area, but you mustn't ask, especially in England. People are offended, whether they are or aren't. There are few honest whores left. Besides, you're often robbed of your wallet or watch—you have to beware of two whores working together. That's a constant problem for me now that I'm getting older and I have to pay so much of the time.

Amsterdam is a fine place. When you're there, look at the Hotel Unique—everyone is queer, they'd hardly let a woman in the door. The C.O.C. is very serious; they have a Sunday tea dance that's really quite funny. The D.O.K. and nightclubs are all full of rent and trade, and there are lots of pretty sinister professionals around, especially on the bridge near the D.O.K.

North Africa is a different story. Every queer I know who's been to Egypt says the thing to do is cruise the banks of the Nile at night. One friend of mine went to a bath in Cairo and received a mass fucking, almost a rape. In Morocco you can pick up boys on the street just like that. I once went to Tangier with two friends for a sex bash, to get as much as possible in a short time. The trip wasn't very successful, really. The Arab boys were wonderful, but I had a very unhappy experience. You see, the Arab boys do it as though they mean it. They kiss you tenderly, they'll go down on you and let themselves be fucked. In England and Europe the professionals are mostly trade, and even many campy, made-up men will refuse to be fucked. So the Arab boys are wonderful. By the way, I think the kind my friends and I picked up aren't professional with their own kind, but I don't know for sure; if you start asking questions about that, they clam up entirely.

Anyway, as I said, I had a very unhappy experience. I met a lovely butch-type Arab engineer. I was getting quite involved with him. I mean, really romantically, so eager to see him again each time. Then, shortly before I was ready to leave, I found that he had lifted my wallet. I didn't want to believe it, but it turned out to be true, because we'd arranged for a last date, and he stood me up.

[*We have finished dinner and are riding in a taxi toward the first pub on Phillip's gay Baedeker of London. On the way, he explains.*] The pickup points are the watering holes—the pubs and the outside lavatories near them. The cruising path tends to be the route between each point and the nearest tube station. If the police crack down and padlock a lavatory, the route disappears, and other cruising paths develop. But if an area has been very well established, it may remain even after the lavatory has been closed. Of course there are a few rather permanent spots—a few are tube stations and their lavatories. Hyde Park is a big one, of course—god, once I picked up a marvelous Portuguese boy of seventeen there. Putney Towpath used to be good, until the police got after it. There's fairly heavy cruising between Leicester Square and Piccadilly. And, of course, there's Piccadilly Circus station, but the characters there are very rough-looking, and it's terribly squalid. You have to be out of your mind to pick up someone there.

[*We get out of the taxi on Colherne Road and enter a large, pleasantly fur-*

*nished, well-lit pub. There is a big oval bar in the center, tables along the walls,
and a flight of stairs leading to a smaller upstairs room. As we go in Phillip says
quietly, "This place is out of bounds to troops." We stand inside the door, looking around. A few people at the bar look us over, but it isn't like the gamut of
haughty, hunting glares in a New York or Chicago gay bar. There are some
eighty men here. The atmosphere is quiet and respectable; in twenty minutes I
do not see two men touch in any way. There's no camping, no shrillness, little
tension. Phillip and I stand at the bar and order drinks. At the far end of the
bar stand eight or ten men wearing white Levis, leather jackets, boots and studded belts. Despite their outfits, they don't have very tough faces. I ask Phillip if
this is known as a leather bar.]*

No, not especially.

Is there one in London?

No, none that's only or mostly that. At least not that I know of. In lots of
queer pubs there's a group of them, like this. Actually, they used to stay
together more, in one corner; now they circulate among the others a little.

[*Two men and two attractive young women enter, talking and laughing. They
receive subdued but clearly hostile attention. I look inquiringly at Phillip.*]
Maybe the girls are queer. Or queer chums. But by the looks of them, they're
just slumming around town.

[*Soon they seem to be forgotten as they talk and drink at their table. Phillip
nods toward a side door leading to the street:*] You see, they're going outside to
use the lavatory there and make pickups. Come on, I'll show you. [*We set
our drinks on the bar, leave by the front exit, and turn the corner. There we see
the door to the lavatory. A young man emerges from the bar and enters it, casting a look back at us.*] He left the door open a bit. It may mean he wants to be
followed in, unless he's gone in after the fellow who preceded him. He was very
nice. I'm sorry, but I'm really tempted. Will you excuse me while I find out? I
hope you'll understand if I buzz off, if it works. You can go on by yourself
tonight, can't you?

[*I nod. Phillip enters the lavatory. A moment later the young man exits. I
stand looking at the leather boys' tooled-up, apehanger cycles parked at the
opposite curb. Phillip rejoins me.*] Well, no luck. What can an old man expect?

[*He turns his head and scans the street for a taxi.*] You see those motorcycles? Leather boys from all around the area gather here at closing time—the
lavatory stays open half an hour later than the pub. Sometimes there are fifty of
them here then. [*He stops a taxi, and we get in.*] We'll go to a very different
sort of place. It's a bit younger and a bit swishier. I hardly ever go there myself.
The crowd there makes me look like an old auntie.

[*We get off on the King's Road in Chelsea, and enter a small, jam-packed bar
on a side street. We slowly work our way through the little Sargasso of elbows
and shoulders to the bar. There is more of the electricity, the air of barely restrained hysteria and predation, found in New York bars on a busy night. And as
Phillip said, the crowd is younger and a little swishy. But in such a bar in Philadelphia or Boston I might be groped or patted by passing hands several times in
the course of a drink. Here, as in the first pub, there is nothing of the sort. Once
or twice I see a slightly lingering handshake or touch on an arm.*

[*Phillip nods toward the door. A pretty, short, round-faced blond boy is
pushing in. He has the appearance of a prissy and slightly puffy adolescent girl,*

with his middy-type pullover and a silk handkerchief tied about his neck. Phillip quietly tells me to look at his throat. The kerchief is slipping on one side, revealing a neat and recent set of teethmarks. Now he nods to the far end of the bar, where a hefty elderly lady is talking and laughing with a mustached old gent.]

She's an old queer's chum. Been around forever. [*He glances around.*] You see the black fellow over there?

[*In the corner is a black in his middle twenties. He isn't obviously effeminate, but he has very liquid eyes and a petulant mouth. He stands aloof, one of the few people here who doesn't scan each new entry and occasionally try to lock eyes with others. People come and talk to him, seek his glance.*] He's an African, in the arts. As you can see, he's very much in demand, and he knows it. Englishmen have the same ideas about blacks and sex that Americans have. He knows it, and he resents it. He wants to go back to his own country. I tried to get to know him, and did him a small favor or so. But it didn't get me anywhere.

[*Another taxi leaves us at Piccadilly Circus. We walk down into the tube station. I remember being here on weekend nights like tonight ten years ago, when I was traveling in Europe as a student. Then the circle at the middle of the big underground station area was ringed with female prostitutes. Now that the police have cracked down on the streetwalkers, most of the prostitutes here, as in the rest of the city, are the male homosexual ones. We walk slowly around the circle. There is one girl, a nervous teenager who, judging by her clothes, is a scared novice just in from a provincial town. In one circuit round we count more than fifteen clearly identifiable male hustlers. One has just picked up a well-dressed man of about fifty and is walking away with him. Phillip leads me down a passageway to the men's lavatory.*]

I don't know why anyone makes a pickup here. It costs at least three pounds, and it's very dangerous. You're likely to be beaten up and robbed if you go off with one of those boys.

[*We enter the big lavatory. A narcotics bust is in progress, and Phillip tells me that the place is used for narcotics sales as much as for hustling. Six or eight policemen are frisking and questioning as many men on one side of the room. A dozen other men, half of them black and most in shabby topcoats, stand at urinals, their eyes wandering everywhere—over the fuzz, each other, Phillip and me—as though awaiting cues. We leave, head down another passageway, and pause at the entrance to a big bar and restaurant. It's a busy night; hundreds of people jam the tables.*]

The homosexuals are almost all at the bar. I'm sure most of the people at the tables don't know what's going on there. [*As we look in, people keep passing whose business might be anything from hustling to drug pushing; their professional badge is less swishiness than an air of shabby illegitimacy.*

[*We go up again to the cold air and dense crowds of Piccadilly. We walk half a dozen blocks, turn into a dark little alley, and enter an unmarked door. A long and almost unlit flight of steps takes us down to another door, and we enter a small reception room where a uniformed man presides over a guest book. Phillip signs and explains that I am a friend whom he feels it would be all right to bring into the club.*

[*We enter a pleasant, posh little private club. It is now about 10 P.M., and only a dozen or fifteen members are there. Looking around, I don't see one whom I'd assume was homosexual if I passed him on the street. They range from about thirty to fifty in age. A few are self-consciously elegant in dress, veering toward sporty high style, but the majority look like any prosperous young-to-middle-aged executives and professionals. One or two older members are in tweeds. Phillip quietly informs me that many of the men here are rather highly placed, distinguished or wealthy.*

[Toward 11 o'clock the room is filling up. A couple of very fey Oriental boys in swishy outfits have arrived; so has a fashion designer who almost matches their style. Phillip says disapprovingly that a few hustlers manage to sneak in once in a while as guests. This club has been here for a long time, and it is careful whom it allows in, but there are slips.

[I talk to a crusty old gentleman in his fifties; he has brought with him a blond, beefily good-looking young man in his middle twenties. Philip tells me in an aside that the older man is a very wealthy country gentleman, which is what I had guessed, and that the boy is his kept fellow. The older man is a bit hostile, but I suspect that it's his usual manner. No attempt to engage the younger man in conversation succeeds; I can't tell whether he's tight-lipped or just utterly obtuse.

[Closing time comes. There is much shouting and debate over where to go now. Phillip and I decide to go on to an after-hours gay club with a couple— a young man Phillip knows and a dapper, middle-aged gentleman who has asked him out for the evening. On the street, the couple walks on ahead, and Phillip asks:]

"If you had to guess the kinkiest person in there tonight, who would it be?"

"I don't think I could guess."

"Remember that blond piece of muscle? He's a laborer, and the older man keeps him. He's the queerest one of all. You know . . . no, you couldn't possibly. There's a special sort of blue silk bloomers that ladies used to wear here in England years and years ago; they were already old-fashioned when I was young. They're made of blue silk, with elastic at the waist and knees. There are only two shops in all London that have them today. Well, that young fellow is a fetishist. Every week when he gets his pay, or when he gets a gift from the old boyfriend, he runs to one of those stores, buys a pair of blue silk bloomers, goes to the nearest men's room, puts them on, and whacks off!"

[We are soon in another downstairs private club. This one is very dim, quiet, rather plush. There is just a little blue light; cushioned seats line the walls, and sling chairs are set about low tables. There's a small room to one side for dancing. A single lesbian is sitting between two young men, but otherwise it is a crowd of well-dressed, restrained males, some in their forties but most in their late teens and twenties. We sit drinking and talking for an hour. There is quiet recorded music, and very restrained, no-touching dancing has begun in the side room. The couple who came with Phillip and me decide to dance. When they are away, Phillip explains that the young man is heartbroken over the end of a romance; the older man is an apparently decent chap who just happened to ask him out tonight, sensed something is not quite right and is being quietly understanding. Phillip himself is looking about the room, trying to pick out in the near-darkness a possible bedmate. I wish him good hunting and say goodnight.]

19

Going for Facts

The twenties and thirties was the first period to call itself modern—as though every era weren't modern as it happened. It was the time of Buck Rogers stories, of foods advertised for their vitamins rather than their taste, of babies bottle-fed on timetables. One would expect that the simultaneous increase of sexual permissiveness and of confidence in science would produce a great leap in sex research. But for three decades only a handful of people followed Magnus Hirschfeld's lead and asked large numbers of people about their sex lives. Around the First World War and after, some studies were done in the United States of male frequencies of coitus and masturbation; they were small, narrowly conceived, and unreliable by modern standards. There was no ambitious effort to find out what people actually do in bed, what is in fact normal, and what is deviant. Scientists, like the rest of their society, thought they knew, that "everyone knows." Only gradually did they realize that common knowledge in such things is usually as reliable as the obvious flatness of the earth. When big behavior studies did appear, they all contained important surprises. The first ones represented a small, awkward leap forward in knowledge and prompted foolhardy conclusions.

Through the twenties there appeared in scientific journals fragments of a study in progress by a social worker and penologist named Katherine Bement Davis. In 1929 the whole work appeared, *Factors in the Sex Life of Twenty-Two Hundred Women*—the first even half-dependable study of sex behavior on a large scale. Katherine Davis had sent questionnaires to twenty thousand women in the New York City area, mostly graduates of Eastern women's colleges and born around or before 1900. She received answers from twelve hundred single and a thousand married women about their experience with intercourse, contraception, masturbation and homosexuality.

Half of the single women and a third of the married ones answered yes to the question whether they'd ever had "intense emotional relationships" with other women. The question is ambiguous, the responses open to almost any sort of interpretation. Many of these relationships, the respondents wrote, were crushes on friends or teachers during their teens and college years. Physical contact, if any, had usually been hugging and kissing, unaccompanied by sexual feelings. Of all twenty-two hundred women, about two hundred were active, overt lesbians. All but eighteen of these were single. Katherine Davis put another two hundred subjects in a border-line group that leaned toward lesbianism in the past or present. In all, said Davis, 10 to 20 per cent of all the women were now or had once been homosexual.

Actually, this figure included many married women who had had passing homosexual episodes or affairs while at girls' colleges. Some of these said they had stopped because they thought it wrong, abnormal, disgusting or harmful. Others said they had stopped because they'd finally become seriously involved with a man. Some recalled their lesbian past with fear or shame; but a large number claimed it had been a good, even beneficial experience, though they had "outgrown it."

The hard-core lesbian group contained some of the most sexually active women of all the twenty-two hundred, and some of the most inhibited. A number had had not only extensive lesbian experience but wide heterosexual experience as well. Among the least active of the whole group were those lesbians engaged in long-lasting, deeply emotional, and relatively nonphysical homosexual affairs. Only about forty of all two hundred lesbians saw their homosexuality as a problem or a source of shame. The majority claimed lesbianism had been good for them, and one of these typically wrote, "It has arisen as an expression of love and made my life inexpressibly richer and deeper." As a group, according to Davis, the lesbians showed surprisingly little sexual disturbance.

Scientists today must discount many of Davis' results. To begin with, her sample were college graduates from eastern schools—at that time, a group heavily weighted with upper-class and upper-middle-class WASPs who had broken with their traditional sex role by preparing for careers and financial independence. Further, a population who in those days would respond to a questionnaire on sex behavior was probably loaded with members of an "enlightened" minority opposed to common mores. On both counts one suspects the presence of a larger than usual number of "masculine protest" types and people with deviant behavior or attitudes.

Also, Davis was psychologically naïve in framing some of her questions and in accepting the answers and self-evaluations. We will never know what distortions occurred in her figures on behavior because she shunned psychologically oriented interviewing. We can guess, though, by the sexual self-evaluations she recorded. Many of the lesbians who claimed to be happy and have no sex problem also expressed repugnance at their own femininity, at menstruation and at men. They spoke of "turning to ice" around males. One woman was a nurse of thirty-eight who had had no sex activity till she began to masturbate at twenty-six, and then felt intense religious guilt. She was now living with another woman and had no desire for men or marriage. Davis faithfully transcribed the woman's summary: "No sex problem." Another woman, forty-one, had stayed single because of her twenty-five-year affair with another woman. She denied having any sex feelings at all. Davis concluded, "She has never had any sex problems in her life."

The high percentage of lesbians, many details of their lives and sexual histories, and their attitudes all become doubtful data under examination. Still, sketchy information was better than none, and when Katherine Davis died in 1935, others were already following her trail, learning from her mistakes and doing better. Even though most of them still failed to turn up results from which one could generalize about most people, a hunt was now on for facts rather than guesses or impressions.

As interest in behavior research grew, money appeared to back it. In 1921 the National Research Council formed a Committee for Research in Sex Problems, heavily financed by the Rockefeller Foundation. It included many famous physicians, psychiatrists, biologists and anthropologists. It backed many major studies of sex behavior through the decades between the wars—including the landmark projects of Dickinson and Beam, Terman and Miles, Landis and finally, beginning in 1938, Kinsey and his associates. They studied what sexual acts people performed, how often, in what way, and sometimes with what feelings and attitudes. Until Kinsey's massive studies were complete, the figures and conclusions were often uncertain or contradictory, but certain trends and rough facts were clear.

Many people had overestimated the twenties sexual revolution, and so did some of the thirties investigators. There was a similar mistaken belief that the change was rolling onward through the thirties. Terman said that now between 35 per cent and 65 per cent of American women experienced premarital sex, as compared to 10 per cent in Davis' sample (he ignored that their samples were from different segments of the population). He admitted that many of these women slept only with their fiancés, but predicted that if things went on this way, no American girl would reach the bridal bed a virgin by 1960.

A few others balanced the picture realistically. Carney Landis studied married couples and found that traditional attitudes sometimes continued beneath the emancipated façade, and even beneath emancipated behavior. Many husbands now deliberately varied sexual techniques and extended intercourse in order to bring their wives to orgasm; the majority of those wives remained "unaware" of these efforts and felt that their husbands cared only about gratifying themselves. Clearly, having a consciously enlightened attitude and reading sex manuals no more solved sex problems than reading karate manuals enables a coward to leap bravely and effectively into a brawl.

Again one must turn to Kinsey's work for the most accurate estimate of what was happening. Kinsey compared the generations that came of age in the twenties and thirties and said flatly that the difference in behavior was barely significant. In the thirties, some young people had first coitus a year or so earlier, began petting comparably sooner, and went farther. Essentially this meant that middle-class patterns of petting and dating behavior, established in the twenties, were becoming entrenched and extended along with other middle-class life patterns. (Working-class patterns were and are more restrictive about masturbation, petting and premarital sex among girls.) After the Second World War, despite boom, bust, war and social and legal reform, American sexual behavior had remained more stable than unstable since the twenties.

As for homosexuality, Kinsey said, "there is at best only a slight substantiation for the oft-repeated assertion that 'sexual perversion' is on the increase." He noted that the gap between his figures and popular opinion was especially odd, because public displays of homosexuality had been more open at the turn of the century, before red-light districts were abolished and police pressure was put on homosexual gathering places. Perhaps, Kinsey guessed, many people hadn't been aware of the homosexuality around them when they were young. As their own awareness increased, they thought they were seeing something new come into existence. Kinsey also turned critical attention to the idea that men segregated together, as in the army, are likely to turn to each other for sexual satisfaction. Men in the army, then, should have more homosexual behavior than they would if they stayed at home. There was no indication that this had happened, nor that lesbianism had increased while men were away in the army.

In 1935 the effort to fill information gaps finally extended specifically to homosexuality. That year a group of scientists formed the Committee for the Study of Sex Variants and underwrote a study. Most of the research and writing fell to Dr. George Henry, a hard-working, earnest and rather unimaginative psychiatrist. As a result, in 1941 he produced a huge two-volume study called *Sex Variants*, and later a book for laymen called *All the Sexes*. Both books are still read, and the paperback edition of the latter is presented as though it were still authoritative. Henry's books were of limited value even when they first appeared.

Like many scientists then, Henry sought a physical basis or predisposition for homosexuality. He got others to help him in extensive physical examinations of his subjects. They concluded that the body-carrying angle of homosexuals of both sexes was "intermediate between male and female" and was often accompanied by "abnormal" pelvic formation and "immature" skeletal development. Looking for genetic clues, Henry made up genealogical charts for his subjects like those of Krafft-Ebing, noting the occurrence in their families of homosexuality, bisexuality, suicide, psychosis, addiction, alcoholism, divorce, promiscuity, tuberculosis and "artistic inclinations." Although he said that in individual cases genetic and environmental factors weren't separable, he summed up case histories by stating a man's "innate effeminacy" or a woman's "innate virility."

When Henry did discuss emotional dynamics, it was often in an avuncular tone, with unenlightening truisms and what were already psychiatric clichés. He presented eighty long, detailed case histories, forty of males and forty of females, for the most part in their own words. This was the book's greatest value. Patterns can be seen in their background, life style and emotional dynamics, though much has to be inferred by the reader, for Henry either didn't see the patterns or was not prepared to speak decisively about them. What *Sex Variants* lacks in conceptual firmness and finesse, it makes up in bulk of material.

In a large proportion of the male and female homosexuals' homes, sex had been utterly ignored—that is, implicitly rejected. Sex education of any kind had been lacking. As children, they had seemed especially prone to nightmares; to fear of the dark, of attack and injury; to prolonged thumb-sucking and bed-wetting. Many had been told by one or both parents that their birth had damaged their mother physically and emotionally. They told Henry, "Mother almost died . . . she was an invalid for years after . . . she decided never to get pregnant again. . . ." The emotional message to the child was, "Look what men do to women, what your father did to your mother—through sex." Thus the mothers (sometimes with the fathers' acquiescence or help) had told the girls that femininity made them vulnerable, told the boys that their maleness could only martyr women and destroy love.

Many of the mothers and fathers had told the homosexual subjects that they had wanted a child of the opposite sex. Even more destructive was the mother telling a boy that his father had wanted a girl, or a father telling a girl that mother had wanted a boy. This was part of the oblique warfare between the parents, their duel to win the child's exclusive sympathy and allegiance. The mothers of both male and female homosexuals were in many cases unhappy, stiff and reserved—withdrawn martyrs who made their children conspirators with them against the man of the house, teaching fear and contempt for him as a brute, a clod and a victimizer.

Some fathers fought back with angry displays or infidelity, making the mothers' judgment come true. Others withdrew, helpless before the mother-child conspiracy, and became ciphers in their families. In some cases, the fathers took as actively destructive a role as the mothers. There were fathers who, like some mothers, acted dramatic, domineering, flaunting their sexuality and suffering to win attention. Others made their daughters allies against a cold, controlling mother. Some were narcissistic Don Juans, seductive even with their own children, making the mother seem dull and undesirable by comparison.

So in various ways, one parent became vivid and glamorous or won the child's solicitude by suffering and being distant. The other parent became unlovable, contemptible or colorless. The homosexual children were veterans of intense parental warfare in which the spoils were control, loyalty and attention. Particularly, many of the male homosexuals had mothers who were martyred or jilted princesses and downgraded their husbands and masculinity. The mother overprotected the boy and made him fastidious. As a result, he felt weak and unmasculine compared to other boys. They were rough and dirty, unacceptable to his mother. He feared undressing before other boys, ashamed of what he was convinced must be a small penis. He became prudish, inhibited, sissified. If his mother had pretensions to gentility and "higher" pursuits, he equated intellect, art and gentility with being lovable to her. In many cases, sisters, aunts and nurses aided the mother in making the boy feel controlled by females and unacceptable if he was sexual and aggressive. He clung to them, trying to win their approval, and felt dominated by them.

Many a mother was openly seductive, presenting herself to him as a sexual object—for instance, by always calling him to help her dress and undress even when a sister was there to do it. As the boy felt more sexual fantasies and impulses, he was torn between his mother arousing his sexuality and rejecting it; between his desires and the revenge he imagined from his "ogre" father. In short, there was a very acute Oedipal conflict. Some boys, unable to salvage their maleness at home, tried to do so by developing crushes on boys or men with whom they identified. Others clung to their mothers, identified with them, and wanted to wear women's clothes. The result was, respectively, a homosexual with a strong male or female identification.

The open or unconscious complicity of the mother with her son's homosexuality was often grotesquely clear. One of Henry's subjects, at thirty-one, lived with his widowed mother, supported her, and wore her wedding ring—she said that since he'd been taking care of her for five years, he might as well have it. She almost surely knew of her son's deviance and wasn't bothered in the least.

In many cases, the deviant went through adolescence feeling self-conscious about his body, fearful, poorly coordinated, and uncomfortable around assertive men. He was preoccupied with sex but felt powerful masturbation guilt. He might tentatively approach a woman, but if she responded, he would "shrivel up" because she "expected something." As a man, he might go to bed with a woman or even marry. If she were responsive and passionate, he would find sex with her unendurably nauseating, and flee. Then he would avoid women altogether, suspecting that they were laughing at him. Perhaps he could tolerate frigid girls or lesbians.

The homes of many of the lesbians, like those of many homosexual men, were broken or unstable. Perhaps one of the parents died or deserted the other when the girl was young. Perhaps she was raised by grandparents, in a convent, at boarding schools. Where both parents were present, they tended to fit a few common patterns, like those seen in the males' histories—a cold mother and seductive father, or a martyr mother and brutal father, or a domineering mother and a passive, withdrawn father. The most striking common factor in all the lesbians' histories was inadequate mothering because of the mother's death, illness, breakdown or withdrawn and rejecting manner.

Just as many male homosexuals insisted that their mothers were very feminine, many lesbians described their fathers as "very masculine." In many cases the father apparently tried to masculinize his daughter. Further, she may have had a prettier sister to compete with. She became a tomboy, felt clumsy, awkward, ugly, gawky or pudgy. She refused dolls and "frills," became competitive and aggressive, prayed to become a boy. As she grew older, she resented menstruation. Warned by her mother's stories of the agony of childbirth, she also feared motherhood. Perhaps she became contemptuous of her martyr mother; she claimed she had never known a strong man, only brutal ones (except perhaps her father). She envied and resented men, became a rabid feminist, and determined never to be helpless or pliant. One of Henry's lesbians wanted to create a home for prostitutes so that they wouldn't have to sell themselves to men.

The girl continued to see herself as physically inadequate in some way—tiny and puny, awkward and flat, fat and shapeless. If sent away to school or camp in her teens, she might find sexualized mothering in bed with an older woman. Many of Henry's lesbians said how important large, beautiful breasts were to them. One said, "Titty calms me. If I can't have it every day I get evil." Even some very butch lesbians admitted special pleasure in being petted and fondled like babies. They used the word "sweetness" a great deal to describe their happiest experiences. They claimed to prefer women to men as lovers because they were more "gentle" and "delicate."

Many of the lesbians went through an aggressive period during their late teens and twenties, but then settled down to a femme pattern or a middle ground between the two. Sometimes the reverse could be seen—a young femme sought older women and then, at thirty, started to seek girls who reminded her of herself at that age. Many lesbians insisted on how "feminine" their lovers were, as male homosexuals spoke of their "masculine" partners.

As adults, the homosexual men and women were a varied group. Some were openly homosexual, some secretive. Some had successful careers and social lives; others displayed depression, career failure, general instability, alcoholism, suicidal urges. Many feared growing old alone, and showed more and more neurotic symptoms through their thirties and forties. Many who married and had children saw their homes dissolved by alcohol and continuing homosexual affairs.

Though Henry's approach was mechanistic and earnestly pedestrian, he did emphasize and document the frequent relationship between homosexuality and aggression-passivity problems, and how this syndrome was passed on through generations of a family. Some case histories showed a cold, domineering grandmother, a withdrawn and antisexual martyr of a mother, and a lesbian daughter—all three personalities revealing distorted ideas of passivity and aggression, dominance and submission. These power struggles seemed a likely explanation of the often-mentioned instability of homosexual couples. Battles for dominance make maintaining any relationship difficult; homosexuals, with special trouble in this area, would probably have a particularly hard time in their love affairs.

Henry thought there might be a genetic basis for this syndrome, but that a neurotic environment made it paramount in personality development. He said that for society to produce fewer homosexuals, it must produce more emotionally healthy parents—fathers who weren't passive or infantile Don Juans, mothers who weren't frigid martyrs or bristling with masculine protest. Finally, despite his talk about genetic and constitutional factors, Henry believed that homosexuals were neurotics, and that like most types of neurotics, they had a good chance of cure.

As behavior studies increased during the thirties and forties, other scientific fields made dramatic progress as well. Newspapers carried utopian predictions based on new developments in endocrinology, genetics and experimental psychology. Much of the work represented a real gain in knowledge, but many people jumped to premature conclusions on the basis of one or two experiments, and half steps and missteps were followed up with headlong enthusiasm. Many still hoped to explain human complexity with a simple formula and thus have a tool for straightening out a sexually misaligned *homme machine*. As usual, some of this "revolutionary hard science" was really tradition in statistical modern dress.

Even the ancient idea of physical constitution as the direct basis of sexual behavior was disinterred. In the early forties, W. S. Sheldon produced two volumes—*The Varieties of Human Physique* and *The Varieties of Human Temperament*—that won wide attention for his system of "constitutional psychology." Sheldon had asked himself, "Do those who look most alike behave most alike? Does a particular sort of temperament go with a definite physique? Can we predict a man's likes and dislikes by measuring his body?" Tradition said that fat men are jolly, lean men dour, short men aggressive—could one picture a skinny Falstaff or a roly-poly Scrooge? Sheldon decided to find out. Unfortunately, it's a rare man who can spend years testing a hypothesis and end with a simple no.

Sheldon took thousands of measurements and photographs of men and women, interviewed them, and then matched their body types and personalities. He divided physiques into three basic categories—endomorph, ectomorph and mesomorph—and said each had its own physiological and psychological characteristics. The endomorph is dominated by his gut; he is soft, round, with massive digestive viscera, gluttonous, convivial, dependent and complacent. The ectomorph is long, thin and fragile, and consequently he has maximum skin surface and nerve tissue for his body mass. Dominated by his brain and nerve endings, he is hypersensitive, tense, inhibited, cerebral, tied up in knots, tending toward symbolic rather than direct action. The mesomorph is hard and rectangular, mostly muscle. He is geared to exertion, self-expression, and loud, energetic, even manic behavior. Few people, said Sheldon, fit perfectly into one category; they blend two or even three types, but usually with one predominant. He created an intricate system of subcategories of all the blends and variations, each represented by a mathematical code representing the "somatotype," or body-build pattern.

Sheldon claimed that body-build and emotional disturbance were related. For instance, he said that "dysplasia" (different patterns in different parts of the body, such as ectomorphic head and neck on mesomorphic trunk and legs) were common in schizophrenics. Manic-depressives showed mixed endomorphy and mesomorphy. Ectomorphs tended to feel overwhelmed by sexual feelings: "Theirs are sensitive bodies, and they are consequently susceptible to the development of masturbational and perversive [*sic*] qualities."

The assumption of a relationship between masturbation, high sexual activity and perversion is typical of Sheldon's dance on Lombroso's grave. Like Lombroso, Sheldon also suspected a relationship between the gifted person, the criminal and the "bisexual." Of homosexuals, Sheldon said, with implied contempt, they were weak, fragile, defenseless and poorly endowed, with physical characteristics of the opposite sex. "Case 73 . . . is a constitutional inferior whose graduation from college reflects the gravest doubt upon the integrity of American higher education. This weak creature has only one strength. That is his helplessness and dependency."

Sheldon implied that conventional mesomorphy was the highest physical, psychological and social value. With his facile formulas, talk of constitutional weaklings and apparent scientific exactitude, he was an Ayn Rand of physical anthropology. It was as though all the tragicomic history of palmistry, phrenology and "criminal anthropology" had left no cautionary message behind. Sheldon became very popular very quickly. National magazines popularized his work, and the terms ectomorph, endomorph and mesomorph entered middle-brow vocabulary along with Jung's introvert and extrovert, Freud's id and libido. Sheldon appealed to many popular prejudices by linking together many kinds of deviant and unconventional people, and praising the current social norm as the greatest natural good.

People have long suspected that there is a relationship between body structure and behavior. There may be one, to some extent, but surely not the simple, one-to-one connection Sheldon described. In fact, there is equal evidence that the emotions shape the body as much as the body molds temperament. But many people were reassured to hear again that hereditary nature, not environment and development, explained psychosexual disturbances.

Competing specialists kept claiming they had discovered other master-keys to mankind. Geneticists in England, Germany, Holland and the United States affirmed over and over between 1930 and 1950 that homosexuality ran in families and was more common among siblings (especially twins) than in the general population. When other scientists argued with their methods and results, geneticists demonstrated with more studies that homosexuals were "intergrades," with an imbalance of male or female genes. These genes remained undiscovered, but their presence, geneticists said, had to be inferred.

The isolation of hormones was one of the most exciting developments in science. People have thought sporadically since the ancient world that the ductless glands might secrete substances vital to life and growth, and in the middle of the nineteenth century a few substantiating discoveries were made. Then in 1889 the seventy-two-year-old physician Brown-Séquard announced in Paris that he had rejuvenated himself with injections of a filtered extract of dog testicles. His solution contained an insignificant amount of testosterone, but the psychological effect on him and the world was immense. Endocrinology immediately became a subject of public fascination and soon a full scientific specialty.

During the next few decades research began uncovering the intricate system of interlocking hormone and nervous-system mechanisms that control much of sexual development and behavior. But the next time most laymen heard about endocrinology was through the claims of the Austrian Eugen Steinach and the Russian Serge Voronoff, who during the twenties grabbed the imagination of everyone from Freud to tabloid journalists. Steinach said he had changed people's sex with hormones and surgery. Voronoff claimed that testicular transplant from ape to man had brought wondrous vigor to older men. Monkey-gland and sex-change jokes became popular, and soon Banting's discovery of the hormone insulin and its role in diabetes gave the whole field a boost in both knowledge and prestige.

Freud hoped that hormones might some day explain homosexuality, and said so in his last revision of *Three Essays* in 1920. In 1927 a psychiatrist named van Ophuisen visited Freud, found him with Steinach, and heard the master saying, "Of course, you know, I am firmly convinced that one day all these disturbances we are trying to understand will be treated by means of hormones or similar substances."

For a while it looked as though this might be true. It was learned that a tumor of the adrenal glands can cause psychosis; that sometimes euphoria, mania, depression and schizoid states rise from endocrine disorders; that hyperthyroidism can produce abnormal mental conditions and masculinize women. There were tentative reports of hormone deficiencies in criminals and of changes in the gonads of schizophrenics. Several scientists claimed that they had shown abnormal amounts of estrogens, or female hormones, in male homosexuals, and androgens, or male hormones, in lesbians (actually, males normally produce small amounts of estrogen, and females small amounts of testosterone). When male homosexuals were treated with estrogen, their homosexual activity slackened; estrogen stops heterosexual activity as well, but that was brushed aside as a cumbersome subtlety. In 1940 Steinach wrote that he had microscopically examined the testicles of five male homosexuals and seen "secreting cells of a female nature." Now, he rejoiced, the answer to the problem of homosexuality had been found, and "the period of presumptions and intuitions has passed."

Many of these findings were partial or incorrect—no one but Steinach subsequently found such cells—but they were gravely announced to the press by scientists as final solutions. People read and presented themselves for treatment. One of George Henry's subjects was a male transvestite, heterosexual most of his life, who had turned himself into a workshop for delirious experimenters. He had asked for and received the Steinach rejuvenation operation, persuaded another doctor to X-ray his testicles to make him sterile, and took female hormones to develop his hips and breasts, with moderate success. Finally he called on Magnus Hirschfeld for an expert diagnosis, only to be told that he was a congenital inverted lesbian.

Soon it became clear to all but zealots that the endocrine system and its relationship to sex behavior is far more complex than had first been thought. If a woman receives a small amount of testosterone, the male sex hormone, it stimulates her ovaries and affects her nervous system in such a way as to increase her sex drive. If she is heterosexual, she will have more desire for heterosexual acts; if homosexual, for homosexual acts. But if the dose of testosterone passes a certain threshold, it inhibits the ovaries, and such secondary sex characteristics as fat deposits and body hair change toward a masculine pattern. If testosterone is given to a man, it will also increase his drive, but it has no influence on his choice of sexual objects. Estrogen, the female sex hormone, will reduce sex drive in a man, but it will not affect his sexual orientation, his preference for men or women. In larger amounts it will produce physical feminization, but still not change orientation. Also, the first announcements of sex change by hormones and surgery had been exaggerated. It was (and still is) impossible to make a really normal female out of a normal male, and vice versa. Those who had been operated on with most success had had some degree of physical hermaphroditism to begin with. Many of the changes produced by hormones and surgery in some people had causes as much psychological as physical—those who asked for such treatment tended to be emotionally unstable. So the results were far from decisive and trustworthy. The eminent psychiatrist Karl Menninger argued (as had Adler before him) that it was just as likely that psychological rejection of femininity altered many lesbians' appearance as that a hormone imbalance had caused the lesbianism and physical masculinization. In other words, emotions and environment influence the neuro-endocrine system, just as hormones influence emotions and behavior.

But the desire for simple medical solutions to sexual problems was strong, and men went on announcing they had total solutions to sexual deviance through surgery, hormones, transplants, prefrontal lobotomy and, most of all, castration. Though evidence against all these things as single solutions was already quite strong by the mid-forties, legislators, judges and the lay public kept up with the simplistic right wing of science by calling for the hypodermic and the knife.

In the 1880s, as in ancient Egypt and Rome, hysterics and epileptics of both sexes were surgically castrated—thousands each year in Paris, hundreds yearly by one doctor alone in the United States. Theories vaguely related convulsive disorders, the gonads and sexual activity. (In the same spirit, cauterization of the clitoris was used to cure "excessive masturbation" in females.) In the 1890s, as degeneracy theories became accepted, the idea spread that castration would solve two problems at once: it would prevent the passing on of tainted genes and, by reducing sexual drive, stop masturbation, rape, child molestation and homosexuality.

In the middle of the 1890s, F. Hoyt Pilcher, head of a Kansas institution for the feeble-minded, allowed four boys and fourteen girls, all "confirmed masturbators," to be castrated. He had no legal authority to do so, but he was convinced, one of his defenders later explained, that it would prevent "excessive masturbation and pervert [*sic*] sexual acts." A public outcry stopped Pilcher, but others had the same idea. In 1898 a Kansas asylum reported that forty-eight young men had been castrated to keep them from fathering idiot children. A doctor at the Hospital for Epileptics in Palmer, Massachusetts, castrated twenty-four males, half of them younger than fourteen, for persistent masturbation and epilepsy. Masturbation, said the doctor, was "unpleasant for a refined woman to see . . . it seemed an absolute necessity to try something we had not tried."

In 1899 Dr. Harry Sharp of Indiana State Reformatory announced that he had not been castrating boys at the institution, but sterilizing them with a new technique he had developed—vasectomy, severing the spermatic ducts. This, he said, produced all the benefits of castration without obvious caponization. By 1909 he had experimented on 236 people and claimed that the subject of vasectomy becomes "of a more sunny disposition, brighter of intellect, ceases excessive masturbation." Now, he felt, society could humanely sieve out hereditary degenerates—most of the insane, epileptic, mentally retarded, alcoholic, criminal and sexually deviant as well as paupers and tramps.

Indiana passed a eugenic sterilization bill in 1907, as did Washington and Oregon and California in 1909. Indiana's law was declared unconstitutional after four years and 873 sterilizations. New York, Connecticut, New Jersey and other states also passed and then expunged such acts. In 1929 there were twenty-two states with such a law in effect—except for Maine, all were in the Midwest, West and border South. In some states it was hardly applied. In others, such as Kansas, Oregon and Wisconsin, it was used on a few hundred people a year. California, excessive as usual, had already sterilized six thousand people.

Asexualization also appeared on European lawbooks. After the turn of the century, castration was used on homosexuals, exhibitionists and child molesters in Switzerland. In 1929 Denmark passed a castration law, and during the next decade it was applied to almost two hundred homosexuals, bisexuals, rapists, fetishists, sado-masochists and psychopaths. By 1956 some six hundred people had been operated on. During the thirties and forties castration laws also appeared in Sweden, Norway, Finland, Holland, Greenland, Iceland and Germany.

Those who supported the practice reported that deviants and psychopaths had been "pacified" and "resocialized" by it and were unlikely to repeat their offense. (Exactly the same claims were made for lobotomy after it was developed in 1936.) Judges, among other laymen, were impressed. When Virginia's sterilization law was appealed in the twenties by a feeble-minded woman with a feeble-minded daughter, Justice Holmes wrote in upholding the statute, "the principle that sustains compulsory vaccination is broad enough to cover cutting the fallopian tubes.... Three generations of imbeciles are enough."

Fortunately, not all scientists were swept away, and not all courts heeded the call of science. As early as 1914 an American scientist reviewed 112 cases of ovarectomy and urged caution because the results were uncertain. Evidence against surgical measures kept piling up, and by the late thirties and early forties it was pretty clear that those who believed in asexualization said it worked, but that those without such faith rarely found it did. The evidence from endocrinology was that aside from sterility, asexualization had varied, unpredictable and often negligible effects on women. The effects on men also varied, and depended partly on psychological factors; they never changed sexual object choice and didn't necessarily stop sexual activity.

Supporters of asexualization probably saw what they hoped for. Studies showed there had been inadequate follow-ups of most of those asexualized. "Success" had been based on a quick judgment soon after surgery. In Norway a study of castrated sex offenders showed that many diagnoses had been doubtful to begin with; many who claimed they were now better had requested castration because of mental instability to begin with; of course castration had in no way changed epileptics; "pacification" and "resocialization" were often missing; in fact, many of those operated on were bitter and had deteriorated psychologically. Finally, since there was no evidence that homosexuality, epilepsy, psychopathy, etc., were caused by hormones or the gonads, there was no reason to expect change after asexualization.

Soon a trend away from asexualization began in Holland and Denmark. One by one, state courts in the United States decided it was of unproved value, denied due process, and was a cruel and unusual punishment. Besides, the "voluntary" castration of many prisoners was often the only alternative a judge offered, quite extralegally, to a long prison sentence. In 1941 there was a national scandal over the fact that six sex offenders at

Ohio State Penitentiary had submitted to emasculation in order to get paroles.

It was also clear that many apparently scientific arguments for emasculation were really disguised sermons of the most traditional and irrational kind against "filth" and "perversion." In practice, asexualization often meant revenge rather than therapy. Oklahoma's asexualization law called for involuntary vasectomy of "habitual criminals" and those who commit "felonies involving moral turpitude," including embezzlement. The man whose appeal overthrew the law in the early forties had been sentenced to vasectomy for two armed robberies and chicken stealing.

The peak of eugenic sterilization, and of vengeful castration under its guise, was in Nazi Germany. In 1933 a law was passed there calling for the sterilization of schizophrenics, epileptics, alcoholics, drug addicts, hysterics, homosexuals and those born blind or with physical malformations. Two years later fifty-six thousand people had been sterilized. In concentration camps all pollutors of society were given inverted triangles of various colors to identify them: green was for lawbreakers, red for political offenders, purple for religious objectors, black for "asocial elements," two yellow triangles making a Star of David for Jews, and a pink triangle for homosexuals—a catch-all for various people the Gestapo wanted out of the way. Many of these groups were liable to sterilization. Jewish sex offenders were sometimes sterilized before being murdered for their religion.

By 1950 proof was overwhelming of the pointlessness of asexualizing almost everyone on whom it had been practiced. Meanwhile, those who wanted to believe in cutting kept doing so, wherever they were still legally able, and reporting good results. The director of the Winfield, Kansas, State Training School argued that year that castration had recently made 330 males at his institution more stable and peaceful, less a "social menace." Eleven states still had involuntary sterilization on their books, and almost twenty more allowed it on a voluntary basis. (Most of these states were still in the Middle and Far West.) Estrogen injections were being advocated as a second-best way of neutralizing deviants, criminals and psychotics here and in Europe. More daring medical minds predicted lobotomy would soon be the ideal preventative for use on moral degenerates.

In its report of 1950, the American Neurological Association Committee for the Investigation of Sterilization was still advocating limited use of asexualization. By now some fifty thousand sterilizations for medico-legal reasons were on record in the United States; there had probably been many, many more. The total in the Western world over the preceding seventy-five years was doubtless in the many hundreds of thousands. And a Kansas physician who had been amazed to find it difficult to get cooperation in carrying out asexualization wrote, "The great reluctance to castration on the part of the male possibly dates back to phallic worship."

PART THREE

20

Genes and Hermaphrodites

The evidence is overwhelming that the genes do not cause homosexuality. Some scientists and many laymen don't believe it. Most homosexuals don't want to. Even many homosexuals who, after psychotherapy, explain how their upbringing caused their homosexuality, will add, "But anyway, as time goes on, I'm more and more convinced it's in the genes." Like most of us, they feel that character and behavior are to some degree transmitted along family lines. The idea of hereditary traits arouses primitive feelings about doom and giftedness; the desire to be like or unlike one's parents; fear of unalterable defects; longing for innate strength and superiority. To blame the genes is to blame fate; to exonerate them seems to affirm the ability to choose.

The genetics of sex is a crucial area of sex research today, but the genetic nature of homosexuality is not its chief problem. Some of the current research relevant to sexology deals with such matters as stress and drive. The most dramatic discoveries deal with hermaphroditism and the way maleness and femaleness are coded in our genes. Like most sciences dealing with man, genetics has shifted from hopefully simple ideas of direct causation to a complex, multifactor view. But before this could happen, the myth of homosexuality being in the genes had to flower and—at least among enlightened geneticists—die.

Until this century it was not known just how parents transmit traits to children. During the seventeeth and eighteenth centuries the microscope revealed that most higher plants and animals reproduce sexually through the union of a sperm from a male and an ovum from a female. (In the eighteenth century, the idea that flowers should do so was considered blasphemous and obscene.) At first people thought that the whole human being existed, fully formed in miniature, within the sperm or egg. Till the nineteenth century, argument continued between ovulists, who believed the homunculus lay in the egg, and those who thought submicroscopic man slept within the sperm. Gradually it became clear that there was no homunculus involved, but rather a biological blueprint for a man, to which both egg and sperm contribute half. They fuse into one cell, which divides and subdivides, traversing the stages of evolutionary development to attain human infancy.

In the 1860s, the Austrian monk Gregor Mendel proved that there are laws of inheritance by which one can predict the transmission of traits. His work went almost unnoticed, and was forgotten after his death in 1884. But at that time Sir Francis Galton in England was also trying to learn how traits are inherited. He invented the pedigree method of genetic study, tracing traits through family trees. He also developed the twinship-study method, comparing the relative frequency of traits in twins and nontwins. Men began to postulate the existence of unseen, submicroscopic particles called genes, and to attribute immense importance to them in human behavior. Galton concluded that "nature prevails enormously over nurture when the differences of nurture do not exceed what is commonly to be found among persons of the same rank of society and in the same country." In 1900 the Mendelian laws were rediscovered, and soon the role of the chromosomes, which bear the genes, was puzzled out.

Genetics was one of those developments that first promised—at least to some people—an explanation for half the facts of life: many believed that genetic "degeneration" or mutation would soon account for everything from intelligence to inversion. Before too long, it was discovered that fairly simple genetic flaws lie behind albinism, hemophilia, Huntington's chorea and Mongolism. For decades attempts were made to show a genetic basis for character traits, intelligence, homosexuality, schizophrenia and depression. Krafft-Ebing's pedigree studies showed such multiple "hereditary flaws" in homosexuals' families as alcoholism and tuberculosis. Hirschfeld said that 35 per cent of male homosexuals have homosexual brothers or other close relatives, proof of a hereditary factor. Between 1900 and the 1950s, many geneticists claimed to have proof of a hereditary basis for homosexuality, male feminization and female masculinization.

Genetics was also said to hold the answer to crime, civilization, racial qualities. Now one could prove that "good stock" pre-elected those one favored, that "bad seed" corrupted those one scorned. Genetics proved the superiority of Nordic man, justified castration of sexual and criminal offenders. Those who hated homosexuals made genetic degeneration the medical equivalent of original sin. Homosexuals and apologists said homosexuality sprang from a harmless or even beneficial mutation. In either case, the homosexual was seen as a victim of his urges, not their creator, and thus potentially their master. Since most laymen's ideas about sex still come directly or indirectly from Havelock Ellis, Krafft-Ebing and other experts of fifty and eighty years ago, they still believe this.

The methods used by Krafft-Ebing, Ellis and Hirschfeld to prove the genetic basis of homosexuality are acceptable to no scientists today. The studies discussed in books on homosexuality now are those of Lang, Slater and Kallmann. Lang's, the first, rose from experiments that discovered the workings of the sex chromosomes.

The nucleus of every cell contains paired bodies called chromosomes. Each kind of plant and animal has a characteristic number of them—the fruit fly eight, the mouse forty, the potato forty-eight, man forty-six. Man's twenty-three pairs of chromosomes bear forty thousand or more genes, long and complex protein molecules in a double helix that bear hereditary information as a computer tape bears instructions for an assembly-line operation. But egg and sperm cells, by a complex process of division, end up containing only one of each pair of chromosomes, to make a total of twenty-three. When an egg and sperm fuse, they join their half-complements of chromosomes to create a new, full complement of forty-six. These forty-six chromosomes contain directions for the growth of the entire human being, probably through the creation of enzymes that in turn trigger other biochemical reactions.

Twenty-two of a human's twenty-three pairs of chromosomes look similar. One pair, the sex chromosomes, are distinctive. In women this pair look alike. In men, one sex chromosome is similar to those in women, but the other is smaller. The large chromosome is called the X chromosome, the smaller one the Y. So the formula for a woman's sex chromosomes is XX, for a man's XY.

Since a woman has two X's in a normal body cell, each of her ova contains one X, so she always contributes an X to her child. Since the male is XY, he produces one sperm cell with an X and one with a Y. If he adds an X to the woman's X, the result is XX, a female. If he adds a Y, the result is XY, a male.

If a person is genetically intersexual, or hermaphroditic, the source should lie in these sex chromosomes. A German geneticist named Goldschmidt, studying intersexuality in gypsy moths in the second and third decades of this century, found apparent males with female (XX) genetic coding. This and other results of his research proved that intersexuality can indeed have its basis in the sex chromosomes. Goldschmidt and others thought this might be the key to human homosexuality. Lang, another German geneticist, picked up Goldschmidt's speculation that female sex chromosomes in a human male were the biological basis for "psychic hermaphroditism." The homosexual, then, was really a female whose body development had been reversed—a modern-dress version of the old idea of a female mind in a male body, with gene substituted for mind.

Lang reasoned that since males and females are born in predictable proportion, the existence of a homosexual in a family is equal to a "missing female." Lang got access to confidential police files in Hamburg and Munich, compiled a list of more than fifteen hundred homosexuals, looked them up, and in 1940 announced that his theory had been correct. These homosexuals had a larger proportion of male siblings than did the population at large. The following year another geneticist, Jensch, repeated Lang's study and confirmed the result.

A different approach was announced by geneticist E. Slater in England in 1962, based on the fact that chromosomal anomalies become more likely as the mother's age increases. If homosexuality is a chromosomal anomaly, it should be more common among males born later in their mothers' lives, and late or last among their siblings. Slater studied some four hundred homosexuals and found that this was so. He concluded that homosexuality is a chromosomal anomaly.

But the study that seemed to wrap things up, when it was announced, was that of the American geneticist F. J. Kallmann. He used the twinship method. There are two types of twins, dizygotic and monozygotic (DZ and MZ for quick reference). DZ twins grow from two ova fertilized by different spermatoza; they are neither more nor less alike than any other brothers or sisters. MZ twins develop from the splitting of a single fertilized egg. They look identical, are of the same gender and blood type, and often have similar fingerprints and other characteristics. Since they have almost identical genetic structure, they are excellent subjects for research. When twins share a heritable trait, they are called concordant for it. So to prove a trait is heritable, one compares the amount of concordance in MZ twins as compared to DZ twins. The comparatively higher the MZ concordance, the greater the proof of a genetic basis for the trait.

Kallmann found eighty-five homosexual men in New York who had twin brothers. He separated them into MZ and DZ twins and tried to track down their brothers. In 1952, he had data on thirty-seven pairs of MZ twins and twenty-six pairs of DZ twins. The DZ twin brothers showed no unusual amount of homosexuality. But of the thirty-seven MZ twin brothers, all had had homosexual activity, and twenty-eight were exclusively or almost exclusively homosexual. That was 100 per cent concordance for homosexual activity, and 86 per cent concordance for predominant or exclusive homosexuality. It sounded almost too perfect to be true, and it was.

Lang's, Slater's and Kallmann's studies have been wholly or partly discredited as proofs of a genetic basis for homosexuality. Several people, including even Slater, have repeated Lang's study, and they simply did not find an undue number of brothers among male homosexuals. Furthermore, if Lang's theory were true, the children of homosexuals should all be female or homosexual, since the fathers are really genetic females; this is not the case. Anyway, even if Lang's figures did hold up, psychological factors could explain them just as well as genetic ones. Having a disproportionate number of older male siblings could be an important environmental pressure favoring homosexuality, according to many psychodynamic theories.

Slater's study has not been duplicated, but it too can be explained just as well by psychological factors. Many psychiatrists have noted that homosexual and other various deviant patterns seem a bit more common among only children and youngest children. There are many reasons for this, as we will see later; an obvious one is that many mothers tend to baby the last male child longer than his older brothers, so that he clings to her more and identifies with her more. Contrary to both Lang and Slater, there are studies maintaining that adopted children in families show about the same rate of sexual difficulty as their step-siblings.

Kallmann's study is the one most mentioned today. A close look at it shows why a large part of scientific literature consists of criticism of research techniques. Kallmann's almost perfectly consistent results, in a matter so complex and lacking in other certainties, are suspect; the study runs counter to the clinical experience of probably the great majority of people who work with homosexuals. J. Lang has reported a case of identical twins with very different sexual patterns—one apparently healthily and happily heterosexual, the other an effeminate homosexual. Since then, a number of other scientists have made similar reports. On the other hand, no one has confirmed Kallmann's study. Kallmann did not show that the MZ twins' fathers and other male relatives are homosexual, which certainly should be the case if a straightforward genetic cause exists. Furthermore, all of Kallmann's twin subjects had been raised together: they shared not only the same genes but the same childhood home. Analysts who have worked with MZ twins say that the emotional bond between them is extraordinarily strong; there is great mutual identification, which could be crucial in encouraging homosexual development. Again, psychological explanations are as likely as genetic ones.

Dr. Judd Marmor, an eminent psychiatrist and editor of a major recent text on homosexuality, pointed out, "Kallmann's scientific objectivity is open to question. He has been an ardent proponent of the basic importance of genetic factors in a wide variety of conditions, and his monozygotic 'twin studies' have shown more than 86 per cent concordance in conditions as disparate as schizophrenia and tuberculosis." Kallmann himself has more moderately said that a complex disturbance involving a large number of genes may give some people a vulnerability to unstable psychosexual development, with many possible outcomes, depending on the environment.

Today relatively few geneticists seek a simple, fixed genetic base for character traits or behavior patterns. Homosexuality, intelligence and schizophrenia are so complex, the results of so many different forces, that one can hardly expect a gene or even a group of genes to control their development. There are many kinds of homosexuals, with different backgrounds, sex-behavior patterns, emotional patterns and life styles. Expecting to find a gene or genes for homosexuality is like expecting to find a gene for temperament. So simple a physical trait as eye color may be caused by many genes scattered on different chromosomes.

Even few physical traits, let alone character traits, are the result of genes alone. Geneticists are now thinking more in terms of "interaction" traits than acquired or inherited ones. For instance, genes, infant care, diet, climate and other factors combine to determine one's height. There is no nature-nurture dichotomy, but interaction between the two. Right- and left-handedness are probably encoded in the genes, but can be overridden by social training. It is now guessed that left- and right-handedness are "permissive" traits: certain combinations of genes are necessary for their existence, but not sufficient to insure them. As even Kallmann now admits, what the genes may contribute toward sexual development is a complex, flexible substratum; it probably determines no specific quality decisively, but helps create a firm or unstable roadbed for development.

Sophisticated research has turned to discovering what the elements of this genetic substratum are. For instance, it is commonly assumed that some people are born with greater sex drive than others. Geneticists found a simple measurement of sex drive: how soon after ejaculation is a male sexually responsive again? Since human sexual behavior is so much influenced by individual adaptation, they turned to rats, guinea pigs and mice, whose sexual behavior is more biologically programed. Through selective breeding, they could produce different strains of mice whose sexual "recovery times" averaged as little as one hour or as long as four days. So it seemed that sex drive, at least in rodents, depended on a genetic given.

But even this apparently simple trait turned out to be the product of several factors. Rodents, like humans, are not just machines acting out a genetic coding; their age, previous sexual experience, isolation from or exposure to other animals, all influence individual sexual-recovery rates. Human handling in the laboratory is a very important factor. It is likely that mice are sexually more active if subjected to large amounts of stress in infancy.

Now attention turned to stress. Selective breeding can produce strains of mice that are labile, easily effected by small amounts of stimulation or of change in their environment. Other strains are stable, and can withstand large amounts of stress. However, various kinds of stress may be determined separately. Tactile stress, for instance, seems independent of aural stress. Selective breeding can produce a disposition to withstand high audio vibrations well or poorly; one strain of mice may be comfortable with high vibrations, while another, subjected to the same frequency, suffers fatal convulsions.

Similar results came from genetic studies of aggression—perhaps the most fashionable new scientific field of the sixties. Male mice have been bred to produce strains that tend to initiate and win fights, others that avoid and lose them. Again, handling by humans and other environmental factors have a strong influence. So there probably is not a simple aggressivity quotient determined by the genes, but a complex of specialized traits, susceptible to the environment, that help develop or inhibit aggressive behavior. This is crucial in the study of human behavior, and human sexuality in particular; inability to handle aggression is probably central to many types of homosexual development. But just as people decades ago announced they had found the key to homosexuality in the genes, some unsophisticated geneticists claim to have found the key to aggression there.

What seems likely is something like this: A person is born with a genetically determined low threshold to tactile and acoustic stress, and to environmental stress in general. He may also have a strike against him genetically in his capacity for developing aggressive behavior patterns. (All these tendencies work through a complex interplay of genes, enzymes, hormones and neurons.) If the person is roughly handled by parents with tense, high-pitched voices, this may contribute to his becoming supersensitive, inclined to overreact, always shrinking back from anticipated jolts to his nervous system. This could be a factor in his becoming a fearful, sissified child. That in turn could make homosexual development more likely for him than for another person. Thus many genes, with specific limited effects, interact with the environment to create a predisposition to maladaptation, with gross symptoms varying from mild neurosis to homosexuality to schizophrenia, depending on dozens of environmental factors.

Some geneticists have hated to give up the grandiose expectations of the pioneer days of their specialty; others have been fascinated by the unexpected complexity of more mature genetic research, and by the contact it brings with other branches of science. Such research is relatively new. Over the next couple of decades, geneticists will work with endocrinologists, neurologists, ethologists and research psychologists and begin to chart the network of minute interaction traits that underlie the development of human personality and behavior. Man's genetic endowment figures in his sexuality as does one color in a large, complicated mosaic.

There has been another thrust in the genetic study of sex during the past decade; it not only gave decisive proof that homosexuality involves no gross genetic defect but opened up a dramatic and sometimes bizarre area of sex research. The groundwork was laid in 1949, when Dr. Murray L. Barr and some colleagues at the University of Western Ontario discovered that a small mass of chromatin exists in the nuclei of most or all female mammals' body cells. In the fifties, he showed that this spot—called the Barr body after him—is present in human females' body cells, but is missing in men; the logical conclusion, which has been supported by subsequent experiments, is that the Barr body is actually a female's second X chromosome coiled up in a tight spiral. At last there was a simple, direct test for gender. One could take cells from any part of a person's body—the most convenient way is a buccal smear, cells scraped from the inside of the cheek—and check for Barr bodies. The cells of a female contain Barr bodies, the cells of a male do not. This technique for determining one's genetic sex is called chromatin sexing. It solved old problems and opened up new ones.

Slater, who had tried to show a genetic basis for homosexuality, had said in 1950, "A much more direct test . . . would presumably be obtained by biopsy and cytological examination of the chromosomes." In other words, if male homosexuals are really disguised genetic females, a direct study of chromosomes would show it. Now, thanks to Barr, it was possible to find out. In 1956 Dr. C. M. B. Pare, at Maudsley Hospital in London, did chromatin-sexing studies of fifty male homosexuals and five male transvestites. All had normal XY sex-chromosome patterns, as indicated by the absence of Barr bodies. Not long after, techniques were developed for viewing all the chromosomes of a cell. No abnormality relating to homosexuality has been found.

There are people, though, whose sex chromosomes are not normal, and the result is not homosexuality but hermaphroditism. Hermaphrodites have fascinated and terrified men for millennia. As we have seen, physical hermaphrodites, who have anatomical traits of both male and female, were feared and destroyed in ancient Greece; but the *idea* of hermaphroditism, the blending of psychological images of male and female, was cultivated. Into this century, Westerners have thought that "psychic hermaphroditism" must be the reason for homosexuality—the mind, soul or brain of one sex in the body of the other. The ability to identify gender by chromosomes has at last begun to clarify the differences between men and women, and the ways maleness and femaleness are mixed in the intersexual. It has led to greater understanding not only of homosexuality but of heterosexuality as well.

In 1938 it was recognized that there is a congenital disorder of women involving genetic sexual endowment. It is variously called Turner's syndrome, ovarian agenesis and gonadal aplasia. The victim is born without ovaries. She is short, sometimes almost dwarfed, perhaps overweight. She may also have a webbed neck, receding chin, defects of the heart and kidneys and low intelligence. At puberty she fails to menstruate and to develop secondary sex characteristics. When chromatin sexing was developed, it turned out that the cells of her body lack Barr bodies; that is, the cells contain forty-five instead of forty-six chromosomes, because one of the female's usual two X chromosomes is missing. An X was received from the mother, but neither the masculinizing Y nor the feminizing X came from the father. This XO person is the closest thing to a human neuter. Victims of Turner's syndrome, who are genetically less than female, show an absence of homosexuality. In fact, these women are clearly feminine and heterosexual in fantasies and self-image.

Four years after the discovery of Turner's syndrome, an equivalent male disorder was defined—Klinefelter's syndrome. The Klinefelter male is born with small infertile testes. His sex drive is low. He appears somewhat eunuchoid, with sparse facial hair and a high-pitched voice. He may be obese and show breast development, but is more likely to become tall and gangly. He may be more prone than average to mental deficiency and schizophrenia; it is still uncertain whether the personality and intelligence deficits of some Turner females and Klinefelter males come from genetic damage or the emotional difficulties of being physically abnormal. The Klinefelter male's cells show a Barr body. Instead of the normal XY pattern, he has one or even two feminizing X chromosomes in addition. He is XXY or XXXY.

The Klinefelter male is a true genetic intersexual, the chromosomal man-woman imagined by Ulrichs, Krafft-Ebing, and several generations of scientists after them. In 1957 a study of thirty-one cases showed that despite physical and psychological problems, almost three quarters had had heterosexual relations by the age of twenty; only two had had homosexual experiences, and those were episodic. A study of thirty-two other Klinefelter males the following year showed that all were heterosexual, though four lacked sexual drive or experience. Since then, Klinefelter males have been discovered who are homosexuals, transvestites and transsexuals, but they are probably a minority, and the sexual problems of some seem part of faulty general emotional adaptation.

Genetics had shown that the idea of homosexuals as a "third sex" did not hold; that in fact there is a genetic "third sex," and its members are not markedly prone to homosexuality. Many other genetic variants have been found; more are being discovered almost every year. It is now thought that many people, apparently normal, bear some degree of mosaicism in their sex chromosomes—a small percentage of cells with abnormal patterns mixed with the normal ones. One of the most interesting discoveries has been that of XXX women and XYY men, who by genetic definition should be supermales and superfemales.

This turns out not to be true. Such patterns are the result of trisomy, a chromosome existing in triplicate instead of duplicate. Trisomy usually produces severe physical and mental disabilities—for instance, trisomy of the twenty-first pair of chromosomes causes Mongolism. XXX women, instead of being superfemales, are often infertile and otherwise physically defective; some are mentally defective as well.

The XYY male has recently received special attention in the press. Just as papers and magazines jumped on the idea of a simple genetic basis for aggression, they found appealing copy in the XYY "supermale." The condition was first discovered in 1962 in Sweden, among "hard-to-manage" cases in mental hospitals. A hunt for XYY men in Scottish hospitals for the criminally insane and maximum-security prisons turned up a surprising number. Studies in the U.S. had similar results. The typical XYY male was pictured as tall, acned, violent, impulsive, with low intelligence and a history of crime, sexual assault, homosexuality and other antisocial behavior. It was said that Richard Speck, slayer of eight nurses in Chicago in 1967, was an XYY. Lawyers in France and Australia pleaded insanity for XYY criminals; they won acquittal in the first country and a reduced sentence in the second. A test case, at this time of writing, is in progress in Los Angeles. Meanwhile, killfish with genetic patterns equivalent to the human XYY had been bred at Downstate Medical Center, in Brooklyn, and they were extraordinarily competitive and combative.

As usual, a little more research showed that a simple key to things as complex as aggression and criminality was not really at hand. Only above-average height has turned out to be consistent in XYY men; impulsive behavior is also quite common, but not thoroughly consistent. So far, all studies have been carried out in prisons and asylums; a study of XYY's in the general population has not yet been done. The French defendant received a lower sentence than usual, but the decision did not say why. The Australian criminal was found unfit for trial on grounds of severe epilepsy and low intelligence, not his XYY condition. It turns out that Richard Speck is not an XYY at all. The chief of research at Atascadero State Hospital in California, where XYY Ray Tanner awaits trail for criminal assault, is Dr. Frank Vanasek. He says that no known behavior traits are caused by chromosomes. "I can see how a potential for aggression, for example, can be inherited, but whether the potential becomes expressed is dependent on a very large number of factors, including environment. This is a far more subtle thing than is being made out." It is a long way from killfish behavior to human behavior. There may well be a link between the XYY syndrome, impulsiveness and criminal behavior, including sexual assaultiveness. But serious research has been going on for only a few years, and the idea of an aggressive supermale is not only a premature but an unlikely conclusion. Late in 1970 the National Institutes of Mental Health released a report, written by psychologist Saleem Shah, to cool off speculations by scientists, policy makers, the press and public about a causal link between the XYY condition and deviance. It said that research is still inconclusive and at most shows that "the individual with an XYY chromosomal anomaly appears to incur some increased risks of developing behavioral problems."

The development of cell genetics during the past decade has made chromatin sexing a standard definition of gender. The International Amateur Athletic Federation, the world governing body for track and field events, insisted on the test for competitors in 1966 because of participation in international events by "ladies" of dubious gender from Eastern Europe. In 1967 three Russian and one Rumanian "female" athletes failed to show up for the European Cup meet. Polish track star Ewa Klobukowska, co-holder of the women's world 100-meter-dash record, was disqualified. The tests had shown "one chromosome too many"—a remark interpreted by one American geneticist to mean that she is probably an XO/XYY mosaic.

If track-and-field officials felt a problem had been solved by chromatin sexing, sex researchers did not. Many hermaphrodites have nothing whatever wrong with their genes. If nongenetic hermaphrodites were as free of homosexuality as sufferers of Turner's and Klinefelter's syndrome, the proof that homosexuality is developmental, not constitutional, would be final. Precisely that evidence has appeared during the past fifteen years. The research was carried on at the Pediatric Endocrine Clinic of Johns Hopkins Hospital. There, during the fifties and sixties, Drs. John Money and Joan and John Hampson reviewed three hundred cases of hermaphroditism described in English-language medical literature, and found seventy-six cases of their own. For purposes of definition, they broke down gender into seven factors, the genetic and six others—a classification that makes sense in terms of physical development.

When an egg and sperm fuse, a person's genetic code is set. At first every fetus, regardless of sex, has the same sort of rudimentary genital tissue. Internally there are undifferentiated gonads, and both a mullerian duct (from which female genitals can develop) and a wolffian duct (from which male genitals can form). Externally, both sexes have a genital groove topped by a small bud of tissue. Around the third month the genes probably trigger a mechanism that starts sexual differentiation. At this point, chromosomes probably stop guiding the process, and the fetus' own hormones take over. In a female, the undifferentiated gonads become ovaries, the mullerian duct develops into female internal organs, and the wolffian duct atrophies. The genital groove becomes a vulva and the bud a clitoris. In a male, the gonads become testes, the wolffian duct turns into male internal structures, and the mullerian duct withers. The genital groove closes to form the scrotum, and the bud grows into a penis.

If the genetic process has been normal, the hormonal may not be. In either case, the result is often incomplete differentiation, an unfinished male or female—perhaps with a penoclitoris and something between an unfinished vulva and an unfinished scrotum. There are other possibilities, but there is never a penis and a clitoris, a vulva and a scrotum, for these are alternative developments of the same basic tissue.

Considering these facts of development, Money and the Hampsons set forth these components of gender: first is chromosomal sex, XX or XY or abnormal. Second is gonadal sex, the presence of ovaries or testicles. Third is hormonal sex, including the physical characteristics hormones produce, such as facial hair in men and breast development in women. (Since each sex produces both male and female sex hormones, and since glands other than the gonads produce hormones affecting sex, hormonal sex is distinct from gonadal sex.) The fourth factor is the accessory internal sex organs—the uterus in women, the prostate in men. Fifth, the external genitals. Sixth is sex of assignment and rearing—being designated male or female at birth and reared accordingly. Last is gender role, a person's own sense of being male or female. In most people, the seven components are consistently male or female. In hermaphroditism, one or several of these components contradict the others.

Some abnormalities of the internal and external sex organs occur for reasons still unknown, without genetic, gonadal or hormonal abnormalities. A man may be born normal except for a penis about the size of a clitoris, which never grows larger. Or he may possess a uterus and fallopian tubes in addition to normal male organs (and never know it). A woman may be born with closure of the vagina. Sometimes the appearance of a baby is ambiguous, with a penoclitoris and a blind vaginal pouch. Sometimes an otherwise normal male develops breasts at puberty. And rarely—only sixty cases recorded in Europe and the United States in a century—there is a so-called true hermaphrodite. This person is usually a genetic female, but possessing a pair of ovaries and a pair of testicles, or else one ovary and one testicle. The body may show various elements of both sexes at birth and after puberty, being predominantly male, predominantly female or ambiguous.

Some people have chromosomal abnormalities but no external or internal sexual abnormalities. But in Klinefelter's and Turner's syndromes, sex-chromosome defects produce sexual and other defects. Or sometimes genetic damage disturbs the function of the gonads, with effects on physical development; one of the commonest forms of hermaphroditism today, the adrenogenital syndrome, has such a cause. A victim of this disorder is female in every way—chromosomes, gonads, hormones, internal sex organs—but externally looks like a male with an empty scrotum. Such a girl is usually labeled male at birth, raised as a boy and brought for treatment when her breasts start developing at puberty. The cause is a gene mistakenly directing the adrenal glands of a fetus to produce male sex hormones instead of cortisone. This masculinizes the fetus' external sex organs only: the labia fuse into an empty scrotum, and the clitoris develops to penile size. The condition often occurs several times in the progeny of one couple. An analogous condition occurred in the fifties, when the hormone progestin was used for a while to prevent miscarriages, and it affected some fetuses as would extra male sex hormones.

There is a male equivalent—male in chromosomes and gonads, but externally female. The reason for this testicular feminizing syndrome, or androgen insensitivity syndrome, may also be genetic; it seems to run in families and to be maternally transmitted. The male fetus is unable to use its own androgen, so it fails to develop external male genitals. The infant looks like an externally normal female; there is a blind vagina, and two lumps in the groin where testicles are hidden. Female development continues at puberty except for lack of menstruation and absence of pubic hair.

There are other kinds of hermaphroditism, combining various degrees of apparent maleness, femaleness and ambiguity. Most people decide a person's sex on the basis of the external genitals at birth. During the past decade, some scientists have relied on the chromosomes alone to assign gender. Both systems can produce ridiculous results. Imagine a girl with the adrenogenital syndrome (and a penis) and a man with testicular feminizing syndrome (and a vagina). Would love and sex between them be "normal"? They look like nearly normal men and women—but genetically the man is a woman, the woman a man. Or if a chromosomal male with testicular feminizing syndrome (and a vagina) loves a Klinefelter's syndrome case (who has a penis and two female X chromosomes)? If an adrenogenital-syndrome female (with a penis) falls in love with a normal female (both are genetic females), is that homosexual? If that female with a penis falls in love with a normal man, and these two people with penises got into bed together, would *that* be homosexual, even though genetically one is a woman?

So no one element, from chromosomes to external sex organs, can be the single criterion for gender. However, the most important two are the nonbiological ones. Money and the Hampsons broke down their seventy-six cases by the seven categories and found that the only factors that almost always agree are gender identity and the sex of assignment and rearing. In other words, whatever people are labeled and raised to be, that is what they think they are and live as—no matter what the genes, gonads or even external genitals indicate to the contrary.

Of the seventy-six intersexual patients, chromosomes disagreed with rearing in nineteen. Hormones and secondary sex characteristics contradicted rearing in twenty-seven. There were twenty-three, said Money, who "had lived for more than two thirds of their lives with a contradiction between external genital morphology and assigned sex. For one reason or another, they did not receive surgical correction of their genital deformity in infancy, but lived with a contradictory genital appearance for at least five and for as many as forty-seven years. In all but one instance, the person had succeeded in coming to terms with his, or her anomaly, and had a gender role and orientation wholly consistent with assigned sex and rearing."

Money and the Hampsons said that gender is mentally fixed so early, so indelibly, that mankind has always assumed it is inborn. But here was proof that in fact it is learned—perhaps by a process, said Money, akin to imprinting in animals. A sense of being male or female, wrote Money, "is built up cumulatively through . . . casual and unplanned learning, through explicit instruction and inculcation, and through spontaneously putting two and two together to make sometimes four and sometimes, erroneously, five."

Let us say a female was masculinized before birth because her mother took progestin to prevent miscarriage. She was born looking like a malformed male, with a penis but no testicles. By the age of eighteen months, she was at a critical peak in learning that she was male. By two and a half, she was fully established psychologically as male: her mannerisms, dreams, daydreams, play preferences, physical self-image, topics of conversation, all were male. With puberty she would grow facial hair, develop strong muscles and a deep voice if given testosterone. Her gender identity, sexual fantasies and sex practices would become more fixedly male, to the extent that this was physically possible.

Such a person could be made female through surgery and hormone treatment. But Money and the Hampsons found that to do so was psychologically risky or even catastrophic. She would still identify as a male, think and feel as a male. Without her penis, she would feel like a male who has been castrated and forced into homosexuality. The only course is to make this person as normally male as possible. In the same way, a male with testicular feminizing syndrome, raised as a female because of his external genitals, is convinced forever of being female. Once he is past early childhood, the only safe medical treatment is to remove his hidden testicles, give him estrogen to make him look more female, and surgically create a vagina for him—though genetically and gonadally this should be called castration.

Eleven of the Johns Hopkins hermaphrodites underwent surgery and hormone treatment to change their sex. The four who were treated when they were younger than nine months showed no adverse psychological effects. The other seven ranged from fifteen months to sixteen years. All but one (changed at twenty-seven months) showed chronic psychological difficulties as a result. Money and the Hampsons concluded that eighteen months is the usual threshold for fixing gender identity; two and a half is probably the point of no return, and four is definitely too late to change a person's sex without leaving permanent conflict. A person who believes he is one sex, changed to look like the other (even if the other is more biologically correct), will feel homosexual or may even have a psychotic break.

For instance, a woman with Turner's syndrome, raised as a female, but lacking an X chromosome and ovaries, usually has normal female identity, with the usual female fantasies of courtship, sex, marriage and motherhood. Dr. Robert Stoller, a Los Angeles psychiatrist who has done important research on sex and gender, has reported two cases of hermaphroditism in which misguided physicians gave biology precedence over the patients' own sense of gender. One was a child brought up without question as a boy, who at six was diagnosed as a normal female except for external genitals—a case of adrenogenital syndrome. If his ovaries, uterus and vagina had been removed, his sense of identity would not have been endangered. But for moralistic reasons medical authorities had his "penis" removed, his "scrotum" split to create labia. At twelve this girl was "a grotesque caricature of a girl," who said she did not ever want to go out with boys, marry or have children, but would like to be a cowboy or auto racer when she grew up.

Stoller also reports a case of Turner's syndrome in which the girl was told at fourteen by a gynecologist that she "might be a boy." When Stoller first saw her she was sixteen, and after two years of increasingly bizarre behavior had been diagnosed schizophrenic. She said such things as "I should have been left to die. I am no good to society. . . . My breasts were given to me for a time. Who knows when they will be taken away? That is my fear. My terrible fear. Not to be like a woman. . . . I must learn appropriate ways to show emotion. It just builds up in me and then I have to escape. All of a sudden I feel very *womanly*. . . . No man can touch me. He will never know my inner self, my personality, because I don't have one. It is too odd. He won't understand." Stoller reassured her that her femininity was not in question, and with treatment her psychosis disappeared.

On the other hand, Stoller treated a girl with Turner's syndrome who had no such problems. At eighteen, like most XO women, she was "unremarkably feminine in her behavior, dress, social and sexual desires, and fantasies, undistinguishable in these regards from other girls in Southern California." She was told she was sterile because of an anatomical defect, and that her undeveloped vagina could be surgically corrected. This was done, and she married. Her grief at not being able to have children passed. Six years later she seemed happy and without serious troubles, excited and gratified by intercourse with her husband. She has never considered herself anything but a woman.

Of all the thirty-one intersexed patients at Johns Hopkins whose hormones contradicted their rearing, all but five felt sure of their assigned gender. The five who were ambivalent, unable to fully accept their imputed gender and live up to it, showed severe psychological disturbance. Money believes that when hermaphrodites are uncertain and disturbed about their gender identity, it is because the parents were unsure and disturbed. In a small number of cases in which the parents accepted the child's intersexuality as such with relative calm, the children did too: they were the few people who had a mixed gender identity without deep disturbances, and who could adjust to sex-change treatment at a later age with relative ease.

John Money has also studied homosexuals, transvestites and transsexuals; as a group, they show nothing unusual in the seven components of gender. Others have duplicated his finding. Neither physical nor "psychic" hermaphroditism has anything to do with homosexuality. In most homosexuals, gender identity is not deeply distorted; though their choice of sex object is homosexual, they are in no doubt about being male or female. If gender identity is something learned—sometimes despite anatomy and physiological functions—then choice of sex object, which is less basic, must be learned as well.

Now that this was established, the way was open to explaining two of the most puzzling and bizarre phenomena of human sexuality—transvestites, who masquerade as the opposite sex, and transsexuals, who actually believe they belong to the opposite sex, and seek surgery and hormones to make their bodies conform to their gender identity. With greater understanding of these people, a new picture begins to develop of maleness and femaleness, heterosexuality and homosexuality.

21

The Erotic Disguise

The Old Testament said that if a man dressed as a woman or a woman as a man, "their blood shall be upon them." A Viking woman could divorce her husband if he wore feminine clothes. In California a person disguised as the opposite sex can and probably will be arrested. In Germany, Sweden and a few other Western countries, it has been legal at various times during the past century to cross-dress if one has a police permit, issued at the direction of a psychiatrist. But in most of the West, and in much of the world, society's mockery, rage and legal vengeance are set in motion by sexual masquerade.

Traditionally, most people have thought that there is some man in every woman, some woman in each man, and increasing amounts of cross-identification progressively cause effeminacy in men and masculinity in women, homosexuality, transvestism and transsexualism. Such thinking fails to account for male homosexuals who are not effeminate or for heterosexual transvestites. One of the major steps in modern sex research has been to start clarifying these various conditions by separating the concepts of sex, gender, gender role and choice of sexual object.

Research with physical hermaphrodites showed that sex (male or female) is biological—the sum of genes, gonads, hormones and sex organs. Gender (masculine or feminine) is psychological, learned during the first two years of life, primarily from one's mother. Gender role—the behavior and characteristics appropriate to each sex—is psychological and social. In most people, sex and gender and gender role all agree. The Hampsons and Money helped make this clear by studying rare cases in which gender was learned in contradiction to sex. Now research with two rare, bizarre conditions, transvestism and transsexualism, is further disentangling the elements of what we take for granted as normal manhood and womanhood.

Identification with both parents is central to the development of gender identity. Some seventy years of psychoanalysis and developmental psychology have produced a paradigm for the process of identification, much of it complex and debatable in detail. But in basic, brief form, it is this:

Every infant's first love is its mother; she can bring him safety or terror, bliss or destruction. The touch of her body, her love and care, create a feeling of literally being one with her. Gradually an infant becomes a child, realizes it is separate from its mother, and develops an independent image of itself. Still, it retains from infancy an image of itself as a female like mother. To a little girl, it is herself as a child version of mother; to a boy, it is himself as a little female. Even as a boy is learning from his mother to be male and masculine, even after he starts separating from her and identifying with his father, part of him is, in fantasy, a female. Every man can remember, if he will, imagining that he had his mother's soft body and soft voice; having breasts, lacking a penis, being pregnant and giving birth. He probably at some time experimented with urinating sitting down; tucked his penis between his legs to imagine himself as a female; wondered whether being fat enough could give him hips and breasts like a woman's. He may have tried on mother's shoes, jewelry and cosmetics; cooked with her in the kitchen, cleaned a room with her, watched her dress and undress, laughed or cried with her, and learned to associate tenderness, emotionality and creative play with her. And since one's past is never lost, only covered over by later strata of experience, a little female remains within each man.

In a similar way, a girl eventually separates somewhat from her mother and begins to identify with her father as well. She adores his physical characteristics, his power and assertiveness, and wants to share in them. She may join him in rough play, athletics, traditionally masculine interests and activities; imitate his physical and emotional toughness and control; try on his coat and shoes; fantasy having a penis; try to urinate standing up; wonder whether being thin and flat could make her a man. All her life, there will be within her an image of herself as a little male.

If a child develops healthily, this identification with the opposite sex causes no major problems. In fact, it produces a diverse and flexible personality. But if a child overidentifies with the parent of the other sex (or excessively fears doing so) there may be mild or acute personality problems as a result. If a girl has a cold or harsh mother, she reaches out to her father with exaggerated need and expectation, hoping he will make up her deficit in parental love. He may encourage her by being unconsciously seductive or by competing with his wife for the girl's love. The girl's love for her father becomes intense, her identification with him overdeveloped. The little boy created in her fantasies becomes a larger part of her; she is tomboyish and grows up to be a masculine woman—competitive, aggressive, controlled, with mannerisms and interests usually seen more in men. She (and others) may suspect herself of inadequate femininity, even of having a "lesbian streak." Though she is likely to have some psychosexual problems, she may be quite heterosexual.

The same early background may cause apparently opposite results. A girls' masculine identification and love for her father may frighten her. If her father is cold, she fears rejection; or if the relationship gets too intimate, she fears incest or, paradoxically, going over the line and becoming predominantly masculine. So to escape incestuous love or loss of femininity, a girl may use denial and reaction formation to bury the little boy within herself. She says there is nothing competitive, hard or domineering about her, nothing male. She is all soft seductiveness, in fact a bitch-princess parody of femininity—fleeing the male within, the little girl in love with her father.

Similar problems lie along the road of a boy's development. If his mother gives him love but also encouragement to separate from her, he accepts a degree of love for her and identification with her, even as he separates and begins to identify more with his father. But if she clings to the boy, he clings to her. If the father is cold, withdrawn or abusive, the boy has further reason to cling to her. If the mother is rejecting and domineering, he may hang on to her in hope of finally wresting more of her frugal love. From clinging and attachment to his mother, a boy develops powerful identification with her. He may grow up to be somewhat effeminate. He is passive, solicitous, maternal, openly emotional, with feminine interests and behavior; and perhaps fully heterosexual, despite others' and his own occasional doubts.

But a boy may be frightened by his increasing identification with his mother. He fears the incestuous love, and the imagined punishment of castration. He fears that if he identifies more, the female within him will take over, he will become female himself. So he tries to deny the girl within by insisting there's nothing soft, emotional and dependent about him. He becomes hyperaggressive, callous, unbendable, a Muscle Beach or barracks-room parody of masculinity—fleeing the girl within, the little boy in love with his mother.

So effeminacy in a man and masculinity in a woman do not necessarily indicate homosexuality; cross-identification can be fairly strong without changing one's choice of sexual object. But because gender role develops along with gender identity, a threat to one seems a threat to the other. This is especially true in males. A boy must wrench himself away from the first object of his love and identification in order to become a man. A woman's final identification is the same as her first—feminine. This is probably why masculinity is more vulnerable to threat, breakdown and distortion than femininity; and therefore why more men than women in every society studied for such things show extreme casualties in psychosexual development—impotence, homosexuality, sado-masochism, fetishism, transvestism, transsexualism.

If a woman's adult identity breaks down under internal or external pressure, she will find herself reliving the fantasies and identity of a little girl. She has lost her adulthood for the moment, but not her femininity. If a man's identity breaks down, he becomes a baby, a nonmale dependent on its mother and identifying with her. His masculinity has collapsed. Society shores up the male in his struggle to identify with his father by equating everything nonmale and labeling it with a big NO—passivity, effeminacy, homosexuality, wearing the clothes or other symbolic trappings of femininity. What seems an almost ubiquitous male fear of homosexuality is really much more a fear of being nonmale—a soft helpless thing, without aggression and self-reliance, a sissy, a mama's boy, a "faggot." A woman who is threatened by the competitive, aggressive and other male aspects of her personality may have emotional and sexual problems; but she is less likely than a man to fear losing her gender, becoming a nonwoman. And she is less likely to equate that loss with homosexuality.

So it is hardly strange that society's anxiety is mobilized, as ridicule or persecution, when people flauntingly reverse the gender identities others work so hard to reach and maintain. No wonder that it is more scorned to be a sissy than a tomboy, to be an effeminate male than a masculine woman; that some countries have laws against male homosexuality and transvestism, but do not restrict women; that men's clothes generally do not resemble women's, but that in some times and places women's clothes have resembled (without quite duplicating) men's.

Since we all harbor some cross-identification, cross-dressing appears widely in children's behavior, in dreams and art, in special social situations in which society allows a brief outlet to this otherwise fearsome reversal. One may safely cross-dress at masquerades, during Carnival, Mardi Gras and Halloween. People flirt with cross-identification by laughing at it in such plays as *Charley's Aunt* and *Some Like It Hot*. In *As You Like It*, the sexual disguise has an eerie loveliness, perhaps arousing early positive feelings of cross-identification, and a narcissistic affection for one's own other-sexed self-image.

There is no simple formula for the various degrees and combinations of cross-identification, cross-dressing, effeminacy in men and masculinity in women, homosexuality, and transsexualism. Most of these phenomena can occur alone or in various combinations. Most homosexuals, like most heterosexuals, have no doubt of their gender. Once gender identity is established, at two, it can be distorted or weakened or overlaid by various neurotic problems—with homosexuality, transvestism or various other symptoms as a result. There may even be wishful attempts to be taken for the other gender. But it is known as a wish. The male homosexual knows he is male; his identity is masculine, and so is the majority of his behavior. He wouldn't want to be a woman in body, clothing or manner, The converse holds true for lesbians. Homosexual camp is nothing like the transvestite's desire to be taken for a woman. It is not female impersonation when a homosexual puts on an item of woman's clothing and does a brief bit of female mimicry; when he flips his hand disdainfully on his wrist and calls his lover Mary; when he wraps a table cloth around his waist and mimes to a Dietrich or Streisand record. It has an air of malice and defiant parody, showing how silly women are, how unadmirable. To the extent that identification is involved, much of it is hostile and negative—what classical psychoanalysis calls "identifying with the aggressor."

Freud said that a child tends to identify more strongly with the parent it most fears. One sees this sort of mechanism at work when an adolescent army trainee apes the swagger of a feared, bullying sergeant. He is saying, "I am me, but I can play your game at least as well as you." And so the homosexual camping it up at a gay party is saying, "You see, ladies, I have the advantages of being a man, and on top of that I can play your game more extravagantly than you!" To capture the inner satisfaction this gives, you might assure a person that you wouldn't speak frankly unless you were a devoted friend, and then say the worst things you can get away with.

A small minority of homosexuals do have very strong cross-identification and act it out. This too is usually a mixture of positive and negative identification. The positive identification leads to mincing effeminacy, involvement in housewifery, and a very Nellie performance as lady of the house—a child's picture of a proper lady. To the extent that the identification is negative, a bitchy Mae West appears, a somewhat spasmodic and ferocious parody of woman as a sexual rather than domestic person. (It is significant that the women homosexuals like to mimic or parody are larger-than-life female stars, themselves almost parodies of sexual femininity and lush emotionality—Mae West, Marlene Dietrich, Diana Dors, Barbra Streisand, Judy Garland.) The effeminate homosexual is saying, "You see, Mother, I can be more of a woman than you!" In the same way, the butch lesbian who crops her hair, swears, bullies and clumps aggressively about is not really anxious to be taken for a man—she fears and hates men as much as the effeminate homosexual fears and hates women. She is saying, symbolically, "I'm more a man than my father, the bastard!" There is as much reproach as true emulation.

The effeminate homosexual and masculine lesbian are not transvestites. At most, they may have a slight transvestic trend. The transvestite's prime, and obsessive, sexual pleasure is masquerading as the opposite sex. Such cross-dressing was long assumed to be merely the farthest extreme of homosexuality. Hirschfeld first pointed it out as a distinct phenomenon, and coined the present name for it; he argued that the transvestite is more likely than not to be heterosexual. Early psychoanalysts said transvestism was just a mask for homosexuality. Neither Hirschfeld nor the classical analysts were quite right.

What I will call the true transvestite emphatically claims to be heterosexual. He is or has been married, and a father. However, he may be potent with women only if he dresses as a woman; he may also lie supine, imagining that the woman above him possesses the penis, and he is the woman. Or he may fantasy being a female having lesbian relations with "another woman." Or even that he is a woman and his wife a man. But although homosexuality might appear in such a fantasy, it is absent from his life. He abhors the idea of homosexuality, avoids homosexuals, and feels he has nothing in common with them. Imagining a male partner is just a natural consequence of his fantasy of female gender. In fact, gender probably matters to him far more than sex acts. He is probably low on all kinds of sexual behavior, even largely asexual. He may merely masturbate while viewing himself in drag in a mirror. Eventually even this may cease. His prime or exclusive pleasure is sexual disguise itself, and the satisfaction is more emotional than orgasmic. He may rationalize his impotence on ethical and religious grounds, and wonder why people attach such importance to mere physical sex experience.

If there is a typical family background for the transvestite, it is a cold, harsh mother and an abusive, withdrawn or absent father. He may have lived with older sisters, aunts or other relatives. Sex wasn't talked about at home. Masculine aggression was discouraged by mother, and demanded in what seemed impossible amounts by father. In some cases, but far from all, an older female relative dressed the boy in girls' clothes, or the father did so to shame him for being effeminate. Most likely, the boy cross-dressed in secret; if discovered, he wasn't strongly hindered by his mother, and the detached father did not intervene.

The transvestite may have begun in childhood with a fetishistic interest in his mother's (or sister's or aunt's) clothes. He masturbated with his mother's underwear or while dressed in it. Perhaps he continued, as he moved toward obsessive interest in female garb and disguise, to have a fetishistic interest in fur or leather or high-heeled shoes or silk panties. He may have had masochistic fantasies of humiliation and submission along with cross-dressing. One transvestite has claimed from his experience and that of his friends that transvestites have fetishistic preferences by which they can be divided into "overs" and "unders." The "overs" begin by fascination with shoes and go on to total impersonation of women as they get older. The "unders" start out fascinated with undergarments, and go through life wearing panties or a bra beneath their masculine clothing, experiencing terrible frustration and tension if deprived of the opportunity.

Actually, the distinctions probably aren't so fine for most transvestites. The transvestite feels tense in male clothes; to be without female garb causes mounting internal pressure, and cross-dressing relieves it. He may say, "When I dress it feels as if I have a continuous orgasm," or he may just describe "a sexual glow," or say, "I feel myself at last." The need to dress has the quality of a compulsion, an addiction. Actually, the man, in his male role, tends to be undistinguished, even shabby or drab, with a timid personality. But he may not be at all effeminate, and no one suspects his transvestism.

When he gets home at night, he can take out his female clothes, underwear, wigs, cosmetics. He assumes his female role, for whom he has a name, and whom he speaks of as another person. He dresses, and he loses his self-consciousness, perhaps his timidity or phobias. He may have electrolysis to remove facial and body hair, estrogen to enlarge his breasts and hips. If the estrogen destroys what potency he had, it may be a relief, for erections only remind him of his male sexuality. Unless one has met and spoken with an accomplished transvestite, it is impossible to imagine how perfectly he can impersonate a woman, from physical appearance to minute body movements—flicking an ash, looking at a watch. The transvestite may look like a glamorous young woman or a suburban matron. He is far from the homosexual's campy parodies, and convinces one thoroughly of the difference.

The transvestite's obsessive interest in feminine garb and role shows in letters written to *Transvestia,* a magazine published in Los Angeles "by, for and about transvestites" by Charles Virginia Prince. One letter describes the exciting venture of shopping at a tall-girls' dress shop. Another discusses whether it is fittingly feminine for a transvestite to wear slacks, as some women do. Another comes from a young soldier in Vietnam who counts with agony amid rocket barrages the days till he can cross-dress again. One letter describes the woman within, and "the exquisite joy of being able to be Dorothy for the evening, manicuring and painting my nails and feeling that everything that I'm wearing is just right. To do so would be reaching the heavenliness that other tv's know so well. . . . Dorothy feels that there still is a great deal more that she can learn to be the best possible kind of lady. . . . A polaroid with a self-timer is helpful but Dorothy has to learn natural poses—proper angles and how to avoid the double-chin look. Really now, dieting is the answer—any girl knows that."

But the transvestite does not want a sex-change operation. He is male and knows it. In fact, the whole point of his behavior is to be a male passing. It is a common fantasy among transvestites to become famous as a female athlete or singer, and then at the height of his glory to reveal his maleness to the world by dropping his voice or his panties. Though some transvestites are incredibly skillful at impersonating women, others produce such grotesque parodies that one can't help thinking they really want their maleness known. Unfortunately, their exhibitionism leaves them torn between being alone with their female roles or taking the risk of walking the streets, being arrested and facing public exposure and total ruin.

The constant fear of discovery is only one of the transvestite's continuing problems. He tends to live a guilty, isolated life. He avoids the gay world because he doesn't want homosexual love-making, but merely to pass as a woman. Other transvestites are as secretive as himself, and difficult to find. He may find a place on the fringe of the theatrical world or the underworld. (The majority of female impersonators, to my knowledge, are effeminate homosexuals with transvestic tendencies, and are quite at home in the gay world.) The transvestite may occasionally go to prostitutes and pay just to dress as a woman and have someone to talk to girl-to-girl. Or he may go to enact a ritual of debasement dressed as a servant girl, ordered to scrub floors and humiliate himself. If he is a very skillful impersonator, he may actually be able to live as a woman undetected—with a driver's license and social security card in a female name and accepted at work as a female.

The transvestite is likely to have an immature and dependent personality. He also sometimes "purges" himself of his deviation and its trappings. When he was a child, he felt fits of guilt, disgust and remorse after wearing or masturbating with his mother's clothes. As an adult he periodically relives them. He throws away his dresses and high-heeled shoes, his wig catalogs and transvestite pornography, his expensive jewelry and perfume. He swears never to cross-dress again. Although he doesn't want to go to bed with men, except perhaps in occasional fantasies, he can't explain his condition to himself except as a form of homosexuality. He may go to a psychotherapist in deep remorse and self-doubt after a purge. But in most cases he leaves treatment as soon as he feels the remorse lifting or gets any reassurance that he is not homosexual. He resumes cross-dressing.

But there is a good chance the transvestite will marry, probably keeping his deviation secret. He can have occasional intercourse and father children, with the aid of fantasies. On holidays, business trips or long visits to the bathroom after dinner he indulges his craving to cross-dress. But the secret will drive a wedge between him and his wife. Not the least problem is his burning envy of her for being able to dress and act like a woman so well, and all the time! Eventually he may confess his transvestism. She may leave him or say that she doesn't care as long as she doesn't have to see it. On the other hand, she may accept his transvestism. There are also women who go out with men and then marry them, knowing that they are transvestites. These women not only accept but even enjoy the man's cross-dressing. They help him learn to dress, make up, walk and speak like a woman. The problem remains of keeping the secret from the rest of the world, including the children. In a few cases, the children are informed so that they won't learn the truth on their own—and spread it around.

Some transvestites combine with their cross-dressing various degrees of fetishism, homosexuality and sado-masochism (especially the "bondage" type, in which a male is the slave-in-petticoats of a domineering woman). There are family resemblances and fine but significant differences between these deviations. Many pioneer psychoanalysts thought transvestism was simply an extension of fetishism, and it is true that in some cases of transvestism the fetishistic element is strong. Fetishism was one of the first sexual deviations to be understood and successfully treated psychodynamically. In simplest terms, the fetishist protected himself as a child from incestuous urges and the fantasied punishment for them by substituting a symbolic object for his real sexual goal. The commonest fetishistic objects are the underwear that conceal a woman's genitals and breasts, and body parts or garments furthest removed from the genitals, such as hair, shoes, feet, gloves. Like many other deviants of all kinds, the fetishist is playing wolf-in-sheep's-clothing with himself, focusing his interest on something less than the real thing. He says, in effect, "You see, Mother, I don't want you. I don't even want to do anything nasty with any woman. I just love shoes. What's dirty about that?" The transvestite's version is, "Mother, how could I be thinking of anything nasty when I'm really a nice girl, not a nasty male?" His version of the wolf-in-sheep's-clothing is the penis in skirts. The thrill of passing, of successfully bearing the phallus intact into the world in a successful deception, is a devious triumph over rejection and castration. The fantasy of revealing his maleness to the world is the ultimate masculine triumph as he dares to conceive it. Like all neuroses, it is an uneconomical solution to life's problems, based on the unnecessary assumption that a leaky boat is better than none.

Theoretically one can make a case for not distinguishing between fetishists, heterosexual transvestites, homosexual transvestites, masochistic transvestites, other masochists and so on. And they do represent, in most cases, variations on one basic theme. But the distinctions teach us more than the similarities. No matter what the similarities, one must still try to make sense of the very different patterns of being a married, heterosexual transvestite and a sado-masochistic homosexual with a strong fetishistic interest in chains. The emotional aura that surrounds fetishism, so beautifully and sensitively described by Stekel half a century ago, is very different from the impression one carries away from a talk with a successful transvestite. Any sensitive novelist would portray two very different emotional climates.

It has been easy for some theorists to lump together very different phenomena in one verbal or intellectual category simply because they refuse to step outside their offices and study the worlds their deviant patients live in. I have seen psychiatrists utterly puzzled by a belated first look at the transvestite or sado-masochistic pornography their patients avidly read. Obviously the pornographers know something about these conditions the doctors don't. One of the most fascinating and convincing analyses of transvestism has been made by Dr. Hugo Beigel, who compared transvestic pornography, the accounts his patients gave of their lives, and his own perceptions of both. The results strike at the core of traditional analytic and behavioral theories about transvestism.

Back in 1921, the analyst Sadger had shrewdly summed up the transvestite's mental formula as being: "As a female, I should be loved more by Mother, and indeed by everyone." Implicit in this formula is the child's interpretation of his family life and his adaptation to it. Yet in even the most recent writings on transvestism, one finds the ancient belief that transvestism is essentially a matter not of adaptation but conditioning: a mother hostile to masculinity cross-dressed her boy. The mothers of some transvestites are, in fact, malignantly envious and hostile to masculinity and did cross-dress their children. Some transvestites were cross-dressed by sisters, aunts or others. But Hugo Beigel says that of twenty-three transvestites he has treated, not one was kept in dresses and curls. Two admitted that, when asked to explain their transvestism, they told the dresses-and-curls story because they knew it would be accepted. Beigel also points out that years ago people kept children of both sexes in dresses till they were a few years old without producing regiments of transvestites; now that the practice has ended, transvestites still exist. Furthermore, the common statement of transvestites that their parents really wanted a girl often turns out on investigation to be a recriminatory conclusion rather than a historical fact. Looking at all the curious differences between his cases and the usual assumptions about transvestites' backgrounds, Beigel concludes, "This conspicuous discrepancy makes one wonder whether researchers, too, have not been misled."

While treating transvestites, Beigel also studied transvestite pornography, to compare the fantasies there with what he was discovering clinically. With co-worker Robert Feldman he examined the books, stories, photographs and cartoon strips on which transvestites spend so much money and time. The first striking characteristic of all the transvestite literature was that the protagonist of the story was always innocent. He never wanted to cross-dress and began against his will. An older powerful woman—stepmother, aunt, unknown woman in a position of authority—gave him the choice of being feminized or suffering a far worse fate. The hero must submit, and this is the turning point of the plot and his life. He has feared and hated the domineering woman, fought the change to female clothes and role. But finally he sees that it is unavoidable, predestined; and when he accepts his feminine role, he and his female subduer mutually accept each other.

There are three common patterns for this in the transvestic literature. In one, the female demands sewing, cleaning and other feminine service from the hero, and punishes any rebellion on his part. He submits, and the mistress initiates him into sex as a reward; she either becomes his lover or presents him with another female as a partner. In a second type of story, the hero gives up his male sex organs along with his male role. He allows himself to be castrated by a female surgeon—perhaps on altruistic grounds, such as idealistic love for a lesbian. Castrated, he becomes the "lesbian" lover of the controlling woman. In the third version, the transvestite's mother is in the story, but on the sidelines. She is aloof and disapproving of her son. He goes off on adventures, posing as a woman (always of necessity, of course) and achieves triumphs impossible had he remained in male garb. To ruin some malevolent plot, he has to pass as a girl and live with young girls, as a nurse in a hospital or as a female soldier in barracks. The chief nurse or superior officer—the domineering woman—knows his real identity. But she forgets about the hero or is replaced. Eventually the girls dress and undress before the hero, consult with him about clothes and underwear. He has no sexual desire for them. At the end of the story, the hero returns to his mother, famous for his exploits. She now accepts him with love.

In a small number of stories, the mother herself persuades the hero to dress as a girl. As a reward she gives love, caresses and gratitude; she dresses and undresses before him and sleeps in the same bed. In another small number of stories, the hero remains resentful of the woman who forced him to be feminine; there is always, in this case, a happy homosexual ending—for instance, the hero, now a female impersonator, marries a man.

As the hero of one of these stories says, "It is the women who hold all the power." They prohibit masculinity, aggression and sexuality; the hero must relinquish these qualities to have love, protection and success in life. He must live as a girl among girls to prove he is just one of them, not a male marauder. Sex is sacrificed for higher reasons, and that wins his mother's love.

Beigel's clinical data now make more sense. During the first few years of life, a boy develops the male gender identity he will never lose. But as he becomes older and more aggressive, his mother may reprove him with comments such as, "You're behaving just like a man!" His sexual awareness and experimentation is upsetting to her. Also, he can no longer stay in his mother's room while she dresses and undresses. He must knock before entering. Especially if a sister is born, and she retains the privileges of intimacy, he becomes convinced that his maleness is robbing him of the old paradisical closeness with his mother. He fingers or wears his mother's clothes, nostalgically trying to recover the old intimacy. He decides that his mother prefers girls. Lack of a warm, strong father, the presence of rival sisters, a mother who encourages or condones effeminacy will make his belief stronger. The boy conceals his debilitating maleness by hiding it with a dress, and relieves his guilt by saying to himself that his mother forced him to do so. He is saying, "Love me as you love my sisters" or "Love me as you would if I weren't a boy."

In transvestite fiction, as in the transvestite's imagination, the hostile mother is split off from the loving mother, to appear as a separate person. In most children's imagination there is a picture of mother as aggressive and sadistic; she is symbolically endowed with the male sex organ. This phallic woman exists in Western folklore as the witch—the destructive female with pointed hat, long nose and broomstick who in the Middle Ages was said to make men impotent by stealing their penises. A boy clinging to a hostile mother and identifying with her has an image of her (and perhaps of himself) as a phallic woman.

This makes clear the bondage element so often associated with cross-dressing. Transvestite bondage pornography shows a tyrannical woman with high-heeled boots, whips, a hard, smooth body with bomblike buttocks and breasts. This phallic witch-mother is enslaving a sweet, innocent, slight, defenseless male, forcing him to feminize himself. He complies, and becomes feminine in everything but having a penis beneath his disguise. He is now made over in the image of his phallic mother. And in fact some transvestites see themselves in dreams as hermaphrodites, with breasts and a penis; many dream of a sexual partner who is a hermaphroditic mirror image of their own double identification.

Some transvestites are homosexual. In almost every transvestite, to the extent that there is cross-identification, there is an urge for a male partner to complete the fantasy, and therefore at least some buried homosexual imagery. Some psychiatric accounts make a good case for the existence of powerful submerged homosexual trends in all transvestites. One tells of a transvestite who said he didn't cross-dress to attract men but was stopped in the street once and kissed by an elderly man (who apparently thought he was a woman); the patient was so shocked to find how much he liked being kissed, that he fled from the man—and soon from therapy as well. One of Robert Stoller's transvestite patients, frightened that he might be homosexual, began to go to gay bars and talk to homosexuals to explore the matter. He became increasingly disturbed. He had his wife dress as a prostitute, attach an artificial penis to herself, and bugger him. He had a paranoid psychotic break as a result, and during the ensuing hours of suicidal and homicidal panic, he said he realized that his transvestism had been an attempt to hide his homosexual desires from himself. Having faced this, he soon stopped cross-dressing, and a year later still had not resumed it; he seemed thoroughly cured.

Even if such content lies buried in most transvestites—which is not certain—it is an oversimplification to call transvestism a mask for homosexuality. Transvestism without homosexual object choice seems to be a distinct syndrome. When transvestism (not just camping) coincides with open homosexuality, the pattern is probably also a distinctive one. There is not enough research to be sure of this, but the homosexual transvestite may tend to be sexually very active, more strikingly infantile in personality than the nonhomosexual transvestite, and usually unable to carry on the same social façade for years. If he is a good passer, he may work as a stage female impersonator, move in homosexual circles, or even support himself as a "female" prostitute. He binds his penis and scrotum, picks men up in bars or on the street, and takes them to a dimly lit room. He claims that he is menstruating, recovering from an abortion, or just prefers "frenching" (fellatio), and offers oral or anal intercourse. The customer is usually none the wiser.

Some of these transvestites pass over the line after a promiscuous youth and young adulthood as a "male" or "female" prostitute and become transsexuals. They save their earnings as prostitutes for sex-change therapy. After the change, they advertise themselves as feminized men; in contrast, the typical transsexual wants to be accepted as a normal woman, his male past forgotten. The gender disturbance of the homosexual transvestite may generally be deeper than that of the nonhomosexual transvestite, but not as deep as the transsexual's. This still requires careful, discriminating research.

Transvestism is very rare in women—compulsive cross-dressing as the prime source of psychosexual satisfaction. (Psychologically there is no female equivalent for the male transvestite's fantasied phallic woman; it would be, logically, a penisless male.) As we have seen, butch lesbians don't really disguise themselves as men or try to pass, however much ambivalent masculine identity they may possess, or however much hostile masculine parody they may carry out. There are lesbians who get added emotional pleasure by cross-dressing, and their background resembles that of many male homosexual cross-dressers—a harsh, cold mother, distant father, envied siblings of the opposite sex. Some have so strong a masculine identification that they will only take the active role in bed, refusing even to let their genitals be touched by their partners. And there is an occasional case that seems equivalent to male transvestism—for instance, a girl who assumed male clothes and a male first name, and who had such contempt for women that she never practiced lesbian relations. Her fantasies were of changing into a man and having homosexual relations with "another man" (like the male transvestite's fantasy of being a woman and having "lesbian" love affairs with women). There have been some historical cases of women passing as men and serving in a profession and even in the army for years without being detected; we are not sure today whether these people were variously transvestites, transsexuals or intersexuals.

Transvestism usually starts early in life and reflects a virulent family background. Stekel and some others have reported cures of transvestites, but there has been general therapeutic pessimism. Recently a few tentative successes with aversion therapy have been reported, but they must be evaluated with caution. Hugo Beigel reports that of twenty-four transvestites whom he has treated with psychotherapy, fourteen dropped out quickly despite (or perhaps because of) early indications of progress. The other ten patients gave up cross-dressing permanently after fewer than fifty therapeutic sessions. Essential to his unusual success, says Beigel, was convincing the transvestites that they were not, as they believed, female souls in male bodies, but people whose childhood experience had made them depreciate maleness and see femaleness as a cure for their unhappiness. In some cases Beigel used hypnotherapy (many transvestites have difficulty producing accurate early memories and examining their emotions). One transvestite who first told Beigel he had cross-dressed for as long as he could remember, revealed under hypnosis that he'd first done so at seventeen or eighteen, after his sister's marriage, which he considered one more proof that girls have it easier in life than boys.

An instructive case of mixed results comes from Beigel's writings about his cases. A transvestite of twenty-four said his first masturbatory experience occurred when he was thirteen, and coincided with his first cross-dressing, in his mother's clothes. Pressed to give more detail, he recalled that just before this event he had been called on by his demanding, critical father to carry out an unexpected and unwanted responsibility. On the day he first cross-dressed, he had been postponing the task. He went to his parents' bedroom, pulled out his mother's nightgown, and put it on. He felt elation, then guilt and anxiety. He put away the nightgown, threw himself on his own bed, cried, and then masturbated.

Now, at twenty-four, recalling the demands that had led to the scene, he wept and repeated, "Why pick on me? Girls needn't go through these ordeals." As he went on recalling more distant layers of his past, he recounted that his mother had spent much time with him when he was small, kissing and cuddling him when she dressed him, praising his good taste when he handed her items of her clothing to put on. With the arrival of a younger brother, this intimacy ceased. When he had trouble dressing himself, his mother now sharply told him to do it himself; he took off all his clothes and threw them out the window. From then on he shrank from his mother's touch.

As a young adult, he longed for female company. But as soon as a girl showed interest in him, he talked about transvestism and offered to demonstrate; this eliminated most of his prospects pretty quickly. His friends were other male transvestites. Still, he hoped to have some girl look at his feminine wardrobe, to help him zip his dress, lend him a necklace.

In therapy, he recalled more and more feelings of pain at losing the symbiotic paradise of his infancy, when he was mother's only baby. He spontaneously began to cut down on transvestism; eventually, with help, he stopped entirely. During the following five years he had no temptation to go back to cross-dressing, and felt alienated from the transvestite world. Finally he married. But the mate he chose could have come from a piece of transvestite fiction. "She" was a male transsexual who had been converted by hormones and surgery to a female.

Robert Stoller has made some interesting observations on the transvestite's women. His mother hates, envies and is destructive to his masculinity. As an adult he may meet women who enjoy dressing men in women's clothes. Like "fag molls," or "fruit flies," these women go out only with men who are effeminate, extremely passive, homosexual, transvestic or otherwise heterosexually impaired. When the transvestite confesses his problem, the girl is sympathetic. She is what Stoller calls the Succorer. She is warm, affectionate, with a need to rescue and help others. She helps the transvestite learn to pass as a woman, "with an air of innocent enthusiasm, as if the acts of putting lipstick on a man, plucking his eyebrows, or stuffing his brassiere were essentially the same action as teaching these artifices to a teenage girl."

In one such case, the woman accepted a man's transvestism and married him. She later said that when he confessed, he had seemed like "a hurt little boy who needs to be held and loved." When this man, says Stoller, who was powerful and violent, displayed a weakness, she felt a warm tenderness "that masked her sense of triumph. She then eagerly encouraged him in his use of her clothes." The transvestite's wife, like his mother, was glad to help him demasculinize himself.

What these women do not know, says Stoller, is that such "happy" transvestite marriages almost always have a built-in scuttling device. When the husband becomes very successful in his transvestism or in his career, and his confidence becomes greater, the wife no longer has a dependent, grateful sufferer. "The fighting will start; neither will understand what has happened, and they will divorce. I have not seen a transvestite who has been married for years where this did not happen; it happens faster or slower depending on how fast the transvestite becomes successful, either as a transvestite or in the world."

In another case, says Stoller, a socially prominent man was ruined when, in the course of his divorce trial, his wife revealed his transvestism. His reputation and fortune fell to a terrible low. He met a Succorer who accepted his transvestism, sympathized, married him, and enthusiastically taught him how to be more perfectly feminine and pass as a woman. He soon became a marked success both as a transvestite and as a businessman. He turned strong, aggressive, more interested in intercourse with her. She ended the marriage, calling him "a con man and the worst kind of criminal." But even then, on the way out of the door, she was referring to his financial dealings, not his sex life.

INTERVIEWS

The psychiatrist who put us in touch by phone said, "All I'll tell you is that Charles Virginia Prince is a physically normal male. You'll find out everything else you want to know by yourself." C. V. Prince and I agree on the phone to meet for lunch outside a Van de Kamp's—one of a chain of big, ersatz-Dutch restaurants in Los Angeles with a tea-room atmosphere. The voice on the phone is high and somewhat feminine—not a man's voice, but not effeminate like that of some homosexuals. "I'll be wearing a white suit and blue accessories." When I arrive at Van de Kamp's, I meet a matronly looking person close to fifty, I would guess, five foot eight or nine, in a white skirt and jacket, rather chic in a matronly way, with blue accessories. Within the first minute I am opening doors and lighting cigarettes for her—for I think of C. V. Prince as "she." It is perfectly natural, for to all appearances and in behavior this is unequivocally a woman. We sit at a table, and I order for us both. Her voice comes from her throat, not her chest; though not exactly chirping, it is feminine. There is no hair on her face or forearms; she wears blue eye make-up and has brown hair streaked with gray; I am only sure it is a wig after half an hour of staring. She wears a wedding ring and rather strong perfume. Later, Nat Lehrman, Playboy editor of the "Playboy Forum" and in charge of liaison with sex researchers for the magazine, will tell me, "When Virginia visited me in my office, I called her in and introduced her to a half dozen editors, male and female. Not one realized she wasn't a normal woman." Virginia has written widely, appeared on television, and is in touch with some of the nation's leading sex researchers. She publishes the magazine Transvestia *and books of interest to transvestites.*

I've been married to females twice, and I had a son. I have a Ph.D.—I was a chemist and owned a good business. I was also cross-dressing. I got dragged through the papers and lost everything I'd accumulated in twenty-five years. It was not over homosexuality. I'm not homosexual—I've never had a homosexual experience in my life. I started *Transvestia* because there are people like me who have nowhere to go, no one to talk to. Because of ignorance and social pressure, they often think they're homosexual, and others label them such. They are more rare, isolated and guilt-ridden than homosexuals. I want them to be able to find me. My organization now has four hundred members all over the world—there are affiliated groups in England and Sweden, and one is on the way to existence in Australia. There are members in Burma, Zambia, Cuba, Kenya and Finland. When chapters meet, they have open house and invite doctors, lawyers, judges, the police, so that they'll understand what transvestism is about.

Some transvestites, though, are homosexual.

Let me use this analogy. In the Middle Ages, fever might be called a disease. Now we know it can be a symptom of diphtheria, malaria, smallpox or a dozen other things. It's not a disease in itself. A person who cross-dresses may be a tranvestite, like myself; or he may be a transsexual, a homosexual, a bank robber or a person at a Halloween party. It's a taxonomic problem. Our society makes heterosexuality and homosexuality its chief distinction. But you can cross-dress if you're either, so using transvestism as a separate category is a bad distinction. I have invented a term for my sort of condition. I call it femmiphilia, and the person who feels it a femmiphile. Femmiphilia is love of the feminine, and this is what characterizes the transvestite, as the person is usually called. Explain this in your book and show why transvestite is a bad word that creates problems. People who look at us see the cross-dressing and say we're homosexual. They don't distinguish gender and sexual object choice.

During the last four months I've cast Charles aside. I live as Virginia. I'm not a female, but I'm a woman. Virginia and Charles used to be separate people, and each existed in its own right. But now I have crossed the boundary from being a transvestite to being a woman. A transvestite is always aware of his maleness, of disguising it. I feel that now the girl within me is becoming the girl without. I discussed this in my magazine, and I went past the understanding of some of my readers; the reader response was five-to-three against. But I preserve my real self despite the visible proof of my maleness, and what more can you do? On the gender level, I'm as much a woman as anyone in this restaurant. The difference is that below the belt they're female, and I'm male. There are male women and female women. Female and male refer to the body; masculine and feminine are gender words, belonging to psychology and sociology—and I'm feminine. Recently I went on a boat trip and shared a cabin with a woman, without revealing myself. I didn't want to. She never felt that I'm not a woman or that I'm physically male.

I went to a drag ball recently with a notebook. I talked to twenty homosexual queens, and they all said, "I do this a few times a year." A tv would say, "I do it whenever I get a chance." I asked what they wore under their dresses. Most said jockey shorts. No tv would say that. He wears female underwear. There's a state law saying you can't dress as the opposite sex with intent to deceive, so men go to bars and drag balls wearing a little sign somewhere that says, "I am a boy." That way the police can't arrest them. No tv would do that. He wants to be a girl. Most tv's wear panties under the male clothes they have to put on at jobs and out in society—it's all they can express then. But none would wear jockey shorts! And when I asked the drag homosexual types whether they wore the clothes when having sex, they gave a very emphatic no. "Well, no. I take these things off. I'm a boy." Not every tv can accomplish it, but he'd like to—to have sex while dressed in women's clothes. I know two rather special cases of people who have female gender identity, cross-dress, and have homosexual object choice. But what would a homosexual get out of it, really? Being as feminine as possible, I mean. I know only one female impersonator who may be heterosexual. When you get around those impersonators and drag queens, you find, as among most homosexuals, that even talk about the weather is saturated with sexual *double entendre*. If a real tv got into that atmosphere, he'd be so disgusted with this sex business, and having to battle off those people, that he'd quit or get seduced and come to like it.

You don't believe tvs are disturbed, in some cases.

It isn't a psychopathological syndrome. It's a social phenomenon. I've done questionnaires on 504 cases for a book I'm writing, and I found that a third had seen a psychiatrist; of these only a third went more than once; of these, only a third said it had done them any good at all. There are no cases in the psychiatric literature of a transsexual being cured. There are piles of things the doctors don't understand about these things. They can't cure it because the tv has found a part of himself that was stolen from him as a child, and he's not about to give it up. Suppose a prince had a treasure, and during the night, when he was a child, someone stole it and hid it somewhere in a cave. Later in life he found it. He'd say, "No one will ever take it from me again." That's the way the tv feels about his femininity, and why he's incurable. Society robbed him of a chance to be his full self by seeing it as a sickness and forbidding it. The clothes are a doorway. When you put on the clothes, they entitle you to behave a certain way. You know my true physical nature, but you opened the door for me when we came in. You're afraid of social guilt. It's the same as in the army. An officer is saluted. If a private puts on the uniform, he'll be saluted the same way.

Why do you think more men than women are transvestites?

Men are asked to pay social usury, more than is reasonable and fair, for the so-called privilege of growing up to become men. Men are asked to give up more than women—60 per cent of themselves. They aren't allowed to express and experience their human, rather than male, potential. Boys don't cry, don't play with dolls. If a boy keeps too clean, avoids rough, competitive sports, he becomes a sissy to his peers. It's not nearly the insult to a woman to be called a tomboy as it is for a boy to be called a sissy. A woman who lacks the usual interest in clothes, jewelry and perfume isn't penalized; she can be an executive and have rewards. Women have more freedom to express themselves in dress and behavior. That's what I meant by social usury.

Tv's wouldn't exist if it weren't for the masculine-feminine polarizing of society. The kids are wiping out some of this, and I think tv-ism may disappear in fifty years. Now women are free economically from their husbands and have the pill. They used to take an inferior position as the price for sperm and protection. Masters and Johnson have shown that women are sexually inexhaustible, but men aren't. Now women, not being dependent on men, may turn to other women for satisfaction. The male will prove that if he's sexually inadequate, he can't "cut the mustard." Men are sexually insecure anyway. They'll withdraw somewhat. Males don't expect as much from each other, and two women are inexhaustible. Now that women are no longer to put up with masculine domination, homosexuality of both sexes will increase.

Hugo G. Beigel practices re-educational therapy and hypnotherapy, largely applied to sexual problems. He has written extensively on the subject in books, professional journals and popular magazines. He is an officer of the Society for the Scientific Study of Sex and the editor of its Journal of Sex Research. *He has written on transvestites, their cure by hypnotherapy and, with Robert Feldman, on the themes and motivation patterns in transvestite pornography. We discuss transvestism, homosexuality and transsexualism, the desire not to disguise one's sex but to surgically change it.*

It used to be that parents dressed kids of both sexes in the same clothes, yet transvestism wasn't common. Today only schizophrenic mothers keep kids in same-sex clothes, even at the age of two, yet there are still transvestites. So clothes are not the simple answer. The transvestite fiction and transvestites' accounts of their mothers dressing them as girls fit the adult transvestite's daydreams. What really happens is that a boy gets into girls' clothes and finds, or believes, that this is what makes him most likable to parents and others—soft, sensitive, unassertive. The transvestite was an unaccepted child—unaccepted by his father, anyway. The father says, "Boys should be sturdy!" and rejects or neglects his troubled son. The boy's crucial relationship, then, is with his mother. He sees that girls are closer to mama than he is. Say he has a younger sister. Mama says he is old enough to take care of himself, she doesn't wipe his ass and wash his penis any more. The old golden intimacy is gone. Now mama brushes his sister's hair. Mama goes naked in front of the little girl, but she has stopped letting the boy see her body. So the boy thinks girls are better off.

Then the transvestite may have had very significant relationships with female siblings?

I've had more than twenty-five transvestites in therapy and talked to more than a hundred others. In most instances, sisters or other close females in the family got preferential treatment. One could call transvestism feminine protest; it runs parallel to the masculine protest in women of which Alfred Adler made us aware. The transvestite shows longing for his father's respect and attachment—expressed as homosexuality.

But most transvestites aren't homosexual.

The majority aren't practicing homosexuals, except *perhaps* if we count the drag queen as a transvestite. The transvestites themselves, of course, don't accept the queen as one of their own. But I believe that the majority of transvestites are repressed homosexuals; a minority are overt homosexuals. Repressed homosexual transvestites may marry and wear high heels or a nightgown when performing heterosexually. Some even tell me that they don't enjoy being beneath the woman, for what that may be worth. Or they may content themselves with masturbation, or they may be completely asexual—they hate their male organs and acts involving them.

I get the impression that transvestites are more preoccupied with gender and their own bodies than with sex.

When you treat transvestites, you find powerful masochism—a girdled feeling, pulling the body in, wanting to be refined and confined. Those who hate sex will try to get rid of it mentally and physically. They'll bind up the penis so it doesn't show or mutilate themselves, saying "You see, I'm not a man at all." When they reach this stage, they are transsexuals, and psychotic. Interestingly, the transvestite cares very much whether females accept him as a female. He may find one woman who accepts him as he is, and he can have sex relations with her—that is your "heterosexual transvestite." But in effect he is his wife's lesbian friend. The joy he still gets from fixing her bra comes from early tending of his mother—helping her, zipping her dress and so on. That tending of his mother ended, it seemed to him, because of his maleness. Now he fixes his wife's hair, zips her dress and gets the same help from her. He is getting from her what his mother stopped giving him in favor of a sister or other female.

Dr. Harry Benjamin says in his book on transsexuals that he has performed a sex-change operation on those who desire it and that generally they're happier.

I don't agree with many of his views, diagnoses and follow-ups. He is essentially an endocrinologist; he isn't psychologically oriented. The only psychological idea he'll grant some validity in regard to transvestism is imprinting. Imprinting means an instinctive drive mobilized by an external object—which is not the cause of transvestism. What he really means is conditioning—which strictly speaking is not the cause of transvestism either. After all, the transvestite makes a choice; it isn't forced on him or even suggested to him by anybody.

I get the impression that there is a polarization in sexology, with Benjamin and some others insisting on the deviant's possible health, and his right to his deviation, with a reaction against this view stressing the deviant's sickness.

Some of this is due to the existing laws. Most of us find them ridiculous and harmful. But as a result, some people become extra sweet to deviants, and find reasons why homosexuals should be homosexual. I disagree. I don't think homosexuality is a sickness *per se*, but I do think it's a sign that one is dealing with a neurotic person. His homosexuality is his way out of his problems in coping with life, and if he is uncomfortable with it, he should be helped. But homosexuality is an easier way to take, so many homosexuals avoid or quickly give up therapy.

You're suggesting that a basic immaturity is the problem.

Immaturity is a basic issue. I had one patient, a Jewish man of forty-five who'd grown up in an Irish neighborhood, unlucky with girls, and late to mature in every way. He had a homosexual experience in high school and became fixated. When he came to see me, he was disappointed with life. He felt, why start with females when men are so easy? I think a person's sexual experiences are important in such cases. I had another patient, a handsome man in his middle thirties, who had been seduced homosexually when he was sixteen. He needed to be made to feel like a man. The fact that homosexuals had and did approach him made him feel he wasn't really male. We managed to make him feel his maleness more in therapy, and he married. I saw him later, and he seemed happy with his heterosexual adjustment. He had been satisfying his wife sexually, and that meant a lot to him.

If the problems underlying homosexuality are cured, the homosexual behavior can often be cured. Especially if the patient is young. Only in some cases homosexuality became an autonomous pattern. It persists despite the cure of the underlying cause, because it has become habitual. This is also true of transvestism. But most transvestites are badly adjusted. For instance, they have trouble holding jobs. The ability to hold a job doesn't exclude other neurotic trends; it can't be taken as an index of adjustment in itself. But inability to hold a job must be taken as maladjustment. So one can't prove the transvestite's "perfect health" by saying that he has no trouble holding a job. This argument has often been used with both transvestites and homosexuals. A great deal depends on the kind of job, in relation to the person's abilities. And even more depends on what else he has made of his life, where he has messed it up, why he doesn't function in social relations—except with other transvestites—or in his sex and love relations. And why he is completely unreliable, drifts along, pursues unrealizable hopes, and so on—as most transvestites do.

What about transsexuals, as opposed to transvestites?

I agree with Burger-Prinz, Burchardt and others who consider the transsexual a psychotic. Others claim to have met transsexuals who aren't deeply disturbed. But let any psychotic live in the world that he has built in his head, and he won't appear deeply disturbed. Take the paranoiac who knows that his neighbors mysteriously observe him through the ceiling. He shifts his bed from one place to another or moves out—only to find that his persecutors have followed him with their observation apparatus. He can hold a job. He can even marry, as long as his wife accepts his idea and his means of dealing with it. Yet he is classified as a psychotic. The transsexual lives in his world as long as he can hope for an operation or has undergone one. Many who could not get one have mutilated themselves. Some threaten suicide. Others are just unhappy and can't fit themselves into the accepted life pattern, are convinced that they are actually women, and so on. Where is the difference between them and the paranoiac? And having been castrated and equipped with a vagina, is this person really a woman now? Only he believes so.

22

Across the Gender Line

For centuries folklore and science agreed that the person who wants to change his or her sex is the "hermaphroditic" extreme of a homosexual continuum. During the twenties and thirties some clumsy attempts were made at sex-change surgery; estrogen and androgen were the only other recourse for the man who wanted to be a woman, the woman who wanted to be a man. Those who in desperation castrated themselves were noticed occasionally in scientific literature, and usually checked off in a vague way as homosexuals who had gone totally mad. In 1949 Dr. David O. Cauldwell described a woman who wanted to be a man and called it a distinct syndrome, which he named *psychopathia transsexualis*. At this time, a team of endocrinologists and surgeons in Denmark, headed by Dr. Christian Hamburger, was starting to perfect techniques of sex change with a combination of surgery and hormones. In 1962 a twenty-six-year-old photographer and ex-GI from Long Island named George Jorgensen quietly went to Denmark to be one of their subjects. He returned as Miss Christine Jorgensen, and soon an avalanche of publicity began.

Letters poured in to Jorgensen, to surgeons and physicians, pleading for sex transformation. Hamburger alone received some five hundred imploring missives. Meanwhile Jorgensen met Dr. Harry Benjamin, an elderly German-born endocrinologist practicing in New York, and from their conversations Benjamin realized that he was learning about a distinctive phenomenon usually unrecognized by scientists. Christine Jorgensen referred her many transsexual correspondents to Dr. Benjamin; soon many of them—the great majority men—began to appear at his office. In 1966 his book *The Transsexual Phenomenon* appeared; it was the first full-length study of transsexualism.

In most cases the male transsexual is physically normal, without disorders of the genes, gonads, hormones or sex organs. But he believes that he is a woman. Unless he is confused about the exact meaning of the terms, he probably denies that he is a transvestite or a homosexual. He probably had strong feelings of being female early in life. A small number of transsexuals manage to go through at least part of their lives with a normal social façade, as some transvestites do; more commonly, the transsexual has a pained, disrupted life—dropping out of school, arrested for transvestism or homosexuality because of his appearance, unable to hold a job, shunned by family and friends, deprived of all social supports except the company of other transsexuals or extreme transvestites he may meet. If, as part of his "femininity," he takes a passive homosexual role, reigning as queen of some jail's gay tank may have been the only happy experience of his life.

When he appears at a doctor's office, he may be dressed as a woman and feminized by estrogens. He may have pleaded with a dozen doctors for sex-change treatment and been refused. He is miserably unhappy; he will discuss nothing but gender, of which he has constantly read, thought and talked. Feeling himself a victim of a society that refuses to allow him to live according to his "true nature," he may have tried to dull his unremitting discomfort with alcohol or narcotics. He may threaten to mutilate himself or commit suicide if he doesn't get what he wants—and he may, in fact, do either. What he wants is a female body, female status under law, recognition as a female by society, and to marry and adopt children. What any woman wants.

The transsexual looks at his body with disgust as one of nature's mistakes. He feels that his penis no more identifies him as male than a sixth finger on one hand would identify him as a nonhuman freak. He is not the most perverse sort of homosexual, but a case of totally reversed gender identity. Some transvestites and effeminate homosexuals take estrogens and talk about sex-change treatment. Despite their flirting with cross-identification, they draw the line at losing their penises; in fact, the whole point of the transvestite's deviation is to maintain it by disguising it—he tends to alternate between a rather normal masculine appearance and an alternate female identity. He knows he is male, as much as he claims to regret it. But the transsexual has no fetishistic interest in women's clothes. At best they give him incidental and partial satisfaction. The transsexual, by definition, is convinced that he is a female, and will endure huge expense and a great deal of pain to get rid of his male sex organs. By ordinary standards, transsexuals are delusional psychotics. But some doctors who have dealt with them say that a number are surprisingly healthy by usual psychiatric standards, apart from their female identification.

In the dozen years after he met Christine Jorgensen, Dr. Benjamin interviewed and treated several hundred transsexuals, and a large number of transvestites with strong transsexual tendencies. He said they were the unhappiest people he had ever met. There is no record of an adult transsexual being cured by psychotherapy; nevertheless, it was almost impossible for them to obtain sex-change therapy. At least four of Benjamin's subjects tried to castrate themselves and partly or fully succeeded. Others attempted suicide, and some succeeded. Benjamin concluded, "Since the mind of the transsexual cannot be adjusted to the body, it is logical and justifiable to attempt the opposite, to adjust the body to the mind." It was admittedly an expedient, but so is a great deal of medical treatment.

Though no law specifically forbids sex-change surgery in the United States, it is almost impossible to obtain. Many doctors and psychotherapists object that the treatment merely makes a delusion a reality. Others say that castration, like suicide and drug addiction, is not a right, but an irresponsible action from which a person should be protected. Other doctors frankly admit fear of malpractice suits, and many district attorneys make clear that they will not approve such treatments. Furthermore, sex-change treatment requires major surgery, and approval by hospital boards is needed. Hospital boards usually include laymen and clergymen; they have been known to veto sex-change treatment on moral and religious grounds even after it has been recommended by several physicians and psychiatrists. Finally, the chief objection to sex transformation is a basic resistance among doctors and laymen alike to destroy reproductive organs and obliterate or alter the insignia of sex and gender.

Transsexualism is so rare that most doctors never see a case; there may be no more than a dozen or so people in the world who have studied transsexuals in any numbers. They are divided on whether sex-change therapy is a wise expedient. It seems that the majority of transsexuals are happier than before if they receive sex transformation—not happy, in some cases, but at least less unhappy, and they are very miserable people indeed to begin with. Even many who oppose transformation admit that the immediate future holds hope of no other help for them. One wonders, finally, if the denial of such treatment is not fearful and punitive in many cases. Considering the number of people who have been involuntarily castrated or sterilized with medical, governmental and judicial approval during the past hundred years, it is difficult to see why this accommodation of a small number of harmless and hopeless people should be opposed so vigorously in carefully selected cases.

Harry Benjamin feels that transformation is better than compelling transsexuals to go on suffering, facing suicide or being the victims of their own or others' varying surgical skills. He selected from the transsexuals he studied seventy-six who were, in his judgment, intelligent, responsible, non-psychotic, and in possession of a well-established female pattern of life. He put them under observation while giving them estrogen. If months later they still seemed highly motivated and sufficiently feminine to adapt well to living as females, he recommended them for transformation. Usually this had to be done abroad. After the Jorgensen case received wide publicity, the Danish techniques of transformation surgery were improved, and others were invented. Sex-change mills, like abortion mills, appeared in Casablanca, Tokyo, Mexico City and Rome. There, for two to five thousand dollars, a good job or a pathetic botch might be made of a desperate transsexual who could raise the necessary money.

There are several sex-change techniques, all at least months long and painful—and none, of course, producing a truly normal or fertile person of the opposite sex. People who claim to have been changed from one sex to another may have been intersexuals of some kind and degree, themselves ignorant of or protected from the exact nature of their original condition. In sex-change surgery, a male's penis and testicles are removed, but the skin from them may be used to create labia and to line an artificial vagina, so that the nerve endings remain to give sexual sensation. The vagina is created from a loop of intestine or, more recently, a plastic pouch. Painful dilations may be necessary to keep the vagina from closing up, especially if it is made of gut. Secondary treatments include shaving down the Adam's apple, electrolysis, silicone injections or plastic implants to enlarge breasts, buttocks and hips, and continuing intake of sex hormones to create secondary sex characteristics.

The transformation of a woman to a man requires a complex, three-stage course of surgery that takes at least six months to a year. The breasts and internal sex organs are removed. A scrotum is made from labial tissue and filled with plastic "testicles." A penis is created in stages; a skin graft from the abdominal wall is built into a tube that hangs down to enclose an artificial urethra. Finally the clitoris is embedded in the artificial penis, so that capacity for orgasm is retained. At best, the penis is not very large or realistic, and it cannot become erect; to penetrate a vagina, it must be given artificial support.

There are now some fifteen hundred to two thousand people in the world who have undergone such surgery, five hundred of them American. About two-thirds are unknown to scientists; after treatment, they vanished into society in their new identities. The majority of Benjamin's seventy-six transformed subjects live more stable lives than before, he says, and are more able to maintain lasting relationships. The lucky ones have been able to have their birth certificates and other documents altered so that they are free from the risk of arrest for transvestism and other social and legal difficulties.

Most of all, the transformed patients wanted to marry. In 1966, sixteen of them had, and some of these had adopted children. Another thirty-three were having heterosexual relations (if one accepts that they are female). A number, in fact, were busy confirming and reconfirming their newfound femaleness through promiscuity or prostitution. From Benjamin's and others' reports, it seems that the transformed men tend to fall into two types, the seductress and the matron—the same clichés of femininity held by many transvestites and effeminate homosexuals.

On the other hand, Benjamin does not explain what he means by "good" or "satisfactory" adjustment. As a group, transsexuals are described as childish, vastly egocentric, obsessed by their gender problem, righteously and vengefully angry at a society that doesn't share their preoccupations or views. Even Dr. Benjamin, who has championed transsexuals' right to transformation, says that "all kinds of objectionable traits may exist. Unreliability, deceitfulness, ingratitude, together with an annoying but understandable impatience, have probably ruined their chances for help in more than a few instances." If after transformation they still tend to have the personalities of exhibitionistic, hysterical women, it is not a surprise, and still represents an improvement.

During the last few years economic and institutional backing have appeared for the first time for systematic study of transsexualism, sex-change and gender problems. The Erickson Educational Foundation has supported The Harry Benjamin Foundation, and in 1966 provided funds for the world's first clinic for gender-reversal problems. The Gender Identity Clinic was formed at Johns Hopkins Hospital despite objections by some resident psychiatrists. The clinic's committee consisted of nine men, including John Money, and was headed by plastic surgeon John Hoopes. They screened applicants, many of them referrals from Dr. Benjamin, and began selecting two each month for transformation and follow-up. Not long after, a gender committee for study and treatment was set up at the University of Minnesota Medical School, and in 1970 two Chicago hospitals began to practice sex-change surgery.

The *what* of the issue was now clear—a distinct transsexual syndrome. Money and his associates had shown *when*—that gender identity is learned during the first two years of life. There still remained the question *how?* Benjamin speaks vaguely of "constitution," and Money, who has made analogies with imprinting, has been criticized for lack of psychological subtlety. In 1968 Dr. Robert Stoller, a psychoanalyst and professor of psychiatry at UCLA, produced the book *Sex and Gender*, the only full-length study of transsexuals other than Benjamin's. For more than a decade he studied eighty-five patients with gender problems, among them transsexuals as young as five, three, even two and one. By studying them and sometimes their mothers as well, Stoller has produced convincing leads about how children get their gender crossed—and, by implication, how normal children get it straight.

The three- and five-year-old transsexual boys dressed in feminine clothes whenever they could. They were not effeminate, but truly feminine, in gestures, inflections, interests, play, conversation. They sat to urinate. They asked their mothers whether their breasts would grow, and why their penises couldn't be removed. By four or five they quite expected to grow up to be women. They were bright, creative, able to form warm relationships with people of both sexes and all ages. In fact, they seemed free of major conflict. Not one had been dressed as a girl by his mother or subjected to the "pinafore punishment." Not one had even been directly encouraged to act girlishly. The mother, it was true, considered the boy's feminine behavior cute, but sometimes feared it was excessive and made feeble attempts to limit it. When he wore her clothes, she might say, "Darling, why don't you put that away for a while? Won't you please?" This oblique encouragement of femininity in the boy, however, seemed to be the by-product of something more important—a totally permissive upbringing by a mother who was extraordinarily intimate with and solicitous toward her baby.

The mother kept the child in constant physical contact with her, always carrying, holding or touching him. He accompanied her when she sat on the toilet, took a bath, dressed and undressed. His wishes were anticipated, and he was not even compelled to be weaned or toilet-trained unless or until he desired it. Speaking of him, the mother always said "we," as of an equal. Obviously this was an only child whose father was physically absent much of the time, and emotionally withdrawn when physically there, so that the mother-child symbiosis wasn't interrupted. The child ended up with the closest possible thing to a continued intrauterine life.

Stoller says that the mother led the child to overidentify with her through the constant physical contact—so much so that the child's ego boundaries remained blurred. Because the boys failed to separate physically, and thus emotionally, they failed to separate their identities. "These women surrounded these babies with their flesh, their breath, their cooing voices, and their enveloping movements. Other loving mothers may do this also, but not, I believe, for as many hours a day. Then, at a time when the normal separation of mother and infant is accelerating, these mothers are still nestling the boys in upon their bodies as much as when they were defenseless infants—and it is this delay in permitting the boys to be free of their mothers' bodies, of their constant cuddling and following eyes, that I feel may be the primary pathology." This turned out to be just the first and less surprising discovery in Stoller's research.

Stoller raised the logical criticism to his own statement—that many people around the world, such as the Eskimos, keep mother and baby in constant skin-to-skin contact for years without creating transsexualism. Contact, then, is not itself the cause. This sort of criticism has been raised about many psychodynamic studies; for instance, if certain conditions produce homosexuality, why in some people and not others? Closer observation and more detailed description may show why. Psychiatrists have tended to sum up complex, subtle patterns with such broad labels as "immature," "passive dependent" and "aggressive" without showing distinctive small differences in degree and manner. They are behind many novelists in pinpointing such differences. When clinicians sense a distinctive "vibration" in a person or behavior, they rarely attempt to find the exact words or mannerisms that give the impression. When Stoller felt that the mothers of child transsexuals behaved in some way differently from other mothers he had seen, he began to observe them—through analytic therapy.

"The problem," said Stoller, "appears to be not that the baby is held but *how* he is held, and the accompanying feelings . . . that bathe him day and night." The intimacy was a bridge for communicating feelings. And the mothers' feelings seemed eerily similar. There was even an obvious similarity in their physical appearance—boyish, almost neuter, without any of the sexual sheen and sparkle one feels from an erotically alive person. They kept their hair short, wore little make-up and dressed in boyish or, at best, plain-Jane styles. But this was of a piece with their over-all drab quality. Beneath a veneer of housewifely activeness, they were generally lackluster people, with a deep sense of emptiness, incompleteness and bleak depression. They also turned out to have similar sexual histories. All had married in their late twenties, without great love or passion. All had been virgins. Not one had willingly had intercourse with her husband more than once a month. None considered her marriage happy, yet none had been unfaithful to her husband. Aside from their relationships with their transsexual sons, they lived deadened and unsensual lives.

Then came the payoff. The mothers of twelve transsexuals in a row revealed, eventually, that they themselves had almost become transsexuals during the so-called "latency years" between six and twelve. They had been tomboys, dressed in boys' clothes, and wanted to become male, dreaming that at puberty they would develop penises. With the "disappointment" of female puberty, they buried the hope of becoming male and lived with façades of disappointing femaleness by default.

Even their lives before and after this pubertal crisis were similar. The mother's mother had been cold or absent. She grew up with a feeling of parched, empty unhappiness. Feeling helpless, hopeless, she smothered her rage at being unmothered and magically hoped that becoming male might cure her sorrow. When this was proved impossible, she became a grudging, minimal female, and to avoid spinsterhood entered a marriage barren of love and sex. When a son was born, she had an immense stake in him. He was dependent on her, and therefore safe to love. He was also a phallus produced of her own flesh, her buried masculine self come true. Further, he created a chance to "make better" her own painful childhood.

So the son became both an extension of the mother and her own security blanket. Questioned about the continual intimacy with her son, one mother said she was "addicted" to him; the warm touch of his body relieved her inner emptiness. Another said she kept him against her because her own mother had failed to show interest in her, and she wanted to be sure her son never suffered that. Another said the contact comforted her inner sadness. When the boy did not separate from her and identified with her even in gender, he was only returning to her the feelings she gave to him.

Stoller felt one last link remained to be proven—that adult transsexuals were results of the same background as the child transsexuals he had studied. So far, he has found this to be true. But the question remained that if his theory were correct, there should be no female transvestites. Lack of separation from the mother would not reverse a girl's gender from normal. But female transsexuals do exist, if in smaller numbers than male ones—the proportion is variously guessed as one to three and one to eight. They dress as men if possible, but this cross-dressing is not episodic; it leads to living uninterruptedly as a man. There is none of the transvestite's urge to reveal the true biological sex. The female transsexual resents her breasts and curves; she binds her breasts flat. She resents menstruation, and is glad to see it cease when she obtains androgen. Her ambition is to lose her female organs and characteristics and gain those of a male. She has almost as much trouble as a man finding a doctor to remove her breasts and her internal organs, let alone try to give her a penis. She may pursue transformation frantically and nurse paranoid hatred toward anyone who prevents her. She wants to live legally and socially as a man, married to a woman and perhaps rearing adopted children—as the father. Nevertheless she denies being homosexual and dislikes lesbians. But she also abhors the idea of being penetrated by a man, which proves her female. She sometimes settles for tribadism—"dyking," or a "rub job," in face-to-face imitation of heterosexual intercourse. She would like to be a truck driver, soldier or policeman but often settles for an office job. As the male transsexual feels his sex organs are a deformity that make him "live a lie," the female transsexual curses nature for not making her true inner maleness manifest.

Of 368 transsexuals and extreme transvestites seen and examined by Benjamin, only twenty-eight were women. Twenty underwent various combinations of androgen and surgical treatment. (Even if such females do not seek or obtain a penis, they obtain testosterone and have their breasts and pelvic sex organs removed.) Six now live as men, legally married to normal women. Others, not having obtained legal status as males, live in illegal "marriages"; among them are some patients who received hormone therapy only. Stoller has also recorded some cases of female transsexualism. They live and work as men, accepted by co-workers as such. One is a tool operator, another a draftsman, a third a research chemist.

Stoller has found a fascinating lead to female transsexualism in one of his young patients. The little girl's mother was absent during a large part of her childhood. The father was a very protective and nurturing man and took care of her a great deal. To a degree, he became to her what the mother is to male transsexuals. Stoller has found some evidence of this in the backgrounds of other female transsexuals. In one case the father took the little girl not only on walks and rides but even to the barber shop and neighborhood tavern. The father may have fed, bathed, changed and rocked the girl a great deal—because of the mother's absence or illness or for other reasons. If female transsexuals are rarer than males, one factor may be that excessive "mothering" and identification between father and daughter naturally occurs more rarely than such mother-son bonds.

Serious study of transsexualism has been going on for only some fifteen years; a great deal remains to be learned. Stoller's work supports the dramatic evidence of the Hampsons and Money with physical hermaphrodites—that gender is learned. The Hampsons and Money have guessed that gender disorders may be due to faulty imprinting, but there is no sure evidence that imprinting exists at all in human beings. Benjamin says that more than a third of transsexuals show "sexual underdevelopment," but gives no data to show how; he has a subjective impression that they are physically feminine in some way, and suggests a genetic-endocrine basis. Stoller, I believe, makes by far the most convincing case. His theory may also explain the relative normality described in some transsexuals.

There are people who maintain that transsexuals are by definition psychotic. Stoller and others maintain that a small number of them are surprisingly healthy and realistic aside from the matter of their gender. Actually, there may be two kinds of transsexuals, conflictual and nonconflictual. The child transsexual Stoller describes has learned he is female by a nonconflictual learning process. He may not run into difficulty until he has to go to school, deal with ridicule and isolation from his peers, and progressively face the demands of adolescence and adulthood. If his sense of femininity and his ego strength are high, he may maintain some sense of worth and be relatively free of severe emotional problems.

Stoller reports having cured child transsexuals by treating both mother and child. (The fathers, predictably, will not participate.) One boy had been fearless, constantly exploring his environment; but he did so in short, quick sprints, always returning to his mother's touch before venturing out again. As treatment made him start losing his femininity, enjoy being male and masculine, he became phobic. As long as his transsexualism was undisturbed, he remained generally undisturbed.

Other cases may be conflictual and involve degrees of transvestism or homosexuality—for instance, the child who learns that he is male during his first two years, but then comes to feel that he must choose between being male and being loved. He wants to regain symbiosis with his mother, yet fears castration and feminization as a result of seeking it. He becomes a transvestite as the result of this conflict. Or perhaps he progresses from fetishism to transvestism to borderline transsexualism. In the latter case, he may become an effeminate homosexual who works as a female impersonator or prostitute; eventually he uses his earnings to obtain sex transformation, but does not try to pass as a normal woman, always advertising that he is a simulated female. Stoller reports a female borderline case between transvestism and transsexualism. She lives as a man, accepted as one by the men at the electronics plant where she works. She wears boots, jeans and a crew cut, and she swears broadly. Her breasts and pelvic organs have been removed, and androgens have given her body and facial hair. She can sit on a beach in men's trunks displaying a flat, hairy chest and speaking in a deep voice. But if questioned, she does not deny that she is a biological female, and some intimate friends know it. She has only mild interest in gaining a phallus—less interest, says Stoller, than the urologist who has promised to create one for her.

Cases of gender disturbance may vary in kind and degree, depending on whether the cross-identification originally arose more out of conditioning or "critical learning" on one hand or out of conflict-ridden adaptation on the other. During the next few decades, more detailed studies may clarify this.

Transsexuals are a very small group, transvestites a larger but still tiny one. The importance of research in such gender disorders is that it eliminates many old assumptions about the normal development of gender identity and sex role. It leads one to the question of how society programs people as male and female and instructs them in choosing a partner for love and sex.

INTERVIEWS

Dr. Robert Stoller is the author of Sex and Gender, *a study of the biological and psychological roots of gender and the first extended work on child transsexuals. The book is the fruit of a dozen years' research on gender. Stoller is a psychoanalyst; he limits his practice to people with gender defects and their families. He teaches psychiatry to medical students and psychiatric residents at UCLA. He is an open, enthusiastic and genial man in his forties. We meet at his house, for he is on a year's sabbatical leave, which is not an unalloyed pleasure to him.*

I'm no longer in touch with my patients, and sometimes I feel as though I'm drying up. After all, they're the ones who give me my ideas. My position on transsexuals or anything else is always subject to change, because sooner or later, when I have things figured out, some patient comes along and ruins everything. He raises new questions, and I'm off looking for data I couldn't even conceptualize before. That's what our work is about.

In fact, that's how I got started working with transsexuals. A colleague of mine had been studying them, and when he gave up the research, he asked me to see one transsexual patient. When the patient walked into my office, I saw what appeared to be a normal man. But I knew the person was biologically female. I thought, how can psychoanalytic theory explain *this*? Analytic theory came more into doubt as we went on with treatment. It basically sees personality development, and especially such a marked aberration as transsexualism, as coming from conflict. But I felt that some of my patients had become transsexual through a relatively nonconflictual process. A behaviorist would say it was conditioning. When I read John Money's work on gender, I found that he and I were working toward the same sort of conclusion—that gender is basically determined psychologically, especially by the parents. John used the word imprinting. I would too, but putting it in quotes, because I'm not sure that's the only thing involved. We don't have proof that it's like imprinting in animals, but we lack a better word.

This led to a larger question—how masculinity and femininity develop in normals. Again, I suspect an old analytic position I used to take. In 1930 Freud wrote a last paper on female sexuality, saying that girls and boys are pretty much the same till they're three or four; then comes traumatic penis envy for the girl, etc. During those first years, both had chiefly loved their mothers, so the male's first love object was heterosexual, the female's homosexual, and this allegedly made males emotionally stronger. Freud was a Victorian, and he saw maleness as the ideal condition. He said that, with luck, the female escapes into a sort of second-rate heterosexuality. But she is fickle, has a defective conscience, and so on. Freud thought femininity is the overcoming of a disappointment.

But all you have to do is look at girls of one or two, and you know this whole theory can't be true. They're already little girls. I think that nontraumatic, nonconflictual events help determine the sense of masculinity and femininity. If the parents, especially the mother, ascribe maleness or femaleness to the child at birth, this isn't basically questioned or changed. If we can find out how the transsexual, without apparent trauma, developed a gender that conflicts with his sex, we may be on the track to learning how masculinity and femininity develop in normal people. I know that I look at maleness and femaleness with bias and take a lot about them for granted. Just as everyone in society does, as Freud did in his time. So studying the wrong learners may be the best way to understand right learning.

The next crucial step in research is looking from the beginning—observing mothers and their children and searching for the biological origins of gender. For instance, there seem to be inborn differences between male and female post-satiation patterns. After little girl infants are fed, they become more alert; little boys go to sleep. This may lead directly into something more psychological as their personalities develop. It certainly sounds like a common sexual satiation pattern. In such ways we may learn to be more exact about what sex and gender are. Masculine and feminine are psychological terms, but at first you can't separate them from male and female, which are biological.

People get very inexact or absolute about such matters. A man may have a reservoir of latent homosexual thought; some classic analysts say such a person is homosexual. Then they say that homosexuality causes schizophrenia, alcoholism, coin collecting, auto racing and heterosexuality! I don't think you should equate homosexual impulses with homosexual identity. In some boys you find feminine interests and identification; there are scientists who say, "He wants to be female." It's not quite true. If his parents think he is a boy, he may be homosexual, heterosexual, anything—but he does *not* question that he's male. He may distort his maleness, pick homosexual love objects, have fragments of identification with females. He may even become a delusional psychotic and think he's a woman. But even the delusional schizophrenic who says "I am a woman" stands up to urinate. Because he knows that really he is male. A male may question whether he's masculine, think that he's feminine, but he does not doubt that he's male. Unless he is a transsexual. From the time a transsexual can sit on a potty, he sits on it to urinate. He doesn't stand. And I'm sure that this is due to parental influence.

Sometimes you have to listen to people for years to really learn about such things. When I first began to see transsexual patients, I said, "I haven't the faintest idea why there are transsexuals." I saw the mother of a transsexual for years, and in the course of her analytic treatment I got the first clue to her son's gender problem. Then I saw it reappear in case after case. The mother had gone through a period, from about eight till the beginning of menstruation and breast development at eleven, when she came close to being transsexual herself. After discovering this in one mother, and knowing to look for it, I found it in eleven more cases in a row. In the thirteenth I didn't. I don't know that case well enough yet to say more about it. The point of psychiatric research is to follow leads but never to force data to fit them or our theories.

It wasn't just that these mothers were athletically competitive when young, that they wore boys' clothes. They actually wanted to be boys. It wasn't the penis envy of normal women. They *really* wanted to be boys. Later, they married men who were psychologically absent, and gave their boy children the most blissful infancies I've ever seen. In most cases, the transsexual was the youngest child. A geneticist might talk about "tired eggs" from an older mother, but a completely different explanation is that the woman sees to it that she has no succeeding child to interrupt the relationship.

What the mother failed to give the child was adequate separation from her body. A good mother has the ability to frustrate her child. R. R. Greenson and I worked with a family; he treated the transsexual boy, and I the mother. Greenson described the mother-child relationship as "a kangaroo baby in its mother's pouch." The child remained emotionally almost intrauterine after birth. This close, unbroken physical contact with his mother led the boy to identify himself as female. No succeeding sibling, no assertive father, interfered with the mother as she overidentified with her child and created overidentification in return. Before treatment, the boy made a drawing he called "Mother and Son." The bodies were literally not separated. The mother was clearly drawn, but the child was only a shmoo-like protuberance, a sort of arm of the mother.

You find excessive mother-son symbiosis in fetishistic transvestites and homosexuals too, but homosexuals usually show more emotional double bind with the mother than transsexuals. The homosexual's mother displayed more hostility and emotional blackmail to the child. The transsexual is more like the normal in nontraumatic development of gender. But even with some homosexuals there may be things done from birth on, not felt as traumatic, that help condition identity to produce a socially deviant pattern. There may be some types of homosexuals who become homosexual partly because of a loving experience with the mother between birth and the age of one and a half to two, as is the case with transsexuals.

Many more transsexuals are male than female. It makes sense, again, only if you reverse the classic psychoanalytic position, which says that boys have it easier because their first love is heterosexual. But that leaves out the baby's first identification. If a little girl identifies strongly with her mother, it should just create a strong female identification, so female transsexuals shouldn't exist at all. But they do, and I have a suggestive case that needs following up. A colleague of mine treated a nine-year-old girl who thought she was a boy. The father more or less took the place of the mother during her early years, in fact mothering her to an extraordinary degree, with constant physical contact. I haven't found this so clearly in past cases of female transsexuals, but it's a hint of something to look for in the future.

Another relevant point, by the way, on which classic analytic thought doesn't hold, in my experience, is the theory that homosexuality causes paranoia. Freud said that paranoia—and that nowadays usually means paranoid schizophrennia—is caused by homosexuality. Theoretically, it should be equally true of males and females. In fact, several studies have shown less hallucinated homosexual accusation in female than in male paranoids. Homosexual accusation is probably the commonest paranoid delusion in males: "People are calling me a cocksucker" and that sort of thing. I've even seen cases where homosexual conflict precipitated a psychotic episode, but that doesn't mean it's the cause. I guess that patients who are paranoid about homosexuality are really trying to handle fear over whether they're masculine.

Their real problem is fear of identity dissolution. They fear they'll fall apart and not *be* at all. One aspect of identity dissolution is the collapse of masculinnity, and this is expressed as fear of being feminine, of homosexuality. Some vulnerable people can be thrown into psychotic episodes by such fear of a homosexual identity. For instance, I saw a strong paranoid reaction in a homosexual when, in the course of treatment, he was faced with the possibility of a heterosexual life. He was faced with dissolution of his personality as he knew it. In this case, he feared his safe, accustomed identity as a homosexual would dissolve.

Homosexuals may sometimes have a solid identity and not be threatened by fragmentation. These are the adjusted homosexuals Hooker and Hoffman write about. But I sometimes wonder whether, if they were pressed in a way they couldn't avoid—say, in therapy aimed at heterosexual adjustment—they might not blow up. Would the same thing happen to some heterosexuals if in treatment they were forced to believe homosexuality is the only way to practice sex?

23

Wired for Gender

In 1956 psychologist Alan E. Fisher injected testosterone into the brain of a male rat, expecting it to go into a frenzy of aggression and sexual excitement. Instead, it acted like a mother. When a female was put in its cage, the male didn't mount her; it tried to pick her up by the tail or the loose skin on her back and carry her across the cage, like a mother rat retrieving a pup. Fisher put rat pups into the cage, and the male tried to build them a nest.

Fisher was working in the new and promising field of neuroendocrine mapping. Normally, the blood carries small amounts of a hormone to the brain, where it releases the impulses programed in the brain cells. Pinpoint injections of hormone concentrate, by provoking exaggerated results, show exactly which area of the brain controls a given feeling or behavior. Fisher had been seeking the neural circuit that controls aggression and copulation. Clearly he hadn't found it.

So Fisher tried again, injecting testosterone at a nearby point. Within minutes he saw what he had expected the first time— an exaggerated show of aggression and sexual arousal. Fisher then tried injecting between the first and second points. The rat acted out a confused mixture of maternal and aggressive behavior. It became sexually excited and tried to retrieve its own tail. When a female was put in its cage, it became excited, but instead of mounting, it "retrieved" her.

Fisher had done something more important than locate two more brain centers and their hormonal triggers. His results suggested that the whole range of rat behavior, male and female, lies programed in every rat, regardless of sex, awaiting selective activation. Normally only the male behavior is triggered in a male, but the dormant maternal behavior can be artificially induced. Later Fisher was able to produce typically male aggression in female rats with similar techniques. Why testosterone, of all things, should make a male act maternal is still a puzzle. It is called a paradoxical effect—which is scientists' way of saying they really don't understand the basic processes involved.

The work of Fisher and many others in the late forties and fifties spurred efforts to discover how males and females are biologically programed. Is

385

there bisexual potential within us all? Are males aggressive and females passive by biological nature or is that a result of cultural conditioning? Do hormones, family relationships or social stereotyping most shape gender and sexuality? The answers have far-reaching effects, from the nursery school to the psychiatric clinic.

As we have seen, sex behavior is programed by the genes, hormones and nervous system. The genes lay down a potential range of traits and responses to the environment. Among other things, they direct the fetus of a higher animal to develop undifferentiated gonads; then at some point (the third month in humans) the Y or second X chromosome directs the gonads to differentiate into testes or ovaries, producing mostly androgens (male) or estrogens (female). Androgens are the cause of many typically male traits and behavior, but they exist in smaller amounts in women, and they heighten sexual excitability in both sexes. Estrogens produce female traits and behavior, but are present in small quantities in men; they lower excitability in both sexes. Calling them sex hormones or male and female hormones is convenient shorthand, but an oversimplification.

Three parts of the brain control much of emotion and sex behavior. The hypothalamus, below the center of the brain, is a sort of biological clock and timing device. In interplay with the endocrine glands, it sends the body signals to begin and end puberty, fertility cycles, perhaps sexual arousal. Along with the thalamus, just above it, and the limbic system that surrounds both, it governs many basic physical and emotional responses. Around 1950, sophisticated techniques began to develop for finding just which parts of the thalamus, hypothalamus and limbic system control various acts and emotions. One is injecting or implanting hormones directly in the brain, as Fisher did. Since 1962, radioactive hormones have been injected into animals' bloodstreams to allow study of selective absorption by brain cells. Another stimulant-probe is a small electric shock given directly to the exposed brain with a fine wire. Depending on where the shock is applied, it can make a placid cat attack a dummy or cower from a mouse; create such hunger in a rat that it eats till it triples its weight; make mother monkeys thrust away their young; elicit erection, grooming and other acts of courtship in cats; relieve pain in ill human beings and stop violence in the mentally disturbed.

The question scientists asked as a result of Fisher's experiments was how a male rat's brain usually "knows" to respond to testosterone with its male program and not its maternal one. The guess was that at an early stage of fetal development, the embryo's own hormones act as organizers on its brain, muting one program and priming the other. To test this idea, certain types of behavior could be used as standards of male and female programing because they are limited to or highly predominant in one sex. For instance, in most higher animals, males mount, threaten and show aggression and rough-and-tumble play far more than females. Females show much more appeasing and submissive posturing and lordosis (the sway-backed crouch that presents the posterior and genitals to the male). It was already known that hormones have a strong influence on these behaviors. If male mice are castrated, they stop fighting; given androgens, they start again. If a female cat is spayed, she stops showing lordosis; if estrogens are implanted in her hypothalamus, lordosis reappears.

The research team of Young, Goy, Phoenix and their associates at Oregon University worked out an ingenious experiment with guinea pigs. Androgen was injected into pregnant females, so that their bloodstreams carried it to the embryos. The male embryos used as much androgen as they needed and ignored the surplus. But the female embryos were masculinized—born not only with male external genitals but with masculine behavior patterns. The androgen had reprogramed not only the genitals but the brain. The Oregon team is now doing further experiments with rhesus monkeys and getting similar results. They have androgenized pregnant females during the critical period of sexual development; the female offspring have male external genitals and behave much like male monkeys—with mounting, threatening gestures and rough-and-tumble play. The eminent Frank Beach is doing similar studies with dogs, with similar preliminary results.

Further support for the idea that fetal hormones organize the brain for male and female behavior comes from several other experiments. It has been found that androgenized females show insensitivity to estrogen injections after birth; the embryo's female program not having been primed to respond, it remained dormant after birth. A female rat's neural organization does not pass the critical stage until five days after birth; if during the first few days of life she is given androgen, the sexual timetable in her hypothalamus is permanently scrambled. At puberty she will become estrous and stay that way instead of going into a monthly cycle; however, she will not only be sterile but without lordosis as well, and therefore unable to copulate.

The question now is whether human programing can be altered by hormone imbalance during gestation. John Money has been able to study human beings who are perfect parallels to the artificially masculinized guinea pigs and monkeys—women with the adrenogenital syndrome. The critical period of neuroendocrine organizing seems to be the second trimester for people; during that time, some fetal females, due to a genetic defect of the adrenal glands, produce large amounts of androgen. And during the fifties, as we saw, many pregnant women took progestin to prevent miscarriage, which had the same effect on the embryos as the adrenogenital syndrome. The children were born with almost normal male genitals, though internally and genetically they were normal females.

Money has studied a number of such females over a period of years. Many received corrective surgery and continuing estrogen treatment, and were raised as normal girls. All are heterosexual and have basically normal female and feminine identities. However, most were tomboys according to themselves and those around them—physically active and aggressive, with many masculine interests and little desire for feminine clothes and play. After puberty, a few showed what Money considers somewhat masculine sexual patterns. Money concludes that there may have been some masculinization of behavior mechanisms before birth.

Robert Stoller, in his work with transsexuals and transvestites, has ended up with doubts about the psychological basis of a few of his cases. He studied an infant who was apparently a normal girl at birth and was raised as a girl, but was always steadfastly convinced she should be a boy. At puberty it was discovered that she was really a biological male, mislabeled because of a deformity of the external genitals. Stoller has seen other patients who were apparently normal boys but insisted that they were girls and became effeminate and transvestic—and later turned out to have Klinefelter's syndrome or other physical male deficiencies. It was as though some hidden drive in their nervous systems told them their true sex despite all evidence to the contrary. Stoller leaves this an open question, a possibility.

Reading about these experiments makes one wonder whether Krafft-Ebing, Magnan and Chevalier mightn't have been right after all, with their talk of male brains in female bodies and vice versa. (The *Life Science Library* book *The Mind* said flatly in 1964 that Fisher's work "suggests that deviant sexual behavior in humans, as well as in animals, may proceed from chemical deficiencies during the period of youth.") Even Stoller and Money, who have done so much to prove that psychological learning can override all the biological factors of sex and gender, allow a future place for some evidence of neural programing as a major factor in adult patterns of sexual identity and behavior.

Nevertheless, the entire field remains tantalizingly primitive. The extent and mechanisms of sex programing lie in still shadowy reaches of cell chemistry. As in the early days of genetics, there are people ready to jump on dramatic but still exploratory experiments. Stoller and Money admit that the relationship of programing to human deviation is still a hypothesis. Furthermore, Money's suggestive study of adrenogenital women is not his best piece of research.* Generally, the trend in neuroendocrine research, like that in modern genetics, is away from simple formulas, unitary drives and mechanical programing. The more research is done, the more behavior breaks down into components. For instance, electrical stimulation shows that there are separate centers in the human nervous system for erection, orgasm and ejaculation; electrical shocks to the right nervous centers can produce each without the other two. So even relatively simple fragments of human sexuality are orchestrations of many sub-behaviors, and sometimes

*I cannot go into a detailed criticism of it here, but the observations are sketchy and the criteria for maleness arguable. For instance, he uses response to visual stimuli as an example of masculinization. The research of Johnson and Masters suggests that it is a cultural variable. And as with MZ-twin studies, psychological factors may just as easily explain some of the behavior as physiological ones.

each has its own genetic range and thermostat type of ON and OFF neuroendocrine switches. These breakthroughs in cell-level research can make one forget that even lower vertebrates have to learn when and how to use what is programed into them. That is, genes and neuroendocrine circuits are only part of a creature's behavior system, and, as one goes up the evolutionary scale, they make up a smaller and smaller proportion of it. Learning and interaction with the environment are needed to complete the program. In fact, when we look at the whole range of animal sexuality, humans almost seem an experiment by nature to see whether sexuality can be left minimally to programing and mostly to learning. This helps explain why homosexuality is uniquely human.

We know that the sexual behavior of birds—like the rest of their behavior—is rigidly programed. For instance, when a male turkey is sexually excited during its mating period, he acts like a combination scanner and computer; when he sees something a certain size, shape and height from the ground, goes behind it, mounts and tries to copulate. The size, shape and height are those of a female turkey's head. If you cut the head off a female turkey and mount it on a stick at the right height, the male, with the rigid efficiency of a machine obeying its taped directions, gets the usual distance behind the head and goes through the motions of mounting and copulating. In fact, if you make a wooden dummy the size and shape of a female turkey's head, it responds again to the right-shape-in-the-right-place. It trots behind the totem and flaps lustfully in the air, trying to mate with the invisible better half of its better half.

Daniel Lehrman, the distinguished experimental psychologist at Rutgers, has shown in detail how the six-to-seven week reproductive cycle of the ring dove is a chain of synchronized feedbacks between male and female. The male affects the female, who responds; her response cues the male to respond with a further step, and so on. For instance, Lehrman wondered what makes a female dove sit on her eggs. He found that if she is isolated, she doesn't do so, but an injection of progesterone will make her begin immediately. If she is around the male, she will begin on schedule without help. In fact, if she can just watch the male through a pane of glass, she secretes her own progesterone and gets on the eggs. Some still unidentified behavior of the male (caused in turn by his own hormones) is her cue. The cues pass back and forth, through courting, mating, nest building, egg laying, incubation and rearing the young, an intricate, complex, genetically determined set of neuroendocrine reactions with each step the starter for the next.

Because birds' behavior is so rigidly programed, humans can easily misprogram it in the laboratory. Lehrman has isolated female doves and stroked their heads for a few minutes each day; after several days they lay eggs in response, and afterward are less likely to do so in response to a male dove. An otherwise normal mandarin drake can be sexually fixated on mallard ducks—interspecies mating is nonexistent or very rare for most animals. When female turkeys see their young hatch from the egg, they are at the height of their aggressiveness. This is good for protecting their eggs and young from predators, but since they cannot recognize their young (or perhaps simply cannot turn off their aggression despite the recognition), the turkey chicks need a way to fend off the mother's hair-trigger wrath. They do so by peeping. When they peep, the mother turkey becomes maternal instead of aggressive. If humans intervene and surgically make mother turkeys deaf, they peck their chicks to death.

The most famous illustration of this sort of behavior is Konrad Lorenz's misprogramed ducks. In his pioneer experiments during the thirties, the great Austrian ethologist guessed that when newly hatched ducklings first see a moving object of certain proportions, they make it "mother" for life. In other words, they are genetically programed so that when they see a-certain-shape-that-waddles, it is "imprinted" in their nervous system. Lorenz waddled before newborn ducklings, and they soon followed in a line. He was their mother from then on. He also got geese to imprint him as mother, and further, to imprint him (and thus humans) as their preferred sexual object. Lorenz also sexually imprinted birds for inanimate objects, such as bowls. The concept of imprinting has become a popular and useful one, for it is a middle ground between the old dichotomy of innate and learned behavior. It is, in effect, being programed to learn something special and important, in a certain way at a certain time. It is one of the ways that wiring, incomplete at birth, is finished through learning after birth.

One can not only misprogram a bird by deliberately giving it something with the characteristics to which it has imprinting sensitivity, one can even improve on nature. Imprinting sensitivity seems often to depend on things such as "as low as possible" or "as high as possible" or "as dark below and as light on top as possible." Nikolaas Tinbergen, once Lorenz's colleague and an equally distinguished ethologist, wanted to discover what made a young gull peck at its mother's beak to move it to dispense food. He made dummy gull heads with different shapes, color contrasts and so on, until he had found the stimulating shape and color-contrast characteristics; then he made a dummy "supergull." The gull chicks would peck at it hundreds of times, even though they never got food as a result.

But even birds have to learn some things; they build on wired-in response with experience. A gosling will imprint the right sort of moving object—in nature, invariably a female goose—during its first day of life. However, for a few days it will follow any such object; only gradually does it learn to recognize its mother and follow only her. A male finch raised in isolation can't give the usual finch song; it has the vocal equipment, but it must learn to organize sounds properly from other finches, as humans must learn speech. What has to be learned and what can be misprogramed varies from species to species. Female mallard ducks can't imprint males of any other species as sexual objects; their sexual response is keyed to the mating plumage of the male mallard, which nothing else begins to approximate. Toads, lower on the evolutionary scale than birds, must learn their eating habits to some degree. A young toad snaps at anything the right size that moves. Only experience teaches it not to snap at moving blades of grass and other inedible things. It may be by a similar process of habituation that birds learn to recognize their mothers, mates and young.

There is no homosexual behavior among birds. Males do not copulate. Misprograming experiments show not that submammalians are potentially ambisexual, as some have wanted to believe, but that they are so rigidly and specifically programed that only the most bizarre human intervention breaks their usual pattern. Furthermore, imprinting so far seems to be chiefly a phenomenon of bird life. Those who want to explain human sexual deviation by pointing to artificially misprogramed mallards should think back to Goldschmidt's intersexual gypsy moths and how little they have to do with drag queens.

The "triumph rite" and subsequent pairing of ganders, as described by Konrad Lorenz, is sometimes referred to as homosexual. Lorenz made clear, though, that such pairing involves no copulation and helps rather than hinders procreation. Such ganders seldom mount each other; if they do, the one on the bottom does not lie flat on the water in a sexually receptive posture. In mating season, the two males usually allow a female to join them, and form a threesome that is biologically very successful—a coalition with high dominance among their own species, capable of winning good nesting territory and of raising many goslings, and with double paternal protection against predators.

As one goes up the evolutionary scale to mammals, all behavior is less automatic and rigid, and more must be learned. No mammal in its natural state (or probably even in captivity) performs homosexual acts in the sense that male seeks male, female seeks female, for sexual satisfaction. Homosexuality has been reported in a large number of mammals, and even submammals; sometimes this is due to anthropomorphic observation, sometimes to plain faulty observation, sometimes to a special use of the term. The commonest confusion is that in many species, same-sex animals may mount each other. There is no intromission, no copulation, though there may be some pelvic-thrusting motions. Some observers have thought or assumed there was copulation. Others, working on the assumptions of classical psychoanalysis, have called *any* same-sex activity homosexually libidinal. Others, especially homosexual apologists, have taken such occurrences as proof of the biologic normality of human homosexuality. In the same way, fragments of other-sex behavior, such as females mounting females or Fisher's male rat acting maternal, have been called bisexual. The terms bisexual and homosexual are misleading in these contexts, for they imply the human sort of bisexual or homosexual contact.

For instance, frogs have been described as bisexual. In the breeding season, a male frog mounts any frog in sight. Step one of its program is, "If it has the right shape, mount it." If it mounts another male, the "homo-sexual" partner chirps in protest and jumps away. Both proceed to leap on frogs till they land on females. Females do not resist. Step two of the pro-gram is, "If it stays still, screw it." Males copulate only with females.

Among mammals, too, same-sex mounting has been called homosexual. In many species both males and females mount and make thrusting motions with any of their kind when sexually excited. A female bitch in heat may mount another female. A male rat or bull may mount another male. What happens is not copulation, just mounting—and sometimes orgasmic accidents occur due to inexperience or chance. This is the case especially in rats and bulls, which are so often used as examples of "animal homosexuality."

The male rat has to make several intromissions to reach orgasm. Some-times he does so with several partners. And like many other animals, he may mount, but not penetrate, another male when sexually excited. So the rat copulates with a series of females, building toward orgasm; and some-times, during the course of this, he briefly mounts another male. If he is close to orgasm, the friction of his thrusting when atop another male may make him ejaculate on the other male's back. Bulls may reach orgasm in a moment, and one brief mount of anything, even an inanimate object, can bring it on. An inexperienced bull will mount anything roughly the right size—a female, a male, a human, a bale of hay covered with canvas. Given a female, he mounts any part that's handy. Gradually, with experience, he learns to mount only females and to orient properly to them. His learning is based on visual cues; if he is blindfolded, he will mount indiscriminately again. I know of no unambiguous accounts of preference for males over females or of anal insertion among animals.

The importance of learning in sex is clear among all the higher animals. Anyone who has watched cats breed knows that they are almost as clumsy in their first attempts as people. If a male cat is castrated and then given testosterone, the degree to which he resumes sex activity depends on how much experience he had before castration. Cats are not born with a com-plete and automatic program of rigidly set cues and feedbacks like those of ring doves. The wired-in behaviors—aggressive display, lordosis, mounting, thrusting—are integrated and synchronized through learning and progres-sive experience. This begins to resemble the path of human experience. An even closer parallel to it appeared in Harry Harlow's famous work with rhesus monkeys at the University of Wisconsin.

Originally Harlow was trying to find out exactly what binds the rhesus infant and mother, and how a deficit in mothering affects development. He isolated young monkeys at birth and raised them with substitute mothers—wire dummies with wooden heads and equipped with feeding bottles. Some wire dummies were left bare, others covered with soft terry cloth. The experiment was set up so that some infant monkeys could feed only from the wire dummy, others only from the cloth-covered one. If a monkey had a choice of either kind of dummy, it always clung to the cloth one and treated it in every way like a mother. If only the wire one was equipped with milk, the infant fed from it and then went back to cling to the softer surrogate. A soft surface to cling to was more important in a "mother" than food. This parallels decades of research with human infants deprived of body warmth and affectionate handling; they are smaller, sicklier and less mentally and emotionally developed despite adequate nutrition.

Harlow put a terrifying object into the monkeys' cages—a wind-up teddy bear that marched and beat a drum. The infants with cloth mothers did what a small human child would do; they ran to mother, clung, felt reassured, and then went forth to investigate the intruder. The monkeys with only wire mothers showed panic and withdrawal; they ran about the room and then froze in a crouch on the floor, hugging themselves with their arms and screaming. They behaved like autistic children, emotionally disturbed by maternal deprivation.

Disruption of the mother-infant bond has a powerful influence on animals' and humans' development in all behavior, including sex. Several years after Harlow's first results were published, when the surrogate-raised monkeys were full-grown, it became clear that they could not mate. In fact, these monkeys couldn't develop any affectional ties with other monkeys. Instead they went on acting like autistic humans—sitting passively in their cages and staring into space, hugging and rocking themselves, biting their own arms till they bled. The males might come out of their withdrawal only to exhibit random outbursts of aggression. They sometimes showed sexual excitement, but they couldn't orient themselves to a female; they would grab her shoulders and thrust against her back or seize her from the side and thrust laterally. The surrogate-raised females wouldn't present their hindquarters and accept the male's weight. Harlow wrote, "We paired our females with the most knowledgeable, patient and gentle normal males. The girls would sit down and look appealingly at their would-be consorts, but nothing fruitful came of it. Their hearts were in the right place, but nothing else was . . . we had developed not a breeding colony, but a brooding colony."

Harlow, his wife and other associates have since done many ingenious experiments to discover what programing male and female monkeys are born with, and how learning and interaction complete the job. Male and female both cling to the mother and learn much basic coordination and social behavior from her. The male shows pelvic thrusting even while a clinging infant; the mother's grooming of him seems to stimulate it. By contrast, the infant female takes a passive, rigid posture. At first the mother is mostly protective. When the infants are about three months old, they become more aggressive—especially the males. The mother responds to increased mobility and aggression by punishing the infant and pushing it away from her; the infant, in turn, moves from briefly exploring its environment to actively playing with other infant monkeys. If it has not had adequate mothering, it makes this step of separating and relating to its peers slowly or not at all, depending on the amount of deprivation.

Between the third and sixth months, sex differences become even clearer. The males show increasing rough-and-tumble play, threatening gestures, mounting, pelvic thrusting and dominant behavior. They are hostile or indifferent to newborn infants. The females exhibit more presenting and submissive behavior, no thrusting, and already show maternal responses to the newborn. A male may chase both males and females; a female will not chase a male. Both sexes develop the male and female techniques of aggression, appeasement, evasion, friendship and threat. To a degree, peer interaction can make up for the lack of mothering caused by isolation. Harlow separated infants from their mothers and let them see each other but not play together. They never set up a dominance hierarchy, and remained socially and sexually infantile. They could not mate when they became adults. But even infants totally deprived of real mothers would develop normally if allowed to play together for a short time each day in a stimulating environment.

As the animals approach full development, their aggressive play becomes real aggression, and the males develop a pecking order. Females learn to present to males and groom them, and not to confuse aggression and sexual approach. Normal adult sexuality follows, with the male dominant and the female submissive. In short, mothering prepares the infant for relating well to peers; peer play (like human preadolescent "chumship") prepares the juvenile for adult social and sexual functioning. All the biological equipment for mating is inborn, but the deprived animal doesn't know when or with whom to use it. The same deficiency runs through all its social behavior.

This sounds like a close parallel to what is seen in the psychiatric clinic and the school. Even closer analogies are the "psychotic" monkey mothers produced by these experiments. With great effort and patience, Harlow got some of his autistic, surrogate-raised females to conceive and bear infants. Not one of the infants would have survived without the help of the researchers. The mothers abused or ignored their offspring. Some beat them, dragged them about and pushed their faces into the wire-mesh cage floor. Others brushed off their babies like flies. The infants, pushed aside or attacked, desperately tried time after time to cling to their mothers. One starved to death. The other three survived, with human protection and help; like many emotionally disturbed human children, they were abnormally sexual and aggressive.

The unmothered monkeys did not know how to give mothering in turn. But their second pregnancies were followed by better results; they were adequate mothers to their second offspring. This shows why nature did something as wasteful and chancey as making mammals have to learn sex and parenthood instead of programing it in. The capacity to learn and adapt allows one to make up deficits, correct errors, learn from experience and improve on the past. Just as warm blood allows an organism to adapt to changes in climate, the learning process makes behavior more flexible and adaptive.

However great the distance between Lehrman's ring doves and Harlow's monkeys, the distance between monkey and man is far greater. There are some physical differences, and even greater ones in learning. Physically, man has the biggest penis of all existing primates. Upright walking position has shifted the vaginal opening toward the ventral aspect of the body, so that the coital position is usually face-to-face rather than from behind. The male is not dependent on female estrus to be sexually excited. Only humans are sexual and orgasmic in both sexes and all year around instead of during one season of the year or one week of the month. Sexual excitability goes on even during pregnancy and lactation and when fertility is past. It is also uncertain that females of any other species experience orgasm. The idea that sexual activity and pleasure are animalistic is topsy-turvy.

So far, the most reasonable explanation of this is the incredible human capacity for learning. Human beings are born with a minimum of programed behavior; they must learn a great deal, coordinate what is programed and what is learned, and do it in interaction with other humans. They also show the greatest neotony of all creatures—the extension of infant characteristics into adulthood, such as hairlessness, curiosity and play. The extended helpless infancy, with great dependence on adults, means that a fairly stable and protective environment has to be provided. Though sex is for reproduction in animals, it serves other vital functions in man, and one is probably to make a bond of pleasure that helps hold together the family every infant needs. Societies have many different sorts of families, but they all have families of some kind, and they invariably involve an intimate, prolonged bond between the infant and the biological mother, and protection and support for them by the biological father and/or other males.

To separate what is programed from what is learned is very difficult in humans, let alone to find the third ground of what one is programed eventually to learn. Learning not only plays an immense role, but it starts just after birth. For instance, training in gender identity begins the moment one is touched and spoken to. Parents speak more softly to a girl, handle a boy more firmly (or sometimes more caressingly), make different cuddling gestures to the two sexes. Myriad daily cues soon make learning and programing so intermingled that no test can separate one from the other. But we do know that learning is so important that it can override all the biological programing not only for sexual choice but for gender. All through life, learned and psychologically adaptive (or maladaptive) factors are prominent. Big doses of androgen may increase sexual excitability, but they won't make the shy and inhibited have coitus. Some physically eunuchoid people are quite normally sexual and aggressive despite their lack of testosterone. As with Harlow's unmothered monkeys, learning capacity can make up for deficits. One of the most dramatic proofs of the primacy of learning is the existence of perversions in a small but quite noticeable minority of humans, while they are nonexistent or infinitesimally rare in the animal world unless humans deliberately tamper. Man seems to be nature's experiment in whether so much can be left to learning instead of programing. Where so much must be learned, there is a proportionate possibility of scrambled learning.

The differences in the programing of men and women are still largely unknown. We cannot, as experimental psychologists do with laboratory animals, deliberately deprive and deform the newborn to find out. Our tradition says that men are aggressive and females submissive and appeasing. This is true among most mammals, and there is similar dimorphism built into humans. How much we don't know—nor how much learned variation on the programing is compatible with good psychosocial functioning. A fascinating study of nursery-school children by Robert Sears at Stanford shows that before age three, boys engage in more large-muscle activity and vigorous play than girls. At three the boys far surpass girls in physical aggression.

The extent to which embryonic hormones organize us as males and females is something science will not answer in the immediate future. We know that to a degree we share the element of programming with other animals, but that we have to learn far, far more than they from parents, peers and society, to synchronize it all and use it appropriately. Our wiring is so much at the service of our total adaptation that it can become almost irrelevant. But some people continue to hope that the key to sexual deviation will be found in our wiring, not our learning. Personally, I wonder whether the haunting mental image of the hermaphrodite—the phallic female or feminized, breasted boy—which seems to lie in all men's minds, accounts for the persistent conviction that there is a "natural," or biological, basis for homosexuality and gender disorders. Many homosexuals hope to find a biological precedent for their sex patterns to relieve them of guilt, fears of abnormality and responsibility. Some scientists bend over backward not to close the door prematurely on the possibility, because they do not want to feed traditional prejudices against homosexuals and give further ground for their persecution.

But the evidence is that we must scrap the biologically rooted concepts of bisexuality and latency. Freud inherited from Krafft-Ebing and others the idea that humans are in some way biologically bisexual; those who still retain the concept point to Fisher's work with rats, the mounting behavior of frogs and bulls, the undifferentiated embryonic gonads, the dual sex organs of earthworms. Earthworms are physically hermaphroditic, or intersexual. Calling them bisexual evokes human *bisexual behavior*, which is something quite different—a physically differentiated creature choosing sex objects of two sexes. Psychiatrist Sandor Rado, in 1940, wrote the classic critique of the human-bisexuality theory and concluded that "using the term bisexuality in the only sense in which it is biologically legitimate, there is no such thing as bisexuality either in man or in any other of the higher vertebrates."

Humans do repeat the undifferentiated state of their evolutionary ancestors in the womb; in fact, they also have gills and fur at various times. But just as they lose their gills and fur, they differentiate fully into males or females, with consistent genitals, hormones, genes—and, usually, behavior, object choice and social role. Differentiation and development may foul up at various points between fetal life and adulthood, for reasons of body chemistry or psychological adaptation. But to call once-undifferentiated gonads and intersexual ancestors the basis of human homosexuality is as farfetched as calling our fetal gills the reason we can swim. Harlow can create autistic monkeys, but we don't call the monkey potentially autistic. Lorenz can fixate ducklings on humans, but we don't call ducks potentially perverse. And though Fisher made male rats act maternal, to call them potentially bisexual is logic-chopping. In nature the monkey is not autistic; the duck imprints its mother; as a rat develops, one potential is submerged or eliminated for the sake of the other. Some humans are born with six fingers, but we don't speak of man as potentially six-fingered. And though some men become homosexual, the assumption of a fully developed homosexual pattern lying latent within him is an intellectual wish. Regular homosexual orgasmic behavior is uniquely human, so the reasons for it do not lie in his biological inheritance.

The idea of bisexual potential and latency arise from the instinct theory on which Freud, in the fashion of his time, tried to explain homosexuality. He conceived of instincts as programed forces that act like flowing streams of energy, and hoped to explain behavior by the vicissitudes of their volatile currents. Such energic concepts of instinct have not been taken seriously in the mainstream of biology for decades. We have seen even such simple instinct concepts as sex drive break down into myriad complex components. But Freud felt that if there is bisexual behavior (the choice of both sexes as erotic objects), and if some behavior seems sex-specific (aggression in men, passivity in women), there must be a unifying, underlying biological force involved. Therefore everything that varied from his own very traditional, culture-bound view of masculinity—passivity, gentleness, timidity, tenderness, creativity, sensitivity, domestic interests—must be due to a female instinct. Females who were ambitious, athletic, aggressive and competitive must also be showing their latent other-sex instinct. Everything from the women's vote to all-male poker games were then knowingly called homosexual. Freud took any fantasy or dream as proof of such a homosexual drive, though it had no basis in behavior, and despite the fact that many homosexuals have next to nothing in common with the opposite sex. Rarely has a scientific idea been cherished by so many people on such slender evidence.

If we all have bisexual potential, the homosexual part must be latent, repressed or sublimated. The idea of bisexuality demanded defense of an equally untenable concept, sublimation—the idea that sexual instinct can be diverted into such "higher" activities as learning, friendship, art, science and religion. Despite Freud's elaboration of the idea in his book on Da Vinci, the fact remains that many creative people are sexually active, and many uncreative people are sexually inactive. As Kinsey said in his volume on the male, sublimation is an academic possibility, not a demonstrated actuality. And like latency, it has been used in so many reductionistic and confusing ways that it is better buried than kept alive.

Since the late thirties, psychiatrists have also questioned the idea of latency. A definitive critique, as convincing as Rado's on bisexuality, has been written by Dr. Leon Saltzman. Latency, as he points out, implies either dormancy or potential. A hibernating bear is a dormant bear, fully developed and waiting to be awakened. An acorn is a potential oak; it must develop under the right conditions. The idea of potential is part of modern biological and psychological thought. Humans are potentially homosexual—this is proved by the simple fact that humans do become homosexual. But humans also develop into heterosexuals, and latent heterosexuality is only spoken of jokingly. Everyone can catch syphilis or tuberculosis, but we don't call man potentially syphilitic or potentially tubercular. We reserve this concept for homosexuality. We reserve it especially for men. When a man does something that deviates from traditional male behavior, he is said to be a latent homosexual. A female who violates the traditional role is accused of masculine protest or penis envy but far less often of homosexuality.

Theoretically, all of us are potentially all that is human. Everyone is a "latent" everything. As Saltzman says, "It explains everything and elucidates very little. . . . The absence of such behavior proves the concept, while the presence of such behavior implies that the latent has become manifest. Consequently it has practically no operational value." What needs study is the set of social and psychological forces that have made so many cherish the idea of latency as dormancy, especially in regard to homosexuality in men. Educated laymen and some scientists still want to believe that homosexuality, full-blown and totally developed, lies dormant behind a wall of repression in us all, and that any female aggression or male passivity is due to this instinctive force bursting into the open. There is such a thing as a suppressed homosexual—the person who feels he is homosexual, has homosexual desires, and restrains himself from sex activity for psychological or social reasons. But that has nothing to do with latency.

There remains the fact, long a puzzle and a source of theoretical argument, that heterosexuals sometimes have homosexual dreams, fantasies and impulses. These things do seem to have direct biological parallels, in the mounting and dominance behavior of animals. The use of sexual gestures for nonsexual purposes in animals is strikingly like recent psychiatric findings about what classic Freudians have called instinctive, latent homosexuality. In humans, too, there are nonsexual uses of sex, and this knowledge has led to a much better chance of curing deviants and relieving heterosexuals of anxiety over what they feared was a latent "homosexual component" in themselves. Examining these observations and concepts that have taken the place of instinct theory will be the task of the next chapter.

INTERVIEWS

Dr. Frank Beach is one of the world's leading researchers on animal sex behavior. For more than two decades he has written monographs, edited texts and acted as a central figure in coordinating interdisciplinary sex research. We meet at his office at UCLA in Los Angeles. He is a ruddy, brisk, husky man who becomes very precise and rigorously skeptical when he talks about his field. He says:

I don't know any authenticated instance of males or females in the animal world preferring a homosexual partner—if by homosexual you mean complete sexual relations, including climax. Now, there is mounting of males by males, but without intromission of the penis or climax. There's also mounting of females by females—I've just finished writing a paper on female mounting behavior. This mounting is homosexual in a very literal, descriptive sense; it's male-to-male and female-to-female behavior. But calling it homosexual in the human sense is an interpretation, and interpretations are tricky. That's why I want to work by just measuring behavior. Before we interpret things, we have to look at them, accurately describe what we see. I'm not even sure we should call mounting sexual. It might be more accurate just to use a descriptive term—mounting behavior. It's questionable that mounting in itself can properly be called sexual.

Then you don't see males mounting males when females are around?

I've never seen it. Males mount males, but they're faster to mount females when there's opportunity. The beagles I'm experimenting with now show male-to-male mounting. And there's one male in the colony who seems to be mounted by other males all the time. I don't know why this happens, but some males seem to be constant objects of mounting behavior.

Is there a difference in mounting between domestic or confined animals and those living under natural conditions?

There may be more homosexual mounting in domesticated species, especially in animals confined in homosexual groups. But it also occurs in nature, so I don't think it makes a great deal of difference.

Does it relate to aggressive or competitive situations?

I've seen nothing to relate mounting and aggression. Whether you want to equate them is primarily a matter of definitions. My own inclination is not to confuse the two conceptions. In general, I'm opposed, for instance, to applying such terms as pecking order and territorial behavior to human activities.

Then you've seen no special context for homosexual mounting?

Well, it often seems to occur in conditions of intense excitement, which have no apparent sexual connotations. The hormonal condition of the individual seems to be another cause. In some species, females mount other females only when they're in heat; but under that circumstance they also mount males.

What research are you doing now that bears on these things?

Stand up and look behind you. [*Pinned to the wall is a photograph of an organ system dissected from an animal's body.*] That's a picture of a dog's genitourinary system. These are the ovaries, and this is the uterus. Here at the end of the tract is a penis. We gave male hormones to pregnant females bearing female fetuses, and this is what happens. The genitals of the offspring are masculinized. Now we want to see whether such a female will lift her leg when she urinates or whether she'll squat. That is, have we also masculinized the nervous system? The answer isn't clear yet, but of course we do know that if we give normal females large amounts of male hormone during childhood, their mounting behavior increases. All this may shed light on whether there are basic differences between the male and female nervous systems—and, if so, what they are. It may also show whether or not there are real morphological or biochemical differences between human heterosexuals and homosexuals. Personally, I tend to doubt it. In fact, I think the chances are one in a thousand.

The volume you edited, Sex and Behavior, *showed not only how the different specialties overlap and contradict each other, but how little they know each other. Why is there so little contact between them?*

There's a basic split. The people who deal with patients and the people who work in the laboratory still tend not to know each other's work.

Harlow's monkeys have become a standard reference, like Pavlov's dogs and Lorenz's geese. At the Primate Research Laboratory in Madison, Wisconsin, Harry Harlow says:

In the monkey, there's no such thing as deviant behavior as we speak of it among humans. At least not in the field. When the adult rhesus monkey mates, the male has to make several successive mounts. In other words, he has to work at it. I've never seen such persistent mounting, with intromission and ejaculation, between two males. I'd guess that male homosexual behavior—if you want to call it that—is transient play or a token sexual gesture as a sign of friendship. Reports of "homosexual mating" are probably old cases of anthropomorphic observation. You got that sort of stuff until about 1925, when people began to ask what mounting means to the monkey, rather than what it evokes in people.

Anthropologists call what monkeys do Brittle Monogamy. I call it the Hollywood Mating. There are only a few minutes or a few days of attachment in the sexual bond, even among anthropoid apes. Humans have relatively permanent love attachments, of which sex is a component part. But no animal has enough of a capacity for lasting, complex love relationships to develop a homosexual pattern. The human's capacity for individualized affection separates him from the so-called lower animals as much as anything else.

Your work suggests basic differences between the male and female, and a foul-up of sex behavior if dependence and aggression patterns are distorted.

We still know very little about how heterosexual behavior develops in primates, but I'm sure it's learned, even at one year of age—especially in females. We're also guessing now that significant male-female differences will show anyway, without contact with other animals. Even as an infant, the male rhesus approaches the female and makes mounting and thrusting motions. In fact, male infants make thrusting motions even when newborn and clinging to the mother's body. There's limited data showing that human babies do the same thing, though mothers tend not to notice or report it. The threat gesture also exists very early in male monkeys. The female infant seems to have inborn rather than learned patterns, too—body rigidity, erection of the tail, passivity. When approached by a male infant, the female infant presents herself dorsally, rigid and passive. This happens even though neither sexual nor aggressive behavior has really developed in the male or female yet.

So the physical gestures are there at birth. What's learned is how and when to use them. Tinbergen has shown a lot about how the male learns to separate sexual and aggressive postures, how the female learns to use rigidity and passivity. We've found that when the male monkey is about a year old, he develops real aggressive behavior; he also learns in what situation to use it, and when to inhibit it. He learns how to approach, seize and clasp a female without threatening her. The female, in turn, learns not to show threat back to the male in a sexual situation, and to accept his weight without retreating.

But if a monkey is deprived of good affectional bonds with its mother and peers, it doesn't learn from them to use these inborn gestures appropriately. A seriously deprived male won't approach females. His aggression has been obliterated, and his fear is overwhelming. The female who failed to learn to relate to other monkeys won't take the passive posture when approached by a male, and she's aggressive instead of affectionate with infants. So the monkey needs the reciprocal affectional systems with its mother and age-mates to learn to play, fight and mate. If either system is fouled up, there's a serious effect on sociosexual development.

So physical sexual dimorphism prepares for sex and dominance behavior. Offhand, I don't know of any human antecedants for sex-posture patterns, but I don't think anyone has studied humans for it yet.

Is the idea of imprinting useful in explaining any of this?

We don't know about imprinting in monkeys. The term originated in the study of submammalians. Ford and Beach were the first to point out that as you go upward in the animal world, toward higher complexity, endocrine factors decrease and neurological factors increase. I think it's wiser to talk about optimal times for learning certain things. Imprinting implies something more mechanical. It also smacks of old-fashioned instinct theory, which said an unsatisfied instinct dies. I think that if something drops out of behavior, something else must be taking its place. For instance, if something allegedly learned by imprinting doesn't develop, maybe social fear has developed in its place.

For instance, we've seen that unmothered monkeys are in turn abusive and indifferent to their own offspring. I'm sure they didn't recognize their offspring as members of their species. They just saw these *things* bothering them, and their aggression was called into play. I'm sure they would have shown such behavior to any monkey, if they thought they could get away with it. So maybe there isn't imprinting in mammals, or even a clear and irreplaceable period for learning something, which leaves a behavioral blank if ignored. Obliteration of one capacity takes place, I think, because a conflicting pattern—such as fear—hinders proper development.

John Money has become a leading figure in sex research through his articles on sexual anomalies, behavior genetics and endocrinology—but especially for his work with anatomical hermaphrodites. We speak at his office at Johns Hopkins Hospital in Baltimore, where he has taught and done research for almost twenty years as a member of the university.

People set me up as a person who says that gender role is determined by environment. I've never been so simpleminded. What I did say in my first reports on hermaphrodites is that psychosexual development is determined after birth, rather than before, to an extraordinary degree. There wasn't any conclusive evidence on that point before my work with hermaphrodites. I think the crucial work that lies immediately ahead in my field is hard laboratory research—most of which will have to be done on animals. The hope is finding the centers that regulate sex in the brain. For instance, Lisk, at Princeton, has found that there is a center to turn off sexual activity as well as one to turn it on. Could that differ in males and females? Soon we may have a clear analysis of sexual dimorphism in the brain—and how much of each sex's behavior is dormant in the brain of the other sex, capable of experimental activation.

None of this points to homosexuality at the present, but we're getting a first peek at the scene of the future in the work of Fisher and Phoenix and Goy. Soon we may find correlations between animal and human findings. We know that girls who were hormonally masculinized before birth have a high level of physical activity. They call themselves tomboys, and so does everyone else. What we don't know yet is what this may have to do with later psychosexual development.

Many psychiatrists and psychologists have written as though they were talking about astral bodies, not creatures with brains, hormones and some amount of programed behavior. Hilda Bruce, at Cambridge, found that female mice can't implant a fertilized egg and become pregnant if they get contaminated by the smell of an alien stud. Henkin, at the National Institute of Health, is one of the few people in the world studying human smell. Now he's finding a relationship between gonadal deficiency and smell deficiency in certain people—presumably on the basis of a deficiency in the pituitary gland and the hypothalamic cells. We don't know what the sense of smell has to do with human sexual development. For all we know, the underarm smell of an infant's father may be crucial in his life! You're laughing, and I'm almost joking. But almost no theory is too wild, as we've been learning. Gorski reported that the effects of testosterone on the brains of fetal rats are canceled out by phenobarbitol and other drugs. How many pregnant women take phenobarbitol, and what effect has it had on their babies?

I've used the word "imprinting" regarding certain things in psychosexual development. Animal-behavior people use the word in a strict Lorenz-Tinbergen sense. It's as clean and simple as spiders knowing where to spin webs—though how simple is that, really? A spider's architectural capacity is very different from a person's, but there's also a commonality. The imprinting idea draws attention to the fact that there is a kind of learning that happens in critical periods—learning of tremendous, long-lasting influence. At a given time, an organism is especially malleable to a certain type of environmental stimulus. If a response takes place, what's learned is hard to lose; if it's missed, there is a gap in learning, and the opportunity is permanently lost.

For example, nobody has ever extinguished a native language, to my knowledge. If it's forgotten, it always revives faster than any other can be learned from scratch. If you don't learn language at the right time, you never make it up well or easily. Imprint for which foods are edible isn't as strong as language imprint. Imprint for gender identity is very strong. So is imprint for falling in love. This is different from the concepts of Pavlovian or operant conditioning, which assume that if something is learned, it can be unlearned or extinguished just as easily. You can use the imprinting idea and still allow that people are a hundred times more flexible developmentally than other animals, and more subject to life-history experiences.

In addition to imprinting, I find the concept of programing useful. The bird is preprogramed as a nest-building architect. In a learned program, rather than one that's built in, there's a greater margin of error. The sexual behavior of some house pets is very peculiar, due to special human intervention in behavior. You scarcely have to bother intervening with humans to make their sexuality peculiar—just let them follow society! Restraining the sexual play of preschool children may be just as risky to good psychosexual development as restraining dogs in theirs.

We've talked mostly about hard research, but of course I'm the first to admit that family influences are important. I know that Stoller says he has transsexuals who seemed to know their correct genetic sex even though the parents ascribed an incorrect sex to them. I wonder! I have patients like Stoller's who fight the gender their parents ostensibly ascribe. However, I think that in practically every case the family—even the family physician, too—lived in equivocation about whether this child would turn out male or female at puberty. Parents protect themselves, and amnesia is a beautiful thing when it works well. I had a hermaphrodite boy of eleven, and the mother claimed to be surprised when I told her that he sat to urinate. It was impossible for him to urinate standing. She really believed that she didn't know anything was wrong. Then the mother's sister came in and said they'd all known perfectly well all along.

I see a bit of daylight coming through from work being done these days in family therapy, simultaneously watching all members of the family. The effect of children on parents is underestimated. A child becomes an autonomous influence in a house, enough even to be a perfect little bastard and have a powerful effect on everyone! I suspect that family therapy will teach us more about how people interact than about etiology. Psychiatry has generally given us good phenomenology but fallen down on etiology. It tells us how, but not really why. Of course the majority of families I see come because of endocrine problems in a child, and there's a good chance with them that a little guidance and counseling will help a lot. They're more flexible than people tied up in neurotic knots.

It's easy to give opinions about these things when you're not dealing with hard evidence. I was asked to write something on the change of sex role in American males. In my first, uncensored draft I began, "The American father fucked the American mother." It's as good a point of view as most of the quasi-anthropology that's around these days. I don't think it matters much what the differences are between the male and female, as long as there *are* differences. And that will be true until babies are produced in some new way. What fouls up a child, for instance, is if a transvestite father dresses and acts like a female after he stood as the model of a father to the child in the past.

I remain most interested in the interaction of physiology, gender and behavior. There are now a dozen or twenty cases in the world of a new antiandrogen being used successfully on sexual psychopaths. They aren't feminized by it, as they would be by estrogen, which was used in such cases in the past. Transsexual males are happy with it because it removes their sex drive. Without any sex drive to bother them, they feel more feminine, and they like that.

The relative hang-ups of various deviants are pretty difficult to estimate. Heterosexuals can get into hang-ups as great as those of a lot of homosexuals. But if I matched homosexuals with transvestites and transsexuals, my impression is that the transvestites and transsexuals would have more hang-ups to destroy their lives. Yet many of them are surprisingly good at finding ways out. I know one person who had a sex-reassignment operation from male to female and now looks like a plain-Jane but adequate woman. As a woman, she got a job where the new femaleness is valued and useful. Some of the transsexuals who've had reassignment surgery were once male prostitutes who picked up "heavy trade." Now some are female prostitutes proving over and over, as they seem to need to, that men will want them. These aren't the majority, though. Many fade away into respectable anonymity in their new lives.

24

Instead of Latency

In a book on quadrupeds published in the 1550s, the naturalist Konrad Gesner said that a younger or weaker male baboon signals his submission to older stronger ones: "And when he is signed to, he presents his arse." Four centuries later, psychiatrist Lionel Ovesey wrote about a heterosexual patient's dream in which the man, after having been humiliated by his boss, left the office on all fours, ass in the air. Ovesey called the dream an expression not of latent homosexuality but of "pseudohomosexuality"—the patient had imitated his primate ancestors by signaling submission with a "feminine" gesture.

This connection between sex and dominance was made only after scientists disentangled their ideas about human emotions and animal behavior. For thousands of years people have ascribed their own feelings and motives to animals. Aesop's *Fables* and the *Panchatantra* made nature a human drama with moral lessons. From medieval bestiaries to Victorian naturalists' theories, animals were seen as examples of fidelity, lust, pride, maternal love, malice, vanity and modesty. With the advent of social Darwinism, nature became a gladitorial arena—as Tennyson put it, red in tooth and claw—where all but the most ruthless were devoured and kept from reproducing. Others, who saw that life also depends on cooperation and mutual dependence, rhapsodized about birds that pair for life and animal mothers that lure the hunter from their young. When Westermarck and Briffault had their controversy on the nature of sex and the family in *homo sapiens*, each could find troves of animal lore to back his own theory.

A more exact, impersonal approach began to appear in the 1890s. The American zoologist Charles Otis Whitman insisted that we can't know what animals feel; we should stop talking about their souls and just scrupulously observe their behavior—what they do. At that time instinct was the favored concept for explaining behavior. Soon experimental psychology, with its laboratory tests of learning and conditioning, brought better results than instinct-theory work. Pavlov's experiments in conditioning were followed by the studies of John Watson, whose book *Behaviorism* appeared in the twenties, applying a blend of learning theory and Pavlovianism to the human psyche. Behaviorism flourished in America, and it produced excesses as silly, in their very different ways, as those of early psychoanalysis. It soon became clear to all but the incurably zealous that human (and even animal) life can't be reduced to a network of reflexes and conditioned responses. But behaviorism had already acted as a needed corrective to moralizing naturalism and self-indulgent psychoanalytic speculation. Behaviorism, like classical analysis, still has some adherents today, but both fields have outgrown the early phase when, as young sciences, they tried to prove their legitimacy by being as prematurely doctrinaire as possible.

In the twenties and thirties, Zuckerman, Yerkes and Carpenter did their pioneer observations of primate behavior. Carpenter was especially influential in getting researchers to stop watching animals in zoos, whose behavior often becomes as abnormal as their habitat; captive and domesticated animals may act as peculiarly as humans who've been in solitary for years. In the 1930s ethology, the study of animal behavior, came into its own as a specialty. Like biology and anthropology at that time, it produced some of the best results through a functional approach—assuming that if behavior exists, it is because it has a purpose in the animal's life.

One of the greatest pioneer ethologists to appear during that period was Konrad Lorenz. Recently American experimental psychologists, with their hard-headed laboratory approach, have criticized him, sometimes justly and sometimes not. It is paltry to deny his brilliance, skill and intellectual daring. The Dutch-born Nikolaas Tinbergen, now at Oxford University, became the second great ethologist of that generation. There followed a lag of research during the forties. Then in the fifties a great surge of activity began in America, Germany, England, Holland and Japan. Now the questions ethologists had been asking were also taken up by biologists, psychologists, and psychiatrists. During the sixties the first popularizations of ethology appeared—*African Genesis, The Territorial Imperative, The Naked Ape, The Human Zoo, Body Language*—some of them useful, others as misleading or silly as many of the first popularizations of psychoanalysis during the twenties. But they are probably a prelude to public interest and support that will allow further, more sophisticated research.

Ethologists found that nothing like human sentiment governs much of animal behavior, no matter how human the behavior seems. Shapes, colors and motions stimulate programed responses through biochemical reactions. Gulls will zealously protect their chicks, but nothing like human maternal feeling is involved; if a chick dies, its calls and movements no longer elicit their parental acts, so they eat it. Nor is foresight usually present. The male dog that licks the vulva of a bitch in heat isn't trying to excite her, he is just responding to an olfactory stimulus; because it does excite her and promote reproduction, the stimulus and response have been programed genetically through natural selection. Understanding this was crucial when ethologists tried to decode the nonverbal "language" of sex and aggression.

Before the First World War, Julian Huxley had noticed that the language of one sequence of behavior can become altered slightly for use in another. He called this ritualization. The signaling motion acquires a formal, slightly exaggerated quality that makes it conspicuous and, in its new context, unambiguous. For instance, a gull chick stimulates its parents to regurgitate and feed it by making a special food-begging noise. When an adult male and female gull do their courting, they use the food-begging call. The adult voice quality, the context and the addition of a peculiar head-tossing motion make clear that now this is not merely a request for food. It brings them closer by eliciting the protective behavior also shown to infants; they drop their aggressive and flight tendencies and become comfortably intimate enough to mate. If the male gull regurgitates and feeds the female, it is a pretty sure sign that they will go on to copulate.

Human beings have a similar behavior that has been ritualized from infant activity—kissing. The adult act derives from nursing, one of the relatively few programed behaviors with which people are born. It has been elaborated to convey meanings that have little or nothing to do with its original purpose. A mother tenderly kisses her baby, a flirt gives a touch of the lips, two lovers kiss at the height of coitus, de Gaulle kisses Adenauer on a state occasion—and two times out of three, anyway, people know what message is being sent.

We don't call most kisses between adults an infantile or suckling activity. We distinguish the fine difference in behavior, motivation and response. But sloppy, anthropomorphic observation and failure to see exactly when in a whole sequence of behavior an act is performed have created many confusions about sex, homosexuality and aggression, in animals and in men. The nonverbal "languages" of these kinds of activity often carry over from one to the other. Disentangling them explained a great deal that used to be accounted for with the concepts of bisexuality and latency. This began when the sexual and nonsexual meanings of mounting, lordosis and presenting became clear. It was during roughly the same time that psychiatrists began to find nonsexual messages behind many sexual (and especially homosexual) fantasies and acts. But before that relationship can be clear, we must see where sex, aggression and their ritualized languages fit in an animal's life.

It used to be thought that most male animals fight for mates, often to the death. This is very rarely true. The expression and control of aggression begins with birth. The newborn animal is relatively or completely helpless. But at breeding time, parents are at the height of their aggressiveness, primed to release their attack mechanism in defense of their young, home and food supply. Therefore the infant needs signals to keep the parents from venting that aggression on them. The cheeping and gaping mouths of fledglings, the nuzzling and licking of wolf pups are ritualizations, respectively, of begging and suckling. They send the parent the message, "Don't hurt me, I'm just a hungry, helpless infant." This causes a chemical reaction in the adult that inhibits aggression and remotivates it to act protective and nurturing.

As the infant grows, it gradually ceases to send the parent "protect and feed me" signals. The young male increasingly expresses aggression; so does the female, though to a markedly lesser extent. This could bring retaliation from adults and peers, so new ways of inhibiting others' aggression develop. The juvenile gull employs a posture that is a reversal of the adult threatening posture. The young male langur monkey makes the adult gesture of dominance but immediately apologizes with a demonstration of infantile dependence; he will mount an adult male (an act of dominance), quickly dismount, run around to face him, embrace him, and bury his face in the adult's chest, squealing tensely.

As animals begin to mature, differences between the sexes in aggression and appeasement become stronger. Males show more threat and attack, especially at breeding time. In most species the male is larger and stronger, and for a female to threaten a male would be suicide. But in most animals there are signals that prevent this from happening. Plumage, coloration or behavior allow many animals to tell the opposite sex on sight, and there is a programed nonaggressive response. A large female emerald lizard will fiercely fight other females, which have no particular throat markings. The male has blue coloration that appears at his throat with maturity, like the fuzz on an adolescent boy's face. If a pugnacious female meets a weak young male only a third her size, she will automatically fall on her belly before him in a submissive posture. This in turn inhibits his aggression toward her.

In some animals, both female and male are aggressive, and there are no distinctive markings by which they recognize each other. This is true among herring gulls, a species in which there is overlap in size between the sexes. Sometimes a male gull will appease a female, but when mating pairs form, it is always a larger male and smaller female, and his dominance is clearly established.

Aggression is paradoxically a help and a hindrance to mating. A male must be aggressive or he is unattractive and may not get to mate; he will also have a hard time defending and feeding himself, his mate and his offspring. On the other hand, since he tends to react to all animals with aggression, his pugnacity stands in the way of mating and rearing young. For reproduction to take place, the female must be able to appease or divert his aggression. However, her tendency to flee also works against mating. To animals, being touched tends to mean being captured or injured; if the female is to accept the courting and body weight of the male, her desire to flee aggression and contact must be lessened. So the aggressive male and the flight-poised female need remotivating if they are to reproduce.

In some species, males are programed not to attack females under any circumstances. (Human beings and domestic chickens are among those species in which males sometimes attack females.) Even when the male does not attack the female, she must be reassured that she is being courted, not assaulted, just as the male must be reassured that his aggression is not being met with aggression or genuine flight. In very few species can a male force a female to copulate against her will. Rape is quite rare in the animal world, and atypical among humans. Mating is an intricately synchronized set of mutual adjustments between male and female. It ends with their becoming habituated to each other, often to a point where the dominance relationship between them is not pronounced.

The male black-headed gull defends its nesting territory against all comers. When a female approaches him, she turns her head so as not to present her black face mask, which is the combat signal in this species. The male then uses ritualized attack gestures, clearly not real attack: this displays his aggressive power harmlessly. The female makes gestures of flight and appeasement without actually running away. Soon they become habituated and mate.

Aggression and appeasement between males of a species is also highly ritualized. As in mating, there are advantages and disadvantages to aggression. It is needed for self-defense and hunting, but it would be disastrous for the species if let loose indiscriminately. So animals rarely actually fight others of their kind; they go through an escalating series of threats until one signals his surrender. ⌊Man is unique in the animal world for being murderously destructive to his own.⌋ But even among people, aggression more often follows a pattern of threat and appeasement than of actual combat, as one can see when two men in a bar go through a ritual of rising threats until one calls the bluff and the other backs down.

Males may fight over territory, to establish a pecking order, or over mates. Their ways of signaling threat and appeasement vary. The red comb and wattles of the cock are his battle flags; the loser in a fight between males turns them from sight. Hunting animals that live in packs, such as wolves, are high in aggression yet must control it in order to live together. Lorenz describes two male wolves battling to a point where the tough, older one is on top, apparently about to kill: "The old wolf has his jaws close, very close, to the young one's throat; and the younger is holding his head turned aside, the curve of his throat, the most vulnerable part of his body, being offered unprotected to the enemy. . . . But the victor doesn't bite. You can see that he would like to, but that he simply cannot do it. A wolf who offers his throat to the opponent in the manner just described is never seriously bitten."

The wolf seems to say in ritual language, "I'm as good as dead." He may also turn off another male's aggression by nuzzling, pawing and licking, as though to say, "I'm just a baby with you." But one of the chief ways higher animals express dominance and appeasement is by borrowing the behavior-language of sex and ritualizing it. As Gesner noted, when two male baboons confront each other and vie for dominance, the loser takes the presenting position with which a female turns off a male's aggression, saying, "I'm just a poor weak woman." The dominant one may mount, as though to say, "You are vanquished and on the bottom, like a female."

Mounting, presenting and displaying or grasping of genitals among males were long considered the strongest evidence of "animal homosexuality." Fifty years ago the dominance behavior of baboons was described as homosexual copulation, with the subordinate reaching back and masturbating the winner. Actually, the dominant baboon mounts and may or may not make a few pelvic thrusts; there is never intromission. The subordinate baboon presents, but not in quite the same way as a female. His posture has a note of cringing and apprehension, even incipient flight, and he looks back with apparent anxiety over his shoulder. He may reach back and touch the dominant's penis, which is a signal of subordinate status in many primates. Lorenz describes such an encounter. The subordinate took the "female" posture, and the dominant stalked off without mounting him. The loser ran after, presenting until the dominant finally mounted and gave a few perfunctory thrusting motions. The subordinate, satisfied at last that his token of subordination had been recognized, went his way, the Adlerian interchange complete.

In some species, females as well as males threaten and fight to establish a dominance hierarchy; then high-ranking females tend to pair with high-ranking males, and low-ranking females with low-ranking males. In other species, females derive their status from their mates. (Among macaques, a high-dominance mother will fight on her son's behalf, and help keep up his dominance status in the troop.) Regardless of its sex, an animal may use the male sex posture as a dominance signal, the female one as a sign of submission. A female will mount another female to show her higher rank, and a male will present to another male to show subordination. Females in many species also mount to express sexual excitement. Mounting has other, still poorly understood ritualized meanings, probably at least as many as the human kiss.

Some male primates show their subordination by touching the other male's penis. It is very like a human kissing a superior's hand, saluting an officer or, as the idiom has it, kissing his ass. The squirrel monkey uses penis display to establish his dominance. He spreads his legs, displays his erect penis, and thrusts it before his opponent's face. The opponent must stay still and duck his head as though dodging a blow or he will be viciously attacked. To find the most dominant member of a squirrel monkey colony, one just picks out the male who displays to everyone, but to whom no one displays in return.

Signals of sex and aggression have gone through very elaborate ritualizations and borrowings in some animals, especially the primates. Since all animals mate most or all the time with the male mounting from behind, the female's primary sexual signal is rearward—for instance, the great red patch that appears on the female baboon's rump when she is fertile. This patch turns off the male's aggression and remotivates him sexually. In some species of baboons, the male has a similar red patch on his rear, an evolutionary adaptation that makes his submissive display to other males more effective. It is a (literally) glaring example of the male borrowing female sex signals to show subordination—and as we shall see, it has parallels in human homosexual imagery and acts. Another development that has human counterparts is the shift of sex signals from the rear to the front of the body. The mandrill has a red penis, and blue scrotal patches on either side of it. His usual body posture hides his genitals from sight, so this signal may go unseen. His face duplicates the pattern—a bright-red nose and blue cheeks—for the benefit of females met head-on. Similarly, the female gelada baboon has a chest patch that imitates the intricate markings around her vulva, and it waxes and wanes along with the vulvar markings during her estrous cycle.

W. S. Gilbert once said that man is just a monkey shaved. Often watching primates makes the idea irresistible. In 1968 Dr. Bryan Robinson implanted electrodes in monkeys' brains so that he could stimulate their aggression with an electronic signal. He put together a dominant male, a subordinate male and a female. The female allied herself with male Number One, and helped him abuse Number Two. Then Robinson, by electrical stimulation, increased Number Two's aggression to such a point that the balance of power shifted. The female promptly switched her allegiance and helped the new Number One attack the former Number One. Robinson concluded, "I refuse to draw conclusions on this about human females."

Tongue in or out of cheek, one must be cautious in deciding what man shares with his biological relatives and how he differs. When Zuckerman's early study of captive baboons' behavior appeared, many people liked to think they had observed something close to the state of "natural man." The troop's ruler, said Zuckerman, was a tyrant male who ruthlessly beat down all male competition to establish a haremlike sexual monopoly. The recent field studies of Washburn, De Vore and others have changed the picture radically.

The male baboon becomes potent and fertile at age five, but he doesn't reach full adult social status until he is ten or eleven. Until then, older males may interfere with his attempts to mate, and females may reject him. His appearance and behavior are still clumsy. He spends these "adolescent" years on the periphery of the troop with the other young males, learning to attack, appease, cooperate. He and other males may compete over females, but that is only a small part of their aggressive behavior. When they do fight, it is usually with threat, appeasement and sparring rather than serious combat. No ladderlike hierarchy forms. Through assertion and social participation, the peripheral young male may finally win a place in the little power establishment at the center of the baboon troop.

The power there is not held by a ruthless, battle-scarred pasha, but by a ruling clique of two or three. This baboon establishment doesn't necessarily consist of the strongest, fiercest males. They are the baboons who have the best balance of aggressive and cooperative behavior; otherwise their coalition could not endure. Their mutual aid enables them to defeat any male who challenges their authority. They have not only status but responsibility. They keep their position more by threat than by actual combat; they also prevent fights and stop bickering among the others. They groom and protect the young. They are not necessarily the males who copulate most often, but females seek them out at the height of their fertile period, so the establishment has a breeding advantage in an evolutionary sense.

Sex takes up a minor part of any baboon's life. The male is excited only by the female's receptivity, which is signaled by her red rump. She is estrous for only a week out of the month, and inactive during pregnancy and lactation. Sex, rather than being the motivating force and cement of baboon society, is a relatively rare and disruptive part of it.

There are similarities in another primate with marked competitive behavior, the macaque. The male Japanese macaque may mount a subordinate to confirm their relative status; or the dominant may let the subordinate mount him in order to groom him. Society polarizes around the more dominant males, as in baboon troops. But there is no pecking order, extensive conflict over sexual partners, or unbridled aggression. The chief males are not simply the most aggressive but the ones best able to cooperate with other males, and most protective with infants. A male gets to join the establishment by social participation—grooming and being groomed, preventing fights, protecting the young—as well as by nerve and strength.

For centuries scientists have wanted to use primates as proof of their view of mankind. One tradition runs from Hobbes through the social Darwinists to Freud, saying that man is a baboon as Zuckerman first described him—grudgingly and incompletely controlling his selfish, lustful and aggressive instincts. In this view, life is battle without quarter, man a creature of conflict within himself and in relation to others. The counterargument runs from Rousseau to A. S. Neill and Erich Fromm, saying that man is loving, nonaggressive and constructive unless kept from being so. (John Dollard, in an age of utopian "permissiveness" and optimism, helped win acceptance for the idea that humans are aggressive only if frustrated; if this were true, it would mean that man has escaped inheriting behavior from the entire vertebrate kingdom.) There are no end of irresponsible popularizers, from Robert Ardrey to "inspirational" authors, who try to show one side or the other as scientific fact.

As Harlow proved, even an unsocialized monkey is functionally no monkey at all. There is certainly no such creature as natural man—man outside society is nonexistent, and society irreversibly molds the plastic biological base of man's behavior. As Ashley Montagu has said, much that people think of as human nature is really second nature. We in the West

look at the baboon and macaque and see parodies of ourselves, for the
West is a very competitive society. Members of other societies might see
themselves better in the gentle mountain gorilla or in the howler monkey
community, where there is less difference in dominance among males and
between the sexes. Even the baboon and macaque are cooperative as well
as aggressive. Man is neither dedicated to predation nor an unsullied
altruist. He is both of these and more. Like all higher animals, he must balance aggression, the need to control it, and the need to cooperate.

There is no exact paradigm for human sex, aggression and signal language in any of the nearly two hundred species of primates. Each has a
unique pattern, and so does man; there are similarities and differences
among them all. Furthermore, humans may vary from culture to culture as
much as primates do from species to species. Seen in an ethological overview, man is a very aggressive, predatory animal, but also a highly cooperative social one; his prolonged early dependence requires a stable web of
supportive social bonds. This means that he has many conflicting needs to
fill without their getting in each other's way. A gull or baboon has programed checks and balances to keep his aggression, sex and dependence
integrated. Man must learn to do so much more than they, and he often
comes up with uneconomical or even bizarre solutions, including neurosis,
psychosis and sexual deviation.

The most striking fact about man's sexuality is its sheer extent. He is
sexually active most of his adult life, regardless of fertility. This is biologically unique. If man were truly, as the maxim says, a wolf to other men,
murder would hardly exist, and war not at all, and the aims of sex would
not extend beyond reproduction. Sex has become a physically pleasureful
and emotionally complex social cement, reinforcing bonds and acting as a
vehicle for nonsexual feelings such as affection, reassurance and power.
This is particularly true within the long-lasting nuclear family. But prolonged intimate contact there allows many disruptive feelings of sex and
aggression to develop. The Oedipal conflict of Western society, and similar
emotional complexes in other societies, seem to result from the need to
control them. The incest taboo has no basis in our biological wiring and
probably little genetic danger, but it exists in every society—apparently
another attempt to accommodate to the peculiar needs of so long a childhood. Family tensions are somewhat eased when human children, like
other mammalian young, start spending more time with their peers. Young
and adolescent males especially group together, and develop their aggressive and cooperative potential in play, clubs and other all-male activities.

Human beings have their own set of sexual and aggressive signals built
into their bodies. The large, rounded, protruding breasts of the female
aren't necessary for milk production, and no other animal has them.
Humans are also the only primates with rounded, protruding buttocks
instead of flat flanks. The breasts seem to be a front-view duplication of the
buttocks, which are the prime sexual stimulus to our evolutionary ances-

tors. Humans' uniquely thick, red lips and rosy breast patches may imitate the red vulva. Underarm hair may reinforce the signal of the pubic thatch. All these front-view signals coincide with the shift to face-to-face sexual approach and coital position—and all of these in turn with the change to upright posture.

The buttocks remain sexually exciting to humans. Considering our red-rumped ancestors, it is significant that an important element of sado-masochistic pornography is the rosiness of buttocks when they are spanked or whipped. The connection of rump and anus with conquest and submission persists in our idioms—being reamed or shafted, a brown nose, an ass-kisser. Similar idioms exist in many other cultures. It is as though the shift of sexual approach from rear to front—and with it ritualized signals of dominance behavior—is only half complete. Old primate rear-approach patterns probably exist as a substratum in our behavior and imagination. We also retain the equation of male activity with dominance and female activity with subordination. We talk about being on top both coitally and nonsexually, of being fucked as being conquered.

Like our ancestors, we have ritualized sexual gestures to express nonsexual meanings, and incorporated nonsexual meanings into our sex behavior. Often we do so through a dimension of expression our ancestors lack—language. Instead of mounting a male competitor, a man "fucks" him verbally or by a nonsexual conquest. The majority of us only fuck our buddies, ream our competitors, kiss our boss's ass and suck off the local bully symbolically. Many homosexuals take the metaphor literally; that is one of the reasons they are so scorned. They make these symbolically charged acts a way of life. This is uniquely human, and could happen only in a species so preoccupied with sex, so prone to use it for nonreproductive purposes. A subhuman will only enact a ritualized fragment of the reproductive cycle to express dominance or submission. A human, in expressing a power relationship, may go through the entire sexual act, including orgasm, and sometimes in a way that cannot further reproduction.

Distorted ideas of aggression and compliance were a major topic in early psychoanalysis; their relationship to sex and to homosexuality in particular was discussed. But instinct theory, with its corollaries of bisexuality and latency, was a trap door through which the discussions fell before they could get very far. During the thirties mistrust of instinct theory grew, and more psychiatrists emphasized adaptation instead. Anatomists had long assumed that a body structure exists because it serves a special purpose—the paw of a sea-going mammal such as the seal has become a flipper to help it swim. Functionalism had taken over in anthropology—a custom exists because it fills a social need. Now human behavior and emotions were interpreted as adaptive, as means to help a person cope with his environment. If people are not instinctively homosexual or bisexual, homosexual behavior must be the best way a person could find to deal with the world as he saw it. Without benefit of parallels from animal behavior, Clara Thompson said that many cases of homosexuality rise from abnormal dependency needs; Karen Horney said homosexuality is a way of acting out the need to conquer and submit. It had already become a psychiatric truism that many male homosexuals had suffered inhibited or misrouted aggression because of competition (real or imagined) with their fathers and brothers, and that many lesbians were still seeking their mothers' breasts or psychologically slithering around family competition problems.

Psychologist A. H. Maslow was one of the first to notice that homosexuality is eerily like the dominance-submission expression of higher animals and of folk language. He had studied primates and worked as a psychotherapist, and he felt that in man, as in his ancestors, there must be a direct relationship between high dominance and high sexual activity. In 1942 he decided to study this in women. He defined high dominance as a feeling of assurance, capability and self-confidence, low dominance as timidity and low self-evaluation. He gathered a group of female subjects, rated them for dominance and began to question them about their sex lives. His suspicions were borne out more dramatically than he'd expected. Every low-dominance woman was a virgin and had never masturbated. He then sought out low-dominance women with sexual experience to balance his sample. The principle still held. High-dominance women tended to have tried everything sexual at least once, liked sex, spoke of it as fun instead of something earnest, and described desirable males in terms of how good they were in bed. Middle-dominance women spoke of sex seriously, surrounded it with romance and sentiment; they praised moral and domestic qualities in men. Low-dominance women just didn't like sex. There were five women in Maslow's group who had had homosexual experience. All were near the top of the dominance scale.

Maslow discussed sexual positions with his subjects, and he concluded that they are linked closely with feelings of dominance. Face to face positions, he said, express more mutuality and less dominance than rear-entry positions. He pointed out that in the Trobriand Islands, a commoner who married a noble woman was not permitted to be above her during coitus. The same equation between "being on top," being more powerful, and being masculine existed among his subjects.

A decade later, Hugo Beigel did a small study of the psychological meanings of coital positions among married couples. Wives who objected to being on top said it was undignified, animalistic, cold, greedy, unfeminine. Men who objected to it called it unnatural and felt that they were relinquishing their initiative and aggressiveness. To both sexes it represented a violation of their sex roles. Beigel found that even more people objected to coitus *a tergo*—from behind, "doggy style." Similar adjectives were used—animalistic, cold, unnatural. Beigel pointed out that rear entry exposes a part of the body considered even more shameful than the genitals; embarrassment about the rectum may persist after genital modesty disappears. Most important, there was a parallel with Maslow's findings. Sexual positions have far-reaching emotional implications, and, as Maslow said, face-to-face gives a great feeling of mutuality as opposed to dominance. The pursuit of sexual pleasure is considered unfeminine in our culture, as emotionality is thought unmasculine. Beigel said that women more than men tend to feel that sex without love is bad. If they kiss, embrace and then slide over into "love making" they can feel they have just accelerated, not shifted gears. (The same feeling is expressed by many women who don't like to use a diaphragm because "stopping to put it in breaks the mood.") With the woman on top, there is more distance, more chance to watch the bodies, less ability to call coitus love rather than sex. Certainly rear entry makes it impossible to say, "This is just my affection gone out of bounds despite myself."

When Maslow wrote again about sex and power in 1960, he pointed out that the concepts of child and adult, weak and strong, ruled and ruler, patient and doctor tend to be equated with femaleness and maleness, and sexual acts become equated with both. He described a lesbian patient of his with strong masculine aspirations, who during her first heterosexual experience found herself atop the man, feeling that she was the thrusting, dominating one. He quoted other female patients with high dominance ratings as saying that sometimes when they got on top during coitus, they imagined the penis was theirs, and they were penetrating their partners. Maslow said that sex and power become mentally interchangeable. A patient feels weak, helpless, without defenses; therefore he or she may have fantasies of sexual attack by the therapist. This is not so much a sexual wish as a sexual metaphor for a power relationship. Much of what has been called transference, said Maslow, may be sexualizing of the dominance aspect of the therapeutic situation.

Male patients, he said, tend to equate being on the bottom with submitting and being feminized. One who'd been having heterosexual problems ran away from his family to hide out in a hotel room while in the grip of a severe panic over the thought that he might be homosexual. During the night he had a deep religious experience of "submitting to God." He returned home, relieved, his sexual difficulties ended, with a religious mission, and his self-acceptance somewhat restored. He had found a symbolic, nonsexual, and therefore acceptable way to admit his inner need to be passive.

Homosexual panic is the cause of many initial visits to psychotherapists. It is common in men in and out of therapy. Sometimes the immediate cause is being solicited or seduced homosexually, sometimes homosexual dreams or fantasies, sometimes sudden irrational fear of appearing effeminate. The patient's identity as a heterosexual male is shaken, and he appears at the doctor's office in a state of terror and impending disorganization. He says, "I'm afraid that I may be homosexual," and waits for an answer, yearning to be proved wrong. Classical psychoanalysts used to explain that he was experiencing an outbreak of the latent homosexuality that lies within us all, and he should accept it. This often tended to increase his anxiety; he was told his doubts were about an ineradicable instinct, so his fear that his "homosexual component" would get out of control increased.

Sandor Rado, Abram Kardiner, Lionel Ovesey, Leon Saltzman, Irving Bieber and many other analysts began to take a different approach. These men, usually loosely called neo-Freudians, kept an analytic view of emotional dynamics but scrapped instinct theory for adaptational ideas. Classic Freudians had assumed that sexual motivation lies behind nonsexual thoughts, but never followed their assumption of "hidden meanings" to the natural conclusion that there might just as easily be nonsexual meanings behind sexual thoughts. During the early and middle fifties, more than a decade after Rado's definitive criticism of Freudian "instinctual bisexuality," detailed studies appeared of homosexual images, impulses and fears in heterosexuals. This "homosexual" content turned out to be symbolic of dominance and dependence—shafting or being shafted, sucking up or being sucked off, becoming a baby or woman to another man.

Before the fifties, psychiatrist Abram Kardiner had been impressed by anthropological hints that social change—depression, war, sudden economic mobility or rigidity—may make it more difficult for men to live up to their masculine roles, and that many adapt to this stress with impotence and homosexual behavior. With one of his younger colleagues at Columbia University, Dr. Lionel Ovesey, Kardiner did a socio-psychiatric study of blacks, *The Mark of Oppression*, to try to find the effects of the ghetto on emotional development and adaptations. He found that the ghetto reduces a man's feeling of potence in the broad sense; this "emasculation" of the black man in racist societies is now common knowledge. Kardiner, then working in a barely explored field, found a relationship between prejudice, deprivation and resulting sexual expressions of dependence and dominance feelings.

One of Kardiner's and Ovesey's subjects was a man from Harlem who suffered premature ejaculation and often feared he might be homosexual. He had a powerful dread of castration evidenced by fear of knives, dreams of being knifed by other men, etc. Kardiner and Ovesey concluded that his apparent sexual troubles with women were really a by-product of his feeling that he couldn't compete socially and sexually with other men. As a child, he had felt beaten down by his strict father, and in constant, fruitless competition with his brothers. He unconsciously perceived assertion as an act of aggression for which stronger males would retaliate. He avoided vocational success when opportunities for it arose (not tempting "the gods" to take revenge). The researchers felt that his anxieties about homosexuality were not really erotic, but symbolic of a wish, unacceptable to him because it seemed feminine, to take a submissive role with stronger, more successful men, like a little boy dependent on his father.

Another subject had an ambitious, violent and sometimes brutal father, whom he saw as an intimidating giant to whom he must submit to survive. As a boy he had been meticulous and fearful; other boys had called him a sissy. As an adult he was competitive and ambitious, but always provoked self-defeating clashes with supervisors. For years he had had a compulsion to glance down and estimate the size of the penis of every man he met— literally testing out the power metaphor "Who has the bigger cock?" He spoke of fears of being homosexual and of people thinking he was effem- inate. Actually he had a masculine appearance and no erotic urges toward other men. He was projecting his own self-accusation ("I am a sissy, a failed male, a faggot") into others' minds.

During the early and middle fifties, Ovesey wrote a series of papers on power and dependence as motives for homosexual thoughts in heterosex- uals. He called them pseudohomosexual because they did not involve erotic excitement. They were as symbolic as the ritualized mounting and present- ing of baboons. Ovesey pointed out that dependence and power-striving are two sides of one coin. The male who fears he can't stand up to the world may deny that he wants to, and make failure and dependence a way of life. On the other hand, his dependent urges may be too damaging to his self- esteem and male identity; he will deny his feeling of being a weak, inade- quate male by a compensatory striving for aggressive conquest.

This sort of problem is especially likely to be acute in a boy who feels at a competitive loss with his father and brothers. He thinks, "Daddy and my brothers push me around as though I were a weak little girl. I'm so mad I could kill them. But if I fight, they'll cut me down, shaft me, kill me." Ideas of dominance, sex and gender become fused. He sees the world as being like his family and assumes that others feel as he does. The world is a jungle where the "real men" "fuck" and destroy the losers. All feelings of success and failure, assertion and inhibition, tend to fall into this groove. To win is to rape and kill, and face retaliation in kind. The alternative is to become a mama's boy, a "faggot."

One of Ovesey's patients was a thirty-year-old man, heterosexual, mar- ried, quite masculine in appearance. He came for help because for two years he had felt irrational resentment at his wife, loss of sexual interest in her, and finally impotence. He had been an only child, with a domineering, overprotective mother who expected top performance in everything, and a distant father who spoke to him only to criticize. He grew up feeling boor- ish and graceless with women. Now he considered himself a vocational fail- ure. He was a trainee at a minimal salary; his boss was a petty tyrant who stole his ideas and presented them to higher-ups as his own. He was the picture of a totally deflated person.

It turned out that his sexual difficulties with his wife began two years before, when she went to work to support them both while he, after a career failure, went back to school. When their socio-economic roles were reversed, their genders began to change in his mind. He began to have an uncanny feeling that his wife looked physically masculine, and his potency waned. Then he got his present job through his wife's relatives. His angry, exploitative boss seemed to him like his father, forcing him into a submissive relationship.

One day, after discussing his difficulty asserting himself, he announced that he would not let his boss intimidate him any more. But the next day, when the time came to speak up, he felt powerless. That night he had a dream. "I tore into his office madder than hell. He was sitting behind his desk. This time I was really going to tell him. He looked up and said, 'What in hell do you want?' I just stood there and couldn't say anything. Then I turned around, but instead of walking away, I crawled away on my hands and feet with my ass up in the air."

He expressed anxiety about homosexuality, but had never felt sexually attracted to other men. Ovesey realized that in the dream, the patient had taken the primate posture of "feminine" submission, putting male-male competition in male-female sex-behavior language. The unconscious reasoning was, "I am a failure = I am not a man = I am castrated = I am a woman = I am a homosexual." The reason for the symptom was an underlying feeling of weakness, and a compensatory striving for power.

Ovesey went on to spell out the various kinds of magical thinking that underlie pseudohomosexual images. Which ones appear will depend on whether dependence or power is the chief emotion at the moment. Dependent feelings make a man feel like a child, wanting to cling to his mother's breast, to be passive, protected, fed. Some inhibited, dependent patients reported to Ovesey dreams in which they appeared as little girls. As a little boy separates somewhat from his mother and begins to relate more to his father, it is first in a chiefly dependent way; the father is then, among other things, a second mother. So the man who feels like a helpless little boy in the face of adult competition may fall back in fantasy to being a baby, a nonmale, a little girl, as he was with his mother, or he may want a stronger male to mother him. This frustration at not being mothered by superiors accounts for the hostility of some men toward their bosses.

In some children's minds, there is a magical association of the father's penis with the mother's nipple: "The thing that sticks out is for feeding." When the child learns about semen, he may equate it with milk. Thus a man in the grip of infantile dependence feelings may have a fellatio fantasy; the penis is the substitute for the breast. One of Ovesey's patients was a young man struggling for worldly success and trying to break his tie with his mother; he dreamed of sucking a penis until it gushed milk.

A man may also dream that he, like his primate ancestors, recognizes another male's dominance by recognizing his penis. A heterosexual medical student told Ovesey about having missed a diagnosis, which was then made correctly by someone else in his group. That night he dreamed of kissing a midget's penis before a crowd that hooted in derision. He interpreted the dream sexually and asked, "Did it mean I was a fairy?" Ovesey interpreted it as feeling "lower than the lowest."

Some men perform apparently passive, receptive homosexual acts in fantasy or even in reality without sexual motivation. Instead of tumbling into total dependency, they imagine a kind of magical repair to their "little" manhood. One way is to incorporate a bigger, stronger male's penis into their own bodies orally or anally. One very competitive and successful businessman who saw Ovesey had been the only short man in a very tall family. During a business crisis, he had fantasies of sucking the penis of an uncle who was six foot three and a great tycoon. It was as though he were imagining a transfusion of masculinity from a "really big man." Sometimes the fantasy is acted out. A number of psychiatrists besides Ovesey have described predominantly heterosexual men who, when feeling anxious and insecure, compulsively seek out men to fellate without any erotic arousal on their own part.

In other men, the striving for power is paramount, not the wish for dependence. Often they project their feelings in paranoid fashion: "I don't want to fuck or deball everyone, they all want to do it to me." As a result, they go around fearing homosexual attack. If the "battle" of life seems hopeless to them, and they fear succumbing, the result may be an acute pseudohomosexual panic.

This sexualized paranoia about assertion is often involved in "success phobia," an outbreak of anxiety and neurotic symptoms when a man is promoted, wins financial success, or otherwise feels himself moving from the "loser" to the "winner" role. The conflict between raging ambition and the need to appease competitors has become acute. This can also happen to the man who falls under the authority of a threatening superior at work or in the army. He expects to be shafted, and fears that his own desire to retaliate in kind will get out of control. The commonest image is being buggered (or punctured or gored) and castrated (slashed, bitten). One very competitive heterosexual patient reported to Ovesey a dream about a giant dog and a puppy. The big dog bent the little one over a sofa and buggered him; then he bit off the puppy's genitals. The patient said the top dog and underdog of the dream made him think of father and son and of therapist and patient.

Another patient, an illustrator, had a set of drawings rejected by a magazine. He then dreamed that the magazine printed them under another artist's name. "Then a bull was attacking me. He had me impaled on his horns and was biting my thumb. . . . I yelled for my cousin to act like a cow so the bull would get interested in him and let me go." Ovesey said the bull represented the man's more successful competitors; and, in reality, the cousin he dreamed of was an unskilled laborer, a vocational failure compared to him. In the dream, the patient was trying to divert his victorious competitor into raping and castrating someone even "less masculine" than himself—a worse "cow" to sate their bullishness.

Pseudohomosexual anxiety may also break out when a patient is first asked to lie down or turn his back to the psychotherapist. Ovesey had a patient who was a successful businessman. As a child he had been brutalized and openly threatened with castration by his father. He entered treatment because, after ousting a crooked partner and taking sole control of his firm, he fell into depression, anxiety and suicidal preoccupations. After a while in treatment, Ovesey suggested that at the next session he might lie down on the couch, not facing the doctor. The patient dreamed before that next session about forcing his penis into the anus of a doctor he knew. On waking, his first thought had been. "By God, if anybody is going to be screwed, it's not going to be me!"

This sort of conflict is sometimes expressed in fears of oral rape or of being forced to perform fellatio. It may suggest babyish suckling; also, the "low posture" of being on one's knees is symbolic of submission, and puts a person on eye level with another's crotch, as when he was a child among adults. A heterosexual patient became preoccupied with Ovesey's income as compared to his own. Then he dreamed that his older brother outfought him, threw him on his back, pinned his arms, pried open his mouth, and forced him to perform fellatio. Oral rape symbolized competitive defeat by the therapist, as it had symbolized defeat by his older brother.

Some patients have images and dreams that show a back-handed triumph through homosexuality. (Again there are echoes of the Adlerian view of motivation and behavior.) They submissively receive the penis in anus or mouth, but then bite or cut it off and keep it, to steal the donor's masculinity. Dr. Irving Bieber reports a case of a homosexual patient who, after performing fellatio, dreamed of having blood on his teeth. An English psychiatrist told me of a dream of a homosexual patient in which he devoured a famous entertainment figure known for his virile, aggressive character, and then felt the he-man, digested, coursing through his veins.

One such classic dream of "incorporation" came from one of Ovesey's patients who was a college instructor and had lost out to a younger rival for promotion. He dreamed of sitting in a theater, waiting for a show to begin. The audience gave a big round of applause to a celebrity among them—his rival. Then the curtain rose, and a burlesque-comedy act began. A little comedian ran out on stage carrying a wooden sword. After him came a bigger man with a bigger sword; then a still bigger one, with yet a bigger sword. The second man goosed the first with his sword, and it pushed out the first man's pants in front like a penis. The audience laughed. The third man goosed the second; the sword, instead of pushing out the second man's pants, came out like a huge penis in the first one's pants. The audience laughed even harder. The patient woke up laughing. In his dream he had envisioned someone being shafted but turning this into a victory by keeping the shaft for himself.

These dreams and interpretations may seem bizarre or farfetched to some people. But they occur commonly in psychiatric treatment, in many interviews with nonpatients and in our idioms. They may exist at some deep level in all or most people in our society. If they do arise from our primate inheritance of programed signal behavior, they exist in all societies. They certainly concur with much animal behavior and with the idioms in Western and other languages. I have heard them spontaneously spoken by many homosexuals. (Phillip—page 316—says he was interested in women's breasts and then switched to men's bottoms. Howard—page 175—spoke on and on in our interview about the nutritive, health-giving value of semen as one of his motives for fellatio.)

These sexual power-dependence metaphors are blended with eroticism in the homosexual. When a heterosexual feels them, they seem alien to his personality. The panic they provoke is an identity panic: "Am I straight? Am I a faggot? Who am I?" Women are not prone to this sort of panic. If they feel like dependent babies, "angry fuckers" or competitive losers, they lose self-esteem, but not usually their basic belief in their femininity. As we have seen, men's route to gender identity may be more arduous, the result more fragile.

Sexualized power-dependence problems are likely to be acute if a woman grows up in rivalry with her male relatives. Like men, she learns from society that competitive success is masculine; that the penis is symbolically an instrument of prowess and domination; that being penetrated means subordination. A family in which males seem to win love and advantage more easily then females makes the idea even stronger. If a woman from such a background retains strong dependency needs, she may wish she had a compensatory penis so that she too could be strong and successful in life, like her father and brothers. The result is the exaggerated penis envy that has motivated some radical feminism. Such a woman blames her failure to reach ambitious goals on her gender, her lack of a penis. Under analytic therapy, it often becomes clear that as a child she believed she once had a penis, and it was taken from her—very commonly, that she was castrated by her mother for sexual misbehavior.

The dependence striving had the upper hand in one of Ovesey's patients, a woman of twenty-six who lived in a daughter-mother relationship with an older lesbian. She wanted to break away and go out with men, but the prospect of being on her own terrified her. She didn't believe she could survive. She had dreams of leaving the woman for wealthy uncles who fed her extravagantly; then she dreamed of marrying her therapist, who in the dream filled all her needs. Then, in a crucially revealing dream, she took her pet cat, a spayed male, to her mother, to exchange it for one with a penis. This finally made her realize that she identified with the castrated animal; she felt that receiving a penis from her mother would enable her to cope with the world.

There is a subtle but important difference between this sort of woman, who feels castrated and in need of penile strength, and the power-driven woman. The power-driven woman fantasies that she has a penis and fears losing it. She fights to keep it, and is the sort of person popularly called a castrating woman. Such a woman considers her own craving for dependence shameful and demeaning; she must deny it and compensate for it, lest she become a slave of her own need. Like the power-driven man, she feels that the penis is the engine of success; that lack of one means inferiority, weakness and humiliating defeat; that winners rape, castrate and destroy their rivals. Since she fantasies that she has a penis and sees relationships as battles, she has an unconscious fear of retaliatory castration. The rape she expects is usually not oral or anal, as in the power-driven male, but vaginal. Therefore the power-driven female does not tend to have pseudo-homosexual panic; instead she has a paranoid fear of rape.

One such patient of Ovesey's went into a deep depression after the birth of her first child. She shunned the baby, refused coitus with her husband, and began to urinate standing up. She had what in men would be typical castration dreams—of being mutilated and cut, of losing races to men because she was crippled, of blood-spattered cars that lacked engine parts. In analysis it became clear to her that motherhood had proved once and for all that she was a woman and had no penis. Beneath her masculine defense was a desire to be a baby or "mere female," dependent and protected.

Career success can bring a woman's power-dependence conflict to a head, just as it can a man's. Though some women consciously reject the idea, most people in our society do consider such success masculine. One of Ovesey's patients was the only female executive in her firm; at thirty-two she still had not formed a lasting relationship with a man. Under treatment, she eventually married. But when she was picked for promotion over a male rival, she went into a success-phobia reaction. Like a man in a success crisis, she equated success with committing castration and rape, and feared them as retaliation. Her vagina became so tight that coitus was impossible. She had dreams that clearly represented cutting off a man's penis and attaching it to herself. Her mental formula was, "I am a failure = I am not a man = I am a woman = I am castrated."

When Ovesey studied male and female homosexuals, he found all these sexual metaphors for dominance and submission, power and dependence, fused with erotic feelings and acted out. In male homosexuals, the kind of sex act a man preferred in a given circumstance depended on whether dominance or dependence was paramount. Dr. Irving Bieber has similarly found that whether a male homosexual wants to be the inserter or insertee often depends on whether he or the partner is considered more masculine. Dr. Thomas Freeman has written that some of his homosexual patients explicitly equate the erect penis with masculinity, and the softness of the female body—especially the flabbiness of a pendulous breast—with a flabby penis and inferiority.

The question of distorted power and dependence feelings became central to psychiatric studies of homosexuality in both sexes through the fifties and sixties. Dr. Daniel Cappon, in Canada, wrote, "A son must rise on the ashes of his father . . . a daughter must see that she is more beautiful and desirable than her mother . . . lack of aggression is the most universal and malignant nonsexual factor in homosexuality." He, Bieber and many others also pointed out that a woman must be capable of a cetain amount of assertion to compete with other women, win and hold a man, and feel self-esteem. If she can't compete with her mother, she may flee into lesbianism; though she consciously believes she is avoiding the male genitals, the source of her behavior is appeasement of her mother. Lesbians tend to pair as husband-wife or mother-daughter. Ovesey believes that if dependency feelings are foremost, a lesbian takes the wife or daughter role; if power strivings are more important, the result is the masculine or mother (really "phallic mother") role.

Ovesey recounts a case of a male who demonstrated perfectly the erotic re-enactment of power conflicts—a thirty-year-old unmarried junior executive who came for help because of anxiety about his career. He was so competitive at his office, especially with male authorities, that his job was in danger. Later, he casually revealed that he was an active homosexual. Why hadn't he mentioned this? He said that his brother was also homosexual and had been told by an analyst that homosexuality was inherited and couldn't be treated. Besides, he said, it had no connection with his work problems. Ovesey said he felt homosexuality was a symptom of neurosis, and a treatable one. The patient seemed confused, anxious and delighted.

He had been the youngest of three boys, with a sharp-tongued, aggressive mother and an intimidated father. Throughout childhood he had felt inadequately competitive and masculine. He had wide hips, and in the army men had taunted him, saying he was built like a woman. His feelings of unmanliness became acute, and he had his first homosexual experience. It was the prototype for all that followed. He masturbated his partner, then buggered him; he did not permit the other man to penetrate him. He played a compensatory dominant role, womanizing his partner.

He had avoided women, but during treatment he gradually realized that because he had seen his mother castrate his father, he feared the same fate. After a few months he began to date girls. Simultaneously he saw that he had been deeply afraid of standing up to his mother. Though his assertiveness increased, he still had dreams of sucking men's penises to acquire their strength; he didn't believe yet that he had enough of his own. He developed a heterosexual pattern over the three years of treatment, and with this came many insights. One was that he had always equated his lack of aggressiveness with femininity. Another was that his old hyperaggressive manner was an attempt to ward off in advance men's retaliation for his normal assertiveness and to deny his wish for dependence on them. He married, and five years later was happy with his wife, less aggressive with men, very successful in his work, and the father of a child. At one point during a career crisis, he had a mild outbreak of homosexual (and pseudo-homosexual) fantasies, but he was sure they would be transitory, and they were.

A consistent picture of a common type of homosexual type of development was emerging from the work of the neo-Freudians—one that also explained homosexual mental content in heterosexuals. A boy is intimidated in expressing aggression and assuming the assertive male role. He fears that if he does so, he will be castrated, feminized, destroyed, by his father and brothers. The inhibition becomes general. As he grows, he feels that sexual assertiveness will be punished especially severely, and he sets up a phobic avoidance of the female genitals. It is like any other phobia: an object that arouses unendurable feelings is avoided and blamed for the trouble. Impotence, fetishism, exhibitionism, and homosexuality are such protective devices in many cases, perhaps the majority. The power, dependence and erotic motivations have become intertwined; they keep interacting and reinforcing each other. Psychotherapy can often cure sexual deviance by treating it like any other phobia. The homosexual learns that he can assume the masculine role and survive. He need not act out magical ideas of incorporation, dependence and conquest. Finally he does what any phobic must learn to do—face the things he fears while dispersing the irrational structures that underlie the avoidance.

Dominance and submission are not the single key to homosexuality. But, as Bieber has said, in many male and female homosexuals such feelings are the psychodynamic hard core of the homosexual trend. New theories of sexual dominance-submission language explain in a better way what Freud called the "inverted Oedipal attachment" between father and son, and what Adler meant by saying that the Jerusalem of every neurosis is, "I want to be a real man." It also explains the often-noted mistrust and hostility in many homosexual relationships; power-dependence conflict is often inherent in the homosexual condition.

Many homosexual patients say they are uneasy with burly, aggressive men and with people in positions of authority. They deride other homosexuals as queens, screamers and fags, but don't feel sure that they themselves are "real men." In many homosexuals, there is a general renunciatory trend in competitive situations of all kinds. Bieber says, "The society of other homosexuals is a haven, not only for the avoidance of sexual arousal by women, but for safety from the threat of aggressive, heterosexual males." Gustav Bychowski, in a well-known analytic paper on homosexuality, said one of his homosexual patients explained that he wouldn't be able to approach women as long as other men didn't acknowledge him as one of them. In many of his patients, the ability to relate sexually to women developed as a homosexual became able to talk freely and as an equal to men he considered virile. The compensatory aggressive, cocksure, antisentimental manner of some homosexuals can switch quickly to passivity or crude masochism, revealing the underlying conflict. Plays about the gay world have shown the verbal bickering and hostility that are so common in it. In interviews with many homosexuals, I have felt that sooner or later most of my efforts had to be directed toward keeping the talk from turning into a series of power plays, a kind of verbal wrestling for who is on top.

This shift of homosexuality into a dominance-dependence perspective is intriguing, and probably a big step toward therapeutic progress. Aggression has become a fashionable scientific subject, but it is often spoken of as a unitary instinctive force, as sex used to be. Further study is needed to break it down—when it is defensive, when it is predatory, when it is instrumental toward some other end, and so on. How much and in what way it is programed into man remains unclear. In man, as compared to gulls or baboons, it easily becomes distorted, because he may parataxically perceive people and situations as threats or project his own aggression onto others. Furthermore, the cultural variations of humanity make man not a single species but, in effect, a collection of species. We don't know how constant aggressive patterns are among various societies, nor enough about how they relate to sexual behavior.

There are other areas of animal behavior that may have strong implications for the clinical psychologist and psychiatrist. One is male-male relationships, and their role in the development of heterosexual capacity. In the past, many psychoanalysts who were themselves uncomfortable in male-male relationships called a patient's ability to relate warmly to other males an expression of latent homosexuality. The all-male groups and activities of our and other societies have loosely been called homosexual in the same way. Much more attention needs to be paid to what Sullivan called "chumship," among preadolescents, adolescents and adults. The explanation may lie as much in ethological study of "male bonding" as in psychiatry and anthropology; Lionel Tiger's book *Men in Groups* is an interesting exploration of the possibility that "the behavior of men in groups in part reflects an underlying biologically transmitted 'propensity' with roots in human evolutionary history." Work such as Harlow's suggests that even in babyhood same-sex relationships may be necessary for learning sex role and heterosexuality, especially aggressive and cooperative behavior.

There are other biological background factors affecting sexuality about which we are starting to learn, such as overcrowding, and stress in general. Both are believed to increase anxiety, sexual difficulties and infertility in men as in animals. In the early sixties, psychologist John B. Calhoun described an experimentally induced "behavior sink" in wild Norway rats, a radical disturbance of behavior caused by extreme overcrowding. All sorts of deviant behavior occurred, such as attempted rape, cannibalism, frenetic activity and pathological withdrawal. Females stopped building nests and neglected their young. Males attacked females and infants. Among the subordinate males a number became pansexual, unable to discriminate between potential sexual partners. They mounted females, males and juveniles. Others became totally withdrawn and ignored the opposite sex.

Even death can result from nonspecific stress in many species—including men, who may become sick (e.g., develop ulcers) or die (from the conviction that they have been bewitched). Studies of reaction to stress are continuing to appear—the most famous so far is by Dr. Hans Selye. Research on maternal attachment, loss and deprivation, such as that of René Spitz and John Bowlby, may eventually be relevant to a larger understanding of stress and adaptation. The specific effects of overcrowding, psychological pressures and other kinds of stress are still largely unknown, but they may eventually tell something about psychosexual problems.

Maslow, in his paper on dominance and human sexuality in 1960, concluded that one of his hopes for psychotherapy is separating the two. Then, he said, a patient learns that "the penis is in fact not a club or a sword or a rending instrument, that the vagina is not a garbage pail or a biting mouth or an engulfing well; that the above or below positon in the sexual act is meaningful only for sexual convenience and pleasure; that taking orders from a superior is not equivalent to being raped; that stronger people need not be made a sexual oblation in order to avert their anger."

Certainly gross distortions of dominance, submission, power and dependence distort sexuality, and all other behavior and relationships. But Maslow almost seems to be hoping for a world without conflict, aggression and submission; that might also be a world without variety and joy. In any case, it is probably wishful thinking. Maslow himself admitted that dominance and sexuality are blended throughout all the entire higher animal world. He guessed that perhaps humans alone could separate them. But Nikolaas Tinbergen once wrote that even if ethological studies didn't tell so much about human psychology, "I am afraid I would not leave them alone. Blood is thicker than water."

INTERVIEWS

Though Niko Tinbergen and Konrad Lorenz are not ancients, they are the grand old men of ethology. Tinbergen is from the Netherlands, and has taught at the University of Leiden, Yale, Columbia and, since the Second World War, Oxford. I visit his office at Oxford; it is cluttered with books, slides, cans of film, letters and book galleys—many of his books on animal behavior and communication are in print in the United States and England now. He is in his early sixties, a slight, sunny man with white hair and a youthful manner.

When Konrad Lorenz and I were young, we were the only ethologists in the world with university appointments—and they were hardly remunerative ones. Now the field has exploded. Books on animal behavior sell to laymen; I get a request to write one literally every week. Lorenz's works, Morris' *Naked Ape* and Robert Ardrey's books have made people aware of what we do, and the value our methods can have some day in understanding human behavior.

Lorenz's book On Aggression *has been criticized for unproven analogies between human and animal behavior. So have Ardrey's work and Morris'.*

Lorenz may overstate his case sometimes, but he's a brilliant and highly critical man, and I think he knows he is overstating. Morris was a student of mine in the early fifties. I'll show you some interesting monographs he wrote then on pseudohomosexual behavior in fish. I think that much of what Lorenz and Morris say is probably true. Now we must find the data. We have to tell people not just what we know, but what we don't know. As I said, what we can offer is a method. Many theories, including some psychoanalytic ones, depend far too much on what subjects say. Subtle nonverbal expressions sometimes tell more, and different things. We used to think, "What a pity animals can't talk." But we've learned to see that animals do express things very specifically without words. So do men, and we should see how. For instance, in all mammals the switch from infant to adult feeding patterns brings biting. Human babies don't bite the nipple when they're hungry, they bite when they're sated. But what do psychoanalysts say? That this post-satiation biting is "aggression," due to frustration. We must battle to get analysts to return to observation. Unfortunately, we still have an old taboo that says, "Oh yes, that may be true of animals, *but . . .*"

Many psychiatrists treat homosexuals successfully by dealing with their sexual pattern as distorted expressions of aggression and submission. Homosexual dreams and fantasies often reproduce the sexual-aggressive gestures of higher animals.

Homosexuality, to my knowledge, is extremely rare in animals in the narrow sense of preference for the same sex. You do get object fixations sometimes—an animal in a zoo learns to copulate with its feeding bowl or some such thing. But it will usually return to its normal pattern if given an acceptable partner.

As for aggression, in all species in which it appears in some context other than sex, it also appears in sex. Whether a species' fear and aggression behavior is expressed in peck order, territoriality, or in relation to predators, it will also appear in courtship and often even in mating. In many animals, the male is stronger and a fighter, and the female must show submissiveness or there is no mating. The positions and gestures that show aggression and fear are also used to show dominance and submission in nonsexual encounters between adults, between parent and child, and between older and younger animals. The male approaches the female with an aggressive gesture. If the two animals are going to mate rather than fight, both must show that they are neither afraid nor dangerous. Remember that a mating animal is in a terribly vulnerable position; during orgasm it has a few moments when it loses all its self-protective awareness. We talk of human females' apprehension about sex and males' castration fear, but there is fear and aggression mixed with sex in very many animals. Both must be allayed in a sexual situation. But the first requirement in mating remains male aggression, to which the female responds by showing that she isn't aggressive in return.

What distinguishes a sexually receptive female from a competitively submissive male?

There are similarities and differences. We've discovered that in black-headed gulls it is some body postures and the brown face mask that are threatening. When two males confront each other in threatening postures, the loser in this battle of bluff will usually switch to submissive postures. When a male and female go through pair formation, they adopt the least aggressive of these threat postures, which mean in male-male context "I won't fight," but in evolution have become friendly postures in the male-female, where they mean "I love you."

Could this have anything to do with the hostility and contempt humans show for effeminate males?

I think this is a complex thing. One aspect has been pointed out by Lorenz. He stressed long ago that animals are more afraid of, and more aggressive toward, a deviant of their own species than toward a member of another species. You can observe gulls attack *en masse* an individual that acts or looks abnormal—say, one that was beaten so badly in a fight that it no longer walks or flies normally. This also occurs among storks and rooks. It's what Lorenz called a spook reaction. Ask a person to draw a spook, and he draws a distorted human. I believe that our rejection of homosexuals, while in part a cultural phenomenon, may have such a deep root. Look at the reaction to stammerers, who distort normal speech behavior. I can always predict when people will laugh while watching films of animals; it happens when they're embarrassed at seeing themselves in distorted forms. When a bird gets angry, and its aggression is thwarted, it stumbles—and people laugh.

Laughter is one of the many means that humans use, as social animals, to control deviance, and it may be a signal system with biological roots. When one's behavior elicits contemptuous laughter, one tries to conform. Even stronger pressure is exerted by ignoring. In England we say that we send a person to Coventry; in Holland we say that we declare someone dead. We need to study subtle communication systems in all social animals more closely. Lorenz with his geese and I with my gulls have seen how sharply animals watch each other, watch even every change in each other's eyes. Gifted novelists are still far ahead of scientists in these matters. And I think urban man has lost a lot of this perceptiveness.

On paper, it's easy to test what relation such animal behavior has to human behavior—that is, whether this behavior of ours is biologically or culturally induced. This deserves more and very serious study, but we don't do nature-versus-nurture experiments with humans for ethical reasons. You just don't raise children in an impoverished environment. So we will learn by inference, and it will take a bit longer.

But if a form of behavior—say, aggression or a signal system—exists through the whole higher animal world, it's unlikely that it has been culturally re-invented by humans. Why should we be the only species that doesn't carry traces of its evolutionary past? I say this tentatively, because evolutionary origins are finally unprovable. But man has always struggled against his nonrational inheritance, and when we ask why something happens, we always eventually hit something irrational.

For instance, I think something like peck order plays an enormous part in social organization. And I think the female must always, at least in certain things, play second fiddle to her husband for a marriage to be successful. But there is also, in all of us, no matter how dominant, a need for a top dog. We learn best from a teacher we respect, no matter how wise we are. Japanese researchers showed that monkeys learn faster from an older or stronger individual. De Vore and Washburn found that the old male baboon is not only feared but trusted—one might say respected. The group wait for him to go into an open place, and then follow when they see that he is confident.

What sort of points bearing on human sexual behavior could be followed up with profit?

The whole matter of sexual signals has hardly been investigated in humans and their nearer evolutionary relatives. For instance, some monkeys and baboons show signal changes—vulvar and rear-end signals moved to the front of the body or the opposite sex. So do we. Privacy is another interesting question. Primates mate among the group, like other mammals. I don't know of a case in which a sexual pair withdraws for coitus. Sometimes a pair of lions do, but it isn't clear yet whether privacy is the reason or it's just that they fall behind the pride while mating.

People are different in crucial ways from other animals; the differences are as important as the similarities. This is especially important in studying aggression. It's very rare for animals to kill others of their species in any number. People probably didn't originally. After all, it's hard to kill someone with your fists. The development of hand weapons and then long-range weapons created a situation unknown in the animal world. Besides, animals aren't ashamed to flee. When they fight, it's over a practical matter, and when one realizes that it's going to lose, it runs away—or, if it's a social animal, it has an appeasement device. But people think, "I'd rather die than do such-and-such." We also seem to be the only species to learn that a dead opponent won't return. So humans die for symbolic things, have the brainwashing of armies that makes them see others as prey, predators, parasites, as well as opponents. No animal does any of that.

About a decade ago Irven De Vore and his teacher, S. L. Washburn, did some of the first fine studies of baboons in the wild. De Vore has recently returned to the Harvard anthropology department from a long field trip to Africa, where he carried these studies further.

Back in 1959, Washburn and I saw that the old idea that sex holds the baboon troop together was ridiculous. First of all, a baboon has only six to ten weeks of sexual activity each year. The female has a twenty-nine- to thirty-day cycle in which her sexual receptiveness crests, levels, and then drops abruptly. While it's on the rise, she mates with juveniles and then subordinate males; at her peak, she mates with the dominant, older males, who therefore give the most genes to the population. Then the female is pregnant for seven months and lactates for three or four months more. Lactation wanes, she has a receptive cycle or two, and bang, she's pregnant again. Just do some simple arithmetic and you see that there have to be more important bonds holding the troop together than sex.

But before coming to conclusions about either baboons or people, you must consider a few other points. One is that primates vary tremendously in sexiness. The gorilla rates very low; when George Schaller did his famous observations, he witnessed only one copulation. When you watch a baboon troop, you may see forty copulations in one morning. But human beings are further, in fact furthest, on the sexy end of the scale. Another point is that primates are very individual, too much so for the elegant, neat work done in ethology on simpler animals. Chimps and baboons show extraordinary individuality. Again, people show most individuality of all—and for the same reason, their long period of socialization, which extends even past sexual maturation and gives each adult a unique personality. This is even more true of males than females, and as a result the male personality, in baboons and humans, seems more fragile; one gets the feeling that no matter what happens, more females can muddle through. It's hard to document, but I think it's so. Certainly the male baboon takes a lot longer to become socially mature. The female starts menstruating at four and a half and becomes a baby factory for life. The male begins mounting at six months and produces sperm at five years, but he doesn't get his big canine teeth, mantle hair and full adult sex behavior till he's eight or nine. He has to learn to challenge, appease and cooperate with other males to become grown up.

And to do so he uses mounting, presenting and erection. But in just what circumstances?

I didn't keep records on when the males have erections, but it often happens during grooming, and it's frequent in juveniles, from one year of age on. I break down presenting into five or six categories. The baboon presents its side or shoulder for grooming; that's the most common presentation. A male may also present its rear for grooming. Females present their rears for grooming, too, when they aren't estrous; this is interesting, because the male doesn't confuse it with sexual presentation, showing that not only posture but color and smell influence the meaning of presentation.

Mounting is an ancient gesture, in the evolutionary sense, and it's come to serve a variety of purposes. In Japanese macaques, when the troop arrives at a feeding place in the morning, one male may mount another. It's always the dominant one who mounts. This is done very calmly, and it seems sort of like shaking hands. Then if a tangerine is thrown between the two males, the subordinate one looks away, and the dominant one eats it. When a second tangerine is thrown, the subordinate takes it, presents his rear to the dominant one, and then eats. I think mounting follows a similar pattern in the rhesus macaque but happens a little less frequently.

In baboons it's another story. First, you have to see how a male sexually mounts a female, and the posture she takes to receive him. The female presents sexually by turning her hindquarters to the male's face; she places her hands apart on the ground, ready to take his weight when he mounts. The male mounts, grabs her haunches with his hands, and grasps her ankles with his feet.

When two males engage in mounting, the context and the behavior are different. The commonest way of stopping tension and fighting is presenting followed by grasping the haunches. A male who's being harassed presents his rear, but it's lowered so that he isn't really in a position to be mounted. The other male grabs his haunches. Often both have erections. The one being grasped looks back over his shoulder at the one grasping him. Both seem very tense.

There's a dramatic break in tension, and harassment ends for about half an hour. This grasping seems to be an independent gesture for stopping fights. Only one time in fifty does it lead to mounting.

The most common situation for mounting is this. A chases B. B mounts C and gives one to three pelvic thrusts, without grabbing C's ankles with his feet. Then B and C turn and threaten A together. Sometimes a harassed male presents his posterior—even a dominant one may do this when others harass him while he's mating.

Is there ever male-male intromission?

Because the baboon is sexy, some people argue that almost everything a baboon does has sexual content. When I first watched them, I thought there was intromission. When they got used to me, and I could watch from eight or nine feet away, I saw it wasn't so. The penis always slides down between the legs or off to one side.

How do the males of the central group join up and form their coalition?

We need a fifteen-year study to answer that one. It involves the whole balance of aggression and cooperation. Let me get to it in a roundabout way, starting with a question I've been very interested in—why male primates don't copulate with their mothers. This is important because it shows the beginning of dominance-submission relationships. You know, Harlow said that he couldn't get his female macaques pregnant if they were dominant over their male partners. Well, the male baboon is twice as large as the female, so there's no chance of a tough female and a small, insecure male joining up, as there is among macaques. But generally in primates there's a striking correlation between male dominance and female submission for successful copulation to take place. The baby baboon is put in a submissive relationship to its mother when it is weaned. Actually, it isn't literally weaning that brings the traumatic break between mother and infant, it's her refusal to let him cling to her back and ride around there—with Harlow's macaques also the key mother-infant bond was clinging, not feeding. Anyway, when the mother rejects the infant, she puts it in a submissive state, and for the young male that is incompatible with copulation. Therefore, no baboon incest.

Incidentally, you see that the primate mother, like the human mother, often affects a young male's dominance after the first separation. In macaques, a low-dominance female is bullied and cringing, and I'm sure this must condition her infant in the course of group life. By comparison, a high-dominance macaque mother helps even a full-grown son put down another male. The macaque equivalent of being born with a silver spoon is to have a dominant mother. The sons of dominant mothers are the future dominant males of the troop. But the top dominant male is dominant over all females, including his mother.

But back to baboons. The young male separates from his mother and begins to act out a juvenile aggressive phase. In fact, the juvenile and young-adult males act much more aggressive than the central males, and less able to cooperate. They neither solicit nor give help very often. They tend to be egocentric and disruptive. The male at the center is sober and calm by comparison. He doesn't take advantage of chinks in relationships between other monkeys to rush in between them. He's protective of the young. The male who signals for help most frequently is usually number one in the central hierarchy. If he's attacked by A, he'll run to B, trying to get his support against A.

I have several years of film on one troop now, and I suspect from it that males who've grown up together have a better chance of cooperating than others. Males do change groups as adults, and if a powerful younger male takes over, he may form a new central group about him. Unalloyed aggression is not the way to do it, though. One baboon, whom I called Curly, was very big and very aggressive, but he lacked the supreme confidence of most central males. He was tense, frustrated, full of displacement behavior, dashing angrily through the females and young. He became part of the central group—himself, A and B. A was dominant over Curly; Curly and B were inseparable. B disappeared, and Curly went way down in status, though he was the biggest baboon by far. He never copulated. No male can force a female to do so, no matter how dominant he is; the female chooses. And the females seem to like the calm and confidence, the lack of fighting, around the central males.

You see in chimps, too, that the male plays a reassuring role. When the group comes to a clearing, the males burst into it screaming and throwing rocks. It becomes clear that it's safe. Then the females and young calm down. They approach the males tentatively and touch their hands. When people see films of this, they say, "Oh, they're holding hands!" Then if the chimps are really getting calm, the male puts his arm around the female's back, and they make like Frenchmen giving medals, touching alternate cheeks. Then people say, "Oh, they're kissing!" Then they reach out and cup each others' genitals, and people say, "My God, what are they doing?" You see, monkeys are a lot like people.

A lot of the primate behavior just begs psychiatric description. I observed an old male whose canines were gone and who had sunk to the bottom of the hierarchy. The others made life miserable for him when he was away from the protection of the central hierarchy. If younger males harassed him, he'd cackle like a female and throw himself on the ground screaming like an infant.

How much could imprinting have to do with dominance and sex behavior?

Social science literature has been cluttered with the idea of imprinting the past five years. It's a very specific phenomenon, limited to precocial rather than altricial animals. Precocial animals can run about and feed themselves at birth. Altricial animals are born helpless, often blind and undeveloped; they have to elicit care, feeding and protection. A hare is precocial; it can run as soon as it's born. A rabbit can't—it's altricial. Birds are largely precocial; they can follow their mothers an hour after birth. So can sheep.

Imprinting occurs in precocial animals, even in the adults to some degree. Imprinting doesn't occur in altricial animals, such as humans. The idea of a critical period of learning makes more sense for them, and that's different from imprinting. J. P. Scott, in his classic work on the genetics and behavior of the dog, found that if a puppy isn't handled by humans between the ages of four and eight weeks—between the opening of the eyes and weaning—it will never really be socialized with people, domesticated. There are probably critical periods for learning in humans, since they're altricial, but to make conclusions about it is to make much of little data. Now that ethology is getting popular, and social scientists are jumping on ideas like territoriality and imprinting, some misleading things are being said.

Actually, our whole vocabulary of inherited versus learned behavior is bad. Most behavior in higher animals can't be polarized that way. In birds it can. Lorenz raised some pigeons in clay tubes, with their wings held in. Pigeons that weren't enclosed tried to fly, and it took till they were a month old. When the ones in tubes were released at about one month, they learned to fly in a short time. The untubed birds just hadn't developed physically to the point where they could fly properly until then. So the tubed birds learned in half an hour rather than ten days. That's programing. But look at Harlow's monkeys. When they were raised in isolation, they could make all the right sounds needed to communicate with other monkeys; they'd inherited them. But they used them in the wrong context when put with other monkeys. They hadn't learned when and how to use them. This combination of programing and learning is true of a lot of higher animals' behavior. Programing is just the beginning of their development.

In fact, we're finding what has to be called culture in some of the primates. A baboon born in captivity is afraid of legless lizards at first sight; it's programed. Some troops of baboons eat legless lizards; hard learning seems to have overcome the inherited behavior and then been socially perpetuated within the troop. The Japanese monkey-researchers have shown that food-washing can be spread by one individual through a whole macaque troop and become standard behavior, passed on by mothers to infants. Washburn and I felt that baboon troops are very different—some always nervous and fighting, others calm. Juveniles raised in a tense group will be tense adults. Anthropologists such as Whiting, Sears and Maccoby are doing long-term correlation work with material on different human societies to show that if the mother is such, and the father is such, the boy will have such-and-such problems. Interestingly, as I said, female children seem to muddle through better.

It's also interesting that a male turns off another male's aggression by using the language of the female or child.

Many human societies have no word for boy. They have one word for men and another that includes women and children, the nonmen.

Dr. Lionel Ovesey is an eminent psychoanalyst and the author of many papers on homosexuality, pseudohomosexuality, success phobia and masculine aspirations in women. He explains how he developed the concept of pseudohomosexuality.

I found that heterosexual men who were in psychotherapy repeatedly had dreams and fantasies of genital contact with other men. Understandably, they concluded from the imagery that they must be homosexual, and got anxious about it. It just made no sense to me, even though Freudian theory agreed with them and interpreted the images as "latent homosexuality."

But most of these men never had any erotic arousal with these images, and they consistently denied any homosexual desires or acts. I reviewed their sexual histories with them, and as far as I could make out there was no question about it, they really were heterosexual. I just couldn't figure it out. Then I decided to throw out the Freudian theory and look for other motivations. And I found them. In every case where there was no homosexual arousal, the fantasies were motivated by dependency needs or power needs. The patient was using the sexual fantasies to achieve dependence and power goals through symbolic use of his genitals. He misinterpreted the images as truly homosexual, but they were only symbolically homosexual. So I named them pseudohomosexual, and the anxiety pseudohomosexual anxiety.

Do all men have these fantasies?

Well, I feel they're universal, at least in our culture—and, I suspect, in most others. I find them regularly in male patients where I have access to the unconscious through free association, fantasies and dream material. It's hard for me to believe they exist only in these patients and in no one else. My inference is that they're universal, but that in most men they're unconscious and rarely or never reach awareness. After all, the symbols are biologically rooted in male anatomy, and they represent success or failure in the masculine role, which is culturally determined. All men have the same anatomy, and they're all subject to the same cultural pressures, so it seems logical to me that unconsciously, when it comes to pseudohomosexuality, they would use the same symbols.

Besides, there have been studies of nonpatients that support such assumptions. I did some with Abram Kardiner in *The Mark of Oppression*. Hendin and Gaylin did a study of nonpatient nurses. And there have been others. Are people different because they become patients? All of psychodynamic theory rests on the assumption that the same mechanisms we see in patients exist in all people, to some degree or in some way.

The difference between homosexuality and pseudohomosexuality, you say, is erotic arousal.

That's right. Homosexual anxiety occurs when a person has homosexual fantasies and is disturbed at being homosexually aroused. Pseudohomosexual anxiety occurs when the same fantasies bother a person, but without arousal. As I said, I think pseudohomosexual fantasies are universal, but they don't cause everyone trouble. They're fantasied solutions to problems of dependency and power, and if a person has a big problem, he'll use them, and they'll bother him. If he doesn't have much of a problem, the fantasies will remain unconscious.

Here's an example. Suppose a guy feels he's a failure as a man—maybe he can't get a job—and he has a fantasy of sucking some great big man's penis. But he doesn't have an erection, feels no arousal, and has no history of homosexuality. Well, how do you explain it? I've found over and over from the patient's own associations that he's trying to repair his failure as a man by sucking masculine strength out of the bigger man's penis. It's a magical solution, so it won't work, and causes further anxiety. But it's a very common mechanism. Psychoanalysis calls it introjection.

Here's another example, this time from the power side. When someone says, "I've been shafted," he shows how pseudohomosexual fantasy exists in folk language. He's telling you that he's been overpowered, but he's expressing it as though he's been subjected to homosexual assault. Most people know they're speaking figuratively. Then along comes someone who has a problem, and he unconsciously reacts to the symbol literally, as though it's a reality. Before he knows what's hit him, he begins to worry that he's a homosexual. That is, he develops a pseudohomosexual anxiety.

But the same fantasies, and the same problems of power and dependence, do play a role in homosexuality?

Yes. In the homosexual act, the person not only satisfies himself sexually, he also acts out his nonerotic fantasies. I feel that homosexuals tend to fall into patterns of sex behavior according to whether dependence or power strivings are predominant. Take a closet queen with a very masculine manner—and paranoid, as many such people are. He tends to seek a partner to subjugate. He will either screw somebody in the ass or will force him to suck him off. He is "trade," as they call it in homosexual society. This rises from his underlying personality structure.

On the other hand, if you look at a dependent, unassertive guy seeking a male protector, you're likely to see him moving to a sexually passive and dependent position. Sometimes both types of behavior occur in the same person, depending on the kind of pressure he's subject to at a given time. If the pressure isn't very great, and his manliness is only deflated a little, he can retrieve it by subjugating another man. But if the pressure is very great, and his manliness is deflated a lot, he can only retrieve it through submission.

Here, I'll show you how it works in an actual case. I had a patient recently who was a bisexual, a muscle man who worked with weights and who also went out with girls. Let's say he makes a pass at a girl, she turns him down, and he feels unmanly. This is a little pressure. So he goes to a bar and picks up a male homosexual who looks as manly as possible and who'll submit to him. He takes the guy home, mounts him *per anum,* and then throws him out. This makes him feel more manly, because he's made a woman out of his partner. Now let's say that another time he's been looking for a job all day, he's been turned down in a half dozen places, and he's pretty depressed. That night he's turned down by a girl too. This is a big pressure. It really makes him feel unmanly, castrated, like a woman. He doesn't feel strong enough to subjugate anybody. The only way he can get his manhood back now is through submission. So he goes back to the bar, picks up another strong guy, but this time he allows himself to be penetrated. He has fantasies of incorporating the stronger guy's penis, and thus his manhood and strength. It's as though he needed a transfusion of masculinity.

Do many patients still hear their homosexual imagery described to them as latent homosexuality?

Not so much any more, at least not in this country. It wasn't unusual fifteen or twenty years ago. Even most so-called Freudians wouldn't say it today unless they could document it and distinguish it from pseudohomosexuality. In the old days, a number of people on whom analysis had failed, and who then came to me for a second try, said that they'd expressed homosexual fantasies and anxieties and been told it was latent homosexuality. They said, "But I'm heterosexual!" Then they were told, "But everyone has to come to terms with his homosexuality." It only intensified their anxiety. I haven't heard this from a patient for several years now. Before, I heard it several times a year.

Then there's no such thing as latent homosexuality?

Of course there's such a thing. But I use the word behaviorally, not instinctually. I use it in the strict dictionary sense, latent as opposed to overt. Any homosexual arousal that isn't acted out is latent, and it can be either conscious or unconscious.

What do you find in following up homosexual patients after therapy?

I've seen homosexuals find equal pleasure in women and then stick with heterosexuality if they marry. Besides sex they have friendship, family and other benefits. But I've never seen a homosexual who didn't drift back to men if he didn't eventually marry, even though he'd managed to become potent with women. This is just an impression, but it would be important if it could be documented. The temptations are too great for a former homosexual without close bonds. Often the failure to make such bonds is the greatest problem in a homosexual's life. In recent years I've been surprised at the number of homosexuals who come for treatment who have or develop heterosexual capability, but who fail to establish a close, lasting relationship with anyone, male or female. Treatment breaks down, and so does heterosexuality, because the person can't sustain intimate relaitonships with women or with people in general.

25

From Outrage to Boredom

Each day the popular wisdom is confirmed: America is in the spasms of a sexual revolution. The mass media and learned journals alike report on crash pads, communes, suburban swapping, homosexuality, kink and teen-agers freed for promiscuity by the pill. Many clinicians believe that premar-ital sex, gender problems and homosexuality are more common than a decade ago. Whether these changes are interpreted as liberation or as social pathology, there is wide agreement that the grunt and mumble of copulaton are becoming the major background noise of the Western world. But in fact, strong evidence has been accumulating that no such thing is happen-ing. What needs explaining is our touching fidelity to the idea.

Before the research of Kinsey and his associates, there were only frag-mentary reports of what people do sexually. It was safe to generalize from none of them. At about the time when ethology was developing and experi-mental psychology growing more sophisticated, Kinsey decided to use with human beings the scrupulous methods of observation that were bringing such good results in other fields. Today his approach seems obvious in con-ception, the need for it self-evident; most great research has that air of simple inevitability in retrospect. But it shocked both popular and learned sensibilities when it appeared, and it launched the present era of sex research.

Alfred C. Kinsey was a zoologist, his research specialty the gall wasp. Over many years of teaching at Indiana University, he regularly received questions about human sexuality from students—a frequent fate of zoology teachers. When he tried to find answers for them, he was shocked to find impassioned muddle, unverified wisdom and an almost total absence of data. More was known about the sexuality of some insects than of man. But this panorama of ignorance hadn't kept biologists, psychologists and anthropologists from holding strong convictions which, for lack of proof to the contrary, they called facts. Psychoanalysts and endocrinologists labeled people "underactive" and "hypersexual" without saying what norm made them so. They talked about clitoral versus vaginal orgasm without having a physiological definition of orgasm. They spoke of "immature" and "deviant" acts without knowing what most adults really do.

A small number of people over the two previous decades had tried to apply the rules of evidence to human sexuality, but their results were mere traces in a wilderness. Some used samples of forty, three hundred and, rarely, a thousand or so; Kinsey had thought it necessary to use 150,000 individuals to learn the morphology of one species of gall wasp. Some studies had used special samples, such as female college graduates (then a more solidly upper-middle-class group than today). Some used questionnaires instead of interviews—rarely a very reliable method in sexology, as anyone knows who has tried both.

What was needed was a taxonomic study—a description of a species by finding the range of variation in its traits. Kinsey performed his first interviews in 1938 with the support of Indiana University. Four years later the Rockefeller Foundation added its support. Kinsey acquired three chief collaborators along the way, Wardell Pomeroy, Clyde Martin and Paul Gebhard. They encountered widespread cooperation from some laymen, threats of prosecution and censorship from others. Scientists, especially during the early years of the project, showed timidity and critical animosity. Some said Kinsey's project shouldn't be carried out; some that only "normal" sex should be studied; others that the results must not be published. Psychoanalysts, gynecologists and testing psychologists objected to a strictly taxonomic approach; Kinsey invited them to add their skills to his project. They declined, saying it would be too long and complicated a job. Later they complained that the study was just taxonomic.

Kinsey spoke to club ladies, farm ladies, prostitutes, prisoners, professors and lumberjacks. To avoid skewed volunteer samples, he got all the members of a club, a congregation, a prison, even a whole small town, to cooperate. Husbands and wives were interviewed separately as checks on each others' accuracy; Kinsey's staff did multiple interviewing and recording of results to check their own accuracy. To establish rapport and win honesty from so many different people is both a gift and a hard discipline; Kinsey's chapter on interviewing in *Sexual Behavior in the Human Male*, describing his attitudes and methods, is a great human and scientific document. As he said there, an interviewer gets results only if he shows genuine interest and compassion, meanwhile combining the skills of a psychotherapist, a lab researcher and a snake-oil salesman. These pages on method anticipated almost every major criticism that has been made of Kinsey's studies; it sometimes seems that many of his severest critics didn't even read the volumes through, let alone this chapter.

Kinsey's over-all plan called for a hundred thousand life histories, with at least three hundred for any given subpopulation (by sex, age, religion, educational level, etc.). After gathering more than eighteen thousand interviews, he decided that the project was the work of more than a lifetime and that he already had so many significant facts that he should publish preliminary reports. He selected some 6,300 male and 5,300 female subjects; others were excluded because they belonged to subgroups of which he still knew too little. In 1948 *Sexual Behavior in the Human Male* appeared, and in 1953 *Sexual Behavior in the Human Female*. They contained something to startle or offend everyone.

Some single statistics were enough to provoke howls. If all existing laws were enforced, some 95 per cent of American men would go to jail for sex offenses. More than one man in three had had a homosexual experience to orgasm. One woman out of two had had coitus before marriage, and one in four had been unfaithful to her husband. Some acts widely called perversions were practiced by 60 or even 75 per cent of certain segments of the population.

There were obvious, seemingly inescapable, conclusions to be drawn from the data. There was a huge gap between official and private morality and still another between private morality and behavior. Girls with premarital sex experience made better, faster sex adjustments in marriage than those without. The college-educated people who talked sexual liberation (and who reviewed Kinsey's volumes) were inhibited late starters in sex. Woman's orgasmic capacity is biologically greater than man's, not less, and is potentially no more slowly mobilized; only social conditioning makes women less or more slowly aroused.

Furthermore, Kinsey's evidence contradicted many treasured truisms of biology and psychoanalysis. Traditional concepts of bisexuality are partly a result of sloppy observation and theory. Sexual behavior simply does not, in fact, proceed from autoerotic to homosexual to heterosexual on the classic Freudian timetable. Sublimation is an unworkable concept.

Kinsey demonstrated, as had no one before him, the immense range of human sex behavior. This range, plus the fact that most people tend to consider their own place in it normal, accounts for much scientific and social controversy. For instance, said Kinsey, when a school board discusses sex education, "it is difficult for an observer to comprehend how objective reasoning can lead to such different conclusions among intelligent men and women. If, however, one has the histories of the educators involved, it may be found that there are persons in the group who are not ejaculating more than once or twice a year, while there may be others . . . experiencing orgasm as often as ten or twenty times per week. . . . The possibility of an individual engaging in sexual activity at a rate remarkably different from one's own is one of the most difficult for even professionally trained persons to understand."

The *New York Times* refused to print an ad for the first Kinsey volume, and later the Rockefeller Foundation withdrew its support. But the book instantly became a best-seller, and discussion of it appeared in the press for years. Kinsey heeded many methodological criticisms and improved his processing of data in the volume on females in 1953. The storm renewed. A clergyman called the second book "statistical filth"; Clare Booth Luce supported a Catholic women's organization in labeling it a "cheap thriller," an insult to the American people and a spur to immorality. Many psychoanalysts and anthropologists distinguished themselves just as little, attacking Kinsey because his data failed to enshrine their old theories. Lionel Trilling, in a famous essay, warned that Kinsey's figures could be misleading, and many scientists joined him in clucking over the possible misinterpretation by laymen of all those statistics. The chief criticism was that Kinsey had ignored feelings and stuck to behavior—which had been his avowed purpose, since feelings about sex had heretofore prevented knowledge of behavior.

But Kinsey was also compared to Darwin, Freud and Copernicus. His data provided the first reliable guidelines for doctors, psychotherapists, clergymen and legislators. Many psychoanalysts and anthropologists, after defending their traditions, praised his work. Experts on polling, statistics and social science generally admired his methods and results. The most positive response of all came from the lay public. A Gallup poll found that five out of six people with opinions about Kinsey's work thought it a good thing. They bore out the faith Kinsey had shown when he argued with scientists who wanted to protect the public from his data. In his 1953 volume he said that the scientist who depends on citizens at large in his work must make the results available to all or he "fails to recognize the sources of his right to investigate. . . . The restriction of sexual knowledge to a limited number of professionally trained persons, to physicians, to priests, or to those who can read Latin, has not sufficiently served the millions of boys and girls, men and women, who need such knowledge to guide them in their everyday affairs."

Among Kinsey's male subjects were people born before 1900 and as late as the 1940s. He found that the biggest determinant of their sex behavior was their educational and occupational level. The differences between grade-school and college graduates were not a result of education itself, for they were present even in early childhood; the educational levels represented life styles in different socioeconomic classes. Men who had graduated from grade school only and worked at blue-collar jobs were the most active of all educational groups. As preadolescents they began sex play earliest; whatever they did from then on, they did it more. Their main source of orgasm was coitus. They began it in their early or mid-teens, and 98 per cent experienced it before marriage. They tended to hold the double standard, separating sex from affection and marriage. After marriage, they expected fidelity from their wives but not from themselves. Only when they reached their thirties did they start settling down to monogamy and a lower plateau of sex activity. Coitus without overture or variation was their favored sex activity. They considered masturbation and petting mere substitutes, even perversions; only 16 per cent ever petted to orgasm. They practiced oral-genital sex and a variety of coital positions least of all groups. Some 6 per cent were mostly or exclusively homosexual for at least three consecutive years of their lives.

A different pattern appeared among male college graduates who entered upper-white-collar or professional careers. They began preadolescent sex play later than lower-level males. During their teens, masturbation was their main sex outlet. Petting was second, practiced by four times as many males as in the grade-school group. Two thirds rather than 98 per cent had premarital coitus, and only 15 per cent with regularity. Many did so only with the girls they eventually married, and few had more than a half dozen partners. They carried oral-centered petting and other coital substitutes into marriage as coital foreplay; to them orality and varied coital positions were not frills or perversions but added pleasures. During their thirties, they gained more assurance and had more extramarital sex. By forty, a good number finally obtained the lack of inhibition and range of partners with which the grade-school group began adult life. A somewhat larger number had at least three years of predominant or exclusive homosexuality than among the grade-school group—more than 9 per cent.

The high school graduates who entered skilled manual or lower-white-collar jobs lay between the other two groups in most things. Twice as many petted to orgasm as compared to grade-schoolers, but half as many as in the college group. They began coitus earlier than the college men and had it more often, but their record did not approach the grade-school group's. However, this turned out to be the group with the largest amount of casual and exclusive homosexuality—14 per cent mostly or totally homosexual for at least three years.

There were other, less important influences on men's sex behavior. One was religion; strong belief and regular religious practice correlated with less sex activity. Urban males had slightly higher incidence and frequency figures for most acts than rural males. Decade of birth made little or no difference. Between the 1890s and 1940s, men's total orgasmic outlet was unchanged; there had been minor shifts in types of activity and choice of partner. As the nation moved from blue to white collar, fewer men had impulsive, aggressive sex behavior; more had upper-level patterns of restraint and substitute activity. The same proportion of men went to prostitutes, but males at higher social levels did so less frequently; instead they petted or had coitus with girls from their own backgrounds. Frequency of marital coitus went down during the twenties, probably because men gave more consideration to their wives' desire (or lack of it). If there had been any change in male sex behavior during the twentieth century, it was hardly an outbreak of wildness. The change had been in women's behavior.

Women's social script for sexual development was more labile, more easily revised, than men's; the sexual revolution that had been talked about since the end of the First World War turned up in the statistics of their behavior. As usual, people judged the world by their own experience; some found Kinsey's figures shockingly high, and fewer found them shockingly low.

Some people were astounded to find in Kinsey's second volume that half of all women experienced coitus before marriage and that a quarter had been unfaithful by the age of forty. But these figures included people—in fact a majority—who had done such things once, rarely, or for a brief time. The median frequency for girls who petted to orgasm was four to six times a year. Nonvirgins under twenty who had premarital coitus averaged once every five to ten weeks. In many such cases there were periods of months or even years without sexual activity. Half the single nonvirgins had had only one partner, usually their fiancés; only one in ten had had six or more partners. Generally, once people began a sex practice, they did it no more frequently than those in previous generations; incidence had changed, but not frequency.

Some critics said Kinsey's female sample was heavily weighted with white, urban, well-educated women from the Northeast. Kinsey had been quite aware of this, and counterweighted his data accordingly. He also pointed out that this made less difference than it would in a male sample, for he had enough lower-level female subjects to show that education and parents' occupation were minor influences for females. The various levels had produced very different patterns of aggression and control in males, but girls of all classes got pretty much the same kind and amount of training in restraint.

Girls who completed college, high school and grade school (and whose families were correspondingly blue collar, white collar and professional) began sex activity at different ages, but they also married at different ages. Adjusting for age of marriage, similar proportions of girls from all backgrounds had similar amounts of premarital petting and coitus—usually in anticipation of marriage. To the extent that there were differences, they were explained by the postponement of marriage for the sake of education, which leaves a longer period as a mature single person. Girls who went to graduate school did finally accumulate a little more premarital experience than grade-school girls; at twenty a third of the grade-school girls were married, but only a tenth of the college group. The upper-level woman, like her male counterpart, eventually developed a wider sexual repertoire; but the lower-level woman resembled her male counterpart in being less restrained, as shown by a slightly higher orgasmic rate.

Religion was more influential than educational level—just the reverse of the male pattern. Belief and observance created restraint. Religiously inactive Roman Catholics had a slight edge over the other nonobserving groups in sexual activity.

By far the most important factor was decade of birth, which had mattered hardly at all for men. As we saw in examining the twenties, Kinsey revealed that the generation of women born between 1900 and 1910 had a leap of five, ten, fifteen or more percentage points for most sex activities at a given age. This cut across all lines of education, religion and class. Now 30 per cent of girls petted to orgasm before marriage instead of 15 per cent; the average age of doing so for the first time dropped from eighteen to sixteen. Petting techniques became more diverse, women took a more active sexual role, and oral taboos loosened. The spinster and unresponsive woman became rarer phenomena. Of women still single at twenty-five, 36 per cent had had coitus rather than 14 per cent. In marriage, more women tried a variety of sexual positions, experienced orgasm, slept nude. The change was significant, but not earthshaking. It leveled off by 1930, and went up at a barely perceptible rate until Kinsey closed his interviewing books two decades later.

In all, the changes added up to a spread of the new middle-class pattern of necking, petting and perhaps coitus within the context of dating and anticipation of marriage. We saw that with the end of arranged matches and closed communities the dating system arose as a means of mate selection, with some limited erotic exploration as part of it. The greatest changes of all were increases in petting at younger ages, petting to orgasm and coitus as the seal of a love match. These changes and a lot of talk made society assume youth was sexually running wild. People pointed out that divorce continued to increase, but so did remarriage; this was another sign of the growing emphasis on marriage as a love bond rather than a social contract, not a symptom of the death of sexual restraint.

Despite all the changes that did take place in female behavior, and the minor shifts in male behavior, there was no increase in male or female homosexuality. Deviance involved the same proportions of people and to the same extent. But this is only one of the deflations of mythology about deviance in Kinsey's reports.

The first surprise was childhood homosexual play. Two fifths of Kinsey's male subjects remembered sex play with girls in preadolescence, usually beginning in the eighth year. But more, two thirds, recalled sex play with other boys, usually starting at nine. Most of this "homosexual play" was exploratory—exhibition, exploration or joint masturbation—in the context of preadolescent chumship. Only 15 per cent of these experiences involved attempts at oral or anal sex.

After puberty 37 per cent of all males had a homosexual contact to orgasm. Kinsey found the figure surprisingly high; he kept rechecking, and it was confirmed again and again. Like that initially startling 50 per cent nonvirginity rate for single girls, it must be qualified. It included every boy who took part in a "circle jerk" at thirteen. Half the males with homosexual experience had it only between twelve and fourteen, and never again. Another third had it by eighteen; much of it was limited to joint or mutual masturbation. But many males had periods of brief or even extended homosexual activity in the course of over-all heterosexual lives, and Kinsey saw that he had to scrap the usual categories of heterosexual, homosexual and bisexual.* In their place he put a seven-point scale based on both physical acts and psychological arousal:

---

*Kinsey gave a detailed, cogent criticism of the term bisexual for a person with both heterosexual and homosexual behavior. Unfortunately, we still have no word to replace it, so I have reluctantly retained it in this book.

0. Exclusively heterosexual, with no homosexual
1. Predominantly heterosexual, only incidentally homosexual
2. Predominantly heterosexual, but more than incidentally homosexual
3. Equally heterosexual and homosexual
4. Predominantly homosexual, but more than incidentally heterosexual
5. Predominantly homosexual, but incidentally heterosexual
6. Exclusively homosexual

About 18 per cent of all males rated between 3 and 6 on the Kinsey scale, at least as much homosexual as heterosexual, for at least three consecutive years of their lives. Some 13 per cent rated between 4 and 6, more homosexual than heterosexual, for at least three years. One man in ten rated 5 or 6, predominantly or exclusively homosexual, for three years. This figure probably represents homosexuality as it is usually referred to by laymen—a sufficiently intense and prolonged homosexual experience to become a consistent problem behavior to the person or, potentially, his society. Only four per cent were exclusively homosexual all their lives, and another 2 per cent nearly so. These figures established two important facts. First, the extent of hard-core male homosexuality is about 4 to 6 per cent, and as a "problem" behavior during at least part of life, a good 10 per cent. Second, a small degree of homosexual behavior is, in the statistical sense, normal, involving about one male in three, especially between puberty and the early twenties.

Equally important was Kinsey's discovery that homosexual men tend to follow the usual sex-behavior patterns of other men, rather than of homosexual or heterosexual women. College-level homosexuals scored lowest in number of orgasms and partners. Grade-school-level homosexuals ranked highest; what they did, they did more. There were fewer low-level homosexuals, and that group's homosexual-orgasm figures were boosted by men who worked in remote rural areas—lumbermen, cattlemen, prospectors, miners, hunters. These men sometimes used each other for sexual release when no women were available, without conflict over their heterosexual identity or capacity. Kinsey guessed this might have been common among pioneers and cowboys in the past.

Some college-level males tolerated homosexual behavior out of conviction; some lower-level men did so because of a *laissez-aller* attitude. The most condemnatory feelings came from the level where there was the most homosexuality, casual and committed—high school graduates who were skilled laborers and low-level white-collar workers. At age nineteen, when one grade-schooler in four and one college male in five had had a homosexual experience to orgasm, the figure was 45 per cent for the high school group. From this class came many men who baited, beat up and rolled homosexuals; it also included many men who worked as male prostitutes, denying they were homosexual but then paying for homosexual contacts themselves when age made them less desirable.

So educational and occupational level was the biggest determinant of sex behavior for homosexual as well as heterosexual men. For homosexual men, too, religion was second in importance. Men of different educational levels but the same religion showed differences of 200 or even 500 per cent in the number of homosexual acts. Within one educational level, religiously active and inactive men differed by only 10 to 50 per cent, but belief was consistently a restraint. Homosexuality was phenomenally rare among Orthodox Jews.

Figures on frequencies and numbers of partners flatly contradicted the traditional idea that young homosexuals are promiscuous and then slip into pathetically near-impotent "aunthood." Many young males are shy, secretive, afraid or ashamed about acting on their homosexual urges. They may go months without sexual contact during their teens and early twenties. Their choice of partner may be narrowed by special tastes in age, appearance, sex role or sex act. But as they get older, their experience and self-assurance grow, and they become more active. The average frequency of contact to orgasm was about once a week at twenty-five and twice a week at thirty-five. At any age, in any segment of society, only one homosexual in twenty had as much sex as the usual married young heterosexual—about every other day.

Kinsey's findings on female homosexuals were just as surprising. Hirschfeld, Bergler and others had thought them more common than male homosexuals. Krafft-Ebing, Ellis and Freud believed them equal in number. Half of Kinsey's males admitted to physical or emotional response to their own sex at some time, 37 per cent to an act leading to orgasm. Only 28 per cent of the women confessed homosexual response, 13 per cent an act to orgasm. One third to half as many women as men were primarily or exclusively homosexual; a comparably smaller number had had intermediate amounts of homosexual experience. The women who rated between 3 and 6 on Kinsey's scale, at least as much homosexual as heterosexual, were 4 to 11 per cent of the single, 1 to 2 per cent of the married, and 5 to 7 per cent of the formerly married. Those with the ratings 5 and 6, mostly or totally homosexual, were half as numerous as among men— altogether a bit more than 2 per cent of all women.

This killed the idea that there was widespread secret homosexuality among married women. To the contrary, marriage almost always put an end to women's homosexuality; not more than one wife in a hundred experienced homosexual contact to orgasm, and in that rare case probably just once or twice. There was more lesbianism among the formerly married. Some women had been divorced because of preexisting lesbianism; others had their first lesbian experience after the end of their marriages. But by far the most homosexuality was among the single and never married.

In homosexuality, as in heterosexuality, fewer women had experience than men, and those who did were less active. Some 15 per cent of preadolescent girls had sex play with boys only, 18 per cent with girls only, and 15 per cent with both; all figures were far lower than those for boys. This play occurred during a shorter period; almost none, as compared to half among boys, was carried on into adolescence. Girls experienced a sharp break in all sex activity at puberty, when family and society put restrictions on them as maturing females.

After puberty, women's homosexual patterns remained similar to those of female heterosexuals, and different from men's. Men had a much greater amount of homosexual exploration during their teens. A similar graph for women shows the line rising gradually from adolescence to about age thirty, when it stood at 17 per cent; it paralleled a woman's general sexual development to a final peak of de-inhibition around or after age thirty.

Much of this homosexual activity was exploratory and limited to a short period—for half the women, a year or less. A third had ten or fewer homosexual experiences, many only one or two. Like heterosexual women, most had fewer partners than a comparable group of men. More than half the lesbians had only one partner, another fifth had only two. Only 4 per cent had ten or more partners, as compared to 22 per cent of male homosexuals. Lasting couples were rare among male homosexuals, but many lesbian pairs lived together domestically for five, ten, or fifteen years.

Like heterosexual women, lesbians might take a while to attain whole-hearted, orgasmic sex lives. Many were sexually inactive for long periods. They reached a peak of activity in their late twenties—once every two and a half weeks. Even some women with long homosexual histories did little more than kiss and hug for years. In time, though, most began stimulating each other's breasts and genitals. Among experienced lesbians, cunnilingus had been practiced by almost four fifths, genital apposition (a grind or rub job) by more than half. Using a penis substitute was very, very rare; the dildo is far more a male fantasy than a female pleasure, and the clitoris remains the chief center of direct erotic satisfaction aside from coitus. In short, lesbians' sex lives were typically feminine, as male homosexuals' were typically masculine.

Religion played the expected role in female homosexuality. The devout among lesbians were more restrained; inactive Catholics were highest in many ratings, and religiously active Jews were remarkably low in homosexuality. Three things stood in relief from the usual female pattern: education, decade of birth and incidence of orgasm.

Educational level had little effect on heterosexual women, and what effect it had seemed mostly a result of deferring marriage. But there was a definite increase in homosexual experience as one went up the educational scale. By age thirty, 9 per cent of grade-school women, 10 per cent of high school graduates, 17 per cent of college and 24 per cent of graduate-school females had had at least one homosexual experience. This may have been a result of class attitudes or of general increased experience and experiment among those who wait to marry. Decade of birth, the most important influence on heterosexual women, had no correlation with lesbianism. There had been no change in incidence or frequency of lesbianism from Kinsey's oldest to youngest subjects, whether the lesbianism was incidental, exclusive or at any point between. And a larger number of lesbians than of women married up to five years experienced orgasm during most or all sex relations. Kinsey guessed this was because one knows best how to stimulate a person of one's own sex.

Kinsey's studies did have failings. They were weak in cross-cultural perspective; in extenuation, one must say that reliable anthropological data were almost nonexistent on many points. Many population categories were omitted, among them ethnic ones; grouping together as Catholics a second-generation Italian-American and a fourth-generation German-American may cloud as much as it explains. Kinsey sometimes emphasized mammalian precedents for human sex behavior at the expense of crucial human differences. Probably most clinicians doubt that women's orgasmic rates are as high as Kinsey's subjects said. Figures on female orgasm prior to the Masters and Johnson research on sexual physiology are doubtful, but Kinsey anticipated their basic findings and even did clinical observations of human sex behavior without cameras or such detailed data. It may still be the clinicians who are wrong. Over-all, the Kinsey studies are remarkable for their probable general accuracy—against all odds. Although some figures may some day be revised, we must consider the trends reliable.

Kinsey himself said these two volumes were just preliminary reports, omitting blacks, enough lower-class women, certain deviants, etc. Even so, they are among the major social documents of the century, the only large body of data on sex behavior, and every subsequent investigator's point of departure. Kinsey's grand research plan is still unfinished, a challenge ignored. When it comes to sex, society follows Bergson's description of it: if it ever changes, it denies that change happened. The selective reading of the Kinsey reports to this day is a case in point.

Everyone noticed or remembered what supported his emotional views and ignored the rest when possible. Some emphasized the 50 per cent nonvirginity rate for women, the 37 per cent homosexual-orgasm statistic for men and any sign of sexual change. Those impressed by the signs of stability in society's scripting of sex pointed to small frequencies and signs of reluctant evolution. Lesbians who wanted to believe that the whole world is gay spoke of the 28 per cent figure of homosexual arousal in women but ignored the data on married women and went on believing that half the wives in America were potential lesbians or "bisexuals." The evidence against some psychoanalytic theories of development and the trenchant argument against such concepts as sublimation were ignored by those who had faith in them; careless experimental workers ignored criticism of their old concepts of biological bisexuality and narrow physical determinism.

Paul Gebhard, now director of the Institute for Sex Research and a co-author of Kinsey's female-behavior volume, says that when people know what they believe about sex, they don't want to be disturbed by facts. Our society now, as in the twenties, has a stake in the popular myth of abrupt sexual change, especially in the increasingly separate subculture of adolescents.

That, at least, was where matters stood in 1967 when one blow for accuracy was struck by the Institute for Sex Research. During the fifties it had been assumed that Kinsey's figures still described American society. During the sixties, talk of sexual revolution began, and the media presented a picture very much like that of "Flaming Youth" in the twenties—hedonistic, guiltless, liberated by technology and a new life-outlook for a grand sensual holiday. It was as though no one had read Kinsey and learned from the trends he demonstrated in his retrospective portrait of the twenties. In several years of interviewing people about sex behavior, I have found that especially among the educated there is a pose of boredom and blasé indifference if one suggests that data are needed about alleged socio-sexual changes. The society that greeted the Kinsey volumes with outrage now assumes an attitude of knowledgeable amusement. A common response is to make jokes and say that we all know about these things without counting heads, or whatever. The rhetoric of sexual enlightenment and the pose of fearless experience are more entrenched than ever. If there has been further "revolution" during the past decade, it is chiefly in attitudes and rationalizations.

The presumed Red Square of American sexuality is the campus. This is doubtful to begin with, since college-level people have long been the most inhibited late starters in sex of all social groups. About half a dozen small studies were made of students' sex behavior in the sixties, most limited to one school and a small sample. None is a basis for generalizations, for campuses vary widely in the backgrounds of their students—by class, religion, region of country, urban-rural origin, etc.* Nevertheless, the majority reveal nothing Kinsey couldn't have predicted twenty years ago. The lines on the graphs of sex behavior, almost level since 1930, began a small upswing in the late fifties and early sixties but certainly not at a rate equaling the twenties. Indicative of the general trend in these studies is that of Dr. Joseph Katz, who studied a few hundred students at Stanford and Berkeley and found that 76 per cent of the girls and 63 per cent of the boys hadn't had coitus by the middle of their junior year. A third of the men and a quarter of the women dated little or not at all even as seniors.

Finally in 1967 sociologists William Simon and John Gagnon, then at the Institute for Sex Research, duplicated Kinsey's sample of twelve hundred college students and studied their behavior. Kinsey said that about 20

*Vance Packard, in *The Sexual Wilderness*, reports that his questionnaire study of college students indicates regional differences in attitudes and behavior. His studies do not, in my opinion, even approach reliability, but regional differences—South, Midwest, Mountain states, etc.—have often been reported as subjective impressions and should be carefully investigated.

per cent of college girls were nonvirgins; now the figure is more like 25 per cent—a bit higher or lower, depending on various background factors. The nonvirginity rate among senior girls is 50 per cent, but the average marriage age for college girls has dropped to twenty-two. Going steady, with petting, begins earlier now, and so does coitus, but most college students have little or no coital experience in high school. The pattern remains one of increasing amounts of sex by girls in return for increasing amounts of love, with monogamous marriage in ultimate view. If there is more casual coitus, there is only a little more. The most significant increase, according to Simon, is a small but distinct shift toward earlier masturbation among girls, indicating an earlier commitment to sexuality.

Back in the thirties, when the peak of change in sex behavior was well past, the famous sexologist Dr. Lewis M. Terman said that if things continued the way they were going, no American girl would reach the bridal bed a virgin in 1960. Most prophets of sexual revolution today will look just as silly a few decades hence. There is a process of slow evolution, amounting usually to a couple of percentage points a decade for a given act in a given group. Some researchers feel that a larger number of young people enjoy sex more, and feel less guilt. But it is significant that now, as in Kinsey's day, no increase in sexual frequencies has been reported along with this alleged de-inhibition.

The majority of journalists, without any background in the psychology, biology or measurement of sex behavior, have crudely sampled the attitude of a minority of youth and have taken at face value what they heard. But, as we have seen, people's talk and lives may stand at odds. What's more, surveys of attitudes have sometimes been confused with surveys of behavior. A study of more than 250 sociology students in Iowa showed that only 59 per cent of those who approved of premarital coitus had ever experienced it.

Members of the liberal and radical youth subculture tend to look with lofty pity at their elders' alleged inhibitions. In 1961 Robert Bell and Jack Buerkle studied the attitudes of 217 female college students and their mothers. All the mothers disapproved of premarital coitus to some degree; only half the daughters considered it "very wrong," and 13 per cent thought it all right. Kinsey's and other studies make it almost certain that the mothers and daughters will end up with similar sexual histories; Bell and Buerkle conclude that the daughters' liberal attitudes may only last till they themselves have daughters. "It is therefore possible that the 'sexual emancipation' of the college girl exists only for a short time in her life span, centering around the time of premarital love and/or engagement." A more recent study by sociologist Robert Walsh of 850 parents and their 425 college-age children showed that 74 per cent of the women students approved of premarital sex behavior beyond kissing, and so did 60 per cent of the mothers—but only 16 per cent of the mothers were seen by the daughters as approving such behavior. In other words, the real "generation gap" was 14 per cent, and the imagined one was 48 per cent.

Beats, hippies, dissident politics, drugs and sexual hedonism have all been lumped together in the media. *Newsweek* assured readers in 1967 that "for the hippies, sex is not a matter of great debate, because as far as they are concerned the sexual revolution is accomplished. There are no hippies who believe in chastity, or look askance at marital infidelity or see even marriage itself as a virtue. Physical love is a delight—to be chewed upon as often and freely as a handful of sesame seeds."

Again, there has been a leap in attitudes, expectations and verbal sophistication, and probably a short hop in behavior. This dissident youth group is really a loose amalgam of many different subgroups sharing similar trappings. Some are lower- and lower-middle-class delinquents who ten years ago might have joined gangs; today they fall into a different delinquent or quasi-delinquent slot which society provides, the hip-rock-drug scene. Others are drop-outs from the upper middle class. Some are drop-outs from small-town life. They themselves are rarely accurate or sophisticated observers of their own peers; that is, they are as prone to ignorance and error as their elders. Members of the loosely defined youth culture that talks a big game of sexual emancipation run a full range of emotional adjustment and sexual expression. My own experience in interviewing them gives me the impression that until new data prove otherwise, they do not fall far outside the predictions one would make for them on the grounds of class and religion, the usual clinical indicators of sexuality, etc. In fact, I often had the sort of experience recounted by journalist Gael Greene in 1964 in her book *Sex and the College Girl*: "A City College of New York freshman chattered away for nearly two hours about her erotic adventures before something she said struck a false note and I prodded her into confessing what was, to her, apparently a disgraceful admission: that she was actually a virgin."

It remains as true now as twenty years ago, Morton Hunt says, that "when the wishful thinking of the young and the envious reminiscences of the old are put aside, the unglamorous truth is that ... nonvirgins under twenty have intercourse only once every five to ten weeks, and those over twenty only once every three weeks or so. In comparison, the stodgily married live in riotous debauchery."

In the twenties people said the automobile was bearing off youth to new orgiastic treats. In the late thirties it was said that penicillin would make the world free for sex. Now the contraceptive pill is supposed to be creating a youthful generation as sexually carefree as rodents. The perfection of the condom and diaphragm, the arrival of the auto and the perfection of antibiotics did not produce a great change in sex behavior. Why the pill should do so, when these other things did not, is unclear. Actually, almost nothing is known about the effects of the pill on behavior. No one knows how many single girls take it (or how many take it for acne or menstrual irregu-larities); whether those who take it have coitus more often or with more partners; whether they enjoy sex more. There is evidence that the pill blocks orgasm and may reduce sex drive in some people (though perhaps it de-inhibits others). But this has not prevented even the learned from assuming that the pill has created a national sex festival.

Many leading sex researchers—Paul Gebhard, Mary Calderone, Ira L. Reiss, Harold Lief—agree that the pill is not changing sex behavior. Fear of pregnancy and venereal disease have rarely kept people out of bed; it just made them worry afterward. As John Gagnon has said, "A doctor with a dirty mind who fits a young woman with a diaphragm can convince him-self that there is a sexual explosion. He talks to the press in the role of marriage counselor and then everyone else thinks so, too. . . . The presence of the pill does not make people decide to have sex. It is after they decide to have sex that they try to get the pill." Those who think inhibitions and traditional views have died should remember that avoidance of contracep-tion is still common. Sometimes it is due to ignorance. Sometimes it is due to sexual guilt, rationalized as "it spoils the mood." Sometimes it is to induce pregnancy and force marriage. The shotgun marriage is still com-monplace in our society, and pregnancy is the precipitating cause of more engagements than we admit.

Cycles of sex-revolution reporting would themselves be interesting sub-jects of social research. When I began writing this book, *Esquire* magazine immediately approached me for an article on kink, which was then the latest piece of fresh copy in the field of baroque sex. Four years later, as I was finishing the book, I was approached by *Playboy* to write about com-munes. At these times, kink and communes were spreading in magazine articles more than in life. There are allegedly many sexual undergrounds—swapping, sado-masochistic, transvestite, group marriage. Most reliable observers say that the members of each variety probably number in four figures, perhaps five, in the United States. They are barely statistically noticeable. People familiar with communes and group-marriage clusters on the West Coast, where they are probably most common, say there are forty to sixty such groups there, most with ten to thirty members each. Many meet only sporadically, and few last as long as a year. But during the couple of decades before the Civil War there were dozens of communities based on shared property and sex partners. There were at least forty Four-ierite and Owenite communes alone. The Oneida group had hundreds of members and lasted for two or three generations. Proportionately, more people may then have been involved in radical sex communities than today, and more successfully.

It is considered common knowledge that there has been a big upsurge in homosexuality. There is much casual talk of it in some radical youth sub-cultures, with rationales taken from Herbert Marcuse and Norman O.

Brown. But Kinsey showed that while a gradual shift took place in much sex behavior, male and female homosexuality stayed stable. No study since Kinsey's even hints at increased homosexuality since his time. Simon and Gagnon, who duplicated his college sample, have written, "The future does not augur an increase in the number of exclusively homosexual men. . . . Female homosexuality will probably remain relatively stable over time, in terms of incidence and the number of adult committed deviants." And as open as sex and homosexuality may seem, there is no toleration for what most major American cities had in the 1890s—an open red-light district with male brothels and male streetwalkers.

English sociologist Michael Schofield says there is probably no more chance of homosexual acts among the young today, just less chance of the stony silence of shame afterward. A well-known homosexual painter commented to me: "My own memory of the attitudes of adolescent boys in bed twenty years ago [at a famous eastern prep school] tells me they were not all that shameful over breakfast. A few, of course, decided they'd matured beyond such things after a while. Now they are mostly divorced, working to be generals or district attorneys or surgeons. Of approximately fourteen . . . lured into bed and primed by Pierre Louys and other literate devices, almost all liked it and continue not to blush when we meet at reunions, etc. Still, I'm not wearing my GAY POWER button to too many affairs. In the next life, maybe, but it's unlikely before."

Again, my experience talking to female students on widely scattered campuses was like that of Gael Greene in 1964. She said: "There was one glaring exception to the rule of candor. The topic of discussion was sex, yet not one of the girls interviewed ever brought up the subject of homosexuality. Often a plot complication of the college novel and a behavior found constant over four decades by Kinsey, homosexuality appears to be a subject the college girl of the sixties finds difficult or impossible to discuss. Although no one *volunteered* comment on the subject, a few had observations to make when the questioner brought it up. Most of the comments were vague, mostly hearsay and gossip, and not enough was learned to justify a discussion of homosexual behavior in this book."

I can add only the observation that during such discussions of lesbianism, girls tended to display subtle signs of increased anxiety such as body tension, arm hugging, averted eyes and flat voices.

For at least three thousand years Westerners have been claiming that there is more sex and more homosexuality than in the past. Obviously, most of them have been wrong. There is only fragmentary evidence about sex behavior in other Western countries. The only broad-scale study in England, by Michael Schofield, is based on interviews with almost nineteen hundred randomly selected teenagers. The "swinging England" of the media did not materialize. He found petting and coital patterns roughly parallel to those in the United States, incidence figures perhaps a bit lower.

Homosexual experience was admitted by 5 per cent of the males and 2 per cent of the girls.

Several recent Swedish studies provide contradictory data. There is a higher nonvirginity rate before marriage than in the United States and England, but this rises partly from an old rural tradition of trial marriage, meant as an assurance of fertility. There is probably less heavy petting among young people and a smaller number of casual partners in petting and coitus. Infidelity and homosexuality are both estimated to be significantly lower than in the United States, but other psychosexual problems are far from rare. "Swedish sin" and other alleged Scandinavian erotic blisses are as much a myth as the carefree hedonism of the Mediterranean world.

There are many trends suggesting that this century's slow evolution toward more and earlier sex activity, before and outside marriage, will continue in the West. Better hygiene and nutrition bring earlier maturation; girls now start menstruating three and a half years earlier than at the turn of the century. The old double standard continues to erode slowly, being replaced by an ethic of sex-with-affection in limited but progressive amounts. The fifties and sixties have seen "going steady," necking, petting and coitus begin at earlier ages; these "coitus substitutes" and masturbation may also be spreading more into lower-income groups along with other essentially middle-class patterns, according to William Simon. And in an increasingly affluent society, a greater proportion of people will lose their blue-collar sexual patterns for white-collar and college-graduate patterns, with their greater verbal sophistication and tolerance for things outside the straight "meat-and-potatoes" concept of sex.

On the other hand, there are contrary pressures. The divorce rate has been stable for more than two decades in the United States and England, with perhaps a slight worldwide urban upswing in the late sixties. While a shift to middle-class patterns means more verbal and social sophistication about sex and eventually the growth of a wider sexual repertoire, it also means increased control and inhibition in males, years of petting rather than coitus for girls. The portrait of our society as wildly hedonistic, with the family breaking down and deviance snowballing, is a fantasy. Coitus without a close emotional bond is still a minority behavior among women, and this can't be expected to change rapidly. The increase in petting, necking and coitus and the earlier age of starting these activities corresponds to a drop in marriage age.

Particularly apt at this point is Kinsey's suggestion that the older generation is always aghast at the young because they themselves, when young, didn't know half of what the adults were really doing. As they grew up, they gradually lost their naïveté and saw through the adult world's studied concealments. They end up shocked at the "increase" in sex around them.

But apart from the combined ignorance and machinations of the media, our society has had a special stake in fantasying a sexual utopia among the young. The West has always considered sex a dangerous chained beast. In the eighteenth century a movement of sexual utopianism began, making sex a beneficent force to be released rather than controlled. As the anti-Victorian reaction mounted, debased Freudianism provided an ideology for it, and many social factors were converging to make a moderate but marked relaxation in sexual restraints. More people than ever believed that if sexual impulses were acted out, society would end war and individuals lose their pimples, sulks, work problems and other debilities. They were convinced that this was in fact starting to happen on a large scale—if not to them, then to someone else, to the young. The young, many of them, believed it too.

Four-letter words, mini-skirts and public nudity don't necessarily mean that many people act very differently in bed. We are less secretive and inhibited than in the past, and some people act more freely than their parents or grandparents, but the basic taboos have only been eroded at the edges. Talking a liberal game of sex doesn't mean living one. It sometimes seems that youth and parents are busy today acting out the psychiatric truism that children always pick up and often act out their parents' hidden fantasies. The young talk the sexual liberation their elders sought with limited success, and the elders, with mixed hope and envy, like to think the young are doing it for them.

Although these changes are real and have some effect, the illusion that a sexual revolution has already taken place is ultimately crippling. Laws controlling sex practices, divorce and abortion need reform; the social restraints that prevent the reform of those laws need examination. The smug cant of progress is itself an evasion, when in fact even many people who have conquered their inner censors still cannot live expressive sexual lives without legal penalties and social obstacles.

The first step, certainly, is data on which to base evaluations of legal, institutional and social processes. Our scientific knowledge of sex is still pitifully small compared to other fields of research, and the reason is simply fear. No one has provided funds for finishing Kinsey's research plan. No one has studied the effects of contraceptive pills. Sex education is still absent, primitive or prudish. When the Institute for Sex Research wanted to study homosexuality, it was turned down by two dozen foundations. Johnson and Masters, trying to learn the mere physiology of sex, had to handle their project like an explosive. Most of the reports in the media are misleading entertainment or axe-grinding, not information. As John Gagnon points out, "It is as if all of the discussion and sexuality were really organized as a form of entertainment rather than as a serious consideration of the kinds of processes that are central to the human condition and the possibilities of human experience." The Kinsey reports no longer create outrage; they evoke pseudo-sophisticated jokes and giggles. In fact, it is still largely nervous laughter.

INTERVIEWS

William Simon is a former member of the Kinsey Institute, where he and John Gagnon replicated Kinsey's study of college-age youth.

Do you think there has been an increase in homosexuality?

The original Kinsey data do tend, in my opinion, to suggest a slight generational increase. But only a slight one. We don't have evidence of a significant increase.

What do you mean, the original data?

Kinsey interviewed eighteen thousand people and used only about a quarter of the cases in his two reports. Some of the data are still on file, but haven't even been coded on the IBM cards for statistical study yet. For instance, when he found people with backgrounds heavy in prostitution or homosexuality, he had them fill out a second questionnaire as long as the first. He also had data on Negroes. The data on Negroes, deviants and prostitutes didn't go into the book because the samples weren't large enough yet.

Why is the material still uncoded?

There's a small grant for coding it, but the biggest problem in sex research is still money. The Rockefeller Foundation was taken to task for supporting Kinsey's work. Most private foundations are still scared, and the bulk of the research money in the past ten years has come from the federal government—the National Institutes for Mental Health.

How many people in this country do you think have had significant homosexual experience?

Kinsey's and other studies would make me guess that 2 to 3 per cent of the male population has a serious, long-term homosexual pattern. Another 7 or 8 per cent have casual or episodic homosexual experience. That makes about 10 per cent of the male population who've had more than fleeting or experimental homosexual events in their lives. By that I mean there have been about fifty experiences to orgasm or twenty different partners. The distinction should be made as to whether a person has orgasm or just brings his partner to orgasm. In a steam bath, a guy can do twenty other guys, have two orgasms and be listed as having had twenty homosexual contacts. Kinsey observed that the majority of homosexual hustling is by lower-class guys who are only trade, and who drift back to heterosexual life. In years of hustling, a guy may never bring another man to orgasm.

Would you make any guesses about prevalence of various kinds of sexual acts in different subpopulations—by ethnic background and so on?

The largest number of homosexuals having orgasms on a given night, as Kinsey showed, are getting it through masturbation. American homosexuals—say, as compared with English—are hung up on fellation. Anal sex hardly competes. I'd guess that anal sex is more common among Negro than white homosexuals in this country, along with greater gender confusion—the ghetto seems generally to promote gender-identity problems. It's interesting, too, that the number of lesbians who've had more than five sexual partners isn't comparatively much greater than the number of heterosexual women who've had more than five sex partners. Homosexual women are still women and follow female patterns for sexual behavior as set down by our society.

You and John Gagnon worked on the Institute's study of homosexuality. How was it different from previous studies?

We wanted to ask the questions Kinsey didn't ask—how does a homosexual find a job, make friends, get on with his parents? By avoiding the question of cause and pathology, we desexualized the subject and put it in a more sophisticated sociological landscape.

We asked how people supported themselves financially and functioned socially, and realized that the question is why so many homosexuals seem to function so well. Most homosexuals meet these pressures.

We found that ideas of a homogeneous life style are naïve. Cycles and crises occur in everyone's life. Aging is a crisis for everyone. For homosexuals, it is a major one and probably occurs earlier than among heterosexuals. Feminizing may be part of a certain segment of the homosexual career, rather than a part of homosexuality per se. I think it usually happens after coming out, confirming the homosexuality that was decided on in a sort of Eriksonian identity crisis. If we can show such developmental processes as the study continues, we'll have learned something important.

You and Gagnon have also done a study of college students' sexual behavior, haven't you?

Yes. We found that 17 to 30 per cent of all girls at campuses are nonvirgins. Of seniors, half were nonvirgins—as compared to a quarter of them two decades ago. But meanwhile, the average marriage age has dropped to twenty-two, and much premarital sex is still within the context of formal or informal engagement. There's nothing like a sexual revolution. I think the most significant change is a slight but clear tendency for girls to begin masturbation younger. It shows great and earlier independent commitment to sexuality.

Have there been changes in male behavior?

To the extent that society scripts our sex lives for us, male sexuality is pretty well scripted. Class, age and gender are important factors determining adult behavior; male behavior varies dramatically in different social classes and educational levels. But men are relatively predictable and relatively unchanged over the decades in comparison to female behavior. Female sexuality differs less from class to class and is more labile, less scripted. Female interest in coitus is increasing; the interest is being created for women. The big break is in women who've attended graduate school. They are, as a group, the most sexually committed and uninhibited. In the strict sense of the word, they're deviant, as homosexuals are. The girl who goes on to graduate school and who has a freedom and commitment in her sexual life was somewhere earlier in life pushed out of the modal socializing process. This probably left some scars. One study shows that most grad-school women began menstruating either earlier or later than usual. They also overidentified with one parent or the other. This is where the question of deviation becomes tricky. Are these girls, whom technically you'd call deviant, to be considered victims of psychosexual or social impairment? I'm not sure deviance necessarily means impairment.

Michael Schofield is a social psychologist, author of The Sexual Behavior of Young People *and* The Sociological Aspects of Homosexuality. *The former is a study of the sex behavior and attitudes of nearly nineteen hundred English teenagers. The latter analyzes 150 homosexuals and 150 nonhomosexuals. I visit Schofield at his home in London.*

There are no broad behavior studies of the Kinsey type anywhere except the United States. Your book on English teenagers is probably the biggest and most recent effort in that direction here. What does it suggest in terms of a comparison between the two countries?

First, let me say that we're all indebted to Kinsey, but we've learned from his mistakes. My teenage group was much like his in America, and the data show a lot of similarities. There are also some smaller American studies in the past decade that help in estimating what changes have or haven't happened since Kinsey. I think that if you did a Kinsey type of study here, you'd probably find the same behavior he did, and the same changes in the twenty years since. Youth are somewhat freer now than before, but premarital sex still isn't the norm in behavior.

Then there's no sweeping generational change?

I think there has been a big change in sexual attitudes, but not a big change in sexual acts. Of course, attitudes change much faster than actual behavior. It's much easier to express an opinion than to put it into practice. I'd say that twenty years ago young people probably had more sex than they would admit to, whereas today teenagers almost certainly have less sex than they claim. If there is an increase in sexual activity, it isn't an increase in sexual promiscuity but perhaps in the number of couples who have intercourse before their wedding day.

The Scandinavian countries are talked about as places where there's sexual freedom. Premarital intercourse is common and occurs early, but in a pretty inflexible pattern. When a girl is sixteen or seventeen, she starts to go with a young man in a serious way. She goes to bed with him, and that fixes the engagement. Marriage takes place at twenty or twenty-two. It makes for a high premarital-sex statistic, but in fact there's not that much of it except with future spouses. One could almost wish for a little more promiscuity.

Do you feel that there has been an increase in homosexuality?

I don't think anyone can say for sure. I doubt that there's a significant change. It's very much the thing today to say, "We're more broad-minded nowadays." And I think that to some degree these young people are. But there remains a gap between what they say and what they do. Maybe if you put two adolescent boys in a double bed tonight, they'd be just as likely or not to have sex as twenty years ago. They'd get up embarrassed tomorrow morning, as they would have twenty years ago. But there's less likely to be the stony silence of utter shame. They wouldn't doubt themselves as much, feel quite so guilty and hide it so carefully. So maybe there's less guilt rather than more acts.

Does the public-school system here really produce much homosexuality?

It's incredible, considering the attitude toward women bred in those schools, that there's so little homosexuality. It proves how difficult it is to make someone homosexual.

I haven't found here the detailed slang, classification and finely categorized subculture among homosexuals that exists in large American cities.

That particular ritualization seems to be more American than English. And, by the way, the landlords of queer pubs here are rarely queer, whereas in America they so often are. But stereotyping does go on here. Many of the pretty young homosexuals I interviewed for my book on homosexuality complained bitterly, "Other queers all expect me to turn over!" Even a boy's partners, who of all people should know better, assume that because he is pretty and somewhat effeminate, he would automatically take the so-called passive role in bed.

Has the law reform here changed much in people's lives?

No. It has changed things only a little. But I think it was vital, and it opens the door to serious change in the future.

I get the impression from your books that you are suspicious of psychodynamic approaches to sex problems. And I feel it's a more common attitude among educated people in England than in the States.

Some people in Britain feel strongly that there's no need for psychiatry, and many remain unimpressed by a number of the so-called cures claimed by it. I think it's fair to say that I'm suspicious too. I regard homosexual acts as noncomformist, but I don't regard nonconformity as a sickness or a psychiatric problem.

The New York Times Magazine *has asked me to write an article about students who are permanently shacked up—living as though married, without ceremony or ring.* Life *and* Newsweek *and* Esquire *have all run articles recently saying that this is a new and rapidly increasing practice. A coed at Boston University has informed a* Times *editor that one out of three students at her college are living in some sort of "arrangement."*

I find that at various campuses situations are very different. At a vast number of them, girls must sign in by 10 P.M., and the lives of many probably wouldn't be very different even if the rules changed. At other colleges there are rules about keeping the door open during visiting hours; the University of Illinois requires that neckers in college buildings keep three of their collective four feet on the ground. Despite this, many students get away to have coitus or shack up during weekends at motels or friends' apartments. There is nothing new in this. Students ten and twenty years ago did so—students at Vassar and Swarthmore and Columbia, at the University of Chicago and at Ohio State University in Columbus. As the school takes a less controlling, parental position, somewhat more students do so. Both behavior studies and my own impressions are that the increase is far from vast.

Students say that "everyone is shacking up or living together." Their definitions turn out to be vague. They are talking about people who go together steadily and sleep together overnight when possible. Only a tiny number of students can and do live in domestic arrangements. Most of them are older undergraduate students at schools with permissive regulations and graduate students in their middle twenties. It is curious that people who are twenty-four or twenty-five and who have lived away from home for many years are considered part of a sexual revolution for having acquired some sexual experience—for even becoming mature enough only to go to bed with people they'd like to have breakfast with.

I am visiting a small liberal-arts college with a radical tradition and a very permissive atmosphere. It has a reputation for extreme sexual freedom. I find that here only a small fraction of the students take advantage of opportunities to live together. There are some coed dorms which, rather than being free and easy, are full of tensions and difficulties about sleeping around. The majority of the students are sheltered, upper-middle-class kids from Scarsdale and Shaker Heights and Winnetka; they have radical rhetoric about sex, but when I have private three- and five-hour interviews with them, I discover that their behavior doesn't match up. They are trying very hard, and usually unsuccessfully, to do what comes naturally to many a fifteen-year-old slum kid.

The rhetoric about sexual deviation is just as radical. There is a great deal of talk about "homosexual experimentation," especially by the boys, and it is made to sound like a joyful dabble in the waters of Marcuse and Brown, all orifices for everybody. Nevertheless, despite the fact that many students talk to me in detail and without reserve, few have anything specific to say about homosexuality on campus. Whatever goes on remains, in detail, quite secret.

FEMALE STUDENT: From what my boyfriend and his friends tell me, I'd guess that about a tenth of the guys have experimented with homosexuality. I think most are in the drug-using crowd. And I think most of them are tense and ashamed about it. You never know any facts for sure. Females? I don't know of any lesbians. I think the girls are more afraid of homosexual experimentation than the boys. Generally this is a horny but guilty campus. There are a lot of tight, tied-up guys. And because a girl still doesn't feel she should just go out with some guy for the sake of plain sex, she develops some kind of relationship first. She forms a relationship for the sake of getting sex, and then afterward she's stuck with the relationship. Also, a lot of half-platonic, half-erotic relationships exist, and people say they're afraid of ruining the relationship with sex.

HEAD OF THE STUDENT GOVERNMENT: I'd say 5 to 10 per cent of the students are homosexual. But I'm not at all sure it's associated with drugs. I hear a lot about it because guys sometimes come to me to discuss the hassles they get into over these things. I can't really talk about it.

MALE STUDENT: There's a lot of homosexual experimentation among the guys. We don't have the hang-ups about sex that your generation had. What do people do? Man, how should I know? My best friend, who's been my roommate for two years, I don't know what he does. That's his private business.

MALE STUDENT: Six months ago I said that there was nothing wrong with homosexual experimentation, that making a big thing out of that sort of thing was a puritanical hang-up. Then the head of a homosexual clique that was here last year almost talked me into going to bed with him one night when we'd been drinking. I didn't, but I really got very shook up by the fact that I almost did. I was almost in a panic. Actually, I haven't had sex with anyone, male or female, for about eight months now. I don't know what's the matter. I just don't want it. I have no desire.

MALE STUDENT: There was an open homosexual clique here last year, half a dozen or a dozen people, centered around one student. He graduated, and you can't identify any homosexual group since then. I've talked to some girls, and none of them is aware of any lesbianism. I do know about a married teacher who got drunk one night recently with a couple of male students and propositioned one of them.

A PROFESSOR: There aren't a great many lesbians, but there are more than most people know. Several have spoken to me about their problems. The school is pretty bad about personal files on students sometimes. I've seen "effeminate" written in some of them.

AN ADMINISTRATOR: If anything, people around here are naïve rather than sophisticated about such things. We had a few glaring cases of homosexuality on the faculty in recent years—not swishy, but anyone with eyes in his head would have known. One of them was picked up eventually by police for a homosexual offense after he went to another college.

DEAN OF STUDENTS: Many homosexual students have come to me to confess and get help. If I think there's a grain of hope for adjusting to a normal life, I help them in that direction. I tell others they should learn to accept it. If they can limit their activity on campus and not exploit other people, we let them finish school. I've done this sometimes despite recommendations to the contrary. I can't recall one case of a student being dismissed because of homosexuality. If his homosexuality got him into trouble, that's something else. Our admission policy is the same. If a kid is shy, was never involved in sports, it's a good indication that he'll have trouble adjusting to life here; it may be part of his homosexuality, but homosexuality is not the issue. Actually, we're much stricter about homosexuality when it comes to teachers, and there have been a few homosexual teachers.

A PROFESSOR: We're so liberal here that the penalty is put on heterosexuality. If a teacher is homosexual, everyone bends over backward not to be punitive and to avoid looking into his personal life. But God help you if you've been healthily diddling one of your twenty-two-year-old female seniors!

THE PRESIDENT: We have few homosexuals, to my knowledge. In any case, we have no fixed policy. Like most schools, we tend to be permissive about such things as long as no problem is created. It isn't our business.

THE COLLEGE PSYCHIATRIST: I wish you could have seen the two couples I had in this office last week. They were here for counseling because the two guys had been having a homosexual affair! The situation results from an over-all problem in emotions and relationships here. A great many guys at this school are passive, unable to deal with anger. They talk about nonexploitative relationships, and they make a real effort to avoid hurting people. But that puts them in a bad bag. If you can't express anger, you can't get close to anyone. If you don't have the one emotion accessible, you don't have the other. This isn't necessarily just an upper-middle-class phenomenon, either. I've heard social workers in lower-class settings describe it over and over. I suppose you'd have to say it's a character disorder, if you're going to use the usual terminology. A guy can't express his anger, turns off his feelings; he has anxiety, but he doesn't live with it because that feeling isn't any more consciously available than the others. There are girls like this too, though I see fewer of them. The girls tend to be more conscious of their feelings and therefore are more aware of their anxiety.

This sort of guy tends to pair up with a girl whose feelings are more accessible. He thinks he's getting a bubbly girl who'll bring him alive. Because of her anxiety, she sees her emotionality as something negative, and she seeks a male who will control it for her. When they get close, they eventually see each other more realistically. He sees that her emotion is often used to control and manipulate. She sees that his apparent strength is really constricted emotion, inability to feel. This kind of neurotic pairing is the one I saw most often as a marriage counselor. But when I came to this college, I thought at first that it was some kind of trick—the same type of couple coming into my office time after time as lovers. The two couples who came to me last week were of this kind. The males had matched up in defense against their girlfriends.

A fair number of kids I see have had homosexual experiences, played around with it. It's always a loaded experiment, and it may produce panic. I think the root problem is that in this country fathers don't know how to be warm to children. Then the kids grow up and say they are at war with materialism, that their fathers wanted money and status, and this gets between them and their fathers. What they don't see at first is that these are fathers who can't bring the warm, nurturing part of themselves together with their sexual and aggressive maleness. When I get the children to analyze their fathers' personalities, they realize that if it hadn't been work, money and status keeping their fathers from them, it would have been something else. Then the kids stop putting down material things so much; they confront their fathers, and thus make contact with them, and build new relationships with them. Finally the kid learns he can be a man, like his father, but different from his father. A common key factor to homosexuality, and to masculinity problems, is a father who won't accept his son in a masculine role and who can't be close to him.

As for why a kid picks homosexuality rather than another neurotic solution, there are many things involved. It's important whether a person has a pattern of withdrawing from anxiety or of trying to immerse himself in it and master it. A kid in a controlling family may be robbed of a chance to develop his controls; a permissive environment makes a kid have to create his own. In any case, I see homosexuality as a developmental obstruction to growth, not a normal thing. If it's someone's choice, and it fills his needs, so be it. But I try to make him see his hassles, choose the things that can let him deal best with life. I go into things that sent him on his route—lacking closeness with his father, thinking sex can give him the closeness he lacked and so on. I try to make him see that he can have closeness without selling his soul. When he can deal with closeness, homosexuality often just drops out of the picture. Of course good experiences with females help. I had a student who went into a two-year period of homosexual experience, and now he's making a heterosexual adjustment.

26

In Other Worlds

Cross-cultural surveys of homosexuality usually come to the conclusion that it is universal, appearing among mankind in all times and places. The same could be said of psychosis, hangnail and heterosexuality. This bland, misleading simplicity results from a century of polemics in which people have tried to make anthropology prove that homosexuality is either a social cancer or a "normal alternative" to normality. This has made it difficult to learn what we must really know for an informed view of sexual deviance and normality in our own society: whether there are universal sexual norms and deviations; how societies define homosexuality (that is, what one must do with whom, and how often, to receive the "homosexual" label); whether any cultures accept labeled homosexuals; why homosexual acts are a capital crime in some, merely ridiculed in others; why homosexual acts are rare in one society and rife in another; and finally how all these things relate to differences in social and family structure, sex role and sex behavior, child rearing, impulse control and over-all patterns of personality development.

For something that occurs in so many societies, homosexuality has received incredibly little study. In the early days of anthropology, it was usually noted only to be condemned. (One early authority, asked about a preliterate people's customs and manners, said, "Customs none, manners beastly.") Only Westermarck and a few others investigated it instead of averting their eyes and keeping the tools of science unsullied. Soon modern methods of scientific anthropology developed, but that brought little new knowledge of deviance. Homosexuality outside the West wasn't examined in depth until the 1930s, when social science and psychoanalysis were combined in research on a long-known and misunderstood type of transvestite who took a female name, married a man, and even faked menstruation, pregnancy and childbirth.

In the 1660s, Father Marquette saw men in the villages of the Illinois and Nadowessie Indians who dressed as women. He said:

> There is some mystery in this, for they never marry, and glory in demeaning themselves to do everything the women do. They go to war, however, but

can use only clubs, and not bows and arrows, which are the weapons proper to men. They are present at all the juggleries, and at the solemn dances in honor of the Calumet; at these they sing, but must not dance. They are summoned to the Councils, and nothing can be decided without their advice. Finally, through their profession of leading an extraordinary life, they pass for Manitous—that is to say, for Spirits—or persons of Consequence.

French explorers called such transvestites *berdaches*, a corruption of a word that had passed into Arabic from Persian and variously meant slave, kept-boy or male prostitute. *Berdaches* were eventually found among the Seminole, the Plains Indians, and many tribes of the West, Southwest and Northwest. In some tribes there were a smaller number of women who dressed as men, did men's work and refused to marry. Many explorers equated these *berdaches* with European homosexuals in drag. In the eighteenth century, Jean Bossu wrote of the Choctaw, "They have, besides, very bad morals, most of them being addicted to sodomy. These defiled men wear long hair and a little petticoat like the women, who despise them very much." The Crow were painted as athletes of perversity too, but careful observers such as Marquette saw that they, like the Illinois, gave *berdaches* a religious function (in this case chopping down the first tree for the Sun Dance Lodge). The Sioux, Sac and Fox also had rites in which *berdaches* were prominent.

As explorers pushed north to Alaska and Siberia, they found transvestites whose religious role was more conspicuous. Among the Aleuts, Yakut, Koryak, Samoyed and others, there were "shamans" with plucked beards, dressed and tattooed as women, who did women's work and became wives or concubines to other men. Many were magicians, healers, priests and visionaries. The source of their special magico-religious status was variously diagnosed by Western scientists as epilepsy, "arctic hysteria," trance states and schizophrenia. Eventually *berdaches* and shamans were found in Central and South Asia, Oceania, Australia, Madagascar, the Sudan, Patagonia and the Amazon region. The two terms became confused and were often used interchangeably, with the emphasis variously on priesthood, transvestism, epilepsy or other characteristics. Generally the word *berdache* is best used to emphasize transvestism, and shamanism to emphasize magic and religion, though sometimes the two overlap.

The ways of becoming a *berdache* or shaman varied. Shamanistic power could be indicated by a caul among the Samoyed, inherited along family lines by the Nez Percé and Klamath. The sea Dyak of Indonesia believed one could become a *manang bali*, or transvestic shaman, through heredity, choice or a revelatory dream. Visions and dreams were the "call" to become a *berdache* for Plains Indians. The Ponca, an Omaha tribe, thought that if a young man dreamed of the man in the moon and had coitus too much in youth, he would be seduced by the evil Deer Woman spirit and become a *berdache*. Among the Siberian Chukchee, a young man might dream of having to choose between the distaff and the bow and arrow; if he chose the distaff, he assumed feminine clothes and role. Some tribes of the American West suspected any child with an unusual personality of being a potential *berdache*. He was placed in a brush shelter, with women's implements on one side, bow and arrow on the other. The shelter was set on fire to frighten him. If under stress he seized the women's tools, it was assumed that he would become a *berdache*.

The *berdache* now went through complete role reversal. He spoke in falsetto, walked like a woman, spent his time with women, assumed a female name, and referred to himself with female pronouns. He might be taken as a wife by a warrior—perhaps a temporary wife or perhaps a secondary wife by someone who already had a female one. Female *berdaches* dressed like men, took male names, hunted, deported themselves like men, called themselves "he," and took female wives.

Transvestism, homosexuality and shamanism existed separately and in all combinations in various societies. In many cultures, the roles of *berdache* and shaman never coincided. Both existed among the Paviotso Indians of the west coast in the United States; neither was common or important in tribal life. Among the Chukchee, there were homosexual transvestites who were not shamans. Some Chukchee shamans dressed transvestically but only for ritual reasons; they had female wives and children. If a Chukchee was both homosexual and a shaman, his homosexuality was tolerated as an unfortunate adjunct to his shamanism; in fact, only his feared magical power kept people from showing open ridicule. The Flathead Indians ascribed no special powers to their *berdaches*; they treated them decently but ridiculed them behind their backs as cowards who didn't want to hunt and fight. The Amhara of Africa said they pitied transvestites as "mistakes of God," but there was enough hostility mixed with their tolerance to make many transvestites go to work in other provinces, away from the comments of village and family.

Many theories about *berdaches* and shamans were made from these facts and all the half-truths that rose about them. Homosexual armchair "anthropologists" such as Edward Carpenter tended to coalesce the reports to produce an archetypal figure who was homosexual, transvestic, a priest and healer—an inverted primitive genius blessed with the gift of tongues. This view has lived on as the myth that homosexuals have special prestige and powers in some societies. At the other extreme, many scientists dismissed all shamans and *berdaches* as perverts and psychotics, which is almost as far from the truth. Better understanding came after Freud and Bronislaw Malinowski forged a fragile marriage between psychiatry and anthropology.

When Freud read in anthropology and the history of religion, he saw correspondences between social institutions and mental processes. Exogamy seemed to him an elaboration of incest fear. The rule of socially avoiding mothers-in-law must rise from their evocation of forbidden mother-son intimacies. Freud connected taboo with phobia, purification rituals with guilt and compulsion. He saw that attitudes toward chiefs and gods were like patients' dreams and children's fantasies about their fathers. Almost every theme, image and mechanism described by psychoanalysis could be found in primitive custom, myth and art.

Freud began to construct the first major theory of society as an expression of inner man rather than as a superorganism that shaped him from without. He dovetailed evolutionary schemes of society with his own theory of the stages of libidinal development. The result, in *Totem and Taboo* and several other books, was a system already out of touch with advanced anthropology when it appeared. (It said, among other things, that the latency period recapitulates the "ice age," and that children's animal phobias are an "infantile return of Totemism.") This sort of stuff soured a lot of social scientists on psychiatry. But Freud's daring and brilliant failure was more fruitful than many more accurate books, and it inspired a few people to start thinking in the same direction. Within a couple of decades anthropologists finally started writing about society as though it were created and re-created by living individuals, and psychiatrists about people as though they developed in a given society.

A few scientists, such as Géza Róheim, tried to apply psychoanalysis directly to non-Western cultures. Some of the results were provocative, but the usual product was a verbal cathedral of libido theory resting on a thin mist of data; by its nature, libido was an imperfect concept for relating psyche and society. The anglicized Pole Bronislaw Malinowski tried to use it, became disillusioned, yet in the process made psychiatry usable to social scientists.

Malinowski was brilliant, witty, argumentative, imaginative, a great teacher, full of passionate conviction, and a model field researcher. Some of his colleagues never forgave all that; even today some say he was little more than an intellectual grandstander drawing on ideas Boas developed before him. Part of his greatness was his dramatic intellectual style, which made many of his colleagues uncomfortable.

Until Malinowski's time, most anthropologists interpreted institutions as fossilized survivals of past practices or as stages between a presumed yesterday and a foreordained tomorrow. Malinowski was the major founder of functionalism, the belief that institutions survive only if they serve a purpose, and that all the institutions of a society interact to help individuals adapt to their environment. This brought to anthropology an approach appearing in other scientific fields, such as psychiatry and ethology. People had always known about slips of the tongue; Freud said they had a meaning and purpose, giving vent to repressed ideas struggling for release. Naturalists had always known that coral fish have gaudy coloration; ethologists would show that these colors are territorial warning flags. Malinowski made anthropologists similarly assume that if something seems isolated, gratuitous, with no place in an over-all adaptive pattern, it probably hasn't been studied enough.

Malinowski read widely in psychoanalysis and hoped it would be the means of showing how institutions and individuals interact. The place to start was the family, for it is the first institution to join a person and his society, his social placenta; furthermore, family relationships were the first ones mapped out in detail by psychoanalysis. Freud concluded that the Oedipus complex, being instinctually based, was universal; so were the psychic mechanisms involved in it, such as repression. If he was right, the key to the socializing process was in hand. Malinowski set out to learn whether "the conflicts, passions and attachments within the family vary with its constitutions, or do they remain the same throughout humanity?" His guess was that Freud's general approach had been right, but that his specific picture of Oedipal conflict and family-society-personality patterns was culture-bound. A matrilinear structure might produce similar but modified results.

Malinowki immersed himself in the matrilinear society of the Trobriand Islanders, living as they did and trying to feel what it was like to be in their skins. His example of the anthropologist as a participant-observer had tremendous influence. He also studied sex in frank detail, which was and still is rare for a social scientist. When he related his findings about sex, family structure, economy, folklore, his guess turned out to be right.

The Trobriand child lived with his mother and her family. His biological father was more a kind, visiting friend than a disciplinarian. His maternal uncle was the male authority who taught him taboos on sex and social behavior. As a result, there was no Oedipal conflict of the Western type, involving lust toward the mother and hostile competition with the father. When Malinowski asked Trobriand males whether they ever dreamed of coitus with their mothers, they laughed with surprise and said only an idiot would dream something like that. However, there was conflict between boy and maternal uncle, and an anxiety-laden taboo on brother-sister coitus. It was the Oedipal triangle, built on different points. When Malinowski asked men whether they had sexual dreams about their sisters, they denied it with angry vehemence, then admitted "other people" did, and finally confessed to such dreams themselves. The themes of conflict with the maternal uncle and of brother-sister incest ran through folklore, magic and many details of daily life. Repression seemed to have the same role in handling these feelings as it did in the Western Oedipal conflict.

Furthermore, these family and psychic patterns were part of a large adaptational web. Economic and environmental forces had helped create the matrilinear system. This matrilinear structure in turn produced a particular emotional complex, which in turn affected customs, folklore, personal development and character. Studying any part of this social network in isolation would distort the picture.

Freud had been wrong in detail. He had considered his society's family configuration universal and insisted that libido and the Oedipal complex shaped all institutions. But he had been right in general by insisting on the crucial nature of nuclear-family relationships, their importance in relating individual and society, and the psychic mechanisms involved. Western psychoanalysis couldn't be transplanted to the study of other societies, but its basic viewpoint and techniques could.

The romance between Malinowski and psychoanalysis went sour. Ernest Jones and other rigid analysts criticized his every deviation from the words of Father Freud. The polemical Malinowski fought back, and though he hardly dented analytic thinking at the time, he discovered many inconsistencies in it while trying. Eventually he claimed to have moved close to a behaviorist point of view. Meanwhile, his work influenced even many who argued with it, and it continued to bear fruit after he had lost sympathy with psychodynamic theories.

In the thirties, a decade after Malinowski's major publications appeared, George Devereux of the University of Pennsylvania used analytic concepts in studying Mohave *berdaches*. He spent many years among the Mohave and wrote of their customs, mores, fantasy and dream life—and, unlike most anthropologists, did detailed studies, with case histories, of incest, suicide, homosexuality and other forms of deviance. Though today he seems a rather traditional Freudian, he was basically curious and flexible, usually willing to adjust his theories to fit the data he found, rather than cramming data into the confines of the theory. His study of Mohave *berdaches* is still the most detailed and reliable one of non-Western homosexuals. It is especially interesting because such *berdaches* have been used as the chief example of the normality and even prestige of homosexuals in some societies.

Devereux described the Mohave as a sunny-tempered yet adventurous warrior culture. Apart from the universal bar against incest, there were so few sex taboos for the Mohave adult that, as Devereux said in a drolly formal way, "it seems inexpedient to differentiate too sharply between a stimulus and an opportunity." They preferred privacy in coitus, but didn't insist on it, so children could observe adult sex. The children had no latency period. Their sex play went on from childhood through puberty. Girls usually lost their virginity at eleven or younger. Men often sodomized girls who were between ten and fourteen, when the rectum was still larger than the vagina. The absence of cunnilingus was explained by aversion to genital odor; Devereux said the Mohave women were careless enough about cleanliness to give the attitude some justice. Almost anything else went. Heterosexual fellatio and sodomy were common. Promiscuous women got into trouble only if they became generally obnoxious through other behavior as well. Pregnancy out of wedlock was lightly regarded, and reprisals for adultery were weak. When asked about female frigidity, people laughed at the idea. Apart from a strong feeling that women shouldn't be above men during coitus, the Mohave were always willing to try out any new or even absurd style of intercourse.

Devereux felt that his data on Mohave sex life were accurate. The

Mohave treated sex with eager, good-humored curiosity. There was a lot of gossip, most of it humorously tolerant rather than vicious or ridiculing. There was little erotic fantasy. The Mohave were too involved with all the real sex around them to spend time on anything imaginary.

Casual sexual play among male children was common and taken for granted. Most of it was group contests in masturbation, urination and penis size. Mutual masturbation and fellatio were unusual. Older boys often forced sodomy on younger playmates, but this too was dismissed as mere childish naughtiness rather than a presage of adult homosexuality. But to call a grown person a homosexual was a fiercely resented insult and a serious matter.

Local gossip claimed that in this community of five hundred there were three adult male (and no female) homosexuals. All three kept their homosexuality as secret as possible, for exclusive homosexuality was shameful in anyone but an *alyhā*, or transvestic homosexual who assumed the female role. White influence had put an end to the *alyhā* initiation rite. There were no such people in the tribe now, and there never would be again. But some *alyhā* were remembered from the fairly recent past; so was one *hwamē*, or female homosexual transvestite. An old singer, said to be the last person who knew the transvestite initiation songs, said:

"From the beginning of the world it was meant that there should be homosexuals, just as it was instituted that there should be shamans." (The shaman in this society was not necessarily a transvestite; shamanism consisted mainly of magic and curing venereal disease.) A child born to be a homosexual was said to seem normal for some years after birth. His nature asserted itself when the time approached for his initiation into such functions of his gender as hunting or cooking—usually by about age ten. In a child not preordained to be an *alyhā*, occasional homosexual acts were thought harmless. A normal person would feel toward his same-sex partner as he did toward a member of the opposite sex.

But the future transvestite tried to duplicate the behavior of the other sex, and to make others feel toward him as though he truly belonged to it. Such a boy played with dolls and kitchen implements, asked for skirts to wear, and might pull his penis between his legs, display himself to women and say, "I am a woman too. I'm just like you." The future *hwamē* threw away her dolls and refused to wear a skirt. Such children might be generally unruly or strange.

Sometimes parents tried to bully such a child into normal behavior—especially a girl, for the *hwamē* was more sociosexually delinquent in Mohave eyes than an *alyhā*. But in either case, said the old singer, the family wasn't proud of having a transvestite in the family, "because transvestites are considered somewhat crazy." But if all efforts failed, the family gave in. The initiation ceremony was seen as a sanction of the inevitable.

In other cases, when the parents were still doubtful (or rather hopeful), the ceremony became a test. If a boy of ten or eleven seemed strange and unmasculine, his family secretly prepared female clothes for him and arranged an *alyhā* initiation rite. The villagers gathered and the boy was brought out. The singer began to perform the transvestite-initiation songs. If the boy refused to dance to them, he was meant to live a normal life, and the ceremony was stopped—to the family's relief. If he "couldn't resist the urge" to dance to them, he was revealed as a born *alyhā*. Women bathed him in the Colorado River and gave him a skirt. He took a female name. From then on he insisted on being referred to as she. He demanded that people call his penis a clitoris, his testicles labia majora, his anus a vagina.

A girl went through the same sort of ceremony to become a *hwamē*. Her name was changed to a male one, and she resented references to her female genitals. People did refer to *alyhā* as she and *hwamē* as he; the sex-role reversal was a social reality to everyone. But they joked at times about the real, hidden genitals, which hadn't changed along with the role. Furthermore, a female could change only her personal name. To adopt a full male name, she would have to alter her gentile name as well, and the lineage it represented was too serious a thing to be dragged into the humorously viewed world of sex, let alone the somewhat ridiculous one of transvestism.

The *alyhā* eventually found a male husband, usually a young man not yet married to a woman or an older one between marriages. The *alyhā*, like transvestites in our society, gloried in carrying the female role to perfection. He was a model homemaker, and hyperfeminine in observing ritual laws. Sexually he took a purely passive role. An account of homosexual married life came from accounts by a man named Kuwal, who had had several female and several *alyhā* wives. He told people that he'd had to keep up the charade of his *alyhā*'s femininity and hide his amusement. He said he could play with the *alyhā*'s penis when it was flaccid, but only if he said as he did so, "Your cunt is so nice and big and your pubic hair is so soft to touch." This made the *alyhā* loll about, giggling with delight at himself and at Kuwal. When the *alyhā* had an erection and it protruded through his bark skirt, he was embarrassed. This happened when he was being buggered. Kuwal said that when this happened with his *alyhā* wives, "I would put my arm about them and play with the erect penis, even though they hated it. I was careful not to laugh aloud, but I chuckled inwardly." Kuwal said that if he dared touch an *alyhā*'s erect penis any other time, he was courting violence.

When the *alyhā* married, he began to imitate menstruation by scratching his legs with a stick till blood flowed. He followed all menstrual taboos and insisted his mate observe those of a husband. Eventually the *alyhā* decided to become pregnant. He stopped menstruating and began observing pregnancy taboos. He did so more rigidly than most women, even conforming to archaic customs. Again, the husband had to observe those that fell on him. The *alyhā* started stuffing rags and bark under his skirt in increasing quantities, preparing a cradle, and boasting of his condition in public. (By comparison, many Mohave women denied pregnancy even when it was visible.) This caused a lot of teasing, but the *alyhā* ignored it. His only violation of the rules governing pregnancy was to keep permitting his husband oral and rectal coitus, probably on the assumption that love can make just so many sacrifices.

As delivery time drew near, the *alyhā* started drinking a concoction of mesquite beans that caused acute constipation. After a while came a day or two of sharp cramps, which were called labor pains. When the colonic backload couldn't be held in any longer, the *alyhā* went into the bushes, took the position of a woman giving birth, and let go of so vast and overdue a load that it caused rectal bleeding.

Now the *alyhā* had to do something with the "baby." A Mohave baby that died after birth was cremated, and such ceremonies were past joking. But stillborn children were buried. The *alyhā* buried the "baby" and returned home, wailing that it had entered the world dead. He went into mourning, clipped his hair, and made his husband share the grief. The cradle was given away.

The *alyhā* was teased, but not persistently or viciously. He had been "born that way," and the Mohave were generally tolerant about sex and about temperamental compulsions. The *alyhā*, in turn, was usually peaceable unless provocatively taunted, in which case he could be vengeful and assaultive. Actually, there would have been more mockery if it weren't for the fact that an *alyhā*, being a man, could really hurt an enemy. The Mohave made the common equation of masculinity, heterosexuality, aggressiveness and sexually being on top. Being underneath, being sodomized, being passive, meant femininity—and for an adult biological male this meant being held in contempt. A heterosexual man whose disposition was unusually sunny, even for a Mohave, was significantly described by his wife as "so stupidly kind that if anyone wanted to sodomize him, he would go down on all fours and spread his buttocks."

The Mohave were as adventurous in fighting as in sex. All men were expected to take part in daring or even suicidal raids. Cowards were deeply despised. The Mohave term for coward derives from the same stem as *alyhā*, and one word was sometimes used for the other. When men returned from battle, old women who had lost relatives in the fight walked through the crowd poking wooden phalluses between the legs of those who had stayed at home, saying, "You aren't a man but an *alyhā*." The *alyhā* themselves joined the old women in doing so.

The Mohave saved stronger taunts for men who took *alyhā* as wives. Their attitude was, "The *alyhā* was born that way, but what's your excuse?" Actually, there were many reasons for marrying a transvestite, some of them practical and domestic. Many young Mohave women were poor housekeepers; men often married older women, even former mothers-in-law, in order to have a good cook and housewife. The *alyhā* kept a model home. *Alyhā* were said to be lucky in gambling and lucky in love; these gifts were supposed to rub off on their mates. Some *alyhā* were also shamans, which principally meant that they were adept in curing venereal disease.

To the man who was heterosexually troubled or insecure at some time in his life, the *alyhā* was a psychologically tolerable substitute. Oral and anal coitus were common heterosexual acts, so what a man got from an *alyhā* was not new or threatening. Sex was generally seen in a joking and adventurous way, so experiment in itself had a positive value. To a degree, everyone viewed the *alyhā* as a functional female. He always took the passive part, maintaining a parody of usual dominant-submissive (and thus male-female) roles. Furthermore, one or even a sequence of homosexual acts didn't give a man the "homosexual" label, as in our society. In short, a brief marriage to an *alyhā* was a domestic and sexual convenience, and a chance to retreat from heterosexuality for a while without undergoing a crisis in male heterosexual role and identity.

Nevertheless, there was a price to pay. The husband of an *alyhā* had to keep up a continual charade and observe husbandly taboos. When he was ready to resume heterosexuality, the *alyhā* might become possessive and violent, and refuse to separate. If the husband politely requested divorce on grounds of barrenness, he discovered that no *alyhā* admitted such a lack. The result was a "pregnancy" to save the marriage.

The community's ridicule did more than anything else to end homosexual marriages. Kuwal, who'd had male and female wives, was a sad example. He had had children by his female wives, but they had all died. When he spoke with regret of his past wives and dead children, people said, "We know all about your beautiful wives. You married those *alyhā* and believed them when they scratched themselves and pretended to be menstruating, or when they were pregnant with a pillow." Or they would kick a pile of animal dung and say, "Those are your children."

Female transvestites, or *hwamē*, were like *alyhā* in their reversal of role. They dressed, rode and hunted like men. At social gatherings they sat with the men and spoke braggingly of their wives' or mistresses' genitals. However, *hwamē* were rarer than *alyhā*, and considered more deviant. They had to court girls carefully for fear of angering the girls' parents; generally, they had a harder time finding spouses. When they did, they were excellent providers. They ignored taboos on their menses, but acted out those of the husband for their wives' periods.

Like any other Mohave, the *hwamē* avoided cunnilingus because of aversion to vaginal odor. She might practice digital intercourse, with her wife beneath, or use a special posture called *hithpan kudhape*, or "split vulvae." Devereux said, "The *hwamē* lies with her head in the opposite direction, one of her legs under the wife's body, the other on top of it. In this posture of interlocking scissors the vulvae touched." The Mohave believed that coitus with a pregnant woman could change the baby's paternity; if a *hwamē* succeeded in making love to a pregnant woman, she could claim to be the baby's father and take care of it. However, the tribe didn't allow change of the baby's gentile name, any more than it had of the *hwamē*'s.

No one had heard of an *alyhā* going to bed with a woman, but some women were said to have become *hwamē* after bearing a child. In fact, painful childbirth was sometimes hinted at as the reason. This may have also led some women to become lovers of *hwamē* without changing sex role themselves. Devereux guessed that homosexual mateship became attractive to some women because they had married lazy, spendthrift men and wanted to be kept in comfort for a change.

Hwamē and their partners were teased more than their male counter-parts. Partly this was because there was less fear of reprisal, partly because there was greater hostility. People said that a woman would only live with a *hwamē* because no man wanted her; it was a self-fulfilling judgment, for men did shun women after their affairs with *hwamē*. This was clear in the story of Sahaykwisa, the only *hwamē* in the community's memory when Devereux studied them. He constructed her biography from many accounts.

Sahaykwisa was a lesbian transvestite, probably the last Mohave to undergo the female-transvestite initiation rite. She was apparently normal physically, and had large breasts. She didn't always dress as a man, for she sometimes worked as a prostitute for whites. She was prosperous from prostitution, industrious farming and hunting, shamanism and finally witch-craft.

Her first wife was quite a pretty girl, whom many men tried to lure away. Finally one succeeded, saying no man would want her afterward if she continued to live with Sahaykwisa. She eloped with him. The abandoned Sahaykwisa took to flirting with girls at dances, which roused animosity and caused people to call her "split vulvae" behind her back, a serious insult. But the wife returned. Sahaykwisa could now take her to the dances, sit with the men and boast of her wife's genitals. Meanwhile, people teased and mocked the girl. Finally she left Sahaykwisa again, and found a second male husband. People went on making fun of her and her new husband. They told him, "Just poke her with your finger, that's what she likes. . . . Don't waste your penis on her!"

Sahaykwisa found a second wife, and both had to endure the same sort of ridicule. People yelled at Sahaykwisa, "The *hwamē* is proud now! She thinks that maybe she has a penis!" The second wife left, apparently unable to take the pressure. Sahaykwisa went to another camp, in pursuit of a married woman there. She was insulted and mocked; then, to most people's surprise, she won the woman away from her husband. They eloped. But this third wife in turn deserted Sahaykwisa. Her husband took her back with hesitation, for she had lowered herself by being the wife of a *hwamē*.

Sahaykwisa was furious. She painted her face black and picked up her bow and arrows, like a man "on the warpath." She lurked about the camp where her former third wife lived with her husband. People warned the husband of her vengefulness and her knowledge of witchcraft. He said, "Let her come! The next time she comes, I will show her what a real penis can do." He caught Sahaykwisa outside the camp, raped her in the bushes and left her there.

This rape changed Sahaykwisa's life, for the fiction of her masculinity had been destroyed. She became an alcoholic and low-level prostitute. She also practiced witchcraft increasingly. Eventually she fell in love with a man much older than herself. He died, allegedly because of her witchery, and she had an affair with his son and then a friend of the son. One day while traveling with the son and friend, she got drunk and bragged that she had bewitched the father. They threw her into the Colorado River to drown. No one did anything about her murder. The Mohave believed that witches long to die so that they can rejoin the spirits of those they loved and bewitched.

Devereux's picture of the *berdache* and his place in society is far out of line with the cliché of "an accepted or honored role." Institutionalized transvestism did create a place for the person unable to maintain the masculine, heterosexual role, but not a very rewarding one. Devereux felt that the chief beneficiaries of the institution were the *berdache*'s lovers and spouses. They were able to live on the outskirts of homosexuality and then return to average tribal life "without the humiliation of a moral Canossa." But the *alyhā*, whose name meant coward, dressed as a woman and poking cowards with a wooden phallus in mockery, "epitomizes the whole, rather sad, picture of the status of the homosexual in almost any society."

One wonders whether any societies approve predominant and exclusive homosexuality or whether it is deviant everywhere. The lack of reliable, detailed studies is astounding. Devereux's paper is one of a small handful that even approach standards for sex research in our own society. Even so, it has intriguing gaps; for instance, just how often is it that boys "often" sodomize younger playmates?

Laymen tend to assume that "scientists know about these things." For two centuries the West has been intrigued with Polynesian sexuality, yet there is little sure knowledge about something as simple as preferred coital positions there. In most anthropological studies, such things are described in a sentence or a paragraph, without any description of research methods, without data, without case histories. Most should be accepted provisionally, at best. However little is known about sex, much less is known about homosexuality. There are dozens of reports about shamanism and *berdaches*, but one precise study like Devereux's throws nine tenths of them in doubt on many points.

One reason for this ignorance is simple squeamishness, which some anthropologists rationalize as fear of destroying rapport with their subjects. Another is the uncertainty of sex research as a way to academic advancement. And still another is the tendency in the past two decades for social science to focus on method, theory and other armchair pursuits while non-Western cultures vanish or change each year, and the irreplaceable is lost.

Even if an anthropologist is willing to do sex research in the field, and can do so without much anxiety or bias, he faces all the problems of a sex researcher in our society, plus several more. He must deal with taboos, mistrust and rules of courtesy that make his subjects fall silent or say what they think is expected. One is tempted to be sympathetic to the profession for this failure because of such problems. But the biggest problems have been irrational anxiety and academic cowardice. When Devereux and some others really wanted to do the job, they have managed quite well. The work of Cora Dubois and Abram Kardiner in Alor in the late thirties provided a fine model for interdisciplinary work in anthropology and psychiatry, relating environment, institutions and individual development. But their kind of research has been more praised than repeated.

There is only one broad cross-cultural survey of sex behavior, summarizing all the information in various ethnological studies. *Patterns of Sexual Behavior* was published in 1951, the joint effort of psychologist Frank Beach and anthropologist Clellan Ford. It was an ambitious and admirable work, but by now it is dated, and some of the sources it draws on are relatively inadequate. Its conclusions on homosexuality are still quoted by most serious writers on the subject; unfortunately this is probably the weakest section of the book. Still more unfortunate is the fact that no one has done better since 1951.

Apart from their findings on homosexuality, Ford and Beach give a general picture of sexual norms and deviance. Their basic points on this are reinforced by other studies before and since and can be taken as cornerstone concepts of sexology. One is that there is a fantastic variety in human sex behavior—so much that there is hardly a generalization to which an exception can't be found in a society or individual somewhere. The second is that nevertheless some sexual restrictions are so widespread they can be called universal.

On the side of variety, one could make a list to fill a chapter. There are societies where modesty calls for hiding body and face, others where it insists that the male hide only his glans penis; where widows commit suicide, and where women have several husbands; where girls commence coitus at eleven, and where they and their lovers are put to death for premarital intercourse; where relatively few women masturbate, and where they do so with a reindeer's leg tendon or with a live mink whose jaws are tied shut; where every male has experienced sodomy at some time in his life, and where one homosexual act may cause ostracism or even execution.

On the other hand, despite some charming fantasies of total sexual freedom, there is no society where people have unlimited sexual access to most potential partners. The most basic restriction is that on incest. Families are defined differently in various societies, and so is incest; but it is always defined, always forbidden, and always involves at least the nuclear family.

Furthermore, heterosexual coitus is the dominant form of sex activity for adults everywhere, in both recommendation and practice. No society accepts as a chief practice homosexuality, masturbation, bestiality or any of the kinkier perversions.

Some other rules and practices are universal or nearly so. In most societies monogamy is the preferred family structure, though the man may be allowed to support another sex partner if he is able. Unlimited sex activity before or outside marriage is practically never encouraged; almost every society has a definition of promiscuity and infidelity, however wide it may be. Furthermore, sex acts with small children or unconsenting young people are never socially permitted; rape of women in one's own community, except in certain special circumstances, is generally discouraged or punished. Face-to-face coital positions are preferred almost everywhere, and more often with the man on top. Exposure of the genitals is also limited in some way in most societies; female exposure is probably universally considered a sexual invitation.

Many sexual sanctions are obviously aimed at preserving the family's integrity and peace, or at encouraging adult heterosexuality while minimizing conflicts about it. Of course incest, rape, homosexuality, child molestation, adultery and adult masturbation all occur, rarely in some societies and less rarely in others. However, they are always condemned in some way when carried on to a great extent. There are even a few exceptions to the incest taboo: brother-sister coitus was allowed in the royal families of Hawaii and ancient Egypt to preserve the purity of the ruling family line. However, many accounts of widespread rule-breaking rise from lack of careful distinctions in observation and description.

Sometimes overt and covert mores disagree; there is a gap between what people publicly say they believe and what they condone in daily life. For instance, a certain amount of adultery may be permitted as long as it is discreet, not chronic, and not believed to involve pregnancy. Some behavior is considered deviant except for a certain age group, sex, caste group or other special category. Our society overtly condemns premarital coitus, but it covertly expects males to acquire sexual experience before marriage, with prostitutes or "bad girls." Pervasive social pressures try to keep sex within rather than outside marriage; this negatively influences premarital sex. Masturbation is universally scorned if done often by an adult or when partners are available, but it may be accepted in children and adolescents. Homosexual acts may be taken for granted among the young; among sexually isolated men or women; between a man and a defined "non-man" such as a prepubescent boy or transvestite. But there is no known society that approves homosexual acts as a chief outlet or, in most circumstances, among adults in general.

So despite some special exceptions and distinctions, all societies share basic, deeply felt limitations on sex. The majority of people live by them the majority of the time. Those who commit incest, who take partners truly indiscriminately, who are predominantly homosexual are deviant everywhere. Society disapproves, ridicules or punishes them. They, in turn, tend to feel inadequacy, shame and social isolation. The fact that deviant acts occur widely does not makes them "natural" in a positive sense. The question is what one must do to acquire a deviant "homosexual" label and how harshly a person thus labeled is treated.

The chapter on homosexuality in Ford and Beach's *Patterns of Sexual Behavior* is ambiguous in language and ambivalent in attitude. The authors felt they had adequate information about seventy-six societies to be able to discuss homosexuality in them. They divided these into two groups: those that approved and those that disapproved of it. Female homosexuality existed in only seventeen, and in those was less common than male homosexuality. Adult homosexual acts were totally absent, very rare or so secret that they stayed unknown in twenty-eight, or roughly a third, of all the societies. Forty-nine societies, the other two thirds, came under the heading "Societies That Approve of Some Forms of Homosexuality."

The heading is badly phrased. The authors don't say whether "homosexuality" means occasional group masturbation by twelve-year-old boys or a fixed adult pattern of oral or anal coitus. Nor whether "approved" means enthusiastically praised, neutrally taken for granted, shrugged off as a misdemeanor, or seen more with pity than anger. They say that "a number of cultures make special provisions for the adult male homosexual, according him a position of dignity and importance and permitting him to live as the 'wife' of some man." They are referring chiefly to shamanistic *berdaches*, apparently confusing the different statuses of the sexual and magico-religious elements, and ignoring such studies as Devereux's.

This lack of fine distinctions is a result of covert bias as much as of scientific neutrality. It is appalling that Ford and Beach are better informed and more careful than most writers of cross-cultural summaries on homosexuality. Though they do say that predominant homosexuality is a preferred pattern in no society, they give a somewhat exaggerated impression of the prevalence and acceptance of homosexuality. They do so by not distinguishing casual homosexual acts from homosexual identity; by loosely defining approval and disapproval; by speaking of homosexuality as similar in humans and animals and as a basic "mammalian potential" and therefore "natural." The interview with Frank Beach in this book shows that he has changed his position since 1951.

One comes away from many such studies with this impression of homosexuality being "universal and natural." Kinsey, Ford, Beach and others have reacted against psychoanalytic and other interpretive theories about sex behavior because they were sometimes laden with traditional values. It has taken almost a century of hard fighting for scientists to shift psychosocial deviance from the "sin" category to the "disease" category—only to see that "disease" becomes in turn a synonym for sin, and "health" a new term for "virtue." Our society's generally negative attitude toward sex, and its harshly punitive one toward homosexuality, have caused persecution and blocked reliable research. Therefore many scientists have bent over backward to make sex, and especially deviant sex, as neutral—as natural and normal—as possible.

In justice, it must be said that scientists have also properly bent over backward to rid their own work of traditional bias. But there remains in many studies not only a hidden bias against popular negative attitudes but a subtle anti-Western bias, a desire to show up our old sanctions as humanly wasteful and destructive. Tacit envy and approval creep into descriptions of ancient Greece, Japan and other cultures where homosexual activity was not so severely punished as in ours. The distinction between homosexual activity and homosexual identity is carefully avoided. Many social scientists and psychiatrists I have interviewed dislike saying that preferred long-term homosexuality is a universal deviance, and try to avoid it, even though most believe it to be true. It is good liberalism but bad science.

It is also an overcorrection to be expected in our society, for we tend to forbid homosexual acts by people of either sex at any age, and sometimes punish them officially or unofficially. One act may be enough to make us apply the deviant label with scorn and anxious hostility. This fearful preoccupation of our society knows no cultural bounds; anthropologists may carry it around the world with them. Burrows and Spiro, writing of the Central Carolines, say that "the people know of no cases of homosexuality or of sexual perversions, nor did I observe any." Yet they say that young men there, by walking hand in hand or arm in arm, show "mild homosexual manifestations." This will doubtless appear in some volume one day as an example of universal human bisexuality, latent homosexuality, and homosexuality approved by a non-Western people. It is difficult to say whether scientific works are distorted more by our homosexual-hunting or by intellectual calisthenics aimed at avoiding it.

Many societies do allow a good bit of homosexual activity—mutual masterbation, fellatio, sodomy, cunnilingus—without applying a deviant label. Probably the commonest unlabeled homosexual acts are those that do not involve two adults. Two boys may experiment; adult male status is not involved. If a grown male has a partner of the same biological sex, it may be a defined "non-man" such as a boy or transvestite. The "non-man" takes the passive role, so the man's dominant, active role—and thus his heterosexual male identity—is not infringed. However, no single rule or theory can account for all homosexual acts and labels.

One popular theory is that homosexuality is more common and feared in patriarchies. Since there are no matriarchies, the theory isn't much use. Attempts to correlate homosexuality with patrilocal and patrilinear societies haven't held up consistently. Probably the most common idea in our educated middle class is that homosexual behavior, if not exclusive homosexuality, increases along with general permissiveness. Our sexual utopianism, by tradition, says that man is bisexual or pansexual, and only cultural inhibitions limit him to heterosexuality primarily or at all.

In a certain literal sense this is true, for humans do have to learn to be sexual, and to be heterosexual. But all societies train people to become at least predominantly heterosexual, which is just as significant as the biological plasticity of man. Furthermore, there are many very permissive societies that show little or no homosexuality, either casual or exclusive. The Andaman Islanders and Ute Indians are permissive, but homosexuality is rare and considered highly deviant among both. Anthropologist Marvin Opler says that when he asked the Ute about homosexuality, it aroused "amusement, disbelief and counterquestioning on American urban culture."

One of the most detailed and apparently reliable studies of non-Western sex behavior is a recent one by Robert Suggs on the Marquesans. He says that the Marquesans make sex their national sport and encourage it from earliest childhood. There is an incest taboo; an aversion to vaginal odor is responded to with strict rules of hygiene rather than avoidance, as among the Mohave. Their definition of promiscuity is probably as loose as any in existence. In many ways, this society evokes the very permissive Mohave. Among the Mohave, adult homosexuals are conspicuous but rare; certain casual or periodic homosexual acts may be practiced without invoking sanctions. But the Marquesans condone homosexual acts in only two situations. One is during early adolescence, when boys are sometimes unable to find partners, for girls their age are more mature physically and socially. Another is when circumstances deprive an adult man of access to women; he may then have homosexual relations with a young boy, who is considered soft and womanish. More than fleeting homosexual contacts, or any with other adult males, make a man a *mahu*, or homosexual. As may be the case in much of Polynesia, there are a small number of *mahu*, and a still smaller number of *mahu'o hiva* ("homosexuals of the ridgepole"), or transvestites who stay around the house and do domestic chores.* So permissiveness is not necessarily a cause of homosexual behavior.

Another common theory is that social pressure against homosexuality has the reverse effect of producing it—the old "blocked conduit" concept. Malinowski's Trobrianders are among the many examples to the contrary. Homosexual acts were thoroughly repugnant to them, "a subject for invective and comic anecdote ... whipped by public contempt." They didn't even use the word for taboo about perversions, for it was absurd to assume any sane person might indulge in them. A homosexual must be mentally and sexually deficient; they thought of him as we would of a man who

---

*Suggs's book contradicts many major points in a famous and important earlier study of Marquesan sexuality by Abram Kardiner and Ralph Linton, *The Individual and Society*. In these two studies of the same society, one can see the different conclusions and interpretations resulting from Suggs's more specific and taxonomic approach and the more impressionistic, interpretive one of Linton and Kardiner.

masturbated at noon on the city hall steps or had an affair with an ostrich.

Malinowski concluded that in this society, which equated homosexuality with general deficiency, homosexuality exsited, if at all, "only in its more spiritual manifestation, that is, in emotional and platonic friendships. . . . Personally I find it misleading to use the term 'homosexuality' in the vague and almost intentionally all-embracing sense that is now fashionable under the influence of psychoanalysis and the apostles of '*Urning*' love . . . male friendships in Trobriands are not homosexual."

A variation on the blocked-conduit theory is that Victorianism—personal and public denial of sexuality—produces perversion. The Dobuans are far more Victorian than our Victorians ever were. They have an extraordinary façade of public propriety and prudery, behind which premarital sex activity is carried on in secrecy and shame. This has produced no noticeable homosexuality among the Dobuans.

The high-caste Hindus of northwestern India, studied by Morris Carstairs of the University of Edinburgh, do seem to bear out the Victorianism-homosexuality correlation. But like the Mohave, they contradict the idea that if homosexuals have an appointed place in society, they are happy and secure. Carstairs says the high-caste Hindus are fantastically prudish. They consider sex animalistic and weakening to body and soul. They enforce their stringent sexual code far better than the Dobuans. They abhor homosexuality. Nevertheless, they talk about it a great deal, and it is said to be fairly common in a secret, guilt-ridden way. However, open homoseuxals become *hinjras*, or mendicant transvestites, and there are one or two in every group of villages. They may come from any caste, but as *hinjras* they are outcaste. Some prostitute themselves; some castrate themselves. They appear at weddings, parody women's songs and dances, expose themselves, and make themselves so obnoxious that people finally throw them money to get rid of them. They have miserable lives, impoverished and despised.

William Davenport of the University of Pennsylvania has done some careful, detailed studies of sex in certain Melanesian communities, and he has described a fascinating society that is quite restrictive about heterosexuality but very permissive about homosexual acts, which are widespread. There is little genital modesty, and no idea that sex can be "excessive" and damaging. However, they marry in their late teens or early twenties; virginity is considered very important, bastardy a social disaster. Although clandestine premarital and extramarital affairs do go on, "social efforts to forestall, to discover, and to punish proven sex offenders are far more vigorous than any that occur even among the most Puritanical segments of our own society. Only murder has more severe punishment than fornication and adultery." Masturbation is urged as a substitute for coitus before marriage for both sexes, and an extensive system of social avoidance between the sexes keeps arousal and opportunity at a minimum.

There is another substitute activity for young males, though. Boys engage in homosexual acts with their friends and brothers, usually beginning a session with mutual masturbation and then taking turns at sodomy. Boys aren't considered homosexual lovers for doing this, just friends accommodating each other's needs. It is assumed that after marriage a man will prefer coitus with his wife to anything else; he gives up masturbation, but not necessarily homosexual acts—in fact, only a small proportion do so entirely. An adult man has relations with a boy between seven and eleven, taking the active role. He must give a present, but it is also something of a duty for the boy to accede to his elder. The pattern is basically that of homosexual contact being permitted between nonadult peers and between grown men and prepubescent boys. For a young man to sodomize a young boy would be presumptuous, for it does not befit his status by age. The adult man does not practice sodomy with other grown men; this too would be deviant.

An exclusively heterosexual man isn't deviant among these Melanesians, but some homosexual behavior is expected from most men as long as it doesn't prevent them from fulfilling their wives sexually. There is privacy in the homosexual act, but no secrecy about it. Boys discuss homosexual acts before friends and parents without shame. Men don't object to a friend using their young sons homosexually, as long as the adult is kind and generous. Sodomy is their only homosexual activity; all men deny fellatio. When Davenport told them this was a common practice among homosexual European men, they thought it was hilarious. However, they didn't grasp the idea of exclusive homosexuality. Davenport asked whether there were any men among them who enjoyed men but didn't desire women. They couldn't comprehend the question, for there was nothing like this in their experience. Davenport explained that there were a number of such European men, and their response was on the order of "Isn't that a shame!" Of twelve men Davenport questioned, ten said heterosexual acts were better, two said heterosexual and homosexual acts were equally satisfying; one of the latter preferred homosexual acts but was not an exclusive homosexual.

There are other societies where many or perhaps all males have experienced homosexual intercourse at some time. This is often alleged of Moslem North Africa and the Near and Middle East (again, the lack of scientific study is astonishing, and in some parts of the "Arab" world homosexual acts are known to be rare). In many societies where homosexual acts are a universal experience, they are associated with highly elaborate initiation ceremonies. These take place in the men's club houses, which have been used by homosexual apologists, misogynists and psychoanalysts as proof of universal "homosexual feeling" or "latent homosexuality," and sometimes to prove the superiority of male-male love to other affections.

Exclusively male organizations exist all over the world, especially in African and Pacific cultures. Men live together in them, may have sexual assignations there, and participate through male secret societies in magical or other special activities. These societies were first written about simultaneously in 1902 by A. E. Crawley, in *The Mystic Rose*, and by German historian Heinrich Schurtz. Both men were antifeminists and misogynists, and believed that men instinctively recoil from women. Crawley said men fear woman as sexually and socially destructive, and dread contagion of their negative qualities through contact with them. They rationalize this as a feeling that sex is shameful and celibacy virtuous; they institutionalize it through taboos controlling coitus, menstruation, birth and incest.

Schurtz, like Crawley, believed men are naturally antagonistic to women and younger males. Women are possessive, domestic, interested in the family but not society. Men are gregarious, in flight from stifling domestic bonds to the joys of hunting, male brotherhood and social participation. Therefore male societies arose as havens from women and the home. After Crawley and Schurtz, the American anthropologist Hutton Webster emphasized the role of initiation rites in male secret societies all over the world. He said that older men haze, terrify and mutilate boys approaching manhood in order to bolster their own prestige against these oncoming rivals.

The entire subject was reinterpreted in a book whose title became a standard part of anthropological thinking—*Les Rites de passages*, by the gallicized Dutch scholar Arnold Van Gennep. He said that society is like a house with many rooms, and special ceremonies mark a person's passage from each to each—first by separating him from the old state, then by purifying him at the threshold, and finally by welcoming him into the new. Such ceremonies occur at birth, puberty and marriage, and give one a new social status. Van Gennep pointed out that initiation rites, in which boys may be circumcised, sodomized and scarified, mark the passage to adult male status and occur not at physical puberty but later. Puberty rites exist in some places, and they are not initiatory.

In his famous study of the Malekula of Melanesia, John Layard described extensive and brutal rites performed when boys were initiated into manhood (not sexual adulthood). These included sodomy. Usually a grown Malekulan man had a young boy as a passive sexual partner before initiation; the man was referred to as the husband, the boy as his wife. The Malekulans said that a boy's penis grew large and strong by his being sodomized by the older male—the idea of absorbing a stronger man's maleness through anal incorporation that is described by Western psychiatrists. The Malekulans believed, in fact, that homosexual acts transmit traditional male power, just as people in some matrilineal societies say the umbilical cord joins all generations to the original ancestress.

The growth of a boy's penis is said to be complete when the time for initiation approaches. Now he must endure a month of seclusion, seeing no females, undergoing circumcision, scarification, painful hazing and buggery by the men. When the initiation period is over, the boy has become a man; he dons the bark belt of the adult male, ceases to be an adult's passive sex object, and takes a boy as a "wife" in turn. On a nearby island there is no homosexuality between men and boys, and it does not occur in the otherwise similar initiation rites. However, each boy has an older male who is formally referred to as his husband, and part of the hazing includes threats that the boys will be sodomized by ancestral ghosts.

Studies of initiation rites have shown that many conform to Van Gennep's theory. Gregory Bateson described the *Naven* ceremony of the Iatmul of New Guinea, where at the beginning boys were treated as though they were women and made to handle the grown men's penises; then they had to brave their way through circumcision and scarification to win adult-male status. Some intricate theories have been worked out relating initiation rites, homosexuality, headhunting (head being symbolically equated with phallus), and the fear and rejection of women. A more modest and perhaps more likely theory, developed by John Whiting of Harvard, is that *rites de passages* including genital operations, seclusion from women, and tests of endurance and courage occur in societies where small boys are very dependent on their mothers and hostile to their fathers. The rite symbolically breaks the boy's dependence on his mother, makes him submit to his father, and finally identify with adult males. This corresponds with certain Western psychiatric concepts, and for the moment is as good as any of several other theories also being debated by social scientists in recent years.

But no single theory can stand up on a broad, cross-cultural basis, explaining the Mohave *alyhā*, the Marquesan who enjoys marital intercourse and sodomy with boys, Malekulan initiation rites, and Arab women of certain Red Sea areas who take black female lovers. But we do know that predominant or exclusive homosexuality is seen negatively everywhere, and that when a society alleged to approve homosexuality is carefully studied, it turns out that homosexual acts are accepted only in special situations or times of life, and to the extent that they do not impair heterosexual functioning or loss of sexual identity. Rejection of one's sex role can be provided with an institutionalized role, as among the Mohave, but that does not imply approval or a happy way of life. Whenever the final limits of heterosexuality and biologically appropriate role are infringed, the result is sanctions that range from death through persecution to harassment and mild contempt.

INTERVIEWS

William Davenport is a professor of anthropology at the University of Pennsylvania. His paper "Sexual Patterns and Their Regulation in a Society of the Southwest Pacific" is a careful account of sex attitudes and behavior in one part of Melanesia. I ask him how difficult it is getting accurate information on sex behavior in non-Western societies.

It varies tremendously. I can give you two examples. The Melanesians I dealt with in that paper are the most concrete people you'd ever want to meet—dour, direct, they'll talk about anything with utter bluntness. Usually it takes a while to start getting private data in the field, but with these people it began on the third day. A couple of men came to me, and one asked whether some Englishmen have penises so long they can wrap them around their waists. I asked him where he'd heard this. He said he used to work for a trader who always told them stories like that, and they didn't know whether or not to believe him. They just came to me matter-of-factly to check it out.

The amount of sex talk among these people was tremendous, and it was always precise and straightforward. A week after I arrived, a pair of dogs got stuck together in the village. There was terrific uproar, and I must have heard the word for copulation a hundred times. Kids ran around yelling it for hours while everyone watched and joked. The men sat up all night talking about it and gossiping about sex. However, this was a society in which a woman is a closely guarded piece of property, and property values apply to her. So despite the tough, direct, concrete talk about sex, there are significant restrictions.

Later I worked in another society a couple of hundred miles away. I gathered that sex behavior was free there; everyone seemed to have been involved at some time with practically everyone else. But even though no one gave a damn what a person did, the big rule was never to talk about it. The first society yielded reliable data. The more permissive one didn't; I don't trust any of my sexual data from there.

Your paper on that first society has sometimes been mentioned as an example of homosexual behavior being considered normal and natural. But isn't exclusive or predominant homosexuality deviant in every society? I mean by that, it's never the desired end of the child-rearing process.

No, it's never the desired end of child rearing. And in that society I wrote about, a married man who prefers men over women when given a choice is deviant, if you put it that way. But they prefer not to probe that area; they have no concept and therefore no word for the exclusive homosexual. Different societies judge you a success or a flop as a man or woman on various grounds, and sex behavior is only one of them. Also, some things we think of as primarily sexual have other meanings in other societies.

For instance, maturation sequences are especially important. In some societies, getting married is a maturational rite; when you get married, you become a grownup. Not to marry means to remain a perpetual adolescent. Or if property is deeply involved in the process, it means remaining a person without goods and status. Some societies fuse the concepts of mother and woman. We don't—we say you can be a woman without being a mother. But in a society where bearing a child means the female has matured, there's a big thing about the first baby. So some celebrations over the first baby are really maturational rites for the mother. Maturation sequences pair off with all sorts of things in different societies. Societies also vary a great deal in tolerance of various sexual patterns—for instance, in tolerance of asexual behavior. We're very tolerant of it, especially in women. We have the benign concept of the spinster, the solitary widow and so on. Some societies don't.

Now, in that Melanesian society I wrote about, no one is labeled a homosexual. There was such a guy there, and god, did they persecute him! But it wasn't because of his homosexuality *per se*. That sexual choice didn't in itself make him a flop as a man, the way it would in our society. He was a flop due to *other* behavior that *arose* from his homosexuality. He was a bad husband, didn't have the correct regard for a wife as property, lacked the usual deep male value on labor and achievement. By failing to become the owner of a wife and household, he appeared to be a perennial adolescent, a non-male. This all flowed from his homosexual pattern, but his sexual choice was never the voiced accusation. The case against him was that he was what we'd call a grown man acting like a schoolboy.

In that society homosexual acts take place between adolescents and between older men and young boys—but not between two grown men. That came under the same charge of immaturity—a man having sex with another man his own age was acting like an adolescent, and therefore he was deviant.

What sort of distinctions are involved in attitudes toward berdaches *and other transvestites?*

Take the *berdache* of the Plains Indians. You can see that the institution was almost a cultural necessity. The Plains Indians put immense value on achievement and competitive success. They idealized the quest for power and made it the test of maleness. Realizing the complete ideal male role was almost impossible—people talk about competitiveness in our society, but among the Cheyenne and such tribes it went far beyond anything we know. There had to be some men to whom that expectation was too much of a threat. So society made a slot for them. They became *berdaches* and dressed like women. It was gender role that was crucial, not sexual behavior. In fact, we simply don't know one way or the other whether they had sex with men or women. *Berdaches* may have been men who were passive but heterosexual, and who opted for that role because they preferred making baskets to fighting for power with other males.

The classic Siberian and Alaskan shaman is a different social phenomenon. I don't know enough to talk as an authority—the best stuff on classical shamanism is in Russian, which I can't read. But apparently some shamans were incipient schizophrenics. Shamanism and dressing as the opposite sex exist in many parts of the world, and they represent different culture complexes in different places. What's interesting is that the West has assumed in all these cases that homosexual acts are involved. We plug our meanings into their systems of symbols. It's the same as Latin Americans who decide North Americans are effeminate because they're deferential to their wives, don't kill bulls out of pity, and so on. To get an accurate picture of a society, you have to see what aspect of gender role is loaded there—property, age-appropriate behavior, choice of sexual object. The last one happens to be most loaded for us.

If you were going to study homosexuality in our society as an anthropologist, what sort of questions would you ask?

I work on the assumption that when a society sees a need, it creates a slot for people in order to handle it. For instance, society may see the inadequacy of gay kids, create a social slot for them, and then afterward many people can enter that slot for various reasons. It isn't safe to assume that there's one personality type involved. When society creates a Don Juan slot, various people may take out stress that way. When living up to the expected gender role is blocked, there has to be an outlet of some kind. Devereux posits a common cultural personality, the way Mead and Benedict do. They say that basic institutions produce a common personality. The question is whether we're talking about common personalities or just agreement on the meaning of certain cultural symbols. I'd say that people adapt pretty flexibly and with variety to what they inherit. I see culture as a communication system, a system of symbols, which allows a lot of individual variety.

Now, if I were examining homosexuality as a subculture, I'd try to see how the system and the subsystem feed back into each other. I'd ask what sends a person into deviance, and then what the problems of adjustment are for him once he is committed to deviance. For instance, in prisons homosexuality might turn out to be as much a question of dominance behavior and labeling as of deviance. In prison, people are socially impotent and undifferentiated. How can you be a big man and obtain a label for your bigness? Sex can express it symbolically. Animal behavior studies provide models for that.

27

Masculine–Feminine

When Twiggy became a famous fashion model in the mid-sixties, the best cultural commentator would have been Alexander Pope. He could have written a satire like *The Rape of the Lock* about the assault on sex-role traditions by editors of ladies' magazines, fashion photographers and publicists, and the counterattack by intellectuals, journalists, comedians and amateur social critics from the typing pool and corner tavern to the academic cocktail party. For instance, columnist Pete Hamill wrote an irate prediction of things to come—a presentation to the press by flaming fags of a "Girl of the Year" named Ralph. Novelist John Fowles took a more benign, balanced view, saying, "it seems ominous that the taste for hermaphrodites has always arisen in decadent periods of culture. The present fad may, as the optimists claim, be no more than a side effect of the healthy tolerance most societies now show toward homosexuality. We all have repressed homosexual desires; and the popularity of the Twiggies may be merely a harmless recognition."

Though Hamill and Fowles have written intelligently and well, Twiggy provoked them to knout-swinging against this evanescent product of media, marketing and publicity. Such critical overkill rises from the uneasy preoccupation with sex role that has long pervaded the West. This worry rose to one of its peaks in the twenties, and another in the sixties, with the usual talk of feminine men, masculine women, deviance, promiscuity, the death of the family and general social decay. Or as psychiatrist Robert Odenwald put it in *The Disappearing Sexes*, we are developing "a population of neutrals with virtually nothing to distinguish them but the shape and size of their breasts and genitals . . . the source of many great social evils—sexual promiscuity, juvenile delinquency, homosexuality and others."

Though such fear about the loss of "real men and women" reflects genuine conflict, it is also an old Western mental habit. We may be repeating Rome's literary traditions as much as its history. Behavior studies show no great increase in homosexuality over seven decades, yet it's spoken of more and more as a bloat to be fought or accommodated. Actually, homosexuality is just a handle for the bigger issue—loss of a positive sexual identity. A certain number or kind of homosexual acts are the most dramatic way to lose the label "real man" or "real woman." However, homosexuality coalesces in people's minds with other sex-role "failures"—competitive women in pants who are sexually aggressive, and passive, compliant men. These "mannish" women and "faggy" men provoke the same image of abnormality and psychosocial failure as homosexuality itself. Furthermore, since sex role is created and maintained by myriad cultural forces, sex-role failure seems evidence of the culture's failure. Apparent evidence of such failure began to mount during the late fifties and early sixties.

Until then, homosexuality had rarely appeared in Western art and entertainment except to be satirized or in pornography. In a short time it became a major subject for such writers as Gore Vidal, James Baldwin, Hubert Selby, Jr., John Rechy and Paul Goodman. The homosexual novel was no longer an occasional scandal; it was a genre. Some writers, such as Goodman and Allen Ginsberg, frankly presented their own homosexual feelings and experiences in public.

The stage and popular film also began admitting sexual deviance as a major theme. It appeared in *The Mark* and *A Taste of Honey* early in the sixties. Between 1967 and 1969 there were more than a dozen films about homosexuals, with such stars as Alec Guinness, Rex Harrison, Richard Burton and Sandy Dennis. Some, like *Staircase*, had been quite successful as plays. Off-Broadway, Off-Off-Broadway and underground films showed an even greater increase in plays about homosexuality.

Between about 1962 and 1965 the turned-on, long-haired boy and the pants-clad girl taking the pill took the same meaning for society as had twenties boys with flasks and cars, girls with cigarettes and turned-down hose. Censorship weakened, and there were nude happenings, erotic-art shows, see-through and topless fashions. Sexual "exploitation" films became a big industry, first heterosexual and then about homosexuality, transvestism and sado-masochism. Enthusiasts and alarm-ringers both agreed that the age of see-all and do-all had arrived, and that as a consequence marriage, family, heterosexuality and sex-role distinctions were on the way out.

Edward Albee's *Who's Afraid of Virginia Woolf?*, with its four-letter words and amatory savagery, was first called evidence of the "new morality." But before long, several critics began complaining that it hadn't gone far enough; it was actually more evasive than free. *Newsweek*'s critic said, "Albee is using his harrowing heterosexual couples as surrogates for homosexual partners having a vicious, narcissistic, delightfully self-indulgent spat. He has not really written about men and women, with a potential for love and sex, however withered the potential may be. He has written about saber-toothed humans who cannot reproduce, and who need to draw buckets of blood before they can feel compassion for others."

This writer apparently wouldn't have liked it as a homosexual play either. But such eminent critics as Stanley Kauffmann and John Simon not only agreed that *Virginia Woolf* was a disguised homosexual play, they said they'd welcome the real thing; there was no reason to disguise half a cast as aging nymphomaniacs and lugubrious virgins. They got their wish; homosexuality became an open theme in films, graphics and fashion as well as theater.

Major shows of erotic art began appearing in Europe and the United States in 1966, and many showed homosexual and s-m (sado-masochistic) acts and fantasies. Larry Rivers' construction *Lamp Man Loves It* showed the act of buggery. English painter Allen Jones made huge pictures of black-stockinged legs on stiletto heels—blow-ups of bondage pornography. Art critic Mario Amaya said, "We begin to find ourselves totally immersed in the artist's own sex fantasies." That is just what bothered a lot of people. Camp and kink had combined with pop as part of the fashionable avant-garde.

Susan Sontag gave camp its first cultural blessing in an essay called "Notes on Camp," in which she called it "the triumph of epicene style . . . love of the unnatural: of artifice and exaggeration."* Like homosexual camp, artistic camp was a genteelly administered dose of acid—parodic, flippant, mocking and obsessed with small things. It defied soup-can labels, Busby Berkely films, comic books and old polychrome household horrors. Pop-camp was exploited by media and marketers; soon people who'd never seen drag or heard of camp as anything but a Shawnee settlement were buying campy clothes and furnishings. Attacking camp became almost as large an industry as the target. One of the more impassioned but sensible commentaries on it was written by Vivian Gornick for the *Village Voice*. In her essay "It's a Queer Hand Stoking the Campfire," she said camp was not, as Sontag claimed, a valuable esthetic vision; it was arch, sly, hysterical, built upon hatred and self-hatred, and relentlessly at grips with the trivial.

Kink followed camp onto the market place, with its armamentarium of whips, chains, boots, leather, vinyl, rubber, high heels, goggles and motorcycles. It had become a major element of Off-Off-Broadway in such plays as *Vinyl*, *Gorilla Queen* and *When Queens Collide*. The underground film was full of lesbians beating each other and of pretty, heavy-bicepped boys in leather. Kenneth Anger's film *Scorpio Rising*, with its s-m fantasies about cyclists, won a Ford Foundation grant for its maker—and the indirect homage of boutique windows decorated with cycles, leather and chains. In 1966 Andy Warhol's film *The Chelsea Girls* was presented successfully in an uptown commercial setting; kink had moved up from the underground. Now it had its greatest effect on society at large through fashion.

*The essay is sometimes itself a piece of unintentional camp (". . . the most refined form of sexual attractiveness . . . consists in going against the grain of one's sex"). For a good brief history of camp as a term in the theater, literature and the homosexual world, see George Frazier's essay in the "Party of One" column in the November 1965 issue of *Holiday*.

A pointed comment on the deviant vision in fashion came from Jack Doroshaw, a transvestite who stages drag beauty contests under the name Flawless Sabrina. In an interview in *Evergreen Review* he said that women are now supposed to look like twelve-year-olds, and traced this back to Twiggy. "Have you seen a picture of her in underwear, no tits, right? and a flat little belly. Well, there's your sight lesson right there. Twiggy is a girl, a desirable girl, and the cretin kissing her in the photograph with the long hair and bangs is a boy, right? It's not only drag queens who don't know where their heads are at."

Early in the sixties, it seemed that the boyish look of the twenties had been revived, with narrow-hipped, flat-chested, thin-legged models wearing straight dresses to reveal limbs but not breasts, hips or waists. Then designer Rudi Gernreich introduced see-through and topless costumes. Many people charged he did so out of indifference or even hostility to the female body. Courrèges brought trousers into high fashion for the first time; again critics questioned the motives, pointing out that stroking a leg clad in tweed or twill isn't very stimulating to either party. It was a short step to space-suit, jumpsuit and look-alike clothing. An ad for Alexander's department store in New York City showed lace pants suits for men and women with the words, "Lace shows who wears the pants . . . for the ultimate in Unisex in the most uninhibited way possible."

The ad didn't point out that lack of inhibition is pointless to a unisexual creature. In any case, the unisex look was not a compromise design. Although men's clothing had acquired some bright colors, ruffles and flowery patterns, the his-and-hers styles basically put women in male clothes. There were occasional exceptions, such as evening skirts for men in the "Clothing for the Emancipated Male" collection of Hess's Department Store in Allentown, Pennsylvania, but they never caught on.

To be precise, women were being dressed not as men but as boys or pubescent androgynes. The words "lean" and "lithe" and "action" became common in fashion copy. The cover model of one leading magazine was so lean and lithe that a rumor went around the publishing trade for months that she was really a he. *Harper's Bazaar* spoke of "ragamuffin chic" and "schoolboy" characteristics in outfits. Journalist Helen Lawrenson pointed out that *Vogue* had become addicted to captions that "read like descriptions of boy athletes or juvenile delinquents." Basically, this fashion trend was a return to the feminist mood of the twenties. It remained true, as so often through Western history, that women may sometimes dress somewhat like males, but a man doesn't dress like a female unless he is deviant.

Lawrenson pointed out another change. Models' faces had gone from haughty to either furious or catatonic. For a long time they had looked as though they'd stepped in something distressing or suffered from chronic gastritis. But their haughty manner still suggested a trace of "Take me, if you're man enough." Now, said Lawrenson, they could "easily be imagined issuing orders for the punishment of recalcitrant serfs . . . her message seems to be, 'Come on, Buster, I'm going to castrate you!' It is a look inviting only to a sado-masochist."

Kink had come in—boots, leather, vinyl, chains, motorcycles and other s-m accessories. Ads showed triumphant, icy women astride motorcycles, wearing hip-hugger pants and leather bras studded with nails. High-fashion photographs presented phalanxes of fierce ladies in leather and vinyl. A pop-camp illustration in a mid-sixties *New York Times Fashion Supplement* contained wistful, breastless creatures whose cartoon thought-bubbles showed fantasies of tank assaults and car crashes. If the relationship of these ads to deviant fantasies seem tenuous to any reader, he should compare the ads to s-m books of photos and cartoons such as those sold on West 42nd Street in New York City. He will see, in many cases, perfect congruence in posture, expression, props and themes.

It may have been accidental that *Vogue* began using such terms as "cut-throat chic," but the October 1968 issue of *Glamour*—a magazine not given to freaky displays—contained explicit kink, until the editors discovered it and stopped the presses. The Paraphernalia clothing shops had an ad that showed a girl wearing a leather dress, kneeling, hands bound behind her, pouting up at the camera. A single line of type said that this was "The Story of O Dress." After printing had begun, one of *Glamour*'s editors learned that *The Story of O* was sado-masochistic pornography recently published by Grove Press. Any reader who had ever seen s-m literature would instantly understand the picture in the ad anyway—the typical s-m heroine, wearing leather, bound and kneeling, waiting to be beaten, buggered or ordered to perform fellatio. *Glamour* stopped the presses; the ad was pulled, and printing resumed. Or at least so the story ran when it was passed about the magazine business.

The acute phase of homosexual and kinky fantasy seems to have passed, but it continues as a major element in fashion. A male transvestite aping high fashion must now consider going back to pants, throwing away his wig, and flattening his hormone-fattened breasts.

Some people have defended these fashions as utilitarian or natural. Utility has never determined fashion as much as fantasy, ideology and economics. Female sodbusters and ranchwives wore cumbersome full dresses; today's "sensible" fashions have all the practical drawbacks of traditional male clothing, which have been enumerated many times. The more revealing rationalization is that of naturalness and freedom.

The desire for self-exposure and self-revelation runs through see-through clothes, see-me novels, T-groups and nude group-therapy marathons, and praise of sincerity as a total way of life (I can't imagine one more dangerous or more cruel). It tends to have a strong feminist bias, like the "unisex" clothing styles. It says people are first of all people, in a genderless sense, rather than female-people and male-people; they become alike because men reduce their aggressiveness, but women increase theirs. It says that any human possibility is natural and therefore to be viewed positively; that restraints and limits are destructive, and the restraints of traditional sex roles most destructive of all. The result of this attitude is often approval of sexual deviance. Actually, the impulse for this is not sexual or even vaguely sensual. Nor is the acceptance of deviance forthright and trustworthy.

Sex is not the motive when *Evergreen Review* shows pictures of a black woman and a white woman making love; when a whole theater troupe strips down to its natural, blemished self; when a cellist performs topless; when Yoko Ono produces a film consisting of 365 buttocks of London artists and intellectuals each on screen for twenty seconds; when the play *Early Morning* presents Queen Victoria as a lesbian having a go with Florence Nightingale, and Gladstone as a sadist running England like a Mafia *capo*. If these were meant to be sensual statements, we should really worry about the psychosexual state of the West. Fortunately, they are only ideological protests against social restraint and tradition in a broad sense. Their use of sex is essentially symbolic and polemical. "See me strip!" and "So call me faggot!" are contemporary equivalents of shredding the Bible on the steps of the town church.

The basic argument of this antisocial protest is that sexual deviance is natural and traditional sex norms are perverse. For instance, Rosalyn Regelson writes in the *New York Times* to explain the anarchy and (alleged) eroticism in the theater of the sixties: "To the bourgeois liberal, in whose cosmology marriage, family and the rigors [*sic*] of successful normal sexuality are a form of religion, homosexuality represents a heresy. ... It is involved with the primordial dream of the Golden Age in which Eros is unshackled from the bonds of procreation and social duty. Straining against the straitjacket of male and female roles in our patriarchal culture, the modern young [question] our outmoded concepts of marriage and psychosocial identity." More briefly, Andrew Sarris, whose column in the *Village Voice* must set a record for inanities on sex and society, writes about "the abiding abnormality of American sexuality."

The fashionable sexual Left do not pursue their stated goal. If they really want to dissolve constraint and break through inhibitions to reach full freedom of body and soul, they should try to dispel anal disgust. Sphincter control is the first major control we learn; it is generally associated with bodily and emotional control, with rigidity and lack of spontaneity. The anus is the most shame-laden part of the Westerner's body; this shame predates genital modesty and usually outlasts it. A truly Living Theater would not just strip bare and display their genitals but bend over, spread their buttocks and drop a load. Fortunately for American drama and the stagehands' union, the sex-protest underground shirks its mission. It merely creates a negative image of traditional restraints and calls that an ideal. It follows a convention as old as Rousseau and just as rigid as its enemy. Its stereotype of "naturalness and freedom" is a reaction against inherited stereotypes, which say that men are competitive and aggressive, females passive and compliant, and sex limited to heterosexual coitus in marriage. Protesters therefore say that man is essentially nonaggressive; that this nonaggressiveness makes most sex-role distinctions false; and that all constraints subvert our birthright of unbounded ambisexuality.

Like many rebels, they are more attached to the enemy than they admit. Many of the very people who shrill "Sexual freedom!" are also ready to yell "Pervert!" at those who disagree with them. If they really believe there is nothing wrong with homosexuality and sodomy, why do they mock opponents as "intellectual fairies" and show what a villain Uncle Sam is by allegorically showing him (in the play *Che*) as a closet queen buggering Castro? Their defense of deviation is often undemocratic, inhumane and fraudulent. It brings to mind whites who idealize blacks on grounds of their superior rhythm, eroticism and razor fights. In short, some of their best friends are homosexual.

Their intellectual justifications are Bachofen, Briffault, old instinct theories and other such anachronisms. Despite their smug ignorance and disingenuous pleading, they may help create a freer sexual climate. Our world is too imperfect for us to reject good things won the wrong way for the wrong reasons. Meanwhile, they have shock value, entertainment value, and therefore commercial value; the media have helped make their views more or less fashionable in some parts of society.

The fashionable sexual Left gets its greatest outside support in its rejection of Western sex-role traditions. The educated middle class tends to agree with them that "Victorian" sex roles are arbitrary and probably destructive. The less doctrinaire and better educated quote not Briffault but Margaret Mead and other pioneers of modern sex-role research.

When Margaret Mead was ready to undertake her first field work, in 1925, science was providing the groundwork for dynamic studies of personality and of society. Psychology had focused closely on early growth and learning. Ego psychology sent men looking for the mechanisms by which personality develops as an adaptation to family, society and physical environment. Functional anthropology showed how myriad social forces interlock to create a social environment. Now it was time for integrative studies, showing the dynamic interplay between continually adapting cultures and continually adapting individuals.

The West was also now experiencing a dramatic change in attitudes toward sex behavior—which in part reflected an even broader change, in ideas of sex role, the family and child rearing. These changes show most in the new mass adolescent subculture, the first in our history. Adolescence was considered a time of special stress, conflict and emotional upheaval; this had been claimed decades ago by Freud and others, and now it became general wisdom. When Margaret Mead was seeking a subject for her first field work, her teacher Franz Boas suggested she study adolescents in a non-Western society to see whether this was true in other cultures.

So Mead went to Samoa to observe child rearing, personality and behavior. She found that Samoan females make a rather slow and tranquil transition from childhood to adulthood, with a period of permitted sexual experimentation before marriage. When her book *Coming of Age in Samoa* appeared in 1928, it implied that Western adolescent conflict was largely due to restraints on a natural maturing process. Greater sexual expressiveness and more preparation for adult sexual life could help turn the teens from a time of crisis to a time of peaceful growth. As in decades past and to come, anthropology tended to reinforce the two great arguments of the feminist movement—that sharp restrictions on sex behavior and sex role create inner and social conflict.

Thanks to Malinowski, Mead and some others, many anthropologists began to relate social institutions, child rearing and adult patterns of personality and behavior. Ruth Benedict said that cultures are "individual psychology thrown large upon the screen, given gigantic proportions and a long time span." Others reversed the emphasis, showing how culture shapes personality. Erik Erikson studied nursing and weaning among the Sioux, and the effect on mother-child relationships. Devereux combined psychoanalytic training, anthropological techniques and hard-data collecting. Irving Hallowell, Clyde Kluckhohn, Cora Dubois, Ralph Linton, Abram Kardiner and many others worked in the same direction. Margaret Mead went on to do photographic studies in Bali of how children are nursed, handled and toilet-trained. She related the way they are sexually teased and then frustrated to the adult pattern of frustration, withdrawal, and proneness to trances and violent outbursts. She and Geoffrey Gorer wrote about the effects of swaddling on Eastern Europeans' temperaments. Many of these studies were grandiose and ambitious, and assumed that a single correlation proves a cause-and-effect situation; for instance, swaddling and certain adult characteristics show a suggestive similarity, but there was no attempt to show the effects of swaddling generally, and thus prove the point. But many such studies remain convincing, and they established the idea that the dynamics of culture and of personality have many links and that child rearing is the main one.

One of the most ambitious studies of all was Mead's *Sex and Temperament in Three Primitive Societies*. Like many great scientific works, it seems to rise from the author's personal involvement with the problem. Mead was the first distinguished woman researcher in her field, in an era of mass female emancipation. It was no surprise that she undertook to see whether men and women are born with different natures, suited for different life styles, or whether social tradition alone dictates the differences. Nor is it a surprise that she found the latter to be true. The case she made in *Sex and Temperament* is still many people's introduction to the scientific study of sex role.

Mead studied three very different peoples in New Guinea. First were the gentle Arapesh. Among them, child care was warm and mild, shared by both parents. All Arapesh, male and female, were tender, sensitive and maternal. They had no tradition of sharp temperamental differences between the sexes. Sex was not thought a strong driving force in either sex, and either might take the gentle initiative. Boys were discouraged from being aggressive. In fact, violent and aggressive people of either sex were considered deviant, and Mead said they tended to be neurotic. An aggressive woman was in constant trouble. An aggressive male might become paranoid and withdrawn. He had one positive option, if he could take it: a few "big men," or aggressive tribal leaders, were needed. Most Arapesh thought this an onerous role, but an aggressive male could assume it to make his deviant personality work to his advantage. The "big men" were the only socially successful exceptions to the cultural ideal, which we would call feminine.

The Mundugumor were headhunters and cannibals, and they had a "masculine" ideal for both sexes—violent, competitive and aggressively sexual. There was rivalry between man and woman, brother and sister, woman and woman. Fathers saw their sons chiefly as potential economic and sexual rivals. Sex was a woman's chief value to a man, and therefore her chief way of making her way in society. Pregnancy took her off the sexual market, and she resented it almost as much as the man. Child rearing was therefore a burden too; the young were raised harshly and perfunctorily. Arrogance, lust for power, rivalry and jealousy were a way of life. The deviants in this society, often troubled and neurotic, were the mild people. Gentle men had difficulty winning money to buy the brides they wanted, and they were generally considered losers in life. Devoted, maternal women weren't prized by successful men. The deviant Arapesh "big man" would have adjusted more easily among the Mundugumor. The gentle Mundugumor failure might have made a fairly successful Arapesh.

The Tchambuli, like us, saw the sexes as temperamentally opposite and complementary, but they reversed our view of them. The men were emotional, vain, dependent and flighty. They spent their time at art, dancing, flute playing, intricate social ceremonies and gossip. Nominally they were the heads of the households, but the real rulers were the women. The women gathered the food that guaranteed survival. They were hardheaded, responsible, impersonal social managers. The men were wary, strained and catty among themselves; the women were open, friendly, efficient and formed a solid front of cooperation. They enjoyed the men but seemed able to get on without them. In this society, neurotic deviants were the aggressive, virile men and passive, timid women.

Mead's work showed that sex role is socially learned to great degree, and varies from society to society. Furthermore, masculine and feminine are not simple opposites, nor are they strictly equivalent to dominance and passivity. Sex role may involve anything from occupation to posture and choice of language. Role standards vary not only from society to society, but over time within a society. A Western Don Juan of two centuries ago might have been wigged, rouged and powdered—hardly the way today.

Many scientists other than Mead went on to show how ideas of what is appropriate for males and females can contradict ours, in large ways or in odd particulars. Among the Andaman Islanders, a man sits on his wife's lap rather than she on his; he may greet friends of either sex by sitting on their laps and crying like an affected Victorian lady—this in a society that puts a premium on heterosexual experiment, prowess and technique. Among the Cubeo Indians, women court men aggressively, and husbands conventionally complain that their wives are too sexually demanding.

Mead said that the feminine Arapesh tended to fall apart when events called for aggression and resourcefulness. The masculine Mundugumor barely kept their society in one piece because of their hostility and competitiveness. The Tchambuli, with their sex-role dichotomy, produced unhappy men but contented women. Finally, she said, "it is hard to judge which seems to us the most utopian and unrealistic behavior, to say that there are no differences between men and women, or to say that both men and women are naturally maternal, gentle, responsive and unaggressive."

In all societies, those who fail to live up to the norm because of their temperaments—or for other reasons—pay a price. Mead believed that sharply defined and demanding sex roles make such suffering common, because in every society there is a wide variation of temperaments among both men and women. "Every time the point of sex-conformity is made, every time the child's sex is invoked as the reason why it should prefer trousers to petticoats, baseball bats to dolls, fisticuffs to tears, there is implanted in the child's mind a fear that indeed, in spite of anatomical evidence to the contrary, it may not really belong to its own sex at all."

A mild example, she said, is our society, where dominant, aggressive women and emotional, submissive men have the hardest time. Because they don't fit the mold, these people form couples that evoke the Tchambuli—bumbling, childish men making bluff shows of authority while their women exercised real strength and control. This was satirized in the *Dagwood and Blondie* cartoons, as it is in television domestic comedies. An extreme example is the Plains Indians, with their rigid and demanding code of male aggression, competition and stoicism. There the institution of the *berdache*, said Mead, was a warning to every father, so that he redoubled "the very pressure which helped to drive a boy to that choice." Ruth Benedict agreed that strongly contrasting sex roles correlate with homosexuality. Kardiner and Linton made a case that among the Tanala of Madagascar, the *sarombavy*, or transvestite, was usually a younger son who'd lost out in the tough emotional and economic competition among the males of the Tanala family. Not every *sarombavy* was homosexual; any man might take the role if he doubted his virility. And since Tanala women openly discussed lovers and jeered at erotic inadequacy, heterosexual failure called for public explanation. Like the transvestic "soft man" of the Siberian Chuckchee, the *sarombavy* had opted out of the demanding male role of his society.

Much of educated America, and of the educated West, was ready to hear the idea that traditional sex roles aren't necessarily natural or good—and to accept the feminist bias with which Mead presented it. The subliminal message of her volume, said anthropologist Ralph Linton, was that "there were no significant differences between the sexes, or at least only such differences as would inspire envy in the male." Somehow, when one has finished *Sex and Temperament*, one feels that all women are potentially happy Tchambuli managers, and that the desperate Western male would be happily relieved to become an Arapesh. It would take a detailed critique to show how this effect is achieved; a few biases and contradictions will serve.

Mead arbitrarily stated (preferred to believe) that genes mechanically fix the same range of temperaments in all people, of both sexes, the world over; but she said that sex role, despite its complex interplay with constitution, is purely a social convention. She avoided dwelling on even basic anatomical sex differences; ignoring that humans are mammals, she said it is just more "convenient" for women than men to raise children. Like most feminists, she directly or indirectly praised lack of aggression in men, and assertiveness in women: she found redeeming virtues in mild Mundugumor males, but few in Arapesh "big men." Most important, she claimed that specialized, contrasting sex roles create deviance and neuroticism. In fact, there is no evidence that this is so—that they cause more deviance, severer deviance or any special kind of deviance. The Plains Indians had *berdaches*—but more than we have homosexuals and transvestites? Devereux found only three among five hundred Mohave, and a study of the Omaha showed scarcely more in a community of 5,000. In the rigid warrior culture of old Montenegro, homosexuality has apparently been almost unheard of. Perhaps what Mead, Benedict and others didn't like about societies with clearly defined, aggressive male roles is that women could not assume that role without being marked severely deviant. In short, Mead and Benedict wouldn't have been happy in them.

Mead viewed sex-role distinctions *a priori* as a burden or psychological imprisonment. To a gifted woman such as herself, they might be. But she failed to point out that when society makes a demand, it doesn't just punish those who fail to meet it; it also rewards and supports those who live up to it. In later years Mead somewhat corrected the bias in her work, saying that the sexes tend to have different gifts to cultivate. She still makes statements, though, that show glee over female aggression and superior pity for males. She says that many American men evoke the Tchambuli-Bumstead type; despite their nominal authority, they "feel they must shout in order to maintain their vulnerable positions." When she recently suggested that women be drafted for military service, she characteristically joked, "I do not believe in using women in combat, because females are too fierce."

Sex and Temperament remains a popular model for thinking about sex roles, but the hard-line feminism it represents has produced subtle changes in attitude rather than a deep change in life style (in this it resembles the drive for sexual freedom, which has changed life a little but attitudes a great deal). Deploring the state of women has become a minor industry, and it usually takes one of three positions. One is to decry the failure of feminism; another is to decry feminism's victories; the third, and most frequent, is to show that women today stand in frustration between feminist and traditional ideas.

The feminist position is defended by such women as Simone de Beauvoir, Betty Friedan, Kate Millet and Alice Rossi. They point out that female emancipation has actually lost ground since 1930. Then one out of every seven people granted a Ph.D. was a woman; today only one in ten is a woman. In 1930 half of all professional and semiprofessional workers were women. Today only a third are women, and the majority of those are teachers, nurses, social workers, librarians, bookkeepers and accountants. Betty Friedan has helped organize NOW, the National Organization for Women, to end all discrimination against women. Like traditional feminists, she gives little attention to woman's maternal, nurturing role; the group intends "to supplement the all-pervasive image of the aproned mother." Alice Rossi wants "a socially androgynous conception of the role of men and women." Leaders of the strong emancipation movement in Sweden are getting public schools to teach cooking to boys and woodworking to girls.

Many others, beginning with psychiatrists Helene Deutsch and Marynia Farnham in the thirties and forties, have warned against the progress of feminism. Generally the popular press and magazines agree. They may say that women should be "independent" and "interesting" rather than docile and dependent, but they usually avoid hard-line feminism—for the simple reason that most people, male and female, are hostile to it. Though many girls in dissident youth subcultures call for the end of sex-role distinctions, many others have gone back to the most traditional role, baking their own bread and generally playing earth-mother.

There is apparently little fear that women are becoming homosexual. But there is belief that conflict between traditional and new assertive roles is making women unhappy and destructive. Mead herself speaks of "an increasing number of American women who clutch unhappily at a dominance that their society has granted them." The usual picture is of a lady with a college degree abandoning her quest for "self-fulfillment" to become a frazzled, frustrated suburban drab; she mourns her blighted aspirations and unconsciously castrates her husband and sons in revenge. However, she continues gradually to assert herself more sexually, financially and socially. This makes her husband back off, abdicate his role, retreat from the children. The wife concentrates her life on them, and as a result the boys are feminized. She ends up a domestic despot, unable to stop herself as she turns the nation into a matriarchy in all but name.

Here again is the Bumsteadized husband. Since Philip Wylie's tirades against momism two decades ago, the American male has been painted in a progressively cringing posture. He is obsessed with mother and breasts, and drifts into a neuter or homosexual state. Made impotent by his increasingly emancipated wife, he flees to overtime on the job, provides his sons with an inadequate male model, and thus makes them even weaker and less effectual than he. The alleged proofs of his emasculation can be found in a spate of books describing the erosion of the male role. They describe with pity how men drink more tea while women switch to beer; how children are given more names of vague gender, such as Jackie; how men use the passive phrase "to get laid." This pseudo-anthropology, pseudo-sociology and pseudo-psychology is practiced with or without academic qualification. Psychiatrist Abram Kardiner has been writing for thirty years about a headlong "flight from masculinity" and increase in homosexuality, despite all evidence to the contrary. Geoffrey Gorer says that frontiersmen put women on pedestals, and we keep them there; the women run primary schools and prepare little boys to be abashed fumblers before their lovers and wives. But the obsequious American male is allegedly only a bit worse off than his *confrères* in the rest of the West, blustering helplessly as women encroach on their fragile preserves of power.

Journalist Gloria Steinem writes that more upper-middle-class homosexual men are now getting married to have a social front, although she doesn't say how many such marriages took place in 1940 and how many take place now, or how she knows. But she does consider it part of a larger trend, and a good one, for "strictly polarized roles are a mark of authoritarian societies, with very little individual subgroup freedom." She isn't the only one to excel Mead in inventing evil consequences of sex-role distinctions. Steinem's article is part of an increased tendency to stop mourning the alleged inch-by-inch castration of the Western male and call it a sign of a happier future.

In *The American Male* Myron Brenton describes "the invisible straitjacket that still keeps him bound to antiquated notions of what he must do or be in order to prove himself a man." Harold Rosenberg, often a brilliant critic, said in *Vogue* that with the disappearance of the frontier, masculinity "lost its outdoor stage setting. . . . Masculinity today is thus largely a myth." Dr. Karl Stern, in *The Flight from Woman*, speaks of his many male patients who are passive or fleeing unconscious passive strivings. Dr. Hendrik Ruitenbeek's *The Male Myth* and H. R. Hays's *The Dangerous Sex: The Myth of Feminine Evil* also call traditional male aggression proud callousness when genuine, and pathetic bluff when forced. According to a *Cosmopolitan* article by Bernard Wolfe, we are ready for "The Step Beyond Muscle."

The argument for, rather than against, the diminished male is something like this: Men no longer shoot it out and wrestle bears. They can't prove their masculinity with brawn; to try to do so produces neurosis, compulsive heterosexuality, and a sense of failure that leads to homosexuality. In our automated, bureaucratized world, the old aggressive male role is anachronistic, for individuals feel socially and politically powerless, alienated. Those old patterns were undemocratic and arbitrary anyway. They have robbed men of emotional warmth. Women are freer, and men must learn to have equalitarian relationships with them, and become more nurturing with their children.

Mead, always ready to let men share the joys of motherhood, says men may soon prefer to stay at home and mind children while their wives work—and, despite her aversion to Bumstead-Tchambuli types, seems to think it a good thing. Steinem frankly equates the old male role with fascism. Dissident youth tells us to make love, not war—as though sex and aggression were incompatible (biology suggests the opposite). Like Mary Wollstonecraft and John Stuart Mill, like Coventry Patmore and Havelock Ellis—like feminists and Victorians of all times and both sexes—these people say in effect that when man is aggressive, he is a brute to women and mankind. From Mead to *Vogue* to campus radicals, there is a call for man to be an Angel in the House.

In all this talk there is little about proven sex differences. And they do exist. As in the study of sex behavior, a heavy undergrowth of conviction has kept research from blossoming. With so much emotionally at stake, people don't want to be distracted by facts. But a start has been made at finding traits physically programed in males and females by genes, hormones and nervous system, and the social forms these programs create.

The Hampsons, Money and a few others say that since people can be raised in a sex role that contradicts anatomy, they must be born with neutral neuro-endocrine "wiring." It is a minority view. Humans are born with less complete wiring than any other creature, and a great deal of learning takes place; but the learning does have a biological underpinning. Wiring and learning proceed in constant interplay until many of the basic "circuits" are completed during the first few years. There are probably critical periods of learning and, despite vulnerability to variant learning, a predisposition to learn certain things.

Some sex differences are clear just after birth—in muscle activity, in response to temperature, satiation and skin contact. Many more probably remain to be found. Other traits can't be measured till later in life, but are probably innate as well—for instance, females have greater acuity of smell, probably because of their estrogens. The relationship between androgens and aggression is unknown in man; it is probably subtle and indirect, but real. The work of Frank Beach and of Young, Goy and Phoenix has shown that prenatal injections of androgen masculinizes female macaques not only genitally but behaviorally. They will initiate play, mount, threaten and engage in rough-and-tumble play like young males; they withdraw and show appeasing behavior less than normal females. Work such as Fisher's suggests that prenatal hormones set up such sex-linked patterns by selectively sensitizing the brain. This probably exists to some degree in humans;

for instance, males may be born with a lower threshold of response to aggression stimuli, and with a greater sense of satisfaction in using their larger muscles.

Harlow's young male macaques began at three months to show more mounting, threat and rough play than females; the females showed innate nurturing behavior toward infants while still quite young themselves. Harlow concludes that "females are innately blessed with better manners; they do not threaten little boy monkeys." Though Harlow is quite cautious about such analogies, he concludes, "I am convinced that these data have an almost total generality in man." Greater male size, aggression and dominance, and greater female appeasement and nurturing are the rule through the whole higher animal world—and as Tinbergen and other ethologists point out, it would be strange if there were no evolutionary trace of this in man. It would be odd indeed if males weren't prepared to use their heavier skeletons and musculature or females to rear young through the longest dependency period in the animal world. It is already pretty safe to infer from laboratory research and ethological parallels that male and female are wired in ways that relate to our traditional sex roles.

There have been theories about males being aggressive because of their protruding sex organ and biological need to penetrate the female. Female characteristics, from passivity to intellectual subjectivity, have been attributed to her sexual innerness, her need to accept penetration and nurture young. These ideas have not yet been verified by studies of body image and body awareness, but they seem likely assumptions in the light of general clinical experience. Freud dramatically said that anatomy is destiny. Scientists who shudder at the dramatic, no matter how accurate, could rephrase this: anatomy is functional, body functions have profound psychological meanings to people, and anatomy and function are often socially elaborated.

Like many primate juveniles, young boys and girls all over the world form same-sex play groups. By then it is already clear that the male is taller and heavier than the female, with a higher muscle-to-fat ratio. Though the sexes overlap in size and dominance, males as a group always exceed females in both. Tinbergen has pointed out that although male and female herring gulls overlap in size, a small male always mates with a still smaller female. I do not know whether cultures other than ours tend to laugh at men who mate with females much larger than themselves, but it wouldn't be surprising.

The human female, like many primate females, matures earlier than the male; she walks and talks earlier, her adult teeth come in sooner, and her bones harden when she is younger. The male's sociosexual maturity also comes later. There are many societies—I know no survey showing how many other than ours—where the male, like the primate male, is slower than the female to take an adult sexual role. There is an adolescent period, while cooperative and aggressive patterns continue to develop; then the male takes a mate, often one younger than himself. As the female becomes a mother, the larger, stronger male assumes the role of protector of the female and her young.

Sex identity is learned by eighteen to twenty-four months; it is irrevocably set by thirty months. During this time, sex role is being learned. Robert Sears, who has done much authoritative research on this, showed that by the age of three sex role has already been established in its basic form. Boys show far more aggression than girls—as groups and, over a long period, as individuals. Boys tend to vent more of their aggression on other boys, and to respond to it with counteraggression. Girls show less aggression. And their aggression is usually prosocial—they state the punishment for breaking a rule. He hits another boy or knocks over a chair; she says angrily, "People who hit or knock things over get spanked, because it isn't nice." She is already pursuing conformity and social approval, oriented to others' cues. This is her way to master her environment and gain self-esteem, as aggression is the way for a boy.

Sears has shown that the kind and degree of aggression vary according to permissiveness, household structure and other factors, and says this is evidence that girls' prosocial-aggression pattern is learned, to a degree. However, he (and almost everyone else who has studied this) says that boys are still more aggressive, venturesome and independent; girls are more obedient, conforming and compliant, on the side of law and order. John Whiting of Harvard, along with his colleagues, has confirmed higher male aggressiveness in a detailed study of six cultures. He says the male-female difference in all of them is sharper at ages three to six than at seven to ten—perhaps suggesting that the difference is innate, and if anything is decreased by social learning. Though the difference varies, it is always there.

Some say that sex-typed behavior is instinctive; some say it is learned through identifying with the same-sex parent; others claim that once sexual identity exists, children try to strengthen it regardless of models or rewards. Possibly all these processes operate in tandem. Another important factor is peers' pressure to conform; children are very punitive toward those among them who deviate from sex-role norms. In our society, at least, each sex tends to say in childhood that it is inherently better than the other; males and females have thorough scorn for each other during preadolescence.

However, more boys claim superiority for their sex than girls. Furthermore, although girls say they are "better" or "nicer" than boys, they give higher status to men than to women and children. The male role, and fathers and men in general, have the highest prestige. Cross-cultural studies have confirmed that men are everywhere seen as stronger than women, less emotionally expressive, more dangerous and punitive, better able to master the world beyond the home and to command in the home itself. Studies of very different cultures show that they agree in associating angularity with males, roundness and smallness with females. (One wonders whether they also, like our society, tend to call a tiger he and a rabbit she.) Children everywhere see that women clean, cook, comfort, nurse and change diapers. And that men are bigger, stronger, more aggressive; they are the presidents, judges, criminals, policemen, supporters of families. Even the fact that this is not the case in a child's own household does not change his image of the sexes. Girls whose mothers work have the same domestic definition of femininity as girls whose mothers stay home and keep house. Boys without fathers have the usual stereotype of masculinity.

In a world ethnographic survey, anthropologist George Murdock showed that of 565 societies, the large majority were patrilocal and patrilinear. But even in the matrilinear and matrilocal, says A. Kimball Romney, another leading scholar in this field, "it is the male in the family who exercises *de jure* authority." The mother's male kin are the real rulers of the home.* Murdock's survey showed that multiple marriage occurred in 431 of the 565 societies; only in four of these could the woman take more than one mate. Everywhere, men are probably more sexually active and aggressive. In every known society, the male is the leader inside and outside the home, and receives greater deference.

Among the Arapesh whom Mead described as feminine, a girl marries an older man in a father-daughter type of pairing. Among the masculine Mundugumor, the men are still more violent and competitive than the women. Cubeo men jokingly complain that their wives are too ardent; but no matter how sexually aggressive the women are, they like to be physically subdued by the man in coitus. Beneath the courtesies and conventions of all civilizations, the fact remains that men can usually enforce their will physically if they feel they must. And women rarely make that necessary—except symbolically, for their own enjoyment. As Mary McCarthy has put it, anyone who says there are no differences between the sexes has never had her wrist twisted by a man.

Furthermore, women everywhere engage in different work than men. In most societies, men fight, hunt, trap, fish and herd. They also tend to do tasks related to these activities, such as working with metal and making weapons. Women cook, tend children and do such related jobs as carrying water, making fires, gathering fuel, preserving food and bearing burdens. There is no biological necessity for some of these tasks being labeled masculine or feminine, but they are logical extensions of work that does depend on male and female physique and physiology.

Some of the *kibbutzim* in Israel have experimented in freeing tasks from sex-typing. Melford Spiro, who has done the authoritative study of them, says they are influenced by the Zionist Youth Movement, whose values are "strongly feminist in orientation. The woman in bourgeois society, it is believed, is subjected to the male and tied to her home and family. This 'biological tragedy of woman' forced her into menial roles, such as house

---

*Murdock and others say that matrilinear and matrilocal legal systems correlate with agriculture-without-cattle economies, where women do all or most of the food gathering and other subsistence labor.

cleaning, cooking and other domestic duties, and prevented her from taking her place beside the man in the fields, the workshop, the laboratory, and the lecture hall." So on the *kibbutzim* women drove tractors, and men worked in kitchens. It soon turned out that women didn't enjoy this emancipation—not when it involved daily, exhausting male labor and responsibilities rather than vague fantasies of attaining masculine prestige and "self-fulfillment." Spiro says that "almost every couple who has left the Kibbutz has done so because of the unhappiness of the woman." Those who remained just weren't up to the heaviest labor, least of all when pregnant and nursing. They found themselves, gradually and of necessity, drifting back to cooking, cleaning, laundering, teaching and caring for children. Spiro concluded, "Apparently a cultural undervaluation of women cannot be corrected by abolishing the female role."

Sweden has continued to try to erase sex-role boundaries, in much the radical feminist spirit of the United States in the twenties. However, the proportion of women on the labor market is no higher than in the United States, and few are in positions of leadership. Neither sex, there or here, takes easily to the idea of working for females in supervisory capacities. Events in Israel, Sweden and the United States suggest that we may have been wrong in saying that men have high prestige because of their activities. It is just as possible that certain activities bring high prestige because they are usually performed by men.

Talk about fading sex distinctions is as much fantasy as talk of the Age of Orgy and the triumph of deviance. In 1964 sociologist Mirra Komarovsky showed in a study of blue-collar marriages that 80 per cent of husbands took no significant part in domestic duties. In a study of all classes, it turned out that 70 per cent of women in all classes do their dishwashing by themselves. Over three decades, studies of marriages evaluated as successful have usually shown greater male dominance, and the wife's high ability to perceive her husband's expectations. Though television situation comedies often show bumbling men and manipulative women, these are satires; it is a situation at which people laugh because it runs counter to usual expectations and values.

A great deal of wealth in the United States is nominally in female hands. Within the family, power of the household budget may be delegated to the wife, but the power is the man's to delegate or keep, for he is usually the only or chief wage earner. Outside the home, much of women's wealth consists of dummy corporations run by their husbands, created for the sake of tax evasion. Women with wealth of their own often put it in the hands of professional (male) managers. There are still few female leaders in business, politics and the professions. And it is still widely thought unfeminine for a woman to be sexually aggressive. When it comes to basics, emancipation tends to go the way of all rhetoric.

Talk about masculinity has been even less realistic. When a couple are assaulted on the streets of a modern, automated, nonfrontier city, they don't flip a coin over who can best defend them. A man who wants to go to bed with women and leaves the initiative up to his prospective partners will end up frustrated. Only boys sure they'll never have to enter an army or even walk into a bar can take the Step Beyond Muscle. No one in the near future will automate loading trucks, collecting garbage or building houses. But the talk about traditional masculinity being passé comes from very protected middle-class people, often those in relatively noncompetitive fields. Professors who insist that corporate life emasculates men should try to hold down even a middle-level corporate job and see just how much competitive aggression it takes compared to teaching.

As Bruno Bettelheim has pointed out, violence does exist, not only in the world about us, but within us. And especially within children. We have replaced Grimm's fairy tales with books about people who live on Happy Street in Pleasant Town; mothers campaign against letting children play with toy weapons. Violence is ignored or treated with contempt. The result, says Bettelheim, is that children don't learn to face violence in themselves and others, and thus to master it.

So far women have not been called on to protect their escorts from delinquents or aggressive drunks; and man's nurturing role will go just so far unless, as the idiom has it, God grows tits on boars. Certain elements of sex role, though traditional, are probably optional for coping with life, and they do change from century to century. Femininity won't disappear if women stop fearing mice, smoke in public, vote and wear pants. Nor if men drink tea and wear ruffles. But fundamental attitudes about sex and sex role are not just arbitrary stereotypes; they are rooted in biology and practical necessity. They must be learned early in childhood, and will remain our social and psychological norms, despite changes in fashion ads.

It is true that deviants in fashion and the arts now capitalize on their fantasies instead of hiding them. But wearing kinky clothes probably never changed anyone's performance as a lover, spouse or parent. These fashions are nevertheless analyzed in ways that would also turn the goldfish eating of the twenties into ritual cannibalism reflecting frustration at the breast, and the canasta parties of the fifties into symbols of aggression deflected by alienation and the Cold War. This may win a doctorate or even a fee from a publisher, but it's otherwise unprofitable. Sex roles are not dying or being radically altered; they are modifying under social and psychological pressures. Some flexibility in them can only help rather than harm, I think.

We do not have broad-scale, accurate studies of sex-typed behavior, and it is useless to guess much about the past. We have a large job ahead learning more about sex differences and sex-role differences, and observing their distribution and expression in our own society in our own time. It now seems that masculine and feminine are not polarized alternatives but loose clusters that may overlap. They vary even within our own society by class, education, ethnic background and family constellation. The important factors affecting them may be the increasingly middle-class style of child rear-

ing, with its greater emphasis on impulse control; that between the late
fifties and late sixties the number of mothers who nursed their babies
dropped by half; that suburbs do not seem to nourish preadolescent chumship, as city blocks did. But first we need good studies of the effects of
nursing, bottle-feeding and chumship. We also need to direct research
away from campus and college-town middle-class samples and study the
sociologically invisible lower middle and lower classes.

There is no doubt that the social environment is changing, and that the
brunt of adapting falls immediately on males, perhaps making their role
behavior more vulnerable. But the great tumult of sex-role discontent for a
century and a half has been about female role. Feminists have further
devalued the already low-valued domestic side of the female role.
Middle-class women are educated to expect adventure, fulfillment, and the
prestige given to successful males. Nevertheless, they are raised without
male competitive attitudes, and usually fail to muster the labor, commitment, persistence and ambition necessary for even middling career success.
Significant success isn't won by most men, because it isn't easy—and they
have been raised to try to achieve it. Most men don't have jobs that deeply
interest and fulfill them; if they wish to do creative things, they probably
do something else for a living and save their evenings and weekends for the
labor of love. Women seem to curse that they too must usually settle for
what a man must—being a wage earner instead of having a creative calling,
plus time and joy to spare. Actually, women have greater freedom and
more extra time than ever; many men envy them their freedom to explore
a creative calling rather than work for success at a job. Many women, with
their fantasies of men being better off, mourn that they don't have even
more freedom, and complain. They will have champagne or nothing.

Interestingly, this attitude seems most common among mothers of the
youth whose passivity is most talked about—middle- and upper-middle-
class college boys. Kenneth Keniston's book *The Uncommitted*, a
study of quasi-hippies in the late fifties and early sixties, shows passive,
insecure young men who will be familiar to anyone who's been around dissident college culture since then. Keniston's subjects had mothers who were
the ambitious Emancipated Women of the twenties. Like most such
women, they ended up being wives and mothers, dropping artistic or
professional ambitions, and inwardly resenting their husbands for not doing
the same. They formed overintimate relationships with their sons, in conspiracy against the fathers. The boys learned to see the fathers as the
mothers presented them—disappointed, frustrated idealists who were weak
and had sold out their early aspirations. The boys rejected the fathers, and
the role and commitment they represented. They had the misfortune to
believe they had won the Oedipal struggle, and remained passive and
dependent, longing to repeat their early childhood relationship with their
mothers. Those who have not read Keniston's book can see the situation
portrayed in the film *The Graduate*, with its passive and uncommitted

young protagonist, its older men who are contemptible in their worldly success, its emotional and dramatic women who give sexualized mothering.

It is of such people that psychologist Eleanore Luckey is talking when she writes, "I am deeply concerned by the number of males on campuses where I have been who are concerned enough about masculinity to wonder if they are homosexual." Psychologist Richard Koenigsberg says, "In the hippie culture each person takes care of another person—like saying 'I'll be your mommy if you'll be my mommy.' " Others agree with him in finding "oral" themes, dependence, avoidance of aggression and other dependent, "feminine" themes in dissident college youth. My own experience confirms this, and on campuses in recent years I have sometimes felt that the most obvious problem one sees is children whose mothers are thwarted feminists.

Many of Keniston's arguments are convincing; they are also perhaps too temptingly easy. Are there really more passive-dependent young men today than fifty years ago, afraid they aren't man enough and expressing this as fear of homosexual potential? Or are we just noticing them more? No one really knows. Keniston guesses, and I believe with reason, that the pattern is at least somewhat more common. Women continue to devalue their traditional role and restlessly expect more; they usually don't get more, and when they do, they tend to feel it's not enough. This must have an effect on their children. Again, we need more studies before we go on speculating.

Meanwhile, a rhetorical call for less aggressive, more nurturing males continues in the media and the educated middle class. A just and necessary drive for more legal and social rights for women goes on as well, but often in the context of contempt for necessarily female tasks. None of this changes the fact that when a male rejects his role, he is rejecting society's basic values. But when a female strives for part of the male role, it is understandable, because it is the preferred role. A woman in pants is cute or a laughing matter, but a man in skirts is a howl. And this social prejudice has roots in biology at least as much as in social traditions.

COMMENTS

"I used to be Superman . . . Wherever you looked I was saving somebody. Then one day I pulled this chick from the river. Do you think she thanked me? No! She just wanted to know why I had this *compulsion* to rescue. . . . She accused me of doubting my masculinity. . . . She took one look at my cape and said I was a latent transvestite."   —Jules Feiffer

LeRoi Jones said he was supporting a boycott of Newark schools by black children because: "We do not want them to grow up to be Marlon Brando. We do not want them to grow up to paint Campbell Soup cans. We do not want them to grow up to think that somehow the celebration of homosexuality is esthetic and profound."

In 1968 Andy Warhol was shot and critically wounded by Valerie Solanis, age twenty-eight, who had appeared in his film *I, A Man* in the role of a lesbian. Friends told reporters that she was not a woman-lover, but a man-hater. In 1967 she formed SCUM, the Society for Cutting Up Men. Her manifesto included the aim of eliminating the male sex, for the male is a "biological accident" and an "emotional cripple." Her program, she said, would "bring about the complete female takeover, eliminate the male sex and begin to create a swinging, groovy, out-of-sight female world."

"John Steinbeck's *Of Mice and Men* was once viewed by most critics as a touching tale of migrant farm laborers. Today Lenny and George come over either as two flaming faggots or as a vegetable keeping company with an oversized phallic symbol."　　　　　　—Andrew Sarris, in *The Village Voice*

In 1968 pacifists set up coffee houses to spread their word near military bases. A Special Force NCO said to a *Newsweek* reporter, "We aren't fighting and dying so these goddam pansies can sit around drinking coffee."

"Anyone who spends any time with the Hell's Angels knows the difference between outlaw motorcyclists and homosexual leather cults. At any bar full of Hell's Angels there will be a row of sleek bikes lined up on the curb outside. At a leather bar there are surrealistic renderings of motorcycles on the wall and perhaps, but not always, one or two huge, accessory-laden Harleys parked outside—complete with windshields, radios and red plastic saddlebags. The difference is as basic as between a professional football player and a rabid fan. One is a performer in a harsh, unique corner of reality; the other is a cultist, a passive worshiper, and occasionally a sloppy emulator of a style that fascinates him because it is so hopelessly remote from the reality he wakes up to every morning. . . .

". . . *Scorpio Rising* [an underground motorcycle-cult film] played in San Francisco. . . . The San Francisco Angels made a pilgrimage to check it out. It didn't groove them at all. They weren't angry, but genuinely offended. One said. 'A lot of people got conned, and now we have to listen to all this crap about us being queers. Shit, did you see the way those punks were dressed? And those silly goddam junkwagon bikes? Man, don't tell me that has any connection with us.' "　　　　　　—Hunter Thompson, in *Hell's Angels*

In 1967 the makers of Captivator shoes for women advertised their product as "blatantly boyish."

"*The Ugliest Girl in Town* is disappearing from TV. The ostensible comedy about a guy who masqueraded as a girl for some unlikely reasons . . . did perform a public service, though: it made people aware of the tide of creeping faggotry of television, heretofore manifested in commercials."　　　—*True* magazine

After Egyptian actor Omar Sharif kissed Jewish actress Barbra Streisand during a rehearsal of the film *Funny Girl*, a Cairo magazine ran a picture of the two and demanded, "Bar this effeminate actor from Arab nationality."

"America's sweethearts like their pants slung low. Belted mean, wide and black."　　　　　　—Fashion copy, *The New York Times Magazine*

"SLAVE to periodic pain."   —Advertisement for Midol, *McCall's*

"Both *Vogue* and the *Bazaar* are addicted to captions that read like descriptions of boy athletes or juvenile delinquents. Their favorite adjectives these days are 'lean' and 'hard,' and one can find reference to clothes that have 'schoolboy spunk' or that make a girl look like 'a tough little Italian boy' . . . the new woman—a lean, lithe, androgynous creature stomping around in her boots."— From "Androgyne, You're a Funny Valentine," by Helen Lawrenson, *Esquire*

"Their hair is short and their chests modishly flat. They wear arrogant trouser suits, earn their own living, and drive their own cars the moment they (or Father) can afford them. They share flats uncomfortably with friends, preferring to be poised on the edge of financial instability, rather than live comfortably but dependently at home."—From "Why Can't a Girl Be Like a Man?" by Alma Birk, *Cosmopolitan*

Editor:
William Redfield's comments on the Presidential campaign, published in your Letters column were excellent. Unfortunately, the references to Mayor Richard Daley as "Mary Daley," "the Mother of Us All," and other such feminine appellations may have given some of your readers the idea that Mayor Daley is, or seems to be, a homosexual.

That mistaken impression needs instant correction. So far as I know (and I am a homosexual, as well as Executive Director of the Mattachine Society, an organization for homosexuals) Mayor Daley is a practicing heterosexual, and as such, belongs in that long list of prominent people reputed to be heterosexuals. Such a list would have to include the following: Adolph Hitler, Josef Stalin, Adolph Eichmann, Lyndon Johnson, Ronald Reagan.

We homosexuals have enough prejudice against us without having to be blamed for including these weirdos in our group. . . . We all know that the Chicago police force is composed only of virile, heterosexual men—after all, what queen would strike or tear-gas women and nice-looking young men?

As a matter of fact, from the havoc wreaked by the known heterosexuals around us, isn't it about time that the National Institutes for Mental Health granted some funds to discover whether murder and mayhem and violence is part of the heterosexual personality, or just a symptom of disturbed heterosexuality?   Dick Leitsch
                                                        —Letter to the Editor, *Playboy*

In the much-publicized murder trial of Mrs. Candace Mossler, accused of murdering her banker-husband, the alleged homosexuality of Mr. Mossler was made a major point by the defense. Mrs. Mossler said he picked up boys in back streets and high school bars. Her attorney, Percy Foreman, said, "Except for the shoe fetish ... Mossler had 'em all—transvestism, masochism, sadism, all the perversions mentioned in *Psychopathia Sexualis*, Krafft-Ebing's great masterpiece." Prosecuting attorney Richard Gerstein was quoted as commenting, "If the jury buys the stuff about Mossler being a homosexual, we're dead." Mr. Mossler's deviance was never proven, but Mrs. Mossler did win an acquittal.

After a clash between hippies and police in New York's Grand Central Station in 1968, a policeman was quoted by the *New York Post* as saying, "Some of the guys said I shoved one of the hippie females too hard. Well, if a woman comes over and kicks you in the groin, how would you react? It's like dealing with any queer pervert, mother raper or any of these other bedbugs we've got crawling around the Village. As a normal human being, you feel like knocking every one of their teeth out."

I am sitting in a cafe on Constitution Square at the center of Athens. A tall, slim man walks past the cafe toward a nearby arcade. He is about forty-five, sandy-haired and deeply tanned, with a tense, self-conscious stride. One assumes at once that he's one of the many well-to-do, middle-aged English or German homosexuals who vacation here. As he nears the arcade, half a dozen young Greek men hanging out on the corner spot him and begin to yell at him. The man passes them, looking straight ahead. They begin to follow, hooting and yelling abuse. All heads in the cafe turn to watch; many spectators are grinning, others remain expressionless. The man walks a little faster, trying to ignore the group that now runs behind, alongside, all around him, like a pack of hounds boxing in their prey. He turns into the arcade, and the pack follows. I ask my Greek acquaintance, "Why are they after him like that?" He says, "Look, every Greek man does things with another man sometimes, but those . . ." He nods toward the arcade with disgust. "We aren't *fairies.*"

28

In the Shadow

Of the two hundred million people in the United States, some ten million are or will become exclusive or predominant homosexuals—more than there are Jews or Latin Americans. People with at least a few years' significant homosexual experience may number more than twenty-five million—more than blacks. Yet there is no "problem" minority of which sociology has learned so little. The avoidance is especially disappointing because the few studies that exist are full of provocative surprises. In order to learn who homosexuals are and how they live, one should begin with a basic ethnography. How many homosexuals are there, where and how do they live, and what jobs do they hold? How do they deal with and feel about family, friends, lovers and society at large? How alcoholic, suicidal or free of gross pathology are they? If there is a homosexual subculture, what are its ways and values, and how does it affect its members?

This peculiar absence is due not to a lack of scientific tools, but to the peculiar history of the science. Sociology began in the nineteenth century, when such men as Comte, Hume, Marx and Durkheim asserted that society acts according to laws, just as chemicals, moving bodies and species do. First they tended to borrow concepts from biology, comparing societies to organisms, institutions to organs, individuals to cells, and history to evolution—tempting analogies that often fall down. Then, accused of being metaphysical and unscientific, sociologists borrowed methods from physical science, reducing people to measurable units by behavior, status and attitudes. Their work became more concrete and accurate; but in an excess of mathematical zeal, they often garnered irrelevant or limited data, acting as though people lacked histories, personalities and motives. The result was a stunted intellectual landscape, as unreal as that produced by classical psychoanalysts who wrote as though a man could live outside mankind.

In the late twenties and thirties, sociology concentrated more on social interaction and on such special milieux as the neighborhood, small town and ghetto. People trained in anthropology and psychiatry added the field method of the participant-observer and applied psychodynamic insights. Out of this rich interdisciplinary approach came some of the masterpieces of modern social science—the Lynds' *Middletown*, William Lloyd Warner's *Yankee City*, John Dollard's *Caste and Class in a Southern Town*, William Whyte's *Street Corner Society*. Kinsey began to quantify sexual behavior and relate it to attitudes, class, education, religion and other social factors.

But "pure" sociology, before and after that period, has tended to avoid the streetcorner and its society, to theorize and do research by questionnaire, to repeat the self-evident in dense jargon, and to shun contamination by outside ideas. This wavering between theory-making and the narrowest empiricism rises from continuing anxiety about scientific respectability, and from scholars' discomfort among people unlike themselves. Howard Becker points out that most of his fellow sociologists know less about criminals than journalists do, because they usually study them from court and prison records; and despite a mountain of writings about delinquents, he says, the best information on them is still found in Frederick Thrasher's *The Gang*, written in 1927. It is significant that sex research is usually done in college and other middle-class communities, where the researchers are most comfortable. We still know relatively little about the sex lives of the poor, the rich and the lower middle class. Sexology, of course, has suffered deeply from sociological avoidance of field study, and the study of deviant sex most of all.

The gathering of basic sociosexual data has only begun. After a significantly long and hard struggle for funds, the Kinsey Institute has started to study the social history and adjustment of twelve hundred male homosexuals. The results will not be analyzed and published for a while yet—though interesting leads appear as they sift the results of a pilot study of five hundred homosexual men. For the moment, our main sources of information are Kinsey's two volumes, the smaller studies of Gordon Westwood and Michael Schofield in England and Hans Giese in Germany, and a handful of fascinating monographs.

When Kinsey's pioneering work appeared in the forties, his figures on the prevalence of homosexual behavior shocked laymen and scientists alike. The shock subsided, and now they are generally accepted. Many scientists elsewhere in the West assume, accurately or not, that such studies in their countries would have the same results (smaller studies than Kinsey's do suggest that this is true of England and Germany). Kinsey also contradicted traditional wisdom when he said that rural areas lag only a little behind cities in homosexuality—in fact, by the same small margin as heterosexual activity. The difference seems due to fewer partners and opportunities in the countryside, for the gap closes at the college-graduate level of society, among people who leave their rural homes for campuses and then professional life. Kinsey's evidence negates the old idea that deviance is a product of city life.

Having lived in small midwestern towns, I suspect that many of them harbor people whose "queer" character is a public secret. Even flagrant effeminacy may be tolerated as long as homosexual acts are kept discreet. In the late forties, the English psychiatrist William O'Connor related the same impression. He said that "the most mincing effeminate homosexuals are to be found not in London, but in small provincial towns . . . everyone knows everyone else, the homosexual's predilections will soon become common knowledge and before long he will have to give up trying to appear normal to his friends and workmates."

Our inherited lore also has it that homosexuals move from small towns to big cities in droves—that homosexuality is an urban phenomenon in actuality if not in origin. Kinsey could not confirm or deny this, for he classified people as rural or urban only according to where they spent their formative years. In *A Minority*, a study of 127 male homosexuals in London published in 1960, Gordon Westwood found some signs of a disproportionate drift to the capital city by homosexual men. So did Michael Schofield in his study *Sociological Aspects of Homosexuality* (which despite its authoritative title is also based on relatively small samples). There is no final evidence yet: the gay may tend to drift to large cities more than the straight, but perhaps not a huge proportion of them. In fact, Schofield noted that many small-town homosexuals would not think of leaving home, and a number stay to care for aged parents, in a manner reminiscent of the spinster daughters of Victorian novels.

Homosexuals may live settled lives in small towns, in unannounced homosexual "marriage" with a roommate or joint homeowner. Others spend weekends and holidays in nearby cities, where they can find bars, parties and other aspects of organized gay life. A town with a population as small as a few thousand, though, may have a rudimentary homosexual subsociety, usually centering around the local "queen"—in this context, the term means an older man with extensive experience in the gay world who provides a meeting place for the local gay set and helps younger homosexuals in trouble.

Paul Gebhard guesses that a city must have about fifty thousand people to support gay bars and other public centers of gay life. Dayton, Ohio, with a population of three hundred thousand, has an extensive and visible gay world, with bars, cruising areas, spots for homosexual prostitution and apartments leased by gay landlords to gay tenants. Urban gay neighborhoods are usually downtown areas with large transient populations— Old Town and the Near North in Chicago, Boston's Beacon Hill and Back Bay, Philadelphia's Rittenhouse Square area, and New Orleans' French Quarter. Parts of Los Angeles are known locally as "the Swish Alps." New York has many such sections—Greenwich Village, Brooklyn Heights, and parts of Manhattan's upper West Side and midtown East Side. These areas have gay parks, restaurants, bookstores, laundries, clothing stores, barbers and even shops with greeting cards for "gay occasions" (gay valentines are a big item). Outside such major cities are resorts where homosexuals gather, roughly according to social class—Fire Island, the Hamptons and Provincetown for middle-class New York homosexuals, and Riis Park and Jones Beach for the less moneyed.

In the largest cities, subworlds exist within the gay world—leather bars for sado-masochists and fetishists on New York's Christopher Street; Muscle Beach in Santa Monica for homosexuals obsessed with body-building; expensive midtown Manhattan bars where secret middle-class homosexuals seek discreet pickups after work; San Francisco Tenderloin joints where transvestite hustlers work at all hours; drag bars in Chicago. European capitals have drag bars and other specialized hangouts, but the largest American cities show a variety and ritualization rare elsewhere.

The inhabitants of these gay worlds come from every class and work in every occupation, from cook to clergyman. Conflicting folklore says that the majority come from among the uninhibited poor or the jaded rich. When William Lloyd Warner studied "Yankee City," the aristocracy of "Hill Streeters" stood at the top of the social ladder and the poor "Riverbrook" fishermen at the bottom. A doctor in town who had taken an interest in the Riverbrookers said, "You've heard people call them 'broken-down Yankees' and accuse them of all the crimes on the calendar. People are always asking me if they all sleep with their daughters. Because there have been one or two cases of homosexuality among them, everyone in Yankee City thinks that all of the Riverbrookers are homosexual. . . . I suspect that aristocrats are more likely to be homosexual than lower-class people." Warner found no justification for the widespread belief that incest and homosexuality were Riverbrook specialties, nor, apparently, for the doctor's reversal of the idea.

When Kinsey broke down his data by class, he showed that the lead in homosexuality clearly belongs to the lower middle class—a surprising fact he couldn't explain and that has provoked strangely little questioning and study. My guess is that lower-middle-class striving for gentility may be involved. Psychiatrists have pointed out that the stress on "niceness" in upward-striving families often takes a toll in children's aggressiveness and sexuality.

Many homosexuals I interviewed said that the gay, as a group, slip down the economic scale from their parents' level. It is a statement some scientists have accepted and then pointed to as proof that homosexuality is psychosocially crippling. Schofield heard the idea expressed by many of his subjects, yet he found no such downward trend among them. He noted that most of those who said it were younger than thirty; few people that age, homosexual or heterosexual, have reached their parents' income level, and they may prematurely generalize on the basis of their own and their friends' lives. We must hope for better information about economic mobility among homosexuals from the Kinsey Institute study. Meanwhile, an interesting lead has appeared in a profile of male homosexuals in a Canadian city by sociologists Maurice Leznoff and William Westley.

Thirteen of Leznoff's and Westley's subjects held professional jobs; all were secret homosexuals. Another thirteen gay men had sales and clerical jobs; nine of these were secret. But nine others, in the arts and service jobs, were overt. This suggests a simple, common-sense interpretation that the overt—and especially the effeminate—homosexual cannot get a good job; he ends up as a counterman, dishwasher, hairdresser, a waiter or salesman in a gay establishment, or in one of a few permissive artistic professions. Overt homosexuals from middle-class families may drift downward vocationally from their origins, but Dr. Gebhard guesses that a good 85 per cent of homosexuals, not being overt, can pass, conform and keep open the door to vocational success.

Schofield and Westwood did find two job characteristics among their subjects—slight tendencies to avoid technical work and to change from manual to nonmanual jobs, even for the same pay. Westwood's men used the word creative frequently; despite this and their avoidance of technical and manual work, they weren't concentrated in artistic professions. This belies twenty-five hundred years of belief that homosexuals are artistic, and artists homosexual. Though a disproportionate number of homosexuals work in some arts, especially performing and graphic arts, they are only tens of thousands out of ten million homosexuals: a minuscule fraction of the gay are in the arts. In some arts it may be not just the proportion of homosexuals that is high, but their visibility, because of tolerance for deviance in these fields. In fact, some homosexuals may opt for the arts because of that tolerance, the way some heterosexuals with creative gifts opt for other professions for the sake of security and respectability.

Technical hobbies are rare among homosexuals, according to Westwood, and cultural hobbies popular. Many psychiatrists and sociologists report a high interest in ballet, opera and theater among the gay. According to Dr. Richard Green and John Money, this may result from a special propensity for role-taking and performance in some homosexuals that goes back to childhood, as well as with a traditional stereotyping of sedentary and artistic interests as feminine.

Because homosexuals predominate or are highly visible in some arts, people have speculated about queenish cabals, homosexual casting couches and a self-serving homosexual freemasonry (as the French call it, the *franc-maçonnerie du trou du cul*). The outraged, from Juvenal to current journalists, say there is a gay conspiracy to erode the social, artistic and political health of civilization. Writer Ian Fleming referred to it as the homintern. Doubtless the gay, like the straight, tend to favor lovers, potential lovers and the like-minded. But my interviews suggest that in most professions, where homosexuals are a secret minority, they avoid or even discriminate against each other. They fear that other homosexuals will expose them accidentally or, if antagonized, deliberately. Some say that given a choice between hiring someone straight and someone gay, they hire the straight for safety's sake.

For a look at homosexual solidarity, one must look not at professions but homosexual associations—or homophile societies, as the American ones call themselves. Such groups have existed in most North European countries on and off throughout this century. The American homophile movement began around 1950 with the founding of the Mattachine Society and the lesbian Daughters of Bilitis in San Francisco. Other groups have sprung up since then, such as the New York Mattachine Society, the Society for Individual Rights (SIR) in San Francisco, ONE in Los Angeles, and the gay power and gay liberation movements in New York. These organizations have chapters in major cities throughout the country, and student homophile leagues have risen (and fallen) on some large university campuses in recent years.

To many people, gay societies suggest hysterical drag balls and shrieking orgies. To the contrary, they are middle-class, genteel, even dowdy. Visiting their offices and meetings gave me the impression that a minority of the members are militant reformists, the majority isolated, timid people seeking a social life and group identity. Homophile groups organize dances, picnics, lectures and social meetings; publish magazines, give members practical and legal advice; try to educate the public about homosexuality. They have had a real, if minor, effect on laws and public policies. They have defended the rights of prosecuted homosexuals in Philadelphia; worked in liaison with police and church groups in San Francisco; picketed federal buildings in Washington, D.C., and elsewhere to oppose sanctions against homosexuals in the civil service and armed forces. Advocates of gay power talk about organizing local and national gay voting blocs to achieve full social and legal equality.

Despite grandiose rhetoric about gay power, few politicians are quaking. The combined membership of all the homophile societies in the United States is only about ten thousand, and their efforts to federate have collapsed in vehement splinter politics. Even in Holland, where the movement is most developed, only a tiny fraction of the country's homosexuals belong to it. Most of the gay lack patriotism about homosexuality or prefer to stay secret. Most heterosexuals with even vaguely liberal views would support many homophile aims, but they and many homosexuals as well are put off by the defensive, aggrieved, even vitriolic tone of some of the societies. These groups occasionally sound quite unrealistic—especially when they claim to be society's most mistreated minority. Even among deviants, they are the only ones sufficiently numerous and accepted by society to be able to organize. Imagine the fate of a national society of sadists, pedophiles or necrophiles.

The reasons for their relative failure to organize can be found in the arguments of those who deny that a homosexual subculture exists. Psychiatrist Stanley Willis says in his book *The Overt Homosexual* that the gay world is just a mixed crowd who hope a group identity will relieve their individual state of alienation. Their kinship-in-misery is self-defeating, he says, for anxiety and loneliness are often felt most strongly in a group—finding expression as waspishness, pettiness and disloyalty. There is some truth in this, as anyone knows who has seen gay parties and bars.

Furthermore, homosexuals are wrong in asserting that they are bound by the same minority-group loyalty as blacks, Jews and other oppressed ethnic groups. A black or Jew is born into a family of people like himself; he often has a neighborhood and larger community to give him support, positive traditions and a sense of loyalty. On the other hand, the homosexual is usually the only one in his family. He grows up keeping his deviance a guilty secret from almost everyone—especially from those closest to him. His sense of differentness, of bearing a guilty secret, does not disappear in gay circles. He lives in fear of exposure by other homosexuals. He finds that many of the gay see themselves as sick or sinful. Furthermore, they are of many classes, backgrounds and personality types. They have varying sexual preferences, which are symbolic of different motives and emotions. In short, they have almost as little in common as a group of men thrown together at random only because of their heterosexuality.

Some homosexual apologists say that because the gay are persecuted, their condition is a leveler. Homosexuals, they claim, disregard conventional biases about class and race, side with all underdogs, and are democratic and liberal. This is like the old Greek argument that homosexuals are a bastion of liberty because they practice fraternal love. My interviewing convinces me that homosexuals have the usual social prejudices for people of their backgrounds, and I have heard this confirmed by many impartial investigators. Like the straights, gay people of different races and classes sometimes go to bed together, but they rarely breakfast together and still less often remain lovers for long.

Social scientists have described musicians, medical students, criminals, drug users and the urban poor as constituting subcultures. Like such groups, homosexuals have shared argot, rituals and attitudes, which are passed on from old members to new. So by the loose definition that social scientists currently use, there are grounds for saying that the gay have a subculture, though it has meager content compared to ethnic subcultures. To be more accurate, there is a cluster of gay subcultures to which some homosexuals belong, during some part of their lives, and to varying degrees.

One of the most accessible and revealing parts of the gay world is its slang. Most gay argot now in use has been around for thirty to sixty years or more, showing remarkable cultural continuity. Like all in-group argots, it affirms the user's identification with the group—an experience known to anyone who has proudly shown his knowledgeability in a special circle by using its secret phrases or salute. It upholds not only the group's differentness, but its dignity and esteem as well; insiders use the positive term *gay* and never, except in self-parody, the contemptuous outsiders' words *queer* and *faggot*. Many tend to describe themselves and others as "bi" (bisexual) on the basis of only a few fleeting or even incomplete heterosexual experiences, thus denying compulsion and "faggotry," and putting themselves on the fringe of the "normal" sexual continuum.

This, however, shows desperation to avoid the label homosexual. Having grown up in straight society, most homosexuals have internalized its attitudes toward homosexuality and unmasculine behavior, so even their stylized in-group behavior contains ambivalence and self-mockery. They call each other "faggot" with precisely the same self-denigration as blacks calling each other "nigger." Camping and drag often parody homosexuals as well as women, with a self-directed sneer. There is a similar tone of self-contempt in much gay use of feminine words, names and pronouns. The commonest gay invective is "bitch." Mary is a general form of address —affectionate but slightly deprecating—and "sister" means a platonic friend. Female pronouns are often used. One man may say of another, "She's a lying bitch. She says she and John are just sisters! Oh Mary, do you believe it!" This sort of talk, while it may reinforce homosexual identification, may also erode self-esteem.

Gay slang is also important to homosexuals in recognizing each other. If a man says with slight emphasis, "I had a gay time last night," and receives gay argot or a significant smile in return, he knows he has found one of his own and can safely reveal himself. Equally important, though, is the nonverbal "language" of gestures and symbols. Some homosexuals wear a pinky ring (so do many straight men, but in a gay setting or along with other signs it has confirming value). In gay cliques one hears that wearing certain colors at certain times—say, green on Thursdays—is a gay signal. In fact, there is a whole homosexual folklore about recognition, and only Gordon Westwood, to my knowledge, has investigated and tested it. His subjects spoke most of recognizing other homosexuals by an expression in their eyes—a haunted, searching look or a heavy-lidded, dreamy one. They also mentioned gestures, voice quality, clothes, left-handedness, small feet and wearing green. None of these things marked many of the group, though. Two thirds of the men claimed they could usually spot other homosexuals, yet 90 per cent considered themselves difficult to identify as gay. Many older, experienced homosexuals admit that after decades in the gay life, they can tell little better than heterosexuals who is gay. In fact, speculation about "who is" and "who isn't" occupies a great deal of homosexual cliques' gossip. The belief that the eyes reveal homosexuality is probably due to the fact that the gay, like the straight, use a lingering or challenging stare as a signal of sexual interest.

There are other kinds of nonverbal communication. In steambaths, patrons waiting in cubicles to be "serviced" by other homosexuals indicate their sexual preferences by lying face up to be fellated, face down to be buggered. Sado-masochistic homosexuals wear key chains on leather belts or loop steel chains over the shoulders of their leather jackets—metal hanging to the left for *M*, to the right for *S*. Drag and swishing can be considered messages, or dramatizations, about one's personality and sexuality. There has been very little thought given to homosexual behavior as a communication system, and careful study in this direction would probably lead to a better understanding of various homosexual roles and of the "scripts" for those roles.

Even study of normal sexual roles and "scripts" is just beginning, for the learning of them is unconscious, the behavior itself taken for granted. Such a perspective would be a good corrective to psychiatric theories of deviance, which tend to explain deviant behavior as resulting from unique, individual fantasies and compulsions. One can see this clearly in the case of shoe fetishism, which psychiatrists usually speak of as arising from childhood experiences. This may be true, but therefore one would expect fetishist pornography to show floppy bedroom slippers or homey scuffed flats, such as fetishists probably saw on their mothers and sisters. However, fetishist pornography always shows red or black spike-heeled shoes, such as few boys ever see in their homes. Somewhere along the way, the fetishist learned to consider the standard pornographic item more exciting—probably from the pornography itself. If there were a shoe fetishist among the Mohave, he would probably be fixated on moccasins; the question is whether exposure to pornography would teach him to find red spike-heeled shoes more exciting.

It is easy for us to see that the Mohave homosexual learned from tribal lore and living examples how to be an *alyhā*—that is, he learned how to act deviant. It is more difficult for us to see that the same learning takes place among us. One important clue is that drag, camping and other such behavior are sporadic among most homosexuals, and done in uniform ways—hardly the characteristics of compulsive idiosyncrasies. A man who goes in full drag to a party on Saturday night, in orange wig, silver nail polish and sequined dress, may act like the straightest of citizens the rest of the week. The leather freak who wears full leather-and-chains regalia to an s-m bar may otherwise be a paragon of mild-mannered normality. So many people could not have spontaneously invented these same props and rituals. And of course some homosexuals never adopt them; they reject or have never been exposed to those deviant scripts.

The three chief male homosexual roles are swish, butch and boyish. The camping and drag style is largely a magnified, distorted version of feminine stereotypes. At the opposite pole in the grossly hypermasculine butch (often s-m) style. Between these extremes is the more common good-little-boy role, less bizarre than the others but just as precisely defined, with its meticulous Peter Pan grooming and absence of stereotyped male aggressiveness. Like the others, it has a prescribed uniform; in the fifties and early sixties it called for tennis shoes, chinos and other casual college styles, but in recent years Levis, mustaches, love beads and some other hippie touches have been added.

Role-playing, in fact, is one of the most important characteristics of the gay world. When a man acts the role of a petulant, flamboyant woman or a swaggering tough or an appeasing little boy, he may create stage settings to support the parts. One feels this in the self-consciously exotic atmosphere of many gay restaurants; in the melodramatic decor of many gay apartments; in gay clothes that are a bit like costumes. The exhibitionistic behavior of some homosexuals is as stereotyped as that of a virgin girl trying to act seductive by imitating old Rita Hayworth movies. The very gayness of the gay is a game of masks, a dramatization. Much of the irritation a straight person feels among the gay is due to the fact that the homosexual's role-playing crowds out authentic behavior. The straight feels as though he is talking to actors who hold to their scripts no matter what he says to them. It is the same irritation one feels when trying to talk to someone at a cocktail party who relentlessly answers everything with cliché witticisms, according to his conception of cocktail-party charm.

Signals, rules and roles exist even in the most rudimentary and seemingly chaotic part of the gay subculture—the public cruising and pickup grounds. At first glance, one sees only a milling and somewhat varied crowd, following a few simple formulas. The gay walk their dogs on New York's Central Park West, and when pets stop to sniff each other out, so do the owners. They cruise and hustle at the "Meat Rack" at Christopher and Greenwich Streets in the West Village. They orgy indiscriminately at steambaths such as the one near St. Mark's Church (a bath known in the gay world as "Our Lady of the Mists"). They gather in Bryant Park behind the New York Public Library and, as the park's supervisor recently said, "make faces at people during lunchtime, and at night occasionally paint the busts of Mr. Goethe and Mr. Dodge with lipstick and rouge." In "tea rooms"—the public toilets in parks, subway stations, bus terminals, movie houses and YMCAs—men stand scrubbing their hands and combing their hair for hours, waiting to catch someone's eyes. They linger before the urinals, fondling their penises and looking at other men's, hoping for a word or long stare. They sit in the cubicles and tap their feet, rap on the partitions or pass notes beneath the dividing walls when someone enters the adjoining compartment. They use "apartment to share" ads in newspapers to invite calls. About the only new partner-hunting technique in decades or perhaps centuries is a gay computer-dating service based in Great Neck, Long Island, called Man-to-Man, Inc., whose ads in gay magazines begin, "How to Meet Mr. Right and Stop Trying to Fit a Round Peg into a Square Hole."

Cruising the tea rooms (or "trolling the cottages," in London) is an unlikely way to meet a lover—and indeed the code of behavior in public cruising grounds calls for brief, anonymous and impersonal encounters. Men quickly fellate or masturbate each other on the spot, in the nearest half-hidden place, or in one of their living quarters (if located nearby). Hardly a word is spoken, and usually names are not asked or given. If a name is offered, it is usually just a first name—and it may be false. As soon as the sex act is over, the men are likely to part at once. If they recognize each other later in some other place, they may act as though they are total strangers.

Some homosexuals never or rarely cruise this way, but they are almost surely a minority. According to Simon and Gagnon, between 10 and 20 per cent of the homosexuals studied by Kinsey often got partners in public terminals, and a larger proportion in other public and semipublic places.

Men who cruise risk propositioning straight men and being humiliated or attacked; being beaten, robbed or blackmailed by toughs and male prostitutes; being entrapped by plainclothesmen and ending up in court, the newspapers and jail. One's first thought is to wonder who takes such risks, and why. Scientists and novelists have said that many kinds of men take part in this public sexual marketplace, in different ways and degrees and for different reasons. Some are gay men who, for long or short periods of time, have a compulsive need for repetitive and impersonal sex. Others are predominantly straight men, some of them married, who occasionally feel driven to homosexual episodes; they tell their wives they are out on business or "with the boys" and cruise or sign into a steambath under a false name. Many such men do not know about gay bars and meeting places or are afraid to be seen in them. Some men cruise habitually, others in rare states of sexual desperation or emotional turmoil.

To stop with such a picture of the cruising scene is to stop where science usually has in the past. Out of this scene of apparent hectic sexual anarchy, sociologist Albert J. Reiss, Jr., isolated two groups of participants, whom he described in 1961 in a monograph called "The Social Integration of Queers and Peers." It is an example of the kind of research needed if we are to understand the complex nature of sex and homosexuality in society. The project took shape when Reiss discovered in a Nashville, Tennessee, reform school a number of boys who had practiced homosexual prostitution but did not consider themselves homosexual—and who, in fact, were not prostitutes or homosexuals in the usual sense.

Almost without exception, these boys had belonged to lower-class delinquent gangs. Not all such gangs practiced male hustling, but some included it in their varied delinquent repertoire. Those that did so allowed members to abstain from hustling without losing face, if it was especially repugnant to them. Reiss found that the gang boys who had hustled had learned how to do so from their peers and stopped when they left or outgrew the gangs. To them, "getting a queer" was just a transitory, part-time element in their antisocial activities, an easier and less risky way to get money than theft. It was done according to very specific rules.

New gang members learned from their pals to make contacts in places where the joint presence of lower-class delinquent "peers" and middle-class adult "queers" drew no attention—parks, transportation depots and movie houses. The adult customer nodded at the boy or used a commonly understood introduction such as "You got the time?" They then went to the man's car or a nearby hotel, where the man fellated the boy. If the queer acted in any way affectionate with the boy, he might be beaten up. He ran the same risk for suggesting sexual alternatives. Reiss asked the boys, "Did they ever want you to do anything besides blow you?" The typical answer was, "Yeah, sometimes . . . like they want me to blow them, but I'd tell them to go to hell and maybe beat them up." But if the queers stuck to the rules, so did the peers. The boys rarely beat up or rolled queers—a common sport for some gangs that do not practice hustling.

A boy's reputation as nonhomosexual was safe within the gang as long as gain rather than pleasure was his chief motive for hustling. He could even admit enjoying it as long as that was secondary. Typically, boys told Reiss, "It's all right, but I like the money best of all." This was consistent with the boys' working-class concept of masculinity, which depended strongly on a dominant, aggressive role; as in many cultures in the world, and in many areas and classes in the West, the insertor role was considered masculine regardless of the partner's gender. "The boys," wrote Reiss, "are very averse to being thought of in a queer role. . . . Fellation is defined as a 'queer' act. Even to ask a boy if he committed fellatio would provoke terrific hostility. To do more than be fellated would, in the gang, be considered acting like a queer. Some are willing to take an active role in sodomy with a boy about the same age, for instance in jail. But never is the receptor role acceptable." The boys beat up queers who used affectionate language to them because it made them feel that they were being put in a girl's role. Despite the aversion many boys felt toward their queer customers, they sensed that anger could be interpreted as emotional involvement, so they only assaulted customers who directly violated their masculine image.

Occasionally a customer gave his phone number to a boy or a boy gave his to a customer. But to maintain a continuing relationship with a queer made the boy "no better than a queer" himself, and he lost his place in the gang. Most of the boys gave up hustling as they reached their later teens. It was kid stuff, like petty theft and vandalism. Now they were young men with jobs or with careers in crime, and with regular girlfriends or wives. No one with money and heterosexual outlets could practice homosexual hustling without being suspect. The boys simply said, "I got a job and don't need that kind of money now."

Reiss concluded by saying that what he had discovered was not merely a local phenomenon. "Discussions of these findings with criminologists in Denmark and Sweden and exploratory investigations in several larger American cities . . . suggest that the description and explanation offered in this paper will hold for other American cities and for some other social systems." A few years later, the English writer Simon Raven described similar hustling by heterosexual gang members—but the "gang" in this case was Her Majesty's Horse Guards and Household Cavalry. Like the Nashville gang delinquents, guardsmen teach the ropes of male hustling to new members, if they choose to take part in it. And like the Nashville boys, most guardsmen apparently give it up when they leave the outfit.

Before Riess's paper, such boys and young men were simply ticked off as so many more homosexuals in the cruising and hustling scene. Unfortunately, Reiss did not get to study the middle-class customers who paid the boys. There are doubtless many other varied types in the cruising crowd, awaiting discovery and description. One large group among cruisers is probably young men who have just "come out" as homosexuals; the gelling of a homosexual identity often generates a total immersion of several years' duration in the gay world's social and sexual whirl.

It is at this time that many people make gay bars a major part of their lives. The bar is most obviously a sexual marketplace, creating what sociologist David Reisman calls a "cosmetic self" that emphasizes youth, physical appearance and glibness. Many of the men sit or stand with their backs to the bar, facing the room and doorway, scrutinizing each person who enters and sizing him up as a potential sexual partner. There is a predatory atmosphere, more intense than that of a heterosexual pick-up bar because the customers are young males, the majority hoping for quick sex without seduction or commitment. It is assumed that men over thirty-five will usually have to pay for partners; prostitutes also hang out in the bars to get their business. The middle-aged men usually stand around self-consciously, trying by dress and manner to seem young, and ending up with the hustlers, most of whom look more butch or more swishy than most of the bar crowd. The majority of patrons are people who in other surroundings probably wouldn't be taken for homosexual; but there is an unmistakable, distinctive quality to them as a group— something tense yet muted and lacking in open aggressiveness. At the same time there is a slightly theatrical and hysterical tone, the manifestation of narcissism, prowling and role-playing.

That, at least, is the most common gay-bar scene. Depending on the type and size of the crowd, the atmosphere may be chattery or ominously quiet. There are many gay bars in large cities, some sixty in Los Angeles and forty each in Chicago and San Francisco. Some are almost purely pickup and hustling bars, some for special types such as transvestites and leather freaks, and others almost like heterosexual neighborhood taverns (gay bars in smaller towns, where only one or a few exist, tend to be of this kind and may also entertain the local lesbian crowd). The majority of bars have a hard core of regular habitués and a changing transient trade. The regulars do not lightly bed-hop within their social clique, and a familiar face does poorly on the sexual market, so many homosexuals use one bar as a social base and seek casual bed partners in other bars in different neighborhoods.

Men try to make pickups in bars because it is safer and less squalid than cruising toilets. There is less danger of police entrapment, blackmail and unpredictably unpleasant partners. However, the bar is not a simple and happy hunting ground. There are secret homosexuals there, afraid of involvements and of being known too well; people at bars, like cruisers, often given only their first names and tell their occupations but not where they work. There is a good chance that one's pickup may want to neck and make love tenderly rather than just reach orgasm as quickly and impersonally as possible; but there is also a good chance of picking up a guilt-ridden person who loathes his partner the moment sex is over. Gay bars are an unhappy experience for many men who are shy, find the meat-rack atmosphere humiliating, and really want emotional warmth more than sex. Psychiatrist Martin Hoffman points out in his book *The Gay World* that even many homosexuals don't understand why so many gay-bar patrons stand for hours eyeing each other in silence or studiously ignoring each other. They are afraid to take the initiative and risk rejection; like shy girls in straight pickup bars, they yearn for some handsome young prince to come and carry them off, and reject any approach that promises less.

During the past decade or so, as sociologists begin to take a look at deviant subcultures, emphasis is being put on the nonsexual functions of the gay bar. It is the major public institution of the gay world—as psychologist Evelyn Hooker says, its "induction, training and integration center"—more complex by far than the cruising sector because it serves more purposes. Here the young man who has come out discovers how many varieties of homosexuals and homosexual life styles there are. He makes friends who become the nucleus of a social clique. He learns gay argot, etiquette, lore and values. He has an island of security in a straight world—the one place, he says, where he can "let my hair down," camp and proclaim his homosexuality as much as he likes. People gossip with and about friends, get the word on patrons who are "dirt" (who beat or rob pickup partners), and reinforce positive attitudes toward homosexuality. It is no wonder that some homosexuals make this haven the focus of their existence. Their sexual identity becomes the chief determinant of their lives, and they are progressively isolated from events outside their private world.

Secret homosexuals keep wider contact with the world at large, but they pay a price in peace and security. Between them and the bar's hard core of overt homosexuals there is little love wasted—though sometimes no little sex. Leznoff and Westley found that the steady bar crowd complained of "closet queers" who would "stoop down to have an affair, cruise us, take us to bed," yet would hesitate to say hello on the street the next day for fear of being publicly revealed.

Scientific investigators are finally realizing that people in gay bars are a small fraction of the homosexual population. Some men avoid bars because they are shy, don't drink, dislike the marketplace atmosphere, or fear to be seen there. The middle-aged feel out of place there and make a social life elsewhere. Steady homosexual couples prefer to avoid the temptations and jealousies of the promiscuous bar life. After the coming-out period and a fling at the bars, men tend to center their social life in cliques of friends and private parties. They subsequently drift back to the bars only occasionally or between affairs.

Gay social cliques consist of friends and couples. They sometimes go to bars and restaurants together, but mostly they meet in each other's homes to talk and drink. Martin Hoffman describes a typical gay party that took place in the suburban home of a homosexual couple who had been "married" for six years. Party presents for the guests were all sexual —tubes of KY Jelly (used as a lubricant in sodomy), pictures of nude males, pornographic drawings. The conversation relied almost entirely on sexual jokes and innuendoes, giving the event an adolescent air—this obsessive concern with sex characterizes gay conversation. There is gossip about sexual exploits, men's physical attractiveness (large penises and butch appearance are highly valued), the alleged latent homosexuality of all the world and especially of famous men (from Jesus Christ to John Wayne). Another common theme is the repulsiveness of the female body; the female genitals are rated as the most disgusting of earthly sights.

This "sex fetishism," as it has been called, leads many to believe that homosexuals are devoted to full-time sexual musical-chairs. Kinsey showed that the reverse is true, and recent studies reveal that in fact there is least action where there is most talk, within social cliques. "In any particular age group," said Kinsey, "in any segment of the population, it is never more than about 5.5 per cent of the males who are having homosexual relations that average more than once every other day (3.5 times per week)." By comparison, 25 per cent of straight men average more than that, and 24 per cent of married males average more than six times per week in their busiest periods. Because of the difficulty of finding acceptable partners and/or emotional inhibitions, homosexual men have a definitely lower level of sexual activity—despite the impression given by talk and by a minority who are promiscuous at certain times in their lives.

Leznoff and Westley say that their subjects believed sex tends to destroy friendship; they carefully kept friends and bed partners separate. This was confirmed in 1967 by anthropologist David Sonenschein when he studied the homosexual community of about a hundred men in a southwestern city and checked the findings against gay groups in five other cities around the country. Homosexuals he interviewed categorized people as "best friends" (usually two to five in number), "good friends" who were liked but not in their intimate cliques, and sexual partners. When asked about sex with good and best friends, the men spoke of " 'knowing them too well to have sex' and/or that sexual needs were amply satisfied from other sources. . . . Whether the category of 'friends' is really a residual category of individuals who did not work out as sexual partners . . . is a matter now set for future research." The splitting of social and sexual life is another new discovery that begs for study and interpretation.

Almost everyone who has written about gay life has called it pretentious, absurd, pitiful or repugnant. The great majority of homosexuals seem to vouch for the accuracy of its depiction in *The Boys in the Band*, a play replete with jealousy, competitiveness, insecurity, malice, tantrums and hysterical mood shifts. To accept all this as a price for companionship, the homosexual must get important rewards from the gay milieu. In a hostile society in which he must guard each word and reaction or become a pariah, the gay world is a refuge of security, warmth and support. It is the one place where he can camp and express his sexual desires and identity, making up for hours, weeks and years when he didn't dare announce "I'm gay!" In this island he is reassured that the whole world is really gay, or would be if it didn't fear its hidden inner self; that homosexuals are a worthy part of humanity; that they are a wronged and perhaps superior minority; that homosexuality is fate, and to resist or try to change it foolish, cowardly, or at best a waste of time and money.

It is understandable that this verbal and behavioral proclamation—"I'm gay!"—should be shrill and a bit frantic, for it is born not just of frustration but of ambivalence. It attempts to drown out another inner voice, which developed before a defensive gay ideology was learned—"I'm queer!" The gay world reflects this ambivalence by pushing down with one hand what it props up with the other. While saying that "gay is good," it puts a premium on butchness, mocks "faggots," and confirms the homosexual's separateness from the straight world. Deep involvement in the gay life tends to heighten alienation from the mainstream of society, which may already be great because of lack of involvement with a family and community.

The happiest, "healthiest" homosexuals, it is often claimed, avoid the gay life entirely and live in homosexual "marriages" that last for years or even decades. The English psychiatrist Renée Liddicoat wrote in 1961 that almost half the homosexuals he had studied had maintained liaisons for more than five years; this is probably the most extravagant claim of gay-marriage stability ever made. West in England, Giese in Germany and countless American scientists and homosexual writers agree with Kinsey's conclusion that long homosexual relationships between men are notably rare. Many homosexuals say they are looking for a lasting affair and are quick to shack up, but in fact have a series of brittle, stormy, short-lived relationships. Schofield, who is often strenuous in trying to show the normality of many homosexuals, says that half of the best-adjusted group of homosexuals he studied had had affairs longer than a year. A one-year affair is no criterion of emotional stability for heterosexuals, and there is no reason to make it one for homosexuals. Homosexuals often argue that straight marriages would last no longer than gay ones were it not for legal sanctions. They seem to think that only constraint could keep families together; my impression is that many, probably because of the families they grew up in, think of a family as an unhappy place from which anyone would try to escape. But the majority of straight men, despite all their grumbling, apparently prefer family responsibilities (and rewards) to bachelorhood; many who don't want family commitment find ways out of it regardless of legal restraints.

Homosexuals have been justified, though, in claiming that the straight world has a distorted picture of gay mateship. The stereotype presents one member as effeminate, the sexually "passive" male "wife" who stays home to do domestic tasks. The other is the "husband," who takes a masculine social and sexual role and supports the couple. Homosexuals have claimed that this is not usually true, and Sonenschein confirmed that only a small proportion of the gay "marriages" he saw fit this description. This minority had a wedding ceremony, acted out dichotomized roles, and had a very romantic conception of ideal, unending love. Their relationships were not very stable or long-lasting. "It seemed that in fact, the ritual, rather than being an attempt to cement the relationship, was more of an excuse for the ever-present and ever-needed party. It seemed in a sense to reintegrate the group in terms of its own values, particularly those that mock the heterosexual world." A psychologist who has counseled many homosexuals said to me, "I find that the more settled homosexual couples, the ones who live together any amount of time, have the same conflicts as heterosexual couples, and some can be helped to reach more harmonious relationships in the same ways. But generally homosexual mateships remind me of the more splenetic heterosexual marriages."

And as Sonenschein accurately pointed out, effeminate behavior is sporadic for the majority of homosexuals, and few take a consistent masculine or feminine role socially or in bed. Among most gay couples, he said, "division of labor in terms of household duties was a matter of personal choice rather than any function of so-called masculine or feminine roles." This commoner, more stable kind of mateship involved the exchange of rings and setting up of a household, but it was based on shared interests and values as much as on ceremony, sex and romance. Couples who thus paired off without fanfare and withdrew from the gay life seemed to have a better chance of staying together.

Sonenschein also noted that the search for a steady partner is not as widespread as many have claimed; younger men especially may be content with sexual adventures or a series of affairs. "It was usually only after 'aging' (about age thirty) that finding a steadier mate became a significant concern." He also warned against assuming that homosexuals who live together are sexually involved. Many become roommates in order to live more cheaply, have companionship, and share each other's social resources. Roommates often fall into the asexual "good friend" category, and split-ups are usually due to conflicts over financial responsibility, domestic matters or personality clashes.

This sounds quite mundane, familiar and normal. Recent social research has tried to demythify the homosexual and show that he does not belong to a separate, bizarre species. He must earn a living, have lovers and friends, cope with family, aging and the other usual phases and crises of life. The question is whether he does so differently from others. Three relatively new concepts have been used to try to find out—career, deviance and stigmatization. Sociologists now use the word career in relation not only to occupation but to any activity running through a person's life. The word deviance is used, as neutrally as possible, for behavior that diverges from social norms. Such sociologists as Edwin Lemart, Erving Goffman and Howard Becker have elaborated the idea of deviant career, claiming there is a common pattern in the lives of such different deviants as homosexuals, drug users, jazz musicians, prostitutes, asylum patients, the physically handicapped and members of some ethnic minorities. They see deviance not as a quality of the deviant person but as a result of interaction between him and society. Putting the idea in its simplest, most extreme form, Becker says, "Whether an act is deviant . . . depends on how other people react to it."

Sociologists of deviance stress labeling and stigmatizing as crucial in deviant career. As Goffman points out, sex is one of the "master status-determining traits" that lie at the heart of a person's public and inner identity. When a person is labeled homosexual, his former identity becomes secondary; it is as though he finally became what he "really" was all along. Homosexuality (like addiction, being black, being an ex-con) is paramount in his identity, outweighing his social class, profession and personal qualities. Society sees the labeled deviant stereotypically and puts him at a distance, saying he is now a basically different kind of person than normals, generally inferior, tainted, dangerous, unable or unwilling to behave like other people. This sociological wisdom was long ago encapsulated in a bar-room joke about a small-town pariah who explained his status to a stranger: "I built a great bridge, and do they call me Pierre the bridge builder? I made a million dollars, and do they call me Pierre the millionaire? No. But just suck one cock. . . ."

According to the sociology of deviance, this stigmatization drives people farther into deviant careers. They identify with the subculture and return society's hostility in a bitter, mocking and supercilious way. One way to show hostility is to flaunt one's stigma by public swishing or by living up to normals' stereotypes—Anatole Broyard calls the latter behavior minstrelization, from the way some Negroes hostilely act out white stereotypes. (Sociologist Ned Polsky illustrates this counterhostility with jazz musicians' view that everything a square does is ridiculous, and tells of one who privately titled his theme song, "If You Don't Like My Queer Ways You Can Kiss My Fucking Ass.") Flaunting provokes more hostility from normals, which in turn confirms the deviant's stigma and anger. This mutual provocation has a built-in regulator—the deviants' own ambivalence. They see themselves through normal eyes and rate a member of their group according to the prominence of his stigma. In fact, they may try to act more normal than normals—stable, masculine, not promiscuous or defensive. "Passing" is considered disloyal to the group, and faggotry brings scorn on it. Therefore deviant views and behavior alternate between bravado and cowering.

Theorists of deviance also point out that various deviant groups have similar ways of bolstering their esteem against the normal's-eye view. They develop an ideology full of historical, psychological, scientific and legal justifications for their way of life, showing that they are "normal" yet different and superior. For instance, sociologists who have done research with prostitutes say that they claim they are like other women but less hypocritical, for wives give sex only to get support; that they are better in bed than wives; that rich and famous men pay just for their conversation and company; that they help preserve the institution of marriage; that customers, being exploiters, should be exploited. This mixture of bitterness with claims of normality and of special good qualities sounds familiar to one who has read the parochial literature of homosexuals and of oppressed ethnic groups.

Like such ethnic groups, homosexuals talk and write about their martyrs and heroes through history, of sufferings at the hands of the majority, and of triumphs over them. Some scientists are re-evaluating gay life in terms of what the psychiatrist Gordon Allport, in his book *On Prejudice*, called traits of victimization—self-hatred, protective clowning, and an attitude of dependence and passivity. Wainwright Churchill, in his sympathetic book on male homosexuals, says that as a group they have "all the vainglorious pride, all the contempt of self, all the chauvinism, all the sense of alienation coupled with a desire for conformity, that are characteristic of any other persecuted minority." In recent years psychiatrists Martin Hoffman and Evelyn Hooker have said that some qualities usually considered psychological components of homosexuality are actually common ego traits among all types of victimized people. The victimized, they believe, tend to be anxious, guarded, withdrawn and obsessive-compulsive.

Homosexuals' notorious preoccupation with sex, according to this view, results from society defining sex as a problem for them—just as black preoccupation with race results from white bigotry.

However, public labeling isn't necessary for a person to experience such feelings: self-labeling and anticipation of labeling are enough. An adolescent boy who develops a homosexual identity can afford honest intimacy only with other homosexuals if he wants to avoid catastrophe in his home, school and neighborhood. If he is religious, he feels a sinner in the eyes of his church. When people tell jokes about faggots, guess who is queer and brag of heterosexual conquests, he has to join in, lying, hating them and hating himself, knowing that he too could be the butt of their laughter and hatred. He must keep his lies consistent, yet always wonder whether he is suspected—like a girl who has lost her virginity and guiltily wonders whether people can tell. As years go by, he must deal with all the problems of passing that face light Negroes, unidentifiable Jews, ex-convicts and former prostitutes. If he does not reveal himself and is then discovered, he is discredited; if he reveals himself, the reaction will probably be negative anyway. He may create a façade of normality—sometimes leading to such bizarre situations as being a policeman or judge and having to arrest or convict people for what he does in secret. The price in paranoia and guilt is large. Westwood says that more than half his subjects tried at least once to stop all homosexual activity, in vain, to suffer depression, remorse and self-loathing. And this was in a relatively well-adjusted group of homosexuals of whom only 10 per cent were markedly effeminate. Even if one creates a heterosexual façade of army service, marriage and family, he himself is likely to feel a hollowness in living up to those role expectations out of shame and fear.

The sociology of deviance is a good scientific and humanitarian influence, stressing what deviants have in common with the rest of society. It has made scientists aware of ways they stereotype deviants and treat them like similar packages with nasty labels rather than as human beings. It emphasizes the high price paid by both the labeled and labelers for such stigmatizing. Furthermore, the concept of homosexual career is starting to enrich and change clinical views. The homosexuals most visible to society, and most often seen as patients, are those in what now seems to be a phase that follows coming-out, when they camp, flit from partner to partner, and adopt social models from the gay world. Such things have often been seen as basic components of homosexuality, though they may be, at least in part, an episode in a psychosocial process.

The tendency to see homosexuality as a career with stages has gone hand in hand with a growing conviction that the pathology of homosexuality has been exaggerated. Simon and Gagnon say that now, "instead of exceedingly vague and somewhat utopian goals, we tend to ask more pragmatic questions: Is the individual self-supporting? Does he manage to conduct his affairs without the intervention of the police or the growing number of mental health authorities? Does he have adequate sources of social support? A positively balanced and adequately developed repertoire for gratification? Has he learned to accept himself?" They conclude from data on 550 homosexuals studied by Kinsey and his associates that most homosexuals cope quite well, considering the "stigmatized and in fact criminal nature of their sexual interests."

Martin Weinberg, looking at results of current Kinsey Institute studies, also suggests that deviants, like other people, manage to deal with the usual problems of life, and often in common, familiar ways. Aging comes sooner to homosexuals than heterosexuals, due to the terrific premium on youth in the gay world. The lonely, aging "auntie," trying to carry a fragile and varnished Peter Pan quality into middle age, is a specter before the eyes of young homosexuals—or as they pungently put it, "Nobody loves you when you're old and gay." The aging homosexual must cope with his new undesirability without support from wife, children or usually even a secure, lasting relationship with another man. Almost everyone who has written about homosexuality speaks of higher-than-average rates of depression and suicide among them, and some of this is attributed to the loneliness of aging.

Weinberg did find that gay men over forty-five had fewer partners and less sex than the young, and were more likely to live alone and without contact with the gay world. However, he found that happiness and good adjustment steadily increased with age among homosexuals. Those over forty-five were less worried about exposure, less prone to psychosomatic illnesses and negative self-image, and more self-accepting and happy than those between twenty-six and thirty-five. Studies of heterosexuals show the same lessening of self-doubt with age. It may be achieved through lowering of youthful aspirations or by adapting realistically to life's possibilities, depending on one's point of view. The young may find this happiness unenviable, and a married straight man may find it difficult to imagine that he could be happy in such a life—but the fact remains that many older homosexuals make their own peace with aging, with their special problems, and with life in general.

There is much to criticize as well as praise in the work of sociologists of deviance and some of those they influence. They emphasize "drift," or gradual chance involvement, as a reason for becoming deviant. They minimize self-labeling and self-destructiveness, laying most of the responsibility for deviants' problems on the nondeviant. They take statements of contentment at face value, studiously ignoring psychodynamic evidence. They claim that homosexuals become isolated and neurotic chiefly because they have been labeled—for instance, Michael Schofield concludes that the male homosexual basically "has few marked differences apart from his choice of sexual partner." After criticizing psychiatrists for lumping all homosexuals together and calling them sick, they tend themselves to lump all homosexuals together and call them healthy or merely victims of social pressure. In short, they have bent over backward to normalize deviants, sometimes so strenuously that one can't help feeling they identify very strongly with their subjects.* The result is a naïve, one-sided and grossly oversimplified picture.

Psychiatrists have made a good case for the theory that some men flaunt and cruise to invite the punishment this behavior may well bring. They suggest that some people latch onto hostile subculture patterns because this provides an outlet for preexisting paranoia and hostility. Homosexuals themselves, despite expressions of contentment with being homosexual, almost all say, sadly or fervently, that if they had children they wouldn't want the children to be homosexual. Martin Weinberg says that most of the homosexuals he interviewed emphatically agreed with the line in the play *The Boys in the Band*, "Show me a happy homosexual and I'll show you a gay corpse." Homosexuality conflicts with every influence, from parental upbringing to broad social attitudes, and most people grow up quite aware of the rewards for heterosexuality, the price of deviance. It makes little sense to see homosexuality other than as a compulsion. As Dr. Gebhard says, "Almost nobody chooses to be homosexual. . . . Anyone who has to live a life that cannot be integrated into society cannot really enjoy it."

We know that there is no society without norms, and none that sanctions adult predominant homosexuality. The sociologists of deviance have made a humane, realistic and scientifically sound effort to humanize deviants. In their zeal, they have sometimes passed off conviction as fact, spoken as though society can exist without norms and sanctions, and unnecessarily polarized the scientific community. But perhaps they will make some people realize that norms need not be as rigid as some of ours dealing with sexual conduct, that deviants need not be stigmatized so severely, and that sanctions need not be excessive and cruel.

The strongest argument against the sociology of deviance is that some of its convincing logic doesn't always hold up in field research. Weinberg, studying the Kinsey Institute's preliminary data on the social adjustment of more than fifteen hundred male homosexuals, does not find that public scandal, stigmatizing and subsequent commitment to overt homosexuality necessarily create greater maladjustment in later life. In fact, most research on deviant career has been done with delinquents, drug users and the handicapped. It may be too ambitious to say that all or even most deviants have similar careers. Much more study will be needed.

This is the note that most talk about homosexuals in society comes back to: more study. We have had endless sociologizing, but little real sociology. There remains a vast unexplored territory for study in sex behavior, roles, learning and attitudes. As little as we know about male

---

* One well-known sociologist of deviance said to me that although he has never studied homosexuals, he thinks they must be pretty healthy. However, he objects to the unscientific prejudices of those who "label" deviants.

homosexuals, we know even less about lesbianism, homosexuality among blacks and other ethnic minority groups, prison homosexuality, sexual offenders, and the rarer deviations. After a look at these subjects, it will be possible to venture some conclusions about the nature of what we call normality.

INTERVIEWS

Don and Dick have shared this apartment in Brooklyn Heights for a couple of months. Don is in his middle twenties, tall, thin and bespectacled, with straight light hair. He is a bit fastidious and prematurely sedate, but not effeminate. One might guess that he is a reserved graduate student in philosophy from an upper-middle-class family. Actually he is in the executive-trainee program of a major corporation, where his homosexuality is unknown. At moments he loses his donnish air and becomes funny in a twinkly, sly way. He had many years of psychotherapy after a suicide attempt in his teens. Dick, his lover, is a few years younger, short, slim, pretty in an almost cherubic way. He is rather swishy and exhibitionistic; his speech is feverishly quick, and it seems impossible for him to sit still for more than a moment. The mutual acquaintance who has put me in touch with Don and Dick has told me that Dick was a hustler on West 42nd Street not too long ago. He and Don are trying to make their relationship last. They are like many couples, homosexual and heterosexual, in that one is controlled and overserious, the other sparkling and funny. But in their case the contrast is extreme, and at moments they bring to mind old comedy skits about a professor and a chorus girl. Edward, a neighborhood friend who has dropped in to visit, is tall, a bit pudgy, and so shyly tense that he seems ready to implode.

After we have chatted for a while, I explain what my book is about. Don says authoritatively:

Read the sociologist Festinger on the theory of cognitive dissonance. It really explains homosexual behavior and attitudes. The concept "homosexual" becomes a person's starting point for developing an identity, and that's what you need to define a group as a minority. Homosexuals are a typical minority group.

[Don turns to Edward for confirmation, but Edward ducks his head, answers with half sentences, and declines to discuss the matter. Don and Dick chide him for lacking wholehearted commitment to a homosexual identity. He becomes even more withdrawn. I feel that all this is quite self-conscious; the ice hasn't been broken. Then there are two long phone calls, one for Don and one for Dick. On the phone, both act progressively campy, make sexual innuendoes, and call the other party Mary. I seem unconcerned, and when we talk on, the atmosphere is more relaxed. I have passed the test: I do not condemn or laugh at them. I now ask them to tell me about distinctions within the gay subculture in New York. They disagree on some points, and it becomes clear that neither knows the gay world authoritatively, any more than most other people have a complete and objective view of their own sector of society.]

DON: The area around Broadway and 71st Street has swishy Spanish [Puerto Rican] fags, some Negroes—very effeminate guys, real trash, very badly educated.

DICK: No, you don't get the point! Those are leather boys hanging around up there, a different bunch from the ones on Christopher Street. Now, the East Fifties bars are another story. Homos and heteros both cruise there in the early evening. Gay executives go if they know it's safe. They aren't really part of gay life. Half the time in those places you can't be sure who's gay and who isn't. A lot of the discothèques have mixed crowds, too. But there aren't any real gay dancing bars left now.

DON: The West Village has people who are younger and more open. Up to about twenty-four, I'd say.

DICK: And prettier. Much prettier boys there. But there are some slightly older professional people there.

DON: Yes, lots of the artsy, full-time homosexuals in their early twenties and late teens, and future professional people. It's a kind of coming-out area for young people, some of whom graduate to uptown lives.

What about ethnic groups? Are they different?

DON: Very different. Most of the Negroes I meet who are gay just toady to whites, want to mix with them.

DICK: They'll fuck anything. But they don't look down on being gay the way whites do. They have their queens—I mean, there are straight men who have women but also have queens they fuck on the side, and they aren't considered homosexual by themselves or other people. Now, the Puerto Ricans aren't like that at all. Their queens are real queens.

DON: Yes, with them you're either *muy macho* or swishy. Just compare the Spanish queens with a gay bar in Oklahoma or the deep Midwest.

EDWARD: A gay bar there looks like a college bar. It's open and friendly, and not swishy at all. People wear very conservative clothes.

DON: It isn't tense and scared, like gay bars in New York. And that's true to a lesser degree of gay bars in, say, Philly or D.C. But look who go to the bars in New York—people who have to dress up in public. But Holland is really the place to be.

DICK: God, yes! It's really like paradise. Very quiet, very free. Now by comparison, let me tell you, I got arrested in the West Village a few months ago. I looked as straight as could be, and there was a girl with us, but the other guys were very swishy types. We were picked up and treated with all sorts of verbal abuse at the station. When we came in, the cop yelled, "Here's another six!" It sounded as though they had a quota to meet. But let me tell you, as soon as I gave my lawyer's name, it changed from "All right, Mary, move your ass!" to "Excuse me, sir!" But you know, it isn't the cops who make life tough, it's the latents.

DON: Yes, and the ones who come to work in your office can reveal you no matter what you do. There was one at mine who kept looking and looking at me. I was sure someone would notice. Finally I sat down across from him at lunch one day and stared right back into his eyes. He got good and scared, and he hasn't even looked at me since.

DICK: The real trouble is that the latents are afraid of being revealed to themselves. My boss at my last job was a real hunk, a real football-player type. He was always asking me questions, like why I didn't go out with girls. I was afraid he'd keep asking questions, and then one day he'd discover his own latent homosexuality. . . .

[*Dick goes on and on about a dreadful but unspecified disaster this would cause. There are many glances at me, to check my reaction. Now and then Don breaks in with subtle digs about the latency of all straights; in fact, the more straight they seem, the more homosexuality they must be fighting. Dick talks faster and faster, working himself into a hysterical spin, more swishy, more feverish, trying to outrage me, put me on and turn me on all at the same time. I just listen, and he keeps escalating. Don and Edward are getting very embarrassed. Dick is giving long descriptions of his sex experiences, with as many details and four-letter words as possible—and the point of it all is still the homosexuality of apparent straights:*]

I fucked him and fucked him, and there I was, with my balls still slapping up against his ass, and all the time he's talking to me over his shoulder, denying that he's really homosexual! . . .

[*Don finally tells him curtly to shut up, but this has only a momentary effect. Dick's wild monologue ends only when we break up for dinner. A month later, I pass Don and Dick in the West Village. They wear chinos, sport shirts and loafers; they look like any rather proper, conservative college boys. We exchange pleasantries. A couple of months later our mutual acquaintance tells me, "Don is doing fine, but Dick is in Bellevue. He cracked up." Two years later I hear that Don has committed suicide.*]

Martin Weinberg is a sociologist on the staff of the Institute for Sex Research. He has written about nudists and other social deviants, and now he is at work summarizing the data of the Institute's preliminary study of homosexuals' social adjustment.

As you know, this data hasn't been completely analyzed yet. But one basic finding is that the more a homosexual becomes involved with other homosexuals, the better adjusted he is. The lonely homosexual hasn't learned to see homosexuality as being at least neutral, let alone positive. Other homosexuals help him to normalize his homosexuality to himself, and to neutralize the negative view nonhomosexuals have of him.

So keeping most of one's social relationships confined to heterosexuals and being a closet queen usually aren't good adjustments. The homosexual who's best off is one who has a homosexual roommate and doesn't feel that others react to him with disgust. What's crucial is whether homosexuality runs too deeply against his old self. Whether he allows himself to be engulfed in the homosexual world, and to draw support from it, depends on what he brings to it—job, social class, church affiliation, values, whether or not he lives with his family, etc. Exactly how these things link up still remain to be examined in the data.

You could say, then, that the homosexual's job is reducing the dissonance in his thinking about homosexuality.

Well, most of us live with a fair amount of dissonance throughout our lives. It's rarely perfectly resolved. For instance, a number of homosexuals are generally pretty well-adjusted people. But when we talk, they mention the play *Boys in the Band*, with its presentation of the suffering, silliness and nastiness you see in some homosexual atmospheres, and they say, "That tells it like it is!" You know, the guy in the play says that there's no such thing as a happy homosexual. Yet when I ask, "Are you happy?" many say, "Yes, I'm not unhappy because of my homosexuality." If you can convince yourself positively that you don't suffer from self-contempt and the contempt of others, it doesn't matter much who dumps on you or what the public thinks of homosexuals.

How much have you found that bears out the idea of deviant career, the step-by-step progression in life and attitudes?

That's an interesting point, because the basic aim of this study was to show how homosexuals adapt to society, and how that adaptation affects them psychologically. Now, Howard Becker, who's written about deviant careers, says that labeling is a crucial factor. If you put a deviant label on a person, or he puts it on himself, it pushes him further along the track of a deviant career. We checked on homosexuals who went through the armed service without trouble as compared with those who received other than honorable discharges because of their homosexuality. There was strong short-term reaction to discharge, but after a relatively brief time they learned to adjust to the label without much difficulty, suffering or rancor. In the long run, the lives and adjustments of the two groups weren't very different, despite the labeling of the less than honorable discharge. It's true that our sample included only those who'd developed a deviant career; it lacked those who stopped short or reversed it. But we did have the officially labeled and unlabeled, and in the long run we found few differences.

What about aging? Did you find the old saying true—"Nobody loves you when you're old and gay"?

That was another surprise. It gets harder to find partners as you grow older, but the older a homosexual is, the better-adjusted he seems to be. Let's face it, everyone makes necessary adaptation as they get older. The older homosexual has less sex than the younger one, but he isn't as hung-up as the younger guy. He's learned to accept his predilections. He definitely isn't the hung-up guy the young homosexual describes when he talks with terror of turning twenty-eight.

Alan Bell, who has been the principal investigator in the Kinsey Institute's second study of homosexuals' social adjustment, explains the plans for the project.

In our first study we found the "many homosexualities" Evelyn Hooker talks about—differences in the kinds of sexual relationship that are sought, in self-concept, attitudes toward one's own and others' homosexuality, degrees of overtness and secrecy. Now we're hoping to measure these various adaptations more precisely. We'll also focus on the experience of psychotherapy, past and present family relationships, and the usual areas of psychological and social adjustment. We'll study not only homosexual men and women, white and black, but parents, siblings and a control group of about a thousand heterosexuals. I'm interested in the psychodynamics and etiology of homosexuality, and I hope that in a study including the interests and methods of psychology, sociology and anthropology we may find out more surely what kinds of backgrounds and homosexual patterns are related to better adjustments than others.

Who's funding this project?

The federal government—the National Institutes of Mental Health. Listen, if you put anything in your book, put in this: we drew up a plan for a study of the psychosexual development of children and adolescents; we approached twenty-five private foundations, and every one said that sex was out of its bailiwick. We wanted to find out about kids' behavior, fantasies, knowledge of sex, stages of development, the influences on them of parents, school, peers, church, mass media. Children have been researched to death in every area but sex. But we still live in a basically erotophobic society. No private foundation would touch the study with a ten-foot pole! People say they want facts, and that sex taboos have broken down. But just try to get money to gather the necessary facts about sex. Even now that sex research has almost become respectable.

Homophile organizations continue to increase and multiply; even though they still represent only a very small proportion of homosexuals, they are making themselves heard socially far beyond their size. Phyllis Lyon was one of the eight founding members of the Daughters of Bilitis, the largest lesbian association in the United States. She is now vice president, under Ted McIlvenna, of the Council on Religion and the Homosexual, with an office at the Glide Foundation in San Francisco. She gives the impression of a cheerful, articulate lady executive in her middle years.

The Daughters of Bilitis began back in the earliest years of the homophile movement. The Mattachine Society, for boys, began in 1953, the first such group in the country. In 1955 there were Mattachine chapters in San Francisco and Los Angeles, and they had started to publish the magazine *One.* That was the year the DOB began, but we knew nothing about Mattachine and *One.* It started as a social club, so that people wouldn't have to meet in bars.

What was the bar scene like then?

San Francisco was more open in the late forties and early fifties than it is now. That was when I came here. There were lots of male and female gay bars and groups around North Beach, and places with male and female impersonators. A lot of women ran around trying to look very butch. My friend and I tried going to bars, and we felt like tourists. We were afraid to strike up conversations with strangers. Today there's less open lesbian life, and less obvious division into butch and femme types. You find that more among kids, and it drops away as they get older. But even then most lesbians felt that nice women don't go to bars alone. What's more, considering most women's salaries, they can't afford going to bars very easily. And you get a rougher element at bars. So how can lesbians meet each other? That's their biggest problem. I think there are as many female as male homosexuals, but they're more scared. They're caught in the same trap as most women—second-class citizens with all the usual hang-ups women are raised with. It isn't easy for them to be aggressive and go hunting partners. They're more concerned than men about what family and friends would say—in fact, they're more afraid of opinion than of the law. And of course they grew up hearing that homosexuality is immoral and sick. So lesbians tend to be secretive, solitary, and in constant terror of being found out. Many DOB members belong under pseudonyms.

Are homosexuals who belong to homophile groups representative?

Some people come to DOB because they see there are things to be accomplished legally and socially. Some join anonymously by mail and can't be gotten out of the woodwork enough to answer anonymous questionnaires. Many come because they need partners but don't dig the bar scene. But DOB was set up so that people with problems would come, find supportive groups or in some cases counseling, and then go out into the big world on their own. These are still a big percentage. DOB's membership remains pretty static, somewhere under a thousand, but the people change. Here in San Francisco there's an almost totally new group of members every few years. I suspect that roughly the same situation exists, to a degree, in lots of homophile groups, male and female.

DOB has many chapters, doesn't it?

Yes, one in New York, of course. Our Philadelphia chapter recently withdrew because they want to be for both boys and girls. SIR, the male homophile group here, tries that. They have about forty girls. But the women don't really get involved. They join a homophile group for different reasons than males. The male groups emphasize the legal side of things—entrapment, enticement, criminal law, VD. The women aren't much involved with criminal law and aren't the least bit interested in VD. Their problems are more in civil law—for instance, how two women can own a home together. Besides, women want to run their own organization, and the men always want them to do the typing. The homosexuals are worse this way than heterosexuals, and the heterosexuals are pretty bad!

DOB and CRH have gotten homosexuals and scientists to meet and talk. What have the results been?

Both sides have learned a great deal. Clergymen and social workers and policemen have talked to homosexuals who aren't sick or criminals, and the homosexuals have spoken to informed experts. They both understand each other better. But I must say, at the last such meeting, when a lot of the lesbians in the audience heard the experts talking about the love-making of lesbians, we just had to laugh. They really don't know.

Antony Grey is the harried, overworked director of the Albany Trust, the only major organization in England dealing with male homosexuality. Besides putting me in touch with individuals who can help me gather information, he spends a few hours and a lunchtime talking to me about the work of the Trust. When we first meet at his office on Shaftesbury Avenue, he explains the origins and activities of the Trust.

This was originally the Homosexual Law Reform Society. It was formed six months after the Wolfenden Report's appearance in 1957. It was not a homosexual organization. Some homosexuals were involved, but so were archbishops, M.P.s, psychiatrists and others. The present legislation still leaves something to be desired, but the main thrust of the Homosexual Law Reform Society achieved its goal. Now the Albany Trust is trying to work on the next major steps—education, guidance, case work, and so on. We have contact with government figures, and some distinguished heterosexual trustees and patrons. In fact, comparatively few homosexuals know of the Albany Trust. It is financed by donations and subscriptions, and we have to work despite the attitude that sex is not a respectable subject, even for academic study.

Then it isn't a homophile organization.

It's still inconceivable that such a group as the Mattachine Society could exist here. There is much less organized homosexual subculture in England, and until recently even few openly homosexual clubs. Here homosexuals guiltily keep their homosexuality split off from the rest of their lives. Few are open enough to even discuss it in public, as American homophile groups do, despite all their imperfections. I'd say it won't happen for at least five years.

Then the change in law hasn't changed people's lives very much.

It's beginning. Witch hunting has ceased gradually over the last five years, and now more advances are possible. Still, the homosexual's sense of isolation from society is his greatest problem in England. We'd like to see integration rather than the development of a homosexual subculture. A lot of popular ignorance will have to disappear first. Police see homosexuality as an infection spread by corruption of the young. While psychiatrists have rather too great a grip in America, they are denigrated somewhat here. Sex education exists in schools only by local assent, and it's not universal. Even among scientists there's often ignorance. I talked to a group of psychiatrists, and the chairman said, "This is a problem most psychiatrists know very little about and rarely come across."

Are there female homophile groups?

There are three in this country. I think lesbians feel even more isolated than male homosexuals. They tend to have a great chip on their shoulder. To be a woman and a lesbian is a double disadvantage.

Do you think there is more homosexuality today in England?

I don't know. In any case, there are more people, and if the old ratio remains, the number of homosexuals is larger. We need a Kinsey type of study here.

What sort of counseling do you offer?

The law reform brought more freedom of discussion, and more people asking for guidance, so we added a social caseworker to our staff a year ago, and requests for counseling snowballed.

What sort of training does she have?

Her experience has been with youth, alcoholism and welfare—mostly practical social work.

No specific training in psychodynamics or sexual deviation?

No, but she's an excellent and understanding caseworker. We feel that if we adjust people's fringe problems, their sexual problems often fall into line. Anxiety makes schooling break down. Then discovery brings a series of sharp rejections, from the Boy Scouts, the church choir, even their families. So we often see a young person out of work and school, away from home, his fringe problems building. We insist that young people tell their parents about themselves. We tell the parents that their child's present sexual orientation may be temporary or permanent; in either case, it's better to accept him, not create a crisis for him, and gentleness helps. We say, "Stop thinking of your needs, and think of his. Even if you hope he'll change, treat him as a whole human being. He is still your child, as before." Often children report improved relationships with the parents. We recently had two boys here, one sixteen and one twenty, and we urged each family to have its son's friend to tea and get to know him.

Mightn't you be, in effect, reinforcing exploratory homosexual relationships?

Everyone is partly homosexual and partly heterosexual. If a person has heterosexual urges, he will experiment with them, I think. Sometimes we recommend psychiatric care, but one must sort out temporary adolescent problems from real ones.

Can most sixteen-year-old boys having homosexual relationships easily experiment and choose? The homosexuality may arise from difficulty relating to girls.

I believe one should experiment and choose, and find one's true balance. Especially at a young age, such traumas can upset people, and we don't want to shake them up more by sending them to psychiatrists. For instance, many young homosexuals don't go to church because of their homosexuality. They're happy if we can guarantee a sympathetic talk for them at their church. This sort of thing can prevent them from becoming psychiatric patients.

Clark Polack has become a nationally known leader in the American homophile movement in recent years. He is executive secretary of the Janus Society and editor-in-chief of the magazine Drum. *He is also founder of the Homosexual Law Reform Society, which has a speakers' bureau and provides legal and financial aid to homosexuals who have been arrested or threatened with loss of their jobs.*

Polack lives in Philadelphia, where he has a book-and-magazine distribution company. Our contact tells me, "He says he isn't sure whether you and he have anything to talk about. He says that if you call him, he'll decide whether he's willing to see you." On the phone I start to explain what my book is about, and he asks abruptly, pugnaciously:

I'd like to ask you a few questions to see whether we have anything to talk about. Do you think homosexuality is a sickness?

I don't think homosexual acts are in themselves pathological, and I don't think a person who's homosexual is necessarily more disturbed than many heterosexuals.

Okay, then maybe we have something to talk about.

[*He gives me his business address. The office is in a big loft full of stacks and cartons of magazines and paperback books. A few of the magazines seem to be girlie magazines, but most are male nudist publications. Several packers and office workers are busy. Polack makes me wait for him for ten or fifteen minutes. When we begin to talk, he seems tense and hostile. I ask about the aims of the Janus Society, and he makes several vague replies. I keep trying to rephrase the question. Finally he says:*]

All homosexual societies have the same aims, solving the legal, social and religious problems of the homosexual. Janus publishes *Drum*. There are about fifteen thousand people associated with *Drum* and Janus in one way or another. Janus doesn't have a strict membership role. It exists all over the world, with members in every state.

Does Janus have activities other than publishing Drum?

Drum is its first activity. Knowing that all the rest of the world is antihomosexual, we present something entertaining and informative for homosexuals from a prohomosexual point of view.

[*I make several attempts to find out more, and learn nothing. He asks to know more about my book.*]

My publisher and I think a book should be done that . . .

That sells! [*He interrupts with a hard smile.*] I know, I'm in the book business. They want a book that sells.

I'm sure they do. I wouldn't mind it myself. But that still leaves a few differ-rent possibilities. I . . .

Why didn't you start with the homophile societies?

[*He seems to be trying to pick a fight, and I try to avoid it.*] *Considering the number of homosexuals in the country, the membership of homophile societies are only one aspect of homosexual society. I have no idea whether they're repre-sentative groups or not. That's one of the things I was hoping you could tell me about.*

You should have started with the homophile societies.

In any case, I'm here now, so . . .

Look, there's only one kind of book that will sell. A good modern thing in the same approach as Daniel Webster Cory's. Something written by a homosexual. As I said, I know, I'm in the book business.

I'm trying to see the agreement and overlaps between various fields of study and compare what's said with what I find myself.

It's been done. Have you read *One in Twenty*? [*He leans forward expectantly in his chair.*]

Yes, and within its limits it's better than most books on the subject. But it doesn't evaluate scientific work at any length.

[*He leans back in his chair and looks at me with scorn.*] Look, you guys are all the same. I hear the same bullshit from you guys every time, and then you go and write the same palaver afterward.

Who are we?

We don't need you heterosexuals coming in and telling us what it's all about. You all say your book is going to be different, and you all have the same bias.

Funny, that's what I think of most of the books written by homosexuals.

Name one!

Cory.

What's wrong with it?

[*He is sitting forward again in his chair, angry but eager. I have finally risen to the bait; I can see hours of argument ahead—in which, if my amateur psychol-ogizing is correct, he will continue to bait me to fight him, and he will run through all his defenses and counterattacks, and end up feeling justified. I de-escalate to my previous bland tone, suspecting, however, that my refusal to argue will make him angrier than any argument I might offer.*]

I'd like to talk about it with you, but I think we could discuss other people's books for hours. Really I came here because I thought you might be able to tell me some things I don't know.

You all do the same thing. Look. This is one faggot who knows the score. I'm writing a book myself. We don't need you to write books for us.

You know, I think maybe you really don't want to talk.

No, I don't think I do.

[*I walk out, feeling that I leave behind a man with a sense of triumph.*]

29

Other Outsiders

The words sexual deviant make people think of slight, pale males rolling their eyes at other males. Aside from the fact that only a minority of homosexual men fit this stereotype, gay men are only one group in a wide spectrum of deviants. Lesbians probably fascinate people more than any other sexual outsiders—except perhaps prostitutes, part of whose allure to the prurient is their reputed homosexuality. The idea of two men in bed does not titillate women, but many men find the sight of two women in bed erotically exciting. Lesbian exhibitions are often requested in brothels, and mutual female love-making is almost obligatory in pornography. (Some psychoanalysts say this interest reflects hidden male homosexuality. Dr. John Money suggested to me, equally sensibly, that two women may simply present a double visual and psychological stimulus.) Even many men who are not especially attracted by lesbianism view it with tolerance or mild amusement; their masculine identity and sense of social righteousness are not as threatened by female as by male homosexuals. This light attitude may be partly responsible for the great lack of study of lesbians. Another reason is lesbians' apparent rarity compared to gay men.

This inconspicuousness has given rise to legends about secret armies of single and married lesbians ("the housewife next door," etc.), but in fact there are just far fewer female than male homosexuals, and a smaller proportion of gay women than gay men live in an organized subculture. As we have seen, Kinsey found that a third to half as many women as men are primarily or exclusively homosexual. He also showed that they resemble other women more than they resemble straight or gay men—for instance, the occupational level of their parents has little influence on their sex lives, but their own level of education does. Among women thirty and older, homosexual response and experience increase along with schooling.

Educational Level	Homosexual Response	Homosexual Contact	Contact to Orgasm
Primary school	10%	9%	6%
High school	18	10	4
College	25	17	10
Postgraduate	33	24	14

Kinsey believed that "moral restraint on premarital heterosexual activity is the most important single factor contributing to the development of a homosexual history, and such restraint is probably most marked among the younger and teenage girls of those social levels that send their daughters to college." In college, he said, girls are further restricted by administrators; this and their delay in marrying interfere with heterosexual development. Furthermore, people in upper educational levels tend to be more frankly accepting of homosexuality. So, Kinsey believed, intellectual liberalism about homosexuality, along with heterosexual restrictions, produce more lesbianism.

There is a lesbian subculture, with its own neighborhoods, gathering places, coffee houses, bars, restaurants and clubs. The majority are within or near areas frequented by gay men, such as the West Village in New York and Fire Island outside New York. Lesbians sometimes go to men's gay bars and parties, especially in small cities, where deviant circles are limited, but they usually prefer all-female groups. Female cruising is quite rare, and lesbian prostitution almost unknown, though rumors sporadically circulate of lesbian brothels in Hollywood, Paris and Capri. There is only one lesbian bar for every dozen male gay bars in major cities. Gay women, like straight women, are raised to consider sexual aggressiveness demeaning, a loss of dignity and worth. Going to bars to pick up or be picked up is as difficult for them as for the straight—perhaps more so, for many lesbians seem moralistic and inhibited. In the last decade or so lesbian clubs have opened, such as the Gateways in London, to provide women with gay meeting places without a hard bar atmosphere.

Conventional feminine attitudes have many effects on the lesbian career and subculture. Simon and Gagnon point out their origin in basic differences in male and female scripts for sex and love. Typically, boys commit themselves to sex at puberty by masturbating; through ensuing years they find love relationships increasingly important. Girls, to the contrary, first learn the rhetoric of love, and then discover themselves sexually during romantic involvements. The majority of women who masturbate begin to do so well after puberty, as a result of sexual response in petting or coitus. This is true of gay women as well, and the result is a later average coming-out than among gay males. Lesbians, committed to romance before sex, may be drawn to women for years before engaging in homosexual acts. According to Kinsey, only 2 to 3 per cent of women who have had homosexual experience to orgasm did so during their teens.

Just as most homosexual men are not markedly effeminate, most lesbians are not grossly masculine in appearance or manner. Changes in women's clothes and life style in recent decades make it even easier for them to live without traditional frills, marriage and dependence on males yet not be labeled deviant. It is also easier for a woman than for a man to live with another person of the same sex and avoid suspicion. Our stereotype of the unmarried male is sexual—the randy bachelor; two grown men living together are likely to be thought of in sexual terms. Our stereotype of the single woman is asexual—the desiccated spinster; two women rouse fewer thoughts of sexual activity.

Furthermore, we do not stigmatize and punish lesbians as harshly as male homosexuals. Few are harassed, and fewer prosecuted. They may even be considered ideal employees. Many of the 195 lesbians studied in the mid-sixties by sociologist Rita Bass-Hass said that their bosses knew they were homosexual but gladly kept them on; it counted in their favor that they had to be self-supporting and were without obligations to husbands or children. Nevertheless, lesbians feel the same shame, isolation and fear of being publicly revealed as gay men. They are as characteristically deviant a subgroup, for they have internalized the dominant society's expectations of women. They experience the same alienation as gay men when they see their friends date, marry and have children. Few take refuge behind a façade of straight marriage; less than 1 per cent of women who have married engage in homosexual acts while wed. A small number of lesbians form maternal, quasi-sexual relationships with gay men, and in a very few cases marry them with the understanding that both will have sex lives outside marriage. A significant number of women have heterosexual marriages, get divorced, and then begin homosexual involvements. Lesbianism remains primarily an activity of single women, and to a lesser degree of the divorced and widowed.

Less is known about the occupations of lesbians than of gay men. They are notoriously overrepresented in the theater, modeling, striptease and the dance, prostitution and the armed forces. There may be large numbers of lesbians among those in the professional careers most open to women, teaching and nursing. In any case, to keep jobs above the lowest occupational level, most lesbians retain a semblance or even a perfect façade of femininity. But after a day's work as a waitress, secretary, teacher or saleslady, many of them remove their make-up, put up their hair, and take part in the gay life.

The gay subculture of women in many ways resembles that of men. It has the same veneer of buoyancy over a bedrock of depression; the same extravagant expectations of relationships, and fear that few will last long; the same sense of alienation from the rest of society; the same defensive, self-flattering ideology. Clubs and bars offer them the same advantages; they can meet partners, drop their heterosexual or asexual masks, flirt without offending the straight, gossip, and have a sense of belonging. One hears the usual prohomosexual ideology and talk of how crude, lustful and untender straights are—that is, straight men. Lesbian love, to the contrary, is portrayed as romantic and sweet. Just as many gay men talk with disgust of women, many lesbians, speaking of men, express cold or vehement revulsion. There is a tendency to close ranks against reporters and curious straights—especially male ones. Lesbian gathering places have the same air of hysteria and obsessive sexuality as male gay spots, but there is an added edge of hostility. A man who walks in may meet anything from silent bristling to physical threats from the bulldykes.

However, lesbians apparently differ from gay men in being even less likely to choose partners from different backgrounds. The well-informed author of the lesbian chapter in *The New London Spy*, a guide to underground London, says that "teachers talk to other teachers, factory workers and petrol pump attendants clan together with lower-paid office workers and bus conductresses." A black lesbian bar crowd studied in St. Louis by Ethel Sawyer of Washington University made fine class distinctions in the gay world. Their first criterion was ability to get along with a mate for a long time, and the second was that a couple should be "trying to get somewhere." At the fifth, or bottom, social level they put "the loud and dirty ones who are boisterous and make trouble." The subjects put themselves a notch higher; they were mostly working class (a few were middle class), openly homosexual and part of a gay-bar crowd, but not drastically antisocial. Above themselves, at the third level, they classed more ambitious and steadily mated people who stayed outside the bar life. At level two were lesbians they considered intelligent and who had more money, such as owners of bars, restaurants and beauty parlors. At the top were teachers, doctors and other professional people, alleged to be so secretive that "no people outside of the life and very few in the life know they are gay." Sawyer's subjects seem to have sought partners mostly in their own circle. When they looked outside it, they turned upward to levels two and three (of the top and bottom extremes, they said, "I know they are there, but I don't know who they are"). Conventional feminine respectability, or at least aspiration to it, was the rule. Bass-Hass's group included both whites and nonwhites; the races mixed socially at their gay bar, but did not form sexual couples or permanent pairs.

The most important difference between the lesbian and gay male worlds is in roles. The words butch and femme do not really correspond to the male butch and queen, nor do the roles they describe. The male butch is normally heterosexual in manner, perhaps hypermasculine. The queen, who takes the opposite-sex role, is scorned; other gay men will say of him, "She's only a queer." In Westwood's homosexual group, although 10 per cent were effeminate, only one preferred effeminate partners; they wanted "real men." But among lesbians, the femme, with the "normal" role, is not the most admired one. Her status is lower or, at best, ambiguous. We have seen that the male role has more prestige among both sexes in most or all societies, and this is true among lesbians. The aggressive, controlled, and controlling dyke has highest prestige. This makes lesbians' role priorities different from gay men's, and they hold to the roles more rigidly. They look down on women who are "kiki"—alternately butch or femme, depending on their lovers. Sawyer's subjects derogatorily called role-switchers "pancakers," suggesting people who can be flipped over from one sexual position to another.

The butch and femme roles correspond to those of a straight couple, and they carry through from sex behavior to social manner and dress. The butch wears fly-front trousers, men's shirts and flat shoes, her clothes conceal her breasts and buttocks, and she may bind her breasts to flatten them. Her hair is cropped short, and she wears cuff links and other male accessories. She always holds the femme's coat, opens doors for her, lights her cigarettes. Sociologist Suzanne Prosin studied twenty lesbian couples and found that it mattered very much to them which partner wore more tailored clothes and shorter hair; if both had long hair, one kept her hair longer or wore a wave in it to mark her as the femme. The typical stud (butch) in Sawyer's group made passes at women in public and generally did everything possible to proclaim her lesbianism. She took pride in "turning out" girls (introducing them to homosexuality), and in winning them away from other studs and from men. She denied she had ever been a fish (femme) and said she wanted nothing to do with men—as one subject said, "There's nothing more hypocritical than a pregnant stud." Actually, some studs had coitus and even bore children after entering "the life," but they tried to keep all heterosexual activity secret. As studs they had achieved the ultimate status in lesbianism, and if they failed to live up to it, they would be scorned as mere pancakers. Having taken the male role, they bragged of their conquests, and often left their fish home at night to go out seeking one-night stands. Studs tended not to struggle to sustain relationships, for they were greatly outnumbered by fish, and the fish competed for the attention of prestigious studs.

Being feminine, the femmes in Bass-Hass's group were competitive about dating and bragged of going steady or having many dates—but they were as anxious not to be considered promiscuous as most straight girls. If they had many one-night stands, they were looked down on as sluts and whores by the entire group, and rejected. In fact, Bass-Hass believes that this attitude is an important reason for many fish turning stud. A fish who slept around could lose the "slut" stigma by switching to the sexually aggressive masculine role and have, in effect, a new start in the gay life.

Ideally, the stud was the protector and financial provider, but in practice it sometimes worked the other way around. Many fish could be lured away by men, and unlike the studs, they did not feel committed to homosexuality or the gay life. They tended to see themselves as victims of their own curiosity rather than "innately" homosexual. They dated men openly and often, and about two thirds said they wanted to marry men eventually. During the sixteen months of Sawyer's study, some fish went back and forth between studs and men several times, disappearing and reappearing on the gay scene. They were generally careful not to reveal their homosexual activities outside the gay bar, and might pretend not to know studs on the street. Unlike many studs, they were publicly unstigmatized and remained steadily employed. Some gave their studs financial help and even became their sole means of support. The studs, in turn, tended to see fish as dabblers in homosexuality, "bisexuals" who were "neither fish nor fowl," and perhaps primarily people from whom to get money.

Of course some fish were quite committed to homosexuality in the femme role; they were considered "definitely homosexual" but "all woman." Many femmes not only keep a conventionally feminine appearance but become little-girlish and dependent. They may permit themselves to be domineered and jealously nagged in return for total support and control. The extreme butch-femme relationship was portrayed in the play *The Killing of Sister George.* Some have objected that this play, like Mart Crowley's *The Boys in the Band,* exaggerates and stereotypes homosexuality. It is true that the average femme does not drink from the toilet bowl at her butch's command, as Childie does for Sister George, and that most gay men's parties do not follow Crowley's script. Nevertheless, the portrayal of roles and personal interaction is basically accurate and fits many homosexuals to a greater or lesser degree. A play about any problem or obsession is likely to emphasize its negative aspects, whether that problem is homosexuality, militarism, middle age, delinquence or America-Firstism. The more a trait dominates a person's life, the more he becomes monochromatic and stereotypic. The two plays do not dehumanize homosexuals and make them tragi-comic any more than some extreme homosexuals do so to themselves.

We still can't be sure how many lesbians take part in the subculture, how many outside "the life" take dichotomized roles, or how many varieties of lesbian career they may follow. Sawyer, in her bar group, found that some of the women had discovered homosexuality as early as fourteen or fifteen, with an intimate friend of equal inexperience. Many of them had been influenced to do so by cousins or older sisters who were already lesbians. There were at least three sets of sisters in the bar group, and Sawyer heard constant reference to mothers, cousins and nieces who were gay. A number of lesbians had been turned out by older women, usually studs. If a stud had been brought out by a fish, the stud had been quite young at the time, and the fish considerably older.

After entering the gay life, says Bass-Hass, girls may be much in demand, but as they approach thirty, they find themselves in keen competition with younger girls appearing on the scene. Like gay men that age, they start to restrict their social life to small groups of friends who meet in private homes. They form cliques that do not easily accept single people, who could create rivalry and disruption among the couples comprising the group. At this time, having dropped out of the gay life, some may act out dichotomized roles less dramatically, both partners showing a mild, almost equal amount of butchness. At forty, the cliques tend to break up, and couples become isolated and out of touch with other lesbians. If relationships end at this time of life, it is very difficult finding new partners. Lesbians in their late forties may, with luck, meet younger divorced women, disappointed and hostile to men after bitter experience with marriage, and good candidates for the protective older lesbian. As psychiatrist Charles Socarides says, "Women can easily regress to a mother-child relationship with another woman who will take care of them at times like first menstruation, first intercourse, a disappointing love affair or a divorce."

Some such couples, Socarides adds, "protect each other and depend on each other; there is often very little actual sexual contact." There are also couples who have sex regularly through their relationship, and most studies agree that by age thirty the majority of lesbians have progressed from kissing and petting to cunnilingus. However, despite the promiscuity of some aggressive butches and participants in the bar life, most lesbians' sexual patterns resemble straight women's. Of the lesbians studied by Kinsey, 71 per cent had had only one or two bed partners (as compared with 51 per cent of gay men with only one or two). Only 4 per cent of lesbians had had more than ten partners (as compared to 22 per cent of gay men). Three quarters of the women who were having homosexual acts to orgasm did so once a week or less—the usual orgasmic frequency of single straight women. Some women had intense sexual activity for days or weeks, then none for months or years; gay and straight women are more able than gay and straight men to undergo long periods of sexual abstinence.

There is general agreement that lesbians are more likely than homosexual men to form stable, lasting relationships. Some stay together for five, ten or fifteen years, and have joint bank accounts and jointly owned homes. In some cases, one has children from a past marriage; the women may keep separate apartments or form a household of mother, children and "aunt." Many childless lesbian households have a stifling hothouse atmosphere; as Bryan Magee said, there are two people with motherly and wifely potential but only each other to give it to.

Sawyer found a high premium put on long relationships, and the same hopeful fantasies many gay men have that "this time it will be the real thing, it will last." Lesbian mateships are long-lasting compared to gay men's, but not compared to heterosexual ones. Sawyer's subjects pointed with pride to couples who had stayed together as long as eight years, but these were exceptions. They agreed that few couples lasted more than three, and even this turned out to be optimistic. When Sawyer ended her research, only one person had the same mate as when the project began. It is true that this observation comes from the bar world of pugnacious studs and flirtatious fish, where friends were often only waiting for the right time to pounce on each other's lovers, and where fights ending in stabbings and suicide attempts might occur between jealous mates and rival studs. The couples who retreat from this world to the privacy of their home and small social circle stay together longer, but probably not, in most cases, for as long as lesbian apologists like to believe.

One of the indications of the existence of a wide variety of lesbian careers was the background difference between Bass-Hass's 125 white and 75 nonwhite subjects. Three quarters of the white lesbians came from very strict homes; many had parents who warned them "how easy it was for a girl to get into trouble," and taunted them when they brought boyfriends home. Most of the whites had seldom or never had a sexual relationship with a man, or even a close nonsexual relationship with one. Only three had had children. On the average, they began having homosexual relationships between seventeen and twenty-two.

The nonwhites presented a different picture. Most grew up in homes where the father was partially or totally absent. The mother was the breadwinner, and therefore away from home a great deal; when home, she openly had sexual involvements with a series of men. The girls dated males extensively in their early teens, and by sixteen they had had considerable experience, usually including coitus. By the time they were in their early twenties, most of their friends had had babies, married or lived "common-law," and had perhaps been abandoned one or more times. Many of the lesbian group had experienced these things themselves. They were determined not to go through life increasingly burdened with children, economic hardship and unsteady men. They saw men as harsh and exploitative, lesbian relationships as secure and companionate. A number of them, while carrying on lesbian relationships, were still living with children, male mates, or both. Their average age of first lesbian relationship was between twenty-three and thirty, five to seven years later than the whites. In short, the black lesbians were far more likely to have tried and retreated from heterosexuality.

Equally important differences are turning up in the first preliminary studies of black male homosexuals. These studies are so significant, and so promising as models for future research, that it is worthwhile to backtrack for a moment to see their origins in the study of the black subculture, and the concepts from which they grew.

For decades people have described the way slavery and racism splintered the black family and emasculated the black man, robbing him of assertion and respect in the eyes of his women, his children, society, and himself. A quarter of the black children in the United States live in homes headed by women, and in urban areas the proportion is half; even where both parents are present, the woman may be the respectable breadwinner, the father struggling against a sense of impotence in society, work and relationships. In 1951 Abram Kardiner and Lionel Ovesey of Columbia University wrote *The Mark of Oppression*, still the classic social-psychiatric study of how the black ghetto shapes emotional development. Predictably, they found in Harlem acute problems of assertion and dependence, often expressed in such symptoms as success phobia, potency problems and pseudohomosexual anxiety. Ovesey went on to write his papers on homosexuality and pseudohomosexuality in men, and masculine aspirations in women, as expressing assertion-dependence conflicts. Dr. Herbert Hendin, a contemporary of Ovesey at Columbia, used this adaptational framework in studying suicide in Scandinavia to see how different social traditions and pressures mold the emotions. This project posed problems that would eventually lead him to undertake the first depth study of male homosexuality in the black ghetto.

In *Suicide and Scandinavia*, in 1964, Hendin showed that Denmark, Sweden and Norway have different frequencies and patterns of suicide, which corollate with different psychosocial climates. In competitive Sweden, where boys are pushed away emotionally by their mothers at a young age and urged to perform socially to win parental acceptance, the suicide rate is high, and people most commonly commit suicide when they fail to achieve their social and career goals. In the cozy, tight-knit society of Denmark, where mothers create great dependence and passivity in their children, suicide is also widespread, and most commonly happens after a dependency loss (divorce, end of a love affair, death of a spouse). In Norway, where there is less emphasis on the patterns found in Sweden and Denmark, suicide is relatively rare; in pietistic, rural Norway, when it does occur, it is often the result of feelings of moral failure. In short, said Hendin, sociologists and psychiatrists should stop trying to find one pattern to explain suicide; there are many kinds of suicide, reflecting different and complex psychosocial forces. In the course of his research, Hendin had noted that homosexuality, like suicide, varied in the three countries and might also be a good barometer of psychosocial tensions.

Hendin said that "it was only in the Danish sample that either overt homosexuality or anxieties connected with homosexual behavior were encountered with any frequency . . . . overt homosexuality or the fear of being homosexual occurred rather infrequently among the Swedish and Norwegian patients, despite the search for both in the two countries. Particularly in Sweden it might be suspected, because of the strong competitive pressures upon the men, the early mother-child separation and deep-seated conflicts between the sexes, that the rate of homosexuality would be high." But this was not the case. In fact, Hendin guessed that homosexuality was less common there than in the United States. "If confirmed by further studies of homosexuality in Scandinavia, this finding would seem to indicate that the passivity shown by Danish male patients tended to be more decisive in determining a homosexual adaptation than Swedish competitiveness or hostility to women."

Hendin then investigated black-white differences in suicide; as he did so, the problem of homosexuality turned out to be more prominent than in his Scandinavian project. Like suicide, sexual conflicts seemed more common and debilitating in the ghetto than in white society. Four of the twelve suicidal men Hendin described in depth in his book *Black Suicide* were homosexual; a comparable white group contained only one homosexual. The samples are very small, but the psychiatric content, and findings by other researchers, suggest that wider studies might show similar differences. Since devoting a chapter to homosexuality in *Black Suicide*, Hendin has been studying more homosexuals in Harlem, in preparation for a book on the subject, So far, he has told me, six further cases bear out what he wrote in *Black Suicide*.

Like Kardiner and Ovesey before him, Hendin found that the need to adapt to a frustrating society and home situation dictated by pervasive racism creates neurotic as well as real problems with competition and passivity. Hendin's homosexual subjects, like Sawyer's black lesbians, grew up in homes where the mother was the overburdened head of the household; she herself had been deprived of nurturing and someone to depend on, and had trouble giving what she hadn't received. The children felt frustration and rage at the maternal deprivation they suffered, and a sense of being domineered by females. The black homosexuals saw their mothers as cold, rejecting and controlling, and blamed them for making them afraid of women. However, they still had an unfulfilled need to depend passively on their mothers, and remained bound to them in anger. One of the suicidal homosexuals tried to kill himself when he learned that his mother planned to marry, and again after having a fight with her and trying to give up homosexuality.

Most of the boys' fathers had been absent a great deal, and violent when present. The boys were intimidated and unable to identify with them. They saw heterosexuality as assaultive and frightening. The idea that blackness is dirty and violent ran through all of Hendin's case histories; the majority of the ten black homosexuals he has so far studied in depth prefer white partners. "For all the black homosexuals in this study homosexuality was an escape from the destructive heterosexuality invariably associated with the brutality of their black father. . . . For them, the homosexual act included a symbolic incorporation of whiteness—a whiteness that signified freedom from anger—and could, if only temporarily, relieve them of the pervasive feeling of being loathesome 'black bugs.'" Of course this reflects the attitude of the dominant white culture, with its fantasies associating blackness, violence and eroticism. Martin Hoffman points out that cities outside the South have few black gay bars; a gay bar that started out black would immediately be invaded by whites seeking sexual transfusions of blackness.

At first this sounds like the family background attributed to many white homosexuals, a domineering mother and absent father. And because of the large proportion of fragmented black families, one could logically expect a larger proportion of black than white homosexuals. However, Hendin points out a crucial difference. The white pattern usually involves an antisexual mother and an absent, detached or passive father. To the contrary, the black homosexuals' mothers were openly sexual—involved, to their sons' deep unhappiness, with a series of men. The father was totally out of the picture for only one of the ten homosexuals, so paternal violence was a recurring threat. Hendin points out that six of the ten had been potent with women, more than one would expect in a similar white group; this brings to mind Sawyer's black lesbians, with their extensive heterosexual experience. We do not know whether in fact there are more homosexuals in the black ghetto than in white society, or whether larger studies would continue to show greater heterosexual elements in the lives of black homosexuals. Nor do we know, if these findings were borne out, whether the reason would be the difference in family background (sexual mother and violent father) or the influence of a sexually permissive peer-group during adolescence. We have only some ingenious and frequently convincing probes in depth, which need validation on a large scale.

Hendin's work in Harlem, like his study showing that there are many kinds of suicide, opens important avenues of research. It suggests that there are many homosexualities, with quantitative and qualitative differences, each reflecting a different psychosocial environment. Dr. Marvin Opler has pointed out different homosexual and schizophrenic patterns in Italian-Americans and Irish-Americans. Kinsey died before he could complete his sociosexual profile of our society and specify such differences behaviorally. No one has picked up the task. However, two other unique homosexualities have been described, each clearly the result of a special environment and begging a multifactor, social-psychiatric research approach. One is homosexuality in men's prisons; the other, anatomized only in the past decade, is homosexuality in women's prisons.

Popular belief says that men in armies and prisons turn to each other for sexual relief—in most cases without becoming permanently homosexual. Kinsey found no increase in homosexual behavior during either world war, so apparently men who engaged in it in the army would have done so anyway. Even in prisons, homosexuality is not the norm. When Donald Clemmer made his classic study of prison culture in the early thirties (*The Prison Community*), he found that 10 per cent of his convict subjects had been homosexual before entering prison. Another 30 per cent had homosexual activity only or mostly in jail. Fully 60 per cent performed no homosexual acts in jail. Subsequent experts on prison life— Kinsey, Fishman, Robert Lindner and others—agreed that only 30 to 45 per cent of prisoners engage in homosexuality; research by the Kinsey Institute showed that those who do so attain frequencies of only one tenth to one fifth of their outside rates. Prison is a sexually dulling and inhibiting environment. In short, prisons do not necessarily make men homosexual; they create pressures to which a minority of prisoners succumb.

Most researchers have found that many of the prisoners who were confirmed homosexuals before entering prison were effeminates; many had been arrested for homosexual prostitution. In many penitentiaries these "fags," "queens" or "screaming bitches" must live in segregated cell blocks and work gangs, usually in the kitchen and laundry. They give feminine touches to their uniforms and use substitutes for rouge, lipstick and eye makeup—the black material on the striking band of a matchbook, mixed with water, takes the place of mascara. They swish about parts of the prison to which they have access, selling themselves for cash or commodities. Some find an inmate to act as a protector and settle down in prison marriage, but many are promiscuous and are a constant source of trouble, provoking jealous fights between other prisoners.

At the other extreme of the prison population are the "wolves," or "jockers." Many come from the disorganized "culture of poverty" that floats below stable working-class life. They have had wide sexual experience before prison, and like so many people from lower social levels, have a strong taboo against masturbation. They may be committed to a rigid code of *machismo*, and a life style built on affirming their masculinity among other men through aggression and domination. Robert Lindner, author of *Rebel Without a Cause* and for years a prison psychiatrist, said that many of these men have psychopathic personalities. They are predatory and impulsive, without empathy or conscience; they view other people as objects to be used or destroyed. The wolf was heterosexual outside prison; on the inside he uses weaker prisoners, dominating them and, in effect, womanizing them and masturbating in their bodies. He expresses no tenderness and takes only the insertor role, affirming his masculinity through violence and conquest. To himself and other prisoners, the fact that he used the body of another man to do so does not compromise his manhood or heterosexuality. His object may be an effeminate or a "punk."

The punk, or "lamb," probably entered prison heterosexual. A con who is young, good-looking and in for the first time is likely to become the object of wolves' campaign to make him a punk. His new stigma as a con threatens to supercede all previous identities. He is not yet con-wise, and feels threatened on all sides. Imprisonment robs him of autonomy and his usual ways of winning status and esteem—achievements, women, money. All this makes him feel helpless, dependent and in a state of general emotional shock.

He finds that in prison, men have fallen back on the adolescent male peer-group code of competition and dominance. One must fight for one's rights and status, refuse to chicken out, and never be a coward, whiner or informer. (This code persists more strongly in adult life in lower social classes, from which most prisoners come.) Wolves threaten the new con, pressure him, mock him, test his courage. He is told he will be gang-sodomized, mutilated or killed if he doesn't submit sexually. Sometimes the wolf alternates threats with gifts and protection; the punk is frightened and in debt. Finally he is told he must "fight or fuck." Lindner quoted a letter from a wolf to a reluctant lamb: "I'm going to give you one more chance. If you know what's good for you you'll follow my advice. You didn't get everything I gave you for nothing. In this world you got to pay for what you get, you know. Which would you rather have stuck into you—my shiv or you know what." Sometimes a group of wolves threaten the new con with gang rape, and another wolf steps in to become his protector—for a predictable price. The newcomer decides it is better to have one partner willingly than three or four unwillingly, in a "gang splash." He does not know that the whole thing was prearranged by the "lone" wolf and his friends.

Now the new con, deprived of old ways to validate his masculinity, threatened with rape and humiliation, may undergo acute homosexual or pseudohomosexual panic, a classic sort of prison breakdown. If he is brave, tough and lucky, he stands up to his pursuers and is left alone afterward, a man in the prison world. If he is unlucky or lacks the requisite toughness, he gives in. If very unlucky, he is subjected to sodomitic rape and as a result feels totally shorn of his manhood, despite his resistance. The young con who becomes a punk is shoved into a feminine role and held in derision along with the fags; it doesn't matter that he was "made that way" rather than "born that way." His degradation and feminine status bring to mind the transvestites of warrior societies. The erosion of masculinity by terror, mockery and assault was vividly shown in the play *Fortune and Men's Eyes*. Not long after it appeared, there was a national scandal about sodomitic rape in Philadelphia jails. However, this was nothing new to people familiar with prison life. This sort of thing takes place in many local prisons and detention houses, perhaps a little less in penitentiaries for long-timers, which are usually less crowded and more strictly supervised.

It seems that sexual deprivation is far from the chief motive for prison homosexuality. Rather, homosexuality becomes an instrument for establishing rank and status, validating masculinity, and creating protective-dependent relationships. (Some long-timers form rather companionate prison marriages, with a parody of parent-child rather than heterosexual roles.) The attitudes and policies of many prison officials and guards are contradictory, ineffectual or outright destructive, alternately punishing and ignoring sex and violence among prisoners. The answer to prison homosexuality is not only conjugal visits, but a way of providing prisoners with a sense of status and manhood in ways less imitative of hostile primates. Unfortunately, we still have no studies of the majority of prisoners who become neither wolves nor lambs. It is likely that personality and sexual patterns established before imprisonment account for prison sex life at least as much as the conditions of confinement. This is even more true in women's prisons, where deprivation of a sense of womanhood creates more bizarre varieties of homosexuality.

In the sixties, psychologists David Ward and Gene Kassebaum studied the inmates of the Frontera penitentiary for women in California and showed that psychological and social needs were far more pressing than sexual ones. Of 293 women who answered a questionnaire, only five said that lack of sex with men was the hardest thing to adapt to in jail. Absence of home and family was given as the chief problem of 120. When asked why girls "turn out" as lesbians in prison, one said, "They need to be loved, everybody has to have someone." Another explained, "There's a lot of homosexuality because women are more emotional. They find in jail that they have to depend on themselves. They need someone to talk to, so they get friendly, which leads to sexual intimacy."

Even more than men, women depend on their erotic and biological nature for fulfillment. In jail they are no longer lovers, wives, mothers, daughters and family members. They lack sources of admiration, love and support. They suffer at least as much fear, ego damage and identity crisis as men, but they do not have men's same-sex peer-group experience to fall back on; men's prison society promotes not only brutality and competition but solidarity and familiar roles and codes of behavior. Women prisoners tend to see each other according to society's usual feminine stereotypes—untrustworthy, devious, less reliable than men. There are no "right guy" and "snitcher" roles among them. Squealing to the authorities is common and goes unpunished by other prisoners, so the new arrivals feel they have no safe place for confidences and support. While men have been brought up to be concerned with the reactions of other men to their conduct, women are more concerned with being cared for and found attractive by one important person. As a result, they are ripe for intimate relationships. In most prisons for long-term inmates—that is, felons and minors—violence and threats aren't needed to induce newcomers to enter sexual partnerships.

It is true that in some local women's prisons there are violent bulldykes who threaten new inmates with beating or disfigurement unless they submit sexually. This seems to occur mostly in overcrowded jails for short-term prisoners, where most inmates are addicts and prostitutes. Some of the very aggressive butches there are both addicts and pimps; on the outside their femme lovers work as prostitutes for men to support both their own and the dykes' drug habits. Some of these "king dykes" are generally psychopathic and assaultive, like wolves in men's prisons. Accounts of New York City's house of detention for women say that such ferocious bulldykes terrorize other prisoners at will because even the guards are afraid of them. Some women do become homosexually involved in jails under pressure, as punks do in men's prisons, but probably fewer, and for shorter periods.

Ward and Kassebaum found that such incidents did not occur at Frontera, yet half of the eight hundred inmates became sexually involved at least once during their sentences there. The roles and behavior resembled those seen in lesbian bars. The butches—a third of those homosexually involved—had high prestige. Many older, con-wise butches had learned that if they dramatized their masculinity too much, it only got them into trouble with the authorities. Only one butch in three, therefore, was a "drag butch." The drag butches cropped their hair in "DA" or pixie style, sat with knees spread wide, held their cigarettes between thumb and forefinger, and didn't shave their legs. They wore pedal-pushers if they could, and stole men's underwear from the laundry (which washed clothes for men's prisons). They acted out the male stereotype of control, strength and independence. Many, the researchers noted, were markedly unattractive—underweight or overweight and afflicted with skin problems. Many, though not all, of the butches had been homosexual before prison. The majority of prison femmes were "JTO's," or jailhouse turnouts; they had been heterosexual before prison and expected to be so again after release. A small number of JTO's became butches. Some of these were very unattractive women for whom this was their only hope of winning prestige and attention; a few were very pretty women who thus continued to win the high status they'd been used to on the outside. Before leaving prison, the JTO who had become butch would "clean herself up"—resume feminine appearance.

A butch began her campaign to turn out a new prisoner by heaping gifts and flattery on her. If the seduction was successful and an alliance was formed, the femme did the butch's sewing, cleaning, laundry and bedmaking; the butch offered protectiveness and commissary goods in return. Usually the butch performed cunnilingus on the femme, but at first allowed no reciprocation. Remaining "untouchable" served many purposes. It made seducing the guilty, inexperienced and hesitant girls much easier. It also put the femme in the butch's debt and under her emotional control. To the butch, it proved that she could satisfy her woman "like a man."

Most important, though, it protected the butch emotionally. She was committed to homosexuality and scorned dabblers who played at lesbian relationships for passing fun or easy profit; actually, she feared committing her emotions and showing her needs to such a person and being hurt. In a third of the lesbian relationships, the butch stayed untouchable for a long time, even remaining completely dressed during sex. Some femmes were relieved at first not to have to reciprocate, but many eventually wanted to do so. This would ease their indebtedness and feeling of being controlled, and demonstrate their feminine ability to please. Eventually, the butch would "give up the works"—ask for reciprocation. This meant giving up power and making herself vulnerable to rejection, and it happened only after trust had developed on her part. Some femmes refused to reciprocate, and that ended the relationship. In this way, butches said, they screened women who had affairs or slept around just for the sake of gifts and other advantages. If the femme returned the butch's sexual favors, it was never spoken of publicly. To admit giving up the works lessened the butch's masculine status, her reputation for control and indifference.

This subordination of sexual pleasure to emotional ends and the re-creation of normal roles is even clearer in prisons for younger women, who feel more disturbed over separation from parental than from conjugal families. Especially where younger and older females are in prison together, pseudofamilies develop that consist entirely of women, reproducing what was left behind on the outside. This was first described in detail in 1966 by Rose Giallombardo as a result of her study of 654 inmates at the Federal Reformatory for Women at Alderson, West Virginia. Only 5 per cent of the women there had been exclusively homosexual on the outside, but three quarters became involved with "families" inside.

The usual lesbian roles were there—the femme wore cosmetics and looked as attractive as possible, and the stud acted like a man in a world without men. The stud was expected to be reliable and not gossip; she had a masculine stride and changed her name from Barbara to Bob, Catherine to Kelly. If she fell for another stud and "dropped the belt" (changed roles), she was looked down on for having failed her role. There was scorn for the "turnabout" who played it either butch or femme, for the "chippie" who slept around, for the "commissary hustler" who turned tricks for goods and gifts. The stud showered a new inmate with candy, cigarettes and flowery love letters (ability to write them was highly prized at Alderson); she showed her the ropes in prison, took her to movies and ball games. Many relationships were fleeting and based on commercial interests; the femme did housework for two, and the stud became a commissary hustler to provide her with gifts. The usual duration of an affair was one to three months. Nevertheless, when an affair began, the couple considered themselves married; often there was an exchange of rings or religious medals. The femme moved to the stud's dormitory and entered a kinship system that linked as many as fifteen people.

Prison families grow out of the roles taken by a couple. The femme is a "mommy," the stud broad a "daddy." If the couple breaks up, the stud may tell the femme, "I feel like a brother to you," and they literally become brother and sister. When the stud takes up with another femme, the new partner finds herself with a sister-in-law—the stud's first femme. Or perhaps when a couple split the stud says, "I'll be your father"; when the femme begins a second affair, her new partner thus acquires a father-in-law. Families keep growing by accretion, and are depleted by releases from prison. Families may grow to include parents, children, siblings, uncles and aunts, nieces and nephews and cousins. (There are a few grandmothers at Alderson, but no grandfathers.) There are even rules for addressing one another. A mother is referred to as "my mother" but addressed as ma, mommy or mama. A parent addresses a child by name except for reasons of discipline or emotional support, at which times the child becomes "my daughter," "my son" or "my child." Sisters and brothers call each other sis and bro (pronounced "bur"). A brother-in-law may be called bro, and cousins address each other as "cous." Roles are first determined by masculine or feminine role, but once a family role is established, it survives later role changes; a femme who is someone's sister may later turn stud, but she remains that person's sister. This is a sign of how seriously family relationships are taken. Families survive the strains caused by "divorces," and parents retain great influence—they are the undisputed leaders among the inmates. Incest rules are scrupulously observed. Giallombardo heard of only one offense, between an uncle and niece. This re-creation of the outside family serves a very important purpose. It is the only force promoting cohesiveness and stability in a life of deprivation, mistrust, jealousy and exploitation.

In studying women's prisons, it again becomes clear that homosexuality is a behavior expressing a variety of motives and environmental forces, and that its forms have roots in normal roles and attitudes. Even homosexual styles that first seem grotesque and rare, irrelevant to most people's lives, turn out to be mirror images of the needs and beliefs of us all. As sophisticated social-psychiatric studies of all the homosexualities proceed, they will continue to force on us a clearer view of the sociosexual forest that straights live in and therefore usually fail to see.

Prostitutes, pedophiles ("child molesters"), exhibitionists, voyeurs and other "sex offenders" are also finally emerging from behind stereotypic masks as new research is done. Prostitutes, for instance, have been spoken of as homosexual since Greek and Roman times, but despite a vast anecdotal and impressionistic literature, there is little reliable information about them.* Various studies over the past century have reported from one quarter to three quarters of prostitutes as having had at least incidental lesbian experience. Psychiatrist Harold Greenwald, in one of the smaller but more reliable investigations, found that fifteen of twenty-six call girls had been to bed with other women. Sociologists Charles McCaghy and James Skipper recently interviewed a group of strippers (like prostitutes, reputed in women's prisons to be prone to lesbianism) and found that a quarter admitted lesbian experience; most of the strippers guessed that the proportion was probably twice that.

It was simplistic to hope that one formula could explain prostitutes' life patterns. Some prostitutes have not had lesbian experience. Some have love affairs only with their male pimps. Some are lesbians, with bulldykes for pimps; in many such cases, the prostitute's earnings may support the drug habit of either or both of the pair. Many probably have only sporadic lesbian contacts. In the past, Krafft-Ebing, Stekel and others said that prostitutes turn to other women because of disenchantment with heterosexuality. McCaghy's and Skipper's strippers bore this out; they saw

---

*Even less is known about pimps, men whose work is so despised that very few will admit practicing it.

lesbianism as a respite from men interested in them only for sexual or financial advantage. "Strippers go gay," said one, "because they have little chance to meet nice guys. They come in contact with a lot of degenerate types. If they do meet a nice guy chances are he will ask them to stop stripping. If he doesn't he's likely to be a pimp. So the girls got to turn to a woman who understands them and their job."

This begs the question of why these women chose a life that could offer them only brutalizing relationships with men. Reversing the "disenchantment" theory, many analysts have said that prostitutes, like Don Juans, are trying to prove they are not homosexual; Edward Glover and Frank Caprio, for instance, wrote that many prostitutes are "frigid" but seek constant coitus as a flight from "unconscious homosexuality." This brings one to a bog of untestable speculation. But it does, by its curious use of the word *frigid* (in this context, nonorgasmic), suggest an interesting hypothesis about why there are fewer female than male homosexuals in every known society. Few male homosexuals would or could choose a life of frequent coitus with women; yet some prostitutes' behavior is overwhelmingly heterosexual, despite an emotional commitment to lesbianism. A man with a high level of anxiety or of repugnance toward heterosexual coitus cannot perform, for he cannot maintain an erection. A woman can give a minimal sexual performance and rationalize it in many ways, from "Women don't enjoy it as much as men" to "I only do this for money." Thus a woman with a high level of antiheterosexuality can keep a distorted or limited heterosexual pattern; perhaps women, as a group, must be more antiheterosexual than men to be forced to a homosexual adjustment.

Prostitution has many motives. In very poor societies, economic hardship may be decisive. In our society, where starvation and prostitution are rarely the only alternatives, there is general agreement that most prostitutes are unhappy, destructive people. Many seem to be alcoholics, addicts, suicidal, anxious, lonely, with severely disturbed family backgrounds and hazy identities. My own talks with prostitutes bear out the suggestion that this fragile or vague self-image accounts in part for their varying object choice. Some were angry, impulsive pansexuals whose relationships with both sexes tended to be either exploitative or sentimentally sisterly. Others struck me as chameleons, ready to become whatever they thought people expected them to be. Suffering acute identity problems, they clung to their pimps like limpets to rocks, for whatever mooring and sense of definition they could get. Many, like those described by Greenwald, combined shallowly felt imitations of seductive feminine stereotypes with neuter or masculine behavior. Some of Greenwald's call girls spent their nonworking hours dressed in such incongruous costumes as frilly blouse, dungarees and high-heeled shoes. A number whom I observed spent their off hours in pants and elaborate wigs, dancing with gay men in gay bars.

Male and female prostitutes both have hierarchies, with street hustlers ("shitkickers") at the bottom, bar hookers higher up, and call girls and their male equivalents at the top. Male hustlers, though, make another caste distinction; they look very differently on the effeminate, who may act as an insertee, than on "trade," who will be only insertors. In *City of Night*, novelist John Rechy describes the latter as an antisocial vagrant who sees his customers as Riess's peers regarded queers. One of them says, "No matter how many queers a guy goes with, if he goes for money, that don't make him queer. You're still straight. It's when you start going for free with other guys, that you start growing wings." Such knowledgeable men as Paul Gebhard believe that most of these hustlers return to predominant heterosexuality, but several recent novels by men who know the hustler's world describe as common the eventual switch to homosexuality—fulfilling the old gay dictum that today's trade is tomorrow's competition.

During the past decade, studies have begun yielding information about other deviants, such as pedophiles. In 1963 Michael Schofield's *Sociological Aspects of Homosexuality* made a revealing comparison of pedophiles with adult-seeking homosexuals and several other deviant and control groups. He found pedophiles more likely to be heterosexually than homosexually oriented, and more interested in children than in boys in particular. In fact, only a fifth were exclusively interested in boys under sixteen. And the homosexual who generally had relations with other adults was rarely interested in children. The typical pedophile was anything but a rabid "sex fiend." To the contrary, he appeared masculine and robust. However, he was religious, moralistic, guilt-laden and lonely. He was socially ineffective and a vocational underachiever. And perhaps most important, he had a low sexual frequency; only half of the pedophiles who had been married when they committed their offenses had had coitus during the previous year. Two thirds of the pedophiles had turned their attention to boys as they approached middle age, were subjected to internal and social stress, and found their adult heterosexuality dwindling. Usually they approached not strangers but the children of friends or neighbors. In many cases the offense was only timidly touching a boy's knee; most commonly, it was fondling a child. This agrees with psychiatrist Stanley Willis' interpretation of the pedophile as a man acting the "good mother" or "good father" to a child; he sees the child as representing himself and showers him with tender affection.

Two years after Schofield's book appeared, the team of Gebhard, Gagnon, Pomeroy and Christenson of the Kinsey Institute produced a detailed and sophisticated study of 1,356 sex offenders. This massive work, entitled *Sex Offenders*, was still far from definitive, but it widened Schofield's picture tremendously. The Gebhard team agreed that many men who committed sex offenses against the young were inhibited, ill at ease with adults, and able to feel in control of a sexual situation only with children, but were rarely violent and were more heterosexual than homosexual. But when the researchers separated their subjects into "offenders vs. children" (under twelve) and "offenders vs. minors" (twelve to fifteen), new patterns appeared alongside the one Schofield had found.

Some of the offenders vs. children actually preferred minors, and only turned to preadolescents if no minors were available. Others were assertive and indiscriminate, "interested primarily in reaching orgasm with any warm-blooded animal . . . operating at a primate level with the philosophy that necessity is the mother of improvisation." A third to half of the offenders vs. minors were hebephiles, especially interested in boys between puberty and the middle teens, and not in children under twelve; most such men were strongly homosexual. And so, as a group, the offenders vs. minors were more homosexually oriented than the offenders vs. children. Others among them, like the offenders vs. children, had turned to young people because they found adult relationships too demanding. And the ones who had used violence, like some of the offenders against children, had been impulsive men who ignored "the wishes and even the gender of their victims." But still others were primarily homosexual with adults and had had a lapse of judgment and control in the face of temptation, as an adult heterosexual might with a pretty adolescent girl. In many cases, it seemed that the youth, not the adult, had been the real seducer.

A great gulf lay between the offenders vs. children and minors on the one hand and offenders vs. adults on the other. The offenders vs. adults were predominantly homosexual, three fifths of them recognizably so. Few were interested sexually in the young. Far from being inhibited and moralistic, they had had many partners—almost two thirds had had more than seventy-five, and some of them hundreds. But like offenders against children and minors, few were especially criminal or dangerous.

All these groups of homosexual offenders—against children, minors and adults—had a higher sexual frequency, whether with partners or through masturbation, than any other sex offenders or than the nonprison control subjects. In fact, their "sex drive" had been distinctly higher throughout their entire lives. The Gebhard team said that perhaps homosexuality results from a child having to cope with strong sexual impulses before society makes heterosexual provisions for them. The majority of offenders vs. minors had shown both heterosexual and homosexual interest until they reached the ages of twelve to fifteen; then a massive displacement of their heterosexuality occurred. The reason, according to *Sexual Offenders,* "is simply that our society inadvertently makes homosexuals by abruptly and powerfully repressing heterosexual behavior (especially in girls) around the age of puberty. . . . A young boy without a great backlog of homosexual conditioning can wait out this period during which he is robbed of girls and can still emerge primarily heterosexual; a male with much previous homosexual conditioning cannot." This is surely inadequate as *the* explanation of homosexuality, but it may be crucial in many cases. The massive behavioral evidence of *Sex Offenders* is a good corrective to etiological studies that focus almost exclusively on family relationships. It is not just families that make heterosexuals and homosexuals, but societies as well.

Other patterns emerged with other types of sex offenders. Incest offenders vs. children tended to be ineffectual and dependent, many of them given to heavy drinking and uneven work records. Incest offenders vs. adults were generally conservative, moralistic and traditional, with little criminality or alcoholism. But in almost every category of sex offense, the commonest pattern still accounted for only about half the group. A third of the men convicted of peeping were shy and sexually inexperienced, their voyeurism a substitute for intercourse; a fifth had simply been caught taking advantage of opportunities few men would ignore. Some groups utterly defied summation.

The study of "problem" sexuality has only begun, and if enough information and insight accumulates, we may be able to start answering some very important questions. Once we understand the backgrounds of problem-ridden people, can potential offenders be recognized and helped? Or does having a fundamentally rewarding sex life depend chiefly on having picked the right parents or on growing up in a less sexually repressive society? Can such a society be modified? Social scientists, especially American ones, tend to hope that solutions to problems are inherent in knowledge about them. Intellectually, our rationalism and social utopianism are at stake. More concretely, the stakes are the lives of thousands or millions of people.

INTERVIEWS

Janice is a rather pretty lesbian about twenty-five years old who is involved in the gay bar life of Boston. I hardly get to ask any questions, for she rattles away disjointedly with tense animation, repeating points, changing subjects, jumping back to them suddenly half an hour later, and usually relating slightly different facts with each retelling of a story.

I was married once, for a very short time, to a gay guy, and I have a kid. I live with a girl, we've been together for five years. I'm butch with her. But I've had a secret affair on the side for the past two years, and with my second lover I'm the femme. Even so, I go out to the bars a lot, just dump my kid— lots of us do that, dump our kids on our parents and run. I don't know, I've got to go out, look for women. Gay women care for their babies, but they can't stand to stay home. I know one couple who wanted to adopt a kid, but they decided not to, and now they have dogs. You know, lots of times a femme will have an illegitimate child. And if you ask them, they'll say they don't want their child to be a lesbian. My lover hates children. She says marriage is only legal prostitution. She says, "Get rid of that thing"—she means my kid—"and I'll set you up for life."

When I was married, which I did on the spur of the moment, my girlfriend wouldn't let us alone. She followed us, threatened us, put sugar in his gas tank. I was afraid of being butchered in bed by her some night. Mostly I didn't have sex with my husband: I let him eat me. But you see, I wanted to get away from my old lover. That bar life is so rough. I got rolled in a bar for the first time when I was eighteen. My girlfriend was very violent—beatings, police, the whole thing. God, I had another girlfriend once, a hooker I met in a bar. I was seventeen then, and she was the first woman I had a climax with. She beat me up all the time, tried to knife me and hit me with bottles. Once she threw peroxide at my eyes. She had forty stitches in her from fights with other dykes. She tried to commit suicide once or twice. You see all that sort of stuff in bars. A dyke will start a girl on junk and then pimp her off. There are lots of one-night stands by the older dykes, but usually a girl needs to have some sort of feeling involved. But you see little femmes fifteen and sixteen who are out on their own on the street who come in and hustle the old dykes for clothes, food, drinks. I want to be dead at thirty, not a lonely hag chasing young girls and paying them off.

What kind of women do I like to make love to? Most of all I like Natalie Wood types, with dark hair and white teeth, slender. [*This is a description of Janice herself.*] I've gone from the femme to the aggressor. I don't want my breasts touched, it's like her being a baby and me being the mother. I'd never breast-feed a child, it's horrible. It sounds like I'm the baby, doesn't it. My grandmother calls me retarded. My parents? My mother's an alcoholic, and my father is nice on the outside, but he always displays sex in an ugly, vulgar form when he talks. It sickened me.

I don't know what I'm going to do. I have migraine and sleeping trouble. I have to have two or three or five people going at once. I have these two lovers, and I go out with four different guys. I can't seem to break up with anyone despite fights. I want to get married now, maybe because I feel in prison with my lover now—we fight, I don't eat, and I get migraine. I'm twenty-five, I feel I should try to go out with guys and look for security. I need a person to take care of me, maybe an old fag or a dyke. I don't have a job, I always quit or got fired. I told the bitches off wherever I worked. Now I'm on welfare, have been for a year and a half. I do a little part-time work sometimes.

Yes, I think I ought to get married. I wouldn't go to bed with a man without marrying him. My mother does it for drinks, for a few bucks. Sometimes guys I go out with try to sleep with me. I told one guy who says he wants to marry me, "Go have an affair, but don't tell me. And don't bring me a disease."

I talk to Ed and Patsy at a gay party in New York. There are a dozen people in the large Village apartment on this Saturday night, most of them between eighteen and twenty-five. All but a few are male. Patsy, one of the girls, agrees to talk to me about herself. With us is her gay friend Ed. I said that I was curious about fag molls and their male counterparts who hang out with lesbians. Ed said, "You should talk to me. I'm a kind of male fag-hag myself." He, Patsy and I go into the kitchen and talk there over coffee at a small round table while the party goes on in the living room.

Patsy is eighteen, heavy, almost obese, with a round face and the expression of a sad little girl. She wears baggy jeans, a big baggy sweater and scuffed flat shoes. Her hair is not cropped but worn at short page-boy length; it is unwashed and scraggly. She is what is sometimes called a "baby butch"—young, butchy, but not yet fully hardened in the role. At first she seems reticent, but eventually she becomes quite talkative and animated. Ed is twenty-one, from Brooklyn, a gentle, dark-haired young man with a restrained and polite manner through which hints of aggression and anger sometimes flash very briefly. Both he and Patsy seem intelligent, serious, likable and in many things quite mature for their ages. At the beginning, Patsy tries to define herself.

PATSY: I'm bisexual. I've had my problems. I saw two analysts, one for two years and the other for a year.

Why did you see them?

PATSY: I tried to commit suicide. I mean, a lot of things were going. I dig writing, that's my thing. I was skipped in school, a special school. My mother died when I was fourteen, but I was already gay then. I was brought out at thirteen and a half. My mother was dying, my grandmother had just died. I was reaching out for friendship, and got it—no sex, just friendship. I got a crush on this chorus girl. Then just as my mother was dying, the girl left for California, and I tried to commit suicide.

What was the rest of your family like?

PATSY: I have a couple of sisters. My father was away from home a lot—he's alcoholic, and he's best when he's drunk. If he lived next door I'd want to visit all the time. He's fond of me, as though I were the girl next door. But he's a very apathetic person. One day he said, "Are you a bull-dagger?" I said, "*You* like girls don't you? So?" He plays around a lot.

What happened when you saw the doctor?

PATSY: He refused to admit I'm gay. He said it was an adolescent stage. I can't conceive of getting emotional fulfillment from a man. I wish I could, I don't like putting myself out on a limb by being homosexual.

What do you think the cause of homosexuality is?

PATSY: Well, with girls, I think it's overattachment to the mother and repulsion from the father. Usually one element is stronger than the other, so you get a butch or femme—I'm butch, I was very attached to my mother, much more in temperament than in looks. I'm quite like her . . . [*she grins*] a nice Jewish girl.

Ed, what about you?

ED: Oh, I come from a middle-class family. I have a sister—she's straight. My mother wore the pants in the family. My aunt, her sister, she sort of adopted me, and enhanced anything gay in me—bought me dolls. My father is a basic baseball-and-bowling guy. He's not exactly crude, but he isn't well educated. He's very afraid to show emotion and very disappointed in me—I mean at the lack of relationship between us. I think my mother knows about me. My parents are broad-minded, but I've wanted to tell them out of revenge, say "You made me this way." You said you weren't going to use anyone's name in your book. Doesn't anyone ever insist on using his name to get even with his family?

Not so far. Did you ever see a therapist?

ED: I saw someone for four months when I was sixteen. The doctor told me to accept homosexuality and be happy within it. He said he didn't see any reason for a homosexual to change. He should be taught to accept it, change doesn't last. I have friends who go to doctors and the doctor tries to get them to go out with girls. I've been gay consciously for four or five years. I've only slept with one person, once. I want something more substantial than sex.

What sort of people do you hang around with?

ED: Like I said, I'm a male fag-hag, I hang out in lesbian bars. Some guys keep gay girls, you know, they have a thing about it.

PATSY: I've met a few straight guys who dig butch chicks and hang out in dyke bars. But they aren't accepted in the bars. If a straight guy comes into a les bar, I think he must be sick, so I'm hostile.

ED: Girls and the girls' clubs are different. There aren't as many one-night stands, the bars and clubs are really clubs, groups of friends. Girls go out longer before getting into bed, but all the girls in a group have slept with each other once or more.

PATSY: With girls it's not so much a sex thing as emotional domination and other things. Drag butches—they're different. I argued the other day with a drag butch about her masculinity complex, and she got so mad she wanted to beat me up. I hate the games lesbians play; they're the same ones heteros play. I usually like to go out with straight girls.

If you go out with straight girls, what do you do for sex?

PATSY: I go to bed with them!

If they go to bed with you, why do you say they're straight?

PATSY: Well, I think some are. I mean, some of them go and live straight lives.

ED: I think that in a way a lot of lesbians are looking for heterosexual relationships with each other. Sometimes they look for a child to raise as their own in a homosexual marriage. I've seen girls stick together for two years, and that's an incredibly long time for guys, but also considerably long for girls. They cheat less than men, they don't have the gang-bangs and orgies the boys have. But the roles are much stronger in public. You see with two girls right off who's wearing the pants. That breaks down in bed, though, the roles tend to drop away. Now, it's the other way around with guys. A guy may take either role in public, depending on the guy. But his role is always the same with any one guy.

PATSY: Yes, that's true. But I'll tell you, I see a lot more bisexuality around, among my friends. Or just with people I meet. I say I'm gay, the others say, "I've tried it a few times." I haven't met anyone in years who doesn't say that.

Could it be that you travel in different circles now than a few years ago?

PATSY: Well, I'm into the hippie drug scene now, and there's lots of everything—heterosexuality, homosexuality, just sex, because they're into the love thing.

When men are around lesbians, is there much feeling of competition or threat?

PATSY: Femmes threaten their lovers with men. And with female rivals too.

ED: I've heard girls say to each other, "I don't care if you go out with a guy, but not with another girl."

PATSY: But only if the girl is absolutely surely lesbian, so then it's no threat.

ED: Or a femme wants to try a guy, and the butch says, "Well, go ahead, I'd like to see you try."

Your voice had a kind of sneering contempt when you said that. Is that how it's said?

ED: Exactly. And the answer back is, "Spit's good, but it doesn't make babies."

You make it sound like a tough life.

PATSY: As a lesbian you must break from the whole structure, everything you're brought up to be—wedding, kids, all that. It's hard for a girl. I mean, life is so much simpler if you're straight. I only know one couple where just the butch works; a woman can't make enough to support two. But it's easier for a gay girl to go to bed with the opposite sex than it is for a gay boy. She doesn't have to be excited. I went to bed with a boy three weeks ago. He's an old friend, and I didn't have anything to do, so we drank. I'm very affectionate, and suddenly I get very motherly and want to hold a person. So we went to bed. I was detached, but he wasn't. I could go through with it, but a fag with the same detachment couldn't. You know, girls are more jealous because a girl always gets offers from men. But men don't get offers from women.

Men don't get sexual offers from women?

PATSY: No, not the same way. But I don't like the whole scene, that's why I go out with straight girls.

ED: Lesbians are forgotten people. When you say queer, girls don't come to mind. But Patsy, aren't you just as queer as I am?

[*Patsy's face goes blank. This happens when specific sexual matters come up or when she is asked about why she calls her girlfriends straight.*]

PATSY: Well, I don't identify as a man. I watch women, they fascinate me. I mean [*she grins*] they're insane! They act so logical, but it's all this Alice in Wonderland, Humpty Dumpty logic. I identify as a butch lesbian, a third sex.

[*The noise from the party in the next room is getting louder: banter, shrieks, giggling. A young man holds up a full-page photo from a magazine of a man and woman embracing, and someone yells scornfully, "Is that supposed to turn me on?" For a few minutes a half dozen of the guys, draped in towels and robes, camp, dance and sing in a chorus line to a record of the wedding march. A little later the party settles down; four boys sit in a row of chairs to give a reading of* Who's Afraid of Virginia Woolf? *The rest of the party are their appreciative audience.*]

Ed, what sort of person attracts you?

ED: Because of my father, until recently I was only attracted to men old enough to be my father. I saw that my parents' marriage was bad, and I decided not to marry. And all girls want to marry eventually. I don't want to marry and have kids, not after seeing what my parents did to me.

What did they do to you?

ED: Like I told you, my father had this masculinity fetish.

Do you think gay people can have stable or happy lives?

PATSY: I think homosexuality is an aberration. All homosexuals have some sort of psychological problem, and social pressure besides.

ED: I don't agree that all homosexuals are neurotics. Many have a problem when they're young but don't as they get older. What if becoming homosexual completely eradicates the problem?

PATSY: But it can't. I'm looking for a mother, and no matter how perfect my homosexual affairs are, it won't work. You only have one mother, you can't get another one afterward.

ED: I'm looking for someone I'm in love with. Someone who will protect me, look after me, care for me. And I want to do that for someone. Just what any heterosexual looks for.

Not everyone would say a good relationship is mutual protection above all else.

ED: I mean, I want someone who will look after me.

PATSY: It is true that half the problems homosexuals have result from it not being socially acceptable.

ED: I think that doesn't matter. I've found the homosexual world, and in it I can do anything a heterosexual can do—hold hands, go to a beach . . .

PATSY: But they're a minority. A gay bar, a gay beach . . .

ED [*defiantly*]: I've told every straight person I'm gay! Every one! I can take a boyfriend around them. As for other people, I don't care. There's no difference between a heterosexual and homosexual except in bed.

PATSY: I do care. Homosexuals are a minority. My girlfriend and I kiss in the subway, and a cop comes over. I think it's a disease. But I refuse to be part of the subculture.

ED: But how can you function, thinking it's a disease? [*He pauses.*] Well, yes, I have my two o'clock depression. I'm in a les or a gay bar, I see where I am, and I ask, "What am I doing here?"

PATSY: The kind of people I meet in a bar aren't usually the kind of people I want to meet. The ones I want to meet are in the library, and they aren't gay.

ED: Meeting people is hard for me.

PATSY: It's hard.

[*The argument of a moment ago has vanished. Patsy has again retreated behind a mask of quiet unhappiness. The talk has played itself out. A minute later I say goodnight and leave quietly, so as not to disturb the second act of* Virginia Woolf.]

Dr. Kurt Konietzko is a Philadelphia psychologist with wide experience in individual and group psychotherapy. He was originally a Rogerian, but many years' work with delinquents, addicts and criminals made him turn to an active, directive approach. It suits his personality, which is brisk, assertive and outgoing. He is in his forties, a short man with wide shoulders, an incipient paunch and a short-cropped full beard that is turning gray. His speech retains an occasional hint of Danzig, where he spent his first fourteen years.

Certain patterns run commonly through all kinds of deviance; it doesn't make sense to deal with homosexuality separately. What happens is that in order to become a living reproof to his parents, a kid picks the pattern that pains them most. I often see homosexuality used by a rebellious kid as a lever against his family.

But why homosexuality in a given case rather than addiction or delinquency?

Every day parents send out little clues to their value systems. For instance, a parent will say, "You're like your Uncle Joe." Maybe Uncle Joe is effeminate, the fairy of the family. The kid gets training in a negative self-concept. Furthermore, he's being accused in advance. When a parent constantly says, "Don't do this," he's suggesting that the child is the sort of person who would do it. As a result, the child may fulfill the parent's prophecy. When the kid comes home, he hears, "What were you doing out at one in the morning?" The parent is implying sexual misbehavior. If a person is blamed in advance, he'll live up to the prediction, out of anger. I've heard kids say this right out—"If I'm going to be blamed for it, I might as well do it."

In other words, the kid is acting out the parents' own hidden expectations.

They aren't even hidden in a lot of cases. They're right out in the open. You'd be surprised how many of these kids have a mother who says, "I'd rather see you dead than an addict" or a homosexual or whatever. Or a father who repeatedly talks about all sex offenders as degenerates in a loathing voice.

I've read reports of studies of addicts' mothers, saying that the vast majority know of their children's addiction and tacitly support it. My interviews with homosexuals make me suspect a similar situation.

Yes, the mother is often a silent conspirator. She covers this by playing a dual role. For instance, the addict's mother presents herself to the world as a victim: "Look what he's doing to us!" She comes off as a martyr and creates guilt. But when the son asks her for money for a haircut, she hands him a five-dollar bill. She knows damn well he's going to use it to buy a nickle bag [five-dollar bag of heroin]; she just can't stand to see him suffer. The same thing goes on between the homosexual and his mother; she stands in the way of his heterosexual attempts, his maleness, but doesn't make it hard for him to act out his homosexuality.

Why doesn't she show her love by trying to get her son to deal with his problems?

If she really faces his problem, she'll have to face her own. Maybe she is afraid of maleness, and in order to keep her son lovable has kept him a dependent little boy. Actually, not just the mother but the whole family has a vital stake in most kids' illness. The kid becomes the family's "identified patient," the one labeled sick, but he reflects all of their problems.

Let me give you a couple of examples. I had a kid who'd committed six auto thefts in four years. He'd take a car on a joy ride and get caught, and his parents would have to bail him out of jails, pay for lawyers and so on. Each time it took a few months to straighten things out. This was the only way he got their attention and care; at the same time, he got even by inflicting worry and expense on them. Or take an eight-year-old I saw recently, whose school phobia had kept her out of class for six months. The mother couldn't understand it, because the girl claimed she liked school and her teachers, and the school was practically right across the street. After six or eight sessions with the girl, it became clear that the mother had left the father once, and the marriage was always on the verge of breaking up. By staying home with a problem, the little girl forced her parents to stay home together and focus their attention on her. She was resolving their conflict.

I'm talking about these cases because the homosexual youngster, like any disturbed person, is usually doing something of this kind. His problem is the family's problem, and his choice of symptoms depends on the paradoxical messages going back and forth in the family relationships.

But what specific elements are involved in a homosexual pattern?

They're well documented in the scientific literature. The mother who keeps her boy dependent sends him into classic flight from incest; every woman is too much of a threat to him, because she arouses his incestuous feelings. Or the boy identifies with his father, seeks his maleness, and in sex hopes to magically absorb his partner's maleness—this is very common. When I get a homosexual who seeks rough, tough partners, I ask him to describe his father, and it's often obvious the partner is the father's spitting image. As a boy, he may have seen his mother give in to the father's sexual approaches, and got the idea that to please a man you have to win him sexually by appeasing, passive, seductive behavior. Anyway, these are a few of the more prominent dynamics.

How many homosexuals are there in your practice, and how do you treat them?

I usually have four to six homosexuals in therapy. I give individual and group treatment, with one or two homosexuals in each group. First we work on their anxieties and nonsexual problems. Then on sex. The vast majority come in saying, "Just adjust me to my homosexuality." And that's what you have to do with the greater number of them. But change is possible, and one of the problems is their resistance to that fact. The existence of one cured homosexual changes the nature of the condition in homosexuals' eyes. It challenges them. So they try to deny it.

The head of an English homosexual organization said that he counsels boys in their teens who have homosexual involvements to experiment and make a free choice. I suggested that a boy of that age who's homosexually involved probably isn't free to try girls with equal ease and success.

Sometimes when a kid tells me that he's experimenting bisexually, I say, "Fine, but if you're bisexual, then really be bisexual. Bring me a scorecard. For every guy you see, take out a chick. For every guy you make it with, make it with a chick." It doesn't take long for him to face his real problem, which is difficulty relating to females. One of the reasons for developing a homosexual pattern is that it's easier to make it with another male.

Then there's been no big sexual revolution to provide a lot of ready partners?

There's a small swell on campuses, in big cities, certain parts of society. But any big change will be in the future. These things change slowly, especially for people in small towns, in religiously oriented institutions and so on. There's also the fact that women are less sexy than men. Males culturally and biologically want more variety of partners—how many bulls does it take to service a herd of cows?

So, given our nature and our culture, it still isn't very easy for most boys to get laid. And to do so, they must take the initiative, ask for dates, try, wait for a yes or no. It's all frustrating, doubtful, demanding. With another guy, there's none of that. Two guys jump into a car, give each other hand jobs, and the whole thing only takes a few minutes.

Inability to delay rewards is the usual definition of an immature personality. What you say implies that homosexuals tend to be immature or disturbed.

We live in a sexually and emotionally disturbed society. Most heterosexuals don't handle relationships well. But theirs is a culturally normal disturbance. I think most homosexuals are far more disturbed. They say they want true love, but they find they can't deal with it. Their basic level of insecurity is higher. Like the heterosexual with troubled relationships, the homosexual keeps repeating his problems with one person after another.

You see, unsolved problems always keep being repeated. When you take an exam, you remember afterward not the problems you solved but the ones that stumped you. Your mind is biologically constructed to solve problems, and like any computer, it keeps flipping around unsolved problems again and again—about sex, marriage, business, anything. Now, an obsessional person spends most of his time doing this. He can't let go of his problem. Let's say that a given homosexual, having a higher level of insecurity, has a better chance of being more obsessional. You can see the trouble he gets into. In fact, his biggest problem is the way his problems take most of his attention. That's why you often treat a character component like obsessiveness first, and the sexual problem second or third.

Sullivan wrote back in the thirties that the boys in one boarding school who became homosexual were those who didn't take part in the homosexual play that was part of a preadolescent chumship. Do you find anything similar in the kids you see?

Yes, the kids in such trouble are often isolated. My questions is, what kept them from participating? They shied away from others because they already thought they were terrible, unlovable people. At about eight, boys find buddies, think their friends know everything, and that their parents are insignificant. At adolescence, the peer-group bond becomes even more intense, its evaluations even more important. But why does a person choose a particular peer group? Why does one particular girl join a gang that demands each new girl screw all twenty boys in it? Why do the isolates try to group together? If you feel like a rejected person, you surround yourself with people who confirm your view of the world and share your own low self-valuation.

What about the teenagers who hang out in Rittenhouse Square? Many of these kids in the hip-drug subculture talk about bisexual experimentation, sexual liberation and so on.

I know a lot of them, and I've treated many. I'd say that maybe one girl in a hundred among them has pleasure, reaches orgasm, and knows what love-making is. A girl may run with three guys, be fucked no end of times, and still have no sense of her body, no idea of a warm sexual relationship. I've seen girls like that finally get involved with homosexuals, trying to straighten them out. They're especially screwed up—finding a guy to mother and dominate.

What's deceptive is that many of these kids have read the right books and can verbalize well. They come here in beads, old dresses and soldier coats, and have beautiful verbal façades, but they don't know how to love or live. Many are schizoid or schizophrenic. They definitely are not living their own lives, opting out of the system by choice. They're very dependent personalities. They can't make a good life on their own, so they join this group for support. Of course, you can get into all sorts of scenes because of faddism—a certain thing becomes part of the special world you've joined. It had a great effect when to be in the scene in the ghetto you had to be hip, dress a certain way, go to certain bars and use drugs.

Do you think many men in our society go down on other men out of casual faddism? Isn't it too loaded for that?

No, I doubt that they do. It's too big a cultural no. By comparison, pot and pills aren't terribly big no's in some parts of society. But when you consider acts involving basic male sexuality, that's something else. I'd say that if bisexual behavior makes you a big stud in your surroundings, it might not be too big a threat—you fuck women and you also fuck other men, who are like girls in relation to you. Your maleness isn't called into question—your aggressiveness and dominance.

Do you think many American college students or kids in the radical youth culture play the bisexual stud?

They're more likely to panic and doubt their maleness. To be otherwise would mean one was beating the most basic social standards. Most of us can't even get over the double standard! The old sexual attitudes may be a little looser, but not much.

Do people who engage in group sex or group marriage beat the values?

Some young singles and divorced people I know live together in a sharing way. Or mean to. But when you get right down to it, they're usually looking for the one important relationship. Not being possessive is almost unheard of; most of us can't be that way about things, let alone people. I doubt the solidity of most couples who swap or share. Are they expressing freedom or showing that they have a pretty crummy relationship? Anyway, it's hard enough to live with one person, let alone two or a dozen. When a group live together, they develop territorial disputes, over everything from who uses the bathroom first in the morning to sexual partners. A lot of this depends on the group members' real rationality. Intellectually the experimenters sound very advanced and liberated, but it usually turns out that they don't really want to share. Soon a relationship forms with one person and then the girl wants to get married. They hassle about it, work through some problems, and then he says, "My god, how long would it take to work out so much with someone else, and get such a close relationship?" Of those I know who've set up a sort of group experiment here, four couples are now about to get married.

30

Cure or Illusion

In 1962 there appeared a ponderously written book laden with statistical tables called simply *Homosexuality*. A subtitle explained that it was a psychoanalytic study of male homosexuals. It presented the results of a decade's research by eight psychoanalysts and a psychologist led by Dr. Irving Bieber, done on their own time with almost no funds. With unhesitating authority they claimed to identify the sources of homosexuality and said that a third of their subjects had become exclusively heterosexual in treatment. The book quickly polarized sex researchers and became a football in several crucial conflicts in the human sciences. Ultra-orthodox analysts, standing by instinct theory and traditional prognostic pessimism about homosexuality, refused to believe the "cures" had happened. Behaviorists, opposed to analysis as fanciful, attacked the work theoretically and claimed that conditioning methods had brought far higher cure rates. A new radical wing of psychiatrists, psychologists and social scientists objected to the Bieber group's notions of deviance, illness and health, and said the very idea of cure was repressive heterosexual conformity. Today experts on deviance often pigeonhole each other ideologically according to each others' opinions of "the Bieber book."

Most psychodynamic studies of homosexuals have been written by lone clinicians. No matter how brilliant, these works are always vulnerable to charges of small samples and subjective interpretations. In 1952 Bieber and other members of the Society of Medical Psychoanalysts formed a research committee to study male homosexuality with analytic tools but using the cross-checks and rules of evidence usually missing in such projects—comparison cases, multiple evaluations, statistical analysis and, when possible, follow-ups. They got seventy colleagues to answer questionnaires about homosexual patients and comparison heterosexual cases. Over the years, Bieber (to make him a collective pronoun for his team) kept sharpening, expanding and readministering his questionnaires, and put the results through ingenious statistical analysis. Finally he had several runs of information on 106 homosexuals and 100 comparisons, the two groups closely matched in age, income, education and even in emotional problems other than homosexuality. No one has ever gathered so much finely discriminating detail on so many homosexuals, treated in depth by so many different doctors, and put through so many evaluations. Bieber reached for Kinseyan objectivity; like Kinsey, he fell short of his goal but produced the most authoritative study of its kind. The critical flap that ensued is largely a tribute to a sometimes discomforting achievement.

When Bieber looked at homosexuals' family backgrounds, he found that a disproportionately large number were only children or only sons. Their mothers tended to get along poorly with women and, if they had daughters, not to favor them. About 70 per cent of the mothers fit a pattern Bieber characterized as "close-binding-intimate," or "CBI." The CBI mother bound one son to her with emotional and physical seductiveness; if she had other sons, she did not wrap them in this same destructive intimacy. She even preferred the son to her husband; in fact, she acted out a "romance" with the boy to compensate for the lacks in her marriage, making him her confidant and involving him in arguments and complaints (including sexual ones) against his father. Thus the males in the family were pitted against each other for her love, with the homosexual preselected as the unfortunate winner.

In some cases the mother's seductiveness was covert; in others it ran from habitually going undressed before the child to banishing her husband to another bedroom and having the son sleep with her. But, having won a monopoly on his attention and desire, she inhibited him with antisexual attitudes. Most of the homosexuals described their mothers as puritanical and frigid. These women strictly prohibited masturbation and interfered with heterosexual activities from early childhood into young adulthood. A normal mother-child relationship has erotic overtones, but the mother neither acts them out nor overreacts by stifling physical affection between herself and her boy. The CBI mother, ridden by old incestuous conflicts of her own, did both; she trapped her son in a hopeless bind between her seductiveness and rigid restrictions. Bieber, like many psychiatrists before him, pointed out that when homosexuals are exposed to heterosexual stimuli, they often feel acute anxiety and immediately seek a homosexual partner—reliving their reaction to a mother who incited sexuality but threatened rejection if it were expressed.*

To keep her son reliant on her, the CBI mother generally babied and overprotected him; but, as in sexuality, she controlled with one hand while indulging with the other. Though she pampered him, she discouraged assertion and masculine behavior, acted overanxious about his health, and was constantly apprehensive about his being injured. When he joined in rough-and-tumble play, she interfered, calling the other boys mere roughnecks. Thus she made him fearful, dependent, and isolated from his age-mates.

Bieber had pinpointed the pathogenic traits in the homosexual's mother,

*Psychiatrist Lawrence Hatterer says that several homosexual patients have told him the busiest day at the gay steambaths is Mother's Day.

but far more striking was his discovery of deep, unremitting pathology on the father's part. Twelve homosexuals (and only four comparison patients) grew up without fathers. Of ninety-four homosexuals' fathers studied, seventy-nine were emotionally detached from the sons. The detached father was not just a lazy or too-busy parent, any more than the CBI mother merely gave too much of a good thing. Nor did paternal absence for work or other such reasons necessarily have a bad effect; a good relationship surmounts such hurdles. The detached father had severe male-rivalry problems and acted them out with the son. If he had a daughter, he was likely to favor her; and if he had more than one son, he did not favor the homosexual one. Not one detached father favored the patient. So the homosexual's unfortunate victory in winning a monopoly on his mother's love was compounded by abysmal failure to get a father's warmth and protectiveness.

A normal father steps in and protects his children from destructive maternal influences. Some of the homosexuals' fathers abdicated and did nothing while their wives tied the boys to them in submission and guilt. They were coolly indifferent and offered the sons meager, barren relationships. But an even larger number of detached fathers actively helped crush their sons' masculinity by being openly hostile, rejecting and minimizing. They stifled attempts at assertion with outbursts of anger, and underscored failure with scorn. The boys feared their fathers, and hated them for abandoning them to their mothers' engulfing grip. They saw the fathers as brutes or as ciphers, no more to be respected or admired than to be loved. They did not rebel, though, fearing to provoke even more hostility. However, they sided with their mothers in parental arguments, probably thus provoking even more competitive anger from their fathers.

Bieber wrote, "We have come to the conclusion that a constructive, supportive, warmly related father *precludes* the possibility of a homosexual son; he acts as a neutralizing protective agent should the mother make seductive or close-binding attempts." Bieber was not the first to stress the father's role in creating homosexuality. In 1959 D. J. West in England had said that in the fifty homosexuals he had studied, "It is the combination of parental relationships that characterized the homosexual groups. . . . Exclusive emphasis on the mother figure . . . is misplaced." The same striking absence of a strong father or any father at all has appeared in the research of Gordon Westwood, Michael Schofield, Eva Bene and a number of other researchers. But no one had shown such thorough and dramatic evidence of this, and the Bieber study can be credited with shifting the psychodynamic emphasis in studying homosexuality—both male and female—during the past decade. The work of Bieber, Eva Bene in England and others points to the lack of a warm, strong, healthy father in the backgrounds of lesbians. Simon and Gagnon, in a pilot interviewing study with lesbians, found that almost all of them had a preference for one parent and an attitude toward the other that went from "condescending neutrality to open hostility." The prehomosexual girl, it seems, often has a critical and competitive mother and a father who is either openly seductive or utterly rejecting and who fails to protect the girl against the mother's destructiveness.

Homosexuality, it became clear, was the result of an entire family constellation, a distinctive wife-husband-child triangle of which each side is distorted. The marriages of the homosexuals' parents differed from those of the control group's parents. The mother and father of the homosexual were more distant emotionally, spent less time together, and shared fewer interests. The mother was more likely to dominate the father and be contemptuous of him. (A dominating spouse was usually a dominating parent; not one detached father was a dominating husband.) The best marriages Bieber observed—judged in terms of the children's development—were those of a small number of the comparison group's parents, where neither spouse was much more powerful than the other. Either there was equality or the husband, though dominating, did not downgrade his wife.

The extreme social snobbery and elegance-seeking of many homosexuals (the "piss-elegant faggot" manner, according to the vernacular) was explained by Bieber as a by-product of parental downgrading. Many a homosexual's mother felt she had married beneath herself, and she scorned her husband's "vulgar" interests and behavior, as compared to her genteel and "esthetic" (nonaggressive) ones. To avoid being humiliated and rejected like his father, the son identified with his mother's "superior" manners, interests and social goals.

To see the reality from which Bieber's clinical abstractions came, here is a condensed excerpt from the case history of one of his subjects with a typical CBI mother and detached-hostile father:

> The patient was outstandingly handsome, of imposing height and muscular development . . . he enjoyed exposing his magnificent physique on the beach for ladies to admire. He attempted heterosexual intercourse for the first time at age twenty-eight and failed. His homosexual practices began with mutual masturbation at seventeen. He had extended periods of sexual inactivity.
>
> His mother was nervous, overprotective, seductive and close-binding-intimate. "She is a bundle of nerves and terror. She considers my father a villain." When the patient was four, his parents quarreled bitterly, and the mother said she would raise the child without the father's help. The father remained an outsider. He was of German extraction, and during World War I the patient was frequently chased off the street by other children and called "Heinie," whereupon his mother would say, "Never mind, come into the house with me—I will teach you how to knit." He learned to knit well.
>
> Between four and seven he had a minor intestinal condition, and his mother kept him in bed most of the time. Her daily ritual was to rub his back, then pat his buttocks and kiss them. When he was seven years old he had an erection while she did this. He was completely terrified, and desperately frightened that she would notice it. He thought that he must hide it, and that this must never happen again. He said that "the back-rub business" made

him so afraid of sexual activity that he had divided himself in half—from the waist down he was numb.

The mother was a "vitamin-conscious" hypochondriac who made her son worry excessively about his health. At eight and nine he had asthma. "My asthma is the story of my attachment and dependency on my mother."

The patient had no playmates during childhood. His mother would criticize him as soon as he "opened up" with others. "It was as if she demanded that I give her all my attention. She criticized my friends and did it so nicely that it hurt more."

The father was like a boarder in the house, and the patient always felt uneasy with him. The father was assiduously protective of his possessions and immaculate in personal habits. He fastidiously avoided drinking out of a glass that either the patient or the mother had used. He never kissed either one on the lips. The patient was never permitted to wear his father's ties, even ones that had been discarded. In fact, the father did not permit the patient to touch anything belonging to him.

When the patient was three and a half he was given a tricycle that was too tall for him. His feet did not reach the pedals. "I got on to ride it, but I started to roll down the hill. My father was standing there—tall, still, dressed very correctly. He watched but did nothing to try to stop me. I was terrified. I went racing down the hill and fell off. My father just continued to stand there."

The patient felt that through his father's prudishness he had become imbued with the idea that sex was filthy and revolting.

The patient never had a feeling of moral support for any assertive acts, but when he ran away from fights his father would harshly accuse him of cowardice. "My father's voice always sounded rough and harsh to me. Whenever I had a boss who had a harsh voice, I would panic."

The patient recalled only one occasion when his father played with him. The mother asked the father to play ball with him, and he complied, but his reluctance provoked the mother to anger. He retaliated by saying that the boy couldn't catch. The patient felt extremely humiliated. Since then, he has experienced anxiety when anyone suggested playing catch.

In a troubled family, a good relationship with a sibling compensated somewhat for parental lacks, and might even tip the scales in favor of heterosexuality. More homosexuals than comparisons wanted to be like a brother, despite the fact that more homosexuals hated their brothers. Apparently identifying with a brother was a desperate attempt to find a male model. Not one homosexual who wanted to be like his brother admired his father, and the seventeen comparisons who wanted to be like males other than their fathers were among the most disturbed of the group. Unfortunately, most of the homosexuals developed distorted relationships with siblings, partly because of parental favoritism. They tended to compete with their brothers for the love of the mother, and with their sisters for the love of the father. Effeminacy, in some homosexuals, seems to have developed as an attempt to rival a sister the father favored. Few of the homosexuals had homosexual siblings; Bieber concluded that when a family produces two homosexual sons, the parents create similar destructive triangles with each in turn.

Not all the homosexuals had CBI mothers and detached fathers. A distinctive group of eight mothers, though covertly seductive, were openly hostile, contemptuous, critical and belittling to their sons. In contrast to CBI mothers, they inspired as much fight as flight, and that aggressiveness made the boys' homosexuality less entrenched: six of the eight were bisexual in behavior; five were exclusively heterosexual after treatment. Another seven mothers, though superficially affable and affectionate, were basically cold and unrelated to their sons. The sons, like Harlow's rejected baby monkeys, never gave up trying to win their mothers' love— and not one became heterosexual. A few homosexuals' fathers were overprotective. Thirteen fathers were not detached; though often rivalrous, destructive and humiliating, they had some positive feelings for their boys as well. Even largely hostile attention was better than none; half the sons of such fathers became heterosexual.

But the most common pattern, the "classic" pattern, was the CBI mother and hostile-detached father. "Paternal hostility and engulfing maternalism," wrote Bieber, "emerge throughout our findings as having the most telling and destructive impact." Only four patients with such parents became heterosexual. Nearly half of all the homosexuals had CBI mothers and detached or absent fathers, and the rest had various combinations of parental favoritism, hostility, seductiveness, indifference and control. Not one had a healthy mother and warm father; not one had a relationship with either parent "that could reasonably be called normal."

If Bieber's ideas on the causes of homosexuality were correct, he would have to explain the fact that thirty-two comparisons had CBI mothers and fifty-four had detached fathers. Why hadn't they too become homosexual? They did, in fact, share a number of problems with the homosexuals, such as anxiety about sexual arousal. But these problems were less acute in the comparisons, and their parents were distinctly *less* CBI and detached than the homosexuals'. They had feared their fathers less as children, felt less babied by their mothers, and avoided physical aggression less. A smaller dose of parental pathology had damaged their maleness, but not decisively.

Bieber selected for special study nine of the thirty-two comparisons whose background and childhood development so resembled the homosexuals' as to be indistinguishable. Each had a seductive, puritanical mother and a detached father whom the mother held in contempt; each showed the typical features of a prehomosexual childhood. Seven of the nine now suffered from impotence and from anxiety over homosexual fantasies and impulses. Still, they had not developed homosexual identities and behavior. A meticulous probing of their histories showed that their mothers had interfered with their heterosexuality less than the CBI mothers of homosexuals. Some of the mothers, though rejecting their husbands, held up one of the boy's uncles or some other male as an admirable man. The fathers, though hostile, ineffectual or indifferent, put up some resistance to the mothers' campaign of infantilization and somehow encouraged their sons' masculinity. In short, one or both parents showed that they valued masculinity and heterosexuality.

Bieber turned from family background to his subjects' childhood development. The mothers' sexual provocations produced precocious and sometimes compulsive sexuality—masturbation and sex play with other children—which in turn created more guilt. Here, it seemed, was the source of the sexual preoccupation of so many homosexuals. However, this hypersexuality did not lead to a healthful reaching out toward others, for it occurred within a pattern of stunted psychosocial growth. The mother's overprotectiveness and the father's disinterest or contempt made the boy feel inadequate with other children. His peers were quick to sense his timidity and to mock him as a sissy. His failure to be a competent, independent, "regular" boy reinforced his feeling of shameful impotence. Three quarters of the homosexuals had been excessively fearful of physical injury as children; 80 per cent avoided competitive sports, and 90 per cent avoided fights. Almost two thirds were lone wolves, and a third played mostly with girls. Half thought of themselves as frail.

Despite thinking themselves frail, the homosexuals as a group had excellent health records; only two had had severe childhood illnesses. Few had judged themselves athletic or well coordinated, and this self-evaluation carried over into adulthood in many cases, sometimes despite courses of body-building. Bieber concluded that feeling clumsy was a result of anxiety and muscle tension in competitive situations. The marked pattern of timidity and defeatism might reflect the fears of overanxious mothers, but Bieber considered another possibility—that it was a façade of fragility to hide competitive strength, which the homosexuals consciously or unconsciously equated with masculinity. This made sense in the light of the common clinical observation that fear of a mother's rejection and of a father's retaliation often created such a denial of one's own strength. Bieber tested the idea by studying frailness, effeminacy, and fear of castration and injury.

He learned that generalized fear of injury and fear of castration tended to exist together in a person, and both were far more common in the homosexuals than in the comparisons. Baseball, the most popular competitive sport, had special symbolic meaning to many of them; they recounted dreams of fast balls hurting their genitals, having the bat splinter in their hands, or hitting the ball weakly. Other patent symbols of castration, injury, weakness and failure were common, and they often went hand in hand with vague apprehensions and phobias.

Such feelings of fear and helplessness did not coincide with having a physically punitive father. They reflected emotional conflict rather than real threat, and they tended to exist along with a special cluster of background items—extreme dependence on a CBI mother, hatred of the father, parental strictures on masturbation, and disgust at the female genitals. These correlations and a wealth of clinical material supported Bieber's guess that fear and timidity were a protective camouflage of assertion rising from Oedipal conflict. The close mother-son bond made the prehomosexual son murderously competitive with his father and proportionately afraid of retaliation. This extended to nonsexual matters. His parents' strict sexual and nonsexual prohibitions reinforced each other in his mind till all behavior suggesting masculinity and aggression caused him acute anxiety. The child's fears were "projected to external sources, sexual and nonsexual, creating a generalized fear of attack. Phobias (fears of mice and insects, etc.) are a common manifestation of such fears." In sexual life, the result was a phobic reaction to the female genitals, a defensive avoidance rising from fear of the consequences of heterosexuality.

If the homosexuals' insistence on being frail, clumsy and ineffective was a denial of their own strength—"I'll cut myself down to size before my father or anyone else can"—the same might be true of effeminacy. A third of Bieber's subjects showed some effeminacy, only two markedly. About the same proportion sometimes had a wish to be women, but more often than not the two phenomena failed to overlap. Only fifteen of the thirty-eight who wanted to be women were effeminate, and the majority of effeminate men did not want to be women. (Rather, the wish to be a woman correlated most strongly with having a distant father and craving his acceptance.) Wanting to be a woman and being effeminate might become intertwined, but the chief function of effeminacy, like "frailness," seemed to be a declaration of nonaggressiveness. This interpretation explains the fact that many effeminate gestures have no relation at all to feminine stereotypes—tightly held shoulders, elbows to the sides, arms not swinging naturally with footsteps. Bieber pointed out that effeminacy is a *sui generis* style, neither masculine nor feminine; shrugging, wrist-breaking and hand-to-hip posturing are bizarre in either sex. (One wonders whether an ethologist would see some of them as displacement of aggression.) Bieber called attention to the fact that most effeminate gestures are confined to small arcs in space and directed toward the midline of the body—the opposite of the easy, outreaching gestures associated with confident assertion. In sum, effeminacy seems to be a misleadingly named body language that combines reversal of masculine signals, nonassertive signs and some elements of burlesqued femininity to announce, "I won't fight, I'm not dangerous—if necessary, not even a man."

The "bisexuals" had fewer potency problems with either sex than the exclusive homosexuals had with men. They were more openly aggressive and competitive, and showed little of the covert competitiveness so common in the homosexuals. Fewer had CBI mothers, few had been lone wolves as children. As a group, they showed less acute emotional disturbance. Their ability to assert themselves sexually and nonsexually went in tandem. Bieber concluded that "every homosexual is, in reality, a 'latent' heterosexual; hence we expected to find evidence of heterosexual striving among the H-patients in our study." And this turned out to be the case. Only a quarter of the comparisons had homosexual dreams, but half the homosexuals had heterosexual dreams. Homosexuality itself, then, appeared to be primarily a phobia, an irrational fear of the female genitals meant to cover a fear of heterosexual assertion. Bieber found that half the homosexual subjects wanted a partner with a large penis, and that this desire usually went along with fear of genital injury and aversion to the female genitals.

Further confirmation of Bieber's views came from a separate study by two members of his team of thirty adolescent homosexuals who were chosen because they were so different from the adult subjects. The adults were mostly middle class, well educated, neurotic, and relatively set in their sexual and emotional patterns. The adolescents, most of them from New York's Bellevue Psychiatric Hospital, were lower class, poorly educated, profoundly disturbed, and at a volatile crisis point in their lives. These boys did show in acute, obvious form the problems Bieber had inferred in the adults' development.

The boys divided rather neatly into two groups, hypermasculine and effeminate. Those keeping up a masculine, heterosexual front showed extreme anxiety, severe conflict, and acting-out of the conflict. Many were preoccupied with body-building and pretended to be Don Juans, but worked as homosexual prostitutes; at first they insisted they did so only for gain, but later admitted this was not so. One boy had robbed all his customers at knife-point. Another had reported about fifty homosexual assaults on himself to the police; many of the men had been arrested and sentenced to jail before the boy's game was discovered. Another broke into houses seeking men's jewelry, which he threw away. He had been institutionalized after setting fire to an apartment where he found no jewelry to steal. He complained bitterly that his father never gave him what he wanted, and when asked how he felt while setting the fire, said that "it was like when I don't get what I want from my father."

The effeminate boys showed no apparent conflict about being homosexual—as long as they could act effeminate. When they were in wards full of tough heterosexual boys and had to drop their mannerisms for safety's sake, they became acutely anxious. One solved the problem by seducing the ward bully and becoming effeminate again while under his protection. This fit the effeminates' usual pattern of becoming "mistresses" to protective partners. But in even the most effeminate boys there were histories, dreams and fantasies of heterosexual activity—admitted only after establishing a relationship of trust with the psychiatrist. (Typically, one effeminate boy told of a night spent at the home of a girlfriend when her parents were away. She got into bed with him, and he became "numb" and "paralyzed"; within a few days he yielded to a compulsion to pick up a homosexual partner.) Desires for heterosexuality and masculinity, when they became conscious, caused the effeminates anxiety; in fact, so did any kind of impulse to sexual assertion. With their bed partners, they usually avoided using their penises; they let themselves be penetrated orally or anally and hoped for spontaneous orgasm. They even tended to avoid masturbation, finding their own excitement disturbing.

The adolescents' parents fit the CBI-and-detached pattern that had appeared in the adult subjects' families; the only difference was that the fathers tended to be even more brutal yet ineffectual. Some of the fathers occasionally tyrannized their homes by violence, especially when bolstered by alcohol, but most of the time the mothers tightly controlled their families. There was not one case of marital love and respect, nor one couple whose sex life was more than minimal. The homosexual sons were isolated and overprotected by their mothers and saw them as protectors against their feared fathers. In some of the families, sibling rivalries developed that were so intense the parents didn't dare leave the children alone together.

The mothers were marvelously unconcerned about their sons' effeminacy, but quite disturbed at the thought that they might be sexually active. The psychiatrists asked the mothers whether their sons masturbated. One said no, she sewed up his pockets to make sure he couldn't. Another became upset, said the question disgusted her, and denied that her boy did such things; she would know if he did, because she always checked his clothes for incriminating evidence. Another gave the extraordinary answer, "If being a boy is to go out and steal and play with yourself, I'm glad L. is the way he is."

When Bieber sifted through all the data on his adult subjects, he found that they, like the adolescents, tended to identify partners with one or more members of their families (father and brother or sister and mother). In fact, there were many correlations between family background, sexual identification, choice of sex partners, and sex behavior. For instance, every homosexual with a CBI mother and a detached-hostile father who downgraded and dominated his wife, identified his sex partners with his feared and hated father. Such correlations suggest consistent psychosexual patterns, logically connecting factors as different as the parents' marriage and the son's preferred sexual acts. Most of these patterns are too complex to be gone into here, but the question of "active" and "passive" sexuality is of special importance.

Bieber began by tossing out the labels; it is questionable that a person sucking someone else's penis is more passive than the partner who lies back and lets himself be serviced. Furthermore, the preferred sexual act of almost half the subjects was mutual masturbation; some others preferred only hugging and cuddling. And many who did prefer oral or anal sex took both roles, depending on partners, mood and circumstance. Therefore Bieber divided his subjects into insertors and insertees. A third preferred inserting in oral and anal sex, a third preferred receiving, and others had no preference.

Contrary to conventional expectations, there were only a few differences between the two groups, but they were important differences. The insertors followed no pattern, but many insertees scored high on a particular cluster of items—a seductive but harshly antisexual mother, strong masturbation guilt, deep fear and submissiveness toward the father, and frailness or effeminacy in childhood. Only one insertor scored high on all these counts. Some insertors sought feminine partners, apparently a covert expression of heterosexual drives. But almost all the insertees sought partners with very masculine characteristics; while being buggered, they often imagined themselves in the female role, with the anus as a vagina. The insertees were more anxious about sex than insertors, had more potency problems, and as a group were more deeply disturbed. Neither insertors nor insertees showed greater potential for heterosexuality, but anal insertees had a poorer chance than oral insertees.

Many of the correlations Bieber found call for further research in the future, with larger samples and extended research methods. But one finding was so provocative that it has tended to overshadow these intricate and important results—the fact that almost 30 per cent of the homosexuals became exclusively heterosexual as a result of treatment. There had been chances to follow up the results three, four or more years after the end of therapy in many cases. When the book appeared, a number of the subjects were still in treatment, and at least a few more could be expected to change; one could assume a final change rate of one in three. A fifth of the exclusive homosexuals had changed, and half of those classified as bisexual (on whatever extent of heterosexual experience). Another fifth of the exclusive homosexuals had become bisexual, and the vast majority of all the subjects had generally improved in nonsexual areas of adjustment. Although Bieber did not spell out his definition of change, it was apparently the usual, stringent one used by most psychoanalysts—not only had homosexual acts ceased and been replaced by regular, pleasurable heterosexual ones, but there were no homosexual impulses, masturbation fantasies or recurring dreams.

As in therapy for all problems, motivation was the biggest single factor in success; though half the subjects had not entered therapy for the purpose of changing their orientation, some of these did eventually change. Bieber presented a profile of the typical (though not the only) homosexual who changed. He began treatment before passing age thirty-five and stuck it out for at least 150 hours (a year to a year and a half), preferably 350 hours or more (three or four years). He was not an only child, and had some positive feelings toward women. His father was at least ambivalent rather than detached, and the boy felt some respect, admiration or affection for him. He acknowledged rivalry with his brothers, reacted to stress with rage, and sometimes had fantasies of violence when sexually excited—all indications of being able to feel and admit his own aggressiveness.

There was, predictably, a direct relationship between change and how exclusive a man's homosexuality was, and how early in life it was set. A man who had had heterosexual contact by sixteen had a good chance of changing; if he had not done so by twenty-one, he wasn't likely even to remain in treatment. Effeminacy was a sign of poor but not hopeless prognosis. Psychiatric diagnosis—schizoid, character disorder, etc.—had no relation to change.

Some scientists greeted Bieber's results with disbelief or even accusations of wishful thinking. Therapeutic pessimism about homosexuality went back to Freud. When his daughter, Dr. Anna Freud, surveyed analytic writing on changing homosexuals in 1951, she found that the same negative tone prevailed. In fact, in 1947 Dr. D. Stanley-Jones had written in England that the goal of change was not only futile but "quite indefensible when regarded in the light of absolute morality: attempted 'treatment' or alteration of the basic personality of an inborn homosexual can only be described as a moral outrage."

Pious adherence to Freudian instinct theory and to Freud himself had created *a priori* skepticism about change—the key word in Stanley-Jones's statement is "inborn." Several decades ago, according to analyst Charles Socarides, "it was unusual for clinics to accept homosexual patients. They were 'too difficult' and the prognosis too uncertain." Nevertheless, Stekel, Bergler, Anna Freud herself and a number of other analysts had been reporting cases of change since the twenties. In advance of Bieber, they said that homosexuality grew from fear of the female genitals and of heterosexuality, and that it could often be successfully treated in the same way as most phobias. In the fifties, as adaptational theories progressively replaced instinctual ones, optimistic reports appeared in greater number. During that decade, as Bieber was just beginning his work, accounts of change came from Drs. Gustav Bychowski, Frank Caprio, Stephen Coates, Albert Ellis, Edward Glover, A. J. Hadfield, Sandor Lorand, J. F. Poe, Ismond Rosen and I. H. Rubinstein. In 1956 Dr. Clifford Allen, in England, said he had seen change in ten of sixteen homosexual patients, some quite mature and set in their homosexual patterns. That same year the American Psychoanalytic Association surveyed its members and found that a third of the homosexuals they treated underwent complete change. Since the appearance of Bieber's book, similar change rates have been reported by Drs. Daniel Cappon, Samuel Hadden, Lawrence Hatterer, Harold Lief and Charles Socarides. I have heard many clinical psychologists say they take for granted that they will get complete change in a third of their sexually deviant patients and partial change in another third.

Nevertheless, most laymen have continued to believe that homosexuals must be "adjusted to their homosexuality"—including many homosexuals. Some behaviorists, orthodox analysts and other scientists keep a stubborn or even vitriolic conviction that such changes just do not take place. This pessimism is greater in England than in the United States, and greater still in Europe; it is greater wherever psychotherapy is strongly polarized into medical and Freudian instinctual schools. In England Drs. D. J. West, Peter Scott and the team of Hemphill, Leitsch and Stuart have remained pessimistic. Drs. Curran and Parr, who were members of the Wolfenden Committee, investigated thirty-eight exclusive homosexuals who underwent psychiatric treatment and found signs of change in only three. It was on the word of such men that the Wolfenden Committee made this extraordinary statement: "We were struck by the fact that none of our medical witnesses were able, when we saw them, to provide any reference in medical literature to complete change." Some committee members, and some of its medical experts, simply chose not to believe reports of change. They obeyed Maier's Law, propounded by psychologist N. R. F. Maier: if one has a theory but the facts oppose it, dispense with the facts.

It is true that there are few systematic studies of homosexual patients with adequate information and follow-ups. Trying to evaluate the evidence for and against change can leave one floundering in a sea of arguments, refutations and counterrefutations. A few examples will give an idea of the problems involved. Curran and Parr, in their case against change, failed to describe the type and goals of treatment in their cases; if many of the doctors merely tried to adjust their patients to homosexuality, it is little wonder that so few changed. Mary Woodward's report of poor results in treating 113 homosexuals at London's Portman Clinic is often quoted as authoritative; it is not always noted that only eighty-one ever came for treatment, and only one received more than 130 hours of treatment (Bieber called for at least 150). On the other hand, the usually scrupulous Bieber was lax in specific data on follow-ups. Furthermore, he never explained his definition of bisexual; it could mean someone with a history of six hundred homosexual contacts and six heterosexual ones or just the reverse. Furthermore, definitions of homosexuality on behavioral grounds are common but doubtful. Some men have mostly heterosexual contacts but depend on homosexual fantasies to do so; Curran and Parr described a man, married for twenty-five years and the father of six, who reached orgasm with his wife only by imagining she was a man. Also, there are inhibited, nearly virginal homosexuals, just as there are "sexless" heterosexuals. Anna Freud was probably right in making the object of masturbation fantasies the final criterion of sexual orientation.

Digging into the vast literature on psychiatric cure, one sees why scientific journals are justifiably filled with mutual criticism of concepts and methods. On the basis of reading alone, one might hesitate to come to conclusions about the questions of treatment methods and change. The matter was resolved for me in the course of interviewing the authors of many of the writings. I found, very simply, that change was claimed by those who thought it possible. It was not produced by those who doubted its likeliness. There were men of intelligence and honesty in both camps, but I found much more doctrinaire and rigid thinking among the deniers of change. Among the men who impressed me most by their general qualities of intellect, imagination and emotional perceptiveness, I found widespread belief in the possibility of change.

In fact, perhaps one should revise the old clinical axiom that the chief prerequisite for cure is the patient's desire for change. It is just as true that cure depends on the skill, personality and expectations of the doctor. Cure or lack of it is often the doctor's self-fulfilling prophecy. Patients sense whether a doctor is basically unsympathetic, uninterested or unhopeful about them. The doctor can unwittingly produce false "cures" as well as false "failures." A famous psychoanalyst tells me that he has treated several former patients of the great Bergler, and a few admitted that they had lied to Bergler about stopping homosexual acts because they felt pressured by his muscular advocacy of change (they claim, at least, that he believed them). On the other hand, I asked one eminent clinician about Bieber's results, and he gave me a wise, tolerant smile and said he would believe such things when he saw them. "I've treated homosexuals for forty years," he said benignly, "and I've never seen one change. I just get them to accept and adjust to their lot." The therapist usually has a quite human ego, and likes no more than anyone else to believe that others succeed where he fails.

There is no doubt that psychotherapy—like surgery, corporate law and original mathematics—is as much an art as a science. In the thirties, when schizophrenics were considered almost impossible to treat, Harry Stack Sullivan became famous for his special, personal gift for gaining rapport with patients no one else could reach. Dr. Bruno Bettelheim has made a similar breakthrough with autistic children, who not long ago were considered untreatable. Some doctors who report high change rates in homosexuals may simply have a gift for dealing with them, or for that matter with people in general. I feel sure this is true of a number of clinicians I have interviewed. Fortunately, psychotherapy, surgery and mathematics are also sciences, and the personal gifts of one creative man can be, within limits, routinized into standard techniques by men who read his ideas and case histories. Thus conditions once considered untreatable become treatable by more and more practitioners.

One reason for doubts about reported cures is general suspicion of psychotherapy itself. Many people say it is not really scientific; therapists are fanciful and patients self-indulgent ("I have a friend who went for years—it was all he talked about, and it didn't do a bit of good"). Some such objections rise from defensive hostility, perhaps a fear of how the critic himself might be evaluated by an analyst. Others are due to magical expectations. We accept that a person may have to wear braces on crooked teeth or a bent back for years to correct a distorted physical pattern. There is no reason to expect lifelong distorted emotional and neurological patterns to vanish in weeks. And just as some people need medical support for years or for life—insulin, eyeglasses, a brace—others need continuing supportive psychotherapy. It is true that there are people who are helped little or not at all by psychotherapy, but the proportion who can be helped has grown, and no one decries medical science for now helping only some of those it could help not at all in the past. It is also true that psychotherapy is expensive and available to too few people, but this is just as true of prolonged specialized physical treatment. And last but not least among the irrational hostilities toward psychotherapy is the feeling that it is weak, self-pampering and contemptible to need help solving one's problems. It is an attitude that could be discussed with a good therapist.

Other objections are due not to hostility but to ignorance of how flexible, ambiguous and complex is even the hardest of "hard" science. Physics and genetics are full of conflicting theories and schools of thought; their histories are strewn with the skeletons of abandoned theories and techniques, once useful but replaced by others more useful. If we can tolerate a Heisenberg and an Einstein in physics, we can live with the complexities of the human sciences, which must deal with infinite variables. Science is not a body of data or of laws; it is a method, and it has been a great help when applied to human behavior over the past century. It is odd to object that psychology and psychiatry, like molecular physics, must progress slowly, by half steps and missteps, and fail to reach perfection.

One of the sorest points in the human sciences today is the question of psychiatric evaluation and results. Some scientists claim that "spontaneous" cures are as common among the neurotic and psychotic as are cures produced by psychotherapy. In arguments for both sides there is too little careful estimation of over-all life patterns. Some of the "spontaneously" cured get rid of a major debilitating symptom only to replace it with another symptom or a second line of psychic defenses—the former phobic becomes a counterphobic mountain climber, the former alcoholic becomes a vengeful antialcohol zealot. Estimates of improvement too often focus on one or two symptoms, such as homosexual behavior or other "problem" behavior, instead of a person's over-all emotional and social flexibility, satisfactions and strengths.

In a thoughtful essay on "results" in psychotherapy—one of many that have been appearing in recent years—L. Börje Löfgren compares the problems of evaluating therapy to studying the effect of various iron drugs on patients who were constantly receiving blood transfusions. "No amount of standardization of the procedures would get [the researcher] out of his difficulties. Since psychology can be regarded as the study of man's constant interaction with his surroundings, every variable that can be described must be regarded as of possible therapeutic influence." He also points out that results are not necessarily a good test of theories. If one group of patients with colds were treated with magical incantations and another according to modern virology, 100 per cent of both groups would probably be cured a couple of weeks later. Would this mean that incantations and virology are equally "good" or "true"? As Löfgren points out, the matter of evaluating psychotherapy is complex and in need of new, more sophisticated approaches. We know too little of factors outside the doctor's office that affect results—a good love affair, a vocational failure. We have not yet pinpointed the things that produce change: therapists with very different theories tend to produce similar success rates with patients, whether Jungian, Adlerian or Rogerian—in fact, they seem to end up dealing with the majority of patients in pretty much the same way as they gain professional experience. Half the analysts in Bieber's study were somewhat traditional Freudians and half were adaptational "culturalists," and their results were the same. Löfgren does consider one interesting possibility, though:

> Let us . . . assume that we have conquered all difficulties and ambiguities in the use of our term [results] and are able exactly to define mental health. Let us then assume that we have two different treatments, one a drug treatment, and the other of a psychoanalytic nature. Both of them will bring the patient to exactly the same state of mental health. There will always be some patients who will choose the one and some who will choose the other method. . . . After that the paths of the two persons will diverge, because one has the experience "I am cured by self-knowledge," and the other the experience "I am cured by a drug." This must result in two quite different attitudes and must influence the future courses of their lives. One will tend in the face of renewed difficulties to turn to drugs, and the other will attempt internalized psychological work.

The harshest critics of analytically oriented therapists have been the behaviorists, whose theories rose from Pavlov's work early in the century. As a result of his classic studies of dogs taught to salivate at the sound of a bell, Pavlov concluded that very few reflexes are innate and that the majority are learned, or conditioned. In fact, he felt that he had created in his dogs conditioned states comparable to what were then called hysteria and neurasthenia in humans. It was a logical if simplistic step to assert that most human experience can be explained as conditioned response, and that what has been conditioned can be deconditioned. John B. Watson, during the second and third decades of this century, laid down the principles of what would be known as behaviorism. His insistence on creating a "purely objective" psychology and his heroic therapeutic aims have remained typical of the school. He rejected the concept of consciousness; thought, he said, was merely the behavior of talking to oneself. The unconscious, of course, he rejected utterly. He said that an analyst might take pride in inducing insight in a patient, but a behaviorist, by refusing to speculate about "something else in addition" to conditioning and behavior, could "almost remake this very intelligent individual in a few weeks' time."

Behaviorism began winning popularity during the twenties, as a scientific fashion and an object of journalistic popularizing. Behaviorists began to try curing people of phobias and alcoholism, most commonly with "aversion therapy," in which electric shock and nauseating drugs such as apomorphine were used to make patients associate their problem behavior with displeasure. During the following decades behaviorists went on to attack addiction, smoking, stuttering, sexual deviations and finally all the disorders of the psychiatric clinic. They often made extravagant claims of success, obviously feeling—as they still do today—that they have a monopoly on the future. Still, behavior therapy for alcoholism was pretty much abandoned, for follow-ups showed it to be no more effective than group therapy or even the drug Antabuse, which makes a person sick if he drinks. Despite this far from overwhelming record of clinical success, behavior therapy not only survived its fall from fashion during the thirties, forties and fifties, but has aroused a new wave of excitement and curiosity during the past decade. One of the reasons for its revival is its recent claims of changing more sexual deviants than analytic therapists, and doing so in a small fraction of the time.

Since Watson's day, behaviorism has been refined by such men as B. F. Skinner of Harvard, H. J. Eysenck of the University of London and Joseph Wolpe of Temple University. Skinner, creator of the famous "Skinner box" and author of *Walden Two,* emphasized not only the extinction of old behavior patterns but the positive encouragement of new ones. H. J. Eysenck has written widely for scientists and laymen about learning theory (as the behaviorists usually prefer to call their work), damning psychodynamic thinking as subjective self-indulgence and looking optimistically to a correctly conditioned world. He says flatly: "Get rid of the symptoms and you have eliminated the neurosis." Wolpe uses muscle relaxation and other forms of "desensitization" to help patients replace anxiety with calm or pleasure in situations they fear. In the usual behaviorist vein, Wolpe writes that "contrary to the popular psychoanalytic conception, a neurosis is 'just' a habit—a persistent habit of unadaptive behavior, acquired by learning."

Louis Max made the first attempt to cure a sexual deviant with behavior therapy in 1935. With somewhat ghoulish detachment he described administering heavy electric shocks to a young fetishistic homosexual while showing him photographs the young man preferred. "Low shock intensities had little effect but intensities considerably higher than those usually employed on human subjects in other studies definitely diminished the emotional value of the stimulus for days after each experimental period." A four-month follow-up showed considerable improvement in the patient's responses, said Max.

This lead was not followed up for almost two decades. Then in 1953 a brief but widely noted résumé appeared in the *International Journal of Sexology* of a paper by the Czech researchers Srnec and Freund. They had treated twenty-five male homosexuals with nausea-inducing apomorphine, and as a result ten showed considerable change. Now a small but growing stream of cases appeared, especially in British journals, and the enthusasm of the behavior therapists was matched by the indignation and disgust of some of their readers. Often the therapy sounded like brutal brainwashing. Patients were kept awake day and night, shocked and dosed with emetics, and subjected to moralistic harangues and derision either by the therapist or from repeating tape loops.

A. J. Cooper, for instance, had a transvestic fetishist dress in his regalia, kept him up without food for seven days and six nights, put him before a mirror and told him to reflect on his "disgusting perversion." The treatment ended then, for the patient broke down. But his cross-dressing ended, Cooper reported, and still had not resumed nine months later. D. F. Clark, also in England, followed a similar program and reported, "At one session, by a particularly happy chance, one of [the patient's] favorite pictures fell into the vomit in the basin so that the patient had to see it every time he puked." A masterpiece of the genre came from Ian Oswald, who had a transvestite dress in female clothes and gave him apomorphine injections. On the fourth day a tape loop was played over a loudspeaker. " 'Dressing up in female clothing makes him sick' (male voice). Vomit noise. Laughter (male and female). 'Him! Trying to be a woman! It's ridiculous!' (female voice). Vomit noise. Laughter. 'Wearing brassieres make him ————' (male voice). Vomit noise. . . . Pause with three clicks and a few roaring noises."

Not all behavior therapy is so strenuous. Of perhaps a couple of hundred behaviorists in England and the United States, a fair number also use positive conditioning and "desensitizing." M. P. Feldman in England gives homosexual patients a degree of control over their own shock therapy, so that they can develop a positive feeling of creating their own relief when shown heterosexual stimuli. Wolpe not only uses desensitization but sometimes employs the "assertive training" devised by New York psychologist Andrew Salter, getting inhibited patients to practice "talking back" to family, friends and employers, and thus developing assertive patterns to supplant their old passive, self-destructive ones.

Wolpe and his associate A. A. Lazarus have spoken of obtaining 80 to 90 per cent cure rates for assorted problems as compared to the usual two-thirds improvement rate claimed by the majority of analysts—in a mean time of merely thirty sessions. There has been as much outside criticism and argument about such claims as about Bieber's, perhaps more. Probably a large majority of psychodynamic therapists suspect that in many cases, even if the obvious neurotic symptom has disappeared, a substitute symptom will take its place, for the underlying neurotic conflict has not been dealt with. Behavior therapists either do not want to think in

such terms or fail to do what an analyst would consider a careful pre-
treatment and post-treatment evaluation of the person's total emotional
functioning. But even in the simpler matter of the presenting symptom,
behavior-therapy results are open to question. Only two large-scale studies
of sexual deviants given behavior therapy have been published; one presents disappointing results, the other questionable results.

In 1958, the Czech researcher Freund wrote a second paper announcing that he had now treated sixty-seven homosexuals; he had given them
emetics and shown pictures of nude men, and then administered testosterone and shown pictures of women. In evaluating the results, he eliminated from his final figures twenty subjects referred to him by courts (such
patients, in any kind of therapy, tend not to be as highly motivated as
volunteers and usually do not respond as well to treatment). Of the remaining forty-seven, twelve reached "heterosexual adaptation" (performed coitus) and had maintained it two years after treatment. This
conclusion is sometimes quoted without further qualifications, though
Freund himself added some important ones. Of the twelve, only one had
lost his homosexual desires entirely; the other eleven all said their homosexual urges still outbalanced the heterosexual ones. A second follow-up
two years later showed that only six of the twelve were still exclusively
heterosexual in behavior. All still had homosexual desires, and three were
practicing homosexual acts fairly frequently. In short, the results were
worse by far than those claimed by analysts with any optimism at all
about treating homosexuality.

In 1967 M. J. MacCulloch and M. P. Feldman wrote in England that
they had given electric-shock aversion therapy to forty-three homosexuals,
of whom thirty-six stuck through the full course of treatment. Follow-ups
a year or more later showed that twenty-five of the thirty-six were "improved," and thirteen were having no homosexual contacts and performed
heterosexual coitus without the help of homosexual fantasies. So roughly a
third of those who finished treatment changed completely, another third
changed somewhat, and a third not at all—the same results Bieber had
found among analysts. Then at the end of MacCulloch's and Feldman's
paper, which seems a scrupulously detailed and statistically sophisticated
piece of work, there occurs an extraordinary juggling of figures. The authors compare their two-third improvement rate with Bieber's one-third
rate of total change, and claim superior success. This sleight-of-hand conclusion has been quoted in at least one widely read and reputable science
magazine.

It is difficult to believe that this misrepresentation rose either from statistical naïveté or from malicious intent to deceive. Nor should such motives be attributed to most other behavior therapists, though their use of
systematic and detailed follow-ups is rare. (A reputable London psychologist tried a few years ago to survey the results of behavior therapy on
sexual deviants; she wrote to about a hundred behavior therapists and

received not one reply.) The very men who most castigate analysis as unscientific and subjective often seem cavalier about scientific method and full of self-fulfilling intellectual prophecies. The explanation, I believe, can be found in the comment of an eminent British analyst, who said to me, "I think some of these men believe so strongly in what they are doing, and the good it will accomplish, that they feel they just don't have time for the proofs they demand of everyone else."

So behavior therapists who make such extravagant claims and produce such sketchy proof are no more cynical frauds than they are sadists. They are men of zeal and often of the highest intentions; they feel that talk about emotional subtleties is obscurantist and muzzy-headed, and too little help for people with day-to-day problems. Unfortunately, they represent a utopian reductionism that insists on the perfectibility of man through simple, direct and rigid means. The tone of Salter's book on assertive therapy constantly evokes Sheldon's paeans to the ideal, narrowly conventional mesomorph, and the papers of many practitioners of behavior therapy resurrect the spirit of the eugenic engineers and lobotomists of three and six decades ago, who, instead of seeking a complex physical substratum for our complex psychic development, reduced the psyche to a set of simple physical events and nothing more.

Analytically oriented therapists, of course, have much to say in return to the behaviorists. They await careful, detailed studies of over-all emotional functioning after treatment. Even if substitute symptoms do not turn up, the "cure" itself must be considered as a possible second line of neurotic defense: the reformed alcoholic who becomes a shouting, full-time crusader against the bottle has merely substituted a less self-destructive dysfunction, which in analytic therapy would be considered only a first step toward full cure. Furthermore, if the successes claimed by behaviorists turn out to be reliable, the method may be useful only for a very special, small range of people. Behavior therapy is rigorous and even agonizing. Psychiatrist A. D. Jonas points out that in any group of patients there are some seeking a "magical cure" through pills, shocks or one-paragraph panaceas; they are very highly motivated to change and are ripe to respond to almost any kind of treatment. The volunteers for behavior therapy may well contain a larger-than-usual proportion of such people. Feldman himself notes the hectoring, moralistic and muscular tone of many behavior therapists, and he suggests that they might "render the whole situation so unpleasant as to force the patient to a 'flight into health.' "

Furthermore, there is little in behavior therapy that cannot be just as well explained psychodynamically. Aversion therapy often includes support, advice and explanations (insight) from the therapist, the same aids given in psychodynamic therapy. Wolpe and other behaviorists deny that "transference" and other such analytic events take place in behavior therapy, but some analysts who have observed behavior-therapy sessions claim they do. Even Ian Oswald, whose tape recording of derision, vomiting sounds and scare noises was quoted earlier, admits, *"The success of aversion therapy is vitally dependent upon personal relationships* [italics his]. The therapist must establish a sufficiently good relationship with the patient first to persuade the patient to start upon what, he must be warned, may be the most terrible experience of his life, and secondly, to sustain the patient throughout the treatment when, as invariably happens, the patient angrily rejects the whole situation and demands his clothes and shoes."

Wolpe and Ian Stevenson wrote a paper in 1960 about successfully using Salter-style assertive therapy on three sexual deviants and finding that the sexual symptom began to fade although it was not being specifically deconditioned. They apparently were not aware of decades of analytic literature about deviance often being symptomatic of low self-esteem and blocked assertion. Many other behaviorists as well tend to sound as though they are proudly discovering the wheel in the twentieth century, and their argument is less with modern psychiatry than with the orthodox Freudianism of fifty years ago. Stekel, the Rogerians and many others have practiced short-term, problem-centered therapy, with emphasis on changed behavior as well as insight, since the earlier decades of psychotherapy. Analysts have known since Freud's day that phobics must eventually be gotten to do the things they fear. Yet only a few years ago Joseph Cautela of Boston College observed with a sense of discovery that some patients to whom he gave behavior therapy spontaneously produced insights like those that emerge in psychoanalysis!

But like many ideologues, the behaviorists will probably in the long run have some positive effect on the mainstream of psychotherapy. They have given a good shake to what remains of the old piety toward Freud's Socratic belief in truth (insight) as being itself the solution to problems. Some therapists do still underestimate how much improved functioning heightens self-esteem, and the extent to which some people can change without extensive insight. More and more analytic therapists are taking cues (rather than borrowing methods) from behaviorism. Dr. Lawrence Hatterer, in his recent book on treating male homosexuals, describes his use of edited taped "capsules" of crucial analytic sessions, which his patients play at home as reminders (or reinforcement, if one wishes) between treatment hours. Albert Ellis, Masters and Johnson and a number of others who treat sexual problems are speeding up the behavior-change aspect of psychological counseling and borrowing concepts from the learning-theory armamentarium.

Doubtless some people respond better to certain kinds of therapy. In my own interviewing, I spoke to a woman who consulted Albert Ellis once but never returned, frightened by his suggestions of immediately changing her sexual behavior. She improved during slow, patient treatment from an analytically oriented therapist who gave her time to gradually relax her emotional defenses and change at her own wary pace. On the other hand,

I have spoken to several people who spent minimally productive years in nondirective therapy and then responded quickly to directive, behavior-oriented therapy with such men as Ellis. Ideally, I believe, both approaches should be within the range of every therapist, to be used in different balances with various patients.

Other techniques as well hold promise in the treatment of sexual deviations. LSD has been used successfully as an adjunct to the analytic therapy of some homosexuals. When group therapy came into use a few decades ago, many clinicians felt it would not help homosexuals and that homosexuals disrupted mixed-problem groups. Now group therapy has become a common adjunct to individual therapy. For decades Dr. Samuel Hadden, a Philadelphia psychiatrist, has been a lonely pioneer in treating groups consisting entirely of homosexuals; now the eminent psychologist Wardell Pomeroy, once a colleague of Alfred Kinsey, is doing so as well. The decades to come will probably see a flexible mixture of clinical methods erode the old fatalism about treating deviations and a new therapeutic optimism rapidly taking its place.

Before leaving the subject of treatment and change, we must look at a view opposing both the analysts and behaviorists, one that has become increasingly popular in scientific circles over the past decade. In 1956 the Group for the Advancement of Psychiatry issued a report calling persisting adult homosexuality a "severe emotional disorder." Evelyn Hooker, a California psychologist, objected that few clinicians examine homosexuals outside of mental-health facilities and prisons. She found thirty homosexuals with at least an average adjustment to life aside from their homosexuality and then gathered a control group of heterosexuals who matched them in age, education and IQ. All sixty took the Rorschach, TAT (Thematic Apperception Test) and MAPS (Make-A-Picture-Story)—all projective tests commonly used as diagnostic aids. Two testing experts evaluated the results "blind," not knowing the subjects or their sexual orientation.

Neither judge did better than chance in telling homosexuals from heterosexuals; general adjustment scores were the same for both groups. One judge said after learning that a certain subject was homosexual, "We talk about a guy sometimes who functions fairly well until you mention 'Republican' or 'Communist,' then you plug in a whole series of paranoid or illusory material; at this point the guy is just crazy. *This* guy has an encapsulated homosexual system. . . . I mean, it's like a guy who has a tic; ordinarily we say he must have a very severe problem. Maybe he does, but if you examine the material of lots of people who have tics, you will find some people who look pretty good. . . . If you want proof that homosexuals can be normal, this record does it."

Hooker concluded that homosexuals may be "very ordinary individuals, indistinguishable, except in sexual pattern, from ordinary individuals who are heterosexual. Or . . . that some *may* be quite superior individuals, not only devoid of pathology (unless one insists that homosexuality itself is a sign of pathology) but also functioning at a superior level." She suggested that homosexuality as a clinical entity does not exist; its forms may be as varied as those of heterosexuality, and compatible with good adjustment in the rest of life.

Hooker's paper appeared at about the same time as many of the influential works by the sociologists of deviance, and her results and the sociologists' theories reinforced each other. Michael Schofield in England produced an ambitiously titled book, *Sociological Aspects of Homosexuality,* in which he came to the conclusion that homosexuals, as a group, may differ from heterosexuals only in their object choice. Hooker, Schofield and others were attempting to humanize and even normalize the sexual deviant, and argued with traditional psychiatric ideas of sickness and health. During the sixties a growing number of scientists have joined them or made a bow in their direction, sometimes earnestly, and sometimes with contrite relish that smacks of "radical chic." Thomas Szasz in the United States and Ronald Laing in England have both written extensively to the point that traditional ideas of sickness and health are tools of social repressiveness at worst and narrow conventionalism at best. Now no representative scientific commission on deviance, sexual or other, would omit Hooker, Schofield, Martin Hoffman, Wainwright Churchill or one of the others who now speak for the existence of the generally adjusted homosexual.

Hooker's methods and interpretations beg for argument. Since all her subjects were carefully selected for their good adjustment, it is no surprise that neither group showed gross pathology. There is much debate about what projective tests reveal; it is often impossible to distinguish men from women by a Rorschach test, let alone homosexuals from heterosexuals. (Despite many attempts to find a characteristic homosexual Rorschach response, none has appeared.) Most such tests are intended as adjuncts to diagnosis; few experts in projective testing, which is a complex specialty in itself, would claim definitive results from blind evaluations. Even Hooker's idea that there are many homosexualities is not new; it has been stated since the thirties by Clara Thompson and many other psychiatrists. Hooker's paper, far from being the final word, is an interesting lead for further research.

But psychiatry and social science have polarized around the work of Bieber and Hooker, and the argument is often blatantly unscientific. Some Hooker enthusiasts equate Bieber's work with conventional, authoritarian or even fascistic attitudes, and fear that his findings will provide one more sanction for the persecution of sexual nonconformists. Some Bieber enthusiasts equate Hooker's camp with homosexual apologetics, and fear that it will be used to fortify deviant patterns in people who might otherwise benefit from treatment. Unfortunately, there is a grain of truth in each charge. Bieber's study bespeaks a pervasive conviction that homosexuality is quite incompatible with a productive and rewarding life, Hooker's a running implication that only the Biebers of this world make homosexuals feel ashamed, unhappy and maladjusted.

I do not see how anyone who has spoken with many homosexuals can say categorically that homosexuals are sick. Some live varied, productive, rewarding lives and seem as happy and successful as many of their heterosexual peers. Though there is one large area of dysfunction in their lives—an inability to relate sexually to the opposite sex and a sexualizing of relationships with their own—most heterosexuals have areas of dysfunction as well, and on the balance seem no more healthy. However, I also feel that only a small minority of homosexuals reach the upper levels of adaptive success. And even if their homosexuality is "encapsulated," one must question the value of encapsulating one's love life. Many well-adjusted homosexuals would probably be even better adjusted without their deviation.

Dr. Judd Marmor commented to me, "Szasz is right in saying that some so-called illness is just socially unacceptable behavior—for instance, some of the delinquencies. But he overstates the case; some people do feel intense dis-ease, and people with psychoses are ill. I agree on not labeling deviants or using psychiatric treatment as a punishment. Homosexuality isn't a disease, but it is deviant, and I think more homosexuals than heterosexuals are unhappy." In the same vein, psychiatrist A. D. Jonas said, "Instead of sickness we should speak of inability to adapt under stress. Sickness *results* from poor adaptation. If a twenty-five-year-old person is immature, he is not sick; but if his life circumstances demand that he behave like an adult, he will begin to show symptoms, and then he is sick. In my experience, most homosexuals fall in a range from the middle to the bottom of the scale of general adaptation, with a very small number toward the top. At the bottom are the pansexuals, the babies and the effeminate queens who cannot deal with stress. You almost never see them come for treatment or stay in it. One step up is the passive-dependent one, who comes to relieve his dysphoria but not to be cured. He is hypersensitive, phobic, can't sustain effort; heterosexuality is an unbearable burden to him. The homosexual with a strong ego, and with good muscle tone and a firm gait may have become homosexual because of incest fear, a seduction, a bad pregnancy; there is good prognosis for treatment. But if you try to change the very passive homosexual with a poor work record and other obvious adaptive problems, there is a good chance he will crack or take out his ego problems elsewhere."

The idea of psychological health (or maturity or any of a dozen other such terms) is nebulous. Freud's dictum that health is the ability to love and to work contains a solid kernel of truth, but it cannot be used literally. Some very paranoid people enter highly competitive professions and, because of their very disorder, become worldly successes. Many people go through life deeply neurotic or even on the edge of psychosis, yet hold jobs, maintain a family life and never become "mental patients"—at least as long as they are not subjected to certain stresses. Hooker and others are unjustified in arguing that psychiatrists see only the sick homosexuals, for some of the sickest never go for treatment. And sociologists of deviance who say homosexuals adjust well because they hold jobs and cope with the usual demands of life are scanting the question of how great a range of human experience such "adjusted" people may block out of their lives. It is equally indefensible for psychiatrists to argue that despite every evidence of general adjustment, a homosexual is sick.

It has taken the better part of a century for the majority of our society to think of sexual behavior in terms of sickness and health rather than virtue and sin. Given some more time, perhaps we can drop those categories in turn and accept the concept of over-all adaptation to life, in which sexual orientation is only one factor. Homosexuality probably does originate in emotional conflict or developmental distortion, but in a minority of homosexuals it seems to be minimally damaging—or at least no more damaging than the conflicts and distortions from which many acceptably "average" heterosexuals suffer. Meanwhile, anachronistic arguments about health and sickness divert attention from the many aspects of homosexuality that need research so that those who want treatment and change will have a better chance.

INTERVIEWS

The leading theoretician of behavior therapy is Professor H. J. Eysenck of the University of London. I have heard scientists variously describe him as a genius and a zealot. He has written widely for scientists and laymen attacking psychodynamic thinking and treatment as unscientific and unhelpful. I find him a pleasant-mannered, coolly genial man in his fifties. I ask him about the people who volunteer for behavior therapy. He says:

We can only treat people who are truly dissatisfied with their state. The one who says he is happy but is in jail or in psychotherapy isn't for us. We only take the ones who really want to change.

Who diagnoses them homosexual, and on what grounds?

You'll have to talk to my assistants about that. They deal with the people. They can tell you better than I.

Do you treat any of the patients?

I'm just a theoretician. My assistants are the ones you should talk to about things like that.

Then you've never treated people at all.

[*An almost shy smile and shake of the head.*] I'm just interested in the theory of learning. See Feldman, my assistant. I do theory, not therapy.

Yes. What were you saying about the subjects?

Homosexuals should be easy to work with, because deviance is conditioned behavior. Therefore it should be easy to decondition. The problem is that because their activity is pleasurable, it's hard to get them to change. We're still just at the beginning of this sort of work, but it's already remarkably successful.

You've written widely attacking psychodynamic treatment for lack of follow-ups, but behavior therapy reports offer equally limited follow-ups.

Long-term follow-ups are rare in all kinds of therapy. It's quite irresponsible, but that's the way it's done. Also, it costs a lot of money, and we haven't the money or facilities here. Actually, I've predicted that you should expect relapse after aversion therapy, because there's no subsequent reinforcement of the newly learned behavior. I suggest booster treatments. It's surprising that relapses aren't more frequent. Spacing out and delaying extinction of the old pattern gives a better chance of cure. So does desensitization, according to Wolpe. He says we should desensitize anxiety in an alcoholic rather than drinking itself, but I don't agree that that's necessarily better. Still, it's too early to be sure about such questions yet. There's a relapse in many kinds of treatment.

I've heard it said that behavior therapy may inhibit homosexual behavior but put nothing in its place. It just conditions out accustomed sexual response.

It's true, the problem isn't just change; we have to create a satisfactory alternative. The problem isn't so much getting rid of the homosexuality, it's relapse because of lack of alternatives. We ought to create a positive feeling for the person, teach him to dance and pick up a girl. Kraft here in London set up social groups and such with alcoholics, and maybe something similar could be done with homosexuals. But you know, there's something wrong with so many of these people anyway.

How so?

I mean, they're poor or ugly or something, inferior in some way. So what choice do they have?

If you don't see patients, how did you find that out?

That's the general impression I get from the workers. Besides, there's something in a paper . . . [*He rummages through a few volumes but cannot find the item, so we resume our talk.*]

Do you put more faith in chemical or electric therapy?

I prefer shock to chemical aversion. We can control the timing better, and chemicals are unnecessarily messy and unpleasant. We don't have to use high-level shock; mild shock is just as effective. Now we're trying to refine the timing and sequence techniques. One idea that came here from America is to do this by computer. If anxiety gets too intense, a button goes on, and the whole process of shock-conditioning goes back to a lower level. We still have a lot to work out in this sort of thing.

You do feel that psychodynamic approaches are worthless.

We have to train people to forget all this psychodynamic nonsense and learn about learning and conditioning. Fortunately, general acceptance of our work has been very wholehearted and quick. Recently a questionnaire was sent to English psychiatrists, and it showed that those over forty were against behavior therapy, and those under forty are almost 100 per cent for it. The young see that it works, and they're impressed. During the last ten years there has been great dissatisfaction because psychotherapy doesn't work. The people now complain that although behavior therapy works, it's comparatively boring.

Analyst Dr. Lionel Ovesey comments on behavior therapy.

All therapies are behavior therapies in the sense that they all try to change behavior. That's just as true of classical analysis, which relies on insight into the unconscious, as it is of pure behavior therapy, which sidetracks the unconscious altogether and relies entirely on learning theory. These are the two extremes. Actually, most psychiatrists, at least in the United States, fall somewhere in the middle and use combinations of both, of uncovering and reconditioning. I do so myself, and I'm an analyst—though I'd say I'm much farther over on the behavioral side than most analysts. But even the most classical analysts use behavioral techniques today—sparingly, of course, but they do use them. They don't call them behavioral, they call them parameters, meaning nonanalytic extensions of pure analysis. I guess that makes it more palatable to them.

But when you say behavior therapy, I assume you mean the current school represented in Europe by Eysenck and in this country by Wolpe. They try to treat everything with reconditioning techniques such as aversion therapy, systematic desensitization and assertive retraining, as they call them. I feel there's promise in their techniques, and I'm all for their experimentation, but I take issue with them when they advocate behavior therapy to the exclusion of all other therapeutic tools. I feel many psychiatric problems are far too complicated for such simplistic approaches, so I'm not ready to throw out insight yet. There's no such thing as a "universal" therapy yet. Eysenck and Wolpe are no better in this respect than the die-hard classical analysts they attack. They plug behavior therapy for everybody. I'm against fanaticism on both sides.

Another thing is that Eysenck and Wolpe are just out of touch in making their criticisms. They're talking about psychoanalysis thirty or forty years ago, not today, and they get hooked on theory, which isn't the same thing as practice. They assume they have a corner on dealing directly with behavior. Many psychiatrists, including analysts, have done so for many years. I hear that Eysenck never sees patients, but sticks to his laboratory and devises techniques, and then his assistants try them out clinically, so we can cross him off. But Wolpe is a clinician, and I know what he does, at least from his writings. It's behavior therapy, all right, and I give him credit for that, but he also does a lot of other things that are standard practice in psychiatry. He gives advice. He is supportive. He sees both parties in a marriage problem. He manipulates the environment.

When Wolpe gets a person with a fear of open places, he has him "desensitize" himself by fantasizing in Wolpe's office about going just outside his door, then to the corner, and so on. Then he has him go out and do all the things he fantasized about. I've never worked with "systematic desensitization" in my office—that's Wolpe's contribution and it may be important. But I wrote years ago about retraining phobic patients in this way. I actually had them meet me outside the door, then at the corner, then across the street, and so on. The same thing in treating erectile failure in men. Wolpe says relax, don't try too hard, etc.—which is just what any psychiatrist says. Christ, practically every psychiatrist I know at Columbia has been doing such things for years. Now Wolpe thinks he's invented it. If anybody invented it, it was Pavlov.

Well, let's get back to your question. There have been reports of successful treatment of homosexuals with aversion therapy. A picture of a nude man is thrown on the screen, and at the same time the patient is given an electric shock. Supposedly, it isn't long before he can't stand men and he begins having intercourse with women. Maybe it works sometimes, I don't know, but I doubt any such cure would last very long. For that matter, it isn't at all unusual for a psychiatrist to get an isolated heterosexual act, even several, out of a homosexual patient, but what does that prove? As I've said, the answer to the problem isn't just the ability to perform sexually with a woman. If the homosexual can't continue to relate positively to a woman in an intimate relationship, treatment will fail. I had a patient once, an exclusive homosexual, who went into a rage over being deserted by a male lover and who then ran over to see a woman and successfully carried off the sex act, which had never happened to him before in his life. After that night he never saw the woman again. He got over this depression and anger and went back to homosexuality.

So I don't think much of such gimmicks as aversion therapy in such a complicated disorder as homosexuality. On the other hand, a behavior therapy consisting of a prolonged period of retraining in bed with a woman in the course of an intimate relationship may very well work. There are some homosexuals who are healthy enough so that with support from the therapist, and some guidance, they can go through such a training program and learn to be heterosexuals without any insight into unconscious motivation at all, and without any attempt by the therapist to instill it. Some of these patients then go on and get married, not necessarily to the same woman they trained with, and you have a good therapeutic result.

There are other homosexuals, however, who are much sicker, and the unconscious obstacles are so formidable they can't surmount them without insight. They require some analysis as a prelude to behavioral change. They can't even embark on a training program without some understanding of the unconscious symbols they're using and what makes them so afraid of women. Just knowing they're afraid isn't enough. But everything I've just said is equally applicable to psychotherapy of any disorder. It isn't limited to homosexuality. I'm trained as a psychiatrist, and I'm an analyst and I do essentially a dynamic therapy, but I'm eclectic and I'll modify it behaviorally in whatever way I think will help the patient solve his problems in the shortest time possible. It isn't a question of either-or; it's what combination you elect to use and how skillfully you use it.

Addicts, alcoholics, prostitutes, compulsive gamblers and others with special problems have been treated in groups by many psychotherapists. Only a few people have tried this with homosexuals, among them the eminent Wardell Pomeroy. But probably the first person to do so was Dr. Samuel B. Hadden, a Philadelphia psychiatrist and former president of the American Group Psychotherapy Association. In his office near Rittenhouse Square, Dr. Hadden—an elderly gentleman with a trim tonsure of white hair and spectacles—explains:

I've had homosexuals together in group therapy for fifteen years. It began in the same way as my starting group therapy with neurotic patients back in 1937—as an individual experiment, not knowing anyone else was doing it. I suppose the idea was planted in 1923, when I was a medical student and saw cases of pulmonary tuberculosis treated in groups to speed their recovery. Then in 1937, when I was in charge of the department of neurology and psychiatry at Presbyterian Hospital in Philadelphia, I was faced with the problem of an over-whelming load of out-patient cases, and I decided to try to treat them in groups. Everyone thought I was crazy then.

Fifteen years ago I realized that putting a few homosexuals in mixed neurotic groups didn't work well. The homosexuals created anxiety in some heterosexuals which they couldn't cope with, and the homosexuals in turn often felt rejected and tended to withdraw emotionally and soon to drop out. So I decided to try groups made up exclusively of homosexuals. Again, everyone said I was crazy. The first time I read a paper on these homosexual groups, professionals were incredulous. They said, "You'll have acting-out, shacking up, all sorts of problems.

Did you have acting-out and shacking up?

Over fifteen years it has come up only twice, to my knowledge. In one case I suspect something was going on, but I'm not sure; they left the group abruptly of their own accord and never came back. Another time three people got involved together, and we warned them that they couldn't do this and belong to the group. Finally we had to ask them to leave.

One of the problems sometimes talked about in one-problem groups is that they may hold each other back. When one member starts to change, the others have a stake in undermining him.

To the contrary, homosexuals in a group keep each other motivated to change. But then, we have no limited goals. We never say it's all right to make peace with being homosexual; our objective is full heterosexual adjustment. However, some who stay in treatment continue to say that they have no thought of being anything but homosexual.

How many change?

About one third. But let me explain that figure. About a third of the homosexuals drop out after six to eight weeks; I don't consider someone who attended only eighteen or twenty sessions really involved in treatment. Twenty sessions hardly accomplishes any change to speak of, but I consider it a threshold of involvement. It usually takes about a year before a person really gets moving, and the usual full treatment span is two to three years. Of all those who go beyond twenty weeks, a third become fully heterosexual. Others have great improvements in their lives generally, but I consider them treatment failures. My criterion is still full heterosexual adjustment.

Is age a factor in prognosis?

I find that the best age is between the middle twenties to thirty-five. You'd think adolescents would be easiest. I often see teenagers heading toward homosexuality who've been forced into treatment for some reason by their parents—they're not impossible to treat, but they're very difficult. Generally, adolescents are hell to work with. Someone between twenty-two and thirty-five has usually spent five or six years as a homosexual, he's been around and been hurt and disillusioned in his homosexual life. The adolescent may not have been hurt by homosexuality yet.

Then involvement in the gay world isn't always prognostically negative?

Those who have steeped in the gay culture have a harder time changing, but some who've been exposed to it benefit, for they see the shallowness of it. Most homosexuals retain some straight contacts, and they become disturbed as they see one friend after another marry and make a home. They may share apartments with other homosexuals and spend their money on nice clothes and furnishings, but nothing seems to give them real satisfaction, and there isn't enough emotional sharing to make them happy.

The sociological theories of labeling and deviant career lead one to expect that entering the gay world and being put in a gay therapy group would only confirm homosexual identity. From what you say, this isn't always the case.

In the group we don't identify people as homosexuals. I make clear that to me there's no such thing as "a homosexual." Homosexuality is a symptom of a maladjusted personality, as are handwashing and having to go back home over and over to make sure the gas is turned off and many other compulsions. Each homosexual has different motivations, and for one person the same homosexual act may have different meanings on different occasions. The people in the group share a symptom. That symptom is determined by experience, so corrective experience can bring about change.

Is there much difference between the dynamics of homosexual groups and mixed neurotic groups?

No. You do notice, though, that the homosexuals are a more traumatized group. They're rejected, bitter and hostile. They are masters of sarcasm, and they can pin each other on the wall with one perfect dart.

Some people say homosexuality may be an encapsulated thing in one's life, so that he is well adjusted, happy and copes well with the world. I get the impression that you don't think so.

Many homosexuals function in a world all their own. That doesn't mean they're happy. For instance, many theater people are homosexual, and they get great satisfaction from playing roles and from being admired. They consider themselves happy. When I talk to them, I don't find them especially happy people. I can't buy the homosexual life as a satisfying one. There are short relationships, traumatic break-ups, and no feeling of responsibility.

I can give you a dramatic example of the extremes of their unhappiness and disturbance. Once I was a consultant to the police, and one day I had to go to the office of the head of the homicide division. He had some pictures in the viewing box of a recent murder victim. He said, "Here, look at these." The man was an awful mess, puncture wounds all over his body. The chief said, "Come on, doc, tell me, who committed this murder? What kind of man was he? What was he like?" Of course I said I didn't know. He said, "Doc, when we come in on a crime like this, we're almost sure that the guy killed was homosexual, and so was the guy who killed him."*

But aside from such extreme cases, there's no doubt that a high percentage of homosexuals are quite bitter people. As a group they remind me at times of the usual epileptic—an angry, rejected person always ready to blow his stack. Homosexuals will often say in group, "We're all cats, we're really catty." They've been aware most of their lives of being misfits. In reviewing life histories, I've

---

*Although homosexuals certainly have no corner on gory homicide, I have heard from several other sources that many bloody and ritualized sadistic killings are by common police knowledge attributed to disturbed homosexuals. Several famous homosexuals in the arts have met such deaths in recent decades.

found that almost every homosexual knew at four or five that he didn't belong. He never fitted into his peer group. Between two and six or seven is a critical age; kids are bubbling over with physical energy. They run, wrestle, tug, and the physical contact, the give and take, make them feel they belong and are part of the gang. Right now I'm trying to work up a statistical summary of more than a hundred homosexuals, and one of the questions I've asked is, "What do you remember about your first day at school?" It's amazing the number who said, "I was miserable. I cried all day." They couldn't take the separation from mother. From that first day, they felt they didn't belong; and since they couldn't take part in sports, they couldn't belong through that. I suspect that the banter, needling and teasing in my homosexual groups takes the place of the physical play that was avoided. The boys learned quite young to compensate for being out of things with other kids. When they found a responsive teacher, they studied hard for him. In high school there was finally an opportunity for organized nonphysical activities—band, theater, debating. Now the kid could find a spot that gave him importance at last.

Some people claim that the data from homosexuals in psychiatric treatment are weighted, that nonpatient homosexuals are a healthier group.

It's true that people come because they're anxious or depressed about something. There are also many who come out of curiosity, for only a small number of visits, and I see no difference between the two groups. Besides, we all know that there are many more people who need psychiatric treatment than get it—this is true for all groups and all problems. Also, we often find after a person has been in therapy for a while that we have the wrong member of the family in treatment, that the real pathology of the family springs mostly from another member. Sometimes I feel that the ones we get are the more intelligent, but also those with weaker egos, who can't tolerate things the way they are any more.

Since you and many others claim solid rates of cure and improvement, why is there still so much therapeutic pessimism?

Two reasons. One is that nobody likes to make a monkey out of his pop. Freud was our intellectual father, and he was very pessimistic about curing homosexuals. It took a long time for his children to say he was wrong. What's more, the average therapist is often hostile to homosexuals, just like other people in this society. If you question him closely, he'll admit it. I've had psychiatrists come up to me at meetings and say, "I have a goddamn homosexual on my hands. Will you take him?" A goddamn homosexual! And you just can't hide from a patient that you basically don't like him and don't enjoy treating his problem. Many doctors tell homosexuals, "I don't think that I or anyone can do anything for you." They're expressing not only traditional pessimism but, in many cases, personal dislike.

Have you treated any transvestites?

A couple. I had one who has undergone complete change. He used to wear frilly underwear and rush home to put on a nightgown. Once he told the group, "I had female cousins next door who never got spanked." He got clobbered all the time at home. He became compliant, and of course he never got spanked any more. This was at age four or five. In group he revealed that at that age he had boosted a girl cousin up to look in a window and saw up her dress. She was wearing tight pants. He said, "I saw that girls are much *neater* than boys." He found it was easier to be a girl, too competitive being a male. You might get hurt. Fear of getting hurt and dirty are very important in the minds of many homosexuals.

I've heard some psychiatrists around campuses say that they find a growing tendency for boys in the radical youth culture to be passive, and for the girls to be controlling and have masculine aspirations. Do you see much of this sort of role change?

I see lots of young people, and in the past few years that pattern has increased. It's related to increasing devaluation of marriage and a change within the family—competition between husband and wife for the dominant role in the family. Being a man is a hell of a chore today, and many young men today are a bit emasculated and have a somewhat feminine orientation. And being a wife is no more attractive to many girls than going to an office nine-to-five is for the boys. Some parents prepare their daughters for marriage by impressing on them the idea that they mustn't be subordinate to any man. I had two sisters here in my office, daughters of a judge. They had gone to a good liberal-arts college, and then their father insisted they spend a year at business college. When they asked why, he said that if their marriages failed, then they needn't be dependent on their husbands and could walk out of their marriage and support themselves. That's a hell of a way to get a woman to think positively of marriage. And sure enough, about two years apart, both girls sat here in my office, both divorced—neither sister knowing the other had consulted me—both resentful that they now had to support themselves! And both realizing that they had been prepared to terminate their marriages as soon as difficulties arose.

Maurice and Joan are in their thirties, and she has a child by a previous marriage. He has only recently chosen decisively for heterosexuality and for marriage and against the gay world. He is in psychotherapy with an eclectic, analytically oriented therapist in Cleveland who also puts a strong emphasis on action and altering old behavior patterns. Joan is now also in treatment with the same doctor. Before Joan joins us, Maurice tells me about his background:

I was a very active homosexual when Joan and I got married five years ago. I came out at thirteen, a couple of years after my father left home. I made the scene with women, but the most important thing in my love life had been one long affair with a guy, which lasted five years, until Joan and I decided to marry.

When Joan and I met, I was still living with this guy. He and I broke up, and I wanted to get away from homosexuality. I felt that if I ever could, it would be with someone like Joan, who knew the score. She wasn't the first girl I'd gone out with or had sex with, but she was the first who knew about my homosexuality. She was in love with me and believed I wasn't a genuine homosexual. She was sure I could make the change. I didn't really believe it myself, that I was homosexual. I thought some day I'd wake up and it would be gone. I hated the gay world, the fickleness, the fear that tomorrow someone would come along for the other person and it would be over for you and him.

But I was really just on the run, not dealing with my problems. Two weeks before the marriage, I attempted suicide and was sent to a psychiatrist. It wasn't much help, and I didn't go for long. When it came to really making the marriage work, we ceased to be friends. There was no sex and no commitment. She read Bergler, and the doctor I saw was a pupil of Bergler. His writings on masochism made a lot of sense. With my masochism as a base, and then my father's absence, it was natural that I became homosexual. I'm still exorcizing the ghost of my father, which has always been around me, causing so much of my trouble. He and I have finally met again recently, after twenty years, and have a fragile relationship. My mother? She hasn't spoken to me since I was twenty-four, when I told her that I was homosexual.

Anyway, after I was married, I went back to men. I had always said I didn't want marriage as a cover-up, so that I could carry on in the old way. But that's just what was happening—not having sex with my wife, and wanting men. But I couldn't just sneak out, because she knew everything about me. After two years, I began an affair with a guy, and it lasted for a year. That's when I started seeing our present therapist, before the break-up of that affair. I realized that I really wanted my family. And it took me a year of therapy to really start working at the sex problem.

Why did your wife marry a homosexual man and consent to living without what's usually considered a normal sex life?

A little less than a year ago, my doctor asked her to come in to his office and we both realized that she had problems too. Sexual and otherwise. In fact, I have a contest with her about who's the bigger masochist. I think I finally have her convinced that she is. She was brought up by the proverbial stepmother, was sent off alone in the world in her teens, and drifted from relative to relative. Her first husband was a near-illiterate with whom she had nothing in common and no communication. He moved back and forth between men and women. They had a daughter, but they never had a sex life that amounted to anything. Finally she decided to leave him.

She had a good friend she was going to marry after that. A homosexual. She could talk to him. She was going to marry him for companionship and help him with his work, so that he'd be free to do his work, which was in the arts. Joan and I met through this guy. Well, her marrying him would have been a masochist's delight. But if you're a masochist, you also have something inside that keeps you from going over the precipice. She broke with him. And I broke with the guy I'd been having a long affair with. Joan and I decided to get married—we'd been great friends for two years. We got married and almost destroyed each other. I still don't know for sure that the marriage will work, but there's a much better chance than before.

It was important for us to both be involved. The burden of the problem in the marriage has always been on me. I was the nut. Now, as we work on the marriage for real, we find other problems, and one of them is that she's a bit of a nut too. I was the sexual deviant, but she has sex hang-ups too. She has had two husbands and a daughter, but to all intents and purposes she remained almost a virgin. Now that I'm improving, she can't go on being nutty in *her* old way. We're trying sex systematically now. There are no rockets bursting in the air, but we've tasted a few flares.

If there was one crucial threshold, it was three months ago. I was trying, but I was still procrastinating about real commitment to the marriage. I had the perfect set-up—a wife, a household, and I could indulge my problem by running off and getting a piece. She had always been afraid of pushing me to a clear choice. And she was right. I might have taken the tested, safe way that I knew. But she finally gave me an ultimatum: split or else stay and commit myself. I decided, and I had a real revelation. I realized that I'd always thought fear of failure was what kept me from success and commitment with a woman. Now I saw that I could succeed sexually, but was still trying to avoid it. So I saw that what I really feared was success. Because success meant having no excuse for copping out of commitment.

[*Joan joins us. She is somewhat tense and uncomfortable at first. We explain what we've been talking about so far. Maurice adds:*] Since three months ago, things have really improved. I had to choose between ways of life. I wasn't strong enough to say no to homosexuality and walk away. Homosexuality is easier. But I knew that if I said no to this marriage, there would never be hetero-sexuality in my life. I'd commit myself by default to a life I'd tried and found incomplete.

JOAN: It really began because we sent our girl to the therapist. Then Maurice went, stopped, and really began to go regularly at last. Then I began to see I had to go.

MAURICE: Because you were nutty too.

JOAN: It was a relief. We finally got it into the open.

Did it produce many arguments? [*They look at each other and smile.*]

MAURICE: She better not argue, or I'll hit her . . . with my pocketbook! [*They both laugh.*]

Joan, why did you marry a man with whom you knew you wouldn't have a satisfactory sex life, at least not for quite a while?

JOAN: It was a gamble. I went into it knowingly. I'd never had a real sexual relationship. Marrying Maurice was maintaining the sexual status quo for me. I wanted sex, but I had no burning desire. If it didn't work, I wouldn't have lost anything I had. But Maurice did do a lot for me in terms of self-confidence generally.

What about his affairs with men?

JOAN: I wasn't disturbed as long as he was just going out to have sex. Only when he fell in love.

MAURICE: You see, to her sex wasn't an area of competition.

JOAN: What caused problems was when he took the role of the aggressor. I'm not experienced, and I'm not comfortable with taking initiative. I'd always pictured . . .

MAURICE: . . . the great white penis on a charger.

JOAN: Well, I was used to a male being aggressive. I didn't expect to have to really take part, just to be there. But I realized that when Maurice really did start to be aggressive, it made me feel inadequate. I didn't know what to do back. So I've been learning. The doctor urges me to be more aggressive. There isn't much real change yet, but we've gotten a big-sized bed, and we're starting to take turns at night about who rolls over first and says hi. The old thing would be for both of us to just get withdrawn, and end in a stalemate. I do want a marriage, and it has to work on the sexual end.

What other changes have taken place as this goes on?

MAURICE: Things have changed with some of our friends. They're mixed, both straight and gay. You can't talk to gay guys about a piece of ass or they'll vomit or walk out of the house. I'm going to legally adopt the little girl, and I'm planning to return to graduate school to prepare for a better profession. And I guess I play lord and master less in the household. And we've set aside a half hour each night for talking.

What do you talk about?

JOAN: Sex, handling the kids, his job.

MAURICE: If this marriage is to work, the key is in communication. It has to be kept open.

31

The Logic of the Law

A homosexual scandal tore apart Boise, Idaho, in 1955. A decade later journalist John Gerassi went there to study the affair from its origins to its aftermath. As a result, he wrote a book called *The Boys of Boise*, an anatomy of a homosexual-hunting crusade and a demonstration of the apparent cruelty, pointlessness and destructive illogic of our formal sanctions against sexual deviance. Typically, the scandal probably began for reasons quite unrelated to sex.

Though Boise has a population of only fifty thousand, it is the capital of Idaho and an important political and economic center. In 1955, according to Gerassi, the city administration and a local power clique were fighting for control of the area. The prosecutions for homosexuality were meant to create an excuse for attacking a member of the City Council through his son—the young man was eventually sentenced to three years in jail for a homosexual act. Some people told Gerassi that the power clique behind this vendetta was also out to get one of its own group, a man referred to only as "The Queen."

The scandal began with the revelation by police and press that Boise high school boys had been prostituting themselves to adult homosexuals. It seems that some were doing the sort of casual, part-time hustling Reiss described in his paper on "queers and peers"; a smaller number may have been seriously engaged in prostitution and blackmail. Under questioning, suspects began to give the names of their sex partners, and more arrests were made. Among those eventually accused of what Idaho law calls "the infamous crime against nature" was a prominent banker. Newspapers whipped up paranoia and a lynch spirit with editorials about perverts corrupting youth from behind their respectable façades. A mood of hysterical outrage swept through the city. Furious phone calls—the majority from women—flooded police and newspaper offices, denouncing neighbors as homosexuals.

The search for "seducers" of high school boys led to a general round-up of homosexuals. Some men promptly resigned from their jobs and left town, fearing exposure as the chain of accusations grew. Many of the accused lost their homes and employment well before going on trial. The city hired an outside investigator to help uncover deviants, a man who had hunted homosexuals for the State Department during the McCarthy days. Police, prosecution and investigation methods were apparently worthy of the late senator; as Gerassi puts it, juvenile prostitutes and stool pigeons were used to send sick men to jail. Police offered suspects psychiatric care instead of exposure and punishment if they would cooperate, give names and plead guilty. Many did so, only to receive jail sentences ranging from six months to life—but no psychotherapy. One man, promised therapy if he pleaded guilty, was paroled from prison nine years later; jail had been his only treatment. And the son of a city councilman, perhaps one of the original targets of the antihomosexual drive, was recalled from West Point and sentenced to three years in a penitentiary for a homosexual act committed three years earlier, during his adolescence.

As more and more men were arrested, ruined and sent to jail, the vengeful spirit ebbed. Too many people, from teenaged boys to respected family men, were being hurt. The city's name was being tarnished less by homosexuality now than by rabid vindictiveness. The investigations were called off. Newspapers that had yelled for purges began talking about unfortunates afflicted with emotional problems. The state legislature promised to start a mental-health program, and the special investigator was told his skills were no longer needed.

When Gerassi arrived in Boise in 1965 to study the history and effects of the affair, he received threatening phone calls, learned that court records were missing, and found many people still reluctant or unwilling to talk. But generally both the town's hatred and its deep remorse had faded. The proposal for a mental-health program had been attacked by conservatives as a communist plot and shelved. On the other hand, prosecutions for homosexual acts were few, and punishments light. In 1963 only two people had been jailed for homosexuality, one for a night and the other for twenty days; the highest fine imposed for a homosexual offense had been $150. Many people now said they wished the whole business of ten years before had never happened. "The Queen," Gerassi was told, still flourished in undisturbed privacy. Though many small fry had been netted to create a plausible context for exposing and ruining him, he was so rich and powerful that he escaped harm.

As homophile societies often point out, the United States has the most severe antihomosexual laws in the West. The Napoleonic Code made adult consensual homosexuality legal in France. Antihomosexual laws were repealed a century ago in Belgium and Holland, a few decades ago in Denmark, Sweden and Switzerland, and in Czechoslovakia and England during the sixties. Similar legal immunity exists not only in Norway and Poland but in such Latin nations as Italy, Spain, Greece, Mexico and Brazil.

West Germany, Austria and Finland still have antihomosexual laws, but West Germany seems likely to repeal its statute within a decade. In many communist countries, traditional mores are reinforced by scientific behaviorism and political conformity, and life is quite difficult for homosexuals. East Germany and Russia denounce homosexuality as bourgeois degeneracy and permit almost no gay life. Only a few years ago homosexuals were rounded up in Cuba and sent to labor camps, a policy described by writer André Schiffrin as "a disastrous blending of thuggish *machismo* and perverted Soviet Pavlovianism." But in none of these nations are penalties as severe as in the majority of the forty-eight American states that still forbid homosexual acts under what are collectively called "sodomy laws."

Our state and municipal statutes against homosexual acts have been patched and rewritten for decades, in some places for centuries. Their definitions and penalties are rooted in English common law, nineteenth-century "degeneracy" theories, or both, and they seem as arbitrary and inconsistent as medieval penitentials. The offense varies in name from state to state. In some it is "sodomy," which may include "oral copulation." In Michigan, anal intercourse is forbidden by one law, fellatio by another. Idaho's "infamous crime against nature" is anal intercourse with man, woman or beast. In New Hampshire, homosexuality falls under the rubric "lascivious acts." Most states make homosexual acts felonies (by rule of thumb, crimes punishable by more than one year in prison); others make them mere misdemeanors. Many states give courts the option of using either felony or misdemeanor charges. Punishments vary from light fines to five, ten, twenty years or even life in prison—in Georgia the life sentence is mandatory for sodomy unless clemency has been recommended. Some twenty states also have "sex psychopath" laws, used to detain and keep registries of sex offenders—not only rapists and sadists but homosexuals, voyeurs and exhibitionists. Pennsylvania's Barr-Walker Act allows indeterminate detention of "sex psychopaths" in mental hospitals, and California law permits detention for a period of from one year to life. Twelve states still provide for compulsory sterilization of "hereditary" criminals, and seven include sex offenders in this category.

Most often, though, homosexuals are not prosecuted under sodomy laws. Courts usually use omnibus misdemeanor laws forbidding sexual solicitation, vagrancy, loitering, "outrageous conduct" and "lewd behavior." And many judges, loath to impose felony penalties for sex offenses, let people plead guilty to lesser, nonsexual charges—rapists to assault, peepers to trespassing, exhibitionists to disturbing the peace, homosexuals to loitering. The misdemeanor punishments usually range from $10 to $10,000 fine and from three to twelve months in jail, often suspended.

But the punishments inflicted on homosexuals go far beyond such laws. Many cities bar deviants from licensed professions such as taxi driving and bartending; for example, ordinances in Miami and Coral Gables, Florida, prohibit homosexuals from working, being served or congregating where alcoholic drinks are sold. Professional societies may act against members who are revealed as homosexuals, and many school systems have general "moral turpitude" clauses in their contracts that can be invoked in such cases. Federal policy has long barred or discharged homosexuals from the armed forces and the civil service. The civil service states that homosexuals are not only security risks but a source of revulsion, apprehension and inefficiency in its offices. The Immigration and Naturalization Service can and does deport people with homosexual histories, and it has been accused of using distasteful and even unconstitutional means of gathering information on suspects.

The way many police departments enforce antihomosexual laws repels even the mildest defenders of civil rights. Since consenting homosexuality is a "crime without victims," arrests depend almost entirely on entrapment, surveillance and admissions wrung from suspects. Many vice squads wire park benches for sound, install peepholes and one-way mirrors in public lavatories, and hide closed-circuit television cameras in the men's rooms of bus depots and department stores. Plainclothesmen work in pairs enticing homosexuals into propositioning them. One, acting as a decoy, stands exposing himself at a urinal or walks along cruising grounds wearing tight trousers and jangling keys or loose change in his pocket. His partner follows to act as a witness, though often too far away to hear what is said by the decoy and the accused; in court it is the defendant's word against the decoy's. In its exhaustive study of homosexuality and the law in 1966, the *UCLA Law Review* said that "no crime is easier to charge or harder to disprove than the sex offense." It concluded that entrapment fosters crime rather than preventing or detecting it. Nevertheless, high-court decisions have upheld entrapment as legitimate on the grounds that it exposes criminal intent.

When the New York City police stopped practicing entrapment in 1966, arrests for homosexual solicitation dropped from more than a hundred a week to almost none, but no outraged crowds appeared in precinct headquarters complaining about homosexual propositions. Few homosexuals are insensitive or foolish enough to solicit people who are obviously not receptive. Many large cities have tended recently to more or less tolerate homosexuality; they suppress only open male prostitution and offensive exhibitionism. They know that homosexuality cannot be eliminated, only more or less contained, and that if a gay gathering place is raided, it is just recreated in a new locale.

Occasional and even systematic raids on bars and pick-up spots continue all the same, sometimes including harassment, shakedowns and perhaps even beatings. The UCLA group questioned fifteen law-enforcement agencies and found that seven—most of them in small towns—admitted regular harassment of homosexuals. Their purpose was not making arrests but getting the gay out of town. The police parked their cars outside gay bars, demanded identification from those who entered, and gave jaywalking tickets to those who left. In some cities the police are believed to keep lists of homosexuals, with or without sanction of laws requiring the registration of "sex psychopaths."

Once a person has been arrested for homosexual soliciting or acts, he is almost compelled to plead guilty to a misdemeanor, for safety's sake. There are lawyers who specialize in defending homosexuals, and many charge their frightened clients excessive fees. Their advice is almost always to plead guilty to lesser charges (before a lenient judge, if possible), and at all costs to avoid pleading innocent and therefore having to face a jury. Juries tend to be more punitive than judges, and in a jury trial the charge is likely to remain a felony. The UCLA study revealed that of 480 men who originally went to court on homosexual felony charges, only eleven pleaded innocent and insisted on jury trials. Of those eleven, only one was acquitted, and only two had their cases dismissed. On the other hand, 95 per cent of those charged with felonies were permitted by judges to plead guilty to misdemeanors. Finally only 1 per cent of them received felony dispositions.

The law is actually one of the least of homosexuals' problems; informal sanctions are often far crueler than legal ones. Many teenagers still beat up and roll homosexuals. Revealed homosexuals may be dismissed by employers and turned out by landlords. A couple of decades ago Lord Jowett told Parliament that while he was Attorney General "at least 95 per cent of all cases of blackmail which came to [my] attention arouse out of homosexuality." This estimate may be high, but even the cautious Wolfenden Report set the figure at 45 per cent. There was good reason, then, for calling the old antihomosexual law a "blackmailer's charter."

Large blackmail rings preying on homosexuals have been discovered regularly in New York City. One was broken up in 1940 and another in 1960. In March 1966 another was uncovered there, consisting of some seventy men who had extorted at least a million dollars from perhaps a thousand victims—among them a congressman, a minister, a surgeon, two university deans, a wealthy midwestern teacher who had paid $120,000 over four years, and a nuclear physicist who had broken security to avoid exposure. A military officer who was victimized by the gang committed suicide the night before he was to testify at a grand-jury hearing. Some men who had refused to pay the blackmailers had been beaten, publicly identified, and lost their jobs and wives. Several studies of homosexuals have shown that as many as 10 to 15 per cent were at some time threatened with blackmail. Twice as many were assaulted or robbed by strangers and by hustlers. Almost all feared to report the incidents to the police, and with good reason. A sadly common incident was reported in *The Guardian* on April 22, 1965, of a homosexual who had sex relations with a young man in his car and was then attacked and told to hand over his money. "Unable to get rid of the assailant he finally drove to the police station and complained. Some weeks later . . . he was charged with indecent assault—the younger man being prosecution witness—and fined £ 50."

Harsh laws, devious enforcement and sometimes cruel penalties have made many people call for an end to antihomosexual laws. Jurists have criticized as unconstitutionally vague the terms immoral, abnormal, perverted, unnatural, psychopathic, indecent, lewd and lascivious. The word psychopath, in regard to homosexuality, was dropped recently from our immigration laws as the result of an appeal to the Supreme Court, but the principle of deporting homosexuals was upheld. Justice William O. Douglas, in a dissenting opinion, wrote that "it is common knowledge that in this country homosexuals have risen in our own public service—both in Congress and in the executive branch—and have served with distinction."

Many legal, religious, medical and psychiatric groups have supported the principle that adult consenting sexual behavior is not the law's concern. When the American Law Institute devised a Model Penal Code in 1955, it made homosexual acts criminal only when they involved force, fraud or a minor; otherwise, said the ALI, homosexuality does "no harm to the secular interests of the community." Some Protestant churches in the United States and Europe, and a scattering of Roman Catholic clergymen as well, have called for a more tolerant attitude toward deviants. After the Walter Jenkins incident, the American Mental Health Foundation wrote to President Lyndon Johnson to oppose "the kind of hysteria that demands that all homosexual persons be barred from any responsible position," since being homosexual does not "per se make him more unstable or more of a security risk than any heterosexual person." In 1969 fourteen experts appointed by the National Institutes of Mental Health to study homosexuality issued a majority report (three members expressed reservations on some of the recommendations) urging states to make adult consensual homosexuality legal. The American Civil Liberties Union has taken the same position.

This attitude is probably becoming acceptable to more people almost from year to year. In 1962 Illinois adopted the Model Penal Code's recommendation on homosexuality and became the first state to make adult consensual homosexuality legal. In 1971 Connecticut took the same course. In other states the old penalities are being lightened. The North Carolina sodomy law (barring anal intercourse and "all kindred acts of bestial character whereby degraded and perverted desires are sought to be gratified") used to call for five to sixty years' imprisonment. In 1962 a man was sentenced to twenty to thirty years for a private, consenting homosexual act, and this aroused such public pity and revulsion that the law was revised, reducing the sentence to four months to ten years.

Many Americans hope that British law reform will be a model for continued relaxation of antihomosexual laws in the United States. The British repeal movement got its impetus from a scandal tinged with hysteria and vengefulness equaling Boise's. In the early fifties the press reported allegations of a homosexual menace to society, and its panicky cry was taken up even by the British Medical Association, which said homosexuals had infiltrated the church, civil service, armed forces, press and Parliament. It claimed that they tended to "place loyalty to one another above loyalty to the institution or government they serve"; that they gave each other preferential treatment; that they required "homosexual seduction as expedient for promotion." This set off a homosexual-hunt that paralleled in time and tone the McCarthy purge in the United States. And like the American purge, it eventually repelled and frightened even many who had first applauded it. After the much-publicized trial of Lord Montagu for homosexuality, public figures began to call such proceedings inhumane and senseless. The Home Secretary appointed a special committee, headed by Sir John Wolfenden of Reading University, to study homosexuality, prostitution and the law, and to make recommendations to the government.

In 1957 the Wolfenden Committee submitted a report calling for relaxation of strictures against adult consenting homosexuality. The next year a poll showed 47 per cent of the public to be against reform, 38 per cent in favor, and 15 per cent undecided. The reform bill failed in the House of Commons in 1960 and 1965, though the latter time it was approved by the House of Lords. Finally in 1967 the bill passed in both houses. Polls then showed almost two thirds of the public in favor of the change, probably because of extensive campaigning and education by scientists, churchmen, distinguished laymen and homosexual organizations.

Those who want such reform in the United States point to the excesses and incongruities of the laws we have inherited and to their irrelevance in an increasingly permissive society. In most states, almost all sex acts are forbidden except marital coitus. The laws apply to all people, including the married; fellatio, for instance, is equally illegal in most states for spouses and for homosexuals. Kinsey estimated that if all our sex laws were enforced, 95 per cent of the nation's men would go to jail. But of course heterosexuals are almost never prosecuted under these laws, even unmarried ones. They are used almost solely against homosexuals. Homosexuals say this reveals the straight majority's prejudice and vengefulness. The complaint is just, but indignant rant about it is like complaints that a lower-class delinquent is punished more harshly for stealing a hubcap than is a wealthy executive for "stealing" a fortune through financial slither. We all admit it is true, and nothing is changed. More humane laws and enforcement will come only from understanding the origins and cultural context of our sexual controls, and acting on the basis of that understanding.

First one should note that relatively few homosexuals are arrested and punished, especially considering how severe our sanctions against homosexuality are. Wolfenden believed there was only one conviction for every twenty-five hundred homosexual acts; that is the highest estimate that has been made. Kinsey estimated one conviction for every thirty thousand acts, Dr. Morris Ploscowe one for every three hundred thousand, and sociologist Edwin Schur one for every six million. A disproportionately large number of those who are convicted belong to a minority of effeminate exhibitionists, prostitutes and sporadic homosexuals who don't know the rules of the gay world. Even in cities where enforcement is tough, and even in times of antihomosexual crusades, prosecution is spotty and affects a small proportion of those who could be hurt. Furthermore, many judges are reluctant to give heavy sentences to those who end up in court. Their chief aim is to prevent public displays, not to gratuitously or vengefully damage those unlucky or careless enough to get caught; they also know that sending a homosexual to jail is like sentencing an alcoholic to a distillery. The UCLA study says that homosexuality trials are characterized by uniformity, routine and pragmatism, and that the attitude of many judges and citizens is wondering sorrow that the defendant was found out. I have seen homosexuals tolerated and even protected in corporations, schools and the army because no one wanted to be the one to cause a deviant to be punished.

There are great gaps, then, between our laws, their enforcement, public attitudes and private attitudes. But that does not mean our system of sex control is capricious and bizarre. We have seen that all societies limit sex according to age, object choice, marital status, gender, social visibility of sex acts and other factors. The West, for instance, considers women less sexual than men, and in danger of psychic and social damage if they become sexually active. When evidence contradicts this assumption, the evidence is ignored. Many Western laws against oral sex, anal sex and homosexuality mention men only. Even where such laws mention women, they are almost never enforced. Kinsey reported that only one woman was convicted of homosexual "sodomy" in New York City during the entire 1930s, and the situation is basically unchanged. Charges of loitering are occasionally used to harass lesbians, and lesbian bars are sometimes raided, but prosecutions of women for homosexuality are very rare. One police department told the UCLA group that although it entrapped male homosexuals, it refused to "degrade" policewomen by using them as decoys to entrap lesbians—again, female sexuality was considered a fragile blossom that must be protected from erotic blasts. It is true that lesbians suffer socially if discharged from the armed forces for homosexuality; they are then unable to get civil service jobs or to work in fields requiring police registration. And obvious, aggressive lesbians may be harassed by hostile men. But very few lesbians have trouble with the law, and many tend to be a bit contemptuous of gay men's preoccupation with legal troubles—the usual female attitude toward "bad boys" and masculine lack of social compliance.

Age also defines permitted sexuality. The West considers children, like women, erotically unawakened and better off that way. Authorities in schools, reformatories and other institutions may feel bound to prevent or punish masturbation, let alone homosexuality. Contact between an adult and a child is severely sanctioned, though the "child" may be the seducer, as many victims of statutory rape prosecutions know. Contact between minors may be dismissed as "experimentation," but it may also arouse anxiety and retribution. Early in 1967 three boys in England were sent to Borstal by a magistrate for private homosexual acts; a fourth boy had committed suicide after being questioned by the police.

Social class also influences the reaction to sex behavior. A middle-class girl who becomes pregnant may be considered emotionally disturbed; a working-class girl may be labeled delinquent and sent to an institution. In criminal actions of all kinds, the respectable and middle class have an easier time; the police may even help them stay out of court, or in cases of homosexuality, to plead guilty to a nonsexual offense such as disturbing the peace. The poor and antisocial have less chance of getting off lightly. Homosexual prostitutes, effeminates and the exhibitionistic are liable to receive harsh treatment. Social visibility is generally important in our sexual code—many people are willing to ignore sex behavior they disapprove of as long as it remains out of sight.

There are bans of varying strength on premarital coitus, adultery, prostitution, sexual violence, homosexual object choice, incest, oral-genital sex and anal-genital sex. All these strictures operate simultaneously, and violation of more than one norm brings stronger sanctions. If a young female is seduced by an older male, she is seen as a victim: both youth and femininity have been violated. But as Kinsey pointed out, if a grown woman seduces a boy, there is "a strong tendency for society to consider the male not as a victim but as an amusingly fortunate exception to the rule." Youth has been violated, but male sexuality has been affirmed, the violation balanced. Homosexual violation of youth is a double violation, and it calls for double retribution. If a person on the borderline between childhood and adulthood is seduced, the social reaction depends on how deviant the sex act was in other ways. Of the Western nations that permit adult homosexuality, all but Italy make the age of consent higher for homosexual than for heterosexual acts.

The enforcement of these strictures has always been inconsistent. Some people believe in various rules more strongly than others, and are more punitive toward offenders. To a degree, such attitudes are shaped by class background. Many policemen come from levels of society that tend to be abusive toward sexual deviants; many judges and journalists come from more tolerant backgrounds. In a pluralistic society, religious and ethnic differences interact with other factors to produce a wide range of complex, even contradictory standards. And beyond all these influences, there remain individual differences of character. So there are people who literally want to kill homosexuals and others who hardly care what anyone else does in bed. Between these poles lie innumerable complexes of values.*

Most of our sexual proscriptions existed long before Christianity and persist among nonbelievers; they are part of our enduring social fabric,

---

*In other words, homosexuality is subject to the same contradictory complex of feelings and ideas as, say, adultery. One person may want "deterrent" laws against adultery, not really want people to go to jail for it, and practice it himself with guiltless zest. His neighbor may condemn all legal limits on consenting sex behavior yet never violate one traditional prohibition himself. Age also influences attitudes. A permissive young single person may think the ban on adultery a pointless "law of sexual property," yet find himself more in accord with tradition ten years later, when he is a spouse and parent. A prim youngster who considers adultery sinful and destructive may be much more tolerant of it after a decade or so of marriage.

rationalized in turn by religion, law and science. Although legal and social tolerance of deviants has increased during this century, the most basic feelings toward them have not. Until those feelings undergo a fundamental revision, law reform will be only a small first step in social equality for deviants. Homosexuality was legalized in France more than a century and a half ago, yet most homosexuals live in shame and secrecy there. Most people to whom I have spoken in England feel that the gay won only a bit more freedom and dignity with law reform. Illinois removed its ban almost a decade ago, but homosexuals are still harassed by police and arrested under loitering and nuisance statutes. And when fifteen men were arrested there in the mid-sixties during a raid on a gay establishment, twelve lost their jobs as a result of their public exposure. In England, Illinois and many other places where homosexual acts are legal, solicitation to commit a homosexual act remains a crime. There is no logic in prosecuting a man for asking someone else to perform a legal act, but of course such logic has little to do with our sanctions. Stronger, more primitive social and psychological forces are involved.

Laws are only the formal aspects of social control, to be called into play when mores and informal sanctions fail to do their job. Therefore the law tends to represent society's harshest judgments and penalties. Usually, little daily snubs, mockeries and humiliations are enough to make the prospect of being homosexual unappealing to most people and to prevent most homosexuals from flaunting their propensity. The same sort of control is used in our white-supremacist society against blacks. If blacks are not cowed by little day-to-day expressions of racism, legal sanctions (such as miscegenation laws) stand in reserve. If neither formal nor informal sanctions are effective, lynch-spirit brutalities are inflicted. The reaction toward a proudly defiant homosexual is somewhat like that toward a proudly assertive black—puzzled pity that he should so test the majority's power to hurt him legally or extralegally.

In periods when mores become superficially more permissive, the laws of a previous period seem a brutal caricature of popular attitudes. But even if these laws are relaxed, millennia-old traditions will survive and be unofficially reinforced. Despite journalistic and even learned gabble about the death of the family and of the sexes, there seems no serious danger to the nuclear family, basic sex-role distinctions and heterosexuality. The family is a universal institution, and homosexuality, like incest, is a universal deviance. The biological substratum that underlies them will go on bolstering these patterns, and custom will still stand behind them as the most socially functional possibilities. Though family and sex-role patterns may change, they will probably do so only slightly. Though homosexuality may become more tolerated, it will probably never be made as easy and rewarding as heterosexuality. (Those who think a "sexual revolution" gives this statement the lie should consider a 1966 CBS poll which revealed that although

70 per cent of the respondents considered homosexuality an illness, more than half still wanted homosexuals to be punished by law.) Homosexual societies are probably taking exactly the wrong course in trying to justify their preference on ethical and logical grounds. I suspect that society will always draw the line precisely at deviants claiming *justification* for their deviance. Society, however, may tolerate them without moral, social or biological justifications. In fact, it may do so only when it realizes that homosexuals are not and can never be a serious threat to the majority way of life. In other words, society can easily afford to be humane toward deviants when it recognizes the hopelessness of their struggle for true equality. To the Rousseauian optimist, this may seem a brutal and pessimistic view. I, too, find it sad that life does not always realize one's best hopes.

Society's problem, then, is not the menace of homosexuality, but the possibility that doubly and triply punishing the deviant robs society of some of its valuable members and taints the quality of life with gratuitous cruelty. We have much evidence that easing formal sanctions is not dangerous. The seduction of children by adult deviants is mostly a bogey; even if it were not, the law is probably not much of a deterrent—as we know, even capital punishment does not reduce crime. The barbarity of long prison sentences in our shameful prison system and of barring deviants from productive jobs and professions harms society as much as it harms the penalized. Society has moments of clarity when it becomes aware of this. When the hatred of the zealous and the fear of the conventional are mobilized in Boise or London or Havana, the witch-hunt rolls on for a while almost independent of its original impetus. Then it burns itself out as people realize that a society with as great a variety of sexual patterns as ours, and as sexually restrictive, simply cannot afford to enforce the most conservative and extreme sanctions without harming itself. Even in their terms, the cure becomes more destructive than the affliction.

Therefore I believe that we should totally revise our sex-control laws. As long as violence and the seduction of very young children are not involved, sex can be left to the control of informal sanctions. There is no sense in refusing jobs or security clearances to avowed homosexuals. Furthermore, sex-control laws should not be handy for the frightened, vengeful or vicious to use. From the *Anecdota* of Procopius through the chronicles of the McCarthy era, charges of homosexuality have rarely been made against people until someone had a political or other ulterior motive for doing so. Sodomy laws are used to blackmail and intimidate people, just as fornication laws are used to disqualify the poor and dark-skinned from welfare rolls. Finally, the homosexual cannot be more or less included in society until sexual deviance is clearly separated from other kinds of deviance. Unlike the traitor and the revolutionary, the homosexual does not really threaten the vitals of his society. And perhaps if we stop seeing the sexual deviant as such a threat, we can afford to see him as a unique human being, in many cases little different from others except in his sexual preference.

Such a profound change in attitudes and in deviance control happens rarely in any society. But once in a while society does change. Slavery was a fact of human life all over the world until a century or two ago. Although many people are still far from free in an ideal sense, there are at least few real human chattel in the world today. Perhaps humanity is ready to begin to allow sexual freedom, now that it has tried to guarantee the integrity and freedom of the person. Society itself can only gain. There is an element of truth in some homosexuals' charge that the straight world persecutes them out of fear of its own nature. This is not because of "latent homosexuality" but because of an emotional need to defend masculinity and femininity, the vulnerability of sex-role performances, and a traditional Western fear that any loss of individual or social control will start a snowballing loss of controls in general.

In interviewing for this book, I was struck over and over by the fact that beneath a façade of confident and fearless familiarity with the facts of sex, the majority of people have some feeling of inadequacy about themselves as men and women. The smallest liberalization of public and private sexuality brings cries about degeneracy, the banalizing of love, and the end of civilization; to the contrary, we have far to go to make sex in our society the source of joy and fulfillment it can be.

The possibility of such sexual satisfaction exists for the same reason deviance exists. Man is the animal whose sexuality is not merely programed to produce offspring but left largely to learning so that sex can fill many purposes—hold together child-rearing units and act as a broad social bond. Because man is a learning animal, a problem-solving animal, an inventive animal, he is capable of splendid triumphs of change and richness of living— and therefore equally vulnerable to maladaptive learning and the special human failures that result, from suicide to mass warfare. Only man can invent a Sistine Chapel, a betatron, romantic love, homosexuality. Leaving so much to learning is perhaps nature's most brilliant and risky experiment. As a result of it, we have produced art, science, altruism; and as a further result, we may pollute, irradiate or just blast ourselves out of existence. We do not yet know whether this peculiar evolutionary twist our species has taken is a success or a failure. The hope is that we will be able to invent solutions to the very problems we create for ourselves. Sexual deviance is uniquely human, and so are the study, understanding and empathy with which it can be met.

A Critical Bibliography

A complete bibliography of all works consulted in writing this book, and of others relevant to it, would be very long, unwieldy and of little practical use. Bibliographies are usually meant to legitimate the text, list major sources and guide readers to further information. Therefore I have made a selective, chapter-by-chapter list of works quoted directly or indirectly, some important background readings, and well-known books the reader is likely to encounter. In many cases I have added brief comments and evaluations, so that someone seeking more background or wondering whether to trust some popular book can have at least one critical opinion.

During my work on this book, there occurred one of the small disasters that haunt writers' bad dreams: some of my reference notes inexplicably disappeared in the course of moving. I have been able to replace most of them, but at press time a handful of sources still could not be tracked down again. Therefore a small number of quotations are not bibliographically accounted for. The majority are in chapters 6 to 9; many of them are from nineteenth-century French books and anonymous French poems and pamphlets of the sixteenth to eighteenth centuries. I read most of these works in the original editions in special collections not quickly accessible to me now, but I expect to be able to consult these collections again and add the missing references in any future edition of this book.

The citations of dates, volume numbers and page numbers in scientific journals have been made as consistent and complete as possible, but the journals themselves are inconsistent in these matters, especially those of fifty and eighty years ago and of special or local circulation.

The following works recur frequently in the bibliography. For convenience they are listed here and are indicated throughout the listing by asterisks.

Beach, Frank A., ed. *Sex and Behavior*. New York: John Wiley & Sons, 1965. Technical; for the scientist, advanced student or very diligent, adventurous layman. Contains monographs and round-table discussions by many of the leading sex-behavior researchers in the world and an excellent introductory essay by the editor.

Brinton, Crane. *A History of Western Morals*. New York: Harcourt, Brace & World, 1959. An intelligent and gracefully written survey of morality and mores in the West.

Ellis, Havelock. *Studies in the Psychology of Sex*, Vol. 2, Part 2. New York: Random House, 1936. Utterly dated scientifically, and in many ways historically superseded, but still indispensable for a student of the history of sex research.

Foster, Jeannette H. *Sex Variant Women in Literature*. New York: Vantage Press, 1956. An exhaustive historical and bibliographical survey.

Hunt, Morton. *The Natural History of Love*. New York: Alfred A. Knopf, 1959. A fine introduction for general readers to the history of sex, love and marriage by probably the best-informed lay writer on the subject.

Kinsey, Alfred C.; Pomeroy, Wardell; and Martin, Clyde. *Sexual Behavior in the Human Male*. Philadelphia: W. B. Saunders, 1948.

Kinsey, Alfred C.; Pomeroy, Wardell; Martin, Clyde; and Gebhard, Paul. *Sexual Behavior in the Human Female*. Philadelphia: W. B. Saunders, 1953. Despite the shortcomings of the two Kinsey volumes, if all the sex-research information in the world were to be thrown away and only one source could be preserved, these would be the items to save.

Marmor, Judd., ed. *Sexual Inversion*. New York: Basic Books, 1965. Papers and essays from all the disciplines that can throw light on the subject, with a fine essay by the editor. A must for the scientist, and recommended for the layman who wants to make the effort. This and the Ruitenbeek anthology listed below contain, between them, half the crucial recent scientific papers on problems in sex and gender. With the Beach anthology, they almost constitute a basic library of important modern monographs in the field.

Ruitenbeek, Hendrik, ed. *The Problem of Homosexuality in Modern Society*. New York: E. P. Dutton, 1963. Ruitenbeek has edited several poor anthologies, but this one, as I noted in my comments on Marmor's *Sexual Inversion*, is excellent.

1 THE MYTH OF THE PATRIARCHS

Bachofen, Johann Jakob. *Myth, Religion, and Mother Right.* Translated by Ralph Manheim. Princeton: Princeton University Press, 1967. The *locus classicus* of "matriarchy" theories and of much feminist ideology.

Beauvoir, Simone de. *The Second Sex.* Translated and edited by H. M. Parshley. New York: Alfred A. Knopf, 1953. An interesting and well-written study of women, very personal, scientifically inaccurate, and laden with feminist polemics.

Bebel, August. *Woman: Past, Present and Future.* New York: Boni & Liveright, 1918.

Briffault, Robert. *The Mothers.* Abridged by Gordon Rattray Taylor. New York: Grosset & Dunlap, 1963. The major modern elaboration of Bachofen's theory.

Bright, John. *A History of Israel.* Philadelphia: Westminster Press, 1959.

Brim, Charles J. *Medicine in the Bible.* New York: Froben Press, 1936.

Brinton, Crane.*

Bulliet, Clarence J. *Venus Castina.* New York: Covici, 1933. A rather off-handedly written and documented history of transvestism and sexual disguise.

Cole, William G. *Sex and Love in the Bible.* New York: Association Press, 1960.

Driver, G. R., and Miles, John. *The Babylonian Laws.* Oxford: Clarendon Press, 1952.

Ellis, Havelock.*

Ellison, John, ed. *Nelson's Complete Concordance of the Revised Standard Version Bible.* New York: Thomas Nelson & Sons, 1957.

Engels, Frederick. *The Origin of the Family, Private Property and the State.* New York: International Publishers, 1942.

Epstein, Louis. *Sex Laws and Customs in Judaism.* New York: Block Publishing Co., 1948.

Ferm, Vergilius, ed. *Forgotten Religions.* New York: Philosophical Library, 1950.

Frazer, Sir James. *Folklore in the Old Testament.* London: Macmillan, 1919.

———. *Golden Bough.* 3rd ed. 12 vols. London: Macmillan, 1951. Both Frazer works are scholarly classics.

Gide, André. *Corydon.* New York: Farrar, Straus, 1950. An elegantly written homosexual apologetic, of literary and historical value only.

Graves, Robert. *The White Goddess.* New York: Farrar, Straus & Giroux, 1966. A brilliant but crankish piece of scholarship in the Bachofen vein.

Gray, John. *I and II Kings.* Philadelphia: Westminster Press, 1963.

———. *The Canaanites.* London: Thames & Hudson, 1964.

Hammurabi. *The Code of Hammurabi.* Translated by Percy Handcock. New York: Macmillan, 1932.

Hartland, E. S. "Concerning the Rite at the Temple of Mylitta." In *Anthropological Essays Presented to Edward B. Taylor.* Oxford: Clarendon Press, 1907.

Hays, H. R. *From Ape to Angel.* New York: Alfred A. Knopf, 1958. An engaging history of anthropology for laymen.

———. *The Dangerous Sex.* New York: Pocket Books, 1965. A sometimes superficial but sometimes fascinating study of what the author calls "The Myth of Feminine Evil," drawing on history, psychiatry, anthropology and literature.

Worth reading.

Henriques, Fernando. *Love in Action.* New York: E. P. Dutton, 1960. An interesting grab-bag of historical and anthropological material.

———. *Prostitution and Society.* New York: Grove Press, 1962. To my knowledge, the best work of its kind, dealing with Western and non-Western societies.

Herodotus. *The Greek Historians*, Vol. 1. Edited by R. B. Francis. Translated by George Rawlinson. New York: Random House, 1942.

The Holy Scriptures, According to the Masoretic Text. Philadelphia: Jewish Publication Society, 1917.

Jewish Encyclopedia. 12 vols. New York: Funk & Wagnalls, 1912.

Kardiner, Abram, and Preble, Edward. *They Studied Man.* Cleveland: World Publishing Co., 1965. A good history of anthropology, less comprehensive than Hays's (above), but more penetrating. Touches on psychiatry and sociology as well.

Kramer, Samuel N. *The Sumerians.* Chicago: University of Chicago Press, 1963.

Lewinsohn, Richard. *A History of Sexual Customs.* Translated by Alexander Layce. New York: Fawcett Books, 1964. Like most general sexual histories for laymen, this is uneven and intellectually uncoordinated, but better researched and better written than most books of its kind.

May, Geoffrey. *Social Control of Sex Expression.* London: Allen & Unwin, 1930. An excellent and indispensable reference.

May, Herbert and Metzger, eds. *The Oxford Annotated Bible: Revised Standard Version.* New York: Oxford University Press, 1962.

The New English Bible, New Testament. London: Oxford University Press; Cambridge. University Press, 1961.

Ollendorff, Robert, Jr. *The Juvenile Homosexual Experience.* New York: Julian Press, 1966. Not recommended.

Patai, Raphael. *Sex and Family in the Bible and the Middle East.* Garden City, N.Y.: Doubleday, 1959. An illuminating comparison of the ancient and modern Middle East.

Pentateuch with Targum Onkelos, Haphtaroth and Rashi's Commentary. Translated by M. Rosenbaum and A. M. Silbermann. 5 vols. New York: Hebrew Publishing Co., n.d.

Plummer, Douglas. *Queer People.* New York: Citadel Press, 1965. Poorly written and inaccurate.

Rattray Taylor, Gordon. *Sex in History.* New York: Vanguard, 1954. Built on a doubtful elaboration of Bachofen's theory, but crammed with useful details and documentation. To be read, but critically.

———. "Historical and Mythological Aspects of Homosexuality." In Marmor.* Like the book listed above, full of fascinating source material and arguable interpretations.

Westermarck, Edvard. *Origin and Development of the Moral Ideas.* 2nd ed. 2 vols. London: Macmillan, 1917. A classic, theoretically dated but still indispensable for its vast range of source material.

Young, Wayland. *Eros Denied.* New York: Grove Press, 1964. Muscularly anti-Victorian and often simplistic, but contains some useful information.

Zerin, Edward. *The Birth of the Torah.* New York: Appleton-Century-Crofts, 1962.

2 THE GREEK REVISION

The quotations from Aeschylus, Ariston, Epicurus, Isocrates, Menander and Solon are from Flacelière's book; most other brief quotations of minor Greek poets are from Licht and the *Greek Anthology*. Brinton, Flacelière and Hunt give the best basic background for the subject.

Alciphron. *Letters from the Country and the Town.* Translated by F. A. Wright. New York: E. P. Dutton, 1923.

Aristophanes. In *The Complete Greek Drama,* cited below.

Aristotle. *The Works of Aristotle.* Edited by W. D. Ross and J. A. Smith. 12 vols. Oxford: Clarendon Press, 1908–52.

Athenaeus. *The Deipnosophists.* Translated by Charles B. Gulik. 7 vols. Vols. 1–5—New York: G. P. Putnam's Sons. Vols. 6–7—Cambridge, Mass.: Harvard University Press. 1927–41.

Avery, Catherine, ed. *Classical Handbook.* New York: Appleton-Century-Crofts, 1962.

Beau, George F. *Aegaean Turkey.* New York: Praeger, 1966.

Brinton, Crane.*

The Complete Greek Drama. Edited by W. J. Oates and Eugene O'Neill, Jr. 2 vols. New York: Random House, 1938.

Delcourt, Marie. *Hermaphrodite.* Translated by Jennifer Nicholson. London: Studio Books, 1961. Excellent study of the hermaphrodite in art, history and the human imagination.

Demosthenes. *Private Orations.* Translated by A. T. Murray. London: Heinemann, 1939.

Dodds, E. R. *The Greeks and the Irrational.* Berkeley: University of California Press, 1968. An important work in the modern re-evaluation of Greek culture.

Epictetus. *Discourses, Fragments, and Encheiridion.* Translated by W. S. Oldfather. New York: G. P. Putnam's Sons, 1926–28.

Finley, Moses I. *The World of Odysseus.* New York: Viking Press, 1954. Good background reading.

Flacelière, Robert. *Love in Ancient Greece.* Translated by James Cleugh. New York: Crown Publishers, 1962. The best general, brief work on the subject.

Foster, Jeannette.*

Garde, Noel I. *Jonathan to Gide.* New York: Vantage Press, 1964. Biographies of homosexuals and alleged homosexuals. Unreliable and uncritical, but it draws on some out-of-the-way sources. To be read with the greatest critical caution, unless one believes that the world's a stage and all the plays and players really gay.

Graves, Robert. *Greek Myths.* 2 vols. Baltimore: Penguin Books, 1955.

The Greek Anthology, Poems from the. Translated by Dudley Fitts. New York: New Directions, 1956. Wonderfully witty translations.

The Greek Anthology. Translated by W. R. Paton. 5 vols. Cambridge, Mass.: Harvard University Press, 1912–26. The old reliable Loeb Classical Library edition of the entire anthology.

Hays, H. R. *The Dangerous Sex.* See Chapter 1.

Henriques, Fernando. *Prostitution and Society.* See Chapter 1.

Herodotus. See Chapter 1.

Hesiod. *The Works and Days; Theogony; The Shield of Herakles.* Translated by Richard Lattimore. Ann Arbor: University of Michigan Press, 1959.

Hippocrates. *Collected Works.* Translated by W. H. S. Jones. 4 vols. Cambridge, Mass.: Harvard University Press, 1923–43.

Homer. *The Iliad.* Translated by E. V. Rieu. Baltimore: Penguin Books, 1966.

———. *Odyssey.* Translated by E. V. Rieu. Baltimore: Penguin Books, 1946.

Hunt, Morton.*

Kinsey, Alfred, *et al. Male.**

Lacroix, Paul. *History of Prostitution.* Chicago: Covici, 1926. A nineteenth-century work that is still useful.

Lewinsohn, Richard. See Chapter 1.

Licht, Hans [Paul Brand]. *Sexual Life in Ancient Greece.* Edited by Lawrence H. Dawson. Translated by J. H. Freese. New York: Barnes & Noble, 1963. The most complete scholarly compendium on the subject; unfortunately, written with a pervasive prohomosexual bias. To be used only as a source book.

Lucian. *Collected Works.* Translated by A. M. Harmon and M. D. Macleod. 8 vols. Vols. 1–2—New York: Macmillan, 1913–15. Vols. 3–4—New York: G. P. Putnam's Sons, 1921–25. Vols. 5–7—Cambridge, Mass.: Harvard University Press, 1936–61. Vol. 8—New York: Macmillan, 1967.

Marrou, H. I. *A History of Education in Antiquity.* Translated by George Lamb. New York: Sheed & Ward, 1956. Excellent background reading.

Maxime de Tyr. *Dissertations.* Translated by J.-J. Combes-DouNous. 2 vols. Paris: Chez Bossange, Masson, et Besson, 1802.

Müller, Karl Otfried. *Doric Race,* Vol. 2. Oxford: Oxford University Press, 1830.

Pausanias. *Description of Greece,* Vols. 2 and 4. Translated by W. H. S. Jones. Vol. 2—New York: G. P. Putnam's Sons, 1926. Vol. 4—Cambridge, Mass.: Harvard University Press, 1935.

Pindar. *Odes.* Translated by Sir John Sandys. New York: Macmillan, 1915.

Plato. *The Portable Plato.* Edited by Scott Buchanan. New York: Viking Press, 1948.

Plutarch. *Plutarch's Lives.* Translated by John Dryden; revised by Arthur Hugh Clough. New York: Modern Library, 1932.

———. *Selected Essays.* New York: New American Library, 1957.

Sappho. *Lyrics.* Translated by Willis Barnstone. Garden City, N.Y.: Doubleday Anchor, 1965.

Seltman, Charles. *Women in Antiquity.* New York: Collier Books, 1962. Argues against the idea of Athenian antifeminism. Contains some useful information.

Strabo. *Geography.* Translated by H. L. Jones. 8 vols. New York: G. P. Putnam's Sons, 1917–32.

Symonds, John Addington. *Studies in Sexual Inversion.* Privately printed, 1931. Includes "A Study in Greek Ethics" and "A Study in Modern Ethics." Finely written and still useful; has a strong prohomosexual bias.

Tarn, William W. *Alexander the Great.* Boston: Beacon Press, 1956.

Theocritus. *The Idylls.* Translated by W. Douglas P. Hill. Eton, Windsor: Shakespeare Head Press, 1959.

Thomson, George. *Aeschylus and Athens.* London: Lawrence & Wishart, 1950.

Thucydides. *Thucydides.* Translated by C. Forster Smith. 4 Vols. Cambridge, Mass.: Harvard University Press, 1958–62.

Weigall, Arthur. *Sappho of Lesbos.* New York: F. A. Stokes, 1932.

Westermarck, Edvard. See Chapter 1.

Xenophon. *Anabasis.* Translated by C. L. Brownson. 2 Vols. New York: G. P. Putnam's Sons, 1922–32.

———. *Cyropaedia.* Translated by W. Miller. 2 vols. New York: Macmillan, 1914.

———. *Scripta Minora.* Translated by E. C. Marchant. New York: G. P. Putnam's Sons, 1925.

3 HOMOSEXUAL AND PANSEXUAL

Apuleius. *The Golden Ass.* Translated by W. Adlington. New York: Horace Liveright, 1943.

Aristotle. See Chapter 2.

Augustine, Saint, Bishop of Hippo. *Confessions.* Translated by R. S. Pine-Coffin. Baltimore: Penguin Books, 1961.

Bloch, Raymond. *The Etruscans.* London: Thames & Hudson, 1958.

Brinton, Crane.*

Carcopino, Jerome. *Daily Life in Ancient Rome.* New Haven: Yale University Press, 1940.

Cato. *Cato, the Censor, on Farming.* Translated by Ernest Brehaut. New York: Columbia University Press, 1933.

Catullus. *The Poems of Catullus.* Translated by Horace Gregory. New York: Grove Press, 1956.

Cicero. *De Republica; De Republica De Legibus.* Translated by C. W. Keyes. New York: G. P. Putnam's Sons, 1928.

———. *Letters to His Friends.* Translated by W. G. Williams. 3 vols. New York: G. P. Putnam's Sons, 1928.

Cles-Reden, Sibylle von. *The Buried People: A Study of the Etruscan World.* Translated by C. M. Woodhouse. London: Rupert Hart-Davis, 1955.

Deiss, Joseph. *Herculaneum.* New York: Thomas Y. Crowell, 1966.

Dio Cassius. *Dio's Roman History.* Translated by Earnest Cary. 9 vols. New York: Macmillan, 1914–27.

Diodorus Siculus. *Diodorus of Sicily.* Translated by C. H. Oldfather. 12 vols. Cambridge, Mass.: Harvard University Press, 1947–67.

Durant, Will and Ariel. *Caesar and Christ.* New York: Simon & Schuster, 1944. Like the Durants' other historical works, this has wide scope, excellent material and some conventional, even cliché evaluations and interpretations.

Foster, Jeannette.*

Frazer, Sir James. See Chapter 1.

Gibbon, Edward. *The Decline and Fall of the Roman Empire.* 6 vols. New York: E. P. Dutton; London: J. M. Dent, 1957–62. Still one of the most valuable sources.

Hays, H. R. *The Dangerous Sex.* See Chapter 1.

Henriques, Fernando. *Prostitution and Society.* See Chapter 1.

Herodotus. See Chapter 1.

Highet, Gilbert. *Juvenal the Satirist.* New York: Oxford University Press, 1961. Excellent collateral reading.

Horace. *The Complete Works.* New York: Modern Library, n.d.

Hunt, Morton.*

Hus, Alain. *The Etruscans.* Translated by Jeanne U. Duell. New York: Grove Press, 1961.

Jerome, Saint. *A Select Library of the Nicene and Post-Nicene Fathers,* 2nd series, Vol. 6. Edited by Philip Schaff and Henry Wace. New York: The Christian Literature Co., 1893.

Juvenal. *The Satires.* Translated by Rolfe Humphries. Bloomington: Indiana University Press, 1958.

Kiefer, Otto. *Sexual Life in Ancient Rome.* Translated by Gilbert and Helen Highet. New York: Barnes & Noble, 1951. Like Licht's book on Greece, necessary for research but short on insight.

Lawrence, D. H. *Etruscan Places.* New York: Viking Press, 1957.

Lecky, W. E. H. *History of European Morals from Augustus to Charlemagne.* New York: George Braziller, 1955. An enduring edifice of nineteenth-century scholarship.

Livy. *Works,* Vol. 11. Translated by E. T. Sage, Cambridge, Mass.: Harvard University Press, 1949.

Lucretius. *On the Nature of Things.* Translated by W. H. D. Rouse. Cambridge, Mass.: Harvard University Press, 1959.

Martial. *Epigrams.* London: Bohn's Classical Library, 1860.

———. *Epigrams.* Translated by Walter C. A. Ker. 2 vols. Cambridge, Mass.: Harvard University Press. 1961.

Ovid. *Art of Love.* Translated by Rolfe Humphries. Bloomington: Indiana University Press, 1957.

Pallotino, M. *The Etruscans.* Translated by J. Cremona. Baltimore: Penguin Books, 1955.

Petronius. *The Satyricon.* Translated by William Arrowsmith. New York: New American Library, 1960.

Plato. See Chapter 2.

Plutarch. *Lives.* See Chapter 2.

Propertius, Sextus Aurelius. *The Poems of Sextus Propertius.* Translated by Constance Carrier. Bloomington: Indiana University Press, 1963.

Sallust. *"The Jugurthine War" and "The Conspiracy of Catilene."* Translated by S. A. Handford. Baltimore: Penguin Books, 1963.

Schaff, Philip, and Wace, Henry, eds. *A Select Library of the Nicene and Post-Nicene Fathers,* 2nd series. New York: The Christian Literature Co., 1891–1916.

Seneca. *Epistulae Morales.* Translated by R. D. Gummere. 3 vols. Cambridge, Mass.: Harvard University Press, 1953.

Strabo. See Chapter 2.

Strato. In *Greek Anthology.* See Chapter 2.

Suetonius. *The Twelve Caesars.* Translated by Robert Graves. Baltimore: Penguin Books, 1957.

Swift, Jonathan. *Poems,* Vol. 2. Edited by Harold Williams. London: Oxford University Press, 1937.

Tacitus. *Annales.* Translated by G. G. Ramsay. 2 vols. London: John Murray, 1904–9.

Tibullus. *Poems.* Translated by Constance Carrier. Bloomington: Indiana University Press, 1968.

Villeneuve, Roland. *Heliogabale, Le César Fou.* Paris: P. Amiot, 1957.

Virgil. *Aeneid. Minor Poems.* Translated by H. R. Fairclough. 2 vols. London: Heinemann, 1925.

Westermarck, Edvard. *Christianity and Morals.* London: Paul, Trench, Trubner, 1939.

4 THE CHRISTIAN BEDROCK

Burchard is quoted in Cleugh's book; Cyprian and Apollonius in Hunt's; de Vitry in the Durants'; Tertullian in the *Ante-Nicene Fathers.* The collections of writings by the Church fathers are, of course, the basic documents on this period. Lea's work on sacerdotal celibacy is also important. The *Horizon* book, Cleugh, Hunt and Henriques are good for the nonspecialist; Waddell and May are necessary for the reader with greater historical background. William Graham Cole's volume can be recommended to any serious reader.

Augustine, Saint, Bishop of Hippo. *Confessions.* See Chapter 3.

———. *The City of God.* Translated by George E. McCracken. Cambridge, Mass.: Harvard University Press, 1957.

Basil, Saint. *Letters and Select Works.* Translated by Rev. B. Jackson. New York: The Christian Literature Co., 1895.

Beowulf. A verse translation by Edwin Morgan. Berkeley: University of California Press, 1964.

Brinton, Crane.*

Cassian, John. In Schaff and Wace, eds., *A Select Library of Nicene and Post-Nicene Fathers,* 2nd series, Vol. 11. See below.

Chrysostom, Saint John. "Letters to Theodore." In *A Select Library of the Nicene and Post-Nicene Fathers.* Edited by Philip Schaff. See below.

Cleugh, James. *Love Locked Out.* New York: Crown Publishers, 1964. Unscholarly in spirit at times, with a gee-whiz tone, but interesting.

Cole, William Graham. *Sex in Christianity and Psychoanalysis.* New York: Oxford University Press, 1966. Good background in history and psychoanalysis from a liberal theological standpoint.

DeFerrari, Roy, and Barr, Sister M. I. *A Complete Index of the Summa Theologica of St. Thomas Aquinas.* Baltimore: Catholic University of America Press, 1958.

Dio Chrysostom. *Discourses*. Translated by J. W. Cohoon and H. L. Crosby. Vol. 1—New York: G. P. Putnam's Sons, 1932. Vols. 2–5—Cambridge, Mass.: Harvard University Press, 1939–51.

Dodd, C. H. *The Moffatt New Testament Commentary: The Epistle of Paul to the Romans*. New York: Harper & Brothers, 1932.

Durant, Will and Ariel. See Chapter 3.

Elder, E. *Concordance to the New English Bible, New Testament*. Grand Rapids, Mich.: Zondervan Publishing House, 1965.

Ellis, Havelock.*

Epton, Nina. *Love and the English*. Cleveland: World Publishing Co., 1960. Charming, well researched and not as lightweight as the title and tone might first suggest.

Eusebius. *The Ecclesiastical History*. Translated by K. Lake. 2 vols. New York: G. P. Putnam's Sons, 1926–32.

Gibbon, Edward. See Chaper 3.

Gwatkin, H. M., *et al.*, eds. *The Cambridge Medieval History*, Vols. 6 and 7. Cambridge: Cambridge University Press, 1957. Probably the best general background reading.

Henriques, Fernando. *Prostitution in Europe and the Americas*. New York: Citadel Press, 1965. Excellent for this and other periods.

Holmes, William G. *The Age of Justinian and Theodore*, Vol. 1. London: G. Bell & Sons, 1912.

The Horizon Book of Christianity. New York: American Heritage Publishing Co., 1964. A good introduction.

Hunt, Morton.*

Jerome, Saint. See Chapter 3.

Justin Martyr, Saint. *The Fathers of the Churches: St. Justin Martyr, First Apology*. Translated by Thomas Falls. New York: Christian Heritage, 1949.

Justinian I. *The Code of Justinian*. In *The Civil Law*, Vol. 15. Edited by S. P. Scott. Cincinnati: The Central Trust Co., 1932.

Klugerman, Charles. "A Psycho-analytic Study of the *Confessions* of St. Augustine." *Journal of the American Psychoanalytic Association*, 3 (July 1957).

Lacroix, Paul. See Chapter 2.

Lea, Henry C. *History of Sacerdotal Celibacy in the Christian Church*. New Hyde Park, N.Y.: University Books, 1966. A standard reference.

Lecky, W. E. H. See Chapter 3.

McNeill, John, and Gamer, Helena, eds. *Medieval Handbooks of Penance*. New York: Columbia University Press, 1938.

Maxime de Tyr. See Chapter 2.

May, Geoffrey. See Chapter 1.

Moffatt, James. *The Moffatt New Testament Commentary: The First Epistle of Paul to the Corin-*

thians. New York: Harper & Brothers, 1928; rpr. 1960.

Procopius. *Works*, Vol. 6. Cambridge, Mass.: Harvard University Press, 1935.

Roberts, Alexander, and Donaldson, James, eds. *The Ante-Nicene Fathers*. New York: Charles Scribner's Sons, 1899–1900.

Salvian. *Governance of God; Letters; Books to the Church*. New York: Cima Publishing Co., 1947.

Schaff, Philip, ed. *A Select Library of the Nicene and Post-Nicene Fathers*. New York: The Christian Literature Co., 1887–1900; rpr. Grand Rapids, Mich.: W. B. Eerdman, 1956.

Schaff, Philip, and Wace, Henry. *A Select Library of the Nicene and Post-Nicene Fathers*. 2nd series. New York: The Christian Literature Co., 1891–1916.

Scott, S. P., ed. *The Civil Law*. 17 vols. Cincinnati: The Central Trust Co., 1932.

The Seven Ecumenical Councils. Edited by H. R. Percival. New York: Charles Scribner's Sons, 1900.

Tacitus. *On Britain and Germany*. Translations of *Agricola* and *Germania* by H. Mattingly. Baltimore: Penguin Books, 1948.

Tarachow, Sidney. "St. Paul And Early Christianity: A Psychoanalytic and Historical Study." In *Psychoanalysis and the Social Sciences*, Vol. 5. Edited by W. Muensterberger and S. Axelrod. New York: International Universities Press, 1955. Has the usual drawbacks of classical psychoanalytic internal criticism, but otherwise interesting and valuable.

Tertullian. In Roberts and Donaldson, eds., *The Ante-Nicene Fathers*, Vols. 3–4. See above.

Theodosius II. *The Theodosian Code and Novels and the Sirmondian Constitutions*. Translated by C. Pharr. Princeton: Princeton University Press, 1952.

Thomas Aquinas, Saint. *Summa Theologiae*. Edited by Thomas Gilby. 2 vols. Garden City, N.Y.: Image Books, 1969.

Toon, Mark. *The Philosophy of Sex According to St. Thomas Aquinas—An Abstract of a Dissertation*. Washington, D.C.: The Catholic University of America Press, 1954.

Verkuyl, Gerrit, ed. *The Holy Bible: The Berkeley Version in Modern English*. Grand Rapids, Mich.: Zondervan Publishing House, 1959.

Waddel, Helen. *The Desert Fathers*. Ann Arbor: University of Michigan Press, 1957. Recommended.

Westermarck, Edvard. *Christianity and Morals*. See Chapter 3.

———. *Origin and Development of the Moral Ideas*. See Chapter 1.

Young, Wayland. See Chapter 1.

5 THE CAPITAL SIN

Andreas Cappelanus. *The Art of Courtly Love*. Translated by John J. Parry. New York: Columbia University Press, 1941.

Backman, E. L. *Religious Dances in the Christian Church and in Popular Medicine*. London: Allen & Unwin, 1952.

Boniface, Saint. *The Letters of Saint Boniface*. Translated by E. Emerton. New York: Columbia University Press, 1940.

Brinton, Crane.*

Campbell, G. A. *The Knights Templars*. London: Duckworth, 1937.

Cleugh, James. See Chapter 4.

Coulton, G. *Life in the Middle Ages*. New York: Macmillan, 1931. For background reading.

DeLille, Alain. *The Complaint of Nature*. Translated by Douglas Moffat. New York: Henry Holt, 1908.

Dingwall, Eric. *The Girdle of Chastity*. London: George Routledge & Sons, 1931.

DuBoys, Albert. *Du Droit Criminel de L'Espagne*. Paris: Durant et Pédonc Lauriel, 1870.

Durant, Will and Ariel. *The Renaissance*. New York: Simon & Schuster, 1953. As noted before, full of good material but predictable and avuncular.

Ellis, Havelock.*

Epton, Nina. *Love and the French*. Cleveland: World Publishing Co., 1959. Not as good as her book on the English, but worth reading.

Garde, Noel I. See Chapter 2.

Hays, H. R. *The Dangerous Sex*. See Chapter 4.

Henriques, Fernando. *Prostitution*. See Chapter 4.

Huizinga, Johan. *The Waning of the Middle Ages*. Garden City, N.Y.: Doubleday, 1954. A splendid book by a great historian and historiographer.

Hunt, Morton.*

John of Salisbury. *Frivolities of Courtiers and Footprints of Philosophers*. Translated by G. B. Pike. Minneapolis: University of Minnesota Press, 1938.

Kamen, Henry. *The Spanish Inquisition*. London: Weidenfeld & Nicolson, 1965.

Kinsey, Alfred, *et al. Female*.*

———. *Male*.*

Lea, Henry Charles. *History of the Inquisition of the Middle Ages*. 3 vols. New York: Harper & Brothers, 1887–88. Still unsurpassed.

———. *The Inquisition in the Spanish Dependencies*. New York: Macmillan, 1922.

———. *History of the Inquisition of Spain*, Vol. 4. New York: Macmillan, 1922.

Legman, George. *The Guilt of the Templars*. New York: Basic Books, 1966. A brilliant book, but highly speculative and, in my opinion, wrongheaded and even crankish in places.

Lewis, C. S. *The Allegory of Love*. London: Oxford University Press, 1951. Along with de Rougemont's book, a basic education in the courtly tradition.

Lewinsohn, Richard. See Chapter 1.

May, Geoffrey. See Chapter 1.

Murray, Margaret. *The Witch-Cult in Western Europe*. London: Oxford University Press, 1962. Argues that witchcraft was part of organized pagan survivals.

Pitcairn, Robert, compiler. *Criminal Trials in Scotland*. 3 vols. Edinburgh: The Maitland Club, 1833.

Rattray Taylor, Gordon. *Sex in History*. See Chapter 1.

Rougemont, Denis de. *Love in the Western World*. New York: Fawcett World Library, 1966. A brilliant, elegant and profound book on *l'amour courtois*. For everyone who reads.

Rule, William Harris. *History of the Inquisition*, Vol. 2. New York: Scribner, Welford, 1874.

Schaff, Philip, ed. See Chapter 4.

Simon, Edith. *The Piebald Standard: A Biography of the Knights Templars*. London: Cassell, 1959.

Sprenger, Jacob, and Krämer, Heinrich. *Malleus Maleficarum*. Translated by Montagu Summers. London: John Rodker, 1928. No summary can do justice to this testament to human fear and frailty.

Stephen, Sir James F. *History of the Criminal Law of England*, Vol. 1. London: Macmillan, 1883.

Troyes, Jean de. *Les Chroniques de . . . Louys de Valois Onzième . . . .* Paris, 1820.

Veith, Ilza. *Hysteria: The History of a Disease*. Chicago: University of Chicago Press, 1965. A thorough and intelligent study with many interesting sidelights on the histories of science and of ideas.

Westermarck, Edvard. *Christianity and Morals*. See Chapter 3.

Zilboorg, Gregory. *A History of Medical Psychology*. New York: W. W. Norton, 1941. Exhaustive, scholarly, yet readable. Highly recommended.

6 THE BISEXUAL GLORY

Brinton is at his best on this period and on the Enlightenment. D'Ewes is quoted in Ellis; Ariosto, Franco and *L'Alcibiade* in Young; the sonnet from W. H. to Shakespeare in Cole; *La Frigarelle* in L'Estoile; the French account of Italy in Henriques' *Prostitution in Europe and America*; Pico della Mirandola in Brantôme.

Aretino, Pietro. *Works*. Translated by Samuel Putnam. Chicago: P. Covici, 1926.

Ascham, Roger. *English Works*. Edited by W. Aldis Wright. Cambridge: Cambridge University Press, 1904.

Aubrey, John. *Brief Lives*. Edited by Oliver Lawson Dick. Ann Arbor: University of Michigan Press, 1957.

Bacon, Francis. *New Atlantis*. Edited by Alfred B. Gough. Oxford: Clarendon Press, 1924.

Bakeless, John. *The Tragicall History of Christopher Marlowe*. Cambridge, Mass.: Harvard University Press, 1942.

Barnfield, Richard. *The Complete Poems*. Edited by A. B. Grosart. London: J. B. Nichols & Sons, 1876.

Boas, Frederick S. *Marlowe and His Circle*. Oxford: Clarendon Press, 1929.

Boccaccio, Giovanni. *Decameron*. Translated by R. Aldington. New York: Covici, Friede, 1930.

Brantôme, Pierre de. *Vies des Dames Galantes*. Paris: Garnier, 1960. English edition—*The Lives of Gallant Ladies*. Translated by Alec Brown. London: Elek Books, 1961.

Brinton, Crane.*

Browne, Sir Thomas. *Works*. Edited by Geoffrey Keynes. New ed. Chicago: University of Chicago Press, 1964.

Burckhardt, Jakob C. *The Civilization of the Renaissance*. New York: Harper Torchbook, 1958. The source of nineteenth- and twentieth-century romanticizing of the Renaissance.

Bussy-Rabutin, Roger. *Histoire Amoureuse des Gaules*. Paris, 1930.

Castiglione, Baldesar. *The Book of the Courtier*. Translated by Charles S. Singleton. Garden City, N.Y.: Doubleday Anchor, 1959.

Cellini, Benvenuto. *The Life of Benvenuto Cellini*. Translated by J. A. Symonds. London: Macmillan, 1924.

Cleugh, James. *The Divine Aretino: A Biography*. New York: Stein & Day, 1966. Like his other books, valuable despite a tendency toward Sunday-supplement prose and fuzzy use of sources.

Cole, William, ed. *Erotic Poetry*. New York: Random House, 1963.

Dante, Alighieri. *The Divine Comedy*. Translated by John Ciardi. New York: New American Library, 1961–62.

D'Aubigné, Agrippa. *Les Tragiques*. Livre 2, *Les Princes*. Baltimore: Johns Hopkins Press, 1953.

Davis, H., and Weaver, J., eds. *Dictionary of National Biography*. London: Oxford University Press, 1921–22.

Durant, Will and Ariel. *Renaissance*. See Chapter 5.

Ellis, Havelock.*

Epton, Nina. *English*. See Chapter 4.

Epton, Nina. *French*. See Chapter 5.

Erasmus, Desiderus. *The Epistles of Erasmus*, Vol. 1. Translated by F. M. Nichols. New York: Russell, 1962.

Fiedler, Leslie. *Love and Death in the American Novel*. Rev. ed. New York: Stein & Day, 1966.

Forberg, Friedrich. *Manual of Classical Erotology*. New York: Grove Press, 1966.

Foster, Jeanette.*

Freud, Sigmund. *Leonardo da Vinci and a Memory of His Childhood*. Translated by Alan Tyson. New York: W. W. Norton, 1964.

Garde, Noel I. See Chapter 2.

Hays, H. R. *The Dangerous Sex*. See Chapter 1.

Henriques, Fernando. *Love in Action*. See Chapter 1.

———. *Prostitution*. See Chapter 2.

Hubler, Edward. *The Riddle of Shakespeare's Sonnets*. 1st ed. New York: Basic Books, 1962. The best single reference on homosexuality and the sonnets.

Huizinga, Johan. See Chapter 5.

Huon of Bordeaux. *The Boke of Duke Huon of Burdeux*. Translated by Lord Berners. London: Trubner & Co., 1884.

Hunt, Morton.*

Jonson, Ben. *Complete Poetry*. Edited by William B. Hunter. New York: New York University Press, 1963.

Kamen, Henry. See Chapter 5.

Knight, G. Wilson. *The Wheel of Fire*. 4th rev. and enl. ed. rpr. with minor corrections. London: Methuen, 1959.

Laurence, John. *A History of Capital Punishment*. New York: Citadel Press, 1960.

Lea, Henry C. See Chapter 5.

LeMacon, Robert. *Les Funerailles de Sodome et de ses filles*. London: R. Field, 1600.

L'Estoile, Pierre de. *Journal des choses memorables advenues durant le regne de Henry III . . . 1621*. Paris: Gallimard, 1943. Packed with fascinating details, including many anonymous short works of the period.

Lithgow, William. *The Totall Discourse, of the Rare Adventures, and Painefull Peregrinations of Long Nineteen Years Travailes.* London: I. Okes, 1640.

MacLysaght, Edward. *Irish Life in the Seventeenth Century.* Oxford: B. H. Blackwell, 1950.

Marlowe, Christopher. *Works.* Edited by R. H. Case, et al. 2nd ed. rev. London: Methuen, 1951.

Middleton, Thomas, and Dekker, Thomas. *The Roaring Girl. Works,* Vol. 4. Edited by A. H. Bullen. Boston and New York: Houghton Mifflin, 1885–86.

Mirabeau, Honoré Gabriel Riqueti, Comte de. *The Secret History of the Court of Berlin.* London: H. S. Nichols, 1895.

Montaigne, Michel de. *Journal of Montaigne's Travels in Italy.* London: John Murray, 1903.

Muggeridge, Malcolm. *The Thirties.* London: H. Hamilton, 1940.

Nash, Thomas. *Works.* Edited by R. B. McKerrow; rpr. ed. by F. P. Wilson. Oxford: B. Blackwell, 1958.

Partridge, Eric. *Shakespeare's Bawdy.* New York: E. P. Dutton, 1960.

Pearson, Hesketh. *A Life of Shakespeare.* London: Carroll & Nicholson, 1949.

Pitcairn, Robert. See Chapter 5.

Rattray Taylor, Gordon. *Sex in History.* See Chapter 1.

Sauerwein, Henry A. *Agrippa d'Aubigné's Les Tragiques: A Study in Structure and Poetic Method.* Baltimore: Johns Hopkins Press, 1953.

Sidney, Philip. *The Countess of Pembroke's Arcadia.* Cambridge: Cambridge University Press, 1912.

Stubbes, Philip. *The Anatomie of Abuses.* London: R. Jones, 1583.

———. *The Second Part of the Anatomie of Abuses.* London: R. Ward for M. Wright, 1583.

Trevor-Roper, H. R. "Witches and Witchcraft." *Encounter,* 28 (May-June 1967):3–25; 13–34. A good short study.

UCLA Law Review. "(Project:) The Consenting Adult Homosexual and the Law." 13 (March, 1966). A painstaking study; basic reference.

Vasari, Giorgio. *Stories of the Italian Artists from Vasari.* Translated by E. L. Seeley. London: Chatto & Windus; New York: E. P. Dutton, 1906.

Wilde, Oscar. "The Portrait of Mr. W. H." In Hubler, cited above.

Willson, David Harris. *King James VI and I.* New York: Oxford University Press, 1967.

Wraight, A. D. *In Search of Christopher Marlowe.* New York: Vanguard Press, 1965.

Young, G. F. *The Medici.* New York: Modern Library, 1933. Good background.

Young, Wayland. See Chapter 1.

7 MARRIEDS AND LIBERTINES

Erikson, Hunt, May and Perry Miller are useful for understanding the period. Rattray Taylor's *The Angel Makers* is a fine and original work that corrects the usual concentration on libertinism in literary and historical studies. Bradford is quoted by Henriques; Higgeson by Powers; Daniel Rogers by Hunt.

Adams, Charles F. *Some Phases of Sexual Morality and Church Discipline in Colonial New England.* Cambridge, Mass.: J. Wilson & Son, 1891.

Bradford, William. *Of Plymouth Plantation.* Edited by Samuel Eliot Morison. New York: Alfred A. Knopf, 1952.

Brantôme, Pierre de. See Chapter 6.

Brinton, Crane.*

Bussy-Rabutin, Roger. See Chapter 6.

Calvin, John. *Institutes of the Christian Religion.* Edited by John T. McNeill. Translated by Ford Lewis Battles, et al. Philadelphia: Westminster Press, 1940.

Chesterfield, Philip Dormer Stanhope, Earl of. *Letters to His Son.* Edited by O. H. Leigh. New York: Tudor Publishing Co., n.d.

Choisy, François Timoléon de. *Mémoirs de l'abbé Choisy.* Edited by Georges Mongrédien. Paris: Mercure de France, 1966.

Durant, Will and Ariel. *The Age of Louis XIV.* New York: Simon & Schuster, 1963.

———. *The Reformation.* New York: Simon & Schuster, 1957.

Elizabeth of Bohemia. *Letters.* Compiled by L. M. Baker. London: Bodley Head, 1953.

Ellis, Havelock.* "Eonism." In *Studies in the Psychology of Sex.* Vol. 3. Though scientifically far surpassed, still valuable for historical material.

Epton, Nina. *English.* See Chapter 4.

———. *French.* See Chapter 5.

Erikson, Erik H. *Young Man Luther.* New York: W. W. Norton, 1958. Brilliant.

Fenichel, Otto. *The Psychoanalytic Theory of Neuroses.* New York: W. W. Norton, 1945.

Hamilton, Count Anthony. *Memoirs of the Count de Grammont.* Translated by Horace Walpole. London: Allen & Unwin, 1926.

Hays, H. R. *The Dangerous Sex.* See Chapter 1.

Hunt, Morton.*

Kessler, Henry H., and Rachlis, Eugene. *Peter Stuyvesant and His New York.* New York: Random House, 1959.

Luther, Martin. *Works,* Vol. 3. Edited by Jaroslav Pelikan. St. Louis, Mo.: Concordia Publishing House, 1961.

Mather, Cotton. *Diary of Cotton Mather (1681–1708).* Massachusetts Historical Society Collections, 7th series, Vols. 7–8. Boston: Published by the Society, 1911.

Maurepas, Jean, Comte de. *Pièces libres, chansons, épigrammes sur divers personnages des siècles de Louis XIV et Louis XV.* 6 vols. Leyde, 1865.

May, Geoffrey. See Chapter 1.

Miller, Perry. *The New England Mind: From Colony to Province.* Cambridge, Mass.: Harvard University Press, 1953. Good background reading.

———. *The New England Mind: The Seventeenth Century.* New York: Macmillan, 1939. Good background reading.

Milton, John. *Complete Prose Works.* Edited by Don M. Wolfe, Ernest Sirluck and Merritt Hughes. 3 vols. New Haven: Yale University Press, 1953–62.

Mirabeau, Honoré. *Erotika Biblion.* Brussels, 1866.

Mitford, Nancy. *The Sun King.* New York: Harper & Row, 1966. Readable and reliable.

Nixon, G. "The Chevalier d'Eon." *History Today,* 14:126–34.

Otway, Thomas. *Venice Preserved. Works,* Vol. 2. Edited by J. C. Ghosh. Oxford: Clarendon Press, 1932.

Pepys, Samuel. *The Diary of Samuel Pepys.* Edited by Robert Latham and William Matthews. Berkeley and Los Angeles: University of California Press, 1970.

Powers, Edwin. *Crime and Punishment in Early Massachusetts: 1620–1692.* Boston: Beacon Press, 1966.

Rattray Taylor, Gordon. *The Angel Makers.* London: Heinemann, 1958. Excellent.

Saint-Simon, Louis de Rouvroy, Duc de. *Memoirs of the duc de Saint-Simon.* Rev. ed. Edited by W. H. Lewis. Translated by Bayle St. John. New York: Macmillan, 1964.

Shadwell, Thomas. *The Virtuoso. Works,* Vol. 3. Edited by Montagu Summers. London: Fortune Press, 1927.

Shellabarger, Samuel. *Lord Chesterfield and His World.* Boston: Little, Brown, 1951.

Spitzka, E. C. "A Historical Case of Sexual Perversion." *Chicago Medical Review,* August 20, 1881, 378–79.

Suckling, Sir John. In *Minor Poets of the Seventeenth Century.* Edited by Robert G. Howarth. New York: E. P. Dutton; London and Toronto: J. M. Dent, 1931.

Vieth, David M. *Attribution in Restoration Poetry.*

New Haven: Yale University Press, 1963.

Visconti, Primi. *Mémoires sur la Cour de Louis XIV.* Translated by Jean Lemoine. Paris: Calmann-Lévy, 1908.

Wilmot, John, Earl of Rochester. *Poems on Several Occasions.* Edited by James Thorpe. Princeton: Princeton University Press, 1950.

8 MOLLIES AND ROARERS

Foucault, Henriques, Hunt and Brinton are helpful. Chamfort is quoted by Hunt; Garrick and Johnson in the edition of Churchill; de Sauvages is cited by Foucault; *The Annual Register* and *Hell Upon Earth* by Rattray Taylor in his essay in Marmor; Taine and *Satan's Harvest Home* are in Rattray Taylor's *Sex in History*; Weyer is quoted by Zilboorg, and the erotic advertisements by Henriques.

Barnes, Harry Elmer, ed. *An Introduction to the History of Sociology.* Chicago: University of Chicago Press, 1948.

Bayne-Powell, Rosamond. *Eighteenth Century Life.* London: J. Murray, 1937.

Berneri, Marie Louise. *Journey through Utopia.* Boston: Beacon Press, 1951.

Bloch, Iwan. *Marquis de Sade: His Life and Works.* New York: Brittany Press, 1948. Poor.

Brinton, Crane.*

Cambridge Modern History, Vol. 5—*The Age of Louis XIV.* Edited by A. W. Ward, G. W. Prothero and Stanley Leathes. Cambridge: Cambridge University Press, 1934.

Casanova, Jacques. *The Memoirs of Jacques Casanova de Seingalt.* Translated by Arthur Machen. 8 vols. New York: A. & C. Boni, 1932.

Chesterfield, Philip Dormer Stanhope, Earl of. See Chapter 7.

Churchill, Charles. *The Poetical Works of Charles Churchill.* Edited by Douglas Grant. Oxford: Clarendon Press, 1956.

Cleland, John. *Fanny Hill.* New York: G. P. Putnam's Sons, 1963.

A Complete Collection of State Trials and Proceedings for High Treason, and Other Crimes from the Reign of Richard I to George I. 2nd ed. 6 vols. London: J. Walthoe, 1730.

Coxe, William. *Account of the Prisons and Hospitals in Russia, Sweden, and Denmark.* London: T. Cadell, 1781.

Desmaze, Charles. *Les Pénalités Anciennes.* Paris: Henri Plon, 1866.

Diderot, Denis. *Oeuvres Romanesques.* Paris: Garnier Frères, 1951.

———. *Rameau's Nephew and Other Works.* Translated by Jacques Barzun and Ralph Bowen. Garden City, N.Y.: Doubleday Anchor, 1956.

———. *Supplement to Bougainville's Voyage.* In *Oeuvres philosophiques.* Paris: Garnier Frères, 1956.

Ellis, Havelock.*

Epton, Nina. *English.* See Chapter 4.

Foucault, Michel. *Histoire de la Folie.* Paris: Librairie Plon, 1961. A fine study, very helpful in understanding Western conceptions of sanity and insanity, health and sickness, normality and deviance. The American edition, published in paperback by Mentor Books, is abridged; much important material (including some used in this chapter) has been omitted. Readers with a knowledge of French should refer to the original edition.

Frye, Northrop. *Utopias and Utopian Thought.* Boston: Houghton Mifflin, 1966.

Goncourt, Edmond and Jules de. *The Woman of the Eighteenth Century.* New York: Minton, Balch & Co., 1927. Still useful.

Gorer, Geoffrey. *The Life and Ideas of the Marquis de Sade.* One of the better books about de Sade. There is none I can recommend wholeheartedly.

Heriot, Angus. *The Castrati in Opera.* London: Secker & Warburg, 1956.

Henriques, Fernando. *Prostitution.* See Chapter 4.

Hobbes, Thomas. *Leviathan.* Edited by Michael Oakeshott. New York: Collier Books, 1967.

Hume, David. *Commentaries on the Law of Scotland,* Vol. 2. Edinburgh: Bell & Bradfute, 1797.

Hunt, Morton.*

Imbert, Guillaume. *La Chronique Scandaleuse.* 2 vols. Paris, 1785.

Laver, James. *Manners and Morals in the Age of Optimism.* New York: Harper & Row, 1966.

Lewis, W. H. *The Splendid Century.* New York: William Sloane Associates, 1954.

Locke, John. *Of Civil Government, Second Treatise.* Chicago: Henry Regnery, 1968.

MacKenzie, Henry. *The Man of Feeling.* New York: W. W. Norton, 1958.

Mairobert, Mathieu. *Bouquet de Monseigneur.*

———. *L'espion anglais, ou Correspondence entre Milord All'Eye et Milord All'Ear,* Vol. 10. London: J. Adamson, 1779.

Maury, J.-F. *Les Enfants de Sodome.* Neuchâtel: La Société des Bibliophiles Cosmopolites, 1873.

Mirabeau, Honoré. See Chapter 6.

Montesquieu, Baron de. *The Spirit of the Laws.* Translated by Thomas Nugent. New York: Hafner Publishing Co., 1962.

O'Donnell, Bernard. *The Old Bailey and Its Trials.* New York: Macmillan, 1951.

Rattray Taylor, Gordon. *Angel Makers.* See Chapter 7.

———. Essay in Marmor.* See Chapter 1.

———. *Sex in History.* See Chapter 1.

Restif de la Bretonne, Nicolas Edme. *Le nuits de Paris.* Paris: Hachette, 1960.

———. *Oeuvres Erotiques Arcanes.* Paris, 1953.

Rousseau, Jean-Jacques. *The Confessions.* Translated by J. M. Cohen. Baltimore: Penguin Books, 1953.

———. *Emile.* Translated by Barbara Foxley. London: J. D. Dent & Sons; New York: E. P. Dutton, 1963.

———. *Julie; or the New Héloïse.* Translated and abridged by Judith H. McDowell. University Park, Pa.: Pennsylvania State University Press, 1968.

———. *The Social Contract and Discourses.* Translated by G. D. H. Cole. New York: E. P. Dutton, 1950.

Rule, William. See Chapter 5.

Sade, Marquis de. *Juliette.* Translated by Austryn Wainhouse. New York: Grove Press, 1968.

———. *Justine, Philosophy in the Bedroom and Other Writings.* Edited and translated by Richard Seaver and Austryn Wainhouse. New York: Grove Press, 1966.

Shellabarger, Samuel. See Chapter 7.

Smollett, Tobias. *Roderick Random.* New York: E. P. Dutton, 1927.

Swift, Jonathan. *Gulliver's Travels.* Edited by R. A. Greenberg. New York: W. W. Norton, 1961.

Tilly, Pierre Alexandre, Comte de. *Souvenirs d'un page de Marie-Antoinette.* Paris: Emile-Paul frères, 1913.

Ward, Ned (Edward). *The London Spy.* Edited by Arthur Hayward. New York: George H. Doran Co., 1927.

Zilboorg, Gregory. See Chapter 5.

9 THE VICTORIANS

Steven Marcus is essential for reinterpretation of the Victorians; Rattray Taylor's *Angel Makers* documents social Victorianism in a traditional way but with painstaking care, and in doing so upsets a few accepted scholarly ideas. Tennyson is quoted by Hunt; Willard and Marryat by Markun. Dr. Gregory, *The Yokel's Preceptor, The Lady's Magazine, Hints on . . . the Prevalence of Vice* and most of the other minor Victorian sources are in *Angel Makers*.

Acton, William. *The Functions and Disorders of the Re-productive Organs in Childhood Youth, Adult Age, and Advanced Life.* London: John Churchill, 1857.
———. *Prostitution.* Edited by Peter Fryer. New York: Praeger, 1969.
Archenholtz, J. W. von. *A Picture of England.* London, 1797.
Brinton, Crane.*
Dingwall, Eric J. *Male Infibulation.* London: John Bale, Sons & Danielsson, 1925.
Frye, Northrop. See Chapter 8.
Fryer, Peter. "Censorship at the British Museum." *Encounter.* 27 (October 1966), 68–77.
Henriques, Fernando. *Prostitution.* See Chapter 1.
Houghton, Walter E. *The Victorian Frame of Mind: 1830–1870.* New Haven: Yale University Press, 1957.
Hunt, Morton.*
Keats, John. *Poetical Works.* Edited by H. W. Garrod. London: Oxford University Press, 1956.
Lafourcade, Georges. *Swinburne: A Literary Biography.* New York: Russell & Russell, 1967.
Lewinsohn, Richard. See Chapter 1.
Markun, Leo. *Mrs. Grundy.* New York: D. Appleton, 1930. Smugly anti-Victorian, but still useful.

Marcus, Steven. *The Other Victorians.* New York: Basic Books, 1964. A first-rate re-evaluation of the Victorians from a literary, historical and psychiatric point of view.
My Secret Life, Vols. 1–11. New York: Grove Press, 1966.
Patmore, Coventry. *Poems.* Edited by F. Page. London: Oxford University Press, 1949.
The Pearl: A Journal of Facetiae and Voluptuous Reading. New York: Grove Press, 1968.
Penrose, Sir C. V., Vice Admiral of the Blue. *Observations Occasioned by Reading a Pamphlet, Entitled "Statement of Certain Immoral Practices Prevailing in His Majesty's Navy."* Bodmin: J. Liddell & Son, 1824.
Rattray Taylor, Gordon. *Angel Makers.* See Chapter 6. A must for this period.
Reader, W. J. *Life in Victorian England.* New York: G. P. Putnam's Sons, 1964.
Robiquet, Jean. *Daily Life in France under Napoleon.* London: Allen & Unwin, 1962.
Statement of Certain Immoral Practices Prevailing in His Majesty's Navy. 2nd ed. London: J. Hatchard & Son, 1822.
Stephen, Sir James F. See Chapter 5.
Ward, Ned. See Chapter 8.
Young, Wayland. See Chapter 1.

10 THE SCIENTIFIC OVERTURE

Ellis remains the best single source on early sexology. Dr. Hare's essay gathers and evaluates a wide variety of material over two centuries' time; it deserves to become a standard reference. Foster, Lewinsohn and Foucault contain useful details. For the history of science see Brinton, Kardiner and Preble, Maus, Murphy and Zilboorg. Caspar is quoted by Ellis.

Abrahamsen, David. *The Mind and Death of a Genius.* New York: Columbia University Press, 1946. On Otto Weininger.
Acton, William. *Prostitution.* See Chapter 9.
Binet, A. "Le fétichisme dans l'amour." *Revue Philosophique,* 24 (1887):143.
Biographisches Lexikon der Hervorragenden Ärzte aller Zeiten und Völker. Berlin and Vienna: Urban & Schwarzenberg, 1932.
Biographisches Lexikon der Hervorragenden Ärzte der Letzten Fünfzig Jahre. Berlin and Vienna: Urban & Schwarzenberg, 1933.
Biographisches Lexikon Hervorragender Ärzte des Neunzehnten Jahrhunderts. Berlin and Vienna: Urban & Schwarzenberg, 1901.
Boch, Ivan. *The Sexual Life of Our Time.* 6th ed. Translated by M. E. Paul. London: Rebman, 1908. Of historical interest.
Boase, Frederic. *Modern English Biography.* 2 vols. Truro: Netherton and Worth, for the author, 1897.
Brinton, Crane.*
Caprio, Frank. *Female Homosexuality.* New York: Citadel Press, 1954. Not recommended.
Chambers's Encyclopedia. New rev. ed. 15 vols.

Oxford-London-Edinburgh-New York-Toronto: Pergamon Press, 1967.
Chevalier, Julien. *Une Maladie de la Personalité: L'Inversion Sexuelle.* Paris: G. Nason, 1893.
Cornevin, C. *Contribution à l'étude de la criminalité chez les animaux; perversion du sens génésique chez un étalon.* Lyon and Paris, 1896.
Darwin, Charles. *The Descent of Man and Selection in Relation to Sex.* 2nd ed. rev. and augm. Akron, Ohio: The Werner Co., n.d.
———. *Expression of the Emotions in Man and Animals.* New York: D. Appleton, 1899.
———. *The Origin of Species.* Rpr. of 6th ed. London: Oxford University Press, 1968.
Ellis, Havelock.* The best single source.
Enciclopedia Universal Ilustrada Europeo-Americana. 80 vols. Madrid and Barcelona: Espasa-Calpe, 1905–33.
Féré, Charles. *Sexual Degeneration in Mankind and in Animals.* Translated by Ulrich van de Horst. New York: Anthropological Press, 1932.
Flexner, Abraham. *Prostitution in Europe.* New York: Century, 1914.
Forberg, Friedrich. See Chapter 6.
Forel, August. *The Sexual Question.* English adap-

tation from the 2nd German ed. rev. and enl. by C. F. Marshall. New York: Rebman, 1908.

Foster, Jeanette. See Chapter 1.

Foucault, Michel. See Chapter 8.

Gordon, David Cole. *Self-Love.* New York: Macmillan, 1970.

Hare, E. H. "Masturbatory Insanity: The History of an Idea." *The Journal of Mental Science,* 108 (January 1962):1–25. A fine monograph with a good bibliography. Highly recommended.

Hays, H. R. *Ape and Angel.* See Chapter 1.

Hirschfeld, Magnus. *Men and Women.* New York: G. P. Putnam's Sons, 1935.

———. *Sexual Anomalies.* New York: Emerson Books, 1956.

———. *Die Transvestiten.* Berlin: Pulvermacher, 1910.

Howard, A. V. *Chambers's Dictionary of Scientists.* New York: E. P. Dutton, 1951.

Hunt, Morton.*

Ireland, Norma O. *Index to Scientists of the World from Ancient to Modern Times.* Boston: F. W. Faxon, 1962.

Irvine, William. *Apes, Angels and Victorians.* New York: McGraw-Hill, 1955.

Kardiner, Abram, and Preble, Edward. *They Studied Man.* See Chapter 2.

Krafft-Ebing, Richard von. "Neue Studien auf dem Gebiete der Homosexualität." *Jahrbuch für sexuelle Zwischenstufen,* 3 (1901):1–36.

———. *Psychopathia Sexualis.* Translated by Harry E. Wedeck. New York: G. P. Putnam's Sons, 1965.

Lewinsohn, Richard. See Chapter 1.

Lombroso, Cesare. *Female Offender.* New York: Philosophical Library, 1958.

———. *L'Homme Criminel.* Paris, 1876.

McMurtrie, Douglas C. "Notes on Homosexuality: An Attempt at Seduction; an Example of Acquired Homosexuality in Prison; a Commentary on the Prevalence of Inversion in Germany." *Vermont Medical Monthly,* 19 (1913):66–68.

———. "Record of a French Case of Sexual Inversion." *Maryland Medical Journal,* 57 (1914):179–81.

———. "Sexual Inversion among Women in Spain." *Urologic and Cutaneous Review,* 18 (1914):308.

———. "Note on Masturbation in Women: Its Re-lation to Sexual Inversion." *Cincinnati Medical News,* 1 (1914):287.

———. "Manifestations of Sexual Inversion in the Female: Conditions in a Convent School, Evidence of Transvestism, Unconscious Homosexuality, Sexuality of Masculine Women, Masturbation under Homosexual Influences, Indeterminate Sexuality in Childhood." *The Urologic and Cutaneous Review,* 18 (1914):424–26.

Malthus, Thomas Robert. *On Population.* Edited by Gertrude Himmelfarb. New York: Modern Library, 1960.

Mantegazza, Paolo. *Physiology of Love.* New York: Eugenics Publishing Co., 1936.

———. *The Sexual Relations of Mankind.* North Hollywood, Calif.: Brandon House, 1966.

Maus, Heinz. *A Short History of Sociology.* New York: Philosophical Library, 1962.

Moll, Albert. *Libido Sexualis.* North Hollywood, Calif.: Brandon House, 1966.

———. *Perversions of the Sexual Instinct.* Newark: Julian Press, 1931.

———. *The Sexual Life of the Child.* New York: Macmillan, 1913.

Montagu, Ashley. *Darwin, Competition and Cooperation.* New York: Abelard-Schuman, 1952.

Murphy, Gardner. *Historical Introduction to Modern Psychology.* Rev. ed. New York: Harcourt, Brace & World, 1949.

Näcke, P. *Le monde homosexuel de Paris.* Lyon, 1905.

Sade, Marquis de. *Justine.* See Chapter 8.

Schrenck-Notzing, Albert. *The Use of Hypnosis in Psychopathia Sexualia.* Translated by C. G. Chaddock. New York: Julian Press, 1956.

Tardieu, A. A. *Etude Medico-légale sur les Attentats aux Moeurs.* Paris: J. B. Bailliere, 1857.

Tarnowsky, Benjamin. *Pederasty in Europe.* North Hollywood, Calif.: Brandon House, 1967.

Tissot, Samuel A. *L'Onanisme.* Lausanne: A. Chapuis, 1760.

Webster's Biographical Dictionary. 1st ed. Springfield, Mass.: G. & C. Merriam, 1948.

Westphal, C. von. "Die conträre Sexualempfindung." *Archiven für Psychiatrie & Nervenkrankheiten,* 2 (1869):73–108.

Whyte, Lancelot Law. *The Unconscious Before Freud.* Garden City, N.Y.: Doubleday, 1962.

Zilboorg, Gregory. See Chapter 5.

11 THE WITCH REBORN

Schopenhauer is quoted by Hays.

Balzac, Honoré de. *The Girl with the Golden Eyes.* Translated by Ernest Dowson. New York: Williams, Belasco & Meyers, 1930.

———. *Vautrin's Last Avatar. Honoré de Balzac in Twenty-Five Volumes: The First Complete Translation into English,* Vol. 11 [Vol. 2]. New York: P. F. Collier & Son, 1900.

Barbey d'Aurevilly, Jules. *The She-Devils.* Translated by Jean Kimber. London and New York: Oxford University Press, 1964.

Baudelaire, Charles. *The Flowers of Evil.* Edited by Marthiel and Jackson Mathews. Norfolk, Conn.: New Directions, 1955.

Bebel, August. See Chapter 9.

Belot, Adolphe. *Mademoiselle Giraud, My Wife.* Chicago: Laird & Lee, 1891.

Berneri, Marie Louise. See Chapter 8.

Daudet, Alphonse. *Sappho.* New York: Modern Library, n.d.

Dingwall, Eric. *The American Woman.* New York: Rinehart, 1957. Superficial.

Ditzion, Sidney. *Marriage, Morals and Sex in America.* New York: Bookman Associates, 1953.

Engels, Frederick. See Chapter 1.

Farnham, Eliza. *Woman and Her Era.* 2 vols. New York: A. J. Davis, 1864.

Foster, Jeanette.*

Gautier, Théophile. *Mademoiselle de Maupin.* New York: Modern Library, n.d.

Gribble, Francis. *George Sand and Her Lovers.* New York: E. P. Dutton, 1928.

Hays, H. R. *The Dangerous Sex.* See Chapter 1.

Holbrook, Stewart H. *Dreamers of the American Dream.* Garden City, N.Y.: Doubleday, 1957. Good background reading.

Hunt, Morton.*

James, H. R. *Mary Wollstonecraft.* London: Oxford University Press, 1932.

James, Henry. *The Bostonians.* New York: Modern Library, n.d.

Johnston, Johanna. *Mrs. Satan: The Incredible Saga of Victoria C. Woodhull.* New York: G. P. Putnam's Sons, 1967.

Keats, John. See Chapter 9.

Louys, Pierre. *The Songs of Bilitis.* Translated by Mitchell S. Buck. New York: Capricorn Books, 1966.

Lundberg, Ferdinand, and Farnham, Marynia. *Modern Woman: The Lost Sex.* New York: Grosset & Dunlap, 1947. A striking combination of good sense and prejudice. Still to be read, but critically.

Maupassant, Guy de. *La Femme de Paul.* In *Oeuvres Complètes.* Paris: Librarie de France, 1934.

Maurois, André. *Lélia: The Life of George Sand.* New York: Harper & Brothers, 1953.

Mendes, Catulle. *Mephistophéla.* Paris: Dentu, 1890.

Mill, John Stuart. *The Subjection of Women.* London: J. M. Dent & Sons, Everyman's Library, 1929.

Musset, Alfred de. *Gamiani.* New York: Universal Publishing & Distributing Corp.; London: Universal Tandem Publishing Co., 1968.

Nugent, Elinor. *The Relationship of Fashion in Women's Dress to Selected Aspects of Social Change.* Baton Rouge: Louisiana State University Press, 1962.

O'Neill, William. *Everyone Was Brave.* Chicago: Quadrangle, 1969. On feminism; good documents but lacks evaluative depth.

Pierson, George W. *Tocqueville and Beaumont in America.* New York: Oxford University Press, 1938.

Praz, Mario. *The Romantic Agony.* New York: Meridian Books, 1956. A scholarly masterpiece.

Sand, George (pseud. of Mme. Dudevant). *Histoire de ma vie.* Adaptation de Noelle Roubaud. Paris: Stock (Delamain et Boutelleau). 1960.

———. *Oeuvres illustrées de George Sand.* Paris:

Michel Lévy Frères, 1853–74.

Seyd, Felizia. *Romantic Rebel: The Life of George Sand.* New York: Viking Press, 1940.

Van de Werker, Ely. "A Gynecological Study of the Oneida Community." *American Journal of Obstetrics and Diseases of Women and Children,* 17 (1884):785–810. An interesting document on the Oneida experiment.

Verlaine, Paul. *Parallèlement.* Paris: 1894.

Wedekind, Frank. *The Lulu Plays.* Translated by Carl Richard Mueller. Greenwich, Conn.: Fawcett Publications, 1967.

Weintraub, Stanley. *Beardsley: A Biography.* New York: George Braziller, 1967. Solid scholarship about a man who has been subject to much biographical silliness.

Wollstonecraft, Mary. *The Rights of Women.* London: J. M. Dent & Sons, Everyman's Library, 1929. The *locus classicus* of feminism.

Zola, Emile. *Nana.* New York: Modern Library, n.d.

12   THE APOLOGISTS

Brecher, Edward. *The Sex Researchers.* Boston: Little, Brown, 1969. Not the book it could have been, but useful and interesting.

Brittain, Vera. *Radclyffe Hall: A Case of Obscenity?* London: Macdonald, 1968.

Brodie, Fawn N. *The Devil Drives: A Life of Sir Richard Burton.* New York: W. W. Norton, 1967.

Burton, Sir Richard. *The Erotic Traveler.* Edited by Edward Leigh. New York: G. P. Putnam's Sons, 1967.

———. *Terminal Essay* in Vol. 3 of his translation of *The Book of the Thousand Nights and a Night.* Heritage Press, 1962; pp. 3746–82.

Calder-Marshall, Arthur. *The Sage of Sex: A Life of Havelock Ellis.* New York: G. P. Putnam's Sons, 1959. A good biography.

Carpenter, Edward. *The Intermediate Sex.* London: Allen & Unwin, 1908.

———. *Intermediate Types among Primitive Folk.* New York: Mitchell Kennerley, 1914.

———. *My Days and Dreams.* 2nd ed. London: Allen & Unwin, 1916. Three works by the Coventry Patmore of homosexuality.

Delisle, Francoise. *Friendship's Odyssey.* London: William Heinemann, 1946. A memoir by Havelock Ellis' second wife.

Ellis, Havelock.*

———. *My Life.* Boston: Houghton Mifflin, 1939.

Farwell, Byron. *Burton.* New York: Avon Books, 1965.

Grosskurth, Phyllis. *John A. Symonds: A Biography.* London: Longmans, 1964.

Hadfield, J. A. "The Cure of Homosexuality." *British Medical Journal,* 2 (1968):1323.

Hall, Radclyffe. *The Well of Loneliness.* New York: Pocket Books, 1950.

Hirschfeld, Magnus. See Chapter 10.

Hunt, Morton.*

Kinsey, Alfred, *et al. Female.**

———. *Male.**

Symonds, John Addington. *The Letters of John Addington Symonds,* Vol. 1, 1844–68. Edited by Herbert Schueller and Robert Peters. Detroit: Wayne State University Press, 1968.

———. *Studies in Sexual Inversion.* See Chapter 2. Still worth reading.

13   BEYOND THE WEST

Sources on this subject are many and scattered. Henriques and Westermarck are the best grab-bags. For early anthropological theory, see Hays, Maus and Penniman. Cavendish, Nuño de Guzman and Purchas are in Burton; Cieza de Leon is in Hoyle; Caron, Kaempfer, Mendoza and Mundy are in Henriques; Matignon is in Ellis.

Bachofen, Johann Jakob. See Chapter 1.

Badensperger, P. J. "Orders of Holy Men in Palestine." In *Palestine Exploration Fund, Quarterly Statement,* January 1894; pp. 22–38.

Barrow, Sir John. *Travels in China.* London: T. Cadell & W. Davies, 1804.

Beauvoir, Simone de. See Chapter 1.

Bousquet, Georges H. *La morale d'Islam et son éthique sexuelle.* Paris: A. Maisonneuve, 1953.

Briffault, Robert. See Chapter 1.

Brinton, Crane.*

Brown, (Mrs.) Kenneth. *Haremlik.* Boston and New York: Houghton Mifflin, 1909.

Burton, Sir Richard. See Chapter 12.

Campbell, C. G. *Tales from the Arab Tribes.* London: Lindsay Drummond, 1949.

Cooper, Elizabeth. *The Harim and the Purdah: Studies of Oriental Women.* New York: The Century Co., 1915.

Cory, Donald Webster, ed. *Homosexuality: A Cross Cultural Approach.* New York: Julian Press, 1966. Does not live up to its title. Reprints

much dated material, such as Symonds and Westermarck.

Das, (Mrs.) Sarangadhar. *Purdah: The Status of Indian Women.* London: Kegan Paul, Trench, Trubner & Co., 1932.

Diaz del Castillo, Bernal. *The Bernal Diaz Chronicles: The True Story of the Conquest of Mexico.* Translated and edited by Albert Idell. Garden City, N.Y.: Doubleday, 1956.

Edwardes, Allen. *Jewel in the Lotus.* New York: Julian Press, 1959. Contains some good source material, but is careless and uncritical.

Ellis, Havelock.*

Field, Claud, ed. *Tales of the Caliphs.* New York: E. P. Dutton, 1909.

Garcilasso de la Vega. *Royal Commentaries of Peru.* Translated by Sir Paul Rycaut. London, 1688.

Gibb, Hamilton, and Bowen, Harold. *Islamic Society and the West.* 2 vols. New York: Oxford University Press, 1950–57.

Goldenweiser, Alexander. *History, Psychology and*

Culture. New York: Alfred A. Knopf, 1933.

Hays, H. R. *From Ape to Angel*. See Chapter 1.

Henriques, Fernando. *Prostitution and Society*. See Chapter 1.

Hibbett, Howard. *The Floating World in Japanese Fiction*. London: Oxford University Press, 1959.

Hoyle, Rafael Larco. *Checan*. New York: Julian Press, 1965. South American erotic art.

Javidan, Princess. *Harem Life*. New York: Dial Press, 1931.

Kluckhohn, Clyde. "As an Anthropologist Views It." In *Sex Habits of American Men: A Symposium on the Kinsey Report*. Edited by Albert Deutsch. New York: Prentice-Hall, 1948.

LaBarre, Weston. *The Aymara Indians of Bolivia*. Edited by J. Alden Mason and Mrs. Dorothy C. Donath. Menasha, Wisc.: American Anthropological Association, 1948.

Lane, Edward William. *The Manners and Customs of the Modern Egyptians*. New York: E. P. Dutton, 1923.

Langsdorf, G. H. von. *Voyages and Travels*. 2 vols. London: Henry Colburn, 1814. An old classic.

Lecky, W. E. H. See Chapter 3.

Legman, George, compiler. *Toward a Bibliography of Homosexuality*. Unpublished. Consists of several thousand entries, in card-catalogue form, in the library of the New York Academy of Medicine. This unfinished project contains many obscure and interesting items from all over the world. A gold mine for some future detailed scholarly study of the history of sexology.

Leonowens, Anna. *Siamese Harem Life*. New York: E. P. Dutton, 1953.

Lisiansky, Urey. *Voyage Round the World*. London: S. Hamilton, 1814.

Lithgow, William. See Chapter 6.

McLennan, John. *Primitive Marriage: An Inquiry into the Origin of the Form of Capture in Marriage Ceremonies*. Edinburgh, 1865.

Maine, Henry. *Ancient Law*. London: J. M. Dent, Everyman's Library; New York: E. P. Dutton, 1954. Another of the grand pyramids of nineteenth-century English scholarship. Still belongs in the serious student's library.

Maus, Heinz. See Chapter 10.

Miller, Barnette. "The Passing of the Turkish Harem." *Asia*, 20 (1920):302–07.

Morgan, Lewis. *Ancient Society*. Cleveland: World Publishing Co., 1963.

———. *Systems of Consanguinity and Affinity of the Human Family*. Washington, D.C.: The Smithsonian Institution, 1871.

Myer, J. J. *Sexual Life in Ancient India*. New York: Barnes & Noble, 1953.

Parsons, Elsie Clews. *Mitla: Town of the Souls*. 2nd ed. Chicago: University of Chicago Press, 1966.

Penniman, T. K. *A Hundred Years of Anthropology*. 2nd ed. rev. London: G. Duckworth, 1952. Good background reading.

Penzer, N. M. *The Harem*. London: George G Harrap, 1936.

Prescott, William H. *The Conquest of Mexico* and *The Conquest of Peru*. New York: Modern Library, 1936. Essential to the historian.

Rycaut, Sir Paul. *The Present State of the Ottoman Empire*. London: John Starkey and Henry Brome, 1670.

Saikaku, Ihara. *The Life of an Amorous Woman and Other Writings*. Translated by Ivan Morris. New York: New Directions, 1963.

———. *Nippon Eitaigura: The Way to Wealth*. Translated by Mizuno. Tokyo: Hokuseido Press, 1955.

———. *Five Japanese Love Stories*. Translated by William Theodore de Bary. London: The Folio Society, 1958. Charming Japanese erotic literature.

Sauer, Martin. *An Account of a Geographical and Astronomical Expedition to the Northern Parts of Russia*. London: A. Strahan, 1802.

Snouck Hurgronje, *Mekka, in the Latter Part of the Nineteenth Century*. London: Luzac, 1931.

Tylor, Sir Edward. *Primitive Culture*. London: Oxford University Press, 1963. Classic.

Van Gulick, R. H. *Sexual Life in Ancient China*. Leiden: Bull, 1961.

Vatsyayna. *The Koka Shastra*. Translated by Alex Comfort. New York: Stein & Day, 1965.

Westermarck, Edvard. *The History of Human Marriage*. 3 vols. New York: Allerton Book Co., 1922.

———. *Origin and Development of the Moral Ideas*. See Chapter 1. Both Westermarck volumes highly valuable, even though theoretically superseded.

14   THE LIFE

Adams, Henry. *The United States in 1800*. Ithaca, N.Y.: Great Seal Books, 1960.

Broad, Lewis. *The Friendships and Follies of Oscar Wilde*. London: Hutchinson, 1954.

Carlier, F. *Lex Deux Prostitutions*. Paris: Dentu, 1889.

Colette, Sidonie Gabrielle. *Claudine at School*. New York: Boni, 1930.

Ellis, Havelock.*

Flexner, Abraham. See Chapter 10.

Foster, Jeanette. See Chapter 1.

Garde, Noel I. See Chapter 2.

Ginzberg, Ralph. *An Unhurried View of Erotica*. New York: Helmsman Press, 1958.

Hirschfeld, Magnus. See Chapter 10.

Holloway, Mark. *Heavens on Earth: Utopian Communities in America, 1680–1800*. London: Turnstile Press, 1951.

Howard, William L. "Sexual Perversion in America." *American Journal of Dermatology and Genito-Urinary Diseases*, 3 (1904):9–14.

Hyde, H. Montgomery. *The Love That Dared Not Speak Its Name*. Boston: Little, Brown, 1970.

———. *The Trials of Oscar Wilde*. London: W. Hodge, 1948.

Krafft-Ebing, Richard von. *Psychopathia Sexualis*. See Chapter 10.

Laver, James. *Manners and Morals in the Age of Optimism 1848–1914*. New York: Harper & Row, 1966. Good background.

Legman, George. See Chapter 13.

Lewinsohn, Richard. See Chapter 1.

Manchester, William. *The Arms of Krupp: 1587–1968*. Boston: Little, Brown, 1968. The definitive study.

Menne, Bernhard. *The Rise of the House of Krupp*. New York: L. Furman, 1938.

Moll, Albert. *Perversions of the Sexual Instinct*. See Chapter 10.

Muhlen, Norbert. *The Incredible Krupps*. New York: Henry Holt, 1959.

Pearson, Hesketh. *Oscar Wilde, His Life and Wit*. New York: Harper & Brothers, 1946.

Peyrefitte, Roger. *The Exile of Capri*. New York: Fleet Publishing Corp., 1965.

Rae, Isabel. *The Strange Story of Dr. James Barry*. London and New York: Longmans, Green, 1958.

Saint Méry, Moreau. *St. Méry's American Journey*. Translated and edited by Kenneth and Anna Roberts. Garden City, N.Y.: Doubleday, 1947.

Tarnowsky, Benjamin. See Chapter 10.

Zola, Emile. See Chapter 11.

15   THE AGE OF IRONY

Breuer, Joseph, and Freud, Sigmund. *Studies in Hysteria*. Translated by A. A. Brill. Boston: Beacon Press, n.d.

Cole, William Graham. *Sex in Christianity and Psychoanalysis*. See Chapter 4.

Freud, Sigmund. *The Interpretation of Dreams*.

Translated by A. A. Brill. New York: Modern Library, 1950.
———. *The Psychopathology of Everyday Life.* Edited by James Strachey. Translated by Alan Tyson. New York: W. W. Norton, 1966.
———. *Sexuality and the Psychology of Love.* Collected Papers, Vol. 8. Edited by Philip Rieff. New York: Collier Books, 1963.
———. *Three Essays on the Theory of Sexuality.* Translated by James Strachey. New York: Avon Books, 1965.
Harper, Robert A. *Psychoanalysis and Psychotherapy.* New York: Prentice-Hall, 1959.

Jones, Ernest. *The Life and Works of Sigmund Freud.* 3 vols. New York: Basic Books, 1953–57.
Lewinsohn, Richard. See Chapter 1.
Moll, Albert. *Sexual Life of the Child.* See Chapter 10.
Thompson, Clara, ed. *An Outline of Psychoanalysis.* New York: Modern Library, 1955.
Veith, Ilza. See Chapter 5.
Zilboorg, Gregory. *A History of Medical Psychology.* See Chapter 5.
———. *Sigmund Freud: His Exploration of the Mind of Man.* New York: Charles Scribner's Sons, 1951.

16 NEW EXPECTATIONS

Foster's book is especially valuable, and Hunt's eminently sensible. The Lynds' *Middletown* is as fresh and informative as when it appeared. Maurois's book on Proust contains the selections from his unpublished journals. Lawrence is quoted by Epton; Ellis and Hurst by Hunt; Pilnyak and Zoshchenko by Sandomirsky.

Blum, Léon. *Du Mariage.* Paris, 1907.
Bourdet, Edward. *The Captive.* Translated by Arthur Hornblow, Jr. New York: Brentano, 1927.
Brinton, Crane.*
Brittain, Vera. See Chapter 12.
Dane, Clemence. *Regiment of Women.* New York: Macmillan, 1917.
Epton, Nina. See Chapter 4.
Foster, Jeanette.*
Gide, André. *Corydon.* See Chapter 1.
———. *If It Die.* Translated by Dorothy Bussy. New York: Modern Library, 1935.
———. *The Immoralist.* Translated by Dorothy Bussy. New York: Alfred A. Knopf, 1961.
Hall, Radclyffe. See Chapter 12.
Hamilton, Gilbert von Tassel. *A Research in Marriage.* New York: A. & C. Boni, 1929.
Kinsey, Alfred, et al. *Female.**
———. *Male.**
Lawrence, D. H. *The Rainbow.* New York: Modern Library, n.d.
Lewinsohn, Richard. See Chapter 1.
Lewis, Wyndham. *The Apes of God.* New York: McBride, 1932.
Lindsey, Ben. B. *The Revolt of Modern Youth.* New York: Boni & Liveright, 1925.
———. and Evans, Wainright. *The Companionate*

Marriage. New York: Boni & Liveright, 1925.
Lynd, Robert S. and Helen M. *Middletown.* New York: Harcourt, Brace & Co., 1929.
McDermott, John, and Taft, Kendall, eds. *Sex in the Arts: A Symposium.* New York: Harper & Brothers, 1932.
Margueritte, Victor. *La Garçonne.* Paris: Flammarion, 1922.
Martin du Gard, Roger. *Recollections of André Gide.* Translated by John Russell. New York: Viking Press, 1953.
Maurois, André. *Proust: Portrait of a Genius.* New York: Harper & Brothers, 1950. Recommended.
Painter, George. *André Gide.* London: Arthur Barker, 1951.
Reich, Wilhelm. *Function of the Orgasm.* New York: The Orgone Institute Press, 1942.
Sandomirsky, Vera, "Sex in the Soviet Union." *Russian Review,* 10 (1951):199–209.
Stopes, Marie. *Married Love.* London: A. C. Fifield, 1918.
Van de Velde, Theodoor H. *Ideal Marriage.* New York: Covici Friede, 1930.
Ware, Caroline. *Greenwich Village: 1920–1930.* Boston: Houghton Mifflin, 1935.

17 INSTINCTS AND ANALYSTS

The psychiatric literature from this period is rich, widely scattered and difficult to summarize. The Ansbachers' selection of Adler's writings should have high priority in reading about the first great revisionists. Horney, Klein, Sullivan and Stekel are also very important. For a good sampling see the book co-edited and the book co-authored by Clara Thompson. If one must select one paper specifically about homosexuality, it should be Thompson's essay in Ruitenbeek. For a good modern look backward, read Socarides.

Adler, Alfred. *Individual Psychology.* 2nd ed. rev. Translated by P. Radin. London: Routledge & Kegan Paul, 1929.
———. *The Individual Psychology of Alfred Adler.* Edited by Heinz L. and Rowena R. Ansbacher. New York: Harper Torchbook, 1964.
Alexander, Franz. *Psychosomatic Medicine.* New York: W. W. Norton, 1950.
Deutsch, Helene. *Psychology of Women.* 2 vols. New York: Grune & Stratton, 1944.
Ferenczi, Sandor. "The Nosology of Male Homosexuality." In Ruitenbeek.* A landmark among

monographs.
Freud, Anna. *The Ego and the Mechanisms of Defense.* Translated by Cecil Baines. New York: International Universities Press, 1946.
Freud, Sigmund. *Collected Papers.* Edited by Ernest Jones. 5 vols. New York: Basic Books, 1959.
———. *The Ego and the Id.* Edited by James Strachey. Translated by Joan Riviére. New York: W. W. Norton, 1961.
———. "Letter to an American Mother." In Ruitenbeek.*
———. *New Introductory Lectures on Psychoanal-*

ysis. Edited and translated by James Strachey. New York: W. W. Norton, 1965.
————. *An Outline of Psychoanalysis*. Rev. ed. Edited and translated by James Strachey. New York: W. W. Norton, 1970.
————. *The Problem of Anxiety*. Translated by Henry Alden Bunker. New York: W. W. Norton, 1936.
Fromm, Erich. *Escape from Freedom*. New York: Farrar & Rinehart, 1941.
————. *Man for Himself*. New York: Rinehart, 1947.
Horney, Karen. *New Ways in Psychoanalysis*. New York: W. W. Norton, 1939.
————. *The Neurotic Personality of Our Time*. New York: W. W. Norton, 1937. Probably the best of her books to read first.
————. *Self-Analysis*. New York: W. W. Norton, 1942.
Jones, Ernest. "Early Development of Female Sexuality." *International Journal of Psychoanalysis*, 8 (1927):459–72.
Jung, Carl Gustav. *Collected Works*. Vols. 7 and 9 (parts I & II). Edited by Herbert Read, Michael Fordham and Gerhard Adler. New York: Pantheon Books, 1953–70.
Klein, Melanie. *The Psychoanalysis of Children*. Translated by Alix Strachey. London: Hogarth Press and The Institute of Psychoanalysis, 1949.
Klein, Viola. *The Feminine Character*. New York: International Universities Press, 1948.
Lorand, Sandor, and Balint, Michael, eds. *Perversions: Psychodynamics and Therapy*. New York: Random House, 1936. A collection of analytic essays, some quite good.
Moll, Albert. *The Sexual Life of the Child*. See Chapter 10.
Mullahy, Patrick. *Oedipus, Myth and Complex*. New York: Hermitage House, 1948.
Nabokov, Vladimir. *Lolita*. Greenwich, Conn.: Fawcett Books, 1955.
Nunberg, Hermann. "Homosexuality, Magic and Aggression." *International Journal of Psychoanalysis*, 19 (1938):1–16.

Reich, Wilhelm. *Character Analysis*. 3rd ed. New York: Orgone Institute Press, 1949.
Ruitenbeek, Hendrik, ed. *Psychoanalysis and Female Sexuality*. New Haven: College and University Press, 1966.
————. *Psychoanalysis and Male Sexuality*. New Haven: College and University Press, 1966.
————. *Psychotherapy of Perversions*. New York: Citadel Press, 1967. All three of these collections contain a few very good papers, and others that could just as well have remained in the stacks.
Socarides, Charles W. *The Overt Homosexual*. New York: Grune & Stratton, 1968. Probably the best recent analytically oriented book on homosexuality. It contains a careful and thoughtful history of analytic theory on the subject, with a full bibliography. Highly recommended to the specialist or to the layman who wants to go beyond the shallow water.
Stekel, Wilhelm. *The Autobiography of William Stekel*. New York: Liveright, 1950. Interesting because Stekel is interesting, but an oddly unrevealing autobiography for a psychoanalyst.
————. *The Homosexual Neurosis*. Translated by James Van Teslaar. New York: Emerson Books, 1950.
————. *Patterns of Psychosexual Infantilism*. New York: Grove Press, 1959.
————. *Sexual Aberration*. 2 vols. New York: Grove Press, 1964.
Sullivan, Harry Stack. *The Interpersonal Theory of Psychiatry*. Edited by Helen Swick Perry and Mary Ladd Garvel. New York: W. W. Norton, 1953.
Thompson, Clara. "Changing Concepts of Homosexuality in Psychoanalysis." In Ruitenbeek.* A must.
————; Mazer, Milton; and Witenberg, Earl, eds. *An Outline of Psychoanalysis*. New York: Modern Library, 1955.
Thompson, Clara, and Mullahy, Patrick. *Psychoanalysis: Evolution and Development*. New York: Grove Press, 1957. A good history.

18   THE LIFE TILL THE FIFTIES

Berrey, Lester V., and Van Den Bark, Melvin. *The American Thesaurus of Slang*. 2nd ed. New York: Thomas Y. Crowell, 1962.
Davidson, Eugene. *The Trial of the Germans: Nuremberg 1945–1946*. New York: Macmillan, 1967.
Gallagher, Richard F. *Nuremberg: The Third Reich on Trial*. New York: Avon Book Division, 1961.
Hellman, Lillian. *Plays*. New York: Random House, 1942.
Henry, George W. *All the Sexes*. New York: Rinehart, 1955.
————. *Sex Variants*. New York: Paul B. Hoeber, 1948.
Kahn, Samuel. *Mentality and Homosexuality*. Boston: Meador Publishing Co., 1937.
Krich, A. M., ed. *The Homosexuals*. New York: Citadel Press, 1954. A mixture of good and useless items.
Larchey, L. *Dictionnaire de l'Argot Parisien*. London: Hutten, 187? (date not certain).

Mencken, H. L. *The American Language*. 4th ed. New York: Alfred A. Knopf, 1963.
Partridge, Eric. *Dictionary of the Underworld*. New York: Macmillan, 1950.
————. *Slang Today and Yesterday*. 3rd ed. New York: Macmillan, 1950.
Schuman, Frederick. *The Nazi Dictatorship: A Study in Social Pathology and the Politics of Fascism*. 2nd ed. New York: Alfred A. Knopf, 1936.
Schwartz, Alan, and Ernst, Morris. *Censorship*. New York: Macmillan, 1964.
Shirer, William L. *The Rise and Fall of the Third Reich*. New York: Simon & Schuster, 1959.
Steiner, Jean-François. *Revolt at Treblinka*. New York: Simon & Schuster, 1967.
Wentworth, Harold, and Flexner, Stuart. *Dictionary of American Slang*. New York: Thomas Y. Crowell, 1960.
Wile, Ira S., ed. *The Sex Life of the Unmarried Adult*. New York: Vanguard Press, 1934.

19   GOING FOR FACTS

Menninger is quoted by Barahal. The comment on "phallic worship" is by Hawke. Pilcher is quoted in innumerable works on legal sterilization.

Barahal, H. S. "Constitutional Factors in Psychotic Male Homosexuals." *Psychiatric Quarterly*, 13 (1939):398.
Barr, Martin W. "Some Notes on Asexualization;

with a Report of Eighteen Cases." *Journal of Nervous and Mental Diseases*, 51 (1920):231–41.
Blacker, C. P. *Voluntary Sterilization*. London: Humphrey Milford, 1934.

Bowman, Karl M. "Review of Sex Legislation and the Control of Sex Offenders in the United States of America." *International Review of Criminal Policy*, 20 (1953):20–39.

———. "The Problem of the Sex Offender." *American Journal of Psychiatry*, 108 (1951): 250–57.

Brecher, Edward. See Chapter 12.

Bremer, Johan. *Asexualization: A Follow-up of 244 Cases*. New York: Macmillan, 1959. An important modern study.

Cleghorn, R. A. "A Short History of the Relationship of Endocrinology to Psychiatry." *International Record of Medicine and General Practice Clinics*, 166 (1953):175–82.

Cohen, Elie. *Human Behavior in the Concentration Camp*. Translated by M. H. Braaksma. New York: W. W. Norton, 1953.

Cook, Walter W. "Eugenics or Ethenics." *Illinois Law Review*, 37 (1943):287–332.

Davis, Katherine Bement. *Factors in the Sex Life of Twenty-Two Hundred Women*. New York: Harper & Brothers, 1929.

Dickinson, Robert Latou, and Beam, L. *A Thousand Marriages*. Baltimore: Williams & Wilkins, 1931.

East, W. Norwood. *Medical Aspects of Crime*. London: J. & A. Churchill, 1936.

Ellis, Havelock.*

"Eugenic Sterilization." *Society of Comparative Legislation Journal*, 23 (1941):191–92.

Freud, Sigmund. *Three Essays*. See Chapter 15.

Golla, F. L., and Hodge, R. Sessions. "Hormone Treatment of the Sexual Offender." *The Lancet*, 256 (1949):1006–07.

Gordon, Alfred. "Nervous and Mental Disturbances Following Castration in Women. *Journal of the American Medical Association*, 63 (1914): 1345–48.

Gosney, E. S., and Popenoe, Paul. *Sterilization for Human Betterment*. New York: Macmillan, 1929.

Hawke, C. C. "Castration and Sex Crimes." *American Journal of Mental Deficiency*, 55 (1950):220–26.

Henry, George W. *All the Sexes*. See Chapter 18.

———. *Sex Variants*. See Chapter 18.

Highleyman, Samuel. *Legal Bibliography on Sterilization, as of January 1, 1957*. New York: Human Betterment Association of America, 1957.

Holman, E. J. "Medicolegal Aspects of Sterilization, Artificial Insemination and Abortion." *Journal of the American Medical Association*, 155 (1954):1309–11.

"Human Sterilization." *Iowa Law Review*, 35 (1950):251–69.

Karst, Georg M. *The Beasts of the Earth*. New York: Albert Unger, 1942.

Kinsey, Alfred, *et al. Female.**

———. *Male.**

Kretschmer, Ernst. *Physique and Character*. New York: Harcourt, Brace, 1925.

Landis, Carney, *et al. Sex in Development*. New York: Paul B. Hoeber, 1940.

LeMaire, Louis. "Danish Experiences Regarding the Castration of Sexual Offenders." *Journal of the American Institute of Criminal Law and Crim-inology*, 47:294–310.

Lewinsohn, Richard. See Chapter 1.

McCullagh, E. P., and Renshaw, J. F. "The Effects of Castration in the Adult Male." *Journal of the American Medical Association*, 103 (1934):1140–43.

May, Geoffrey. See Chapter 1.

Mirsky, I. A. "Psychologic and Endocrinologic Interrelations." *International Record of Medicine and General Practice Clinics*, 166 (1953):204–10.

Myerson, Abraham. "Sterilization," *Atlantic Monthly*, 186 (1950):52–57.

"Regierungstrat: The German Sterilization Law." *Eugenics Review*, 26 (1934):137–40.

Scharrer, Ernst and Berta. *Neuroendocrinology*. New York: Columbia University Press, 1963.

Sharp, H. C. "The Sterilization of Degenerates." Indiana Board of State Charities: reprint of a paper read before the American Prison Association at Chicago, 1909.

Sheldon, W. H. *The Varieties of Human Physique*. New York: Harper & Brothers, 1940.

———. *The Varieties of Delinquent Youth*. New York: Harper & Brothers, 1949.

———. *The Varieties of Temperament*. New York: Harper & Brothers, 1944.

Slater, Eliot. "German Eugenics in Practice." *Eugenics Review*, 27 (1936):285–95.

Steinach, Eugen. *Sex and Life*. New York: Viking Press, 1940.

Stürup, Georg K. "Sexual Offenders and Their Treatment in Denmark and the Other Scandinavian Countries." *International Review of Criminal Policy*, 1 (1953). Major study.

Sutherland, E. H. "Critique of Sheldon's 'Varieties of Delinquent Youth.' " *American Journal of Sociology*, 57 (1951):10–13.

Tappan, Paul W. "Sex Offender Laws and Their Adminstration." *Federal Probation*, 14 (1950): 32–37.

———. "Treatment of the Sex Offender in Denmark." *American Journal of Psychiatry*, 108 (1951):241–49.

Terman, L. M, *et al. Psychological Factors in Marital Happiness*. New York: McGraw-Hill, 1938.

United States Reports. *Cases Adjudged in the Supreme Court at October Term, 1926*. Washington, D.C.: U.S. Government Printing Office, 1928, Vol. 274.

———. *Cases Adjudged in the Supreme Court at October Term, 1941*. Washington, D.C.: U.S. Government Printing Office, 1943, Vol. 316.

Van Ophuijsen, J. H. W. "A New Phase in Clinical Psychology, Part I and Introduction, Endocrinologic Orientation to Psychiatric Disorders." *Journal of Clinical and Experimental Psychopathology*, 12 (1951):1–4.

Veith, Ilza. *Hysteria*. See Chapter 5.

Westwood, Gordon. *Society and the Homosexual*. New York: E. P. Dutton, 1953.

Williams, Robert H., ed. *Textbook of Endocrinology*. 3rd ed. Philadelphia and London: W. B. Saunders, 1962.

Woodside, Moya. *Sterilization in North Carolina: A Sociological and Psychological Study*. Chapel Hill: University of North Carolina Press, 1950.

20 GENES AND HERMAPHRODITES

Good basic readings are Albert Ellis' essay, John Money's *Sex Errors of the Body*, Perloff's essay and Amram Scheinfeld's volume. Stoller's book will be a basic reference for many years to come. The text by Fuller and Thompson is the only thorough work of its kind.

Arieti, Silvano, ed. *American Handbook of Psychiatry*. 3 vols. New York: Basic Books, Vols. 1 and 2, 1959; Vol. 3, 1966. Contains several useful essays.

Barr, M. L., and Hobbs, G. E. "Chromosomal Sex in Transvestites." *The Lancet*, 266 (1954):1109–10.

Beach, Frank, A., ed.* Contains many important papers on this subject.

Beigel, Hugo, ed. *Advances in Sex Research*. New York: Hoeber, 1963. Contains several useful essays.

Briggs, Donald K. "Chromosomal Anomalies in Hermaphroditism and Other Sexual Disorders." In Beigel, *Advances in Sex Research*. See above.

Drake, R. A. "Heredity as an Etiological Factor in Homosexuality." *Journal of Nervous and Men-

tal Diseases, 107 (1948):251–68.
Dobzhansky, Theodosius. *Mankind Evolving.* New Haven: Yale University Press, 1962. Good background reading.
Ellis, Albert. "Constitutional Factors in Homosexuality." In Beigel, *Advances in Sex Research.* See above. An excellent and comprehensive essay.
Ellis, Havelock.*
Erhardt, Anke A., and Money, John. "Progestin-induced Hermaphroditism: IQ and Psychosexual Identity in a Study of Ten Girls." *Journal of Sex Research,* 3 (1967):83–100.
Essen-Möller, Erik. "Twin Research Psychiatry." In *Current Issues in Psychiatry.* New York: Science House, 1967.
Fuller, John, and Thompson, William. *Behavior Genetics.* New York: John Wiley & Sons, 1960. Essential reference work.
Ginsburg, Benson E. "Coaction of Genetical and Non-Genetical Factors Influencing Sexual Behavior." In Beach.*
Goldschmidt, R. *Physiological Genetics.* New York: McGraw-Hill, 1938.
Hampson, John L. "Determinants of Psychosexual Orientation." In Beach.*
Kallman, Franz. "Comparative Twin Studies on the Genetic Aspects of Male Homosexuality." *Journal of Nervous and Mental Diseases,* 115 (1952):238–98. The famous paper.
———. "Genetic Aspects of Sex Determination and Sexual Maturation Potentials in Man." In *Determinants of Human Sexual Behavior.* Edited by G. Winokur. Springfield, Ill.: Charles C. Thomas, 1963.
———. "The Genetics of Mental Illness." In Arieti, Vol. 1. See above.
———. "Twin and Sibship Study of Overt Male Homosexuality." *American Journal of Human Genetics,* 4 (1952):136–46.
Kety, S. S. "Biochemical Theories of Schizophrenia." *Science,* 129 (1959):1528–32; 1559–96.
Kinsey, Alfred, *et al. Female.**
———. *Male.**
Krafft-Ebing, Richard von. See Chapter 10.
Lang, Theo. "Studies on the Genetic Determination of Homosexuality." *Journal of Nervous and Mental Diseases,* 92 (1940):55–64.
McGill, Thomas E. "Studies of the Sexual Behavior of Male Laboratory Mice: Effects of Genotype, Recovery of Sex Drive, and Theory." In Beach.*
Marmor, Judd, ed.*
———.* Introduction. A good summary essay.
Money, John. "Factors in the Genesis of Homosexuality." In *Determinants of Human Sexual Behavior.* Edited by George Winokur, *et al.* Springfield, Ill.: Charles C. Thomas, 1962.
———. "Hermaphroditism and Pseudohermaphroditism." In *Textbook of Gynecologic Endocrinology.* Edited by Jay J. Gold. New York: Hoeber, 1968.
———. *Sex Errors of the Body.* Baltimore: Johns Hopkins Press, 1968. Recommended.
———. "Sexual Dimorphism and Homosexual Gender Identity." *Psychological Bulletin,* 74 (1970):425–40. A good survey of the subject with an up-to-date bibliography.
———, ed. *Sex Research: New Developments.* New York: Holt, Rinehart & Winston, 1965.
Money, John; Hampson, J. G.; and Hampson, J. L. "An Examination of Some Basic Sexual Concepts: The Evidence of Human Hermaphroditism." *Bulletin of Johns Hopkins Hospital,* 97

(1955):301–19.
———. "Hermaphroditism: Recommendations Concerning Assignment of Sex, Change of Sex, and Psychological Management." *Bulletin of Johns Hopkins Hospital,* 97 (1955):284–300.
Moody, Paul Amos. *Genetics of Man.* New York: W. W. Norton, 1967. Good basic text.
Moore, K. L.; Graham, M. A.; and Barr, M. L. "The Detection of Chromosomal Sex in Hermaphrodites from a Skin Biopsy." *Surgery, Gynecology and Obstetrics,* 96 (1953):641–48.
Moore, K. L., and Barr, M. L. "Nuclear Morphology According to Sex in Human Tissues." *Acta Anatomica,* 21 (1954):197–208.
Nelson, Harry. "The XYY Factor." *The Philadelphia Inquirer,* February 16, 1969.
Pare, C. M. B. "Etiology of Homosexuality: Genetics and Chromosomal Aspects." In Marmor.*
———. "Homosexuality and Chromosomal Sex." *Journal of Psychosomatic Research,* 1 (1956): 247–51.
Pasqualini, R. Q.; Vidal, G.; and Bur, G. E. "Psychopathology of Klinefelter's Syndrome." *The Lancet,* 2 (1957):164–67.
Perloff, William H. "Hormones and Homosexuality." In Marmor.* An informative essay.
Robach, J., and Nedoma, J. "Sex Chromatin and Sexual Behavior." *Psychosomatic Medicine,* 20 (1958):55–59.
Robinson, R. *Genetics of the Norway Rat.* New York: Pergamon Press, 1965.
Scheinfeld, Amram. *Your Heredity and Environment.* Philadelphia: Lippincott, 1965. A good introduction.
Scott, J. P., and Fuller, J. L. *Genetics and the Social Behavior of the Dog.* Chicago: University of Chicago Press, 1965. The greatest single project in behavior genetics; a model for future study.
"Sex Test Disqualifies Athlete." *The New York Times,* September 16, 1967.
Shaffer, John W. "Masculinity-Femininity and Other Personality Traits in Gonadal Aplasia." In Beigel, *Advances in Sex Research.* See above.
Shah, Seleem. "Report on the XYY Chromosomal Abnormality." Washington, D.C.: U.S. Government Printing Office, 1970.
Silcock, Byron. "Of Crime and Chromosomes." *New York Post,* December 4, 1968.
Slater, E. "Birth Order and Maternal Age of Homosexuals." *The Lancet,* 1 (1962):69–71.
Stock, Robert. "The XYY and the Criminal." *The New York Times Magazine,* October 20, 1968.
Stoller, Robert J. *Sex and Gender.* New York: Science House, 1968. An excellent and original book on the physical and psychological basis of sexuality. Has already become a basic reference work.
"Twilight People." *Newsweek,* October 2, 1967.
Wendt, Herbert. *The Sex Life of the Animals.* Translated by Richard and Clara Winston. New York: Simon & Schuster, 1965. Not up to date or reliable in a number of places, but charmingly written and full of fascinating information on the history of biology.
West, D. J. *Homosexuality.* 2nd rev. ed. Harmondsworth, Middlesex: Penguin Books, 1968. In American terms, a bit conservative and therapeutically pessimistic, but as thorough, intelligent, readable and accurate as anything written for laymen.

21   THE EROTIC DISGUISE

Baker, Roger. *Drag: A History of Female Impersonation on the Stage.* London: Macdonald, 1968.
Barahal, H. "Female Transvestism and Homosexuality." *Psychiatric Quarterly,* 27 (1953):390–438.
Barr, M. L., and Hobbs, G. E. See Chapter 20.
Beigel, Hugo. "Three Transvestites under Hypnosis." *Journal of Sex Research,* 3 (1967):149–62.
———. "A Weekend in Alice's Wonderland." *Journal of Sex Research,* 5 (1969):108–22. An account of a weekend at a transvestite gathering.
———. "Wives of Transvestites." *Sexology,* 29:814–16.

———, ed. See Chapter 20. All of Beigel's writings on transvestism are worth reading.
Beigel, Hugo, and Feldman, Robert. "The Male Transvestite's Motivation in Fiction, Research and Reality." In Beigel, ed., see Chapter 20. An imaginative study providing a new lead in sex research that should be pursued.
Benjamin, Harry. *The Transsexual Phenomenon.* New York: Julian Press, 1966. Interpretations doubtful, but a basic source for factual material.
———. "Transvestism and Transsexualism in the Male and Female." *Journal of Sex Research,* 3

(1967):107–28.

Bruce, Virginia. "The Expression of Femininity in the Male." *Journal of Sex Research,* 3 (1967): 129–40.

Bulliet, Clarence J. See Chapter 1.

Ellis, Havelock. "Eonism." See Chapter 7.

Fenichel, Otto. "The Psychology of Transvestism." *In Collected Papers,* Vol. 1. New York: W. W. Norton, 1953.

Gelder, M. G., and Marks, I. M. "Aversion Treatment in Transvestism and Transsexualism." In Green and Money. See below.

Green, Richard, and Money, John, eds. *Transsexualism and Sex Reassignment.* Baltimore: Johns Hopkins Press, 1969. The most comprehensive and recent book on the subject. Specialized papers, indispensable for close scientific understanding of transsexualism and its treatment. An exhaustive bibliography.

Greenson, R. R. "A Transvestite Boy and a Hypothesis." *International Journal of Psychoanalysis,* 47 (1966):396–403.

Lukianowicz. N. "Survey of Various Aspects of Transvestism in the Light of Our Present Knowledge." *Journal of Nervous and Mental Diseases,* 128 (1959):36–64.

Money, John. "Cytogenics of Transvestism and Transsexualism." *Journal of Sex Research,* 3 (1967):141–44.

Prince, "Charles" Virginia. *The Transvestite and His Wife.* Los Angeles: Argyle Books, 1967.

Rosen, Ismond, ed. *The Pathology and Treatment of Sexual Deviation.* London: Oxford University Press, 1964. The best modern British collection of papers on sexual deviation. Highly recommended.

Rubinstein, L. H. "The Role of Identification in Homosexuality and Transvestism in Men and Women." In Rosen. See above.

Ruitenbeek, Hendrik. *Psychotherapy of Perversions.* See Chapter 17.

Smith, D. R., and Davidson, W. M., eds. *Symposium on Nuclear Sex.* London: Heinemann, 1958.

Stoller, Robert. "Pornography and Perversion." *Archives of General Psychiatry,* 22 (1970):490–500.

———. "Transvestites' Women." *American Journal of Psychiatry,* 124 (1967):333–39.

———. "Passing and the Continuum of Gender Identity." In Marmor.*

Storr, Anthony. *Sexual Deviation.* Baltimore: Penguin Books, 1964. The best brief explanation for laymen from a modern psychiatric standpoint. Highly recommended.

Strzyzewski, Janus, and Maria Zierhofer. "Aversion Therapy in a Case of Fetishism with Transvestitic Components." *Journal of Sex Research,* 3 (1967): 163–68.

Thorne, Melvin, and Sales, Barbara. "Marital and LSD Therapy with a Transvestite and His Wife." *Journal of Sex Research,* 3 (1967):169–78.

"Transvestism-Transsexualism." *Journal of Sex Research,* 3 (May 1967). A special issue of the journal, with interesting papers by Benjamin, Beigel, Money and others. Recommended.

22 ACROSS THE GENDER LINE

The volume of papers edited by Green and Money is the most up-to-date single work on transsexualism, and it has an extensive bibliography, including important European monographs. Stoller's volume and Benjamin's, each within its self-imposed limits, are very useful.

Benjamin, Harry. See Chapter 21.

Buckley, Tom. "The Transsexual Operation." *Esquire,* April 1967.

Cauldwell, David, ed. *Transvestism: Men in Female Dress.* New York: Sexology Corporation, 1956.

"A Change of Gender." *Newsweek,* December 5, 1966.

"A Changing of Sex by Surgery Begun at Johns Hopkins." *The New York Times,* November 21, 1966.

"Chicago Offers Sex Surgery." *New York Post,* May 12, 1970.

"Dawn's New Day." *Newsweek,* December 2, 1968.

Green, Richard, and Money, John. See Chapter 21.

———; Stoller, R.; and MacAndrews, C. "Attitudes Toward Sex Transformation Procedures." *Archives of General Psychiatry,* 15 (1966):178.

Greenson, Ralph. "On Homosexuality and Gender Identity." In *Psychoanalysis and Male Sexuality.* Edited by Hendrik Ruitenbeek. See Chapter 17.

Hamburger, C. "Desire for Change of Sex as Shown by Personal Letters from 465 Men and Women." *Acta Endocrinologica,* 14 (1953):361–75.

Hamburger, C.; Sturrup, G.; and Dahl-Iversen, E. "Transvestism." *Journal of the American Medical Association,* 152 (1953):391–96.

Jorgensen, Christine. *A Personal Autobiography.* New York: Bantam Books, 1967.

Journal of Sex Research. "Transvestism-Transsexualism" issue. See Chapter 21.

Kirkham, George L., and Sagarin, Edward. "Transsexuals in a Formal Organizational Setting." *Journal of Sex Research,* 5 (1969):90–107.

Newman, Lawrence E. "Transsexualism in Adolescence." *Archives of General Psychiatry,* 23 (1970):112–21.

Pauly, I. "The Current Status of the Change of Sex Operation." *Journal of Nervous and Mental Disease,* 147 (1968):460–71.

Stoller, Robert. See Chapter 20.

Transvestia, 9 (August 1968).

Waldiner, Jan. *Transsexualism: A Study of Forty-Three Cases.* Goteberg, Sweden: Scandinavian University Books, 1967.

Williams, Robert H. See Chapter 19.

23 WIRED FOR GENDER

The layman can begin by reading the nontechnical work of Lorenz, Tinbergen and Harlow, and the John Wilson book about the mind. For a deeper look into the subject, he can try Bowlby, Salzman, Rado, Scott, P. Sears, R. Sears, the volume by Ford and Beach, and the one edited by Beach.

Beach, Frank A., ed.* Much of the volume is informative on the subjects covered in this chapter. See especially the editor's essay.

———. "Experimental Studies of Mating Behavior

in Animals." In Money, ed., *Sex Research*. An excellent essay summarizing recent research.

Beeman, Elizabeth A. "The Effect of Male Hormone on Aggressive Behavior in Mice." *Physiological Zoology*, 20 (1947):373–405.

Bliss, E. L., ed. *Roots of Behavior*. New York: Harper & Row, 1962. Contains many valuable papers.

Bowlby, John. *Attachment and Loss*, Vol. 1, *Attachment*. New York: Basic Books, 1969. A first-rate work dealing with the earliest stages of human behavior and development.

——. *Maternal Care and Mental Health; Deprivation of Maternal Care: A Reassessment of Its Effects*. New York: Shocken Books, 1967.

Broadhurst, P. L. *The Science of Animal Behaviour*. Baltimore: Penguin Books, 1963. A handy introduction.

Chamove, A.; Harlow, H. F.; and Mitchell, G. "Sex Differences in the Infant-Directed Behavior of Preadolescent Rhesus Monkeys." *Child Development*, 38 (1967):329–35. See note under Harlow, below.

Comfort, Alex. *The Nature of Human Nature*. New York: Harper & Row, 1966.

——. *Sex in Society*. New York: Citadel Press, 1966. These two books by Comfort view sex within a broad biological, anthropological and psychological perspective. Arguable in places, but intelligent and stimulating.

Denniston, R. H. "Ambisexuality in Animals." In Marmor.* Argues for human ambisexuality.

Ehrhardt, Anke A.; Epstein, Ralph; and Money, John. "Fetal Androgens and Female Gender Identity in the Early-Treated Adrenogenital Syndrome." *Johns Hopkins Medical Journal*, 122 (1968):160–67.

Ehrhardt, Anke A.; Evers, Kathryn; and Money, John. "Influence of Androgen and Some Aspects of Sexually Dimorphic Behavior in Women with the Late-Treated Adrenogenital Syndrome." *Johns Hopkins Medical Journal*, 123 (1968):115–22.

Ehrhardt, Anke A., and Money, John. See Chapter 20. This and the two papers listed above suggest that human females may be psychologically masculinized by prenatal androgens.

Fisher, A. "Chemical and Electrical Stimulation of the Brain in the Male Rat." In R. A. Gorski and R. E. Whalen, eds., *Brain and Behavior*. Vol. 3, *The Brain and Gonadal Function*. Berkeley: University of California Press, 1966.

Ford, Clellan, and Beach, Frank. *Patterns of Sexual Behavior*. New York: Ace Books, 1951. Though dated and slightly biased in places, this book has not yet been superseded. Indispensable.

Freud, Sigmund. *Three Theories*. See Chapter 15.

Fuller, John, and Thompson, William. See Chapter 20.

Goy, R. "Organizing Effects of Androgen in the Behavior of Rhesus Monkeys." In *Proceedings of the London Conference: Endocrines and Human Behavior*. Edited by R. P. Michael. London: Oxford University Press, 1968. An important paper.

Harlow, Harry F. "Love in Infant Monkeys." *Scientific American*, 200 (June, 1959):68–74.

——. "Of Love in Infants." *Natural History*, 69 (1960):19–23.

——. "Sexual Behavior in the Rhesus Monkey." In Beach.*

Harlow, Harry F. and Margaret K. "A study of Animal Affection." *Natural History*, 70 (1961): 48–54.

——. "The Effect of Rearing Conditions on Behavior." In Money, ed., *Sex Research*. See below.

——. "Social Deprivation in Monkeys." *Scientific American*, 207 (November, 1962):136–46.

Harlow, Harry F., and Zimmerman, Robert R. "Affectional Responses in the Infant Monkey." *Science*, 130 (1959):421–32. Harlow's papers are masterpieces of contemporary psychology, a must for specialists and laymen alike.

Hinde, R. A. "Interaction of Internal and External Factors in Integration of Canary Reproduction." In Beach.*

Kagan, Jerome, and Beach, Frank. "Effects of Early Experience on Mating Behavior in Male Rats." *Journal of Comparative and Physiological Psychology*, 46 (1953):204–8.

Kinsey, Alfred, *et al. Female.**

——. *Male.**

Lehrman, Daniel. "Interaction Between Internal and External Environments in the Regulation of the Reproductive Cycle of the Ring Dove." In Beach.* Excellent technical paper.

——. "Interaction of Hormonal and Experiential Influences on Development of Behavior." In Bliss, ed. See above.

Levine, S. "Sex Differences in the Brain." *Scientific American*, 214 (April 1966):84–92.

Lisk, R. D. "Testosterone-Sensitive Centers in the Hypothalamus of the Rat." *Acta Endocrinologica*, 41 (1962):195–204.

Lorenz, Konrad. *Evolution and Modification of Behavior*. Chicago: University of Chicago Press, 1965. Theoretical.

——. *King Solomon's Ring*. New York: Thomas Y. Crowell, 1952. For laymen, charming and informative.

——. *On Aggression*. New York: Harcourt, Brace & World, 1966. Facts and speculations about aggression, by one of the greatest investigators of the subject.

Michael, Richard. "Biological Factors in the Organization and Expression of Sexual Behavior." In Rosen. See below.

Money, John, ed. *Sex Research*. See Chapter 20. A useful collection of technical papers by Beach; Harlow; Hooker; Money; Young, Goy and Phoenix; and others. With discussions and critiques.

Money, John; Ehrhardt, Anke A.; and Masica, Daniel N. "Fetal Feminization Induced by Androgen Insensitivity in the Testicular Feminizing Syndrome: Effect on Marriage and Maternalism." *Johns Hopkins Medical Journal*, 123 (1968): 105–14.

Pfaff, D. W. "Cerebral Implantation and Autoradiographic Studies of Sex Hormones." In Money, ed., *Sex Research*. See Chapter 20.

Phoenix, C. H.; Goy, R. W.; Gerall, A. A.; and Young, W. C. "Organizing Action of Prenatally Administered Testosterone Propionate on the Tissues Mediating Mating Behavior in the Female Guinea Pig." *Endocrinology*, 65 (1959): 369–382.

Rado, Sandor. "A Critical Examination of the Concept of Bisexuality." In Marmor.* The definitive refutation of Freud's libido theory.

Rheingold, Harriet, ed. *Maternal Behavior in Mammals*. New York: Wiley, 1963.

Robbins, Bernard S. "The Myth of Latent Emotions: A Critique of the Theory of Repression." *Psychotherapy*, 1 (1955):3–30.

Rosen, Ismond, ed. *The Pathology and Treatment of Sexual Deviation*. London: Oxford University Press, 1964. The best British collection of scientific papers on the subject. Highly recommended.

Rosenblatt, Jay. "Effects of Experience on Sexual Behavior in Male Cats." In Beach.*

Salzman, Leon. "'Latent' Homosexuality." In Marmor.* A little modern classic of psychiatric theory, to be read with Rado's essay on bisexuality.

Scharrer, Ernst and Berta. *Neuroendocrinology*. New York and London: Columbia University Press, 1963. A good basic text.

Schein, M. W., and Hale, E. B. "Stimuli Eliciting Sexual Behavior." In Beach.*

Schutz, F. "Sexuelle Prägung bei Antiden." *Tierpsychologie*, 22 (1965):50–103. On mallard duck imprinting.

——. "Homosexualität und Prägung." *Psychologische Forschung*, 28 (1965):439–63. On "homosexual" imprinting in the mallard.

Scott, John Paul. *Aggression*. Chicago: University of Chicago Press, 1958. Now somewhat dated, and takes the position of Dollard on frustration as the chief cause of aggression. But carefully and well written by a distinguished researcher, and still worth reading.

——. and Fuller, J. L. *Genetics and Social Behavior of the Dog*. Chicago: University of Chicago Press, 1965. A major study.

Sears, Pauline. "Doll Play Aggression in Normal Young Children." *Psychological Monographs*, 65 (1951):3–42. Good.

Sears, Robert. "Development of Gender Role." In Beach.* Good.

"Sexless." *Newsweek*, January 16, 1961. On Harlow's monkeys.

Stoller, Richard. See Chapter 20.

Thorpe, W. H. *Learning and Instinct in Animals.* 2nd ed. London: Methuen, 1963.

Tinbergen, Nikolaas. *The Herring Gull's World.* New York: Doubleday Anchor, 1967. Delightful and instructive.

——. *Social Behavior in Animals with Special Reference to Vertebrates.* London: Methuen, 1965. A must in the field.

——. "Aggression and Fear in the Normal Sexual Behavior of Some Animals." In *The Pathology and Treatment of Sexual Deviation.* Edited by Ismond Rosen. London: Oxford University Press, 1964. Shows clearly the relationship between sexual and aggressive behavior in a species.

Van Gennep, Arnold. *The Rites of Passage.* Translated by Monika B. Vizedom and Gabrielle L. Caffee. Chicago: University of Chicago Press, 1960.

Wilson, John R. *The Mind.* New York: Time, Inc., 1964. A good introduction to experimental neurology, but mechanistic in interpretation.

Young, William C.; Goy, Robert W.; and Phoenix, Charles H. "Hormones and Sex Behavior." In Money, ed., *Sex Research.* See Chapter 20. A fine essay.

Young, W. C., ed. *Sex and Internal Secretions.* Baltimore: Williams & Wilkins, 1961. Useful.

24 INSTEAD OF LATENCY

Anthony Storr's book is best for someone starting to read about human aggression, Tinbergen and Lorenz on animal aggression. Ardrey should be read with great caution, Morris with the thought that much of his popular writing is speculative. Lionel Ovesey's monographs are indispensable. I also recommend Calhoun, Beigel's interesting paper, Kardiner, Maslow, Selye, Tiger, Tinbergen and Wynne-Edwards. For the history of ethology I am indebted to an unpublished essay by Nikolaas Tinbergen and an essay by C. G. Beer. Gesner is quoted by Wendt.

Ardrey, Robert. *African Genesis.* New York: Atheneum, 1961.

——. *The Territorial Imperative.* New York: Atheneum, 1966. These books of Ardrey's have stimulated much of the new popular interest in ethology and its human implications, but they make scientists tear their hair over the one-sided selection of material and facile, simplistic interpretations. To be read with extreme caution.

Barnett, S. A. "Rats." *Scientific American,* 216 (January 1967):78–85.

Beigel, Hugo G. "The Meaning of Coital Postures." In DeMartino, ed., *Sexual Behavior.* See below. Interesting exploration of an oddly ignored subject.

Bieber, Irving. "Clinical Aspects of Male Homosexuality." In Marmor.* An excellent monograph.

Bychowski, Gustav. "The Ego and the Object of the Homosexual." *International Journal of Psycho-Analysis,* 42 (1961):255–59.

——. "The Structure of Homosexual Acting Out." *Psychoanalytic Quarterly,* 23 (1954):48–61. Two of the major analytic papers on the subject.

Calhoun, J. B. "A Behavioral Sink." In Bliss, ed., *Roots of Behavior.* See Chapter 23.

——. "Population Density and Social Pathology." *Scientific American,* 206 (February 1962):139–48.

Campbell, Bernard. *Human Evolution.* Chicago: Aldine, 1967. A useful summary including recent discoveries and theories.

Cappon, Daniel. *Toward an Understanding of Homosexuality.* Englewood Cliffs, N.J.: Prentice-Hall, 1965. Fundamentally, mostly sound, but sometimes disturbing in its athletic advocacy of cure.

Carrighar, Sally. "War Is Not in Our Genes." *The New York Times Magazine,* September 10, 1967. *Contra* Lorenz and Ardrey.

Comfort, Alex. *Sex in Society.* See Chapter 23.

DeMartino, Manfred F., ed. *Sexual Behavior and Personality Characteristics.* New York: Grove Press, 1966. Does not quite live up to its title, but contains some good papers.

DeVore, Irven. "Male Dominance and Mating Behavior in Baboons." In Beach.* Excellent.

——, ed. *Primate Behavior: Field Studies of Monkeys and Apes.* New York: Holt, Rinehart & Winston, 1965. Good anthology.

Dollard, J.; Doob, L. W.; Miller, N. E.; Mowrer, O. H.; and Sears, R. R. *Frustration and Aggression.* New Haven: Yale University Press, 1939. The source of several decades of thinking
about aggression being caused by frustration rather than innate programing.

Fox, Robin. "The Evolution of Human Sexual Behavior." *The New York Times Magazine,* March 24, 1968.

Harlow, Harry F. See Chapter 23.

Hinde, Robert A. *Animal Behavior: A Synthesis of Ethology and Comparative Psychology.* New York: McGraw-Hill, 1966. By an eminent researcher.

——. "The Nature of Aggression." *New Society,* 9 (1967):231.

Hoagland, Hudson. "Cybernetics of Population Control." *Bulletin of the Atomic Scientists,* 20 (February 1964):2–6.

Kardiner, Abram, and Ovesey, Lionel. *The Mark of Oppression.* New York and Cleveland: Meridian Books, 1962. A classic of social psychiatry.

Kempf, Edward J. "The Social and Sexual Behavior of Infrahuman Primates with Some Comparable Facts in Human Behavior." *Psychoanalytic Review,* 4 (1917):127–54. Of historical interest.

Lorenz, Konrad. See Chapter 23.

Maslow, A. H. "Love in Self-Actualizing People." In DeMartino, ed., *Sexual Behavior.* See above.

——. "Self-esteem (Dominance-Feeling) and Sexuality in Women." In DeMartino, ed., *Sexual Behavior.* See above.

——; Rand, H.; and Newman, S. "Some Parallels Between Sexual and Dominance Behavior of Infra-Human Primates and the Fantasies of Patients in Psychotherapy." In DeMartino, ed., *Sexual Behavior.* See above. This and the two papers above are original and suggestive.

Montagu, Ashley M. F. *The Biosocial Nature of Man.* New York: Grove Press, 1956.

——. *On Being Human.* New York: Hawthorn Books, 1966. Montagu's books argue for innate cooperative instincts rather than aggressive and competitive ones. As one-sided, in his way, as his opponents.

Morris, Desmond. *The Naked Ape.* New York: Dell Publishing Co., 1969. Full of interesting speculations but occasionally simplistic in its lack of cultural and psychological depth.

——, ed. *Primate Ethology.* Garden City, N.Y.: Doubleday Anchor, 1969. A very useful collection of scientific papers.

——. "The Causation of Pseudofemale and Pseudomale Behaviour: A Further Comment." *Behaviour,* 8 (1955):46–56.

——. "Homosexuality in the Ten-Spined Stickleback." *Behaviour*, 4 (1952):233–61.

———. and Ramona. *Men and Apes*. New York: Bantam Books, 1968. Well written and informative.

Ovesey, Lionel. "Fear of Vocational Success." *Archives of General Psychiatry*, 7 (1962):30–40.

———. "The Homosexual Conflict: An Adaptational Analysis." *Psychiatry*, 17 (1954):243–50.

———. *Homosexuality and Pseudohomosexuality*. New York: Science House, 1969. Contains most of the monographs listed here.

———. "Masculine Aspirations in Women." *Psychiatry*, 19 (1956):341–51.

———. "Pseudohomosexuality and Homosexuality in Men: Psychodynamics as a Guide to Treatment." In Marmor.*

———. "The Pseudohomosexual Anxiety." *Psychiatry*, 18 (1955):17–25.

———. "Pseudohomosexuality, the Paranoid Mechanism, and Paranoia." *Psychiatry*, 18 (1955): 163. Ovesey's papers are crucial to the modern reinterpretation of sex, aggression and deviance. A must for the scientist, and recommended to the serious lay reader as well.

Pavlov, Ivan. *Conditioned Reflexes*. New York: Dover Publications, 1960.

Rado, Sandor. "An Adaptational View of Sexual Behavior." In *Psychosexual Development in Health and Disease*. Edited by Paul Hoch and Joseph Zubin. New York: Grune & Stratton, 1949. A major paper in adaptational analysis.

Salzman, Leon. See Chapter 23.

Schrier, A. M.; Harlow, H. F.; and Stollnitz, F., eds. *Behavior of Nonhuman Primates*. New York: Academic Press, 1965.

"Scientist Reports He Made Bosses of Timid Monkeys." *The New York Times*, July 4, 1968.

Scott, John Paul. *Aggression*. See Chapter 23.

Selye, Hans. *The Stress of Life*. New York: McGraw-Hill, 1956. Already a standard reference on the biological underpinnings of human behavior.

Southwick, Charles H., ed. *Primate Social Behavior*. Princeton, N.J.: Van Nostrand, 1963. A good collection of papers covering a wide range of information.

Spitz, R. A. *The First Year of Life*. New York: International Universities Press, 1965. Along with John Bowlby's work, essential for understanding early human development.

Storr, Anthony. *Human Aggression*. New York: Atheneum, 1968. Like his book on sexual deviation, distinguished in grasp, humanity and clarity. Highly recommended; probably the best single book on the subject for laymen.

Thompson, Clara. "Changing Concepts of Homosexuality in Psychoanalysis." In Ruitenbeek.*

Tiger, Lionel. *Men in Groups*. New York: Random House, 1969. An interesting book speculating, and I believe correctly, that there is a genetic basis for human male bonding. Written in the usual academic jargon, but worth plowing through.

Tinbergen, Nikolaas. *Social Behavior in Animals*. See Chapter 23.

Washburn, S. L. *The Early Social Life of Man*. New York: Wenner-Gren Foundation, 1962. Recommended.

Watson, John B. *Behavior*. New York: Holt, Rinehart & Winston, 1914.

———. *Behaviorism*. Rev. ed. Chicago: University of Chicago Press, 1930. Along with Pavlov's work, the foundation of modern behaviorism.

Wendt, Herbert. See Chapter 20.

Wickler, Wolfgang. "Socio-Sexual Signals and Their Intra-Specific Imitation Among Primates." In Morris, *Primate Ethology*. A fascinating paper that touches on human sexual signals.

Wynne-Edwards, V. C. *Animal Dispersion in Relation to Social Behaviour*. Edinburgh: Oliver & Boyd, 1962. A major work.

Yerkes, R. M. *Chimpanzees: A Laboratory Colony*. New Haven: Yale University Press, 1943. A landmark in early primatology.

Zuckerman, S. *The Social Life of Monkeys and Apes*. New York: Harcourt, Brace & World, 1932. Of historical interest.

25 FROM OUTRAGE TO BOREDOM

Aberle, Sophie D., and Corner, George. *Twenty-five Years of Sex Research*. Philadelphia: W. B. Saunders, 1953.

"Anything Goes: Taboos in Twilight." *Newsweek*, November 13, 1967.

Auken, Kirsten. *Unge Kvinders Sexuelle Adfaerd*. Copenhagen: Rosenkilde og Babber, 1953. On sex behavior in Denmark. Includes an English summary.

Bell, Robert R. *Premarital Sex in a Changing Society*. Englewood Cliffs, N.J.: Prentice-Hall, 1966. A much-used reference.

——— and Buerkle, Jack V. "Mother and Daughter Attitudes to Premarital Sexual Behavior." *Marriage and Family Living*, 23 (1961):390–92. An interesting little study supporting one of Kinsey's speculations about attitudes.

Brecher, Ruth and Edward. *An Analysis of Human Sexual Response*. New York: Signet Books, 1966.

Brody, Jane E. "Sex and the College Girl." *The New York Times*, January 8, 1968.

Burgess, Ernest, and Wallin, Paul. *Courtship, Engagement and Marriage*. Philadelphia: J. B. Lippincott, 1953.

Chesser, Eustace. *The Sexual, Marital and Family Relationships of the English Woman*. New York: Roy Publishers, 1957.

Christensen, H. T. "Scandinavian and American Sex Norms." *Journal of Social Issues*, 22 (1966): 60–75.

Cuber, John, and Harroff, Peggy. *Sex and the Significant Americans*. Baltimore: Penguin Books, 1965. A limited but provocative sociological study.

"Draft Rejections Show Rise in Homosexuals." *Providence Evening Bulletin*, August 24, 1966.

Ehrmann, Winston. *Premarital Dating Behavior*. New York: Holt, Rinehart & Winston, 1959.

Freedman, Mervin B. "The Sexual Behavior of American College Women: An Empirical Study and an Historical Survey." *Merrill-Palmer Quarterly*, 11 (1965):33–48.

Gagnon, John, and Simon, William. "Sexual Deviance in Contemporary America." *Annals of the American Academy of Political and Social Science*, 376 (1968):106–22.

———, eds. *The Sexual Scene*. New York: Aldine Publishing, 1970. Gathers some interesting papers in one volume.

Geddes, Donald, ed. *An Analysis of the Kinsey Reports*. New York: New American Library, 1954. An informative group of articles, essays and criticism.

Greene, Gael. *Sex and the College Girl*. New York: Dell, 1964. Impressionistic but informative.

Hofmann, Hans. *Sex Incorporated*. Boston: Beacon Press, 1967. Not recommended.

Holbrook, Stewart. See Chapter 11.

Hunt, Morton.*

Karlen, Arno. "Speaking Out: The Sexual Revolution Is a Myth." *Saturday Evening Post*, January 11, 1968.

———. "The Unmarried Marrieds on Campus." *The New York Times Magazine*, January 26, 1969. Interviews with "the new youth."

Kinsey, Alfred, et al. *Female*.*

———. *Male*.*

Kirkendall, Lester A. *Premarital Intercourse and Interpersonal Relationships*. New York: Julian Press, 1961. Much referred to, somewhat useful.

Linnér, Birgitta. *Sex and Society in Sweden*. New York: Pantheon Books, 1967. Reliable.

———. *Society and Sex in Sweden*. Stockholm: The Swedish Institute, n.d. A pamphlet.

McWhirter, William. "The 'Arrangement' at College." *Life*, May 31, 1968.

Marcuse, Herbert. *Eros and Civilization*. Boston: Beacon Press, 1955.

Moskin, Robert J. "Sweden's New Battle Over Sex." *Look*, November 15, 1966.

"The Necker Checkers." *Newsweek*, May 8, 1967.

Packard, Vance. *The Sexual Wilderness*. New York: David McKay, 1968. Contains much information, but relies on questionnaires of limited reliability and seems, finally, more an undigested mass of data than a conclusive study.

"Pill Doesn't 'Encourage' Sex, M.D. Says." *New York Post*, May 31, 1968.

"The Pleasures and Pain of the Single Life." *Time*, September 15, 1967.

Reiss, Ira L. *Premarital Sexual Standards in America*. New York: The Free Press, 1964. Widely used.

———. "America's Sex Standards—How and Why They're Changing." *Trans-Action*, March 1968, pp. 26–32.

Rollin, Betty. "Early to Wed." *Look*, September 20, 1966.

Rubin, Isadore. "Sex and Morality." *Redbook*, October 1966.

Schofield, Michael. *The Sexual Behaviour of Young People*. London: Longmans, Green, 1965. An important behavioral study.

"Sex 'Revolution' Is Called a Myth." *The New York Times*, December 15, 1968.

Sherwin, Robert, and Keller, George. "Sex on the Campus." *Columbia College Today*, Fall 1967. A good article.

Shorris, Earl. "Sex Is Dead in Southern California." *Esquire*, September 1968. Some interesting comments on the West Coast "sexual underground."

Silberman, Arlene. "The Pregnant Bride." *Redbook*, November 1966.

"A U.S. Sex Revolt? It's Mostly Talk." *The New York Times*, July 11, 1966.

Von Hoffman, Nicholas. *The Multiversity*. New York: Holt, Rinehart & Winston, 1966.

Walsh, Robert H. Quoted in "Findings" column, *Behavior Today Supplement*, September 2, 1970.

Whiting, John. "Menarcheal Age and Infant Stress." In Beach.*

26 IN OTHER WORLDS

Langsdorf is quoted in Crawley, and Marquette in Kenton. The basic readings remain Devereux's monographs and the volume by Ford and Beach.

Ammar, Hamed. *Growing Up in an Egyptian Village*. London: Routledge & Kegan Paul, 1954.

Barclay, Harold B. *Buurri Al Lamaab: A Suburban Village in the Sudan*. Ithaca, N.Y.: Cornell University Press, 1964.

Bateson, Gregory. *Naven*. 2nd ed. Stanford: Stanford University Press, 1958. A classic ethnological study of the Iatmul.

——— and Mead, Margaret. *Balinese Character*. New York: Publications of the New York Academy of Science, 1942. A fine piece of research and methodological innovation.

Benedict, Ruth. *The Chrysanthemum and the Sword*. Boston: Houghton Mifflin, 1946. On Japanese culture and personality.

———. *Patterns of Culture*. New York: New American Library, 1946. Takes an extreme relativist position on deviance.

Bettelheim, Bruno. *Symbolic Wounds*. Glencoe, Ill.: Glencoe Free Press, 1954. Psychoanalytic interpretation of initiation rites.

Bogoras, W. *The Chukchee Religion*. Memoirs of the American Museum of Natural History, Vol. 11. Leiden: E. J. Brill, 1907.

Bossu, Jean B. *Travels Through That Part of North America Formerly Called Louisiana*. 2 vols. London: Printed for T. Davies, 1771.

Burrows, Edwin G., and Spiro, Melford E. *An Atoll Culture: Ethnography of Ifaluk in the Central Carolines*. New Haven: Human Relations Area Files, 1957.

Burton, R. V., and Whiting, J. W. M. "The Absent Father and Cross-Sex Identity." *Merrill-Palmer Quarterly of Behavior and Development*, 7 (1961):85–95.

Carpenter, Edward. See Chapter 12.

Carstairs, G. Morris. *The Twice Born: A Study of a Community of High-Caste Hindus*. London: Hogarth Press, 1957.

———. "Cultural Differences in Sexual Deviation." In Ismond Rosen, ed., see Chapter 23.

Cline, Walter. *Notes on the People of Siwah and El Garah in the Libyan Desert*. General Series of Anthropology, No. 4. Menasha, Wisc.: George Banta, 1936.

Cohen, Y. A. "Establishment of Identity in a Social Nexus: The Special Case of Initiation Ceremonies." *American Anthropologist*, 66 (1964): 529–52.

Comfort, Alex. *Sex in Society*. See Chapter 23.

Crawley, Ernest. *The Mystic Rose*. New York: Meridian, 1960. Of historical interest.

Czaplicka, M. *Aboriginal Siberia*. Oxford: Clarendon Press, 1914.

Danielsson, B. *Love in the South Seas*. London: Allen & Unwin, 1956.

Davenport, William. "Sexual Patterns and Their Regulation in a Society of the Southwest Pacific." In Beach.* An important and much-quoted study.

Devereux, George. "Institutionalized Homosexuality of the Mohave Indians." In Ruitenbeek.* The best paper on non-Western homosexuality. A must.

———. "Mohave Ethnopsychiatry and Suicide: The Psychiatric Knowledge and Psychic Disturbances of an Indian Tribe." In *Smithsonian Institution Bureau of American Ethnology*, Bulletin 175. Washington, D.C.: U.S. Government Printing Office, 1961.

Dickson, H. R. P. *The Arab of the Desert*. 2nd ed. London: Allen & Unwin, 1951.

Dorsey, J. O. *Omaha Sociology*. In U.S. Bureau of American Ethnology Third Annual Report, 1884.

DuBois, Cora. *The People of Alor*. Cambridge, Mass.: Harvard University Press, 1960. Still a model study in social psychiatry and anthropology.

Eliade, Mircea. *Shamanism*. New York: Pantheon Books, 1964. Definitive. With an exhaustive bibliography on works in several languages.

Ellis, Havelock.*

Erikson, Erik H. *Childhood and Society*. New York: W. W. Norton, 1950. A classic anthropological-psychoanalytic study.

Ford, Clelland, and Beach, Frank A. See Chapter 23.

Fortune, R. F. *Sorcerers of Dobu: The Social Anthropology of the Dobu Islanders of the Western Pacific*. New York: E. P. Dutton, 1963.

Freud, Sigmund. *Moses and Monotheism*. New York: A. A. Knopf, 1939.

———. *Totem and Taboo*. Edited and translated by James Strachey. New York: W. W. Norton, 1952.

Gladwin, Thomas, and Sarason, Seymour B. *Truk: Man in Paradise*. New York: Wenner-Gren Foundation, 1963.

Goldman, Irving. *The Cuebo Indians of the Northwest Amazon*. Illinois Studies in Anthropology, No. 2. Urbana: University of Illinois Press, 1963.

Green, Richard. "Mythological, Historical and Cross-Cultural Aspects of Transsexualism." In *Transsexualism and Sex Reassignment*. Edited by Richard Green and John Money. Baltimore: Johns Hopkins Press, 1969.

Hays, H. R. *Ape to Angel*. See Chapter 1.

———. *The Dangerous Sex*. See Chapter 1.

Hoebel, E. Anderson. *Man in the Primitive World*. New York: McGraw-Hill, 1958.

Howard, James. *The Ponca Tribe*. Smithsonian Institution, Bureau of American Ethnology, Bulletin 195. Washington, D.C.: U.S. Government Printing Office, 1965.

Kardiner, Abram. *The Individual and His Society*. New York. Columbia University Press, 1939. Intelligent, useful and opinionated.

―――― and Preble, Edward. See Chapter 1.

Kenton, Edna, ed. *The Jesuit Relations and Allied Documents*. New York: Vanguard Press, 1954.

Kinsey, Alfred, et al. *Female.**

――――. *Male.**

Kluckhohn, Clyde. "As an Anthropologist Views It." In *Sex Habits of American Men: A Symposium of the Kinsey Report*. Edited by Albert Deutsch. New York: Prentice-Hall, 1948.

Layard, J. W. *Stone Men of Mulekula*. London: Chatto & Windus, 1942. On initiation rites in Melanesia. A classic.

Lessa, William A. *Ulithi: A Micronesian Design for Living*. New York: Holt, Rinehart & Winston, 1966.

Linton, Ralph. *Culture and Mental Disorders*. Springfield, Ill. Charles C. Thomas, 1956.

――――. "Marquesan Culture." In Kardiner, *The Individual and His Society*. See above.

Lowie, Robert H. *The Crow Indians*. New York: Rinehart, 1956.

McCoy, Isaac. *History of Baptist Indian Missions*. Washington: William M. Morrison; New York: H. & S. Raynor, 1840.

Malinowski, Bronislaw. *Sex and Repression in Savage Society*. New York: Meridian Books, 1955.

――――. *The Sexual Life of Savages*. 3rd ed. London: George Routledge & Sons, 1932. Malinowski still warrants reading.

Messing, Simon David. *The Highland-Plateau Amhara of Ethiopia*. Ph.D. dissertation, University of Pennsylvania, 1957.

Mischel, Walter. "Father-Absence and Delay of Gratification: Cross-Cultural Comparisons." *Journal of Abnormal Psychology*, 63 (1961):116–24.

Norbeck, E.; Walker, D. E.; and Cohen, M. "The Interpretation of Data: Puberty Rites." *American Anthropologist*, 64 (1962):463–85. An inter-

pretation of initiation rites that contradicts Whiting's.

Opler, Marvin K. "Anthropological and Cross-Cultural Aspects of Homosexuality." In Marmor.* A very good essay. Recommended.

――――. "The Southern Ute Indians in Colorado." In *Acculturation in Seven American Indian Tribes*. Edited by Ralph Linton. New York: Appleton-Century-Crofts, 1940.

Park, Willard Z. "Paviotso Shamanism." In *The North American Indians: A Sourcebook*. Edited by Roger C. Own, James J. F. Deetz, and Anthony D. Fisher. New York: Macmillan, 1967.

Patai, Raphael. See Chapter 1.

Radcliffe-Brown, A. R. *The Andaman Islanders*. New York: Free Press, 1948.

Róheim, Géza. *Psychoanalysis and Anthropology*. New York: International Universities Press, 1950. Of limited usefulness but historically important.

Suggs, Robert. *Marquesan Sexual Behavior*. New York: Harcourt, Brace & World, 1966. A convincing and detailed study of non-Western sex behavior, with a taxonomic approach; contradicts previous studies and has an air of authority in doing so. Recommended.

Tiger, Lionel. *Men in Groups*. See Chapter 24.

Turney-High, Harry Holbert. *Ethnography of the Kutenai*. In *Memoirs of the American Anthropological Association*, No. 56. Menasha, Wisc.: American Anthropological Association, 1941.

――――. *The Flathead Indians of Montana*. In *Memoirs of the American Anthropological Association*, No. 48. Menasha, Wisc.; American Anthropological Association, 1937.

Webster, Hutton. *Primitive Secret Societies*. New York: Macmillan, 1932. Dated but still interesting.

Westermarck, Edvard. See Chapter 1.

Whiting, J.; Kluckhohn, R.; Anthony, A. "The Function of Male Initiation Ceremonies at Puberty." In *Readings in Social Psychology*. Edited by E. E. Maccoby, T. M. Newcomb and E. L. Hartley, 3rd ed. New York: Holt, Rinehart & Winston, 1958.

Young, Frank W. *Initiation Ceremonies*. New York: Bobbs-Merrill, 1965.

27 MASCULINE-FEMININE

Doroshaw is quoted in "Notes from the Underground," Luckey in Packard, Mead on fierceness in "People." The interracial lesbian photographs appeared in the September 1968 issue of *Evergreen Review*.

Anastasi, Anne. *Differential Psychology*. 3rd ed. New York: Macmillan, 1958.

"Andy Warhol Fighting for Life." *New York Post*, June 4, 1968.

Barry, H.; Bacon, M. K.; and Child, I. L. "A Cross-Cultural Survey of Some Sex Differences in Socialization." *Journal of Abnormal Psychology*, 55 (1957): 327–32.

Bates, Alan, and Babchuk, Nicholas. "The Primary Relations of Middle-Class Couples: A Study of Male Dominance." *American Sociological Review*, 28 (1963):377–84.

Beauvoir, Simone de. See Chapter 1.

Benedict, Ruth. See Chapter 26.

Bernard, Jessie. *Academic Women*. University Park, Pa.: Pennsylvania State University Press, 1964.

Bettelheim, Bruno. "Speaking Out: Children Should Learn About Violence." *Saturday Evening Post*, March 11, 1967. Good short essay.

Blood, Robert, and Wolfe, Donald. *Husbands and Wives*. New York: Free Press of Glencoe, 1960.

Brenton, Myron. *The American Male*. New York: Coward-McCann, 1966. Not recommended.

"Coffee for the Army." *Newsweek*, August 26, 1968.

Davis, Douglas. "The New Eroticism." *Evergreen Review*, September 1968. Kink in the art world.

DeMille, Agnes. "Whatever Has Become of Mommy?" *Horizon*, 8 (Summer 1966), 5–16. Inter-

esting historical essay.

Fashions of the Times. *The New York Times*, March 7, 1965 and February 26, 1967.

Fowles, John. "Here Comes Twiggy!!!" *Cosmopolitan*, April 1967.

Frazier, George. "Party of One!" *Holiday*, November 1965. A good short history of camp.

Friedan, Betty. *The Feminine Mystique*. New York: W. W. Norton, 1963. Mystique is hardly the word. A book of minor historical interest.

Garai, J. E., and Scheinfeld, Amram. "Sex Differences in Mental and Behavioral Traits." Pratt Institute, *Genetic Psychology Monographs*, 77 (1968):169–299.

Gesell, A., et al. *The First Five Years of Life*. New York: Harper & Row, 1940.

Goldman, George D., and Milman, Donald S., eds. *Modern Woman: Her Psychology and Sexuality*. Springfield, Ill.: Charles C. Thomas, 1969.

Goldman, Irving. See Chapter 26.

Gorer, Geoffrey, *The American People*. New York: W. W. Norton, 1948. An odd mixture of insight and unsupported generalizations.

Gornick, Vivian. "It's a Queer Hand Stoking the Campfire." *Village Voice*, April 7, 1966.

Harlow, Harry, and Zimmerman, Robert. See Chapter 23.

Harrington, Stephanie, and Sabol, Blair. "Outside Fashion: Hexes." *Village Voice*, February 1, 1968.

Hays, H. R. *Ape to Angel*. See Chapter 1.

Henry, Jules. *Culture Against Man*. New York: Random House, 1963. An interesting book blending observation of American youth and cultural theory.

"Hippie Home Life Is Studied Here." *The New York Times*, August 6, 1967.

Hunt, Morton. *Her Infinite Variety*. New York: Harper & Row, 1962. Though already a bit dated and weak in certain scientific areas, an intelligent, balanced overview of woman in nature and in society. Recommended to laymen, with the proviso that further reading is needed.

Jahoda, G. "Sex Differences in Preferences for Shapes: A Cross-Cultural Replication." *British Journal of Psychology*, 47 (1956):126–32.

Jennison, Sandra. "Little Boy Lovers." *Cosmopolitan*, May 1966.

Kagan, Jerome. "Check One: Male, Female." *Psychology Today*, 3 (July 1969):39–41. A good short essay, for both laymen and specialists, by a distinguished researcher.

——— and Moss, H. *Birth to Maturity*. New York: Wiley, 1962. Recommended.

Kardiner, Abram. *Sex and Morality*. London: Routledge & Kegan Paul, 1955. Like Kardiner's other nonresearch works, worthwhile—if sometimes only to argue with.

Keniston, Kenneth. *The Uncommitted*. New York: Dell, 1967. A searching book, worth more than stacks of magazine articles and learned monographs about American youth during the late 1950s and 1960s.

Komarovsky, Mirra. *Blue-Collar Marriage*. New York: Random House, 1962. Recommended.

LaBarre, Weston. *The Human Animal*. Chicago: University of Chicago Press, 1954. Though a little dated now, still one of the best general books on man from a medical-psychiatric viewpoint.

Lawrenson, Helen. "Androgyne, You're a Funny Valentine." *Esquire*, March 1965. A clever article.

LeShan, Eda. "The 'Perfect' Child." *The New York Times Magazine*, August 27, 1967.

Lester, Elenore. "From Underground: Kenneth Anger Rising." *The New York Times*, February 19, 1967.

Lewis, M., and Kagan, Jerome. "Studies in Attention." *Merrill-Palmer Quarterly*, 11 (1965):95–127. On male-female differences.

Lifton, Robert J., ed. *The Woman in America*. Boston: Houghton Mifflin, 1965.

Lundberg, Ferdinand, and Farnham, Marynia. *Modern Woman: The Lost Sex*. See Chapter 11.

McElroy, W. A. "A Sex Difference in Preferences for Shapes." *British Journal of Psychology*, 45 (1954): 209–16.

McNeill, Don. "Run, Do Not Walk, to the Nearest Exit." *Village Voice*, May 23, 1968.

Maccoby, Eleanor, ed. *The Development of Sex Differences*. Stanford: Stanford University Press, 1966. A fine collection of scientific essays, with an extensive critical bibliography. Highly recommended.

Mead, Margaret. *Coming of Age in Samoa*. New York: Morrow, 1966.

———. *Male and Female*. New York: New American Library, 1955.

———. *Sex and Temperament in Three Primitive Societies*. New York: William Morrow, 1963. Mead's books are always worth reading, and worth rereading critically.

——— and Bateson, Gregory. *Balinese Character*. See Chapter 26, under Bateson.

Murdock, G. P. "Comparative Data on the Division of Labor by Sex." *Social Forces*, 15 (1953):551–53. Good.

———. *Social Structure*. New York: Macmillan, 1949. A standard work.

"Notes from the Underground." *Evergreen Review*, June 1967.

Odenwald, Robert. *The Disappearing Sexes*. New York: Random House, 1965. Not recommended.

O'Neill, William. See Chapter 11.

"Out on a Limb." *Newsweek*, September 11, 1967.

Packard, Vance. See Chapter 25.

"People." *Time*, December 16, 1966.

"Pop." *Newsweek*, April 25, 1966.

Radcliffe-Brown, A. R. See Chapter 26.

Regelson, Rosalyn. "Up the Camp Staircase." *The New York Times*, March 3, 1968.

Rodman, Hyman. "Marital Power in France, Greece, Yugoslavia and the United States." *Journal of Marriage and the Family*, 29 (1967): 320–24.

Romney, A. Kimball. "Variations in Household Structure as Determinants of Sex-Typed Behavior." In Beach.*

Rosenberg, Harold. "Masculinity: Real and Put On." *Vogue*, November 15, 1967.

Rossi, Alice. "Equality Between the Sexes: An Immodest Proposal." *Daedalus*, 93 (Spring 1964): 607–652.

Ruitenbeek, Hendrik M. *The Male Myth*. New York: Dell, 1967. Not recommended.

Sarris, Andrew. "Films." *Village Voice*, November 30, 1967.

Schott, Webster. "One Side of the Erotic Street." *The New York Times Book Review*, January 4, 1968.

Scott, John Paul. *Aggression*. See Chapter 23.

Sears, P. See Chapter 23.

Sears, Robert. "Development of Gender Role." In Beach.* Recommended.

Sennett, Richard. "The Brutality of Modern Families." *Trans-Action*, 7 (September 1970): 29–37. An interesting essay on the American family.

Sexton, Patricia Cayo. *The Feminized Male*. New York: Vintage Books, 1969. Contains questionable generalizations, but provocative.

Simon, John. " 'The Boys in the Band' as Object Lesson." *New York*, May 8, 1968.

Simpson, George. *People in Families: Sociology, Psychoanalysis and the American Family*. Cleveland: World Publishing, 1966.

Sontag, Susan. "Notes on 'Camp.' " *Partisan Review*, 31 (1964), 515–30. The source of much silliness.

Spiro, M. E. *Children of the Kibbutz*. Cambridge, Mass.: Harvard University Press, 1958.

———. *Kibbutz: Venture in Utopia*. Cambridge, Mass.: Harvard University Press, 1956.

Stern, Karl. *Flight from Woman*. New York: Farrar, Straus & Giroux, 1967. Of limited usefulness, often literary where it should be scientific.

Stoller, Robert. *Sex and Gender*. See Chapter 20.

Storr, Catherine. "The Logic of See-Through." *Cosmopolitan*, November 1968. Rather good journalism.

Terman, L. M., and Miles, Catherine C. *Sex and Personality*. New York: McGraw-Hill, 1936. An old classic of psychology.

Tiger, Lionel. See Chapter 26.

———. "Male Dominance? Yes, Alas. A Sexist Plot? No." *The New York Times Magazine*, October 25, 1970.

White, Ted. "Masochism of the Month." *The Realist*, December 1968.

Whiting, Beatrice, ed. *Six Cultures: Studies of Child Rearing*. New York: John Wiley & Sons, 1963. Interesting.

"Who's Afraid . . ." *Newsweek*, July 4, 1966.

Winick, Charles E. *The New People: Desexualization in American Life*. New York: Pegasus, 1968. Disappointing blend of sociology and sociologizing, but contains some interesting details.

Wolfe, Bernard. "The Step after Muscle." *Cosmopolitan*, February 1966.

28 IN THE SHADOW

Allport, Gordon. *The Nature of Prejudice*. Cambridge, Mass.: Addison-Wesley, 1954. Becoming dated.

Becker, Howard S., ed. *The Other Side: Perspectives in Deviance*. New York: The Free Press, 1964. Contains some useful essays.

——. *Outsiders*. New York: The Free Press, 1963. Interesting theory about deviant career, but unsupported by field work with homosexuals.

Churchill, Wainwright. *Homosexual Behavior Among Males*. New York: Hawthorn Books, 1967. Argumentative and one-sided, apparently bent on normalizing homosexuality.

"Columbia Charters Homosexual Group." *The New York Times*, May 3, 1967.

Cory, Donald Webster. *The Homosexual in America*. New York: Paperback Library, 1951. About being homosexual, by a homosexual.

Crowley, Mort. *The Boys in the Band*. New York: Farrar, Straus & Giroux, 1968.

Ellis, Albert. "Homosexuality: The Right to Be Wrong." *Journal of Sex Research*, 4 (1968):96–107. Recommended.

Festinger, Leon. *A Theory of Cognitive Dissonance*. Stanford: Stanford University Press, 1957. A sociological theory that touches tangentially the nature of deviant ideology and attitudes.

Forsythe, Reginald. "Why Can't 'We' Live Happily Ever After, Too?" *The New York Times*, February 23, 1969.

Frankenheimer, Anna. "A Much-Needed Upbraiding of Long-Hair Music." *Fact*, November-December, 1964.

Freed, Louis F. *The Problem of European Prostitutes in Johannesburg*. Cape Town: Juta, 1949.

Gagnon, John, and Simon, William. "Homosexuality: The Formulation of a Sociological Perspective." *Journal of Health and Social Behavior*, 8 (1967):177–85.

——. "Sexual Deviance in Contemporary America." See Chapter 25. Both essays recommended.

——, eds. *Sexual Deviance*. New York: Harper & Row, 1967. Contains useful papers.

Garfinkle, Harold. "Conditions of Successful Degradation Ceremonies." *American Journal of Sociology*, 5 (1956):61.

" 'Gay Is Good,' or Is It?" *Philadelphia Inquirer*, November 4, 1968.

Giese, Hans, ed. *Die sexuelle Perversion*. Frankfurt: Akademische Verlagsgesellschaft, Akademische Reihe, 1967. German studies that support, in the main, major American and British studies of deviance.

Goffman, Erving. *Stigma*. Englewood Cliffs, N.J.: Prentice-Hall, 1963. One of the basic texts in the sociology of deviance. Recommended.

Green, Richard, and Money, John. "Stage-Acting, Role-Taking, and Effeminate Impersonation During Boyhood." *Archives of General Psychiatry*, 15 (1966):535–38. An interesting exploratory investigation; it implies not that homosexuals are drawn to acting and role-playing but that a propensity for role-playing may be a factor in homosexuality.

Harrington, Stephanie. "League at Columbia. Homosexual Sortie: An Anonymous Crusade." *Village Voice*, May 25, 1967.

Hauser, Richard. *The Homosexual Society*. London: The Bodley Head, 1962. Sketchy and undocumented. Not recommended.

Helmer, William J. "New York's 'Middle-Class' Homosexuals." *Harper's*, March 1963.

Hoffman, Martin. *The Gay World*. New York: Basic Books, 1968. The author says he intends to produce an ethnology of the homosexual subculture. Although he reaches no such ambitious goal, he does make some interesting comments on the gay life. Influenced by the Hooker viewpoint (see below).

"Homosexuals Ask Candidates' Ideas." *The New York Times*, August 19, 1968.

Hooker, Evelyn. "The Adjustment of the Male Overt Homosexual." In Ruitenbeek.*

——. "The Homosexual Community." In Gagnon and Simon, eds., *Sexual Deviance*. See above.

——. "Male Homosexuals and Their 'Worlds.' " In Marmor.* Hooker's papers have become influential and should be read. The one in Marmor's volume is as good as any if a reader wants to pick one.

"Hoving Calls a Meeting to Plan for Restoration of Bryant Park." *The New York Times*, June 22, 1966.

Humphreys, Laud. *Tearoom Trade: Impersonal Sex in Public Places*. Chicago: Aldine Publishing, 1970. Some details on lavatory sex-hunting.

Jackman, Norman R.; O'Toole, Richard; and Geis, Gilbert. "The Self-Image of the Prostitute." In Gagnon and Simon, eds., *Sexual Deviance*. See above. Interesting.

Kinsey, Alfred, *et. al. Male*.*

Leznoff, Maurice. "Interviewing Homosexuals." *American Journal of Sociology*, 62 (1956):204.

—— and Westley, William. "The Homosexual Community." In Ruitenbeek.* A good paper, recommended.

Lindner, Robert. "Homosexuality and the Contemporary Scene." In Ruitenbeek.*

Magee, Bryan. *One in Twenty*. London: Secker & Warburg, 1966. One of the better once-over-lightly books on homosexuality, journalistically competent but lacking scientific depth.

Masters, R. E. L. *The Homosexual Revolution*. New York: Julian Press, 1962. A history of the homophile movement until the 1960s.

Polsky, Ned. *Hustlers, Beats, and Others*. Garden City, N.Y.: Doubleday, 1969.

Raven, Simon. "Boys Will Be Boys." In Ruitenbeek.* On male prostitutes.

Reiss, Albert J. "The Social Integration of Queers and Peers." In Ruitenbeek.* An important paper.

Rubington, Earl, and Weinberg, Martin, eds. *Deviance: The Interactionist Perspective*. New York: Macmillan, 1968. Too many short snippets, but contains useful material.

Ruitenbeek, Hendrik. "Men Alone: The Male Homosexual and the Disintegrated Family." In Ruitenbeek.*

Sagarin, Edward. *Odd Man In*. Chicago: Quadrangle Books, 1969. On deviance of many kinds.

Schofield, Michael. *Sociological Aspects of Homosexuality*. Boston: Little, Brown, 1965. A real contribution to scientific knowledge, but subject to many methodological criticisms and not as far-reaching as the title implies.

Schur, Edwin M. *Crimes Without Victims*. Englewood Cliffs, N.J.: Prentice-Hall, 1965. One of the more moderate and important works in the "sociology of deviance."

Skir, Leo. "The Gay World." In *The New York Spy*. Edited by Alan Rinzler. New York: D. White, 1967.

Sonnenschein, David. "The Ethnography of Male Homosexual Relations." *Journal of Sex Research*, 4 (1968):69–83. A good study.

Star, Jack. "The Sad 'Gay' Life." *Look*, January 10, 1967.

Stearn, Jess. *The Sixth Man*. New York: Macfadden Books, 1965. Not recommended.

"Student Homophile League." *Gay Power*, Vol. 1, No. 4.

"Trees in a Queens Park Cut Down as Vigilantes Harass Homosexuals." *The New York Times*, July 1, 1969.

Ullerstam, Lars. *The Erotic Minorities*. Translated by Anselm Hollo. New York: Grove Press, 1966. Loud and silly.

Walker, Gerald. *Cruising*. New York: Stein & Day, 1970. An interesting novel about the violent antihomosexual.

Walker, Kenneth, and Fletcher, Peter. *Sex and Society*. Baltimore: Penguin Books, 1965. Not recommended.

Weinberg, Martin S. "The Aging Male Homosexual." *Medical Aspects of Human Sexuality*, 3 (1969):66–72.

——. "The Male Homosexual: Age-Related Variations in Social and Psychological Characteristics." *Social Problems*, 17 (1970):527–37. Interesting papers on how homosexuals cope with aging.

——. "Homosexual Samples: Differences and Similarities. *Journal of Sex Research*, 6 (1970): 312–25.

Welch, Paul. "The 'Gay' World Takes to the City Streets." *Life*, June 26, 1964.

West, D. J. See Chapter 20.

Westwood, Gordon. *A Minority*. London: Longmans, Green, 1960.

——. *Society and the Homosexual*. New York: E. P. Dutton, 1953. These books, especially the one published in 1960, are solid little studies. The use of direct quotations from the interviews is helpful.

"When Celibacy Fails: A Study." *New York Post*, May 14, 1970.

Willis, Stanley E. *Understanding and Counseling the Male Homosexual.* Boston: Little, Brown, 1967. An excellent psychiatric study. Recommended.

29 OTHER OUTSIDERS

Achilles, Nancy. "The Development of the Homosexual Bar as an Institution." In Gagnon and Simon, eds. *Sexual Deviance.* See Chapter 28.

Bass-Hass, Rita. "The Lesbian Dyad." *Journal of Sex Research,* 4 (1968):108–26.

Benjamin, Harry, and Masters, R. H. L. *Prostitution and Morality.* New York: Julian Press, 1964.

Bernard, Jessie. *Marriage and Family Among Negroes.* Englewood Cliffs, N.J.: Prentice-Hall, 1966.

"Call Me a Prison-Made Homosexual." *Dayton Daily News,* September 20, 1968.

Caprio, Frank. See Chapter 10.

Clark, Kenneth B. "Explosion in the Ghetto." *Psychology Today,* 1 (September 1967):30–38; 62–71.

Clemmer, Donald. *The Prison Community.* New York: Holt, Rinehart, 1958. A standard reference.

Cory, D. W. *The Lesbian in America.* New York: Citadel Press, 1964. Of limited value.

Cressey, Donald, ed. *The Prison.* New York: Holt, Rinehart & Winston, 1961. Widely read.

Crowley, Mort. See Chapter 28.

Curran, Frank J., and Levine, M. "A Body Image Study of Prostitutes." *Journal of Criminal Psychopathology,* (1942):93–116.

Davies, Hunter, ed. *The New London Spy.* London: Anthony Blond, 1966.

DeMartino, Manfred. *The New Female Sexuality.* New York: Julian Press, 1969. On female nudists and lesbianism.

Dippolitino, Gloria. "The Women's Army Corps: Life Among the Funny-Bunnies." *Fact,* May-June, 1966.

Fishman, Joseph E. *Sex in Prison.* New York: National Library Press, 1934.

"Forum Newsfront: Sodomy Factories." *Playboy,* January, 1969.

Gagnon, John, and Simon, William, eds. *Sexual Deviance.* See Chapter 28.

Gagnon, John, and Simon, William. "Femininity in the Lesbian Community." *Social Problems,* 15 (1967):212–21.

———. "Homosexuality." See Chapter 28.

———. "The Lesbians: A Preliminary Overview." In Gagnon and Simon, eds., *Sexual Deviance.* See Chapter 28.

———. "The Social Meaning of Prison Homosexuality." *Federal Probation,* 32 (March, 1968): 23–29. The papers of Gagnon and Simon are recommended.

Gebhard, Paul; Gagnon, John; Pomeroy, Wardell; and Christenson, Cornelia. *Sex Offenders.* New York: Bantam Books, 1967. The most complete and reliable study of its kind. Highly recommended.

Giallombardo, Rose. *Society of Women.* New York: John Wiley & Sons, 1966. An excellent book describing lesbian prison "families."

Glover, Edward. "The Abnormality of Prostitutes." In *Women.* Edited by A. M. Krich. New York: Dell, 1953.

———. *The Psychopathology of Prostitution.* London: I.S.T.D. Publications, 1945.

Greenwald, Harold. *The Call Girl.* New York: Ballantine Books, 1958. Recommended.

Halleck, Seymour, and Hersko, Marvin. "Homosexual Behavior in a Correctional Institution for Adolescent Girls." *American Journal of Orthopsychiatry,* 32 (1962):911–17.

Harris, Sara. *Hell-Hole.* New York: E. P. Dutton, 1967. On the New York House of Detention for Women; good journalism.

Hendin, Herbert. *Black Suicide.* New York: Basic Books, 1969.

———. *Suicide and Scandinavia.* Garden City, N.Y.: Doubleday, 1964. Both of Hendin's books are highly recommended.

———; Gaylin, Willard; and Carr, Arthur. *Psychoanalysis and Social Research: The Psychoanalytic Study of the Non-Patient.* Garden City,

N.Y.: Doubleday, 1965. Important in the dispute over patient and nonpatient samples. Makes a good case for there being little significant difference.

Henriques, Fernando. *Prostitution and Society.* See Chapter 2.

Herbert, John. *Fortune and Men's Eyes.* New York: Grove Press, 1967. A vivid and accurate play on prison homosexuality.

Jersild, Jens. *Boy Prostitution.* Copenhagen: G. E. C. Gad, 1956. Contains interesting material.

Kinsey, Alfred, *et al. Female.**

———. *Male.**

Kobler, John. "The Sex Criminal." *Saturday Evening Post,* January 28, 1967.

Konopka, Gisela. *The Adolescent Girl in Conflict.* Englewood Cliffs, N.J.: Prentice-Hall, 1966.

Lamott, Kenneth. *Chronicles of San Quentin.* New York: David McKay, 1961.

Lindner, Robert. "Sexual Behavior in Penal Institutions." In Deutsch, ed., *Sex Habits of American Men.* New York: Prentice-Hall, 1948.

——— and Seliger, Robert V., eds. *Handbook of Correctional Psychology.* New York: Philosophical Library, 1947.

McCaghy, Charles H., and Skipper, James K., Jr. "Lesbian Behavior as an Adaptation to the Occupation of Stripping." *Social Problems,* 17 (1969):262–70. A good study.

Magee, Bryan. See Chapter 28.

Marcus, Frank. *The Killing of Sister George.* New York: Random House, 1967.

Moynihan, Daniel. "The Discarded Third." *Look,* May 17, 1966.

Murtagh, John M., and Harris, Sara. *Cast the First Stone.* New York: McGraw-Hill, 1957. On prostitution, by a judge and a journalist.

Opler, M. K. "The Influence of Ethnic and Class Subcultures on Child Care." *Social Problems,* 3 (1955):12–21.

———. "Cultural Perspectives in Research on Schizophrenics." *Psychiatric Quarterly,* 33 (1959): 506–24. Two good monographs.

Parker, Tony. *Women in Crime.* New York: Delacorte Press, 1965. Journalistic account of female deviants.

Polsky, Howard. *Cottage Six.* New York: Russell Sage Foundation, 1962. On reformatory life.

Poussaint, Alvin. "A Negro Psychiatrist Explains the Negro Psyche." *The New York Times Magazine,* August 20, 1967.

Prosin, Suzanne. "The Concept of the Lesbian, a Minority in Reverse." *The Ladder,* 6 (July, 1962).

Rechy, John. *The City of Night.* New York: Grove Press, 1963.

Ruitenbeek, Hendrik, ed. *Psychoanalysis and Social Science.* New York: E. P. Dutton, 1962. Not a very good collection.

Sawyer, Ethel. *A Study of a Public Lesbian Community.* Unpublished thesis. Washington University, St. Louis, Missouri, 1965. A good study.

Schofield, Michael. See Chapter 28.

Schur, Edwin M. See Chapter 28.

Selby, Hubert, Jr. *Last Exit to Brooklyn.* New York: Grove Press, 1957.

Socarides, Charles W. *The Overt Homosexual.* New York: Grune & Stratton, 1968. A good psychoanalytic study, with a review of analytic theory and many case histories. Deals with female as well as male homosexuality. Recommended.

Stearn, Jess. *The Grapevine.* Garden City, N.Y.: Doubleday, 1964. Not recommended.

Streetwalker. London: The Bodley Head, 1959. An anonymous autobiography.

Sykes, Gresham. *The Society of Captives.* New York: Atheneum, 1965.

Ward, David, and Kassebaum, Gene. *Women's Prison.* Chicago: Aldine, 1965. This and Giallombardo's book are the only thorough and

reliable modern studies of prison lesbianism.
Ward, Jack L. "Homosexual Behavior of the Institutionalized Delinquent." *Psychiatric Quarterly Supplement*, 32 (1958):301–14.
Warner, W. Lloyd, and Lunt, Paul S. *The Social*

Life of a Modern Community. New Haven: Yale University Press, 1941. Justly, a sociological classic.
Westwood, Gordon. See Chapter 28.
Willis, Stanley E. See Chapter 28.

30 CURE OR ILLUSION

Abarbanel-Brandt, Albert. "Homosexuals in Hypnotherapy." *Journal of Sex Research*, 2 (1966): 127–32.
Abramson, Harold A. "Lysergic Acid Diethylamide (LSD-25):III. As an Adjunct to Psychotherapy with Elimination of Fear of Homosexuality." *Journal of Psychology*, 39 (1955):127–55.
Allen, Clifford. *Homosexuality: Its Nature, Causation, and Treatment*. London: Staples Press, 1958. Not a work of tremendous depth and detail, but sound.
Babkin, B. P. *Pavlov*. Chicago: University of Chicago Press, 1949. A biography.
Ball, J. R., and Armstrong, Jean. "The Use of LSD 25 (D-Lysergic Acid Diethylamide) in the Treatment of Sexual Perversions." *Canadian Psychiatric Association Journal*, 6 (1961):231–35.
Bene, Eva. "On the Genesis of Female Homosexuality." *British Journal of Psychiatry*, 3 (1965): 815–21.
———. "On the Genesis of Male Homosexuality." *British Journal of Psychiatry*, 3 (1965):803–813. Two good studies supporting Bieber's research and stressing the importance of the father in the backgrounds of both male and female homosexuals.
Berg, Charles, and Allen, Clifford. *The Problem of Homosexuality*. New York: Citadel Press, 1958. A bit dated, but basically good. Contains the work of Allen listed above.
Bergler, Edmund. *Homosexuality: Disease or Way of Life?* New York: Collier Books, 1967.
———. *Counterfeit-Sex*. 2nd enl. ed. New York: Grove Press, 1961. Bergler's writings, though often useful, now seem old-fashioned and a bit cranky in places. Not to be read without some critical background.
Bieber, Irving. "The Meaning of Masochism." *American Journal of Psychotherapy*, 7 (1953): 433–48. A fine paper with implications for the understanding and treatment of other sexual deviations.
———. "Speaking Frankly on a Once Taboo Subject." *The New York Times Magazine*, August 23, 1964. Some interesting comments on lesbianism.
——— *et al. Homosexuality*. New York: Random House, 1962. A must. The most important modern psychiatric study.
Bychowski, Gustav. See Chapter 24.
Cappon, Daniel. See Chapter 24.
Caprio, Frank. *Variations in Sexual Behavior*. New York: Grove Press, 1955. Not recommended.
Chang, Judy, and Block, Jack. "A Study of Identification in Male Homosexuals." *Journal of Consulting Psychology*, 24 (1960):307–10.
Clark, D. F. "Fetishism Treated by Negative Conditioning." *British Journal of Psychiatry*, 109 (1963):404–08.
Coates, Stephen. "Clinical Psychology in Sexual Deviation." In Rosen. See Chapter 23. Contains sound criticism of behaviorist methods.
———. "Homosexuality and the Rorschach Test." *British Journal of Medical Psychology*, 35 (1962): 177–90. A good survey of the subject.
Cooper, A. J. "A Case of Fetishism and Impotence Treated by Behaviour Therapy." *British Journal of Psychiatry*, 109 (1963):649–52.
Curran, Desmond, and Parr, Denis. "Homosexuality: An Analysis of 100 Male Cases." *British Medical Journal* (April 6, 1957):797–801.
Davids, A.; Joelson, M.; and McArthur, C. "Rorschach and TAT Indices of Homosexuality in Overt Homosexuals, Neurotics, and Normal Males." *Journal of Abnormal and Social Psychology*, 53 (1956):161–72.
Dengrove, Edward. "Behavior Therapy of the

Sexual Disorders." *Journal of Sex Research*, 3 (1967):49–61.
Ellis, Albert. *Homosexuality: Its Causes and Cure*. New York: Lyle Stuart, 1965. Contains some excellent chapters and, unlike many therapists' works, transcripts of doctor-patient sessions. Though Ellis' method of treatment is a bit special, this is worth attention.
Erikson, Erik. *Identity: Youth and Crisis*. New York: W. W. Norton, 1968. Recommended as background for the general problem of identity-formation and identity crisis.
Evans, Jean. *Three Men*. New York: Alfred A. Knopf, 1950. Contains a good fictionalized portrait of a disturbed homosexual.
Eysenck, Hans J. *Fact and Fiction in Psychology*. Baltimore: Penguin Books, 1965.
———. *The Structure of the Human Personality*. London: Methuen; New York: John Wiley & Sons, 1953.
———. *Uses and Abuses of Psychology*. London: Penguin Books, 1953.
———, ed. *Behaviour Therapy and the Neuroses*. Oxford: Pergamon Press, 1960. Eysenck represents the behaviorist position at its extreme.
Feldman, M. P. "Aversion Therapy for Sexual Deviations: A Critical Review." *Psychological Bulletin*, 65 (1966):65–79. Useful survey of behavior-therapy literature.
——— and McCulloch, M. J. "Aversion Therapy in Management of 43 Homosexuals." *British Medical Journal*, 2 (1967):594–97. Probably the most important single behavior-therapy paper on homosexuality; contains a bit of figure-juggling. To be read critically.
Fraiberg, Selma. "Homosexual Conflicts." In *Adolescents: Psychoanalytic Approach to Problems and Therapy*. Edited by Sandor Lorand and Henry I. Schneer. New York: Harper & Row, 1961. A revealing case of an adolescent in conflict over homosexuality.
Freeman, T. "Clinical and Theoretical Observations on Male Homosexuality." *International Journal of Psychoanalysis*, 36 (1955):335–47.
Freud, Anna. "Homosexuality." *Bulletin of the American Psychoanalytic Association*, 7 (1951): 117–18.
Freud, K. "Some Problems in the Treatment of Homosexuality." In Eysenck, ed. *Behaviour Therapy and the Neuroses*. See above.
Freund, D., and Srnec, D. "Treatment of Male Homosexuality through Conditioning." *International Journal of Sexology*, 7 (1953):92–93. This and the paper above are important in the literature of behavior therapy.
Hadden, Samuel B. "Group Psychotherapy for Sexual Maladjustments." *American Journal of Psychiatry*, 125 (1968):327–32.
———. "Group Psychotherapy of Male Homosexuals." *Current Psychiatric Therapies*, 6 (1966): 177–86.
———. "Treatment of Male Homosexuals in Groups." *International Journal of Group Psychotherapy*, 16 (1966):13–22.
———. "A Way Out for Homosexuals." *Harper's*, March 1967. At least one of these papers should be read by the specialist; the last item is recommended to laymen.
Hadfield, J. A. "The Cure of Homosexuality." *British Medical Journal*, 1 (1958):1323–26.
Hammer, Emanuel F. "Symptoms of Sexual Deviation: Dynamics and Etiology." *Psychoanalytic Review*, 55 (1968):5–27.
Harper, Robert A. See Chapter 15.
Hatterer, Lawrence. *Changing Homosexuality in the Male*. New York: McGraw-Hill, 1970. An interesting book on the results of a clinician's own practice, with some therapeutic innovations

Hemphill, R. E.; Leitch, A.; and Stuart, J. R.; "A Factual Study of Male Homosexuality." *British Medical Journal*, (June 7, 1958):1317–23.

Hooker, Evelyn. "The Adjustment of the Male Overt Homosexual." See Chapter 28.

———. "Male Homosexuality in the Rorschach." *Journal of Projective Techniques*, 22 (1958):33–54. Hooker's work, especially her original paper on the Rorschach, has an important place in modern scientific literature, but should be read critically.

Hunt, Morton. "A Neurosis Is 'Just' a Bad Habit." *The New York Times Magazine*, June 4, 1967. On behavior therapy. A good introduction for laymen.

James, Basil. "Case of Homosexuality Treated by Aversion Therapy." *British Medical Journal* (March 17, 1962):768–70.

Kahn, M. Masud R. "The Role of Infantile Sexuality and Early Object Relations in Female Homosexuality." In Rosen. See Chapter 23. Classical analytic approach, but useful.

Kolb, L. C., and Johnson, A. M. "Etiology and Therapy of Overt Homosexuality." *Psychoanalytic Quarterly*, 24 (1955):506–15.

Kraft, T. "A Case of Homosexuality Treated by Systematic Desensitization." *American Journal of Psychiatry*, 21 (1967):815.

Krich, A. M., ed. *The Homosexuals*. New York: Citadel Press, 1964. Contains some interesting snippets, but hardly a complete, balanced or up-to-date anthology.

Liddicoat, Renée. "A Study of Non-Institutionalized Homosexuals." *Journal of the National Institute of Personnel Research*, 8 (1961):217–49.

Lief, Harold, and Mayerson, Peter. "Psychotherapy of Homosexuals: A Follow-up Study of Nineteen Cases." In Marmor.* One of the few systematic follow-ups of analytically treated homosexuals. Recommended to the specialist.

Litman, R. E. "Psychotherapy of a Homosexual Man in a Heterosexual Group." *International Journal of Group Psychotherapy*, 16 (1965):13–22.

Löfgren, L. Börje. "Difficulties and Ambiguities in Using 'Results' as an Evaluating Norm in Psychiatry." *British Journal of Medical Psychology*, 33 (1960):95–103. A very good essay.

Lowen, Alexander. *Love and Orgasm*. New York: New American Library, 1965.

———. *The Physical Dynamics of Character Structure*. New York: Grune & Stratton, 1958. Lowen's approach is a bit too whole-heartedly Reichian, but his sense of body image, body language and body awareness is very valuable. Not to be swallowed whole, but excellent if read critically as an adjunct to, say, Bieber, Willis or Socarides. For laymen as well as specialists.

McCord, William; McCord, Joan; and Verden, Paul. "Family Relationships and Sexual Deviance in Lower-Class Adolescents." *International Journal of Social Psychiatry*, 8 (1962):165–79. Interesting sidelights on family background and sex-role attitudes.

Martensen-Larsen, O. "The Family Constellation and Homosexualism." *Acta Genetica et Statistica Medica*, 7 (1957):445–46. Based on a Danish sample.

Max, Louis William. "Breaking Up a Homosexual Fixation by the Conditioned Reaction Technique." *Psychological Bulletin*, 32 (1935):734.

Oswald, Ian. "Induction of Illusory and Hallucinatory Voices with Considerations of Behaviour Therapy." *Journal of Mental Science*, 108 (1962): 196–212.

Patterson, C. H. *Theories of Counseling and Psychotherapy*. New York: Harper & Row, 1966.

Pavlov, Ivan. See Chapter 24.

Poe, J. S. "The Successful Treatment of a 40-Year-Old Passive Homosexual Based on an Adaptational View of Sexual Behavior." *Psychoanalytic Review*, 29 (1952):23–36.

Rachman, S. "Sexual Disorders and Behavior Therapy." *American Journal of Psychiatry*, 118 (1961):35–40.

Reik, Theodor. *Psychiatry of Sex Relations*. New York: Grove Press, 1966. Not recommended.

Rogow, Arnold. *The Psychiatrists*. New York: G. P. Putnam's Sons, 1970. A good, readable study of the profession and its members.

Rosen, Ismond. "The Basis of Psychotherapeutic Treatment of Sexual Deviation." *Proceedings of the Royal Society of Medicine*, 61 (1968):793–96.

———. See Chapter 23.

Rubinstein, L. H. "Psychotherapeutic Aspects of Male Homosexuality." *British Journal of Medical Psychology*, 31 (1958):74–78.

Salter, Andrew. *Conditional Reflex Therapy*. New York: Capricorn Books, 1961. Largely an example of what science should not be.

Scott, Peter. "Definition, Classification, Prognosis and Treatment." In Ismond Rosen, ed. See Chapter 23.

Shoben, Edward J., Jr. "Psychotherapy as a Problem in Learning Theory." *Psychological Bulletin*, 46 (1949):366–92.

Slavson, S. R. *A Textbook in Analytic Group Psychotherapy*. Cambridge, Mass.: Harvard University Press, 1964.

Socarides, Charles. See Chapter 17.

Stanley-Jones, D. "Royal Society of Medicine Symposium on Homosexuality." *Medical Press*, September 1947.

Stekel, Wilhelm. See Chapter 17.

Stevenson, Ian, and Wolpe, Joseph. "Recovery from Sexual Deviations Through Overcoming Non-Sexual Neurotic Responses." *American Journal of Psychiatry*, 116 (1960):737–42.

Stone, Walter; Schenger, John; and Seifried, E. Stanley. "The Treatment of a Homosexual Woman in a Mixed Group." *International Journal of Group Psychotherapy*, 16 (1966):425–33.

Storms, Lowell, and Sigal, John. "Eysenck's Personality Theory with Special Reference to the Dynamics of Anxiety and Hysteria." *British Journal of Medical Psychology*, 31 (1958):228–46.

Szasz, Thomas. *Law, Liberty and Psychiatry*. New York: Macmillan, 1963.

———. *The Myth of Mental Illness*. New York: Hoeber-Harper, 1961. An extreme relativist position on mental health and social normality.

Watson, John. See Chapter 24.

West, D. J. See Chapter 20.

Wilbur, Cornelia. "Clinical Aspects of Female Homosexuality." In Marmor.*

Willis, Stanley E. See Chapter 28.

Wolberg, Lewis R. "Hypnotherapy." In *Six Approaches to Psychotherapy*. Edited by James McCary. New York: Dryden Press, 1955.

The Wolfenden Report. New York: Stein & Day, 1963.

Wolpe, Joseph. *Psychotherapy by Reciprocal Inhibition*. Stanford: Stanford University Press, 1958.

——— and Lazarus, A. *Behavior Therapy Techniques*. New York: Pergamon Press, 1966. Important in the behavior-therapy literature.

Woodward, Mary. "The Diagnosis and Treatment of Homosexual Offenders." *British Journal of Delinquency*, 9 (1958):44–59.

31 THE LOGIC OF THE LAW

The *UCLA Law Review* has the best over-all study of antihomosexual legislation and enforcement. The book on sex offenders by Paul Gebhard and his associates is also very good. Jowitt is quoted by D. J. West.

The Armed Forces and Homosexuality. San Francisco: The Society for Individual Rights, n.d.

"Bisexual Leanings Are Called No Bar to U.S. Citizenship." *The New York Times*. March 1,

1969.

"Blackmail Paid by Congressman." *The New York Times*, May 17, 1967.

"Britain: Homosexual Acts." *Newsweek*, January 2, 1967.

"California: Spots on Mr. Clean." *Newsweek*, November 13, 1967. About Ronald Reagan's staff.

The Challenge and Progress of Homosexual Law Reform. San Francisco: The Council on Religion and the Homosexual, 1968.

"City Would Ease Curbs on Tenants." *The New York Times*, August 21, 1966.

"Commons Adopts a Bill to Modify Penalty for Adult Homosexuality." *The New York Times*, July 5, 1967.

"Court Will Rule on Homosexuals." *The New York Times*, November 8, 1966.

Daniel, Marc. "Sex, Law and Society in France Today." In *Man and Society*, Journal of the Albany Trust, 5 (Winter, 1966):23–29.

"Detective Accused as a Top Extorter." *The New York Times*, June 30, 1966.

"Extortionist Gets Maximum Five Years." *The New York Times*, July 12, 1967.

"Federal Job Barriers on Homosexuals Falling." *New York Post*, September 10, 1969.

"Forum: Psychopathic Homosexuals." *Playboy*, December 1967.

Gall, Norman. "Cuba Libre." *The New York Times Book Review*, July 14, 1968.

Gebhard, Paul, et al. *Sex Offenders*. See Chapter 29.

Gerassi, John. *The Boys of Boise*. New York: Macmillan, 1966. Though liable to some criticism, an informative piece of journalism.

"Government Upheld on Right to Fire Homosexuals." *New York Post*, April 20, 1970.

"Great Britain: Shame Is Enough." *Time*, July 14, 1967.

"High Court Denies Homosexual Plea." *The New York Times*, May 23, 1967.

"The Homosexual: Newly Visible, Newly Understood." *Time*, October 31, 1969.

Kinsey, Alfred, et al. *Female*.*

———. *Male*.*

Klimmer, Rudolf. "Homosexuality in East Germany." *Man and Society*, 5 (Winter, 1966):30–33.

Lapham, Lewis. "The Trials of Candy and Mel."

Saturday Evening Post, September 10, 1966.

"The Law: Immigration." *Time*, July 22, 1966.

"Medicine: Legal Castration." *Newsweek*, February 23, 1970.

"Pickets Aid Homosexuals." *The New York Times*, July 5, 1967.

"The Playboy Forum." *Playboy*, September 1968.

Ploscowe, Morris. *Sex and the Law*. New York: Prentice-Hall, 1951.

"Police Forbidden to Entrap Homosexuals." *The New York Times*, May 10, 1966.

Roberts, Gene. "The Case of Jim Garrison and Lee Oswald." *The New York Times Magazine*, May 21, 1967.

Rovere, Richard H. *Senator Joe McCarthy*. New York: Harcourt, Brace, 1959.

Sanford, David. "Boxed In." *New Republic*, May 21, 1966.

Schiffrin, André. "Publishing in Cuba." *The New York Times Book Review*, March 17, 1968.

Schofield, Michael. See Chapter 28.

Schott, Webster. "A 4-Million Minority Asks for Equal Rights." *The New York Times Magazine*, November 12, 1967. Good journalistic survey but lacks depth.

Schur, Edwin M. See Chapter 28.

"Sexual Offences Act, 1967." London: Published by Her Majesty's Stationery Office, 1967.

"S.L.A. Won't Act Against Bars Refusing Service to Deviates." *The New York Times*, April 26, 1966.

Slovovenko, Ralph. *Sexual Behavior and the Law*. Springfield, Ill.: Charles C. Thomas, 1965.

"3 Deviates Invite Exclusion by Bars." *The New York Times*, April 22, 1966.

"U.S. Appeals Court Backs Order Deporting Alien as Homosexual." *The New York Times*, July 9, 1966.

Van Horne, Harriet. "Homosexuals: A Brave Study." *World Journal Tribune*, March 8, 1967.

West, D. J. See Chapter 20.

Westwood, Gordon. See Chapter 28.

"The Woman Homosexual: More Assertive, Less Willing to Hide." *The New York Times*, November 17, 1969.

Wortis, Joseph. *Soviet Psychiatry*. Baltimore: Williams & Wilkins, 1950. On Russian laws and official attitudes.

Index